Alan Greenwood and his wife, Cleo, are the publishers of *Vintage Guitar* magazine, which they launched in 1986. *Vintage Guitar* is the largest monthly publication for guitar collectors, enthusiasts, and dealers. They also publish *Vintage Guitar®* Online at www.vintageguitar.com, and *The Official Vintage Guitar Magazine Price Guide*. His collection includes several vintage instruments from the '50s, '60s and '70s, as well as newer production and custom-made guitars and amps. He lives in Bismarck, North Dakota.

Gil Hembree began collecting guitars in 1966 as a college student working at Kitt's Music in Washington, DC. He holds a BSBA from American University and a MBA from Midwestern State University. He worked for General Motors Corporation in Flint and Detroit, Michigan for over 30 years as a Financial Administrator and Supervisor of Corporate Audit. During that time he played music semi-professionally and has continued collecting guitars and amps. Since 1992 he has written for several guitar publications, and is a contributing writer for *Vintage Guitar* magazine penning his "401K Guitars" column. He is also the author of *Gibson Guitars: Ted McCarty's Golden Era: 1948–1966* (Hal Leonard Corp) which was released in 2007. Gil and his wife Jane live in Austin, Texas.

The Official Vintage Guitar® Magazine Price Guide
By Alan Greenwood and Gil Hembree

Vintage Guitar Books
An imprint of Vintage Guitar Inc., PO Box 7301, Bismarck, ND 58507, (701) 255-1197, Fax (701) 255-0250, publishers of *Vintage Guitar®* magazine and Vintage Guitar® Online at www.vintageguitar.com. Vintage Guitar is a registered trademark of Vintage Guitar, Inc.

ISBN-10: 1-884883-20-6
ISBN-13: 978-1-884883-20-0

Cover and Back photos: (Front Cover) 1958 Gibson ES-335 with sunburst finish, '64 Gibson ES-335 in Golden Mist Poly, '60s Gibson ES-335 in Pelham Blue: VG Archive. Guitars courtesy Dave Rogers. Gibson ES-335 in Cherry Red: VG Archive. Guitar courtesy of Gil Southworth. 1961 Fender Band-Master, '64 Fender Telecaster in Ice Blue Metallic, '65 Fender Stratocaster in Ice Blue Metallic.
Photo courtesy Phil Winfield.

Cover Design: Doug Yellow Bird/Vintage Guitar, Inc.

Printed in the United States of America

EXCLUSIVELY DISTRIBUTED BY
HAL•LEONARD® CORPORATION
7777 W. BLUEMOUND RD. P.O. BOX 13819
MILWAUKEE, WISCONSIN 53213

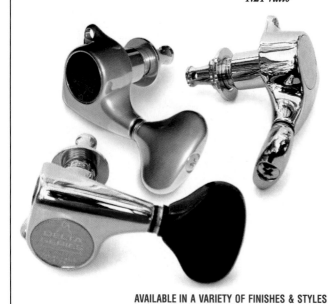

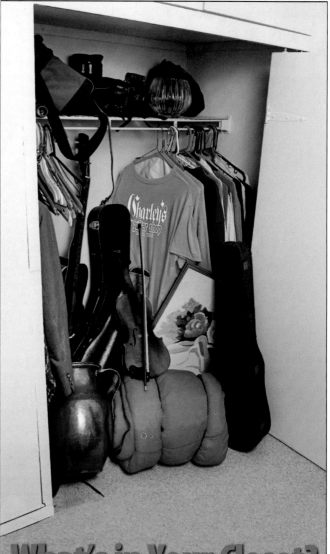

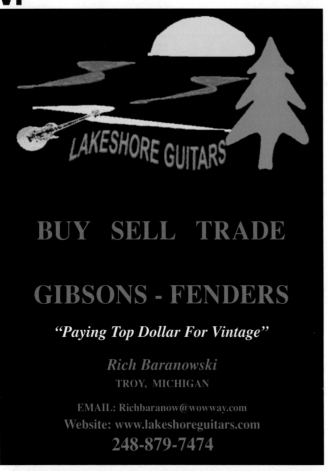

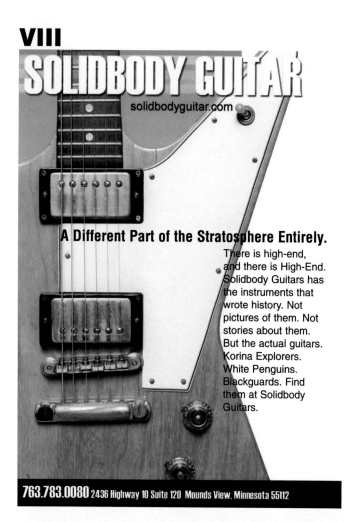

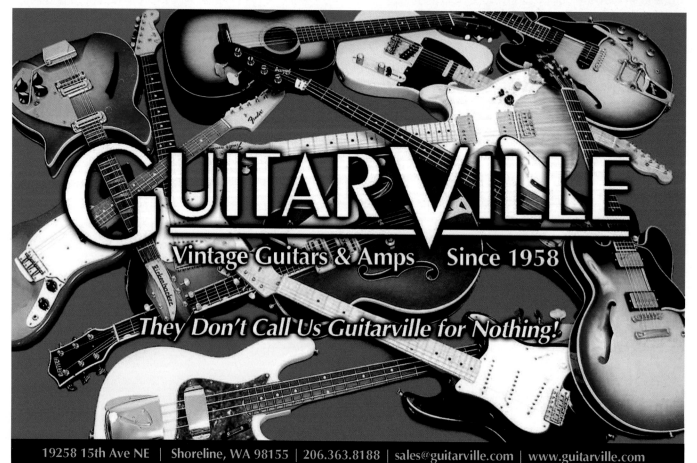

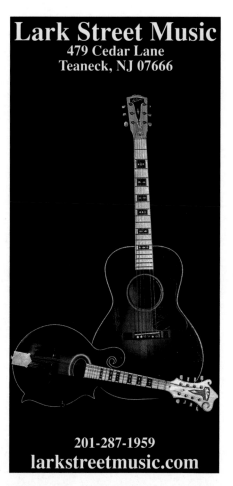

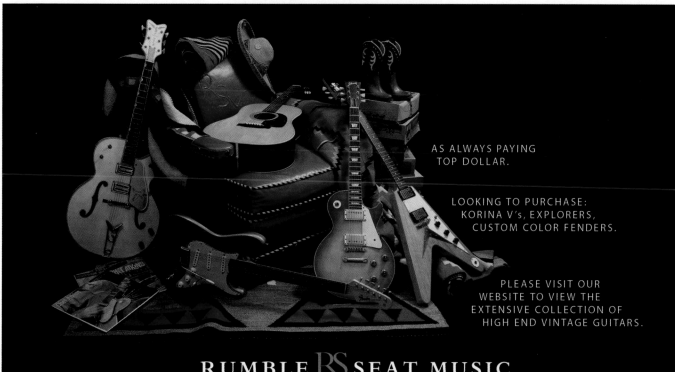

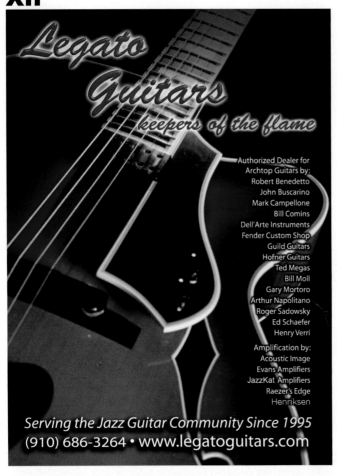

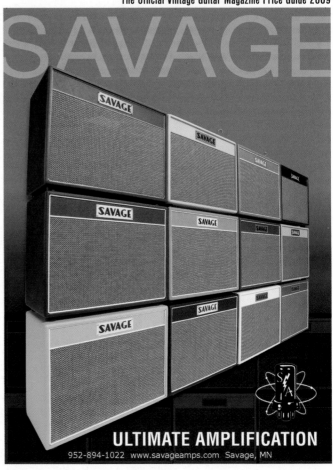

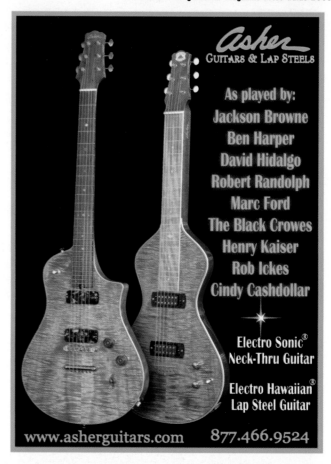

1959 Fender Esquire. Photo: VG Archive. Guitar courtesy Chris Meeker.

Table of Contents

THE
BURST BROTHERS

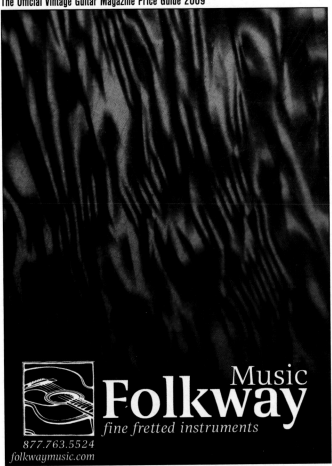

Using The Guide

Understanding the Values

The values presented in *The Official Vintage Guitar Price Guide* are for excellent-condition, all-original instruments. Our definition of excellent condition allows for some wear, but the instrument should be well-maintained, with no significant blemishes, wear, repairs, or damage. All-original means the instrument has the parts and finish it had when it left the factory. Replacement parts and refinishes can greatly affect value, as can the appropriate case (or cover) in excellent condition. In many instances, a "wrong" case will not greatly affect value, but with the top-dollar collectibles, it can.

We use a range of excellent-condition values, as there is seldom agreement on a single price point for vintage and used instruments. A tighter range suggests there is a general consensus, while a wide range means the market isn't in strict agreement. A mint-condition instrument can be worth more than the values listed here, and anything in less-than-excellent condition will have a reduced value. And, of course, when dealing with high-end collectibles, values can quickly change.

Repairs affect value differently. Some repair is necessary to keep an instrument in playable condition. The primary concern is the level of expertise displayed in the work and an amateurish repair will lower the value more than one that is obviously professional. A refinished guitar, regardless of the quality of the work, is generally worth 50% or less of the values shown in *The Guide*. A poorly executed neck repair or significant body repair can mean a 50% reduction in a guitar's value. A professional re-fret or minor, nearly invisible body repair will reduce a guitar's value by only 5%.

The values in the *The Guide* are for unfaded finishes. Slight color fade reduces the value by only 5%, but heavily faded examples can reduce the value by 25% to 50%.

Finding the Information

The table of contents shows the major sections and each is organized in alphabetical order by brand, then by model. In a few instances, there are separate sections for a company's most popular models, especially when there is a large variety of similar instruments. Examples include Fender's Stratocasters, Telecasters, Precision and Jazz basses, and Gibson's Les Pauls. The outer top corner of each page uses a dictionary-type header that tells the models or brands on that page. This provides a quick way to navigate each section. The index at the back shows the page numbers for each type of instrument, by brand, and is a great place to start when looking for a specific model or brand.

The Guide has excellent brand histories and in most cases the guitar section has the most detailed information for each brand. When possible, *The Guide* lists each model's years of availability and any design changes that affect values.

More information on many of the brands covered in *The Guide* is available in the pages of *Vintage Guitar* magazine and on the "Brand Pages" section of our website, www.vintage-guitar.com.

The authors of *The Guide* always appreciate your help, so if you find any errors, or have additional information on certain brands or models, we'd like to hear from you. We are especially looking for info on any brand not yet listed. Whatever you may have to contribute, feel free to drop us a line at al@vguitar.com.

New Retail Pricing Information

The Guide continues to add information on individual luthiers and smaller shops. It's difficult to develop values on used instruments produced by these builders because much of their output is custom work, production is low, and/or they haven't been producing for a period of time sufficient to see their instruments enter the used/resale market. To give you an idea about their instruments, we've developed five grades of retail values for new instruments. These convey only the prices charged by the builder, and are not indicative of the quality of construction. *The Guide* applies this scale to all builders and manufacturers of new instruments.

The five retail-price grades are:
Budget - up to $250,
Intermediate - $251 to $1,000,
Professional - $1,001 to $3,000,
Premium - $3,001 to $10,000,
Presentation - more than $10,000.

The Guide uses the terms "production" and "custom" to differentiate between builders who do true custom work versus those who offer standard production models. "Production" means the company offers specific models, with no variations. "Custom" means they do only custom orders, and "production/custom" indicates they do both. Here's an example:

Shea Guitars
1965-present. Luthier Jeanine Shea builds her premium-grade, custom, archtop guitars in Bismarck, North Dakota. She also builds mandolins.

This tells who the builder is, the type of instruments they build, where they build them, how long they've been operating under that brand, that they do only custom work, and that they ask between $3,000 and $10,000 for their guitars (premium-grade).

We've applied the retail price grades and production and/or custom labels to most new-instrument manufacturers.

Introduction

As we mark the 20th anniversary of the creation of the monthly "Price Guide" column in *Vintage Guitar* magazine, we're reminded that each year, this book is purchased by thousands of people for many reasons. Music stores and pawn brokers find *The Guide* to be a handy, reliable source of pricing information on used and vintage instruments. Thrift shoppers who hit flea markets and garage sales often keep one copy in their car and another at home. Guitar dealers wouldn't think about attending a guitar show without one, and in most booths you'll see a *Guide* on the table. Many buy *The Guide* because they own one or more of the guitars listed and simply feel comfortable having documentation of what their prizes are worth. Others love the pictures of gear and the info about the instrument builders.

The Guide lists almost every conceivable type of fretted instrument, and values listed range from $50 to $350,000. Though there is a lot of interest in the expensive vintage guitars costing more than $20,000, we get more questions on reasonably priced used guitars, many of which were made in the '90s – an era now considered by many to be the start of the "Second Golden Era" and customers often ask specifically that we include as many of its instruments as possible.

Much of the news in the guitar-collecting community concerns high-end/iconic vintage instruments made from 1930 to 1965. *The Guide* has been studying these instruments since 1991 and developed a way to demonstrate what is happening in that market segment. The demonstration is The 42-Guitar Index.

This year, The 42-Guitar Index shows a 7 percent decline from 2008 to 2009. Some may be surprised with this, but those close to the market have been expecting a correction in market values. The decline in the Index from '08 to '09 was across the board, with Fenders losing 10 percent, Gibsons dropping 7 percent, and Martins declining 4 percent. Of the 42 guitars in the Index, 25

THE 42 INDEX

FROM FENDER
1952 blond Precision Bass
1952 blond Esquire
1953 blond Telecaster
1956 sunburst Stratocaster
1958 sunburst Jazzmaster
1958 blond Telecaster
1960 sunburst Stratocaster
1961 sunburst, stack knob, Jazz Bass
1962 sunburst, 3-knob, Jazz Bass
1963 sunburst Telecaster Custom
1963 sunburst Esquire Custom
1964 Lake Placid Blue Jaguar
1964 sunburst Precision Bass
1966 Candy Apple Red Stratocaster

FROM GIBSON
1952 sunburst ES-5
1952 Les Paul Model
1954 Les Paul Jr.
1958 sunburst EB-2 Bass
1958 Les Paul Custom
1958 natural ES-335

1958 Super 400CES
1959 Les Paul Jr.
1959 J-160E
1961 sunburst ES-355
1961 Les Paul SG
1964 sunburst Thunderbird II Bass
1965 EB-3 Bass
1969 sunburst Citation

FROM MARTIN
1931 OM-28
1932 00-28 special order
1935 D-18
1944 scalloped-brace 000-28
1944 D-28
1950 D-28
1958 000-18
1959 D-18
1959 D-28E
1962 D-28
1967 GT-75
1968 000-18
1969 N-20
1969 D-45

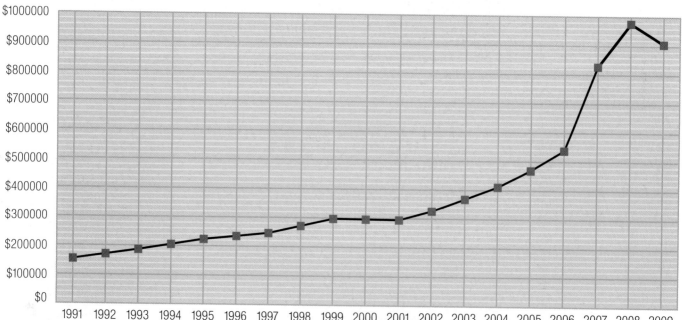

The 42 Guitar Index 1991 - 2009

Jensen
loudspeakers

Fender

The Vintage Legend

In the 1950s Fender and Jensen came together to create a sound that forever changed the music industry. Even today, Fender uses Jensen Vintage Alnico and Ceramic Special Design reissue speakers in the new reproductions of their classic amplifiers from the 50s and 60s.

Modern with a Touch of English

The Jensen MOD line was developed to bring the British sound to a player's amp while maintaining the integrity of the amplifier's tone. The player holds the power with the Jensen Mod Series.

Hear the Future

The Neo line of speakers is both clear and soulful, demonstrating Jensen's innovation through its use of Neodymium magnets. Daring to lead the way, the Neo allows the musician to lighten the load without limiting the sound.

First in Class

The premier Jensen Jet line shares the same sense of groundbreaking tradition as the original Jensen musical instrument speakers. Knowing what players want and utilizing the finest materials, Jensen continues its tradition of producing speakers with unparalleled tone.

jensentone.com

dropped in value, 7 did not change, and 10 increased in value. Remember, most of them are expensive – the average value of a guitar in the Index is $21,570. Guitars that were not in the Index or were in less-expensive segments did not necessarily drop in value.

Is the 7 percent decline in Index value a concern? No. It reflects only the activity in a small portion of the high-end market – guitars costing more than $25,000 represent roughly 1.4 percent of the vintage guitars that are bought, sold, and traded.

The 42 Guitar Index shows general market trends for higher-end instruments. But what specifically happened to Gibson Les Paul goldtops and Fender Stratocasters? To report on those iconic models, we've prepared a new chart that tracks and compares the values of four '50s Les Pauls and four '50s Stratocasters.

The Les Paul Index included models made between 1953 and '56; all have P-90 pickups and either wraparound or Tune-O-Matic bridges. The index presents the combined value of all four. The chart tracks how the combined value (the index) has changed from 2001 to '09. The Stratocaster Index included four sunburst models, all with maple necks and vibratos, made between '55 and '58. As with the Gibson Index, the Fender Index represents the combined value of all four Fenders.

This chart shows that the Les Paul and Stratocaster indices both showed declines in value more significant than The 42-Guitar Index. The '50s Gibson goldtops trend shows a bubble and a correction. Fifties goldtops are down 25 percent from last year, and 32 percent from their 2007 high. The '50s Stratocasters show a more modest correction, but one that exceeded The 42-Guitar Index cor-

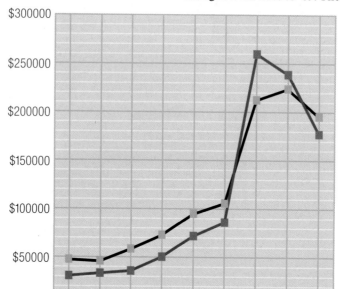

1950s Les Paul (Goldtop) vs. 1950s Stratocaster

Legend: ▇ Les Paul ▇ Stratocaster

XXX

Authors Gil Hembree and Alan Greenwood.

rection of 7 percent. Stratocasters are down 13 percent from their high point in '08.

For most of their history, '50s Stratocasters have been more valuable than '50s goldtop Les Pauls. But as the chart shows, in 2007 and '08, Les Pauls were more highly valued. Why? When goldtops jumped past Strats in '07, we asked some of the industry's best vintage guitar dealers to explain the change. The consensus suggested fewer goldtops were made in the '50s and prices reflected old-fashioned supply and

demand. Dealers also felt that a goldtop was a higher-quality guitar. They didn't say a goldtop was a "better" guitar, but with its bound top and set neck, it was seen as a higher-quality design. But goldtops did not rule for long; today, '50s goldtops have returned to a more normal position in the market and are valued slightly below '50s Stratocasters.

Charles Krauthammer, a foreign/domestic policy and politics op-ed columnist for the *Washington Post*, recently wrote a piece entitled "At $4, Everybody Gets Rational." The subject was $4/gallon gasoline and how the price transformed the world.

"So now we know," he wrote. "The price point is $4. At $3 a gallon, Americans just grin and bear it, suck it up, and while complaining profusely, keep driving like crazy. At $4, it is a world transformed. Americans become rational creatures. Mass transit ridership is at a 50-year high. Driving is down 4 percent. Any U.S. decline is something close to a miracle. Hybrids and compacts are flying off the lots. SUV sales are in free fall. The wholesale flight from gas guzzlers is stunning in its swiftness, but utterly predictable. Everything has a price point."

He goes on to list rapid changes that directly relate to the price of gas. Other writers and pundits have discussed this, as well, noting how everything from food to air travel to imported goods are increasing rapidly in price.

With all of this in mind, I posed a question to several respected vintage guitar dealers: "Are high-end guitars just

too expensive?" In other words, has the market hit a "point of change" in regard to price.

Most dealers felt interest in excellent, all-original vintage guitars was still remarkably strong. However, quality and rarity is more important than ever. In particular, 1930s and '40s golden-era flat-top guitars are enjoying a surge in popularity. Why? Once again, it's supply and demand. A small number of golden-era flat-tops were made and their chances of surviving in excellent condition was significantly less than guitars from later eras, specifically solidbody Fenders and Gibsons from the '50s. So a "price point of change" may not exist in the golden-era acoustic market.

The golden-era solidbody market is stable for many instruments in excellent, all original condition, and especially good for any rare items such as those with custom colors. But variation from originality detracts significantly. Same goes for too much wear. The value of less-than-excellent-condition instruments is dropping from recent historic highs. And there's no shortage of marginal-quality solidbody instruments.

The second most prevalent thought from vintage dealers involves how the economy is affecting the overall vintage guitar market. With real estate values and the stock market in decline, and the low value of the U.S. dollar creating inflation at the gas pump and grocery store, consumers may curtail spending – including on vintage guitars. Dealers point out that not only is the vintage-guitar market affected by the economy, but so are boutique builders.

Vallis Kolbeck, owner of GuitarVille, a music store in Seattle, compared the current U.S. economy to what Japan experienced in the 1980s.

"A Japanese guitar-collector market that at one time would seemingly pay any price for good-quality vintage instruments suddenly made an about face," he said. "But then the value of the yen plummeted and a layer of investors was revealed that had no musical talent but had put a lot of money in the latest 'can't miss' investment. Like investors in the U.S. and other countries who bought because of articles in *Forbes* and *Money*, they knew little about the market or the instruments, but invested at its peak. New real estate investors and developers in the Western U.S. are dealing with similar problems," he added. "The lesson for us, historically, is that all investment markets ebb and flow. We need to learn when to buy and what to buy – even if certain crystal ball questions are pretty much unanswerable."

Richard Friedman, We Buy Guitars, agrees the economy is the culprit. "Many people are losing their jobs and their houses," he noted. "But the best of the best vintage guitars are still selling."

"The economy seems to be the issue with everything, not just the guitar market," added Eliot Michael, Rumble Seat Music. "When people see an increase in anything, they get scared and stop spending, or simply become more cautious about spending money. Once the fear subsides or boredom sets in, they start to spend again. People are still buying in

every market if the product is good or fairly priced. We have people call us as soon as we put up a new cool guitar for sale in every price range."

Nate Westgor, owner of Willie's American Guitars, agrees, but reverses the process by suggesting, "I've always said that if vintage guitar values tank, look out because the rest of the economy will be in bad shape, too. Clean, original vintage guitars still rule the day, and they will pull away from the less-clean guitars with 'stories.'"

Jim Singleton, of Jim's Guitars, goes a bit further. "Now is the time to buy a vintage guitar. Things have cooled a bit, but compared to housing values, fine vintage guitars are still a great buy. If more people would ignore the talking heads with their gloom and doom every morning because gas goes up a few pennies, we'd all be in better shape. Whether you're weeding and feeding a collection or looking for the 'best one,' outstanding examples are not in short supply and prices are great with respect to where we will be 10 years up the road. Gas has been $7 a gallon in Europe for years, it's $11 a

1978 Dean Z Standard

gallon in London. So what? Life goes on. If more people would get back to business as usual, the economy would turn around overnight. The thing to do in times like these is spend money. Fear breeds economic downturn more than gas prices, housing values, or any other factor. Vintage guitars are a finite collectable. We'll look back on these times and think, 'I wish I'd bought that guitar back in 2008.'"

While some Les Paul goldtops, Strats, and other high-end models may be mired down, other brands are ready to spring forward. Examples include vintage B.C. Rich, Hamer, Dean, and Charvel guitars. Purists will say there is no such thing as a vintage B.C. Rich, but B.C. Rich collectors consider the company's heyday to be 1973 to '85, when the guitars were hand-built, starting with the Seagull, then the Eagle, Mockingbird, and Bich. Circa 1985, new shapes were introduced to compete with Jackson and Charvel models of the time. These are less sought-after in today's market.

Another nouveau vintage brand is Dean. From 1973 to

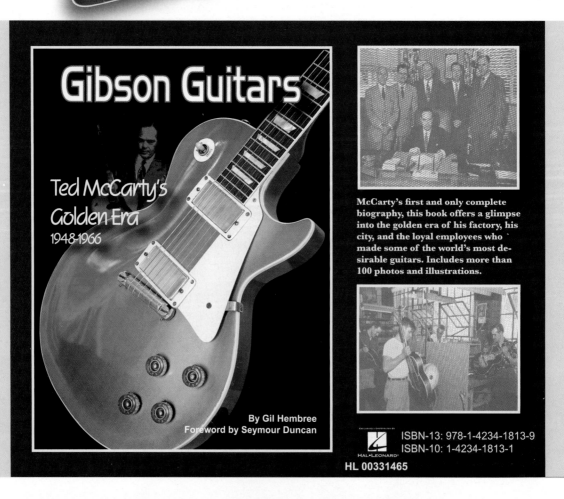

'86, American companies like Paul Reed Smith, Jackson, Charvel, Kramer, and Dean were created in part because their founders felt they could build a better guitar. Dean Zelinsky started building while enrolled in a high school co-op at a local guitar repair shop. In 1976 he rented a building and filled it with machinery under the name of Dean Guitars. His vision was to take the best of '50s Gibsons and upgrade them with more powerful pickups and fancy appointments. While Zelinsky favored Gibson styles, he also advanced their designs by altering body thickness and string tension, giving his guitars their own sound. Zelinsky combined design quality with quality construction and a trendy/sexy ad campaign to achieve success.

The future of guitar collecting may well hold riches in this segment, with names like Jackson, Charvel, Kramer, Travis Bean, and B.C Rich. If you were born before 1960, you're more likely part of the Les Paul/Strat crowd. But if you were born later, you might be ready to chase vintage "nouveau vintage" brands.

Guitar innovation didn't stop after the '70s and '80s. In the '90s, some would argue, Parker Guitars represented the next great innovation in guitar making. Co-founders Ken Parker and Larry Fishman used the 1992 NAMM show to introduce their Super Fly guitar, and its very light weight and acoustic properties left an immediate and sizable impression. By July of 1993 the Parker Fly Deluxe was in production, thanks to help from Korg, which committed nearly $1 million

Is the Parker Fly really just another guitar?

1959: Gibson Les Paul Standard
*Curved top and curly maple.
No ordinary plank o' wood.*

1954: Fender Stratocaster
*Solid as a rock and
ready for the jet age.*

Now: Parker Fly
*Just another moment in history.
Carved from wood.*

A 1995 Parker ad that challenged the best of the best.

dollars. Initially, the Fly found a market and performed well as an electric solidbody. But, up against not only a reinvigorated Fender and Gibson, he faced faced competition from another relative new comer in Paul Reed Smith, whose PRS

Guitar Dealer Participants

The information refined on these pages comes from several sources, including the input of many knowledgeable guitar dealers. Without the help of these individuals, it would be very hard for us to provide the information here and in each issue of *Vintage Guitar* magazine. We deeply appreciate the time and effort they provide.

Andy Eder
Andy's Guitars

Bob Page & Steve Mendoza
Buffalo Brothers

Norm Moren
Cold Springs Electrical Works

Stan Werbin & S.J. "Frog" Forgey
Elderly Instruments

David Brass
Fretted Americana

Dave Hussong
Fretware Guitars

Richard Johnston
Gryphon Strings

Dave Belzer & Drew Berlin
Guitar Center

Vallis Kolbeck
GuitarVille (Seattle)

Kennard Machol & Leonard Coulson
Intermountain Guitar & Banjo

Jim Singleton
Jim's Guitars

Dave Hinson
Killer Vintage

Timm Kummer
Kummer's Vintage Instruments

Buzzy Levine
Lark Street Music

Larry Wexer
Laurence Wexer, Ltd.

Chuck Mahar
Mahar's Vintage Guitars

Stan Jay
Mandolin Brothers

Bob November
McKenzie River Music

Lowell Levinger
Players Vintage Instruments

Mike Reeder
Mike's Music

Eliot Michael
Rumble Seat Music

Bruce Barnes
Solidbodyguitar.com

Fred Oster
Vintage Instruments

Richard Friedman & David Davidson
We Buy Guitars

Nate Westgor
Willie's American Guitars

guitars blended traditional Fender and Gibson elements. When the competitive dusts settled, Fender, Gibson, and PRS were prospering at the expense of Parker Guitars.

By 1998, a used '93 Parker Fly Deluxe that sold new for about $1,200 could be bought for $800. Today, a '90s Fly Deluxe model can be found from $925 to $1,300, or about $1,100 on average. What else will $1,100 buy? Early-'90s guitars in that price range include the B.C. Rich Bich, ESP Horizon Classic (figured maple top), G&L Comanche VI, Hamer Steve Stevens 1, Heritage H-157 Ultra, Fender Robert Cray Stratocaster (Custom Shop), Fender Yngwie Malmsteen Stratocaster, Fender '52 Telecaster, Gibson Chet Atkins SST, Gibson ES-135, Gibson Flying V reissue, Jackson Soloist SL (USA), Jackson Warrior (USA), Music Man Silhouette, Peavey Vandenberg Quilt Top, Rickenbacker Model 320 and Model 320/12.

How does a used $1,100 Parker Fly Deluxe stack up against a similar dated Les Paul, Strat, or PRS? A '92 PRS Custom (Custom 24) fetches about $2,000, a '92 PRS CE 22 brings about $1,200, a '92 Fender American Standard runs $750, a '92 '57 Stratocaster (USA) brings $1,200, '92 Set-Neck Stratocaster (Custom Shop) runs $1,350, '92 Gibson Les Paul Standard (regular production) fetches $1,650, '92 '56 Gibson Les Paul Goldtop brings $2,150, and a '92 '59 Gibson Les Paul Flametop (R-9) fetches $3,750.

The *Vintage Guitar Price Guide* uses precedent selling prices, reflecting the prices that guitars are being sold for in the market. Precedent-value theory stipulates that the next guitar to be sold in the market will be sold at a price equal to the most recently sold similar guitar (same model, color, and condition). Precedent value in the guitar market is not unlike the real-estate market, where a house is often listed for sale at a price equal to the average value of three equivalent houses that were recently sold.

The Guide does not forecast values. Historically, the average classic vintage guitar's annual increase is about 11 percent a year. *The Guide* does not assume this will recur in the future. Experience, especially in 2009, proves that prices do not consistently go up, and prices go up and down differently on various brands and models.

The data that is used to develop precedent values is taken from everywhere. It surveys some of the industry's best dealers, studies prices at the major guitar shows, examines advertised prices in *Vintage Guitar* magazine, visits internet sites, follows auction house actual-sales data, etc. But the final value shown for each line item in *The Guide* is not based on a

The Travis Bean brand is one of the hot brands in the 2009 market.

simple arithmetic average – it does not average data! Rather, it examines each make and model, considers it origin, and uses experience to develop the precedent price, favoring dealer pricing on solidbody instruments that comes from electric solidbody experts and acoustic-specialist info as lead data when pricing acoustics. All data is considered, including prices on electric solidbodies provided by an acoustic seller. This is useful very useful, because it represents a different point of view, which is important because the market is heavily influenced by anecdotal evidence – guitar dealers and sellers tend to stick with their personal experiences, and personal experiences in Detroit can be notably different from experiences in Denver, Dallas, Duluth, or anywhere.

The pricing data shown in *The Guide* is conservative. When considering prices from internet auctions, for instance, it takes into account "winner's curse," which can occur when an auction winner pays so much for a guitar that he will be unable to sell it, except most likely at a loss. *The Guide* requires a number of sellers to set a consistent selling price over a reasonable period of time, thereby avoiding an anomaly.

Market sophistication and specialization tend to create an upward bias in valuation. This applies to all makes and models. Over the long run, market specialists tend to set values; 1930s Martin D-45 specialists tend to have an upward pricing bias for D-45s versus '59 Gibson Les Paul Standards, and visa versa. Sophisticated buyers and sellers who have an upward-value bias tend to establish the high end of a value range. These upward biases are generally accurate.

Vintage retailers, using their own anecdotes, generally base their selling prices on precedent value. *The Guide* is very useful in this endeavor because there are just too many guitars to keep tabs on, and we don't know of any dealers who do not reference our book for guidance. But sometimes dealers will price an excellent all-original guitar higher than what is shown in *The Guide*.

Most dealers, after referencing *The Guide*, use old-fashioned "rule of thumb" pricing, which takes into account a seller's profit expectation and overhead, their purchase cost of the instrument, and an expected turnover rate. A vintage dealer will typically set a selling price for his instrument which is near the instrument's precedent value if that value is justified by "rule of thumb" factors. "Rule of thumb" pricing is a critical part of market mechanics. For most of the history of the market, dealers have had to occasionally break precedent by increasing the price of an instrument above the level shown in *The Guide*. This is

often driven by increasing costs when buying inventory. And, of course, when dealing with high-end collectibles, values can quickly change.

Sellers can also lower prices. This happened in portions of the high-end market between 2008 and '09, where there was notable rejection of high retail prices. In '08, some customers stayed on the sidelines, unwilling to pay high asking prices. In reaction, some sellers lowered prices, establishing lower precedent prices for '09.

What's hot in 2009? While some higher-end instruments have dropped in value, items appreciating in value can be found! Here are some of the "hottest" collectibles at the moment: '50s Gibson BR-4 and BR-6 lap steels, Sunn Concert Bass and Concert Lead amplifiers, '66 Fender Mustang Bass with Competition finish, '59 Gibson ES-225, U.S.-made BC Rich Warlock bass, USA BC Rich Bich 8-string bass, 1978 Dean ML Standard, '79-2007 Rickenbacker Model 4003 Basses, mid-'60s Gibson SG Specials, Fender Telecaster Basses, late-1940s and 1950s Gibson SJ Southern Jumbo, Gibson LG-3 guitars, Vox Mark VI XII guitars, Travis Bean guitars and basses, Martin 0-18 and 0-28 guitars, Gibson EH Series amplifiers, to mention a few. Look for your favorite axe in *The Guide*, you might be surprised.

And of course *The Guide* isn't just about basses and guitars. It also lists banjos, mandolins, steels, lap steels, amplifiers, ukuleles, and effects pedals. It's all here, and we've done the research so you don't have to! So, sit back and enjoy finding your favorite models in *The Official Vintage Guitar Price Guide 2009*.

More Information

VintageGuitar.com, the official website of *Vintage Guitar* magazine, is updated continuously from the magazine's article archive. This ever-expanding resource includes interviews with noted guitarists, reviews of new gear and recordings, and historical information on many of the brands and models covered in this book. Of course, you can read more on classic guitars and your favorite players each month in *Vintage Guitar*.

If a model is missing from *The Guide*, or if you'd like something clarified, please drop a line to gil@vguitar.com. If you are a builder and would like to be included, would like to amend your info, or have information on your favorite brand, drop a line to al@vguitar.com.

Acknowledgments

The Official Vintage Guitar Price Guide is a massive undertaking that requires the talents of many people. We use many sources to determine the values, but the vintage instrument dealers who give their time and expertise to provide market information play an important role. Many provide info on brands and models, and they are acknowledged on page XXXIII.

Randy Klimpert provided the information and photos in the ukulele section. Many of the brand histories used in this edition are based on the work of longtime *VG* columnist Michael Wright. Robert Hartman, author of *The Larson's Creations*, provided most of the biographical information on the various brands built by the Larson Brothers. Stan Werbin of Elderly Instruments, along with his photographer, Dave Matchette provided many of the photos in the banjo section. Thanks go out to all of them.

Several people at *VG* played an important role, as well. Doug Yellow Bird designs the cover and lays out the inside pages. Jeanine Shea assists with proofreading and, with James Jiskra, compiles the ads and dealer directory. Ward Meeker helps with the photos and editing. Wanda Huether entered much of the data. We thank all of them for their usual fine work.

We always welcome suggestions, criticisms, and ideas to improve future editions of *The Guide*. Contact us at Vintage Guitar, Inc., PO Box 7301, Bismarck, ND 58507, or by e-mail to gil@vguitar.com or al@vguitar.com.

Thank you,

Alan Greenwood and Gil Hembree

Builder Updates and Corrections

If you produce instruments for sale and would like to be included in the next *VG Price Guide*, send your information to al@vguitar.com. Include info on the types of instruments you build, model names and prices, yearly production, the year you started, where you are located and a short bio about yourself.

If you spot errors in the information about brands and models in this guide, or have information on a brand you'd like to see included, please contact us at the above email address. Your help is appreciated.

Guitars

A Fuller Sound Steel String

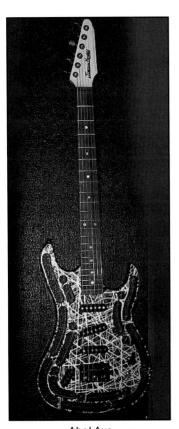

Abel Axe

MODEL		EXC. COND.	
YEAR	FEATURES	LOW	HIGH

A Fuller Sound

1998-present. Professional and premium grade, custom nylon and steel-string flat-tops built by Luthier Warren Fuller in Oakland, California.

Abel

1994-present. Custom aircraft-grade aluminum body, wood neck, guitars built by twins Jim and Jeff Abel in Evanston, Wyoming. They offered the Abel Axe from '94-'96 and 2000-'01, and still do custom orders. They also made the Rogue Aluminator in the late '90s.

Axe

1994-1996. Offset double-cut aluminum body with dozens of holes in the body, wood neck, various colors by annodizing the aluminum body. Abel Axe logo on the headstock.

1994-1996	Non-trem or Trem	$1,000	$1,250

Abilene

Budget and intermediate grade, production, acoustic and electric guitars imported by Samick.

Abyss

1997-present. Luthier Kevin Pederson builds his premium grade, production/custom, hollowbody and solidbody guitars in Forest City, Iowa.

Acme

1960s. Imported inexpensive copy electric guitar models for the student market.

Acoustic

Ca. 1965-ca. 1987, present. Mainly known for solidstate amps, the Acoustic Control Corp. of Los Angeles, California, did offer guitars and basses from around '69 to late '74. The brand was revived by Samick a few years ago on a line of amps.

Black Widow

1969-1970, 1972-1974. Both versions featured a unique black equal double-cut body with German carve, 2 pickups, a zero fret, and a protective spider design pad on back. The early version (called the AC500 Black Widow) had 22 frets, an ebonite 'board, and pickups with 1 row of adjustable polepieces. The later version was 24 frets, a rosewood 'board, and humbuckers with 2 rows of adjustable pole pieces (some '72s have the older style pickup). The jack and 4 control knobs were configured differently on the 2 versions, Acoustic outsourced the production of the guitars, possibly to Japan, but final 200 or so guitars produced by Semie Moseley. The AC700 Black Widow 12-string was also available for '69-'70.

1969-1970		$900	$1,100
1972-1974		$850	$1,050

Agile

1985-present. Budget grade, production, acoustic and electric guitars imported by Rondo Music of Union, New Jersey. They also offer mandolins.

MODEL		EXC. COND.	
YEAR	FEATURES	LOW	HIGH

Aims

Ca. 1974-ca. 1976. Aims instruments, distributed by Randall Instruments in the mid-'70s, were copies of classic American guitar and bass models. Randall also offered a line of Aims amps during the same time.

Airline

Ca. 1958-1968, 2004-present. Airline originally was a brand used by Montgomery Ward on acoustic, electric archtop and solidbody guitars and basses, amplifiers, steels, and possibly banjos and mandolins. Instruments manufactured by Kay, Harmony and Valco. In '04, the brand was revived on a line of imported intermediate grade, production, reissues from Eastwood guitars (see that listing for new info).

Acoustic Archtop (Lower-End)

1950s		$150	$175
1960s		$150	$175

Acoustic Archtop (Higher-End)

1950s		$575	$700
1960s		$575	$700

Acoustic Res-O-Glas Resonator

Res-o-glas, coverplate with M-shaped holes, asymmetrical peghead.

1964		$750	$900

Amp-In-Case Model

1960s. Double-cut, single pickup, short scale guitar with amplifier built into the case, Airline on grille.

1960s		$450	$550

Electric Hollowbody

1950s	Kay Barney		
	Kessel Artist copy	$650	$800
1960s	ES-175 copy	$500	$600
1960s	Harmony H-54		
	Rocket II copy	$450	$550
1960s	Harmony H-75 copy	$500	$600
1960s	Harmony H-76 Rocket III, 3 pu	$600	$725

Electric Res-O-Glas

Res-o-glas is a form of fiberglass. The bodies and sometimes the necks were made of this material.

1960s	Jack White's Red Jetson style	$1,600	$2,000
1960s	JB Hutto, red	$1,700	$2,125
1960s	Other style, 1 & 2 pu	$800	$1,000

Electric Res-O-Glas Resonator

Res-o-glas is a form of fiberglass. These models have resonator cones in the body.

1960s		$825	$1,000

Electric Solidbody (Standard Lower-End)

1960s		$325	$400

Electric Solidbody (Deluxe Higher-End)

Appointments may include multiple pickups, block inlays, additional logos, more binding.

1950s		$725	$900
1960s		$575	$700

MODEL YEAR	FEATURES	EXC. COND. LOW	HIGH
Flat-Top (Higher-End)			
1960s	14"-15" body	$325	$400
Flat-Top (Lower-End)			
1960s	13" body	$100	$125

Alamo

1947-1982. Founded by Charles Eilenberg, Milton Fink, and Southern Music, San Antonio, Texas, and distributed by Bruno & Sons. Alamo started out making radios, phonographs, and instrument cases. In '49 they added amplifiers and lap steels. From '60 to '70, the company produced beginner-grade solidbody and hollow-core body electric Spanish guitars. The amps were all-tube until the '70s. Except for a few Valco-made examples, all instruments were built in San Antonio.

Electric Hollowbody

1960-1970		$275	$325

Electric Solidbody

1960-1970		$275	$325

Alamo Guitars

1999-2008. The Alamo brand was revived for a line of handcrafted, professional grade, production/custom, guitars by Alamo Music Products, which also offers Robin and Metropolitan brand guitars and Rio Grande pickups.

Tonemonger

1999-2008. Ash or African Fakimba offset double cut solidbody, 3 single coils, tremolo.

1999-2008		$900	$1,100

Alan Carruth

1970-present. Professional and premium grade, production/custom, classical and archtop guitars built by luthier Alan Carruth in Newport, New Hampshire. He also builds violins, harps and dulcimers. He started out building dulcimers and added guitars in '74.

Albanus

Late 1950s-1973. Luthier Carl Albanus Johnson built around 100 high quality archtop guitars in Chicago, Illinois. He died in '73. He also built violins.

Alberico, Fabrizio

1998-present. Luthier Fabrizio Alberico builds his premium grade, custom, flat-top and classical guitars in Cheltenham, Ontario.

Alden

1960s. Alden department store private branded by Chicago builders such as Harmony.

H-45 Stratotone

1960s. Alden's version of the H45 Stratotone Mars model, single plain cover pickup.

1960s		$375	$450

Alembic

1969-present. Premium and presentation grade, production/custom, guitars, baritones, and 12-strings built in Santa Rosa, California. They also build basses. Established in San Francisco by Ron and Susan Wickersham, Alembic started out as a studio working with the Grateful Dead and other bands on a variety of sound gear. By '70 they were building custom basses, later adding guitars and cabinets. By '73, standardized models were being offered.

California Special

1988-present. Double-cut neck-thru solidbody, six-on-a-side tuners, various colors.

1988-2006		$1,800	$2,100

Orion

1990-present. Offset double-cut glued neck solidbody, various colors.

1990-2006		$1,700	$1,900

Series I

Early-1970s-present. Neck-thru, double-cut solidbody, bookmatched koa, black walnut core, 3 pickups, optional body styles available, natural.

1970-1980s 12-string		$3,200	$4,000
1970-1980s 6-string		$2,900	$3,200

Alfieri Guitars

1990-present. Luthier Don Alfieri builds his premium and presentation grade, custom/production, acoustic and classical guitars in Long Island, New York.

Alhambra

1930s. The Alhambra brand was most likely used by a music studio (or distributor) on instruments made by others, including Regal-built resonator instruments.

Allen Guitars

1982-present. Premium grade, production resonators, steel-string flat-tops, and mandolins built by Luthier Randy Allen, Colfax, California.

Alleva-Coppolo

1995-present. Professional and premium grade, custom/production, solidbody electric guitars built by luthier Jimmy Coppolo in Dallas, Texas, for '95-'97, and since in New York City. He also builds basses.

Aloha

1935-1960s. Private branded by Aloha Publishing and Musical Instruments Company, Chicago, Illinois. Made by others. There was also the Aloha Manufacturing Company of Honolulu which made musical instruments from around 1911 to the late '20s.

Alosa

1947-1958. Luthier Alois Sandner built these acoustic archtop guitars in Germany.

Airline Super III Res-O-Glas

Alamo Tonemonger

Alternative Guitar and Amplifier Company Smiling Bull

Alvarez RD20 BK

Alpha

1970s. One of the brand names of guitars built in the Egmond plant in Holland.

Alray

1967. Electrics and acoustics built by the Holman-Woodell guitar factory in Neodesha, Kansas, who also marketed similar models under the Holman brand.

Alternative Guitar and Amplifier Company

2006-present. Intermediate grade, custom/production, solidbody electric guitars made in Piru, California, by luthiers Mal Stich and Sal Gonzales and imported from Korea under the Alternative Guitar and Amplifier Company, and Mal n' Sal brands. They also build basses and have future plans for amps.

Alvarez

1965-present. Intermediate and professional grade, production, acoustic guitars imported by St. Louis Music. They also offer lap steels, banjos and mandolins. Initially high-quality handmade guitars Yairi made by K. (Kazuo) Yairi were exclusively distributed, followed by lower-priced Alvarez line. In '90 the Westone brand used on electric guitars and basses was replaced with the Alvarez name; these Alvarez electrics were offered until '02. Many Alvarez electric models designed by luthier Dana Sutcliffe; several models designed by Dan Armstrong.

Classic I, II, III
1994-1999. Designs based on classic solidbody American models.

MODEL YEAR	FEATURES	EXC. COND. LOW	HIGH
1994-1999		$225	$275

Flat-Top (Lower-End)
1966-present. Beginner-grade instruments, solid or laminate tops, laminate back and sides, little or no extra appointments. Some are acoustic/electric.

1970s		$75	$90
1980s		$80	$100
1990s		$90	$110

Flat-Top (Mid-Level)
1966-present. Solid tops, laminated back and sides, lower appointments such as bound 'boards and headstocks, nickel hardware and pearl inlay.

1970s		$150	$180
1980s		$150	$180
1990s		$150	$180

Flat-Top (Mid-to-Higher-End)
1966-present. Solid spruce tops, solid mahogany or rosewood backs, laminated mahogany or rosewood sides, may have scalloped bracing, mid-level appointments like abalone headstock inlay, soundhole rosettes and herringbone body binding.

1970s		$375	$450
1980s		$375	$450
1990s		$375	$450

Flat-Top (Higher-End)
1966-present. Solid rosewood and/or mahogany backs and sides, solid spruce tops, may have dovetail neck joint, highest appointments like abalone inlay and real maple binding.

MODEL YEAR	FEATURES	EXC. COND. LOW	HIGH
1980s		$500	$625
1990s		$500	$625

Fusion Series (With Piezo and EQ)
1981-present. Single-cut, acoustic/electrics with EQ and transducer/piezo pickups. Earlier models had spruce tops with spruce or mahogany back and sides. More recent models have maple tops, backs and sides.

1981-2000		$325	$400

Alvarez Yairi

1966-present. Alvarez Yairi guitars are handcrafted and imported by St. Louis Music.

Flat-Top (Mid-Level)
Solid top of cedar or spruce, depending on model, mid-level appointments.

1970s		$350	$425
1980s		$375	$450
1990s		$425	$525
2000s		$425	$525

Flat-Top (Higher-End)
Solid top of cedar or spruce, depending on model, higher-end appointments.

1970s		$650	$800
1980s		$675	$825
1990s		$750	$925
2000s		$800	$1,000

Flat-Top 9-String (DY-58)
Flat-top acoustic with 9 strings (doubles on the 3 high strings).

1989	Natural	$725	$900

Fusion Series (With Piezo and EQ)
1998-2002. Piezo bridge with volume and tone controls, higher-end appointments.

1998-2002		$725	$900

Alvarez, Juan

1952-present. Professional and premium grade, production/custom, classical and flamenco guitars made in Madrid, Spain, originally by luthier Juan Alvarez Gil and now by son Juan Miguel Alvarez.

American Acoustech

1993-2001. Production steel string flat-tops made by Tom Lockwood (former Guild plant manager) and Dave Stutzman (of Stutzman's Guitar Center) as ESVL Inc. in Rochester, New York.

American Archtop Guitars

1995-present. Premium and presentation grade, custom 6- and 7-string archtops by luthier Dale Unger, in Stroudsburg, Pennsylvania.

MODEL YEAR	FEATURES	EXC. COND. LOW	HIGH

American Conservatory (Lyon & Healy)

Late-1800s-early-1900s. Guitars and mandolins built by Chicago's Lyon & Healy and sold mainly through various catalog retailers. Mid-level instruments above the quality of Lyon & Healy's Lakeside brand, and generally under their Washburn brand.

Style G Series Harp Guitar

Early-1900s. Two 6-string necks with standard tuners, 1 neck fretless, rosewood back and sides, spruce top, fancy rope colored wood inlay around soundhole, sides and down the back center seam.

1917	Natural	$3,100	$3,800

Tenor Guitar

1920s. Four-string tenor, pear-shaped body.

1920s		$625	$725

American Showster

1986-2004. Established by Bill Meeker and David Haines, Bayville, New Jersey, building guitars shaped like classic car tailfins or motorcycle gas tanks. The Custom Series was made in the U.S.A., while the Standard Series (introduced in '97) was made in Czechoslovakia. They also made a bass.

AS-57 Classic (Original '57)

1987-2004. Body styled like a '57 Chevy tail fin, basswood body, bolt-on neck, 1 humbucker or 3 single-coil pickups, various colors.

1987-2004		$2,500	$3,100

Ampeg

1949-present. Founded in '49 by Everett Hull as the Ampeg Bassamp Company in New York and has built amplifiers throughout its history. In '62 the company added instruments with the introduction of their Baby Bass and from '63 to '65, they carried a line of guitars and basses built by Burns of London and imported from England. In '66 the company introduced its own line of basses. In '67, Ampeg was acquired by Unimusic, Inc. From '69-'71 contracted with Dan Armstrong to produce lucite "see-through" guitars and basses with replaceable slide-in pickup design. In '71 the company merged with Magnavox. Beginning around '72 until '75, Ampeg imported the Stud Series copy guitars from Japan. Ampeg shut down production in the spring of '80. MTI bought the company and started importing amps. In '86 St. Louis Music purchased the company, which is now part of LOUD Technologies. In '97 Ampeg introduced new and reissue American-made guitar and bass models. They discontinued the guitar line in '01, but offered the Dan Armstrong guitar again starting in '05.

AMG1

1999-2001. Dan Amstrong guitar features, but with mahogany body with quilted maple top, 2 P-90-style or humbucker-style pickups.

1999-2001	Humbuckers, gold hardware	$875	$1,000
1999-2001	Kent Armstrong pickups	$400	$500
1999-2001	P-90s, standard hardware	$400	$500

Dan Armstrong Lucite Guitar

1969-1971. Clear plexiglas solidbody, with interchangable pickups, Dan Armstrong reports that around 9,000 guitars were produced, introduced in '69, but primary production was in '70-'71, reissued in '98.

1969-1971		$3,800	$4,200
1969-1971	Opaque black, few made	$5,000	$6,000

Dan Armstrong Plexi Guitar

1998-2001, 2006-present. Reissue of Lucite guitar, produced by pickup designer Kent Armstrong (son of Dan Armstrong), offered in smoked (ADAG2) or clear (ADAG1). Latest version is Japanese-made ADA6.

1998-2005	Clear or smoke	$900	$1,100

Heavy Stud (GE-150/GEH-150)

1973-1975. Import from Japan, single-cut body, weight added for sustain, single-coils or humbuckers (GEH).

1973-1975		$450	$550

Sonic Six (By Burns)

1964-1965. Solidbody, 2 pickups, tremolo, cherry finish, same as the Burns Nu-Sonic guitar.

1964-1965		$525	$650

Stud (GE-100/GET-100)

1973-1975. Import from Japan, double-cut, inexpensive materials, weight added for sustain, GET-100 included tremolo.

1973-1975		$450	$525

Super Stud (GE-500)

1973-1975. Double-cut, weight added for sustain, top-of-the-line in Stud Series.

1973-1975		$475	$575

Thinline (By Burns)

1963-1964. Semi-hollowbody, 2 f-holes, 2 pickups, double-cut, tremolo, import by Burns of London, same as the Burns TR2 guitar.

1963-1964		$700	$850

Wild Dog (By Burns)

1963-1964. Solidbody, 3 pickups, shorter scale, tremolo, sunburst finish, import by Burns of London, same as the Burns Split Sound.

1963-1964		$800	$1,000

Wild Dog De Luxe (By Burns)

1963-1964. Solidbody, 3 pickups, bound neck, tremolo, sunburst finish, import by Burns of London, same as the Burns Split Sonic guitar.

1963-1964		$850	$1,050

Andersen Stringed Instruments

1978-present. Luthier Steve Andersen builds premium and presentation grade, production/custom flat-tops and archtops in Seattle, Washington. He also builds mandolins.

1973 Ampeg Heavy Stud

1973 Ampeg Super Stud

Applegate SJ

Aria Pro II RS-750

Andreas

1995-present. Luthier Andreas Pichler builds his aluminum-necked, solidbody guitars and basses in Dollach, Austria.

Andy Powers Musical Instrument Co.

1996-present. Luthier Andy Powers, builds his premium and presentation grade, custom, archtop, Flat top, and, semi-hollow electric guitars in Oceanside, California. He also builds ukes and mandolins.

Angelica

Ca. 1967-1972. Entry-level guitars and basses imported from Japan.

Electric Solidbodies

Model Year	Features	Low	High
1967-1972		$200	$225

Angus

1976-present. Professional and premium grade, custom-made steel and nylon string flat-tops built by Mark Angus in Laguna Beach, California.

Antares

1980s-1990s. Korean-made budget electric and acoustic guitars imported by Vega Music International of Brea, California.

Double Neck 6/4

1990s. Cherry finish double-cut.

Model Year	Features	Low	High
1990s		$400	$500

Solidbody

Model Year	Features	Low	High
1980-1990s	Various models	$150	$175

Antique Acoustics

1970s-present. Luthier Rudolph Blazer builds production/custom flat-tops, 12 strings, and archtops in Tubingen, Germany.

Antonio Hermosa

2006-present. Imported budget grade, production, acoustic and acoustic/electric classical guitars from The Music Link.

Antonio Lorca

Intermediate and professional grade, production, classical guitars made in Valencia, Spain.

Apollo

Ca. 1967-1972. Entry-level guitars imported by St. Louis Music. They also offered basses and effects.

Electric

1967-1972. Japanese imports.

Model Year	Features	Low	High
1967-1972	Advanced model, 4 pickups	$375	$450
1967-1972	Standard model, less features	$150	$175

Applause

1976-present. Budget and intermediate grade, production, acoustic and acoustic/electric guitars. They also offer basses, mandolins and ukes. Kaman Music's entry-level Ovation-styled brand. The instruments were made in the U.S. until around '82, when production was moved to Korea. On the U.S.-made guitars, the back of the neck was molded Urelite, with a cast aluminum neck combining an I-beam neck reinforcement, fingerboard, and frets in one unit. The Korean models have traditional wood necks.

AA Models

1976-1990s. Acoustic, laminate top, plastic or composition body. Specs and features can vary on AA Models.

Model Year	Features	Low	High
1976-1981	U.S.-made	$150	$175
1980s	Import	$100	$125
1990s	Import	$100	$125

AE Models

1976-1990s. Acoustic/electric, laminate top, plastic or composition body. Specs and features can vary on AE Models.

Model Year	Features	Low	High
1976-1981	U.S.-made	$200	$225
1980s	Import	$175	$200
1990s	Import	$175	$200

Applegate

2001-present. Premium grade, production/custom, acoustic and classical guitars built by luthier Brian Applegate in Minneapolis, Minnesota.

APS Custom

2005-present. Luthier Andy Speake builds his production/custom, professional and premium grade, solidbody guitars in Victoria, British Columbia, Canada.

Arbor

1983-present. Budget and intermediate grade, production, classical, acoustic, and solid and semi-hollow body electric guitars imported by Musicorp (MBT). They also offer basses.

Acoustic

Model Year	Features	Low	High
1980s		$100	$125
1990s		$100	$125

Electric

Model Year	Features	Low	High
1980s		$150	$175
1990s		$125	$150

Arch Kraft

1933-1934. Full-size acoustic archtop and flat-top guitars. Budget brand produced by the Kay Musical Instrument Company and sold through various distributors.

Acoustic (Archtop or Flat-top)

Model Year	Features	Low	High
1933-1934		$300	$375

Aria Diamond

1960s. Brand name used by Aria in the '60s.

MODEL YEAR	FEATURES	EXC. COND. LOW	HIGH

Electric
1960s. Various models and appointments in the '60s.

| 1960s | | $400 | $500 |

Aria/Aria Pro II
1960-present. Budget, intermediate nad professional grade, production, electric, acoustic, acoustic/electric, and classical guitars. They also make basses, mandolins, and banjos. Aria was established in Japan in '53 and started production of instruments in '60 using the Arai, Aria, Aria Diamond, and Diamond brands. The brand was renamed Aria Pro II in '75. Aria Pro II was used mainly on electric guitars, with Aria used on others. Over the years, they have produced acoustics, banjos, mandolins, electrics, basses, amplifiers, and effects. Around '87 production of cheaper models moved to Korea, reserving Japanese manufacturing for more expensive models. Around '95 some models were made in U.S., though most contemporary guitars sold in U.S. are Korean. In '01, the Pro II part of the name was dropped altogether.

Early Arias don't have serial numbers or pot codes. Serial numbers began to be used in the mid '70s. At least for Aria guitars made by Matsumoku, the serial number contains the year of manufacture in the first one or two digits (Y##### or YY####). Thus, a guitar from 1979 might begin with 79####. One from 1981 might begin with 1#####. The scheme becomes less sure after 1987. Some Korean- made guitars use a serial number with year and week indicated in the first four digits (YYWW####). Thus 9628#### would be from the 28th week of 1996. However, this is not the case on all guitars, and some have serial numbers which are not date-coded.

Models have been consolidated by sector unless specifically noted.

Acoustic Solid Wood Top
1960s-present. Steel string models, various appointments, generally mid-level imports.

| 1970-2006 | | $275 | $300 |

Acoustic Veneer Wood Top
1960s-present. Steel string models, various appointments, generally entry-level imports.

| 1970-2006 | | $150 | $175 |

Classical Solid Wood Top
1960s-present. Various models, various appointments, generally mid-level imports.

| 1970-2006 | | $225 | $275 |

Classical Veneer Wood Top
1960s-present. Various models, various appointments, generally entry-level imports.

| 1970-2006 | | $125 | $150 |

Fullerton Series
1995-2000. Various models with different appointments and configurations based on the classic offset double-cut solidbody.

| 1995-2000 | | $225 | $275 |

Herb Ellis (PE-175/FA-DLX)
1978-1987 (Model PE-175) and 1988-1993 (Model FA-DLX). Archtop hollowbody, ebony 'board, 2 humbuckers.

| 1977-1987 | | $450 | $550 |

Solidbody
1960s-present. Various models, various appointments, generally mid-level imports.

| 1980-2005 | | $325 | $400 |

Titan Artist TA Series
1967-present. Double cut, semi-hollow bodies, 2 pickups, various models.

| 1980-2005 | | $475 | $575 |

ARK - New Era Guitars
2006-present. Luthier A. R. Klassen builds his professional and premium grade, production/custom, reproductions of vintage Larson Brothers instruments in Chesterton, Indiana.

Armstrong, Rob
1971-present. Custom steel- and nylon-string flat-tops, 12 strings, and parlor guitars made in Coventry, England by luthier Rob Armstrong. He also builds mandolins and basses.

Arpeggio Korina
1995-present. Professional, premium and presentation grade, production/custom, korina wood solidbody guitars built by luthier Ron Kayfield in Pennsylvania.

Art & Lutherie
Budget and intermediate grade, production, steel- and nylon-string acoustic and acoustic/electric guitars. Founded by luthier Robert Godin, who also has the Norman, Godin, Seagull, and Patrick & Simon brands of instruments.

Artesano
Intermediate and professional grade, production, classical guitars built in Valencia, Spain, and distributed by Juan Orozco. Orozco also made higher-end classical Orozco Models 8, 10 and 15.

Artinger Custom Guitars
1997-present. Luthier Matt Artinger builds his professional and premium grade, production/custom, hollow, semi-hollow, and chambered solidbody guitars in Emmaus, Pennsylvania. He also builds basses.

Artur Lang
1949-1975. German luthier Artur Lang is best known for his archtops, but did build classicals early on. His was a small shop and much of his output was custom ordered. The instruments were mostly unbranded, but some have L.A. engraved on the headstock.

Aria Pro II PE-450

Artinger Chambered Solidbody

Atkin OM

Baker RF

MODEL		EXC. COND.	
YEAR	FEATURES	LOW	HIGH

Asama

1970s-1980s. Some models of this Japanese line of solidbody guitars featured built-in effects. They also offered basses, effects, drum machines and other music products.

Ashborn

1848-1864. James Ashborn, of Wolcottville, Connecticut, operated one of the largest guitar making factories of the mid-1800s. Models were small parlor-sized instruments with ladder bracing and gut strings. Most of these guitars will need repair. Often of more interest as historical artifacts or museum pieces versus guitar collections.

Model 2

1848-1864. Flat-top, plain appointments, no position markers on the neck, identified by Model number.

1855	Fully repaired	$600	$750

Model 5

1848-1864. Flat-top, higher appointments.

1855	Fully repaired	$1,350	$1,650

Asher

1982-present. Luthier Bill Asher builds his professional grade, production/custom, solidbody electric guitars in Venice, California. He also builds lap steels.

Astro

1963-1964. The Astro AS-51 was a 1 pickup kit guitar sold by Rickenbacker. German luthier Arthur Strohmer also built archtops bearing this name.

Asturias

Professional and premium grade, production, classical guitars built on Kyushu island, in Japan.

Atkin Guitars

1993-present. Luthier Alister Atkin builds his production/custom steel and nylon string flat-tops in Canterbury, England. He also builds mandolins.

Atlas

Archtop guitars, and possibly other types, built in East Germany.

Atomic

2006-present. Production/custom, intermediate and professional grade, solidbody electric guitars built by luthiers Tim Mulqueeny and Harry Howard in Peoria, Arizona. They also build basses.

Audiovox

Ca. 1935-ca. 1950. Paul Tutmarc's Audiovox Manufacturing, of Seattle, Washington, was a pioneer in electric lap steels, basses, guitars and amps. Tutmarc was a talented Hawaiian steel guitarist and ran a music school.

MODEL		EXC. COND.	
YEAR	FEATURES	LOW	HIGH

Austin

1999-present. Budget and intermediate grade, production, acoustic, acoustic/electric, resonator, and electric guitars imported by St. Louis Music. They also offer basses, mandolins and banjos.

Acoustic Flat-Top

1999-2007	Various models	$125	$150

Solidbody Electric

1999-2007	Various models	$150	$175

Austin Hatchet

Mid-1970s-mid-1980s. Trademark of distributor Targ and Dinner, Chicago, Illinois.

Hatchet

1981. Travel guitar.

1981		$350	$425

Solidbody Electric

1970s-1980s. Various classic designs.

1980s		$200	$250

Avalon

1920s. Instruments built by the Oscar Schmidt Co. and possibly others. Most likely a brand made for a distributor.

Avante

1997-2007. Intermediate grade, production, imported sharp cutaway acoustic baritone guitars designed by Joe Veillette and Michael Tobias and offered by MusicYo. Originally higher priced instruments offered by Alvarez, there was the baritone, a 6-string and a bass.

AV-2 Baritone

1997-2007. Baritone guitar tuned B to B, solid spruce cutaway top, mahogany sides and back.

1997-2007		$300	$350

Avanti

1964-late 1960s. Italian-made guitar brand imported by European Crafts, of Los Angeles. Earlier models were plastic covered; later ones had paint finishes.

Electric Solidbody

1960s. Solidbody, 3 single-coils, dot markers.

1960s		$200	$225

Avar

Late-1960s. Import copy models from Japan, not unlike Teisco, for the U.S. student market.

Solidbody Electric

1969		$275	$325

Aztec

1970s. Japanese-made copy guitars imported into Germany by Hopf.

Babicz

2004-present. Started by luthier Jeff Babicz and Jeff Carano, who worked together at Steinberger, the company offers intermediate, professional, and premium grade, production/custom, acoustic and acoustic/electric guitars made in Poughkeepsie, New York, and overseas.

The *Vintage Guitar Price Guide* shows low to high values for items in all-original excellent condition, and, where applicable, with original case or cover.

MODEL YEAR	FEATURES	EXC. COND. LOW	HIGH

Bacon & Day

Established in 1921 by David Day and Paul Bacon, primarily known for fine quality tenor and plectrum banjos in the '20s and '30s. Purchased by Gretsch ca. '40.

Belmont
1950s. Gretsch era, 2 DeArmond pickups, natural.

1950s		$1,450	$1,800

Flat-Top
1930s-1940s. Large B&D headstock logo, higher-end appointments.

1930s	Includes 'rare' models	$2,700	$3,300
1940s		$2,400	$3,000

Ramona Archtop
1938-1940. Sunburst.

1938-1940		$1,150	$1,400

Senorita Archtop
1940. Lower-end, sunburst, mahogany back and sides.

1940		$1,150	$1,400

Style B Guitar Banjo (Bacon)
1920s. 6-string guitar neck on a banjo-resonator body.

1920s	Fancy appointments	$2,800	$3,500
1920s	Plain appointments	$1,600	$2,000

Sultana I
1930s. Large 18 1/4" acoustic archtop, Sultana engraved on tailpiece, block markers, bound top and back, sunburst.

1938		$3,400	$3,900

Baker U.S.A.

1997-present. Professional and premium grade, production/custom, solidbody electric guitars. Established by master builder Gene Baker after working at the Custom Shops of Gibson and Fender, Baker produced solid- and hollowbody guitars in Santa Maria, California. They also built basses. Baker also produced the Mean Gene brand of guitars from '88-'90. In September '03, the company was liquidated and the Baker U.S.A. name was sold to Ed Roman. Gene Baker is no longer involved with Baker U.S.A.

B1/B1 Chambered/B1 Hollow
1997-present. Double-cut mahogany body, maple top, with a wide variety of options including chambered and hollowbody construction, set-neck. Gene Baker era USA-made until 2003, Ed Roman era import after.

1997-2003	USA	$2,250	$2,800
2004-2005	Import	$1,000	$1,250

BJ/BJ Hollow
1997-2003. Double-cut mahogany body, P-90-type pickups, several options available, set-neck.

1997-2003		$1,800	$2,200

BNT
1997-2000. Mahogany solidbody, maple top, neck-thru body, with various finishes and options.

1997-2000		$2,000	$2,500

Baldwin

1965-1970. Founded in 1862, in Cincinnati, when reed organ and violin teacher Dwight Hamilton Baldwin opened a music store that eventually became one of the largest piano retailers in the Midwest. By 1965, the Baldwin Piano and Organ company was ready to buy into the guitar market but was outbid by CBS for Fender. Baldwin did procure Burns of London in September '65, and sold the guitars in the U.S. under the Baldwin name. Baldwin purchased Gretsch in '67. English production of Baldwin guitars ends in '70, after which Baldwin concentrates on the Gretsch brand.

Baby Bison (Model 560 by Mid-1966)
1966-1970. Double-cut solidbody, V headstock, 2 pickups, shorter scale, tremolo, black, red or white finishes.

1965-1966		$750	$850
1966-1970	Model 560	$650	$750

Bison (Model 511 by Mid-1966)
1965-1970. Double-cut solidbody, scroll headstock, 3 pickups, tremolo, black or white finishes.

1965-1966		$1,100	$1,300
1966-1970	Model 511	$1,000	$1,200

Double Six (Model 525 by Mid-1966)
1965-1970. Offset double-cut solidbody, 12 strings, 3 pickups, green or red sunburst.

1965-1966		$1,350	$1,450
1966-1970	Model 525	$1,250	$1,350

G.B. 65
1965-1966. Baldwin's first acoustic/electric, single-cut D-style flat-top, dual bar pickups.

1965-1966		$750	$875

G.B. 66 De Luxe
1965-1967. Same as Standard with added density control on treble horn, golden sunburst.

1965-1967		$850	$950

G.B. 66 Standard
1965-1966. Thinline Electric archtop, dual Ultra-Sonic pickups, offset cutaways, red sunburst.

1965-1966		$800	$900

Jazz Split Sound/Split Sound (Model 503 Mid-1966)
1965-1970. Offset double-cut solidbody, scroll headstock, 3 pickups, tremolo, red sunburst or solid colors.

1965-1966		$750	$875
1966-1970	Model 503	$750	$875

Marvin (Model 524 by Mid-1966)
1965-1970. Offset double-cut solidbody, scroll headstock, 3 pickups, tremolo, white or brown finish.

1965-1966		$1,300	$1,500
1966-1970	Model 524	$1,200	$1,300

Model 706
1967-1970. Double-cut semi-hollowbody, scroll headstock, 2 pickups, 2 f-holes, no vibrato, red or golden sunburst.

1967-1970		$750	$900

Model 706 V
1967-1970. Model 706 with vibrato.

1967-1970		$775	$950

Babicz Identity Spider

Baldwin Virginian

GUITARS

Ballurio Artist

Bashkin Placenia

MODEL YEAR	FEATURES	EXC. COND. LOW	HIGH

Model 712 R Electric XII
1967-1970. Double-cut semi-hollow body with regular neck, red or gold sunburst.

1967-1970		$625	$750

Model 712 T Electric XII
1967-1970. Model 712 with thin neck, red or gold sunburst.

1967-1970		$625	$750

Model 801 CP Electric Classical
1968-1970. Grand concert-sized classical with transducer based pickup system, natural pumpkin finish.

1968-1970		$750	$850

Nu-Sonic
1965-1966. Solidbody electric student model, 6-on-a-side tuners, black or cherry finish.

1965-1966		$475	$575

Vibraslim (Model 548 by Late-1966)
1965-1970. Double-cut semi-hollowbody, 2 pickups, tremolo, 2 f-holes, red or golden sunburst. Notable spec changes with Model 548 in '66.

1965-1966		$900	$1,100
1966-1970	Model 548	$800	$900

Virginian (Model 550 by Mid-1966)
1965-1970. Single-cut flat-top, 2 pickups (1 on each side of soundhole), scroll headstock, tremolo, natural.

1965-1966		$825	$1,000
1966-1970	Model 550	$775	$950

Ballurio
2000-present. Luthier Keith Ballurio builds his intermediate, professional, and premium grade, production/custom, solidbody and chambered guitars in Manassas, Virginia.

Baltimore
2007-present. Budget grade, production, solidbody electric guitars imported by The Music Link.

Baranik Guitars
1995-present. Premium grade, production/custom steel-string flat-tops made in Tempe, Arizona by luthier Mike Baranik.

Barclay
1960s. Thinline acoustic/electric archtops, solidbody electric guitars and basses imported from Japan. Generally shorter scale beginner guitars.

Electric Solidbody
1960s. Various models and colors.

1960s		$180	$225

Barcus-Berry
1964-present. Founded by John Berry and Les Barcus introducing the first piezo crystal transducer. Martin guitar/Barcus-Berry products were offered in the mid-'80s. They also offered a line of amps from around '76 to ca. '80.

Barrington
1988-1991. Imports offered by Barrington Guitar Werks, of Barrington, Illinois. Models included solidbody guitars and basses, archtop electrics, and acoustic flat-tops. Barrington Music Products is still in the music biz, offering LA saxophones and other products.

Acoustic/Electric
1988-1991. Acoustic/electric, flat-top single-cut with typical round soundhole, opaque white.

1988-1991		$150	$185

Solidbody
1988-ca 1991. Barrington's line of pointy headstock, double-cut solidbodies, black.

1988-1991		$125	$150

Bartell of California
1964-1969. Founded by Paul Barth (Magnatone) and Ted Peckles. Mosrite-inspired designs.

Electric 12
1967. Mosrite-style body.

1967		$1,150	$1,350

Bartolini
1960s. European-made (likely Italian) guitars made for the Bartolini Accordion Company. Similar to Gemelli guitars, so most likely from same manufacturer. Originally plastic covered, they switched to paint finishes by the mid '60s.

Solidbody

1960s		$500	$625

Bashkin Guitars
1998-present. Luthier Michael Bashkin builds his premium grade, custom, steel-string acoustics in Fort Collins, Colorado.

Basone Guitars
1999-present. Luthier Chris Basaraba builds his custom, professional grade, solid and hollowbody electric guitars in Vancouver, British Columbia, Canada. He also builds basses.

Bauer, George
1894-1911. Luthier George Bauer built guitars, mandolins, and banjos in Philadelphia, Pennsylvania. He also built instruments with Samuel S. Stewart (S.S. Stewart).

Baxendale & Baxendale
1975-present. Luthiers Scott Baxendale (father) and John Baxendale (son) build their professional and premium grade, custom, steel-string acoustic and solidbody electric guitars in Denver, Colorado. They were previously located in Tennessee and Texas.

Bay State
1865-ca.1910. Bay State was a trademark for Boston's John C. Haynes Co.

MODEL YEAR	FEATURES	EXC. COND. LOW	HIGH

Parlor Guitar
1900s. Small parlor size, mahogany body with salt & pepper binding.

1965-1910		$900	$1,100

B.C. Rich

Ca. 1966/67-present. Budget, intermediate, and premium grade, production/custom, import and U.S.-made, electric and acoustic guitars. They also offer basses. Founded by Bernardo Chavez Rico in Los Angeles, California. As a boy he worked for his guitar-maker father Bernardo Mason Rico (Valencian Guitar Shop, Casa Rico, Bernardo's Guitar Shop), building first koa ukes and later, guitars, steel guitars and Martin 12-string conversions. He started using the BC Rich name ca. '66-'67 and made about 300 acoustics until '68, when first solidbody electric made using a Fender neck.

Rich's early models were based on Gibson and Fender designs. First production instruments were in '69 with 10 fancy Gibson EB-3 bass and 10 matching Les Paul copies, all carved out of single block of mahogany. Early guitars with Gibson humbuckers, then Guild humbuckers, and, from '74-'86, DiMarzio humbuckers. Around 150 BC Rich Eagles were imported from Japan in '76. Ca. '76 or '77 some bolt-neck guitars with parts made by Wayne Charvel were offered. Acoustic production ended in '82 (acoustics were again offered in '95).

For '83-'86 the BC Rich N.J. Series (N.J. Nagoya, Japan) was built by Masan Tarada. U.S. Production Series (U.S.-assembled Korean kits) in '84. From '86 on, the N.J. Series was made by Cort in Korea. Korean Rave and Platinum series begin around '86. In '87, Rich agrees to let Class Axe of ....New Jersey market the Korean Rave, Platinum and N.J. Series. Class Axe (with Neal Moser) introduces Virgin in '87 and in '88 Rave and Platinum names are licensed to Class Axe. In '89, Rico licensed the BC Rich name to Class Axe. Both imported and American-made BC Riches are offered during Class Axe management. In 2000, BC Rich became a division of Hanser Holdings.

During '90-'91, Rico begins making his upscale Mason Bernard guitars (approx. 225 made). In '94, Rico resumes making BC Rich guitars in California. He died in 1999.

First 340-360 U.S.-built guitars were numbered sequentially beginning in '72. Beginning in '74, serial numbers change to YYZZZ pattern (year plus consecutive production). As production increased in the late-'70s, the year number began getting ahead of itself. By '80 it was 2 years ahead; by '81 as much as 4 years ahead. No serial number codes on imports.

Assassin
1986-1998. Double-cut body, 2 humbuckers, maple thru-neck dot markers, various colors.

1986-1989	1st Rico era	$775	$825
1989-1993	Class Axe era, neck-thru	$725	$775

1994-1998	2nd Rico era		
	USA, neck-thru	$725	$775
2000s	Includes QX & PX	$300	$375

B-28 Acoustic
Ca.1967-1982. Acoustic flat-top, hand-built, solid spruce top, rosewood back and sides, herringbone trim, pearl R headstock logo.

1970-1982		$750	$925

B-30 Acoustic
Ca.1967-1982. Acoustic flat-top.

1960s		$800	$950

B-38 Acoustic
Ca.1967-1982. Acoustic flat-top, cocobolo back and sides, herringbone trim.

1960s		$850	$1,000

B-41 Acoustic
1970s. Brazilian rosewood.

1970s		$1,600	$2,000

B-45 Acoustic
Hand-built, D-style rosewood body.

1970s		$2,300	$2,800

Beast (U.S.A. Custom Shop)
1999-present. Exaggerated four point cutaway body, flamed or quilted top.

1999-2006		$1,200	$1,500

Bich (U.S.A. Assembly)
1978-1998. Four-point sleek body, came in Standard top or Supreme with highly figured maple body and active EQ.

1978-1979	Supreme	$1,800	$2,200
1980-1989	Standard	$1,500	$1,900
1980-1989	Supreme	$1,600	$2,000
1989-1993	Class Axe era	$1,000	$1,200
1994-1998	2nd Rico era		
	USA, bolt-on	$900	$1,000
1994-1998	2nd Rico era		
	USA, neck-thru	$1,150	$1,300

Bich 10-String
1978-present. Doubles on 4 low strings.

1978-1982		$3,600	$4,500

Black Hole
1988. Bolt neck, rosewood 'board, integrated pickup design, Floyd Rose.

1988		$225	$275

Body Art Collection
2003-2006. Imports with different exotic graphics on different models issued each month from January '03 to March '04, 25th Anniversary model available into '06, headstock logo states Body Art Collection.

2003	Boris Beast	$250	$300
2003	Skull Pile	$275	$325
2003	Space Face Ironbird	$275	$325
2003	Spiro Light	$250	$300
2003	Torchy ASM	$250	$300
2004	40 Lashes Mockingbird	$275	$325
2004	Umethar Jr. V	$250	$300

Bronze Series
2001-2007. Made in China. Includes 2 models; Mockingbird and Warlock.

2001-2007		$100	$125

1900 Bay State Parlor Guitar

B.C. Rich Umethar Jr. V

B.C. Rich Mockingbird

1979 B.C. Rich Mockingbird

MODEL YEAR	FEATURES	EXC. COND. LOW	HIGH
Doubleneck Models			

Doublenecks were sporadically made and specs (and values) may vary.

MODEL YEAR	FEATURES	LOW	HIGH
1980s	Bich	$3,000	$3,900
1980s	Eagle	$3,500	$4,300
1980s	Iron Bird		
	custom order	$2,000	$2,800
1980s	Mockingbird	$3,500	$4,300
1980s	Seagull		
	custom order	$4,000	$5,300
1990s	6-12 double-cut	$900	$1,000

Eagle (U.S.A)

1977-1996, 2000-2004. Curved double-cut solidbody, neck-thru. Models included are the Standard, Deluxe, Special and Supreme which is a highly figured, higher end model.

1977-1979	Standard	$2,400	$2,900
1977-1979	Supreme	$2,900	$3,500
1977-1982	Special	$2,100	$2,600
1980-1982	Standard, 3-on-a-side tuners	$1,500	$1,800
1980-1982	Supreme	$2,200	$2,700
2000-2004	Supreme	$2,100	$2,600

Elvira

2001. Elvira (the witch) photo on black Warlock body, came with Casecore coffin case.

2001		$475	$525

Exclusive EM1

1996-2004. Offset double-cut, bound top, 2 humbuckers.

1996-2004		$175	$200

Gunslinger

1987-1999. Inverted headstock, 1 (Gunslinger I) or 2 (Gunslinger II) humbuckers, recessed cutout behind Floyd Rose allows player to pull notes up 2 full steps.

1987-1989	Standard finish	$650	$750
1987-1989	Various graphic designs	$700	$800
1989-1993	Class Axe era	$600	$650
1994-1999	2nd Rico era, bolt-on	$600	$650
1994-1999	2nd Rico era, neck-thru	$600	$650

Ironbird

1983-2004. Pointy body and headstock.

1983-1984		$1,000	$1,250

Kerry King Wartribe1 Warlock

2004-present. Tribal Fire finish, 2 pickups.

2004-2006		$225	$250

Mockingbird

1976-present. Includes Standard and Supreme (fancier features) models, bolt or neck-thru.

1976	Earlier short horn	$2,800	$3,500
1976-1978	Supreme, short horn	$2,750	$3,400
1977-1978	Earlier short horn	$2,750	$3,400
1979-1983	Later long horn	$2,400	$3,000
1979-1983	Supreme	$2,550	$3,200
1984-1989	Last of 1st Rico era	$2,000	$2,500

MODEL YEAR	FEATURES	EXC. COND. LOW	HIGH
1994-1999	2nd Rico era, bolt-on	$1,500	$1,800
1994-1999	2nd Rico era, Supreme	$1,800	$2,100

Mockingbird Ice Acrylic

2004-2006. See-thru acrylic body.

2004-2006		$250	$300

Nighthawk

1978-ca.1982. Eagle-shaped body with bolt neck.

1978-1982		$725	$800

NJ Series

1983-1985. Earlier models made in Japan. Made in Korea '86 forward. Models include Assassin, Beast, Bich, Ironbird, Mockingbird, Outlaw, ST III, Virgin, Warlock.

1983-1985		$300	$825

NJ Series/NJC Series

1986-present. Made in Korea, earlier models were made in Japan. Models include Assassin, Beast, Bich, Ironbird, Mockingbird, Outlaw, ST III, Virgin, Warlock. C for Classic added in '06.

1986-2006		$325	$400

Phoenix

1977-ca.1982. Mockingbird-shaped with bolt neck.

1977-1982		$725	$800

Platinum Series

1986-2006. Lower-priced import versions including Assassin, Beast, Bich, Ironbird, ST, Warlock.

1986-2006		$300	$375

Rave Series

1986-ca. 1990. Korean-made down-market versions of popular models.

1986-1990		$125	$150

Seagull/Seagull II/Seagull Jr.

1972-1977. Solidbody, neck-thru, 2 humbuckers, Seagull ('72-'75) is single-cut, II and Jr. ('75-'77) double-cut.

1972-1975	Initial design	$2,400	$3,000
1972-1975	Supreme	$2,800	$3,500
1975-1977	II & Jr.	$2,400	$3,000

Stealth I Series

1983-1989. Includes Standard (maple body, diamond inlays) and Series II (mahogany body, dot inlays), 2 pickups.

1983-1989	Series II	$1,725	$2,150
1983-1989	Standard	$1,725	$2,150

ST-III (U.S.A.)

1987-1998. Double-cut solidbody, hum/single/single or 2 humbucker pickups, Kahler tremolo.

1987-1989	Bolt-on	$675	$800
1987-1989	Neck-thru	$800	$900
1989-1993	Class Axe era	$650	$800
1994-1998	New Rico era, neck-thru & bolt-on	$650	$800

The Mag

2000. U.S. Handcrafted Series Mockingbird Acoustic Supreme, solid spruce top, quilt maple back and sides, pickup with preamp and EQ optional, dark sunburst.

2000		$875	$950

The *Vintage Guitar Price Guide* shows low to high values for items in all-original excellent condition, and, where applicable, with original case or cover.

MODEL YEAR	FEATURES	EXC. COND. LOW	HIGH

Warlock (U.S.A.)
1981-present. Four-point sleek body style with widow headstock.

1981-1989	Standard	$1,200	$1,400
1981-1989	Supreme	$1,550	$1,900
1994-1999	2nd Ric era, bolt-on	$950	$1,000
1994-1999	2nd Rico era, neck-thru	$1,150	$1,400

Warlock Ice Acrylic
2004-2006. See-thru acrylic body.

2004-2006		$250	$300

Wave
1983. U.S.-made, very limited production based upon the Wave bass.

1983		$2,100	$2,500

Bear Creek Guitars
1995-present. Luthier Bill Hardin worked for OMI Dobro and Santa Cruz Guitar before introducing his own line of professional and premium grade, custom-made Weissenborn-style guitars, made in Kula, Hawaii. He also builds ukes.

Beardsell Guitars
1996-present. Production/custom flat-tops, classical and electric solidbody guitars built by luthier Allan Beardsell in Toronto, Ontario.

Behringer
1989-present. The German professional audio products company added budget, production, solidbody guitars in '03, sold in amp/guitar packages. They also offer effects and amps.

Beltona
1990-present. Production/custom metal body resonator guitars made in New Zealand by Steve Evans and Bill Johnson. Beltona was originally located in England. They also build ukes.

Beltone
1920s-1930s. Acoustic and resonator guitars made by others for New York City distributor Perlberg & Halpin. Martin did make a small number of instruments for Beltone, but most were student-grade models most likely made by one of the big Chicago builders. They also made mandolins.

Resonator Copy
1930s-1940s. Resonator copy but without a real resonator, rather just an aluminum plate on a wooden top, body mahogany plywood.

1938		$350	$425

Beltone (Import)
1950s-1960s. Japan's Teisco made a variety of brands for others, including the Beltone line of guitars, basses and amps. Carvin sold some of these models in the late 1960s. Italy's Welson guitars also marketed marble and glitter-finished guitars in the U.S. under this brand.

Benedetto
1968-present. Premium and presentation grade, production/custom archtop and chambered solid-body guitars, built by luthier Robert Benedetto. He has also built a few violins and solidbodies. He was located in East Stroudsburg, Pennsylvania, up to '99; in Riverview, Florida, for '00-'06; and in Savanah, Georgia, since '07. He is especially known for refining the 7-string guitar. From '99 to '06 he licensed the names of his standard models to Fender (see Benedetto FMIC); during that period, Benedetto only made special order instruments. In '06, Howard Paul joined Benedetto as President of the company to begin manufacturing a broader line of more affordable professional instruments.

Benny
1990s. Electric semi-hollow, 14 1/2" body, cutaway, chambered Sitka spruce top, natural.

1990s		$3,500	$4,500

Benny Deluxe
1990s. Electric semi-hollow, chambered spruce top, abalone inlays, deluxe version of the Benny, sunburst.

1990s		$5,500	$6,900

Cremona
1988-1991. Acoustic/electric archtop, single-cut, 17" body, natural.

1988-1991		$18,000	$22,000

Fratello
1988-1999. Acoustic archtop, single-cut, 17" body, blond or sunburst.

1988-1989		$11,000	$11,800
1990s		$11,000	$11,800
2000s		$11,000	$11,800

La Venezia
1990s. Acoustic archtop, single-cut, 17" body, sunburst.

1990s		$13,000	$15,000

Limelite Custom
1990s. Single-cut, neck pickup, select aged wood, blond.

1990s		$23,000	$27,000

Manhattan
1989-1999. Archtop with 16" body, neck pickup, blond.

1989-1999		$11,000	$12,000

Manhattan Custom
1990s. Carved 17" body, blond.

1990s		$13,000	$14,000

Benedetto (FMIC)
1999-2006. Premium and presentation, production/custom, acoustic and electric archtops. From '99 to '06, Bob Benedetto had an agreement with Fender (FMIC) to build Benedetto guitars under his guidance and supervision. The guitars were originally built in the FMIC Guild Custom Shop in Nashville, and later in Fender's Corona, California, facility.

BC Rich Seagull

Beardsell 4G

1952 Bigsby Grady Martin Doubleneck

Blade Texas Vintage

MODEL		EXC. COND.	
YEAR	FEATURES	LOW	HIGH

Artist/Artist Award
2000-2003. Full body, rounded cutaway, single neck pickup, natural or sunburst.

| 2000-2003 | | $4,000 | $4,500 |

Fratello
2000-2006. Single-cut archtop, block inlays, mini-humbucker.

| 2000-2006 | | $7,000 | $8,700 |

Manhattan
2000-2006. 17" single-cut archtop (3" deep), suspended mini-humbucking pickup.

| 2000-2006 | | $10,000 | $10,500 |

Benedict
1988-present. Founded by Roger Benedict. Professional and premium grade, production/custom, solid and semi-hollow body guitars built by luthier Bill Hager in Cedar, Minnesota. He also builds basses.

Bennett Music
Mid-1970s. Bennett Music Labs, originally founded in the mid-'70s by Bruce Bennett who studied under Terry Atkins (re: Tacoma Guitars) from '82-'85, then worked for Gibson's Steinburger Tobias Division from '92-'94, then moved on to design the first Warrior line of instruments with co-partners J.D. Lewis, M.S. Terrel, and W. Fix.

Bently
ca.1985-1998. Student and intermediate grade copy style acoustic and electric guitars imported by St. Louis Music Supply. Includes the Series 10 electrics and the Songwriter acoustics (which have a double reversed B crown logo on the headstock). St. Louis Music replaced the Bently line with the Austin brand.

Berkowitz Guitars
1995-present. Luthier David D. Berkowitz builds his premium grade, custom/production, steel string and baritone guitars in Washington, DC.

Bernie Rico Jr. Guitars
Professional and premium grade, production/custom, solidbody electrics built by luther Bernie Rico, Jr., the son of BC Rich founder, in Hesperia, California. He also makes basses.

Bertoncini Stringed Instruments
1995-present. Luthier Dave Bertoncini builds his premium grade, custom, flat-top guitars in Olympia, Washington. He has also built solidbody electrics, archtops, mandolins and banjos.

Beyond The Trees
1976-present. Luthier Fred Carlson offers a variety of innovative designs for his professional and presentation grade, production/custom 6- and 12-string flat-tops in Santa Cruz, California. He

also produces the Sympitar (a 6-string with added sympathetic strings) and the Dreadnautilus (a unique shaped headless acoustic).

Bigsby
1946-present. Pedal steel guitars, hollow-chambered electric Spanish guitars, electric mandolins, doublenecks, replacement necks on acoustic guitars, hand vibratos, all handmade by Paul Arthur Bigsby, machinist and motorcycle enthusiast (designer of '30s Crocker motorcycles), in Downey, California. Initially built for special orders.

Bigsby was a pioneer in developing pedal steels. He designed a hand vibrato for Merle Travis. In '48, his neck-through hollow electrics (with Merle Travis) influenced Leo Fender, and Bigsby employed young Semie Moseley. In '56, he designed the Magnatone Mark series guitars and 1 Hawaiian lap steel. He built less than 50 Spanish guitars, 6 mandolins, 125 to 150 pedal steels and 12 or so neck replacements. SN was stamped on the end of fingerboard: MMDDYY. In '65, the company was sold to Gibson president Ted McCarty who moved the tremolo/vibrato work to Kalamazoo. Bigsby died in '68. Fred Gretsch purchased the Bigsby company from Ted McCarty in '99. A solidbody guitar and a pedal steel based upon the original Paul Bigsby designs were introduced January, 2002. These were modeled on the 1963 Bigsby catalog, but look very similar to the typical Bigsby solidbodys made since the early 1950s. Early Bigsby guitars command high value on the collectible market.

Solidbody
Late-1940s-early-1950s, 2002. Solidbody, natural. Reissue offered in '02

| 1948-1952 | | $32,000 | $39,000 |
| 2002 | Reissue | $3,000 | $3,500 |

Bil Mitchell Guitars
1979-present. Luthier Bil Mitchell builds his professional and premium grade, production/custom, flat-top and archtop guitars originally in Wall, New Jersey, and since '02 in Riegelsville, Pennsylvania.

Birdsong Guitars
2001-present. Luthiers Scott Beckwith and Jamie Hornbuckle build their professional grade, production/custom, solidbody guitars in Wimberley, Texas. They also build basses.

Bischoff Guitars
1975-present. Professional and premium-grade, custom-made flat-tops built by luthier Gordy Bischoff in Eau Claire, Wisconsin.

Bishline
1985-present. Luthier Robert Bishline, of Tulsa, Oklahoma, mainly builds banjos, but did build flat-tops and resonators in the past, and still does occasionally.

MODEL YEAR	FEATURES	EXC. COND. LOW	HIGH

Black Jack

1960s. Violin-body hollowbody electric guitars and basses, possibly others. Imported from Japan by unidentified distributor. Manufacturers unknown, but some may be Arai.

Blackshear, Tom

1958-present. Premium and presentation grade, production, classical and flamenco guitars made by luthier Tom Blackshear in San Antonio, Texas.

Blade

1987-present. Intermediate and professional grade, production, solidbody guitars from luthier Gary Levinson and his Levinson Music Products Ltd. located in Switzerland. He also builds basses.

California Custom
1994-present. California Standard with maple top and high-end appointments.

1994-2007		$850	$1,000

California Deluxe/Deluxe
1994-1995. Standard with mahogany body and maple top.

1994-1995		$650	$800

California Hybrid
1998-1999. Standard with piezo bridge pickup.

1998-1999		$550	$675

California Standard
1994-2007. Offset double-cut, swamp ash body, bolt neck, 5-way switch.

1994-2007		$400	$475

R 3
1988-1993. Offset double-cut maple solidbody, bolt maple neck, 3 single-coils or single/single/humbucker.

1988-1993		$650	$800

R 4
1988-1993. R 3 with ash body and see-thru color finishes.

1988-1992		$750	$900

Texas Series
2003-present. Includes Standard (3 single-coils) and Deluxe (gold hardware, single/single/hum pickups).

2003-2005	Deluxe	$500	$625
2003-2005	Special	$475	$575
2003-2005	Standard	$450	$550

Blanchard Guitars

1994-present. Luthier Mark Blanchard builds premium grade, custom steel-string and classical guitars originally in Mammoth Lakes, California, and since May '03, in northwest Montana.

Blount

1985-present. Professional and premium grade, production/custom, acoustic flat-top guitars built by Luthier Kenneth H. Blount Jr. in Sebring, Florida.

Blue Star

1984-present. Luthier Bruce Herron builds his production/custom guitars in Fennville, Michigan. He also builds mandolins, lap steels, dulcimers and ukes.

Bluebird

1920s-1930s. Private brand with Bluebird painted on headstock, built by the Oscar Schmidt Co. and possibly others. Most likely made for distributor.

13" Flat-Top

1930s		$175	$200

Blueridge

Early 1980s-present. Intermediate and professional grade, production, solid-top acoustic guitars distributed by Saga. In '00, the product line was redesigned with the input of luthier Greg Rich (Rich and Taylor guitars).

Bluesouth

1991-present. Custom electric guitars built by luthier Ronnie Knight in Muscle Shoals, Alabama. He also built basses.

Boaz Elkayam Guitars

1985-present. Presentation grade, custom steel, nylon, and flamenco guitars made by luthier Boaz Elkayam in Chatsworth, California.

Bohmann

1878-ca. 1926. Acoustic flat-top guitars, harp guitars, mandolins, banjos, violins made in Chicago Illinois, by Joseph Bohmann (born 1848, in Czechoslovakia). Bohmann's American Musical Industry founded 1878. Guitar body widths are 12", 13", 14", 15". He had 13 grades of guitars by 1900 (Standard, Concert, Grand Concert sizes). Early American use of plywood. Some painted wood finishes. Special amber-oil varnishes. Tuner bushings. Early ovalled fingerboards. Patented tuner plates and bridge design. Steel engraved label inside. Probably succeeded by son Joseph Frederick Bohmann.

Ca. 1896 12" body faux rosewood, 13", 14" and 15" body faux rosewood birch, 12", 13", 14" and 15" body sunburst maple, 12", 13", 14" and 15" body rosewood. By 1900 Styles 0, 1, 2 and 3 Standard, Concert and Grand Concert maple, Styles 1, 2, 3, 4, 5, 6, 7, 8, 9, 10, 11 and 12 in Standard, Concert, and Grand Concert rosewood.

14 3/4" Flat-Top
Solid spruce top, veneered Brazilian rosewood back and sides, wood marquetry around top and soundhole, natural. Each Bohmann should be valued on a case-by-case basis.

1896-1900	Brazilian	$1,400	$1,600
1896-1900	Other woods	$500	$600

Harp Guitar

1896-1899	All styles	$3,600	$4,500

Blanchard Bristlecone

Blueridge BR-40CE

*Boulder Creek
Solitaire Series R3N*

Bourgeois Country Boy

Bolin

1978-present. Professional and premium grade, production/custom, solidbody guitars built by luthier John Bolin in Boise, Idaho. Bolin is well-known for his custom work. His Cobra guitars are promoted and distributed by Sanderson Sales and Marketing as part of the Icons of America Series.

NS

1996-present. Slot-headstock, bolt-on neck, single-cut solidbody, Seymour Duncan passive pickups or EMG active, from '96 to the fall of 2001 custom-built serial numbers to 0050 then from the fall of '01 to the present production model build starting with SN 0051.

MODEL YEAR	FEATURES	EXC. COND. LOW	HIGH
1996-2001	Custom-built	$1,400	$1,700
2001-2003	Standard production	$725	$900

Bolt

1988-1991. Founded by luthier Wayne Bolt and Jim Dala Pallu in Schnecksville, Pennsylvania, Bolt's first work was CNC machined OEM necks and bodies made for Kramer and BC Rich. In '90, they started building solidbody Bolt guitars, many with airbrushed graphics. Only about 100 to 125 were built, around 40 with graphics.

Bond

1984-1985. Andrew Bond made around 1,400 Electraglide guitars in Scotland. Logo says 'Bond Guitars, London.'

ElectraGlide

1984-1985. Black carbon graphite 1-piece body and neck, double-cut, 3 single-coils (2 humbuckers were also supposedly available), digital LED controls that required a separate transformer.

1984-1985		$1,100	$1,350

Boulder Creek

2007-present. Intermediate and professional grade, production, imported dreadnought, classical, and 12-string guitars distributed by Morgan Hill Music of Morgan Hill, California. They also offer basses.

Bourgeois

1993-1999, 2000-present. Luthier Dana Bourgeois builds his professional and premium grade, production/custom, acoustic and archtop guitars in Lewiston, Maine. Bourgeois co-founded Schoenberg guitars and built Schoenberg models from '86-'90. Bourgeois' 20th Anniversary model was issued in '97. Bourgeois Guitars, per se, went of business at the end of '99. Patrick Theimer created Pantheon Guitars, which included 7 luthiers (including Bourgeois) working in an old 1840s textile mill in Lewiston, Maine and Bourgeois models continue to be made as part of the Pantheon organization.

Country Boy

1990s-present. Pre-war D-style model designed for Ricky Skaggs with Sitka spruce top, select mahogany back and sides, Bourgeois script logo headstock inlay, individually labeled with a Ricky Skaggs label, natural.

1990-2000s		$1,800	$2,200

Country Boy Deluxe

2000-present. Country Boy with Adirondack spruce top.

2000-2005		$2,000	$2,500

D-20th Anniversary

1997. 20 made, bearclaw spruce top, rosewood back and sides, mother-of-pearl 'board, ornate abalone floral pattern inlay, abalone rosette and border, natural.

1997		$3,100	$3,300

JOM

1990s-present. Jumbo Orchestra Model flat-top, 15 5/8". Model includes one with cedar top, mahogany back and sides, and one with spruce top, Brazilian rosewood back and sides.

1990s	Brazilian rosewood	$3,200	$3,600
1990s	Indian rosewood	$1,900	$2,100
1990s	Mahogany	$1,150	$1,400

JR-A

1990s. Artisan Series, 15 5/8", spruce top, rosewood back and sides.

1990s		$1,000	$1,300

Martin Simpson

1997-2003. Grand auditorium with unusual cutaway that removes one-half of the upper treble bout, Englemann spruce top, Indian rosewood back and sides, natural.

1997-2003		$2,200	$2,400

OM Soloist

1990s-present. Full-sized, soft cutaway flat-top, Adirondack spruce top, figured Brick Red Brazilian rosewood back and sides, natural.

1990s		$4,600	$4,900

Slope D

1993-present. D-size, 16", spruce top, mahogany back and sides.

1993-2004		$2,100	$2,300

Vintage D

2000s. Adirondack spruce (Eastern red spruce) top, optional rosewood back and sides.

2000s	Brazilian rosewood	$3,900	$4,100
2000s	Indian rosewood	$2,000	$2,200

Vintage OM

2005. Madagascar rosewood and Italian spruce top.

2005		$2,700	$3,000

Bown Guitars

1981-present. Luthier Ralph Bown builds custom steel-string, nylon-string, baritone, and harp guitars in Walmgate, England.

MODEL YEAR	FEATURES	EXC. COND. LOW	HIGH

Bozo

1964-present. Bozo (pronounced Bo-zho) Padunovac learned instrument building in his Yugoslavian homeland and arrived in the United States in '59. In '64 he opened his own shop and has built a variety of high-end, handmade, acoustic instruments, many being one-of-a-kind. He has built around 570 guitars over the years. There were several thousand Japanese-made (K. Yairi shop) Bell Western models bearing his name made from '79-'80; most of these were sold in Europe. He currently builds premium and presentation grade, production/custom guitars in East Englewood, Florida.

Acoustic 12-String
1970-1980s. Indian rosewood.

1970-1980s		$1,600	$2,000

Classical

1969	Limited production	$2,000	$2,500

Cutaway 12-String
1977-1998. Often old world Balkan ornamentation, generally Sitka spruce top, Indian rosewood back and sides, widow-style headstock, ornamentation can vary (standard or elaborate).

1977	Standard	$1,600	$2,000
1993	Elaborate	$3,200	$4,000
1998	Elaborate custom	$4,000	$5,000

Bradford

Mid-1960s. Brand name used by the W.T. Grant Company, one of the old Five & Ten style retail stores similar to F.W. Woolworth and Kresge. Many of these guitars and basses were made in Japan by Guyatone.

Acoustic Flat-Top
1960s. Various colors.

1960s		$150	$175

Electric Solidbody
1960s. Various colors.

1960s		$175	$200

Bradley

1970s. Budget Japanese copy models imported by Veneman's Music Emporium

Brawley Basses

Headquartered in Temecula, California, and designed by Keith Brawley, offering solidbody guitars made in Korea. They also made basses.

Breedlove

1990-present. Founded by Larry Breedlove and Steve Henderson. Intermediate, professional, premium, and presentation grade, production/custom, steel and nylon string flat-top and chambered electric guitars built in Tumalo, Oregon and imported. They also build mandolins. Several available custom options may add to the values listed here.

AD20/SM (Atlas Series)
2004-present. Imported solid spruce top, solid mahogany back and sides, pinless bridge.

2004-2006		$275	$300

C1 (C10)
1990-present. Shallow concert-sized flat-top, non-cut, solid spruce top, mahogany back and sides, natural.

1990-2006		$1,600	$1,800

C2 (C22)
1990-2004. Highly figured walnut body with sitka spruce top, large sloping cutaway.

1990-2004		$2,100	$2,200

C5/Northwest
1995-present. Grand concert with large soft cutaway, sitka spruce top, figured myrtlewood body.

2000-2007		$2,200	$2,300

C15/R
1990-2004. Concert-size C1 with soft rounded cutaway, and optional cedar top and rosewood back and sides, gold tuners.

1990-2004		$1,900	$2,100

C-20
1990s-2004. Concert series, mahgoany back and sides, sitka spruce top.

2000-2004		$1,900	$2,100

C25 Custom
1990s-present. Custom koa body, sitka spruce top.

2000-2007		$2,500	$2,700

CM
1990s-present. Unusual double-cut style, walnut body and top.

1990s		$3,600	$3,800

D20
2002-present. Sitka spruce top, mahogany body, non cut.

2002-2006		$2,000	$2,100

D25/R
2002-present. Cutaway, sitka spruce top, Indian rosewood back and sides.

2002-2007		$2,100	$2,250

Ed Gerhard
1997-present. Shallow jumbo, soft cut, Indian rosewood body.

1997-2006	Custom	$2,300	$2,600
1997-2006	Signature	$2,100	$2,500

J Series (Jumbo)
1990s-present. Spruce top, myrtlewood body.

2000-2007	J25	$2,500	$2,600

Myrtlewood Limited 01
1990s-2003. Acoustic/electric, D-size, solid spruce top, solid myrtlewood back and sides.

1995-2003		$1,700	$1,900

N25E
2000-2004. Acoustic/electric version of N25.

2000-2004		$1,700	$1,800

N25R
2000-2004. Classical, Western red cedar top, solid Indian rosewood back and sides.

2000-2004		$1,800	$2,000

Bourgeois OM Soloist

Breedlove CM Classic

Breedlove Ed Gerhard

Briggs Avatar

MODEL YEAR	FEATURES	EXC. COND. LOW	HIGH

RD20 X/R
1999. Indian rosewood back and sides, sitka spruce top, winged bridge, abalone soundhole rosette.

1999		$1,700	$1,800

SC Series

1990-2004	SC20, Brazilian	$2,500	$2,900
1990-2007	SC20, other	$1,600	$1,800
1990-2007	SC25, other	$1,800	$2,000
1999	SC20 -Z Custom (Zircote)	$1,700	$1,900

SJ20-12 W
1995-2004. 12-string, walnut (W) back and sides.

1995-2004		$1,500	$1,700

SJ25 Series

2003	Woods vary	$1,200	$1,400

Brentwood
1970s. Student models built by Kay for store or jobber.

K-100
1970s. 13" student flat-top, K-100 label inside back, K logo on 'guard.

1970s		$40	$50

Brian Moore
1992-present. Founded by Patrick Cummings, Brian Moore and Kevin Kalagher in Brewster, New York; they introduced their first guitars in '94. Initially expensive custom shop guitars with carbon-resin bodies with highly figured wood tops; later went to all wood bodies cut on CNC machines. The intermediate and professional grade, production, iGuitar/i2000series was introduced in 2000 and made in Korea, but set up in the U.S. Currently the premium grade, production/custom, Custom Shop Series guitars are handcrafted in La Grange, New York. They also build basses and electric mandolins.

C-45
1999-2001. Solidbody, mahogany body, bolt neck, 2 P-90-type pickups, natural satin.

1999-2001		$1,100	$1,350

C-55/C-55P
1997-2004. Solidbody, burl maple body, bolt neck, currently produced as a limited edition. C-55P indicates Piezo option.

1997-2004		$1,100	$1,350

C-90/C-90P
1996-present. Solidbody, figured maple top, mahogany body, bolt neck, hum-single-hum pickups, red sunburst. C-90P has Piezo option.

1996-2004	USA	$1,325	$1,625

DC-1/DC-1P
1997-present. Quilted maple top, 2 humbuckers, single-cut, gold hardware. DC-1P has Piezo option.

1997-1998		$1,800	$2,500

iGuitar Series

2000-2006	2.13	$900	$1,000
2000-2006	2P	$700	$825
2000-2006	8.13 & 81.13	$450	$550
2000-2006	i1	$575	$700

MODEL YEAR	FEATURES	EXC. COND. LOW	HIGH

MC1
1994-present. High-end model, quilted maple top, various pickup options including piezo and midi, gold hardware, currently produced as a limited edition. Should be evaluated on a case-by-case basis.

1994-1999		$1,600	$2,000

Brian Stone Classical Guitars
Luthier Brian Stone builds his classical guitars in Corvallis, Oregon.

Briggs
1999-present. Luthier Jack Briggs builds his professional and premium grade, production/custom, chambered and solidbody guitars in Raleigh, North Carolina.

Broman
1930s. The Broman brand was most likely used by a music studio (or distributor) on instruments made by others, including Regal-built resonator instruments.

Bronson
1930s-1950s. George Bronson was a steel guitar instructor in the Detroit area and his instruments were made by other companies. They were mainly lap steels, but some other types were also offered.

Honolulu Master Hawaiian

1938		$4,600	$5,700

Student Hawaiian

1930s	13" flat-top	$225	$275

Brook Guitars
1993-present. Simon Smidmore and Andy Petherick build their production/custom Brook steel-string, nylon-strings, and archtops in Dartmoor, England.

Brown's Guitar Factory
1982-present. Mainly known for basses, luthier John Brown also builds professional and premium grade, production/custom, solidbody guitars in Inver Grove Heights, Minnesota.

Bruné, R. E.
1966-present. Luthier Richard Bruné builds his premium and presentation grade, custom, classical and flamenco guitars in Evanston, Illinois. He also offers his professional and premium grade Model 20 and Model 30, which are handmade in a leading guitar workshop in Japan. Bruné's Guitars with Guts column appears quarterly in Vintage Guitar magazine.

Bruno and Sons
1834-present. Established in 1834 by Charles Bruno, primarily as a distributor, Bruno and Sons marketed a variety of brands, including their own. Currently part of Kaman Music.

MODEL YEAR	FEATURES	EXC. COND. LOW	HIGH
Harp Guitar			
1924		$2,500	$3,100
Hollowbody Electric			
1960s-1970s. Various imported models.			
1960s		$375	$450
Parlor Guitar			
1880-1920. Various woods used on back and sides.			
1880-1920	Birch	$400	$500
1880-1920	Brazilian rosewood	$1,000	$1,200
1880-1920	Mahogany	$500	$625

Bunker

1961-present. Founded by guitarist Dave Bunker, who began building guitars with his father. He continued building custom guitars and basses while performing in Las Vegas in the '60s and developed a number of innovations. Around '92 Bunker began PBC Guitar Technology with John Pearse and Paul Chernay in Coopersburg, Pennsylvania, building instruments under the PBC brand and, from '94-'96, for Ibanez' USA Custom Series. PBC closed in '97 and Bunker moved back to Washington State to start Bunker Guitar Technology and resumed production of several Bunker models. In early 2002, Bunker Guitars became part of Maple Valley Tone Woods of Port Angeles, Washington. Currently Bunker offers intermediate, professional, and premium grade, production/custom, guitars and basses built in Port Angeles. Most early Bunker guitars were pretty much custom-made in low quantities.

Electric Solidbody or Archtop
1960-1990s. Various colors.

MODEL YEAR	FEATURES	LOW	HIGH
1960-1990s		$1,000	$1,250
2000-2007	Custom Shop	$1,500	$1,800

Burly Guitars

2007-present. Luthier Jeff Ayers builds his professional and premium grade, custom, solid and semi-hollowbody guitars in Land O' Lakes, Wisconsin. He plans on adding basses.

Burns

1960-1970, 1974-1983, 1992-present. Intermediate and professional grade, production, electric guitars built in England and Korea. They also build basses.

Jim Burns began building guitars in the late-'50s and established Burns London Ltd in '60. Baldwin Organ (see Baldwin listing) purchased the company in '65 and offered the instruments until '70. The Burns name was revived in '91 by Barry Gibson as Burns London, with Jim Burns' involvement, offering reproductions of some of the classic Burns models of the '60s. Jim Burns passed away in August '98.

Baby Bison
1965. Double-cut solidbody, scroll headstock, 2 pickups, shorter scale, tremolo.

1965		$900	$1,000

Bison
1964-1965, 2003-present. Double-cut solidbody, 3 pickups, tremolo, black or white, scroll-headstock, replaced flat headstock Black Bison. Has been reissued with both types of headstocks.

1964-1965		$1,300	$1,500
2003-2007	Reissue	$400	$425

Brian May Signature - Red Special
2001-2005. Replica of May's original 'Red Special' but with added whammy-bar, red finish. Korean-made.

2001-2005		$775	$950

Cobra
2004-present. Double-cut solid, 2 pickups.

2004-2005		$150	$175

Double Six
1964-1965, 2003-present. Solidbody 12-string, double-cut, 3 pickups, greenburst. Has been reissued.

1964-1965		$1,450	$1,550
2003-2007	Reissue	$325	$375

Flyte
1974-1977. Fighter jet-shaped solidbody, pointed headstock, 2 humbucking pickups, silver, has been reissued.

1974-1977		$750	$900

GB 66 Deluxe
1965. Like 66 Standard, but with bar pickups and add Density control.

1965		$925	$1,000

GB 66 Deluxe Standard
1965. Offset double-cut, f-holes, 2 Ultra-Sonic pickups.

1965		$875	$950

Jazz
1962-1965. Offset double-cut solid, shorter scale, 2 pickups.

1962-1965		$750	$875

Jazz Split Sound
1962-1965. Offset double-cut solid, 3 pickups, tremolo, red sunburst.

1962-1965		$825	$1,000

Marquee
2000-present. Offset double-cut solid, 3 pickups, scroll headstock

2000-2007		$225	$275

Marvin
1964-1965. Offset double-cut solidbody, scroll headstock, 3 pickups, tremolo, white.

1964-1965		$1,500	$1,700

Nu-Sonic
1964-1965. Solidbody, 2 pickups, tremolo, white or cherry, has been reissued.

1964-1965		$525	$650

Sonic
1960-1964. Double shallow cut solid, 2 pickups, cherry.

1962-1964		$500	$600

Split Sonic
1962-1964. Solidbody, 3 pickups, bound neck, tremolo, red sunburst.

1962-1964		$875	$1,050

Burns Bison

Burns Flyte

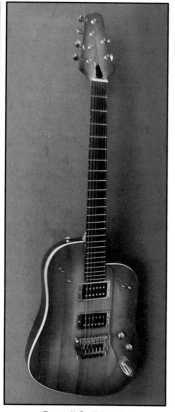

Burrell Solidbody

Campbell American Precix

MODEL YEAR	FEATURES	EXC. COND. LOW	HIGH

Steer
2000-present. Semi-hollowbody, sound-hole, 2 pickups, non-cut and single-cut versions.

2000-2007		$350	$400

TR-2
1963-1964. Semi-hollow, 2 pickups, red sunburst.

1963-1964		$975	$1,100

Vibraslim
1964-1965. Double-cut, f-holes, 2 pickups, red sunburst.

1964-1965		$1,000	$1,200

Virginian
1964-1965. Burns of London model, later offered as Baldwin Virginian in '65.

1964-1965		$900	$1,100

Vista Sonic
1962-1964. Offset double-cut solid, 3 pickups, red sunburst.

1962-1964		$775	$850

Burnside
1987-1988. Budget solidbody guitars imported by Guild.

Solidbody Electric/Blade
1987-1988. Solidbody, fat pointy headstock.

1987-1988		$275	$325

Burns-Weill
1959. Jim Burns and Henry Weill teamed up to produce three solidbody electric and three solidbody bass models under this English brand.

Burny
1980s-present. Solidbody electric guitars from Fernandes and built in Japan, Korea or China.

Burrell
1984-present. Luthier Leo Burrell builds his professional grade, production/custom, acoustic, semi-hollow, and solidbody guitars in Huntington, West Virginia. He also builds basses.

Burton Guitars
1980-present. Custom classical guitars built by luthier Cynthia Burton in Portland, Oregon.

Buscarino Guitars
1981-present. Luthier John Buscarino builds his premium and presentation grade, custom archtops and steel-string and nylon-string flat-tops in Franklin, North Carolina.

Solidbody Electric - Custom-Built
1981-1990s.

1981-1990s		$1,300	$1,500

Byers, Gregory
1984-present. Premium grade, custom classical and Flamenco guitars built by luthier Gregory Byers in Willits, California.

C. Fox
1997-2002. Luthier Charles Fox built his premium grade, production/custom flat-tops in Healdsburg, California. In '02 he closed C. Fox Guitars and move to Portland, Oregon to build Charles Fox Guitars.

C. P. Thornton Guitars
2004-present. Luthier Chuck Thornton builds his professional and premium grade, production/custom, semi-hollow electric guitars in Turner, Maine. From '85 to '96 he built basses and guitars under the C. P. Thornton Basses brand.

CA (Composite Acoustics)
1999-present. Professional grade, production, carbon fiber composite guitars built in Lafayette, Louisiana.

Califone
1966. Six and 12-string guitars and basses made by Murphy Music Industries (maker of the Murph guitars) for Rheem Califone-Roberts which manufactured tape recorders and related gear. Very few made.

Callaham
1989-present. Professional, production/custom, solidbody electric guitars built by luthier Bill Callaham in Winchester, Virginia. They also make tube amp heads.

Camelli
1960s. Line of solidbody electric guitars imported from Italy.

Solidbody Electric

1960s		$525	$650

Campbell American Guitars
2005-present. Luthier Dean Campbell builds his intermediate and professional grade, production/custom, solidbody guitars originally in Pawtucket, Rhode Island, and currently in Westwood, Massachusetts. From '02 to '05, he built guitars under the Greene & Campbell brand.

Campellone
1978-present. Luthier Mark Campellone builds his premium grade, custom archtops in Greenville, Rhode Island. He also made electrics and basses in the '70s and '80s, switching to archtops around '90.

Deluxe
1990-present. 16" to 18" archtop, middle of the company product line, blond or sunburst.

1990-1995		$4,000	$5,000

Special
1994-present. 16" to 18" archtop, top of the company product line, carved spruce top, carved flamed maple back, flamed maple sides, blond or sunburst.

1994-2003		$5,900	$6,400

MODEL YEAR	FEATURES	EXC. COND. LOW	HIGH

Standard
16" to 18" archtop, lower of the 3 model lines offered.

2000-2006		$3,000	$3,400

Canvas
2004-present. Budget and intermediate grade, production, solid and semi-hollow body guitars imported from China by American Sejung Corp. They also offer basses.

Carbonaro
1974-present. Luthier Robert Carbonaro builds his premium grade, production/custom, archtop and flat-top guitars in Santa Fe, New Mexico.

Carl Fischer
1920s. Most likely a brand made for a distributor. Instruments built by the Oscar Schmidt Co. and possibly others.

Carlos
ca.1976-late 1980s. Imported copies of classic American acoustics distributed by Coast Wholesale Music.

Model 240
1970s. D copy with mahogany (laminate?) back and sides, spruce top, natural.

1978		$225	$275

Model 275
1970s. D copy with rosewood (laminate?) sides and three-piece back, spruce top, natural.

1978		$275	$325

Carvin
1946-present. Intermediate and professional grade, production/custom, acoustic and electric guitars. They also offer basses and amps. Founded in Los Angeles by Hawaiian guitarist and recording artist Lowell C. Kiesel as the L.C. Kiesel Co. making pickups for guitars. Bakelite Kiesel-brand electric Hawaiian lap steels are introduced in early-'47. Small tube amps introduced ca. '47. By late-'49, the Carvin brand is introduced, combining parts of names of sons Carson and Gavin. Carvin acoustic and electric Spanish archtops are introduced in '54. Instruments are sold by mail-order only. The company relocated to Covina, California in '49 and to Escondido, California in '68. Two retail stores opened in Hollywood and Santa Ana, California in '91.

Approx. 2,000-4,000 guitars made prior to '70 with no serial number. First serial number appeared in '70, stamped on end of fingerboard, beginning with #5000. All are consecutive. Later SN on neck plates.

Approximate SN ranges include:
1970: First serial number #5000 to 10019 ('79).
'80-'83: 10768 to 15919.
'84-'87: 13666 to 25332.
'88-'90: 22731 to 25683.

'91-'94: 25359 to 42547.
'95-'99: 45879 to 81427.
'00-present: 56162 upward.

Casa Montalvo
1987-present. Intermediate and professional grade, production/custom flamenco and classical guitars made in Mexico for George Katechis of Berkeley Musical Instrument Exchange.

Casio
1987-1988. Line of digital guitars imported from Japan, sporting plastic bodies and synthesizer features.

DG1
1987.

1987		$60	$70

DG10
1987. Self-contained digital guitar.

1987		$175	$200

DG20
1987. Midi-capable digital guitar.

1987		$275	$325

PG-300
1987. Similar to PG-380, but with less features.

1987		$375	$450

PG-310
1987. Similar to PG-380, but with less features.

1987		$475	$575

PG-380
1987. Guitar synth, double-cut, over 80 built-in sounds, midi controller capable.

1987		$725	$900

Champion
Ca. 1894-1897. Chicago's Robert Maurer built this brand of instruments before switching to the Maurer brand name around 1897.

Chandler
1984-present. Intermediate and professional grade, production/custom, solidbody electric guitars built by luthiers Paul and Adrian Chandler in Chico, California. They also build basses, lap steels and pickups. Chandler started making pickguards and accessories in the '70s, adding electric guitars, basses, and effects in '84.

555 Model
1992-present. Sharp double-cut, 3 mini-humbuckers, TV Yellow.

1992-2004		$800	$1,000

Austin Special
1991-1999. Resembles futuristic Danelectro, lipstick pickups, available in 5-string version.

1991-1999		$625	$725

Austin Special Baritone
1994-1999. Nicknamed Elvis, gold metalflake finish, mother-of-toilet-seat binding, tremolo, baritone.

1994-1999		$625	$725

Campellone Special

1966 Carvin Doubleneck

Chandler Lectra-Slide

Charis Acoustic

MODEL YEAR	FEATURES	EXC. COND. LOW	HIGH

LectraSlide
2001-present. Single-cut, Rezo pickguard, 2 pickups.

2001-2007		$800	$1,000

Metro
1995-2000. Double-cut slab body, P-90 in neck position and humbucker in the bridge position.

1995-2000		$550	$675

Telepathic
1994-2000. Classic single-cut style, 3 models; Basic, Standard, Deluxe.

1994-2000	Basic	$475	$575
1994-2000	Deluxe 1122 Model	$650	$775
1994-2000	Standard	$575	$700

Chantus
1984-present. Premium grade, production/custom, classical and flamenco guitars built in Austin, Texas, by luthier William King. He also builds ukes.

Chapin
Professional and premium grade, production/custom, semi-hollow, solidbody, and acoustic electric guitars built by luthiers Bill Chapin and Fred Campbell in San Jose, California.

Chapman
1970-present. Made by Emmett Chapman, the Stick features 10 strings and is played by tapping both hands. The Grand Stick features 12 strings.

Stick
10 or 12 strings, touch-tap hybrid electric instrument.

1970-1999	10-string	$1,500	$1,600
1970-1999	12-string	$1,600	$2,000
2000-2003	10-string	$1,600	$1,700

Charis Acoustic
1996-present. Premium grade, custom/production, steel-string guitars built by luthier Bill Wise in Bay City, Michigan.

Charles Fox Guitars
1968-present. Luthier Charles Fox builds his premium and presentation grade, custom, steel and nylon string guitars in Portland, Oregon. He also produced GRD acoustic and electric guitars for '78-'82 and C. Fox acoustic guitars for '97-'02. He also operates The American School of Lutherie in Portland.

Charles Shifflett Acoustic Guitars
1990-present. Premium grade, custom, classical, flamenco, resonator, and harp guitars built by luthier Charles Shifflett in High River, Alberta. He also builds basses and banjos.

MODEL YEAR	FEATURES	EXC. COND. LOW	HIGH

Charvel
1976 (1980)-present. Intermediate and professional grade, production, solidbody electric guitars. They also build basses. Founded by Wayne Charvel as Charvel Manufacturing in '76, making guitar parts in Asuza, California. Moved to San Dimas in '78. Also in '78 Grover Jackson bought out Charvel. In '79 or early '80 Charvel branded guitars are introduced. U.S.-made to '85, a combination of imports and U.S.-made post-'85. Charvel also manufactured the Jackson brand.

Charvel licensed its trademark to IMC (Hondo) in '85. IMC bought Charvel in '86 and moved the factory to Ontario, California. On October 25, 2002, Fender Musical Instruments Corp. (FMIC) took ownership of Jackson/Charvel Manufacturing Inc.

Pre-Pro (Pre-Production) Charvels began in November 1980 and ran until sometime in 1981. These are known as 'non-plated' indicating pre-production versus a production neck plate. Production serialized neck plates are considered to be San Dimas models which have a Charvel logo, serial number, and a PO Box San Dimas notation on the neck plate. These Serialized Plated Charvels came after Pre-Pros. Late '81 and '82 saw the early serialized guitars with 21-fret necks; these are more valuable. During '82 the 22-fret neck was introduced. The so-called Soft Strat-, Tele-, Flying V-, and Explorer-style headstocks are associated with the early San Dimas Charvel models. In late '82 the pointy headstock, called the Jackson style, was introduced. In '82 the Superstrat style with a neck plate was introduced. Superstrats with a Kahler tailpiece have a lower value than the Pre-Pro models (with Fender-style trem tailpiece).

Collectors of vintage Charvels look for the vintage Charvel 3-on-a-side logo. This is a defining feature and a cutoff point for valuations. Bogus builders are replicating early Charvels and attempting to sell them as originals so fakes can be a problem for Charvel collectors, so buyer beware.

Other electric guitar manufacturing info:

1986-1989	Japanese-made Models 1 through 8
1989-1991	Japanese-made 550 XL, 650 XL/Custom, 750 XL (XL=neck-thru)
1989-1992	Japanese-made Models 275, 375, 475, 575
1990-1991	Korean-made Charvette models
1992-1994	Korean-made Models 325, 425

Early Charvel serial numbers (provided by former Jackson/Charvel associate Tim Wilson):
The first 500 to 750 guitars had no serial number, just marked "Made In U.S.A." on their neckplates. Five digit serial numbers were then used until November '81 when 4-digit number adopted, starting with #1001.

1981	1001-1095
1982	1096-1724
1983	1725-2938
1984	2939-4261
1985	4262-5303
1986	5304-5491

MODEL YEAR	FEATURES	EXC. COND. LOW	HIGH

Pre-Pro

November 1980-1981. Pre-Pros came in different configurations of body styles, pickups, and finishes. There are five basic Pre-Pro formats: the Standard Body, the Bound Body, the Graphic Body, the Flamed Top, and the Matching Headstock. It is possible to have a combination, such as a Bound Body and Matching Headstock. Line items are based on body style and can feature any one of four neck/headstock-styles used: the so-called Tele-headstock, Strat-headstock, Flying V headstock, and Explorer headstock. Finishes included white, black, red, metallic Lake Placid Blue, and special graphics. All original parts adds considerable value and it is often difficult to determine what is original on these models, so expertise is required. An original Fender brass trem tailpiece, for example, adds considerable value. The Pre-Pro models were prone to modification such as added Kahler and Floyd Rose trems. Price ranges are wide because this is a relatively new market without mature pricing.

1980-1981	Bound body	$3,000	$4,500
1980-1981	Flamed top, stained body	$4,000	$6,500
1980-1981	Graphic body	$3,500	$5,500
1980-1981	Matching headstock and body	$4,500	$6,000
1980-1981	Standard body	$2,500	$3,500

275 Deluxe Dinky

1989-1991. Made in Japan, offset double-cut solidbody, 1 single-coil and one humbucker ('89), 3 stacked humbuckers ('90-'91), tremolo.

1989	1 single, 1 humbucker	$425	$525
1990-1991	Stacked humbuckers	$425	$525

325SL

1992-1994. Dot inlays.

1992-1994		$425	$525

325SLX

1992-1994. Surfcaster-like thinline acoustic/electric, dual cutaways, f-hole, on-board chorus, shark inlays, made in Korea.

1992-1994		$425	$525

375 Deluxe

1989-1992. Maple or rosewood 'board, dot inlays, single-single-humbucker.

1989-1992		$425	$525

475

1989-1992. Humbucker-single-single configuration, bolt-on neck, dot markers.

1989-1992		$400	$500

475 Deluxe/Special

1989-1992. Introduced as Special, changed to Deluxe, bound rosewood board, shark tooth inlays, 2 oval stacked humbuckers and 1 bridge humbucker.

1989-1992		$425	$525

525

1989-1994. Acoustic-electric, single-cut.

1989-1994		$425	$525

550XL

1989-1990. Neck-thru (XL), dot markers, single rail humbucker and single bridge humbucker.

1989-1990		$600	$675

625-C12

1993-2000. Acoustic-electric cutaway 12-string, spruce top.

1993-2000		$300	$325

625F/625ACEL

1993-1995. Acoustic-electric cutaway, figured maple top.

1993-1995		$300	$325

650XL/Custom

1989-1991. Introduced as neck-thru XL and discontinued as Custom, shark fin markers, 2 stacked oval humbuckers and 1 bridge humbucker, custom version of 550XL.

1989-1991		$600	$725

750XL Soloist

1989-1990. Introduced as neck-thru XL, shark fin markers, carved alder archtop body, 2 humbuckers (1 neck/1 bridge), large Charvel logo.

1980s		$725	$900

Avenger

1990-1991. Randy Rhoads-style batwing-shaped solidbody, 3 stacked humbuckers, tremolo, made in Japan.

1990-1991		$300	$350

Charvette

1989-1992. Charvette Series made in Korea, superstrat-style, model number series 100 through 300.

1990-1991		$225	$250

Custom Shop Kit

1976-1980. Includes kits that were built from aftermarket necks, bodies, and pickups. Most early-Charvel collectors do not consider these to be true Charvel branded instruments.

1976-1980		$500	$2,000

EVH Art Series

2004-2007. Offset double-cut solidbody, 1 humbucker, striped finish.

2004-2007		$1,500	$1,800

Fusion Deluxe

1989-1991. Double-cut solidbody, tremolo, 1 humbucker and 1 single-coil pickup, made in Japan.

1989-1991		$300	$350

Fusion Standard/AS FX 1

1993-1996. Double-cut solidbody, tremolo, 1 regular and 2 mini humbuckers, made in Japan, also named AS FX1.

1993-1996		$275	$325

Model 1/1A/1C

1986-1989. Offset double-cut solidbody, bolt-on maple neck, dot inlays, 1 humbucker, tremolo, made in Japan. Model 1A has 3 single-coils. Model 1C has 1 humbucker and 2 single-coils.

1986-1989		$325	$400

Model 2

1986-1989. As Model 1, but with rosewood 'board.

1986-1989		$325	$400

Model 3/3A/3DR/3L

1986-1989. As Model 2, but with 1 humbucker, 2 single coils. Model 3A has 2 humbuckers. Model 3DR has 1 humbucker and 1 single-coil.

1986-1989		$325	$400

Charvel EVH

1987 Charvel Model 3

1986 Charvel Model 4

1986 Charvel Model 5

MODEL YEAR	FEATURES	EXC. COND. LOW	HIGH

Model 4/4A
1986-1989. As Model 2, but with 1 regular humbucker and 2 stacked humbuckers mounted in the body (no pickguard), and with active electronics, shark-fin inlays. Model 4A has 2 regular humbuckers and dot markers.

1986-1989		$425	$525

Model 5/5A
1986-1989. As Model 4A, but is neck-thru construction, with JE1000TG active eltronics. Model 5A is single humbucker and single knob version of Model 5, limited production, made in Japan.

1986-1989		$450	$550

Model 6
1986-1989. As Model 4, but with shark's tooth 'board inlays, standard or various custom finishes.

1986-1989		$500	$600

Model 7
1988-1989. Single-cut solidbody, bound top, reversed headstock, 2 single-coils, made in Japan.

1988-1989		$500	$600

Model 88 LTD
1988. Double-cut solidbody, 1 slanted humbucker, shark fin inlay, 1000 built, made in Japan.

1988		$550	$675

San Dimas LTD 25th Anniversary
2006. About 100 made, 25th Anniversary logo on neck plate with production number, highly figured top, high-end appointments.

2006		$1,800	$2,200

San Dimas Reissue (FMIC)

2005-2006		$600	$700

San Dimas Serialized Plated
1981-1986, 1995-1997. U.S.-made with San Dimas neck plate, bolt neck, rounded headstock early production, pointy headstock later, reissued in mid-'90s.

1981-1982	Soft headstock	$3,000	$3,700
1982-1986	Pointy headstock	$1,500	$1,800
1995-1997	Soft headstock	$800	$1,000

ST Custom
1990-1992. Offset double-cut ash solidbody, 2 single-coils and 1 humbucker, rosewood 'board, tremolo, made in Japan.

1990-1992		$350	$400

ST Deluxe
1990-1992. Same as ST Custom but with maple 'board.

1990-1992		$325	$350

Standard
2002-2003. Typical offset double-cut Charvel body, 2 Seymour Duncan humbucker pickups, various opaque colors.

2002-2003		$225	$300

Star
1980-1981. The Star is considered by early-Charvel collectors to be Charvel's only original design with its unique four-point body.

1980-1981		$2,500	$3,000

MODEL YEAR	FEATURES	EXC. COND. LOW	HIGH

Surfcaster
1991-1994. Offset double-cut, f-hole, various pickup options, bound body, tremolo, made in Japan.

1991-1994	1 single-coil, 1 humbucker	$675	$800
1991-1994	2 single-coils	$725	$900
1991-1994	3 single-coils	$775	$950
1991-1994	Optional custom color & features	$800	$1,000

Surfcaster 12
1991-1995. 12-string version of Surfcaster, no tremolo, made in Japan.

1991-1995		$725	$900

Surfcaster Double Neck
1992. Very limited production, 6/12 double neck, Charvel logo on both necks, black.

1992		$1,600	$1,900

Surfcaster HT (Model SC 1)
1992-1996. Made in Japan. Hard Tail (HT) non-tremolo version of Surfcaster, has single-coil and bridge humbucker.

1992-1996	Custom color & features	$925	$1,000
1992-1996	Standard colors & features	$825	$925

Chiquita
1979-present. Intermediate grade, production guitars made by Erlewine Guitars in Austin, Texas (see that listing). There was also a mini amp available.

Travel Guitar
1979-present. Developed by Mark Erlewine and ZZ Top's Billy Gibbons, 27" overall length solidbody.

1980s	Blond, natural or yellow	$325	$400
1980s	Red, 1 pickup	$300	$325
1980s	Red, 2 pickups	$325	$400

Chris George
1966-present. Professional and premium grade, custom, archtop, acoustic, electric and resonator guitars built by luthier Chris George in Tattershall Lincolnshire, UK.

Chrysalis Guitars
1998-present. Luthier Tim White builds his premium grade, production/custom Chrysalis Guitar System, which includes interchangeable components that can be quickly assembled into a full-size electric/acoustic guitar, in New Boston, New Hampshire. A variety of instruments may be created, including 6- and 12-string electrics and acoustics, electric and acoustic mandocello and acoustic basses.

Cimar/Cimar by Ibanez
Early-1980s. Private brand of Hoshino Musical Instruments, Nagoya, Japan, who also branded Ibanez. Headstock with script Cimar logo or Cimar by Ibanez, copy models and Ibanez near-original models such as the star body.

MODEL YEAR	FEATURES	EXC. COND. LOW	HIGH

Cimar

1982	Star body style	$175	$200

Cimarron

1978-present. Luthiers John Walsh and Clayton Walsh build their professional grade, production/custom, flat top acoustic guitars in Ridgway, Colorado. Between '94 and '98 they also produced electric guitars.

Cipher

1960s. Solidbody electric guitars and basses imported from Japan by Inter-Mark. Generally strange-shaped bodies.

Electric Solidbody

1960s. For any student-grade import, a guitar with any missing part, such as a missing control knob or trem arm, is worth much less.

1960s		$175	$200

Citron

1995-present. Luthier Harvey Citron builds his professional and premium grade, production/custom solidbody guitars in Woodstock, New York. He also builds basses. In '75, Citron and Joe Veillette founded Veillette-Citron, which was known for handcrafted, neck-thru guitars and basses. That company closed in '83.

Clifford

Clifford was a brand manufactured by Kansas City, Missouri instrument wholesalers J.W. Jenkins & Sons. First introduced in 1895, the brand also offered mandolins.

Coleman Guitars

1976-1983. Custom made presentation grade instruments made in Homosassa, Florida, by luthier Harry Coleman. No headstock logo, Coleman logo on inside center strip.

Collings

1986-present. Professional, premium, and presentation grade, production/custom, flat-top, archtop and electric guitars built in Austin, Texas. They also build mandolins. Bill Collings started with guitar repair and began custom building guitars around '73. In '80, he relocated his shop from Houston to Austin and started Collings Guitars in '86. In '06 they moved to a new plant in southwest Austin.

00-2H

1999. Indian rosewood.

1999		$2,400	$3,000

00-41

2001. Premium Brazilian rosewood back and sides, Adirondack spruce top, abalone top purfling.

2001		$6,500	$8,000

MODEL YEAR	FEATURES	EXC. COND. LOW	HIGH

000-1

1990s-2000s. Mahogany body, spruce top.

1990s	000-1	$2,300	$2,700
1990s	000-1A Adirondack	$2,900	$3,100
2000s	000-1A Adirondack	$2,900	$3,100

000-2H

1994-present. 15" 000-size, Indian rosewood back and sides, spruce top, slotted headstock, 12-fret neck, dot markers. AAA Koa back and sides in '96.

1994-1995	Indian rosewood	$2,500	$3,000
1996	AAA Koa	$2,900	$3,500

000-41

1990s. Indian rosewood sides and back, Sitka spruce top, slotted headstock.

1999		$3,100	$3,800

C-10

1994-present. 000-size, mahogany back and sides, spruce top, natural.

1995		$2,500	$3,100

C-10 Deluxe

1994-present. Indian rosewood or flamed maple back and sides, natural.

1994-2002	Flamed maple	$3,200	$3,600
1994-2002	Indian rosewood	$3,200	$3,600
1994-2002	Koa	$3,400	$3,600

C-100

1986-1995. Quadruple 0-size, mahogany back and sides, spruce top, natural, replaced by CJ Jumbo.

1986-1995		$2,200	$2,700

CJ Jumbo

1995-present. Quadruple 0-size, Indian rosewood back and sides, spruce top, natural.

1995-2001		$3,000	$3,100

D-1 Gruhn

1989. Short run for Gruhn Guitars, Nashville, Gruhn script logo on the headstock instead of Collings, signed by Bill Collins, Indian rosewood back and sides, sitka spruce top.

1989		$3,000	$3,700

D-1/D-1SB/D-1A Custom

1994-present. D-size, 15 5/8", mahogany back and sides, spruce top, natural. D-1SB is sunburst option. D-1A Custom upgrades to Adirondack spruce top and higher appointments, natural.

1995-2003	D-1	$2,500	$2,900
1999-2002	D-1A Custom	$2,700	$3,300
2001	D-1SB	$2,500	$2,900

D-2

1986-1995. D-1 with Indian rosewood back and sides, natural.

1986-1995		$2,800	$3,400

D-2H

1986-present. Dreadnought, same as D-2 with herringbone purfling around top edge.

1986-2001		$2,700	$3,300

D-2H/D-2HBZ

1994-2001. Grade AA Brazilian rosewood, spruce top.

1994-2001		$5,500	$6,200

1975 Cimar

Collings C-10

GUITARS

Comins Chester Avenue

Conklin Jazz 8

MODEL		EXC. COND.	
YEAR	FEATURES	LOW	HIGH

D-3
1990-present. Similar to D-2H but with abalone purfling/rosette.

1990s	Brazilian rosewood	$5,500	$6,900
2000s	Indian rosewood	$3,000	$3,500

D-42
2000s. Brazilian rosewood back and sides, fancy.

2000s		$6,200	$7,000

DS-41
1995. Indian rosewood, abalone top trim, snowflake markers.

1995		$4,800	$5,500

OM-1/OM-1A
1994-present. Grand concert, sitka spruce top, mahogany back and sides, natural. OM-1A includes Adirondack spruce upgrade.

1990s	OM-1	$2,650	$3,100
1990s	OM-1A	$2,900	$3,400

OM-2H
1990-present. Indian rosewood back and sides, herringbone binding.

1990-2005		$2,750	$3,000

OM-2HAV
1998. Adirondack spruce top, Brazilian rosewood back and sides, ivoroid-bound body.

1998		$5,500	$6,900

OM-3
1998-present. Brazilian rosewood back and sides, Adirondack spruce top, fancy rosette, later Indian rosewood and figured maple.

1998	Brazilian rosewood	$6,000	$6,500
2002	Indian rosewood	$3,200	$4,000
2003	Figured maple	$3,300	$4,100

OM-3HC
1986. Single rounded cutaway, 15", Indian rosewood back and sides, spruce top, herringbone purfling.

1986		$3,400	$4,200

OM-42B
2000. Brazilian rosewood back and sides, Adirondack spruce top, fancy rosette and binding.

2000		$6,700	$7,700

SJ
1986-present. Spruce top, quilted maple back and sides or Indian rosewood (earlier option).

1990s	Indian rosewood	$3,500	$3,800
2000s	Maple	$3,500	$3,800

SJ-41
1996. Brazilian rosewood back and sides, cedar top.

1996		$6,700	$7,700

Winfield
2005-2006. D-style, Brazilian rosewood back and sides, Adirondack spruce top, mahogany neck, ebony board.

2005-2006		$4,300	$4,400

Comins
1992-present. Premium and presentation grade, custom archtops built by luthier Bill Comins in Willow Grove, Pennsylvania. He also offers a combo amp built in collaboration with George Alessandro.

MODEL		EXC. COND.	
YEAR	FEATURES	LOW	HIGH

Commander
Late 1950s-early 1960s. Archtop acoustic guitars made by Harmony for the Alden catalog company.

Concertone
Ca. 1914-1930s. Concertone was a brand made by Chicago's Slingerland and distributed by Montgomery Ward. The brand was also used on other instruments such as ukuleles.

Conklin
1984-present. Intermediate, professional and premium grade, production/custom, 6-, 7-, 8-, and 12-string solid and hollowbody electrics, by luthier Bill Conklin. He also builds basses. Originally located in Lebanon, Missouri, in '88 the company moved to Springfield, Missouri. Conklin instruments are made in the U.S. and overseas.

Conn Guitars
Ca.1968-ca.1978. Student to mid-quality classical and acoustic guitars, some with bolt-on necks, also some electrics. Imported from Japan by band instrument manufacturer and distributor Conn/Continental Music Company, Elkhart, Indiana.

Acoustic
1968-1978. Various models.

1968-1978		$125	$150

Classical
1968-1978. Various student-level models.

1968-1978		$125	$150

Solidbody Electric
1970s. Various models.

1970s		$175	$200

Connor, Stephan
1995-present. Luthier Stephan Connor builds his premium grade, custom nylon-string guitars in Waltham, Massachusetts.

Conrad Guitars
Ca. 1968-1978. Mid- to better-quality copies of glued-neck Martin and Gibson acoustics and bolt-neck Gibson and Fender solidbodies. They also offered basses, mandolins and banjos. Imported from Japan by David Wexler and Company, Chicago, Illinois.

Acoustic 12-String
1970s. Dreadnought size.

1970s		$125	$150

Acoustical Slimline (40080/40085)
1970s. Rosewood 'board, 2 or 3 DeArmond-style pickups, block markers, sunburst.

1970s		$225	$275

Acoustical Slimline 12-String (40100)
1970s. Rosewood 'board, 2 DeArmond-style pickups, dot markers, sunburst.

1970s		$225	$275

MODEL YEAR	FEATURES	EXC. COND. LOW	HIGH

Bison (40035/40030/40065/40005)
1970s. 1 thru 4 pickups available, rosewood 'board with dot markers, six-on-side headstock.

1970s		$200	$250

Bumper (40223)
1970s. Clear Lucite solidbody.

1970s		$325	$375

De Luxe Folk Guitar
1970s. Resonator acoustic, mahogany back, sides and neck, Japanese import.

1970s		$225	$275

Master Size (40178)
1972-1977. Electric archtop, 2 pickups.

1972-1977		$275	$325

Resonator Acoustic
1970s. Flat-top with wood, metal resonator and 8 ports, round neck.

1970s		$375	$450

Violin-Shaped 12-String Electric (40176)
1970s. Scroll headstock, 2 pickups, 500/1 control panel, bass side dot markers, sunburst.

1970s		$225	$275

Violin-Shaped Electric (40175)
1970s. Scroll headstock, 2 pickups, 500/1 control panel, bass side dot markers, vibrato, sunburst.

1970s		$275	$325

White Styrene 1280
1970s. Solid maple body covered with white styrene, 2 pickups, tremolo, bass side dot markers, white.

1970s		$250	$300

Contessa
1960s. Acoustic, semi-hollow archtop, solidbody and bass guitars made in Italy and imported by Hohner. They also made banjos.

Electric Solidbody
1967. Various models.

1967		$350	$425

Contreras
See listing for Manuel Contreras and Manuel Contreras II.

Coral
1967-1969. In '66 MCA bought Danelectro and in '67 introduced the Coral brand of guitars, basses and amps.

Firefly
1967-1969. Double-cut, f-holes, 2 pickups, with or without vibrato.

1967-1969		$1,000	$1,250

Hornet 2
1967-1969. Solidbody, 2 pickups, with or without vibrato.

1967-1969		$1,000	$1,250

Sitar
1967-1969. Six-string guitar with 13 drone strings and 3 pickups (2 under the 6 strings, 1 under the drones), kind of a USA-shaped body.

1967-1969		$2,700	$3,300

MODEL YEAR	FEATURES	EXC. COND. LOW	HIGH

Córdoba
Line of classical guitars handmade in Portugal and imported by Guitar Salon International.

Classical

1999	1A India	$1,900	$2,100
2000s	Gipsy King	$850	$1,050
2000s	Higher-end	$500	$625
2000s	Mid-level	$400	$500
2000s	Student-level	$225	$275

Cordova
1960s. Classical nylon string guitars imported by David Wexler of Chicago.

Grand Concert Model WC-026
1960s. Highest model offered by Cordova, 1-piece rosewood back, laminated rosewood sides, spruce top, natural.

1960s		$250	$300

Corey James Custom Guitars
2005-present. Luthier Corey James Moilanen builds his professional and premium grade, production/custom solidbody guitars in Davisburg, Michigan. He also builds basses.

Coriani, Paolo
1984-present. Production/custom nylon-string guitars and hurdy-gurdys built by luthier Paolo Coriani in Modeila, Italy.

Cort
1973-present. North Brook, Illinois-based Cort offers budget, intermediate and professional grade, production/custom, acoustic and solidbody, semi-hollow, hollow body electric guitars built in Korea. They also offer basses. Cort was the second significant Korean private-label (Hondo brand was the first) to come out of Korea. Jack Westheimer, based upon the success of Tommy Moore and Hondo, entered into an agreement with Korea's Cort to do Cort-brand, private-label, and Epiphone-brand guitars.

Crafter
2000-present. Line of intermediate and professional grade, production, acoustic and acoustic/electric guitars from Hohner. They also offer mandolins and a bass.

Crafter USA
1986-present. Crafter offers budget and intermediate grade, production, classical, acoustic, acoustic/electric, and electric guitars made in Korea. They also build basses and amps. From '72 to '86 they made Sungeum classical guitars.

Crafters of Tennessee
See listing under Tennessee.

1987 Cort Dragon StoStrat

Crafter USA D-6/N

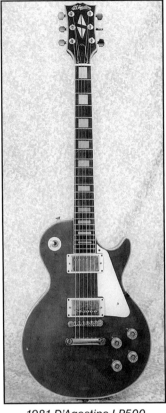

1981 D'Agostino LP500

D'Agostino Bench Mark

MODEL YEAR	FEATURES	EXC. COND. LOW	HIGH

Cranium

1996-present. Professional grade, production/custom, hollow, semi-hollow, and solidbody electrics built by luthier Wayne O'Connor in Peterborough, Ontario.

Crescent Moon

1999-present. Professional grade, production/custom, solidbody guitars and basses built by luthier Craig Muller in Baltimore, Maryland.

Crestwood

1970s. Copies of the popular classical guitars, flat-tops, electric solidbodies and basses of the era, imported by La Playa Distributing Company of Detroit.

Electric

1970s. Various models include near copies of the 335 (Crestwood model 2043, 2045 and 2047), Les Paul Custom (2020), Strat (2073), Jazzmaster (2078), Tele (2082), and the SG Custom (2084).

1970s		$250	$300

Cromwell

1935-1939. Budget model brand built by Gibson and distributed by mail-order businesses like Grossman, Continental, and Richter & Phillips.

Acoustic Archtop

1935-1939. Archtop acoustic, f-holes, pressed mahogany back and sides, carved and bound top, bound back, 'guard and 'board, no truss rod.

1935-1939		$700	$875
1935-1939	With 1930s era pickup	$1,500	$1,800

Acoustic Flat-Top

1935-1939	G-2 (L-00)	$1,100	$1,350

Tenor Guitar (Flat-Top)

1935-1939	GT-2	$700	$850

Crossley

2005-present. Professional grade, production/custom, solidbody and chambered electric guitars built in Melbourne, Victoria, Australia by luthier Peter Crossley.

Crown

1960s. Violin-shaped hollowbody electrics, solidbody electric guitars and basses, possibly others. Imported from Japan.

Acoustic Flat-Top

1960s. 6-string and 12-string.

1960s		$125	$150

Electric Archtop

Double pointed cutaways, 2 humbucking pickups, laminated top, full-depth body.

1960s		$375	$450

Electric Solidbody/Semi-Hollow

1960s. Student-level Japanese import.

1960s	Pointy violin-shaped body	$275	$325
1960s	Standard body styles	$150	$175

Crucianelli

Early 1960s. Italian guitars imported into the U.S. by Bennett Brothers of New York and Chicago around '63 to '64. Accordion builder Crucianelli also made Imperial, Elite, PANaramic, and Elli-Sound brand guitars.

CSR

1996-present. Father and daughter luthiers Roger and Courtney Kitchens build their premium grade, production/custom, archtop guitars in Byron, Georgia. They also build basses.

Cumpiano

1974-present. Professional and premium grade, custom steel-string and nylon-string guitars, and acoustic basses built by luthier William Cumpiano in Northampton, Massachusetts.

Curbow String Instruments

1994-present. Premium grade, production/custom, solidbody guitars built by luthier Doug Somervell in Morganton, Georgia. Founded by Greg Curbow who passed away in '05. They also make basses.

Custom

1980s. Line of solidbody guitars and basses introduced in the early '80s by Charles Lawing and Chris Lovell, owners of Strings & Things in Memphis, Tennessee.

Custom Kraft

Late-1950s-1968. A house brand of St. Louis Music Supply, instruments built by Valco and others. They also offered basses.

Electric Solidbody

1950s-1960s. Entry-level, 1 pickup.

1950-1960s		$175	$200

Sound Saturator

1960s	12-string	$325	$400

Super Zapp

1960s		$350	$400

D.J. Hodson

1994-2007. Luthier David J. Hodson built his professional and premium grade, production/custom, acoustic guitars in Loughborough, Leicestershire, England. He also built ukes. He passed away in '07.

Daddy Mojo String Instruments Inc.

2005-present. Luthiers Lenny Piroth-Robert and Luca Tripaldi build their intermediate and professional grade, production/custom, solidbody electric, resonator and cigar box guitars in Montreal, Quebec, Canada.

MODEL		EXC. COND.	
YEAR	FEATURES	LOW	HIGH

D'Agostino

1976-early 1990s. Acoustic and electric solidbody guitars and basses imported by PMS Music, founded in New York City by former Maestro executive Pat D'Agostino, his brother Steven D'Agostino, and Mike Confortti. First dreadnought acoustic guitars imported from Japan in '76. First solidbodies manufactured by the EKO custom shop beginning in '77. In '82 solidbody production moved to Japan. Beginning in '84, D'Agostinos were made in Korea. Overall, about 60% of guitars were Japanese, 40% Korean. They also had basses.

Acoustic Flat-Top
1976-1990. Early production in Japan, by mid-'80s, most production in Korea.

1976-1990		$175	$200

Electric Semi-Hollowbody
1981-early 1990s. Early production in Japan, later versions from Korea.

1981-1990		$225	$275

Electric Solidbody
1977-early 1990s. Early models made in Italy, later versions from Japan and Korea.

1981-1990		$225	$275

Daily Guitars

1976-present. Luthier David Daily builds his premium grade, production/custom classical guitars in Sparks, Nevada.

Daion

1978-1985. Mid- to higher-quality copies imported from Japan. Original designs introduced in the '80s. They also had basses.

Acoustic
1978-1985. Various flat-top models.

1978-1985		$400	$500

Electric
1978-1985. Various solid and semi-hollow body guitars.

1978-1985		$550	$675

Daisy Rock

2001-present. Budget and intermediate grade, production, full-scale and 3/4 scale, solidbody, semi-hollow, acoustic, and acoustic/electric guitars. Founded by Tish Ciravolo as a Division of Schecter Guitars, the Daisy line is focused on female customers. Initial offerings included daisy and heart-shaped electric guitars and basses.

D'Ambrosio

2001-present. Luthier Otto D'Ambrosio builds his premium grade, custom/production, acoustic and electric archtop guitars in Providence, Rhode Island.

Dan Armstrong

Dan Armstrong started playing jazz in Cleveland in the late-'50s. He moved to New York and also started doing repairs, eventually opening his own store on 48th Street in '65. By the late-'60s he was designing his Lucite guitars for Ampeg (see Ampeg for those listings). He moved to England in '71, where he developed his line of colored stomp boxes. He returned to the States in '75. Armstrong died in '04.

Wood Body Guitar
1973-1975. Sliding pickup, wood body, brown.

1973-1975		$1,600	$2,000

Dan Kellaway

1976-present. Production/custom, premium grade, classical and steel string guitars built by luthier Dan Kellaway in Singleton NSW, Australia. He also builds mandolins and lutes.

Danelectro

1946-1969, 1996-present. Founded in Red Bank, New Jersey, by Nathan I. (Nate or Nat) Daniel, an electronics enthusiast with amplifier experience. In 1933, Daniel built amps for Thor's Bargain Basement in New York. In '34 he was recruited by Epiphone's Herb Sunshine to build earliest Electar amps and pickup-making equipment. From '35 to '42, he operated Daniel Electric Laboratories in Manhattan, supplying Epiphone. He started Danelectro in '46 and made his first amps for Montgomery Ward in '47. Over the years, Danelectro made amplifiers, solidbody, semi-hollow and hollowbody electric guitars and basses, electric sitar, and the Bellzouki under the Danelectro, Silvertone, and Coral brands. In '48, began supplying Silvertone amps for Sears (various coverings), with his own brand (brown leatherette) distributed by Targ and Dinner as Danelectro and S.S. Maxwell. He developed an electronic vibrato in '48 on his Vibravox series amps. In '50 he developed a microphone with volume and tone controls and outboard Echo Box reverb unit. In the fall of '54, Danelectro replaced Harmony as provider of Silvertone solidbody guitars for Sears.

Also in '54, the first Danelectro brand guitars appeared with tweed covering, bell headstock, and pickups under the pickguard. The Coke bottle headstock debuts as Silvertone Lightning Bolt in '54, and was used on Danelectros for '56 to '66. The company moved to Red Bank, New Jersey in '57, and in '58 relocated to Neptune, New Jersey. In '59, Harmony and Kay guitars replace all but 3 Danelectros in Sears catalog. In '66, MCA buys the company (Daniel remains with company), but by mid-'69, MCA halts production and closes the doors. Some leftover stock is sold to Dan Armstrong, who had a shop in New York at the time. Armstrong assembled several hundred Danelectro guitars as Dan Armstrong Modified with his own pickup design.

Rights to name acquired by Anthony Marc in late-'80s, who assembled a number of thinline hollowbody guitars, many with Longhorn shape, using Japanese-made bodies and original Danelectro

Danelectro '63

Danelectro Convertible

Danelectro Doubleneck

1957 Danelectro U-1

necks and hardware. In '96, the Evets Corporation, of San Clemente, California, introduced a line of effects bearing the Danelectro brand. Amps and guitars, many of which were reissues of the earlier instruments, soon followed. In early 2003, Evets discontinued offering guitar and amps, but revived the guitar and bass line in '05.

MCA-Danelectro made guitars were called the Dane Series. Dane A model numbers start with an A (e.g. A2V), Dane B models start with a B (e.g. B3V), Dane C (e.g. C2N), and Dane D (e.g. D2N). The least expensive series was the A, going up to the most expensive D. All Dane Series instruments came with 1, 2 or 3 pickups and with hand vibrato options. The Dane Series were made from '67 to '69. MCA did carry over the Convertible, Guitarlin 4123, Long Horn Bass-4 and Bass-6 and Doubleneck 3923. MCA also offered the Bellzouki Double Pickup 7021. Each Dane Series includes an electric 12-string. Danelectro also built the Coral brand instruments (see Coral).

Baritone 6-String Reissue
1999-2003. Single cutaway, 6-string baritone tuning.

MODEL YEAR	FEATURES	EXC. COND. LOW	HIGH
1999-2003		$400	$500
2008		$200	$250

Baritone Model 1449
1963. Double-cut, baritone tuning, 3-on-a-side tuners, 2 lipstick pickups, Coke bottle headstock shape with large verticle Danelectro logo.

1963		$1,400	$1,600

Bellzouki
1961-1969. 12-string electric, teardrop-shaped body, single pickup, sunburst. Vincent Bell model has modified teardrop shape with 2 body points on both treble and bass bouts and 2 pickups.

1960s	Single pickup	$850	$950
1960s	Vincent Bell, 2 pickups	$950	$1,150

Convertible
1959-1969. Acoustic/electric, double-cut, guitar was sold with or without the removable single pickup.

1950s	Pickup installed, natural	$500	$625
1960s	Acoustic, no pickup, natural	$400	$500
1960s	Pickup installed, natural	$500	$600
1960s	Pickup installed, rare color	$725	$900

Convertible Reissue
1999-2000.

1999-2000		$200	$225

Dane A Series
1967-1969. 1 and 2 pickup models, solid wood slab body, hard lacquer finish with 4 color options.

1967-1969		$500	$600

Dane B Series
1967-1969. 1 and 3 pickup models, semi-solid Durabody.

1967-1969		$550	$650

Dane C Series
1967-1969. 2 and 3 pickup models, semi-solid Durabody with 2-tone Gator finish.

MODEL YEAR	FEATURES	EXC. COND. LOW	HIGH
1967-1969		$550	$650

Dane D Series
1967-1969. 2 and 3 pickup models, solid wood sculptured thinline body, 'floating adjustable pickguard-fingerguide', master volume with 4 switches.

1967-1969		$550	$650

59-DC/'59 Dano (Standard Double Pickup Reissue)
1998-1999, 2007. Shorthorn double-cut, 2 pickups, seal-shaped pickguard, Coke bottle headstock, '07 version called '59 Dano.

1998-1999		$175	$200

DC-12/Electric XII
1999-2003. 12-string version of 59-DC.

1999-2003		$325	$400

Deluxe Double Pickup (6026/6027/6028)
1960s. Double-cut, 2 pointer knobs, 2 pickups, standard-size pickguard, master control knob, white (6026), dark walnut (6027), honey walnut (6028).

1960s		$900	$1,100

Deluxe Triple Pickup (6036/6037/6038)
1960s. Double-cut, 3 pointer knobs, 3 pickups, standard-size pickguard, master control knob, white (6036), dark walnut (6037), honey walnut (6038).

1960s		$1,100	$1,350

Doubleneck (3923)
1959-1969. A shorthorn double-cut, bass and 6-string necks, 1 pickup on each neck, Coke bottle headstocks, white sunburst.

1959-1969		$2,000	$2,500

Doubleneck Reissue
1999-2003. Baritone 6-string and standard 6-string double neck, shorthorn body style, or the 6-12 model with a 6-string and 12-string neck. Price includes $75 for a guitar case, but many sales do not seem to include a guitar case because of unusual body size.

1999-2003		$500	$575

Electric Sitar
1967-1969. Traditional looking, oval-bodied sitar, no drone strings as on the Coral Sitar of the same period.

1967-1969		$2,000	$2,500

Guitaralin (4123)
1963-1969. The Longhorn guitar, with 2 huge cutaways, 32-fret neck, and 2 pickups.

1963-1969		$2,000	$2,500

Hand Vibrato Double Pickup (4021)
1960s. Double-cut, 2 pickups, batwing headstock, simple design vibrato, black.

1960s		$700	$850

Hand Vibrato Single Pickup (4011)
1960s. Double-cut, 1 pickup, batwing headstock, simple design vibrato, black.

1960s		$600	$750

Model C
1955-ca.1958. Single-cut, 1 pickup.

1955-1958		$650	$750

Pro 1
1963-ca.1964. Odd-shaped double-cut electric with squared off corners, 1 pickup.

1963-1964	$700	$800

Pro Reissue
2007. Based on '60s Pro 1, but with 2 pickups.

2007	$200	$225

Standard Single Pickup
1958-1967. A Shorthorn double-cut, 1 pickup, 2 regular control knobs, seal-shaped pickguard, Coke bottle headstock.

1958-1967	$650	$750

Standard Double Pickup
1959-1967. A shorthorn double-cut, 2 pickups, 2 stacked, concentric volume/tone controls, seal-shaped 'guard, Coke bottle headstock, black version of this guitar is often referred to as the Jimmy Page model because he occasionally used one. Reissued in 1998 as 59-DC.

1959-1967	$1,100	$1,200

U-1
1956-ca.1960. Single-cut, 1 pickup, Coke bottle headstock.

1956-1960	Custom color	$1,100	$1,300
1956-1960	Standard color	$750	$925

U-1 '56 Reissue
1998-1999. Single-cut semi-hollow, masonite top and bottom, bolt-on neck, reissue of '56 U-1, with single 'lipstick tube' pickup, various colors.

1998-1999	$170	$210

U-2
1956-1959. Single-cut, 2 pickups, stacked concentric volume/tone controls, Coke bottle headstock.

1956-1959	Custom color	$1,500	$1,800
1956-1959	Standard color	$1,125	$1,400

U-2 '56 Reissue
1998-2003. 2 pickup U-1.

1998-2003	$180	$220

U-3
1957-1959. Single-cut, 3 pickups.

1957-1959	$1,500	$1,675

U-3 '56 Reissue
1999-2003. Single-cut reissue of '56 U-3 with 3 'lipstick tube' pickups, various colors.

1999-2003	$225	$275

D'Angelico
John D'Angelico built his own line of archtop guitars, mandolins and violins from 1932 until his death in 1964. His instruments are some of the most sought-after by collectors.

D'Angelico (L-5 Snakehead)
1932-1935. D'Angelico's L-5-style with snakehead headstock, his first model, sunburst.

1932-1935	$14,000	$16,000

Excel/Exel (Cutaway)
1947-1964. Cutaway, 17" width, 1- and 3-ply bound f-hole, Larry Wexer noted from '50-'57, D'Angelico guitars suffer from severe binding problems and many have replaced bindings. Replaced bindings make the guitar non-original and these repaired guitars have lower values.

1947-1949	Natural, original binding	$40,000	$47,000
1947-1949	Sunburst, original binding	$39,000	$44,000
1950-1959	Natural, original binding	$38,000	$41,000
1950-1959	Sunburst, original binding	$36,000	$39,000
1960-1964	Natural	$37,000	$40,000
1960-1964	Sunburst	$35,000	$38,000

Excel/Exel (Non-Cutaway)
1936-1949. Non-cut, 17" width, 1- and 3-ply bound f-hole, natural finishes were typically not offered in the '30s, non-cut Excels were generally not offered after '49 in deference to the Excel cutaway.

1936-1939	Sunburst, straight f-hole	$18,000	$20,000
1938-1939	Sunburst, standard f-hole	$18,000	$20,000
1940-1949	Natural	$19,000	$21,000
1940-1949	Sunburst, standard f-hole	$18,000	$20,000

New Yorker (Cutaway)
1947-1964. Cutaway, 18" width, 5-ply-bound f-hole, New Yorker non-cut orders were overshadowed by the cut model orders starting in '47, all prices noted are for original bindings, non-original (replaced) bindings will reduce the value by 33%-50%.

1947-1949	Natural, 4 made	$58,000	$66,000
1947-1949	Sunburst	$48,000	$55,000
1950-1959	Natural	$57,000	$65,000
1950-1959	Sunburst	$47,000	$54,000
1960-1964	Natural	$56,000	$64,000
1960-1964	Sunburst	$47,000	$54,000

New Yorker (Non-Cutaway)
1936-1949. Non-cut, 18" width, 5-ply-bound f-hole, New Yorker non-cut orders were overshadowed by the cut model orders starting in '47, all prices noted are for original bindings, non-original (replaced) bindings will reduce the value by 33%-50%.

1936-1939	Sunburst	$24,000	$25,000
1940-1949	Natural	$29,000	$30,000
1940-1949	Sunburst	$27,000	$28,000

New Yorker Special
1947-1964. Also called Excel New Yorker or Excel Cutaway New YorkerCutaway, 17" width, New Yorker styling, prices are for original bindings, non-original (replaced) bindings reduce values by 33%-50%, not to be confused with D'Angelico Special (A and B style).

1947-1964	Natural	$42,000	$45,000
1947-1964	Sunburst	$37,000	$41,000

Special
1947-1964. Generally Style A and B-type instruments made for musicians on a budget, plain specs with little ornamentation, not to be confused with New Yorker Special.

1947-1964	Natural	$15,000	$17,000
1947-1964	Sunburst	$14,000	$16,000

1947 D'Angelico New Yorker

D'Angelico New Yorker NYL-2

D'Aquisto Custom Oval-Hole

D'Aquisto New Yorker Classic

MODEL YEAR	FEATURES	EXC. COND. LOW	HIGH

Style A
1936-1945. Archtop, 17" width, unbound f-holes, block 'board inlays, multi-pointed headstock, nickel-plated metal parts.

1936-1939	Sunburst	$10,500	$12,500
1940-1945	Sunburst	$10,000	$12,000

Style A-1
1936-1945. Unbound f-holes, 17" width, arched headstock, nickel-plated metal parts.

1936-1939	Sunburst	$9,500	$11,500
1940-1945	Sunburst	$9,500	$11,500

Style B
1933-1948. Archtop 17" wide, unbound F-holes, block 'board inlays, gold-plated parts.

1936-1939	Sunburst	$14,000	$16,000
1940-1948	Sunburst	$11,000	$13,500

Style B Special
1933-1948. D'Angelico described variations from standard features with a 'Special' designation, Vintage dealers may also describe these instruments as 'Special'.

1936-1939	Sunburst	$15,000	$17,500
1940-1948	Sunburst	$14,000	$16,500

D'Angelico (D'Angelico Guitars of America)
1988-present. Intermediate and professional grade, production/custom, archtop, flat-top, and solidbody guitars made in South Korea and imported by D'Angelico Guitars of America, of Colts Neck, New Jersey. From 1988 to '04, they were premium and presentation grade instruments built in Japan by luthier Hidesato Shino and Vestax.

New Yorker NYL-2
2001-2004. Japanese 17" single-cut archtop, spruce top, figured maple back and sides.

2001-2004		$2,100	$2,500

D'Angelico (Lewis)
1994-present. Luthier Michael Lewis builds presentation grade, custom/production, D'Angelico replica guitars in Grass Valley, California, under an agreement with the GHS String Company, which owns the name in the U.S. He also builds guitars and mandolins under the Lewis name.

D'Angelico II
Mid-1990s. Archtops built in the U.S. and distributed by Archtop Enterprises of Merrick, New York. Mainly presentation grade copies of Excel and New Yorker models, but also made lower cost similar models.

Jazz Classic
1990s. Electric archtop, cutaway, carved spruce top, figured maple back and sides, single neck pickup, transparent cherry.

1990s		$3,400	$4,000

Daniel Friederich
1955-present. Luthier Daniel Friederich builds his custom/production, classical guitars in Paris, France.

MODEL YEAR	FEATURES	EXC. COND. LOW	HIGH

D'Aquisto
1965-1995. James D'Aquisto apprenticed under D'Angelico until the latter's death, at age 59, in '64. He started making his own brand instruments in '65 and built archtop and flat top acoustic guitars, solidbody and hollowbody electric guitars. He also designed guitars for Hagstrom and Fender. He died in '95, at age 59.

Avant Garde
1987-1994. 18" wide, non-traditional futuristic model, approximately 5 or 6 instruments were reportedly made, because of low production this pricing is for guidance only.

1990	Blond	$80,000	$100,000

Centura/Centura Deluxe
1994 only. 17" wide, non-traditional art deco futuristic archtop, approximately 10 made, the last guitars made by this luthier, due to the low production this pricing is for guidance only.

1994	Blond	$75,000	$94,000

Excel (Cutaway)
1965-1992. Archtop, 17" width, with modern thin-logo started in '81.

1965-1967	Blond	$44,000	$53,000
1965-1967	Sunburst	$42,000	$51,000
1968-1979	Blond	$36,000	$44,000
1968-1979	Sunburst	$31,000	$38,000
1980-1989	Blond	$41,000	$50,000
1980-1989	Sunburst	$33,000	$40,000
1990-1992	Blond	$41,000	$50,000
1990-1992	Sunburst	$35,000	$40,000

Excel (Flat-Top)
1980s. Flat-top, 16", flamed maple back and sides, Sitka spruce top, about 15 made, narrow Excel-style headstock, oval soundhole, D'Aquisto script logo on headstock.

1980s		$19,000	$22,000

Hollow Electric
Early model with bar pickup, D'Aquisto headstock, '70s model with humbuckers.

1965	Sunburst	$12,000	$14,000
1972	Sunburst	$12,000	$14,000

Jim Hall
Hollow-body electric, carved spruce top, 1 pickup.

1965	Laminate top	$12,000	$14,000
1978	Solid top	$12,000	$14,000

New Yorker Classic (Solidbody)
1980s. Only 2 were reported to be made, therefore this pricing is for guidance only.

1980s		$18,000	$22,000

New Yorker Deluxe (Cutaway)
1965-1992. Most are 18" wide.

1965-1967	Blond	$57,000	$59,000
1965-1967	Sunburst	$52,000	$54,000
1968-1979	Blond	$57,000	$51,000
1968-1979	Sunburst	$46,000	$50,000
1980-1989	Blond	$49,000	$51,000
1980-1989	Sunburst	$49,000	$50,000
1990-1992	Blond	$52,000	$54,000
1990-1992	Sunburst	$51,000	$53,000

MODEL YEAR	FEATURES	EXC. COND. LOW	HIGH
New Yorker Special (7-String)			
1980s. Limited production 7-string, single-cut.			
1980s	Sunburst	$46,000	$48,000
New Yorker Special (Cutaway)			
1966-1992. Most are 17" wide.			
1966-1967	Blond	$56,000	$58,000
1966-1967	Sunburst	$51,000	$53,000
1968-1979	Blond	$46,000	$49,000
1968-1979	Sunburst	$45,000	$48,000
1980-1989	Blond	$48,000	$50,000
1980-1989	Sunburst	$48,000	$49,000
1990-1992	Blond	$51,000	$53,000
1990-1992	Sunburst	$50,000	$52,000
Solo/Solo Deluxe			
1992-1993. 18" wide, non-traditional non-cut art deco model, only 2 reported made, because of low production this pricing is for guidance only.			
1992-1993	Blond	$75,000	$94,000

D'Aquisto (Aria)

May 2002-present. Premium grade, production, D'Aquisto designs licensed to Aria of Japan by D'Aquisto Strings, Inc., Deer Park, New York.

DQ-CR
2002-present. Similar to D'Aquisto Centura.

2002-2006		$1,900	$2,300

Dauphin

1970s-present. Classical and flamenco guitars built in Spain.

Classical
Solid spruce top, rosewood back and sides.

1980-2000		$450	$550

Dave King Acoustics

1980-present. Premium grade, custom/production, acoustic and resonator guitars built by luthier Dave King in Reading, Berkshire, U.K.

Dave Maize Acoustic Guitars

1991-present. Luthier Dave Maize builds his professional and premium grade, production/custom, flat-tops in Cave Junction, Oregon. He also builds basses.

David Rubio

1960s-2000. Luthier David Spink built his guitars, lutes, violins, violas, cellos and harpsichords first in New York, and after '67, in England. While playing in Spain, he acquired the nickname Rubio, after his red beard. He died in '00.

David Thomas McNaught

1989-present. Professional, premium, and presentation grade, custom, solidbody guitars built by luthier David Thomas McNaught and finished by Dave Mansel in Locust, North Carolina. In '97, they added the production/custom DTM line of guitars.

MODEL YEAR	FEATURES	EXC. COND. LOW	HIGH
Solidbody (Higher-End)			
2000s. High-end solidbody with indepth inlay (rhino, moonscape), heavily figured wood, various styles.			
2000s		$4,000	$5,000
Vintage (Double-Cut)			
Classic/modern offset double-cut, figured maple top, 2 exposed humbuckers.			
2002		$3,200	$3,600
Vintage Standard			
2003		$3,200	$3,600

Davis, J. Thomas

1975-present. Premium and presentation grade, custom, steel-string flat-tops, 12-strings, classicals, archtops, Irish citterns and flat-top Irish bouzoukis made by luthier J. Thomas Davis in Columbus, Ohio.

Davoli

See Wandre listing.

DBZ

2008-present. Solidbody electric guitars from Dean B. Zelinsky, founder of Dean Guitars, and partners Jeff Diamant and Terry Martin.

de Jonge, Sergei

1972-present. Premium grade, production/custom classical and steel-string guitars built by luthier Sergei de Jonge originally in Oshawa, Ontario, and since '04 in Chelsea, Quebec.

De Paule Stringed Instruments

1969-1980, 1993-present. Custom steel-string, nylon-string, archtop, resonator, and Hawaiian guitars built by luthier C. Andrew De Paule in Eugene, Oregon.

Dean

1976-present. Intermediate, professional and premium grade, production/custom, solidbody, hollowbody, acoustic, acoustic/electric, and resonator guitars made in the U.S., Korea, the Czech Republic and China. They also offer basses, banjos, mandolins, and amps. Founded in Evanston, ... Illinois, by Dean Zelinsky. Original models were upscale versions of Gibson designs with glued necks, fancy tops, DiMarzio pickups and distinctive winged headstocks (V, Z and ML), with production beginning in '77. In '80 the factory was relocated to Chicago. Dean's American manufacturing ends in '86 when all production shifts to Korea. In '91 Zelinsky sold the company to Tropical Music in Miami, Florida. For '93-'94 there was again limited U.S. (California) production of the E'Lite, Cadillac and ML models under the supervision of Zelinsky and Cory Wadley.

Korean versions were also produced. In '95, Elliott Rubinson's Armadillo Enterprises, of Clear-

Dave King Classic

David Thomas McNaught Signature Series

1983 Dean Bel-Air

1978 Dean Z Standard

water, Florida, bought the Dean brand. In '97 and '98, Dean offered higher-end USA Custom Shop models. In '98, they reintroduced acoustics. From 2000 to '08, Zelinsky was once again involved in the company.

Baby ML
1982-1986, 2000-present. Downsized version of ML model.

MODEL YEAR	FEATURES	EXC. COND. LOW	HIGH
1980s	Import	$400	$450
1980s	U.S.-made	$600	$750

Baby V
1982-1986, 2000-present. Downsized version of the V model.

1980s	Import	$375	$425
1980s	U.S.-made	$575	$700

Baby Z
1982-1986, 2000-present. Downsized version of the Z model.

1980s	Import	$375	$425
1980s	U.S.-made	$600	$750

Bel Aire
1983-1984. Solidbody, possibly the first production guitar with humbucker/single/single pickup layout, U.S.-made, an import model was introduced in '87

1980s	Import	$325	$375
1983-1984	U.S.-made	$600	$750

Budweiser Guitar
Ca.1987. Shaped like Bud logo.

1987	$300	$375

Cadillac (U.S.A.)
1979-1985. Single long treble horn on slab body.

1979-1985	$1,700	$2,100

Cadillac 1980
2006-present. Block inlays, 2 humbuckers, gold hardware.

2006-2007	$400	$450

Cadillac Deluxe (U.S.A.)
1993-1994, 1996-1997. Made in U.S., single longhorn shape, various colors.

1993-1994	$1,300	$1,600
1996-1997	$1,300	$1,600

Cadillac Reissue (Import)
1992-1994. Single longhorn shape, 2 humbuckers, various colors.

1992-1994	$400	$475

Cadillac Standard
1996-1997. Slab body version.

1996-1997	$1,600	$2,000

Dime O Flame (ML)
2005-present. ML-body, Dimebuckers, burning flames finish, Dime logo on headstock.

2005-2007	$450	$550

Eighty-Eight (Import)
1987-1990. Offset double-cut solidbody, import.

1987-1990	$225	$275

E'Lite
1978-1985, 1994-1996. Single-horn shape.

1978-1985	$1,400	$1,700
1994-1996	$1,300	$1,600

E'Lite Deluxe
Single-horn shape.

MODEL YEAR	FEATURES	EXC. COND. LOW	HIGH
1980s		$1,450	$1,800

Golden E'Lite
Single pointy treble cutaway, fork headstock, gold hardware, ebony 'board, sunburst.

1980		$1,450	$1,800

Hollywood Z (Import)
1985-1986. Bolt-neck Japanese copy of Baby Z, Explorer shape.

1985-1986		$175	$215

Jammer (Import)
1987-1989. Offset double-cut body, bolt-on neck, dot markers, six-on-a-side tuners, various colors offered.

1987-1989		$175	$215

Mach I (Import)
1985-1986. Limited run from Korea, Mach V with six-on-a-side tunes, various colors.

1985-1986		$175	$215

Mach V (Import)
1985-1986. Pointed solidbody, 2 humbucking pickups, maple neck, ebony 'board, locking trem, various colors, limited run from Korea.

1985-1986		$175	$215

Mach VII (U.S.A.)
1985-1986. Mach I styling, made in America, offered in unusual finishes.

1985-1986		$1,400	$1,750

ML (Import)
1983-1990. Korean-made.

1983-1990		$450	$475

ML (ML Standard/U.S.A.)
1977-1986. There is a flame model and a standard model.

1977-1981	Burst flamed top	$1,900	$2,100
1977-1981	Burst plain top	$1,800	$2,000
1977-1981	Common opaque finish	$1,700	$2,000
1977-1981	Less common finish	$2,000	$2,200
1982-1986	Burst flamed top	$1,600	$1,900
1982-1986	Burst plain top	$1,500	$1,800
1982-1986	Common opaque finish	$1,500	$1,700
1982-1986	Less common finish	$1,800	$2,000

V Standard (U.S.A.)
1977-1986. V body, there is a standard and a flame model offered.

1977-1981	Burst flamed top	$1,900	$2,100
1977-1981	Burst plain top	$1,800	$2,000
1977-1981	Common opaque finish	$1,700	$2,000
1977-1981	Less common finish	$2,000	$2,200
1982-1986	Burst flamed top	$1,600	$1,900
1982-1986	Burst plain top	$1,500	$1,800
1982-1986	Common opaque finish	$1,500	$1,700
1982-1986	Less common finish	$1,800	$2,000

| MODEL | | EXC. COND. | |
YEAR	FEATURES	LOW	HIGH

Z Autograph (Import)

1985-1987. The first Dean import from Korea, offset double-cut, bolt neck, dot markers, offered in several standard colors.

1985-1987		$275	$350

Z Coupe/Z Deluxe (U.S.A. Custom Shop)

1997-1998. Mahogany body offered in several standard colors, Z Deluxe with Floyd Rose tremolo.

1997-1998		$1,150	$1,400

Z Korina (U.S.A. Custom Shop)

1997-1998. Z Coupe with korina body, various standard colors.

1997-1998		$1,300	$1,400

Z LTD (U.S.A. Custom Shop)

1997-1998. Z Coupe with bound neck and headstock, offered in several standard colors.

1997-1998		$1,300	$1,400

Z Standard (U.S.A.)

1977-1986. Long treble cutaway solidbody, 2 humbuckers.

1977-1983	Common finish	$1,600	$2,000
1977-1983	Less common finish	$2,000	$2,200

Dean Markley

The string and pickup manufacturer offered a limited line of guitars and basses for a time in the '80s. They were introduced in '84.

DeArmond Guitars

1999-2004. Solid, semi-hollow and hollow body guitars based on Guild models and imported from Korea by Fender. They also offered basses. The DeArmond brand was originally used on pickups, effects and amps built by Rowe Industries.

Electric

1999-2004. Various import models, some with USA electronic components.

1999	M-72 (Bluesbird)	$400	$450
1999-2004	Jet Star (Polara style)	$400	$450
1999-2004	M-75/M-75T (Bluesbird)	$325	$400
1999-2004	Starfire (Double-cut)	$450	$550
1999-2004	Starfire Special (Single-cut)	$325	$400
1999-2004	X155 (Duane Eddy style)	$450	$550
2000-2004	Baja Jet Baritone	$450	$550

Dearstone

1993-present. Luthier Ray Dearstone builds his professional and premium grade, custom, archtop and acoustic/electric guitars in Blountville, Tennessee. He also builds mandolin family instruments and violins.

DeCava Guitars

1983-present. Professional and premium grade, production/custom, archtop and classical guitars built by luthier Jim DeCava in Stratford, Connecticut. He also builds ukes, banjos, and mandolins.

Decca

Mid-1960s. Acoustic, solid and hollow body guitars made in Japan by Teisco and imported by Decca Records, Decca headstock logo, student-level instruments. They also offered amps and a bass.

Acoustic Flat-Top

1960s. Decca label on the inside back.

1960s		$135	$165

DeGennaro

2003-present. Premium grade, custom/production, acoustic, archtop, semi-hollow and solidbody guitars built by luthier William Degennaro in Grand Rapids, Michigan. He also builds basses and mandolins.

Del Pilar Guitars

1956-1986. Luthier William Del Pilar made his classical guitars in Brooklyn, New York.

Classical (Mahogany)

1980s. Mahogany back and sides, spruce top, red and green rosette.

1980s		$1,300	$1,500

Classical (Rosewood)

1950s. Brazilian rosewood back and sides, cedar top, quilt rosette, 9-ply top binding.

1950s		$3,300	$4,000

Del Vecchio

1902-present. Casa Del Vecchio builds a variety of Spanish instruments including acoustic and resonator guitars in São Paulo, Brazil.

Dell'Arte

1997-present. Production/custom Maccaferri-style guitars from John Kinnard and Alain Cola. In '96, luthier John Kinnard opened a small shop called Finegold Guitars and Mandolins. In '98 he met Alain Cola, a long time jazz guitarist who was selling Mexican-made copies of Selmer/Maccaferri guitars under the Dell'Arte brand. Cola wanted better workmanship for his guitars, and in October '98, Finegold and Dell'Arte merged. As of May '99 all production is in California.

Anouman Custom

1990s		$1,400	$1,750

Delta Guitars

2005-present. Acoustic, acoustic/electric, and solidbody electric guitars from Musician's Wholesale America, Nashville, Tennessee.

Dennis Hill Guitars

1991-present. Premium and presentation grade, production/custom, classical and flamenco guitars built by luthier Dennis Hill in Panama City, Florida. He has also built dulcimers, mandolins, and violins.

DeArmond Starfire

DeGennaro Dynasty

DeVoe Archtop

1916 Ditson Style 1 Standard

MODEL YEAR	FEATURES	EXC. COND. LOW	HIGH

Desmond Guitars

1991-present. Luthier Robert B. Desmond builds his premium grade, production/custom classical guitars in Orlando, Florida.

DeTemple

1995-present. Premium grade, production/custom, solidbody electric guitars built by luthier Michael DeTemple in Sherman Oaks, California. He also builds basses.

DeVoe Guitars

1975-present. Luthier Lester DeVoe builds his premium grade, production/custom flamenco and classical guitars in Nipomo, California.

Diamond

Ca. 1963-1964. Line of sparkle finish solidbody guitars made in Italy for the Diamond Accordion company.
Ranger
Ca. 1963-1964. Rangers came with 1, 2, 3, or 4 pickups, sparkle finish.

1960s		$525	$650

Dick, Edward Victor

1975-present. Luthier Edward Dick currently builds his premium grade, custom, classical guitars in Denver, Colorado (he lived in Peterborough and Ottawa, Ontario until '95). He also operates the Colorado School of Lutherie.

Dickerson

1937-1947. Founded by the Dickerson brothers in '37, primarily for electric lap steels and small amps. Instruments were also private branded for Cleveland's Oahu company, and for the Gourley brand. By '47, the company changed ownership and was renamed Magna Electronics (Magnatone).

Dillion

1996-present. Dillion, of Cary, North Carolina, offers intermediate grade, production, acoustic, acoustic/electric, hollow-body and solidbody guitars made in Korea and Vietnam. They also have basses and mandolins.
Electric Solidbody
1996-present. Includes various models.

1996-2007		$300	$375

Dillon

1975-present. Professional and premium grade, custom, flat-tops built by luthier John Dillon originally in Taos, New Mexico ('75-'81), then in Bloomsburg, Pennsylvania ('81-'01), and since 2001 back in Taos. He also builds basses.

Dino's Guitars

1995-present. Custom, professional grade, electric solidbody guitars built by a social co-op company founded by Alessio Casati and Andy Bagnasco, in Albisola, Italy. It also builds effects.

DiPinto

1995-present. Intermediate and professional grade, production retro-vibe guitars from luthier Chris DiPinto of Philadelphia, Pennsylvania. He also builds basses. Until late '99, all instruments built in the U.S., since then all built in Korea.

Ditson

1916-1930. Ditson guitars were made by Martin and sold by the Oliver Ditson Company of Boston. The majority of production was from '16 to '22 with over 500 units sold in '21.
Concert Models
1916-1922. Similar in size to Martin size 0. Models include Style 1, Style 2 and Style 3.

1916-1922	Style 1	$4,000	$5,000
1916-1922	Style 2	$4,900	$6,100
1916-1922	Style 3	$5,500	$6,900

Standard Models
1916-1922. Small body similar to Martin size 3, plain styling. Models include Style 1, Style 2 and Style 3.

1916-1922	Style 1	$2,500	$3,000
1916-1922	Style 2	$3,000	$3,700
1916-1922	Style 3	$4,200	$5,200

Style 111 Dreadnought
Dreadnought-sized exceeding the Martin 000 size, initially intended to be a 6-string bass guitar, fan bracing on the top generally requires extensive restoration.

1916-1922		$5,600	$7,000

D'Leco Guitars

1991-present. Luthier James W. Dale builds his premium grade, production/custom archtops in Oklahoma City, Oklahoma.
DM Darling Guitars
2006-present. Luthier Denis Merrill builds his professional and premium grade, custom, acoustic, classical, resonator and solidbody guitars in Tacoma, Washington. From 1978 to '06 he built under his own name and Merrill Custom Shop. He also builds mandolin family instruments.

Dobro

1929-1942, ca. 1954-present. Currently, professional and premium grade, production, wood and metal body resophonic guitars offered by Gibson. Founded 1929 in Los Angeles by John Dopyera, Rudy Dopyera, Ed Dopyera and Vic Smith (Dobro stands for Dopyera Brothers). Made instruments sold under the Dobro, Regal, Norwood Chimes, Angelus, Rex, Broman, Montgomery Ward, Penetro, Bruno, Alhambra, More Harmony, Orpheum, and Magn-o-tone brands.

Dobro instruments have a single cone facing outward with a spider bridge structure and competed with National products. Generally, model names are numbers referring to list price and therefore materials and workmanship (e.g., a No. 65 cost $65). Because of this, the same model number may apply to various different instruments. However, model numbers are never identified on instruments!

In '30, the company name was changed to Dobro Corporation, Ltd. In '32, Louis Dopyera buys Ted Kleinmeyer's share of National. Louis, Rudy and Ed now hold controlling interest in National, but in '32 John Dopyera left Dobro to pursue idea of metal resophonic violin. In December of '34 Ed Dopyera joins National's board of directors (he's also still on Dobro board), and by March of '35 Dobro and National have merged to become the National Dobro Corporation. Dobro moves into National's larger factory but continues to maintain separate production, sales and distribution until relocation to Chicago is complete. Beginning in early-'36 National Dobro starts relocating its offices to Chicago. L.A. production of Dobros continues until '37, after which some guitars continue to be assembled from parts until '39, when the L.A. operations were closed down.

All resonator production ended in '42. Victor Smith, Al Frost and Louis Dopyera buy the company and change the name to the Valco Manufacturing Company. The Dobro name does not appear when production resumes after World War II. In mid-'50s - some sources say as early as '54 - Rudy and Ed Dopyera began assembling wood-bodied Dobros from old parts using the name DB Original. In about '59, some 12-fret DB Originals were made for Standel, carrying both DB Original and Standel logos. In around '61, production was moved to Gardena, California, and Louis Dopyera and Valco transferred the Dobro name to Rudy and Ed, who produce the so-called Gardena Dobros. At this time, the modern Dobro logo appeared with a lyre that looks like 2 back-to-back '6s'. Dobro Original debuts ca. '62. In late-'64 the Dobro name was licensed to Ed's son Emil (Ed, Jr.) Dopyera. Ed, Jr. designs a more rounded Dobro (very similar to later Mosrites) and has falling out with Rudy over it.

In '66 Semi Moseley acquires the rights to the Dobro brand, building some in Gardena, and later moving to Bakersfield, California. Moseley introduced Ed, Jr's design plus a thinline double-cutaway Dobro. Moseley Dobros use either Dobro or National cones. In '67 Ed, Sr., Rudy and Gabriella Lazar start the Original Music Instrument Company (OMI) and produce Hound Dog brand Dobros. In '68 Moseley goes bankrupt and in '70 OMI obtains the rights to the Dobro brand and begins production of OMI Dobros. In '75 Gabriella's son and daughter, Ron Lazar and Dee Garland, take over OMI. Rudy Dupyera makes and sells Safari brand resonator mandolins. Ed, Sr. dies in '77 and Rudy in '78. In '84 OMI was sold to Chester and Betty Lizak. Both wood and metal-bodied Dobros produced in Huntington Beach, California. Chester Lizak died in '92. Gibson purchased Dobro in '93 and now makes Dobros in Nashville, Tennessee.

Dobros generally feature a serial number which, combined with historical information, provides a clue to dating. For prewar L.A. guitars, see approximation chart below adapted from Gruhn and Carter's Gruhn's Guide to Vintage Guitars (Miller Freeman, 1991). No information exists on DB Originals.

Gardena Dobros had D prefix plus 3 digits beginning with 100 and going into the 500s (reportedly under 500 made). No information is available on Moseley Dobros.

OMI Dobros from '70-'79 have either D prefix for wood bodies or B prefix for metal bodies, plus 3 or 4 numbers for ranking, space, then a single digit for year (D XXXX Y or B XXX Y; e.g., D 172 8 would be wood body #172 from '78). For '80-'87 OMI Dobros, start with first number of year (decade) plus 3 or 4 ranking numbers, space, then year and either D for wood or B for metal bodies (8 XXXX YD or 8 XXX YB; e.g., 8 2006 5B would be metal body #2008 from '85). From '88-'92, at least, a letter and number indicate guitar style, plus 3 or 4 digits for ranking, letter for neck style, 2 digits for year, and letter for body style (AX XXXX NYYD or AX XXX NYYB).

L.A. Guitars (approx. number ranges, not actual production totals)

1929-30	900-2999
1930-31	3000-3999
1931-32	BXXX (Cyclops models only)
1932-33	5000-5599
1934-36	5700-7699

Angelus
1933-1937. Wood body, round or square neck, 2-tone walnut finish, continues as Model 19 in Regal-made guitars.

MODEL YEAR	FEATURES	LOW	HIGH
1933-1937	Round neck	$1,300	$1,600
1933-1937	Square neck	$1,450	$1,800

Artist M-16
1934-1935. German silver alloy body, engraved.

1934-1935	H square neck	$3,900	$4,100
1934-1935	M round neck	$6,500	$7,000

Columbia D-12
1967-1968. Acoustic 12-string, typical Dobro resonator with spider style bridge, made during Dobro-Moseley era.

1967-1968		$900	$1,100

Cyclops 45
1932-1933. Bound walnut body, 1 screen hole.

1932-1933	Round neck	$2,800	$3,400
1932-1933	Square neck	$2,800	$3,400

D-40 Texarkana
1965-1967. Mosrite-era (identified by C or D prefix), traditional Dobro style cone and coverplate, dot inlays, Dobro logo on headstock, sunburst wood body. Red and blue finishes available.

1965-1967	Sunburst, square neck	$1,100	$1,450

D-40E Texarkana
1965-1967. D-40 electric with single pickup and 2 knobs.

1965-1967		$1,300	$1,550

DM-33 California Girl/DM-33H
1996-2006. Chrome-plated bell brass body, biscuit bridge, spider resonator, rosewood 'board. Girl or Hawaiian-scene (H) engraving.

1996-2006		$1,400	$1,750

1977 Dobro

Dobro DM-33H

GUITARS

Dobro Josh Graves

1967 Domino Baron

Dobro/Regal 46/47
1935-1938 Dobro/Regal 46, renamed 47 1939-1942. Made by Regal of Chicago, aluminum body, round neck, 14 frets, slotted peghead, silver finish. Degraded finish was a common problem with the Dobro/Regal 47.

MODEL YEAR	FEATURES	EXC. COND. LOW	HIGH
1935-1938	Model 46	$1,300	$1,600
1939-1942	Model 47, degraded finish	$600	$700
1939-1942	Model 47, original finish	$1,850	$2,100

Dobro/Regal 62/65
1935-1938 Dobro/Regal 62, continued as Dobro/Regal 65 for 1939-1942. Nickel-plated brass body, Spanish dancer etching, round or square neck. Note: Dobro/Regal 65 should not be confused with Dobro Model 65 which discontinued earlier.

1935-1938	Model 62, round neck	$2,700	$3,300
1935-1938	Model 62, square neck	$3,000	$3,500
1939-1942	Model 65, round neck	$2,700	$3,300
1939-1942	Model 65, square neck	$3,000	$3,500

Dobro/Regal Tenor 27-1/2
1930. Tenor version of Model 27.

1930		$750	$825

Dobrolektric
1998-2005. Resonator guitar with single-coil neck pickup, single-cut.

1998-2005		$900	$1,100

DS-33/Steel 33
1995-2000. Steel body with light amber sunburst finish, resonator with coverplate, biscuit bridge.

1995-2000		$1,200	$1,250

DW-90C
2001-2006. Single sharp cutaway, wood body, metal resonator, f-hole upper bass bout.

2001-2006		$825	$1,025

F-60/F-60 S
1980s-2006. Round neck (60, discontinued '00)) or square neck (60 S), f-holes, brown sunburst.

1980s-2006		$900	$1,100

Hula Blues
1980s-1990s. Dark brown wood body (earlier models have much lighter finish), painted Hawaiian scenes, round neck.

1985-1990s		$875	$1,100

Josh Graves
1996-2006. Single bound ample body, spider cone, nickel plated.

1996-2006	Unsigned	$1,500	$1,875

Leader 14M/14H
1934-1935. Nickel plated brass body, segmented f-holes.

1934-1935	H square neck	$2,200	$2,700
1934-1935	M round neck	$1,800	$2,200

Model 27 (OMI)

1980s		$1,200	$1,300

Model 27 Cyclops
1932-1933.

MODEL YEAR	FEATURES	EXC. COND. LOW	HIGH
1932-1933	Round neck	$2,000	$2,500
1932-1933	Square neck	$2,100	$2,600

Model 27 Deluxe
1996-2005. Square neck

1996-2005		$1,700	$2,100

Model 27/27G
1933-1937. Regal-made, wooden body.

1933-1937	Round neck	$1,500	$1,800
1933-1937	Square neck	$2,100	$2,300

Model 32
1939-1941. Regal-made, wooden body.

1939-1941		$1,800	$1,900

Model 33 (Duolian)
1972. Only made in '72, becomes Model 90 in '73.

1972		$900	$1,100

Model 33 H
1973-1997 (OMI & Gibson). Same as 33 D, but with etched Hawaiian scenes, available as round or square neck.

1980s	Round neck	$1,350	$1,675
1980s	Square neck	$1,350	$1,675

Model 36
1932-1937. Wood body with resonator, round or square neck.

1932-1937	Round neck	$1,600	$1,850
1932-1937	Square neck	$2,200	$2,600

Model 36 S
1970-1980s. Chrome-plated brass body, square neck, slotted headstock, dot markers, engraved rose floral art.

1970-1980s		$1,450	$1,600

Model 37
1933-1937. Regal-made wood body, mahogany, bound body and 'board, round or square 12-fret neck.

1933-1937	Round neck	$1,800	$2,200

Model 37 Tenor
1933-1937 (Regal). Tenor version of No. 37.

1933-1937		$1,300	$1,600

Model 55/56 Standard
1929-1931 Model 55 Standard, renamed 56 Standard 1932-1934. Unbound wood body, metal resonator, bound neck, sunburst.

1929-1931	Model 55	$2,000	$2,300
1932-1934	Model 56	$2,000	$2,300

Model 60
1933-1936. Similar to Model 66/66B.

1933-1936	Round neck	$5,000	$5,500
1933-1936	Square neck	$7,000	$7,500

Model 60 Cyclops
1932-1933.

1932-1933		$4,700	$5,500

Model 60/60 D (OMI)/60 DS
1970-1993. Wood body (laminated maple) with Dobro resonator cone, model 60 until '73 when renamed 60 D, and various 60 model features offered, post-'93 was Gibson-owned production.

1970-1980s	Model 60 Series	$1,150	$1,400

MODEL YEAR	FEATURES	EXC. COND. LOW	HIGH

Model 65/66/66 B
1920s-1930s. Wood body with sandblasted ornamental design top and back, metal resonator, sunburst. Model 66 B has bound top.

1929-1931	Model 65	$3,200	$4,000
1932-1933	Model 66	$3,200	$4,000
1932-1933	Model 66 B	$3,200	$4,000

Model 66 Cyclops
1978	$1,200	$1,300

Model 90 (Duolian) (OMI)
1972-1995. Chrome-plated, f-holes, etched Hawaiian scene.

1972-1995	$1,325	$1,525

Model 90 (Woodbody)/WB90 G/WB90 S
1994-2005. Maple body with upper bout f-holes or sound holes, round neck, metal resonator with spider bridge, sunburst.

1994-2005	$1,200	$1,500

Model 125 De Luxe
1929-1934. Black walnut body, round or square neck, Dobro De Luxe engraved, triple-bound top, back and 'board, nickel-plated hardware, natural.

1929-1934	Round neck	$7,200	$9,000
1929-1934	Square neck	$12,000	$15,000

Professional 15M/15H
1934-1935. Engraved nickel body, round (M) or square (H) neck, solid peghead.

1934-1935	H square neck	$3,200	$3,500
1934-1935	M round neck	$2,700	$3,000

Dodge
1996-present. Luthier Rick Dodge builds his intermediate and professional grade, production, solidbody guitars with changeable electronic modules in Tallahassee, Florida. He also builds basses.

Doitsch
1930s. Acoustic guitars made by Harmony most likely for a music store or studio.

Domino
Ca. 1967-1968. Solidbody and hollowbody electric guitars and basses imported from Japan by Maurice Lipsky Music Co. of New York, New York, previously responsible for marketing the Orpheum brand. Models are primarily near-copies of EKO, Vox, and Fender designs, plus some originals. Models were made by Arai or Kawai. Earlier models may have been imported, but this is not yet documented.

Electric
1967-1968. Various models include the Baron, Californian, Californian Rebel, Dawson, and the Spartan.

1967-1968	$325	$400

Dommenget
1978-1985, 1988-present. Luthier Boris Dommenget (pronounced dommen-jay) builds his premium grade, custom/production, solidbody, flat-top, and archtop guitars in Balje, Germany. From '78 to '85

he was located in Wiesbaden, and from '88-'01 in Hamburg. He and wife Fiona also make pickups.

Don Musser Guitars
1976-present. Custom, classical and flat-top guitars built by luthier Don Musser in Cotopaxi, Colorado.

Doolin Guitars
1997-present. Luthier Mike Doolin builds his premium grade, production/custom acoustics featuring his unique double-cut in Portland, Oregon.

Dorado
Ca. 1972-1973. Six- and 12-string acoustic guitars, solidbody electrics and basses. Brand used briefly by Baldwin/Gretsch on line of Japanese imports.

Acoustic Flat-Top/Acoustic Dobro
1972-1973. Includes folk D, jumbo Western, and grand concert styles (with laminated (?) rosewood back and sides), and Dobro-style.

1972-1973	Higher-end models	$200	$250
1972-1973	Lower-end models	$100	$125
1972-1973	Mid-level models	$150	$175

Solidbody Electric
1972-1973. Includes Model 5985, a double-cuty with 2 P-90-style pickups.

1972-1973	$175	$200

Douglas Ching
1976-present. Luthier Douglas J. Ching builds his premium grade, production/custom, classical, acoustic, and harp guitars currently in Chester, Virginia, and previously in Hawaii ('76-'89) and Michigan ('90-'93). He also builds ukes, lutes and violins.

D'Pergo Custom Guitars
2002-present. Professional, premium, and presentation grade, production/custom, solidbody guitars built in Windham, New Hampshire. Every component of the guitars is built by D'Pergo.

Dragge Guitars
1982-present. Luthier Peter Dragge builds his custom, steel-string and nylon-string guitars in Ojai, California.

Dragonfly Guitars
1994-present. Professional grade, production/custom, sloped cutaway flat-tops, semi-hollow body electrics, and dulcitars built by luthier Dan Richter in Roberts Creek, British Columbia.

Drive
2000s-present. Student imports. Budget grade, production, import solidbody electric guitars. They also offer solidstate amps.

Don Musser dreadnought

D'Pergo Aged Vintage Classic

GUITARS

Eastwood Wandre

Ed Claxton E/M

MODEL		EXC. COND.	
YEAR	FEATURES	LOW	HIGH

DTM

1997-present. See David Thomas McNaught listing.

Duesenberg

1995-present. Professional and premium grade, production/custom, solid and hollow body electric guitars built by luthier Dieter Goelsdorf in Hannover, Germany. They also build basses. Rockinger had a Duesenberg guitar in the 1980s.

Dunwell Guitars

1996-present. Professional and premium grade, custom, flat-tops built by luthier Alan Dunwell in Nederland, Colorado.

Dupont

Luthier Maurice Dupont builds his classical, archtop, Weissenborn-style and Selmer-style guitars in Cognac, France.

Dwight

See info under Epiphone Dwight guitar.

Dyer

1902-1939. The massive W. J. Dyer & Bro. store in St. Paul, Minnesota, sold a complete line of music related merchandise though they actually built nothing but a few organs. The Larson Brothers of Chicago were commissioned to build harp guitar and harp mandolin pieces for them somewhat following the harp guitar design of Chris Knutsen, until 1912 when the Knutsen patent expired. Although the body design somewhat copied the Knutsen patent the resulting instrument was in a class by itself in comparison. These harp guitars have become the standard by which all others are judged because of their ease of play and the tremendous, beautiful sound they produce. Many modern builders are using the body design and the same structural ideas evidenced in the Larson originals. They were built in Styles 4 (the plainest), 5, 6, 7 and 8. The ornamentation went from the no binding, dot inlay Style 4 to the full treatment, abalone trimmed, tree-of-life fingerboard of the Style 8. All had mahogany back and sides with ebony fingerboard and bridge. There are also a very few Style 3 models found of late that are smaller than the standard and have a lower bout body point. Other Dyer instruments were built by Knutsen. Dyer also carried Stetson brand instruments made by the Larson Brothers.

Harp Guitar

1920s	Style 4, no binding	$4,000	$9,000
1920s	Style 5, bound top	$5,000	$10,000
1920s	Style 6, bound top/bottom	$6,000	$11,000
1920s	Style 7, fancy inlays	$7,000	$12,000
1920s	Style 8, tree-of-life	$12,000	$25,000

Dynacord

1950-present. Dynacord is a German company that makes audio and pro sound amps, as well as other electronic equipment. In 1966-'67 they offered solidbody guitars and basses from the Welson Company of Italy. They also had the Cora guitar and bass which is the center part of a guitar body with a tube frame in a guitar outline. They also offered tape echo machines.

Earthwood

1972-1985. Acoustic designs by Ernie Ball with input from George Fullerton. One of the first to offer acoustic basses.

Eastman

1992-present. Professional and premium grade, production, archtop and flat-top guitars mainly built in China, with some from Germany and Romania. Beijing, China-based Eastman Strings started out building violins and cellos. They added guitars in '02 and mandolins in '04.

Eastwood

1997-present. Mike Robinson's company imports budget and intermediate grade, production, solid and semi-hollowbody guitars, many styled after 1960s models. They also offer basses and mandolins.

Eaton, William

1976-present. Luthier William Eaton builds custom specialty instruments such as vihuelas, harp guitars, and lyres in Phoenix, Arizona. He is also the Director of the Robetto-Venn School of Luthiery.

Ed Claxton Guitars

1972-present. Premium grade, custom flat-tops made by luthier Ed Claxton, first in Austin, Texas, and currently in Santa Cruz, California.

Eduardo Duran Ferrer

1987-present. Luthier Eduardo Duran Ferrer builds his premium grade, classical guitars in Granada, Spain.

Edward Klein

1998-present. Premium grade, custom, guitars built by luthier Edward Klein in Mississauga, Ontario, Canada.

Egmond

1935-1972. Founded by Ulke Egmond, building acoustic, archtop, semi-hollow and solidbody guitars originally in Eindhoven, later in Best Holland. They also made basses. Egmond also produced instruments under the Orpheum (imported into U.S.) Rosetti (England), Miller, Wilson and Lion brand names.

MODEL YEAR	FEATURES	EXC. COND. LOW	HIGH

Electric
1960s. Solid or semi-hollow bodies.

1960s		$325	$400

Ehlers

1968-present. Luthier Rob Ehlers builds his premium grade, production/custom, flat-top acoustic guitars, originally in Oregon and since '06, in Veracruz, Mexico.

15 CRC
Cutaway, Western red cedar top, Indian rosewood back and sides.

1996		$2,700	$3,250

15 SRC
Cutaway, European spruce top, Indian rosewood back and sides.

1998		$2,800	$3,350

16 BTM
European spruce top, mahogany back and sides, Troubadour peghead, black lacquer finish.

1998		$2,800	$3,500

16 SK Concert
16" lower bout, relatively small upper bout, small waist, European spruce top, flamed koa back and sides, diamond markers, natural.

1993		$2,500	$3,000

16 SM
European spruce top, mahogany back and sides.

1999		$2,300	$2,600

16 SSC
Cutaway, European spruce top, English sycamore back and sides.

1996		$2,500	$3,100

25 C
Limited Edition Anniversary Model, European spruce top, Indian rosewood back and sides, abalone top border.

2001		$3,700	$4,500

GJ (Gypsy Jazz)

2000s	D-style	$2,300	$2,800

Eichelbaum Guitars

1994-present. Luthier David Eichelbaum builds his premium grade, custom, flat-tops in Santa Barbara, California.

EKO

1959-1985, 2000-present. Originally acoustic, acoustic/electric, electric thinline and full-size archtop hollowbody, solidbody electric guitars and basses built by Oliviero Pigini and Company in Recanati, Italy, and imported by LoDuca Brothers, Milwaukee, Radio and Television Equipment Company in Santa Ana, California and others. First acoustic guitars followed by sparkle plastic-covered electrics by '62. Sparkle finishes are gone ca. '66. Pigini dies ca. '67. LoDuca Bros. phases out in early-'70s. By '75 EKO offers some copy guitars and they purchased a custom shop to make other brands by '78.

Since about 2000, budget and intermediate grade, production, classical, acoustic, acoustic/electric, solidbody, solidbody, and hollowbody EKO guitars are again available and made in Asia. They also make basses and amps.

Barracuda/Barracuda 12-String
1966-ca.1978. Double-cut semi-hollow, 2 pickups, 6- or 12-string.

1966-1978	6- and 12-string	$450	$550

Cobra I/II/III/XII
1966-1978. Double-cut solidbody, 2 knobs. Cobra I has 1 pickup, II 2 pickups and III 3 pickups. 12-string Cobra XII offered '67-'69, has 2 pickups.

1966-1978	Cobra I	$350	$400
1966-1978	Cobra II	$400	$450
1966-1978	Cobra III	$400	$500
1967-1969	Cobra XII	$400	$500

Condor
1966-ca.1969. Double-cut solidbody with 3 or 4 pickups.

1966-1969		$500	$550

Dragon
1967-ca.1969. Single-cut archtop, 2 f-holes, 3 pickups, tremolo.

1967-1969		$550	$650

Flat-Top Acoustic
1960s. Various student-level flat-top acoustic models.

1960s		$200	$250

Florentine
1964-ca.1969. Double-cut archtop, 2 pickups.

1964-1969		$450	$550

Kadett/Kadett XII
1967-ca.1978. Double-cut solidbody with point on lower bass side of body, 3 pickups, tremolo. 12-string Kadett XII offered '68-'69.

1967-1978	Kadett	$450	$550
1968-1969	Kadett XII	$450	$550

Lancer
1967-ca.1969. Double-cut solidbody, 2 pickups.

1967-1969		$275	$325

Lark I/II
1970. Thin hollow cutaway, sunburst. Lark I has 1 pickup and Lark II 2.

1970	Lark I	$350	$425
1970	Lark II	$350	$425

Model 180
1960s. Cutaway acoustic archtop.

1960s		$275	$325

Model 285 Modello
1960s. Thinline single-cut, 1 pickup.

1962		$300	$350

Model 300/375
1962. Copy of Hofner Club-style electric, single-cut, 2 pickups, set-neck.

1962		$600	$750

Model 500/1 / 500/1V
1961-1964. Plastic covered solidbody, 1 pickup. 500/1 no vibrato, 1V with vibrato.

1961-1964	500/1	$500	$625
1961-1964	500/1V	$575	$675

Eichelbaum Guitars Slope Shoulder Dreadnought

1982 EKO CO-2 Cobra

EKO 500/3V

1960s EKO 500/4V

Model 500/2 / 500/3V
1961-1964. Plastic covered solidbody, plastic sparkle finish. 500/2 no vibrato, 2 pickups. 3V with vibrato, 3 pickups.

MODEL YEAR	FEATURES	EXC. COND. LOW	HIGH
1961-1964	500/2	$550	$675
1961-1964	500/3V	$625	$725

Model 500/4 / 500/4V
1961-1964. Plastic covered solidbody, 4 pickups. 500/4 no vibrato, 4V with vibrato.

1961-1964	500/4	$650	$800
1961-1964	500/4V	$700	$875

Model 540 (Classical)
1960s. Nylon-string classical guitar.

1960s		$200	$250

Model 700/3V
1961-1964. Map-shape/tulip-shape body, 3 pickups, vibrato, woodgrain plastic finish.

1961-1964		$900	$1,100

Model 700/4V
1961-1967. Map-shape/tulip-shape body, 4 pickups, multiple switches, vibrato.

1961-1967	Red, blue, silver sparkle	$1,100	$1,350
1961-1967	Standard finish	$900	$1,100

Ranger 6/12
1967-ca.1982. D-size flat-top acoustic, large 3-point 'guard, dot inlays, EKO Ranger label. Ranger 12 is 12-string.

1967-1982	Ranger 12	$400	$475
1967-1982	Ranger 6	$400	$475

Rocket VI/XII (Rokes)
1967-ca.1969. Rocket-shape design, solidbody, 6-string, says Rokes on the headstock, Rokes were a popular English band that endorsed EKO guitars, marketed as the Rocket VI in the U.S.; and as the Rokes in Europe, often called the Rok. Rocket XII is 12-string.

1967-1969	Rocket VI	$600	$750
1967-1969	Rocket XII	$600	$750

El Degas
Early-1970s. Japanese-made copies of classic America electrics and acoustics, imported by Buegeleisen & Jacobson of New York, New York.
Solidbody
Early-1970s. Copies of classic American models, including the Let's Play model.

1970s		$275	$325

Electar
See Epiphone listing.

Electra
1971-1984. Imported from Japan by St. Louis Music. Most instruments made by Matsumoku in Matsumoto, Japan. The Electra line replaced SLM's Japanese-made Apollo and U.S.-made Custom Kraft lines. First guitar, simply called The Electra, was a copy of the Ampeg Dan Armstrong lucite guitar and issued in '71, followed quickly by a variety of bolt-neck copies of other brands. In '75 the

Tree-of-Life guitars debut with a leaf pattern carved into the top, and the Electra line expanded to 25 models. Open-book headstocks changed to wave or fan shape by '78. By around '81 ties with Matsumoku further solidified and decision eventually made to merge SLM's Electra brand with Matsumoku's Westone brand. Some Korean production begins in early-'80s. In the fall of '83, the Electra Brand becomes Electra Phoenix. By beginning of '84, the brand becomes Electra-Westone and by the end of '84 just Westone. Matsumoku-made guitars have serial number in which first 1 or 2 digits represent the year of manufacture. Thus a guitar with a serial number beginning in 0 or 80 would be from 1980.
Concert Professional
Late 1970s. Howard Roberts style, single-cut electric flat-top with oval sound hole, single humbucking pickup, fancy markers.

1977		$650	$750

Custom
1970s. Double-cut solidbody, 2 pickups, Custom logo on truss rod, cherry finish.

1970s		$425	$525

Elvin Bishop
1976-ca.1980. Double-cut semi-hollow body, tree-of-life inlay.

1976-1980		$650	$800

Flying Wedge
1970s. V body, six-on-a-side tuners.

1970s		$350	$425

MPC Outlaw
1976-1983. Has separate modules that plug in for different effects.

1976-1983		$500	$600
1976-1983	MPC plug in module	$75	$100

Omega
1976-ca. 1980. Single-cut solidbody, block inlays, Omega logo on truss rod, black with rosewood neck, or natural with figured top and maple neck.

1976-1980		$350	$425

Phoenix
1980-1984. Classic offset double-cut solidbody, Phoenix logo on headstock.

1980-1984		$200	$250

Rock
1971-1973. Single cut solidbody, becomes the Super Rock in '73.

1971-1973		$400	$475

Super Rock
1973-ca.1978. Renamed from Rock ('71-'73).

1973-1978		$400	$500

X145 60th Anniversary
1982. Classic offset double-cut only made one year, Anniversary plate on back of headstock, single/single/hum pickups.

1982		$225	$275

Electric Gypsy
See listing under Teye.

MODEL YEAR	FEATURES	EXC. COND. LOW	HIGH

Electro

1964-1975. The Electro line was manufactured by Electro String Instruments and distributed by Radio-Tel. The Electro logo appeared on the headstock rather than Rickenbacker. Refer to the Rickenbacker section for models.

Electromuse

1940s-1950s. Mainly known for lap steels, Electromuse also offered acoustic and electric hollowbody guitars. They also had tube amps usually sold as a package with a lap steel.

Elite

1960s. Guitars made in Italy by the Crucianelli accordion company, which made several other brands.

Elk

Late-1960s. Japanese-made by Elk Gakki Co., Ltd. Many were copies of American designs. They also offered amps and effects.

Elliott Guitars

1966-present. Premium and presentation grade, custom, nylon-string classical and steel-string guitars built by luthier Jeffrey Elliott in Portland, Oregon.

Ellis

2000-present. Luthier Andrew Ellis builds his production/custom, premium grade, steel string acoustic and resophonic guitars in Perth, Western Australia. In 2008 he also added lap steels.

Elli-Sound

1960s. Guitars made in Italy by the Crucianelli accordion company, which made several other brands.

Ellsberry Archtop Guitars

2003-present. Premium and presentation grade, custom/production, acoustic and electric archtops built by luthier James Ellsberry in Torrance, California.

Emperador

1966-1992. Guitars and basses imported from Japan by Westheimer Musical Instruments. Early models appear to be made by either Teisco or Kawai; later models were made by Cort.

Acoustic

1960s	Archtop or flat-top	$125	$150

Electric Solidbody

1960s		$150	$175

Empire

1997-present. Professional and premium grade, production/custom, solidbody guitars from Lee Garver's GMW Guitarworks of Glendora, California.

Encore

Late 1970s-present. Budget grade, production, classical, acoustic, and electric guitars imported by John Hornby Skewes & Co. in the U.K. They also offer basses.

English Electronics

1960s. Lansing, Michigan, company named after owner, some private branded guitars and amps by Valco (Chicago), many models with large English Electronics vertical logo on headstock.

Tonemaster

1965. National Val-Pro 84 with neck pickup and bridge mounted pickup, black.

1965		$650	$750

Epiphone

Ca. 1873-present. Budget, intermediate and professional grade, production, solidbody, archtop, acoustic, acoustic/electric, resonator, and classical guitars made in the U.S. and overseas. They also offer basses, amps, mandolins, ukes and banjos. Founded in Smyrna, Turkey, by Anastasios Stathopoulos and early instruments had his label. He emigrated to the U.S. in 1903 and changed the name to Stathoupoulo. Anastasios died in '15 and his son, Epaminondas ("Epi") took over. The name changed to House of Stathopoulo in '17 and the company incorporated in '23. In '24 the line of Epiphone Recording banjos debut and in '28 the company name was changed to the Epiphone Banjo Company. In '43 Epi Stathopoulo died and sons Orphie and Frixo took over. Labor trouble shut down the NYC factory in '51 and the company cut a deal with Conn/Continental and relocated to Philadelphia in '52. Frixo died in '57 and Gibson bought the company. Kalamazoo-made Gibson Epiphones debut in '58. In '69 American production ceased and Japanese imports began. Some Taiwanese guitars imported from '79-'81. Limited U.S. production resumed in '82 but sourcing shifted to Korea in '83. In '85 Norlin sold Gibson to Henry Juszkiewicz, Dave Barryman and Gary Zebrowski. In '92 Jim Rosenberg became president of the new Epiphone division.

AJ Masterbilt Series

2004-present. Sloped shoulder D size, solid spruce tops, solid rosewood or mahogany (M) back and sides.

2004-2006	AJ-500	$400	$500

Alleykat

2000-present. Single cut small body archtop, 1 humbucker and 1 mini-humbucker.

2000-2006		$375	$400

B.B. King Lucille

1997-present. Laminated double-cut maple body, 2 humbuckers, Lucille on headstock.

1997-2006		$475	$550

Barcelona CE

1999-2000. Classical, solid spruce top, rosewood back and sides, EQ/preamp.

1999-2000		$350	$400

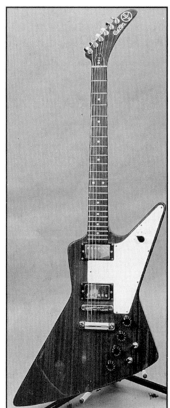

1981 Electra MPC X910

Ellsberry de Lutan

Epiphone Biscuit

Epiphone Broadway

MODEL YEAR	FEATURES	EXC. COND. LOW	HIGH

Barcelone (Classical)
1963-1968. Highest model of Epiphone '60s classical guitars, maple back and sides, gold hardware.

| 1963-1964 | | $900 | $1,000 |
| 1965-1968 | | $800 | $900 |

Bard 12-String
1962-1969. Flat-top, mahogany back and sides, natural or sunburst.

| 1962-1964 | | $1,700 | $2,100 |
| 1965-1969 | | $1,400 | $1,700 |

Biscuit
1997-2000, 2002-present. Wood body resonator, biscuit bridge, round neck.

| 1997-2005 | | $250 | $300 |

Blackstone
1931-1950. Acoustic archtop, f-holes, sunburst.

1933-1934	Masterbilt	$1,000	$1,250
1935-1937		$850	$1,075
1938-1939		$750	$975
1940-1941		$675	$900
1948-1949		$575	$900

Broadway (Acoustic)
1931-1958. Non-cut acoustic archtop.

1931-1938	Sunburst, walnut body	$2,350	$2,900
1939-1942	Sunburst, maple body	$2,700	$2,850
1946-1949	Natural	$2,300	$2,500
1946-1949	Sunburst	$2,000	$2,400
1950-1958	Sunburst	$1,950	$2,300

Broadway Regent (Acoustic Cutaway)
1950-1958. Single-cut acoustic archtop, sunburst.

| 1950-1958 | | $2,300 | $2,800 |

Broadway (Electric)
1958-1969. Gibson-made electric archtop, single-cut, 2 New York pickups (mini-humbucking pickups by '61), Frequensator tailpiece, block inlays, sunburst or natural finish with cherry optional in '67 only.

1958-1959	Natural	$3,300	$3,800
1958-1959	Sunburst	$3,150	$3,700
1960-1964	Natural	$3,225	$3,600
1960-1964	Sunburst	$3,000	$3,500
1965	Natural	$3,150	$3,425
1965	Sunburst	$3,000	$3,250
1966-1967	Natural, cherry	$3,050	$3,300
1966-1967	Sunburst	$2,900	$3,150
1968-1969	Natural, cherry	$3,000	$3,250
1968-1969	Sunburst	$2,800	$3,050

Broadway Reissue
1997-present. Full depth acoustic-electric single cut archtop, 2 humbuckers

| 1997-2006 | | $600 | $675 |

Broadway Tenor
1937-1953. Acoustic archtop, sunburst.

| 1930s | | $900 | $1,100 |
| 1950s | | $725 | $875 |

Byron
1949-ca.1955. Acoustic archtop, mahogany back and sides, sunburst.

| 1949-1955 | | $375 | $475 |

MODEL YEAR	FEATURES	EXC. COND. LOW	HIGH

Caiola Custom
1963-1970. Introduced as Caiola, renamed Caiola Custom in '66, electric thinbody archtop, 2 mini-humbuckers, multi-bound top and back, block inlays, walnut or sunburst finish (walnut only by '68).

1963-1964		$3,300	$4,000
1965		$3,150	$3,800
1966-1967		$3,000	$3,600
1968-1970		$2,900	$3,500

Caiola Standard
1966-1970. Electric thinbody archtop, 2 P-90s, single-bound top and back, dot inlays, sunburst or cherry.

| 1966-1967 | | $2,600 | $3,200 |
| 1968-1970 | | $2,500 | $3,000 |

Casino (1 Pickup)
1961-1970. Thinline hollowbody, double-cut, 1 P-90 pickup, various colors.

1961		$2,900	$3,400
1962-1964		$2,700	$3,300
1965-1966		$2,200	$2,700
1967-1968		$2,100	$2,600
1969-1970		$2,000	$2,400

Casino (2 Pickups)
1961-1970. Two pickup (P-90) version, various colors. '61-'63 known as Keith Richards model, '64-'65 known as Beatles model.

1961		$4,700	$5,300
1962-1964		$3,600	$4,500
1965-1966		$3,100	$3,600
1967-1970		$3,000	$3,500

Casino J.L. U.S.A. 1965
2003-2006. 1,965 made.

| 2003-2006 | | $1,900 | $2,000 |

Casino Reissue
1995-present. Sunburst.

| 1995-1999 | | $450 | $525 |
| 2000-2005 | | $400 | $500 |

Casino Revolution
1999. Limited production 1965 reissue model, sanded natural.

| 1999 | | $2,100 | $2,200 |

Century
1939-1970. Thinline archtop, non-cut, 1 pickup, trapeze tailpiece, walnut finish, sunburst finish available in '58, Royal Burgundy available '61 and only sunburst finish available by '68.

1939-1948	Oblong shape pickup	$1,350	$1,650
1949	Large rectangular pickup	$1,300	$1,600
1950	New York pickup	$1,250	$1,550
1951-1957	Sunburst	$1,200	$1,500
1958-1959	Sunburst, P-90 pickup	$1,500	$1,800
1960-1964	Sunburst, P-90 pickup	$1,400	$1,700
1965-1967	Sunburst, cherry	$1,250	$1,500
1968-1970	Sunburst	$1,200	$1,475

MODEL YEAR	FEATURES	EXC. COND. LOW	HIGH
Classic (Classical)			
1963-1970.			
1963-1964		$700	$800
1965-1970		$600	$700
Collegiate			
2004-2005. Les Paul-style body, 1 humbucker, various college graphic decals on body.			
2004-2005		$150	$175
Coronet (Electric Archtop)			
1939-1949. Electric archtop, laminated mahogany body, 1 pickup, trapeze tailpiece, sunburst, name continued as an electric solidbody in '58.			
1939-1949		$1,000	$1,250
Coronet (Solidbody)			
1958-1969. Solidbody electric, 1 New York pickup ('58-'59), 1 P-90 ('59-'69), cherry or black finish, Silver Fox finish available by '63, reintroduced as Coronet USA '90-'94, Korean-made '95-'98.			
1958-1959		$3,500	$4,100
1960-1964	Various colors	$3,000	$3,600
1965	Custom color (3 options)	$4,000	$4,600
1965	Standard color	$2,600	$3,200
1966-1967	Various colors	$2,400	$2,500
1968-1969	Various colors	$2,100	$2,200
Coronet U.S.A.			
1990-1994. Made in Nashville, reverse banana headstock, typical Coronet styled body, single-coil and humbucker.			
1990-1994		$650	$800
Coronet (Import)			
1995-1998. Import version.			
1995-1998		$275	$300
Crestwood Custom			
1958-1970. Solidbody, 2 New York pickups ('58-'60), 2 mini-humbuckers ('61-'70), symmetrical body and 3+3 tuners ('58-'62), asymmetrical and 1x6 tuners ('63-'70), slab body with no Gibson equivalent model.			
1958-1960	Cherry, New York pickups, 3+3	$4,000	$4,500
1959-1960	Sunburst, New York pickups	$4,000	$4,500
1961-1962	Cherry, mini-humbuckers	$3,900	$4,400
1961-1962	White, mini-humbuckers	$4,200	$5,500
1963-1964	Cherry, 1x6	$3,300	$3,700
1963-1964	Custom color (3 options)	$6,000	$7,500
1965	Cherry	$2,800	$3,500
1965	Custom color (3 options)	$5,000	$6,000
1966-1967	Cherry	$2,800	$3,400
1966-1967	Custom color (3 options)	$4,000	$5,000
1968-1970	Cherry, white	$2,600	$3,200
Crestwood Deluxe			
1963-1969. Solidbody with 3 mini-humbuckers, block inlay, cherry, white or Pacific Blue finish, 1x6 tuners.			
1963-1964	Cherry	$4,300	$5,000

MODEL YEAR	FEATURES	EXC. COND. LOW	HIGH
1963-1964	Custom color (3 options)	$8,800	$11,000
1965	Cherry	$4,200	$4,900
1965	Custom color (3 options)	$7,000	$8,000
1966-1967	Cherry	$3,700	$4,400
1966-1967	Custom color (3 options)	$5,500	$6,000
1968-1969	Cherry, white	$3,600	$4,300
De Luxe			
1931-1957. Non-cut acoustic archtop, maple back and sides, trapeze tailpiece ('31-'37), frequensator tailpiece ('37-'57), gold-plated hardware, sunburst or natural finish.			
1931-1934	Sunburst	$4,500	$5,000
1935-1939	Sunburst	$4,300	$4,700
1939	Natural, 1st year option	$4,800	$5,300
1940-1944	Natural	$4,600	$5,100
1940-1944	Sunburst	$4,300	$4,700
1945-1949	Natural	$4,200	$4,500
1945-1949	Sunburst	$3,500	$4,000
1950-1957	Natural	$3,400	$4,200
1950-1957	Sunburst	$3,100	$3,600
De Luxe Regent (Acoustic Archtop)			
1948-1952. Acoustic cutaway archtop, high-end appointments, rounded cutaway, natural finish, renamed De Luxe Cutaway in '53.			
1948-1952		$4,000	$5,000
De Luxe Cutaway/Deluxe Cutaway			
1953-1970. Renamed from De Luxe Regent, cataloged Deluxe Cutaway by Gibson in '58, special order by '64 with limited production because acoustic archtops were pretty much replaced by electric archtops.			
1953-1957	Epiphone NY-made	$3,800	$4,700
1958-1959		$5,000	$6,000
1960-1965	Gibson Kalamazoo, rounded cutaway	$5,000	$6,000
1965-1970	Special order only	$4,000	$6,000
De Luxe Electric (Archtop)			
1954-1957. Single-cut electric archtop, 2 pickups, called the Zephyr De Luxe Regent from '48-'54. Produced with a variety of specs, maple or spruce tops, different inlays and pickup combinations.			
1954-1957	Natural	$3,600	$4,400
1954-1957	Sunburst	$3,200	$3,900
Del Ray			
1995-2000. Offset double-cut body, 2 blade humbuckers, dot markers, tune-o-matic, flamed maple top.			
1995-2000		$325	$375
Devon			
1949-1957. Acoustic archtop, non-cut, mahogany back and sides, sunburst finish, optional natural finish by '54.			
1950-1953	Sunburst	$1,200	$1,500
1954-1957	Natural	$1,400	$1,750
1954-1957	Sunburst	$1,200	$1,500

1965 Epiphone Casino

Epiphone Crestwood

Epiphone SQ-180 Don Everly

Epiphone Elitist '63 Dot

MODEL YEAR	FEATURES	EXC. COND. LOW	HIGH

Don Everly (SQ-180)
1997-2004. Jumbo acoustic reissue, large double 'guard, black gloss finish.

| 1997-2004 | | $500 | $600 |

Dot (ES-335 Dot)/Dot Archtop
2000-present. Dot-neck ES-335.

| 2000-2007 | | $275 | $325 |

Dot Studio
2004-present. Simplified Dot, 2 control knobs, black hardware.

| 2004-2007 | | $225 | $250 |

Dwight
1963, 1967. Coronet labeled as Dwight and made for Sonny Shields Music of St. Louis, 75 made in '63 and 36 in '67, cherry. National-Supro made Dwight brand lap steels in the '50s.

| 1963 | | $2,600 | $3,200 |
| 1967 | | $1,900 | $2,300 |

EA/ET/ES Series (Japan)
1970-1979. Production of the Epiphone brand was moved to Japan in '70. Models included the EA (electric thinline) and ET (electric solidbody).

1970-1975	ET-270	$350	$400
1970-1975	ET-275	$350	$425
1970s	EA-250	$375	$450
1972	ES-255 Casino	$450	$500
1975-1979	ET-290 Crestwood	$450	$500

El Diablo
1994-1995. Offset double-cut acoustic/electric, onboard piezo and 3-band EQ, composite back and sides, spruce top, cherry sunburst.

| 1994-1995 | | $300 | $350 |

Electar Model M
1935-1939. Epiphone's initial entry into the new electric guitar market of the mid-'30s, 14 3/4" laminate maple archtop, horseshoe pickup, trap door on back for electronics, Electar logo on headstock, oblong pickup replaces horseshoe in late-'37.

| 1935-1936 | 2 control knobs | $1,200 | $1,300 |
| 1937-1939 | 3 control knobs | $1,200 | $1,300 |

Electar Model M Tenor
1937-1939. 4-string electric tenor with Electar specs.

| 1937-1939 | 3 knobs, natural | $1,200 | $1,300 |

Elitist Series
2003-present. Made in Japan, higher-grade series, using finer woods and inlays and U.S.-made Gibson pickups.

2003-2004	J-200	$900	$1,100
2003-2005	1961 SG Standard	$500	$600
2003-2005	Les Paul Studio	$525	$650
2003-2007	1963 ES-335 Dot	$900	$1,100
2003-2007	Broadway	$900	$1,100
2003-2007	Byrdland/L5	$900	$1,100
2003-2007	Casino	$900	$1,100
2003-2007	Les Paul Custom	$700	$800
2003-2007	Les Paul Standard '57 Goldtop	$700	$800
2003-2007	Les Paul Standard/Plus	$700	$800
2003-2007	Sheraton	$1,000	$1,225

MODEL YEAR	FEATURES	EXC. COND. LOW	HIGH

2003-2007	Texan	$900	$1,000
2005	Chet Atkins		
	Country		
	Gentleman	$900	$1,100

Emperor (Acoustic Archtop)
1935-1954. Acoustic archtop, non-cut, maple back and sides, multi-bound body, gold-plated hardware, sunburst, optional natural finish by '39.

1935-1938	Sunburst	$5,500	$6,000
1939-1949	Natural	$5,800	$6,400
1939-1949	Sunburst	$5,000	$5,500
1950-1954	Natural	$4,600	$5,100
1950-1954	Sunburst	$4,200	$4,700

Emperor (Thinline Electric)
1958-1969. Single-cut, thinline archtop, 3 New York pickups in '58-'60, 3 mini-humbuckers '61 on, multi-bound, gold-plated hardware, sunburst or natural finish until '65 when only sunburst was made.

1958-1969	Natural	$11,000	$13,000
1958-1969	Sunburst	$10,000	$13,000
1960-1962	Natural	$10,000	$13,000
1960-1962	Sunburst	$9,000	$11,000
1963-1964	Special order only	$9,000	$11,000
1965-1969	Special order only	$7,500	$9,200

Emperor Cutaway
1953-1957. Renamed from Emperor Regent, acoustic archtop, single-cut, maple back and sides, multi-bound body, gold-plated hardware, sunburst or natural.

| 1953-1957 | Natural | $5,800 | $6,400 |
| 1953-1957 | Sunburst | $5,000 | $5,500 |

Emperor Electric
1953-1957. Archtop, single-cut, 3 pickups, multi-bound body, sunburst, called the Zephyr Emperor Regent in '50-'53.

| 1953-1957 | | $3,400 | $3,700 |

Emperor Regent
1948-1953. Acoustic archtop with rounded cutaway, renamed Emperor Cutaway in '53.

| 1948-1953 | Natural | $6,100 | $6,800 |
| 1948-1953 | Sunburst | $4,500 | $6,500 |

Emperor/Emperor II
1982-1994. Single-cut archtop jazz guitar, 2 humbuckers, blocks, gold hardware. II added to name in '93, became Joe Pass Emperor II (see that listing) in '95, although his name was on the guitar as early as '91.

| 1982-1994 | | $500 | $625 |

Entrada (Classical)
1963-1968. Classical, natural.

| 1963-1964 | | $700 | $800 |
| 1965-1968 | | $600 | $700 |

Espana (Classical)
1962-1968. Classical, maple back and sides, U.S.-made, natural, imported in '69 from Japan.

| 1962-1964 | | $750 | $850 |
| 1965-1968 | | $650 | $750 |

MODEL YEAR	FEATURES	EXC. COND. LOW	HIGH

Exellente
1963-1969, 1994-1995. Flat-top, rosewood back and sides, cloud inlays. Name revived on Gibson Montana insturment in '90s.

1963-1964		$6,500	$7,100
1965		$5,100	$6,000
1966-1967		$4,500	$5,100
1968-1969		$3,800	$4,600

1958 Gothic Explorer/Flying V
2002-present. Flat black finish.

2002-2007		$350	$425

1958 Korina Explorer
1998-present. Explorer with typical appointments, korina body. This guitar was produced with a variety of specs, ranging from maple tops to spruce tops, different inlay markers were also used, different pickup combinations have been seen, natural or sunburst finish.

1998-2007		$400	$500

Firebird
1995-2000. Two mini-humbuckers, Firebird Red, dot markers.

1995-2000		$375	$425

1963 Firebird VII/Firebird VII
2000-2005. Three mini-humbuckers, gold hardware, Maestro-style vibrato, block markers, Firebird Red, reverse body. 1963 added after first year.

2000-2005		$325	$400

Firebird 300
1986-1988. Korean import, Firebird Red.

1986-1988		$300	$350

Firebird 500
1986-1988. Korean import, Firebird Red.

1986-1988		$300	$375

Flamekat
1999-2005. Archtop, flame finish, double dice position markers, 2 mini-humbuckers, Epiphone Bigsby.

1999-2005		$425	$500

Flying V/'67 Flying V
1989-1998, 2003-2005. '67 or '58 specs, alder body, natural.

1989-1998	'67 specs	$375	$450
2003-2005	'58 specs	$400	$475

1958 Korina Flying V
1998-present. Typical Flying V configuration, korina body.

1998-2007		$425	$550

FT 30
1941-1949. Acoustic flat-top, brown stain, mahogany back and sides, reintroduced as Gibson-made FT 30 Caballero in '58.

1941-1949		$1,100	$1,350

FT 30 Caballero
1958-1970. Reintroduced from Epiphone-made FT 30, Gibson-made acoustic flat-top, natural, all mahogany body, dot inlay, tenor available '63-'68.

1958-1959		$925	$1,100
1960-1964		$750	$900
1965		$600	$750
1966-1967		$600	$725
1968-1970		$525	$650

FT 45
1941-1948. Acoustic flat-top, walnut back and sides, cherry neck, rosewood 'board, natural top, reintroduced as Gibson-made FT 45 Cortez in '58.

1941-1948		$1,400	$1,750

FT 45 Cortez
1958-1969. Reintroduced from Epiphone-made FT 45, Gibson-made acoustic flat-top, mahogany back and sides, sunburst or natural top (sunburst only in '59-'62).

1958-1959	Sunburst	$1,450	$1,800
1960-1964	Sunburst or natural	$1,400	$1,700
1965	Sunburst or natural	$1,100	$1,300
1966-1967	Sunburst or natural	$1,000	$1,200
1968-1969	Sunburst or natural	$900	$1,000

FT 79
1941-1958. Acoustic 16" flat-top, square shoulder dreadnought, walnut back and sides until '49 and laminated maple back and sides '49 on, natural, renamed FT 79 Texan by Gibson in '58.

1941-1949	Walnut back & sides	$2,700	$3,400
1949-1958	Laminated pressed maple body	$2,600	$2,900

FT 79 Texan
1958-1970, 1993-1995. Renamed from Epiphone FT 79, Gibson-made acoustic flat-top, mahogany back and sides, sunburst or natural top, Gibson Montana made 170 in '93-'95.

1958-1959		$3,500	$4,100
1960-1964		$3,200	$3,800
1965		$3,000	$3,600
1966-1967		$2,700	$3,300
1968-1970		$2,500	$3,000

FT 85 Serenader 12-String
1963-1969. 12 strings, mahogany back and sides, dot inlay, natural.

1963-1964		$1,300	$1,600
1965-1966		$1,150	$1,250
1967-1969		$950	$1,150

FT 90 El Dorado
1963-1970. Dreadnought flat-top acoustic, mahogany back and sides, multi-bound front and back, natural.

1963-1964		$2,300	$2,800
1965		$2,100	$2,600
1966-1967		$2,000	$2,500
1968-1970		$1,900	$2,300

FT 95 Folkster
1966-1969. 14" small body, mahogany back and sides, natural, double white 'guards.

1966-1967		$650	$775
1968-1969		$550	$675

FT 98 Troubadour
1963-1969. 16" square shouldered drednought, maple back and sides, gold-plated hardware, classical width 'board.

1963-1964		$1,600	$1,900
1965-1969		$1,500	$1,600

Epiphone Flamekat

Epiphone FT 79 Texan

Epiphone G 400 Tony Iommi

Epiphone Les Paul LP-100

MODEL YEAR	FEATURES	EXC. COND. LOW	HIGH
FT 110			
1941-1958. Acoustic flat-top, natural, renamed the FT 110 Frontier by Gibson in '58.			
1941-1949	Square shoulder	$2,800	$3,500
1949-1954	Round shoulder	$2,700	$3,300
1954-1958	Mahogany neck	$2,600	$3,200
FT 110 Frontier			
1958-1970, 1994. Renamed from FT 110, acoustic flat-top, natural or sunburst, Gibson Montana made 30 in '94.			
1958-1959		$3,200	$3,500
1960-1964		$3,100	$3,400
1965		$2,900	$3,300
1966-1967		$2,600	$3,200
1968-1970	Maple	$2,400	$2,800
FT Series (Flat-Tops Japan)			
1970s. In '70 Epiphone moved production to Japan. Various models were made, nearly all with bolt necks and small rectangular blue labels on the inside back.			
1970s	FT 120	$60	$75
1970s	FT 130, 132, 133, 140	$100	$125
1970s	FT 135	$200	$225
1970s	FT 145, 146, 160 12-string, 160N	$150	$200
1970s	FT 150, 165 12-string	$200	$300
1970s	FT 155	$250	$325
1970s	FT 200 Monticello	$200	$250
1970s	FT 350 El Dorado, 565 12-string	$300	$350
1970s	FT 550	$300	$375
1970s	FT 570SB Super Jumbo	$350	$400
G 310			
1989-present. SG-style model with large 'guard and gig bag.			
1989-2007		$200	$225
G 400			
1989-present. SG-style, 2 humbuckers, crown inlays.			
1989-2007		$250	$300
G 400 Custom			
1998-2000, 2003-present. 3 humbucker version, gold harware, block inlays.			
1998-2007		$400	$450
G 400 Deluxe			
1999-2007. Flame maple top version of 2 humbucker 400.			
1999-2007		$325	$400
G 400 Limited Edition			
2001-2002. 400 with Deluxe Maestro lyra vibrola, cherry red.			
2001-2002		$350	$425
G 400 Tony Iommi			
2003-present. SG-style model with cross 'board inlay markers, black finish.			
2003-2006		$450	$500
G 1275 Custom Double Neck			
1996-present. 6- & 12-string, SG-style alder body, maple top, mahogany neck, cherry red, set neck. Also offered as bolt-neck Standard for '96-'98.			
1996-2007		$675	$825

MODEL YEAR	FEATURES	EXC. COND. LOW	HIGH
Genesis			
1979-1980. Double-cut solidbody, 2 humbuckers with coil-taps, carved top, red or black, available as Custom, Deluxe, and Standard models, Taiwan import.			
1979-1980		$450	$550
Granada (Non-cutaway Thinbody)			
1962-1969. Non-cut thinline archtop, 1 f-hole, 1 pickup, trapeze tailpiece, sunburst finish.			
1962-1965		$1,000	$1,250
1966-1969		$950	$1,150
Granada (Cutaway)			
1965-1970. Single-cut version.			
1965-1966		$1,300	$1,400
1967-1970		$1,000	$1,200
Howard Roberts Standard			
1964-1970. Single-cut acoustic archtop, bound front and back, cherry or sunburst finish, listed in catalog as acoustic but built as electric.			
1964		$2,700	$3,100
1965-1967		$2,200	$2,400
1968-1970		$1,800	$2,100
Howard Roberts Custom			
1965-1970. Single-cut archtop, bound front and back, 1 pickup, walnut finish (natural offered '66 only).			
1965-1967		$2,800	$3,400
1968-1970		$2,300	$2,800
Howard Roberts III			
1987-1991. Two pickups, various colors.			
1987-1991		$550	$600
Joe Pass/Joe Pass Emperor II			
1995-present. Single-cut archtop jazz guitar, 2 humbuckers, blocks, gold hardware, renamed from Emperor II (see that listing).			
1995-2006		$400	$475
Les Paul Ace Frehley			
2001. Les Paul Custom 3-pickups, Ace's signature on 22nd fret, lightening bolt markers.			
2001		$650	$700
Les Paul Black Beauty 3			
1997-present. Classic styling with three gold plated pickups, black finish, block markers.			
1997-2007		$450	$475
Les Paul Classic			
2003-2005. Classic Les Paul Standard specs, figured maple top, sunburst.			
2003-2005		$425	$450
Les Paul Custom			
1989-present. Various colors.			
1989-2007		$425	$475
Les Paul Custom Plus (Flame Top)			
1998-present. Flamed maple top version of 2 pickup Custom, gold hardware, sunburst.			
1998-2007		$450	$550
Les Paul Deluxe			
1998-2000. Typical mini-humbucker pickups.			
1998-2000		$350	$400

The *Vintage Guitar Price Guide* shows low to high values for items in all-original excellent condition, and, where applicable, with original case or cover.

MODEL YEAR	FEATURES	EXC. COND. LOW	HIGH

Les Paul ES Limited Edition
1999-2000. Les Paul semi-hollow body with f-holes, carved maple top, gold hardware, cherry sunburst and other color options.

| 1999-2000 | Custom | $700 | $775 |
| 1999-2000 | Standard | $600 | $675 |

Les Paul LP-100
1993-present. Affordable single-cut Les Paul, bolt-on neck.

| 1993-2007 | | $150 | $175 |

Les Paul Slash
1997-2000. Slash logo on body.

| 1997-2000 | | $600 | $650 |

Les Paul Sparkle L.E.
2001. Limited Edition LP Standard, silver, purple, red (and others) glitter finish, optional Bigsby.

| 2001 | | $375 | $450 |

Les Paul Special
1994-2000. Double-cut, bolt neck.

| 1994-2000 | | $150 | $200 |

Les Paul Special II
1996-present. Economical Les Paul, 2 pickups, single-cut, various colors.

| 1996-2007 | Guitar only | $120 | $130 |
| 1996-2007 | Player Pack with amp | $140 | $160 |

Les Paul Special Limited Edition/TV Special
2006. Copy of single-cut late '50s Les Paul Special with TV finish.

| 2006 | | $450 | $550 |

Les Paul Standard
1989-present. Solid mahogany body, carved maple top, 2 humbuckers.

| 1989-2007 | | $350 | $425 |

Les Paul Standard Baritone
2004-2005. 27-3/4" long-scale baritone model.

| 2004-2005 | | $325 | $400 |

Les Paul Standard Plus FMT
2003-present. LP Standard figured curly maple sunburst top.

| 2003-2007 | | $325 | $400 |

Les Paul Studio
1995-present. Epiphone's version of Gibson LP Studio.

| 1995-2007 | | $325 | $400 |

Les Paul Ultra
2005-present. LP Standard with chambered and contoured body, quilted maple top.

| 2005-2007 | | $350 | $400 |

Les Paul XII
1998-2000. 12-string solidbody, trapeze tailpiece, flamed maple sunburst, standard configuration.

| 1998-2000 | | $450 | $550 |

Madrid (Classical)
1962-1969. Classical, natural.

| 1962-1964 | | $575 | $625 |
| 1965-1969 | | $525 | $575 |

Melody Tenor
1931-1937. 23" scale, bound body.

| 1931-1937 | Masterbilt | $1,300 | $1,400 |

Moderne
2000. Copy of '58 Gibson Moderne design, dot markers, Moderne script logo on 'guard, black.

| 2000 | | $650 | $800 |

Navarre
1931-1940. Flat-top, mahogany back and sides, bound top and back, dot inlay, brown finish.

| 1931-1937 | Hawaiian,
Masterbilt label | $1,800 | $2,000 |
| 1938-1940 | Hawaiian,
standard label | $1,600 | $1,800 |

Nighthawk Standard
1995-2000. Epiphone's version of the Gibson Nighthawk, single-cut, bolt neck, figured top.

| 1995-2000 | | $300 | $375 |

Noel Gallagher Union Jack/Super Nova
1997-2005. Limited edition, higher-end ES-335. Union Jack with British flag finish (introduced '99) or Supernova in solid blue.

| 1997-2005 | | $500 | $575 |

Olympic (3/4 Scale Solidbody)
1960-1963. 22" scale, sunburst.

| 1960-1963 | | $925 | $1,150 |

Olympic (Acoustic Archtop)
1931-1949. Mahogany back and sides.

| 1931-1939 | | $800 | $900 |
| 1940-1949 | | $750 | $850 |

Olympic Double (Solidbody)
1960-1969. Slab body, the same as the mid-'60s Coronet, Wilshire and Crestwood Series, single-cut '60-'62, asymmetrical-cut '63-'70, 2 Melody Maker single-coils, vibrato optional in '64 and standard by '65.

1960-1962	Sunburst, single-cut	$1,750	$2,100
1963-1964	Sunburst, double-cut	$1,300	$1,600
1965-1969	Cherry or sunburst	$950	$1,175

Olympic Single (Solidbody)
1960-1970. Slab body, the same as the mid-'60s Coronet, Wilshire and Crestwood Series, single-cut '60-'62, asymmetrical double-cut '63-'70, 2 Melody maker single-coil pickups, vibrato optional in '64 and standard by '65.

1960-1962	Sunburst, single-cut	$1,450	$1,800
1963-1964	Sunburst, double-cut	$1,100	$1,300
1965-1970	Cherry or sunburst	$800	$1,000

Olympic Special (Solidbody)
1962-1970. Short neck with neck body joint at the 16th fret (instead of the 22nd), single Melody Maker-style single-coil bridge pickup, small headstock, double-cut slab body, dot markers, Maestro or Epiphone vibrato optional '64-'65, slab body contour changes in '65 from symmetrical to asymmetrical with slightly longer bass horn, sunburst.

1962-1964	Symmetrical	$1,300	$1,600
1965	Asymmetrical	$900	$1,100
1966-1967		$800	$1,000
1968-1970		$600	$800

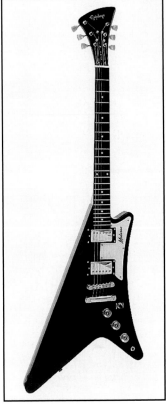

Epiphone Moderne

1965 Epiphone Olympic

1966 Epiphone Riviera

Epiphone SG Special

MODEL YEAR	FEATURES	EXC. COND. LOW	HIGH

PR-200 (EA-20)
1992-2000. Imported dreadnought, spruce top, satin finish, mahogany back and sides, natural.

| 1992-2000 | | $150 | $225 |

PR-350
1984-2000. Acoustic flat-top, mahogany body, also available with a pickup.

| 1984-2000 | | $200 | $250 |

PR-350 CE
1989-2000. Cutaway 350, also available with a pickup.

| 1989-2000 | | $275 | $325 |

PR-600 ACS/ASB/N
1980-1985. Import 000-size flat-top, glued bridge, dot markers, sunburst.

| 1980-1985 | | $350 | $400 |

PR-755S
1980-1985. Flat-top, single-cut, solid spruce top, laminate rosewood body, set mahogany neck, block markers, gold hardware, natural.

| 1980-1985 | | $275 | $325 |

Pro 1
1989-1996. Solidbody, double-cut, 1 single-coil and 1 humbucking pickup, bolt-on neck, various colors.

| 1989-1996 | | $325 | $400 |

Pro 2
1995-1998. Higher-end Pro I with Steinberger DB bridge, set-neck, 2 humbuckers, various colors.

| 1995-1998 | | $350 | $400 |

Professional
1962-1967. Double-cut, thinline archtop, 1 pickup, mahogany finish.

1962-1964	With matching Professional Amp	$2,200	$3,000
1965	With matching Professional Amp	$1,900	$2,300
1966-1967	With matching Professional Amp	$1,800	$2,100

Recording A
1928-1931.

| 1928-1931 | Standard 6-string | $1,900 | $2,300 |
| 1928-1931 | Tenor 4-string | $1,600 | $2,000 |

Recording B
1928-1931. Asymmetrical body, cutaway bouts, flat-top, arched back, laminated maple back.

| 1928-1931 | | $2,500 | $3,100 |

Recording C
1928-1931.

| 1928-1931 | | $2,900 | $3,400 |

Recording D
1928-1931.

| 1928-1931 | | $3,400 | $3,900 |

Recording E
1928-1931.

| 1928-1931 | | $4,600 | $4,900 |

Riviera
1962-1970, 1993-1994. Double-cut thinline archtop, 2 mini-humbuckers, Royal Tan standard finish changing to sunburst in '65, cherry optional by '66-'70, additional 250 were made in Nashville in '93-'94, a Riviera import was available in '82 and for '94-'06.

1962-1964	Tan or custom cherry	$4,000	$4,300
1965	Sunburst or cherry	$3,700	$4,000
1966-1967	Burgundy Mist	$3,500	$4,200
1966-1967	Sunburst or cherry	$3,300	$3,900
1967-1968	Walnut	$3,200	$3,500
1968-1970	Sunburst or cherry	$3,000	$3,300

Riviera Reissue (Korea)
1994-2006. Korean-made contemporary reissue, natural.

| 1994-2006 | | $375 | $450 |

Riviera 12-String
1965-1970. Double-cut, 12 strings, thinline archtop, 2 mini-humbuckers, sunburst or cherry.

1965		$2,800	$2,900
1966-1967		$2,300	$2,600
1968-1970		$2,200	$2,500

Riviera 12-String Reissue (Korea)
1997-2000. Korean-made reissue, natural.

| 1997-2000 | | $475 | $575 |

Royal
1931-1935. 15 1/2" acoustic archtop, mahogany back and sides, dot markers, sunburst, bound top, back and neck, Masterbilt headstock logo.

| 1931-1935 | | $2,400 | $2,800 |

S-900
1986-1989. Neck-thru-body, locking Bender tremolo system, 2 pickups with individual switching and a coil-tap control.

| 1986-1989 | | $350 | $425 |

SC350
1976-1979. Mahogany solidbody, scroll bass horn, rosewood 'board, dot inlays, bolt neck, 2 humbuckers, made in Japan.

| 1976-1979 | Mahogany | $350 | $400 |

SC450
1976-1979. Like SC350, but with maple body, glued neck, and coil tap.

| 1976-1979 | Maple | $350 | $400 |

SC550
1976-1979. Like SC450, but with gold hardware, block inlays, neck and body binding, and ebony 'board.

| 1976-1979 | Maple, gold hardware | $375 | $450 |

Seville EC-100 (Classical)
1938-1941, 1961-1969 (Gibson-made). Classical guitar, mahogany back and sides, natural, the '61-'63 version also available with a pickup.

| 1961-1964 | | $700 | $800 |
| 1965-1969 | | $600 | $700 |

The *Vintage Guitar Price Guide* shows low to high values for items in all-original excellent condition, and, where applicable, with original case or cover.

MODEL YEAR	FEATURES	EXC. COND. LOW	HIGH

SG Special
2000-present. SG body, dot markers, 2 open-coil humbuckers.

2000-2007	Guitar only	$100	$125
2000-2007	Players Pack with amp	$125	$150

Sheraton
1958-1970, 1993-1994. Double-cut thinline archtop, 2 New York pickups '58-'60, 2 mini-humbuckers '61 on, frequensator tailpiece, multi-bound, gold-plated hardware, sunburst or natural finish with cherry optional by '65.

1958-1959	Natural, New York pickups	$8,300	$9,500
1960	Natural, New York pickups	$7,300	$8,500
1961-1964	Natural, mini-humbuckers	$7,300	$8,500
1961-1964	Sunburst, mini-humbuckers	$6,500	$7,000
1965	Cherry	$5,500	$6,500
1965	Natural	$6,000	$7,000
1965	Sunburst	$5,400	$6,400
1966	Sunburst or cherry	$5,300	$6,200
1967	Sunburst or cherry	$4,800	$5,800
1968	Sunburst or cherry	$4,600	$5,600
1969-1970	Sunburst or cherry	$4,500	$5,500

Sheraton (Japan)
1978-1983. Early reissue, not to be confused with Sheraton II issued in late-'90s, natural or sunburst.

1978-1983		$450	$550

Sheraton (Reissue U.S.A.)
1993-1994. An additional 250 American-made Sheratons were built from '93-'94.

1993-1994		$450	$550

Sheraton II (Reissue)
1994-present. Contemporary reissue, natural or sunburst.

1994-2007		$450	$550

Slasher
2001. Reverse offset double cut solidbody, bolt neck, six-on-a-side tuners, 2 pickups, dot markers.

2001		$275	$300

Sorrento (1 pickup)
1960-1970. Single-cut thinline archtop, 1 pickup in neck position, tune-o-matic bridge, nickel-plated hardware, sunburst, natural or Royal Olive finish, (cherry or sunburst by '68).

1960-1964		$1,900	$2,200
1965-1966		$1,700	$2,000
1967-1970		$1,600	$2,000

Sorrento (2 pickups)
1960-1970. Single-cut thinline archtop, 2 pickups, tune-o-matic bridge, nickel-plated hardware, sunburst, natural or Royal Olive finish, (cherry or sunburst by '68).

1960-1964		$2,300	$2,700
1965-1966		$2,200	$2,400
1967-1970		$2,000	$2,200

Sorrento (Reissue)
1997-2000.

1997-2000		$400	$475

Spartan
1934-1949. Acoustic archtop, multi-bound, trapeze tailpiece, sunburst.

1934-1939		$650	$800
1940-1949		$525	$650

Special/SG Special (U.S.A.)
1979-1983. SG Special body style, dot markers, 2 exposed humbuckers, Special logo on truss rod cover.

1979-1983		$650	$750

Spider/The Spider
1997-2000. Wood body resonator, spider bridge, square neck.

1997-2000		$250	$300

Spirit
1979-1983. U.S.-made electric solidbody, Spirit logo on truss rod cover and new Epiphone U.S.A. designated script logo on headstock, double-cut, carved top with 2 humbuckers, various colors.

1979-1983		$650	$750

Trailer Park Troubadour Airscreamer
2003-2005. Airstream trailer-shaped body, identifying logo on headstock.

2003-2005		$400	$500

Triumph
1931-1957. 15 1/4" '31-'33, 16 3/8" '33-'36, 17 3/8" '36-'57, walnut back and sides until '33, laminated maple back and sides '33, solid maple back and sides '34, natural or sunburst.

1931-1932	Sunburst, laminated walnut body	$1,500	$1,850
1933	Sunburst, laminated maple body	$1,500	$1,850
1934-1935	Sunburst, solid maple body	$1,600	$2,000
1936-1940	Sunburst 17 3/8" body	$1,900	$2,100
1941-1949	Natural	$1,900	$2,100
1941-1949	Sunburst	$1,800	$2,000
1950-1957	Natural	$1,800	$2,000
1950-1957	Sunburst	$1,300	$1,600

Triumph Regent (Cutaway)
1948-1969. Acoustic archtop, single-cut, F-holes, renamed Triumph Cutaway in '53, then Gibson listed this model as just the Triumph from '58-'69.

1948-1952	Triumpt Regent, natural	$2,500	$2,800
1948-1952	Triumpt Regent, sunburst	$2,400	$2,600
1953-1957	Triumph Cutaway, natural	$2,500	$2,700
1953-1957	Triumph Cutaway, sunburst	$2,300	$2,600
1958-1959	Sunburst	$3,000	$3,500
1960-1964	Sunburst	$2,900	$3,400
1965	Sunburst	$2,500	$3,000
1966-1967	Sunburst	$2,300	$2,800
1968-1969	Sunburst	$2,200	$2,700

Epiphone Sheraton II (reissue)

Epiphone Wildkat

To get the most from this book, be sure to read "Using **The Guide**" in the introduction.

Epiphone Zephyr Emporer Regent

ESP Eclipse

MODEL YEAR	FEATURES	EXC. COND. LOW	HIGH

USA Map Guitar
1982-1983. U.S.-made promotional model, solid-body electric, mahogany body shaped like U.S. map, 2 pickups, natural.

1982-1983		$2,000	$2,200

Vee-Wee (Mini Flying V)
2003. Mini Flying V student guitar, Flying V shape with single bridge pickup, gig bag, solid opaque finish.

2003		$100	$125

Wildkat
2001-present. Thinline, single-cut, hollow-body, 2 P-90s, Bigsby tailpiece.

2001-2005		$275	$300

Wilshire
1959-1970. Double-cut solidbody, 2 pickups, tune-o-matic bridge, cherry.

1959	Symmetrical body	$5,000	$5,500
1960-1962	Thinner-style body, P-90s	$4,500	$5,000
1962	Mini-humbuckers	$4,000	$4,500
1963-1964	Asymmetrical body	$3,500	$4,000
1965-1966	Custom color (3 options)	$4,100	$4,600
1965-1966	Standard color	$3,100	$3,500
1967-1970		$2,500	$3,000

Wilshire 12-String
1966-1968. Solidbody, 2 pickups, cherry.

1966-1967		$2,600	$3,000
1968		$2,500	$3,000

Wilshire II
1984-1985. Solidbody, maple body, neck and 'board, 2 humbuckers, 3-way switch, coil-tap, 1 tone and 1 volume control, various colors.

1984-1985		$275	$300

Windsor (1 Pickup)
1959-1962. Archtop, 1 or 2 pickups, single-cut thinline, sunburst or natural finish.

1959-1960	New York pickup, natural	$2,100	$2,300
1959-1960	New York pickup, sunburst	$2,000	$2,200
1961-1962	Mini-humbucker, natural	$2,000	$2,200
1961-1962	Mini-humbucker, sunburst	$1,900	$2,100

Windsor (2 Pickups)
1959-1962. Archtop, 1 or 2 pickups, single-cut thinline, sunburst or natural finish.

1959-1960	New York pickup, natural	$2,600	$2,800
1959-1960	New York pickup, sunburst	$2,500	$2,700
1961-1962	Mini-humbucker, natural	$2,500	$2,700
1961-1962	Mini-humbucker, sunburst	$2,400	$2,600

X-1000
1986-1989. Electric solidbody, Korean-made, various colors.

1986-1989		$250	$300

Zakk Wylde Les Paul Custom
2003-present. Bull's-eye graphic, block markers, split diamond headstock inlay.

2002-2005		$525	$625

Zenith
1931-1969. Acoustic archtop, bound front and back, f-holes, sunburst.

1931-1933		$1,000	$1,100
1934-1935	Larger 14 3/4" body	$1,000	$1,100
1936-1949	Still larger 16 3/8" body	$1,000	$1,100
1950-1957		$800	$950
1958-1959		$775	$950
1960-1969		$675	$825

Zephyr
1939-1957. Non-cut electric archtop, 1 pickup, bound front and back, blond or sunburst (first offered '53), called Zephyr Electric starting in '54.

1939-1940	Natural, 16 3/8", metal handrest pickup	$1,500	$1,800
1941-1943	Natural, no metal handrest	$1,500	$1,800
1944-1946	Natural, top mounted pickup	$1,500	$1,800
1947-1948	17 3/8", metal covered pickup	$1,500	$1,800
1949-1952	Natural, New York pickup	$1,400	$1,700
1953-1957	Natural, New York pickup	$1,400	$1,700
1953-1957	Sunburst, New York pickup	$1,300	$1,600

Zephyr Regent
1950-1953. Single-cut electric archtop, 1 pickup, natural or sunburst, called Zephyr Cutaway for '54-'57.

1950-1953	Natural	$1,500	$1,800
1950-1953	Sunburst	$1,400	$1,700

Zephyr Cutaway
1954-1957. Cutaway version of Zephyr, called Zephyr Regent for 1950-'53.

1954-1957	Natural	$1,800	$2,700
1954-1957	Sunburst	$1,700	$2,500

Zephyr Electric (Cutaway)
1958-1964. Gibson-made version, thinline archtop, single-cut, 2 pickups, natural or sunburst.

1958-1959	Natural	$2,600	$2,800
1958-1959	Sunburst	$2,400	$2,600
1960-1964	Natural	$2,400	$2,600
1960-1964	Sunburst	$2,200	$2,400

Zephyr De Luxe (Non-cutaway)
1941-1954. Non-cut electric archtop, 1 or 2 pickups, multi-bound front and back, gold-plated hardware, natural or sunburst.

1941-1942	Natural	$2,300	$2,700
1945-1949	Natural, 1 pickup	$2,300	$2,700
1945-1949	Natural, 2 pickups	$2,600	$3,100
1950-1954	Natural, 2 pickups	$2,400	$2,600
1950-1954	Sunburst, 2 pickups	$2,100	$2,300

Zephyr De Luxe Regent (Cutaway)
1948-1954. Single-cut electric archtop, 1 or 2 pickups until '50, then only 2, gold-plated hardware, sunburst or natural finish. Renamed Deluxe Electric in '54.

		LOW	HIGH
1948-1949	Natural, 1 pickup	$3,100	$3,800
1948-1949	Natural, 2 pickups	$4,000	$5,000
1948-1949	Sunburst, 1 pickup	$2,900	$3,600
1948-1949	Sunburst, 2 pickups	$3,600	$4,500
1950-1954	Natural, 2 pickups	$3,900	$4,800
1950-1954	Sunburst, 2 pickups	$3,500	$4,000

Zephyr Emperor Regent
1950-1954. Archtop, single rounded cutaway, multi-bound body, 3 pickups, sunburst or natural finish, renamed Emperor Electric in '54.

		LOW	HIGH
1950-1954	Natural	$4,000	$5,000
1950-1954	Sunburst	$3,600	$4,500

Zephyr Tenor
1940. Natural, figured top.

	LOW	HIGH
1940	$1,800	$2,000

Erlewine
1979-present. Professional and premium grade, production/custom guitars built by luthier Mark Erlewine in Austin, Texas. Erlewine also produces the Chiquita brand travel guitar.

ESP
1983-present. Intermediate, professional, and premium grade, production/custom, Japanese-made solidbody guitars and basses. Hisatake Shibuya founded Electronic Sound Products (ESP), a chain of retail stores, in '75. They began to produce replacement parts for electric guitars in '83 and in '85 started to make custom-made guitars. In '87 a factory was opened in Tokyo. In '86 ESP opened a sales office in New York, selling custom guitars and production models. In the '90s, ESP opened a California-based custom shop and in '96, they introduced the Korean-made LTD brand. Hisatake Shibuya also operated 48th Street Custom Guitars during the '90s but he closed that shop in 2003.

20th Anniversary
1995. Solidbody, double-cut, ESP95 inlaid at 12th fret, gold.

	LOW	HIGH
1995	$1,000	$1,100

Eclipse Custom (U.S.A.)
1998-2000. U.S. Custom Shop-built, single-cut, mahogany body and maple top, various colors offered.

	LOW	HIGH
1998-2000	$625	$775

Eclipse Custom/Custom T (Import)
1986-1988, 2003-present. Single-cut mahogany solidbody, earliest model with bolt dot marker neck, 2nd version with neck-thru and blocks, the Custom T adds locking trem. Current has quilt maple top.

		LOW	HIGH
1986-1987	Bolt, dots	$500	$625
1987-1988	Neck-thru, blocks	$600	$675
1987-1988	Neck-thru, Custom T	$525	$650

Eclipse Deluxe
1986-1988. Single-cut solidbody, 1 single-coil and 1 humbucker, vibrato, black.

	LOW	HIGH
1986-1988	$500	$600

Eclipse Series
1995-present. Recent Eclipse models.

		LOW	HIGH
1995-2000	Eclipse (bolt neck, mahogany)	$500	$600
1996-2000	Eclipse Archtop	$500	$625
2004-2006	Eclipse II (set neck, maple)	$800	$1,000

Horizon
1986, 1996-2001. Double-cut neck-thru, bound ebony 'board, 1 single-coil and 1 humbucker, buffer preamp, various colors, reintroduced '96-'01with bolt neck, curved rounded point headstock.

	LOW	HIGH
1986	$400	$500
1996-2001	$300	$350

Horizon Classic (U.S.A.)
1993-1995. U.S.-made, carved mahogany body, set-neck, dot markers, various colors, optional mahogany body with figured maple top also offered.

		LOW	HIGH
1993-1995	Figured maple top	$1,100	$1,200
1993-1995	Standard mahogany body	$1,200	$1,400

Horizon Custom (U.S.A.)
1998-present. U.S. Custom Shop-made, mahogany body, figured maple top, bolt-on neck, mostly translucent finish in various colors.

	LOW	HIGH
1998-2006	$1,100	$1,200

Horizon Deluxe (Import)
1989-1992. Horizon Custom with bolt-on neck, various colors.

	LOW	HIGH
1989-1992	$600	$700

Hybrid I (Import)
1986 only. Offset double-cut body, bolt maple neck, dots, six-on-a-side tuners, vibrato, various colors.

	LOW	HIGH
1986	$325	$400

Hybrid II (Import)
Offset double-cut, rosewood 'board on maple bolt neck, lipstick neck pickup, humbucker at bridge, Hybrid II headstock logo.

	LOW	HIGH
1980s	$375	$450

Maverick/Maverick Deluxe
1989-1992. Offset double-cut, bolt maple or rosewood cap neck, dot markers, double locking vibrola, six-on-a-side tuners, various colors.

	LOW	HIGH
1989-1992	$325	$400

Metal I
1986 only. Offset double-cut, bolt maple neck, rosewood cap, dots, various colors.

	LOW	HIGH
1986	$325	$400

Metal II
1986 only. Single horn V body, bolt on maple neck with rosewood cap, dot markers, various colors.

	LOW	HIGH
1986	$350	$425

Metal III
1986 only. Reverse offset body, bolt maple neck with maple cap, dot markers, gold hardware, various colors.

	LOW	HIGH
1986	$375	$450

M-I Custom
1987-1994. Offset double-cut thru-neck body, offset block markers, various colors.

	LOW	HIGH
1987-1994	$600	$700

ESP Horizon Custom

ESP LTD Viper

GUITARS

1986 ESP Traditional

*Evergreen Mountain
Tenor Guitar*

MODEL YEAR	FEATURES	EXC. COND. LOW	HIGH
M-I Deluxe	*1987-1989. Double-cut solidbody, rosewood 'board, 2 single-coils and 1 humbucker, various colors.*		
1987-1989		$500	$600
M-II	*1989-1994, 1996-2000. Double-cut solidbody, reverse headstock, bolt-on maple or rosewood cap neck, dot markers, various colors.*		
1989-1994		$650	$750
M-II Custom	*1990-1994. Double-cut solidbody, reverse headstock, neck-thru maple neck, rosewood cap, dot markers, various colors.*		
1990-1994		$850	$900
M-II Deluxe	*1990-1994. Double-cut solidbody, reverse headstock, Custom with bolt-on neck, various colors.*		
1990-1994		$750	$850
Mirage Custom	*1986-1990. Double-cut neck-thru solidbody, 2-octave ebony 'board, block markers, 1 humbucker and 2 single-coil pickups, locking trem, various colors.*		
1986-1990		$600	$700
Mirage Standard	*1986 only. Single pickup version of Mirage Custom, various colors.*		
1986		$300	$400
Phoenix	*1987 only. Offset, narrow waist solidbody, thru-neck mahogany body, black hardware, dots.*		
1987		$450	$550
Phoenix Contemporary	*Late-1990s. 3 pickups vs. 2 on the earlier offering.*		
1998		$800	$850
S-454/S-456	*1986-1987. Offset double-cut, bolt maple or rosewood cap neck, dot markers, various colors.*		
1986-1987		$350	$425
S-500	*1991-1993. Double-cut figured ash body, bolt-on neck, six-on-a-side tuners, various colors.*		
1991-1993		$500	$600
Traditional	*1989-1990. Double-cut, 3 pickups, tremolo, various colors.*		
1989-1990		$500	$600
Vintage/Vintage Plus S	*1995-1998. Offset double-cut, bolt maple or rosewood cap neck, dot markers, Floyd Rose or standard vibrato, various colors.*		
1995	20th Anniversary Edition, gold	$750	$900
1995-1998		$650	$750

Espana

Early-1960s-early-1970s. Distributed by catalog wholesalers. Built in Sweden.

MODEL YEAR	FEATURES	EXC. COND. LOW	HIGH
Classical	*Early-1960s-early-1970s. Guitars with white spruce fan-braced tops with either walnut, mahogany, or rosewood back and sides.*		
1970s		$150	$175
EL-36	*1969-early-1970s. Thin hollow double-cut, 2 pickups, natural.*		
1970s		$200	$225
Jumbo Folk	*1969-early-1970s. Natural.*		
1970s		$150	$175

Essex (SX)

1985-present. Budget grade, production, electric and acoustic guitars imported by Rondo Music of Union, New Jersey. They also offer basses.

MODEL YEAR	FEATURES	EXC. COND. LOW	HIGH
Solidbody Electric	*1980s-1990s. Copies of classic designs like the Les Paul and Telecaster.*		
1980s		$100	$125

Este

1909-1939. Luthier Felix Staerke's Este factory built classical and archtop guitars in Hamburg, Germany. They also built high-end banjos. The plant ceased instrument production in '39 and was destroyed in WW II.

Euphonon

1930-1944. A Larson brothers brand from Maurer & Company. A recent find dates the first Euphonon at 1930 but most of them date from 1934-'44. The early ones still had the slotted peghead and the 12-fret-to-body neck. The conversion to the larger body, 14-fret guitars started in '34 and guitars built during this time could have any of the old and new ideas together in any combination (for example, a 12-fret body with solid headstock or a 14-fret body with a slotted peghead). Many early Euphonons have an elevated off-the-body pickguard, followed by the usual Larson style inset in the top. Body sizes range from 13 ½" to the 19" and 21" super jumbos. The larger body 14-fret neck sizes have body woods of Brazilian rosewood, mahogany, maple and a few rare oak models. The ornamentation used went from a very plain stripe style purfling to abalone trimmed beauties with engraved fret markers. Due to rarity as well as the high quality of craftsmanship and tonal values, these guitars are very sought after. Ornamentation and features are as important as rosewood vs. mahogany.

MODEL YEAR	FEATURES	EXC. COND. LOW	HIGH
Dreadnought	*Late-1930s. Brazilian rosewood, pearl trim.*		
1930s		$25,000	$40,000
Standard 13"-15"	*1934-1944. Brazilian rosewood, mid-level to high-end trim.*		
1934-1944		$10,000	$20,000

MODEL YEAR	FEATURES	EXC. COND. LOW	HIGH

Standard 16"
1934-1944. Dreadnought, Brazilian rosewood, high-end trim.

1934-1944		$20,000	$30,000

Standard 17"
Late-1930s. Brazilian rosewood, mid-level to high-end trim.

1930s		$15,000	$30,000

Super Jumbo 19"
Late-1930s. Brazilian rosewood, high-end trim.

1930s		$25,000	$40,000

Everett Guitars
1977-present. Luthier Kent Everett builds his premium and presentation grade, production/custom, steel-string and classical guitars in Atlanta, Georgia. From '01 to '03, his Laurel Series guitars were built in conjunction with Terada in Japan and set up in Atlanta. He has also built archtops, semi-hollow and solidbody electrics, resonators, and mandolins.

Evergreen Mountain
1971-present. Professional grade, custom, flat-top and tenor guitars built by luthier Jerry Nolte in Cove, Oregon. He also builds basses and mandolins and built over 100 dulcimers in the '70s.

Everly Guitars
1982-2001. Luthier Robert Steinegger built these premium grade, production/custom flat-tops in Portland, Oregon (also see Steinegger Guitars).

Excelsior
The Excelsior Company started offering accordions in 1924 and had a large factory in Italy by the late '40s. They started building guitars around '62, which were originally plastic covered, switching to paint finishes in the mid '60s. They also offered classicals, acoustics, archtops and amps. By the early '70s they were out of the guitar business.

Dyno and Malibu
1960s. Offset, double cut, 2 or 3 pickups, vibrato.

1960s	Dyno I	$175	$200
1960s	Dyno II	$200	$225
1960s	Malibu I	$200	$250
1960s	Malibu II	$225	$275

Fairbuilt Guitar Co.
2000-present. Professional and premium grade, custom/production, archtop and flattop acoustic guitars built by luthiers Martin Fair and Stuart Orser in Loudoun County, Virginia. They also build mandolins and banjos.

Falk
Custom archtop guitars built by luthier Dave Falk, originally in Independence, Missouri, and currently in Amarillo, Texas. He also builds mandolins and dulcimers.

Farnell
1989-present. Luthier Al Farnell builds his professional grade, production, solidbody guitars in Ontario, California. He also offers his intermediate grade, production, C Series which is imported from China. He also builds basses.

Favilla
1890-1973. Founded by the Favilla family in New York, the company began to import guitars in 1970, but folded in '73. American-made models have the Favilla family crest on the headstock. Import models used a script logo on the headstock.

Acoustic Classical
1960s-1973. Various nylon-string classical models.

1960s-1969		$375	$450
1970-1973	Import	$300	$375

Acoustic Flat-Top
1960s-1973. Various flat-top models, 000 to D sizes, mahogany to spruce.

1960s-1969	U.S.-made, Crest logo	$700	$875
1970-1973	Import, Script logo	$575	$700

Fender
1946 (1945)-present. Budget, intermediate, professional and premium grade, production/custom, electric, acoustic, acoustic/electric, classical, and resonator guitars built in the U.S. and overseas. They also build amps, basses, mandolins, bouzoukis, banjos, lap steels, violins, and PA gear.

Ca. 1939 Leo Fender opened a radio and record store called Fender Radio Service, where he met Clayton Orr 'Doc' Kauffman, and in '45 they started KF Company to build lap steels and amps. In '46 Kauffman left and Fender started the Fender Electric Instrument Company. By '50 Fender's products were distributed by F.C. Hall's Radio & Television Electronics Company (Radio-Tel, later owners of Rickenbacker). In '53 Radio-Tel is replaced by the Fender Sales Company which was ran by Don Randall.

In January '65 CBS purchased the company for $13 million and renamed it Fender Musical Instruments Corporation. The CBS takeover is synonymous with a decline in quality - whether true or not is still debated, but the perception persists among musicians and collectors, and Pre-CBS Fenders are more valuable. Fender experienced some quality problems in the late-'60s. Small headstock is enlarged in '65 and the 4-bolt neck is replaced by the 3-bolt in '71. With high value and relative scarcity of Pre-CBS Fenders, even CBS-era instruments are now sought by collectors. Leo Fender was kept on as consultant until '70 and went on to design guitars for Music Man and G&L.

Bill Schultz and Dan Smith were hired from Yamaha in '81. In '82 Fender Japan is established to produce licensed Fender copies for sale in Japan. Also in '82, the Fender Squier brand debuts on Japanese-made instruments for the European market and by '83 they were imported into U.S. In '85,

Farnell GC-2

Favilla Dreadnought

GUITARS

Fender Avalon

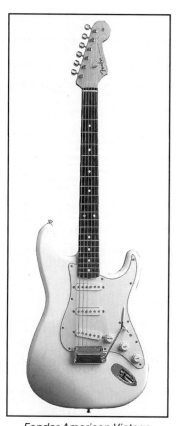

*Fender American Vintage
'62 Stratocaster*

MODEL		EXC. COND.	
YEAR	FEATURES	LOW	HIGH

the company was purchased by an investor group headed by Bill Schultz but the purchase does not include the Fullerton factory. While a new factory was being established at Corona, California, all Fender Contemporary Stratocasters and Telecasters were made either by Fender Japan or in Seoul, Korea.

U.S. production resumes in '86 with American Standard Stratocaster. The Fender Custom Shop, run by Michael Stevens and John Page, opens in '87. The Mexican Fender factory is established in '90. In '95, Fender purchased the Guild guitar company. On January 3, 2002, Fender Musical Instruments Corporation (FMIC) announced the sale of holdings in the company. FMIC recapitalized a minority portion of the common stock. The recapitalization partners included Roland Corporation U.S. (Los Angeles) and Weston Presidio, a private equity firm (San Francisco). As of January 1, 2003, Fred Gretsch Enterprises, Ltd granted Fender the exclusive rights to develop, produce, market and distribute Gretsch guitars worldwide. Around the same time, Fender also acquired the Jackson/Charvel Guitar Company. In October, '04, Fender acquired Tacoma Guitars. In April, '05, William Mendello succeeded Bill Schultz as CEO. On January 1, '08, Fender acquired Kaman Music Corporation and the Hamer, Ovation, and Genz Benz brands. The Groove Tubes brand was purchased by Fender in June, '08.

Dating older Fender guitars is an imprecise art form at best. While serial numbers were used, they were frequently not in sequence, although a lower number will frequently be older than a substantially higher number. Often necks were dated, but only with the date the neck was finished, not when the guitar was assembled. Generally, dating requires triangulating between serial numbers, neck dates, pot dates, construction details and model histories.

From '50 through roughly '65, guitars had more-or-less sequential numbers in either 4 or 5 digits, though some higher numbers may have an initial 0 or - prefix. These can range from 0001 to 99XXX.

From '63 into '65, some instruments had serial numbers beginning with an L prefix plus 5 digits (LXXXXX). Beginning in '65 with the CBS takeover into '76, 6-digit serial numbers were stamped on F neckplates roughly sequentially from 10XXXX to 71XXXX. In '76 the serial number was shifted to the headstock decal. From '76-'77, the serial number began with a bold-face 76 or S6 plus 5 digits (76XXXXX).

From '77 on, serial numbers consisted of a 2-place prefix plus 5 digits (sometimes 6 beginning in '91): '77 (S7, S8), '78 (S7, S8, S9), '79 (S9, E0), '80-'81 (S9, E0, E1), '82 (E1, E2, E3), '84-'85 (E4), '85-'86 (no U.S. production), '87 (E4), '88 (E4, E8), '89 (E8, E9), '90 (E9, N9, N0), '91 (N0), '92 (N2).

Serial numbers on guitars made by Fender Japan consist of either a 2-place prefix plus 5 digits or a single prefix letter plus 6 digits: '82-'84 (JV), '83-'84

(SQ), '84-'87 (E), '85-'86+ (A, B, C), '86-'87 (F), '87-'88+ (G), '88-'89 (H), '89-'90 (I, J), '90-'91 (K), '91-'92 (L), '92-'93 (M).

Factors affecting Fender values: The sale to CBS in '65 is a major point in Fender instrument values as CBS made many changes that collectors feel affected quality. The '70s introduced the 3-bolt neck and other design changes that aren't that popular with guitarists. Custom color instruments, especially Strats from the '50s and early-'60s, can be valued much more than the standard sunburst finishes. In '75 Fender dropped the optional custom colors and started issuing the guitars in a variety of standard colors. The various Telecaster and Stratocaster models are grouped under those general headings.

A custom color is worth more than a standard color. For a Stratocaster, Telecaster Custom and Esquire Custom the standard color is sunburst, while the Telecaster and Esquire standard color is blond. The first Precision Bass standard color was blond but changed to sunburst in the late 1950s. The Jazz Bass standard color is sunburst. The Telecaster Thinline standard color is natural. To understand a custom color, you need to know what the standard color is. Some custom colors are more rare than others. Below is a list of the custom colors offered in 1960 by Fender.

They are sorted in ascending order with the most valuable color, Shell Pink, listed last. In this list, Black and Blond are the least valuable and Shell Pink is the most valuable. A Fiesta Red is typically worth 12% more than a Black or Blond. In the rare color group a Foam Green is normally worth 8% more than a Shoreline Gold. The two very rare colors are often worth 30% more than a Shoreline Gold. In our pricing information we will list the standard color, then the relative value of a common custom color, and then the value of a rare custom color. Remember that the amount of fade also affects the price. These prices are for custom colors with slight or no fade. Fade implies a lighter color, but with custom colors a faded example can also be much darker in color. Blue can fade to dark green. White can fade to deep yellow.

The Price Guide lists the standard color, plus the value of a common color and the value of a rare color. The list below defines which group a color falls into for 1960, and again it is in ascending order so, for example, a Daphne Blue should be considered more valuable than a Lake Placid Blue, assuming they are in equal condition.

Common Color

Black, Blond, Olympic White, Lake Placid Blue, Dakota Red, Daphne Blue, and Fiesta Red

Rare Color

Shoreline Gold, Inca Silver, Burgundy Mist, Sherwood Green, Sonic Blue, and Foam Green

Rare (Very Rare) Color

MODEL YEAR	FEATURES	EXC. COND. LOW	HIGH

Surf Green and Shell Pink

Fender changed their color options in the 1960s. Below is a list of what was offered.

1960-1962
Black, Blond, Burgundy Mist, Dakota Red, Daphne Blue, Fiesta Red, Foam Green, Inca Silver, Lake Placid Blue, Olympic White, Shell Pink, Sherwood Green, Shoreline Gold, Sonic Blue, Sunburst, and Surf Green

1963-1964
Black, Blond, Burgundy Mist, Candy Apple Red, Dakota Red, Daphne Blue, Fiesta Red, Foam Green, Inca Silver, Lake Placid Blue, Olympic White, Sherwood Green, Shoreline Gold, Sonic Blue, Sunburst, and Surf Green

1965-1969
Black, Blond, Blue Ice, Candy Apple Red, Charcoal Frost, Dakota Red, Fiesta Red, Firemist Gold, Firemist Silver, Foam Green, Lake Placid Blue, Ocean Turquoise, Olympic White, Sonic Blue, Sunburst, and Teal Green

1970-1971
Black, Blond, Candy Apple Red, Firemist Gold, Firemist Silver, Lake Placid Blue, Ocean Turquoise, Olympic White, Sonic Blue, and Sunburst

1972
Black, Blond, Candy Apple Red, Lake Placid Blue, Olympic White, Sonic Blue, and Sunburst

1973
Black, Blond, Candy Apple Red, Lake Placid Blue, Natural, Olympic White, Sunburst, and Walnut

1974-1977
Black, Blond, Natural, Olympic White, Sunburst, and Walnut

1978-1979
Antigua, Black, Blond, Natural, Olympic White, Sunburst, Walnut, and Wine

Avalon
1984-1995. Acoustic, 6-on-a-side tuners, mahogany neck, back and sides (nato after '93), spruce top, various colors.

1984-1992		$225	$275

Broadcaster
Mid-1950-early-1951. For a short time in early-'51, before being renamed the Telecaster, models had no Broadcaster decal; these are called No-casters by collectors.

1950	Blond	$90,000	$115,000
1951	Clipped decal, "No Caster"	$70,000	$95,000

Broadcaster Leo Fender Custom Shop
1999 only. Leo Fender script logo signature replaces Fender logo on headstock, Custom Shop Certificate signed by Phyllis Fender, Fred Gretsch, and William Schultz, includes glass display case and poodle guitar

case.

1999		$8,500	$10,000

'50s Relic/'51 NoCaster Custom Shop
1995-present. Called the '50s Relic NoCaster for '96-'99, and '51 NoCaster in NOS, Relic, or Closet Classic versions at present, with the Relic Series being the highest offering. From June '95 to June '99 Relic work was done outside of Fender by Vince Cunetto and included a certificate noting model and year built, an instrument without the certificate is worth less than the value shown.

1995-1996	1st Cunetto era	$2,500	$3,100
1997-1999	Cunetto era NOS & Closet Classic	$1,700	$1,900
1997-1999	Cunetto era Relic	$1,700	$1,900
2000-2006	NOS & Closet Classic	$1,700	$1,900
2000-2006	Relic	$1,750	$1,950

Bronco
1967-1980. Slab solidbody, 1 pickup, tremolo, red.

1967-1969		$700	$800
1970-1980		$600	$675

Bullet
1981-1983. Solidbody, came in 2- and 3-pickup versions (single-coil and humbucker), and single- and double-cut models, various colors. Becomes Squire Bullet in '85.

1981-1983	2 pickups	$350	$425
1981-1983	3 pickups	$400	$475

CG (Classical Guitar) Series
1995-2005. Various nylon-string classical acoustic and acoustic/electric models, label on the inside back clearly indicates the model number, back and sides of rosewood, mahogany or other woods.

1995-2005	Rosewood back and sides	$175	$200

Concert
1963-1970. Acoustic flat-top slightly shorter than King/Kingman, spruce body, mahogany back and sides (optional Brazilian or Indian rosewood, zebrawood or vermillion), natural, sunburst optional by '68.

1963-1965	Natural	$800	$950
1966-1968	Natural or sunburst	$700	$850
1969-1970	Natural or sunburst	$600	$750

Concord
1987-1992. Dreadnought flat-top, 6-on-a-side headstock, natural.

1987-1992		$150	$175

Coronado I
1966-1969. Thinline semi-hollowbody, double-cut, tremolo, 1 pickup, single-bound, dot inlay.

1966-1967	Blue custom color	$1,125	$1,350
1966-1967	Cherry Red	$775	$900
1966-1967	Orange custom color	$1,125	$1,300
1966-1967	Sunburst	$875	$900
1966-1967	White (unfaded)	$1,050	$1,300
1968-1969	Sunburst	$675	$800

1951 Fender Broadcaster

1981 Fender Bullet Deluxe

GUITARS

Fender Coronado II

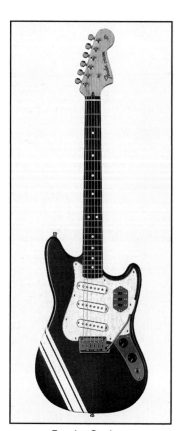

Fender Cyclone

MODEL YEAR	FEATURES	EXC. COND. LOW	HIGH

Coronado II

1966-1969 (Antigua finish offered until '70). Thinline semi-hollowbody, double-cut, tremolo optional, 2 pickups, single-bound, block inlay, available in standard finishes but special issues offered in Antigua and 6 different Wildwood finishes (labeled on the pickguard as Wildwood I through Wildwood VI to designate different colors). Wildwood finishes were achieved by injecting dye into growing trees.

MODEL YEAR	FEATURES	LOW	HIGH
1966-1967	Blue or orange custom colors	$1,400	$1,600
1966-1967	Cherry Red	$1,200	$1,300
1966-1967	Olympic White custom color	$1,250	$1,500
1966-1967	Silver custom color	$1,350	$1,600
1966-1967	Sunburst	$1,200	$1,300
1966-1967	Wildwood (unfaded)	$1,500	$1,850
1967-1969	Antigua	$1,400	$1,700
1968-1969	Cherry Red	$1,100	$1,200
1968-1969	Orange custom color	$1,250	$1,500
1968-1969	Sunburst	$1,100	$1,200
1968-1969	Wildwood (unfaded)	$1,400	$1,750
1970	Antigua	$1,250	$1,400
1970-1973	Cherry Red	$750	$925
1970-1973	Sunburst	$750	$925

Coronado XII

1966-1969 (Antigua finish offered until '70). Thinline semi-hollowbody, double-cut, 12 strings, 2 pickups, block inlay, standard, Antigua and Wildwood finishes available.

MODEL YEAR	FEATURES	LOW	HIGH
1966-1967	Blue or orange custom colors	$1,400	$1,600
1966-1967	Cherry Red	$1,200	$1,300
1966-1967	Sunburst	$1,200	$1,300
1966-1967	Wildwood	$1,500	$1,850
1968-1969	Antigua	$1,400	$1,700
1968-1969	Cherry Red	$1,100	$1,200
1968-1969	Orange custom color	$1,250	$1,500
1968-1969	Sunburst	$1,100	$1,200
1968-1969	Wildwood (unfaded)	$1,400	$1,750

Custom

1969-1971. Six-string solidbody that used up parts from discontinued Electric XII, asymmetrical-cut, long headstock, 2 split pickups, sunburst. Also marketed as the Maverick.

MODEL YEAR	FEATURES	LOW	HIGH
1969-1971		$2,300	$2,700

Cyclone

1998-2006. Mexican import, solidbody, contoured offset waist, poplar body, various colors.

MODEL YEAR	FEATURES	LOW	HIGH
1998-2006	Various options	$400	$500

D'Aquisto Elite

1984, 1989-1994, 1994-2002. Part of Fender's Master Series, archtop, single-cut, glued neck, 1 pickup, gold-plated hardware, made in Japan until '94, in '94 the Fender Custom Shop issued a version that retailed at $6,000, various colors.

MODEL YEAR	FEATURES	LOW	HIGH
1984		$2,100	$2,400
1989-1994		$1,850	$2,300

MODEL YEAR	FEATURES	EXC. COND. LOW	HIGH

D'Aquisto Standard

1984 (Serial numbers could range from 1983-1985). Part of Fender's Master Series, archtop, single-cut, glued neck, 2 pickups, made in Japan, various colors.

MODEL YEAR	FEATURES	LOW	HIGH
1984		$1,600	$1,900

D'Aquisto Ultra

1994-2000. USA Custom Shop, made under the supervision of James D'Aquisto, flamed maple back and sides, spruce top, ebony tailpiece, bridge and 'guard, all hand carved.

MODEL YEAR	FEATURES	LOW	HIGH
1994-2000		$6,000	$7,000

DG Series

1995-1999, 2002-present. Various acoustic and acoustic/electric models, label on inside indicates the model. Made in China.

MODEL YEAR	FEATURES	LOW	HIGH
2002-2006	Various lower-end	$75	$150

Duo-Sonic

1956-1969. Solidbody, 3/4-size, 2 pickups, Desert Sand ('56-'61), sunburst ('61-'63), blue, red or white after, short- and long-scale necks, short-scale necks listed here (see Duo-Sonic II for long-scale), reissued Mexican-made in '94.

MODEL YEAR	FEATURES	LOW	HIGH
1956-1958	Maple neck	$1,400	$1,700
1959-1963	Rosewood 'board	$1,200	$1,400
1964-1965		$1,050	$1,300
1966-1969		$900	$1,100

Duo-Sonic II

1965-1969. Solidbody, 2 pickups, blue, red or white, long-scale neck, though the long-scale neck Duo-Sonic was not known as the Duo-Sonic II until '65, we have lumped all long-scales under the II for the purposes of this Guide.

MODEL YEAR	FEATURES	LOW	HIGH
1965-1969		$1,200	$1,500

Duo-Sonic Reissue

1993-1997. Made in Mexico, black, red or white.

MODEL YEAR	FEATURES	LOW	HIGH
1993-1997		$190	$210

Electracoustic

2007. Thin body acoustic-electric, available with Jazzmaster, Stratocaster and Telecaster body and neck shapes, spruce top, maple sides and back, Fishman Classic IV MB electronics with top-mounted pickup, sunburst and various color options.

MODEL YEAR	FEATURES	LOW	HIGH
2007	Jazzmaster	$375	$425
2007	Stratocaster	$375	$425
2007	Telecaster	$375	$425

Electric XII

1965-1969. Solidbody, 12 strings, long headstock, 2 split pickups. Custom colors can fade or become darker; for example Lake Placid Blue changes to green. The price ranges below are for instruments that are relatively unfaded. Many older guitars have some color fade and minor fade is factored into these values. Each custom color should be evaluated on a case-by-case basis.

Custom color Fenders can be forged and bogus finishes have been a problem. As the value of custom color Fenders has increased, so has the problem of bogus non-original finishes. The prices in the Guide are for factory original finishes in excellent condition. The prices noted do not take into account market

MODEL YEAR	FEATURES	EXC. COND. LOW	HIGH

factors such as fake instruments, which can have the effect of lowering a guitar's market value unless the guitar's provenance can be validated. Please refer to the Fender Guitar Intro Section for details on Fender color options.

1965-1966	Common colors	$4,500	$5,000
1965-1966	Rare colors	$5,000	$6,200
1965-1966	Sunburst, blocks	$2,600	$3,100
1965-1966	Sunburst, dots	$2,700	$3,200
1967-1969	Common colors	$3,500	$4,000
1967-1969	Rare colors	$4,000	$5,000
1967-1969	Sunburst	$2,500	$3,000

ESD (Ensenada) Series
2005-2007. Made in Mexico, D-style, solid spruce top, solid back and sides, on-board electronics.

| 2005-2007 | ESD-10 (solid wood) | $375 | $475 |

Esprit Elite
1983-1985. Part of the Master Series, made in Japan, double-cut, semi-hollow, carved maple top, 2 humbuckers, bound rosewood 'board, snowflake inlays, sunburst.

| 1983-1984 | | $1,200 | $1,400 |

Esprit Standard
1983-1985. Part of the Master Series, made in Japan, double-cut, semi-hollow, carved maple top, 2 humbuckers, bound rosewood 'board, dot inlays, sunburst.

| 1983-1985 | | $1,100 | $1,300 |

Esprit Ultra
1984. Part of the Master Series, made in Japan, double-cut, semi-hollow, carved spruce top, 2 humbuckers, bound rosewood 'board, split-block inlays, sunburst, gold hardware.

| 1984 | | $1,300 | $1,500 |

Esquire
1950-1970. Ash body, single-cut, 1 pickup, maple neck, black 'guard '50-'54, white 'guard '54 on. Please refer to the Fender Guitar Intro Section for details on Fender color options.

1950	Black	$70,000	$93,000
1950	Blond, black 'guard	$34,000	$43,000
1951	Blond, black 'guard	$33,000	$40,000
1952	Blond, black 'guard	$30,000	$37,000
1953	Blond, black 'guard	$29,000	$36,000
1954	Blond, black 'guard	$27,000	$32,000
1954	Blond, white 'guard	$22,000	$27,000
1955	Blond, white 'guard	$22,000	$26,000
1956	Blond	$20,000	$24,500
1957	Blond	$19,000	$23,500
1958	Blond, backloader	$19,000	$23,500
1958	Blond, frontloader	$18,000	$21,000
1959	Blond, maple 'board	$18,000	$20,500

MODEL YEAR	FEATURES	EXC. COND. LOW	HIGH
1959	Blond, rosewood 'board	$16,000	$18,000
1960	Blond	$16,000	$18,000
1960	Sunburst	$16,000	$18,000
1961	Blond	$16,000	$18,000
1961	Custom colors	$20,000	$33,000
1961	Sunburst	$16,000	$18,000
1962	Blond, curved 'board	$12,000	$15,000
1962	Blond, slab 'board	$13,500	$16,500
1962	Custom colors	$18,000	$28,000
1962	Sunburst, curved 'board	$12,000	$15,000
1962	Sunburst, slab 'board	$13,500	$16,500
1963-1964	Blond	$11,000	$14,000
1963-1964	Common colors	$13,000	$19,000
1963-1964	Rare colors	$19,000	$26,000
1963-1964	Sunburst	$11,000	$14,000
1965-1966	Blond	$9,000	$11,000
1965-1966	Common colors	$11,000	$16,000
1965-1966	Rare colors	$16,000	$21,000
1965-1966	Sunburst	$9,000	$11,000
1967	Blond, smuggler cavity	$8,500	$10,000
1967-1970	Blond	$6,000	$7,500
1967-1970	Common colors	$5,500	$10,500
1967-1970	Rare colors	$8,000	$13,500
1967-1970	Sunburst	$6,000	$7,500

Esquire/'50s Esquire (Japan)
1985-1994. Made in Japan, '54 specs.

| 1985-1994 | | $575 | $700 |

'50s Esquire (Mexico)
2005-present. Maple neck, ash body.

| 2005-2007 | | $300 | $375 |

'59 Esquire
2003-present. Custom Shop model.

| 2003-2006 | Closet Classic | $1,650 | $1,750 |
| 2003-2006 | Relic | $1,900 | $2,100 |

Jeff Beck Tribute Esquire (Custom Shop)
2006. Also called Beck Artist Esquire or Tribute Series Jeff Beck Esquire, specs include an extremely lightweight 2-piece offset ash body with Beck's original contours, distressed for an appearance like Beck's original Esquire that was used on many Yardbird records.

| 2006 | | $8,500 | $9,000 |

Esquire Custom
1959-1970. Same as Esquire, but with bound alder sunburst body and rosewood 'board.

1959	Sunburst	$28,000	$35,000
1960	Custom colors	$35,000	$60,000
1960	Sunburst	$23,000	$26,000
1961-1962	Custom colors	$28,000	$50,000
1961-1962	Sunburst	$21,000	$25,000
1963-1964	Custom colors	$25,000	$40,000
1963-1964	Sunburst	$18,000	$22,000
1965-1966	Custom colors	$16,000	$28,000
1965-1966	Sunburst	$12,000	$18,000
1967	Sunburst	$11,000	$14,000

1963 Fender Duo-Sonic

1957 Fender Esquire

Fender Jag-Stang

Fender Jaguar 1963

MODEL YEAR	FEATURES	EXC. COND. LOW	HIGH
1968	Sunburst	$9,000	$13,000
1969	Sunburst	$8,000	$11,000
1970	Sunburst	$7,000	$10,000

Esquire Custom (Import)
1983. Made in Japan with all the classic bound Esquire features, sunburst.

1983-1986		$800	$1,125
1987-1994		$650	$850

Esquire Custom GT/Celtic/Scorpion
2003. Made in Korea, single-cut solidbody, 1 humbucker, 1 knob (volume), set-neck, solid colors.

2003		$275	$325

Flame Elite
1984-1988. Part of the Master Series, made in Japan, neck-thru, offset double-cut, solidbody, 2 humbuckers, rosewood 'board, snowflake inlays.

1984-1988		$1,200	$1,400

Flame Standard
1984-1988. Part of the Master Series, made in Japan, neck-thru, offset double-cut, solidbody, 2 humbuckers, rosewood 'board, dot inlays.

1984-1988		$1,000	$1,300

Flame Ultra
1984-1988. Part of the Master Series, made in Japan, neck-thru, double-cut, solidbody, 2 humbuckers, rosewood 'board, split block inlays (some with snowflakes), gold hardware.

1984-1988		$1,300	$1,500

FR-48 Resonator
2003-present. Made in Korea, chromed steel body.

2003-2007		$375	$425

F-Series Dreadnought Flat-Top
1969-1981. The F-Series were Japanese-made flat-top acoustics, included were Concert- and Dreadnought-size instruments with features running from plain to bound necks and headstocks and fancy inlays, there was also a line of F-Series classical, nylon-string guitars. A label on the inside indicates the model. FC-20 is a classical with Brazilian rosewood. There was also an Asian (probably Korean) import Standard Series for '82-'90 where the models start with a F.

1969-1981	Higher-end solid top	$125	$250
1969-1981	Lower-end laminated	$100	$150
1972-1981	FC-20 Classical	$150	$275

GC (Grand Concert) Series
1997-present. Various grand concert models, an oval label on the inside back clearly indicates the model number.

1997-2007		$200	$250

Gemini Series
1983-1990. Korean-made flat-tops, label on inside indicates model. I is classical nylon-string, II, III and IV are dreadnought steel-strings, there is also a 12-string and an IIE acoustic/electric.

1983-1987	Gemini II	$125	$175
1983-1988	Gemini I	$100	$150
1987-1990	Gemini III/IV	$150	$225

GN-45SCE (Grand Nylon) Series
2001-2007. Cutaway, nylon string, Fishman electronics.

2001-2007		$400	$450

MODEL YEAR	FEATURES	EXC. COND. LOW	HIGH

Harmony-Made Series
Early-1970s-mid-1970s. Harmony-made with white stencil Fender logo, mahogany, natural or sunburst.

1970s		$50	$125

Jag-Stang
1996-2003. Japanese-made, designed by Curt Cobain, body similar to Jaguar, tremolo, 1 pickup, oversize Strat peghead, Fiesta Red or Sonic Blue.

1996	1st issue, 50th Anniv. Label	$550	$675
1997-2003		$525	$650

Jaguar
1962-1975. Reintroduced as Jaguar '62 in '95-'99. Custom colors can fade and often the faded color has very little similarity to the original color. The values below are for an instrument that is relatively unfaded. Each custom color should be evaluated on a case-by-case basis. As the value of custom color Fenders has increased, so has the problem of bogus non-original finishes. The prices in the Guide are for factory original finishes in excellent condition. Please refer to the Fender Guitar Intro Section for details on Fender color options.

1962	Common colors	$5,500	$6,500
1962	Rare colors	$7,000	$8,500
1962	Sunburst	$3,300	$3,600
1963-1964	Common colors	$5,000	$6,000
1963-1964	Rare colors	$6,500	$8,000
1963-1964	Sunburst	$3,000	$3,500
1965	Common colors	$4,500	$5,500
1965	Rare colors	$5,500	$7,500
1965	Sunburst	$2,900	$3,500
1966	Common colors	$4,000	$5,000
1966	Rare colors	$5,000	$7,000
1966	Sunburst, block markers	$2,200	$2,750
1966	Sunburst, dot markers	$2,700	$3,200
1967-1970	Common colors	$3,500	$4,000
1967-1970	Rare colors	$4,000	$6,000
1967-1970	Sunburst	$2,200	$2,700
1971-1975	Common colors	$2,500	$3,000
1971-1975	Rare colors	$3,000	$5,000
1971-1975	Sunburst	$2,000	$2,500

Jaguar '62
1994-present. Reintroduction of Jaguar, Japanese-made until '99, then U.S.-made, basswood body, rosewood 'board, various colors.

1994-1999	Import	$650	$700
1999-2007	U.S.A.-made	$1,000	$1,100

Jaguar Baritone Special HH
2005-present. Baritone Special logo on headstock, humbucker pickups, black.

2005-2007		$550	$600

Jaguar HH
2005-present. Two humbucking pickups.

2005-2007		$400	$475

Jazzmaster
1958-1980. Contoured body, 2 pickups, rosewood 'board, clay dot inlay, reintroduced as Japanese-made Jazzmaster '62 in '96. Custom color Fenders can be

forged and bogus finishes have been a problem. As the value of custom color Fenders has increased, so has the problem of bogus non-original finishes. The prices in the Guide are for factory original finishes in excellent condition. Please refer to the Fender Guitar Intro Section for details on Fender color options.

MODEL YEAR	FEATURES	EXC. COND. LOW	HIGH
1958	Sunburst	$8,000	$8,400
1958	Sunburst, rare maple 'board	$8,500	$9,000
1959	Custom colors, includes rare	$13,000	$18,000
1959	Sunburst	$7,200	$8,300
1960	Common colors	$9,000	$11,000
1960	Rare colors	$11,000	$18,000
1960	Sunburst	$6,000	$7,000
1961	Common colors	$8,500	$10,000
1961	Rare colors	$10,000	$17,000
1961	Sunburst	$5,500	$6,500
1962	Common colors	$8,000	$9,500
1962	Rare colors	$9,500	$16,000
1962	Sunburst	$5,300	$6,400
1963-1964	Common colors	$6,500	$8,000
1963-1964	Rare colors	$8,000	$15,000
1963-1964	Sunburst	$4,400	$5,400
1965	Common colors	$5,500	$7,000
1965	Rare colors	$7,000	$12,000
1965	Sunburst	$4,200	$4,800
1966	Common colors	$5,000	$6,000
1966	Rare colors	$6,000	$11,000
1966	Sunburst, block markers	$3,500	$4,000
1966	Sunburst, dot markers	$3,800	$4,400
1967-1970	Common colors	$4,500	$5,500
1967-1970	Rare colors	$5,500	$10,000
1967-1970	Sunburst	$3,200	$3,900
1971-1975	Custom colors	$3,000	$4,000
1971-1975	Sunburst	$2,400	$3,000
1976-1980	Custom colors	$2,700	$3,300
1976-1980	Sunburst	$2,500	$2,700

Jazzmaster '62
1994-present. Japanese-made reintroduction of Jazzmaster, basswood body, rosewood 'board, U.S.-made from '99, various colors.

1994-1999	Import	$650	$700
2000-2007	U.S.A.-made	$1,000	$1,100
2000s	Import	$650	$750

Jazzmaster The Ventures Limited Edition
1996. Japanese-made, ash body, 2 pickups, block inlay, transparent purple/black.

1996		$900	$1,100

JZM Deluxe
2007-present. Acoustic/electric, Jazzmaster/Jaguar body styling, Fishman and Tele pickups.

2007		$325	$425

Katana
1985-1986. Japanese-made wedge-shaped body, 2 humbuckers, set neck, triangle inlays, black

1985-1986		$325	$400

King
1963-1965. Full-size 15 5/8" wide acoustic, natural. Renamed Kingman in '65.

1963-1965		$1,000	$1,200

Kingman
1965-1971, 2006-present. Full-size 15 5/8" wide acoustic, slightly smaller by '70, offered in 3 Wildwood colors, referred to as the Wildwood acoustic which is a Kingman with dyed wood.

1965-1968		$900	$1,100
1969-1971		$800	$1,000

Lead I
1979-1982. Double-cut solidbody with 1 humbucker, maple or rosewood 'board, black or brown.

1979-1982		$400	$475

Lead II
1979-1982. Lead with 2 pickups, black or brown.

1979-1982		$450	$550

Lead III
1982. Lead with 2 split-coil humbuckers, 2 3-way switches, various colors.

1982		$600	$700

LTD
1969-1975. Archtop electric, single-cut, gold-plated hardware, carved top and back, 1 pickup, multi-bound, bolt-on neck, sunburst.

1969-1975		$4,000	$5,000

Malibu
1965-1971, 1983-1992, 2006-present. Flat top, spruce top, mahogany back and sides, black, mahogany or sunburst. Name used on Asian import model in '80s.

1965-1971		$525	$600

Marauder
1965 only. The Marauder has 3 pickups, and some have slanted frets, only 8 were made, thus it is very rare. 1st generation has hidden pickups, 2nd has exposed.

1965	1st generation	$10,000	$12,500
1965	2nd generation	$6,700	$8,300

Montego I/II
1968-1975. Electric archtop, single-cut, bolt-on neck, 1 pickup (I) or 2 pickups (II), chrome-plated hardware, sunburst.

1968-1975	I	$2,500	$2,900
1968-1975	II	$2,700	$3,100

Musiclander
1969-1972. Also called Swinger and Arrow, solidbody, 1 pickup, arrow-shaped headstock, no model name on peghead, red, white, and blue.

1969-1972		$1,600	$1,800

Musicmaster
1956-1980. Solidbody, 1 pickup, short-scale (3/4) neck, Desert Sand ('56-'61), sunburst ('61-'63), red, white or blue after. Regular-scale necks were optional and are called Musicmaster II from '64 to '69, after '69 II is dropped and Musicmaster continues with regular-scale neck.

1956-1959	Blond	$1,400	$1,700
1960-1964	Blond	$1,300	$1,600
1964-1969	Red, white, blue	$1,200	$1,500
1970-1980	Red, white, blue	$750	$850

Fender Marauder

1964 Fender Musicmaster

Fender Showmaster HH

Fender Squier '51

MODEL YEAR	FEATURES	EXC. COND. LOW	HIGH
Musicmaster II			
1964-1969. Solidbody, 1 pickup, long regular-scale neck version of Musicmaster, red, white, or blue.			
1964-1969		$1,200	$1,500
Mustang			
1964-1982, 1997-1998. Solidbody, 2 pickups. Reissued as '69 Mustang in 1990s, name changed back to Mustang '97-'98. Dakota Red, Daphne Blue and Olympic White with Competition Red, Blue and Orange finishes added ca. '69-'72. Competition finishes featured a racing stripe on the front of the body.			
1964-1965	Blue (unfaded)	$1,900	$2,100
1964-1965	Red or white	$1,800	$2,000
1966-1969	Blue (unfaded)	$1,800	$2,000
1966-1969	Red or white	$1,700	$1,900
1969	Competition colors	$1,900	$2,100
1970-1979	Various colors	$1,400	$1,500
1980-1982	Various colors	$1,100	$1,400
Mustang '65 Reissue			
2006-present. Made in Japan.			
2006-2008		$400	$525
Mustang '69 Reissue			
1994-1998, 2005. Japanese-made, blue or white.			
1994-1998		$500	$525
Newporter			
1965-1971, 1983-1992. Acoustic flat-top, mahogany back and sides. Name used on Asian import model in '80s.			
1965-1968	Spruce top	$400	$525
1968-1971	Mahogany top	$300	$425
Palomino			
1968-1971. Acoustic flat-top, spruce top, mahogany back and sides, triple-bound, black or mahogany.			
1968-1971		$575	$600
Performer			
1985-1986. Imported Swinger-like body design, 2 slanted humbuckers.			
1985-1986		$800	$950
Prodigy			
1991-1993. Electric solidbody, double-cut, chrome-plated hardware, 2 single-coil and 1 humbucker pickups, blue or black.			
1991-1993		$450	$550
Redondo			
1969-1971, 1983-1990. Mid-size flat-top, 14 3/8" wide, replaces Newport spruce top model. Name used on Asian import model in '80s.			
1969-1971		$425	$525
Robben Ford			
1989-1994. Symmetrical double-cut, 2 pickups, glued-in neck, solidbody with tone chambers, multi-bound, gold-plated hardware, sunburst. After '94 made in Fender Custom Shop.			
1989-1994		$1,200	$1,400
1995	Custom Shop	$2,200	$2,700
Shenandoah 12-String			
1965-1971. Acoustic flat-top, spruce top, mahogany back and sides.			
1965-1968	Antigua	$900	$1,125
1965-1968	Blond	$750	$800
1969-1971	Antigua	$850	$1,050
1969-1971	Blond	$600	$750

MODEL YEAR	FEATURES	EXC. COND. LOW	HIGH
Showmaster FMT (Custom Shop)			
2000-present. Bound figured maple top (FMT), 2 single-coil pickups and a bridge position humbucker, maple neck, Custom Shop certificate.			
2000-2006		$1,300	$1,450
Showmaster (Import)			
2003-2007. Off-set double-cut solidbody, set neck, various models.			
2004-2006	3 single coils	$325	$400
2003	Celtic, 1 bridge humbucker	$225	$275
2003-2007	HH, 2 humbuckers	$350	$425
Squier '51			
2004-2006. Korean-made, Strat-style body with a Tele-style neck, various colors.			
2004-2006		$75	$150
Squier Bullet			
1985-1988, 2000-2006. Fender Japan was established in '82, Squier production began in '83, production was shifted to Korea in '87. Name revived in '06.			
1985-1988	Sunburst, humbuckers	$175	$250
1985-1988	White	$175	$250
2000-2006		$50	$125
Squier Katana			
1985-1986. Korean-made version, 1 humbucker, bolt neck, dot inlays, black.			
1985-1986		$200	$250
Squier Showmaster			
2002. 20th Anniversary (1982-2002), made in China.			
2002		$75	$150
Squier Stagemaster HH			
1999-2002. 2 humbuckers.			
1999-2002		$125	$175
Starcaster			
1974-1980. Double-cut, thinline semi-hollowbody, 2 humbuckers, various colors. Fender currently uses the Starcaster name on a line of budget guitars sold through Costco stores.			
1974-1980	Blond, highly flamed maple	$3,000	$3,700
1974-1980	Sunburst, moderate flame	$2,900	$3,500
Starcaster Acoustic			
2000s. Acoustic flat-top with on-board electronics for student market.			
2000s		$80	$120
Starcaster by Fender			
2000s. Student economy pack guitar, Strat body with pointed-arrow headstock, Starcaster by Fender logo.			
2000s	Guitar only	$70	$80
2000s	Pack with guitar, amp, stand	$85	$100

The *Vintage Guitar Price Guide* shows low to high values for items in all-original excellent condition, and, where applicable, with original case or cover.

Stratocaster

The following are all variations of the Stratocaster. The first five listings are for the main American-made models and the '85 interim production Japanese model. All others are listed alphabetically after that in the following order.

Stratocaster
Standard Stratocaster (includes "Smith Strat")
American Standard Stratocaster
American Series Stratocaster
21st Century Limited Edition Stratocaster
25th Anniversary Stratocaster
35th Anniversary Stratocaster
40th Anniversary Stratocaster
'50s Stratocaster (Import)
'50s Stratocaster Relic
50th Anniversary 1954 Stratocaster
50th Anniversary American Deluxe Strat (USA)
50th Anniversary Stratocaster
50th Anniversary Stratocaster (Mexico)
50th Anniversary Stratocaster Relic
'54 Stratocaster
'54 Stratocaster FMT
'56 Stratocaster
'57 Special Stratocaster
'57 Stratocaster
'57 Stratocaster (USA)
'57 Vintage Stratocaster (Japan)
'58 Stratocaster
'58 Stratocaster (Dakota Red)
'60 FMT Stratocaster
'60 Stratocaster
'60s Stratocaster (Japan)
'60s Stratocaster Relic
'62 Stratocaster (Japan)
'62 Stratocaster (USA)
'65 Stratocaster
'66 Stratocaster
'68 Reverse Strat Special (USA)
'68 Stratocaster
'68 Stratocaster (Japan)
'69 Stratocaster
'70s Stratocaster (Mexico)
'72 Stratocaster (Japan)
Acoustasonic Stratocaster
Aerodyne Stratocaster
Aluminum Stratocaster
American Classic Holoflake Stratocaster
American Classic Stratocaster
American Deluxe Fat Stratocaster
American Deluxe HSS Stratocaster
American Deluxe Stratocaster
American Vintage '57 Commemorative Stratocaster
American Vintage '62 Commemorative Stratocaster
Antigua Stratocaster
Big Apple Stratocaster
Big Block Stratocaster
Bill Carson Stratocaster
Blackie Stratocaster
Blackie Stratocaster (Custom Shop 1987)

Blackie Stratocaster (Custom Shop)
Blue Flower Stratocaster
Bonnie Raitt Stratocaster
Bowling Ball/Marble Stratocaster
Buddy Guy Stratocaster (Mexico)
Buddy Guy Stratocaster (Signature)
California Stratocaster
California Fat Stratocaster
Classic Player Stratocaster
Collector's Edition Stratocaster ('62 Reissue)
Contemporary Stratocaster
Contemporary Stratocaster (Import)
Crash Stratocaster
Custom 1960 Stratocaster
Deluxe Players Special Edition Stratocaster
Deluxe Players Stratocaster
Deluxe Strat Plus
Deluxe Vintage Player '62 Stratocaster
Dick Dale Stratocaster
Elite Stratocaster
Eric Clapton Gold Leaf Stratocaster
Eric Clapton Stratocaster
Eric Clapton Stratocaster (CS)
Eric Johnson Stratocaster
Floyd Rose Classic Relic Stratocaster
Floyd Rose Classic Stratocaster
Foto Flame Stratocaster
Freddy Tavares Aloha Stratocaster
Gold Elite Stratocaster
Gold Stratocaster
Gold Stratocaster (CS)
Hank Marvin 40th Anniversary Stratocaster
Hank Marvin Stratocaster
Harley-Davidson 90th Anniversary Stratocaster
Hellecaster Stratocaster
Highway One Stratocaster/HSS
HM Stratocaster (USA/Import)
Homer Haynes HLE Stratocaster
Hot Wheels Stratocaster
HRR Stratocaster
HSS Stratocaster
Ike Turner Tribute Stratocaster
Jeff Beck Stratocaster
Jerry Donahue Hellecaster Stratocaster
Jimi Hendrix Monterey Pop Stratocaster
Jimi Hendrix Tribute Stratocaster
Jimi Hendrix Voodoo Stratocaster
Jimmie Vaughan Tex-Mex Stratocaster
John Jorgenson Hellecaster Stratocaster
John Mayer Stratocaster
Koa Stratocaster
Kon Tiki Stratocaster
Lenny Stratocaster
Lone Star Stratocaster
Mark Knopfler Stratocaster
Milonga Deluxe Stratocaster
Moto Limited Edition Stratocaster
Moto Set Stratocaster
Paisley Stratocaster
Playboy 40th Anniversary Stratocaster
Powerhouse/Powerhouse Deluxe Stratocaster
Proud Stratocaster

Fender American Deluxe Strat

Fender Jimmie Vaughan Tex-Mex Stratocaster

1956 Fender Stratocaster

1964 Fender Stratocaster

Richie Sambora Stratocaster
Roadhouse Stratocaster
Robert Cray Stratocaster
Robin Trower Signature Stratocaster
Roland Ready Stratocaster
Rory Gallagher Tribute Stratocaster
Set-Neck Stratocaster
Short-Scale (7/8) Stratocaster
So-Cal Speed Shop L.E. Stratocaster
Special Edition Stratocaster
Splatter Stratocaster
Squier II Stratocaster
Squier Stratocaster Standard
Squier Stratocaster Standard (Affinity Series)
Squier Stratocaster Standard (Double Fat Strat)
Squier Stratocaster Standard (Floyd Rose)
Standard Fat Stratocaster
Standard HH Stratocaster
Standard Stratocaster (Mexico)
Standard Stratocaster Satin Finish
Stevie Ray Vaughan Stratocaster
Stevie Ray Vaughan Tribute #1 Stratocaster
Strat Plus
Stratacoustic
Stratocaster HSS/HH
Stratocaster Junior
Stratocaster Special
Stratocaster XII
Strat-o-Sonic
Sub Sonic Stratocaster
Super/Deluxe Super Stratocaster
Tanqurey Tonic Stratocaster
Texas Special Stratocaster
The Strat
Tie-Dye Stratocaster
Tree of Life Stratocaster
Turquoise Sparkle Stratocaster
U.S. Ultra / Ultra Plus Stratocaster
Ventures Limited Edition Stratocaster
VG Stratocaster
Walnut Stratocaster
Walnut Elite Stratocaster
Western Stratocaster
Yngwie Malmsteen Stratocaster

Stratocaster

1954-1981. Two-tone sunburst until '58, 3-tone after. Custom color finishes were quite rare in the '50s and early-'60s and are much more valuable than the standard sunburst finish. By the '70s, color finishes were much more common and do not affect the value near as much. In '75 Fender dropped the optional custom colors and started issuing the guitars in a variety of standard colors (sunburst, blond, white, natural, walnut and black).

Custom color Fenders can be forged and bogus finishes have been a problem. As the value of custom color Fenders has increased, so has the problem of bogus non-original finishes. The prices in the Guide are for factory original finishes in excellent condition. One color, Shell Pink, is notable because many vintage authorities wonder if a Shell Pink Strat even exists? An ultra-rare custom color should have strong documented provenance and be verifiable by at least one (preferable two or more) well-known vintage authorities. Please refer to the Fender Guitar Intro Section for details on Fender color options.

Three-bolt neck '72-'81, otherwise 4-bolt. Unless noted, all Stratocasters listed have the Fender tremolo system. Non-tremolo models (aka hardtails) typically sell for less. Many guitarists feel the tremolo block helps produce a fuller range of sound. On average, many more tremolo models were made. One year, '58, seems to be a year where a greater percentage of non-tremolo models were made. Tremolo vs. non-tremolo valuation should be taken on a brand-by-brand basis; for example, a pre-'65 Gibson ES-335 non-tremolo model is worth more than a tremolo equipped model.

MODEL YEAR	FEATURES	EXC. COND. LOW	HIGH
1954	Sunburst	$60,000	$75,000
1955	Sunburst	$50,000	$62,000
1956	Blond, nickel hardware	$52,000	$63,000
1956	Mary Kaye, gold hardware	$56,000	$69,000
1956	Sunburst, alder body	$45,000	$48,000
1956	Sunburst, ash body	$50,000	$61,000
1956	Sunburst, non-trem	$37,000	$45,000
1957	Blond, nickel hardware	$46,000	$55,000
1957	Custom colors	$46,000	$70,000
1957	Mary Kaye, gold hardware	$55,000	$68,000
1957	Sunburst, bakelite knobs	$40,000	$47,000
1957	Sunburst, plastic knobs	$38,000	$46,000
1958	Blond, nickel hardware	$46,000	$55,000
1958	Custom colors	$46,000	$70,000
1958	Mary Kaye, gold hardware	$55,000	$68,000
1958	Sunburst 2-tone	$38,000	$45,000
1958	Sunburst 2-tone, non-trem	$34,000	$42,000
1958	Sunburst 3-tone	$33,000	$39,000
1958	Sunburst 3-tone, non-trem	$27,000	$32,000
1959	Blond, nickel hardware	$46,000	$53,000
1959	Custom colors	$46,000	$70,000
1959	Mary Kaye, gold hardware	$50,000	$62,000
1959	Sunburst, maple 'board Sunburst, non-trem, slab	$27,000	$32,000
1959	Sunburst, slab 'board	$30,000	$37,000
1960	Common colors	$40,000	$56,000
1960	Rare colors	$56,000	$69,000
1960	Sunburst	$28,000	$36,000
1961	Common colors	$40,000	$55,000

MODEL YEAR	FEATURES	EXC. COND. LOW	HIGH
1961	Rare colors	$55,000	$68,000
1961	Sunburst	$27,000	$33,000
1962	Common colors, curve	$28,000	$39,000
1962	Common colors, slab, 2 pat. Logo	$37,000	$45,000
1962	Common colors, slab, 3 pat. Logo	$31,000	$40,000
1962	Rare color, curve	$39,000	$55,000
1962	Rare color, slab, 2 pat. Logo	$45,000	$67,000
1962	Rare color, slab, 3 pat. Logo	$40,000	$57,000
1962	Sunburst, curve	$23,000	$28,000
1962	Sunburst, slab, 2 pat. Logo	$27,000	$33,000
1962	Sunburst, slab, 3 pat. Logo	$26,000	$31,000
1962	Sunburst, slab, tortoise 'guard	$28,000	$34,000
1963	Common colors	$28,000	$38,000
1963	Rare colors	$38,000	$50,000
1963	Sunburst	$23,000	$28,000
1964	Common colors	$28,000	$35,000
1964	Rare colors	$35,000	$46,000
1964	Sunburst, spaghetti logo	$23,000	$28,000
1964	Sunburst, transition logo	$23,000	$27,000
1965	Common colors	$20,000	$28,000
1965	Rare colors	$28,000	$40,000
1965	Sunburst, F-plate	$14,000	$17,500
1965	Sunburst, green 'guard	$19,000	$25,000
1965	Sunburst, white 'guard	$16,500	$20,000
1966	Common colors	$20,000	$25,000
1966	Rare colors	$25,000	$30,000
1966	Sunburst	$13,000	$15,000
1967	Common colors	$15,000	$19,000
1967	Rare colors	$19,000	$23,000
1967	Sunburst, maple cap	$14,000	$16,000
1967	Sunburst, rosewood cap	$13,000	$15,000
1968	Common colors	$15,000	$18,000
1968	Rare colors	$18,000	$23,000
1968	Sunburst, maple cap	$14,000	$16,000
1968	Sunburst, rosewood cap	$13,000	$15,000
1969	Common colors	$15,000	$18,000
1969	Rare colors	$18,000	$22,000
1969	Sunburst, maple cap	$12,000	$15,000
1969	Sunburst, rosewood cap	$11,000	$13,800
1970	Common colors	$11,000	$13,000
1970	Rare colors	$14,000	$20,000
1970	Sunburst, maple cap	$10,000	$11,000
1970	Sunburst, rosewood cap	$9,000	$10,000
1971	Common colors	$9,000	$12,000
1971	Rare colors	$12,000	$19,000
1971	Sunburst	$7,500	$9,000
1972	Common colors, 3-bolt	$5,000	$7,000
1972	Rare colors, 3-bolt	$8,000	$10,000
1972	Sunburst, 3-bolt	$4,000	$5,000
1973	Color option	$4,800	$6,000
1973	Natural	$3,400	$3,700
1973	Sunburst	$3,600	$4,500
1973	Walnut	$3,400	$3,700
1974	Black, blond, Olympic White	$4,000	$5,000
1974	Natural	$2,700	$3,200
1974	Sunburst	$3,400	$4,200
1974	Walnut	$2,700	$3,200
1975	Black, blond, Olympic White	$3,300	$4,100
1975	Natural	$2,300	$2,900
1975	Sunburst, black parts	$2,300	$2,800
1975	Sunburst, white parts	$3,000	$3,700
1975	Walnut	$2,300	$2,900
1976	Black, blond, Olympic White	$2,400	$3,000
1976	Natural	$2,200	$2,500
1976	Sunburst	$2,300	$2,800
1976	Walnut	$2,200	$2,500
1977	Black, blond, Olympic White	$2,400	$2,900
1977	Natural	$2,000	$2,300
1977	Sunburst	$2,200	$2,700
1977	Walnut	$2,000	$2,300
1978	Antigua	$2,200	$2,600
1978	Black, blond, Olympic White, Wine	$2,100	$2,600
1978	Natural	$1,900	$2,200
1978	Sunburst	$1,950	$2,500
1978	Walnut	$1,900	$2,300
1979	Antigua	$2,100	$2,500
1979	Black, blond, Olympic White, Wine	$2,000	$2,500
1979	Natural	$1,800	$2,200
1979	Sunburst	$1,900	$2,300
1979	Walnut	$1,800	$2,200
1980	Antigua	$2,100	$2,500
1980	Black, Olympic White, Wine	$1,650	$2,050
1980	Natural	$1,500	$1,800
1980	Sunburst	$1,575	$1,975
1981	Black, Olympic White, Wine	$1,400	$1,750
1981	International colors	$1,500	$2,000
1981	Sunburst	$1,300	$1,600

1965 Fender Stratocaster

1979 Fender Stratocaster

To get the most from this book, be sure to read "Using *The Guide*" in the introduction.

Fender '56 Stratocaster

Fender '62 Stratocaster (American Series)

Standard Stratocaster (includes "Smith Strat")

1981-1984. Replaces the Stratocaster. Renamed the American Standard Stratocaster for '86–'00 (see next listing). Renamed American Series Stratocaster in '00. From '81/'82 to mid-'83, 4 knobs same as regular Strat but with 4-bolt neck. In August '81, Dan Smith was hired by Bill Schultz and Fender produced an alder body, 4-bolt neck, 21-fret, small headstock Standard Stratocaster that has been nicknamed the Smith Strat (made from Dec. '81–'83). Mid-'83 to the end of '84 2 knobs and 'guard mounted input jack. Not to be confused with current Standard Stratocaster, which is made in Mexico.

MODEL YEAR	FEATURES	EXC. COND. LOW	HIGH
1981	Smith Strat, 4-bolt, 3-knob	$1,500	$1,850
1982	Smith Strat, rare colors	$1,900	$2,350
1982	Smith Strat, various colors	$1,500	$1,850
1983	Smith Strat, various colors	$1,200	$1,700
1983-1984	Sunburst, 2-knob	$900	$1,125
1983-1984	Various colors, 2-knob	$900	$1,125

Standard Stratocaster (Japan)

1985. Interim production in Japan while the new Fender reorganized, standard pickup configuration and tremolo system, 3 knobs with switch, traditional style input jack, traditional shaped headstock, natural maple color.

MODEL YEAR	FEATURES	EXC. COND. LOW	HIGH
1985	Black or red, white 'guard	$475	$575

American Standard Stratocaster

1986-2000. Fender's new name for the American-made Strat when reintroducing it after CBS sold the company. The only American-made Strats made in 1985 were the '57 and '62 models. See Stratocaster and Standard Stratocaster for earlier models, renamed American Series

MODEL YEAR	FEATURES	EXC. COND. LOW	HIGH
1986-1989	Various colors	$875	$1,100
1989	Mary Kaye Limited Edition	$900	$1,150
1990-1999	Various colors	$700	$800
1995	Limited Edition matching headstock	$900	$1,150

American Series Stratocaster

2000-2007. Ash or alder body, rosewood 'board, dot markers, 3 staggered single-coil pickups, 5-way switch, hand polished fret edges. Renamed the American Standard Stratocaster again in '08.

MODEL YEAR	FEATURES	EXC. COND. LOW	HIGH
2000-2007	Alder body	$650	$750
2000-2007	Ash body	$675	$775
2000-2007	Ash body, hardtail	$625	$725
2000-2007	Limited Edition colors	$750	$800
2000-2007	Limited Edition matching headstock	$775	$950
2006-2007	Non-veneer body, new routings	$650	$800

21st Century Limited Edition Stratocaster

2000. Custom Shop model, one of first 100 to leave Fender in 2000, certificate with CEO William C. Schultz, 21st logo on headstock.

MODEL YEAR	FEATURES	EXC. COND. LOW	HIGH
2000		$1,150	$1,350

25th Anniversary Stratocaster

1979-1980. Has ANNIVERSARY on upper body horn, silver metallic or white pearlescent finish.

MODEL YEAR	FEATURES	EXC. COND. LOW	HIGH
1979	White, 1st issue, flaking	$1,075	$1,300
1979	White, 1st issue, no flaking	$1,650	$1,850
1979-1980	Silver, faded to gold	$1,200	$1,500
1979-1980	Silver, unfaded	$2,000	$2,500

35th Anniversary Stratocaster

1989-1991. Custom Shop model, 500 made, figured maple top, Lace Sensor pickups, Eric Clapton preamp circuit.

MODEL YEAR	FEATURES	EXC. COND. LOW	HIGH
1989-1991		$2,700	$2,900

40th Anniversary Stratocaster

1994 only. American Standard model (not Custom Shop model), plain top, appearance similar to a '54 maple-neck Stratocaster, sunburst. Not to be confused with the Custom Shop 40th Anniversary Diamond Edition.

MODEL YEAR	FEATURES	EXC. COND. LOW	HIGH
1994	Japan, '62 specs	$600	$700
1994	U.S.A.	$1,600	$1,700

'50s Stratocaster (Import)

1991-present.

MODEL YEAR	FEATURES	EXC. COND. LOW	HIGH
1991-2007		$450	$500

'50s Stratocaster Relic

1996-1999. Custom Shop model, reproduction of ca. '57 Strat with played-in feel, gold hardware is +$100, see-thru Mary Kaye ash body is +$100, replaced by '56 Strat.

MODEL YEAR	FEATURES	EXC. COND. LOW	HIGH
1996-1999	Various colors	$1,450	$1,800

50th Anniversary 1954 Stratocaster

2004-2005. Custom Shop, celebrates 50 years of the Strat, 1954 specs and materials, replica form-fit case, certificate, Fender took orders for these up to December 31, 2004.

MODEL YEAR	FEATURES	EXC. COND. LOW	HIGH
2004-2005		$3,000	$3,200

50th Anniversary American Deluxe Strat (USA)

2004. U.S.-made, Deluxe series features, engraved neck plate, tweed case.

MODEL YEAR	FEATURES	EXC. COND. LOW	HIGH
2004		$1,250	$1,450

50th Anniversary Stratocaster

1995-1996. Custom Shop model, flame maple top, 3 vintage-style pickups, gold hardware, gold 50th Anniversary (of Fender) coin on back of the headstock, sunburst, 2500 made.

MODEL YEAR	FEATURES	EXC. COND. LOW	HIGH
1995-1996		$1,450	$1,600

50th Anniversary Stratocaster (Mexico)

2004. Made in Mexico, Aztec gold finish, no logo on guitar to indicate 50th Anniv., CE on neck plate to indicate import.

MODEL YEAR	FEATURES	EXC. COND. LOW	HIGH
2004		$525	$575

MODEL YEAR	FEATURES	EXC. COND. LOW	HIGH

50th Anniversary Stratocaster Relic

1995-1996. Custom Shop Relic model, aged played-in feel, diamond headstock inlay, Shoreline Gold finish, 200 units planned.

1995-1996		$2,700	$3,300

'54 Stratocaster

1992-1998 (Custom Shop Classic reissue), 1997-present. Ash body, Custom '50s pickups, gold-plated hardware.

1992-1998	Various options	$1,700	$2,000

'54 Stratocaster FMT

1992-1998. Custom Classic reissue, Flame Maple Top, also comes in gold hardware edition.

1992-1998		$1,800	$2,000
1992-1998	Gold hardware option	$1,900	$2,050

'56 Stratocaster

1996-present. Custom Shop model, most detailed replica (and most expensive to date) of '56 Strat, including electronics and pickups, offered with rosewood or maple 'board, gold hardware is +$100.

1996-1998	Cunetto built relic	$2,700	$3,300
1997-1998	Cunetto era (staff built)	$1,800	$2,200
1999-2006	Closet Classic	$1,700	$1,900
1999-2006	NOS	$1,600	$1,800
1999-2006	Relic	$1,900	$2,100

'57 Special Stratocaster

1992-1993. Custom Shop model, flamed maple top, birdseye maple neck, run of 60 made, sunburst.

1992-1993		$1,700	$1,900

'57 Stratocaster

Mid-1990s. Custom Shop model, replaced by the more authentic, higher-detailed '56 Custom Shop Stratocaster by '99, Custom Shop models can be distinguished by the original certificate that comes with the guitar.

1994-1996	Various colors	$1,300	$1,600

'57 Stratocaster (USA)

1982-present. U.S.A.-made at the Fullerton, California plant ('82-'85) and at the Corona, California plant ('85-present).

1982-1984	Rare colors	$2,500	$3,000
1982-1984	Various colors	$1,500	$2,500
1986-1989	Blond, ash body	$1,500	$1,600
1986-1989	Various colors	$1,200	$1,400
1990-1999	Blond, ash body	$1,300	$1,500
1990-1999	Rare colors	$1,300	$1,500
1990-1999	Various colors	$1,100	$1,300
2000-2006	Various colors	$1,100	$1,200

'57 Vintage Stratocaster (Japan)

1984-1985. Japanese-made, various colors.

1984-1985		$550	$675

'58 Stratocaster

1996-1999. Custom Shop model, ash body, Fat '50s pickups, chrome or gold hardware (gold is +$100.), Custom Shop models can be distinguished by the original certificate that comes with the guitar.

1996-1999	Various colors	$1,500	$1,800

'58 Stratocaster (Dakota Red)

1996. Custom Shop model, run of 30 made in Dakota Red with matching headstock, maple neck, Texas special pickups, gold hardware.

1996		$1,500	$1,800

'60 FMT Stratocaster

1997-1999. Custom Shop model, flame maple top.

1997-1999		$1,600	$1,800

'60 Stratocaster

1992-present. Custom Shop model, '92-'99 version with Texas Special pickups, later version is more detailed replica (and most expensive to date) of '60 Strat, including electronics and pickups, gold hardware is +$100. The price includes the original Certificate of Authenticity, which for the '92-'98 early models indicates the model as 1960 Stratocaster along with the year of manufacture, a guitar without the original certificate is worth less than the values shown.

1992-1998	1st issue	$1,500	$1,700
1996-1998	Cunetto built relic	$2,700	$3,300
1997-1998	Cunetto era (staff built)	$1,800	$2,200
1999-2007	Closet Classic	$1,700	$1,900
1999-2007	NOS	$1,600	$1,800
1999-2007	Relic	$1,900	$2,100
1999-2007	Various "rare" colors	$2,100	$2,400

'60s Stratocaster (Import)

1991-present. Basswood body, U-neck, rosewood 'board, trem, various colors. Originally made in Japan, now in Mexico.

1991-1999	Foto-flame	$575	$700
1991-1999	Various colors	$600	$750
2000-2007	Various colors	$500	$700

'60s Stratocaster Relic

1996-1999. Custom Shop model, reproduction of '60s Strat with played-in feel, gold hardware is +$100, see-thru Mary Kaye ash body is +$100, replaced by '60 Relic.

1996-1999	Various colors	$1,300	$1,800

'62 Stratocaster (Japan)

1984-1985	Various colors	$550	$675

'62 Stratocaster (USA)

1982-present. Made at Fullerton plant ('82-'85) then at Corona plant ('86-present).

1982-1984	Various colors	$1,500	$2,500
1982-1984	Rare colors	$2,500	$3,000
1986-1989	Blond, ash body	$1,500	$1,600
1986-1989	Various colors	$1,200	$1,400
1990-1999	Blond, ash body	$1,300	$1,500
1990-1999	Rare colors	$1,300	$1,500
1990-1999	Various colors	$1,100	$1,300
2000-2006	Various colors	$1,100	$1,200

'65 Stratocaster

2003-present. Custom Shop model, '65 small-headstock specs, rosewood or maple cap 'board, transition logo, offered in NOS, Relic, or Closet Classic versions.

2003-2007	Closet Classic	$1,700	$1,900
2003-2007	NOS	$1,600	$1,800
2003-2007	Relic	$1,900	$2,100

Fender '60s Relic Stratocaster

Fender '65 Closet Classic Stratocaster

Fender Big Block Stratocaster

Fender Blackie Stratocaster (Custom Shop)

MODEL YEAR	FEATURES	EXC. COND. LOW	HIGH
'66 Stratocaster			
2004-present. Custom Shop model, offered in Closet Classic, NOS or Relic versions.			
2004-2007	Closet Classic	$1,700	$1,900
2004-2007	NOS	$1,600	$1,800
2004-2007	Relic	$1,900	$2,100
'68 Reverse Strat Special (USA)			
2001-2002. With special reverse left-hand neck, large headstock (post-CBS style).			
2001-2002		$900	$1,200
'68 Stratocaster			
1990s. Custom Shop model, Jimi Hendrix-style, maple cap neck.			
1990s		$1,600	$1,900
'68 Stratocaster (Japan)			
1996-1999. '68 specs including large headstock, part of Collectables Series, sunburst, natural, Olympic White.			
1996-1999		$600	$700
'69 Stratocaster			
1997-present. Custom Shop model, large headstock, U-shaped maple neck with rosewood or maple cap options, '69-style finish, gold hardware is +$100, since 2000, offered in NOS, Relic, or Closet Classic versions.			
2000-2006	Closet Classic	$1,700	$1,900
2000-2006	NOS	$1,600	$1,800
2000-2006	Relic	$1,900	$2,100
'70s Stratocaster (Mexico)			
1999-present. Made in Mexico, large headstock, white pickups and knobs, rosewood 'board.			
1999-2007		$550	$600
'72 Stratocaster (Japan)			
1985-1996. Basswood body, maple 'board, large headstock.			
1985-1996		$600	$700
Acoustasonic Stratocaster			
2003-present. Hollowed out alder Strat body with braceless graphite top, 3 in-bridge Fishman piezo pickups, acoustic sound hole.			
2003-2006		$525	$550
Aerodyne Stratocaster			
2004-present. Import Strat with Aerodyne body profile, bound body, black.			
2004-2006		$500	$550
Aluminum Stratocaster			
1994-1995. Aluminum-bodied American Standard with anodized finish in blue marble, purple marble or red, silver and blue stars and stripes. Some with 40th Anniversary designation. There is also a Custom Shop version.			
1994-1995	Marble patterns	$2,500	$3,000
1994-1995	Red-silver-blue flag option	$3,000	$3,500
American Classic Holoflake Stratocaster			
1992-1993. Custom Shop model, splatter/sparkle finish, pearloid 'guard.			
1992-1993		$1,550	$1,900

MODEL YEAR	FEATURES	EXC. COND. LOW	HIGH
American Classic Stratocaster			
1992-1999. Custom Shop version of American Standard, 3 pickups, tremolo, rosewood 'board, nickel or gold-plated hardware, various colors.			
1992-1999	See-thru blond ash body	$1,450	$1,600
1992-1999	Various colors and options	$1,350	$1,500
American Deluxe Fat Stratocaster			
1998-2003. Made in USA, Fender DH-1 bridge humbucker for fat sound, premium alder or ash body.			
1998-2003	Ash body, transparent finish	$925	$1,075
1998-2006	Various colors	$850	$900
American Deluxe HSS Stratocaster			
2004-present. Deluxe features, hum/single/single pickups.			
2004		$875	$975
American Deluxe Stratocaster			
1998-present. Made in USA, premium alder or ash body, noiseless pickups.			
1998-2004	Ash body, transparent finish	$925	$1,100
1998-2006	Various colors	$875	$975
American Vintage '57 Commemorative Stratocaster			
2007. Limited production, part of American Vintage Series, 1957-2007 Commemorative logo neckplate.			
2007-2008		$1,100	$1,300
American Vintage '62 Commemorative Stratocaster			
2007. Limited production, part of American Vintage Series, 1957-2007 Commemorative logo neckplate.			
2007-2008		$1,100	$1,300
Antigua Stratocaster			
2004. Made in Japan, limited-edition reissue, '70s features and antigua finish.			
2004		$550	$675
Big Apple Stratocaster			
1997-2000. Two humbucking pickups, 5-way switch, rosewood 'board or maple neck, non-tremolo optional.			
1997-2000	Various colors	$725	$800
Big Block Stratocaster			
2005-2006. Pearloid block markers, black with matching headstock, 2 single coils (neck, middle) 1 humbucker (bridge), vintage style trem.			
2005-2006		$575	$650
Bill Carson Stratocaster			
1992. Based on the '57 Strat, birdseye maple neck, Cimarron Red finish, 1 left-handed and 100 right-handed produced, serial numbers MT000-MT100, made in Fender Custom Shop, and initiated by The Music Trader (MT) in Florida.			
1992		$2,000	$2,200
Blackie Stratocaster			
1989-2005. Production model, Blackie decal and Eric Clapton's signature decal on headstock.			
1989-2000	Lace pickups	$1,100	$1,200
2001-2005	Standard pickups	$1,200	$1,350

The **Vintage Guitar Price Guide** shows low to high values for items in all-original excellent condition, and, where applicable, with original case or cover.

MODEL YEAR	FEATURES	EXC. COND. LOW	HIGH

Blackie Stratocaster (Custom Shop 1987)
1987. 12 made, includes Certificate of Authenticity.

1987		$2,500	$2,700

Blackie Stratocaster (Custom Shop)
November 2006. 185 instruments for U.S. market, 90 made for export, original retail price $24,000.

2006		$18,000	$20,000

Blue Flower Stratocaster
1988-1993, 2003-2004. Made in Japan, '72 Strat reissue with a reissue '68 Tele Blue Floral finish.

1988-1993		$600	$1,000
2003-2004	Reissue	$500	$550

Bonnie Raitt Stratocaster
1995-2000. Alder body, often in blueburst, Bonnie Raitt's signature on headstock.

1995-2000		$1,000	$1,100

Bowling Ball/Marble Stratocaster
Ca.1983-1984. Standard Strat with 1 tone and 1 volume control, jack on 'guard, called Bowling Ball Strat due to the swirling, colored finish.

1983-1984		$2,400	$3,000

Buddy Guy Stratocaster (Mexico)
1996-present. Maple neck, polka-dot finish.

1996-2006		$425	$475

Buddy Guy Stratocaster (Signature)
1995-present. Maple neck, 3 Gold Lace Sensor pickups, ash body, signature model, blond or sunburst.

1995-2007		$1,000	$1,100

California Stratocaster
1997-1999. Made in the U.S., painted in Mexico, 2 pickups, various colors.

1997-1999		$575	$625

California Fat Stratocaster
1997-1998. Humbucker pickup in bridge position.

1997-1998		$450	$550

Classic Player Stratocaster
2000. Custom Shop model, Standard Stratocaster with useful 'player-friendly features' such as noiseless stacked single-coil pickups and factory Sperzel locking tuners, made in the Custom Shop, black, gold anodized 'guard.

2000		$1,250	$1,450

Collector's Edition Stratocaster ('62 Reissue)
1997. Pearl inlaid '97 on 12th fret, rosewood 'board, alder body, gold hardware, tortoise 'guard, nitro finish, sunburst, 1997 made.

1997		$1,350	$1,500

Contemporary Stratocaster
1989-1998. U.S.-made Custom Shop model, 7/8 scale body, hum/single/single pickups, various colors.

1989-1998		$1,150	$1,400

Contemporary Stratocaster (Import)
1985-1987. Import model used while the new Fender reorganized, black headstock with silver-white logo, black or white 'guard, 2 humbucker pickups or single-coil and humbucker, 2 knobs and slider switch.

1985-1987		$450	$525

Crash Stratocaster
2005. Master Built Custom Shop model, hand painted by John Crash Matos, approximately 50, comes with certificate, the original certificate adds value, the prices shown include the certificate.

2005		$8,000	$10,000

Custom 1960 Stratocaster
1994. Short run of 20 custom ordered and specified instruments that have 1960 specs along with other specs such as a pearloid 'guard, came with Certificate of Authenticity, matching headstock color.

1994		$3,000	$3,400

Deluxe Players Special Edition Stratocaster
2007. Made in Mexico, Special Edition Fender oval sticker on back of headstock along with 60th Anniversary badge.

2007		$375	$450

Deluxe Players Stratocaster
2004-present. Made in Mexico.

2004-2006		$300	$400

Deluxe Strat Plus
1987-1998. Three Lace Sensor pickups, Floyd Rose, alder (poplar available earlier) body with ash veneer on front and back, various colors, also see Strat Plus.

1987-1998		$900	$1,100

Deluxe Vintage Player '62 Stratocaster
2005-2006. Design blends vintage and modern features based upon '62 specs including vintage style tuners, bridge and aged plastic parts. Updates include 3 Samarium Cobalt Noiseless pickups and Deluxe American Standard electronics, limited edition, Olympic White or Ice Blue Metallic.

2005-2006		$975	$1,050

Dick Dale Stratocaster
1994-present. Custom Shop signature model, alder body, reverse headstock, sparkle finish

1994-2007		$1,700	$1,875

Elite Stratocaster
1983-1984. The Elite Series feature active electronics and noise-cancelling pickups, push buttons instead of 3-way switch, Elite script logo on 4-bolt neck plate, various colors. Also see Gold Elite Stratocaster and Walnut Elite Stratocaster.

1983-1984	Standard colors	$1,000	$1,125
1983-1984	Stratoburst option(s)	$1,125	$1,250

Eric Clapton Gold Leaf Stratocaster
2004. Custom Shop model, special build for Guitar Center, 50 made, 23k gold leaf finish/covering.

2004		$4,600	$5,700

Eric Clapton Stratocaster
1988-present. U.S.-made, '57 reissue features, had Lace Sensor pickups until '01, when switched to Vintage. Black became an option in '91.

1988-1989		$975	$1,200
1990-2007		$950	$1,150

Fender Crash Stratocaster

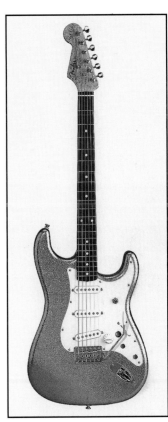
Fender Dick Dale Stratocaster

Fender Koa Stratocaster

Fender Lenny Stratocaster

MODEL YEAR	FEATURES	EXC. COND. LOW	HIGH

Eric Clapton Stratocaster (CS)
2004. Custom Shop model, re-creation of Clapton's personal guitar, standard non-active single-coil pickups, black or blue finish.

2004		$1,550	$1,750

Eric Johnson Stratocaster
2005. Custom Shop model, lightweight '57 spec body, '57 soft-v-neck profile, special design Custom Shop Eric Johnson pickups, vintage tremolo with 5-springs.

2005		$1,100	$1,350

Floyd Rose Classic Relic Stratocaster
1998-1999. Custom Shop model, late '60s large headstock, 1 humbucker and 1 Strat pickup.

1998-1999		$1,700	$1,800

Floyd Rose Classic Stratocaster
1992-1997. Two single-coils, bridge humbucker, Floyd Rose tremolo, various colors.

1992-1997		$1,000	$1,250

Foto Flame Stratocaster
1994-1996, 2000. Japanese-made Collectables model, alder and basswood body with Foto Flame (simulated woodgrain) finish on top cap and back of neck.

1994-1996		$575	$700
2000		$550	$625

Freddy Tavares Aloha Stratocaster
1993-1994. Custom Shop model, hollow aluminum body with hand engraved Hawaiian scenes, custom inlay on neck, 153 made.

1993-1994		$4,500	$5,200

Gold Elite Stratocaster
1983-1984. The Elite series feature active electronics and noise-cancelling pickups, the Gold Elite has gold hardware and pearloid tuner buttons, also see Elite Stratocaster and Walnut Elite Stratocaster.

1983-1984		$1,200	$1,350

Gold Stratocaster
1981-1983. Gold metallic finish, gold-plated brass hardware, 4-bolt neck, maple 'board, skunk strip, trem.

1981-1983		$1,200	$1,500

Gold Stratocaster (CS)
1989. Custom Shop model, 500 made, gold finish with gold anodized and white 'guards included.

1989		$1,800	$2,100

Hank Marvin 40th Anniversary Stratocaster
1998. Custom Shop logo with '40 Years 1958-1998' marked on back of headstock, Fiesta Red, only 40 made, Custom Shop certificate.

1998		$5,900	$7,300

Hank Marvin Stratocaster
1995-1996. Custom Shop model, Feista Red.

1995-1996		$1,500	$1,800

Harley-Davidson 90th Anniversary Stratocaster
1993. Custom Shop, 109 total made, Harley-Davidson and Custom Shop V logo on headstock (Diamond Edition, 40 units), 9 units produced for the Harley-Davidson company without diamond logo, 60 units

were not Diamond Edition, chrome-plated engraved metal body, engraved 'guard, Custom Shop Certificate important attribute.

1993		$8,000	$10,000

Hellecaster Stratocaster
1997. Custom Shop model, gold sparkle 'guard, gold hardware, split single-coils, rosewood 'board.

1997		$1,450	$1,575

Highway One Stratocaster/HSS
2002-present. U.S.-made, alder body, satin lacquer finish, HSS version has humbucker/single/single pickups.

2002-2006		$550	$600

HM Stratocaster (USA/Import)
1988-1992 ('88 Japanese-made, '89-'90 U.S.- and Japanese-made, '91-'92 U.S.-made). Heavy Metal Strat, Floyd Rose, regular or pointy headstock, black hardware, 1 or 2 humbuckers, 1 single-coil and 1 humbucker, or 2 single-coils and 1 humbucker. Later models have choice of 2 humbuckers and 1 single-coil or 2 single-coils and 1 humbucker.

1988-1990	Bud Dry logo finish	$325	$400
1988-1990	Import	$300	$375
1989-1992	U.S.	$450	$550

Homer Haynes HLE Stratocaster
1988-1989. Custom Shop model, '59 Strat basics with gold finish, gold anodized guard, and gold hardware, limited edition of 500.

1988-1989		$1,600	$2,000

Hot Wheels Stratocaster
2003. Custom Shop model commissioned by Hot Wheels, 16 made, orange flames over blue background, large Hot Wheels logo.

2003		$2,800	$3,400

HRR Stratocaster
1990-1995. Japanese-made, hot-rodded vintage-style Strat, Floyd Rose tremolo system, 3 pickups, maple neck, Foto Flame, black, Olympic White or sunburst.

1990-1995		$400	$450

HSS Stratocaster
2006-present. Made in Mexico, humbucker and 2 singles, Floyd Rose tremolo bridge.

2006-2007		$300	$350

Ike Turner Tribute Stratocaster
2005. Custom Shop model, 100 made, replica of Ike Turner's Sonic Blue Strat.

2005		$1,850	$2,000

Jeff Beck Stratocaster
1994-present. Alder body, Lace Sensor pickups, special designed tremolo, various colors but mostly Surf Green.

1994-2007	Standard model, common colors	$1,000	$1,100
1994-2007	Standard model, rare colors	$1,050	$1,400

Jerry Donahue Hellecaster Stratocaster
1997. Made in the Fender Japan Custom Shop as one part of the 3-part Hellecasters Series, limited edition, Seymour Duncan pickups, maple, blue with blue sparkle guard.

1997		$950	$1,250

MODEL YEAR	FEATURES	EXC. COND. LOW	HIGH

Jimi Hendrix Monterey Pop Stratocaster
1997-1998. Custom Shop model, near replica of Monterey Pop Festival sacrifice guitar, red psychedelic-style finish.
| 1997-1998 | | $6,500 | $8,000 |

Jimi Hendrix Tribute Stratocaster
1997-2000. Left-handed guitar strung right-handed, maple cap neck, Olympic White finish.
| 1997-2000 | | $1,400 | $1,700 |

Jimmie Hendrix Voodoo Stratocaster
1997-2002. Right-handed body with reverse peghead, maple neck, sunburst, Olympic White, or black.
| 1997-1998 | 1st year | $1,600 | $2,000 |
| 1999-2002 | | $1,400 | $1,600 |

Jimmie Vaughan Tex-Mex Stratocaster
1997-present. Poplar body, maple 'board, signature on headstock, 3 Tex-Mex pickups, various colors.
| 1997-2007 | | $475 | $525 |

John Jorgenson Hellecaster Stratocaster
1997. Made in the Fender Japan Custom Shop as one part of the 3-part Hellecasters Series, limited edition, special Seymour Duncan pickups, gold sparkle 'guard, gold hardware, split single-coils, rosewood 'board.
| 1997 | | $1,100 | $1,300 |

John Mayer Stratocaster
2005-present. Custom Shop model alder body, special scooped mid-range pickups, vintage tremolo, special design gigbag with pocket for laptop computer.
| 2005-2007 | | $1,000 | $1,100 |

Koa Stratocaster
2006-present. Made in Korea, sunburst over koa veneer top, plain script Fender logo, serial number on back of headstock with.
| 2006-2007 | | $450 | $500 |

Kon Tiki Stratocaster
2003. Custom Shop model, limited run of 25, Tiki Green including Tiki 3-color art work on headstock.
| 2003 | | $1,350 | $1,500 |

Lenny Stratocaster
Introduced Dec. 12, 2007 by Guitar Center stores, Custom Shop model, 185 guitars made, initial product offering price was 17K.
| 2007 | | $13,000 | $15,000 |

Lone Star Stratocaster
1996-2000. Alder body, 1 humbucker and 2 single-coil pickups, rosewood 'board or maple neck, various colors.
| 1996-2000 | | $825 | $900 |

Mark Knopfler Stratocaster
2003-present. '57 body with '62 maple neck.
| 2003-2007 | | $1,100 | $1,350 |

Milonga Deluxe Stratocaster
2005. Special Edition made in Mexico, Vintage Noiseless pickups, rosewood 'board, Olympic White, gold hardware.
| 2005 | | $400 | $425 |

Moto Limited Edition Stratocaster
1990s. Custom Shop model, pearloid cover in various colors, includes Certificate of Authenticity, not to be confused with white pearloid Moto Strat which is part of a guitar and amp set (as listed below).
| 1990s | | $1,500 | $1,700 |

Moto Set Stratocaster
1995-1996. Custom Shop set including guitar, case, amp and amp stand, white pearloid finish.
| 1995-1996 | Red (few made) | $4,100 | $4,300 |
| 1995-1996 | White | $3,800 | $4,100 |

Paisley Stratocaster
1988-1995, 2003-2004. Japanese-made '72 Strat reissue with a reissue '68 Tele Pink Paisley finish.
| 1988-1995 | | $600 | $1,000 |

Playboy 40th Anniversary Stratocaster
1994. Custom Shop model, nude Marilyn Monroe graphic on body.
| 1994 | | $5,500 | $6,800 |

Powerhouse/Powerhouse Deluxe Stratocaster
1997-present. Made in Mexico, Standard Strat configuration with pearloid 'guard, various colors.
| 1997-2007 | | $325 | $400 |
| 2005 | Powerbridge, TRS stereo | $500 | $600 |

Proud Stratocaster
2003. Custom Shop model, only 3 made to commemorate a United Way and Rock & Roll Hall of Fame project, with only 3 made the value becomes more subjective and collector value may far exceed intrinsic value of similar Custom Shop instruments, the body was painted in detail by Fender's artist.
| 2003 | | $3,200 | $3,900 |

Richie Sambora Stratocaster
1993-2002. Alder body, Floyd Rose tremolo, maple neck, sunburst. There was also a cheaper Richie Sambora Standard Stratocaster in blue or white.
| 1993-2002 | USA | $1,150 | $1,400 |
| 1994-2002 | Import | $475 | $550 |

Roadhouse Stratocaster
1997-2000. U.S.-made, poplar body, tortoise shell 'guard, maple 'board, 3 Texas Special pickups, various colors.
| 1997-2000 | | $850 | $900 |

Robert Cray Stratocaster
1991-present. Custom Shop signature model, rosewood 'board, chunky neck, lighter weight, non-tremolo, alder body, gold-plated hardware, various colors. There is also a chrome hardware Robert Cray Standard Stratocaster model.
| 1991-2005 | | $1,100 | $1,250 |

Robin Trower Signature Stratocaster
2004-2006. Custom Shop model, 100 made, large headstock (post '65-era styling), with '70s logo styling, post '71 3-bolt neck, bullet truss rod, white.
| 2004-2006 | | $1,900 | $2,100 |

Roland Ready Stratocaster
1998-present. Made in Mexico, single synth pickup and 3 single-coils.
| 1998-2007 | | $400 | $475 |

Fender So-Cal Speed Shop Stratocaster

Fender Paisley Stratocaster

GUITARS

*Fender SRV Tribute #1
Stratocaster*

Fender VG Stratocaster

MODEL YEAR	FEATURES	EXC. COND. LOW	HIGH

Rory Gallagher Tribute Stratocaster
2005. Custom Shop model, heavily distressed '61 model based on Gallagher's guitar, price includes the original Custom Shop certificate, a model without the certificate is worth less, Rory Gallagher logo signature on back of headstock.

| 2005 | | $2,200 | $2,300 |

Set-Neck Stratocaster
1992-1999. Custom Shop model, mahogany body and figured maple top, 4 pickups, glued-in neck, active electronics, by '96 ash body.

| 1992-1999 | | $1,200 | $1,500 |

Short-Scale (7/8) Stratocaster
1989-1995. Similar to Standard Strat, but with 2 control knobs and switch, 24" scale vs. 25" scale, sometimes called a mini-Strat, Japanese import, various colors.

| 1989-1995 | | $525 | $625 |

So-Cal Speed Shop L.E. Stratocaster
2005-2006. Limited edition for Musician's Friend, custom red, white, and black So-Cal paint job over basswood body and rosewood 'board, 1 humbucker, So-Cal Speed Shop decal.

| 2005-2006 | | $500 | $625 |

Special Edition Stratocaster
2004-present. Special Edition oval logo on back of headstock, import model, various styles offered, '50s or '60s vintage copy specs, maple fretboard, ash or koa body, see-thru or opaque finish.

| 2004-2007 | | $400 | $500 |

Splatter Stratocaster
2003. Made in Mexico, splatter paint job, various color combinations, with gig bag.

| 2003 | | $300 | $375 |

Squier II Stratocaster
1989-1990. Import from India.

| 1989-1990 | | $100 | $125 |

Squier Stratocaster Standard
1982-present. Low-cost Stratocaster Standard version of the Squier line. Fender Japan was established in '82 with Squier production beginning in '83. Production was shifted to Korea in '87 and later allocated to China, India (Squier II '89-'90) and Mexico.

1982-1989		$250	$400
1990-1999		$150	$250
2000-2007	Indonesia	$125	$150

Squier Stratocaster Standard (Affinity Series)
1997-present. Made in China.

| 1997-2007 | | $75 | $125 |

Squier Stratocaster Standard (Double Fat Strat)
2000-2006. Made in China, 2 humbucker pickups.

| 2000-2006 | | $100 | $125 |

Squier Stratocaster Standard (Floyd Rose)
1995-1996. Floyd Rose tailpiece, fotoflame finish, large Fender script logo.

| 1995-1996 | | $175 | $275 |

Standard Fat Stratocaster
2000-2006. Made in Mexico (vs. California Fat Strat).

| 2000-2006 | | $325 | $375 |

Standard HH Stratocaster
2006. Tex Mex Fat Strat humbucker pickups, 1 volume and 2 tone control knobs.

| 2006 | | $225 | $275 |

Standard Stratocaster (Mexico)
1990-present. Fender Mexico started guitar production in '90. Not to be confused with the American-made Standard Stratocaster of '81-'84. High end of range includes a hard guitar case, while the low end of the range includes only a gig bag, various colors.

1990-1999		$325	$375
2000-2006		$300	$350
2006-2007	Thicker bridge block	$300	$325

Standard Stratocaster Satin Finish
2003-2006. Basically Mexico-made Standard with satin finish.

| 2003-2006 | | $200 | $275 |

Stevie Ray Vaughan Stratocaster
1992-present. U.S.-made, alder body, sunburst, gold hardware, SRV 'guard, lefty tremolo, Brazilian rosewood 'board (pau ferro by '93).

| 1992-2006 | | $1,000 | $1,150 |

Stevie Ray Vaughan Tribute #1 Stratocaster
2004. Custom Shop model limited edition recreation of SRV's #1 made by Master Builder John Cruz in the Custom Shop, 100 made, $10,000 MSRP, includes flight case stenciled "SRV - Number One," and other goodies.

| 2004 | | $21,000 | $26,000 |

Strat Plus
1987-1999. Three Lace Sensor pickups, alder (poplar available earlier) body, tremolo, rosewood 'board or maple neck, various colors. See Deluxe Strat Plus for ash veneer version.

| 1987-1989 | All colors | $725 | $900 |
| 1990-1999 | All colors | $725 | $875 |

Stratacoustic
2000-2006. Thinline acoustic/electric, single-cut, spruce top, fiberglass body.

| 2000-2006 | | $200 | $250 |

Stratocaster HSS/HH
2004-present. Made in U.S., HSS has humbucker/single/single pickups, HH has 2 humbuckers.

| 2004-2006 | Alder body | $675 | $725 |
| 2004-2006 | Ash body, transparent finish | $700 | $775 |

Stratocaster Junior
2004-2006. Import, short 22.7" scale, Alder body, non-trem hardtail bridge.

| 2004-2006 | | $250 | $275 |

Stratocaster Special
1993-1995. Made in Mexico, a humbucker and a single-coil pickup, 1 volume, 1 tone.

| 1993-1995 | | $275 | $325 |

MODEL YEAR	FEATURES	EXC. COND. LOW	HIGH

Stratocaster XII
1988-1995. Alder body, maple neck, 21-fret rosewood 'board, 3 vintage Strat pickups, Japanese-made, various colors.

1988-1995		$625	$775

Strat-o-Sonic
2003-2006. American Special Series, Stratocaster-style chambered body, includes Strat-o-Sonic Dove I (1 pickup, '03 only), Dove II/DV II (2 black P-90s, '03-'06) and HH (2 humbuckers, '05-'06).

2003-2006		$650	$725

Sub Sonic Stratocaster
2000-2001. Baritone model tuned B-E-A-D-G-B, single-single-hum pickup configuration, Strat-styling.

2000-2001		$750	$900

Super/Deluxe Super Stratocaster
1997-2003. Import made in Mexico, part of Deluxe Series, Standard Strat features with maple neck.

1997-2003		$275	$300

Tanqurey Tonic Stratocaster
1988. Made for a Tanqurey Tonic liquor ad campaign giveaway in '88; many were given to winners around the country, ads said that they could also be purchased through Tanqurey, but that apparently didn't happen.

1988	Tanqurey Tonic Green	$750	$925

Texas Special Stratocaster
1991-1992. Custom Shop model, 50 made, state of Texas map stamped on neck plate, Texas Special pickups, maple fretboard, sunburst.

1991-1992		$1,750	$1,950

The Strat
1980-1983. Alder body, 4-bolt neck, large STRAT on painted peghead, gold-plated brass hardware, various colors.

1980-1983	Common colors	$950	$1,100
1980-1983	Rare colors	$1,200	$1,400

Tie-Dye Stratocaster
2004-2005. Single-coil neck and humbucker bridge pickups, Band of Gypsies or Hippie Blue tie-dye pattern poly finish.

2004-2005	Band of Gypsies	$300	$350

Tree of Life Stratocaster
1993. Custom Shop model, 29 made, tree of life fretboard inlay, 1-piece quilted maple body.

1993		$7,000	$8,000

Turquoise Sparkle Stratocaster
2001. Custom Shop model, limited run of 75 for Mars Music, turquoise sparkle finish.

2001		$1,200	$1,400

U.S. Ultra / Ultra Plus Stratocaster
1990-1997. Alder body with figured maple veneer on front and back, single Lace Sensor pickups in neck and middle, double Sensor at bridge, ebony 'board, sunburst.

1990-1997		$1,000	$1,100

Ventures Limited Edition Stratocaster
1996. Japanese-made tribute model, matches Jazzmaster equivalent, black.

1996		$925	$1,000

VG Stratocaster
2007-present. Modeling technology using Fender's classic Strat design and Roland VG circuitry, 5 guitar tone banks deliver 16 sounds.

2007		$900	$1,100

Walnut Stratocaster
1981-1983. American black walnut body and 1-piece neck and 'board.

1981-1983		$1,725	$2,075

Walnut Elite Stratocaster
1983-1984. The Elite Series features active electronics and noise-cancelling pickups, Walnut Elite has a walnut body and neck, gold-plated hardware and pearloid tuner buttons. Also see Elite Stratocaster and Gold Elite Stratocaster.

1983-1984		$1,825	$2,175

Western Stratocaster
1995. Custom Shop model, only 5 made, featured in Fender Custom Shop book from the 1990s.

1995		$9,500	$11,500

Yngwie Malmsteen Stratocaster
1988-present. U.S.-made, maple neck, scalloped 'board, 3 single-coil pickups, blue, red, white.

1988-2007		$1,000	$1,250

TC-90
2004. Semi-hollow thinline, double-cut, Duncan SP-90 pickups stop bar and tune-o-matic tailpiece.

2004		$400	$475

Fender TC-90

Telecaster
The following are all variations of the Telecaster. The first five listings are for the main American-made models and the '85 interim production Japanese model. All others are listed alphabetically after that in the following order. Broadcaster and Nocaster models are under Broadcaster.

Telecaster
Standard Telecaster
Standard Telecaster (Japan)
American Standard Telecaster
American Series Telecaster
40th Anniversary Telecaster
'50s Telecaster (Import)
50th Anniversary Spanish Guitar Set Custom Shop
50th Anniversary Telecaster
'52 Telecaster
'60s Telecaster Custom
'60s Telecaster Relic
60th Anniversary Telecaster
'62 Custom Telecaster (Import)
'62 Custom Telecaster (U.S.A.)
'63 Custom Telecaster Relic
'63 Telecaster
'69 Tele/Telecaster Thinline (Import)
'72 Telecaster Custom (Import)
'72 Telecaster Thinline
'90s Tele Thinline
'90s Telecaster Deluxe (Foto-Flame)
Aerodyne Telecaster
Albert Collins Telecaster

1952 Fender Telecaster

GUITARS

GUITARS

1956 Fender Telecaster

1964 Fender Telecaster

MODEL YEAR	FEATURES	EXC. COND. LOW	HIGH
	Aluminum Telecaster		
	American Classic Holoflake Telecaster		
	American Classic Telecaster		
	American Deluxe Power Telecaster		
	American Deluxe Telecaster		
	Antigua Telecaster		
	Big Block Telecaster		
	Bigsby Telecaster		
	Black and Gold Telecaster		
	Blue Flower Telecaster		
	Buck Owens Limited Edition Telecaster		
	California Fat Telecaster		
	California Telecaster		
	Chambered Mahogany Telecaster		
	Classic Series Telecaster		
	Collector's Edition Telecaster		
	Contemporary Telecaster (Import)		
	Danny Gatton Telecaster		
	Deluxe Nashville Telecaster (Mexico)		
	Deluxe Telecaster (USA)		
	Elite Telecaster		
	Foto Flame Telecaster		
	G.E. Smith Telecaster		
	Highway One Telecaster/Texas Telecaster		
	HMT Telecaster		
	J5 Triple Telecaster Deluxe		
	James Burton Telecaster		
	Jerry Donahue JD Telecaster		
	Jerry Donahue Telecaster		
	Jim Root Telecaster		
	Jimmy Bryant Tribute Telecaster		
	John Jorgenson Telecaster		
	Jr. Telecaster		
	Matched Set Telecaster		
	Moto Limited Edition Telecaster		
	Nashville Telecaster		
	Nashville Telecaster (Mexico)		
	NHL Premier Edition Telecaster		
	Nokie Edwards Telecaster		
	Paisley Telecaster		
	Plus/Plus Deluxe Telecaster		
	Rosewood Telecaster		
	Rosewood Telecaster (Japan)		
	Set-Neck Telecaster		
	Sparkle Telecaster		
	Special Telecaster/Telecaster Special		
	Squier Telecaster		
	Squier Telecaster Affinity		
	Squier Telecaster Custom		
	Squier Thinline Telecaster		
	Standard Telecaster (Mexico)		
	Telecaster Custom		
	Telecaster Custom (2nd Edition)		
	Telecaster Custom (Japan)		
	Telecaster Custom HH FMT (Korea)		
	Telecaster Stratocaster Hybrid		
	Telecaster Thinline (Custom Shop)		
	Telecaster Thinline/Thinline II		
	Telecoustic Deluxe		
	Tele-Sonic		
	Texas Special Telecaster		

MODEL YEAR	FEATURES	EXC. COND. LOW	HIGH
	Will Ray Jazz-A-Caster		
	Will Ray Telecaster		
Telecaster			

1951-1982. See Standard Telecaster (following listing) for '82-'85, American Standard Telecaster for '88-2000 and American Series Telecaster for 2000-'07. Renamed American Standard Telecaster again in '08. In the late '60s and early '70s Fender began to increase their use of vibrato tailpieces. A vibrato tailpiece for this period is generally worth about 13% less than the values shown. Please refer to the Fender Guitar Intro Section for details on Fender color options.

MODEL YEAR	FEATURES	EXC. COND. LOW	HIGH
1951	Blond, black 'guard	$60,000	$70,000
1952	Blond, black 'guard	$50,000	$60,000
1953	Blond, black 'guard	$48,000	$55,000
1954	Blond, black 'guard	$41,000	$50,000
1954	Blond, white 'guard	$25,000	$30,000
1955	Blond, white 'guard	$24,000	$29,000
1956	Blond	$24,000	$29,000
1957	Blond	$24,000	$29,000
1957	Custom colors	$45,000	$65,000
1958	Black	$45,000	$53,000
1958	Blond, backloader	$24,000	$29,000
1958	Blond, top loader	$23,000	$28,000
1958	Fiesta Red	$45,000	$53,000
1958	Sunburst, backloader	$28,000	$35,000
1958	Sunburst, top loader	$24,000	$30,000
1959	Blond, maple	$23,000	$28,500
1959	Blond, slab	$22,000	$27,500
1959	Custom colors	$30,000	$52,000
1959	Sunburst, maple	$24,000	$30,000
1959	Sunburst, slab	$23,000	$28,500
1960	Blond	$20,000	$25,000
1960	Common colors	$27,500	$34,000
1960	Rare colors	$35,000	$50,000
1960	Sunburst	$22,000	$27,500
1961	Blond	$20,000	$24,000
1961	Common colors	$27,000	$33,000
1961	Rare colors	$33,000	$48,000
1961	Sunburst	$22,000	$27,000
1962	Blond, curved	$15,000	$18,000
1962	Blond, slab	$16,000	$20,000
1962	Common colors	$20,000	$25,000
1962	Rare colors	$25,000	$43,000
1962	Sunburst, curved	$15,000	$18,000
1962	Sunburst, slab	$16,000	$20,000
1963	Blond	$15,000	$18,000
1963	Common colors	$18,000	$22,000
1963	Rare colors	$22,000	$40,000
1963	Sunburst	$15,000	$18,000
1964	Blond	$15,000	$18,000
1964	Common colors	$18,000	$22,000
1964	Rare colors	$22,000	$40,000

MODEL YEAR	FEATURES	EXC. COND. LOW	HIGH
1964	Sunburst	$15,000	$18,000
1965	Blond	$11,500	$14,500
1965	Common colors	$14,500	$18,000
1965	Rare colors	$18,000	$30,000
1965	Sunburst	$11,500	$14,500
1966	Blond	$9,600	$12,000
1966	Common colors	$12,000	$15,000
1966	Rare colors	$15,000	$23,000
1966	Sunburst	$9,600	$12,000
1967	Blond	$8,800	$10,800
1967	Blond, smuggler	$13,000	$14,000
1967	Common colors	$10,800	$11,500
1967	Rare colors	$11,500	$14,000
1967	Sunburst	$8,800	$10,800
1968	Blond	$7,500	$8,500
1968	Blue Floral	$10,000	$15,000
1968	Common colors	$8,500	$10,000
1968	Pink Paisley	$10,000	$15,000
1968	Rare colors	$9,500	$12,000
1968	Sunburst	$7,500	$8,500
1969	Blond	$6,000	$7,500
1969	Blue Floral	$11,000	$14,000
1969	Common colors	$7,500	$8,500
1969	Pink Paisley	$11,000	$14,000
1969	Rare colors	$8,500	$10,500
1969	Sunburst	$6,000	$7,500
1970	Blond	$5,500	$6,500
1970	Common colors	$6,500	$8,500
1970	Rare colors	$8,500	$9,500
1970	Sunburst	$5,500	$6,500
1971	Blond	$4,500	$5,000
1971	Common colors	$6,500	$8,500
1971	Rare colors	$8,500	$9,500
1971	Sunburst	$4,500	$5,000
1972	Blond	$3,500	$4,200
1972	Common colors	$4,200	$5,200
1972	Rare colors	$5,200	$8,000
1972	Sunburst	$3,500	$4,200
1973	Black, blond, Lake Placid Blue, Olympic White	$3,500	$4,500
1973	Natural	$2,800	$3,500
1973	Sunburst	$3,000	$4,100
1973	Walnut	$2,800	$3,500
1974	Black, Olympic White	$2,900	$3,700
1974	Blond	$2,900	$4,000
1974	Natural	$2,300	$3,200
1974	Sunburst	$3,400	$4,200
1974	Walnut	$2,300	$3,000
1975	Black, Olympic White	$2,400	$3,000
1975	Blond	$2,400	$3,000
1975	Natural	$2,200	$2,500
1975	Sunburst	$2,300	$2,800
1975	Walnut	$2,200	$2,500
1976	Black, Olympic White	$2,400	$3,000
1976	Blond	$2,400	$3,000
1976	Natural	$2,200	$2,500
1976	Sunburst	$2,300	$2,800

MODEL YEAR	FEATURES	EXC. COND. LOW	HIGH
1976	Walnut	$2,200	$2,500
1977	Black, Olympic White	$2,400	$2,900
1977	Blond	$2,400	$2,900
1977	Natural	$2,000	$2,300
1977	Sunburst	$2,200	$2,700
1977	Walnut	$2,000	$2,300
1978	Antigua	$2,200	$2,600
1978	Black, Olympic White, Wine	$2,100	$2,600
1978	Blond	$2,000	$2,500
1978	Natural	$1,900	$2,200
1978	Sunburst	$1,950	$2,500
1978	Walnut	$1,900	$2,300
1979	Antigua	$2,100	$2,500
1979	Black, blond, Olympic White, Wine	$2,000	$2,500
1979	Natural	$1,800	$2,200
1979	Sunburst	$1,900	$2,300
1979	Walnut	$1,800	$2,200
1980	Antigua	$2,100	$2,500
1980	Black, Olympic White, Wine	$1,650	$2,050
1980	Blond	$1,575	$1,975
1980	Natural	$1,500	$1,800
1980	Sunburst	$1,575	$1,975
1981	Black, Olympic White, Wine	$1,400	$1,750
1981	International colors	$1,500	$2,000
1981	Sunburst	$1,250	$1,500

Standard Telecaster

1982-1984. See Telecaster for '51-'82, and American Standard Telecaster (following listing) for '88-2000. Not to be confused with the current Standard Telecaster, which is made in Mexico.

1982-1984	Blond, Sunburst	$1,000	$1,500

Standard Telecaster (Japan)

1985. Interim production in Japan while the new Fender reorganized.

1985		$475	$575

American Standard Telecaster

1988-2000. Name used when Fender reissued the standard American-made Tele after CBS sold the company. The only American-made Tele available for '86 and '87 was the '52 Telecaster. See Telecaster for '51-'81, and Standard Telecaster for '82-'84. All '94 models have a metal 40th Anniversary pin on the headstock, but should not be confused with the actual 40th Anniversary Telecaster model (see separate listing), all standard colors, renamed the American Series Telecaster in 2000.

1988-1989		$850	$1,100
1990-2000		$700	$800

American Series Telecaster

2000-2007. See Telecaster for '51-'81, Standard Telecaster for '82-'84, and American Standard for '88-'99. Renamed American Standard again in '08.

2000-2007	Typical colors	$650	$750
2000-2007	Unusual colors	$750	$800

1966 Fender Telecaster (Lake Placid Blue)

1968 Fender Telecaster (Pink Paisley)

GUITARS

Fender '52 Telecaster

Fender Albert Collins Telecaster

MODEL YEAR	FEATURES	EXC. COND. LOW	HIGH

40th Anniversary Telecaster
1988, 1999. Custom Shop model limited edition run of 300, 2-piece flamed maple top, gold hardware ('88), flamed maple top over ash body, gold hardware ('99).

| 1988 | 1st run, higher-end | $2,500 | $3,100 |
| 1999 | 2nd run, plain top | $1,500 | $1,800 |

'50s Telecaster (Import)
1982-present.

| 1982-2007 | | $450 | $500 |

50th Anniversary Spanish Guitar Set Custom Shop
1996. 50 sets made, Tele Prototype reproduction with similar era copy of woodie amp.

| 1996 | | $6,500 | $8,100 |

50th Anniversary Telecaster
1995-1996. Custom Shop model, flame maple top, 2 vintage-style pickups, gold hardware, sunburst, gold 50th Anniversary coin on back of the headstock, 1250 made.

| 1995-1996 | | $1,450 | $1,600 |

'52 Telecaster
1982-present. Ash body, maple neck or rosewood 'board.

1982	1st year export market	$1,500	$1,800
1982	1st year U.S.A., with certificate	$1,500	$1,800
1983		$1,450	$1,750
1983-1990	Blond	$975	$1,125
1984		$1,400	$1,700
1985		$1,350	$1,650
1986		$1,300	$1,600
1987		$1,250	$1,550
1988		$1,200	$1,500
1989		$1,150	$1,400
1990		$1,100	$1,350
1990-1999	Blond	$975	$1,100
1990-1999	Copper (limited number)	$975	$1,100
1991		$1,100	$1,300
1992		$1,075	$1,275
1993		$1,025	$1,250
1994		$1,000	$1,225
1995		$975	$1,200
1996		$975	$1,200
1997		$975	$1,175
1998		$975	$1,175
1999		$975	$1,150
2000-2005	Blond	$975	$1,000

'60s Telecaster Custom
1997-1998. U.S. Custom Shop model, bound alder body, black or custom colors.

| 1997-1998 | | $1,350 | $1,650 |

'60 Telecaster Custom
2003-2004. Custom Shop model, alder body, offered in NOS, Closet Classic and Relic versions.

| 2003-2004 | Relic | $1,500 | $1,800 |

60th Anniversary Telecaster
2006. Special Edition commemorating Fender's 60th year with banner 60th logo on headstock, neck plate reads Diamond Anniversary 1946-2006, made in U.S.A., sunburst.

| 2006 | | $725 | $775 |

'62 Custom Telecaster (Import)
1984-1999. Made in Japan, bound top and back, rosewood 'board, sunburst or red.

| 1984-1999 | | $550 | $700 |

'62 Custom Telecaster (U.S.A.)
1999-present. American Vintage Series, rosewood board.

| 1999-2005 | Standard colors | $1,100 | $1,300 |

'63 Telecaster Custom Relic LTD
2006. Custom Shop model.

| 2006 | | $1,900 | $2,100 |

'63 Telecaster
1999-present. Custom Shop model, alder body (or blond on ash), original spec pickups, C-shaped neck, rosewood 'board.

| 1999-2006 | Closet Classic | $1,700 | $1,900 |
| 1999-2006 | NOS | $1,600 | $1,800 |

'69 Tele/Telecaster Thinline (Import)
1986-present. Import, 2 Tele pickups, natural.

| 1986-2006 | | $475 | $575 |

'72 Telecaster Custom (Import)
1986-present. Import, 1 humbucker, 1 single-coil.

| 1986-1999 | Japan | $600 | $700 |
| 2000-2005 | Mexico | $500 | $600 |

'72 Telecaster Thinline
1988-present. Import, 2 humbuckers, f-hole.

| 1988-2005 | | $475 | $575 |

'90s Tele Thinline
1997-2000. Bound semi-hollow ash body, f-hole, 2 single-coils.

| 1997-2000 | | $1,200 | $2,000 |

'90s Telecaster Deluxe (Foto-Flame)
1995-1998. Import, 1 Tele-style bridge pickup and 2 Strat-style pickups, rosewood 'board, Foto Flame '95-'97 and standard finishes '97-'98.

| 1995-1997 | Foto-Flame | $575 | $700 |
| 1997-1998 | Standard finish | $600 | $750 |

Aerodyne Telecaster
2004-present. Imported Tele with Aerodyne body profile, bound body, black.

| 2004-2006 | | $450 | $475 |

Albert Collins Telecaster
1990-present. U.S.-made Custom Shop signature model, bound swamp ash body, humbucker pickup in neck position.

| 1990-1999 | Natural | $1,250 | $1,350 |
| 1995 | Silver sparkle | $1,350 | $1,450 |

Aluminum Telecaster
1994-1995. Aluminum-bodied American Standard with anodized finish in blue marble, purple marble or red, silver and blue stars and stripes.

| 1994-1995 | Marble patterns | $2,000 | $3,000 |
| 1994-1995 | Red-silver-blue flag option | $2,500 | $3,500 |

MODEL YEAR	FEATURES	EXC. COND. LOW	HIGH

American Classic Holoflake Telecaster
1996-1999. Custom Shop model, splatter/sparkle finish, pearloid 'guard.

1996-1999		$1,550	$1,900

American Classic Telecaster
1996-1999. Custom Shop model, handcrafted version of American Standard, thin lacquer-finished ash body, maple or rosewood 'board, various options and colors, earlier versions had gold hardware and custom-color options.

1996-1999		$1,350	$1,500

American Deluxe Power Telecaster
1991-2001. With Fishman power bridge piezo pick-ups.

1999-2001		$1,300	$1,400

American Deluxe Telecaster
1998-present. Premium ash or alder body with see-thru finishes.

1998-1999	Alder	$875	$975
1998-1999	Ash	$925	$1,100
2000-2003	Ash	$900	$1,000

Antigua Telecaster
2004. Made in Japan, limited-edition (400 made) reissue, '70s features and antigua finish.

2004		$550	$600

Big Block Telecaster
2005-2006. Pearloid block markers, black with matching headstock, 3 single-coils with center pickup reverse wound.

2005-2006		$575	$650

Bigsby Telecaster
2003. Made in Mexico, standard Tele specs with original Fender-logo Bigsby tailpiece.

2003		$500	$700

Black and Gold Telecaster
1981-1982. Black finish, gold-plated brass hardware.

1981-1982		$1,300	$1,400

Blue Flower Telecaster
1986-1993, 2003-2004. Import, Blue Flower finish.

1986-1993	1st issue	$1,000	$1,200
2003-2004	2nd issue	$500	$550

Buck Owens Limited Edition Telecaster
1998. Red, white and blue sparkle finish, gold hardware, gold 'guard, rosewood 'board.

1998-2002		$1,125	$1,375

California Fat Telecaster
1997-1998. Alder body, maple fretboard, Tex-Mex humbucker and Tele pickup configuration.

1997-1998		$450	$550

California Telecaster
1997-1998. Alder body, maple fretboard, sunburst, Tex-Mex Strat and Tele pickup configuration.

1997-1998		$575	$625

Chambered Mahogany Telecaster
2006. US-made, chambered mahogany body, Delta Tone System.

2006		$975	$1,050

Classic Series Telecaster
2006. Made in Mexico.

2006		$500	$550

Collector's Edition Telecaster
1998. Mid-1955 specs including white 'guard, offered in sunburst with gold hardware (which was an option in '55), 1,998 made.

1998		$1,350	$1,500

Contemporary Telecaster (Import)
1985-1987. Japanese-made while the new Fender reorganized, 2 or 3 pickups, vibrato, black chrome hardware, rosewood 'board.

1985-1987		$350	$425

Danny Gatton Telecaster
1990-present. Custom Shop model, like '53 Telecaster, maple neck, 2 humbuckers.

1990s	Frost Gold	$2,100	$2,200

Deluxe Nashville Telecaster (Mexico)
1997-present. Made in Mexico, Tex-Mex Strat and Tele pickup configuration, various colors.

1997-2006		$525	$575

Deluxe Telecaster (USA)
1972-1981. Two humbucker pickups, various colors.

1972-1974		$2,800	$3,200
1975-1978		$2,500	$3,000
1978-1979	Antigua	$2,100	$2,600
1979-1981		$1,700	$2,100

Elite Telecaster
1983-1985. Two active humbucker pickups, 3-way switch, 2 volume knobs, 1 presence and filter controls, chrome hardware, various colors.

1983-1985		$1,000	$1,125

Foto Flame Telecaster
1994-1996. Import, sunburst or transparent.

1994-1996		$575	$700

G.E. Smith Telecaster
2007-present. Swamp ash body, vintage style hardware, U-shaped neck, oval and diamond inlays.

2007		$1,200	$1,400

Highway One Telecaster/Texas Telecaster
2003-present. U.S.-made, alder body, satin lacquer finish, Texas version (introduced in '04) has ash body and Hot Vintage pickups.

2003-2007		$550	$600

HMT Telecaster
1990-1993. Japanese-made Metal-Rock Tele, available with or without Floyd Rose tremolo, 1 Fender Lace Sensor pickup and 1 DiMarzio bridge humbucker pickup, black.

1990-1993		$300	$375

J5 Triple Telecaster Deluxe
2007-present. John 5 model, made in Mexico, 3 humbuckers, medium jumbo frets.

2007		$625	$650

Fender Danny Gatton Telecaster

Fender G.E. Smith Telecaster

*1965 Fender Telecaster
Custom*

*1971 Fender Rosewood
Telecaster*

MODEL YEAR	FEATURES	EXC. COND. LOW	HIGH

James Burton Telecaster
1990-present. Ash body, 3 Fender Lace pickups, available in black with Gold Paisley, black with Candy Red Paisley, Pearl White, and Frost Red until '05. In '06 in black with red or blue flame-shaped paisley, or Pearl White.

1990-2005	Black and gold paisley, gold hardware	$1,100	$1,350
1990-2005	Black and red paisley, black hardware	$1,200	$1,450
1990-2007	Frost Red or Pearl White	$775	$950
2006-2007	Paisley flames	$1,000	$1,125

Jerry Donahue JD Telecaster
1993-1999. Made in Japan, Custom Strat neck pickup and Custom Tele bridge pickup, basswood body, special "V" shaped maple neck.

1993-1999		$650	$750

Jerry Donahue Telecaster
1992-2001. Custom Shop model designed by Donahue, Tele bridge pickup and Strat neck pickup, birdseye maple neck, top and back, gold hardware, passive circuitry, there was also a Japanese JD Telecaster.

1992-1999	Sunburst	$1,400	$1,600
1992-1999	Transparent Crimson or Sapphire Blue	$1,600	$1,800

Jim Root Telecaster
2007-present. Made in Mexico, black hardware, mahogany body, goes to 11.

2007		$550	$650

Jimmy Bryant Tribute Telecaster
2004-2005. Custom Shop model, hand-tooled leather 'guard overlay with JB initials.

2004-2005		$1,900	$2,100

John Jorgenson Telecaster
1998-2000. Custom Shop model, double-coil stacked pickups, sparkle or black finish, korina body.

1998-2000	Sparkle	$1,600	$2,000

Jr. Telecaster
1994, 1997-2000. Custom Shop model, transparent blond ash body, 2 P-90-style pickups, set neck, 11 tone chambers, 100 made in '94, reintroduced in '97.

1994		$1,650	$1,900

Matched Set Telecaster
1994. Matching Tele and Strat Custom Shop models, model name on certificate is "Matched Set Telecaster", 3 sets were built, each set has serial number 1, 2, or 3.

1994		$3,000	$3,500

Moto Limited Edition Telecaster
1990s. Custom Shop model, pearloid cover in various colors. There were also Strat and Jag versions.

1990s		$1,500	$1,700

Nashville Telecaster
1995. Custom Shop model, 3 pickups.

1995		$1,700	$1,900

Nashville Telecaster (Mexico)
2003. Made in Mexico, 2 traditional Tele pickups, 1 Strat pickup in middle position.

2003		$500	$575

NHL Premier Edition Telecaster
1999-2000. Limited edition of 100 guitars with NHL hockey art logo on the top.

1999-2000		$1,400	$1,600

Nokie Edwards Telecaster
1996. Made in Japan, limited edition, book matched flamed top, multi-lam neck, Seymour Duncan pickups, gold hardware, zero fret, tilted headstock.

1996		$1,800	$2,000

Paisley Telecaster
1986-1998, 2003-2004. Import, Pink Paisley finish.

1986-1989		$600	$1,000
1990-1998		$550	$1,000
2003-2004	Reissue	$500	$550

Plus/Plus Deluxe Telecaster
1990-1997. Tele with Strat 3-pickup combination, Deluxe has added Strat-style tremolo system, various colors.

1990-1997		$900	$1,100

Rosewood Telecaster
1969-1972. Rosewood body and neck.

1969-1972		$7,000	$8,700

Rosewood Telecaster (Japan)
1986-1996. Japanese-made reissue, rosewood body and neck.

1986-1996		$1,700	$2,100

Set-Neck Telecaster
1990-1996. Glued-in neck, Custom Shop, 2 humbucking pickups, Set-Neck CA (Country Artist) has 1 humbucker and 1 Tele pickup, various colors.

1990-1996		$1,200	$1,500

Sparkle Telecaster
1993-1995. Custom Shop model, poplar body, white 'guard, sparkle finish: champagne, gold, silver.

1993-1995		$1,400	$1,600

Special Telecaster/Telecaster Special
2004. Made in Mexico, Special Edition logo with star logo sticker on back of headstock, special features like 6-way bridge and modern tuners.

2004		$400	$450

Squier Telecaster
1983-present. Fender Japan was established in '82 with Squier production beginning in '83. Production was shifted to Korea in '87 and later allocated to China, India (Squier II '89-'90) and Mexico. This model is the low-cost version of the Telecaster for Squier.

1983-1984	Blond, 1st year '70s-style logo	$275	$375
1985-1989	Black or blond	$225	$325

MODEL YEAR	FEATURES	EXC. COND. LOW	HIGH

Squier Telecaster Affinity
1998-present. Standard Telecaster styling, made in China, various colors.

| 1998-2007 | | $60 | $75 |

Squier Telecaster Custom
2003-present. Made in Indonesia.

| 2003-2007 | | $90 | $110 |

Squier Thinline Telecaster
2004. Made in China, Thinline body with f-hole.

| 2004 | | $175 | $250 |

Standard Telecaster (Mexico)
1990-present. Guitar production at the Mexico facility started in '91. High end of range includes a hard guitar case, while the low end of the range includes only a gig bag, various colors.

1990-1999		$325	$375
2000-2005		$300	$350
2006-2007		$300	$325

Telecaster Custom
1959-1972. Body bound top and back, rosewood 'board, 2 Tele pickups, see Telecaster Custom (2nd Edition) for the 1 Tele/1 humbucker version. Please refer to the Fender Guitar Intro Section for details on Fender color options.

1959	Sunburst, maple	$35,000	$43,000
1960	Custom colors	$40,000	$69,000
1960	Sunburst	$32,000	$39,000
1961	Custom colors	$40,000	$68,000
1961	Sunburst	$30,000	$36,000
1962	Custom colors	$33,000	$58,000
1962	Sunburst	$27,000	$33,000
1963	Custom colors	$28,000	$50,000
1963	Sunburst	$25,000	$26,000
1964	Custom colors	$28,000	$46,000
1964	Sunburst	$23,000	$26,000
1965	Custom colors	$20,000	$40,000
1965	Sunburst	$16,000	$23,000
1966	Custom colors	$20,000	$30,000
1966	Sunburst	$13,000	$16,000
1967	Custom colors	$15,000	$23,000
1967	Sunburst	$13,000	$16,000
1968	Custom colors	$15,000	$23,000
1968	Sunburst	$11,000	$14,000
1968	Sunburst, rosewood	$10,000	$13,000
1969	Custom colors	$14,000	$23,000
1969	Sunburst	$10,000	$14,000
1970	Custom colors	$11,000	$20,000
1970	Sunburst	$8,000	$11,000
1971	Custom colors, 3-bolt	$5,000	$7,000
1971	Custom colors, 4-bolt	$10,000	$18,000
1971	Sunburst, 3-bolt	$4,000	$5,000
1971	Sunburst, 4-bolt	$7,000	$9,000
1972	Custom colors, 3-bolt	$5,000	$10,000
1972	Sunburst, 3-bolt	$3,500	$5,000

MODEL YEAR	FEATURES	EXC. COND. LOW	HIGH

Telecaster Custom (2nd Edition)
1972-1981. One humbucking and 1 Tele pickup, standard colors, see above for 2 Tele pickup version. Also called Custom Telecaster.

1972-1974		$2,800	$3,400
1975-1978		$2,500	$3,000
1979-1981		$2,000	$2,400

Telecaster Custom (Japan)
1985. Made in Japan during the period when Fender suspended all USA manufacturing in '85, Tele Custom specs including bound body.

| 1985 | | $500 | $625 |

Telecaster Custom HH FMT (Korea)
2003-present. Part of Special Series, Korean-made, flamed maple top, 2 humbuckers.

| 2003-2006 | | $425 | $475 |

Telecaster Stratocaster Hybrid
2006. Custom Shop model, Tele body shape, Strat pickup system and wiring, Strat headstock shape, dot markers on rosewood board, reissue tremolo, includes Custom Shop Certificate that reads "Telecaster Stratocaster Hybrid".

| 2006 | | $2,350 | $2,500 |

Telecaster Thinline (Custom Shop)
1990s. Custom Shop version.

| 1990s | | $1,450 | $1,700 |

Telecaster Thinline/Thinline II
1968-1980. Semi-hollowbody, 1 f-hole, 2 Tele pickups, ash or mahogany body, in late-'71 the tilt neck was added and the 2 Tele pickups were switched to 2 humbuckers. Please refer to the Fender Guitar Intro Section for details on Fender color options.

1968	Common colors	$7,000	$8,700
1968	Natural ash	$5,500	$6,800
1968	Natural mahogany	$5,500	$6,800
1968	Rare colors	$8,000	$11,000
1968	Sunburst	$6,500	$8,000
1969	Common colors	$6,800	$8,500
1969	Natural ash	$5,300	$6,500
1969	Natural mahogany	$5,300	$6,500
1969	Rare colors	$7,500	$10,000
1969	Sunburst	$6,400	$8,000
1970	Common colors	$6,500	$8,500
1970	Natural ash	$4,500	$5,600
1970	Natural mahogany	$4,500	$5,600
1970	Rare colors	$7,500	$9,500
1970	Sunburst	$6,500	$8,000
1971	Color option, 3-bolt	$5,000	$6,000
1971	Color option, 4-bolt	$6,000	$9,000
1971	Natural ash, 3-bolt	$3,500	$4,300
1971	Natural ash, 4-bolt	$4,400	$5,500
1971	Natural mahogany, 3-bolt	$3,500	$4,300
1971	Natural mahogany, 4-bolt	$4,400	$5,500
1971	Sunburst, 3-bolt	$4,000	$5,000
1971	Sunburst, 4-bolt	$6,500	$8,000

1972 Fender Telecaster Thinline

1974 Fender Telecaster Thinline

Fender Toronado

Fontanilla Classical

MODEL YEAR	FEATURES	EXC. COND. LOW	HIGH
1972-1974	Color option	$3,500	$4,300
1972-1974	Mahogany, humbuckers	$3,400	$3,800
1972-1974	Natural ash, humbuckers	$3,200	$3,700
1972-1974	Sunburst, humbuckers	$3,200	$4,000
1975-1978	Color option	$3,000	$3,700
1975-1978	Natural ash, humbuckers	$2,200	$2,700
1975-1978	Sunburst, humbuckers	$2,200	$2,700

Telecoustic Deluxe
2007. Deluxe model, design includes upgrades.
2007		$325	$400

Tele-Sonic
1998-2000. U.S.A., chambered Telecaster body, 2 DeArmond pickups, dot markers, upper bass bout 3-way toggle switch.
1998-2000		$750	$850

Texas Special Telecaster
1991. Custom Shop model, 60 made, state of Texas outline on the 'guard, ash body with Texas Orange transparent finish, large profile maple neck.
1991		$1,750	$1,950

Will Ray Jazz-A-Caster
1997. Made in the Fender Japan Custom Shop as one part of the three part Hellecasters Series, Strat neck on a Tele body with 2 soap-bar Seymour Duncan Jazzmaster-style pickups, gold leaf finish, limited edition.
1997		$1,200	$1,500

Will Ray Telecaster
1998-2001. Custom Shop, ash body, flamed maple Strat neck, locking tuners, rosewood 'board, skull inlays, double coil pickups, optional Hipshot B bender.
1998-2001		$3,000	$3,300

Toronado/Toronado Deluxe
1999-2006. Contoured offset-waist body.
1999-2001	Atomic humbuckers	$400	$500
1999-2001	DE-9000 P-90s	$400	$475
2002-2006	GT with racing stripes, humbuckers	$400	$500

Villager 12-String
1965-1969. Acoustic flat-top, spruce top, mahogany back and sides, 12 strings, natural.
1965-1969		$550	$675

Violin - Electric
1958-1976. Sunburst is the standard finish.
1958-1959		$1,450	$1,600
1960-1969		$1,350	$1,500
1970-1976		$1,150	$1,400

Wildwood
1963-1971. Acoustic flat-top with Wildwood dyed top.
1966-1971	Various (faded)	$1,000	$1,250
1966-1971	Various (unfaded)	$1,500	$1,850

Fernandes
1969-present. Established in Tokyo. Early efforts were classical guitars, but they now offer a variety of intermediate grade, production, imported guitars and basses.
Nomad Travel/Nomad Deluxe
1998-present. Unusual body style, extra large banana headstock, built-in effects, built-in amp and speaker. Deluxe models have added features. Standard discontinued in '05.
1998-2005	Standard	$125	$150
2000-2006	Deluxe	$250	$450

Fina
Production classical and steel-string guitars built at the Kwo Hsiao Music Wooden Factory in Huiyang City, Guang Dong, mainland China. They also build acoustic basses.

Fine Resophonic
1988-present. Professional and premium grade, production/custom, wood and metal-bodied resophonic guitars (including reso-electrics) built by luthiers Mike Lewis and Pierre Avocat in Vitry Sur Seine, France. They also build ukes and mandolins.

First Act
1995-present. Budget and professional grade, production/custom, acoustic, solid and semi-hollow body guitars built in China and in their Custom Shop in Boston. They also make basses, violins, and other instruments.

Firth Pond & Company
1822-1867. Firth and Pond was an east coast retail distributor that had Martin Guitars and Ashborn Guitars private brand instruments. The company operated as Firth and Hall from 1822-1841, also known as Firth, Hall & Pond, the company operated in New York City and Litchfield, Connecticut. Most instruments were small parlor size (11" lower bout) guitars, as was the case for most builders of this era. Brazilian rosewood sides and back instruments fetch considerably more than most of the other tone woods and value can vary considerably based on condition.

Guitars from the 1800s are sometimes valued more as antiques than working vintage guitars. In 1867 Firth & Sons sold out to Oliver Ditson, a company which went on to become an important progressive force in the guitar distributor retailer business. Sometimes the inside back center seam will be branded Firth & Pond.

Flammang Guitars
1990-present. Premium grade, custom/production, steel string guitars built by luthier David Flammang in Greene, Iowa and previously in East Hampton and Higganum, Connecticut.

MODEL		EXC. COND.	
YEAR	FEATURES	LOW	HIGH

Flaxwood

2004-present. Professional grade, production/custom, solid and semi-hollow body guitars built in Finland, with bodies of natural fiber composites.

Fleishman Instruments

1974-present. Premium and presentation grade, custom flat-tops made by luthier Harry Fleishman in Sebastopol, California. He also offers basses and electric uprights. Fleishman is the director of Luthiers School International.

Fletcher Brock Stringed Instruments

1992-present. Custom flat-tops and archtops made by luthier Fletcher Brock originally in Ketchum, Idaho, and currently in Seattle, Washington. He also builds mandolin family instruments.

Flowers Guitars

1993-present. Premium grade, custom, archtop guitars built by luthier Gary Flowers in Baltimore, Maryland.

Floyd Rose

2004-2006. Floyd Rose, inventor of the Floyd Rose Locking Tremolo, produced a line of intermediate and professional grade, production, solidbody guitars from '04 to '06. They continue to offer bridges and other accessories.

Foggy Mountain

2005-present. Intermediate grade, production, steel and nylon string acoustic and acoustic/electric guitars imported from China.

Fontanilla Guitars

1987-present. Luthier Allan Fontanilla builds his premium grade, production/custom, classical guitars in San Francisco, California.

Fouilleul

1978-present. Production/custom, classical guitars made by luthier Jean-Marie Fouilleul in Cuguen, France.

Frame Works

1995-present. Professional grade, production/custom, steel- and nylon-string guitars built by luthier Frank Krocker in Burghausen, Germany. The instruments feature a neck mounted on a guitar-shaped frame. Krocker has also built traditional archtops, flat-tops, and classicals.

Framus

1946-1977, 1996-present. Professional and premium grade, production/custom, guitars made in Markneukirchen, Germany. They also build basses, amps, mandolins and banjos. Frankische Musikindustrie (Framus) founded in Erlangen, Germany by Fred Wilfer, relocated to Bubenreuth

MODEL		EXC. COND.	
YEAR	FEATURES	LOW	HIGH

in '54, and to Pretzfeld in '67. Begun as an acoustic instrument manufacturer, Framus added electrics in the mid-'50s. Earliest electrics were mostly acoustics with pickups attached. Electric designs begin in early-'60s. Unique feature was a laminated maple neck with many thin plies. By around '64-'65 upscale models featured the organtone, often called a spigot, a spring-loaded volume control that allowed you to simulate a Leslie speaker effect. Better models often had mutes and lots of switches.

In the '60s, Framus instruments were imported into the U.S. by Philadelphia Music Company. Resurgence of interest in ca. '74 with the Jan Akkermann hollowbody followed by original mid-'70s design called the Nashville, the product of an alliance with some American financing. The brand was revived in '96 by Hans Peter Wilfer, the president of Warwick, with production in Warwick's factory in Germany.

Atilla Zoller AZ-10

Early-1960s-late-1970s. Single-cut archtop, 2 pickups, neck glued-in until the '70s, bolt-on after, sunburst. Model 5/65 (rounded cutaway) and Model 5/67 (sharp cutaway).

| 1960s | Model 5/65 | $650 | $750 |
| 1960s | Model 5/67 | $650 | $800 |

Atlantic 5/110

1960s. Thin body electric archtop, 2 pickups, tremolo, sunburst or blackrose finish options, in the original price list it was one of the lower level thin body electrics in the line.

| 1960s | | $500 | $600 |

Big 18 Doubleneck

Late 1960s. Model 5/200 is a solidbody and Model 5/220 is acoustic.

| 1960s | Model 5/200 | $650 | $750 |
| 1960s | Model 5/220 | $650 | $750 |

Caravelle 5/117

Ca.1965-1977. Double-cut archtop, tremolo, 2 pickups, cherry or sunburst.

| 1960s | | $600 | $700 |

Gaucho 5/194

1960s. Lowest model offered in the flat-top line, small concert size body, spruce top, mahogany sides and back, rosewood bridge and 'board, offered in shaded sunburst or natural finish.

| 1960s | | $200 | $250 |

Jan Akkerman

1974-1977. Single-cut semi-hollowbody, 2 pickups, gold hardware.

| 1974-1977 | | $375 | $450 |

Jumbo 5/197

1960s. Jumbo size flat-top, spruce top, mahogany sides and back, shaded or natural finish options.

| 1960s | | $375 | $450 |

Jumbo 12-String 5/297

1960s. Jumbo size 12-string, spruce top, mahogany sides and back, shaded or natural finish options.

| 1960s | | $400 | $500 |

Floyd Rose Redmond

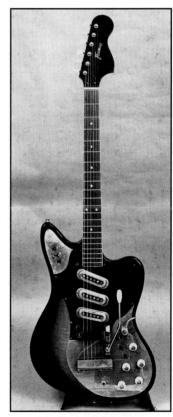

Framus Strato de Luxe

Fritz Brothers Super Deluxe

Fukuoka FN Standard

MODEL YEAR	FEATURES	EXC. COND. LOW	HIGH

Missouri 5/60 (E Framus Missouri)
Ca.1960-1977. Non-cut acoustic archtop until '65, single-cut archtop with 2 pickups after, natural or sunburst.

1960s		$350	$425

New Sound Series
1960s. Double-cut semi-hollowbody. Model 5/116 I has 2 pickups and Model 5/116 II has 3.

1960s	Model 5/115/54	$650	$800
1960s	Model 5/116/52	$600	$750

Sorella Series
Ca.1955-1977. Model 5/59 is single-cut acoustic archtop, Model 5/59/50 is electric 1-pickup, Model 5/59/52 is electric 2-pickup.

1959-1965	Model 5/59	$400	$475
1959-1966	Model 5/59/50	$450	$550
1959-1967	Model 5/59/52	$475	$575

Sorento
Ca.1965-1970. Oversized semi-hollowbody, single-cut, 2 pickups, organ effect, F-holes.

1960s	Model 5/112/52	$450	$550

Strato de Luxe Series
Ca.1964-1972. 1, 2, or 3 pickups, some models have gold hardware. Model 5/068 is 12-string, 2 pickups, tremolo.

1960s	Model 5/068	$500	$600
1960s	Model 5/168/52, 2 pickups	$575	$650
1960s	Model 5/168/52, 3 pickups	$650	$825

Strato Super
1960s. Economy version of Strato de Luxe.

1960s	Model 5/155/52, 3 pickups	$475	$575

Studio Series
1960s. Model 5/51 is acoustic archtop, cutaway and Model 5/51E is electric, 1 pickup.

1960s	Model 5/51	$250	$300
1960s	Model 5/51E	$325	$400

Television Series
1960s. Offset double-cut, thinline hollowbody, cherry or sunburst. Model 5/118/52 has 2 pickups and Model 5/118/54 3 pickups.

1960s	Model 5/118/52	$550	$650
1960s	Model 5/118/54	$650	$750

Texan Series
1960s. Sunburst or natural, 6- or 12-string.

1960s	Natural, 12-string	$325	$400
1960s	Natural, 6-string	$325	$400
1960s	Sunburst, 12-string	$325	$400
1960s	Sunburst, 6-string	$325	$400

Western 5/195
1960s. Grand concert size, 2nd lowest model in the flat-top line, spruce top, maple sides and back, shaded or natural finish options.

1960s		$275	$325

Fresher
1973-1985. The Japanese-made Fresher brand models were mainly copies of popular brands and were not imported into the U.S., but they do show up at guitar shows. They also made basses.

Solidbody Electric
1970s. Import from Japan.

1970s		$275	$325

Fritz Brothers
1988-present. Premium grade, production/custom, acoustic, semi-hollow, and solidbody guitars built by luthier Roger Fritz, originally in Mobile, Alabama, currently in Mendocino, California. He also builds basses.

Froggy Bottom Guitars
1970-present. Luthier Michael Millard builds his premium and presentation grade, production/custom flat-tops in Newfane, Vermont (until '84 production was in Richmond, New Hampshire).

Fukuoka Musical Instruments
1993-present. Custom steel- and nylon-string flat-tops and archtops built in Japan.

Furnace Mountain Guitar Works
1995-1999. Instruments built by luthier Martin Fair in New Mexico. He currently builds under the Fairbuilt Guitar Co. brand.

Fury
1962-present. Founded by Glenn McDougall in Saskatoon, Saskatchewan, Fury currently offers production, solidbody electrics. They also build basses. They have built hollow and semi-hollow body guitars in the past.

Futurama
1957-mid to late 1960s. Futurama was a brand name used by Selmer in the United Kingdom. Early instruments made by the Drevokov Cooperative in Czechoslovakia, models for '63-'64 made by Sweden's Hagstrom company. Some later '60s instruments may have been made in Japan. Hobbyists will recognize the brand name as Beatle George Harrison's first electric.

Futurama/Futurama II
1960s. Offset double-cut, 2- or 3-pickup versions available, large Futurama logo on headstock with the reverse capital letter F.

1960s		$525	$650

Fylde Guitars
1973-present. Luthier Roger Bucknall builds his professional and premium grade, production/custom acoustic guitars in Penrith, Cumbria, United Kingdom. He also builds basses, mandolins, mandolas, bouzoukis, and citterns.

MODEL YEAR	FEATURES	EXC. COND. LOW	HIGH

G & L

1980-present. Intermediate and professional grade, production/custom, solidbody and semi-hollowbody electric guitars made in the U.S. and overseas. They also make basses. Founded by Leo Fender and George Fullerton following the severance of ties between Fender's CLF Research and Music Man. Company sold to John MacLaren and BBE Sound, when Leo Fender died in '91. In '98 they added their Custom Creations Department. In '03 G & L introduced the Korean-made G & L Tribute Series.

ASAT

1986-1998. Called the Broadcaster in '85. Two or 3 single-coil or 2 single-coil/1 humbucker pickup configurations until early-'90s, 2 single-coils after.

1986		$775	$850
1987	Leo sig. on headstock	$775	$900
1988-1991	Leo sig. on body	$875	$1,000
1992-1998		$775	$850

ASAT 20th Anniversary

2000. Limited Edition of 50, ash body, tinted birdseye maple neck, 2-tone sunburst.

2000		$1,300	$1,500

ASAT '50

1999. Limited edition of 10.

1999		$1,000	$1,200

ASAT Bluesboy Limited Edition

1999. Limited edition of 20.

1999		$1,075	$1,325

ASAT Bluesboy Semi-Hollow Limited Edition

1999. Limited edition of 12, thin semi-hollow.

1999		$1,050	$1,250

ASAT Classic

1990-present. Two single-coil pickups, individually adjustable bridge saddles, neck-tilt adjustment and tapered string posts.

1990-1991	Leo sig. on neck	$875	$1,000
1992-1997	3-bolt neck	$775	$875
1997-2007	4-bolt neck	$700	$875

ASAT Classic B-Bender

1997. 12 made with factory-original B-Bender.

1997		$1,000	$1,200

ASAT Classic Bluesboy

2001-present. Humbucker neck pickup, single-coil at bridge.

2001-2007		$775	$975

ASAT Classic Bluesboy Semi-Hollow

1997-present. Chambered Classic with f-hole.

1997-2007		$925	$1,000

ASAT Classic Commemorative

1991-1992. Leo Fender signature and birth/death dating.

1991-1992	Australian lace-wood, 6 made	$4,500	$5,500
1991-1992	Cherryburst, 350 made	$2,200	$2,600

ASAT Classic Custom

1996-1997, 2002-present. Large rectangular neck pickup, single-coil bridge pickup

1996-1997	1st version	$850	$950
2002-2007	2nd version, 4-bolt neck	$750	$850

ASAT Classic Custom Semi-Hollow

2002-present. Custom with f-hole.

2002-2007		$700	$875

ASAT Classic Semi-Hollow

1997-present. With f-hole.

1997-2007		$850	$950

ASAT Classic Three

1998. Limited Edition of 100 units.

1998		$1,100	$1,375

ASAT Custom

1996. No pickguard, 25 to 30 made.

1996		$800	$950

ASAT Deluxe

1997-present. Two humbuckers, flamed maple top, bound body.

1997	3-bolt neck, less than 100 made	$1,150	$1,350
1997-2007	4-bolt neck	$1,050	$1,150

ASAT Deluxe Semi-Hollow

1997-present. Two humbuckers.

1997-2007		$1,050	$1,300

ASAT III

1988-1991, 1996-1998. Single-cut body, 3 single-coil pickups.

1988-1991	1st version, Leo era, 150 made	$950	$1,150
1996-1998	Post Leo era	$750	$850

ASAT JD-5

2004-2007. Single-cut solidbody, 2 single-coils, maple 'board.

2004-2007		$1,500	$2,000

ASAT Junior Limited Edition

1998-1999. Single-cut semi-hollowbody, 2 single-coils, run of 250 units.

1998-1999		$950	$1,100

ASAT S-3

1998-2000. Three soap-bar single-coil pickups, limited production.

1998-2000		$700	$875

ASAT Semi-Hollow

1997-present. Semi-hollow version of ASAT Special.

1997-2007		$700	$850

ASAT Special

1992-present. Like ASAT, but with 2 larger P-90-type pickups, chrome hardware, various colors.

1992-1997	3-bolt neck	$850	$900
1997-1999	4-bolt neck	$700	$800
2000-2007	4-bolt neck	$600	$700

ASAT Special Deluxe

2001-present. No 'guard version of the Special with figured maple top.

2001-2007		$875	$950

G&L ASAT 3

G&L Classic Blues Boy

G&L Invader Plus

G&L Legacy

MODEL YEAR FEATURES	EXC. COND. LOW	HIGH
ASAT Z-2 Limited Edition		
1999. Limited edition of 10 instruments, semi-hollow construction, natural ash, tortoise bound, engraved neckplate.		
1999	$925	$1,075
ASAT Z-3		
1998-present. Three offset-style Z-3 high output pickups, sunburst.		
1998-2007	$925	$1,075
ASAT Z-3 Semi-Hollow		
1998-present. F-hole version of Z-3.		
1998-2007	$950	$1,100
Broadcaster		
1985-1986. Solidbody, 2 single-coils with adjustable polepieces act in humbucking mode with selector switch in the center position, black parts and finish, name changed to ASAT in early-'86.		
1985-1986 Signed by Leo, ebony board	$1,900	$2,200
1985-1986 Signed by Leo, maple board	$2,000	$2,300
Cavalier		
1983-1986. Offset double-cut, 2 humbuckers, 700 made, sunburst.		
1983-1986	$700	$875
Climax		
1992-1996. Offset double-cut, bolt maple neck, six-on-a-side tuners, double locking vibrato, blue.		
1992-1996	$650	$800
Climax Plus		
1992-1996. Two humbuckers replace single-coils of the Climax, plus 1 single-coil.		
1992-1996	$700	$850
Climax XL		
1992-1996. Two humbuckers only.		
1992-1996	$700	$875
Comanche V		
1988-1991. Solidbody, 3 Z-shaped single-coil humbuckers, maple neck in choice of 3 radii, rosewood 'board, vibrato, fine tuners, Leo Fender's signature on the body, sunburst.		
1988-1991	$900	$1,100
Comanche VI		
1990-1991. Leo Fender's signature on the body, 6 mini-toggles.		
1990-1991	$1,000	$1,250
Comanche (Reintroduced)		
1998-present. Reissue with either swamp ash or alder body, bolt-on maple neck, 3 Z-coil pickups, standard or premium finish options.		
1998-2003 Premium finish, flame top	$1,000	$1,100
1998-2003 Standard finish	$650	$800
2004-2007 Standard finish	$650	$725
Commemorative		
1992-1997. About 350 made, Leo Fender signature on upper bass bout.		
1992-1997 Sunburst	$1,950	$2,400

MODEL YEAR FEATURES	EXC. COND. LOW	HIGH
F-100 (Model I and II)		
1980-1986. Offset double-cut solidbody, 2 humbuckers, natural. Came in a I and II model - only difference is the radius of the 'board.		
1980-1986	$900	$1,000
F-100 E (Model I and II)		
1980-1982. Offset double-cut solidbody, 2 humbuckers, active electronics, pre-amp, natural. Came in a I and II model - only difference is the radius of the 'board.		
1980-1982	$900	$1,000
G-200		
1981-1982. Mahogany solidbody, maple neck, ebony 'board, 2 humbucking pickups, coil-split switches, natural or sunburst, 209 made.		
1981-1982	$950	$1,175
GBL-LE (Guitars by Leo Limited Edition)		
1999. Limited edition of 25, semi-hollowbody, 3 pickups.		
1999	$1,000	$1,250
George Fullerton Signature		
1995-2007. Double-cut solidbody, sunburst.		
1995-1997 3-bolt neck	$950	$1,175
1997-2007 4-bolt neck	$850	$1,050
HG-1		
1982-1983. Offset double-cut, 1 humbucker, dot inlays. Very rare as most were made into HG-2s.		
1982-1983	$1,900	$2,100
HG-2		
1982-1984. 2-humbucker HG, body changes to classic offset double-cut in '84.		
1982-1984	$1,050	$1,300
Interceptor		
1983-1991. To '86 an X-shaped solidbody (about 70 made), either 3 single-coils, 2 humbuckers, or 1 humbucker and 2 single-coils, '87-'89 was an offset double-cut solidbody (about 12 made).		
1983-1985 1st X-body	$1,000	$1,200
1985-1986 2nd X-body	$1,300	$1,500
1988-1991 Double-cut	$700	$875
Invader		
1984-1991, 1998-present. Double-cut solidbody, 2 single-coil and 1 humbucker pickups.		
1984-1991 1st version	$800	$975
1998-2007 2nd version	$900	$1,100
Invader Plus		
1998-present. Two humbuckers and single blade pickup in the middle position.		
1998-2005	$750	$925
John Jorgenson Signature Model ASAT		
1995. About 190 made, Silver Metalflake finish.		
1995	$875	$1,200
Legacy		
1992-present. Classic double-cut configuration, various colors.		
1992-1994 3-bolt neck, Duncan SSLs	$575	$700
1995-1997 3-bolt neck, Alnicos	$550	$675
1997-2007 4-bolt neck, Alnicos	$525	$650

MODEL YEAR	FEATURES	EXC. COND. LOW	HIGH
Legacy 2HB			
2001-present. Two humbucker pickups.			
2001-2007		$600	$750
Legacy Deluxe			
2001-present. No 'guard, figured maple top.			
2001-2007		$700	$875
Legacy HB			
2001-present. One humbucker pickup at bridge position plus 2 single-coil pickups.			
2001-2007		$675	$825
Legacy Special			
1993-present. Legacy with 3 humbuckers, various colors.			
1992-1997	3-bolt neck	$675	$750
1998-2007	4-bolt neck	$525	$650
Nighthawk			
1983. Offset double-cut solidbody, 3 single-coil pickups, 269 made, sunburst, name changed to Skyhawk in '84.			
1983		$650	$800
Rampage			
1984-1991. Offset double-cut solidbody, hard rock maple neck, ebony 'board, 1 bridge-position humbucker pickup, sunburst.			
1984-1991		$625	$775
Rampage (Reissue)			
2000. Limited Edition of 70 units, supplied with gig bag and not hard case, ivory finish.			
2000		$550	$675
S-500			
1982-present. Double-cut mahogany or ash solidbody, maple neck, ebony or maple 'board, 3 single-coil pickups, vibrato.			
1982-1987	No mini-toggle	$900	$975
1988-1991	Mini-toggle, Leo sig. on body	$1,000	$1,075
1992-1997	3-bolt neck	$750	$925
1997-2007	4-bolt neck	$700	$875
S-500 Deluxe			
2001-present. Deluxe Series features, including no 'guard and flamed maple top, natural.			
2001-2007		$800	$975
SC-1			
1982-1983. Offset double-cut solidbody, 1 single-coil pickup, tremolo, sunburst, 250 made.			
1982-1983		$400	$500
SC-2			
1982-1983. Offset double-cut solidbody, 2 MFD soapbar pickups, about 600 made.			
1982-1983	Shallow cutaway	$350	$425
1983	Deeper, pointed cutaway	$350	$400
SC-3			
1982-1991. Offset double-cut solidbody, 3 single-coil pickups, tremolo.			
1982-1983	Shallow cutaway	$400	$500
1984-1987	Deeper cutaway, no 'guard	$400	$500
1988-1991	Deeper cutaway, 'guard	$575	$700

MODEL YEAR	FEATURES	EXC. COND. LOW	HIGH
Skyhawk			
1984-1991. Renamed from Nighthawk, offset double-cut, 3 single-coils, signature on headstock '84-'87, then on body '88-'91.			
1984-1987		$700	$800
1988-1991		$800	$850
Superhawk			
1984-1987. Offset double-cut, maple neck, ebony 'board, G&L or Kahler tremolos, 2 humbuckers, signature on headstock.			
1984-1987		$650	$750
Tribute Series			
2003-present. Import versions of regular models.			
2003-2007	S-500 Tribute	$225	$275
Will Ray Signature Model			
2002-present. Will Ray signature on headstock, 3 Z-coil pickups, Hipshot B-Bender.			
2002-2007		$650	$900

G.L. Stiles

1960-1994. Built by Gilbert Lee Stiles (b. October 2, 1914, Independence, West Virginia; d. 1994) primarily in the Miami, Florida area. First solidbody, including pickups and all hardware, built by hand in his garage. Stiles favored scrolls, fancy carving and walnut fingerboards. His later instruments were considerably more fancy and refined. He moved to Hialeah, Florida by '63 and began making acoustic guitars and other instruments. His acoustics featured double stressed (bent) backs for increased tension. He later taught for the Augusta Heritage Program and Davis and Elkins College in Elkins, West Virginia. Only his solidbodies had consecutive serial numbers. Stiles made approximately 1000 solidbodies and 500 acoustics.

Gabriel's Guitar Workshop

1979-present. Production/custom steel- and nylon-stringed guitars built by luthier Gabriel Ochoteco in Germany until '84 and in Brisbane, Australia since.

Gadotti Guitars

1997-present. Luthier Jeanfranco Biava Gadotti builds his premium grade, custom/production, nylon- and steel-string, carved, chambered solidbodies in Orlando, Florida.

Gadow Guitars

2002-present. Luthier Ryan Gadow builds his professional and premium grade, custom/production, solid and semi-hollow body guitars in Durham, North Carolina. He also builds basses.

Gagnon

1998-present. Luthier Bill Gagnon builds his premium and presentation grade, production/custom, archtop guitars in Beaverton, Oregon.

1986 G&L S-500

G&L Will Ray Signature Tribute

Gallagher A-70

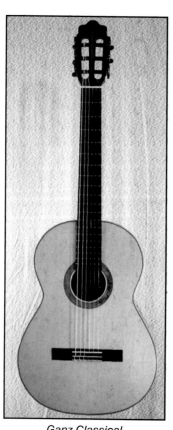

Ganz Classical

MODEL YEAR	FEATURES	EXC. COND. LOW	HIGH

Galanti
Ca.1962-ca.1967. Electric guitars offered by the longtime Italian accordion maker. They may have also offered acoustics.
Electric
1962-1967. Solidbody or hollowbody.

1962-1967		$575	$700

Galiano
New Yorkers Antonio Cerrito and Raphael Ciani offered guitars under the Galiano brand during the early part of the last century. They used the brand both on guitars built by them and others, including The Oscar Schmidt Company. They also offered mandolins.

Gallagher
1965-present. Professional and premium grade, production/custom, flat-top guitars built in Wartrace, Tennessee. J. W. Gallagher started building Shelby brand guitars in the Slingerland Drum factory in Shelbyville, Tennessee in '63. In '65 he and his son Don made the first Gallagher guitar, the G-50. Doc Watson began using Gallagher guitars in '68. In '76, Don assumed operation of the business when J. W. semi-retired. J. W. died in '79.
71 Special
1970-present. Rosewood back and sides, spruce top, herringbone trim, bound ebony 'board, natural.

1970s		$1,600	$1,900

A-70 Ragtime Special
1978-present. Smaller auditorium/00 size, spruce top, mahogany back and sides, G logo, natural.

1980s		$1,400	$1,650

Custom 12-String
Introduced in 1965. Mahogany, 12-fret neck, natural.

1965		$1,200	$1,500

Doc Watson
1974-present. Spruce top, mahogany back and sides, scalloped bracing, ebony 'board, herringbone trim, natural.

1974-1979		$1,700	$2,000
1980-1989		$1,600	$1,900
1990-1999		$1,500	$1,800
2000-2008		$1,500	$1,700

Doc Watson (Cutaway)
1975-present. Spruce top, mahogany back and sides, scalloped bracing, ebony 'board, herringbone trim, natural.

1980s		$1,700	$2,000

Doc Watson 12-String
1995-2000. Natural.

1995-2000		$1,600	$1,900

Doc Watson Signature
2000-2008. Signature inlay 12th fret.

2000-2008		$1,700	$1,900

G-45
1970-present. Mahogany back and sides, spruce top, ebony 'board, natural.

1980s		$1,100	$1,200

G-50
1980s-present. Mahogany back and sides, spruce top, ebony 'board, natural.

1980s		$1,300	$1,500

G-65
1980s-present. Rosewood back and sides, spruce top, ebony 'board, natural.

1980s		$1,600	$1,900

G-70
1978-present. Rosewood back and sides, herringbone purfling on top and soundhole, mother-of-pearl diamond 'board inlays, bound headstock, natural.

1980s		$1,800	$2,100

G-71
1970s. Indian rosewood, gold tuners.

1970s		$1,900	$2,300

Gallagher, Kevin
1996. Kevin Gallagher, luthier, changed name brand to Omega to avoid confusion with J.W. Gallagher. See Omega listing.

Gallotone
1950s-1960s. Low-end foreign brand similar to 1950s Stellas, the Gallotone Champion, a 3/4 size student flat top, is associated with John Lennon as his early guitar.

Galloup Guitars
1994-present. Luthier Bryan Galloup builds his professional and premium grade, production/custom flat-tops in Big Rapids, Michigan. He also operates the Galloup School of Lutherie and The Guitar Hospital repair and restoration business.

Galveston
Budget and intermediate grade, production, imported acoustic, acoustic/electric, resonator and solidbody guitars. They also offer basses and mandolins.

Gamble & O'Toole
1978-present. Premium grade, custom classical and steel string guitars built by luthier Arnie Gamble in Sacramento, California, with design input and inlay work from his wife Erin O'Toole.

Ganz Guitars
1995-present. Luthier Steve Ganz builds his professional grade, production/custom classical guitars in Bellingham, Washington.

Garcia
Made by luthier Federico Garcia in Spain until late-1960s or very early-'70s when production moved to Japan.
Classical
1960s-1970s. Mid-level, '60s model is solid spruce top with solid mahogany, rosewood or walnut back and sides, '70s model is Spanish pine top with walnut back and sides.

1960s	Mahogany	$200	$250

MODEL YEAR	FEATURES	EXC. COND. LOW	HIGH
1960s	Rosewood	$450	$550
1960s	Walnut	$250	$300
1970s	Spanish pine/ Brazilian rosewood	$650	$800
1970s	Spanish pine/walnut	$250	$300

Garrison

2000-present. Intermediate and professional grade, production, acoustic and acoustic/electric guitars designed by luthier Chris Griffiths using his Active Bracing System (a single integrated glass-fiber bracing system inside a solid wood body). He started Griffiths Guitar Works in 1993 in St. John's, Newfoundland, and introduced Garrison guitars in 2000. In '07, Garrison was acquired by Gibson.

G Series
2000-present.

2000-2007		$400	$500

Gary Kramer

2006-present. Intermediate and professioanl grade, production/custom, solidbody electric guitars built by luthier Gary Kramer in El Segundo, California, and imported. Kramer was one of the founders of the Kramer guitar company in the '70s.

Gauge Guitars

2002-present. Luthier Aaron Solomon builds custom, professional and premium grade, solidbody and semi-solid electric guitars in New Jersey.

Gemelli

Early 1960s-ca. 1966. European-made (likely Italian) guitars. Similar to Bartolini guitars, so most likely from same manufacturer. Originally plastic covered, they switched to paint finishes by around '65.

Gemunder

1870s-1910s. New York shop that specialized in re-production-aged violins, but also made parlor-sized guitars that were similar to Martin guitars of the era. An original label on the inside back identifies August Gemunder and Sons, New York.

Parlor
1870s-1910s. Style 28 appointments, rosewood body, spruce top.

1870-1910s		$1,300	$1,500

George

See listing under Chris George.

German Guitars

2001- present. Luthier Greg German builds his premium grade, custom/production, acoustic archtop guitars in Broomfield, Colorado.

Giannini

1900-present. Classical, acoustic, and acoustic/electric guitars built in Salto, SP, Brazil near Sao Paolo. They also build violas, cavaquinhos and mandolins. Founded by guitar-builder Tranquillo Giannini, an Italian who traveled to Brazil in 1890 and discovered the exotic woods of Brazil. The company was producing 30,000 instruments a year by '30. They began exporting their acoustic instruments to the U.S. in '63. They added electric guitars in '60, but these weren't imported as much, if at all. Gianninis from this era used much Brazilian Rosewood.

Classical
Early-1970s. Nylon string import, small body.

1970s		$150	$175

CraViolia
1970s. Kidney bean-shaped rosewood body, acoustic, natural, line included a classical, a steel string, and a 12-string.

1972-1974		$275	$325

CraViolia 12-String
Early-1970s. Kidney bean-shaped body, 12 strings.

1972-1974		$300	$375
2004		$175	$200

Gibson

1890s (1902)-present. Intermediate, professional, and premium grade, production/custom, acoustic and electric guitars made in the U.S. They also build basses, mandolins, amps, and banjos under the Gibson name. Gibson also offers instruments under the Epiphone, Kramer, Steinberger, Dobro, Tobias, Valley Arts, Garrison, Slingerland (drums), Baldwin (pianos), Trace Elliot, Electar (amps), Maestro, Gibson Labs, Oberheim, and Echoplex brands.

Founded in Kalamazoo, Michigan by Orville Gibson, a musician and luthier who developed instruments with tops, sides and backs carved out of solid pieces of wood. Early instruments included mandolins, archtop guitars and harp guitars. By 1896 Gibson had opened a shop. In 1902 Gibson was bought out by a group of investors who incorporated the business as Gibson Mandolin-Guitar Manufacturing Company, Limited. The company was purchased by Chicago Musical Instrument Company (CMI) in '44. In '57 CMI also purchased the Epiphone guitar company, transferring production from Philadelphia to the Gibson plant in Kalamazoo. Gibson was purchased by Norlin in late-'69 and a new factory was opened in Nashville, Tennessee in '74. The Kalamazoo factory ceased production in '84. In '85, Gibson was sold to a group headed by Henry Juskewiscz. Gibson purchased the Flatiron Company in '87 and built a new factory in '89, moving acoustic instrument production to Bozeman, Montana.

The various models of Firebirds, Flying Vs, Les Pauls, SGs, and Super 400s are grouped together

Garrison G-41

German archtop

GUITARS

1981 Gibson 335S Deluxe

1965 Gibson B-25-12 N

MODEL YEAR	FEATURES	EXC. COND. LOW	HIGH

under those general headings. Custom Shop and Historic instruments are listed with their respective main model (for example, the '39 Super 400 Historical Collection model is listed with the Super 400s).

335 S Custom

1980-1981. Solidbody, 335-shaped, mahogany body, unbound rosewood 'board, 2 exposed Dirty Finger humbuckers, coil-tap, TP-6 tailpiece.

1980-1981	Sunburst	$1,000	$1,125

335 S Deluxe

1980-1982. Same as 335 S Custom but with bound ebony 'board, brass nut.

1980-1982	Cherry	$1,100	$1,200
1980-1982	Silverburst	$1,250	$1,350
1980-1982	Sunburst	$1,150	$1,250

335 S Standard

1980-1981. Solidbody, 335-shaped, maple body and neck, 2 exposed split-coil humbuckers, stop tailpiece, no coil-tap, unbound 'board.

1980-1981	Sunburst	$900	$975

Advanced Jumbo

1936-1940. Dreadnought, 16" wide, round shoulders, Brazilian rosewood back and sides, sunburst, reintroduced '90-'97.

1936-1940		$45,000	$65,900

Advanced Jumbo Reissue/AJ Special Edition

1990-1999, 2001-2007. Issued as a standard production model, but soon available only as a special order for most of the '90s; currently offered as standard production. Renamed 1936 Advanced Jumbo for '97-'98. There were also some limited-edition AJs offered during the '90s.

1990-1999	Reissue	$1,600	$1,900
1990-1999	Special Ed. Flamed maple	$2,500	$3,000
1994	Machiche, Mexican rosewood	$3,000	$3,500
2001-2005	Brazilian, Luthier's choice CS	$3,500	$4,300
2001-2007	Reintroduced	$1,700	$1,800
2001-2006	Special Ed. Indian rosewood	$1,700	$2,100

B.B. King Custom

1980-1988. Lucille on peghead, 2 pickups, multibound, gold-plated parts, Vari-tone, cherry or ebony, renamed B.B. King Lucille in '88.

1980-1988		$1,700	$1,900

B.B. King Lucille

1988-present. Introduced as B.B. King Custom, renamed B.B. King Lucille. Lucille on peghead, 2 pickups, multi-bound, gold-plated parts, Vari-tone, cherry or ebony.

1988-1999		$1,800	$2,100

B.B. King Standard

1980-1985. Like B.B. King Custom, but with stereo electronics and chrome-plated parts, cherry or ebony.

1980-1985		$1,800	$2,000

MODEL YEAR	FEATURES	EXC. COND. LOW	HIGH

B.B. King Commemorative ES-355 Lucille

2006. Limited edition of 80 guitars, price includes matching serial number/certificate number, matching B.B. King script logo case.

2006		$4,300	$5,200

B-15

1967-1971. Mahogany, spruce top, student model, natural finish.

1967-1969		$600	$700
1970-1971		$500	$600

B-25

1962-1977. Flat-top, mahogany, bound body, cherry sunburst (natural finish is the B-25 N).

1962-1964		$1,300	$1,600
1965-1966		$1,150	$1,250
1967-1969		$1,050	$1,250
1970-1977		$850	$1,000

B-25 N

1962-1977. Flat-top, mahogany, bound body, natural (cherry sunburst finish is the B-25).

1962-1964		$1,300	$1,600
1965-1966		$1,150	$1,250
1967-1969		$1,050	$1,250
1970-1977		$850	$1,000

B-25 3/4

1962-1968. Short-scale version, flat-top, mahogany body, cherry sunburst (natural finish is the B-25 3/4 N).

1962-1964		$1,000	$1,200
1965-1966		$800	$950
1967-1968		$750	$900

B-25 N 3/4

1966-1968. Short-scale version, flat-top, mahogany body, natural (cherry sunburst finish is the B-25 3/4).

1966-1968		$800	$900

B-25-12

1962-1970. Flat-top 12-string version, mahogany, bound body, cherry sunburst (natural finish is the B-25-12 N).

1962-1964		$1,450	$1,800
1965-1966		$1,100	$1,300
1967-1968		$975	$1,100
1969-1970		$875	$1,000

B-25-12 N

1962-1977. Flat-top 12-string version, mahogany, bound body, natural (cherry sunburst is the B-25-12).

1962-1964		$1,450	$1,800
1965-1966		$1,100	$1,300
1967-1969		$975	$1,100
1970-1977		$875	$1,100

B-45-12

1961-1979. Flat-top 12-string, mahogany, round shoulders for '61, square after, sunburst (natural finish is the B-45-12 N).

1961-1962	Round shoulder	$1,950	$2,300
1962-1964	Square shoulder	$1,750	$2,100
1965-1966	Non-pin bridge introduced	$1,450	$1,700
1967-1969		$1,450	$1,700

MODEL YEAR	FEATURES	EXC. COND. LOW	HIGH
1970-1979	Pin bridge reintroduced	$950	$1,100

B-45-12 N

1962-1979. Flat-top 12-string, mahogany, natural (cherry sunburst finish is the B-45-12).

1962	Round shoulder	$1,950	$2,300
1962-1964	Square shoulder	$1,750	$2,100
1965-1966	Non-pin bridge introduced	$1,450	$1,700
1967-1969		$1,450	$1,700
1970-1979	Pin bridge reintroduced	$950	$1,100

B-45-12 Limited Edition

1991-1992. Limited edition reissue with rosewood back and sides, natural.

1991-1992		$950	$1,175

Barney Kessel Custom

1961-1973. Double-cut archtop, 2 humbuckers, gold hardware, cherry sunburst.

1961		$4,300	$4,500
1962		$4,200	$4,400
1963		$4,100	$4,300
1964		$4,000	$4,200
1965		$3,700	$3,900
1966		$3,600	$3,800
1967-1969		$3,500	$3,700
1970-1973		$2,700	$2,900

Barney Kessel Regular

1961-1974. Double-cut archtop, 2 humbuckers, nickel hardware, cherry sunburst.

1961		$3,200	$3,900
1962		$3,200	$3,800
1963		$3,100	$3,700
1964		$3,000	$3,700
1965		$2,900	$3,500
1966		$2,800	$3,500
1967-1969		$2,700	$3,300
1970-1973		$2,400	$2,700

Blue Ridge

1968-1979, 1989-1990. Flat-top, dreadnought, laminated rosewood back and sides, natural finish, reintroduced for '89-'90.

1968-1969		$800	$1,000
1970-1979		$775	$950

Blue Ridge 12

1970-1978. Flat-top, 12 strings, laminated rosewood back and sides, natural finish.

1970-1978		$775	$950

Blueshawk

1996-2006. Small Les Paul single-cut-type body with f-holes, 2 single-coil hum cancelling Blues 90 pickups, 6-way Varitone rotary dial.

1996-2006		$700	$875

B-SJ Blue Ridge

1989. Model name on label is B-SJ, truss rod covers logo is Blue Ridge, SJ appointments but with narrow peghead shape.

1989		$1,500	$1,700

MODEL YEAR	FEATURES	EXC. COND. LOW	HIGH

Byrdland

1955-1992. Thinline archtop, single-cut (rounded until late-'60, pointed '60-late-'69, rounded after '69, rounded or pointed '98-present), 2 pickups, now part of the Historic Collection.

1956-1957	Natural, P-90s	$9,000	$10,000
1956-1957	Sunburst, P-90s	$7,500	$8,400
1958	Natural, PAFs	$12,500	$14,000
1958	Sunburst, PAFs	$10,500	$11,900
1959	Natural, PAFs	$12,400	$13,900
1959	Sunburst, PAFs	$10,500	$11,900
1960	Natural, PAFs	$10,500	$11,900
1960	Sunburst, PAFs	$8,700	$10,000
1961	Natural, PAFs	$10,500	$11,900
1961	Sunburst, PAFs	$8,500	$9,900
1962	Natural, PAFs	$10,500	$11,900
1962	Sunburst, PAFs	$8,400	$9,800
1963-1964	Natural, pat. #	$8,500	$9,000
1963-1964	Sunburst, pat. #	$8,000	$8,200
1965-1966	Natural	$7,000	$7,900
1965-1966	Sunburst	$6,200	$7,100
1967-1969	Natural	$6,100	$6,700
1967-1969	Sunburst	$5,600	$6,200
1970-1979	Various colors	$4,500	$5,600
1980-1992	Various colors	$4,100	$5,100

Byrdland Historic Collection

1993-present. Various colors.

1993-2006	Natural	$4,500	$5,500
1993-2006	Sunburst	$4,000	$5,000
1993-2006	Wine Red	$3,500	$4,000

C-0 Classical

1962-1971. Spruce top, mahogany back and sides, bound top, natural.

1962-1964		$575	$650
1965-1971		$450	$550

C-1 Classical

1957-1971. Spruce top, mahogany back and sides, bound body, natural.

1957-1961		$650	$725
1962		$650	$700
1963		$650	$675
1964		$525	$650
1965-1971		$500	$625

C-1 D Laredo

1963-1971. Natural spruce top, mahogany sides and back, upgrade to standard C-1.

1963-1964		$700	$800
1965		$600	$700

C-1 E Classical Electric

1960-1967. C-1 with ceramic bridge pickup, catalog notes special matched amplifier that filters out fingering noises.

1960-1964		$750	$850
1965-1967		$650	$750

C-1 S Petite Classical

1961-1966. Petite 13 1/4" body, natural spruce top, mahogany back and sides.

1961-1964		$600	$700
1965-1967		$550	$600

Late '60s Gibson B-45-12

1959 Gibson Byrdland

1957 Gibson C-2

1984 Gibson Corvus

MODEL YEAR FEATURES	EXC. COND. LOW	HIGH
C-2 Classical		
1960-1971. Maple back and sides, bound body, natural.		
1960-1964	$750	$850
1965-1971	$650	$750
C-4 Classical		
1962-1968. Maple back and sides, natural.		
1962-1964	$900	$1,000
1965-1968	$800	$900
C-5 Classical		
1957-1960. Rosewood back and sides, previously named GS-5 Classical in '54-'56.		
1957-1960	$950	$1,150
C-6 Classical		
1958-1971. Rosewood back and sides, gold hardware, natural.		
1958-1964	$1,450	$1,800
1965-1971	$1,150	$1,400
C-8 Classical		
1962-1969. Rosewood back and sides, natural.		
1962-1964	$1,900	$2,300
1965-1969	$1,600	$2,000
C-100 Classical		
1971-1972. Slotted peghead, spruce top, mahogany back and sides, ebony 'board, Gibson Master Model label, non-gloss finish.		
1971-1972	$375	$450
C-200 Classical		
1971-1972. C-100 with gloss finish.		
1971-1972	$550	$650
C-300 Classical		
1971-1972. Similar to C-100, but with rosewood 'board, wider soundhole ring.		
1971-1972	$600	$700
C-400 Classical		
1971-1972. Rosewood sides and back, spruce top, high-end appointments, chrome hardware.		
1971-1972	$950	$1,050
C-500 Classical		
1971-1972. C-400 with gold hardware.		
1971-1972	$1,100	$1,200
CF-100		
1950-1958. Flat-top, pointed cutaway, mahogany back and sides, bound body, sunburst finish.		
1950-1958	$2,500	$3,100
CF-100 E		
1951-1958. CF-100 with a single-coil pickup.		
1950-1958	$3,300	$4,100
Challenger I		
1983-1985. Single-cut Les Paul-shaped solidbody, 1 humbucker pickup, bolt-on maple neck with rosewood 'board and dot markers, silver finish standard.		
1983-1985	$425	$525
Challenger II		
1983-1985. Single-cut Les Paul-shaped solidbody, 2 humbucker pickups, bolt-on maple neck with rosewood 'board and dot markers, various colors.		
1983-1985	$475	$575

MODEL YEAR FEATURES	EXC. COND. LOW	HIGH
Chet Atkins CE		
1981-1995. CE stands for Classical Electric, single-cut, multi-bound body, rosewood 'board with standard width nut, gold hardware, various colors. In '95, the Atkins CE and CEC were consolidated into the Chet Atkins CE/CEC, with an ebony 'board with a standard (CE) and classical (CEC) nut. That model was discontinued in '06.		
1981-1995	$1,000	$1,200
Chet Atkins CEC		
1981-1995. Same as CE but with ebony 'board and 2" classical width nut, black or natural.		
1981-1995	$1,200	$1,350
Chet Atkins Country Gentleman		
1987-2005. Thinline archtop, single rounded cutaway, 2 humbuckers, multi-bound, gold hardware, Bigsby. Part of Gibson's Custom line.		
1987-1995	$2,300	$2,600
2003	$2,300	$2,600
Chet Atkins SST		
1987-2006. Steel string acoustic/electric solidbody, single-cut, bridge transducer pickup, active bass and treble controls, gold hardware.		
1986-2001	$1,000	$1,200
Chet Atkins SST-12		
1990-1994. 12-string model similar to 6-string, mahogany/spruce body, preamp circuit controls single transducer pickup, natural or ebony finish.		
1990-1994	$1,400	$1,650
Chet Atkins Tennessean		
1990-2005. Single rounded cutaway archtop, 2 humbuckers, f-holes, bound body. Part of Gibson's Custom line.		
1990-2005	$1,200	$1,400
Chicago 35		
1994-1995. Flat-top dreadnought, round shoulders, mahogany back and sides, prewar script logo.		
1994-1995 Factory electronics	$900	$1,100
Citation		
1969-1971. 17" full-depth body, single-cut archtop, 1 or 2 floating pickups, fancy inlay, natural or sunburst. Only 8 shipped for '69-'71, reissued the first time '79-'83 and as part of the Historic Collection in '93.		
1969-1971	$15,000	$20,000
Citation (1st Reissue)		
1979-1983. Reissue of '69-'71 model, reintroduced in '93 as part of Gibson's Historic Collection.		
1979-1983 Sunburst or natural	$13,000	$15,000
Citation (2nd Reissue)		
1993-present. Limited production via Gibson's Historic Collection, natural or sunburst.		
1994-2000 Natural	$11,000	$12,000
1994-2002 Sunburst	$11,000	$12,000
2003-2006 Sunburst	$9,700	$11,800
CJ-165 Maple		
2006-present. Classic small body non-cutaway flat top, solid spruce top, maple back and sides.		
2006-2008	$1,600	$1,650

MODEL YEAR	FEATURES	EXC. COND. LOW	HIGH

CJ-165 Rosewood
2007-present. Scaled down jumbo non-cutaway flat top, solid spruce top, Indian rosewood back and sides.

| 2007-2008 | | $1,700 | $1,750 |

CL-20/CL-20+
1997-1998. Flat-top, laminated back and sides, 4-ply binding with tortoiseshell appointments, abalone diamond inlays.

| 1997-1998 | | $1,100 | $1,200 |

CL-30 Deluxe
1997-1998. J-50 style dreadnought, solid spruce top, bubinga back and sides, factory electronics.

| 1997-1998 | | $950 | $1,050 |

CL-35 Deluxe
1997-1998. Single cutaway CL-30.

| 1997-1998 | | $1,000 | $1,100 |

CL-50
1999. Custom Shop model, D-style body, higher-end appointments, offered with Brazilian rosewood.

| 1999 | Brazilian rosewood | $3,400 | $3,600 |

Corvus I
1982-1984. Odd-shaped solidbody with offset V-type cut, bolt maple neck, rosewood 'board, 1 humbucker, standard finish was silver gloss, but others available at an additional cost.

| 1982-1984 | | $475 | $525 |

Corvus II
1982-1984. Same as Corvus I, but with 2 humbuckers, 2 volume controls, 1 master tone control.

| 1982-1984 | | $550 | $600 |

Corvus III
1982-1984. Same as Corvus I, but with 3 single-coil pickups, master volume and tone control, 5-way switch.

| 1982-1984 | | $600 | $700 |

Crest Gold
1969-1971. Double-cut thinline archtop, Brazilian rosewood body, 2 mini-humbuckers, bound top and headstock, bound f-holes, gold-plated parts.

| 1969-1971 | | $4,800 | $5,500 |

Crest Silver
1969-1972. Silver-plated parts version of Crest.

| 1969-1972 | | $4,300 | $5,000 |

CS Series
2002-present. Scaled down ES-335 body style, made in Custom Shop.

2002-2003	CS-356 (plain top)	$1,900	$2,100
2002-2007	CS-336 (plain top)	$1,700	$2,000
2002-2007	CS-336F (figured top)	$1,900	$2,300
2002-2007	CS-356F (figured top)	$2,300	$2,500

Dove
1962-1996, 1999-2003. Flat-top acoustic, maple back and sides, square shoulders.

1962	Natural	$4,700	$5,800
1962	Sunburst	$4,200	$5,200
1963	Natural	$4,600	$5,700
1963	Sunburst	$4,100	$5,100
1964	Natural	$4,500	$5,600
1964	Sunburst	$4,000	$5,000
1965	Natural	$3,700	$4,600
1965	Sunburst	$3,500	$4,500
1966	Natural	$3,300	$4,100
1966	Sunburst	$3,200	$4,000
1967	Natural	$3,100	$3,800
1967	Sunburst	$3,000	$3,600
1968	Natural	$3,000	$3,700
1968	Sunburst	$2,900	$3,600
1969-1970	Natural	$2,500	$2,950
1969-1970	Sunburst	$2,500	$2,750
1971-1984	Natural	$2,400	$2,650
1971-1984	Sunburst	$2,200	$2,550
1984-1989	Various colors	$1,700	$2,100
1990-1996	Various colors	$1,500	$1,850
1999-2003	Reissue model	$2,000	$2,200

'60s Dove
1997-1999. Spruce top, maple back and sides, Dove appointments.

| 1997-2004 | | $1,700 | $2,000 |

Dove Commemorative
1994-1996. Heritage or Antique Cherry finish.

| 1994-1996 | | $1,800 | $2,100 |

Doves In Flight
1996-present. Gibson Custom model, maple back and sides, doves in flight inlays.

| 1996-2007 | | $2,800 | $3,100 |

EAS Deluxe
1992-1994. Single-cut flat-top acoustic/electric, solid flamed maple top, 3-band EQ.

| 1992-1994 | Vintage Cherry Sunburst | $750 | $925 |

EBS(F)-1250 Double Bass
1962-1970. Double-cut SG-type solidbody, double-neck with bass and 6-string, originally introduced as the EBSF-1250 because of a built-in fuzztone, which was later deleted, only 22 made.

1962-1964		$10,000	$12,500
1965-1966		$8,000	$10,000
1967-1969		$7,000	$8,000
1970		$5,500	$7,500

EC-10 Standard
1997-1998. Jumbo single-cut, on-board electronics, solid spruce top, maple back and sides.

| 1997-1998 | | $750 | $925 |

EC-20 Starburst
1997-1998. Jumbo single-cut, on-board electronics, solid spruce top, maple back and sides, renamed J-185 EC in '99.

| 1997-1998 | | $1,500 | $1,700 |

EC-30 Blues King Electro (BKE)
1997-1998. Jumbo single-cut, on-board electronics, solid spruce top, figured maple back and sides, renamed J-185 EC in '99.

| 1997-1998 | | $1,600 | $1,800 |

EDS-1275 Double 12
1958-1968, 1977-1990. Double-cut doubleneck with one 12- and one 6-string, thinline hollowbody until late-'62, SG-style solidbody '62 on.

| 1958 | Black, cherry, sunburst, white | $16,500 | $20,700 |

1974 Gibson Dove

Gibson Doves In Flight

1957 Gibson ES-5 Switchmaster

1962 Gibson ES-125TDC

MODEL YEAR	FEATURES	EXC. COND. LOW	HIGH
1959	Black, cherry, sunburst, white	$16,500	$20,500
1960	Black, cherry, sunburst, white	$15,500	$18,900
1961	Black, cherry, sunburst, white	$15,500	$18,800
1962	Black, cherry, sunburst, white	$15,500	$18,700
1963	Black, cherry, sunburst, white	$15,000	$18,400
1964	Black, cherry, sunburst, white	$15,000	$17,800
1965	Black, cherry, sunburst, white	$12,000	$13,900
1968	Black or cherry	$7,000	$8,700
1968	Jimmy Page exact specs	$9,500	$11,700
1968	White	$7,000	$8,700
1977-1979	Various colors	$2,800	$3,200
1977-1979	White	$3,000	$3,500
1980-1991	Various colors	$2,000	$2,800
1995-2005	Various colors	$2,000	$2,300

EDS-1275 Double 12 (Historic Collection)
1991-1994. Historic Collection reissue.

1991-1994	White	$1,900	$2,200

EDS-1275 Double 12 Centennial
1994. Guitar of the Month (May), gold medallion on back of headstock, gold hardware.

1994	Cherry	$1,900	$2,200

EMS-1235 Double Mandolin
1958-1968. Double-cut, doubleneck with 1 regular 6-string and 1 short 6-string (the mandolin neck), thinline hollowbody until late-1962, SG-style solidbody '62-'68, black, sunburst or white, total of 61 shipped.

1958		$16,500	$20,500
1959		$16,400	$20,400
1960		$16,300	$20,300
1961		$16,200	$20,200
1962		$13,000	$16,000
1963		$12,900	$15,900
1964		$12,800	$15,800
1965		$7,200	$9,000
1966		$6,600	$8,200
1967-1968		$6,500	$8,000

ES-5
1949-1955. Single-cut archtop, 3 P-90 pickups, renamed ES-5 Switchmaster in '55.

1949	Natural	$8,700	$10,500
1949	Sunburst	$7,300	$8,300
1950	Natural	$8,600	$10,400
1950	Sunburst	$7,200	$8,200
1951	Natural	$8,500	$10,300
1951	Sunburst	$7,100	$8,100
1952	Natural	$8,400	$10,200
1952	Sunburst	$7,000	$7,500
1953	Natural	$8,300	$10,100
1953	Sunburst	$7,000	$7,500
1954	Natural	$8,200	$10,000
1954	Sunburst	$6,900	$7,500
1955	Natural	$8,100	$9,900
1955	Sunburst	$6,800	$7,500

ES-5 Switchmaster
1956-1962. Renamed from ES-5, single-cut (rounded until late-'60, pointed after) archtop, 3 P-90s until end of '57, humbuckers after, switchmaster control. The PAF pickups in this model are worth as much as the rest of the guitar. We have listed a non-original '58 with replaced pickups to demonstrate how value is reduced when the original PAFs are removed.

1956	Natural, P-90s	$9,600	$10,500
1956	Sunburst, P-90s	$8,600	$9,500
1957	Natural, humbuckers	$12,700	$15,900
1957	Natural, P-90s	$9,500	$10,400
1957	Sunburst, humbuckers	$12,400	$15,500
1957	Sunburst, P-90s	$8,400	$9,400
1958	Natural, humbuckers	$12,600	$15,800
1958	Sunburst, humbuckers	$12,300	$15,400
1959	Natural, humbuckers	$12,600	$15,700
1959	Sunburst, humbuckers	$12,200	$15,300
1960	Natural, humbuckers	$12,500	$15,600
1960	Sunburst, humbuckers	$12,200	$15,200
1960	Pointed Florentine cutaway	$12,100	$15,100
1961	Pointed Florentine cutaway	$12,000	$15,000
1962	Pointed Florentine cutaway	$12,000	$14,900

ES-5/ES-5 Switchmaster Custom Shop Historic
1995-2006.

1995-2002	ES-5, P-90s, sunburst	$3,000	$3,500
1995-2002	Switchmaster, humbuckers, Wine Red	$3,000	$3,500
1995-2006	Switchmaster, natural option, humbuckers	$3,300	$3,800

ES-100
1938-1941. Archtop, 1 pickup, bound body, sunburst, renamed ES-125 in '41.

1938-1941		$1,200	$1,400

ES-120 T
1962-1970. Archtop, thinline, 1 f-hole, bound body, 1 pickup, sunburst.

1962-1965		$1,150	$1,200
1966-1970		$800	$1,000

ES-125
1941-1943, 1946-1970. Archtop, non-cut, 1 pickup, sunburst, renamed from ES-100.

1941-1943	Blade pickup	$1,400	$1,500
1947-1950	1st non-adj., P-90s	$1,400	$1,600
1951-1959	Adj. P-90s with poles	$1,300	$1,600

MODEL YEAR	FEATURES	EXC. COND. LOW	HIGH
1960-1964		$1,300	$1,500
1965		$1,200	$1,300
1966-1970		$1,100	$1,300

ES-125 C
1966-1970. Wide body archtop, single pointed cutaway, 1 pickup, sunburst.

1965		$1,250	$1,550
1966-1970		$1,150	$1,400

ES-125 CD
1966-1970. Wide body archtop, single-cut, 2 pickups, sunburst.

1965		$1,600	$1,900
1966-1970		$1,500	$1,800

ES-125 D
1957. Limited production (not mentioned in catalog), 2 pickup version of thick body ES-125, sunburst.

1957		$1,600	$1,900

ES-125 T
1956-1969. Archtop thinline, non-cut, 1 pickup, bound body, sunburst.

1958		$1,600	$2,100
1959		$1,500	$2,000
1960-1964		$1,500	$1,800
1965-1969		$1,200	$1,400

ES-125 T 3/4
1957-1970. Archtop thinline, short-scale, non-cut, 1 pickup, sunburst.

1957-1959		$1,450	$1,550
1960-1964		$1,400	$1,500
1965-1970		$1,000	$1,250

ES-125 TC
1960-1970. Archtop thinline, single pointed cutaway, bound body, 1 P-90 pickup, sunburst.

1960-1964		$2,000	$2,200
1965-1966		$1,800	$2,000
1967-1970		$1,500	$1,800

ES-125 TD
1957-1963. Archtop thinline, non-cut, 2 pickups, sunburst.

1957-1959		$2,200	$2,450
1960-1963		$2,100	$2,400

ES-125 TDC or ES-125 TCD
1960-1971. Archtop thinline, single pointed cutaway, 2 P-90 pickups, sunburst.

1960-1964		$2,700	$2,900
1965-1966		$2,300	$2,600
1967-1971		$2,100	$2,300

ES-130
1954-1956. Archtop, non-cut, 1 pickup, bound body, sunburst, renamed ES-135 in '56.

1954-1956		$1,600	$1,700

ES-135
1956-1958. Renamed from ES-130, non-cut archtop, 1 pickup, sunburst, name reused on a thin body in the '90s.

1956-1958		$1,300	$1,500

ES-135 (Thinline)
1991-2002. Single-cut archtop, laminated maple body, 2 humbuckers or 2 P-90s, chrome or gold hardware, sunburst.

1991-2002	Stop tail	$1,150	$1,200
1991-2002	Trapeze	$1,050	$1,100

MODEL YEAR	FEATURES	EXC. COND. LOW	HIGH

ES-137 Classic
2002-present. Thin-body electric single cut, trapezoid inlays, 2 humbuckers, f-holes, gold hardware.

2002-2006		$1,100	$1,250
2007		$1,150	$1,250

ES-137 Custom
2002-present. Like Classic, but with split-diamond inlays and varitone.

2002-2006		$1,200	$1,500

ES-137 P
2002-2005. Like Classic, but with exposed humbuckers, chrome hardware and very small trapezoid inlays.

2002-2005		$850	$950

ES-140 (3/4)
1950-1956. Archtop, single-cut, 1 pickup, bound body, short-scale.

1950-1956	Natural option	$1,800	$2,000
1950-1956	Sunburst	$1,600	$1,800

ES-140 3/4 T
1957-1968. Archtop thinline, single-cut, bound body, 1 pickup, short-scale, sunburst.

1956-1964		$1,400	$1,700
1965-1968		$1,300	$1,600

ES-140TN (3/4)
1956-1958. Natural finish option, low run production, 57 made.

1956-1958		$1,600	$2,000

ES-150
1936-1942, 1946-1956. Historically important archtop, non-cut, bound body, Charlie Christian bar pickup from '36-'39, various metal covered pickups starting in '40, sunburst.

1936-1939	Charlie Christian pickup	$4,000	$4,800
1940-1942	Metal covered pickup	$3,100	$3,800
1946-1956	P-90 pickup	$1,600	$1,800

ES-150 DC
1969-1975. Archtop, double rounded cutaway, 2 humbuckers, multi-bound.

1969-1975	Cherry or walnut	$2,200	$2,400
1969-1975	Natural	$2,300	$2,600

ES-165 Herb Ellis Model
1991-present. Single pointed cut hollowbody, 1 humbucker, gold hardware.

1991-2005		$1,600	$1,900

ES-175
1949-1971. Archtop, single pointed cutaway, 1 pickup (P-90 from '49-early-'57, humbucker early-'57-'71), multi-bound.

1949	Sunburst	$4,000	$5,000
1949-1951	Natural	$4,500	$5,500
1950	Sunburst	$3,900	$4,500
1951	Sunburst	$3,800	$4,500
1952	Natural, P-90	$4,000	$4,500
1952	Sunburst, P-90	$3,500	$4,300
1953	Natural, P-90	$3,900	$4,500
1953	Sunburst, P-90	$3,400	$4,200
1954	Natural, P-90	$3,800	$4,500
1954	Sunburst, P-90	$3,300	$4,100

Gibson ES-135 (Thinline)

1958 Gibson ES-175

1959 Gibson ES-225

Gibson ES-225 TDN

MODEL YEAR	FEATURES	EXC. COND. LOW	HIGH
1955	Natural, P-90	$3,700	$4,500
1955	Sunburst, P-90	$3,200	$4,000
1956	Natural, P-90	$3,600	$4,500
1956	Sunburst, P-90	$3,100	$3,800
1957	Sunburst, humbucker	$5,700	$7,100
1957-1959	Natural, humbucker	$6,500	$7,200
1958-1959	Sunburst, humbucker	$5,700	$6,400
1960	Sunburst	$5,900	$6,000
1961	Sunburst	$5,200	$5,800
1962	Sunburst	$4,900	$5,400
1963	Sunburst	$4,700	$5,200
1964	Sunburst	$4,300	$4,800
1965	Sunburst	$3,900	$4,200
1966	Sunburst	$3,800	$4,100
1967-1969	Black	$4,100	$4,900
1967-1969	Sunburst	$3,100	$3,900
1970-1971	Various colors	$2,600	$3,000

ES-175 CC
1979 (possibly some made as late as '81). 1 Charlie Christian pickup, sunburst or walnut.

1979		$3,000	$3,300

ES-175 D
1951-present. Archtop, single-cut, 2 pickups (P-90s from '53-early-'57, humbuckers early-'57 on). Humbucker pickups were converted from PAF-stickers to Pat. No.-stickers in '62. Different models were converted at different times. An ES-175 model, made during the transitional time, with PAFs, will fetch more. In some of the electric-archtop models, the transition period may have been later than '62. Cataloged as the ES-175 Reissue in the '90s, Currently as the ES-175 under Gibson Custom.

1952	Natural	$6,000	$7,400
1952	Sunburst	$5,500	$6,500
1953	Natural	$5,800	$7,200
1953	Sunburst	$5,400	$6,500
1954	Natural	$5,700	$7,000
1954	Sunburst	$5,300	$6,500
1955	Natural	$5,600	$6,800
1955-1956	Sunburst	$5,200	$6,500
1956	Natural	$5,500	$6,700
1957-1959	Natural, humbuckers	$12,000	$14,000
1957-1959	Sunburst, humbuckers	$10,000	$11,500
1960	Natural	$9,000	$10,500
1960	Sunburst	$8,000	$9,500
1961	Natural	$7,000	$8,000
1961	Sunburst	$6,500	$7,000
1962	Natural	$6,500	$7,000
1962	Sunburst	$6,000	$6,500
1963	Natural	$6,000	$6,500
1963	Sunburst	$5,900	$6,400
1964	Natural	$5,900	$6,400
1964	Sunburst	$5,500	$6,000
1965	Natural	$4,300	$5,300
1965	Sunburst	$4,200	$5,200
1966	Natural	$4,200	$5,200

MODEL YEAR	FEATURES	EXC. COND. LOW	HIGH
1966	Sunburst	$4,100	$5,100
1967-1969	Black	$4,900	$5,500
1967-1969	Various colors	$4,000	$5,000
1970-1972	Various colors	$3,100	$3,500
1973-1979	Various colors	$2,900	$3,100
1980-1989	Various colors	$2,400	$2,700
1990-1999	Various colors	$2,400	$2,600
2000-2006	Various colors	$2,100	$2,400

ES-175 T
1976-1980. Archtop thinline, single pointed cutaway, 2 humbuckers, various colors.

1976-1980	Natural	$3,000	$3,300
1976-1980	Sunburst	$2,900	$3,100

ES-175 Steve Howe
2001-present. Maple laminate body, multi-bound top, sunburst.

2001-2007		$2,100	$2,400

ES-225 T
1955-1959. Thinline, single pointed cutaway, 1 P-90 pickup, bound body and neck, sunburst or natural.

1955	Natural	$2,200	$2,500
1955	Sunburst	$2,000	$2,300
1956	Natural	$2,100	$2,500
1956	Sunburst	$1,900	$2,300
1957	Natural	$2,100	$2,400
1957	Sunburst	$1,800	$2,300
1958	Natural	$2,000	$2,400
1958-1959	Sunburst	$1,800	$2,300
1959	Natural	$2,000	$2,300

ES-225 TD
1956-1959. Thinline, single-cut, 2 P-90s, bound body and neck.

1956-1959	Natural	$3,100	$3,800
1956-1959	Sunburst	$2,700	$3,200

ES-250
1939-1940. Archtop, carved top, special Christian pickup, multi-bound, high-end appointments.

1939-1940	Natural	$17,700	$21,000
1939-1940	Sunburst	$8,500	$10,500

ES-295
1952-1958. Single pointed cutaway archtop, 2 pickups (P-90s from '52-late-'58, humbuckers after), gold finish, gold-plated hardware.

1952	P-90s	$7,300	$8,800
1953-1957	P-90s	$7,200	$8,700
1957-1958	Humbuckers	$17,000	$19,000

ES-295 Reissue
1990-1993. Gold finish, 2 P-90 pickups, Bigsby.

1990-1993		$2,000	$2,500

ES-295 '52 Historic Collection
1993-2000. Higher-end reissue, Antique Gold finish, 2 P-90 pickups, Bigsby.

1993-2000		$2,700	$3,300

ES-300
1940-1942, 1945-1953. Archtop, non-cut, f-holes, had 4 pickup configurations during its run, sunburst or natural.

1940	Natural, oblong diagonal pickup	$4,600	$5,000
1940	Sunburst, oblong diagonal pickup	$4,200	$4,500

MODEL YEAR	FEATURES	LOW	HIGH
1941-1942	Natural, 1 pickup	$3,700	$4,500
1941-1942	Sunburst, 1 pickup	$3,200	$3,500
1945	Black, 1 pickup	$3,400	$4,000
1945-1949	Sunburst, 1 pickup	$3,100	$3,400
1949-1953	ES-300N, natural, 2 pickups	$4,100	$4,900
1949-1953	Sunburst, 2 pickups	$3,300	$3,800

ES-320 TD
1971-1974. Thinline archtop, double-cut, 2 single-coil pickups, bound body, cherry, natural, or walnut.

1971-1974		$1,000	$1,200

ES-325 TD
1972-1978. Thinline archtop, double-cut, 2 mini-humbuckers, 1 f-hole, bound body, cherry or walnut.

1972-1978		$1,125	$1,400

ES-330 T
1959-1963. Double rounded cutaway, thinline, 1 pickup, bound body and neck, in the '60s came with either an original semi-hard case (better than chip board) or a hardshell case. Prices quoted are for hard-shell case; approximately $100 should be deducted for the semi-hard case.

1959-1961	Natural	$4,000	$5,000
1959-1961	Sunburst	$3,000	$3,300
1961	Cherry	$2,800	$3,300
1962-1963	Cherry or sunburst	$2,700	$3,200

ES-330 TD
1959-1972. Double rounded cutaway, thinline, 2 pickups, bound body and neck, in the '60s came with either an original semi-hard case (better than chip board) or a hardshell case. Prices noted for the hard-shell case; approximately $100 should be deducted for the semi-hard case.

1959-1960	Natural	$5,500	$6,500
1959-1960	Sunburst	$5,000	$5,500
1960	Cherry	$5,000	$5,500
1961	Cherry or sunburst	$4,900	$5,500
1962-1964	Cherry or sunburst	$4,000	$4,500
1965	Cherry or sunburst	$3,200	$3,500
1966	Cherry or sunburst	$3,100	$3,500
1967-1968	Burgundy Metallic (unfaded)	$3,200	$3,500
1967-1968	Cherry or sunburst	$2,900	$3,400
1968	Walnut option	$3,000	$3,400
1969-1972	Various colors, long neck	$3,000	$3,400

ES-333
2002-2005. Economy ES-335, no 'guard, no head-stock inlay, exposed coils, stencil logo, satin finish.

2002-2005		$825	$900

ES-335/ES-335 TD
1958-1981. The original design ES-335 has dot 'board inlays and a stop tailpiece. Block inlays re-placed dots in mid-'62, in late-'64 the stop tailpiece was replaced with a trapeze tailpiece. Replaced by the ES-335 DOT in '81.

1958	Natural, unbound neck	$65,000	$70,000
1958	Natural, unbound neck, Bigsby	$41,000	$50,000

MODEL YEAR	FEATURES	LOW	HIGH
1958	Sunburst, bound neck	$41,000	$50,000
1958	Sunburst, bound neck, Bigsby	$33,000	$40,000
1958	Sunburst, unbound neck	$38,000	$45,000
1958	Sunburst, unbound neck, Bigsby	$27,000	$32,000
1959	Natural, bound neck	$70,000	$85,000
1959	Natural, bound neck, Bigsby	$52,000	$64,000
1959	Sunburst	$45,000	$55,000
1959	Sunburst, factory Bigsby	$34,000	$41,000
1960	Cherry, factory Bigsby	$26,000	$31,000
1960	Cherry, factory stop tail	$34,000	$42,000
1960	Natural, factory Bigsby	$33,000	$41,000
1960	Natural, factory stop tail	$45,000	$55,000
1960	Sunburst, factory Bigsby	$26,000	$31,000
1960	Sunburst, factory stop tail	$34,000	$42,000
1961	Cherry, factory Bigsby	$22,000	$25,000
1961	Cherry, factory stop tail	$27,000	$33,000
1961	Sunburst, factory Bigsby	$22,000	$25,000
1961	Sunburst, factory stop tail	$27,000	$33,000
1962	Cherry, blocks, PAFs	$27,000	$31,000
1962	Cherry, blocks, pat. #	$26,000	$30,000
1962	Cherry, dots, PAFs	$27,000	$31,000
1962	Cherry, vibrola tailpiece	$19,000	$23,000
1962	Sunburst, blocks, PAFs	$27,000	$31,000
1962	Sunburst, blocks, pat. #	$26,000	$30,000
1962	Sunburst, dots, PAFs	$27,000	$31,000
1962	Sunburst, dots, pat. #	$26,000	$30,000
1962	Sunburst, vibrola tailpiece	$19,000	$23,000
1963-1964	Cherry, factory Bigsby	$19,000	$22,000
1963-1964	Cherry, factory Maestro	$19,000	$22,000
1963-1964	Cherry, factory stop tailpiece	$24,000	$29,000

1959 Gibson ES-330 TD

1960 Gibson ES-335

GUITARS

Gibson ES-335 Dot Reissue

1960 Gibson ES-345TD

MODEL YEAR	FEATURES	EXC. COND. LOW	HIGH
1963-1964	Sunburst, factory Bigsby	$19,000	$22,000
1963-1964	Sunburst, factory Maestro	$19,000	$22,000
1963-1964	Sunburst, factory stop tail	$24,000	$29,000
1965	Cherry or sunburst, trapeze or tremolo	$6,800	$8,500
1966	Burgundy Metallic (unfaded)	$6,500	$8,000
1966	Cherry or sunburst, trapeze or tremolo	$5,500	$7,000
1966	Pelham Blue (unfaded)	$7,500	$9,000
1967	Black	$5,500	$6,500
1967	Burgundy Metallic (unfaded)	$6,000	$7,000
1967	Cherry or sunburst trapeze or tremelo	$5,000	$6,000
1967	Pelham Blue (unfaded)	$7,000	$8,000
1968	Burgundy Metallic (unfaded)	$5,000	$6,000
1968	Cherry or sunburst trapeze or tremolo	$5,000	$5,500
1968	Pelham Blue (unfaded)	$6,500	$7,500
1969	Cherry or sunburst, trapeze or tremolo	$4,000	$5,000
1969	Walnut finish option	$3,500	$4,000
1970	Cherry or sunburst, trapeze or tremolo	$3,200	$4,000
1970	Walnut finish option	$3,200	$3,500
1971-1976	Cherry or sunburst, trapeze or tremolo	$3,000	$3,750
1971-1976	Walnut finish option	$3,000	$3,600
1977-1979	Various colors, coil tap	$2,600	$3,000
1980-1981	Various colors	$2,300	$2,800

ES-335 Dot

1981-1990. Reissue of 1960 ES-335 and replaces ES-335 TD. Name changed to ES-335 Reissue. Various color options including highly figured wood.

1981-1984	Natural	$2,300	$2,800
1981-1990		$1,850	$2,300

ES-335 Dot CMT (Custom Shop)

1983-1985. Custom Shop ES-335 Dot with curly maple top and back, full-length center block, gold hardware, various colors.

1983-1985		$2,800	$3,000

ES-335 Reissue

1991-present. Replaced the ES-335 DOT, dot inlays, various color options including highly figured wood. Renamed the 1959 ES-335 Dot Reissue in '98. A block inlay version, called the 1963 ES-335 Block Reissue also became available in '98.

1991-1997		$2,000	$2,300
2000-2005	Blond option	$2,000	$2,300

MODEL YEAR	FEATURES	EXC. COND. LOW	HIGH
2000-2005	Sunburst (standard)	$2,000	$2,100
2006	Memphis, updated block	$1,800	$1,900
2007	Wood and finish options	$1,900	$2,400

ES-335-12

1965-1971. 12-string version of the 335.

1965		$3,000	$3,400
1966-1967	Various colors	$2,800	$3,100
1968-1971		$2,600	$3,000

ES-335 '59 Historic Collection

1998-2000, 2002-present. Historical Series based upon 1959 ES-335 dot neck, figured maple top, nickel hardware.

1998-2000	Dot marker	$3,000	$3,400
2002-2007	Dot marker	$3,000	$3,400

ES-335 '60s Block Inlay

2007. Made in Memphis facility, plain maple top, small block markers.

2007		$2,300	$2,400

ES-335 '63 Historic Collection

1998-2000, 2002-present. Historical Series based upon 1963 ES-335 with small block markers, figured maple top, nickel hardware.

1998-2000	1st release	$2,700	$3,000
2002-2007	2nd release	$2,800	$3,300

ES-335 Alvin Lee

2006-present. Custom Division Nashville, 50 made, features reflect Alvin Lee's Big Red ES-335 complete with decal art, cherry red, includes certificate of authenticity (if missing value is reduced). There is also an unlimited version without certificate.

2006-2007	With certificate	$2,800	$3,500

ES-335 Artist

1981. Off-set dot markers, large headstock logo, metal truss rod plate, gold hardware, 3 control knobs with unusual toggles and input specification.

1981		$2,200	$2,500

ES-335 Centennial

1994. Centennial edition, gold medallion in headstock, diamond inlay in tailpiece, cherry.

1994		$3,500	$4,000

ES-335 Custom Shop

1980s-1990s. Gibson Custom Shop logo on the back of the headstock, various color options including highly figured wood.

1980s		$2,600	$2,900
1990s		$2,500	$2,800

ES-335 Custom Shop Dot

2007. Custom Shop limited edition, ES-335 specs with P90s replacing humbucker pickups, stop tailpiece.

2007	P-90s	$2,100	$2,200

ES-335 Diamond Edition

2006. Trini Lopez style diamond f-holes, Bigsby tailpiece option, gold hardware, Pelham Blue, pearl white or black pearl.

2006		$2,150	$2,250

The *Vintage Guitar Price Guide* shows low to high values for items in all-original excellent condition, and, where applicable, with original case or cover.

MODEL YEAR	FEATURES	EXC. COND. LOW	HIGH

ES-335 Eric Clapton Crossroads '64 reissue

2005. Reissue of EC's, with certificate

2005		$9,500	$11,800

ES-335 Jimmy Wallace Reissue

| 1980 | Blond | $2,700 | $3,000 |

ES-335 Larry Carlton

2006-present. Mr. 335 logo on truss rod cover, block neck like Larry's guitar, vintage (faded) sunburst.

| 2006-2007 | | $2,300 | $2,600 |

ES-335 Limited Edition

2001. ES-335 style crown inlay on headstock, P-90 pickups.

| 2001 | | $2,200 | $2,300 |

ES-335 Pro

1979-1981. Two humbucking pickups with exposed coils, bound 'board, cherry or sunburst.

| 1979-1981 | | $1,850 | $2,050 |

ES-335 Roy Orbison

2006. About 70 made, RO serial number, black finish.

| 2006 | | $2,800 | $3,100 |

ES-335 Satin Finish

2007-present. Dot neck reissue style with satin finish on plain maple.

| 2007 | | $1,400 | $1,500 |

ES-335 Showcase Edition

1988. Guitar of the Month series, limited production, transparent white/beige finish, black gothic-style hardware, EMG pickups.

| 1988 | | $2,300 | $2,500 |

ES-335 Studio

1986-1991. No f-holes, 2 Dirty Finger humbuckers, bound body, cherry or ebony.

| 1986-1991 | | $1,250 | $1,500 |

ES-335 TD CRR

1979. Country Rock Regular, 2 stereo pickups, coil-tap, sunburst.

| 1979 | | $2,500 | $3,000 |

ES-336

1996-1998. Custom Shop smaller sized ES-335 with smaller headstock, dot markers.

| 1996-1998 | All options | $1,700 | $2,300 |

ES-340 TD

1968-1973. The 335 with a laminated maple neck, master volume and mixer controls, various colors.

| 1968-1969 | | $2,800 | $3,200 |
| 1970-1973 | | $2,700 | $3,000 |

ES-345 TD

1959-1983. The 335 with Vari-tone, stereo, 2 humbuckers, gold hardware, double parallelogram inlays, stop tailpiece '59-'64 and '82-'83, trapeze tailpiece '65-'82.

1959	Cherry, Bigsby	$17,000	$20,000
1959	Cherry, stud tail	$22,000	$25,000
1959	Natural, Bigsby	$28,000	$35,000
1959	Natural, stud tail	$35,000	$45,000
1959	Sunburst, Bigsby	$17,000	$20,000
1959	Sunburst, stud tail	$22,000	$25,000
1960	Cherry, Bigsby	$16,000	$19,000
1960	Cherry, stud tail	$20,000	$24,000
1960	Natural, Bigsby	$27,000	$33,000
1960	Natural, stud tail	$34,000	$43,000
1960	Sunburst, Bigsby	$16,000	$19,000
1960	Sunburst, stud tail	$20,000	$24,000
1961	Cherry, Bigsby	$15,000	$18,000
1961	Cherry, stud tail	$19,000	$23,000
1961	Sunburst, Bigsby	$15,000	$18,000
1961	Sunburst, stud tail	$19,000	$23,000
1962-1964	Bigsby	$12,000	$15,000
1962-1964	Stud tail	$16,000	$19,000
1965	Various colors	$4,500	$6,000
1966	Various colors	$4,000	$5,000
1967	Various colors	$3,900	$4,800
1968	Various colors	$3,500	$4,000
1969	Various colors	$3,200	$3,900
1970	Various colors	$3,100	$3,800
1971-1976	Various colors	$3,000	$3,700
1977-1979	Various colors	$2,900	$3,600
1980-1983	Various colors	$2,300	$2,800

ES-345 Reissue

2002-present. ES-345 features with 6-position Varitone selector, gold hardware, stop tailpiece, various colors.

| 2002-2007 | | $2,200 | $2,500 |

ES-347 TD/ES-347 S

1978-1993. 335-style with gold hardware, tune-o-matic bridge, 2 Spotlight double-coil pickups, coil-tap, bound body and neck, S added to name in '87.

| 1978-1984 | | $2,000 | $2,200 |
| 1987-1993 | | $2,000 | $2,200 |

ES-350

1947-1956. Originally the ES-350 Premier, full body archtop, single-cut, 1 P-90 pickup until end of '48, 2 afterwards.

1947-1948	Natural, 1 pickup	$6,000	$7,500
1947-1948	Sunburst, 1 pickup	$5,500	$6,500
1949-1956	Natural, 2 pickups	$7,000	$8,500
1949-1956	Sunburst, 2 pickups	$6,000	$7,000

ES-350 T

1955-1963. McCarty era, called the ES-350 TD in early-'60s, thinline archtop, single-cut (round '55-'60 and '77-'81, pointed '61-'63), 2 P-90 pickups '55-'56, humbuckers after, gold hardware.

1956	Natural, P-90s	$7,500	$8,300
1956	Sunburst, P-90s	$5,500	$6,300
1957-1959	Natural, humbuckers	$10,500	$12,800
1957-1959	Sunburst, humbuckers	$9,000	$11,000
1960-1963	Natural	$9,000	$10,000
1960-1963	Sunburst	$7,000	$8,500

ES-350 T (2nd Issue)

1977-1981. Norlin era, second issue of ES-350 T.

| 1977-1981 | Natural | $3,500 | $4,000 |
| 1977-1981 | Sunburst | $3,000 | $3,500 |

1996 Gibson ES-335 Custom Shop

Gibson ES-345 reissue

Gibson ES-355

1961 Gibson ETG-150

MODEL YEAR	FEATURES	EXC. COND. LOW	HIGH

ES-350 Centennial
1994. ES-350 with all the Centennial Custom Shop appointments.

1994		$3,600	$4,000

ES-350 T Limited Edition Reissue
1990s. Special medallion on back of headstock.

1990s		$3,200	$3,600

ES-355 TD
1958-1970. A 335-style with large block inlays, multi-bound body and headstock, 2 humbuckers, the 355 model was standard with a Bigsby, sideways or Maestro vibrato, non-vibrato models were an option. The prices shown assume a vibrato tailpiece, a factory stop tailpiece was considered an advantage and will fetch more. Early examples have factory Bigsby vibratos, early '60s have sideways vibratos, and late '60s have Maestro vibratos, cherry finish was the standard finish.

1958	Cherry, PAFs, stop tail	$25,000	$30,000
1958-1960	Cherry, PAFs, vibrato	$19,000	$23,500
1959	Cherry, PAFs, stop tail	$24,000	$30,000
1960	Cherry, PAFs, stop tail	$24,000	$29,000
1961	Cherry, PAFs, stop tail	$23,000	$29,000
1961	Cherry, PAFs, vibrato	$18,000	$22,000
1962	Cherry, PAFs, stop tail	$23,000	$28,000
1962	Cherry, PAFs, vibrato	$17,000	$21,000
1963-1964	Cherry, pat. #, vibrato	$13,000	$16,000
1965	Burgundy Metallic (unfaded)	$7,000	$8,500
1965	Cherry or sunburst	$6,500	$7,800
1966	Burgundy Metallic (unfaded)	$6,000	$6,500
1966	Cherry or sunburst	$5,500	$6,000
1967	Burgundy Metallic (unfaded)	$5,000	$5,500
1967	Cherry or sunburst	$4,500	$5,000
1968	Various colors	$4,500	$5,000
1969-1970		$3,500	$4,500

ES-355 TD Limited Custom Shop
2006-present. Mono, Bigsby or stop tail.

2006-2007		$3,000	$3,400

ES-355 Centennial
1994. Custom Shop Guitar of the Month in June '94, high-end custom appointments, gold-plated hardware, sunburst.

1994		$3,500	$4,000

ES-355 TDSV
1959-1982. Stereo version of ES-355 with Vari-tone switch, a mono version was available but few were made, the 355 model was standard with a Bigsby, sideways or Maestro vibrato, non-vibrato models were an option. The prices shown assume a vibrato tailpiece.

MODEL YEAR	FEATURES	EXC. COND. LOW	HIGH

A factory stop tailpiece was considered an advantage and will fetch more, early examples have factory Bigsby vibratos, early-'60s have sideways vibratos and late-'60s have Maestro vibratos, cherry finish was standard, walnut became available in '69.

1959-1960	Bigsby	$19,000	$21,000
1961-1962	Sideways, late PAFs	$15,000	$17,000
1962	Maestro, late PAFs	$15,000	$17,000
1963-1964	Maestro, pat. #	$11,000	$13,500
1965	Burgundy Metallic (unfaded), Maestro	$6,500	$8,000
1965	Cherry or sunburst, Maestro	$6,000	$7,500
1966	Burgundy Metallic (unfaded) Maestro	$5,500	$6,000
1966	Cherry or sunburst, Maestro	$5,000	$5,500
1967	Cherry or sunburst, Maestro	$4,000	$4,500
1968	Various colors, Maestro	$4,000	$4,500
1969	Various colors, Bigsby	$3,500	$4,500
1970-1982	Various colors, Bigsby	$3,500	$4,000

ES-355 TDSV/79
1980. Offered with stereo or monaural circuitry and dual output jacks.

1980		$3,700	$4,200

ES-369
1982. A 335-style with 2 exposed humbucker pickups, coil-tap, sunburst.

1982		$1,700	$2,100

ES-446
1999-2003. Single cut semi-hollow, 2 humbuckers, Bigsby, Custom Shop.

1999-2003	Various colors	$2,000	$2,250

ES-775
1990-1993. Single-cut hollowbody, 2 humbuckers, gold hardware, ebony, natural or sunburst.

1990-1993		$2,300	$2,700

ES-Artist
1979-1985. Double-cut thinline, semi-hollowbody, no f-holes, 2 humbuckers, active electronics, gold hardware, ebony, fireburst or sunburst.

1979-1985		$2,300	$2,500

EST-150 (Tenor)
1937-1940. Tenor version of ES-150, renamed ETG-150 in '40, sunburst.

1937-1940		$3,000	$3,500

ETG-150 (Tenor)
1940-1942, 1947-1971. Renamed from EST-150, tenor version of ES-150, 1 pickup, sunburst.

1937-1942		$3,000	$3,500
1947-1959		$2,400	$2,500
1960-1964		$2,400	$2,500
1965-1971		$2,000	$2,200

The *Vintage Guitar Price Guide* shows low to high values for items in all-original excellent condition, and, where applicable, with original case or cover.

MODEL YEAR	FEATURES	EXC. COND. LOW	HIGH

Everly Brothers

1962-1972. Jumbo flat-top, huge double 'guard, star inlays, natural is optional in '63 and becomes the standard color in '68, reintroduced as the J-180 Everly Brothers in '86.

1962-1964	Black	$9,000	$10,000
1963	Natural option	$9,000	$10,000
1965-1966	Black	$7,000	$7,500
1967	Black	$6,500	$7,000
1968-1969	Natural replaces black	$4,500	$5,000
1970-1972	Natural	$4,000	$4,500

Explorer

1958-1959, 1963. Some '58s shipped in '63, korina body, 2 humbuckers. The Explorer market is a very specialized and very small market, with few genuine examples available and a limited number of high-end buyers. The slightest change to the original specifications can mean a significant drop in value. The narrow price ranges noted are for all original examples that have the original guitar case.

1958-1959		$255,000	$305,000
1963		$200,000	$250,000

Explorer (Alder body)

1983-1989. Alder body, 2 humbuckers, maple neck, ebony 'board, dot inlays, triangle knob pattern, referred to as Explorer 83 in '83.

1983-1989	Custom colors limited run	$1,200	$1,500
1983-1989	Standard finishes	$1,000	$1,200

Explorer (Mahogany body)

1976-1982. Mahogany body, 2 humbucking pickups.

1976		$2,300	$2,800
1977		$2,100	$2,600
1978		$2,000	$2,500
1979		$1,900	$2,200
1980-1982		$1,800	$2,200

Explorer '76/X-plorer

1990-present. Mahogany body and neck, rosewood 'board, dot inlays, 2 humbucking pickups, name changed to X-plorer in 2002.

1990-1999	Standard finish	$650	$800
1998	Sunburst or natural limited run	$900	$1,100
2000-2006	Various colors	$725	$900
2007	Explorer '76	$725	$800

Explorer 90 Double

1989-1990. Mahogany body and neck, 1 single-coil and 1 humbucker, strings-thru-body.

1989-1990		$900	$1,100

Explorer Centennial

1994 only. Les Paul Gold finish, 100 year banner inlay at 12th fret, diamonds in headstock and gold-plated knobs, Gibson coin in rear of headstock, only 100 made.

1994		$3,600	$4,500

Explorer CMT/The Explorer

1981-1984. Flamed maple body, bound top, exposed-coil pickups, TP-6 tailpiece.

1981-1984		$1,500	$1,875

Explorer Gothic

1998-2003. Gothic Series with black finish and hardware.

1998-2003		$700	$850

Explorer Heritage

1983. Reissue of '58 Explorer, korina body, gold hardware, inked serial number, limited edition.

1983	Black	$2,400	$3,000
1983	Natural	$2,900	$3,500
1983	White	$2,400	$3,000

Explorer II (E/2)

1979-1983. Five-piece maple and walnut laminate body sculptured like V II, ebony 'board with dot inlays, 2 humbucking pickups, gold-plated hardware, natural finish.

1979-1983	Figured maple top option	$1,700	$2,100

Explorer III

1984-1985. Alder body, 3 P-90 pickups, 2 control knobs.

1984-1985	Chrome hardware	$775	$950
1984-1985	Chrome hardware, locking trem	$750	$900
1985	Black hardware, Kahler	$750	$900

Explorer (Limited Edition Korina)

1976. Limited edition korina body replaces standard mahogany body, natural.

1976		$2,700	$3,300

Explorer Korina

1982-1984. Korina body and neck, 2 humbucking pickups, gold hardware, standard 8-digit serial (versus the inked serial number on the Heritage Explorer of the same era).

1982-1984		$3,400	$3,600

X-plorer V New Century

2006-2007. Full-body mirror 'guard, mahogany body and neck, 2 humbuckers, mirror truss rod cover.

2006-2007		$600	$700

X-plorer Pro

2007-2008. Explorer model updated with smaller, lighter weight mahogany body, 2 humbuckers, ebony or natural.

2007-2008		$700	$800

F-25 Folksinger

1963-1971. 14-1/2" flat-top, mahogany body, most have double white 'guard, natural.

1963-1964		$1,200	$1,400
1965-1966		$900	$1,100
1967-1969		$800	$1,000
1970-1971		$800	$1,000

Firebird I

1963-1969. Reverse body and 1 humbucker '63-mid-'65, non-reversed body and 2 P-90s mid-'65-'69.

1963	Sunburst, reverse	$9,000	$12,000
1964	Cardinal Red, reverse	$11,000	$14,000
1964	Sunburst, reverse	$7,000	$9,000
1965	Cardinal Red, reverse	$10,000	$13,000

1959 Gibson Explorer

1964 Gibson Firebird I

1965 Gibson Firebird III

1964 Gibson Firebird VII

MODEL YEAR	FEATURES	EXC. COND. LOW	HIGH
1965	Custom colors, non-reverse	$8,000	$10,000
1965	Sunburst, non-reverse, 2 P-90s	$3,500	$4,200
1965	Sunburst, reverse	$6,500	$8,500
1966-1967	Custom colors, non-reverse	$6,400	$7,000
1966-1967	Sunburst, non-reverse	$3,200	$3,400
1968-1969	Sunburst, non-reverse	$3,000	$3,200

Firebird I 1963 Reissue Historic Collection

1999-2006. Neck-thru, reverse body, Firebird logo on 'guard, various colors including sunburst and Frost Blue.

1999-2006		$2,100	$2,600

Firebird I Custom Shop

1991-1992. Limited run from Custom Shop, reverse body, 1 pickup, gold-plated, sunburst.

1991-1992		$2,100	$2,500

Firebird 76

1976-1978. Reverse body, gold hardware, 2 pickups.

1976	Bicentennial, red/white/blue Firebird logo	$2,900	$3,500
1977-1978		$2,200	$2,700

Firebird I/ Firebird 76

1980-1982. Reintroduced Firebird 76 but renamed Firebird I.

1980-1982		$2,600	$2,700

Firebird II/Firebird 2

1981-1982. Maple body with figured maple top, 2 full size active humbuckers, TP-6 tailpiece.

1981-1982		$1,800	$2,200

Firebird III

1963-1969. Reverse body and 2 humbuckers '63-mid-'65, non-reversed body and 3 P-90s mid-'65-'69.

1963	Cardinal Red	$16,000	$22,000
1963	Golden Mist	$16,000	$22,000
1963	Polaris White	$15,000	$20,000
1963	Sunburst	$11,500	$13,500
1964	Cardinal Red, reverse	$15,000	$20,000
1964	Golden Mist, reverse	$15,000	$20,000
1964	Pelham Blue	$15,000	$20,000
1964	Polaris White, reverse	$14,000	$19,000
1964	Sunburst, reverse	$11,000	$13,000
1965	Frost Blue, non-reverse	$11,000	$15,000
1965	Frost Blue, reverse	$14,000	$18,000
1965	Inverness Green, non-reverse	$11,000	$15,000
1965	Iverness Green, reverse	$14,000	$18,000
1965	Sunburst, non-reverse, 3 P-90s	$4,000	$5,200

MODEL YEAR	FEATURES	EXC. COND. LOW	HIGH
1965	Sunburst, reverse, 2 P-90s (trans. model)	$4,000	$5,500
1965	Sunburst, reverse, mini humbuckers	$8,000	$11,000
1966	Pelham Blue	$10,000	$13,700
1966-1967	Frost Blue	$10,000	$13,700
1966-1967	Sunburst, non-reverse	$3,700	$4,800
1967	Pelham Blue	$10,000	$13,000
1968	Pelham Blue	$5,300	$7,000
1968	Sunburst	$3,500	$4,700
1969	Pelham Blue	$5,000	$6,000
1969	Sunburst	$3,300	$4,300

Firebird III '64 Reissue (Custom Shop)

2000-present. Maestro, includes color option.

2000-2007		$1,400	$1,700

Firebird Non-Reverse Reissue

2002. Non-reverse body, 2 humbucker pickups.

2002		$1,400	$1,500

Firebird Studio/Firebird III Studio

2004-present. Two humbuckers, dot markers, tune-o-matic and bar stoptail, reverse body, dark cherry finish.

2004-2008		$800	$900

Firebird V

1963-1969, 1994-present. Two humbuckers, reverse body '63-mid-'65, non-reversed body mid-'65-'69.

1963	Pelham Blue	$23,000	$29,000
1963	Sunburst	$14,000	$19,000
1964	Cardinal Red, reverse	$22,000	$27,000
1964	Sunburst, reverse	$14,000	$17,000
1965	Cardinal Red, reverse	$20,000	$25,000
1965	Sunburst, non-reverse	$5,100	$6,500
1965	Sunburst, reverse	$10,000	$13,000
1966-1967	Cardinal Red, non-reverse	$14,000	$16,000
1966-1967	Sunburst, non-reverse	$5,000	$6,300
1968-1969	Sunburst	$5,000	$6,000

Firebird V Celebrity Series

1990-1993. Reverse body, gold hardware, 2 humbuckers, various colors.

1990-1993		$1,300	$1,600

Firebird V Guitar Trader Reissue

1982. Guitar Trader commissioned Firebird reissue, only 15 made, sunburst or white.

1982		$2,600	$2,900

Firebird V Limited Edition Zebrawood

2007. Limited edition from Gibson USA, 400 made, zebrawood reverse body.

2007		$1,300	$1,400

Firebird V Medallion

1972-1973. Reverse body, 2 humbuckers, Limited Edition medallion mounted on body.

1972-1973		$6,000	$7,000

MODEL YEAR	FEATURES	EXC. COND. LOW	HIGH
Firebird V Reissue			

1990-present. Reverse body, 2 humbuckers.

| 1990-1999 | Various colors | $1,200 | $1,500 |
| 2000-2007 | | $1,200 | $1,300 |

Firebird V-12

1966-1967. Non-reverse Firebird V-style body with standard six-on-a-side headstock and split diamond headstock inlay (like ES-335-12 inlay), dot markers, special twin humbucking pickups (like mini-humbuckers).

| 1966-1967 | Custom colors | $10,000 | $13,900 |
| 1966-1967 | Sunburst | $4,700 | $6,500 |

Firebird VII

1963-1969. Three humbuckers, reverse body '63-mid-'65, non-reversed body mid-'65-'69, sunburst standard.

1963	Sunburst	$18,000	$24,000
1964	Sunburst	$17,000	$22,000
1965	Custom colors	$19,000	$26,000
1965	Sunburst, non-reverse	$7,500	$10,000
1965	Sunburst, reverse	$15,000	$18,000
1966-1967	Sunburst, non-reverse	$8,000	$10,000
1968	Custom colors	$9,000	$12,000
1968	Sunburst, non-reverse	$6,100	$7,600
1969	Sunburst, non-reverse	$5,800	$7,200

Firebird VII (Historic/Custom Shop)

1997-present. Historic Collection, standard color is Vintage Sunburst, other colors available.

| 1997-2004 | Custom colors | $3,000 | $3,500 |
| 1997-2004 | Sunburst | $2,600 | $3,000 |

Firebird VII Centennial

1994 only. Headstock medallion, sunburst.

| 1994 | | $3,600 | $4,500 |

Firebird VII Reissue

2003-present. Reverse body, 3 mini-pickups, block markers, vibrola, matching headstock finish.

2003-2007	Blue Mist	$1,450	$1,550
2003-2007	Cherry (dark see-through)	$1,450	$1,550
2003-2007	Firebird Red	$1,450	$1,550
2003-2007	Sunburst	$1,450	$1,550

FJ-N Jumbo Folk Singer

1963-1967. Square shoulders, jumbo flat-top, natural finish with deep red on back and sides.

| 1963-1964 | | $2,900 | $3,300 |
| 1965-1967 | | $2,500 | $2,800 |

Flamenco 2

1963-1967. Natural spruce top, 14 3/4", cypress back and sides, slotted headstock, zero fret.

| 1963-1964 | | $1,800 | $2,200 |
| 1965-1967 | | $1,600 | $2,000 |

Flying V

1958-1959, 1962-1963. Only 81 shipped in '58 and 17 in '59, guitars made from leftover parts and sold in '62-'63, natural korina body, string-thru-body design.

As with any ultra high-end instrument, each instrument should be evaluated on a case-by-case basis. The

Flying V market is a very specialized market, with few untouched examples available, and a limited number of high-end buyers. The price ranges noted are for all-original, excellent condition guitars with the original Flying V case. The slightest change to the original specifications can mean a significant drop in value.

| 1958-1959 | | $150,000 | $225,000 |

Flying V (Mahogany)

1966-1970, 1975-1980. Mahogany body, around 200 were shipped for '66-'70. Gibson greatly increased production of Flying Vs in '75. See separate listing for the '71 Medallion V version.

1966	Cherry or sunburst	$15,000	$18,500
1967-1970	Cherry or sunburst	$12,200	$15,200
1975	Various colors	$3,600	$4,200
1976	Various colors	$3,500	$4,100
1977	Various colors	$3,300	$3,500
1978	Various colors	$2,900	$3,300
1979	Silverburst	$3,800	$4,500
1979	Various colors	$2,800	$3,200
1980	Various colors	$2,500	$3,000
1979-1980	Silverburst	$3,700	$4,500

Flying V (Mahogany string-through-body)

1981-1982. Mahogany body, string-thru-body design, only 100 made, most in white, some red or black possible.

| 1981-1982 | Black, red or white | $2,600 | $2,900 |

Flying V Heritage

1981-1982. Limited edition based on '58 specs, korina body, 4 colors available.

| 1981-1982 | Natural | $4,400 | $4,600 |
| 1981-1982 | Various colors | $4,000 | $4,400 |

Flying V (Korina)

1983. Name changed from Flying V Heritage, korina body, various colors.

| 1983 | | $3,400 | $3,600 |

Flying V Reissue/'67 Flying V/V Factor X

1990-present. Called Flying V Reissue first year, then '67 Flying V until '03, then V Factor X, mahogany body.

1990-2004	Rare colors	$1,000	$1,250
1990-2004	Various colors	$800	$975
2005-2007		$825	$850

Flying V '58 (Historic/Custom Shop)

1991-present. Historic Collection, based on '58/'59 Flying V, gold hardware, natural korina.

| 1991-2007 | | $4,500 | $5,100 |

Flying V '67 (Historic/Custom Shop)

1997-2004. Historic Collection, '67 Flying V specs, korina body, natural or opaque colors.

| 1997-2004 | | $3,000 | $3,500 |

Flying V '90 Double

1989-1990. Mahogany body, stud tailpiece, 1 single-coil and 1 double-coil humbucker, Floyd Rose tremolo, ebony, silver or white.

| 1989-1990 | | $1,000 | $1,250 |

1968 Gibson Flying V

1979 Gibson Flying V (mahogany)

GUITARS

Gibson Flying V Hendrix Psychedelic

1970s Gibson Heritage

MODEL YEAR / FEATURES	EXC. COND. LOW	HIGH
Flying V '98		
1998. Mahogany body, '58 style controls, gold or chrome hardware.		
1998	$950	$1,000
Flying V Centennial		
1994 only. 100th Anniversary Series, all gold, gold medalion, other special appointments.		
1994	$3,600	$4,500
Flying V CMT/The V		
1981-1985. Maple body with a curly maple top, 2 pickups, stud tailpiece, natural or sunburst.		
1981-1985	$1,500	$1,850
Flying V Custom (Limited Edition)		
2002. Appointments similar to Les Paul Custom, including black finish, only 40 made.		
2002	$3,500	$3,800
Flying V Designer Series		
1983-1984. Custom paint finish.		
1983-1984	$950	$1,150
Flying V Gothic/'98 Gothic		
1998-2003. Satin black finish, black hardware, moon and star markers.		
1998-2003	$600	$750
Flying V Hendrix Hall of Fame		
Late-1991-1993. Limited Edition (400 made), numbered, black.		
1991-1993	$2,200	$2,300
Flying V Hendrix Psychedelic		
2005-present. Hand-painted 1967 Flying V replica, 300 made, includes certificate, instruments without the certificate are worth less than the amount shown.		
2005-2006	$7,000	$8,000
Flying V I/V '83/Flying V (no pickguard)		
1981-1988. Introduced as Flying V I, then renamed Flying V '83 in 1983, called Flying V from '84 on. Alder body, 2 exposed humbuckers, maple neck, ebony 'board, dot inlays, black rings, no 'guard, ebony or ivory finish, designed for lower-end market.		
1981-1988	$850	$1,050
Flying V II		
1979-1982. Five-piece maple and walnut laminate sculptured body (1980 catalog states top is either walnut or maple), ebony 'board with dot inlays, 2 V-shaped pickups (2 Dirty Fingers humbuckers towards end of run), gold-plated hardware, natural.		
1979-1982	$1,900	$2,300
Flying V Lenny Kravitz		
2002. Custom Shop, 125 made.		
2002	$2,600	$2,800
Flying V Lonnie Mack		
1993-1994. Mahogany body with Lonnie Mack-style Bigsby vibrato, cherry.		
1993-1994	$3,500	$4,300
Flying V Medallion		
1971. Mahogany body, stud tailpiece, numbered Limited Edition medallion on bass side of V, 350 made in '71 (3 more were shipped in '73-'74).		
1971-1974	$6,000	$7,500

MODEL YEAR / FEATURES	EXC. COND. LOW	HIGH
Flying V New Century		
2006-2007. Full-body mirror 'guard, mahogany body and neck, 2 humbuckers, Flying V style neck profile, mirror truss rod cover.		
2006-2007	$600	$700
Flying V Primavera		
1994. Primavera (light yellow/white mahogany) body, gold-plated hardware.		
1994 Natural yellow/white	$1,600	$2,000
1994 Various special colors	$1,500	$1,850
Flying V Rudolph Schenker		
1993. Only 103 made, black and white body and headstock, signature on 'guard.		
1993	$2,400	$2,500
Flying V Voodoo		
2002-2003. Black finish, red pickups.		
2002-2003	$1,000	$1,200
Futura		
1982-1984. Deep cutout solidbody, 2 humbucker pickups, gold hardware, black, white or purple.		
1982-1984	$825	$1,025
GB-1		
1922-1930s. Guitar-banjo, 6-string neck, walnut, renamed GB-5 in '23.		
1920-1930s Diamond flange	$1,600	$2,000
1920-1930s Thick rim (Mastertone-style)	$1,600	$2,000
GB-3		
1923-1931. Style 4 appointments, maple.		
1920-1931 Archtop (Mastertone-style)	$2,300	$2,600
1920-1931 Two-piece flange	$2,300	$2,600
GB-4		
1923-1931. Style 4 appointments, 14" rim.		
1923-1931	$3,500	$4,000
Gospel		
1973-1979. Flat-top, square shoulders, laminated maple back and sides, arched back, Dove of Peace headstock inlay, natural.		
1973-1979	$750	$925
Gospel Reissue		
1992-1997. Flat-top, laminated mahogany back and sides and arched back, natural or sunburst.		
1992-1997	$900	$1,100
GS-1 Classical		
1950-1956. Mahogany back and sides.		
1950-1956	$1,000	$1,200
GS-2 Classical		
1950-1956. Maple back and sides.		
1950-1959	$1,000	$1,200
GS-5 Classical		
1954-1956. Rosewood back and sides, renamed C-5 Classical in '57.		
1954-1959	$1,600	$1,900
GS-35 Classical/Gut String 35		
1939-1942. Spruce top, mahogany back and sides, only 39 made.		
1939-1942	$2,400	$2,800

MODEL YEAR	FEATURES	EXC. COND. LOW	HIGH
GS-85 Classical/Gut String 85			
1939-1942. Rosewood back and sides.			
1939-1942		$4,700	$5,800
GY (Army-Navy)			
1918-1921. Slightly arched top and back, low-end budget model.			
1918-1921	Sheraton Brown	$750	$925
Harley Davidson Limited Edition			
1994-1995. Body 16" wide, flat-top, Harley Davidson in script and logo, 1500 sold through Harley dealers to celebrate 100th Anniversary of Harley.			
1994-1995	Black	$2,300	$2,650
Heritage			
1964-1982. Flat-top dreadnought, square shoulders, rosewood back and sides (Brazilian until '67, Indian '68 on), bound top and back, natural finish.			
1964	Brazilian rosewood	$2,000	$2,300
1965-1966	Brazilian rosewood	$1,400	$1,600
1967-1969	Brazilian rosewood	$1,300	$1,500
1969-1982	Indian rosewood	$1,000	$1,300
Heritage-12			
1968-1970. Flat-top dreadnought, 12 strings, Indian rosewood back and sides, bound top and back, natural finish.			
1968-1970		$1,300	$1,500
HG-00 (Hawaiian)			
1932-1942. Hawaiian version of L-00, 14 3/4" flat-top, mahogany back and sides, bound top, natural.			
1932-1947		$2,900	$3,500
HG-20 (Hawaiian)			
1929-1933. Hawaiian, 14 1/2" dreadnought-shaped, maple back and sides, round soundhole and 4 f-holes.			
1929-1933		$2,900	$3,500
HG-22 (Hawaiian)			
1929-1932. Dreadnought, 14", Hawaiian, round soundhole and 4 f-holes, white paint logo, very small number produced.			
1929-1932		$3,500	$4,200
HG-24 (Hawaiian)			
1929-1932. 16" Hawaiian, rosewood back and sides, round soundhole plus 4 f-holes, small number produced.			
1929-1932		$7,300	$9,100
HG-Century (Hawaiian)			
1937-1938. Hawaiian, 14 3/4" L-C Century of Progress.			
1937-1938		$3,000	$3,700
Howard Roberts Artist			
1976-1980. Full body single-cut archtop, soundhole, 1 humbucking pickup, gold hardware, ebony 'board, various colors.			
1976-1980		$2,400	$2,700
Howard Roberts Artist Double Pickup			
1979-1980. Two pickup version of HR Artist.			
1979-1980		$2,500	$2,800
Howard Roberts Custom			
1974-1981. Full body single-cut archtop, soundhole, 1 humbucking pickup, chrome hardware, rosewood 'board, various colors.			
1974-1981		$2,300	$2,700

MODEL YEAR	FEATURES	EXC. COND. LOW	HIGH
Howard Roberts Fusion			
1979-1988. Single-cut, semi-hollowbody, 2 humbucking pickups, chrome hardware, ebony 'board, TP-6 tailpiece, various colors, renamed Howard Roberts Fusion IIL in '88.			
1979-1988		$1,900	$2,300
Howard Roberts Fusion III			
1991-present. Renamed from Howard Roberts Fusion IIL, same specs except for finger-style tailpiece and gold hardware, ebony or sunburst.			
1991-1999		$1,800	$2,200
2000-2005		$1,700	$2,000
Hummingbird			
1960-present. Flat-top acoustic, square shoulders, mahogany back and sides, bound body and neck.			
1960	Cherry Sunburst, 156 shipped	$3,700	$4,600
1961-1962	Cherry Sunburst, 1000 shipped	$3,500	$4,300
1962-1963	Cherry Sunburst, maple option	$3,400	$4,200
1963-1964	Cherry Sunburst, 2700 shipped	$3,300	$4,100
1965	Cherry Sunburst	$3,000	$3,600
1966	Cherry Sunburst or natural	$2,900	$3,500
1967-1968	Screwed 'guard	$2,500	$3,100
1969	Natural or sunburst	$2,400	$2,900
1970	Natural or sunburst	$2,100	$2,700
1971-1980	Double X, block markers	$2,000	$2,400
1981-1983	Non-volute neck	$1,700	$2,000
1984	Double para. Markers	$1,500	$1,700
1985-1988	Single X	$1,500	$1,700
1989-1999	25 1/2" scale	$1,500	$1,750
1994	100 Years 1894-1994 label	$1,600	$1,800
2000-2008		$1,600	$1,750
Hummingbird Custom			
2001. Highly flamed koa back and sides, spruce top, gloss finish.			
2001		$4,100	$4,300
Invader			
1983-1988. Single cutaway solid mahogany body, two humbucker pickups, four knobs with three-way selector switch, stop tailpiece, bolt-on maple neck.			
1983-1988	Black, red, white	$525	$650
1983-1988	Silverburst	$550	$675
J-25			
1983-1985. Flat-top, laminated spruce top, synthetic semi-round back, ebony 'board, natural or sunburst.			
1983-1985		$400	$475
J-30			
1985-1993. Dreadnought-size flat-top acoustic, mahogany back and sides, sunburst, renamed J-30 Montana in '94.			
1985-1993		$1,000	$1,100

1974 Gibson Howard Roberts

1968 Gibson Hummingbird

'40s Gibson J-45

1973 Gibson J-50 Deluxe

J-30 Montana

1994-1997. Renamed from J-30, dreadnought-size flat-top acoustic, mahogany back and sides, sunburst.

MODEL YEAR	FEATURES	EXC. COND. LOW	HIGH
1994-1997		$900	$1,100

J-30 RCA Limited Edition

1991. Limited edition for RCA Nashville, RCA logo on headstock.

1991		$1,300	$1,400

J-40

1971-1982. Dreadnought flat-top, mahogany back and sides, economy satin finish.

1971-1982	Natural satin finish	$1,000	$1,100

J-45

1942-1982, 1984-1993, 1999-present. Dreadnought flat-top, mahogany back and sides, round shoulders until '68 and '84 on, square shoulders '69-'82, sunburst finish (see J-50 for natural version) then natural finish also available in '90s, renamed J-45 Western in '94, renamed Early J-45 in '97 then renamed J-45 in '99. The prices noted are for all-original crack free instruments. A single professionally repaired minor crack that is nearly invisible will reduce the value only slightly. Two or more, or unsightly repaired cracks will devalue an otherwise excellent original acoustic instrument. Repaired cracks should be evaluated on a case-by-case basis.

1942	Sunburst, banner logo	$6,000	$6,900
1943	Sunburst, banner logo	$5,300	$6,400
1944	Sunburst, banner logo	$5,200	$6,300
1945	Sunburst, banner logo	$5,100	$6,200
1945	Sunburst, rare maple body	$6,000	$6,100
1946	Sunburst, banner logo	$5,000	$6,000
1947	Sunburst	$4,500	$5,600
1948	Sunburst	$4,400	$5,500
1949	Sunburst	$4,400	$5,400
1950	Sunburst	$4,300	$5,300
1951	Sunburst	$4,300	$5,200
1952	Sunburst	$4,300	$5,100
1953	Sunburst	$4,300	$5,000
1954	Sunburst	$4,200	$5,000
1955	Sunburst	$4,300	$4,900
1956	Sunburst	$3,900	$4,500
1957	Sunburst	$3,900	$4,400
1958	Sunburst	$3,700	$4,200
1959	Sunburst	$3,700	$4,100
1960	Sunburst	$3,400	$3,700
1961	Sunburst	$3,400	$3,600
1962	Sunburst	$3,300	$3,600
1963	Sunburst	$2,800	$3,400
1964	Sunburst	$2,700	$3,100
1965	Sunburst	$2,400	$2,700
1966	Sunburst	$2,200	$2,700
1967	Sunburst	$1,800	$2,200

MODEL YEAR	FEATURES	EXC. COND. LOW	HIGH
1968	Black, round shoulders	$1,700	$2,100
1968	Sunburst, Gibson 'guard	$1,700	$2,100
1969	Sunburst, round shoulders	$1,600	$2,000
1969	Sunburst, square shoulders	$1,600	$2,000
1970	Sunburst, square shoulders	$1,600	$1,900
1971	Sunburst	$1,600	$1,800
1972	Sunburst	$1,500	$1,700
1973	Sunburst	$1,300	$1,500
1974	Sunburst	$1,200	$1,400
1975-1981	Sunburst	$1,100	$1,300
1984-1993	Various colors	$1,050	$1,300
1999-2006	Sunburst	$1,100	$1,400

J-45/Early J-45

1997-1998. J-45 model name for '97 and '98.

1997-1998		$1,050	$1,300

J-45 1968 Reissue

2004. Special run using '68 specs including Gibson logo 'guard, black finish.

2004		$1,700	$1,800

J-45 Buddy Holly Limited Edition

1995-1996. 250 made.

1995-1996		$1,700	$2,000

J-45 Celebrity

1985. Acoustic introduced for Gibson's 90th anniversary, spruce top, rosewood back and sides, ebony 'board, binding on body and 'board, only 90 made.

1985		$1,700	$2,000

J-45 Custom

2001. Custom Shop decal, double bound slope shoulder, solid spruce top, figured maple sides and back.

2001		$1,600	$1,800

J-45 Rosewood

1999-present. Rosewood body, spruce top.

1999-2006		$1,700	$1,900

J-45 Vine

2003. Custom Shop model, D-size with sloped shoulders, Indian rosewood sides and back, fancy pearl and abalone vine inlay in ebony 'board, pearl Gibson logo and crown, natural gloss finish.

2003		$2,600	$3,300

J-45 Western

1994-1997. Previously called J-45, name changed to Early J-45 in '97.

1994-1997		$1,200	$1,700

J-50

1942, 1945-1981, 1990-1995, 1998-present. Dreadnought flat-top, mahogany back and sides, round shoulders until '68, square shoulders after, natural finish (see J-45 for sunburst version).

1945		$5,100	$6,200
1946		$5,000	$6,000
1947		$4,500	$5,600
1948		$4,400	$5,500
1949		$4,400	$5,400
1950		$4,300	$5,300

MODEL YEAR	FEATURES	EXC. COND. LOW	HIGH
1951		$4,300	$5,200
1952		$4,300	$5,100
1953		$4,300	$5,000
1954		$4,200	$5,000
1955		$4,300	$4,900
1956		$3,900	$4,500
1957		$3,900	$4,400
1958		$3,700	$4,200
1959		$3,700	$4,100
1960		$3,400	$3,700
1961		$3,400	$3,600
1962		$3,300	$3,600
1963		$2,800	$3,400
1964		$2,700	$3,100
1965		$2,400	$2,700
1966		$2,200	$2,700
1967		$1,800	$2,200
1968	Sunburst, Gibson 'guard	$1,700	$2,100
1969	Round shoulders	$1,600	$2,000
1969	Square shoulders	$1,600	$2,000
1970	Square shoulders	$1,600	$1,900
1971		$1,600	$1,800
1972		$1,500	$1,700
1973		$1,300	$1,500
1974		$1,200	$1,400
1975-1981		$1,100	$1,300
1990-1995		$1,000	$1,300
1998-2000s		$1,100	$1,400

J-55 (Jumbo 55) Limited Edition
1994 only. 16" flat-top, spruce top, mahogany back and sides, 100 made, sunburst.

1994		$1,500	$1,700

J-55 (Reintroduced)
1973-1982. Flat-top, laminated mahogany back and sides, arched back, square shoulders, sunburst. See Jumbo 55 listing for '39-'43 version.

1973-1982		$1,000	$1,250

J-60
1992-1999. Solid spruce top dreadnought, square shoulders, Indian rosewood back and sides, multiple bindings, natural or sunburst.

1992-1999		$1,300	$1,400

J-60 Curly Maple
1993 and 1996. Curly maple back and sides, limited edition from Montana shop, natural.

1993		$1,600	$1,900
1996		$1,600	$1,900

J-100
1970-1974, 1985-1997. Flat-top jumbo, multi-bound top and back, black 'guard, dot inlays, mahogany back and sides, '80s version has maple back and sides, dot inlays and tortoise shell 'guard, current model has maple back and sides, no 'guard, and J-200 style block inlays.

1972-1974	Mahogany	$1,300	$1,500
1985-1989	Maple	$1,300	$1,500
1990-1997		$1,300	$1,500

J-100 Xtra
1991-1997, 1999-2004. Jumbo flat-top, mahogany back and sides, moustache bridge, dot inlays, various colors, J-100 Xtra Cutaway also available, reintroduced in '99 with maple back and sides and single-bound body.

1991-2004		$1,450	$1,550

J-150
1999-2005. Super jumbo body, solid spruce top, figured maple back and sides (later rosewood), MOP crown inlays, moustache bridge with transducer.

1999-2005		$1,775	$1,825

J-160E
1954-1979. Flat-top jumbo acoustic, 1 bridge P-90 pickup, tone and volume controls on front, sunburst finish, reintroduced as J-160 in '90.

MODEL YEAR	FEATURES	EXC. COND. LOW	HIGH
1954	19 frets, large bridge dots	$5,200	$6,200
1955	20 frets	$5,000	$6,000
1956-1959		$5,000	$6,000
1960		$4,500	$5,500
1961		$4,700	$5,700
1962	Beatles' vintage June '62	$4,800	$6,000
1963		$4,800	$6,000
1964	Lennon's 2nd model	$4,500	$6,000
1965		$3,300	$4,100
1966		$3,200	$4,000
1967		$2,900	$3,500
1968		$2,600	$3,100
1969		$2,100	$2,500
1970		$1,600	$1,900
1971-1979		$1,450	$1,700

J-160E Reissue
1991-1997, 2003-present. Reintroduced J-160E with spruce top, solid mahogany back and sides.

2003-2007	Also called Peace	$1,450	$1,500

J-180 Special Edition
1993. Gibson Bozeman, only 36 made, Everly Brother specs, large double white pearloid 'guard.

1993		$2,600	$2,700

J-180/Everly Brothers/The Everly Brothers
1986-2005. Reissue of the '62-'72 Everly Brothers model, renamed The Everly Brothers ('92-'94), then The Everly ('94-'96), then back to J-180, black.

1986-2005		$1,400	$1,600

J-185 EC Blues King
1999-present. Acoustic/electric, rounded cutaway, flamed maple back and sides, sunburst.

1999-2008		$1,600	$1,900

J-185 EC Rosewood
1999-present. Acoustic/electric, rounded cutaway, Indian rosewood back and sides.

2002-2008		$1,700	$1,900

J-185 Reissue
1990-1995, 1999-present. Flat-top jumbo, figured maple back and sides, bound body and neck, natural or sunburst, limited run of 100 between '91-'92.

1990-1995		$1,600	$1,900
1999-2008		$1,600	$1,900

1987 Gibson J-180

Gibson J-185 EC

Gibson J-200

1961 Gibson Johnny Smith

MODEL YEAR	FEATURES	EXC. COND. LOW	HIGH

J-185 Vine
2005-present. 185 with vine fretboard inlay.

2005-2006		$2,600	$3,300

J-185/J-185N
1951-1959. Flat-top jumbo, figured maple back and sides, bound body and neck, sunburst (185) or natural (185N).

1951-1959	Natural	$13,000	$18,000
1951-1959	Sunburst	$11,000	$14,000

J-185-12
2000-2005. 12-string J-185, flamed maple sides and back.

2000-2005		$1,600	$1,900

J-190 EC Super Fusion
2001-2004. Jumbo single cut acoustic/electric, spruce top, curly maple back and sides, neck pickup and Fishman Piezo,

2001-2004		$1,500	$1,700

J-200/SJ-200/J-200N/SJ-200N
1947-present. Labeled SJ-200 until ca.'54. Super Jumbo flat-top, maple back and sides, see Super Jumbo 200 for '38-'42 rosewood back and sides model, called J-200 Artist for a time in the mid-'70s, renamed '50s Super Jumbo 200 in '97 and again renamed SJ-200 Reissue in '99. Currently again called the SJ-200. 200N indicates natural option.

1947-1949	Natural option	$16,000	$17,000
1947-1949	Sunburst	$14,500	$16,000
1950-1959	Natural option	$10,000	$14,000
1950-1959	Sunburst	$9,000	$11,000
1960	Natural option	$9,000	$10,000
1960	Sunburst	$8,000	$9,000
1961	Natural option	$7,000	$9,000
1961	Sunburst	$6,000	$8,500
1962	Natural option	$7,000	$9,000
1962	Sunburst	$6,000	$8,500
1963	Natural option	$7,000	$9,000
1963	Sunburst	$6,000	$8,500
1964	Natural option	$6,700	$8,700
1964	Sunburst	$5,900	$8,400
1965	Natural or sunburst	$4,500	$6,000
1966	Natural or sunburst	$3,600	$4,500
1967-1969	Natural or sunburst	$3,500	$3,600
1970-1979	Natural or sunburst	$2,600	$3,000
1980-1989	Natural or sunburst	$2,500	$2,800
1990-1999	Natural or sunburst	$2,000	$2,500
2000-2003	Natural or sunburst	$2,200	$2,500
2004-2007	Natural or sunburst	$2,200	$2,300

J-200 Celebrity
1985-1987. Acoustic introduced for Gibson's 90th anniversary, spruce top, rosewood back, sides and 'board, binding on body and 'board, sunburst, only 90 made.

1985-1987		$2,600	$3,100

J-200 Koa
1994. Figured Hawaiian Koa back and sides, spruce top, natural.

1994		$2,600	$2,900

J-250 R
1972-1973, 1976-1978. A J-200 with rosewood back and sides, sunburst, only 20 shipped from Gibson.

1972-1973		$2,500	$3,100
1976-1978		$2,500	$3,100

J-1000
1992. Jumbo cutaway, spruce top, rosewood back and sides, on-board electronics, diamond-shape markers and headstock inlay.

1992		$2,000	$2,100

J-2000/J-2000 Custom/J-2000 R
1986, 1992-1999. Cutaway acoustic, rosewood back and sides (a few had Brazilian rosewood or maple bodies), ebony 'board and bridge, Sitka spruce top, multiple bindings, sunburst or natural. Name changed to J-2000 Custom in '93 when it became available only on a custom-order basis.

1986	J-2000 R, rosewood	$2,800	$3,400
1986	J-2000, maple	$2,800	$3,400
1992	Rosewood	$2,800	$3,400
1993-1996	J-2000 Custom	$2,800	$3,400
1999	J-2000 Custom		
Cutaway	$3,400		$3,700

JG-0
1970-1972. Economy square shouldered jumbo, follows Jubilee model in '70.

1970-1972		$775	$950

JG-12
1970. Economy square shouldered jumbo 12-string, follows Jubilee-12 model in '70.

1970		$775	$950

Johnny A Signature Series
2004-present. Thinline semi-hollow, sharp double-cut, flamed maple top, humbucking pickups, Johnny A truss rod cover, gold plated hardware, Bigsby vibrato (part of his signature style), sunburst, includes certificate of authenticity.

2004-2007	Includes rare color option	$2,500	$3,000

Johnny Smith
1961-1989. Single-cut archtop, 1 humbucking pickup, gold hardware, multiple binding front and back, natural or sunburst. By '80 cataloged as JS model.

1961		$9,000	$9,400
1962		$9,000	$9,300
1963		$8,500	$8,900
1964		$8,500	$8,900
1965		$7,700	$7,900
1966		$7,000	$7,700
1967-1969		$6,500	$7,300
1970-1979		$6,000	$6,800
1980-1989		$5,800	$6,300

Johnny Smith Double
1963-1989. Single-cut archtop, 2 humbucking pickups, gold hardware, multiple binding front and back, natural or sunburst. By '80 cataloged as JSD model.

1961		$9,500	$10,300
1962		$9,400	$10,200

MODEL YEAR	FEATURES	EXC. COND. LOW	HIGH
1963		$9,100	$9,400
1964		$9,000	$9,300
1965		$7,900	$8,100
1966		$7,200	$7,900
1967-1969		$6,700	$7,500
1970-1979		$6,200	$7,000
1980-1989		$6,000	$6,500

Jubilee

1969-1970. Flat-top, laminated mahogany back and sides, single bound body, natural with black back and sides.

1969-1970		$700	$875

Jubilee Deluxe

1970-1971. Flat-top, laminated rosewood back and sides, multi-bound body, natural finish.

1970-1971		$875	$1,075

Jubilee-12

1969-1970. Flat-top, 12 strings, laminated mahogany back and sides, multi-bound, natural.

1969-1970		$875	$1,075

Jumbo

1934-1936. Gibson's first Jumbo flat-top, mahogany back and sides, round shoulders, bound top and back, sunburst, becomes the 16" Jumbo 35 in late-'36.

1934		$20,000	$25,000
1935		$19,000	$21,000
1936		$18,000	$20,000

Jumbo 35/J-35

1936-1942. Jumbo flat-top, mahogany back and sides, silkscreen logo, sunburst, reintroduced as J-35, square-shouldered dreadnought, in '83.

1936		$14,500	$17,000
1937		$14,000	$15,000
1938		$11,500	$14,000
1939		$9,500	$11,500
1940-1942		$8,000	$10,000

Jumbo 55/J-55

1939-1943. Flat-top dreadnought, round shoulders, mahogany back and sides, pearl inlaid logo, sunburst, reintroduced in '73 as J-55.

1939		$18,000	$20,000
1940-1943		$17,000	$19,000

Jumbo Centennial Special

1994. Reissue of 1934 Jumbo, natural, 100 made.

1994		$2,100	$2,300

Junior Pro

1987-1989. Single-cut, mahogany body, KB-X tremolo system 1 humbucker pickup, black chrome hardware, various colors.

1987-1989		$400	$500

Kalamazoo Award Model

1978-1981. Single-cut archtop, bound f-holes, multi-bound top and back, 1 mini-humbucker, gold-plated hardware, woodgrain 'guard with bird and branch abalone inlay, highly figured natural or sunburst.

1978-1981	Natural	$12,800	$14,000
1978-1981	Sunburst	$11,800	$13,000

L-0

1926-1933, 1937-1942. Acoustic flat-top, maple back and sides '26-'27, mahogany after.

1926-1933		$3,500	$4,100
1937-1942		$3,500	$4,100

MODEL YEAR	FEATURES	EXC. COND. LOW	HIGH
L-00			

1932-1946. Acoustic flat-top, mahogany back and sides, bound top to '36 and bound top and back '37 on.

1932-1939		$4,400	$4,500
1940-1946		$3,900	$4,300

L-00/Blues King

1991-1997, 1999-present. Reintroduced as L-00, called Blues King L-00 for '94-'97, back as L-00 for '99-'02, called Blues King '03-present.

1991-1997	L-00/Blues King	$1,200	$1,250
2003-2008	Blues King	$1,300	$1,400

L-1 (Archtop)

1902-1925. Acoustic archtop, single-bound top, back and soundhole, name continued on flat-top model in '26.

1902-1907	Standard 12.5" body	$1,400	$1,500
1908-1925	Standard 13.5" body	$1,500	$1,600

L-1 (Flat-Top)

1926-1937. Acoustic flat-top, maple back and sides '26-'27, mahogany after.

1926-1927	13 1/2" maple body, 12 frets	$4,000	$4,500
1928-1930	13 1/2" mahogany body, 12 frets	$4,000	$4,500
1931	14 3/4" mahogany body	$4,000	$4,500
1932-1937	14 frets	$4,000	$4,500

L-2 (Archtop)

1902-1926. Round soundhole archtop, pearl inlay on peghead, 1902-'07 available in 3 body sizes: 12.5" to 16", '24-'26 13.5" body width.

1902-1907	Standard 12.5" body	$1,500	$1,600
1924-1926	Standard 13.5" body	$1,600	$1,700

L-2 (Flat-Top)

1929-1935. Acoustic flat-top, rosewood back and sides except for mahogany in '31, triple-bound top and back, limited edition model in '94.

1929-1930	Natural, 14 3/4" body, 13 frets	$5,500	$5,700
1931	Argentine Gray, 13 frets	$5,000	$5,200
1932-1933	Natural, 13 frets	$5,000	$5,200
1934-1935	Natural, 14 frets	$5,000	$5,200

L-2 1929 Reissue

1993.

1993		$1,900	$2,100

L-3 (Archtop)

1902-1933. Acoustic archtop, available in 3 sizes: 12 1/2", 13 1/2", 16".

1902-1907	Standard 12.5" body	$1,700	$2,100
1908-1926	Standard 13.5" body	$1,800	$2,200
1927-1929	Oval soundhole	$2,100	$2,400

1965 Gibson Johnny Smith Double

1929 Gibson L-1

1915 Gibson L-4

1933 Gibson L-5

MODEL YEAR	FEATURES	EXC. COND. LOW	HIGH
L-4			
1912-1956. Acoustic archtop, 16" wide.			
1912-1927	Oval soundhole	$3,500	$4,000
1928-1934	Round soundhole	$3,500	$4,000
1935-1939	F-holes	$3,500	$4,000
1940-1945	F-holes	$2,700	$2,900
1946-1956	Crown peghead inlay, triple bound	$2,600	$2,800
L-4 A			
2003-2005. 15 3/4" lower bout, mid-size jumbo, rounded cutaway, factory electronics with preamp			
2003-2005		$1,150	$1,400
L-4 C/L-4 CN			
1949-1971. Single-cut acoustic archtop.			
1949-1959	Natural	$3,600	$4,500
1949-1959	Sunburst	$3,500	$4,200
1960-1964	Natural	$3,200	$4,000
1960-1964	Sunburst	$3,000	$3,700
1965-1966	Natural or sunburst	$2,800	$3,500
1967-1969	Natural or sunburst	$2,700	$3,300
1970-1971	Natural or sunburst	$2,500	$3,000
L-4 CES			
1958, 1969, 1986-present. Single pointed cutaway archtop, 2 humbuckers, gold parts, natural or sunburst, now part of Gibson's Custom Collection.			
1958	Natural, PAF humbuckers	$11,000	$13,000
1958	Sunburst, PAF humbuckers	$10,000	$12,000
1969	Natural	$4,500	$5,600
1969	Sunburst	$3,500	$4,300
1986-1989	Natural or sunburst	$2,600	$3,000
1990-1999	Natural or sunburst	$2,600	$3,000
2000s	Natural or sunburst	$2,600	$3,000
L-4 Special Tenor/Plectrum			
Late-1920s. Limited edition 4-string flat-top.			
1929		$2,400	$3,000
L-5			
1922-1958. Acoustic archtop, non-cut, multiple bindings, Lloyd Loar label until '24, 17" body by '35, Master Model label until '27, sunburst with natural option later.			
1922-1923	Loar era	$45,000	$55,000
1924	Lloyd Loar signed (Mar-Dec)	$49,000	$60,000
1924	Loar era, not signed	$45,000	$55,000
1925-1927	Master Model label	$27,000	$34,000
1928	Last dot markers	$19,000	$23,000
1929	Early 1929	$10,500	$13,500
1929-1930	Block markers	$10,400	$13,000
1931-1932	Kaufman vibrola	$11,000	$14,000
1931-1932	Standard trapeze	$10,000	$11,500
1933-1934	16" body	$8,500	$10,500
1935-1940	17" body	$7,500	$8,000
1939-1940	Natural option	$8,000	$9,000

MODEL YEAR	FEATURES	EXC. COND. LOW	HIGH
1946-1949	Natural option	$7,000	$8,000
1946-1949	Sunburst	$6,000	$7,000
1950-1958	Natural	$6,500	$8,000
1950-1958	Sunburst	$5,500	$7,000
L-5 '34 Non-Cutaway Historic			
1994. 1934 specs including block pearl inlays, bound snakehead peghead, close grained solid spruce top, figured solid maple sides and back, Cremona Brown sunburst finish, replica Grover open back tuners.			
1994		$5,000	$5,500
L-5 C			
1948-1982. Renamed from L-5 Premier (L-5 P), single rounded cutaway acoustic archtop, sunburst.			
1948	Natural	$14,000	$17,000
1948	Sunburst	$13,000	$15,000
1949	Natural	$13,000	$16,000
1949	Sunburst	$12,000	$14,000
1950-1955	Sunburst	$11,000	$13,000
1950-1959	Natural	$12,000	$15,000
1956-1959	Sunburst	$11,000	$12,500
1960-1962	Natural	$10,000	$12,500
1960-1962	Sunburst	$9,000	$11,200
1963-1964	Natural	$9,500	$12,000
1963-1964	Sunburst	$8,500	$11,500
1965-1966	Natural	$8,000	$10,000
1965-1966	Sunburst	$7,500	$9,300
1967-1969	Natural	$7,500	$9,300
1967-1969	Sunburst	$7,000	$8,700
1970-1972	Natural	$6,000	$7,500
1970-1972	Sunburst	$5,000	$6,200
1973-1975	Natural	$5,700	$6,000
1973-1975	Sunburst	$4,700	$5,000
1976-1982	Natural	$4,600	$5,700
1976-1982	Sunburst	$4,000	$4,700
L-5 CES			
1951-present. Electric version of L-5 C, single round cutaway (pointed mid-'60-'69), archtop, 2 pickups (P-90s '51-'53, Alnico Vs '54-mid-'57, humbuckers after), now part of Gibson's Historic Collection.			
1951-1957	Natural, single coils	$20,000	$24,000
1951-1957	Sunburst, single coils	$18,000	$21,000
1958-1959	Natural, PAFs	$27,000	$32,000
1958-1959	Sunburst, PAFs	$21,000	$26,000
1960-1962	Natural, PAFs	$22,000	$27,000
1960-1962	Sunburst, PAFs	$17,000	$21,000
1963-1964	Natural, pat. #	$14,000	$17,000
1963-1964	Sunburst, pat. #	$11,000	$13,500
1965-1966	Natural	$7,300	$9,100
1965-1966	Sunburst	$6,500	$8,100
1967-1969	Natural	$7,000	$8,500
1967-1969	Sunburst	$6,500	$7,500
1970-1972	Natural	$6,500	$7,500
1970-1972	Sunburst	$6,300	$6,900
1973-1975	Natural	$6,300	$7,000
1973-1975	Sunburst	$6,000	$6,800
1976-1979	Natural or sunburst	$6,000	$6,600
1980-1984	Kalamazoo made	$6,000	$6,500
1985-1992	Nashville made	$4,800	$5,600

MODEL YEAR	FEATURES	EXC. COND. LOW	HIGH

L-5 CES Custom Shop Historic Collection
1990s. Historic Collection Series, sunburst or natural.

1990s	100th Anniv., black	$5,100	$6,100
1990s	Natural, highly figured back	$5,000	$6,000
1990s	Sunburst	$4,800	$5,600

L-5 CT (George Gobel)
1959-1961. Single-cut, thinline archtop acoustic, some were built with pickups, cherry.

1959-1961		$19,000	$21,000

L-5 CT Reissue
1998-present. Historic Collection, acoustic and electric versions, natural, sunburst, cherry.

1998-2007		$5,200	$6,200

L-5 Premier/L-5 P
1939-1947. Introduced as L-5 Premier (L-5 P) and renamed L-5 C in '48, single rounded cutaway acoustic archtop.

1939-1940	Natural option	$18,000	$22,000
1939-1940	Sunburst	$16,000	$20,000

L-5 S
1972-1985, 2004-2005. Single-cut solidbody, multi-bound body and neck, gold hardware, 2 pickups (low impedence '72-'74, humbuckers '75 on), offered in natural, cherry sunburst or vintage sunburst. 1 humbucker version issued in '04 from Gibson's Custom, Art & Historic

1972-1974	Natural, gold hardware, low impedence pickups	$3,300	$3,800
1972-1974	Sunburst, low impedence pickups	$3,200	$3,700
1975-1980	Natural or sunburst, humbuckers	$4,000	$4,400
1975-1980	Natural, gold hardware, humbuckers	$4,100	$4,600

L-5 Studio
1996-2000. Normal L-5 dual pickup features, marble-style 'guard, translucent finish, dot markers.

1996-2000		$2,000	$2,250

L-5 Wes Montgomery Custom Shop
1993-present. Various colors.

1993-1999		$4,800	$5,600
2000-2006		$4,800	$5,600

L-6 S
1973-1975. Single-cut solidbody, 2 humbucking pickups, 6 position rotary switch, stop tailpiece, cherry or natural, renamed L-6 S Custom in '75.

1973-1975	Cherry or natural	$1,000	$1,200

L-6 S Custom
1975-1980. Renamed from the L-6 S, 2 humbucking pickups, stop tailpiece, cherry or natural.

1975-1980		$1,000	$1,200
1978-1979	Silverburst option	$1,600	$1,950

L-6 S Deluxe
1975-1981. Single-cut solidbody, 2 humbucking pickups, no rotary switch, strings-thru-body design, cherry or natural.

1975-1981		$1,050	$1,250

L-7
1932-1956. Acoustic archtop, bound body and neck, fleur-de-lis peghead inlay, 16" body '32-'34, 17" body X-braced top late-'34.

1932-1934	16" body	$2,600	$3,100
1935-1939	17" body, X-braced	$2,700	$3,200
1940-1950	Natural	$2,900	$3,500
1940-1950	Sunburst	$2,500	$3,000
1951-1956	Natural	$2,600	$3,000
1951-1956	Sunburst	$2,400	$2,800

L-7 C
1948-1972. Single-cut acoustic archtop, triple-bound top, sunburst or natural finish. Gibson revived the L-7 C name for a new acoustic archtop in 2002.

1948-1949	Natural	$5,000	$5,500
1948-1949	Sunburst	$4,200	$5,000
1950-1959	Natural	$5,000	$5,500
1950-1959	Sunburst	$4,200	$5,000
1960-1962	Natural	$4,100	$4,800
1960-1962	Sunburst	$3,900	$4,600
1963-1964	Natural	$3,900	$4,600
1963-1964	Sunburst	$3,300	$3,900
1965-1966	Natural	$3,300	$3,900
1965-1966	Sunburst	$3,200	$3,600
1967-1969	Natural	$3,300	$3,600
1967-1969	Sunburst	$2,900	$3,200
1970-1971	Natural or sunburst	$2,900	$3,200

L-10
1923-1939. Acoustic archtop, single-bound body and 'board.

1923-1934	Black, 16" body	$3,500	$4,000
1935-1939	Black or sunburst, 17" body, X-braced	$3,500	$4,000

L-12
1930-1955. Acoustic archtop, single-bound body, 'guard, neck and headstock, gold-plated hardware, sunburst.

1930-1934	16" body	$3,200	$3,900
1935-1939	17" body, X-braced	$3,200	$4,000
1940-1941	Parallel top braced	$3,000	$3,500
1946-1949	Post-war	$2,800	$3,500
1950-1955		$2,700	$3,100

L-12 Premier/L-12 P
1947-1950. L-12 with rounded cutaway, sunburst.

1947-1950		$5,300	$5,700

L-30
1935-1943. Acoustic archtop, single-bound body, black or sunburst.

1935-1943		$1,200	$1,500

L-37
1937-1941. 14-3/4" acoustic archtop, flat back, single-bound body and 'guard, sunburst.

1937-1941		$1,300	$1,600

L-48
1946-1971. 16" acoustic archtop, single-bound body, mahogany sides, sunburst.

1946-1949		$1,375	$1,500
1950-1959		$1,300	$1,450
1960-1964		$1,150	$1,300
1965		$900	$1,100
1966		$900	$1,075
1967-1971		$800	$900

1952 Gibson L-7

Gibson L-5 CT reissue

Gibson L-50

Gibson L-C Century of Progress

MODEL YEAR	FEATURES	EXC. COND. LOW	HIGH

L-50
1932-1971. 14 3/4" wide acoustic archtop, flat or arched back, round soundhole or f-holes, pearl logo pre-war, decal logo post-war, maple sides, sunburst.

1932-1934	14 3/4" body	$1,450	$1,700
1934-1943	16" body	$1,675	$1,900
1946-1949		$1,650	$1,900
1950-1960		$1,450	$1,800
1961-1964		$1,350	$1,450
1965		$1,000	$1,200
1966		$1,000	$1,175
1967-1971		$900	$1,000

L-75
1932-1939. 14 3/4" archtop with round soundhole and flat back, size increased to 16" with arched back in '35, small button tuners, dot markers, lower-end style trapeze tailpiece, pearl script logo, sunburst.

1932-1934	14 3/4" body	$1,700	$2,100
1934-1939	16" body	$2,200	$2,600

L-130
1999-2005. 14 7/8" lower bout, small jumbo, solid spruce top, solid bubinga back and sides, factory electronics with preamp.

1999-2005	$1,100	$1,200

L-200 Emmylou Harris
2002-present. SJ-200/J-200 reissue, L-series smaller and thinner than standard jumbo body, solid Sitka spruce top, flamed maple sides and back, gold hardware, crest markers, natural or sunburst.

2002-2007	$1,300	$1,500

L-C Century
1933-1941. Curly maple back and sides, bound body, white pearloid 'board and peghead (all years) and headstock (until '38), sunburst.

1933-1939	$4,750	$5,000
1940-1941	$4,350	$4,800

L-C Reissue
1994. Pearloid headstock and 'board.

1994	$2,350	$2,500

LC-1 Cascade
2002-2006. Acoustic/electric, advanced L-00-style, solid cedar top, quilted maple back and sides.

2002-2006	$1,200	$1,400

LC-2 Sonoma
2002-2006. Acoustic/electric, advanced L-00-style, solid cedar top, walnut back and sides.

2002-2006	$1,400	$1,700

LC-3 Caldera
2003-2004. Acoustic/electric, solid cedar top, solid flamed Koa back and sides, fancy appointments.

2003-2004	$1,950	$2,000

Le Grande
1993-present. Electric archtop, 17", formerly called Johnny Smith.

1993-2005	$6,000	$6,100

Les Paul
Following are models bearing the Les Paul name, beginning with the original Les Paul Model. All others are listed alphabetically as follows:

Les Paul Model
'52 Les Paul Goldtop
'54 Les Paul Goldtop
'56 Les Paul Goldtop
'57 Les Paul Goldtop
'57/'58 Les Paul Jr.
'58 Les Paul Flametop/Reissue/Standard
'59 Les Paul Flametop/Reissue/Standard
'60 Les Paul Corvette
'60 Les Paul Flametop/Standard
'60 Les Paul Jr.
'60 Les Paul Special
Les Paul (All Maple)
Les Paul 25/50 Anniversary
Les Paul 25th Silver Anniversary (Guitar Center)
Les Paul 30th Anniversary
Les Paul 40th Anniversary (from 1952)
Les Paul 40th Anniversary (from 1959)
Les Paul 55
Les Paul Ace Frehley Signature
Les Paul Artisan and Artisan/3
Les Paul Artist/L.P. Artist/Les Paul Active
Les Paul Bird's-Eye Standard
Les Paul Centennial ('56 LP Standard Goldtop)
Les Paul Centennial ('59 LP Special)
Les Paul Class 5
Les Paul Classic
Les Paul Classic Custom
Les Paul Classic Plus
Les Paul Classic Premium Plus
Les Paul Cloud 9 Series
Les Paul Custom
Les Paul Custom 20th Anniversary
Les Paul Custom 35th Anniversary
Les Paul Custom '54
Les Paul Custom Historic '54
Les Paul Custom Historic '57 Black Beauty
Les Paul Custom Historic '68
Les Paul Custom Lite
Les Paul Custom Lite (Show Case Ed.)
Les Paul Custom Mick Ronson '68
Les Paul Custom Music Machine
Les Paul Custom Plus
Les Paul Dale Earnhardt
Les Paul Dale Earnhardt Intimidator
Les Paul DC Pro
Les Paul DC Standard (Plus)
Les Paul DC Studio
Les Paul Deluxe
Les Paul Deluxe 30th Anniversary
Les Paul Deluxe '69 Reissue
Les Paul Deluxe Hall of Fame
Les Paul Deluxe Limited Edition
Les Paul Dickey Betts Goldtop
Les Paul Dickey Betts Red Top
Les Paul Elegant
Les Paul Florentine Plus
Les Paul Gary Moore Signature
Les Paul Goddess

Les Paul GT
Les Paul Guitar Trader Reissue
Les Paul HD.6-X Pro Digital
Les Paul Heritage 80
Les Paul Heritage 80 Award
Les Paul Heritage 80 Elite
Les Paul Indian Motorcycle
Les Paul Jim Beam
Les Paul Jimmy Page Signature
Les Paul Jimmy Page Signature Custom Shop
Les Paul Jimmy Page (Custom Authentic)
Les Paul Jimmy Wallace Reissue
Les Paul Joe Perry Signature
Les Paul Jr.
Les Paul Jr. 3/4
Les Paul Jr. Billie Joe Armstrong Signature
Les Paul Jr. Double Cutaway
Les Paul Jr. Special
Les Paul Jr. Tenor/Plectrum
Les Paul Jumbo
Les Paul KM (Kalamazoo Model)
Les Paul Leo's Reissue
Les Paul Limited Edition (3-tone)
Les Paul LP295 Goldtop
Les Paul Melody Maker
Les Paul Menace
Les Paul Music Machine 25th Anniversary
Les Paul Music Machine Brazilian Stinger
Les Paul Old Hickory
Les Paul Pee Wee
Les Paul Personal
Les Paul Pro Deluxe
Les Paul Pro Showcase Edition
Les Paul Professional
Les Paul Recording
Les Paul Reissue Flametop
Les Paul Reissue Goldtop
Les Paul Richard Petty LTD
Les Paul SG '61 Reissue
Les Paul SG Standard Authentic
Les Paul SG Standard Reissue
Les Paul Signature/L.P. Signature
Les Paul Slash Signature
Les Paul SmartWood Exotic
Les Paul SmartWood Standard
Les Paul SmartWood Studio
Les Paul Special
Les Paul Special (Reissue)
Les Paul Special 3/4
Les Paul Special Centennial
Les Paul Special Custom Shop
Les Paul Special Double Cutaway
Les Paul Special Tenor
Les Paul Spider-Man
Les Paul Spotlight Special
Les Paul Standard (Sunburst)
Les Paul Standard (SG body)
Les Paul Standard (reintroduced)
Les Paul Standard '58
Les Paul Standard '82
Les Paul Standard Lite
Les Paul Standard Plus
Les Paul Standard Premium Plus

Les Paul Standard Sparkle
Les Paul Strings and Things Standard
Les Paul Studio
Les Paul Studio Baritone
Les Paul Studio BFD
Les Paul Studio Custom
Les Paul Studio Faded
Les Paul Studio Gem
Les Paul Studio Gothic
Les Paul Studio Lite
Les Paul Studio Plus
Les Paul Studio Premium Plus
Les Paul Studio Swamp Ash/Swamp Ash Studio
Les Paul Supreme
Les Paul Tie Dye (St. Pierre)
Les Paul Tie Dye Custom Shop
Les Paul TV
Les Paul TV 3/4
Les Paul Ultima
Les Paul Vixen
Les Paul Voodoo/Voodoo Les Paul
Les Paul XR-I/XR-II/XR-III
Les Paul Zakk Wylde Signature
The Les Paul
The Paul
The Paul Firebrand Deluxe
The Paul II

Gibson Le Grande

Les Paul Model

1952-1958. The Goldtop, 2 P-90 pickups until mid-'57, humbuckers after, trapeze tailpiece until late-'53, stud tailpiece/bridge '53-mid-'55, Tune-o-matic bridge '55-'58, renamed Les Paul Standard in '58. All gold option add +10% if the neck retains 90% of the gold paint. All gold option with ugly green wear on the neck is equal to or below the value of a standard paint job. Some instruments had all mahogany bodies which did not have the maple cap. These instruments are of lower value than the standard maple on mahogany bodies. The all mahogany version, although more rare, has a 10% lower value. A factory installed Bigsby tailpiece will reduce value by 30%. A non-factory installed Bigsby will reduce value up to 50%.

MODEL YEAR	FEATURES	EXC. COND. LOW	HIGH
1952	1st made, un-bound neck	$31,000	$38,000
1952	5/8" knobs, bound neck	$22,000	$27,000
1953	1/2" knobs, trapeze tailpiece	$22,000	$26,000
1953	1/2" knobs, late-'53 stud tailpiece	$30,000	$38,000
1954	Stud tailpiece, wrap-around	$35,000	$45,000
1955	Stud tailpiece, wrap-around, early-'55	$38,000	$47,000
1955	Tune-o-matic tailpiece, late-'55	$49,000	$60,000
1956	Tune-o-matic tailpiece	$49,000	$60,000
1957	P-90s, early-'57	$49,000	$60,000

1952 Gibson Les Paul model

1957 Gibson Les Paul model

Gibson '59 Les Paul Standard VOS

MODEL YEAR	FEATURES	EXC. COND. LOW	HIGH
1957	PAF humbuckers, black plastic	$110,000	$140,000
1957	PAF humbuckers, white plastic	$115,000	$150,000
1958	PAF humbuckers	$115,000	$150,000

'52 Les Paul Goldtop
1997-2002. Goldtop finish, 2 P-90s, '52-style trapeze tailpiece/bridge.

1997-2002		$1,900	$2,250
1997-2002	Murphy aged	$2,300	$2,700

'54 Les Paul Goldtop
1998-2003. Goldtop finish, 2 P-90s, '53-'54 stud tailpiece/bridge.

1990s		$2,000	$2,300
2001	R-4 (very accurate)	$2,000	$2,300
2003	Brazilian rosewood, with certificate	$2,700	$3,300
2005-2007		$2,000	$2,300

'56 Les Paul Goldtop
1991-present. Renamed from Les Paul Reissue Goldtop. Goldtop finish, 2 P-90 pickups, now part of Gibson's Historic Collection.

1991-2005		$2,000	$2,300
2003	Brazilian rosewood, with certificate	$2,700	$3,300
2006-2007	V.O.S.	$2,000	$2,300

'57 Les Paul Goldtop
1993-present. Goldtop finish, 2 humbuckers, now part of Gibson's Historic Collection.

1993-1999		$2,100	$2,400
2000-2006	With certificate	$2,100	$2,400
2003	Brazilian rosewood, with certificate	$2,800	$3,400
2006-2007	V.O.S.	$2,100	$2,400
2007	R-7 wrap-around tailpiece	$2,100	$2,400

'57/'58 Les Paul Jr.
1998-present. Historic Collection reissue of slab body, double-cut Les Paul Jr. Originally labeled '57, changed to '58 in early 2000s.

1998-2004		$1,575	$1,700

'58 Les Paul Flametop/Reissue/Standard
1996-1998, 2001-present. Less top figure than '59 Reissue, also offered in plain top version ('94-'98), name changed to '58 Les Paul Reissue in '01, and '58 Les Paul Standard in '03. Now called the 1958 Les Paul Standard VOS. Part of Gibson's Historic Collection, sunburst.

1996-2005		$2,700	$3,300
2003	Brazilian rosewood, with certificate	$4,000	$5,000
2006-2007	V.O.S.	$2,100	$2,400
2006-2007	V.O.S. (chambered)	$2,800	$3,300
2007	V.O.S. Plain Top	$2,000	$2,100

'59 Les Paul Flametop/Reissue/Standard
1991-present. Renamed from Les Paul Reissue Flametop, for 2000-'05 called the 1959 Les Paul Reissue, in '06 this model became part of Gibson's Vintage Original Spec series and is called the '59 Les Paul Standard. Flame maple top, 2 humbuckers, thick '59-style neck, sunburst finish, part of Gibson's Historic

Collection, the original certificate authenticity adds value, an instrument without the matching certificate has less value. By '98 Gibson guaranteed only AAA Premium grade maple tops would be used.

1991-2003	R-9	$3,500	$4,000
1994	Murphy aged	$4,000	$4,500
2000	Murphy aged, highly flamed	$4,000	$5,000
2003	Brazilian rosewood, figured top	$6,000	$7,500
2003	Brazilian rosewood, Murphy aged	$6,000	$7,500
2003	Brazilian rosewood, plain top	$4,400	$5,500
2004	Limited run transparent color, certificate	$3,400	$3,900
2004-2005	Figured top	$3,500	$4,300
2004-2005	Murphy aged	$3,500	$4,500
2006-2007	LPR-9, Murphy aged	$3,500	$4,500
2007	VOS, R-9, highly flamed, certificate	$3,500	$4,300

'60 Les Paul Corvette
1995-1996. Custom Shop Les Paul, distinctive Chevrolet Corvette styling from '60, offered in 6 colors.

1995-1996		$4,500	$5,500

'60 Les Paul Flametop/Standard
1991-present. Renamed from Les Paul Reissue Flametop, flame maple top, 2 humbuckers, thinner neck, sunburst finish, part of Gibson's Historic Collection, in '06 this model became part of Gibson's Vintage Original Spec series and is called the '60 Les Paul Standard VOS.

1991-2005		$3,500	$4,000
2003	Brazilian rosewood, figured top	$6,000	$7,500
2003	Brazilian rosewood, Murphy aged	$6,000	$7,500
2004-2005	Murphy aged	$3,500	$4,500
2006-2007	VOS	$3,500	$4,500

'60 Les Paul Jr.
1992-2003. Historic Collection reissue.

1992-2003		$1,525	$1,700

'60 Les Paul Special
2005. Historic Collection reissue.

2005		$1,600	$1,800

Les Paul (All Maple)
1984. Limited run, all maple body, Super 400-style inlay, gold hardware.

1984		$3,100	$3,400

Les Paul 25/50 Anniversary
1978-1979. Regular model with 25/50 inlay on headstock, sunburst.

1978-1979	Moderate flame	$2,700	$3,100
1978-1979	Premium flame	$3,100	$3,800

The *Vintage Guitar Price Guide* shows low to high values for items in all-original excellent condition, and, where applicable, with original case or cover.

MODEL YEAR	FEATURES	EXC. COND. LOW	HIGH

Les Paul 25th Silver Anniversary (Guitar Center)

1978. Special order of 50 Les Paul Customs with metallic silver top, back, sides and neck, commissioned by Guitar Center of California, most have 25th Anniversary etched in tailpiece.

1978		$2,500	$2,700

Les Paul 30th Anniversary

1982-1984. Features of a 1958 Les Paul Goldtop, 2 humbuckers, 30th Anniversary inlay on 19th fret.

1982-1984		$2,500	$2,700

Les Paul 40th Anniversary (from 1952)

1991-1992. Black finish, 2 soapbar P-100 pickups, gold hardware, stop tailpiece, 40th Anniversary inlay at 12th fret.

1991-1992		$2,450	$2,650

Les Paul 40th Anniversary (from 1959)

1999. Reissue Historic, humbuckers, highly figured top.

1999		$3,600	$3,900

Les Paul 55

1974, 1976-1981. Single-cut Special reissue, 2 pickups. By '78 the catalog name is Les Paul 55/78.

1974	Sunburst	$1,500	$1,800
1974	TV limed yellow	$2,000	$2,500
1976-1981	Sunburst or Wine Red	$1,400	$1,700

Les Paul Ace Frehley Signature

1997-2001. Ace's signature inlay at 15th fret, 3 humbuckers, sunburst.

1997	1st year	$3,200	$3,300
1998-2001		$2,800	$3,200

Les Paul Artisan and Artisan/3

1976-1982. Carved maple top, 2 or 3 humbuckers, gold hardware, hearts and flowers inlays on 'board and headstock, ebony, sunburst or walnut.

1976-1982	2 pickups	$2,700	$3,000
1976-1982	3 pickups	$2,800	$3,200

Les Paul Artist/L.P. Artist/Les Paul Active

1979-1982. Two humbuckers (3 optional), active electronics, gold hardware, 3 mini-switches, multibound.

1979-1982	Fireburst, ebony or sunburst	$2,100	$2,400

Les Paul Bird's-Eye Standard

1999. Birdseye top, gold hardware, 2 humbucking pickups, transparent amber.

1999		$1,900	$2,200

Les Paul Centennial ('56 LP Standard Goldtop)

1994. Part of the Guitar of the Month program commemorating Gibson's 100th year, limited edition of 100, Goldtop Les Paul mahogany body with '56-style configuration, gold hardware, gold truss rod plate, gold medallion, engraved light-gold 'guard, with certificate of authenticity.

1994		$4,200	$5,200

Les Paul Centennial ('59 LP Special)

1994. Part of the Guitar of the Month program commemorating Gibson's 100th year, limited edition of 100, slab body Les Paul Special-style configuration, gold hardware, P-90 pickups, gold medallion, commemorative engraving in 'guard, cherry, with certificate of authenticity.

1994		$3,700	$4,400

Les Paul Class 5

2001-2005. Highly flamed or quilt top, or special finish, 1960 profile neck, weight relieved body, Burst Bucker humbucking pickups, several color options, Custom Shop.

2001-2006		$2,500	$2,800
2001-2006	Stars and Stripes, 50 made	$3,000	$4,000

Les Paul Classic

1990-1998, 2001-2008. Early models have 1960 on pickguard, two exposed humbucker pickups, Les Paul Model on peghead until '93, Les Paul Classic afterwards.

1990-1998	All gold neck and body	$1,500	$1,800
1990-1998	Various colors, plain top	$1,400	$1,650
2001-2008	Various colors	$1,400	$1,550

Les Paul Classic Custom

2007-present. Custom with two exposed pickups, black finish, gold hardware.

2007		$1,900	$2,200

Les Paul Classic Plus

1991-1996, 1999-2000. Les Paul Classic with fancier maple top, 2 exposed humbucker pickups.

1991-1996	Price depends on top figure	$1,700	$1,950
1999-2000	Price depends on top figure	$1,700	$1,950

Les Paul Classic Premium Plus

1993-1996, 2001-2002. Les Paul Classic with AAA-grade flame maple top, 2 exposed humbucker pickups.

1993-1996	Price depends on top figure	$2,100	$2,300

Les Paul Cloud 9 Series

2003-2006. Special lightweight Les Paul series run for three dealers, Music Machine, Dave's Guitar Shop, and Wildwood Guitars, '59 Les Paul body specs, CR serial series number, '59 or '60 neck profile options, various colors, other reissue models available.

2003	'59 or '60 models	$3,500	$3,700
2003-2004	'52, '54, '56, '57, '58 models	$2,900	$3,200

Les Paul Custom

1953-1963 (renamed SG Custom late '63), 1968-present. Les Paul body shape except for SG body '61-'63, 2 pickups (3 humbuckers mid-'57-'63 and '68-'70, 3 pickups were optional various years after), '75 Price List shows a Les Paul Custom (B) model which is equipped with a Bigsby tailpiece versus a wraparound. By '80 offered as Les Paul Custom/Gold Parts and / Nickel Parts, because gold plating wears more quickly

Gibson Les Paul Ace Frehley Signature

Gibson Les Paul Class 5

GUITARS

1956 Gibson Les Paul Custom

*Gibson Les Paul
Dale Earnhardt*

MODEL YEAR	FEATURES	EXC. COND. LOW	HIGH
	*and is therefore less attractive there is no difference in price between an '80s Gold Parts and Nickel Parts instrument.*
1954-1957	Single coils	$38,000	$47,000
1954-1957	Single coils, factory Bigsby	$33,000	$41,000
1957-1960	2 Humbuckers	$90,000	$100,000
1957-1960	2 Humbuckers, factory Bigsby	$70,000	$94,000
1957-1960	3 Humbuckers	$90,000	$100,000
1957-1960	3 Humbuckers, factory Bigsby	$70,000	$94,000
1961	Early '61, 3 PAFs, single-cut	$90,000	$100,000
1961-1963	Black option, SG body, factory stop tail	$28,000	$36,000
1961-1963	Black option, SG body, side-pull vibrato	$22,000	$26,000
1961-1963	White, SG body, factory stop tail	$28,000	$36,000
1961-1963	White, SG body, Maestro vibrola	$22,000	$26,000
1961-1963	White, SG body, Maestro, ebony block	$22,000	$26,000
1961-1963	White, SG body, side-pull vibrato	$22,000	$26,000
1968-1969	Black, 1-piece body	$10,000	$14,000
1968-1969	Black, 3-piece body	$7,000	$9,000
1970-1972	Volute, 2 pickups	$3,300	$4,100
1970-1972	Volute, 3 pickups	$3,600	$4,200
1973-1974	Volute, 2 pickups	$2,800	$3,500
1973-1974	Volute, 3 pickups	$3,300	$4,000
1975-1976	Maple fretboard option	$2,700	$3,300
1975-1976	Maple fretboard option, blond	$2,700	$3,300
1975-1976	Volute, 2 pickups	$2,500	$3,000
1975-1976	Volute, 3 pickups	$3,000	$3,400
1977-1978	Maple fretboard option, blond, 2 pickups	$2,700	$3,300
1977-1978	Volute, 2 pickups	$2,500	$3,000
1977-1978	Volute, 3 pickups	$2,900	$3,300
1979-1982	2 pickups	$2,300	$2,500
1979-1982	3 pickups	$2,325	$2,525
1979-1982	Silverburst, volute, 2 pickups	$2,500	$2,800
1983-1985	2 pickups	$2,300	$2,500
1983-1985	3 pickups	$2,325	$2,525
1986	2 pickups	$2,300	$2,500
1986	3 pickups	$2,325	$2,525
1987-1989	Various colors	$2,000	$2,500
1990-1999	Limited Edition color series	$2,200	$2,500
1990-1999	Various colors	$1,800	$2,200

MODEL YEAR	FEATURES	EXC. COND. LOW	HIGH
2000	Silverburst, 300 made	$2,200	$2,500
2000-2005	Various colors	$2,000	$2,500
2003	Silverburst	$2,200	$2,500
2007	Silverburst re-issue, certificate	$2,200	$2,500

Les Paul Custom 20th Anniversary
1974. Regular 2-pickup Custom, with 20th Anniversary inlay at 15th fret, black or white.

1974		$3,200	$4,000

Les Paul Custom 35th Anniversary
1989. Gold hardware, 3 pickups, carved, solid mahogany body and neck, 35th Anniversary inlay on headstock, black.

1989		$3,300	$4,100

Les Paul Custom '54
1972-1973. Reissue of 1954 Custom, black finish, Alnico V and P-90 pickups.

1972-1973		$4,500	$5,900

Les Paul Custom Historic '54
1991-present. Historic Collection, 1954 appointments and pickup configuration, black, gold hardware.

1991-2005		$2,300	$2,800

Les Paul Custom Historic '57 Black Beauty
1991-present. Black finish, gold hardware, 2 or 3 humbucker pickups, part of Gibson's Historic Collection.

1991-2006	2 pickups	$2,800	$3,500
1991-2006	3 pickups	$3,100	$3,700

Les Paul Custom Historic '68
2003-2007. Historic Collection, ebony block marked fretboard, gold hardware, flamed maple top available, 2 pickups.

2003-2007		$2,500	$3,000

Les Paul Custom Lite
1987-1990. Carved maple top, ebony 'board, pearl block inlays, gold hardware, PAF pickups, bound neck, headstock and body.

1987-1990		$2,000	$2,300

Les Paul Custom Lite (Show Case Ed.)
1988. Showcase Edition, only 200 made, gold top.

1988		$2,100	$2,500

Les Paul Custom Mick Ronson '68
2007. Custom Shop, includes certificate and other authentication material.

2007		$3,600	$4,000

Les Paul Custom Music Machine
2003. Custom run for dealer Music Machine with special serial number series, chambered body style for reduced body weight, quilt tops.

2003		$3,400	$3,800

Les Paul Custom Plus
1991-1998. Regular Custom with figured maple top, sunburst finish or colors.

1991-1998		$2,000	$2,500

Les Paul Dale Earnhardt
1999. 333 made, Dale's image and large number 3 on the front and headstock, Dale Earnhardt signature script on fretboard, chrome hardware, several pieces of literature and an original certificate are part of the

MODEL YEAR	FEATURES	EXC. COND. LOW	HIGH

overall package, lack of an original matching serial number certificate will reduce the value, a lower serial number may add value.

| 1999 | | $3,300 | $4,000 |

Les Paul Dale Earnhardt Intimidator
2000. 333 made, Dale's 'Goodwrench' car on the front of the body, The Intimidator inlay on the fretboard, includes certificate, chrome hardware.

| 2000 | | $3,300 | $4,000 |

Les Paul DC Pro
1997-1998. Custom Shop, body like a '59 Les Paul Junior, carved highly figured maple top, various options. Name revived in '07.

| 1997-1998 | | $1,800 | $1,900 |

Les Paul DC Standard (Plus)
1998-1999, 2001-2006. Double-cut, highly flamed maple top, mahogany set-neck, translucent lacquer finishes in various colors, typical Les Paul Model stencil logo on headstock and 'Standard' notation on truss rod cover, reintroduced as Standard Lite in '99 but without Les Paul designation on headstock or truss rod cover.

| 1998-1999 | | $1,100 | $1,300 |
| 2001-2006 | | $1,200 | $1,400 |

Les Paul DC Studio
1997-1999. DC Series double-cut like late '50s models, carved maple top, 2 humbucker pickups, various colors.

| 1997-1999 | | $750 | $900 |

Les Paul Deluxe
1969-1985. In 1969, the Goldtop Les Paul Standard was renamed the Deluxe. Two mini-humbuckers (regular humbuckers optional in mid-'70s). Mid-'70s sparkle tops, made at the request of the Sam Ash chain, are worth more than standard finishes. The market slightly favors the Goldtop finish, but practically speaking condition is more important than finish, such that all finishes fetch about the same amount (with the exception of the sparkle finish). Initially, the Deluxe was offered only as a Goldtop and the first year models are more highly prized than the others. Cherry sunburst was offered in '71, cherry in '71-'75, walnut in '71-'72, brown sunburst in '72-'79, natural in '75, red sparkle in '75 only, blue sparkle in '75-'77, wine red/see-thru red offered '75-'85. In '99, the Deluxe was reissued for its 30th anniversary.

1969	Goldtop	$4,500	$5,500
1970	Goldtop	$4,000	$5,000
1971-1975	Goldtop	$3,400	$4,200
1971-1975	Natural	$2,200	$2,700
1971-1975	Red (solid)	$2,400	$2,700
1971-1975	Sunburst	$2,300	$3,200
1971-1975	Wine	$2,400	$2,700
1975	Red sparkle, fewer made	$3,900	$4,400
1975-1977	Blue sparkle, more made	$2,900	$3,400
1976-1979	Goldtop	$2,700	$3,000
1976-1979	Various colors	$2,200	$2,700
1980-1985	Various colors	$2,000	$2,500

Les Paul Deluxe 30th Anniversary
1999. 30th Anniversary of the 1969 introduction of the Les Paul Deluxe, Limited Edition logo on the lower back of the headstock neck, Deluxe logo on truss rod cover, Wine Red.

| 1999 | | $1,700 | $2,000 |

Les Paul Deluxe '69 Reissue
2000-2005. Mini-humbuckers, gold top

| 2000-2005 | | $1,400 | $1,500 |

Les Paul Deluxe Hall of Fame
1991. All gold finish.

| 1991 | | $1,800 | $2,000 |

Les Paul Deluxe Limited Edition
1999-2002. Limited edition reissue with Les Paul Standard features and Deluxe mini-humbuckers, black.

| 1999-2002 | | $1,800 | $2,000 |

Les Paul Dickey Betts Goldtop
2001-2003. Aged gold top.

| 2001-2003 | | $4,500 | $5,500 |

Les Paul Dickey Betts Red Top
2003. Transparent red, gold hardware.

| 2003 | | $3,000 | $3,500 |

Les Paul Elegant
1996-2004. Custom Shop, highly flamed maple top, abalone crown markers and Custom Shop headstock inlay.

| 1996-2004 | | $2,400 | $2,800 |

Les Paul Florentine Plus
1997. Custom Shop model, hollowbody with f-holes, higher-end appointments.

| 1997-2001 | | $3,200 | $3,850 |

Les Paul Gary Moore Signature
2000-2002. Signature Series model, Gary Moore script logo on truss rod cover, flamed maple top.

| 2000-2002 | | $2,000 | $2,100 |

Les Paul Goddess
2006-2007. Maple carved top, trapezoid inlays, smaller body, 2 humbuckers, 2 controls, tune-a-matic bridge.

| 2006-2007 | | $1,200 | $1,300 |

Les Paul GT
2007. Includes over/under dual truss rods, GT logo on truss rod cover, several specs designed to add durability during heavy professional use.

| 2007 | | $1,800 | $2,000 |

Les Paul Guitar Trader Reissue
1982-1983. Special order flametop Les Paul by the Guitar Trader Company, Redbank, New Jersey. Approximately 47 were built, the first 15 guitars ordered received original PAFs, all were double black bobbins (except 1 Zebra and 1 double white), 3 of the guitars were made in the '60-style. The PAF equipped models were based on order date and not build date. The serial number series started with 9 1001 and a second serial number was put in the control cavity based upon the standard Gibson serial number system, which allowed for exact build date identification. Gibson's pickup designer in the early-'80s was Tim Shaw and the pickups used for the last 32 guitars have been nicknamed Shaw PAFs. After Gibson's short run for

Gibson Les Paul DC Classic

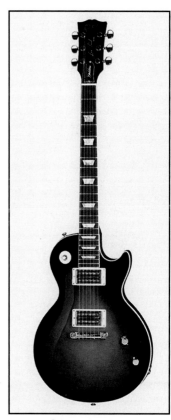

Gibson Les Paul Goddess

GUITARS

*Gibson Les Paul
Jimmy Page Signature*

*Gibson Les Paul
Joe Perry Signature*

Guitar Trader, 10 non-Gibson replica Les Pauls were made. These guitars have a poorly done Gibson logo and other telltale issues.

MODEL YEAR	FEATURES	EXC. COND. LOW	HIGH
1982-1983	Actual PAFs installed	$8,000	$8,500
1982-1983	Shaw PAFs, highly flamed	$4,100	$5,100
1982-1983	Shaw PAFs, low flame	$3,250	$4,000
1983	Non-Gibson Les Paul	$1,600	$2,400

Les Paul HD.6-X Pro Digital
2008-present. Digital sound system, hex pickups.

2008		$2,500	$3,000

Les Paul Heritage 80
1980-1982. Copy of '59 Les Paul Standard, curly maple top, mahogany body, rosewood 'board, sunburst. In '80 cataloged as Les Paul Standard-80 without reference to Heritage, the catalog notes that the guitar has the distinctive Heritage Series truss rod cover.

1980-1982	Figuring can vary	$3,000	$4,000

Les Paul Heritage 80 Award
1982. Ebony 'board, 1-piece mahogany neck, gold-plated hardware, sunburst.

1982	Figuring can vary	$3,500	$4,500

Les Paul Heritage 80 Elite
1980-1982. Copy of '59 Les Paul Standard, quilted maple top, mahogany body and neck, ebony 'board, chrome hardware, sunburst. In '80 cataloged as Les Paul Standard-80 Elite without reference to Heritage, the catalog notes that the guitar has the distinctive Heritage Series truss rod cover.

1980-1982	Quilting can vary	$3,000	$4,000

Les Paul Indian Motorcycle
2002. 100 made, has Indian script logo on fretboard and chrome cast war bonnet on the body, crimson red and cream white.

2002		$3,000	$3,700

Les Paul Jim Beam
2000. Jim Beam logo art on top of guitar, award-ribbon-style B Bean logo on headstock, white background with logo, JBLP serial number series, Custom Shop.

2000		$1,000	$1,300

Les Paul Jimmy Page Signature
1995-1999. Jimmy Page signature on 'guard, mid-grade figured top, push-pull knobs for phasing and coil-tapping, Grover tuners, gold-plated hardware. This is not the '04 Custom Shop Jimmy Page Signature Series Les Paul (see separate listing).

1995	Highly figured, 1st year	$4,500	$5,400
1995	Low to moderate figure, 1st year	$3,900	$4,300
1996-1999	Highly figured	$4,000	$4,500
1996-1999	Low to moderate figure	$3,100	$3,700

Les Paul Jimmy Page Signature Custom Shop
2004. Introduced at the January '04 NAMM Show, 175 planned production, the first 25 were person-

ally inspected, played-in, and autographed by Jimmy Page. Initial retail price for first 25 was $25,000, the remaining 150 instruments had an initial retail price of $16,400. Cosmetically aged by Tom Murphy to resemble Page's No. 1 Les Paul in color fade, weight, top flame, slab cut attribution on the edges, neck size and profile.

2004	1st 25 made	$18,000	$22,000
2004	Factory order 25-150	$14,000	$17,000

Les Paul Jimmy Page (Custom Authentic)
2004-2006. Custom Shop, includes certificate.

2004-2006		$4,500	$5,600

Les Paul Jimmy Wallace Reissue
1978-1997. Les Paul Standard '59 reissue with Jimmy Wallace on truss rod cover, special order by dealer Jimmy Wallace, figured maple top, sunburst.

1978-1983	Kalamazoo-made, highly flamed	$4,100	$5,100
1978-1983	Kalamazoo-made, low flame	$3,250	$4,000
1983-1989	Nashville-made	$3,000	$3,700
1990-1997		$2,900	$3,600

Les Paul Joe Perry Signature
1997-2001. Unbound slab body with push-pull knobs and Joe Perry signature below bridge, Bone-Yard logo model with typical Les Paul Standard bound body, configuration and appointments.

1997-2001	Bone-Yard option with logo	$2,200	$2,700
1997-2001	Unbound standard model	$1,800	$2,100

Les Paul Junior
1954-1963, 1986-1992, 2001-2002, 2005-present. One P-90 pickup, single-cut solidbody '54-mid-'58, double-cut '58-early-'61, SG body '61-'63, renamed SG Jr. in '63, reintroduced as single-cut for '86-'92, reissued as the 1957 Les Paul Jr. Single Cutaway in '98. Current version from Musician's Friend. Headstock repair reduces the value by 40% - 50%. Reinstalled tuners reduces the value by 5% to 10%. Replaced tuner buttons reduces the value by 5% to 10%.

1954	Sunburst, single-cut	$8,500	$10,000
1955	Sunburst, single-cut	$8,500	$9,000
1956	Sunburst, single-cut	$8,500	$9,000
1957	Sunburst, single-cut	$8,000	$9,000
1958	Cherry, early double-cut	$7,700	$9,000
1958	Sunburst, single-cut	$7,800	$9,000
1959	Cherry, double-cut	$7,500	$8,500
1960	Cherry, double-cut	$7,500	$8,000
1961	Cherry, double-cut	$7,000	$7,500
1961	Cherry, SG body	$4,500	$5,500
1962	Cherry, SG body	$4,500	$5,500
1963	Cherry, SG body	$4,500	$5,500
1986-1992	Sunburst, single-cut, Tune-o-matic	$800	$900

MODEL YEAR	FEATURES	EXC. COND. LOW	HIGH
1998-2005	Sunburst, single-cut, stop tail	$450	$650

Les Paul Junior 3/4

1956-1961. One P-90 pickup, short-scale, single-cut solidbody '54-mid-'58, double-cut '58-early-'61.

1956-1958	Sunburst, single-cut	$5,000	$6,000
1958-1960	Cherry, double-cut	$5,000	$6,000
1961	Cherry, double-cut	$4,000	$5,000

Les Paul Junior Billie Joe Armstrong Signature

2007-present. 1956 LP Jr. Specs.

2007		$1,000	$1,100

Les Paul Junior Double Cutaway

1986-1992, 1995-1996. Copy of '50s double-cut Jr., cherry or sunburst, reissued as the 1957 Les Paul Jr. Double Cutaway in '98.

1986-1992		$875	$1,000

Les Paul Junior. Special

1999-2004. LP Junior single-cut slab body with 2 P-90s (making it a Special) instead of the standard single P-90, double pickup controls, cherry, tinted natural or sunburst.

1999-2004		$800	$950

Les Paul Junior Tenor/Plectrum

Late-1950s. Four string neck on Junior body, cherry.

1959		$3,300	$3,900

Les Paul Jumbo

1969-1970. Single rounded cutaway, flat-top dreadnought acoustic/electric, 1 pickup, rosewood back and sides, natural.

1969-1970		$2,400	$2,600

Les Paul KM (Kalamazoo Model)

1979. Regular Les Paul Standard with 2 exposed humbuckers, KM on headstock, sunburst, approximately 1500 were made in the Kalamazoo plant.

1979		$2,300	$2,800

Les Paul Leo's Reissue

1980-1985. Special order from Gibson's Nashville facility for Leo's Music, Oakland, California. Identified by serial number with L at the beginning, flamed maple top. About 800 guitars were made, with about 400 being exported to Japan. Kalamazoo-made Leo's have a 2nd serial number in the control cavity, Nashville-made Leo's do not have a 2nd serial number.

1980-1983	Kalamazoo-made, highly flamed	$4,100	$5,100
1980-1983	Kalamazoo-made, lower-level flame	$3,250	$4,000
1983-1985	Nashville-made	$3,200	$4,000

Les Paul Limited Edition (3-tone)

1997. Limited Edition stamped on the back of the headstock, Les Paul Standard configuration with cloud inlay markers, 2-piece 3-tone sunburst finish over non-figured maple top.

1997		$1,950	$2,150

Les Paul LP295 Goldtop

2008. Guitar of the Month (April, '08), limited run of 1000, Les Paul body style, goldtop, 2 humbuckers, ES-295 appointments such as 'guard and fretboard markers, Bigsby tailpiece option.

2008		$2,000	$2,500

Les Paul Melody Maker

2003-2006. Slab body single-cut solidbody, P-90, dot markers, cherry finish.

2003-2006		$325	$375

Les Paul Menace

2006-2007. Carved mahogany body, 2 humbucker pickups.

2006-2007		$650	$700

Les Paul Music Machine 25th Anniversary

2002. Custom run for dealer Music Machine with special serial number series, 14 flame top and 14 quilt top instruments were produced, Music Machine 25th Anniversary logo on truss rod cover, special cherry sunburst finish.

2002	Flame top	$3,800	$4,200
2002	Quilt top	$4,000	$4,500

Les Paul Music Machine Brazilian Stinger

2003. Custom run for dealer Music Machine with special serial number series, Brazilian rosewood 'board, black stinger paint on back of neck-headstock, '59 or '60 reissue body and neck profile options, highly figured flame or quilt top options, other reissue options available.

2003	'54, '56 or '58, figured flame or quilt	$4,000	$5,000
2003	'54, '56 or '58, goldtop	$3,000	$3,700
2003	'59 or '60, figured flame or quilt	$6,500	$7,500
2003	'59 or '60, plain top	$4,000	$5,000

Les Paul Old Hickory

1998 only. Limited run of 200, tulip poplar body wood from The Hermitage, Custom-style trim.

1998		$3,500	$4,200

Les Paul Pee Wee

1999. 3/4" sized Les Paul Jr. style guitar, included battery-powered amp.

1999		$400	$475

Les Paul Personal

1969-1972. Two angled, low impedence pickups, phase switch, gold parts, walnut finish.

1969-1972		$1,700	$1,900

Les Paul Pro Deluxe

1978-1982. Chrome-plated hardware, Pro engraved on truss rod cover, 2 P-90 pickups, various colors.

1978-1982		$1,700	$1,900

Les Paul Pro Showcase Edition

1988. Goldtop 1956 specs, Showcase Edition decal, 200 made.

1988		$1,800	$1,900

Les Paul Professional

1969-1971, 1977-1979. Single-cut, 2 angled, low impedence pickups, carved top, walnut finish.

1969-1971		$1,900	$2,000

1959 Gibson Les Paul Junior

Gibson Les Paul Old Hickory

*1956 Gibson
Les Paul Special*

*Gibson Les Paul Slash
Signature*

MODEL		EXC. COND.	
YEAR	FEATURES	LOW	HIGH

Les Paul Recording
1971-1980. Two angled, low impedence pickups, high/low impedence selector switch, various colors.

| 1971-1980 | | $1,800 | $2,200 |

Les Paul Reissue Flametop
1983-1990. Flame maple top, 2 humbuckers, thicker '59-style neck, sunburst finish, renamed '59 Les Paul Flametop in '91.

| 1983-1990 | Highly figured | $4,100 | $5,100 |

Les Paul Reissue Goldtop
1983-1991. Goldtop finish, 2 P-100 pickups, renamed '56 Les Paul Goldtop in '91.

| 1983-1989 | | $2,000 | $2,500 |
| 1990-1991 | | $2,000 | $2,500 |

Les Paul Richard Petty LTD
2003. Richard Petty's image on front and back, 'The King' inlay on fretboard.

| 2003 | | $3,100 | $3,800 |

Les Paul SG '61 Reissue
1993-2003. Renamed the Les Paul SG '61 Reissue from SG '62 Reissue, early '60s Les Paul Standard SG specs with small guard, trapezoid markers, heritage cherry finish, by 2003 the Les Paul script marking was not on the truss rod cover, renamed to SG '61 Reissue.

| 1993-2003 | Stud tail | $1,300 | $1,400 |

Les Paul SG Standard Authentic
2005. SG '61 specs, small guard, Les Paul truss rod logo, stud tailpiece.

| 2005 | | $2,000 | $2,100 |

Les Paul SG Standard Reissue
2000-2004. Reissue of early-'60s specs including Deluxe Maestro vibrato with lyre tailpiece and Les Paul script truss rod logo, small pickguard, holly head veneer, rosewood 'board with tapezoid markers, available with stop bar tailpiece, extra slim low action '60 profile neck, small neck to body heel, standard color faded cherry, available in Classic White or TV Yellow, becomes the SG Standard Reissue by '05.

| 2000-2004 | | $2,000 | $2,300 |

Les Paul Signature/L.P. Signature
1973-1978. Thin semi-hollowbody, double-cut, 2 low impedance pickups, f-holes, various colors. The Price List refers to as L.P. Signature.

| 1973-1978 | | $2,900 | $3,600 |

Les Paul Slash Signature
2007. Slash logo on truss rod, SL serial number series.

| 2007 | | $2,800 | $3,000 |

Les Paul SmartWood Exotic
1998-2001. Full-depth Les Paul-style built with eco-friendly woods, Muiracatiara (or Muir) top, mahogany back, Preciosa 'board, pearloid dots.

| 1998-2001 | | $800 | $850 |

Les Paul SmartWood Standard
1996-2002. Smartwood Series, figured maple top, mahogany body, Smartwood on truss rod cover, antique natural.

| 1996-2002 | | $900 | $1,100 |

Les Paul SmartWood Studio
2002-present. Muiracatiara (Muir) top and mahogany back, Preciosa (Prec) 'board, Studio appointments including pearl-style dot markers.

| 2002-2006 | | $750 | $925 |

Les Paul Special
1955-1959. Slab solidbody, 2 pickups (P-90s in '50s, P-100 stacked humbuckers on later version), single-cut until end of '58, double in '59, the '89 reissue is a single-cut, renamed SG Special in late-'59.

| 1955-1959 | TV Yellow | $18,000 | $20,000 |
| 1959 | Cherry (mid- to late-'59) | $10,600 | $13,000 |

Les Paul Special (Reissue)
1989-1998. Briefly introduced as Les Paul Junior II but name changed to Special in the first year, single-cut, 2 P-100 stacked humbucking pickups, tune-o-matic bridge, TV Yellow, in '90 there was a run of 300 with LE serial number, renamed Special SL in '98.

| 1989-1998 | 2 P-100 stacked humbuckers | $800 | $1,000 |
| 1989-1998 | 490R and 496T humbuckers | $800 | $1,000 |

Les Paul Special 3/4
1959. Slab solidbody, 2 P-90 pickups, double-cut, short-scale, cherry finish, renamed SG Special 3/4 in late-'59.

| 1959 | | $8,000 | $10,000 |

Les Paul Special Centennial
1994 only. 100 made, double-cut, cherry, 100 year banner at the 12th fret, diamonds in headstock and in gold-plated knobs, gold-plated Gibson coin in back of headstock.

| 1994 | | $3,300 | $4,000 |

Les Paul Special Custom Shop
1999-present. 1960 Special, offered in single- or double-cut version. Currently a VOS model.

| 1999-2005 | | $1,500 | $1,700 |
| 2006-2007 | VOS | $1,500 | $1,700 |

Les Paul Special Double Cutaway
1976-1979, 1993-1998. Double-cut, 2 pickups (P-90s in '70s, P-100 stacked humbuckers in later version), various colors.

| 1976-1979 | | $1,400 | $1,600 |
| 1993-1998 | | $1,325 | $1,600 |

Les Paul Special Tenor
1959. Four-string electric tenor, LP Special body, TV Yellow.

| 1959 | | $9,600 | $12,000 |

Les Paul Spider-Man
Released December 3, 2002. Custom Art & Historic division's rendering with the superhero depicted on the body, red spider logo, gold hardware, Standard appointments. 15 guitars were produced as a Gibson/Columbia TriStar Home Entertainment/Tower Records promotion, while a larger batch was sold at retail.

| 2002 | | $3,500 | $3,900 |

MODEL YEAR	FEATURES	EXC. COND. LOW	HIGH

Les Paul Spotlight Special

1983-1984. Curly maple and walnut top, 2 humbuckers, gold hardware, multi-bound top, Custom Shop Edition logo, natural or sunburst.

MODEL YEAR	FEATURES	EXC. COND. LOW	HIGH
1983-1984		$3,500	$4,300

Les Paul Standard (Sunburst)

1958-1960, special order 1972-1975. Les Paul Sunbursts from '58-'60 should be individually valued based on originality, color and the amount and type of figure in the maple top, changed tuners or a Bigsby removal will drop the value. Approximately 15% came with the Bigsby tailpiece. The noted price ranges are guidance valuations. Each '58-'60 Les Paul Standard should be evaluated on a case-by-case basis. As is always the case, the low and high ranges are for an all original, excellent condition, undamaged guitar. About 70% of the '58-'60 Les Paul Standards have relatively plain maple tops. The majority of '58-'60 Les Paul Standards have moderate or extreme color fade.

Wider fret wire was introduced in early-'59. White bobbins were introduced in early- to mid-'59. Double ring Kluson Deluxe tuners were introduced in late-'60. It has been suggested that all '58-'60 models have 2-piece centerseam tops. This implies that 1-piece tops, 3-piece tops and off-centerseam tops do not exist.

The terminology of the 'Burst includes: arching medullary grain, swirling medullary grain, ribbon-curl, chevrons, Honey-Amber, receding red aniline, pinstripe, bookmatched, double-white bobbins, zebra bobbins, black bobbins, fiddleback maple, sunburst finish, Honeyburst, lemon drop, quarter sawn, blistered figure, width of gradation, flat sawn, Teaburst, Bigsby-shadow, rift sawn, heel size, aged clear lacquer, 3-dimensional figure, intense fine flame, tag-shadow, red pore filler, Eastern maple fleck, medium-thick flame, shrunk tuners, wave and flame, flitch-matched, elbow discoloration, ambered top coat, natural gradation, grain orientation, script oxidation, asymmetrical figure Tangerineburst, Greenburst, and birdseye.

The bobbins used for the pickup winding were either black or white. The market has determined that white bobbin PAFs are the most highly regarded. Generally speaking, in '58 bobbins were black, in '59 the bobbin component transitioned to white and some guitars have 1 white and 1 black bobbin (aka zebra). In '60, there were zebras and double blacks returned.

Rather than listing separate line items for fade and wood, the Guide lists discounts and premiums as follows. The price ranges shown below are for instruments with excellent color, excellent wood, with the original guitar case. The following discounts and premiums should be considered.

An instrument with moderate or total color fade should be discounted about 10%.

One with a factory Bigsby should be discounted about 10%-15%.

Original jumbo frets are preferred over original small frets and are worth +10%.

MODEL YEAR	FEATURES	EXC. COND. LOW	HIGH
1958	Figured top	$255,000	$305,000
1958	Plain top, no figuring	$125,000	$157,000
1959	Figured top	$290,000	$350,000
1959	Figured top	$130,000	$168,000
1960	Highly flamed, strong color	$285,000	$350,000
1960	Plain top, no figuring	$127,000	$163,000

Les Paul Standard (SG body)

1961-1963 (SG body those years). Renamed SG Standard in late-'63.

MODEL YEAR	FEATURES	EXC. COND. LOW	HIGH
1961-1962	Cherry, side vibrola, PAFs	$20,000	$25,000
1962	Ebony block, SG, PAFs, deluxe vibrola	$20,000	$25,000
1962	Ebony block, SG, pat. #, deluxe vibrola	$17,000	$22,000
1963	Cherry, side vibrola, pat. #	$17,000	$21,000

Les Paul Standard (reintroduced then renamed)

1968-1969. Comes back as a goldtop with P-90s for '68-'69 (renamed Les Paul Deluxe, '69), available as special order Deluxe '72-'76.

MODEL YEAR	FEATURES	EXC. COND. LOW	HIGH
1968	P-90s, small headstock	$15,000	$19,000
1968-1969	P-90s, large headstock	$10,000	$15,000

Les Paul Standard (reintroduced)

1976-present. Available as special order Deluxe '72-'76, reintroduced with 2 humbuckers '76-present. The '75 Price List shows a Les Paul Standard (B) model which is equipped with a Bigsby tailpiece versus a wraparound, also shows a Les Paul Standard (B) with palm pedal. Renamed Les Paul Standard 2008 in '08.

MODEL YEAR	FEATURES	EXC. COND. LOW	HIGH
1971	Early special order goldtop, P-90s	$9,000	$12,000
1972-1974	Special order goldtop, P-90s	$4,500	$5,900
1972-1974	Special order sunburst, P-90s	$4,400	$5,400
1974-1975	Special order sunburst, humbuckers	$4,000	$4,300
1976	Sunburst, 4-piece pancake body	$2,100	$2,600
1976	Wine Red or natural	$2,100	$2,600
1977	Sunburst	$2,075	$2,550
1977	Various colors	$2,075	$2,550
1978	Natural	$2,075	$2,500
1978	Sunburst	$2,075	$2,500
1978	Various colors	$2,075	$2,500
1979	Brown Sunburst	$2,075	$2,500
1979	Cherry Sunburst	$2,075	$2,500
1979	Goldtop	$2,300	$2,600
1979	Natural	$2,075	$2,500
1979	Wine Red	$2,075	$2,500

1960 Gibson
Les Paul Standard

1962 Gibson Les Paul Standard

GUITARS

2004 Gibson Les Paul Standard

Gibson Les Paul Studio

MODEL YEAR	FEATURES	EXC. COND. LOW	HIGH
1980	Black	$2,075	$2,500
1980	Natural	$2,075	$2,500
1980	Sunburst	$2,075	$2,500
1980	Sunburst, mild flame	$2,100	$2,600
1980	Wine Red	$2,075	$2,500
1981	Sunburst	$2,000	$2,500
1981	Wine Red	$2,000	$2,500
1982	Black	$2,075	$2,500
1982	Brown Sunburst	$2,075	$2,500
1982	Candy Apple Red, gold hardware, LD	$2,075	$2,500
1982	Cherry Sunburst	$2,075	$2,500
1982	Goldtop	$2,050	$2,550
1982	Natural	$2,075	$2,500
1982	Wine Red	$2,075	$2,500
1983	Black	$1,900	$2,300
1983	Natural	$2,075	$2,300
1983	Sunburst	$1,900	$2,300
1984	Sunburst	$1,800	$2,200
1985	Black	$1,950	$2,100
1985	Sunburst	$1,950	$2,100
1985	Wine Red	$1,950	$2,100
1986	Sunburst	$1,950	$2,100
1987	Various colors	$1,950	$2,100
1988	Heavily-figured flame	$2,000	$2,400
1988	Various colors	$1,850	$2,000
1989	Various colors	$1,700	$1,800
1990-1993	Limited Edition colors with sticker	$1,950	$2,400
1990-1999	Various colors	$1,400	$1,900
2000-2006	Various colors, includes figured wood	$1,550	$1,850

Les Paul Standard '58
1971-1975. Goldtop, called the '58, but set up like a '54 Goldtop with 2 soapbar pickups and wraparound bridge.

1971-1975		$4,100	$4,900

Les Paul Standard '82
1982. Standard 82 on truss rod cover, made in Kalamazoo, Made in USA stamp on back of the headstock, generally quilted maple tops.

1982		$2,800	$3,500

Les Paul Standard Lite
1999-2001. A member of DC body-style, renamed from DC Standard in '99, reintroduced as Les Paul Standard DC Plus in 2001, various translucent finishes, available in 2004 under this name also.

1999-2001		$1,100	$1,400

Les Paul Standard Plus
1995-1997, 2002-2003. Cherry sunburst standard with mid-level flame.

2002-2003		$1,700	$2,000

Les Paul Standard Premium Plus
2001-2008. Premium plus flamed maple top.

2001-2008		$1,900	$2,300

Les Paul Standard Sparkle
2001. Sparkle holoflake top, reflective back, Standard logo on truss rod.

2001		$2,000	$2,400

Les Paul Strings and Things Standard
1975-1978. Special order flamed maple top Les Paul Standard model, built for Chris Lovell, owner of Strings and Things, a Gibson dealer in Memphis, approximately 28 were built, authentication of a Strings and Things Les Paul is difficult due to no diffinitive attributes, valuation should be on a case-by-case basis, sunburst.

1975	2-piece top	$4,800	$6,000
1975	3-piece top	$3,500	$4,300
1976	2-piece top	$4,700	$5,900
1976	3-piece top	$3,000	$3,300
1977	2-piece top	$4,600	$5,800
1977	3-piece top	$2,700	$3,200
1978	2-piece top	$4,500	$5,700
1978	3-piece top	$2,500	$3,000

Les Paul Studio
1983-present. Alder body, 2 humbuckers, various colors.

1983-1989		$800	$1,000
1990-1999		$825	$1,025
2000-2007		$850	$950

Les Paul Studio Baritone
2004-2006. 28" baritone scale.

2004-2006		$850	$950

Les Paul Studio BFD
2007. Studio specs but with BFD electronics.

2007		$550	$650

Les Paul Studio Custom
1984-1985. Alder body, 2 humbucking pickups, multi-bound top, gold-plated hardware, various colors.

1984-1985		$900	$1,000

Les Paul Studio Faded
2005-2007. Faded sunburst tops.

2005-2007		$500	$600

Les Paul Studio Gem
1996-1998. Limited edition with Les Paul Studio features, but using P-90 pickups instead of humbucker pickups, plus trapezoid markers and gold hardware.

1996-1998		$900	$1,000

Les Paul Studio Gothic
2000-2001. Gothic Black.

2000-2001		$650	$750

Les Paul Studio Lite
1987-1998. Carved maple top, mahogany back and neck, 2 humbucker pickups, various colors.

1987-1998		$800	$1,000

Les Paul Studio Plus
2002-present. Two-piece AA flamed unbound top, gold hardware, Desert Burst or see-thru black.

2002-2007		$1,000	$1,125

Les Paul Studio Premium Plus
2006-2008. AAA flamed-maple top.

2006-2008		$1,250	$1,350

GUITARS

MODEL YEAR	FEATURES	EXC. COND. LOW	HIGH
Les Paul Studio Swamp Ash/Swamp Ash Studio			
2004-2007. Studio model with swamp ash body.			
2004-2007		$700	$800
Les Paul Supreme			
2003-present. Highly figured AAAA maple top and back on translucent finishes only, custom binding, deluxe split style pearl inlay markers, chambered mahogany body, globe logo on headstock, solid colors available by '06.			
2003-2006	AAAA top	$2,300	$2,500
2003-2006	Various colors	$2,000	$2,200
2007	Les Paul signed, Goldtop	$2,300	$2,500
Les Paul Tie Dye (St. Pierre)			
1996-1997. Hand colored by George St. Pierre, just over 100 made.			
1996-1997		$2,500	$3,100
Les Paul Tie Dye Custom Shop			
2002. Limited series of one-off colorful finishes, Custom Shop logo.			
2002		$1,600	$2,000
Les Paul TV			
1954-1959. Les Paul Jr. with limed mahogany (TV Yellow) finish, single-cut until mid-'58, double-cut after, renamed SG TV in late-'59.			
1955-1958	Single-cut	$16,000	$20,000
1958-1959	Double-cut	$14,000	$18,000
Les Paul TV 3/4			
1954-1957. Limed mahogany (TV Yellow) Les Paul Jr. 3/4, short-scale, single-cut.			
1954-1957		$7,000	$12,000
Les Paul Ultima			
1996-present. Custom Shop model, flame or quilted sunburst top, fancy abalone and mother-of-pearl tree of life, harp, or flame fingerboard inlay, multi abalone bound body.			
1996-2007		$5,500	$7,500
Les Paul Vixen			
2006-2007. Les Paul Special single-cut slab body, dot markers, 2 humbuckers, 2 controls, wrap-around bridge.			
2006-2007		$550	$650
Les Paul Voodoo/Voodoo Les Paul			
2004-2005. Single-cut, swamp ash body, 2 exposed humbuckers, black satin finish.			
2004-2005		$1,000	$1,200
Les Paul XR-I/XR-II/XR-III			
1981-1983. No frills model with Dirty Finger pickups, dot markers, Les Paul stencil logo on headstock, goldburst, silverburst and cherryburst finishes.			
1981-1983	XR-I, goldburst	$750	$850
1981-1983	XR-II	$750	$850
1981-1983	XR-III	$750	$850
Les Paul Zakk Wylde Signature			
2003-present. Custom shop, black and antique-white bullseye graphic finish.			
1999	Black/white bullseye	$2,800	$3,500
2003-2007	Black/white bullseye	$2,600	$2,800
2003-2007	Green Camo bullseye option	$2,600	$2,800

MODEL YEAR	FEATURES	EXC. COND. LOW	HIGH
The Les Paul			
1976-1980. Figured maple top, 2 humbuckers, gold hardware, rosewood binding, 'guard, 'board, knobs, cover plates, etc., natural or rosewood finishing, natural only by '79.			
1976-1980	Natural or rosewood	$11,000	$14,000
The Paul			
1978-1982. Offered as The Paul Standard with solid walnut body and The Paul Deluxe with solid mahogany body, 2 exposed humbuckers.			
1978-1982		$825	$1,000
The Paul Firebrand Deluxe			
1980-1982. Single-cut mahogany solidbody, rough natural finish, Gibson branded in headstock, 2 exposed humbuckers.			
1980-1982	Black	$600	$750
1980-1982	Pelham Blue	$700	$875
1980-1982	Rough natural	$600	$750
The Paul II			
1996-1998. Mahogany body, 2 humbucking pickups, rosewood dot neck, renamed The Paul SL in '98.			
1996-1998		$500	$600
LG-0			
1958-1974. Flat-top acoustic, mahogany, bound body, rosewood bridge '58-'61 and '68-'74, plastic bridge '62-'67, natural.			
1958-1961	Rosewood bridge	$975	$1,100
1962-1964	Plastic bridge	$800	$950
1965-1966	Plastic bridge	$675	$825
1967-1969	Rosewood bridge	$650	$800
1970-1974		$600	$725
LG-1			
1943-1968. Flat-top acoustic, spruce top, mahogany back and sides, bound body, rosewood bridge '43-'61, plastic bridge after, examples seen to '74, sunburst.			
1943		$2,000	$2,200
1944		$1,900	$2,100
1945		$1,800	$2,000
1946		$1,700	$1,800
1947-1949		$1,500	$1,700
1950-1961	Rosewood bridge	$1,400	$1,600
1962-1964	Plastic bridge	$1,000	$1,200
1965-1966		$900	$1,100
1967-1968		$800	$900
LG-12 (12-string)			
1967-1973. 14-1/8" wide, mahogany back and sides, bound top, natural.			
1967-1969	Adjustable saddle	$800	$1,000
1970-1974	Set saddle	$800	$900
LG-2			
1942-1962. Flat-top acoustic, spruce top, mahogany back and sides (some with maple '43-'46), banner headstock '42-'46, bound body, X-bracing, sunburst finish, replaced by B-25 in '62.			
1942		$3,100	$3,600
1943		$3,000	$3,500
1944		$2,900	$3,400
1945		$2,800	$3,300
1946		$2,700	$3,300

1950s Gibson Les Paul TV

Gibson Les Paul Zakk Wylde Signature

1985 Gibson Map

1970 Gibson Melody Maker

MODEL YEAR	FEATURES	EXC. COND. LOW	HIGH
1947-1949		$2,500	$2,800
1950-1955		$2,300	$2,700
1956		$2,200	$2,600
1957		$2,200	$2,500
1958-1960		$2,200	$2,400
1961	Rosewood bridge	$2,150	$2,400
1962	Ajustable bridge	$1,650	$2,000

LG-2 3/4

1949-1962. Short-scale version of LG-2 flat-top, wood bridge, sunburst.

1949-1961		$1,900	$2,300
1962		$1,800	$2,200

LG-2 H

1945-1955. Flat-top, Hawaiian, natural or sunburst.

1944		$2,900	$3,400
1945		$2,800	$3,300
1946		$2,700	$3,300
1947-1949		$2,500	$2,800
1950-1955		$2,300	$2,700

LG-3

1942-1964. Flat-top acoustic, spruce top, mahogany back and sides, bound body, natural finish, replaced by B-25 N.

1942		$3,400	$4,000
1943		$3,300	$3,900
1944		$3,200	$3,800
1945		$3,100	$3,700
1946		$3,000	$3,400
1947		$2,900	$3,200
1948		$2,800	$3,200
1949		$2,700	$3,200
1950-1951		$2,500	$2,900
1952-1955		$2,500	$2,800
1956-1961	Rosewood bridge	$2,400	$2,700
1962-1964	Plastic bridge	$1,750	$2,200

M III Series

1991-1996. Double-cut solidbody with extra long bass horn, six-on-a-side tuners on a reverse pointy headstock, dot markers, reverse Gibson decal logo.

1991-1992	Deluxe	$1,600	$2,000

Mach II

1990-1991. Renamed from U-2, offset double-cut, 2 single coils and 1 humbucking pickup.

1990-1991		$775	$850

Map Guitar

1983, 1985. Body cutout like lower 48, 2 humbuckers, limited run promotion, '83 version in natural mahogany or red, white and blue, '85 version red, white and blue stars and stripes on a white background.

1983	Natural	$2,700	$2,900
1983	Red, white and blue	$2,900	$3,200

Marauder

1975-1980. Single-cut solidbody, pointed headstock, 2 pickups, bolt-on neck, various colors.

1975-1980		$625	$725

Melody Maker

1959-1971. Slab solidbody, 1 pickup, single-cut until '61, double '61-'66, SG body '66-'71, reintroduced as single-cut in '86-'93. A single-cut Les Paul Melody Maker was offered from '03-'07.

MODEL YEAR	FEATURES	EXC. COND. LOW	HIGH
1959	Sunburst, single-cut	$1,800	$1,900
1960	Sunburst, single-cut	$1,600	$1,700
1961	Sunburst, single-cut	$1,500	$1,600
1962	Sunburst or cherry, double-cut	$1,300	$1,400
1963	Sunburst or cherry, double-cut	$1,200	$1,300
1964	Cherry, double-cut	$1,100	$1,200
1965	Cherry, double cut	$1,000	$1,100
1966	Cherry, double cut	$900	$1,000
1966-1969	Blue, burgundy or red, SG body	$1,300	$1,700
1968-1971	Walnut, SG body	$1,200	$1,600

Melody Maker 12

1967-1971. SG-style solidbody, 12 strings, 2 pickups, red, white or Pelham Blue.

1967-1969		$1,600	$1,900
1970-1971		$1,550	$1,900

Melody Maker 3/4

1959-1970. Short-scale version.

1959-1965	Melody Maker body	$975	$1,200
1966-1970	SG body	$1,200	$1,500

Melody Maker D

1960-1970. Two pickup version of Melody Maker, reintroduced as Melody Maker Double in '77.

1960	Sunburst, single-cut	$2,200	$2,400
1961	Sunburst, single-cut	$1,800	$2,100
1962	Sunburst or cherry, double-cut	$1,700	$2,000
1963	Sunburst or cherry, double-cut	$1,600	$2,000
1964	Sunburst or cherry, double-cut	$1,600	$2,000
1965-1966	Sunburst or cherry, double-cut	$1,200	$1,500
1966	Blue, SG body	$1,800	$2,200
1966	Burgundy or red, SG body	$1,700	$2,100
1967-1969	Blue, SG body	$1,600	$1,900
1967-1969	Burgundy or red, SG body	$1,600	$1,900
1968-1970	Walnut, SG body	$1,400	$1,700

Melody Maker Double

1977-1983. Reintroduction of Melody Maker D, double-cut solidbody, 2 pickups, cherry or sunburst.

1977-1983		$875	$1,075

Melody Maker Faded

2003. Les Paul Jr. styling, single-cut, 1 P-90 style pickup, Nashville tune-o-matic bridge, black satin finish.

2003		$350	$400

Melody Maker III

1967-1971. SG-style double-cut solidbody, 3 pickups, various colors.

1967-1969		$1,850	$2,300
1970-1971		$1,650	$2,050

MODEL YEAR	FEATURES	EXC. COND. LOW	HIGH

Melody Maker Single Coil
2007. Les Paul Jr. styling, single bridge P-90 pickup, or 2 pickup option.

| 2007 | 2 pickups option | $300 | $350 |
| 2007 | US-made | $250 | $300 |

MK-35
1975-1978. Mark Series flat-top acoustic, mahogany back and sides, black-bound body, natural or sunburst, 5226 made.

| 1975-1978 | | $750 | $800 |

MK-53
1975-1978. Mark Series flat-top acoustic, maple back and sides, multi-bound body, natural or sunburst, 1424 made.

| 1975-1978 | | $800 | $850 |

MK-72
1975-1978. Mark Series flat-top acoustic, rosewood back and sides, black-bound body, chrome tuners, natural or sunburst, 1229 made.

| 1975-1978 | | $850 | $950 |

MK-81
1975-1978. Mark Series flat-top acoustic, rosewood back and sides, multi-bound body, gold tuners, high-end appointments, natural or sunburst, 431 made.

| 1975-1978 | | $900 | $1,000 |

Moderne Heritage
1981-1983. Limited edition, korina body, 2 humbucking pickups, gold hardware.

| 1981-1983 | Black or white | $2,600 | $3,000 |
| 1981-1983 | Natural | $3,800 | $4,400 |

Nick Lucas
1928-1938. Flat-top acoustic, multi-bound body and neck, sunburst, reintroduced in '91 and '99. Also known as Nick Lucas Special and Gibson Special.

1928	Mahogany, 12-fret, 13 1/3"	$8,000	$16,000
1928	Rosewood, 12-fret, 13 1/2"	$9,000	$18,000
1929-1933	Rosewood, 13-fret, 14 3/4"	$14,000	$28,000
1934-1938	Maple, 14-fret, 14 3/4"	$9,000	$18,000

Nick Lucas Reissue
1991-1992, 1999-2004. Limited edition flat-top acoustic, sunburst.

| 1991-1992 | | $2,200 | $2,500 |
| 1999-2004 | | $2,000 | $2,100 |

Nighthawk Custom
1993-1998. Flame maple top, ebony 'board, gold hardware, fireburst, single/double/mini pickups.

| 1993-1998 | | $1,500 | $1,825 |

Nighthawk Special
1993-1998. Single-cut solidbody, figured maple top, double-coil and mini-pickup or with additional single-coil options, dot marker inlay, cherry, ebony or sunburst.

| 1993-1998 | | $800 | $850 |

Nighthawk Standard
1993-1998. Single-cut solidbody, figured maple top, 2 or 3 pickups, double-parallelogram inlay, amber, fireburst or sunburst.

| 1993-1998 | | $900 | $1,000 |

Nouveau NV6T-M
1986-1987. A line of Gibson flat-tops with imported parts assembled and finished in the U.S., acoustic dreadnought, bound maple body, natural.

| 1986-1987 | | $400 | $450 |

Original Jumbo (Custom Shop)
2003. 16" jumbo body, Adirondack (red) spruce top, mahogany sides and back, Gotoh vintage-style tuners with butterbean buttons, deep sunburst finish on complete body, Custom Art Historic.

| 2003 | | $2,200 | $2,300 |

Pat Martino Model
2003-2005. Sharp single-cut, thinline with Les Paul shape, f-holes, 2 humbucker pickups, flamed cherry sunburst top, small snakehead style headstock, Pat Martino logo on truss rod cover.

| 2003-2005 | | $2,500 | $2,800 |

Q-100
1985-1986. Offset double-cut solidbody, Kahler trem, 6-on-a-side tuners, 1 humbucker, black hardware.

| 1985-1986 | | $475 | $575 |

Q-200/Q2000
1985-1986. Like Q-100, but with 1 single-coil and 1 humbucker, black or chrome hardware.

| 1985-1986 | | $525 | $650 |

Q-300/Q3000
1985-1986. Like Q-100, but with 3 single-coils, black or chrome hardware.

| 1985-1986 | | $550 | $675 |

RD Artist/77
1980. The 77 model has a 25.5" scale versus 24.75".

| 1980 | | $1,525 | $1,900 |

RD Artist/79
1978-1982. Double-cut solidbody, 2 humbuckers, TP-6 tailpiece, active electronics, ebony 'board, block inlays, gold-plated parts, various colors, called just RD (no Artist) in '81 and '82.

| 1978-1982 | | $1,600 | $1,875 |

RD Custom
1977-1979. Double-cut solidbody, 2 humbuckers, stop tailpiece, active electronics, dot inlays, maple 'board, chrome parts, natural or walnut.

| 1977-1979 | | $1,500 | $1,675 |

RD Standard
1977-1979. Double-cut solidbody, 2 humbuckers, stop tailpiece, rosewood 'board, dot inlays, chrome parts, natural, sunburst or walnut.

| 1977-1979 | | $1,300 | $1,400 |

Roy Smeck Radio Grande Hawaiian
1934-1939. Dreadnought acoustic flat-top, rosewood back and sides, bound body and neck, natural.

| 1934-1939 | | $10,000 | $12,500 |

Roy Smeck Radio Grande Hawaiian Reissue
1996. Part of SmartWood Series, Grenadillo back and sides.

| 1996 | | $2,300 | $2,600 |

Gibson Melody Maker 3/4

1977 Gibson RD Custom

1976 Gibson S-1

1963 Gibson SG Custom

MODEL YEAR	FEATURES	EXC. COND. LOW	HIGH

Roy Smeck Stage Deluxe Hawaiian
1934-1942. Dreadnought acoustic flat-top, mahogany back and sides, bound body, natural.

1934-1942		$6,000	$7,500

S-1
1976-1980. Single-cut solidbody, pointed headstock, 3 single-coil pickups, similar to the Marauder, various colors.

1976-1980		$700	$825

SG
Following are models, listed alphabetically, bearing the SG name.

SG '61 Reissue
2003-present. Renamed from Les Paul SG '61 Reissue, no Les Paul script on truss rod, small 'guard, stop bar tailpiece (no Deluxe Maestro vibrato), '60 slim-taper neck profile.

2003-2008		$1,250	$1,300

SG '62 Reissue/SG Reissue
1986-1991. Trapezoid markers, stop bar, 2 humbuckers, called SG Reissue '86-'87, SG '62 Reissue '88-'91. Reintroduced as Les Paul SG '61 Reissue for '93-'03 and SG '61 Reissue '03-present, cherry.

1986-1991		$1,300	$1,400

SG '62 Reissue Showcase Edition
1988. Guitar of the Month, bright blue opaque finish, 200 made.

1988		$1,200	$1,400

'63 Corvette Sting Ray
1995-1996. Custom Shop SG-style body carved to simulate split rear window on '63 Corvette, Sting Ray inlay, 150 instruments built, offered in black, white, silver or red.

1995-1996		$3,500	$4,500

SG Classic
1999-present. Late '60s SG Special style, 'Classic' noted on truss rod cover, large 'guard, black soapbar single-coil P-90s, dot markers, stop bar tailpiece, cherry or ebony stain. Offered by Musician's Friend since '03.

1999-2008		$725	$775

SG Custom
1963-1980. Renamed from Les Paul Custom, 3 humbuckers, vibrato, made with Les Paul Custom plate from '61-'63 (see Les Paul Custom), white finish until '68, walnut and others after.

1963	White, pat. #	$18,000	$22,000
1964	White	$18,000	$22,000
1965	White	$14,500	$17,000
1966	White	$9,500	$12,000
1967	White	$9,000	$12,000
1968	White	$8,500	$10,000
1969-1970	Walnut, Lyre	$5,000	$6,200
1969-1970	White, Lyre	$6,500	$7,500
1970-1973	Walnut	$3,600	$4,500
1970-1973	White option	$4,500	$5,500
1974-1976	Various colors	$2,900	$3,300
1977-1980	Various colors	$2,500	$2,900

SG Custom '67 Reissue/Les Paul SG '67 Custom
1991-1993. The SG Custom '67 Reissue has a wine red finish, the Les Paul SG '67 Custom ('92-'93) has a wine red or white finish.

1991-1993		$1,700	$2,000

SG Custom Reissue
1999-present. 1961 specs, SG body style, 3 humbuckers, Deluxe Maestro vibrato or stud with tune-o-matic bridge, white.

1999-2007		$1,800	$2,500

SG Deluxe
1971-1972, 1980-1985, 1998-1999. The '70s models were offered in natural, cherry or walnut finishes, reintroduced in '98 with 3 Firebird mini-humbucker-style pickups in black, Ice Blue or red finishes.

1971-1972	Cherry	$1,300	$1,600
1971-1972	Natural or walnut	$1,250	$1,500
1980-1999	Various colors	$975	$1,200

SG Elegant
2004-present. Custom Shop, quilt maple top, gold hardware.

2004-2007		$2,550	$2,750

SG Exclusive
1979. SG with humbuckers, coil-tap and rotary control knob, block inlay, pearl logo (not decal), black/ebony finish.

1979		$1,800	$2,400

SG Firebrand
1980-1982. Double-cut mahogany solidbody, rough natural finish, Gibson branded in headstock, 2 exposed humbuckers, Firebrand logo on The SG (Standard) model.

1980-1982		$775	$900

SG Goddess
2007. SG Goddess logo on truss rod cover, only 2 control knobs versus standard 4, exposed humbuckers.

2007		$925	$1,025

SG Gothic
2000-2003. SG Special with satin black finish, moon and star marker on 12th fret, black hardware.

2000-2003		$600	$800

SG GT
2006-2007. '61 SG Standard reissue specs with racing stripes paint job and removable tailpiece hood scoop, locking tuners, dual truss rod system, Candy Apple Red, Daytona Blue, or Phantom Black.

2006-2007		$1,250	$1,300

SG I
1972-1977. Double-cut, mahogany body, 1 mini-humbucker (some with SG Jr. P-90), cherry or walnut.

1972-1977		$825	$900

SG II
1972-1976. 2 mini-humbuckers (some in '75 had regular humbuckers), cherry or walnut.

1972-1976		$975	$1,200

SG III
1972-1974. The sunburst version of the II, some shipped as late as '79.

1972-1974		$975	$1,200

MODEL YEAR	FEATURES	EXC. COND. LOW	HIGH

SG Junior
1963-1971, 1991-1994. One pickup, solidbody. Prices are for an unfaded finish, cherry finish faded to brown reduces the value by 30%.

1963	Cherry	$3,600	$4,500
1963	White	$4,500	$5,500
1964	Cherry	$3,300	$4,000
1964	White	$3,700	$4,600
1965	Early-'65 cherry	$3,200	$3,900
1965	Late-'65 cherry	$2,600	$3,200
1965	Pelham Blue	$5,100	$6,300
1965	White	$3,200	$4,000
1966	Cherry	$2,600	$3,200
1966	White	$3,000	$3,500
1967	Cherry	$2,400	$2,800
1967	White	$2,900	$3,100
1968	Cherry	$2,300	$2,700
1968	White	$2,800	$3,400
1969	Cherry	$2,100	$2,250
1970	Cherry	$1,600	$2,100
1971	Cherry or walnut	$1,300	$1,600
1991-1994	Various colors	$675	$725

SG Junior P-90
2007. Single P-90 pickup, large 'guard, stop tail, cherry finish.

2007		$500	$525

SG Les Paul Custom
1986-1992. Called the SG '62 Custom in '86 and SG '90 Les Paul Custom in '90-'92 and SG '67 Custom Shop (300 made) towards the end of its run, 3 humbuckers.

1986-1989	Antique Ivory	$1,700	$2,100
1990-1992	White	$1,700	$2,100
1992	Burgundy	$1,700	$2,100

SG Les Paul Custom Reissue
1999-present. 1961 specs, SG body style, 3 humbuckers, Deluxe Maestro vibrato or stud with tune-o-matic bridge, white..

1999-2007	White or silver	$1,600	$2,000

SG Les Paul Custom 30th Anniversary
1991. SG body, 3 humbuckers, gold hardware, TV Yellow finish, 30th Anniversary on peghead.

1991		$2,000	$2,200

SG Menace
2006-2007. Carved mahogany body, 2 exposed humbuckers, flat black finish, black hardware, single brass knuckle position marker, gig bag.

2006-2007		$575	$625

SG Music Machine Stinger
2003. Custom run for dealer Music Machine, special serial number series, SG Custom with 2 pickups and SG Standard models available, black stinger paint job on neck/headstock, various colors.

2003	SG Custom	$2,800	$3,000
2003	SG Standard	$2,400	$2,600

SG Pete Townshend Signature (Historic/ Custom Shop)
2000-2003. SG Special with '70 specs, large 'guard, 2 cases, cherry red.

2000-2003	Includes certificate	$2,000	$2,400

SG Platinum
2005. A mix of SG Special and SG Standard specs, platinum paint on the body, back of neck, and head-stock, no crown inlay, Gibson stencil logo, exposed humbucker pickups, large plantium-finish 'guard, special plantium colored Gibson logo guitar case.

2005		$600	$950

SG Pro
1971-1973. Two P-90 pickups, tune-o-matic bridge, vibrato, cherry, mahogany or walnut.

1971-1973	Cherry	$1,400	$1,500
1971-1973	Mahogany or walnut	$1,200	$1,400

SG Select
2007. Made in Nashville, TN, carved solid book-matched AAA flame maple, 3-piece flamed maple neck, described as the most exquisite SG offered to date, 2 humbuckers, gold hardware.

2007		$2,200	$2,300

SG Special
1959-1978, 1985-present. Rounded double-cut for '59-'60, switched to SG body early-'61, 2 P-90s '59-'71, 2 mini-humbuckers '72-'78, 2 regular humbuckers on current version, reintroduced in '85. Prices are for an unfaded finish, cherry finish faded to brown reduces the value by 20%-30%. Instruments with stop tailpieces vs. Maestro tailpiece have the same value.

1959	Cherry, slab, high neck pickup	$11,100	$13,900
1960	Cherry, slab, lower neck pickup	$11,100	$13,900
1961	Cherry, SG body	$9,100	$10,400
1962	Cherry	$5,600	$6,900
1962	White	$7,100	$8,900
1963	Cherry	$5,500	$6,500
1963	White	$7,000	$8,000
1964	Cherry	$5,500	$6,500
1964	White	$7,000	$8,000
1965	Cherry	$5,000	$6,000
1965	White	$5,500	$6,500
1966	Cherry, large 'guard	$3,800	$4,000
1966	Cherry, small 'guard	$4,000	$5,000
1966	White, large 'guard	$4,000	$4,300
1966	White, small 'guard	$4,300	$5,300
1967	Cherry	$3,800	$4,000
1967	White	$4,000	$4,300
1968-1971	Cherry	$1,800	$2,500
1972-1975	Cherry or walnut	$1,400	$1,550
1976-1978	Cherry or walnut	$1,200	$1,350
1986-1999	Common colors	$750	$800
1986-1999	Rare colors	$800	$950
2000-2007	Common colors	$675	$800

SG Special 3/4
1961. Only 61 shipped.

1961		$8,000	$9,000

Gibson SG Pete Townshend Signature

Gibson SG Select

1965 Gibson SG Standard

1969 Gibson SG Standard

SG Special Faded (3 pickups)
2007. Made in Nashville, 3 exposed humbuckers, dot markers, stop tail, SG initials on truss rod cover, 2 knobs and 6-position selector switch, hand-worn satin finish.

Year	Features	Low	High
2007		$475	$550

SG Special Faded/Faded SG Special
2002-present. Aged worn cherry finish.

| 2002-2005 | Half moon markers | $550 | $650 |
| 2003-2007 | Dot markers | $450 | $500 |

SG Special II EMG
2007. EMG humbucker pickups, no position markers, standard 4-knob and 3-way toggle switch SG format, black satin finish over entire guitar, black hardware.

| 2007 | | $800 | $850 |

SG Special New Century
Introduced in 2007. Dramatic full-body mirror 'guard, mahogany body and neck, 490R and 498T humbuckers, classic '60s neck profile, mirror truss rod cover, dot markers.

| 2007 | | $600 | $700 |

SG Standard
1963-1981, 1983-present. Les Paul Standard changes to SG body, 2 humbuckers, some very early models have optional factory Bigsby. Prices are for an unfaded finish, a cherry finish faded to brown reduces the value by 30% or more.

1963	Cherry, small 'guard, deluxe vibrato	$16,000	$21,000
1964	Cherry, small 'guard, deluxe vibrato	$16,000	$21,000
1964	Pelham Blue, small 'guard, deluxe vibrato	$20,000	$25,000
1965	Cherry, small 'guard, deluxe vibrato	$15,000	$17,000
1965	Pelham Blue, small 'guard, deluxe vibrato	$18,000	$22,000
1966	Cherry, large 'guard	$7,000	$8,000
1967	Burgundy Metallic	$7,000	$8,500
1967	Cherry	$6,500	$8,000
1967	White	$7,000	$8,500
1968	Cherry, engraved lyre	$6,500	$8,000
1969	Engraved lyre, 1-piece neck	$6,500	$8,000
1969	Engraved lyre, 3-piece neck	$4,000	$4,500
1970	Cherry, non-lyre tailpiece	$2,400	$2,700
1970	Engraved lyre, 3-piece neck	$3,500	$4,000
1970	Walnut, non-lyre tailpiece	$2,200	$2,400
1971	Cherry, non-lyre tailpiece	$2,100	$2,400
1971	Engraved lyre, 3-piece neck	$2,800	$3,000
1971-1975	New specs, block markers	$2,000	$2,300
1976-1981	New color line-up	$1,600	$1,700
1983-1987		$975	$1,200
1988-1999	New specs	$900	$1,100
2000-2007	Standard colors, large 'guard, stoptail	$850	$1,000
2006-2007	Silverburst, 400 made	$1,400	$1,450

SG Standard Angus Young Signature
2000-present. Late-'60s specs with large 'guard, Deluxe Maestro lyre vibrato with Angus logo, late-'60s style knobs, Angus logo on headstock, aged cherry finish.

| 2000-2008 | | $1,550 | $1,650 |

SG Standard Celebrity Series
1991-1992. SG Standard with large 'guard, gold hardware, black finish.

| 1991-1992 | | $1,450 | $1,550 |

SG Standard Gary Rossington Signature
2004. '63-'64 SG Standard specs with Deluxe Maestro vibrola, '60 slim taper neck, limited edition, faded cherry aged by Tom Murphy.

| 2004 | | $2,800 | $3,000 |

SG Standard Korina
1993-1994. Korina version of SG Standard, limited run, natural.

| 1993-1994 | | $1,900 | $2,100 |

SG Standard Reissue
2004-present. Reissue of near '63-'64 specs with Deluxe Maestro lyre vibrato and small 'guard, also offered with stop bar tailpiece, cherry finish, '60 slim taper neck, smooth neck heel joint, trapezoid markers, unmarked truss rod cover without Les Paul designation, formerly called Les Paul SG Standard Reissue, by 2005 part of Gibson's 'Vintage Original Spec' Custom Shop series.

| 2004-2007 | | $2,000 | $2,400 |

SG Supreme
2004-2007. '57 humbuckers, flamed maple top, split-diamond markers, various colors.

| 2004-2007 | | $1,450 | $1,500 |

SG Tommy Iommi Signature (Historic/ Custom Shop)
2001-2003. Custom Shop higher-end, signature humbuckers without poles, cross inlays, ebony or Wine Red.

| 2001-2003 | | $3,800 | $4,700 |

SG TV
1959-1968. Les Paul TV changed to SG body, double rounded cutaway solidbody for '59-'60, SG body '61-'68, 1 pickup, limed mahogany (TV yellow) finish. Prices are for unfaded finish, a faded finish reduces the value by 20%-30%.

| 1959-1961 | TV Yellow, slab body | $14,000 | $18,000 |
| 1961-1963 | White, SG body | $5,000 | $6,000 |

The *Vintage Guitar Price Guide* shows low to high values for items in all-original excellent condition, and, where applicable, with original case or cover.

MODEL YEAR	FEATURES	EXC. COND. LOW	HIGH
SG Voodoo/Voodoo SG			
2004-2005. Black satin finish.			
2004-2005		$900	$1,100
SG-3			
2007-present. SG styling with 3 gold humbuckers, 1 rotor switch, 2 knobs, SG Standard appointments, stop tail.			
2007		$1,100	$1,150
SG-90 Double			
1988-1990. SG body, updated electronics, graphite reinforced neck, 2 pickups, cherry, turquoise or white.			
1988-1990		$600	$650
SG-90 Single			
1988-1990. SG body, updated electronics, graphite reinforced neck, 1 humbucker pickup, cherry, turquoise or white.			
1988-1990		$550	$600
SG-100			
1971-1972. Double-cut solidbody, 1 pickup, cherry or walnut.			
1971-1972	Melody Maker pickup	$550	$900
1971-1972	P-90 pickup option	$1,000	$1,200
SG-200			
1971-1972. Two pickup version of SG-100 in black, cherry or walnut finish, replaced by SG II.			
1971-1972	Melody Maker pickups	$650	$1,100
SG-250			
1971-1972. Two-pickup version of SG-100 in cherry sunburst, replaced by SG III.			
1971-1972	Melody Maker pickups	$750	$1,200
SG-400/SG Special 400			
1985-1987. SG body with 3 toggles, 2 knobs (master volume, master tone), single-single-humbucker pickups, available with uncommon opaque finishes.			
1985-1987		$750	$900
SG-R1/SG Artist			
1980-1982. Active RD-era electronics. SG style but thicker body, no 'guard, ebony 'board, black finish, dot markers, renamed SG Artist in '81.			
1980	SG-R1	$850	$1,150
1981-1982	SG Artist	$850	$1,150
SG-X (All American)			
1995-1999. Renamed the SG-X in '98, previously part of the all American series, SG body with single bridge humbucker, various colors.			
1995-1999		$550	$650
The SG			
1979-1983. Offered as The SG Standard with solid walnut body and The SG Deluxe with solid mahogany body, normal SG specs, ebony 'board, 2 humbuckers, model name logo on truss rod.			
1979-1983	Walnut or mahogany	$900	$1,000
SJ (Southern Jumbo)			
1942-1969,1991-1996. Flat-top, sunburst standard, natural optional starting in '54 (natural finish version called Country-Western starting in '56), round			

MODEL YEAR	FEATURES	EXC. COND. LOW	HIGH
shoulders (changed to square in '62), catalog name changed to SJ Deluxe in '70, refer to that listing.			
1942-1944		$7,700	$11,000
1948		$5,700	$8,200
1949		$5,600	$8,100
1950		$5,500	$7,900
1951		$5,400	$7,700
1952		$5,300	$7,500
1953		$5,000	$6,200
1954	Natural option	$4,700	$5,800
1954	Sunburst	$4,400	$5,700
1955	Natural option	$4,600	$5,800
1955	Sunburst	$4,300	$5,600
1956	Natural option	$4,500	$5,700
1956	Sunburst	$4,200	$5,600
1957		$4,100	$5,500
1958		$4,000	$5,500
1959		$3,900	$5,400
1960		$3,800	$5,400
1961-1962	Round shoulder	$3,800	$5,300
1962-1963	Square shoulder	$3,000	$3,400
1964	Square shoulder	$2,900	$3,300
1965		$2,600	$2,800
1966		$2,300	$2,600
1967-1968		$2,100	$2,500
1969	Below belly bridge	$1,800	$2,200
SJ (Southern Jumbo) 1942 Reissue			
2000. Custom Shop, mahogany back and sides, '42 SJ appointments, 'Only A Gibson is Good Enough' banner logo.			
2000		$2,400	$2,900
SJ (Southern Jumbo) Hank Williams Jr. Hall of Fame			
1997. Custom Shop, mahogany back and sides, SJ appointments.			
1997		$2,300	$2,500
SJ (Southern Jumbo) Reissue			
2003-present. Sunburst.			
2003-2007		$1,450	$1,600
SJ (Southern Jumbo) Woody Guthrie			
2003-present. Single-bound round shoulder body, mahogany back and sides, parallelogram inlays.			
2003-2008		$1,800	$2,000
SJ Deluxe (Southern Jumbo)			
1970-1978. SJ name changed to SJ Deluxe in catalog, along with a series of engineering changes.			
1970-1971	Non-adj. saddle	$1,400	$1,700
1972-1973	Unbound 'board	$1,000	$1,500
1974-1978	4-ply to binding	$900	$1,100
SJN (Country-Western)			
1956-1969. Flat-top, natural finish version of SJ, round shoulders '56-'62, square shoulders after that, called the SJN in '60 and '61, the SJN Country Western after that, catalog name changed to SJN Deluxe in '70, refer to that listing.			
1956	Round shoulder	$3,900	$5,700
1957	Round shoulder	$3,800	$5,600
1958	Round shoulder	$3,700	$5,500
1959	Round shoulder	$3,600	$5,400
1960	Round shoulder	$3,500	$5,300
1961	Round shoulder	$4,500	$5,700

Gibson SG Standard Angus Young Signature

Gibson SG Tony Iommi Signature

GUITARS

Gibson Songwriter Deluxe

Gibson Style U

MODEL YEAR	FEATURES	EXC. COND. LOW	HIGH
1962	Square shoulder	$3,100	$3,800
1963	Square shoulder	$3,000	$3,700
1964	Square shoulder	$2,900	$3,600
1965	Square shoulder	$2,700	$3,000
1966	Square shoulder	$2,400	$3,000
1967-1968	Square shoulder	$2,200	$2,700
1969	Below belly bridge, SJN logo	$1,900	$2,400

SJN Deluxe (Country-Western Jumbo)
1970-1978. SJN name changed to SJN Deluxe in catalog, along with a series of engineering changes.

1970-1971	Non-adj. saddle	$1,700	$1,900
1972-1973	Unbound 'board	$1,300	$1,600
1974-1978	4-ply to binding	$1,000	$1,200

SJ-100 1939 Centennial
1994. Acoustic flat-top, limited edition, sunburst

1994		$1,900	$2,100

SJ-200 Elvis Presley Signature
2001. 250 made, large block letter Elvis Presley name on 'board, figured maple sides and back, gloss natural spruce top, black and white custom designed 'guard after one of Presley's personal guitars.

2001		$3,400	$3,600

SJ-200 Ray Whitley/J-200 Custom Club
1994-1995. Based on Ray Whitley's late-1930s J-200, including engraved inlays and initials on the truss rod cover, only 37 made, one of the limited edition models the Montana division released to celebrate Gibson's 100th anniversary.

1994-1995		$7,700	$8,800

Sonex-180 Custom
1980-1982. Two Super humbuckers, coil-tap, maple neck, ebony 'board, single-cut, body of Multi-Phonic synthetic material, black or white.

1980-1982		$650	$700

Sonex-180 Deluxe
1980-1984. Hardwood neck, rosewood 'board, single-cut, body of Multi-Phonic synthetic material, 2 pickups, no coil-tap, various colors.

1980-1984	Ebony	$650	$700
1982-1984	Red or Fireburst	$725	$800
1982-1984	Silverburst	$725	$800

Sonex-180 Standard
1980. Dirty-fingers pickups, rosewood 'board, ebony finish.

1980		$650	$700

Songbird Deluxe
1999-2003. Square shoulder flat top, Indian rosewood back and sides and 'board, on-board electronics.

1999-2003		$1,325	$1,400

Songwriter Deluxe
2003-present. Square shoulder flat top, Indian rosewood back and sides, on-board electronics

2003-2008	Cutaway	$1,325	$1,350
2003-2008	Non-cutaway	$1,275	$1,300

Spirit I
1982-1988. Double rounded cutaway, 1 pickup, chrome hardware, various colors.

1982-1988		$500	$650

MODEL YEAR	FEATURES	EXC. COND. LOW	HIGH

Spirit II XPL
1985-1987. Double-cut solidbody, Kahler tremolo, 2 pickups, various colors.

1985-1987		$600	$675

SR-71
1987-1989. Floyd Rose tremolo, 1 humbucker, 2 single-coil pickups, various colors, Wayne Charvel designed.

1987-1989		$600	$675

Star
1992. Star logo on headstock, star position markers, single sharp cutaway flat-top, sunburst.

1991-1992		$1,200	$1,400

Style O
1902-1925. Acoustic archtop, oval soundhole, bound top, neck and headstock, various colors.

1910-1925		$5,000	$6,200

Style U Harp Guitar
1902-1939. Acoustic 6-string, with 10 or 12 sub-bass strings, maple back and sides, bound soundhole, black.

1915-1919		$6,500	$7,500

Super 300
1948-1955. Acoustic archtop, non-cut, bound body, neck and headstock, sunburst.

1948		$5,500	$6,000
1949		$5,000	$6,000
1950		$4,500	$5,500
1951		$4,400	$5,400
1952		$4,300	$5,300
1953		$4,200	$5,200
1954		$4,100	$5,100
1955		$4,000	$5,000

Super 300 C
1954-1958. Acoustic archtop, rounded cutaway, bound body, neck and headstock, sunburst with natural option.

1954-1958	Sunburst	$5,000	$6,500

Super 400
1934-1941, 1947-1955. Acoustic archtop, non-cut, multi-bound, f-holes, sunburst (see Super 400 N for natural version).

1934	Super L-5 Deluxe (intro. Model)	$25,000	$30,000
1934-1935		$15,000	$18,000
1936-1941		$12,000	$15,000
1947-1949		$11,000	$12,000
1950-1955		$9,000	$11,000

Super 400 N
1940, 1948-1955. Natural finish version of Super 400, non-cut, acoustic archtop.

1940		$14,000	$15,000
1948		$14,000	$15,000
1949		$13,000	$14,000
1950-1955		$12,000	$13,000

Super 400 P (Premier)
1939-1941. Acoustic archtop, single rounded cutaway, '39 model 'board rests on top, sunburst finish.

1939		$25,000	$30,000
1940-1941		$25,000	$30,000

MODEL YEAR	FEATURES	EXC. COND. LOW	HIGH

Super 400 PN (Premier Natural)
1939-1940. Rounded cutaway, '39 'board rests on top, natural finish.

| 1939 | | $30,000 | $40,000 |
| 1940 | | $30,000 | $35,000 |

Super 400 C
1948-1982. Introduced as Super 400 Premier, acoustic archtop, single-cut, sunburst finish (natural is called Super 400 CN).

1948-1949		$13,000	$16,000
1950-1951		$12,000	$14,000
1952-1959		$12,000	$13,000
1960-1964		$11,000	$12,000
1965-1966		$8,000	$10,000
1967-1969		$7,000	$9,000
1970-1974		$6,000	$8,000
1975-1979		$5,500	$7,000
1980-1982		$5,000	$7,000

Super 400 CN
1950-1987. Natural finish version of Super 400 C.

1950-1951		$15,000	$19,000
1952-1958		$14,000	$16,000
1959		$14,000	$15,000
1960-1962		$13,000	$15,000
1963-1964		$12,000	$14,000
1965-1966		$10,000	$12,000
1967-1969		$9,000	$11,000

Super 400 CES
1951-present. Electric version of Super 400 C, archtop, single-cut (round '51-'60 and '69-present, pointed '60-'69), 2 pickups (P-90s '51-'54, Alnico Vs '54-'57, humbuckers '57 on), sunburst (natural version called Super 400 CESN), now part of Gibson's Historic Collection.

1951-1953	P-90s	$13,000	$18,000
1954-1957	Alnico Vs	$14,000	$20,000
1957-1959	PAFs	$25,000	$30,000
1960	PAFs	$22,000	$28,000
1961-1962	PAFs, sharp cut intro.	$13,000	$20,000
1963-1964	Pat. #	$12,000	$14,000
1965-1966		$9,000	$11,000
1967-1969		$7,000	$9,000
1970-1974		$6,000	$8,000
1975-1979		$6,000	$7,000
1980-1987		$6,000	$6,500

Super 400 CESN
1952-present. Natural version of Super 400 CES, now part of Gibson's Historic Collection.

1952-1953	P-90s	$20,000	$25,000
1954-1956	Alnico Vs	$22,000	$26,000
1957-1959	PAFs	$30,000	$35,000
1960	PAFs	$25,000	$34,000
1961-1962	PAFs, sharp cut intro.	$18,000	$22,000
1963-1964	Pat. #	$14,000	$16,000
1965-1966		$11,000	$13,000
1967-1969		$9,000	$11,000
1970-1974		$7,000	$9,000
1975-1979		$6,000	$7,500
1980-1987		$6,000	$7,000

'39 Super 400
1993-1997. Reissue of non-cut '39 version. Part of Gibson's Historic Collection, various colors.

| 1993-1997 | | $6,800 | $7,200 |

Super Jumbo 100
1939-1943. Jumbo flat-top, mahogany back and sides, bound body and neck, sunburst, reintroduced as J-100 with different specs in '84.

| 1939-1941 | Stairstep peghead | $30,000 | $35,000 |
| 1941-1943 | Standard peghead | $25,000 | $30,000 |

Super Jumbo/Super Jumbo 200
1938-1947. Initially called Super Jumbo in '38 and named Super Jumbo 200 in '39. name then changed to J-200 (see that listing) by '47 (with maple back and sides) and SJ-200 by the '50s. Named for super large jumbo 16 7/8" flat-top body, double braced with rosewood back and sides, sunburst finish.

| 1938-1939 | | $65,000 | $75,000 |
| 1940-1942 | | $63,000 | $73,000 |

Super V BJB
1978-1983. A Super V CES but with a single floating pickup.

| 1978-1983 | | $6,500 | $7,500 |

Super V CES
1978-1993. Archtop, L-5 with a Super 400 neck, 2 humbucker pickups, natural or sunburst.

| 1978-1993 | | $6,500 | $7,500 |

Tal Farlow
1962-1971, 1993-2006. Full body, single-cut archtop, 2 humbuckers, triple-bound top, reintroduced '93, now part of Gibson's Historic Collection.

1962-1964	Viceroy Brown	$7,600	$9,300
1965-1966	Viceroy Brown	$7,000	$8,600
1967-1969	Viceroy Brown	$6,500	$7,800
1970-1971	Viceroy Brown	$5,000	$6,500
1993-2000	Cherry or Viceroy Brown	$2,600	$3,100
1993-2000	Natural, figured wood	$3,000	$3,400

TG-0 (L-0 based)
1927-1933. Acoustic tenor based on L-0, mahogany body, light amber.

| 1927-1933 | | $1,350 | $1,500 |

TG-0 (LG-0 based)
1960-1974. Acoustic tenor based on LG-0, mahogany body, natural.

1960-1964		$700	$800
1965-1966		$600	$650
1967-1969		$550	$600
1970-1974		$450	$500

TG-00 (L-00 based)
1932-1943. Tenor flat-top based on L-00.

| 1932-1943 | | $1,450 | $1,600 |

TG-1/L-1 Tenor/L-4 Tenor (and Plectrum)
1927-1937. Acoustic flat-top, tenor or plectrum guitar based on L-1, mahogany back and sides, bound body, sunburst.

| 1927-1933 | | $1,550 | $2,000 |
| 1934-1937 | | $1,550 | $2,000 |

Gibson Super 400

1959 Gibson Super 400 CES

To get the most from this book, be sure to read "Using *The Guide*" in the introduction.

MODEL YEAR	FEATURES	EXC. COND. LOW	HIGH

TG-7
1934-1940. Tenor based on the L-7, sunburst.

| 1934-1940 | | $3,000 | $3,600 |

TG-25/TG-25 N
1962-1970. Acoustic flat-top, tenor guitar based on B-25, mahogany back and sides, sunburst or natural (25 N).

1962-1964		$800	$950
1965-1966		$700	$850
1967-1970		$600	$750

TG-50
1934-1958. Acoustic archtop, tenor guitar based on L-50, mahogany back and sides, sunburst.

1934-1940		$1,500	$1,850
1947-1949		$1,400	$1,750
1950-1958		$1,300	$1,600
1961		$1,250	$1,550
1963		$1,200	$1,500

Traveling Songwriter CE
2007-present. Solid spruce top, solid mahogany sides and back, soft cutaway, on-board electronics and EQ.

| 2007-2008 | | $1,450 | $1,600 |

Trini Lopez Deluxe
1964-1970. Double pointed cutaway, thinline archtop, 2 humbuckers, triple-bound, sunburst.

1964		$4,000	$4,600
1965		$3,100	$4,100
1966		$3,000	$4,100
1967-1970		$2,900	$3,100

Trini Lopez Standard
1964-1970. Double rounded cutaway, thinline archtop, 2 humbuckers, tune-o-matic bridge, trapeze tailpiece, single-bound, cherry, sparkling burgundy and Pelham Blue finishes.

1964	Cherry	$3,200	$3,900
1965	Cherry	$2,500	$3,100
1965	Sparkling Burgundy, Pelham Blue	$2,700	$3,400
1966	Cherry	$2,500	$3,000
1966	Sparkling Burgundy, Pelham Blue	$2,700	$3,300
1967-1970	Cherry	$2,400	$2,700
1967-1970	Sparkling Burgundy, Pelham Blue	$2,600	$3,000

U-2
1987-1989. Double-cut, 1 humbucker and 2 single-coil pickups, ebony or red, renamed Mach II in '90-'91.

| 1987-1991 | | $650 | $800 |

U-2 Showcase Edition
1988. November 1988 Guitar of the Month series, 250 made.

| 1988 | | $750 | $850 |

US-1/US-3
1986-1991. Double-cut maple top with mahogany back, 3 humbucker pickups (US-1), or 3 P-90s (US-3), standard production and Custom Shop.

| 1986-1991 | | $600 | $750 |

MODEL YEAR	FEATURES	EXC. COND. LOW	HIGH

Vegas Standard
2006-2007. Flat top semi-hollowbody thinline, slim neck, 2 humbuckers, f-holes, split diamond inlays.

| 2006-2007 | | $1,100 | $1,300 |

Vegas High Roller
2006-2007. Upgraded version, AAA maple top, gold hardware and frets, block inlays.

| 2006-2007 | | $1,300 | $1,500 |

Victory MV II (MV 2)
1981-1984. Asymetrical double-cut with long horn, 3-way slider, maple body and neck, rosewood 'board, 2 pickups.

| 1981-1984 | | $600 | $750 |

Victory MV X (MV 10)
1981-1984. 3 humbuckers, 5-way switch, various colors.

| 1981-1984 | | $700 | $900 |

XPL Custom
1985-1986. Explorer-like shape, exposed humbuckers, locking tremolo, bound maple top, sunburst or white.

| 1985-1986 | | $600 | $650 |

Giffin
1977-1988, 1997-present. Professional and premium grade, production/custom, hollow-, semi-hollow-, and solidbody guitars built by luthier Roger Giffin in West San Fernando Valley, California. For '77-'88, Giffin's shop was in London. From '88 to '93, he worked for the Gibson Custom Shop in California as a Master Luthier. In '97, Giffin set up shop in Sweden for a year, moving back to California in the Spring of '98. He also built small numbers of instruments during '67-'76 and '94-'96 (when he had a repair business).

Gigliotti
2000-present. Premium grade, production/custom, electric guitars with a metal plate top and tone chambers and designed by Patrick Gigliotti in Tacoma, Washington.

Gila Eban Guitars
1979-present. Premium grade, custom, classical guitars built by luthier Gila Eban in Riverside, Connecticut.

Gilbert Guitars
1965-present. Custom classical guitars by luthiers John Gilbert and William Gilbert in Paso Robles, California. Son William has handled all production since 1991.

Gilet Guitars
1976-present. Luthier Gerard Gilet builds production/custom, premium grade, acoustic, classical, flamenco, and wooden bodied resonator guitars in Botany, Sydney, New South Wales, Australia. He also builds lap steels.

Gibson Trini Lopez Standard

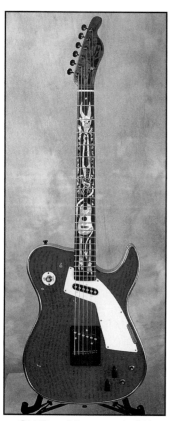

Girl Brand Crossroads Girl

MODEL YEAR	FEATURES	EXC. COND. LOW	HIGH

Girl Brand Guitars

1996-present. Premium-grade, production/custom, guitars built by luthier Chris Larsen in Tucson, Arizona.

Gitane

2003-present. Intermediate and professional grade, production, classic Selmer-Maccaferri style jazz guitars made in China for Saga.

Gittler

1974-ca.1985. Minimalistic electric guitar designed by Allan Gittler, consisting basically of a thin rod with frets welded to it. A total of 560 were built, with Gittler making the first 60 in the U.S. from '74 to the early '80s. The remainder were made around '85 in Israel by the Astron corporation under a licensing agreement. Three Gittler basses were also built. Gittler emigrated to Israel in the early '80s and changed his name to Avraham Bar Rashi. He died in 2002. An U.S.-made Gittler is the only musical instrument in the Museum of Modern Art in New York.

Metal Skeleton
1971-1999.

1971-1982		$2,100	$2,600
1982-1999		$1,800	$2,100

Glendale

2004-present. Professional grade, production/custom, solidbody guitars built by luthier Dale Clark in Arlington, Texas.

GLF

1991-1997. Solidbody electric guitars built by luthier Kevin Smith in Minnesota. In '97 he started building his ToneSmith line of guitars.

Glick Guitars

1996-present. Premium grade, production/custom, acoustic and electric archtop, and acoustic guitars built in Santa Barbara, California by luthier Mike Glick.

Global

Late-1960s-1970s. Budget copy models, not unlike Teisco, imported from Asia for the student market. They also offered amps.

Electric Solidbody
Late-1960s-1970s.

1960s		$175	$200

GMP

1990-2005. Professional and premium grade solidbody electric guitars built by GM Precision Products, Inc. of San Dimas, California. Original owners were Gary and Cameron Moline, Dave Pearson and Glenn Matejzel. Many guitars featured fancy tops or custom graphics. They also made basses. Overall production is estimated at 1120 guitars and basses. GMP was set to reopen in '09 under new ownership.

GMW

1998-present. Professional grade, production/custom, solidbody guitars from Lee Garver's GMW Guitarworks of Glendora, California.

Godin

1987-present. Intermediate and professional grade, production, solidbody electrics and nylon and steel string acoustic/electrics from luthier Robert Godin. They also build basses and mandolins. Necks and bodies are made in La Patrie, Quebec with final assembly in Berlin, New Hampshire. Godin is also involved in the Seagull, Norman, Art & Lutherie, and Patrick & Simon brand of guitars.

Acousticaster 6
1987-2004. Thin line single-cut chambered maple body, acoustic/electric, maple neck, 6-on-a-side tuners, spruce top.

1987-1999		$425	$525
2000-2004		$450	$525

Acousticaster 6 Deluxe
1994-present. Acousticaster 6 with mahogany body.

1994-2007		$500	$625

Artisan ST I/ST I
1992-1998. Offset double-cut solidbody, birdseye maple top, 3 pickups.

1992-1998		$450	$500

Flat Five X
2002-2004. Single-cut, semi-hollow with f-holes, 3-way pickup system (magnetic to transducer).

2002-2004		$725	$900

G-1000/G-2000/G-3000
1993-1996. Offset double-cut solidbody, extra large bass horn, various pickup options.

1993-1996		$275	$325

Glissentar A11
2000-present. Electric/acoustic nylon 11-string, solid cedar top, chambered maple body, fretless, natural.

2000-2007		$450	$550

Jeff Cook Signature
1994-1995. Quilted maple top, light maple back, 2 twin rail and 1 humbucker pickups.

1994-1995		$525	$650

LG/LGT
1995-present. Single-cut carved slab mahogany body, 2 Tetrad Combo pickups ('95-'97) or 2 Duncan SP-90 pickups ('98-present), various colors, satin lacquer finish. LGT with tremolo.

1997-2007		$300	$375

LGX/LGXT/LGX-SA
1996-present. Single-cut maple-top carved solidbody, 2 Duncan humbuckers, various quality tops offered. LGXT with tremolo.

1996-2007	Standard top	$650	$750
1997-2007	SA synth access	$900	$1,000
1998-2007	AA top	$750	$850
1998-2007	AAA top	$900	$1,100

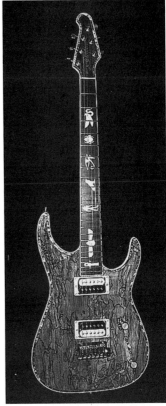

GMW Solidbody

1933 Godin LGX

1974 Grammer S-20

1960 Greco

MODEL YEAR	FEATURES	EXC. COND. LOW	HIGH

Montreal
2004-present. Chambered body carved from solid mahogany, f-holes, 2 humbuckers, saddle transducer, stereo mixing output.

2004-2006		$900	$975

Multiac Series
1994-present. Single-cut, thinline electric with solid spruce top, RMC Sensor System electronics, available in either nylon string or steel string versions, built-in EQ, program up/down buttons.

1994-2007	Duet Nylon, classical	$700	$850
1994-2007	Steel string	$850	$1,025
2000-2007	Jazz SA	$850	$1,025

Radiator
1999-present. Single-cut, dual pickup, pearloid top, dot markers.

1999-2007		$200	$250

Solidac - Two Voice
2000-present Single-cut, 2-voice technology for electric or acoustic sound.

2000-2007		$350	$400

TC Signature
1987-1999. Single-cut, quilted maple top, 2 Tetrad Combo pickups.

1987-1999		$500	$600

Gold Tone
1993-present. Wayne and Robyn Rogers build their intermediate and professional grade, production/custom guitars in Titusville, Florida. They also build basses, lap steels, mandolins, ukuleles, banjos and banjitars.

Golden Hawaiian
1920s-1930s. Private branded lap guitar most likely made by one of the many Chicago makers for a small retailer, publisher, cataloger, or teaching studio.

Guitars

1920-1930s	Sunburst	$400	$500

Goldentone
1960s. Guitars made by Ibanez most likely in the mid to late '60s. Often have a stylized I (for Ibanez) on the tailpiece or an Ibanez logo on the headstock.

Goldon
German manufacturer of high-quality archtops and other guitars before and shortly after WW II. After the war, they were located in East Germany and by the late 1940s were only making musical toys.

Goodall
1972-present. Premium grade, custom flat-tops and nylon-strings, built by luthier James Goodall originally in California and, since '92, in Kailua-Kona, Hawaii.

MODEL YEAR	FEATURES	EXC. COND. LOW	HIGH

Standard
1980s-2000s. Jumbo-style with wide waist, mahogany back and sides, sitka spruce top.

1980-2000s		$2,000	$2,500

Goodman Guitars
1975-present. Premium grade, custom/production, archtop, flat top, classical, and electric guitars built by luthier Brad Goodman in Brewster, New York. He also builds mandolins.

Gordon-Smith
1979-present. Intermediate and professional grade, production/custom, semi-hollow and solidbody guitars built by luthier John Smith in Partington, England.

Gower
1955-1960s. Built in Nashville by Jay Gower, later joined by his son Randy. Gower is also associated with Billy Grammer and Grammer guitars.

G-55-2 Flat-Top
1960s. Square shoulder-style flat-top, triple abalone rosette, abalone fretboard trim, small block markers, natural.

1960s		$800	$1,000

G-65 Flat-Top
1960s. Square shoulder-style flat-top, lower belly bridge with pearl dots on bridge, dot markers, sunburst.

1960s		$600	$750

Solidbody Electric
1960s. Mosrite influenced odd-shaped body, 2 single-coils, bolt neck, Bigsby bridge.

1960s		$500	$625

Goya
1955-present. Brand initially used by Hershman Musical Instrument Company of New York City, New York, in mid-'50s for acoustic guitars made in Sweden by Levin, particularly known for its classicals. From '58 to '61 they imported Hagstrom- and Galanti-made electrics labeled as Goya.

By '63 the company had become the Goya Musical Instrument Corporation, marketing primarily Goya acoustics. Goya was purchased by Avnet, Inc., prior to '66, when Avnet purchased Guild Guitars. In '69, Goya was purchased by Kustom which offered the instruments until '71. Probably some '70s guitars were made in Japan. The brand name was purchased by C.F. Martin in the mid-'70s, with Japanese-made acoustic guitars, solidbody electric guitars and basses, banjos and mandolins imported in around '78 and continuing through the '80s. The brand is currently used on Korean-made acoustic and acoustic/electric guitars, banjos and mandolins.

Model 80/Model 90
1959-1962. Single-cut body, replaceable modular pickup assembly, sparkle top.

1959-1962		$700	$750

MODEL		EXC. COND.	
YEAR	FEATURES	LOW	HIGH

Panther S-3
1960s. Double-cut solidbody, 3 pickups, Panther S-3 Goya logo, volume and tone knobs with 6 upper bass bout switches, bolt-on neck.

1960s		$600	$700

Rangemaster
1967-1969. Double-cut with 2 offset double-coil pickups and lots of buttons, made by EKO, sunburst.

1967-1969		$600	$700

Graf
See listing under Oskar Graf Guitars.

Grammer
1965-1970. Founded by Bill Grammer then sold to Ampeg.

G-10
1965-1970. Solid Brazilian rosewood back and sides, solid spruce top, large crown-shaped bridge, pearl dot markers, natural.

1965-1970		$1,400	$1,600

G-20
1965-1970. Natural.

1965-1970		$1,400	$1,600

G-30
1965-1970. Natural.

1965-1970		$1,400	$1,600

G-50
1965-1970. Top-of-the-line Grammer, Brazilian rosewood back and sides, Adirondack spruce top.

1965-1970		$2,100	$2,400

S-30
1965-1970. Solid spruce top, solid ribbon mahogany back and sides.

1965-1970		$1,300	$1,400

Granada
1970s-1980s. Japanese-made acoustic, electric solid, semi-hollow and hollowbody guitars, many copies of classic American models. They also offered basses.

Acoustic
1970s. Import from Japan, various copy models.

1970s		$125	$150

Electric
1970s. Import from Japan, various copy models.

1970s		$150	$175

Granata Guitars
1989-present. Luthier Peter Granata builds his professional grade, custom, flat-top and resonator guitars in Oak Ridge, New Jersey.

Graveel
Production/custom, solidbody guitars built by luthier Dean Graveel in Indianapolis, Indiana.

Grazioso
1950s. Grazioso was a brand name used by Selmer in England on instruments made in Czechoslovakia. They replaced the brand with their Futurama line of guitars.

GRD
1978-1982. High-end acoustic and electric guitars produced in Charles Fox's Guitar Research & Design Center in Vermont. GRD introduced the original thin-line acoustic-electric guitar to the world at the '78 Winter NAMM show.

Greco
1960s-present. Brand name used in Japan by Fuji Gen Gakki, maker of many Hoshino/Ibanez guitars; thus often Greco guitars are similar to Ibanez. During the '70s the company sold many high-quality copies of American designs, though by '75 they offered many weird-shaped original designs, including the Iceman and carved people shapes. By the late-'70s they were offering neck-through-body guitars. Currently owned by Kanda Shokai and offering solidbody, hollowbody and acoustic guitars, including models licensed by Zemaitis.

Green, Aaron
1990-present. Premium and presentation grade, custom, classical and flamenco guitars built by luthier Aaron Green in Waltham, Massachusetts.

Greene & Campbell
2002-2005. Luthier Dean Campbell builds his intermediate and professional grade, production/ custom, solidbody guitars in Westwood, Massachusetts. Founding partner Jeffrey Greene left the company in '04; Greene earlier built guitars under his own name. In '05, Campbell changed the name to Campbell American Guitars.

Greene, Jeffrey
2000-2002. Professional grade, production/ custom, electric solidbody guitars built by luthier Jeffrey Greene in West Kingston, Rhode Island. He went to work with Dean Campbell building the Greene & Campbell line of guitars.

Greenfield Guitars
1996-present. Luthier Michael Greenfield builds his production/custom, presentation grade, acoustic steel string, concert classical and archtop guitars in Montreal, Quebec, Canada.

Gretsch
1883-present. Currently Gretsch offers intermediate, professional, and premium grade, production, acoustic, solidbody, hollowbody, double neck, resonator and Hawaiian guitars. They also offer basses, amps and lap steels.

Previous brands included Gretsch, Rex, 20th Century, Recording King (for Montgomery Ward), Dorado (Japanese imports). Founded by Friedrich Gretsch in Brooklyn, New York, making drums, banjos, tambourines, and toy instruments which were sold to large distributors including C. Bruno and Wurlitzer. Upon early death of Friedrich, son Fred Gretsch, Sr. took over business at age 15. By the turn of the century the company was

Green Concert Classical

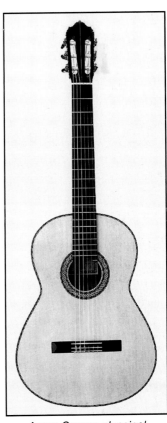
Aaron Greene classical

GUITARS

1966 Gretsch Astro-Jet

Gretsch G6136TBK
Black Falcon

also making mandolins. In the '20s, they were distributing Rex and 20th Century brands, some made by Gretsch, some by others such as Kay. Charles "Duke" Kramer joined Gretsch in '35. In '40 Gretsch purchased Bacon & Day banjos. Fred Gretsch, Sr. retired in '42 and was replaced by sons Fred, Jr. and Bill. Fred departs for Navy and Bill runs company until his death in '48, when Fred resumes control. After the war the decision was made to promote the Gretsch brand rather than selling to distributors, though some jobbing continues. Kramer becomes Chicago branch manager in '48.

In '67 Baldwin of Cincinnati buys Gretsch. During '70-'72 the factory relocates from Brooklyn to Booneville, Arkansas and company headquarters moves to Cincinnati. A '72 factory fire drastically reduces production for next two years. In '78 Baldwin buys Kustom amps and sells Gretsch to Kustom's Charlie Roy, and headquarters are moved to Chanute, Kansas. Duke Kramer retires in '80. Guitar production ends '80-'81. Ca. '83 ownership reverts back to Baldwin and Kramer was asked to arrange the sale of the company. In '84 Fred Gretsch III was contacted and in '85 Gretsch guitars came back to the Gretsch family and Fred Gretsch Enterprises, Ltd (FGE). Initial Gretsch Enterprise models were imports made by Japan's Terada Company. In '95, some U.S.-made models were introduced.

As of January 1, 2003, Fred Gretsch Enterprises, Ltd granted Fender Musical Instruments Corporation the exclusive rights to develop, produce, market and distribute Gretsch guitars worldwide where FMIC is responsible for all aspects of the Gretsch stringed instrument product lines and brands, including development of new products. Fred Gretsch consulted during the changeover and on product development and quality control.

12-String Electric Archtop (6075/6076)
1967-1972. 16" double-cut, 2 Super Tron pickups, 17" body option available, sunburst (6075) or natural (6076).

1967-1972	Natural	$2,000	$2,400
1967-1972	Sunburst	$1,900	$2,300

12-String Flat-Top (6020)
1969-1972. 15 1/5" body, mahogany back and sides, spruce top, slotted headstock, dot markers.

1969-1972		$800	$975

Anniversary (6124/6125)
1958-1971, 1993-1999. Single-cut hollowbody archtop, 1 pickup (Filtron '58-'60, Hi-Lo Tron '61 on), bound body, named for Gretsch's 75th anniversary. 6124 is 2-tone greeen with 2-tone tan an option, 6125 sunburst. Model numbers revived in '90s.

1958-1959	Green 2-tone	$2,000	$2,400
1958-1959	Sunburst	$1,900	$2,200
1960-1961	2-tone green or tan	$2,000	$2,500
1960-1961	Sunburst	$1,800	$2,100
1962-1964	2-tone green or tan	$1,900	$2,300
1962-1964	Sunburst	$1,700	$2,000
1965-1966	Various colors	$1,300	$1,600

1967-1969	Various colors	$1,200	$1,500
1970-1971	Various colors	$1,100	$1,350

Anniversary (6117/6118)
1993-present. 2 pickup like Double Anniversary, 6118 in 2-tone green with (T) or without Bigsby, 6117 is sunburst.

1993-2005	Various colors	$1,100	$1,350

Astro-Jet (6126)
1965-1967. Solidbody electric, double-cut, 2 pickups, vibrato, 4/2 tuner arrangement, red top with black back and sides.

1965-1967		$2,500	$3,000

Atkins Axe (7685/7686)
1976-1980. Solidbody electric, single pointed cutaway, 2 pickups, ebony stain (7685) or red rosewood stain (7686), called the Super Axe with added on-board effects.

1976-1980		$1,250	$1,500

Atkins Super Axe (7680/7681)
1976-1981. Single pointed cutaway solidbody with built-in phaser and sustain, five knobs, three switches, Red Rosewood (7680) or Ebony (7681) stains.

1976-1981		$1,900	$2,200

Bikini (6023/6024/6025)
1961-1962. Solidbody electric, separate 6-string and bass neck-body units that slide into 1 of 3 body butterflies - 1 for the 6-string only (6023), 1 for bass only (6024), 1 for double neck (6 and bass - 6025). Components could be purchased separately.

1961-1962	6023/6024, single neck	$825	$1,025
1961-1962	6025, double neck	$1,600	$1,900

Black Falcon (6136BK/TBK/DSBK)
1992-1997, 2003-present. Black version of Falcon, single-cut, 2.75" body, oversize f-holes, G tailpiece, DSBK with DynaSonic pickups replaces Filter'Tron BK in '06. Had the Limited Edition 1955 designation for '96-'97. Bigsby-equipped TBK offered '04-present.

1992-1997		$1,875	$2,000

Black Falcon (7594BK)
1992-1998. Black version of G7594 Falcon, double-cut, 2" thick body, Bigsby.

1992-1998		$1,875	$2,000

Black Falcon I (7593BK)
1993-1998, 2003-2005. G63136BK with Bigsby and standard f-holes. Came back in '03 as Black Falcon I with wire handle Gretsch Bigsby tailpiece.

1993-1998		$1,875	$2,000

Black Hawk (6100/6101)
1967-1972. Hollowbody archtop, double-cut, 2 pickups, G tailpiece or Bigsby vibrato, bound body and neck, sunburst (6100) or black (6101).

1967-1969	6100, sunburst	$2,000	$2,500
1967-1969	6101, black	$2,000	$2,500
1970-1972	6100, sunburst	$1,900	$2,200
1970-1972	6101, black	$1,800	$2,100

Black Penguin (G6134B)
2003-present. Jet black version.

2003-2007		$2,300	$2,600

Bo Diddley (G1810/G5810)

2000-present. Korean-made version.

MODEL YEAR	FEATURES	EXC. COND. LOW	HIGH
2000-2007		$200	$225

Bo Diddley (G6138)

1999-present. Reproduction of rectangle-shaped, semi-hollow guitar originally made for Diddley by Gretsch, Firebird Red.

1999-2007		$1,400	$1,600

Brian Setzer Hot Rod (6120SHx)

1999-present. Like SSL, but with only pickup switch and 1 master volume control, Hot Rod red.

1999-2007		$1,700	$1,800

Brian Setzer Nashville (6120SSL, etc.)

1993-present. Hollowbody electric, double-cut, 2 Alnico PAF Filtertron pickups, based on the classic Gretsch 6120.

1993-2007	Western Orange	$1,800	$1,900

Broadkaster (Hollowbody)

1975-1980. Double-cut archtop, hollowbody, 2 pickups, natural or sunburst.

1975-1977	7603, Bigsby, natural	$1,000	$1,150
1975-1977	7604, Bigsby, sunburst	$1,000	$1,100
1975-1977	7607, G tail-piece, natural	$900	$1,000
1975-1977	7608, G tail-piece, sunburst	$900	$1,000
1977-1980	7609, red	$900	$1,000

Broadkaster (Solidbody)

1975-1979. Double-cut, maple body, 2 pickups, bolt-on neck, natural (7600) or sunburst (7601).

1975-1979		$700	$825

BST 1000 Beast

1979-1980. Single-cut solidbody, bolt-on neck, mahogany body, available with 1 pickup in walnut stain (8210) or red stain (8216) or 2 pickups in walnut (7617, 8215, 8217) or red stain (8211).

1979-1980		$575	$625

BST 2000 Beast

1979. Symmetrical double-cut solidbody of mahogany, 2 humbucking pickups, bolt-on neck, walnut stain (7620 or 8220) or red stain (8221).

1979		$625	$700

BST 5000 Beast

1979-1980. Asymmetrical double-cut solidbody, neck-thru, walnut and maple construction, 2 humbucker pickups, stud tailpiece, natural walnut/maple (8250).

1979-1980		$675	$750

Burl Ives (6004)

1949-1955. Flat-top acoustic, mahogany back and sides, bound body, natural top (6004).

1949-1955		$425	$525

Chet Atkins Country Gentleman (6122/7670)

1957-1981. Hollowbody, single-cut to late-'62 and double after, 2 pickups, painted f-holes until '72, real after, mahogany finish (6122). Model number changes to 7670 in '71. Guitars made during and after '64 might have replaced body binding which reduces the value shown by about 10% or more.

MODEL YEAR	FEATURES	EXC. COND. LOW	HIGH
1957-1959		$10,000	$12,000
1960		$9,500	$11,800
1961		$7,500	$8,000
1962-1963	George Harrison specs	$7,500	$9,300
1964		$4,500	$6,000
1965		$4,500	$5,500
1966		$4,000	$4,500
1967-1970		$3,000	$3,700
1971-1981	7670	$2,500	$3,000

Chet Atkins Country Gentleman (6122-1962)

2007-present. Double-cut, double muffler (mutes) system, Filter'Trons.

2007		$2,100	$2,400

Chet Atkins Hollowbody (6120)

1954-1966. Archtop electric, single-cut to '61, double after, 2 pickups, vibrato, f-holes (real to '61 and fake after), G brand on top '54-'56, orange finish (6120). Renamed Chet Atkins Nashville in '67.

1954-1955	G brand	$13,000	$16,000
1955-1956	No G brand	$11,000	$13,000
1957-1959	No G brand	$10,000	$12,000
1960		$9,500	$11,800
1961	Single-cut	$6,500	$8,000
1961-1966	Double-cut	$4,000	$5,000

Chet Atkins Junior

1970. Archtop, single-cut, 1 pickup, vibrato, open f-holes, double-bound body, orange stain.

1970		$1,100	$1,300

Chet Atkins Nashville (6120/7660)

1967-1980. Replaced Chet Atkins Hollowbody (6120), electric archtop, double-cut, 2 pickups, amber red (orange). Renumbered 7660 in '72, reissued in '90 as the Nashville 6120.

1967-1971	6120	$2,500	$3,000
1972-1980	7660	$2,400	$2,900

Chet Atkins Solidbody (6121)

1955-1963. Solidbody electric, single-cut, maple or knotty pine top, 2 pickups, Bigsby vibrato, G brand until '57, multi-bound top, brown mahogany, orange finish (6121).

1955-1956		$14,000	$16,000
1957	G brand	$13,000	$15,000
1957	No G brand	$12,000	$14,000
1958-1959		$10,000	$12,500
1960		$8,000	$10,000
1961-1963		$7,500	$9,000

Chet Atkins Tennessean (6119/7655)

1958-1980. Archtop electric, single-cut, one pickup until '61 and 2 after, vibrato. Renumbered as the 7655 in '71.

1958		$3,000	$3,600
1959		$2,900	$3,500
1960-1961	1 pickup	$2,800	$3,400
1961-1964	2 pickups	$2,800	$3,400
1965		$2,600	$3,200
1966-1967		$2,400	$3,000
1968-1970		$2,300	$2,600
1971-1980	7655	$2,200	$2,400

Gretsch BST 2000 Beast

Gretsch Chet Atkins 6120

1966 Gretsch Country Club

*1959 Gretsch
Double Anniversary*

MODEL YEAR	FEATURES	EXC. COND. LOW	HIGH

Clipper (6185/6186/6187/7555)

1958-1975. Archtop electric, single-cut, sunburst, 1 pickup (6186) until '72 and 2 pickups (6185) from '72-'75, also available in 1 pickup natural (6187) from '59-'61.

1958-1961	6186	$1,000	$1,250
1959-1961	6187	$1,200	$1,400
1962-1967	6186	$975	$1,200
1968-1971	6186	$875	$1,000
1972-1975	7555	$1,000	$1,200

Committee (7628)

1977-1980. Neck-thru electric solidbody, double-cut, walnut and maple body, 2 pickups, 4 knobs, natural.

1977-1980		$900	$1,000

Constellation

1955-1960. Renamed from Synchromatic 6030 and 6031, archtop acoustic, single-cut, G tailpiece, humped block inlay.

1955-1956		$2,000	$2,200
1957-1958		$1,900	$2,100
1959-1960		$1,700	$2,000

Convertible (6199)

1955-1958. Archtop electric, single-cut, 1 pickup, multi-bound body, G tailpiece, renamed Sal Salvadore in '58.

1955-1958		$3,200	$3,700

Corsair

1955-1960. Renamed from Synchromatic 100, archtop acoustic, bound body and headstock, G tailpiece, available in sunburst (6014), natural (6015) or burgundy (6016).

1955-1959		$900	$1,100
1960-1965		$800	$1,000

Corvette (Hollowbody)

1955-1959. Renamed from Electromatic Spanish, archtop electric, 1 pickup, f-holes, bound body, Electromatic on headstock, non-cut, sunburst (6182), natural or Jaguar Tan (6184), and ivory with rounded cutaway (6187).

1955-1959	6182, sunburst	$1,100	$1,350
1955-1959	6184, Jaguar Tan	$1,400	$1,700
1955-1959	6184, natural	$1,400	$1,700
1957-1959	6187, ivory	$1,400	$1,700

Corvette (Solidbody)

1961-1972, 1976-1978. Double-cut slab solidbody. Mahogany 6132 and cherry 6134 1 pickup for '61-'68. 2 pickup mahogany 6135 and cherry 7623 available by '63-'72 and '76-'78. From late-'61 through '63 a Twist option was offered featuring a red candy stripe 'guard. Platinum gray 6133 available for '61-'63 and the Gold Duke and Silver Duke sparkle finishes were offered in '66.

1961-1962	Mahogany, cherry	$900	$1,100
1961-1963	Platinum gray	$1,400	$1,700
1961-1963	Twist 'guard	$1,600	$1,900
1963-1965	Custom color	$1,200	$1,500
1963-1965	Mahogany, cherry, 1 pickup	$900	$1,100
1963-1965	Mahogany, cherry, 2 pickups	$1,200	$1,500

1966	Gold Duke	$1,400	$1,700
1966	Silver Duke	$1,400	$1,700
1966-1968	Mahogany, cherry, 1 pickup	$700	$875
1966-1968	Mahogany, cherry, 2 pickups	$1,000	$1,300
1969-1972	Mahogany, cherry, 2 pickups	$1,000	$1,250
1976-1978	7623, 2 pickups	$650	$800

Country Classic I/II (6122 Reissue)

1989-2006. Country Gentleman reissue in '58 (I) and '62 (II) specs. Also cataloged as G6122-1958 and G6122-1962 Country Classic.

1989-2006	'58, single-cut	$1,000	$1,150
1989-2006	'62, double-cut	$1,000	$1,150

Country Classic II Custom Edition (6122)

2005. Reissue of George Harrison's 2nd 6122 Country Gentleman, the Custom Edition has TV Jones Filtertron pickups.

2005		$1,750	$1,850

Country Club

1954-1981. Renamed from Electro II Cutaway, archtop electric, single-cut, 2 pickups (Filter Trons after '57), G tailpiece, multi-bound, various colors.

1954-1956	Cadillac Green or natural	$4,800	$5,400
1954-1956	Sunburst	$3,000	$3,700
1957-1958	Cadillac Green or natural	$4,900	$6,000
1957-1958	Sunburst	$3,700	$4,500
1959	Cadillac Green or natural	$4,700	$5,800
1959	Sunburst	$3,500	$4,100
1960	Cadillac Green	$4,500	$4,900
1960	Sunburst	$3,500	$3,900
1961	Cadillac Green or natural	$4,300	$4,700
1961	Sunburst	$3,300	$3,700
1962	Cadillac Green or natural	$4,000	$4,400
1962-1963	Sunburst	$3,200	$3,600
1964	Cadillac Green	$4,000	$4,300
1964	Sunburst	$2,800	$3,400
1965-1969	Sunburst or walnut	$2,600	$2,800
1970-1972	Various colors	$2,400	$2,700
1973-1981	Various colors	$2,200	$2,500

Country Club 1955 (6196-1955)(FGE)

1995-1999. U.S.-made reissue of Country Club, single-cut, 2 DeArmond pickups, hand-rubbed lacquer finish.

1995-1999		$2,300	$2,700

Country Roc (7620)

1974-1978. Single-cut solidbody, 2 pickups, belt buckle tailpiece, western scene fretboard inlays, G brand, tooled leather side trim.

1974-1978		$2,200	$2,300

Deluxe Chet (7680/7681)

1972-1974. Electric archtop with rounded cutaway, Autumn Red (7680) or brown walnut (7681) finishes.

1972-1974		$2,500	$3,000

Deluxe Flat-Top (7535)

1972-1978. 16" redwood top, mahogany back and sides.

MODEL YEAR	FEATURES	EXC. COND. LOW	HIGH
1972-1978		$1,800	$2,100

Double Anniversary Mono (6117/6118)

1958-1976. Archtop electric, single-cut, 2 pickups, stereo optional until '63, sunburst (6117) or green 2-tone (6118). Reissued in '93 as the Anniversary 6117 and 6118.

MODEL YEAR	FEATURES	EXC. COND. LOW	HIGH
1958-1959	Green 2-tone	$2,900	$3,500
1958-1959	Sunburst	$2,800	$3,100
1960-1961	Green 2-tone	$2,700	$3,300
1960-1961	Sunburst	$2,600	$2,900
1962-1964	Green 2-tone	$2,300	$2,900
1962-1964	Sunburst	$1,900	$2,400
1963	Tan 2-tone	$2,300	$2,850
1965-1966	Various colors	$1,900	$2,350
1967-1969	Various colors	$1,800	$2,250
1970-1974	Various colors	$1,700	$2,100
1975-1976	Various colors	$1,600	$1,800

Double Anniversary Stereo (6111/6112)

1961-1963. One stereo channel/signal per pickup, sunburst (6111) or green (6112).

MODEL YEAR	FEATURES	EXC. COND. LOW	HIGH
1961-1963	Green	$3,300	$3,800
1961-1963	Sunburst	$3,100	$3,400

Duane Eddy (6210DE)

1997-2002. Import, 6120 style, 2 DeArmond single coils, Bigsby, orange.

MODEL YEAR	FEATURES	EXC. COND. LOW	HIGH
1997-1998		$2,000	$2,200

Duo-Jet (6128)

1953-1971. Solidbody electric, single-cut until '61, double after, 2 pickups. black (6128) with a few special ordered in green, sparkle finishes were offered '63-'66, reissued in '90.

MODEL YEAR	FEATURES	EXC. COND. LOW	HIGH
1953-1956	Black	$5,600	$7,000
1956-1957	Cadillac Green	$8,000	$10,000
1957	Black	$5,600	$7,000
1958-1960	Black	$5,600	$7,000
1961-1964	Black	$4,800	$6,000
1963-1966	Sparkle-gold, champagne, burgundy or tangerine	$5,600	$7,000
1964-1966	Silver sparkle	$5,600	$7,000
1965-1967	Black	$3,600	$4,400
1968-1971	Black	$3,200	$4,000

Duo-Jet Reissue (6128)

1990-present. Reissue of the '50s solidbody, black, optional Bigsby (G6128T).

MODEL YEAR	FEATURES	EXC. COND. LOW	HIGH
1990-2006		$1,200	$1,400

Duo-Jet Tenor

1959-1960. Electric tenor, 4 strings, block inlays, black.

MODEL YEAR	FEATURES	EXC. COND. LOW	HIGH
1959-1960		$3,500	$4,300

Eldorado (6038/6039)

1959-1968. The smaller 17" version, named Fleetwood from '55 to '58, sunburst (6038) or natural (6039), also available as a full body non-cutaway.

MODEL YEAR	FEATURES	EXC. COND. LOW	HIGH
1959-1963	Natural	$1,900	$2,300
1959-1963	Sunburst	$1,800	$2,100
1964-1965	Natural	$1,700	$2,100
1964-1965	Sunburst	$1,500	$1,850
1966-1968	Natural	$1,600	$2,000
1966-1968	Sunburst	$1,500	$1,800

Eldorado (6040/6041)

1955-1970, 1991-1997. This is the larger 18" version, renamed from Synchromatic 400, archtop acoustic, single-cut, triple-bound fretboard and peghead, sunburst (6040) or natural (6041). Reintroduced in '91, made by Heritage in Kalamazoo, as the G410 Synchromatic Eldorado in sunburst or natural (G410M).

MODEL YEAR	FEATURES	EXC. COND. LOW	HIGH
1955-1959	Natural	$3,000	$3,200
1955-1959	Sunburst	$2,700	$3,000
1960-1963	Natural	$2,600	$2,800
1960-1963	Sunburst	$2,300	$2,600
1964-1965	Natural	$2,300	$2,600
1964-1965	Sunburst	$2,100	$2,400
1966-1967	Natural	$2,200	$2,500
1966-1967	Sunburst	$2,000	$2,300
1968-1969	Sunburst	$1,900	$2,200
1991-1997	Natural	$2,100	$2,400
1991-1997	Sunburst	$1,800	$2,100

Electro Classic (6006/6495)

1969-1973. Classical flat-top with piezo pickup.

MODEL YEAR	FEATURES	EXC. COND. LOW	HIGH
1969-1970	6006	$750	$925
1971-1973	6495	$650	$800

Electro II Cutaway (6192/6193)

1951-1954. Archtop electric, single-cut, Melita bridge by '53, 2 pickups, f-holes, sunburst (6192) or natural (6193). Renamed Country Club in '54.

MODEL YEAR	FEATURES	EXC. COND. LOW	HIGH
1951-1954	Natural	$3,500	$4,100
1951-1954	Sunburst	$2,500	$3,000

Electromatic Spanish (6185/6185N)

1940-1955. Hollowbody, 17" wide, 1 pickup, sunburst (6185) or natural (6185N). Renamed Corvette (hollowbody) in '55.

MODEL YEAR	FEATURES	EXC. COND. LOW	HIGH
1940-1949	Sunburst	$1,500	$1,700
1950-1955	Natural	$1,800	$2,000
1950-1955	Sunburst	$1,500	$1,700

Fleetwood (6038/6039)

1955-1958. Named Synchronmatic prior to '55, single-cut, sunburst (6038) or natural (6039). Renamed Eldorado in '59, available by custom order.

MODEL YEAR	FEATURES	EXC. COND. LOW	HIGH
1955-1958		$2,300	$2,700

Folk/Folk Singing (6003/7505/7506)

1963-1975. Lower-model of Gretsch flat-tops, 14 1/4", mahogany back and sides. Renamed from Jimmie Rodgers model, renamed Folk Singing in '63.

MODEL YEAR	FEATURES	EXC. COND. LOW	HIGH
1963-1965		$675	$750
1966-1969		$575	$700
1970-1975		$525	$625

Golden Classic (Hauser Model/Model 6000)

1961-1969. Grand Concert body size, nylon-string classical, 14 1/4" spruce top, mahogany back and sides, multiple inlaid sound hole purfling, inlaid headstock.

MODEL YEAR	FEATURES	EXC. COND. LOW	HIGH
1961-1969		$600	$750

Grand Concert (6003)

1955-1959. Lower-model of Gretsch flat-tops, 14 1/4", mahogany back and sides. Renamed from Model 6003 and renamed Jimmie Rodgers in '59.

MODEL YEAR	FEATURES	EXC. COND. LOW	HIGH
1955-1959		$700	$825

1956 Gretsch Duo Jet

1954 Gretsch Electro-II

Gretsch Jet Firebird Reissue

Gretsch Monkees

MODEL YEAR	FEATURES	EXC. COND. LOW	HIGH

Jet 21
Late-1940s. 16" acoustic archtop, Jet 21 engraved logo on headstock, bound top and back, white 'guard, jet black finish.

1947-1948		$500	$600

Jet Firebird (6131)
1955-1971, 1990-present. Solidbody electric, single-cut until '61, double '61-'71, 2 pickups, black body with red top.

1955-1956		$4,000	$5,200
1957		$3,900	$5,100
1958-1960		$3,700	$4,800
1961-1964		$3,400	$4,500
1965-1967		$2,800	$3,700
1968-1971	Super Trons	$2,400	$3,000

Jet Firebird Reissue (6131/6131T)
1989-1997, 2003-present. Based on single-cut '58 specs, red top, 2 FilterTrons, thumbprint markers, gold hardware for '91-'05, currently chrome. Bigsby available (T). Non-Bigsby 6131 ends in '05. DynaSonic-equipped TDS starts in '05.

2003-2005		$1,250	$1,350

Jimmie Rodgers (6003)
1959-1962. 14" flat-top with round hole, mahogany back and sides, renamed from Grand Concert and renamed Folk Singing in '63.

1959-1962		$700	$800

Jumbo Synchromatic (125F)
1947-1955. 17" flat-top, triangular soundhole, bound top and back, metal bridge anchor plate, adjustable wood bridge, natural top with sunburst back and sides or optional translucent white-blond top and sides.

1947-1955	Natural	$2,300	$2,800
1947-1955	White-blond	$2,500	$3,100

Model 25 (Acoustic)
1933-1939. 16" archtop, no binding on top or back, dot markers, sunburst.

1933-1939		$675	$800

Model 30 (Acoustic)
1939-1949. 16" archtop, top binding, dot markers, sunburst.

1939-1949		$750	$900

Model 35 (Acoustic)
1933-1949. 16" archtop, single-bound top and back, dot markers, sunburst.

1933-1949		$850	$1,000

Model 50/50R (Acoustic)
1936-1939. Acoustic archtop, f-holes. Model 50R has round soundhole.

1936-1939		$950	$1,150

Model 65 (Acoustic)
1933-1939. Archtop acoustic, bound body, amber.

1933-1939		$1,000	$1,250

Model 75 Tenor (Acoustic)
1933-1939.

1933-1939		$600	$750

Model 6003
1951-1955. 14 1/4", mahogany back and sides, renamed Grand Concert in '55.

1951-1954		$700	$850

MODEL YEAR	FEATURES	EXC. COND. LOW	HIGH

Monkees
1966-1969. Hollowbody electric, double-cut, 2 pickups, Monkees logo on 'guard, bound top, f-holes and neck, vibrato, red.

1966-1969		$2,900	$3,000

New Yorker
Ca.1949-1970. Archtop acoustic, f-holes, sunburst.

1949-1951		$700	$825
1952-1954		$650	$775
1955-1959		$600	$725
1960-1965		$550	$675
1966-1970		$500	$625

Ozark/Ozark Soft String (6005)
1965-1968. 16" classical, rosewood back and sides.

1965-1968		$750	$925

Princess (6106)
1963. Corvette-type solidbody double-cut, 1 pickup, vibrato, gold parts, colors available were white/grape, blue/white, pink/white, or white/gold, often sold with the Princess amp.

1963		$1,900	$2,300

Rally (6104/6105)
1967-1969. Archtop, double-cut, 2 pickups, vibrato, racing stripe on truss rod cover and pickguard, green or yellow.

1967-1969		$2,300	$2,500

Rambler (6115)
1957-1961. Small body electric archtop, single-cut, 1 pickup, G tailpiece, bound body and headstock.

1957-1961		$1,500	$1,700

Rancher
1954-1980. Flat-top acoustic, triangle soundhole, Western theme inlay, G brand until '61 and '75 and after, Golden Red (orange), reissued in '90.

1954-1955	G brand	$3,000	$4,000
1956-1957	G brand	$2,900	$3,800
1958-1961	G brand	$2,800	$3,500
1962-1964	No G brand	$2,700	$3,300
1965-1966	No G brand	$2,500	$2,800
1967-1969	No G brand	$2,300	$2,500
1970-1974	No G brand	$2,000	$2,300
1975-1980	G brand	$1,800	$2,000

Roc I/Roc II (7635/7621)
1974-1976. Electric solidbody, mahogany, single-cut, Duo-Jet-style body, 1 pickup (7635) or 2 pickups (7621), bound body and neck.

1974-1976	Roc I	$1,100	$1,300
1974-1977	Roc II	$1,300	$1,500

Roc Jet
1969-1980. Electric solidbody, single-cut, 2 pickups, adjustamatic bridge, black, cherry, pumpkin or walnut.

1970-1972		$2,100	$2,400
1973-1976		$1,500	$1,800
1977-1980		$1,200	$1,500

Round-Up (6130)
1954-1960. Electric solidbody, single-cut, 2 pickups, G brand, belt buckle tailpiece, maple, pine, knotty pine or orange. Reissued in '90.

1954-1956	Knotty pine		
	(2 knots)	$18,000	$22,000

MODEL YEAR	FEATURES	EXC. COND. LOW	HIGH
1954-1956	Knotty pine (4 knots)	$21,000	$25,000
1954-1956	Mahogany (few made)	$14,000	$17,500
1954-1956	Maple	$14,000	$17,500
1954-1956	Pine	$16,000	$20,000
1957-1960	Orange	$14,000	$16,000

Round-Up Reissue (6121/6121W)

1989-1995, 2003-2006. Based on the '50s model, Western Orange, G brand sticker (some '05s have actual branded G).

1989-2005	Decal G brand	$1,400	$1,500
2005-2006	Real G brand	$1,600	$1,700

Sal Fabraio (6117)

1964-1968. Double-cut thin electric archtop, distinctive cats-eye f-holes, 2 pickups, sunburst, ordered for resale by guitar teacher Sal Fabraio.

1964-1968		$2,100	$2,600

Sal Salvador (6199)

1958-1968. Electric archtop, single-cut, 1 pickup, triple-bound neck and headstock, sunburst.

1958-1959		$3,400	$4,000
1960-1962		$2,900	$3,500
1963-1964		$2,400	$3,000
1965-1966		$2,300	$2,600
1967-1968		$2,000	$2,400

Sho Bro (Hawaiian/Spanish)

1969-1978. Flat-top acoustic, multi-bound, resonator, lucite fretboard, Hawaiian version non-cut, square neck and Spanish version non- or single-cut, round neck.

1969-1978	Hawaiian	$900	$1,000
1969-1978	Spanish	$900	$1,000

Silver Classic (Hauser Model/Model 6001)

1961-1969. Grand Concert body size, nylon-string classical. Similar to Golden Classic but with less fancy appointments.

1961-1969		$400	$500

Silver Falcon (6136SL-1955)

1995-1999, 2003-present. Black finish and silver features single cut version, G tailpiece. Had the 1955 designation in the '90s.

1995-1999		$1,900	$2,300

Silver Falcon (7594SL)

1995-1999. Black finish and silver features, double-cut, 2" thick body.

1995-1999		$1,800	$2,200

Silver Jet (6129)

1954-1963. Solidbody electric, single-cut until '61, double '61-'63, 2 pickups, Duo-Jet with silver sparkle top, reissued in '90. Optional sparkle colors were offered but were not given their own model numbers; refer to Duo-Jet listing for optional colors.

1954-1956		$8,500	$10,500
1957		$8,000	$10,000
1958-1960		$7,700	$9,500
1961-1963	Double-cut	$7,000	$8,700

Silver Jet 1957 Reissue (6129-1957)

1990-present. Reissue of single-cut '50s Silver Jet, silver sparkle.

1990-2006		$1,300	$1,500

Songbird (Sam Goody 711)

1967-1968. Standard body thinline double cutaway with G soundholes, offered by Sam Goody of New York.

1967-1968		$2,300	$2,800

Southern Belle (7176)

1983. Electric archtop, walnut, parts from the late-'70s assembled in Mexico and U.S., 5 made with all original parts, several others without pickguard and case.

1983		$1,300	$1,500

Sparkle Jet (6129)

1994-present. Electric solidbody, single-cut, 2 pickups, Duo-Jet with sparkle finish.

1995-2005		$1,100	$1,300

Streamliner Double Cutaway (6102/6103)

1968-1973. Reintroduced from single-cut model, electric archtop, double-cut, 2 pickups, G tailpiece, cherry or sunburst.

1968-1969		$1,500	$1,850
1970-1973		$1,400	$1,750

Streamliner Single Cutaway (6189/6190/6191)

1955-1959. Electric archtop, single-cut, maple top, G tailpiece, 1 pickup, multi-bound, Bamboo Yellow (6189), sunburst (6190), or natural (6191), name reintroduced as a double-cut in '68.

1955-1959		$1,600	$2,000

Sun Valley (6010/7515/7514)

1959-1977. Flat-top acoustic, laminated Brazilian rosewood back and sides, multi-bound top, natural or sunburst.

1959-1964		$800	$1,000
1965-1969		$700	$850
1970-1977		$550	$675

Super Chet (7690/7690-B/7691/7691-B)

1972-1980. Electric archtop, single rounded cutaway, 2 pickups, gold hardware, mini control knobs along edge of 'guard, Autumn Red or walnut.

1972-1976		$2,400	$2,900
1977-1980		$2,300	$2,700

Supreme (7545)

1972-1978. Flat-top 16", spruce top, mahogany or rosewood body options, gold hardware.

1972-1978	Mahogany	$1,200	$1,500
1972-1979	Rosewood	$1,600	$1,900

Synchromatic (6030/6031)

1951-1955. 17" acoustic archtop, becomes Constellation in '55.

1951-1955		$1,700	$2,100

Synchromatic (6038/6039)

1951-1955. 17" acoustic archtop, single-cut, G tailpiece, multi-bound, sunburst (6038) or natural (6039), renamed Fleetwood in '55.

1951-1955	Sunburst	$1,800	$2,200

Gretsch Rancher

1955 Gretsch Roundup (6130)

1940s Gretsch Synchromatic 400

1958 Gretsch White Falcon

MODEL YEAR	FEATURES	EXC. COND. LOW	HIGH

Synchromatic 75
1939-1949. Acoustic archtop, f-holes, multi-bound, large floral peghead inlay.

1939-1949		$1,300	$1,400

Synchromatic 100
1939-1955. Renamed from No. 100F, acoustic archtop, double-bound body, amber, sunburst or natural, renamed Corsair in '55.

1939-1949	Natural	$1,300	$1,600
1939-1949	Sunburst	$1,000	$1,250
1950-1955	Natural	$975	$1,200

Synchromatic 160 (6028/6029)
1939-1943, 1947-1951. Acoustic archtop, cats-eye soundholes, maple back and sides, triple-bound, natural or sunburst.

1939-1943	Sunburst	$1,850	$2,100
1947-1951	Sunburst	$1,800	$2,000
1948-1951	Natural	$1,700	$2,100

Synchromatic 200
1939-1949. Acoustic archtop, cats-eye soundholes, maple back and sides, multi-bound, gold-plated hardware, amber or natural.

1939-1949		$2,000	$2,400

Synchromatic 300
1939-1955. Acoustic archtop, cats-eye soundholes until '51 and f-holes after, multi-bound, natural or sunburst.

1939-1949	Natural	$3,000	$3,400
1939-1949	Sunburst	$2,500	$2,900
1950-1955	Natural	$2,500	$2,900
1950-1955	Sunburst	$2,300	$2,600

Synchromatic 400
1940-1955. Acoustic archtop, cats-eye soundholes until '51 and f-holes after, multi-bound, gold hardware, natural or sunburst.

1940-1949	Natural	$6,000	$7,500
1940-1949	Sunburst	$5,500	$6,400
1950-1955	Natural	$5,500	$6,400
1950-1955	Sunburst	$5,000	$5,900

Synchromatic 400F/6042 Flat Top
1947-1955. 18" flat top, renamed 6042 in the late '40s.

1947-1948	400F	$4,500	$5,300
1949-1959	6042	$4,000	$4,800

Synchromatic Limited (450/450M)
1997. Acoustic archtop, hand carved spruce (G450) or maple (G450M) top, floating pickup, sunburst, only 50 were to be made.

1997	Maple	$1,150	$1,400
1997	Spruce	$1,050	$1,300

Synchromatic Sierra
1949-1955. Renamed from Synchromatic X75F (see below), acoustic flat-top, maple back and sides, triangular soundhole, sunburst.

1949-1955		$1,200	$1,450

Synchromatic X75F
1947-1949. Acoustic flat-top, maple back and sides, triangular soundhole, sunburst, renamed Synchromatic Sierra in '49.

1947-1949		$1,200	$1,450

MODEL YEAR	FEATURES	EXC. COND. LOW	HIGH

TK 300 (7624/7625)
1977-1981. Double-cut maple solidbody, 1 humbucker, bolt-on neck, six-on-a-side tuners, hockey stick headstock, Autumn Red or natural.

1977-1981		$700	$800

Town and Country (6021)
1954-1959. Renamed from Jumbo Synchromatic 125 F, flat-top acoustic, maple back and sides, triangular soundhole, multi-bound.

1954-1959		$1,800	$2,100

Traveling Wilburys (TW300T)
1988-1990. Promotional guitar, solidbody electric, single-cut, 1 and 2 pickups, 6 variations, graphics.

1988-1990		$400	$450

Van Eps 7-String (6079/6080)
1968-1978. Electric archtop, single-cut, 2 pickups, 7 strings, sunburst or walnut.

1968-1978		$2,400	$3,000

Viking (6187/6188/6189)
1964-1975. Electric archtop, double-cut, 2 pickups, vibrato, sunburst (6187), natural (6188) or Cadillac Green (6189).

1964-1967	Cadillac Green	$3,400	$4,200
1964-1967	Natural	$3,400	$4,200
1964-1967	Sunburst	$2,950	$3,500
1968-1970	Cadillac Green	$2,700	$3,300
1968-1970	Natural	$2,700	$3,300
1968-1970	Sunburst	$2,500	$3,000
1971-1972	Various colors	$2,100	$2,600
1973-1975	Various colors	$1,900	$2,300

Wayfarer Jumbo (6008)
1969-1971. Flat-top acoustic dreadnought, non-cut, maple back and sides, multi-bound.

1969-1971		$900	$1,100

White Falcon Mono (6136/7595)
1955-1981. Includes the single-cut 6136 of '55-'61, the double-cut 6136 of '62-'70, and the double-cut 7594 of '71-'81.

1955	Single-cut 6136	$22,000	$27,000
1956		$21,500	$26,500
1957		$22,000	$26,000
1958		$21,500	$25,500
1959-1961		$20,000	$25,000
1962-1963	Double-cut 6136	$9,600	$12,000
1964		$8,000	$10,000
1965		$6,800	$8,500
1966		$6,500	$8,100
1967-1969		$6,000	$7,500
1970		$5,500	$6,800
1971-1972	Model 7594	$5,400	$6,600
1973-1979		$5,000	$6,200
1980-1981		$4,800	$6,000

White Falcon Stereo (6137/7595)
1958-1981. Features Project-O-Sonic Stereo, includes Includes the single-cut 6137 of '58-'61, the double-cut 6137 of '62-'70, and the double-cut 7595 of '71-'81.

1958	Early stereo specs	$24,000	$30,000
1959-1961	Single-cut 6137	$22,000	$27,000
1962-1963	Double-cut 6137	$11,000	$13,700

MODEL YEAR	FEATURES	EXC. COND. LOW	HIGH
1964		$10,000	$12,500
1965		$7,000	$8,700
1966		$6,900	$8,600
1967-1969		$6,500	$8,100
1970		$6,000	$7,500
1971-1972	Model 7595	$5,900	$7,400
1973-1979		$5,500	$6,800
1980-1981		$5,200	$6,500

White Falcon I (6136)
1991-present. Single-cut, white, 2.75" thick body, Cadillac G tailpiece. Called the White Falcon I for '91-'92 (not to be confused with current White Falcon I G7593). See Black and Silver Falcons under those listings.

1991-2005		$2,300	$2,600

White Falcon II (7594)
1991-2006. Double-cut, white, 2" thick body, Bigsby. Called the White Falcon II for '91-'92, the G7594 for '93-ca. '02, and White Falcon II G7594 after.

1991-2005		$2,200	$2,500

White Falcon (6136T-LTV)
2007-present. 6136 with TV Jones Classic pickups, Grovers.

2007		$2,700	$2,800

White Falcon (7593/7593 I)
1993-present. G6136 with added Bigsby. Currently sold as G7593 White Falcon I.

1991-1999		$2,300	$2,600

White Falcon Custom U.S.A. (6136-1955)
1995-1999. U.S.-made, single-cut, DynaSonic pickups, gold sparkle appointments, rhinestone embedded knobs, white. In '04, Current U.S. model called G6136CST is released. The import White Falcon has sometimes been listed with the 1955 designation and is not included here.

1995-1999		$4,000	$5,000

White Penguin (6134)
1955-1964. Electric solidbody, single-cut until '62, double '62-'64, 2 pickups (DeArmond until '58 then Filter Tron), fewer than 100 made, white, gold sparkle bound, gold-plated parts. More than any other model, there seems a higher concern regarding forgery.

1956-1958		$80,000	$85,000
1959-1960		$75,000	$80,000
1961-1962		$74,000	$78,000
1962-1964		$55,000	$60,000

White Penguin (G6134)
1993, 2003-present. White, single-cut, metalflake binding, gold hardware, jeweled knobs, Cadillac G tailpiece.

2003-2006		$2,800	$3,000

Greven
1969, 1975-present. Luthier John Greven builds his premium grade, production/custom, acoustic guitars in Portland, Oregon.

Griffin String Instruments
1976-present. Luthier Kim Griffin builds his professional and premium grade, production/custom, parlor, steel-string, and classical guitars in Greenwich, New York.

Grimes Guitars
1972-present. Premium and presentation grade, custom, flat-tops, nylon-strings, archtops, semi-hollow electrics made by luthier Steve Grimes originally in Port Townsend, Washington, and since '82 in Kula, Hawaii. He also made mandolins early on.

Grinnell
Late 1930s-early 1940s. Private brand made by Gibson for Grinnell Music of Detroit and Southeast Michigan, which at the time, was the largest music chain in the Detroit area.

KG-14
1940. Gibson-made L-0/L-00 style with maple sides and back, tortoise-style binding on top and back, ladder bracing.

1940		$1,500	$1,600

Groehsl
1890-1921. Chicago's Groehsl Company made guitars for Wards and other mass-marketers. In 1921 the company became Stromberg-Voisinet, which in turn became the Kay Musical Instrument Company.

Groove Tools
2002-2004. Korean-made, production, intermediate grade, 7-string guitars that were offered by Conklin Guitars of Springfield, Missouri. They also offered basses.

Grosh, Don
1993-present. Professional and premium grade, production/custom, solid and semi-hollow body guitars built by luthier Don Grosh in Santa Clarita, California. He also builds basses. Grosh worked in production for Valley Arts from '84-'92. Guitars generally with bolt necks until '03 when set-necks were added to the line.

Classical Electric
1990s. Single-cut solidbody with nylon strings and piezo-style hidden pickup, highly figured top.

1990s		$1,350	$1,550

Custom S Bent Top
Offset double-cut, figured maple carved top, 2 pickups.

2003		$1,350	$1,550

Custom T Carve Top
Single-cut, figured maple carved top, 2 pickups.

2003		$1,350	$1,550

Retro Classic
1993-present. Offset double-cut, 3 pickups.

2001		$1,350	$1,550

Retro Vintage T
1993-present. Single-cut, black 'guard.

2001		$1,350	$1,550

Gretsch White Penguin

Don Grosh Retro Classic

GUITARS

1969 Guild Bluegrass Jubilee D-40

Guild Aristocrat M-75

MODEL		EXC. COND.	
YEAR	FEATURES	LOW	HIGH

Gruen Acoustic Guitars

1999-present. Luthier Paul Gruen builds his professional grade, custom steel-string guitars in Chapel Hill, North Carolina. His speciality is his E.Q. model, which features 5 soundholes, 4 of which can be plugged with wooden stoppers to give different tonal balances.

Gruggett

Mid 1960s-present. In the 1960s, luthier Bill Gruggett worked with Mosrite and Hallmark guitars as well as building electric guitars under his own name in Bakersfield, California. He still makes his Stradette model for Hallmark guitars.

Guernsey Resophonic Guitars

1989-present. Production/custom, resonator guitars built by luthier Ivan Guernsey in Marysville, Indiana.

Guild

1952-present. Professional and premium grade, production/custom, acoustic and acoustic/electric guitars. They have built solid, hollow and semi-hollowbody guitars in the past. Founded in New York City by jazz guitarist Alfred Dronge, employing many ex-Epiphone workers. The company was purchased by Avnet, Inc., in '66 and the Westerly, Rhode Island factory was opened in '68. Hoboken factory closed in '71 and headquarters moved to Elizabeth, New Jersey. Company was Guild Musical Instrument Corporation in '86 but was in bankruptcy in '88. Purchased by Faas Corporation, New Berlin, Wisconsin, which became the U.S. Musical Corporation. The brand was purchased by Fender Musical Instrument Corporation in '95. In '05, Fender moved Guild production to their newly-acquired Tacoma plant in Washington. In '08, production moved to the Ovation/Hamer plant in New Hartford, Connecticut.

In 2001 Fender moved the Guild factory into its state-of-the-art factory in Corona, California where floorspace was allocated specifically for Guild guitars. Bob Benedetto and Fender veteran Tim Shaw (who previously ran the Nashville-based custom shop) created a line of Guild acoustic guitars that were primarily based on vintage Guild Hoboken designs.

Designs of Tacoma-built Guild product were nothing like Tacoma guitars. The new Guilds were dovetail neck based with nitrocellulose finishes. Later, FMIC Guild introduced the Contemporary Series giving the Tacoma factory another line in addition to the vintage-based F and D model Traditional Series.

A-50

1994-1996. Original A-50 models can be found under the Cordoba A-50 listing, the new model drops the Cordoba name, size 000 flat top, spruce top, Indian rosewood body.

1994-1996		$950	$1,175

MODEL		EXC. COND.	
YEAR	FEATURES	LOW	HIGH

Aragon F-30

1954-1986. Acoustic flat-top, spruce top, laminated maple arched back (mahogany back and sides by '59), reintroduced as just F-30 in '98.

1954-1959		$1,700	$1,875
1960-1969		$1,600	$1,750
1970-1986		$1,100	$1,350

Aragon F-30 NT

1959-1985. Natural finish version of F-30.

1959-1969		$1,700	$2,000
1970-1985		$1,100	$1,350

Aragon F-30 R

1973-1995. Rosewood back and sides version of F-30, sunburst.

1973-1979		$1,200	$1,500

Aristocrat M-75

1954-1963. Electric archtop, routed semi-hollow single-cut body, 2 pickups, sunburst, natural (added '59) or cherry (added '61), reintroduced as Bluesbird M-75 in '67.

1954-1959		$2,800	$3,400
1960-1963		$2,400	$3,000

Aristocrat M-75 Tenor

Mid-late 1950s. Tenor version of 6-string Aristocrat electric, dual soapbar pickups, 4 knobs.

1950s		$2,800	$3,300

Artist Award

1961-1999. Renamed from Johnny Smith Award, single-cut electric archtop, floating DeArmond pickup (changed to humbucker in '80), multi-bound, gold hardware, sunburst or natural.

1961-1969		$4,500	$5,500
1970-1979		$4,300	$5,200
1980-1989		$4,000	$4,500
1990-1999		$3,900	$4,400

Artist F-312 12-String

1963-1973. Flat-top, rosewood back and sides, spruce top, no board inlay (but some in '72 may have dots).

1964-1968	Brazilian rosewood	$2,800	$3,100
1969-1973	Indian rosewood	$1,700	$2,100

Bluegrass D-25/D-25 M

1968-1999. Flat-top, mahogany top until '76, spruce after, mahogany back and sides, various colors, called Bluegrass D-25 M in late-'70s and '80s, listed as D-25 in '90s.

1968-1979		$800	$925
1980-1989		$775	$875
1990-1999		$775	$875

Bluegrass D-25-12

1987-1992, 1996-1999. 12-string version of D-25.

1987-1992		$775	$875
1996-1999		$775	$875

Bluegrass D-35

1966-1988. Acoustic flat-top, spruce top and mahogany back and sides, rosewood 'board and bridge, natural.

1966-1969		$800	$1,000
1970-1979		$775	$875
1980-1988		$775	$875

Bluegrass F-40

1954-1963, 1973-1983. Acoustic flat-top, spruce top, maple back and sides, rosewood 'board and bridge, natural or sunburst.

		LOW	HIGH
1954-1956	F-40	$2,100	$2,600
1957-1963	F-40	$1,850	$2,300
1973-1983	Bluegrass F-40	$1,300	$1,600

Bluegrass F-47

1963-1976. 16" narrow-waist style, mahogany sides and back, acoustic flat-top, spruce top, mahogany back and sides, bound rosewood 'board and bridge, natural.

1963-1969		$1,850	$2,300
1970-1976		$1,700	$2,100

Bluegrass Jubilee D-40

1963-1992. Acoustic flat-top, spruce top, mahogany back and sides, rosewood 'board and bridge, natural. Has been reissued.

1963-1969		$1,450	$1,800
1970-1979		$1,300	$1,600
1980-1992		$1,200	$1,500

Bluegrass Jubilee D-40 C

1975-1991. Acoustic flat-top, single Florentine cutaway, mahogany back and sides, rosewood 'board and bridge, natural.

1975-1979		$1,100	$1,600
1980-1991		$1,000	$1,400

Bluegrass Jubilee D-44

1965-1972. Acoustic flat-top, spruce top, pearwood back and sides, ebony 'board, rosewood bridge.

1965-1969		$1,200	$1,700
1970-1972		$1,100	$1,500

Bluegrass Jubilee D-44 M

1971-1985. Acoustic flat top, spruce top, maple back & sides, ebony fingerboard, rosewood bridge.

1971-1979		$1,200	$1,700
1980-1985		$1,100	$1,500

Bluegrass Special D-50

1963-1993. Acoustic flat-top, spruce top, rosewood back and sides, ebony fretboard, multi-bound.

1963-1968	Brazilian rosewood	$3,600	$4,500
1969-1979	Indian rosewood	$1,600	$2,000
1980-1993	Indian rosewood	$1,200	$1,500

Bluegrass Special D-50 (Reissue)/D-50

2003-present. Also available with pickup system, initially listed as D-50.

2003-2007		$1,300	$1,450

Blues 90

2000-2002. Bluesbird single-cut, chambered body, unbound rosewood board, dots, 2 Duncan 2 P-90s.

2000-2002		$1,000	$1,250

Bluesbird M-75 (Hollowbody)

1967-1970. Reintroduced from Aristocrat M-75, thinbody electric archtop of maple, spruce ('67) or mahogany, single-cut, 2 pickups, Deluxe has gold hardware, Standard chrome. A solidbody Bluesbird was also introduced in '70.

1967-1970		$1,700	$2,100

Bluesbird M-75 (Solidbody)

1970-1978. Solidbody version of Bluesbird M-75, mahogany body, rounded cutaway, 2 pickups.

1970-1978	CS, plain top, chrome hardware	$1,200	$1,500
1970-1978	GS, flamed top, gold hardware	$1,900	$2,200

Bluesbird (Reintroduced)

1997-2003. Single-cut chambered solidbody, 2 humbuckers, block inlays, available with AAA flamed top.

1998-2001		$1,250	$1,475
2002-2003		$1,150	$1,350

Brian May BHM-1

1984-1987. Electric solidbody, double-cut, vibrato, 3 pickups, bound top and back, red or green, Brian May Pro, Special and Standard introduced in '94.

1984-1987		$2,600	$3,200

Brian May Pro

1994-1995. Electric solidbody, double-cut, vibrato, 3 pickups, bound top and back, various colors.

1994-1995		$2,200	$2,700

CA-100 Capri

1956-1973. Acoustic archtop version of CE-100, sharp Florentine cutaway, solid spruce top, laminated maple back and sides, rosewood 'board and bridge, nickel-plated metal parts, natural or sunburst.

1956-1959		$1,050	$1,250
1960-1969		$1,050	$1,200
1970-1973		$900	$1,100

Capri CE-100

1956-1985. Electric archtop, single Florentine cutaway, 1 pickup (2 pickups by '83), maple body, Waverly tailpiece, sunburst, in '59-'82 CE-100 D listed with 2 pickups.

1956-1959		$1,200	$1,450
1960-1969		$1,100	$1,450
1970-1979		$1,100	$1,350
1980-1985		$1,100	$1,350

Capri CE-100 D

1956-1982. Electric archtop, single Florentine cutaway, 2 pickups, maple body, sunburst, Waverly tailpiece (D dropped, became the Capri CE-100 in '83).

1956-1959		$1,400	$1,700
1960-1969		$1,300	$1,600
1970-1979		$1,200	$1,500
1980-1982		$1,200	$1,500

Capri CE-100 T Tenor

1950s. Electric-archtop Capri 4-string tenor guitar, sunburst.

1956		$1,000	$1,250

Cordoba A-50

1961-1972. Acoustic archtop, lowest-end in the Guild archtop line, named Granda A-50 prior to '61.

1961-1965		$575	$700
1966-1972		$500	$625

Cordoba T-50 Slim

1961-1973. Thinbody version of Cordoba X-50.

1961-1964		$1,250	$1,500
1965-1973		$975	$1,150

Guild Brian May Pro

Guild CE-100D Capri

Guild D-25 M

Guild D-35

Cordoba X-50
1961-1970. Electric archtop non-cut, laminated maple body, rosewood 'board, 1 pickup, nickel-plated parts.

Year	Features	Low	High
1961-1970		$950	$1,175

Custom F-412 12-String
1968-1986. Special order only from '68-'74, then regular production, 17" wide body 12-string version of F-50 flat-top, spruce top, maple back and sides, arched back, 2-tone block inlays, gold hardware, natural finish.

Year	Features	Low	High
1968-1969		$2,000	$2,400
1970-1979		$1,800	$2,200
1980-1986		$1,700	$2,100

Custom F-512 12-String
1968-1986, 1990. Rosewood back and sides version of F-412. See F-512 for reissue.

Year	Features	Low	High
1968-1969		$2,000	$2,400
1970-1979		$1,800	$2,200
1980-1986		$1,700	$2,100

Custom F-612 12-String
1972-1973. Acoustic 12-string, similar to Custom F-512, but with 18" body, fancy mother-of-pearl inlays, and black/white marquee body, neck and headstock binding.

Year	Features	Low	High
1972-1973	Brazilian rosewood	$2,900	$3,400
1972-1973	Indian rosewood	$2,000	$2,500

Custom Shop 45th Anniversary
1997. Built in Guild's Nashville Custom Shop, all solid wood, spruce top, maple back and sides, with high-end appointments.

Year	Features	Low	High
1997	Natural, gold hardware	$2,100	$2,500

D-4 Series
1991-2002. Dreadnought flat-top, mahogany sides, dot markers.

Year	Features	Low	High
1991-2002	6-String	$475	$525
1992-1999	12-String	$525	$625

D-6 (D-6 E/D-6 HG/D-6 HE)
1992-1995. Flat-top, 15 3/4", mahogany back and sides, natural satin non-gloss finish, options available.

Year	Features	Low	High
1992-1995		$600	$700

D-15 Mahogany Rush
1983-1988. Dreadnought flat-top, mahogany body and neck, rosewood 'board, dot inlays, stain finish.

Year	Features	Low	High
1983-1988		$550	$650

D-16 Mahogany Rush
1984-1986. Like D-15, but with gloss finish.

Year	Features	Low	High
1984-1986		$600	$700

D-17 Mahogany Rush
1984-1988. Like D-15, but with gloss finish and bound body.

Year	Features	Low	High
1984-1988		$650	$750

D-25/D25 M/GAD-25
2003, 2006-present. Solid mahogany body. Refer to Bluegrass D-25 for earlier models. Reintroduced in '06 as GAD-25.

Year	Features	Low	High
2003		$575	$650

D-30
1987-1999. Acoustic flat top, spruce-top, laminated maple back and solid maple sides, rosewood 'board, multi-bound, various colors.

Year	Features	Low	High
1987-1989		$925	$1,000
1990-1999		$825	$925

D-40
1999-2003. Solid spruce top, mahogany back and sides, rosewood 'board. See earlier models under Bluegrass Jubilee D-40.

Year	Features	Low	High
1999-2000		$850	$975

D-46
1980-1985. Dreadnought acoustic, ash back, sides and neck, spruce top, ebony 'board, ivoroid body binding.

Year	Features	Low	High
1980-1985		$850	$1,000

D-55
1968-1987, 1990-present (Special Order 1968-1973, regular production after). Dreadnought-size acoustic, spruce top, rosewood back and sides, scalloped bracing, gold-plated tuners, called the TV Model in earlier years, sunburst or natural.

Year	Features	Low	High
2000-2005		$1,500	$1,700

D-60
1987-1990, 1998-2000. Renamed from D-66, rosewood back and sides, 15 3/4", scalloped bracing, multi-bound top, slotted diamond inlay, G shield logo.

Year	Features	Low	High
1987-1990		$1,700	$1,950
1998-2000		$1,600	$1,900

D-64
1984-1986. Maple back and side, multi-bound body, notched diamond inlays, limited production.

Year	Features	Low	High
1984-1986		$1,550	$1,850

D-66
1984-1987. Amber, rosewood back and sides, 15 3/4", scalloped bracing, renamed D-60 in '87.

Year	Features	Low	High
1984-1987		$1,600	$1,900

D-70
1981-1985. Dreadnought acoustic, spruce top, Indian rosewood back and sides, multi-bound, ebony 'board with mother-of-pearl inlays.

Year	Features	Low	High
1981-1985		$2,000	$2,200

D-100
1999. Top-of-the-line dreadnought-size acoustic, spruce top, rosewood back and sides, scalloped bracing.s.

Year	Features	Low	High
1999		$2,200	$2,300

D-212 12-String
1981-1983. 12-string version of D-25, laminated mahogany back and sides, natural, sunburst or black, renamed D-25-12 in '87, reintroduced as D-212 '96-present.

Year	Features	Low	High
1981-1983		$725	$900

D-412 12-String
1990-1997. Dreadnought, 12 strings, mahogany sides and arched back, satin finished, natural.

Year	Features	Low	High
1990-1997		$850	$1,000

DCE True American
1993-2000. Cutaway flat-top acoustic/electric, 1 with mahogany back and sides, 5 with rosewood.

Year	Features	Low	High
1993-2000	DCE1	$400	$650
1994-2000	DCE5	$450	$700

MODEL YEAR	FEATURES	EXC. COND. LOW	HIGH

Del Rio M-30
1959-1964. Flat-top, 15", all mahogany body, satin non-gloss finish.

1959-1964		$1,050	$1,300

Detonator
1987-1990. Electric solidbody, double-cut, 3 pickups, bolt-on neck, Guild/Mueller tremolo system, black hardware.

1987-1990		$450	$525

Duane Eddy Deluxe DE-500
1962-1974, 1984-1987. Electric archtop, single rounded cutaway, 2 pickups (early years and '80s version have DeArmonds), Bigsby, master volume, spruce top with maple back and sides, available in blond (BL) or sunburst (SB).

1962	Natural	$6,500	$7,500
1962	Sunburst	$5,500	$6,500
1963	Natural	$6,300	$7,300
1963	Sunburst	$5,300	$6,300
1964	Natural	$6,100	$7,100
1964	Sunburst	$5,000	$5,900
1965	Natural	$5,500	$6,100
1965	Sunburst	$4,500	$5,500
1966	Natural	$5,000	$5,500
1966	Sunburst	$4,500	$5,000
1967-1969	Various colors	$4,000	$4,800
1970-1974	Various colors	$3,500	$4,000
1984-1987	Various colors	$3,000	$3,500

Duane Eddy Standard DE-400
1963-1974. Electric archtop, single rounded cutaway, 2 pickups, vibrato, natural or sunburst, less appointments than DE-500 Deluxe.

1963	Natural	$4,000	$5,000
1963	Sunburst	$3,500	$4,000
1964	Natural	$3,800	$4,700
1964	Sunburst	$3,200	$3,800
1965	Natural	$3,500	$4,300
1965	Sunburst	$3,000	$3,600
1966	Natural	$3,200	$4,000
1966	Sunburst	$2,800	$3,300
1967-1969	Various colors	$2,450	$2,700
1970-1974	Various colors	$2,100	$2,500

DV Series
1992-1999, 2007-present. Acoustic flat-top, spruce top, solid mahogany or rosewood back and sides, ebony or rosewood 'board and bridge, mahogany neck, satin or gloss finish.

1993-1999	DV-52, rosewood, satin	$1,000	$1,200
1993-1999	DV-62, rosewood	$1,500	$1,875
1993-1999	DV-72, limited edition	$1,800	$2,200
1996-1999	DV-6, mahogany, satin	$800	$900

Economy M-20
1958-1965, 1969-1973. Mahogany body, acoustic flat-top, natural or sunburst satin finish.

1958-1965		$1,250	$1,500
1969-1973		$1,100	$1,350

F-4 CEHG
1992-2002. High Gloss finish, single-cut flat-top, acoustic/electric.

1992-2002		$700	$850

F-5 CE
1992-2001. Acoustic/electric, single cutaway, rosewood back and sides, dot inlays, chrome tuners.

1992-2001		$975	$1,100

F-30 R-LS
1990s. Custom Shop model, other F-30 models are listed under Aragon F-30 listing, rosewood sides and back, bearclaw spruce top, limited production.

1990s		$950	$1,150

F-45 CE
1983-1992. Acoustic/electric, single pointed cutaway, active EQ, preamp, spruce top, mahogany back and sides, rosewood 'board, natural finish.

1983-1992		$825	$925

F-47 RCE Grand Auditorium
1999-2003. Cutaway acoustic/electric, solid spruce top, solid maple back and sides, block inlays.

1999-2003		$1,000	$1,250

F-50
2002-present. Jumbo, solid spruce top, solid maple sides, arched laminated maple back, abalone rosette. See Navarre F-50/F-50 for earlier models.

2002-2005		$1,000	$1,250

F-65 CE
1992-2001. Acoustic/electric, single cutaway, rosewood back and sides, block inlay, gold tuners.

1992-2001		$1,350	$1,450

F-212 12-String
1964-1982. Acoustic flat-top jumbo, 12 strings, spruce top, mahogany back and sides, 16" body.

1964-1969		$1,400	$1,750
1970-1979		$1,000	$1,250
1980-1982		$900	$1,100

F-212 XL 12-String
1966-1986, 1998-2000. Acoustic flat-top, 17" body, 12 strings, spruce top, mahogany back and sides, ebony fingerboard.

1966-1969		$1,400	$1,750
1970-1979		$1,000	$1,250
1980-1986		$900	$1,100
1998-2000		$1,000	$1,100

F-412
2002-present. Solid spruce top, solid maple back and sides, block inlays, 12-string. See Custom F-412 for earlier models.

2002-2005		$1,075	$1,300

F-512
2002-2007. Solid spruce top, rosewood back and sides, 12-string. See Custom F-512 for earlier models.

2005-2007		$1,125	$1,350

Freshman M-65
1958-1973. Electric archtop, single-cut, mahogany back and sides, f-holes, 1 single-coil (some with 2), sunburst or natural top.

1958-1959		$1,250	$1,450
1960-1969		$1,150	$1,300
1970-1973		$1,100	$1,250

1997 Guild D-55

Guild Duane Eddy Deluxe DE-500

Guild George Barnes AcoustiLectric

1955 Guild Manhattan X-175

MODEL YEAR	FEATURES	EXC. COND. LOW	HIGH
Freshman M-65 3/4			
1958-1973. Short-scale version of M-65, 1 pickup.			
1958-1959	Natural or sunburst	$900	$1,100
1960-1969	Cherry, natural or sunburst	$800	$1,000
1970-1973	Cherry or sunburst	$700	$900
FS-46 CE			
1983-1986. Flat-top acoustic/electric, pointed cutaway, black, natural or sunburst.			
1983-1986		$650	$750
G-5 P			
1988-ca.1989. Handmade in Spain, cedar top, gold-plated hardware.			
1988-1989		$600	$650
G-37			
1973-1986. Acoustic flat-top, spruce top, laminated maple back and sides, rosewood 'board and bridge, sunburst or natural top.			
1973-1986		$900	$1,000
G-41			
1974-1978. Acoustic flat-top, spruce top, mahogany back and sides, rosewood 'board and bridge, 20 frets.			
1975-1978		$900	$1,000
G-75			
1975-1977. Acoustic flat-top, 3/4-size version of D-50, spruce top, rosewood back and sides, mahogany neck, ebony 'board and bridge.			
1975-1977		$950	$1,150
G-212 12-String			
1974-1983. Acoustic flat-top 12-string version of D-40, spruce top, mahogany back and sides, natural or sunburst.			
1974-1983		$950	$1,175
G-212 XL 12-String			
1974-1983. Acoustic flat-top, 12 strings, 17" version of G-212.			
1974-1983		$1,000	$1,250
G-312 12-String			
1974-1987. Acoustic flat-top 12-string version of the D-50, spruce top, rosewood back and sides.			
1974-1987		$1,150	$1,400
George Barnes AcoustiLectric			
1962-1972. Electric archtop, single-cut, solid spruce top, curly maple back and sides, multi-bound, 2 humbuckers, gold-plated hardware, sunburst or natural finish.			
1962-1972		$3,000	$3,500
GF-30			
1987-1991. Acoustic flat-top, maple back, sides and neck, multi-bound.			
1987-1991		$900	$950
GF-50			
1987-1991. Acoustic flat-top, rosewood back and sides, mahogany neck, multi-bound.			
1987-1991		$950	$1,100
GF-60 R			
1987-1991. Jumbo size, rosewood sides and back, diamond markers.			
1987-1991		$1,050	$1,200

MODEL YEAR	FEATURES	EXC. COND. LOW	HIGH
Granda A-50 (Acoustic Archtop)			
1956-1960. Lowest-end acoustic archtop in the Guild line, renamed Cordoba A-50 in '61.			
1956-1960		$600	$750
Granda X-50			
1954-1961. Electric archtop, non-cut, laminated all maple body, rosewood 'board and bridge, nickel-plated metal parts, 1 pickup, sunburst. Renamed Cordoba X-50 in '61.			
1955-1959		$1,150	$1,400
1960-1961		$1,000	$1,250
GV Series			
1993-1995. Flat-top, rosewood back and sides, various enhancements.			
1993-1995	GV-52, jumbo, rosewood	$875	$925
1993-1995	GV-70, abalone soundhole ring	$925	$975
1993-1995	GV-72, herringbone, extra trim	$975	$1,025
Jet Star S-50			
1963-1970. Electric solidbody, double-cut, mahogany or alder body, 1 pickup, vibrato optional by '65, asymmetrical headstock until '65, reintroduced as S-50 in '72-'78 with body redesign.			
1963-1965	3-on-side tuners, single-coil	$1,050	$1,400
1966-1970	6-in-line tuners, single-coil	$900	$1,100
JF-30			
1987-2004. Jumbo 6-string acoustic, spruce top, laminated maple back, solid maple sides, multi-bound.			
1987-1999		$800	$1,000
2000-2004		$800	$1,000
JF-30 E			
1994-2004. Acoustic/electric version.			
1994-2004		$900	$1,100
JF-30-12			
1987-2004. 12-string version of the JF-30.			
1987-1999		$850	$1,050
JF-50 R			
1987-1988. Jumbo 6-string acoustic, rosewood back and sides, multi-bound.			
1987-1988		$1,200	$1,500
JF-55			
1989-2000. Jumbo flat-top, spruce top, rosewood body.			
1989-2000		$1,400	$1,700
JF-55-12			
1991-2000. 12-string JF-55.			
1991-2000		$1,450	$1,750
JF-65 R/J-65 M			
1987-1994. Renamed from Navarre F-50, Jumbo flat-top acoustic, spruce top, R has rosewood back and sides and M has maple.			
1987-1994	Maple	$1,500	$1,700
1987-1994	Rosewood	$1,600	$1,900
JF-65 R-12			
1987. Rosewood body version of JF-65-12.			
1987		$1,300	$1,400

GUITARS

MODEL YEAR	FEATURES	EXC. COND. LOW	HIGH

JF-65-12
1987-2001. 12-string, version of maple JF-65.

| 1987-2001 | | $1,200 | $1,300 |

Johnny Smith Award
1956-1961. Single-cut electric archtop, floating DeArmond pickup, multi-bound, gold hardware, sunburst or natural, renamed Artist Award in '61.

| 1956-1961 | | $7,500 | $8,000 |

Johnny Smith Award Benedetto
2004-2006. 18 custom made instruments under the supervision of Bob Benedetto, signed by Johnny Smith, with certificate of authenticity signed by Smith and Benedetto.

| 2004-2006 18 made | | $5,600 | $6,600 |

Liberator Elite
1988. Limited Edition, top-of-the-line, set-neck, offset double-cut solidbody, 2-piece figured maple top, mahogany body, rising-sun inlays, 3 active Bartolini pickups, 2 knobs and 4 toggles, last of the Guild solidbodies.

| 1988 | | $900 | $1,100 |

M-80 CS
1975-1984. Solidbody, double-cut, 2 pickups, has M-80 on truss rod cover, called just M-80 from '80-'84.

| 1975-1984 | | $700 | $775 |

Manhattan X-170 (Mini-Manhattan X-170)
1985-2002. Called Mini-Manhattan X-170 in '85-'86, electric archtop hollowbody, single rounded cutaway, maple body, f-holes, 2 humbuckers, block inlays, gold hardware, natural or sunburst.

| 1985-1989 | | $1,500 | $1,650 |
| 1990-2002 | | $1,300 | $1,500 |

Manhattan X-175 (Sunburst)
1954-1985. Electric archtop, single rounded cutaway, laminated spruce top, laminated maple back and sides, 2 pickups, chrome hardware, sunburst.

1954-1959		$2,100	$2,400
1960-1969		$1,800	$2,100
1970-1985		$1,500	$1,900

Manhattan X-175 B (Natural)
1954-1976. Natural finish X-175.

1954-1959		$2,300	$2,600
1960-1969		$2,200	$2,500
1970-1976		$1,900	$2,200

Mark I
1961-1972. Classical, Honduras mahogany body, rosewood 'board, slotted headstock.

| 1961-1969 | | $500 | $575 |
| 1970-1973 | | $400 | $450 |

Mark II
1961-1987. Like Mark I, but with spruce top and body binding.

1961-1969		$550	$700
1970-1979		$525	$650
1980-1987		$400	$525

Mark III
1961-1987. Like Mark II, but with Peruvian mahogany back and sides and floral soundhole design.

1961-1969		$700	$750
1970-1979		$600	$650
1980-1987		$475	$600

Mark IV
1961-1985. Like Mark III, but with flamed pearwood back and sides (rosewood offered in '61, maple in '62).

1961-1969	Pearwood	$875	$950
1970-1979	Pearwood	$775	$850
1980-1985	Pearwood	$725	$800

Mark V
1961-1987. Like Mark III, but with rosewood back and sides (maple available for '61-'64).

1961-1968	Brazilian rosewood	$1,500	$2,000
1969-1979	Indian rosewood	$1,000	$1,200
1980-1987	Indian rosewood	$950	$1,100

Mark VI
1962-1973. Rosewood back and sides, spruce top, wood binding.

| 1962-1968 | Brazilian rosewood | $1,900 | $2,350 |
| 1969-1973 | Indian rosewood | $1,300 | $1,500 |

Mark VII Custom
1968-1973. Special order only, spruce top, premium rosewood back and sides, inlaid rosewood bridge, engraved gold tuners.

| 1962-1968 | Brazilian rosewood | $2,000 | $2,500 |
| 1969-1973 | Indian rosewood | $1,550 | $1,900 |

Navarre F-48
1972-1975. 17", mahogany, block markers.

| 1972-1975 | | $1,250 | $1,350 |

Navarre F-50/F-50
1954-1986, 1994-1995, 2002-present. Acoustic flat-top, spruce top, curly maple back and sides, rosewood 'board and bridge, 17" rounded lower bout, laminated arched maple back, renamed JF-65 M in '87. Reissued in '94 and in '02.

1954-1956		$3,600	$4,000
1957-1962	Pearl block markers added	$3,000	$3,200
1963-1969	Ebony 'board added	$2,800	$3,000
1970-1975		$2,200	$2,600
1976-1979		$1,800	$2,200
1980-1986		$1,750	$2,175
1994-1995		$1,500	$1,700

Navarre F-50 R/F-50 R
1965-1987, 2002-present. Rosewood back and side version of F-50, renamed JF-65 R in '87. Reissued in '02.

1965-1968	Brazilian rosewood	$4,000	$5,000
1969-1975	Indian rosewood	$2,400	$2,900
1976-1979		$2,250	$2,600
1980-1987		$2,000	$2,400

Nightbird
1985-1987. Electric solidbody, single sharp cutaway, tone chambers, 2 pickups, multi-bound, black or gold hardware, renamed Nightbird II in '87.

| 1985-1987 | | $1,500 | $1,850 |

Nightbird I
1987-1988. Like Nightbird but with chrome hardware, less binding and appointments, 2 pickups, coil-tap, phaser switch.

| 1987-1988 | | $1,300 | $1,600 |

Guild Mark V

Guild F-50 R

1976 Guild S-100

Guild Savoy X-150

MODEL YEAR	FEATURES	EXC. COND. LOW	HIGH

Nightbird II

1987-1992. Renamed from Nightbird, electric solidbody, single sharp cut, tone chambers, 2 pickups, multi-bound, black hardware, renamed Nightbird X-2000 in '92.

1987-1992		$1,500	$1,850

Nightbird X-2000

1992-1996. Renamed from Nightbird II.

1992-1996		$1,300	$1,600

Polara S-100

1963-1970. Electric solidbody, double-cut, mahogany or alder body, rosewood 'board, 2 single coil pickups, built-in stand until '70, asymmetrical headstock, in '70 Polara dropped from title (see S-100), renamed back to Polara S-100 in '97.

1963-1964	2 pickups	$1,000	$1,250
1965-1970	3 pickups	$1,000	$1,250

Roy Buchanan T-200

1986. Single-cut solidbody, 2 pickups, pointed six-on-a-side headstock, poplar body, bolt-on neck, gold and brass hardware.

1986		$600	$725

S-50

1972-1978. Double cut solidbody, 1 single-coil (switched to humbucker in '74), dot inlay.

1972-1973	Single-coil	$750	$850
1974-1978	Humbucker	$700	$875

S-60/S-60 D

1976-1981. Double-cut solidbody, 1 pickup, all mahogany body, rosewood 'board. Renamed S-60 D in '77 with 2 DiMarzio pickups.

1976-1980	S-60, 1 humbucker	$550	$675
1977-1981	S-60 D, 2 single-coil	$550	$675

S-65 D

1980-1981. Electric solidbody, double-cut, 3 DiMarzio pickups, rosewood 'board.

1980-1981	1 humbucker	$600	$750

S-70 D/S-70 AD

1979-1981. Solidbody (mahogany D, ash AD), rosewood 'board, 3 single-coils.

1979-1981	D-70AD, ash	$800	$925
1979-1981	S-70D, mahogany	$700	$825

S-90

1972-1977. Double-cut SG-like body, 2 humbuckers, dot inlay, chrome hardware.

1972-1977		$700	$850

S-100

1970-1978, 1994-1996. S-100 Standard is double-cut solidbody, 2 humbuckers, block inlays. Deluxe of '72-'75 had added Bigsby. Standard Carved of '74-'77 has acorns and oakleaves carved in the top.

1970-1978	Standard	$975	$1,225
1972-1975	Deluxe	$975	$1,225
1974-1977	Standard Carved	$1,000	$1,275

S-100 Reissue

1994-1997. Renamed Polara in '97.

1994-1997		$775	$825

MODEL YEAR	FEATURES	EXC. COND. LOW	HIGH

S-250

1981-1983. Double-cut solidbody, 2 humbuckers.

1981-1983		$700	$750

S-261

Ca.1985. Double-cut, maple body, black Kahler tremolo, 1 humbucker and 2 single-coil pickups, rosewood 'board.

1985		$450	$700

S-270 Runaway

1985. Offset double-cut solidbody, 1 humbucker, Kahler.

1985		$450	$700

S-271 Sprint

1986. Replaced the S-270.

1986		$450	$700

S-275

1982-1983. Offset double-cut body, 2 humbuckers, bound figured maple top, sunburst or natural.

1982-1983		$450	$700

S-280 Flyer

1983-1984. Double-cut poplar body, 2 humbuckers or 3 single-coils, maple or rosewood neck, dot markers.

1983-1984		$475	$700

S-281 Flyer

1983-1988. Double-cut poplar body S-280 with locking vibrato, optional pickups available.

1983-1988		$475	$650

S-284 Starling/Aviator

1984-1988. Starling (early-'84) and Aviator (late-'84-'88), double-cut, 3 pickups.

1984	Starling	$575	$700
1984-1988	Aviator	$575	$700

S-285 Aviator

1986. Deluxe Aviator, bound 'board, fancy inlays.

1986		$575	$700

S-300 Series

1976-1983. Double-cut mahogany solidbody with larger bass horn and rounded bottom, 2 humbuckers. S-300 A has ash body, D has exposed DiMarzio humbuckers.

1976-1983	S-300	$800	$1,000
1977-1982	S-300 D	$800	$1,000
1977-1983	S-300 A	$825	$1,025

S-400/S-400 A

1980-1981. Double-cut mahogany (400) or ash (400 A) solidbody, 2 humbuckers.

1980-1981		$975	$1,200

Savoy A-150

1958-1973. Acoustic archtop version of X-150, available with floating pickup, natural or sunburst finish.

1958-1961	Natural	$1,700	$1,800
1958-1961	Sunburst	$1,600	$1,700

Savoy X-150

1954-1965, 1998-2005. Electric archtop, single rounded cutaway, spruce top, maple back and sides, rosewood 'board and bridge, 1 single-coil pickup, sunburst, blond or sparkling gold finish.

1954	Sunburst	$2,100	$2,400
1955-1959	Sunburst	$2,000	$2,300
1960-1961	Sunburst	$1,800	$2,200

The *Vintage Guitar Price Guide* shows low to high values for items in all-original excellent condition, and, where applicable, with original case or cover.

Slim Jim T-100

1958-1973. Electric archtop thinline, single-cut, laminated all-maple body, rosewood 'board and bridge, Waverly tailpiece, 1 pickup, natural or sunburst.

MODEL YEAR	FEATURES	EXC. COND. LOW	HIGH
1958-1960		$1,500	$1,850
1961-1964		$1,400	$1,750
1965-1973		$1,100	$1,350

Slim Jim T-100 D

1958-1973. Semi-hollowbody electric, single Florentine cutaway, thinline, 2-pickup version of the T-100, natural or sunburst.

1958-1960		$1,700	$2,100
1961-1964		$1,600	$2,000
1965-1969		$1,300	$1,600
1970-1973		$1,200	$1,500

Songbird/S-4

1984-1991. Designed by George Gruhn, flat-top, mahogany back, spruce top, single pointed cutaway, pickup with preamp, multi-bound top, black, natural or white. Renamed S-4 later in run.

1984-1991		$825	$900

Standard F-112 12-String

1968-1982. Acoustic flat-top, spruce top, mahogany back, sides and neck.

1968-1969		$1,100	$1,250
1970-1979		$975	$1,225
1980-1982		$850	$1,050

Starfire I

1960-1964. Electric archtop, single-cut thinline, laminated maple or mahogany body, bound body and neck, 1 pickup.

1960-1961	Starfire Red	$1,100	$1,325
1962-1964		$1,000	$1,225

Starfire II

1960-1976, 1997-2001. Electric archtop, single-cut thinline, laminated maple or mahogany body, bound body and rosewood neck, 2 pickups.

1960-1961	Sunburst	$1,400	$1,700
1962	Emerald Green	$2,000	$2,500
1962-1966	Special color options	$2,000	$2,500
1962-1966	Sunburst, Starfire Red	$1,400	$1,700
1967-1969	Sunburst, Starfire Red	$1,300	$1,600
1970-1975	Sunburst, Starfire Red	$1,000	$1,250
1997-2001	Reissue model	$1,000	$1,100

Starfire III

1960-1974, 1997-2005. Electric archtop, single-cut thinline, laminated maple or mahogany body, bound body and rosewood neck, 2 pickups, Guild or Bigsby vibrato, Starfire Red.

1960-1961		$1,500	$1,800
1962-1966		$1,500	$1,800
1967-1969		$1,400	$1,750
1970-1974		$1,100	$1,350
1997-2005	Reissue model	$1,200	$1,250

Starfire IV

1963-1987, 1991-2005. Thinline, double-cut semi-hollowbody, laminated maple or mahogany body, f-holes, 2 humbuckers, rosewood 'board, cherry or sunburst.

MODEL YEAR	FEATURES	EXC. COND. LOW	HIGH
1963-1966		$2,000	$2,200
1967-1969		$1,900	$2,100
1970-1975		$1,800	$2,000
1976-1979		$1,600	$1,800
1980-1987		$1,400	$1,600
1991-2005	Reissue model	$1,200	$1,500

Starfire IV Special (Custom Shop)

2001-2002. Nashville Custom Shop.

2001-2002		$2,000	$2,200

Starfire V

1963-1973, 1999-2002. Same as Starfire IV but with block markers, Bigsby and master volume, natural or sunburst finish, reissued in '99.

1963-1966		$2,500	$3,000
1967-1969		$2,300	$2,800
1970-1973		$2,000	$2,400

Starfire VI

1964-1979. Same as Starfire IV but with higher appointments such as ebony 'board, pearl inlays, Guild/Bigsby vibrato, natural or sunburst.

1964-1966		$3,000	$3,500
1967-1969		$2,900	$3,400
1970-1975	Sunburst or blond	$2,800	$3,300
1976-1979		$2,600	$3,000

Starfire XII

1966-1973. Electric archtop, 12-string, double-cut, maple or mahogany body, set-in neck, 2 humbuckers, harp tailpiece.

1966-1967		$2,000	$2,500
1968-1969		$1,900	$2,300
1970-1973		$1,800	$2,100

Stratford A-350

1956-1973. Acoustic archtop, single rounded cutaway, solid spruce top with solid curly maple back and sides, rosewood 'board and bridge (changed to ebony by '60), sunburst.

1956-1959		$2,300	$2,650
1960-1965		$2,200	$2,550
1966-1969		$2,100	$2,450
1970-1973		$2,000	$2,350

Stratford A-350 B

1956-1973. A-350 in blond/natural finish option.

1956-1959		$2,500	$2,850
1960-1965		$2,400	$2,750
1966-1969		$2,300	$2,650
1970-1973		$2,200	$2,550

Stratford X-350

1954-1965. Electric archtop, single rounded cutaway, laminated spruce top with laminated maple back and sides, rosewood 'board, 6 push-button pickup selectors, sunburst finish (natural finish is X-375).

1954-1959		$2,650	$3,200
1960-1965		$2,550	$2,900

Guild Starfire II

Guild Starfire III

To get the most from this book, be sure to read "Using *The Guide*" in the introduction.

GUITARS

1954 Guild Stratford X-375

Guild X-79 Skyhawk

MODEL YEAR	FEATURES	EXC. COND. LOW	HIGH

Stratford X-375/X-350 B
1954-1965. Natural finish version of X-350, renamed X-350 B in '58.

| 1954-1959 | X-375 | $2,900 | $3,300 |
| 1960-1965 | X-350 B | $2,700 | $3,150 |

Stuart A-500
1956-1969. Acoustic archtop single-cut, 17" body, A-500 sunburst, available with Guild logo, floating DeArmond pickup.

1956-1959		$2,500	$2,850
1960-1965		$2,400	$2,750
1966-1969		$2,300	$2,650

Stuart A-550/A-500 B
1956-1969. Natural blond finish version of Stuart A-500, renamed A-500 B in '60.

1956-1959		$2,800	$3,000
1960-1965		$2,700	$2,900
1966-1969		$2,600	$2,800

Stuart X-500
1953-1995. Electric archtop, single-cut, laminated spruce top, laminated curly maple back and sides, 2 pickups, sunburst.

1953-1959		$3,150	$3,350
1960-1964		$2,900	$3,200
1965-1969		$2,700	$3,000
1970-1979		$2,300	$2,700
1980-1995		$2,400	$2,600

Stuart X-550/X-500 B
1953-1995. Natural blond finish Stuart X-500, renamed X-500 B in '60.

1953-1959		$3,300	$3,700
1960-1964		$3,100	$3,500
1965-1969		$2,900	$3,300
1970-1979		$2,700	$3,100
1980-1995		$2,500	$2,900

Studio 301/ST301
1968-1970. Thinline, semi-hollow archtop Starfire-style but with sharp horns, 1 pickup, dot inlays, cherry or sunburst.

| 1968-1969 | Single-coil | $1,000 | $1,225 |
| 1970 | Humbucker | $1,100 | $1,325 |

Studio 302/ST302
1968-1970. Like Studio 301, but with 2 pickups.

| 1968-1969 | Single-coils | $1,300 | $1,550 |
| 1970 | Humbuckers | $1,400 | $1,650 |

Studio 303/ST303
1968-1970. Like Studio 301, but with 2 pickups and Guild/Bigsby.

| 1968-1969 | Single-coils | $1,400 | $1,650 |
| 1970 | Humbuckers | $1,500 | $1,750 |

Studio 402/ST402
1969-1970. Inch thicker body than other Studios, 2 pickups, block inlays.

| 1969-1970 | Humbuckers | $1,700 | $1,950 |
| 1969-1970 | Single-coils | $1,600 | $1,850 |

T-250
1986-1988. Single-cut body and pickup configuration with banana-style headstock.

| 1986-1988 | | $600 | $750 |

MODEL YEAR	FEATURES	EXC. COND. LOW	HIGH

Thunderbird S-200
1963-1968. Electric solidbody, offset double-cut, built-in rear guitar stand, AdjustoMatic bridge and vibrato tailpiece, 2 humbucker pickups until changed to single-coils in '66.

| 1963-1965 | Humbuckers | $3,800 | $4,500 |
| 1966-1968 | Single-coils | $2,800 | $3,500 |

Troubador F-20
1956-1987. Acoustic flat-top, spruce top with maple back and sides (mahogany '59 and after), rosewood 'board and bridge, natural or sunburst.

1956-1959		$1,050	$1,300
1960-1964		$1,000	$1,250
1965-1969		$900	$1,100
1970-1979		$850	$1,050
1980-1987		$750	$900

TV Model D-55/D-65/D-55
1968-1987, 1990-present (special order only for 1968-1973). Dreadnought acoustic, spruce top, rosewood back and sides, scalloped bracing, gold-plated tuners, renamed D-65 in '87. Reintroduced as D-55 in '90.

1968-1969		$2,000	$2,400
1970-1975		$1,900	$2,300
1976-1979		$1,700	$2,100
1980-1987		$1,650	$1,900
1988-1989	D-65	$1,600	$1,900
1990-1999		$1,600	$1,800

Willy Porter Signature
2007-present. Production started in '07 in FMIC's Guild Tacoma facility, based on acoustic stylist Willy Porter's guitar, AAA sitka spruce top, solid flamed maple sides and back, special appointments, Fishman Ellipse Matrix Blend pickup system.

| 2007 | | $1,500 | $1,600 |

X-79 Skyhawk
1981-1986. Four-point solidbody, 2 pickups, coil-tap or phase switch, various colors.

| 1981-1986 | | $850 | $1,050 |

X-80 Skylark/Swan
1982-1986. Solidbody with 2 deep cutaways, banana-style 6-on-a-side headstock, renamed Swan in '85.

| 1983-1986 | | $850 | $1,050 |

X-88 Flying Star Motley Crue
1984-1986. Pointy 4-point star body, rocketship meets spearhead headstock on bolt neck, 1 pickup, optional vibrato.

| 1984-1986 | | $775 | $950 |

X-92 Citron
1984. Electric solidbody, detachable body section, 3 pickups.

| 1984 | | $675 | $800 |

X-100/X-110
1953-1954. Guild was founded in 1952, so this is a very early model, 17" non-cut, single-coil soapbar neck pickup, X-100 sunburst finish, X-110 natural blond finish.

| 1953-1954 | X-100 | $1,300 | $1,600 |
| 1953-1954 | X-110 | $1,400 | $1,800 |

MODEL		EXC. COND.	
YEAR	FEATURES	LOW	HIGH

X-160 Savoy
1989-1993. No Bigsby, black or sunburst.

1989-1993		$1,275	$1,375

X-161/X-160B Savoy
1989-1993. X-160 Savoy with Bigsby, black or sunburst.

1989-1993		$1,300	$1,475

X-200/X-220
1953-1954. Electric archtop, spruce top, laminated maple body, rosewood 'board, non-cut, 2 pickups. X-200 is sunburst and X-220 blond.

1953-1954	X-200	$1,550	$1,900
1953-1954	X-220	$1,800	$2,200

X-300/X-330
1953-1954. No model name, non-cut, 2 pickups, X-300 is sunburst and X-330 blond. Becomes Savoy X-150 in '54.

1953-1954	X-300	$1,550	$1,900
1953-1954	X-330	$1,800	$2,200

X-400/X-440
1953-1954. Electric archtop, single-cut, spruce top, laminated maple body, rosewood 'board, 2 pickups, X-400 in sunburst and X-440 in blond. Becomes Manhattan X-175 in '54.

1953-1954	X-400	$2,100	$2,500
1953-1954	X-440	$2,300	$2,700

X-600/X-660
1953. No model name, single-cut, 3 pickups, X-600 in sunburst and X-660 in blond. Becomes Statford X-350 in '54.

1953	X-600	$2,900	$3,200
1953	X-660	$3,200	$3,700

X-700
1994-1999. Rounded cutaway, 17", solid spruce top, laminated maple back and sides, gold hardware, natural or sunburst.

1994-1999		$2,100	$2,400

Guillermo Roberto Guitars
2000-present. Professional grade, solidbody electric bajo quintos made in San Fernando, California.

Guitar Mill
2006-present. Luthier Mario Martin builds his production/custom, professional grade, semi-hollow and solidbody guitars in Murfreesboro, Tennessee. He also builds basses.

Gurian
1965-1981. Luthier Michael Gurian started making classical guitars on a special order basis, in New York City. In '69, he started building steel-string guitars as well. 1971 brought a move to Hinsdale, Vermont, and with it increased production. In February, '79 a fire destroyed his factory, stock, and tools. He reopened in West Swanzey, New Hampshire, but closed the doors in '81. Around 2,000 Gurian instruments were built.

MODEL		EXC. COND.	
YEAR	FEATURES	LOW	HIGH

CL Series
1970s. Classical Series, mahogany (M), Indian rosewood (R), or Brazilian rosewood (B).

1970s	CLB, Brazilian rosewood	$1,800	$2,000
1970s	CLM, mahogany	$1,300	$1,500
1970s	CLR, Indian rosewood	$1,500	$1,600

FLC
1970s. Flamenco guitar, yellow cedar back and sides, friction tuning pegs.

1970s		$1,350	$1,550

JM/JMR
1970s. Jumbo body, mahogany (JM) or Indian Rosewood (JMR), relatively wide waist (versus D-style or SJ-style).

1970s	JM	$1,600	$1,700
1970s	JMR	$1,700	$1,800

JR3H
1970s. Jumbo, Indian rosewood sides and back, 3-piece back, herringbone trim.

1970s		$1,600	$1,950

S2M
1970s. Size 2 guitar with mahogany back and sides.

1970s		$1,300	$1,400

S2R/S2R3H
1970s. Size 2 with Indian rosewood sides and back, R3H has 3-piece back and herringbone trim.

1970s	S2R	$1,500	$1,600
1970s	S2R3H	$1,800	$1,900

S3M
Mahogany.

1970s		$1,500	$1,600

S3R/S3R3H
1970s. Size 3 with Indian Rosewood, S3R3H has has 3-piece back and herringbone trim.

1970s	S3R	$1,600	$1,700
1970s	S3R3H	$1,900	$2,000

Guyatone
1933-present. Made in Tokyo by Matsuki Seisaku-jo, founded by Hawaiian guitarists Mitsuo Matsuki and Atsuo Kaneko (later of Teisco). Guya brand Rickenbacker lap copies in '30s. After a hiatus for the war ('40-'48), Seisakujo resumes production of laps and amps as Matsuki Denki Onkyo Kenkyujo. In '51 the Guyatone brand is first used on guitars, and in '52 they changed the company name to Tokyo Sound Company. Guyatones are among the earliest U.S. imports, branded as Marco Polo, Winston, Kingston and Kent. Other brand names included LaFayette and Bradford. Production and exports slowed after '68.

Guild X-700 Stuart

1966 Guyatone Lafayette

Hagstrom HL-550

Hahn Model 228

MODEL YEAR	FEATURES	EXC. COND. LOW	HIGH

Hagenlocher, Henner

1996-present. Luthier Henner Hagenlocher builds his premium grade, custom, nylon-string guitars in Granada, Spain.

Hagstrom

1958-1983, 2004-present. Intermediate, professional, and premium grade, production/custom, solidbody, semi-hollowbody and acoustic guitars made in the U.S. and imported. Founded by Albin Hagström of Älvdalen, Sweden, who began importing accordions in 1921 and incorporated in '25. The name of the company was changed to A.B. Hagström, Inc. in '38, and an American sales office was established in '40. Electric guitar and bass production began in '58 with plastic-covered hollowbody De Luxe and Standard models. The guitars were imported into the U.S. by Hershman Music of New York as Goya 90 and 80 from '58-'61. Bass versions were imported in '61. Following a year in the U.S., Albin's son Karl-Erik Hagström took over the company as exclusive distributor of Fender in Scandinavia; he changed the U.S. importer to Merson Musical Instruments of New York (later Unicord in '65), and redesigned the line. The company closed its doors in '83. In 2004 American Music & Sound started manufacturing and distributing the Hagstrom brand under license from A.B. Albin Hagstrom.

Corvette/Condor
1963-1967. Offset double-cut solidbody, 3 single-coils, multiple push-button switches, spring vibrato, called the Condor on U.S. imports.

1963-1967		$900	$1,100

D'Aquisto Jimmy
1969, 1976-1979. Designed by James D'Aquisto, electric archtop, f-holes, 2 pickups, sunburst, natural, cherry or white. The '69 had dot inlays, the later version had blocks. From '77 to '79, another version with an oval soundhole (no f-holes) was also available.

1976-1979		$1,000	$1,200

Deluxe (D-2H)
2004-present. Carved single-cut mahogany body, set-neck, 2 humbuckers, sparkle tops or sunburst.

2004-2007		$200	$250

F-20 (China)
2004-present. Offset double-cut basswood body, 2 humbuckers, trem.

2001-2007		$125	$150

F-300 Series (China)
2004-present. Offset double-cut basswood body, 300 has 3 single-coils, 301 is single/single/hum.

2004-2007 F-300		$125	$150
2004-2007 F-301		$150	$175

H-12 Electric
1965-1967. Double-cut, 2 pickups, 12 strings.

1965-1967		$600	$725

H-22 Folk
1965-1967. Flat-top acoustic.

1965-1967		$425	$475

Impala
1963-1967. Two-pickup version of the Corvette, sunburst.

1963-1967		$775	$950

Model I
1965-1971. Small double-cut solidbody, 2 single-coils, early models have plastic top.

1965-1971	Rare finish	$725	$900
1965-1971	Standard finish	$525	$650

Model II/F-200 Futura/H II
1965-1972, 1975-1976. Offset double-cut slab body with beveled edge, 2 pickups, called F-200 Futura in U.S., Model II elsewhere, '75-'76 called H II. F-200 reissued in 2004.

1965-1972		$650	$675

Model III/F-300 Futura/H III
1965-1972, 1977. Offset double-cut slab body with beveled edge, 3 pickups, called F-300 Futura in U.S., Model III elsewhere, '77 called H III.

1965-1972		$600	$725
1977		$550	$675

Swede
1970-1982, 2004-present. Bolt-on neck, single-cut solidbody, black, cherry or natural, '04 version is set-neck.

1979-1982		$725	$900

Super Swede
1979-1983, 2004-present. Glued-in neck upgrade of Swede, '04 version is maple top upgrade of Swede.

1979-1983		$1,000	$1,100
1979-1983	Custom color, blue	$1,500	$1,800
2004-2007	Reissue	$350	$400

Viking/V1
1965-1967, 1972-1979, 2004-present. Double-cut thinline, 2 f-holes, chrome hardware, dot inlays, also advertised as the V-1. '60s had 6-on-side headstock, '70s was 3-and-3.

1965-1967		$950	$1,100
1972-1979		$650	$800
2004-2007	Reissue	$300	$375

Viking II/Viking Deluxe
1967-1968, 2004-present. Upscale version, gold hardware, block inlays, bound headstock and f-holes. Current version upgrades are blocks and flame maple.

1967-1968		$1,000	$1,200

Viking XII
1967. 12-string version.

1967		$950	$1,200

Hahn

2007-present. Professional and premium grade, custom electric guitars built by luthier Chihoe Hahn in Garnervile, New York.

Hallmark

1965-1967, 2004-present. Imported and U.S.-made, intermediate and premium grade, production/custom, guitars from luthiers Bob Shade and Bill Gruggett, and located in Greenbelt, Maryland. They also make basses. The brand was originally

MODEL YEAR	FEATURES	EXC. COND. LOW	HIGH

founded by Joe Hall in Arvin, California, in '65. Hall had worked for Semie Moseley (Mosrite) and had also designed guitars for Standel in the mid-'60s. Bill Gruggett, who also built his own line of guitars, was the company's production manager. Joe Hall estimates that less than 1000 original Hallmark guitars were built. The brand was revived by Shade in '04.

Sweptwing
1965-1967. Pointed body, sort of like a backwards Flying V.

1965-1967		$1,000	$1,250

Hamer

1974-present. Intermediate, professional and premium grade, production/custom, electric guitars made in the U.S. and overseas. Hamer also makes basses and the Slammer line of instruments. Founded in Arlington Heights, Illinois, by Paul Hamer and Jol Dantzig. Prototype guitars built in early-'70s were on Gibson lines, with first production guitar, the Standard (Explorer shape), introduced in '75. Hamer was purchased by Kaman Corporation (Ovation) in '88. The Illinois factory was closed and the operations were moved to the Ovation factory in Connecticut in '97. On January 1, '08, Fender acquired Kaman Music Corporation and the Hamer brand. In '90, they started the Korean-import Hamer Slammer series which in '97 became Hamer Import Series (no Slammer on headstock). In '05 production was moved to China and name changed to XT Series (in '07 production moved to Indonesia). The U.S.-made ones have U.S.A. on the headstock. The less expensive import Slammer brand (not to be confused with the earlier Slammer Series) was introduced in '99 (see that listing).

Artist/Archtop Artist/Artist Custom
1995-present. Similar to Sunburst Archtop with semi-solid, f-hole design, named Archtop Artist, then renamed Artist (with stop tailpiece)/Artist Custom in '97.

1995-2007	Sunburst	$1,100	$1,400

Blitz
1982-1984 (1st version), 1984-1990 (2nd version). Explorer-style body, 2 humbuckers, three-on-a-side peghead, dot inlays, choice of tremolo or fixed bridge, second version same except has angled six-on-a-side peghead and Floyd Rose tremolo.

1982-1984	3-on-a-side peghead	$675	$825
1984-1990	6-on-a-side peghead	$625	$750

Californian
1987-1997. Solidbody double cut, bolt neck, 1 humbucker and 1 single-coil, Floyd Rose tremolo.

1987-1989		$675	$825
1990-1997		$625	$750

Californian Custom
1987-1997. Downsized contoured body, offset double-cut, neck-thru-body, optional figured maple body, Duncan Trembucker and Trem-single pickups.

1987-1989		$675	$825
1990-1997		$625	$750

Californian Elite
1987-1997. Downsized contoured body, offset double-cut, optional figured maple body, bolt-on neck, Duncan Trembucker and Trem-single pickups.

1987-1989		$825	$1,025
1990-1997		$800	$1,000

Centaura
1989-1995. Contoured body of alder or swamp ash, offset double-cut, bolt-on neck, 1 humbucker and 2 single-coil pickups, Floyd Rose tremolo, sunburst.

1989-1995		$600	$750

Chaparral
1985-1987 (1st version), 1987-1994 (2nd version). Contoured body, offset double-cut, glued maple neck, angled peghead, 1 humbucker and 2 single-coils, tremolo, second version has bolt neck with a modified peghead.

1985-1987	Set-neck	$750	$875
1987-1994	Bolt-on neck	$650	$725

Daytona
1993-1997. Contoured body, offset double-cut, bolt maple neck, dot inlay, 3 single-coils, Wilkinson VSV tremolo.

1993-1997		$675	$775

Diablo
1992-1997. Contoured alder body, offset double-cut, bolt maple neck, rosewood 'board, dot inlays, reversed peghead '92-'94, 2 pickups, tremolo.

1992-1997		$550	$650

DuoTone
1993-2003. Semi-hollowbody, double-cut, bound top, glued-in neck, rosewood 'board, 2 humbuckers, EQ.

1993-2003		$525	$650

Echotone/Echotone Custom
2000-2002. Thinline semi-hollow archtop, f-holes, 2 humbuckers, trapezoid inlays, gold hardware.

2000-2002		$225	$275

Eclipse
1994-2003. Asymmetrical double-cut slab mahogany body, glued neck, three-on-a-side peghead, rosewood 'board, dot inlays, 2 Duncan Mini-Humbuckers, cherry.

1994-2003		$650	$800

FB I
1986-1987. Reverse Firebird-style body, glued-in neck, reverse headstock, 1 pickup, rosewood 'board with dot inlays, also available in non-reverse body.

1986-1987		$500	$625

FB II
1986-1987. Reverse Firebird-style, glued-in neck, ebony 'board with boomerang inlays, angled headstock, 2 humbuckers, Floyd Rose tremolo, also available as a 12-string.

1986-1987		$600	$675

Korina Standard
1995-1996. Limited run, Korina Explorer-type body, glued-in neck, angled peghead, 2 humbuckers.

1995-1996		$1,100	$1,300

Hallmark Sweptwing Vintage

Hamer Duo-Tone Custom

Hamer Standard Flametop

Hamer Scarab

MODEL YEAR	FEATURES	EXC. COND. LOW	HIGH

Maestro
1990. Offset double-cut, 7 strings, tremolo, bolt-on maple neck, 3 Seymour Duncan rail pickups.

1990		$725	$900

Miller Music Guitar
1985-1986. Miller (Beer) Music graphic art (white letters on red background), shaped like Miller bottle label. There was a matching bass. Trapezoid-shaped Miller Genuine Draft guitars and basses were offered in '87.

1985-1986		$575	$700

Mirage
1994-1998. Double-cut carved figured koa wood top, transparent flamed top, initially with 3 single-coil pickups, dual humbucker option in '95.

1994-1998		$800	$1,000

Monaco Elite
2003-present. Single-cut solidbody, 2 humbuckers, 3-in-a-line control knobs, tune-o-matic style bridge, mother-of-pearl inlaid 'victory' position markers, carved flamed maple cap over mahogany body, flamed maple sunburst.

2003-2007		$900	$1,100

Phantom A5
1982-1884, 1985-1986 (2nd version). Contoured offset double-cut, glued neck, 3-on-a-side peghead, 1 triple-coil and 1 single-coil pickup, second version same but with 6-on-a-side peghead and Kahler tremolo.

1982-1984		$650	$750

Phantom GT
1984-1986. Contoured body, offset double-cut, glued-in fixed neck, six-on-a-side peghead, 1 humbucker, single volume control.

1984-1986		$575	$700

Prototype
1981-1985. Contoured mahogany body, double-cut with 1 splitable triple-coil pickup, fixed bridge, three-on-a-side peghead, Prototype II has extra pickup and tremolo.

1981-1985		$825	$925

Scarab I
1984-1986. Multiple cutaway body, six-on-a-side peghead, 1 humbucker, tremolo, rosewood or ebony 'board, dot inlays.

1984-1986		$550	$650

Scarab II
1984-1986. Two humbucker version of the Scarab.

1984-1986		$600	$750

Scepter
1986-1990. Futuristic-type body, ebony 'board with boomerang inlays, angled six-on-a-side peghead, Floyd Rose tremolo.

1986-1990		$950	$1,100

Special
1980-1983 (1st version), 1984-1985 (Floyd Rose version), 1992-1997 (2nd version). Double-cut solidbody, flame maple top, glued neck, 3-on-a-side peghead, 2 humbuckers, Rose version has mahogany body with ebony 'board, the second version is all mahogany and has tune-o-matic bridge, stop tailpiece and Duncan P-90s, cherry red.

1980-1983	1st version	$850	$950
1984-1985	With Floyd Rose	$800	$900
1992-1997	2nd version	$750	$850

Special FM
1993-1997. Special with flamed maple top, 2 humbuckers, renamed the Special Custom in '97.

1993-1999		$900	$1,100

Standard
1974-1985, 1995-1999. Futuristic body, maple top, bound or unbound body, glued neck, angled headstock, either unbound neck with dot inlays or bound neck with crown inlays, 2 humbuckers. Reissued in '95 with same specs but unbound mahogany body after '97. Higher dollar Standard Custom still available.

1974-1975	Pre-production, about 20 made	$4,500	$9,000
1975-1977	Production, about 50 made, PAFs	$4,500	$9,000
1977-1979	Dimarzio PAF-copies	$2,500	$4,000
1980-1985		$2,000	$2,500
1995-1999		$1,300	$1,600

Stellar 1
1999-2000. Korean import, double-cut, 2 humbuckers.

1999-2000		$150	$200

Steve Stevens I
1984-1992. Introduced as Prototype SS, changed to Steve Stevens I in '86, contoured double-cut, six-on-a-side headstock, dot or crown inlays, 1 humbucker and 2 single-coil pickups.

1984-1992		$1,000	$1,200

Steve Stevens II
1986-1987. One humbucker and 1 single-coil version.

1986-1987		$1,100	$1,300

Studio
1993-present. Double-cut, flamed maple top on mahogany body, 2 humbuckers, cherry or natural.

1993-2007		$850	$1,000

Sunburst
1977-1983, 1990-1992. Double-cut bound solidbody, flamed maple top, glue-in neck, bound neck and crown inlays optional, 3-on-a-side headstock, 2 humbuckers.

1977-1979		$1,700	$2,100
1980-1983	Arlington Heights built	$1,400	$1,700
1990-1992		$1,150	$1,400

Sunburst (Import)
1997-present. Import version of Sunburst, flat or arch top, 2 pickups.

1997-2007		$200	$250

Sunburst Archtop
1991-present. Sunburst model with figured maple carved top, 2 humbuckers, offered under various names:

Standard - unbound neck and dot inlays, tune-o-matic and stop tailpiece '91-'93.

Custom - a Standard with bound neck and crown inlays '91-'93.

Archtop - bound neck with crown inlays '94-'97.

Studio Custom - bound neck with crown inlays '97-present.

MODEL YEAR	FEATURES	EXC. COND. LOW	HIGH

Studio - unbound body, by '95 stud wrap-around tailpiece '93-present.
Archtop GT - Gold top with P-90 soapbar-style pickups '93-'97.

| 1991-1997 | | $1,150 | $1,400 |

T-51
1993-1997. Classic single-cut southern ash body, 2 single-coils.

| 1993-1997 | | $600 | $750 |

T-62
1991-1995. Classic offset double-cut solidbody, tremolo, pau ferro 'board, Lubritrak nut, locking tuners, 3-band active EQ, various colors.

| 1991-1995 | | $675 | $775 |

TLE
1986-1992. Single-cut mahogany body, maple top, glued neck, 6-on-a-side headstock, rosewood 'board, dot inlays, 3 pickups.

| 1986-1992 | | $675 | $775 |

TLE Custom
1986-1992. Bound, single-cut solidbody with maple top, glued-in neck, angled headstock, ebony 'board with boomerang inlays, 3 pickups.

| 1986-1992 | | $675 | $775 |

Vector
1982-1985. V-style body (optional flame maple top), 3-on-a-side peghead, rosewood 'board, 2 humbuckers, Sustain Block fixed bridge (Kahler or Floyd Rose tremolos may also be used).

| 1982-1985 | Maple top | $800 | $1,000 |
| 1982-1985 | Regular top | $775 | $875 |

Vector Limited Edition Korina
1997. 72 built in Hamer's Arlington Heights, IL shop, price includes original Hamer Certificate of Authenticity with matching serial number, Flying-V Vector style body, gold hardware, natural finish.

| 1997 | | $1,800 | $1,900 |

Harden Engineering

1999-present. Professional grade, custom, solid-body guitars built by luthier William Harden in Chicago, Illinois. He also builds effects pedals.

Harmony

1892-1976, late 1970s-present. Huge, Chicago-based manufacturer of fretted instruments, mainly budget models under the Harmony name or for many other American brands and mass marketers. Harmony was at one time the largest guitar builder in the world. In its glory days, Harmony made over one-half of the guitars built in the U.S., with '65 being their peak year. But by the early-'70s, the crash of the '60s guitar boom and increasing foreign competition brought an end to the company. The Harmony brand appeared on Asian-built instruments starting in the late '70s to the '90s with sales mainly is mass-retail stores. In 2000, the Harmony brand was distributed by MBT International. In '02, former MBT International marketing director Alison Gillette announced the launch of Harmony Classic Reissue Guitars and Basses.

Many Harmony guitars have a factory order number on the inside back of the guitar which often contains the serial number. Most older Harmony acoustics and hollowbodies have a date ink-stamped inside the body. DeArmond made most of the electronic assemblies used on older Harmony electrics, and they often have a date stamped on the underside.

Archtone H1215/H1215 Tenor
1950s. Lower-end archtop, sunburst.

| 1950-1960s | 4-string tenor | $350 | $425 |
| 1950-1960s | 6-string | $150 | $175 |

Blond H62
1950s-1960s. Thin body, dual pickup archtop, curly maple back and sides, spruce top, blond.

| 1950s | | $550 | $675 |
| 1960s | | $450 | $550 |

Bob Kat H14/H15
1968. Replaces Silhouette solidbody, H14 has single pickup and two knobs, H15 has 2 pickups. When vibrato is added it becomes the H16 model.

| 1968 | H14 | $200 | $275 |
| 1968 | H15 | $300 | $375 |

Brilliant Cutaway H1310/H1311
1962-1965. 16 1/2" body (Grand Auditorium), acoustic archtop cutaway, block markers, sunburst.

| 1962-1965 | | $525 | $625 |

Broadway H954
1930s-1971. 15-3/4" body, acoustic archtop, dot markers, sunburst.

| 1960s | | $225 | $275 |

Buck Owens
Acoustic flat-top, red, white and blue.

| 1969 | | $600 | $750 |

Cremona
1930s-1952. Full-size archtop line, Harmony and Cremona logo on headstock, natural. Cutaways became available in '53.

| 1940s | | $275 | $350 |

Espanada H63/H64
1950s-1960s. Thick body, single-cut, jazz-style double pickups, black finish with white appointments.

| 1950s | | $700 | $800 |
| 1960s | | $600 | $700 |

Grand Concert H165
1960s. Flat-top, all mahogany body.

| 1960s | | $200 | $250 |

H60 Double Cutaway Hollowbody
1970. Thinline double-cut, 2 pickups, trapeze tailpiece, sunburst.

| 1970 | | $700 | $775 |

H66 Vibra-Jet
1962-1966. Thinline single-cut, 2 pickups, built-in tremolo circuit and control panel knobs and selection dial, sunburst.

| 1962-1966 | | $525 | $650 |

H72/H72V Double Cutaway Hollowbody
1966-1971. Two pickups, multiple bindings, cherry red, H72V has Bigsby.

| 1966-1971 | | $450 | $550 |

Harmony Broadway

Harmony Buck Owens

Harmony H-62

Harmony H-75

MODEL YEAR	FEATURES	EXC. COND. LOW	HIGH

H73 Double Cutaway Hollowbody
Double cutaway, 2 pickups.

| 1960s | | $450 | $550 |

H74
1964. Thinline, partial cutaway on bass bout, full cutaway on treble bout, 2 pickups.

| 1964 | | $500 | $625 |

H75 Double Cutaway Hollowbody
1960-1970. Three pickups, multi-bound body, 3-part f-holes, block inlays, bolt neck, brown sunburst.

| 1960-1970 | | $450 | $550 |

H76 Double Cutaway Hollowbody
Late-1960s. H75 with Bigsby.

| 1960s | | $600 | $700 |

H77 Double Cutaway Hollowbody
1964-1970. Same as H75, but in cherry sunburst.

| 1964-1970 | | $600 | $700 |

H78 Double Cutaway Hollowbody
Late-1960s. H78 with Bigsby.

| 1960s | | $600 | $700 |

H79 Double Cutaway Hollowbody 12-String
1966-1970. Unique slotted headstock, cherry finish.

| 1966-1970 | | $700 | $800 |

H910 Classical
1970s. Beginner guitar, natural.

| 1970s | | $125 | $150 |

H1270 12-String Flat-Top
1965. 16" deluxe acoustic 12-string flat-top, spruce top, mahogany sides and back, dot markers.

| 1965 | | $500 | $600 |

H4101/Flat Top Tenor
1972-1976. Mahogany body, 4-string.

| 1972-1976 | | $350 | $400 |

Holiday Rocket
Mid-1960s. Similar to H59 Rocket III but with push-button controls instead of rotary selector switch, 3 Goldentone pickups, pickup trim rings, Holiday logo on 'guard, higher model than standard Rocket.

| 1964 | | $700 | $875 |

Hollywood H37/H39/H41
Auditorium-sized 15 3/4" non-cut electric archtop, H37 has a single pickup and bronze finish, H39 has a single pickup and brown mahogany shaded finish, H41 has dual pickups and brown finish.

| 1960s | | $300 | $350 |

Lone Ranger
1950-1951. Lone Ranger headstock stencil, Lone Ranger and Tonto stencil on brown body. This model was first introduced in 1936 as the Supertone Lone Ranger with same stencil on a black body.

| 1950-1951 | | $300 | $375 |

Master H945
1965-1966. 15" (Auditorium) acoustic archtop, block markers, music note painted logo on headstock, sunburst.

| 1965-1966 | | $275 | $325 |

MODEL YEAR	FEATURES	EXC. COND. LOW	HIGH

Meteor H70/H71
1958-1966. Single rounded cutaway 2" thin body, 2 pickups, 3-part f-holes, block inlays, bolt neck, H70 sunburst, H71 natural (ended '65), lefty offered '65-'66, reintroduced as H661 and H671 (without Meteor name) in '72-'74.

| 1958-1965 | H71 | $550 | $675 |
| 1958-1966 | H70 | $500 | $600 |

Monterey H950/H952/H1325/H1456/H1457/H6450
1930s-1974. Line of Auditorium and Grand Auditorium acoustic archtop models.

1950s	H952 Colorama	$275	$325
1960s		$250	$300
1970s	H6450	$150	$200

Patrician
1932-1973. Model line mostly with mahogany bodies and alternating single/double dot markers (later models with single dots), introduced as flat-top, changed to archtop in '34. In '37 line expanded to 9 archtops (some with blocks) and 1 flat-top. Flat-tops disappeared in the '40s, with various archtops offered up to '73.

| 1940s-1973 | | $300 | $400 |

Rebel H81
1968-1971. Single pickup version of Rebel, brown sunburst.

| 1968-1971 | | $250 | $300 |

Rebel H82/H82G
Listed as a new model in 1971. Thin body, hollow tone chamber, double-cut, 2 pickups, H82 sunburst, H82G greenburst avocado shading (renumbered as H682 and H683 in '72).

| 1970s | H82 | $550 | $650 |
| 1970s | H82G | $600 | $725 |

Rocket H53/H54/H56/H59
1959-1973. Single-cut, f-holes, dot inlays, 2-tone brown sunburst ('59-'62) or red sunburst ('63 on), came with 1 pickup (Rocket I H53 '59-'71), 2 pickups (Rocket II H54 has 2 pickups, Rocket VII H56 has 2 pickups and vibrato, Rocket III H59 has 3 pickups. Rockets were single-cut, brown sunburst in the early-'60s and double-cut red sunburst in the early-'70s.

1959-1973	1 pickup	$350	$400
1959-1973	2 pickups	$500	$600
1959-1973	3 pickups	$650	$800

Roy Rogers H600
1954-1958. 3/4 size, stencil, sold through Sears.

| 1954-1958 | | $275 | $325 |

Roy Smeck
1963-1964. Electric hollowbody archtop, Roy Smeck logo on headstock or upper bass bout, single neck position silver bar-style pickup or 2 Harmony pickups, standard 4 knobs and toggle, pickup without poles.

| 1963-1964 | | $575 | $700 |

Silhouette De Luxe Double H19
1965-1969. Double-cut solidbody, deluxe pickups, block markers, advanced vibrato, sunburst.

| 1965-1969 | | $425 | $500 |

GUITARS

MODEL YEAR	FEATURES	EXC. COND. LOW	HIGH

Silhouette H14/H15/H17
1964-1967. Double-cut solidbody, H14 single pickup, H15 dual pickup, H17 dual with vibrato (offered until '66).

1965-1966	H17	$350	$425
1965-1967	H14	$225	$275
1965-1967	H15	$325	$400

Singing Cowboys H1057
Western chuck-wagon scene stencil top, Singing Cowboys stenciled on either side of upper bouts, brown background versus earlier Supertone version that had black background.

| 1950s | | $300 | $375 |

Sovereign Jumbo H1260
1960s-1970s. Jumbo shape, 16" wide body, natural.

| 1960s | | $450 | $550 |
| 1970s | | $400 | $500 |

Sovereign Jumbo Deluxe H1266
1960s-1970s. Jumbo nearly D-style, 16" wide body with out-size 'guard, natural.

| 1960s | | $500 | $600 |
| 1970s | | $450 | $550 |

Sovereign Western Special Jumbo H1203
1960s-1970s. 15" wide body, 000-style.

| 1960s | | $525 | $600 |

Stratotone H44
1954-1957. First edition models had small bodies and rounded cutaway, 1 pickup with plain cover using 2 mounting rivets, sometimes called Hershey Bar pickup, '60s models had slightly larger bodies and sharp cutaways, some with headstock logo Harmony Stratotone with atomic note graphic.

| 1954-1957 | | $550 | $700 |

Stratotone Deluxe Jupiter H49
1960s. Single-cut, tone chamber construction, 2 pickups, bound spruce top, curly maple back and 6 control knobs.

| 1960s | | $550 | $675 |

Stratotone Mars Electric H45/H46
1958-1968. Single-cut, tone chamber construction, sunburst finish, H45 with 1 pickup, H46 with 2 pickups.

| 1960s | H45 | $400 | $475 |
| 1960s | H46 | $425 | $500 |

Stratotone Mercury Electric H47/H48
1958-1968. Single-cut, tone chamber construction, H47 with 1 pickup, block inlay and curly maple sunburst top, H48 is the same with a blond top.

| 1960s | H47 | $425 | $525 |
| 1960s | H48 | $450 | $550 |

TG1201 Tenor
Spruce top, two-on-a-side tuners, Sovereign model tenor, natural.

| 1950s | | $350 | $400 |

Harptone
1893-ca. 1975. The Harptone Manufacturing Corporation was located in Newark, New Jersey. They made musical instrument cases and accessories and got into instrument production from 1934 to '42, making guitars, banjos, mandolins, and tiples. In '66 they got back into guitar production, making the Standel line from '67 to '69. Harptone offered flat-tops and archtops under their own brand until the mid-'70s when the name was sold to the Diamond S company, which owned Micro-Frets.

Acoustic
1966-mid 1970s. Various models.

| 1966-1970s | | $1,050 | $1,300 |

Electric
1966-mid 1970s. Various models.

| 1966-1970s | | $1,200 | $1,500 |

Harwood
Harwood was a brand introduced in 1885 by Kansas City, Missouri instrument wholesalers J.W. Jenkins & Sons (though some guitars marked Harwood, New York). May have been built by Jenkins until circa 1905, but work was later contracted out to Harmony.

Parlor
1890s. Slotted headstocks, most had mahogany bodies, some with Brazilian rosewood body, considered to be well made.

| 1890s | Brazilian rosewood | $1,000 | $1,200 |
| 1890s | Mahogany | $525 | $650 |

Hascal Haile
Late 1960s-1986. Luthier Hascal Haile started building acoustic, classical and solidbody guitars in Tompkinsville, Kentucky, after retiring from furniture making. He died in '86.

Hayes Guitars
1993-present. Professional and premium grade, production/custom, steel and nylon string guitars made by luthier Louis Hayes in Paonia, Colorado.

Hayman
1970-1973. Solid and semi-hollow body guitars and basses developed by Jim Burns and Bob Pearson for Ivor Arbiter of the Dallas Arbiter Company and built by Shergold in England.

Haynes
1865-early 1900s. The John C. Haynes Co. of Boston also made the Bay State brand.

Heartfield
1989-1994. Founded as a joint venture between Fender Musical Instrument Corporation (U.S.A.) and Fender Japan (partnership between Fender and distributors Kanda Shokai and Yamano Music) to build and market more advanced designs (built by Fuji Gen-Gakki). First RR and EX guitar series and DR Bass series debut in '90. Talon and Elan guitar series and Prophecy bass series introduced in '91. The brand was dead by '94.

Harmony Rocket

'50s Harmony Stratotone

Heiden dreadnought

HenBev S2

MODEL YEAR	FEATURES	EXC. COND. LOW	HIGH

Elan
1989-1994. Carved-style bound double-cut body, flamed top, 2 humbuckers, offset headstock.

1989-1994		$450	$525

EX
1990-1994. 3 single-coils, Floyd Rose tremolo.

1990-1994		$350	$375

Talon
1989-1994. Offset double-cut, wedge-triangle headstock, dot markers, hum/single/hum pickups.

1989-1994		$350	$375

Heiden Stringed Instruments
1974-present. Luthier Michael Heiden builds his premium grade, production/custom, flat-top guitars in Chilliwack, British Columbia. He also builds mandolins.

Heit Deluxe
Ca. 1967-1970. Imported from Japan by unidentified New York distributor. Many were made by Teisco, the most famous being the Teisco V-2 Mosrite copy. They also had basses.

Acoustic Archtop
1967-1970. Various models.

1967-1970		$175	$225

Electric Solidbody
1967-1970. Various models.

1967-1970		$175	$225

Hemken, Michael
1993-present. Luthier Michael Hemken builds his premium grade, custom, archtops in St. Helena, California.

HenBev
2005-present. Premium grade, production, solid and hollow body electric guitars built by luthier Scotty Bevilacqua in Oceanside, California. He also builds basses.

Heritage
1985-present. Professional, premium, and presentation grade, production/custom, hollow, semi-hollow, and solidbody guitars built in Kalamazoo, Michigan. They have also made banjos, mandolins, flat-tops, and basses in the past.
Founded by Jim Deurloo, Marvin Lamb, J.P. Moats, Bill Paige and Mike Korpak, all former Gibson employees who did not go to Nashville when Norlin closed the original Gibson factory in '84.

Eagle
1986-present. Single rounded cut semi-hollowbody, mahogany body and neck, 1 jazz pickup, f-holes, sunburst or natural.

1986-1999		$1,550	$1,700
2000-2007		$1,650	$1,900

MODEL YEAR	FEATURES	EXC. COND. LOW	HIGH

Eagle Custom
Eagle with custom inlays.

2001		$2,200	$2,400

Gary Moore Model
1989-1991. Single-cut solidbody, 2 pickups, chrome hardware, sunburst.

1989-1991		$1,600	$1,900

Golden Eagle
1985-present. Single-cut hollowbody, back inlaid with mother-of-pearl eagle and registration number, multi-bound ebony 'board with mother-of-pearl cloud inlays, bound f-holes, gold-plated parts, ebony bridge inlaid with mother-of-pearl, mother-of-pearl truss rod cover engraved with owner's name, 1 Heritage jazz pickup, multi-bound curly maple 'guard.

1985-1999		$2,300	$2,600
2000-2007		$2,500	$2,800

H-137
2006-present. Single-cut solidbody, 2 P-90s.

2006-2007		$1,000	$1,150

H140/H-140 CM
1985-2005. Single pointed cutaway solidbody, bound curly maple ('85-'04) or solid gold top ('94-'05), 2 humbuckers, chrome parts.

1985-1994	Curly maple	$800	$850
1985-1994	Goldtop	$775	$825
2001	Flamed maple	$875	$900

H-147
1990-1991. Single-cut solidbody, 2 humbuckers, mahogany body, mother-of-pearl block inlays, black with black or gold hardware.

1990-1991		$700	$850

H-150 C/H-150 CM
1985-present. Single rounded cutaway solidbody, curly maple top, 2 pickups, chrome parts, cherry sunburst.

1985-1999		$925	$1,050
2000-2007		$950	$1,050

H-157 Ultra
1993-1994. Single-cut solidbody, large block markers, highly figured maple top.

1993-1994		$1,200	$1,400

H-170
1980s. Double-cut solidbody, 2 humbuckers, bound carved top, was also a later curly maple top version (H-170CM).

1980s		$1,200	$1,300

H-204 DD
1986-1989. Single-cut solidbody of mahogany, curly maple top, 1-piece mahogany neck, 22-fret rosewood 'board.

1986-1989		$500	$600

H-207 DD
1986-1989. Double-cut solidbody of mahogany, curly maple top, 1-piece mahogany neck, 22-fret rosewood 'board.

1986-1989		$500	$600

H-357
1989-1994. Asymmetrical solidbody, neck-thru.

1989-1994		$1,900	$2,100

The *Vintage Guitar Price Guide* shows low to high values for items in all-original excellent condition, and, where applicable, with original case or cover.

MODEL YEAR	FEATURES	EXC. COND. LOW	HIGH
H-535			
1987-present. Double-cut semi-hollowbody archtop, rosewood 'board, 2 humbucker pickups.			
1987-1999		$1,100	$1,300
1987-1999	Flamed maple top	$1,100	$1,300
2000-2007		$1,200	$1,400
H-550			
1990-present. Single-cut hollowbody, laminated maple top and back, multiple bound top, white bound 'guard, f-holes, 2 humbuckers.			
1990-2007		$1,600	$1,800
H-555			
1989-present. Like 535, but with maple neck, ebony 'board, pearl and abalone inlays, gold hardware.			
1989-2007		$1,700	$1,850
H-575			
1987-present. Single sharp cut hollowbody, solid maple top and back, cream bound top and back, wood 'guard, f-holes, 2 humbuckers.			
1987-2007		$1,300	$1,500
H-576			
1990-2004. Single rounded cut hollowbody, laminated maple top and back, multiple bound top, single bound back and f-holes and wood 'guard, 2 humbuckers.			
1990-2004		$1,200	$1,400
HFT-445			
1987-2000. Flat-top acoustic, mahogany back and sides, spruce top, maple neck, rosewood 'board.			
1987-2000		$650	$800
Johnny Smith			
1989-2001. Custom hand-carved 17" hollowbody, single-cut, f-holes, 1 pickup.			
1989-2001	Optional colors	$2,900	$3,300
1989-2001	Sunburst	$2,600	$3,000
Millennium Eagle 2000			
2000-present. Single-cut semi-solidbody, multiple bound curly maple top, single-bound curly maple back, f-holes, 2 humbuckers.			
2000-2007		$1,700	$1,900
Millennium SAE			
2000-present. Single-cut semi-solidbody, laminated arch top, single cream bound top and back, f-holes, 2 humbuckers.			
2000-2007		$1,100	$1,200
Parsons Street			
1989-1992. Offset double-cut, curly maple top on mahogany body, single/single/hum pickups, pearl block markers, sunburst or natural.			
1989-1992		$800	$950
Roy Clark			
1992-present. Thinline, single-cut semi-hollow archtop, gold hardware, 2 humbuckers, block markers, cherry sunburst.			
1992-2007		$1,600	$1,900
SAE Custom			
1992-2000. Single-cut maple semi-hollow body, f-holes, 2 humbuckers and 1 bridge pickup.			
1992-2000		$1,000	$1,100

MODEL YEAR	FEATURES	EXC. COND. LOW	HIGH
Super Eagle			
1988-present. 18" body, single-cut electric archtop, 2 humbuckers.			
1989-2007	Optional colors	$2,800	$3,000
1989-2007	Sunburst	$2,500	$3,000
Sweet 16			
1987-present. Single-cut maple semi-hollowbody, spruce top, 2 pickups, pearl inlays.			
1987-2007	Optional colors	$2,100	$2,600
1987-2007	Sunburst	$2,000	$2,400

Hermann Hauser

Born in 1882, Hauser started out building zithers and at age 23 added classical guitars and lutes, most built in his shop in Munich, Germany. He died in 1952. His son and grandson and great-granddaughter, Hermann II and III and Kathrin, continued the tradition. The Hermann Hauser's legacy is based on his innovative approach to bracing and top thickness which gave his instruments their own voice. Hermann I Era instruments are linked with Andres Segovia who used them. Hermann II Era instruments are linked with modern players like Julian Bream. Hermann III builds Segovia style and custom-made instruments. Kathrin Hauser, daughter of Hermann III, is a fourth generation builder. The original Hauser shop in Munich was destroyed by Allied bombing in 1946 and was moved to Reisbach in the Bavaria region, where the shop remains. Hauser instruments used paper labels on the inside back. The labels often stipulate the city of construction as well as the Hermann Hauser name. Labels are easily removed and changed, and an original instrument should be authenticated. Beautiful violin-like clear varnish finish ends in '52, approximately 400 instruments were made by Hermann I. Under Hermann II, nitrocellulose lacquer spray replaces varnish in '52, bracing patterns change in the '60s, which was a welcome change for modern players. Instruments should be evaluated on a case by case basis.

Hermann Hauser II

1952-1988. Born in 1911 and the son of Hermann Hauser I, he built between 500 and 600 classical guitars in Germany during his career. He died in 1988.

Hermann Hauser III

1988-present. Hermann III started build guitars in '74, and took over the family business upon the death of his father in '88. He continues to build builds Segovia style and custom-made classical guitars in Munich, Germany.

Hess

1872-ca. 1940. Located in Klingenthal, Germany, Hess built acoustic and harp guitars, as well as other stringed instruments and accordions.

Heritage H-140

1937 Hermann Hauser

MODEL YEAR	FEATURES	EXC. COND. LOW	HIGH

HML Guitars

Hewett Guitars

1994-present. Luthier James Hewett builds his professional and premium grade, custom/production, steel string, archtop jazz, solidbody and harp guitars in Panorama Village, Texas.

Hill Guitar Company

1972-1980, 1990-present. Luthier Kenny Hill builds his professional and premium grade production/custom, classical and flamenco guitars in Felton, California and Michoacan, Mexico.

Hirade Classical

1968-present. Professional grade, production, solid top, classical guitars built in Japan by Takamine. The late Mass Hirade was the founder of the Takamine workshop. He learned his craft from master luthier Masare Kohno. Hirade represents Takamine's finest craftsmanship and material.

H-5

1986-1996. Acoustic or acoustic/electric, solid cedar top, laminate rosewood body.

1980s	Acoustic/electric	$900	$1,100
1987-1996	Acoustic	$800	$1,000

H-8

1987-1996. Acoustic or acoustic/electric, solid spruce top, solid rosewood body.

1987-1996	Acoustic	$1,000	$1,200
1989-1996	Acoustic/electric	$1,050	$1,300

HML Guitars

1997-present. Howard Leese custom-designs premium grade, electric guitars, which are built by luthier Jack Pimentel in Puyallup, Washington.

Hoffman Guitars

1971-present. Premium grade, custom flat-tops and harp guitars built by luthier Charles Hoffman in Minneapolis, Minnesota.

Höfner

1887-present. Budget, intermediate, professional and premium grade, production, solidbody, semi-hollow, archtop, acoustic, and classical guitars built in Germany and the Far East. They also produce basses and bowed-instruments. Founded by Karl Hofner in Schonbach, Germany. The company was already producing guitars when sons Josef and Walter joined the company in 1919 and '21 and expanded the market worldwide. They moved the company to Bavaria in '50 and to Hagenau in '97.

Beatle Electric Model 459TZ

1966-1967. Violin-shaped 500/1 body, block-stripe position markers, transistor-powered flip-fuzz and treble boost, sunburst.

1966-1967		$1,600	$1,700

1967 Höfner Committee

Beatle Electric Model 459VTZ

1966-1967. Violin-shaped 500/1 body, same as Model 459TZ except with vibrato tailpiece, brown (standard) or blond option.

1966-1967	Blond option	$1,900	$2,300
1966-1967	Brown	$1,700	$1,800

Beatle Electric Model G459TZ Super

1966-1967. Violin-shaped 500/1 body, deluxe version of Model 459TZ, including flamed maple sides, narrow grain spruce top, gold hardware, elaborate inlays and binding, natural blond.

1966-1967		$1,800	$1,900

Beatle Electric Model G459VTZ Super

1966-1967. Violin-shaped 500/1 body, same as G459TZ Super but with vibrato tailpiece, narrow grain spruce top, gold hardware, natural blond.

1966-1967		$1,800	$1,900

Club Model 126

1954-1970. Mid-sized single-cut solidbody, dot markers, flamed maple back and sides, spruce top, sunburst. Listed with Hofner Professional Electric Series.

1954-1958		$800	$900

Committee Model 4680 Thin Electric

1961-1968. Thinline single-cut archtop, 2 pickups, split-arrowhead markers, no vibrato, sunburst.

1961-1968		$1,300	$1,600

Deluxe Model 176

1964-1983. Double-cut, 3 pickups, polyester varnished sunburst finish, vibrola tailpiece, similar to Model 175 polyester varnished red and gold version.

1964-1969		$600	$700
1970-1983		$500	$600

Galaxy Model 175

1963-1966. Double-cut, 3 pickups, red and gold vinyl covering, fancy red-patch 'guard, vibrola, similar to Model 176 polyester varnished sunburst version.

1963-1966	Red and gold vinyl	$1,300	$1,500
1963-1966	Sunburst	$1,200	$1,400

Golden Hofner

1959-1963. Single-cut archtop, blond, 2 pickups, f-holes.

1959-1963		$1,900	$2,300

Jazzica Custom

2000-present. Full body, single soft cutaway, acoustic/electric archtop, carved German spruce top, sunburst.

2000-2007		$1,400	$1,700

Model 172 II (R) (S) (I)

1962-1963. Double-cut body, polyester varnished wood (S) or scuff-proof red (R) or white (I) vinyl, 2 pickups, vibrato.

1962-1963		$500	$575

Model 173 II (S) (I)

1962-1963. Double-cut body, polyester varnished wood (S) or scuff proof vinyl (I), 3 pickups, vibrato.

1962-1963	Gold foil vinyl	$550	$650
1962-1963	White vinyl	$550	$650

MODEL		EXC. COND.	
YEAR	FEATURES	LOW	HIGH

Model 178
1967-ca. 1969. Offset double-cut solidbody, 2 pickups with an array of switches and push button controls, fancy position markers, vibrola, sunburst. 178 used on different design in the '70s.

| 1967-1969 | | $600 | $700 |

Model 180 Shorty Standard
1982. Small-bodied, single-cut, solidbody, 1 pickup, travel guitar, the Shorty Super had a built-in amp and speaker.

| 1982 | | $300 | $375 |

Model 450S Acoustic Archtop
Mid-1960s. Economy single-cut acoustic archtop in Hofner line, dot markers, Hofner logo on 'guard, sunburst.

| 1960s | | $600 | $650 |

Model 456 Acoustic Archtop
1950s. Full body acoustic archtop, f-holes, laminated maple top, sides, back, large pearloid blocks, two color pearloid headstock laminate.

| 1950s | | $500 | $625 |

Model 457 President
1959-1972. Single-cut thinline archtop, 2 pickups, non-vibrato.

| 1959-1972 | | $875 | $975 |

Model 462 Acoustic Archtop
1950s. Similar to Model 456 except cutaway, natural.

| 1950s | | $700 | $750 |

Model 470SE2 Electric Archtop
1961-1993. Large single rounded cutaway electric archtop on Hofner's higher-end they call "superbly flamed maple (back and sides), carved top of best spruce," 2 pickups, 3 control knobs, gold hardware, pearl inlay, natural finish only.

| 1961-1993 | | $1,200 | $1,300 |

Model 471SE2 Electric Archtop
1969-1977. Large single pointed cutaway electric archtop, flamed maple back and sides, spruce top, black celluloid binding, ebony 'board, pearl inlays, sunburst version of the 470SE2.

| 1969-1977 | | $1,200 | $1,300 |

Model 490 Acoustic
Late 1960s. 16" body, 12-string, spruce top, maple back and sides, dot markers, natural.

| 1960s | | $325 | $400 |

Model 490E Acoustic Electric
Late 1960s. Flat-top 12-string with on-board pickup and 2 control knobs.

| 1960s | | $450 | $550 |

Model 491 Flat-Top
1960s-1970s. Slope shoulder body style, spruce top, mahogany back and sides, shaded sunburst.

| 1970s | | $400 | $450 |

Model 492 Acoustic
Late 1960s. 16" body, 12-string, spruce top, mahogany back and sides, dot markers.

| 1960s | | $400 | $500 |

Model 492E Acoustic Electric
Late 1960s. Flat-top 12-string with on-board pickup and 2 control knobs.

| 1960s | | $400 | $500 |

Model 496 Jumbo Flat-Top
1960s. Jumbo-style body, selected spruce top, flamed maple back and sides, gold-plated hardware, vine pattern 'guard, sunburst.

| 1960s | | $950 | $1,100 |

Model 514-H Classical Concert
1960s. Concert model, lower-end of the Hofner classical line, natural.

| 1960s | | $250 | $275 |

Model 4560 Thin Electric
1960s. Single-cut thinline, 2 pickups, 2 knobs and 3 sliders located on lower treble bout control plate.

| 1960s | | $500 | $600 |

Model 4600/V2 (Professional Extra Thin)
1968-1970. Thinline acoustic, double-cut, 2 pickups, vibrato arm, dot markers, sunburst.

| 1968-1970 | | $650 | $800 |

Model 4575VTZ/Verythin (Professional Extra Thin)
1960s. Extra-thinline acoustic, double-cut with shallow rounded horns, 2 or 3 pickups, vibrato arm, treble boost and flip-fuzz, straight-line markers. The Verythin Standard was reintroduced in '01.

| 1960s | 2 pickups | $800 | $900 |
| 1960s | 3 pickups | $900 | $1,000 |

Model 4578TZ President
1959-1970. Double-cut archtop.

| 1959-1965 | | $900 | $1,000 |
| 1966-1970 | | $700 | $875 |

Model 4680/4680 V2 Thin Electric
1960s. Single-cut thinline electric, 2 pickups, 3-in-a-line control knobs, ornate inlays, spruce top, V2 with vibrato.

| 1960s | 4680 | $1,100 | $1,350 |
| 1960s | 4680 V2 (vibrato) | $1,200 | $1,450 |

Senator Acoustic Archtop
1958-1960s. Floating pickup option available, full body archtop, f-holes, made for Selmer, London.

| 1958-1960 | | $575 | $700 |

Senator E1
1961. Senator full body archtop with single top mounted pickup and controls.

| 1961 | | $850 | $950 |

Verythin Standard
2000-present. Update of the 1960s Verythin line.

| 2000-2007 | Reissue Verythin | $750 | $850 |

Hohner
1857-present. Budget and intermediate grade, production, acoustic and electric guitars. They also have basses, mandolins, banjos and ukuleles. Matthias Hohner, a clockmaker in Trossingen, Germany, founded Hohner in 1857, making harmonicas. Hohner has been offering guitars and basses at least since the early '70s. HSS was founded in 1986 as a distributor of guitars and other musical products. By 2000, Hohner was also offering the Crafter brands of guitars.

Höfner Verythin

Hohner G3T Headless

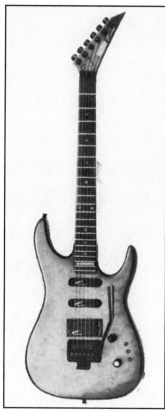

Hohner ST Custom

Holst K100

MODEL YEAR FEATURES	EXC. COND. LOW	HIGH
Alpha Standard		
Designed by Klaus Scholler, solidbody, stereo outputs, Flytune tremolo.		
1987	$225	$275
G 2T/G 3T Series		
1980s-1990s. Steinberger-style body, 6-string, neck-thru, locking tremolo.		
1980-1990s	$200	$250
Jacaranda Rosewood Dreadnought		
Flat-top acoustic.		
1978	$200	$250
Jack		
1987-1990s. Mate for Jack Bass. Headless, tone circuit, tremolo, 2 single-coils and 1 humbucker.		
1987-1992	$225	$275
L 59/L 75 Series		
Late-1970s-1980s. Classic single-cut solidbody, 2 humbuckers, glued neck, sunburst, 59 has upgrade maple body with maple veneer top.		
1970s	$275	$300
Miller Beer Guitar		
Solidbody, shaped like Miller beer logo.		
1985	$275	$300
Professional		
1980s. Single-cut solidbody, maple neck, extra large 'guard, natural.		
1980s	$250	$300
Professional Series - TE Custom		
1980s-1990s. Single-cut solidbody, bolt neck.		
1980-1990s	$850	$1,050
Professional Series - TE Prinz		
Late 1980s-early 1990s. Based on Prince's No. 1 guitar, 2 single-coils, bolt neck, Professional The Prinz headstock logo, natural.		
1989-1990	$850	$1,050
SE 35		
1989-mid-1990s. Semi-hollow thinline, 2 humbuckers, natural.		
1989	$375	$450
SG Lion		
1980s-1990s. Offset double-cut, pointy headstock, glued neck.		
1980-1990s	$225	$275
ST Series		
1986-1990s. Includes the bolt neck ST 57, ST Special, ST Special S, Viper I, Viper II (snakeskin finish option), ST Victory, ST Metal S, and the ST Custom.		
1986-1992	$180	$225
Standard Series - EX Artist		
1970s-1980s. Solidbody, 2 humbuckers, gold hardware, neck-thru, solid maple body, rosewood 'board, tremolo.		
1970-1980s	$225	$275
Standard Series - RR Custom		
1970s-1980s. Randy Rhoads V body, 2 humbuckers, chrome hardware, glued neck, mahogany body, rosewood 'board, tremolo.		
1970-1980s	$225	$275

MODEL YEAR FEATURES	EXC. COND. LOW	HIGH
Standard Series - SR Heavy		
1970s-1980s. Hybrid body, 2 humbuckers, neck-thru, solid maple body, rosewood 'board, tremolo.		
1970-1980s	$225	$275

Holiday

1960s. Student-level, private-branded similar to Stella but may have solid tops.

Silhouette Bobcat

1964-1967. Private branded solidbody electric made by Harmony, similar to Harmony Silhouette, offset double-cut, 2 pickups, toggle switch, 4-in-a-row control knobs, 6-on-a-side tuner.

1964-1967	$300	$375

Hollenbeck Guitars

1970-2008. Luthier Bill Hollenbeck builds his premium grade, production/custom, hollow and semi-hollow body acoustics and electric guitars in Lincoln, Illinois. Bill passed away in '08.

Hollingworth Guitars

1995-present. Luthier Graham Hollingworth builds his production/custom, premium grade, electric, acoustic and archtop guitars in Mermaid Beach, Gold Coast, Queensland, Australia. He also builds lap steels.

Holman

1966-1968. Built by the Holman-Woodell guitar factory in Neodesha, Kansas. The factory was started to build guitars for Wurlitzer, but that fell through by '67.

Holst

1984-present. Premium grade, custom, archtop, flat top, semi-hollow, and classical guitars built in Creswell, Oregon by luthier Stephen Holst. He also builds mandolins. Until '01 he was located in Eugene, Oregon.

Hondo

1969-1987, 1991-present. Budget grade, production, imported acoustic, classical and electric guitars. They also offer basses, banjos and mandolins. Originally imported by International Music Corporation (IMC) of Fort Worth, Texas, founded by Jerry Freed and Tommy Moore and named after a small town near San Antonio, Texas. Early pioneers of Korean guitar making, primarily targeted at beginner market. Introduced their first electrics in '72. Changed brand to Hondo II in '74. Some better Hondos made in Japan '74-'82/'83. In '85 IMC purchases major interest in Jackson/Charvel, and the Hondo line was supplanted by Charvels. 1987 was the last catalog before hiatus. In '88 IMC was sold and Freed began Jerry Freed International and in '91 he revived the Hondo name. Acquired by MBT International in '95, currently part of Musicorp.

MODEL YEAR FEATURES	EXC. COND. LOW	HIGH
Acoustic Flat-Top		
1969-1987, 1991-present.		
1970s	$100	$150
Electric Hollowbody		
1969-1987, 1991-present.		
1980s	$275	$325
Electric Solidbody		
1969-1987, 1991-present.		
1969-1987	$225	$275
1991-1999	$150	$200
2000s	$50	$100
H 752 Fame		
1990s. Single-cut solidbody, black single-ply 'guard, maple neck, blond.		
1990s	$200	$225
H 756 BTS Fame		
1990s. Double-cut solidbody, white 'guard, maple body, rosewood or maple 'board, natural or sunburst.		
1990s	$200	$225
Longhorn 6/12 Doubleneck Copy		
1970s-1980s. Copy of Danelectro Longhorn 6/12 Doubleneck guitar, Dano coke bottle-style headstock, white sunburst.		
1980s	$700	$800
Longhorn Copy		
Ca. 1978-1980s. Copy of Danelectro Long Horn guitar, Dano Coke bottle-style headstock, brown-copper.		
1970s	$350	$425
M 16 Rambo-Machine Gun		
1970s-1980s. Machine gun body-style, matching machine gun-shaped guitar case, black or red. Price includes original case which is long and slender and has form-fit interior, an instrument without the case is worth as much as 40% less.		
1970-1980s	$575	$650

Hopf

1906-present. Intermediate, professional, premium, and presentation grade, production/custom, classical guitars made in Germany. They also make basses, mandolins and flutes.

The Hopf family of Germany has a tradition of instrument building going back to 1669, but the modern company was founded in 1906. Hopf started making electric guitars in the mid-'50s. Some Hopf models were made by others for the company. By the late-'70s, Hopf had discontinued making electrics, concentrating on classicals.

MODEL YEAR FEATURES	EXC. COND. LOW	HIGH
Explorer Standard		
1960s. Double-cut semi-hollow, sharp horns, center block, 2 mini-humbuckers.		
1960s	$525	$650
Saturn Archtop		
1960s. Offset cutaway, archtop-style soundholes, 2 pickups, white, says Saturn on headstock.		
1960s	$650	$800
Super Deluxe Archtop		
1960s. Archtop, 16 3/4", catseye soundholes, carved spruce top, flamed maple back and sides, sunburst.		
1960s	$675	$825

Horabe

Classical and Espana models made in Japan.

MODEL YEAR FEATURES	EXC. COND. LOW	HIGH
Model 25 Classical		
1960s. Solid top.		
1960s	$400	$500
Model 40 Classical		
1960s. Solid cedar top, rosewood back and sides.		
1960s	$600	$750
Model 60 Classical		
1980s. German spruce top, solid Indian rosewood rims.		
1980s	$800	$1,000

House Guitars

2004-present. Luthier Joshua House builds his production/custom, premium grade, acoustic guitars and guitar-bouzoukis in Goderich, Ontario, Canada.

Howe-Orme

1897-ca. 1910. Elias Howe and George Orme's Boston-based publishing and distribution business offered a variety of mandolin family instruments and guitars and received many patents for their designs. Many of their guitars featured detachable necks.

Hoyer

1874-present. Intermediate grade, production, flat-top, classical, electric, and resonator guitars. They also build basses. Founded by Franz Hoyer, building classical guitars and other instruments. His son, Arnold, added archtops in the late-1940s, and solidbodies in the '60s. In '67, Arnold's son, Walter, took over, leaving the company in '77. The company changed hands a few times over the following years. Walter started building guitars again in '84 under the W.A. Hoyer brand, which is not associated with Hoyer.

MODEL YEAR FEATURES	EXC. COND. LOW	HIGH
Acoustic		
1960s. Acoustic archtop or flat-top.		
1960s	$200	$300
Junior		
Early-1960s. Solidbody with unusual sharp horn cutaway, single neck pickup, bolt-on neck, dot markers, Arnold Hoyer logo on headstock, shaded sunburst.		
1960s	$450	$550
Soloist Electric		
Single-cut archtop, 2 pickups, teardrop f-holes, sunburst.		
1960-1962	$525	$650

Humming Bird

1947-ca.1968. Japanese manufacturer. By 1968 making pointy Mosrite inspirations. Probably not imported into the U.S.

MODEL YEAR FEATURES	EXC. COND. LOW	HIGH
Electric Solidbody		
1950s	$125	$200

Late-'70s Hondo Allstar

Hoyer archtop

GUITARS

Huss and Dalton 00

Ibanez Joe Satriani Y2K

MODEL YEAR	FEATURES	EXC. COND. LOW	EXC. COND. HIGH

Humphrey, Thomas

1970-present. Premium and presentation grade, custom, nylon-string guitars built by luthier Thomas Humphrey in Gardiner, New York. In 1996 Humphrey began collaborating with Martin Guitars, resulting in the Martin C-TSH and C-1R. Often the inside back label will indicate the year of manufacture.

Classical

1976-1984. Brazilian or Indian rosewood back and sides, spruce top, traditionally-based designs evolved over time with Millenium becoming a benchmark design in 1985, values can increase with new designs. Valuations depend on each specific instrument and year and type of construction, price ranges are guidance only; each instrument should be evaluated on a case-by-case basis.

1976-1984		$6,500	$8,000

Millennium (Classical)

1985-present. Professional performance-grade high-end classical guitar with innovative taper body design and elevated 'board, tops are generally spruce (versus cedar) with rosewood back and sides.

1995-2007		$9,700	$12,000

Huss and Dalton Guitar Company

1995-present. Luthiers Jeff Huss and Mark Dalton build their professional and premium grade flat-tops and banjos in Staunton, Virginia.

Acoustic

2000s	D-RH	$1,800	$2,200
2000s	OM	$1,900	$2,300

Ibanez

1932-present. Budget, intermediate, and professional grade, production/custom, acoustic and electric guitars. They also make basses, amps, mandolins, and effects.

Founded in Nagoya, Japan, by Matsujiro Hoshino as book and stationary supply, started retailing musical instruments in 1909. He began importing instruments in '21. His son Yoshitaro became president in '27 and began exporting. Manufacturing of Ibanez instruments began in '32. The company's factories were destroyed during World War II, but the business was revived in '50. Junpei Hoshino, grandson of founder, became president in '60; a new factory opened called Tama Seisakusho (Tama Industries). Brand names by '64 included Ibanez, Star, King's Stone, Jamboree and Goldentone, supplied by 85 factories serving global markets. Sold acoustic guitars to Harry Rosenblum of Elger Guitars ('59-ca.'65) in Ardmore, Pennsylvania, in early-'60s. Around '62 Hoshino purchased 50% interest in Elger Guitars, and ca. '65 changed the name to Ibanez.

Jeff Hasselberger headed the American guitar side beginning '73-'74, and the company headquarters were moved to Cornwells Heights, Pennsylvania in '74. By '75 the instruments are being distributed by Chesbro Music Company in Idaho Falls, Idaho, and Harry Rosenblum sells his interest in Hoshino shortly thereafter. Ca. '81, the Elger Company becomes Hoshino U.S.A. An U.S. Custom Shop was opened in '88.

Most glued-neck guitars from '70s are fairly rare.

Dating: copy guitars begin ca. '71. Serial numbers begin '75 with letter (A-L for month) followed by 6 digits, the first 2 indicating year, last 4 sequential (MYYXXXX). By '88 the month letter drops off. Dating code stops early-'90s; by '94 letter preface either F for Fuji or C for Cort (Korean) manufacturer followed by number for year and consecutive numbers (F4XXXX=Fuji, C4XXXX=Cort, 1994).

AE Series

1983-present. Acoustic/electrics.

1994	AE40	$300	$350

AH10 (Allan Holdsworth)

1985-1987. Offset double-cut solidbody, bolt neck, bridge humbucker, dots, various colors.

1985-1987		$350	$425

AM50 Stagemaster

1983-1984. Small double-cut semi-hollow body, 2 humbuckers, no pickguard.

1983-1984		$500	$600

AM70

1985-1987. Small double-cut semi-hollow body, f-holes, 2 humbuckers.

1985-1987		$550	$675

AM75/AM75T

1985-1987. Small double-cut semi hollow body, vibrato, 2 humbuckers.

1985-1987		$600	$750

AM100 Stagemaster

1983-1984, 1989-1990. Small double-cut semi-hollow body, 2 humbuckers. Model name used again, without Stagemaster in '89-'90.

1983-1984		$500	$625

AM200 Artstar

1990. Small ES-335 style with large f-holes, block markers, Artstar logo on headstock, AM200 logo on truss rod.

1990		$600	$725

Artist 2640/AR1200 Doubleneck

1977-1984. Double-cut solidbody, set 6/12 necks, 4 humbuckers, gold hardware. Called 2640 until '79 when changed to AR1200.

1977-1984		$1,100	$1,350

Artist AR50

Late-1970-1980. Double-cut solidbody, dot markers, 2 humbuckers.

1978-1980		$450	$550

Artist AR100

1979-1984. Set neck double-cut maple top solidbody, 2 humbuckers.

1979-1984		$450	$550

Artist AR300

1979-1982. Symmetrical double-cut, carved maple top.

1979-1982		$525	$650

MODEL YEAR FEATURES	EXC. COND. LOW	HIGH

Artist AR2622 Artist EQ (Steve Miller)
1977-1979. Symmetrical double-cut, carved maple top, 5 knobs with EQ-control.

| 1977-1979 | $775 | $950 |

Artist AS100/AS100
1979-1982, 1989-1990. Double-cut set neck semi-hollow body, sunburst, dots, replaced Artist 2629. Artist dropped from name when it becomes hollowbody archtop in '82.

| 1979-1982 | $1,100 | $1,200 |

Artist AS200/AS200
1979-1981. Double cut flame maple semi-hollow body, block markers, gold hardware, 2 humbuckers, replaced Artist 2630. Artist dropped from name when model becomes hollowbody archtop in '82.

| 1979-1981 | $1,200 | $1,300 |

Artist Model 2612
1974-1975. Rounded double-cut solidbody, black finish, birch top, gold hardware, bound rosewood 'board, 2 humbuckers, fleur-de-lis inlay.

| 1974-1975 | $650 | $800 |

Artist Model 2613
1974-1975. Natural version of 2612.

| 1974-1975 | $650 | $800 |

Artist Model 2617
1976-1980. Pointed double-cut natural ash solidbody, set-neck, German carved top, spilt block inlays, bound ebony 'board, 2 humbuckers, later would evolve into the Professional model.

| 1976-1980 | $825 | $1,025 |

Artist Model 2618
1976-1979. Like 2617, but with maple and mahogany body and dot markers. Becomes AR200 in '79.

| 1976-1979 | $825 | $1,025 |

Artist Model 2619
1976-1979. Like 2618, but with split block markers. Becomes AR300 in '79.

| 1976-1979 | $825 | $1,025 |

Artist Model 2630 Artist Deluxe
1976-1979. Double cut semi-hollow body, sunburst, name changed to AS200 in '79.

| 1976-1979 | $1,300 | $1,450 |

AS50 Artstar
1998-1999. Laminated maple body, bound rosewood 'board, dot inlays, 2 humbuckers.

| 1998-1999 | $600 | $750 |

AS80 Artstar
1994-2002. Double cut semi-hollow body, dots, 2 humbuckers.

| 1994-2002 | $600 | $750 |

AS180 Artstar
1997-1999. Double cut semi-hollow body, block inlays, 2 humbuckers.

| 1997-1999 | $700 | $850 |

AW Artwood Series
1979-present.

| 1996-1998 | AW300 | $275 | $325 |

Blazer Series
1980-1982, 1997-1998. Offset double-cut, 10 similar models in the '80s with different body woods and electronic configurations. Series name returns on 3 models in late '90s.

| 1980-1982 | Various models | $300 | $350 |

Bob Weir Model 2681
1975-1980, 1995. Double-cut solidbody of carved solid ash, maple neck, ebony 'board with tree-of-life inlay, gold-plated Super 70 pickups, produced in limited numbers. Reintroduced as a limited run in '95.

| 1975-1980 | $1,700 | $2,100 |

Bob Weir Standard Model 2680
1976-1980. Double-cut solidbody of carved solid ash, maple neck, ebony 'board, dot markers, gold-plated Super 70 pickups, production model.

| 1976-1980 | $1,000 | $1,250 |

Concert CN100 Standard
1978-1979. Double-cut solidbody, set neck, 2 humbuckers, chrome hardware, dot markers.

| 1978-1979 | $250 | $275 |

Concert CN200 Custom
1978-1979. Carved maple top, mahogany body, 7 layer black/white binding, bolt-on neck, gold hardware, block inlays, 2 Super 80 pickups.

| 1978-1979 | $450 | $550 |

Concert CN250
1978-1979. Like CN200 but with vine inlay.

| 1978-1979 | $475 | $575 |

Concord 673
1974-1978. D-style flat-top, laminated spruce top, laminated maple and jacaranda body, maple 'board, natural finish, gold tuners. Just the 673 for '74-'75, Concord added to name in '76.

| 1974-1978 | $375 | $450 |

Destroyer DTX120
2000. Known as the Millennium Destroyer, 2 humbuckers.

| 2000 | $250 | $300 |

Destroyer II DT50
1980-1982. 1 humbucker, bolt neck, thick paint.

| 1980-1982 | $400 | $500 |

Destroyer II DT150
1982-1984. Birch/basswood, 1 humbucker, bolt neck.

| 1982-1984 | $400 | $500 |

Destroyer II DT350
1984-1987. Flamed maple.

| 1984-1987 | $400 | $500 |

Destroyer II DT400
1980-1982. Basswood body, set-neck, 2 pickups, cherry sunburst. Model changed to DT500 in '82.

| 1980-1982 | $400 | $500 |

Destroyer II DT500
1982-1984. Replaced the DT400.

| 1982-1984 | $400 | $500 |

Destroyer II DT555 Phil Collen
1983-1987. Bound basswood solidbody, 3 humbuckers, vibrato, black.

| 1983-1987 | $400 | $500 |

Ibanez Artist 2616

1977 Ibanez Artist Professional

GUITARS

Ibanez George Benson GB10

1979 Ibanez Iceman PS10

MODEL YEAR	FEATURES	EXC. COND. LOW	HIGH

EX Series
1988-1993. Double cut solidbodies with long thin horns, various models, all models may not be included.

1991-1993	EX370	$175	$225
1992-1993	EX1700	$175	$225
1992-1993	EX3700FM maple top	$200	$250

FA-100
1978-1982. Hollowbody, single-cut, 2 pickups, f-holes, block inlays.

1978-1982		$900	$1,100

FG-360S
1973-1974. Single-cut solidbody, bolt neck, trapezoid markers, maple top, sunburst.

1973-1974		$375	$450

GAX Series
1998-present. Symmetrical double-cut (Gibson SG style) with 2 humbuckers.

1998-2007		$125	$150

George Benson GB10
1977-present. Single-cut, laminated spruce top, flame maple back and sides, 2 humbuckers, 3-piece set-in maple neck, ebony 'board.

1977-1979	Blond	$1,600	$1,800
1977-1979	Sunburst	$1,500	$1,700
1980-1989	Blond	$1,500	$1,700
1980-1989	Sunburst	$1,400	$1,600
1990-1999	Blond	$1,400	$1,600
1990-1999	Sunburst	$1,300	$1,500

George Benson GB20
1978-1982. Larger than GB10, laminated spruce top, flame maple back and sides.

1978-1982		$1,800	$2,200

George Benson GB100 Deluxe
1993-1996. GB-10 with flamed maple top, pearl binding, sunburst finish 'guard, pearl vine inlay tailpiece, gold hardware.

1993-1996		$2,200	$2,700

Iceman 2663/2663 TC/2663 SL
1975-1978. The original Iceman Series models, called the Flash I, II and III respectively, I has 2 humbuckers, II (TC) and III (SL) have 1 triple-coil pickup.

1975-1978		$600	$750

Iceman Series
1975-present. Ibanez unique body styles with hooked lower treble horn body.

1978	IC210	$950	$1,050
1978-1979	IC250	$900	$1,100
1978-1979	IC300 (Korina)	$700	$800
1978-1982	IC400	$800	$950
1978-1990	IC200	$700	$800
1981	IC400 CS	$900	$1,000
1994	IC500	$850	$900
1994-2003	IC300	$325	$400
1995-1996	IC350	$325	$400

Iceman PS10 Paul Stanley
1978-1981. Limited edition Paul Stanley model, abalone trim, Stanley's name engraved at 21st fret, reissued in '95 with upgraded model names.

1978-1981	Korina finish	$2,700	$3,300
1978-1981	Sunburst or black	$2,700	$3,300

MODEL YEAR	FEATURES	EXC. COND. LOW	HIGH

Iceman PS10 II Paul Stanley
1995-1996. Reissue of original PS-10.

1995-1996	Black	$1,400	$1,700

IMG-2010 Guitar Controller MIDI
1985-1987. Similar to Roland GR-707, slim triangle-wedge body with treble horn.

1985-1987		$500	$600

JEM7D
1999-2003. JEM with black drip finish.

1999-2003		$1,500	$1,700

JEM7V
1993-present. White, vine inlay, gold hardware.

1993-2006		$800	$900

JEM 77 Series
1988-1999, 2003-present. Basswood body, monkey grip handle, 3 pickups, 'board with tree of life or pyramids inlay, finishes include floral pattern or multicolor swirl. Current version has dot inlays and solid finish. The JEM 77BRMR Bad Horsie was introduced in '05 with a mirror

1980s	Floral	$1,600	$1,900
1980s	Multicolor	$1,600	$1,900
2005-2007	77BRMR "Bad Horsie"	$1,600	$1,900

JEM 555
1994-2000. Basswood, dots and vine inlay, 3 pickups.

1994-2000		$600	$650

JEM 777 Series
1987-1996. Basswood body, monkey grip 3 pickups, pyramids or vine inlay.

1987	LG Loch Ness Green, limited edition	$1,600	$1,750
1988-1987	SK Shocking Pink, pyramids	$1,150	$1,400
1988-1996	DY Desert Sun Yellow, pyramids	$1,600	$1,750
1989-1993	VBK black, vines	$1,150	$1,400
1989-1993	VDY yellow, vines	$1,600	$1,750
1989-1993	White	$1,600	$1,800
1991	BF Blue Floral	$1,500	$1,600

JEM 10th Anniversary
1996. Limited Edition signature Steve Vai model, bolt neck, vine metal 'guard, vine neck inlays and headstock art.

1996		$1,600	$2,000

JEM 20th Anniversary
2007. Steve Vai 20th Anniversary JEM model, green acrylic illuminating body, celebrates the 20th year (1987-2007) of the Ibanez JEM series, limited edition.

2007		$3,600	$4,400

JEM 90th Anniversary
1997. Limited Edition signature Steve Vai model, textured silver finish, chrome 'guard.

1997		$1,700	$1,900

JEM Y2KDNA (Limited Edition)
2000. Red Swirl marble finish using Steve Vai's blood in the paint.

2000		$3,500	$4,000

MODEL YEAR	FEATURES	EXC. COND. LOW	HIGH

Joe Pass JP20

1981-1990. Full body, single-cut, 1 pickup, abalone and pearl split block inlay, JP inlay on headstock.

| 1981-1990 | Sunburst | $1,300 | $1,600 |

Joe Satriani JS100

1994-present. Offset double cut basswood body, 2 humbuckers, vibrato, red, black, white or custom finish.

| 1994-2007 | Custom finish | $550 | $675 |
| 1994-2007 | Standard finish | $450 | $500 |

Joe Satriani JS1000

1994-1996, 1998-present.

1994-1996	BP pearl black	$850	$1,000
1998	BP pearl black	$800	$975
1998-2001	WH white	$800	$975
2001-2007	BTB Europe & Asia market	$800	$975

Joe Satriani JS1200

2004-present. Candy apple red.

| 2004-2007 | | $950 | $1,150 |

Joe Satriani Y2K

2000. Clear see-thru plexi-style body.

| 2000 | | $1,900 | $2,300 |

JPM100 John Petrucci/JPM100P3

1997. Offset double-cut solidbody, 2 pickups, multi-color art finish.

| 1997 | | $1,700 | $2,000 |

JPM100P4 John Petrucci

1998. Like P3 but with cammo graphic.

| 1998 | | $1,800 | $1,900 |

Lee Ritenour LR10

1981-1987. Flame maple body, bound set neck, Quick Change tailpiece, 2 pickups, dark red sunburst, foam-filled body to limit feedback.

| 1981-1987 | | $1,050 | $1,300 |

M340

1978-1979. Flat-top, spruce top, flamed maple back and sides, maple 'board.

| 1978-1979 | | $375 | $450 |

Maxxas

1987-1988. Solidbody (MX2) or with internal sound chambers (MX3, '88 only), 2 pickups, all-access neck joint system.

| 1987-1988 | MX2 | $850 | $1,000 |
| 1988 | MX3 | $1,100 | $1,350 |

Model 600 Series

1974-1978. Copy era acoustic flat-tops with model numbers in the 600 Series, basically copies of classic American square shoulder dreadnoughts. Includes the 683, 684, 693, and the six-on-a-side 647; there were 12-string copies as well.

| 1974-1978 | | $400 | $500 |

Model 700 Series

1974-1977. Upgraded flat-top models such as the Brazilian Scent 750, with more original design content than 600 Series.

| 1974-1977 | | $400 | $500 |

Model 1453

1971-1973. Copy of classic single-cut hollowbody, replaced by Model 2355 in '73.

| 1971-1973 | | $950 | $1,175 |

Model 1800 Series

1962-1963. Offset double-cut solidbody (Jazzmaster-style), models came with bar (stud) or vibrato tailpiece, and 2, 3 or 4 pickups.

1962-1963	1830, 2 pickups, bar	$175	$300
1962-1963	1850, 3 pickups, bar	$225	$400
1962-1963	1860, 2 pickups, vibrato	$200	$325
1962-1963	1880, 3 pickups, vibrato	$250	$425

Model 1912

1971-1973. Double-cut semi-hollow body, sunburst finish.

| 1971-1973 | | $975 | $1,200 |

Model 2020

1970. Initial offering of the copy era, offset double-cut, 2 unusual rectangular pickups, block markers, raised nailed-on headstock logo, sunburst.

| 1970 | | $575 | $700 |

Model 2240M

Early 1970s. Thick hollowbody electric copy, single pointed cutaway, double-parallelogram markers, 2 humbuckers, natural finish.

| 1971-1973 | | $1,200 | $1,400 |

Model 2336 Les Jr.

1974-1976. Copy of classic slab solidbody, TV Lime.

| 1974-1976 | | $500 | $600 |

Model 2340 Deluxe '59er

1974-1977. Copy of classic single-cut solidbody, flametop, Hi-Power humbuckers.

| 1974-1977 | | $625 | $775 |

Model 2341 Les Custom

1974-1977. Copy of classic single-cut solidbody.

| 1974-1977 | | $600 | $750 |

Model 2342 Les Moonlight/Sunlight Special

1974-1977. Copy of classic slab solidbody, black (Moonlight) or ivory (Sunlight).

| 1974-1977 | | $525 | $625 |

Model 2343 FM Jr.

1974-1976.

| 1974-1976 | | $475 | $575 |

Model 2344

1974-1976. Copy of classic Double-cut solidbody.

| 1974-1976 | | $450 | $500 |

Model 2345

1974-1976. Copy of classic sharp double-cut solidbody, set neck, walnut or white, vibrato, 3 pickups.

| 1974-1976 | | $650 | $750 |

Model 2346

1974. Copy of classic sharp double-cut solidbody, vibrato, set neck, 2 pickups.

| 1974 | | $650 | $750 |

Model 2347

1974-1976. Copy of classic sharp double-cut solidbody, set-neck, 1 pickup.

| 1974-1976 | | $550 | $650 |

Ibanez JEM 777

1988 Ibanez Maxxas

168

GUITARS

Ibanez Model 2375

Ibanez Model 2384

MODEL YEAR	FEATURES	EXC. COND. LOW	HIGH

Model 2348 Firebrand
1974-1977. Copy of classic reverse solidbody, mahogany body, bolt neck, 2 pickups.

| 1974-1977 | | $700 | $750 |

Model 2350 Les
1971-1977. Copy of classic single-cut solidbody, bolt neck, black, gold hardware, goldtop version (2350G Les) also available. A cherry sunburst finish (2350 Les Custom) was offered by '74.

| 1971-1977 | | $650 | $750 |

Model 2351
1974-1977. Copy of classic single-cut solidbody, gold top, 2 pickups.

| 1974-1977 | | $650 | $750 |

Model 2351DX
1974-1977. Copy of classic single-cut solidbody, gold top, 2 mini-humbuckers.

| 1974-1977 | | $650 | $700 |

Model 2352 Telly
1974-1978. Copy of early classic single-cut solidbody, 1 bridge pickup, white finish.

| 1974-1978 | | $600 | $725 |

Model 2352CT
1974-1978. Copy of classic single-cut solidbody, single-coil bridge and humbucker neck pickup.

| 1974-1978 | | $600 | $725 |

Model 2352DX Telly
1974-1978. Copy of classic single-cut solidbody, 2 humbuckers.

| 1974-1978 | | $600 | $725 |

Model 2354
1974-1977. Copy of classic sharp double-cut solidbody, 2 humbuckers, vibrato.

| 1974-1977 | | $600 | $725 |

Model 2354S
1972-1977. Stop tailpiece version of 2354.

| 1972-1977 | | $600 | $725 |

Model 2355/2355M
1973-1977. Copy of classic single-cut hollowbody, sunburst or natural maple (M).

| 1973-1977 | | $1,250 | $1,400 |

Model 2356
1973-1975. Copy of classic double pointed cutaway hollowbody, bowtie markers, sunburst. There was another Model 2356 in '74, a copy of a different hollowbody.

| 1973-1975 | | $875 | $1,075 |

Model 2363R
1973-1974. Cherry finish copy of classic varitone double-cut semi-hollow body.

| 1973-1974 | | $900 | $1,000 |

Model 2364 Ibanex
1971-1973. Dan Armstrong see-thru Lucite copy, 2 mounted humbuckers.

| 1971-1973 | | $850 | $950 |

Model 2368 Telly
1973-1978. Copy of classic single-cut thinline, chambered f-hole body, single coil pickup, mahogany body.

| 1973-1978 | | $575 | $700 |

Model 2368F
1973-1974. Classic single-cut black 'guard copy.

| 1973-1974 | | $600 | $750 |

Model 2370
1972-1977. Sunburst version of Model 2363R.

| 1972-1977 | | $1,000 | $1,100 |

Model 2372 Les Pro/2372DX Les Pro
1972-1977. Copy of classic single-cut solidbody, bolt neck, low impedance pickups, DX with gold hardware available for '73-'74.

| 1972-1977 | | $650 | $750 |

Model 2374 Crest
1974-1976. Copy of classic double-cut semi-hollow body, walnut finish.

| 1974-1976 | | $950 | $1,150 |

Model 2375 Strato
1971-1978. Copy of classic offset double-cut solidbody, 3 single-coils, sunburst.

| 1971-1978 | | $550 | $650 |

Model 2375ASH Strato
1974-1978. 2375 with ash body.

| 1974-1978 | | $575 | $700 |

Model 2375WH/N/BK Strato
1974-1978. 2375 in white (WH), natural (N), and black (BK) finishes.

| 1974-1978 | | $550 | $650 |

Model 2377
1974-1975. Copy of classic double sharp-cut solidbody, short production run, dot markers.

| 1974-1975 | | $400 | $500 |

Model 2380
1973-1977. Copy of LP Recording, single-cut solidbody, low impedence pickups, small block markers.

| 1973-1977 | | $550 | $675 |

Model 2383
1974-1976. Copy of classic double sharp cut solidbody, white or walnut, 3 humbuckers, gold hardware.

| 1974-1976 | Walnut | $525 | $625 |
| 1974-1976 | White | $600 | $750 |

Model 2384 Telly
1974-1976. Copy of classic single-cut, f-holes, 2 humbuckers, ash body.

| 1974-1976 | | $525 | $650 |

Model 2387 Rocket Roll/Rocket Roll Sr.
1975-1977. Copy of classic v-shaped solidbody, set-neck, dot markers, gold-covered pickups.

| 1975-1977 | | $1,125 | $1,400 |

Model 2390
1974-1976. Copy of classic double-cut semi-hollow body, maple 'board, walnut finish.

| 1974-1976 | | $850 | $1,000 |

Model 2394
Ca. 1974-ca. 1976. SG style, 2 humbuckers, maple 'board, black block inlays.

| 1974-1976 | | $650 | $750 |

Model 2395
1974-1976. Natural finished 2390.

| 1974-1976 | | $850 | $1,000 |

MODEL		EXC. COND.	
YEAR	FEATURES	LOW	HIGH

Model 2397
1974-1976. Double-cut semi-hollow body, low impedance electronics, trapezoid markers, goldtop.

1974-1976		$850	$1,000

Model 2399DX Jazz Solid
1974-1976. Single-cut solidbody, sunburst, set-neck, gold hardware.

1974-1976		$750	$900

Model 2401 Signature
1974-1976. Double-cut semi-hollow archtop, gold top, bolt neck.

1974-1976		$850	$1,000

Model 2402/2402DX Double Axe
1974-1977. Double sharp cut solidbody 6/12 doubleneck, cherry or walnut, DX model has gold hardware and white finish.

1974-1977		$1,125	$1,400

Model 2404 Double Axe
1974-1977. Double sharp cut solidbody guitar/bass doubleneck copy, walnut, white available '75 only.

1974-1977		$1,125	$1,400

Model 2405 Custom Agent
1974-1977. Single-cut solidbody, set neck, scroll headstock, pearl body inlay, 2 humbuckers.

1974-1977		$1,150	$1,400

Model 2406 Double Axe
1974-1977. Double sharp cut solidbody doubleneck, two 6-strings, cherry or walnut.

1974-1977		$1,125	$1,400

Model 2407 Strato Jazz
1974-1976. Offset double-cut solidbody doubleneck.

1974-1976		$1,100	$1,375

Model 2451
1974-1977. Single-cut solidbody, maple 'board, black or natural, set neck.

1974-1977		$700	$875

Model 2453 Howie Roberts
1974-1977. Single-cut archtop, round soundhole, maple body, set neck, rosewood 'board, block markers, 1 pickup, gold hardware, burgundy or sunburst.

1974-1977		$750	$900

Model 2454
1974-1977. Copy of classic double-cut semi-hollow body, set-neck, small block markers, cherry finish over ash.

1974-1977		$850	$1,000

Model 2455
1974-1977. Copy of classic single-cut archtop, 2 pickups, natural.

1974-1977		$1,200	$1,500

Model 2459 Destroyer
1975-1977. Korina finished mahogany body.

1975-1977		$1,000	$1,300

Model 2460
1975-1977. Copy of classic single-cut archtop, natural.

1975-1977		$1,200	$1,500

Model 2461
1975-1977. Copy of classic single-cut archtop, laminated spruce top, curly maple body, set-neck, ebony 'board, pearl blocks, 2 pickups, gold hardware, sunburst or natural.

1975-1977		$1,200	$1,500

Model 2464
1975-1977. Copy of classic single-cut thinline archtop, natural.

1975-1977		$1,200	$1,500

Model 2469 Futura
1976-1977. Korina finished futuristic model copy.

1976-1977		$1,300	$1,600

Model 2801 Classical
1975-1977. Nylon string.

1975-1977		$175	$200

MTM-1 Mick Thompson
2006. Seven logo on fretboard, MTM1 logo on back of headstock.

2006		$775	$875

Musician MC Series
1978-1982. Solidbodies, various models.

1978-1980	MC-500, carved top	$1,400	$1,500
1978-1980	Neck-thru body	$525	$725
1978-1982	Bolt neck	$500	$700

Performer PF100 Standard
1978-1979. Single-cut solidbody, plain birch top, mahogany body, bolt neck, dot inlays, 2 humbuckers.

1978-1979		$400	$500

Performer PF200 Custom
1978-1979. Maple top PF100.

1978-1979		$450	$550

Performer PF300
1978-1980. Single-cut solidbody, maple top, mahogany body, set neck, 2 humbuckers, Tri-Sound.

1978-1980		$550	$600

Performer PF400
1978-1979. Single cut solidbody, flame maple top, alder body, set neck, block inlays, 2 humbuckers, Tri-Sound.

1978-1979		$575	$650

PF Performance Series Acoustics
1987-present. Line of mostly dreadnought size flattops, various models.

1987-1999	PF-10	$200	$300
1987-1999	PF1012 12-string	$350	$425

PGM Paul Gilbert
1992-present. Superstrat body style, painted f-holes, appointments vary with model numbers.

1998	PGM 90th	$1,500	$1,700

PM Pat Metheny
1996-present. Acoustic-electric archtops, single or single/half cutaway, 1 or 2 humbuckers.

1996-2005	PM100	$1,000	$1,200
1997-1999	PM20	$900	$1,100
2000-2007	PM120	$1,100	$1,300

Pro Line Series
1985-1987. Pro Line models have a PL or PR suffix.

1985	PR1660	$325	$400
1985-1987	PL1770/PLZ1770	$375	$450
1986	PL2550/PLZ2550	$450	$550

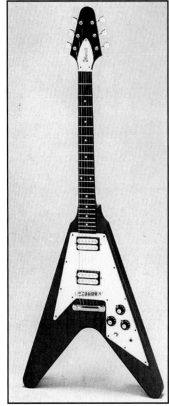
Ibanez Model 2387 Rocket Roll

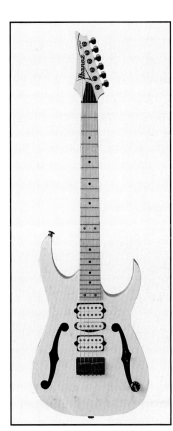
Ibanez PGM Paul Gilbert

To get the most from this book, be sure to read "Using **The Guide**" in the introduction.

Ibanez RG350DX

Ibanez RT 650

MODEL YEAR	FEATURES	EXC. COND. LOW	HIGH

RG Series

1992-present. A large family of guitar models whose model identification starts with RG prefix. Some RG models belong to the Roadstar Standard Series and Roadstar Deluxe Series which are listed under those specific series name.

| 1992-2007 | Various models | $200 | $700 |

Roadstar Deluxe Series

1986-1991. Offset double cut basswood (or maple top) solidbodies, various models, higher appointments than original series, but still says Roadstar II on headstock.

1986	RG530		
	(2 hum, maple)	$350	$550
1986-1887	RG440 (h\s\s)	$400	$650
1986-1987	RG410 (1 hum)	$300	$500
1986-1987	RG420 (2 hum)	$350	$550
1986-1987	RG430 (3 SC)	$400	$650

Roadstar Standard Series

1986-1988. Various offset double-cut solidbodies, says Roadstar II on headstock

1986-1987	RG120/135/140	$225	$300
1987	RG240		
	(more features)	$250	$325
1987	RG250 (flame maple)	$275	$350

Roadster

1979-1983. Offset double-cut, maple 'board, bolt neck, replaced by Roadstar series in '83.

| 1979-1983 | | $275 | $375 |

Rocket Roll II RR550

1982-1984. Flying V body, six-on-side headstock, pearloid blocks, cherry sunburst, maple top, set neck.

| 1982-1984 | | $900 | $1,100 |

RT Series

1992-1993. Offset double-cut, bolt neck, rosewood 'board, dot markers, hum/single/hum pickups. 150 has lower pickup quality, 650 has flamed top.

1992-1993	RT150	$225	$325
1992-1993	RT420	$275	$375
1992-1993	RT450	$325	$450
1992-1993	RT650	$400	$500

RX Series

| 1994-1997 | RX20 | $125 | $225 |
| 1994-1997 | RX240 | $125 | $225 |

S Models

1987-present. In '87 Ibanez introduced a new line of highly tapered, ultra-thin body, offset double-cut guitars that were grouped together as the S Models. Initially the S Models were going to be called the Sabre models but that name was trademarked by Music Man and could not be used.

1987	Pro540S	$500	$550
1988-1994	540S	$500	$550
1989-1998	540SLTD/S540LTD	$525	$625
1991-1998	540SFM/S540FM	$525	$625
1992-1995	470S	$325	$400
2003-2007	S470	$325	$400

MODEL YEAR	FEATURES	EXC. COND. LOW	HIGH

Studio ST50 Jr.

1979-1981. Set-neck, small offset sharp double-cut mahogany solidbody, 2 exposed pickups.

| 1979-1981 | | $350 | $425 |

Studio ST300

1978-1980. Maple/ash body, active tone system, tri-sound switch, natural, gold hardware, 2 humbuckers.

| 1978-1980 | | $450 | $550 |

STW Double

1999. Double neck with 7-string and 6-string neck, limited edition.

| 1999 | | $1,800 | $1,900 |

Talman Series

1994-1998. TC or TV suffix.

1995-1996	TC620	$275	$400
1995-1997	TC420	$375	$450
1995-1997	TC630	$375	$550

Universe UV7/UV7P/UV77

1990-1997. Basswood 7-strings, hum/single/hum pickups. The '90-'93 white 7P and multi-colored 77 have pyramid inlays, the black '90-'97 7 has dots.

| 1990-1993 | 7P | $1,000 | $1,100 |
| 1990-1997 | 7 and 77 | $1,200 | $1,300 |

Universe UV777 Series

1991-1993. Basswood 7-string, pyramid inlays, maple 'board, hum/single/hum pickups.

| 1991-1993 | 777GR | $1,900 | $2,100 |

USRG-10 (U.S.A.)

1994-1995. RG style guitars built in the U.S. by PBC Guitar Technology.

| 1994-1995 | | $1,000 | $1,100 |

V300

1978-1991. Vintage Series acoustic dreadnought, spruce top, mahogany back and sides, sunburst or various colors.

| 1978-1991 | | $225 | $325 |

XV500

1985-1987. Sharply pointed X-body with scalloped bottom.

| 1985-1987 | | $350 | $600 |

Ibanez, Salvador

1875-1920. Salvador Ibanez was a Spanish luthier who operated a small guitar-building workshop. In the early 1900s he founded Spain's largest guitar factory. In 1929 Japan's Hoshino family began importing Salvador Ibanez guitars. Demand for the Salvador Ibanez guitars became so great that the Hoshino family began building their own guitars, which ultimately became known as the Ibanez brand. Guitars from 1875-1920 were mostly classical style and often can be identified by a label on the inside back which stipulates Salvador Ibanez.

Ignacio Fleta

1970s. Classical guitar builder from Barcelona, Spain.

Classical

1971. Higher-end guitar.

| 1971 | | $18,000 | $22,000 |

MODEL YEAR	FEATURES	EXC. COND. LOW	HIGH

Ignacio Rozas

1987-present. Luthier Ignacio M. Rozas builds his classical and flamenco guitars in Madrid, Spain. He also offers factory-made guitars built to his specifications.

Illusion Guitars

1992-present. Luthier Jeff Scott builds his premium grade, production/custom, solidbody guitars in Fallbrook, California.

Imperial

Ca.1963-ca.1970. Imported by the Imperial Accordion Company of Chicago, Illinois. Early guitars made in Italy by accordion builder Crucianelli. By ca. '66 switched to Japanese guitars. They also made basses.

Electric Solidbody

1963-1968. Italian-made until '66, then Japanese-made, includes the Tonemaster line.

1963-1968		$200	$225

Infeld

2003-2005. Solidbody guitars and basses offered by string-maker Thomastik-Infeld of Vienna.

Infinox

1980s. Infinox by JTG, of Nashville, offered a line of 'the classic shapes of yesterday and the hi tech chic of today'. Classic shapes included copies of many classic American solidbody designs with the block letter Infinox by JTG logo on headstock, special metallic grafted paint finish, space-age faux graphite-feel neck, Gotoh tuning machines, Gotoh locking nut tremolo with fine tuners, all models with 1 or 2 humbucker pickups.

Interdonati

1930s. Guitars built by luthier Philip Interdonati, of Staten Island, New York, originally professional grade, luthier's label is on the inside back.

Size 000 Flat-Top

1920s-1930s.

1920-1930s		$4,800	$6,000

Italia

1999-present. Intermediate grade, production, solid, semi-solid, and hollow body guitars designed by Trevor Wilkinson and made in Korea. They also build basses.

J Backlund Design

2008-present. Luthier Bruce Bennett builds professional and premium grade, production/custom, electric guitars designed by J. Backlund in Chattanooga, Tennessee. He also offers basses.

J Burda Guitars

Flat-top guitars built by luthier Jan Burda in Berrien Springs, Michigan.

J. Frog Guitars

1978-present. Professional and premium grade, production/custom, solidbody guitars made in Las Vegas, Nevada by Ed Roman.

J.B. Player

1980s-present. Budget and intermediate grade, production, imported acoustic, acoustic/electric, and solidbody guitars. They also offer basses, banjos and mandolins. Founded in United States. Moved production of guitars to Korea but maintained a U.S. Custom Shop. MBT International/Musicorp took over manufacture and distribution in '89.

J.R. Zeidler Guitars

1977-2002. Luthier John Zeidler built premium and presentation grade, custom, flat-top, 12-string, and archtop guitars in Wallingford, Pennsylvania. He also built mandolins. He died in '02 at age 44.

J.T. Hargreaves Basses & Guitars

1995-present. Luthier Jay Hargreaves builds his premium grade, production/custom, classical and steel string guitars in Seattle, Washington. He also builds basses.

Jack Daniel's

2004-present. Acoustic and electric guitar models, some with custom Jack Daniel's artwork on the body and headstock, built by Peavey for the Jack Daniel's Distillery. There is also an amp model and a bass.

Jackson

1980-present. Currently Jackson offers intermediate, professional, and premium grade, production, electric guitars. They also offer basses. In '78 Grover Jackson bought out Charvel Guitars and moved it to San Dimas. Jackson made custom-built bolt-on Charvels. In '82 the pointy, tilt-back Jackson headstock became standard. The Jackson logo was born in '80 and used on a guitar designed as Randy Rhoad's first flying V. Jacksons were neck-through construction. The Charvel trademark was licensed to IMC in '85. IMC moved the Jackson factory to Ontario, California in '86. Grover Jackson stayed with Jackson/Charvel until '89 (see Charvel). On October 25, 2002, Fender Musical Instruments Corp (FMIC) took ownership of Jackson/Charvel Manufacturing Inc.

DR3

1996-2001. Dinky Reverse, double-cut solidbody, reverse headstock, triangle markers, 2 humbuckers, locking vibrato, made in Japan, flamed maple top available.

1996-2001		$275	$325

Italia Mondial custom

J. Frog Vampira 900

Jackson Randy Rhoads

Jackson Soloist

DR5
1996 only. Offset double-cut solidbody, 2 Kent Armstrong humbuckers, rosewood 'board, dot markers.

1996	$275	$325

Fusion Pro
Late 1980s-early 1990s. Import from Japan.

1990s	$375	$450

JSX94
1994-1995. Offset double-cut solidbody, single/single/hum, rosewood 'board, dot markers.

1994-1995	$275	$325

Kelly Custom
1984-early 1990s. Solidbody, Kahler tremolo, 2 humbuckers, ebony 'board with shark's tooth inlays, bound neck and headstock.

1984-1985	$1,400	$1,700
1986-1993	$1,200	$1,500

Kelly Pro
1994-1995. Pointy-cut solidbody, neck-thru, 2 humbuckers, bound ebony 'board, shark fin inlays.

1994-1995	$600	$800

Kelly Standard
1993-1995. Pointy cutaway solidbody, bolt neck, 2 humbuckers, dot markers.

1993-1995	$500	$700

Kelly U.S.A. (KE2)
1998-present. Alder solidbody, flame maple top, neck-thru.

1998-2007	$1,000	$1,200

Kelly XL
1994-1995. Pointy cutaway solidbody, bolt neck, 2 humbuckers, bound rosewood 'board, shark fin inlays.

1994-1995	$600	$800

King V (KV2)
2003-present. King V Pro reissue, neck-thru, shark-fin markers, Floyd Rose, U.S.-made.

2003-2007	$600	$700

King V Pro
1993-1995. Soft V-shaped neck-thru solidbody, shark fin markers, 2 humbuckers.

1993-1995	$500	$700

King V STD
1993-1995. Bolt neck version of King V.

1993-1995	$300	$350

Phil Collen
1989-1991, 1993-1995. Offset double-cut maple neck-thru solidbody, six-on-a-side tuners, 1 volume, bound ebony 'board, U.S.-made, early version has poplar body, 1 humbucker; later version with basswood body, 1 single-coil and 1 humbucker.

1993-1995	$1,050	$1,200

Phil Collen PC1 (U.S.A.)
1996-present. Quilt maple top, bolt-on maple neck, maple board, koa body '96-'00, mahogany body '01-present, 1 humbucker and 1 single coil '96-'97, humbucker, stacked humbucker, and single coil '98-present.

1996-2007	$1,175	$1,400

Phil Collen PC3 (Import)
1996-2001. Downscale version of Collen model, poplar body, bolt neck, humbucker\single\single.

1996-2001	$450	$525

PS Performers Series
1994-2003. Some with PS model number on truss rod cover.

1994-1999	PS3 Rhoads body	$200	$275
1994-2003	PS2 Dinky body h/s/h	$175	$250
1995-2001	PS4 Dinky body h/s/h	$200	$275
1995-2001	PS7 h/s/s	$200	$300
1997-2001	PS6/PS6T Kelly body	$200	$250

Randy Rhoads (U.S.A.)
1983-present. V-shaped neck-thru solidbody, 2 humbuckers, originally made at San Dimas plant, serial numbers RR 0001 to RR 1929, production moved to the Ontario plant by '87, serial numbers RR 1930 to present in sequential order.

1983	Early serial #, no trem	$2,500	$2,800
1983-1986	Kahler trem	$1,500	$1,800
1983-1986	Rose trem or string-thru	$1,800	$2,200
1987-1989	Early Ontario-built	$1,500	$1,800
1990-1992		$1,400	$1,700
1993-1999		$1,300	$1,500
2000-2002		$925	$1,100
2002-2007	FMIC	$725	$900

Randy Rhoads (Import)
1992-present. Bolt neck import version.

1992-2007	$325	$400

Randy Rhoads Custom Shop
1999. U.S.-made Custom Shop, special features.

1999	$1,150	$1,250

Randy Rhoads Custom Shop RR1T
2002 only. U.S.-made Custom Shop, only 50 made, Randy Rhoads body.

2002	$1,450	$1,700

Randy Rhoads Limited Edition
1992 only. Shark fin-style maple neck-thru body, gold hardware, white with black pinstriping, block inlays, six-on-a-side tuners, U.S.-made, only 200 built.

1992	$2,500	$3,500

San Dimas Serialized Plated
1980-1982. Various custom-built solidbody models, values vary depending on each individual instrument. The values are true for so-called "Serialized Plated" with Jackson neck plate, Jackson logo and serial number.

1980-1982	$4,000	$5,000

Soloist
1984-1990. U.S.-made, double-cut, neck-thru, string-thru solidbody, 2 humbuckers, bound rosewood 'board, standard vibrato system on Soloist is Floyd Rose locking vibrato, a guitar with Kahler vibrato is worth less. Replaced by the Soloist USA in '90.

1984-1986	Custom order features	$1,800	$2,000

MODEL YEAR	FEATURES	EXC. COND. LOW	HIGH
1984-1986	San Dimas-built	$1,600	$1,850
1986-1990	Custom order features	$1,700	$1,950
1986-1990	Ontario-built	$1,400	$1,700

Soloist Custom

1993-1995. Double-cut, neck-thru solidbody, 1 humbucker and 2 single-coils, bound ebony 'board, shark's tooth inlays, U.S.-made.

1993-1995		$1,000	$1,100

Soloist Student J1 (U.S.A.)

1984-1999. Double-cut neck-thru solidbody, Seymour Duncan single-single-hum pickups, rosewood 'board, dot inlays, no binding.

1984-1986	San Dimas-built	$950	$1,000
1986-1999	Ontario-built	$900	$950

Soloist USA/SL Series

1990-1995. Replaces Soloist, shark fin markers, single-single-hum.

1990-1995		$1,000	$1,250

Stealth EX

1992-late 1990s. Offset double-cut, pointed headstock, H/S/S pickups, offset dot markers, tremolo, Jackson Professional logo.

1990s		$275	$325

Surfcaster SC1

1998-2001. Jackson logo on headstock, Charvel Surfcaster styling.

1998-2001		$750	$800

Warrior Pro (Import)

1990-1992. Japanese version.

1990-1992		$350	$450

Warrior USA

1990-1992. Four point neck-thru solidbody, 1 humbucker and 1 single-coil, triangle markers, active electronics, U.S.-made, the Warrior Pro was Japanese version.

1990-1992	Red	$1,000	$1,300

Y2KV Dave Mustaine Signature

2000-2002. V-shaped body, shark tooth markers, neck-thru, 2 humbuckers.

2000-2002		$2,000	$2,400

Jackson-Guldan/Jay G Guitars

1920s-1960s. The Jackson-Guldan Violin Company, of Columbus, Ohio, mainly built inexpensive violins, violas, cellos, etc. but also offered acoustic guitars in the 1950s and early '60s, some of which were distributed by Wards. Their sales flyers from that era state - Made in America by Jackson-Guldan Craftsman. Very similar to small (13"-14") Stella economy flat-tops. Jay G name with quarter-note logo is sometimes on the headstock. They also offered lap steels and small tube amps early on.

Jacobacci

1930s-1994. Founded in France by Italian Vincent Jacobacci and originally building basso-guitars, banjos, and mandolins. Sons Roger and Andre joined the company and encouraged pop to add lap steels and electric and regular acoustic guitars

around '52. The guitars are sometimes labeled as Jaco and, from ca. '54 to ca. '66, as Jaco Major. In '58 the company introduced aluminum neck models, and in '59 their first solidbodies. In the '60s they also made instruments branded Royal, Texas, Ohio, Star and made instruments for Major Conn and other companies. By the mid '60s, they were producing mainly jazz style guitars.

James R. Baker Guitars

1996-present. Luthier James R. Baker builds his premium grade, custom, archtops in Shoreham, New York.

James Tyler

Early 1980s-present. Luthier James Tyler builds his professional and premium grade, custom/production, solidbody guitars in Van Nuys, California, and also has a model built in Japan. He also builds basses.

Janofsky Guitars

1978-present. Production classical and flamenco guitars built by luthier Stephen Janofsky in Amherst, Massachusetts.

Jaros

1995-present. Professional and premium grade, production/custom, solidbody and acoustic/electric guitars originally built by father and son luthiers Harry and Jim Jaros in Rochester, Pennsylvania. In '01 Ed Roman in Las Vegas, bought the brand. He sold it in '04 to Dave Weiler in Nashville, Tennessee.

Jasmine

1994-present. Budget and intermediate grade, production, steel and classical guitars offered by Takamine Jasmine or Jasmine by Takamine. Student level instruments.

Jay Turser

1997-present. Budget and intermediate grade, production, imported acoustic, acoustic/electric, electric and resonator guitars. They also offer basses and amps. Designed and developed by Tommy Rizzi for Music Industries Corp.

JD Bluesville

2005-present. John Schappell and luthier Davis Millard build their professional grade, custom/production, solidbody electric guitars in Allentown, Pennsylvania.

Jeff Traugott Guitars

1991-present. Premium and presentation grade, custom, flat-top, nylon-string, and acoustic/electric guitars built by luthier Jeff Traugott, in Santa Cruz, California.

Jackson Warrior USA

James Tyler Studio Elite

Jet Earlwood Plus

1968 Kalamazoo KG--1

MODEL		EXC. COND.	
YEAR	FEATURES	LOW	HIGH

Jeremy Locke Guitars

1985-present. Premium grade, production/custom, classical and flamenco guitars built by luthier Jeremy Locke in Coomera, South East Queensland, Australia.

Jeronimo Pena Fernandez

1967-present. Luthier Jeronimo Pena Fernandez started building classical guitars in Marmolejo, Spain, in the '50s. In '67, he went full-time and soon became well-known for his fine work. He is now retired, but still builds a few guitars a year.

Classical

Late 1960s-1990s. Brazilian rosewood back and sides, cedar top, full-size classical guitar, higher-end luthier.

1960-1990s		$6,000	$7,000

Jerry Jones

1981-present. Intermediate grade, production, semi-hollow body electric guitars and sitars from luthier Jerry Jones, built in Nashville, Tennessee. They also build basses. Jones started building custom guitars in '81, and launched his Danelectro-inspired line in '87.

Electric Models

Various models include Baritone 6-string ('89-present); Electric Sitar ('90-present) with buzz-bar sitar bridge, individual pickup for sympathetic strings and custom color gator finish; Longhorn Guitarlin ('89-'00, '05-present) with large cutaway Guitarlin-style body, 24 frets in '89 and 31 after; and the Neptune 12-string ('81-present) single-cut with 3 pickups.

1990s	Baritone 6-string	$600	$800
1990s	Electric Sitar	$600	$750
1990s	Longhorn Guitarlin	$600	$750
1990s	Neptune Electric 12-string	$600	$750
1990s	Shorthorn	$500	$600

Jersey Girl

1991-present. Premium grade, production/custom, solidbody guitars made in Japan. They also build effects.

JET

1998-present. Premium grade, custom/production, chambered solidbody electric guitars built by luthier Jeffrey Earle Terwilliger in Raleigh, North Carolina.

Jewel

1920s. Instruments built by the Oscar Schmidt Co. and possibly others. Most likely a brand made for a distributor.

JG Guitars

1991-present. Luthier Johan Gustavsson builds his premium and presentation grade, production/custom, solidbody electric guitars in Malmö, Sweden.

MODEL		EXC. COND.	
YEAR	FEATURES	LOW	HIGH

Jim Dyson

1972-present. Intermediate, professional and premium grade, production/custom electric guitars built by luthier Jim Dyson in Torquay, Southern Victoria, Australia. He also builds basses and lap steels.

Jim Redgate Guitars

1992-present. Luthier Jim Redgate builds his premium grade, custom, nylon-string classical guitars in Belair, Adelaide, South Australia.

John Le Voi Guitars

1970-present. Production/custom, gypsy jazz, flat-top, and archtop guitars built by luthier John Le Voi in Lincolnshire, United Kingdom. He also builds mandolin family instruments.

John Page Guitars

2006-present. Luthier John Page builds his custom, premium grade, chambered and solidbody electric guitars in Sunny Valley, Oregon.

John Price Guitars

1984-present. Custom classical and flamenco guitars built by luthier John Price in Australia.

Johnson

Mid-1990s-present. Budget, intermediate and professional grade, production, acoustic, classical, acoustic/electric, resonator and solidbody guitars imported by Music Link, Brisbane, California. Johnson also offers basses, amps, mandolins, ukuleles and effects.

Jon Kammerer

1995-present. Luthier Jon Kammerer builds his professional grade, custom, acoustic and electric guitars in Keokuk, Iowa. He also builds the Sinister Custom Shop Bass for Sinister Guitars.

Jones

See TV Jones listing.

Jordan

1981-present. Professional and premium grade, custom, flat-top and archtop guitars built by luthier John Jordan in Concord, California. He also builds electric violins and cellos.

Jose Oribe

1962-present. Presentation grade, production, classical, flamenco, and steel-string acoustic guitars built by luthier Jose Oribe in Vista, California.

Jose Ramirez

See listing under Ramirez, Jose.

MODEL		EXC. COND.	
YEAR	FEATURES	LOW	HIGH

K & S

1992-1998. Hawaiian-style and classical guitars distributed by George Katechis and Marc Silber and handmade in Paracho, Mexico. A few 16" wide Leadbelly Model 12-strings were made in Oakland, California by luthier Stewart Port. K & S also offered mandolins, mandolas and ukuleles. In '98, Silber started marketing guitars under the Marc Silber Guitar Company brand and Katechis continued to offer instruments under the Casa Montalvo brand.

Kakos, Stephen

1972-present. Luthier Stephen Kakos builds his premium grade, production/custom, classical guitars in Mound, Minnesota.

Kalamazoo

1933-1942, 1965-1970. Budget brand built by Gibson. Made flat-tops, solidbodies, mandolins, lap steels, banjos and amps. Name revived for a line of amps, solidbodies and basses in '65-'67.

KG-1/KG-1 A

1965-1969. Offset double-cut (initial issue) or SG-shape (second issue), 1 pickup, Model 1 A with spring vibrato, red, blue or white.

1965-1969	Early Mustang body	$200	$300
1965-1969	Later SG body	$250	$350

KG-2/KG-2 A

1965-1970. Offset double-cut (initial shape) or SG-shape, 2 pickups, Model 2 A with spring vibrato, red, blue or white.

1965-1970	Early Mustang body	$250	$350
1965-1970	Later SG body	$300	$400

KG-11

1933-1941. Flat-top, all mahogany, 14" with no 'guard, sunburst.

1933-1941		$700	$875

KG-14

1936-1940. Flat-top L-0-size, mahogany back and sides, with 'guard, sunburst.

1936-1940		$900	$1,100

KG-16

1939-1940. Gibson-made archtop, small body, f-hole.

1939-1940		$600	$750

KG-21

1936-1941. Early model 15" archtop (bent, not curved), dot markers, bound top, sunburst.

1936-1941		$600	$750

KG-22

1940-1942. Early model 16" archtop.

1940-1942		$700	$850

KG-31

1935-1940. Archtop L-50-size, 16" body, non-carved spruce top, mahogany back and sides.

1935-1940		$700	$850

KG-32

1939-1942. Archtop, 16" body.

1939-1942		$725	$850

MODEL		EXC. COND.	
YEAR	FEATURES	LOW	HIGH

KHG-00/KHG-14

1939. Acoustic Hawaiian guitar (HG), some converted to Spanish set-up.

1939		$1,600	$1,900

KTG-14 Tenor

1936-1940. Flat-top L-0-size tenor, mahogany back and sides, bound top, sunburst.

1936-1940		$450	$550

Kamico

Brand started in 1947. Flat-top acoustic guitars. Low-end budget brand made by Kay Musical Instrument Company and sold through various distributors.

Kapa

Ca. 1962-1970. Begun by Dutch immigrant and music store owner Koob Veneman in Hyattsville, Maryland whose father had made Amka guitars in Holland. Kapa is from K for Koob, A for son Albert, P for daughter Patricia, and A for wife Adeline. Crown shield logo from Amka guitars. The brand included some Hofner and Italian imports in '60. Ca. '66 Kapa started offering thinner bodies. Some German Pix pickups ca. '66. Thinlines and Japanese bodies in '69. Kapa closed shop in '70 and the parts and equipment were sold to Micro-Frets and Mosrite. Later Veneman was involved with Bradley copy guitars imported from Japan. Approximately 120,000 Kapa guitars and basses were made.

Electric Guitars

1962-1970. Various models include Challenger with 3-way toggle from '62-'66/'67 and 2 on/off switches after; Cobra with 1 pickup; Continental and Continental 12-string; Minstrel and Minstrel 12-string with teardrop shape, 3 pickups; and the Wildcat, mini offset double-cut, 3

1962-1970	Various models	$325	$475

Karol Guitars

2001-present. Luthier Tony Karol builds his custom, premium grade, acoustic and electric guitars in Mississauga, Ontario, Canada.

Kasha

1967-1997. Innovative classical guitars built by luthier Richard Schneider in collaboration with Dr. Michael Kasha. Schneider also consulted for Gibson and Gretsch. Schneider died in '97.

Kathy Wingert Guitars

1996-present. Luthier Kathy Wingert builds her premium grade, production/custom, flat-tops in Rancho Palos Verdes, California.

Kawai

1927-present. Kawai is a Japanese piano and guitar maker. They started offering guitars around '56 and they were imported into the U.S. carrying many different brand names, including Kimberly and Teisco. In '67 Kawai purchased Teisco. Odd-shaped

Kalamazoo KG--14

Kathy Wingert flat-top

Kay Square Neck

Kay 573 Speed Demon

MODEL YEAR	FEATURES	EXC. COND. LOW	HIGH

guitars were offered from late-'60s through the mid-'70s. Few imports carrying the Kawai brand until the late-'70s; best known for high quality basses. By '90s they were making plexiglass replicas of Teisco Spectrum 5 and Kawai moon-shaped guitar. Kawai quit offering guitars and basses around 2002.

Acoustic
1956-2002.

1956-2002		$200	$350

Electric
1956-2002.

1956-2002	Common model	$250	$500
1956-2002	Rare model	$500	$1,000

Kay

Ca. 1931 (1890)-present. Originally founded in Chicago, Illinois as Groehsl Company (or Groehsel) in 1890, making bowl-backed mandolins. Offered Groehsl, Stromberg, Kay Kraft, Kay, Arch Kraft brand names, plus made guitars for S.S.Maxwell, Old Kraftsman (Spiegel), Recording King (Wards), Supertone (Sears), Silvertone (Sears), National, Dobro, Custom Kraft (St.Louis Music), Hollywood (Shireson Bros.), Oahu and others.

In 1921 the name was changed to Stromberg-Voisinet Company. Henry Kay "Hank" Kuhrmeyer joined the company in '23 and was secretary by '25. By the mid-'20s the company was making many better Montgomery Ward guitars, banjos and mandolins, often with lots of pearloid. First production electric guitars and amps are introduced with big fanfare in '28; perhaps only 200 or so made. Last Stromberg instruments seen in '32. Kuhrmeyer becomes president and the Kay Kraft brand was introduced in '31, probably named for Kuhrmeyer's middle name, though S-V had used Kay brand on German Kreuzinger violins '28-'36. By '34, if not earlier, the company is changed to the Kay Musical Instrument Company. A new factory was built at 1640 West Walnut Street in '35. The Kay Kraft brand ends in '37 and the Kay brand is introduced in late-'36 or '37.

Violin Style Guitars and upright acoustic basses debut in '38. In '40 the first guitars for Sears, carrying the new Silvertone brand, are offered. Kamico budget line introduced in '47 and Rex flat-tops and archtops sold through Gretsch in late-'40s. Kuhrmeyer retires in '55 dies a year later. New gigantic factory in Elk Grove Village, Illinois opens in '64. Seeburg purchased Kay in '66 and sold it to Valco in '67. Valco/Kay went out of business in '68 and its assets were auctioned in '69. The Kay name went to Sol Weindling and Barry Hornstein of W.M.I. (Teisco Del Rey) who began putting Kay name on Teisco guitars. By '73 most Teisco guitars are called Kay. Tony Blair, president of Indianapolis-based A.R. Musical Enterprises Inc. (founded in '73) purchased the Kay nameplate in '79 and currently distributes Kay in the U.S. Currently Kay offers budget and intermediate grade, production,

MODEL YEAR	FEATURES	EXC. COND. LOW	HIGH

acoustic, semi-hollow body, solidbody, and resonator guitars. They also make amps, basses, banjos, mandolins, ukuleles, and violins.

Barney Kessel Artist
1957-1960. Single-cut, 15 1/2" body, 1 (K6701) or 2 (K6700) pickups, Kelvinator headstock, sunburst or blond.

1957-1960		$1,200	$1,400

Barney Kessel Pro
1957-1960. 13" hollowbody, single-cut, Kelvinator headstock, ebony 'board with pearl inlays, white binding, 1 or 2 pickups, sunburst.

1957-1960		$1,400	$1,600

K20
1939-1942. 16" archtop, solid spruce top, maple back and sides, sunburst.

1939-1942		$250	$300

K22
1947-1956. Flat-top similar to Gibson J-100 17", spruce top, mahogany back and sides.

1947-1956		$500	$600

K26
1947-1951. Flat-top, block markers, natural.

1947-1951		$575	$700

K27
1952-1956. 17" Jumbo, fancy appointments.

1952-1956		$1,000	$1,250

K44
1947-1951. Non-cut archtop, solid spruce top, 17" curly maple veneered body, block markers, sunburst.

1947-1951		$400	$500

K45
1952-1954. Non-cut archtop, 17" body, engraved tortoiseshell-celluloid headstock, large block markers, natural.

1952-1954		$450	$550

K45 Travel Guitar
1981. Made in Korea, known as the 'rifle guitar', 'travel guitar', or 'Austin-Hatchet copy', circle K logo.

1981		$300	$500

K46
1947-1951. Non-cut archtop, solid spruce top, 17" curly maple-veneered body, double-eighth note headstock inlay, sunburst.

1947-1951		$475	$575

K48 Artist
1947-1951. Non-cut archtop, 17" solid spruce top with figured maple back and sides, split block inlays, sunburst or black.

1947-1951		$900	$1,100

K48/K21 Jazz Special
Late-1960s. Slim solidbody with 3 reflective pickups, garden spade headstock, fancy position Circle K headstock logo.

1968	White	$400	$500

K100 Vanguard
1961-1966. Offset double-cut slab solidbody, genuine maple veneered top and back over hardwood body, sunburst.

1961-1966		$200	$250

MODEL YEAR	FEATURES	EXC. COND. LOW	HIGH

K102 Vanguard
1961-1966. Double pickup version of the K100, sunburst.

1961-1966		$275	$300

K136 (a.k.a. Stratotone)
1955-1957. Small single-cut slab solidbody electric, similar to Harmony Stratotone style, 1 pickup, trapeze tailpiece, triangle paint graphic in Spring Green and White Mist, matching green headstock, attractive finish adds value to this otherwise lower-end student model.

1955-1957		$1,300	$1,500

K142 (aka Stratotone)
1955-1957. Small slab solidbody, introduced in '55 along with the K136, offered with 1 pickup or 2 pickups (more rare), trapeze tailpiece, copper finish.

1955-1957	1 pickup	$1,100	$1,200
1955-1957	2 pickups	$1,200	$1,500

K161 Thin Twin "Jimmy Reed"
1952-1958. Cutaway semi-hollow, 2 pickups, birds-eye maple, often called the Jimmy Reed, sunburst.

1952-1958		$700	$875

K300 Double Cutaway Solid Electric
1962-1966. Two single-coils, block inlays, some with curly maple top and some with plain maple top, natural.

1962-1966		$500	$600

K535
1961-1965. Thinline double-cut, 2 pickups, vibrato, sunburst.

1961-1965		$500	$600

K571/K572/K573 Speed Demon
1961-1965. Thinline semi-acoustic/electric, single pointed cutaway, some with Bigsby vibrato, with 1 (K571), 2 (K572) or 3 (K573) pickups. There was also a Speed Demon solidbody.

1961-1965	K571	$375	$450
1961-1965	K572	$450	$550
1961-1965	K573	$525	$650

K580 Galaxy
1963. Thinline, single-cut, 1 pickup.

1963		$400	$450

K592
1962-1966. Thinline semi-acoustic/electric, double Florentine cut, 2 or 3 pickups, Bigsby vibrato, pie-slice inlays, cherry.

1962-1966		$525	$625

K672/K673 Swingmaster
1961-1965. Single rounded cutaway semi-hollow-body, with 2 (K672) or 3 (K673) pickups.

1961-1965	K672	$950	$1,175
1961-1965	K673	$1,100	$1,250

K775 Jazz II
1960-1963. Electric thinline archtop, double-cut, standard Bigsby vibrato, 2 Gold K pickups, 4 knobs with toggle controls.

1960-1963		$1,000	$1,200

K797 Acoustic Archtop
1930s. Full size student-intermediate acoustic archtop, 3-on-a-strip tuners, dot markers, sunburst.

1935-1937		$250	$300

K1160 Standard
1957-1964. Small 13" (standard) flat-top, laminated construction.

1957-1964		$50	$60

K1961/K1962/K1963
1960-1965. Part of Value Leader line, thinline single-cut, hollowbody, identified by single chrome-plated checkered, body-length guard on treble side, laminated maple body, maple neck, dot markers, sunburst, with 1 (K1961), 2 (K1962) or 3 (K1963) pickups.

1960-1965	K1961	$400	$500
1960-1965	K1962	$500	$550
1960-1965	K1963	$525	$650

K1982/K1983 Style Leader/Jimmy Reed
1960-1965. Part of the Style Leader mid-level Kay line. Sometimes dubbed Jimmy Reed of 1960s. Easily identified by the long brushed copper dual guard plates on either side of the strings. Brown or gleaming golden blond (natural) finish, laminated curly maple body, simple script Kay logo, with 2 (K1982) or 3 (K1983) pickups.

1960-1965	K1982	$500	$575
1960-1965	K1983	$525	$650

K3500 Student Concert
1966-1968. 14 1/2" flat-top, solid spruce top, laminated maple back and sides.

1966-1968		$75	$90

K5113 Plains Special
1968. Flat-top, solid spruce top, laminated mahogany back and sides.

1968		$150	$175

K5160 Auditorium
1957-1965. Flat-top 15" auditorium-size, laminated construction.

1957-1965		$100	$125

K6100 Country
1950s-1960s. Jumbo flat-top, spruce x-braced top, mahogany back and sides, natural.

1957-1962		$350	$425

K6116 Super Auditorium
1957-1965. Super Auditorium-size flat-top, laminated figured maple back and sides, solid spruce top.

1957-1965		$200	$250

K6120 Western
1960s. Jumbo flat-top, laminated maple body, pinless bridge, sunburst.

1962		$175	$200

K6130 Calypso
1960-1965. 15 1/2" flat-top with narrow waist, slotted headstock, natural.

1960-1965		$250	$300

K6533/K6535 Value Leader
1961-1965. Value Leader was the budget line of Kay, full body archtop, with 1 (K6533) or 2 (K6535) pickups, sunburst.

1961-1965	K6533	$300	$350
1961-1965	K6535	$350	$400

1960 Kay 6980 Upbeat

1960 Kay K8995 Upbeat

GUITARS

Ken Franklin Madison

Kevin Ryan Rosewood

MODEL YEAR	FEATURES	EXC. COND. LOW	HIGH
K7000 Artist	*1960-1965. Highest-end of Kay classical series, fan bracing, spruce top, maple back and sides.*		
1960-1965		$400	$450
K7010 Concerto	*1960-1965. Entry level of Kay classical series.*		
1960-1965		$75	$100
K7010 Maestro	*1960-1965. Middle level of Kay classical series.*		
1960-1965		$225	$275
K8110 Master	*1957-1960. 17" master-size flat-top which was largest of the series, laminated construction.*		
1957-1960		$150	$175
K8127 Solo Special	*1957-1965. Kay's professional grade flat-top, narrow waist jumbo, block markers.*		
1957-1965		$450	$550
K8995 Upbeat	*1958-1960. Less expensive alternative to Barney Kessel Jazz Special, 2 pickups, sunburst.*		
1958-1960		$850	$1,050
Wood Amplifying Guitar	*1934. Engineered after Dobro/National metal resonator models except the resonator and chamber on this model are made of wood, small production.*		
1934		$2,850	$2,900

Kay Kraft

1927-1937. First brand name of the Kay Musical Instrument Company as it began its transition from Stromberg-Voisinet Company to Kay (see Kay for more info).

MODEL YEAR	FEATURES	EXC. COND. LOW	HIGH
Recording King			
1931-1937		$400	$500
Venetian Archtop	*1930s. Unique Venetian cutaway body style, acoustic with round soundhole, flower-vine decal art on low bout.*		
1930s		$625	$700

KB

1989-present. Luthier Ken Bebensee builds his premium grade, custom, acoustic and electric guitars in North San Juan, California. He was located in San Luis Obispo from '89-'01. He also builds basses and mandolins.

Kel Kroydon (by Gibson)

1930-1933. Private branded budget level instruments made by Gibson. They also had mandolins and banjos. The name has been revived on a line of banjos by Tom Mirisola and made in Nashville, Tennessee.

MODEL YEAR	FEATURES	EXC. COND. LOW	HIGH
KK-1	*1930-1933. 14 3/4" L-0 style body, colorful parrot stencils on body.*		
1930-1933		$2,800	$3,500

Keller Custom Guitars

1994-present. Professional grade, production/custom, solidbody guitars built by luthier Randall Keller in Mandan, North Dakota.

Keller Guitars

1975-present. Premium grade, production/custom, flat-tops made by luthier Michael L. Keller in Rochester, Minnesota.

Ken Franklin

2003-present. Luthier Ken Franklin builds his premium grade, production/custom, acoustic guitars in Ukiah, California.

Kendrick

1989-present. Premium grade, production/custom, solidbody guitars built in Texas. Founded by Gerald Weber in Pflugerville, Texas and currently located in Kempner, Texas. Mainly known for their handmade tube amps, Kendrick added guitars in '94 and also offers speakers and effects.

Kent

1961-1969. Imported from Japan by Buegeleisen and Jacobson of New York, New York. Manufacturers unknown but many early guitars and basses were made by Guyatone and Teisco.

MODEL YEAR	FEATURES	EXC. COND. LOW	HIGH
Acoustic Flat-Top	*1962-1969.*		
1962-1969		$125	$150
Acoustic/Electric			
1962-1969		$150	$175
Electric 12-String	*1960s. Thinline electric, double pointy cutaways, 12 strings, slanted dual pickup, sunburst.*		
1965-1969		$275	$325
Semi-Hollow Electric	*1960s. Thinline electric, offset double pointy cutaways, slanted dual pickups, various colors.*		
1962-1969		$275	$325
Solidbody Electric	*1962-1969. Models include Polaris I, II and III, Lido, Copa and Videocaster.*		
1962-1969		$150	$175

Kevin Ryan Guitars

1989-present. Premium grade, custom, flat-tops built by luthier Kevin Ryan in Westminster, California.

Kiesel

See Carvin.

Kimberly

Late-1960s-early-1970s. Private branded import made in the same Japanese factory as Teisco. They also made basses.

MODEL YEAR	FEATURES	EXC. COND. LOW	HIGH

May Queen
1960s. Same as Teisco May Queen with Kimberly script logo on headstock and May Queen Teisco on the 'guard.

1960s		$525	$650

Kinal
1969-present. Production/custom, professional and premium grade, solid body electric and archtop guitars built and imported by luthier Michael Kinal in Vancouver, British Columbia, Canada. He also builds basses.

Kingsley
1960s. Early Japanese imports, Teisco-made.
Solidbody Electric
1960s. Four pickups with tremolo.

1960s		$275	$325

Kingslight Guitars
1980-present. Luthier John Kingslight builds his premium grade, custom/production, steel string guitars in Portage, Michigan (in Taos, New Mexico for '80-'83). He also builds basses.

Kingston
Ca. 1958-1967. Guitars and basses imported from Japan by Jack Westheimer and Westheimer Importing Corporation of Chicago, Illinois. Early examples made by Guyatone and Teisco. They also offered mandolins.
Electric
1958-1967. Various models include: B-1, soldibody, 1 pickup; B-2T/B-3T/B-4T, solidbodies, 2/3/4 pickups and tremolo; SA-27, thin hollowbody, 2 pickups, tremolo.

1958-1967		$125	$400

Kinscherff Guitars
1990-present. Luthier Jamie Kinscherff builds his premium grade, production/custom, flat-top guitars in Austin, Texas.

Kleartone
1930s. Private brand made by Regal and/or Gibson.
Small Flat-Top

1930s		$575	$700

Klein Acoustic Guitars
1972-present. Luthiers Steve Klein and Steven Kauffman build their production/custom, premium and presentation grade flat-tops in Sonoma, California. They also build basses.

Klein Electric Guitars
1988-present. Steve Klein added electrics to his line in '88. In '95, he sold the electric part of his business to Lorenzo German, who continues to produce professional grade, production/custom, solidbody guitars in Linden, California. He also builds basses.

Klira
1887-1980s. Founded by Johannes Klira in Schoenbach, Germany, mainly made violins, but added guitars in the 1950s. The guitars of the '50s and '60s were original designs, but by the '70s most models were similar to popular American models. The guitars of the '50s and '60s were aimed at the budget market, but workmanship improved with the '70s models. They also made basses.
Hollowbody Electric

1960s		$250	$300

Solidbody Electric

1960s		$175	$200

Knutsen
1890s-1920s. Luthier Chris J. Knutsen of Tacoma and Seattle, Washington, experimented with and perfected Hawaiian and harp guitar models. He moved to Los Angeles, California around 1916, where he also made steels and ukes.
Convertible
1909-1914. Flat-top model with adjustable neck angle that allowed for a convertible Hawaiian or Spanish setup.

1909-1914		$3,600	$4,000

Harp Guitar
1900s. Normally 11 strings with fancy purfling and trim.

1900-1910		$4,500	$5,500

Knutson Luthiery
1981-present. Professional and premium grade, custom, archtop and flat-top guitars built by luthier John Knutson in Forestville, California. He also builds basses, lap steels and mandolins.

Kohno
1960-present. Luthier Masaru Kohno built his classical guitars in Tokyo, Japan. When he died in '98, production was taken over by his nephew, Masaki Sakurai.
Classical
Brazilian rosewood back and sides, spruce top.

1970s		$2,500	$3,000

Koll
1990-present. Professional and premium grade, custom/production, solidbody, chambered, and archtop guitars built by luthier Saul Koll, originally in Long Beach, California, and since '93, in Portland, Oregon. He also builds basses.

Kona
1910s-1920s, 2001-present. Acoustic Hawaiian guitars sold by C.S. Delano and others, with later models made by the Herman Weissenborn Co. Weissenborn appointments are in line with style number, with thicker body and solid neck construction. Since '01, the Kona name is now used on an import line of budget grade, production, acoustic and electric guitars and basses. They also offer banjos and amps.

Kingslight Jumbo Cutaway

Koll Duo Glide

MODEL YEAR	FEATURES	EXC. COND. LOW	HIGH
Style 3			
1920s	Koa	$3,600	$4,000
Style 4			
1920s	Brown koa	$3,900	$4,500

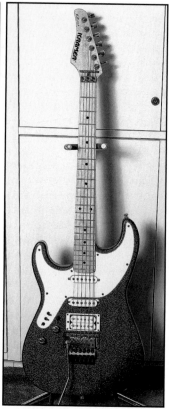

Kramer Elliot Easton Pro

Koontz

1970-late 1980s. Luthier Sam Koontz started building custom guitars in the late '50s. Starting in '66 Koontz, who was associated with Harptone guitars, built guitars for Standel. In '70, he opened his own shop in Linden, New Jersey, building a variety of custom guitars. Koontz died in the late '80s. His guitars varied greatly and should be valued on a case-by-case basis.

Kramer

1976-1990, 1995-present. Currently Kramer offers budget and intermediate grade, production, imported acoustic, acoustic/electric, semi-hollow and solidbody guitars. They also offer basses, amps and effects.

Founded by New York music retailer Dennis Berardi, ex-Travis Bean partner Gary Kramer and ex-Norlin executive Peter LaPlaca. Initial financing provided by real estate developer Henry Vaccaro. Parent company named BKL Corporation (Berardi, Kramer, LaPlaca), located in Neptune City, New Jersey. The first guitars were designed by Berardi and luthier Phil Petillo and featured aluminum necks with wooden inserts on back to give them a wooden feel. Guitar production commenced in late-'76. Control passed to Guitar Center of Los Angeles for '79-'82, which recommended a switch to more economical wood necks. Aluminum necks were phased out during the early-'80s, and were last produced in '85. In '89, a new investment group was brought in with James Liati as president, hoping for access to Russian market, but the company went of business in late-'90. In '95 Henry Vaccaro and new partners revived the company and designed a number of new guitars in conjunction with Phil Petillo. However, in '97 the Kramer brand was sold to Gibson. In '98, Henry Vaccaro released his new line of aluminum-core neck, split headstock guitars under the Vacarro brand.

Non-U.S.-made models include the following lines: Aerostar, Ferrington, Focus, Hundred (post-'85 made with 3 digits in the 100-900), Showster, Striker, Thousand (post-'85 made with 4 digits in the 1000-9000), XL (except XL-5 made in '80s).

Serial numbers for import models include:

Two alpha followed by 4 numbers: for example AA2341 with any assortment of letters and numbers.

One alpha followed by 5 numbers: for example B23412.

Five numbers: for example 23412.

Model number preceding numbers: for example XL1-03205.

The notation "Kramer, Neptune, NJ" does indicate U.S.A.-made production.

Kramer Focus

Most post-'85 Kramers were ESP Japanese-made guitars. American Series were ESP Japanese components that were assembled in the U.S.

The vintage/used market makes value distinctions between U.S.-made and import models. **Headstock and logo shape can help identify U.S. versus imports as follows:**

Traditional or Classic headstock with capital K as Kramer: U.S.A. '81-'84.

Banana (soft edges) headstock with all caps KRAMER: U.S.A. American Series '84-'86.

Pointy (sharp cut) headstock with all caps KRAMER: U.S.A. American Series '86-'87.

Pointy (sharp cut) headstock with downsized letters Kramer plus American decal: U.S.A. American Series '87-'94.

Pointy (sharp cut) headstock with downsized letters Kramer but without American decal, is an import.

1984 Reissue
2007. Various color options.

2007		$475	$500

250-G Special
1977-1979. Offset double-cut, tropical woods, aluminum neck, dot markers, 2 pickups.

1977-1979		$600	$700

350-G Standard
1976-1979. Offset double-cut, tropical woods, aluminum neck, tuning fork headstock, ebony 'board, zero fret, 2 single coils, dot inlays. The 350 and 450 were Kramer's first models.

1976-1979		$800	$900

450-G Deluxe
1976-1980. Like 350-G, but with block inlays, 2 humbuckers. Became the 450G Deluxe in late '77 with dot inlays.

1976-1980		$850	$1,000

650-G Artist
1977-1980. Aluminum neck, ebonol 'board, double-cut solidbody, 2 humbuckers.

1977-1980		$1,300	$1,400

Baretta
1984-1990. Offset double-cut, banana six-on-a-side headstock, 1 pickup, Floyd Rose tremolo, black hardware, U.S.A.-made.

1984	1st style, larger headstock	$1,350	$1,650
1984-1985	2nd style, angled headstock	$850	$1,050
1985-1987	3rd style, ESP neck	$575	$700
1985-1987	With graphics	$650	$800
1988-1990	Standard opaque	$700	$875
1988-1990	With graphics	$800	$1,000
1990	Baretta III hybrid	$575	$700

Baretta II/Soloist
1986-1990. Soloist sleek body with pointed cutaway horns.

1986-1990		$425	$500

MODEL YEAR	FEATURES	EXC. COND. LOW	HIGH

Classic Series

1986-1987. Solidbody copies of the famous Southern California builder, including offset contoured double-cut (Classic I) and slab body single-cut designs (Classic II and Classic III).

1986-1987	Classic I	$500	$600
1986-1987	Classic II	$475	$575
1986-1987	Classic III	$475	$550

Condor

1985-1986. Futuristic 4-point body with large upper bass horn and lower treble horn.

| 1985-1986 | | $450 | $550 |

DMZ Custom Series

1978-1991. Solidbody double-cut with larger upper horn, bolt-on aluminum T-neck, slot headstock, models include the 1000 (super distortion humbuckers), 2000 (dual-sound humbuckers), 3000 (3 SDS single-coils), 6000 (dual-sound humbuckers, active DBL).

1978-1991	DMZ-1000	$600	$875
1978-1991	DMZ-2000	$650	$925
1978-1991	DMZ-3000	$525	$800
1978-1991	DMZ-6000	$800	$1,025

Duke Custom/Standard

1981-1982. Headless aluminum neck, 22-fret neck, 1 pickup, Floyd Rose tremolo.

| 1981-1982 | | $500 | $600 |

Duke Special

1982-1985. Headless aluminum neck, two pickups, tuners on body.

| 1982-1985 | | $525 | $650 |

Eliot Easton Pro I

1987-1988. Designed by Elliot Easton, offset double-cut, six-on-a-side headstock, Floyd Rose tremolo, 2 single-coils and 1 humbucker.

| 1987-1988 | | $625 | $700 |

Eliot Easton Pro II

1987-1988. Same as Pro I, but with fixed-bridge tailpiece, 2 single-coils.

| 1987-1988 | | $525 | $600 |

Ferrington

1985-1990. Acoustic-electric, offered in single- and double-cut, bolt-on electric-style neck, transducers, made in Korea.

| 1985-1990 | | $350 | $425 |

Focus/F Series (Import)

1983-1989. Kramer introduced the Focus series as import copies of their American-made models like the Pacer, Baretta, Vanguard (Rhoads-V), and Voyager (star body). Model numbers were 1000-6000, plus the Focus Classic I, II, and III. Most models were offset, double-cut solidbodies. In '87 the Focus line was renamed the F-Series. In '88 a neck-through body design, which is noted as NT, was introduced for a short time. The Classic series was offered with over a dozen color options.

1983	Focus 4000, Pacer	$225	$325
1983-1984	Focus 1000, Pacer Special	$200	$250
1983-1987	Focus 2000, Pacer Imperial	$200	$250
1983-1987	Focus 3000, Pacer Deluxe	$250	$325
1983-1987	Focus 6000, Pacer Custom	$225	$325
1984-1986	Focus 1000, Baretta	$300	$375
1984-1986	Focus 4000, Vanguard	$225	$325
1986-1987	Focus 5000, Voyager	$225	$325
1987-1989	Focus 1000/F1000	$275	$325
1987-1989	Focus Classic I, 3 pickups	$200	$300
1987-1989	Focus Classic II	$200	$300
1987-1989	Focus Classic III	$200	$300
1988	Focus 1000/F1000 NT	$350	$425
1988	Focus 2000/F2000 NT	$250	$325
1988-1989	Focus 2000/F2000	$175	$225
1988-1989	Focus 3000/F3000	$200	$300
1988-1989	Focus 6000/F6000	$200	$300
1989	Focus 1000/F1000	$275	$325

Gene Simmons Axe

1980-1981. Axe-shaped guitar, aluminum neck, 1 humbucker, slot headstock, stop tailpiece, 25 were made.

| 1980-1981 | | $2,700 | $3,300 |

Gorky Park (Import)

1986-1989. Triangular balalaika, bolt-on maple neck, pointy droopy six-on-a-side headstock, 1 pickup, Floyd Rose tremolo, red with iron sickle graphics, tribute to Russian rock, reissued in late-'90s.

| 1986-1989 | | $300 | $350 |

Hundred Series

1988-1990. Import budget line, most with offset double-cut 7/8th solidbody.

1988-1989	615, bound 610	$275	$325
1988-1990	110, 1 pickup	$200	$250
1988-1990	120	$250	$300
1988-1990	210, 2 pickups	$225	$275
1988-1990	220	$250	$300
1988-1990	310, 3 pickups	$225	$275
1988-1990	410	$225	$275
1988-1990	420, V-body	$275	$325
1988-1990	610, sleek body, 3 pickups	$250	$300
1988-1990	620	$250	$300
1989-1990	111, 2 pickups	$225	$275
1989-1990	112, carved 111	$250	$300
1989-1990	612	$250	$300
1989-1990	710	$250	$300
1989-1990	720, revised 710	$250	$300

Liberty '86 Series

1986-1987. Offset double cut arched-top solidbody, pointy head, 2 humbuckers, black, white or flame-maple bound body.

| 1986-1987 | Black or white | $575 | $700 |
| 1986-1987 | Flame maple | $650 | $800 |

Metalist/Showster Series

1989-1990. Korean-made offset double-cut solidbody, metal trim in body design, pointy droopy six-on-a-side headstock, various pickup options, Floyd Rose.

| 1989-1990 | | $400 | $500 |

Kramer Focus

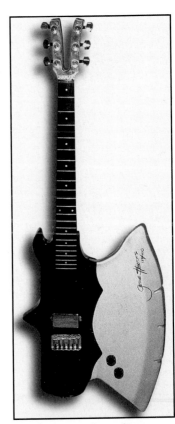

1980 Kramer Gene Simmons Axe

Kramer Vanguard

1967 La Baye 2x4

Nightswan

1987-1990. Offset double-cut, six-on-a-side headstock, 2 Duncan humbuckers, Floyd Rose tremolo, blue metallic.

MODEL YEAR	FEATURES	EXC. COND. LOW	HIGH
1987-1990		$850	$1,000
1987-1990	Custom color or finish	$950	$1,150

Pacer Series

1981-1987. Offset double-cut, six-on-a-side headstock, various pickup options, bolt-on maple neck.

1981	Pacer, 2 pickups, soft headstock	$750	$925
1981-1986	Custom	$625	$775
1982	Special, 1 pickup	$550	$650
1982-1984	Pacer, 2 pickups	$600	$750
1982-1985	Carerra, 2 pickups	$625	$775
1982-1987	Imperial	$575	$675
1983-1986	Deluxe	$600	$700
1987	Custom II	$575	$675

Paul Dean

1986-1988. Offset double cut, neck-thru, hum/single/single pickups, droopy pointy head.

1986-1988		$750	$925

ProAxe (U.S.A.)

1989-1990. U.S.A.-made, offset double-cut, sharp pointy headstock, dot markers, 2 or 3 pickups, smaller 7/8ths size body, 3 models offered with slightly different pickup options. The model was discontinued when Kramer went out of business in 1990.

1989-1990	Deluxe	$550	$700
1989-1990	Special	$525	$650
1989-1990	Standard	$500	$625

Richie Sambora

1987-1989. Designed by Sambora, mahogany offset double-cut, maple neck, pointy droopy 6-on-a-side headstock, gold hardware, Floyd Rose, 3 pickups, 2 coil-taps.

1987-1989		$725	$900

Ripley Series

1984-1987. Offset double-cut, banana six-on-a-side headstock, 22 frets, hexophonic humbucker pickups, panpots, dual volume, Floyd Rose tremolo, black hardware, stereo output, pointy droopy headstock in '87.

1984-1987		$700	$850

Savant/Showster Series

1989-1990. Offset double-cut solidbody, pointy headstock, various pickup options.

1989-1990		$350	$425

Stagemaster Deluxe (U.S.A.)

U.S.-made version.

1981		$1,150	$1,300

Stagemaster Series (Import)

1983-1987. Offset double-cut neck-thru solidbody models, smaller 7/8th body, built by ESP in Japan.

1983-1987	Custom/Custom I	$550	$675
1983-1987	Deluxe/Deluxe I	$525	$650
1983-1987	Imperial	$500	$625
1983-1987	Special	$475	$575
1983-1987	Standard/Standard I	$500	$625
1987	Deluxe II	$450	$550

Striker Series (Import)

1984-1989. Korean imports, offset double-cut, various pickup options, series included Striker 100, 200, 300, 400, 600 and 700 Bass.

MODEL YEAR	FEATURES	EXC. COND. LOW	HIGH
1984-1989	100ST, 1 pickup	$175	$200
1984-1989	200ST, 2 pickups	$200	$250
1984-1989	300ST, 3 pickups	$200	$250
1985-1989	400ST, Rhoads-body	$200	$250
1985-1989	500ST, Star-body	$225	$275
1986-1989	600ST, 3 pickups	$250	$300
1988-1989	605ST, 3 pickups, bound	$275	$325

Sustainer

1989. Offset double-cut solidbody, reverse pointy headstock, Floyd Rose tremolo.

1989		$800	$900

Vanguard Series

1981-1986, 1999-present. U.S.-made or American Series (assembled in U.S.). V shape, 1 humbucker, aluminum (Special '81-'83) or wood (Custom '81-'83) neck. Added for '83-'84 were the Imperial (wood neck, 2 humbuckers) and the Headless (alum neck, 1 humbucker). For '85-'86, the body was modified to a Jackson Randy Rhoads style V body, with a banana headstock and 2 humbuckers. In '99 this last design was revived as an import.

1981-1983	Custom	$600	$750
1981-1983	Special	$550	$675
1983-1984	Imperial, wood neck	$550	$675
1985-1986	Rhoads V-body	$600	$750

Voyager

1982-1985. Wood neck, classic headstock, rosewood 'board, 1 pickup (2 optional), Floyd Rose tremolo, black.

1982-1985	Imperial	$450	$550

XKG-10

1980-1981. Aluminum neck, V-shaped body.

1980-1981		$525	$650

XKG-20

1980-1981. More traditional double-cut body with small horns.

1980-1981		$500	$575

XL Series

1980-1981 and 1987-1990. The early-'80s U.S.-made models were completely different than the late-'80s model. The late-'80s models were inexpensive imports.

1980-1981	XL-5, 2 humbuckers, aluminum neck	$800	$1,000
1987-1990	XL-1, 2 pickups, wood neck	$125	$150
1987-1990	XL-6, 3 pickups, wood neck	$125	$150
1989	XL-2, 2 humbuckers, wood neck	$125	$150
1989	XL-3, 3 pickups, wood neck	$125	$150

MODEL YEAR	FEATURES	EXC. COND. LOW	HIGH

ZX Aero Star Series (Import)
1986-1989. Offset double-cut solidbodies, pointy six-on-a-side headstock. Models include the 1 humbucker ZX-10, 2 humbucker ZX-20, 3 single coil ZX-30, and hum/single/single ZX-30H.

1986-1989		$75	$100

Kramer-Harrison, William
1977-present. Luthier William Kramer-Harrison builds his premium grade, custom, classical and flat-top guitars in Kingston, New York.

KSM
1988-present. Luthier Kevin S. Moore builds his premium grade, custom/production, solidbody electric guitars in Logan, Utah.

Kubicki
1973-present. Kubicki is best known for their Factor basses, but did offer a few guitar models in the early '80s. See Bass section for more company info.

Kustom
1968-present. Founded by Bud Ross in Chanute, Kansas, and best known for the tuck-and-roll amps, Kustom also offered guitars from '68 to '69. See Amp section for more company info.

Electric Hollowbody
1968-1969. Hollowed-out 2-part bodies; includes the K200A (humbucker, Bigsby), the K200B (single-coils, trapeze tailpiece), and the K200C (less fancy tuners), various colors.

1960s		$950	$1,100

Kyle, Doug
1990-present. Premium grade, custom, Selmer-style guitars made by luthier Doug Kyle in England.

L Benito
2001-present. Professional grade, steel and nylon string acoustics from luthier Lito Benito and built in Chile.

La Baye
1967. Designed by Dan Helland in Green Bay, Wisconsin and built by the Holman-Woodell factory in Neodesha, Kansas. Introduced at NAMM and folded when no orders came in. Only 45 prototypes made. A few may have been sold later as 21st Century. They also had basses.

2x4 6-String
1967. Narrow plank body, controls on top, 2 pickups, tremolo, 12-string version was also made.

1967		$1,200	$1,500

La Mancha
1996-present. Professional and premium grade, production/custom, classical guitars made in Mexico under the supervision of Kenny Hill and Gil Carnal and distributed by Jerry Roberts of Nashville.

Style F Classical
1996-present. Solid cedar top, solid rosewood back and sides.

1996-2007		$1,900	$2,100

La Patrie
Production, classical guitars. Founded by luthier Robert Godin, who also has the Norman, Godin, Seagull, and Patrick & Simon brands of instruments.

La Scala
Ca. 1920s-1930s. La Scala was another brand of the Oscar Schmidt Company of New Jersey, and was used on guitars, banjos, and mandolins. These were often the fanciest of the Schmidt instruments. Schmidt made the guitars and mandolins; the banjos were made by Rettberg & Lang.

Lace Music Products
1979-present. Intermediate and professional, production, electric guitars from Lace Music Products, a division of Actodyne General Inc. which was founded by Don Lace Sr., inventor of the Lace Sensor Pickup. In '96 Lace added amplifiers and in 2001 they added guitars. In '02, they also started offering the Rat Fink brand of guitars.

Lacey Guitars
1974-present. Luthier Mark Lacey builds his premium and presentation archtops and flat-tops in Nashville, Tennessee.

Lado
1973-present. Founded by Joe Kovacic, Lado builds professional and premium grade, production/custom, solidbody guitars in Lindsay, Ontario. Some model lines are branded J. K. Lado. They also build basses.

Lafayette
Ca. 1963-1967. Sold through Lafayette Electronics catalogs. Early Japanese-made guitars and basses from pre-copy era, generally shorter scale beginner instruments. Many made by Guyatone, some possibly by Teisco.

Acoustic Thinline Archtop
1963-1967. Various models.

1963-1967		$150	$250

Laguna
2008-present. Guitar Center private label, budget and intermediate grade, production, imported electric and acoustic guitars.

Lakeside (Lyon & Healy)
Early-1900s. Mainly catalog sales of guitars and mandolins from the Chicago maker. Marketed as a less expensive alternative to the Lyon & Healy Washburn product line.

Lace Twister

Lacey Arch Nouveau

GUITARS

Lakewood M-14

Larrivee L-19

MODEL YEAR	FEATURES	EXC. COND. LOW	HIGH

Harp Guitar

Early-1900s. Spruce top, rosewood finished birch back and sides, two 6-string necks with standard tuners, 1 neck is fretless without dot markers, rectangular bridge.

1917	Various models	$2,000	$2,500

Lakewood

1986-present. Luthier Martin Seeliger builds his professional and premium grade, production/custom, steel and nylon string guitars in Giessen, Germany. He has also built mandolins.

Langdon Guitars

1997-present. Luthier Jeff Langdon builds his professional and premium grade, production/custom, flat top, archtop, and solidbody guitars in Eureka, California.

Langejans Guitars

1971-present. Premium grade, production/custom, flat-top, 12-string, and classical guitars built by luthier Delwyn Langejans in Holland, Michigan.

Larrivee

1968-present. Professional and premium grade, production/custom, acoustic, acoustic/electric, and classical guitars built in Vancouver, British Columbia and, since '01, in Oxnard, California. Founded by Jean Larrivee, who apprenticed under Edgar Monch in Toronto. He built classical guitars in his home from '68-'70 and built his first steel string guitar in '71. Moved company to Victoria, BC in '77 and to Vancouver in '82. In '83, he began building solidbody electric guitars until '89, when focus again returned to acoustics.

Up to 2002, Larrivee used the following model designations: 05 Mahogany Standard, 09 Rosewood Standard, 10 Deluxe, 19 Special, 50 & 60 Standard (unique inlay), 70 Deluxe, and 72 Presentation. Starting in '03 designations used are: 01 Parlor, 03 Standard, 05 Select Mahogany, 09 Rosewood Artist, 10 Rosewood Deluxe, 19 California Anniv. Special Edition Series, 50 Traditional Series, 60 Traditional Series, E = Electric, R = Rosewood.

00-10

2000s. 00-size 14" lower bout, spruce top, rosewood back and sides, gloss finish.

2000s		$1,400	$1,500

C-10 Deluxe

Late-1980s-1990s. Sitka spruce top, Indian rosewood back and sides, sharp cutaway, fancy binding.

1980s		$1,600	$1,900

C-72 Presentation

1990s. Spruce top, Indian rosewood back and sides, non-cut Style D, ultra-fancy abalone and pearl hand-engraved headstock.

1990s	Jester headstock	$2,000	$2,500

MODEL YEAR	FEATURES	EXC. COND. LOW	HIGH

C-72 Presentation Cutaway

1990s. Spruce top, Indian rosewood back and sides, sharp cutaway, ultra-fancy abalone and pearl hand-engraved headstock.

1990s	Mermaid headstock	$2,500	$2,900

D-10 Deluxe

1990s-present. Spruce top, rosewood rims, abalone top and soundhole trim.

1995-2007		$1,650	$1,900

D-70 Deluxe

1992		$1,550	$1,900

D-Style Classical

1970s. Rosewood body, unicorn inlays.

1970s		$1,450	$1,800

J-05 12

2000s. Jumbo acoustic-electric 12-string, spruce top, mahogany back and sides.

2000s		$1,100	$1,300

J-70

1990s. Jumbo, Sitka spruce top, solid Indian rosewood back and sides, presentation grade fancy appointments, limited production.

1994		$1,800	$2,000

JV-05 Mahogany Standard

2000s		$1,000	$1,200

L-0 Standard Series

1980s-2000s. Models include L-03 (satin finish), L-05 (mahogany) and L-09 (Indian rosewood).

1980s	L-05	$800	$1,000
1983-1987	L-09	$900	$1,100
1990s	L-03	$600	$700
2000s	L-05	$800	$1,000

L-50

1990s. Solid spruce, solid Indian rosewood.

1990s		$1,600	$1,700

L-72 Presentation Custom

Mid- to late-1990s. Spruce top, Indian rosewood rims, ornate vase and vine inlays.

1996		$3,000	$3,500

OM Series

1990s-2000s.

1990s	OM-10 Custom, rosewood	$1,800	$1,900
2000s	OM-09K	$1,600	$1,700
2000s	OM-V-50	$1,500	$1,600

Parlor Walnut

Early 2000s. Spruce top, solid walnut back and sides.

2002		$500	$600

RS-4 CM Carved Top

1988-1989. Carved top solidbody, curly maple top, single-single-humbucker pickups, sunburst or translucent finishes.

1988-1989		$1,000	$1,250

Larson Brothers

1900-1944. Carl and August Larson emigrated from Sweden to Chicago in the 1880s and apprenticed under E. J. Cubley and Robert Maurer before buying the Maurer & Company out in 1900. They

MODEL		EXC. COND.	
YEAR	FEATURES	LOW	HIGH

built guitars and mandolin orchestra instruments under the Maurer name until the company's demise in 1944. Their house brands were Maurer, Prairie State and Euphonon and they also built for agents Wm. C. Stahl and W. J. Dyer & Bro., adding their brands to the list, including Stetson, a house brand of Dyer. The Larson shop was a two-man operation that was a custom shop, as well as building their standard line of products. One-of-a-kinds are occasionally found. See listings for each brand. For Larson brands serial number lists see The Larsons' Creations Guitars and Mandolins, Centennial Edition.

Laskin

1973-present. Luthier William "Grit" Laskin builds his premium and presentation grade, custom, steel-string, classical, and flamenco guitars in Toronto, Ontario. Many of his instruments feature extensive inlay work.

Laurie Williams Guitars

1983-present. Luthier Laurie Williams builds his premium and presentation grade, custom/production, steel string, classical and archtop guitars on the North Island of New Zealand. He also builds mandolins.

Leach Guitars

1980-present. Luthier Harvey Leach builds his professional and premium grade, custom, flattops, archtops, and solidbody electrics and travel guitars in Cedar Ridge, California. He also builds basses.

Lehmann Stringed Instruments

1971-present. Luthier Bernard Lehmann builds his professional and premium grade, production/custom, flat-top, archtop, classical and Gypsy guitars in Rochester, New York. He also builds lutes, vielles and rebecs.

Lehtela

1993-present. Professional and premium grade, custom/production, acoustic, acoustic/electric, archtop, and solidbody guitars built by luthier Ari Lehtela in Newell, North Carolina. He also builds basses.

Lentz

1975-present. Luthier Scott Lentz builds his professional, premium, and presentation grade, custom/production, solidbody electric guitars in San Marcos, California.

Les Stansell Guitars

1980-present. Luthier Les Stansell builds his premium grade, custom, nylon-string guitars in Pistol River, Oregon.

Levin

1900-1973. Founded by Herman Carlson Levin and located in Gothenburg, Sweden, Levin was best known for their classical guitars, which they also built for other brands, most notably Goya from ca. 1955 to the mid '70s. They also built mandolins and ukes.

Levy-Page Special

1930s. Acoustic guitars likely built by Gibson, having many features of Kalamzoo guitars of the era. Possibly made for a distributor.

Lewis

1981-present. Luthier Michael Lewis builds his premium and presentation grade, custom/production, archtop guitars in Grass Valley, California. He also builds mandolins. Since '94 he has also built guitars under the D'Angelico name.

Linc Luthier

Professional and premium grade, custom/production, electric and acoustic guitars built by luthier Linc Luthier in Upland, California. He also builds basses and double-necks.

Lindberg

Ca. 1950s. Line of guitars produced by Hoyer for Germany's Lindberg music store.

Lindert

1986-present. Luthier Chuck Lindert makes his intermediate and professional grade, production/custom, Art Deco-vibe electric guitars in Chelan, Washington.

Line 6

1996-present. Professional grade, production, imported solidbody and acoustic modeling guitars able to replicate the tones of a variety of instruments. Line 6 also builds effects and amps.

Lion

1960s. One of the brand names of guitars built for others by Egmond in Holland.

Lipe Guitars USA

1983-1989, 2000-present. Custom, professional grade, guitars built in Sunvalley, California by luthier Michael Lipe. He also builds basses.

Liscombe

1992-present. Professional grade, production and limited custom, chambered electric guitars built by luthier Ken Liscombe in Burlington, Ontario, Canada.

Loar

2005-present. Professional grade, production, imported archtop acoustic guitars designed by Greg Rich for The Music Link, which also has Johnson and other brands of instruments.

Leach Franconia

Line 6 Variax 600

Lowden D-32

Maccaferri G-40

MODEL YEAR	FEATURES	EXC. COND. LOW	HIGH

Lollar

1979-present. Luthier Jason Lollar builds his premium grade, production/custom, solidbody and archtop guitars in Vashon, Washington.

Lopez, Abel Garcia

1985-present. Luthier Abel Garcia Lopez builds his premium grade, custom, classical guitars in Mexico.

Loprinzi

1972-present. Professional and premium grade, production/custom, classical and steel-string guitars built in Clearwater, Florida. They also build ukes. Founded by Augustino LoPrinzi and his brother Thomas in New Jersey. The guitar operations were taken over by AMF/Maark Corp. in '73. LoPrinzi left the company and again started producing his own Augustino Guitars, moving his operations to Florida in '78. AMF ceased production in '80, and a few years later, LoPrinzi got his trademarked name back.

Classical
Various models.

1970s	Brazilian rosewood	$1,400	$1,600
1970s	Indian rosewood	$1,050	$1,250
1970s	Mahogany	$700	$850

Lord

Mid-1960s. Acoustic and solidbody electric guitars imported by Halifax.

Acoustic or Electric Soldibody

1960s	Various models	$90	$150

Lotus

Late-1970s-2004. Budget grade acoustic and electric guitars imported originally by Midco International, of Effingham, Illinois, and most recently by Musicorp. They also made basses, banjos and mandolins.

Louis Panormo

Early to mid-1800s. Spanish guitars made in London, England by luthier Louis (Luis) Panormo. He was born in Paris in 1784, and died in 1862.

Lowden

1973-present. Luthier George Lowden builds his premium and presentation grade, production/custom, steel and nylon string guitars in Downpatrick, Northern Ireland. From '80 to '85, he had some models made in Japan.

Flat-Tops
1980s-2000s. Standard models include D, F, O, and S sizes and models 10 thru 32.

1980s	Premium 6-string	$2,000	$2,500
2000s	12-string	$1,400	$1,750
2000s	Premium 6-string	$2,100	$2,500
2000s	Standard 6-string	$1,325	$1,600

MODEL YEAR	FEATURES	EXC. COND. LOW	HIGH

LSR Headless Instruments

1988-present. Professional and premium grade, production/custom, solidbody headless guitars made in Las Vegas, Nevada by Ed Roman. They also make basses.

LTD

1995-present. Intermediate grade, production, Korean-made solidbody guitars offered by ESP. They also offer basses.

Lucas Custom Instruments

1989-present. Premium and presentation grade, production/custom, flat-tops built by luthier Randy Lucas in Columbus, Indiana.

Lucas, A. J.

1990-present. Luthier A. J. Lucas builds his production/custom, classical and steel string guitars in Lincolnshire, England.

Luis Feu de Mesquita

2000-present. Professional and premium grade, custom, acoustic and flat top guitars including Spanish, classical and flamenco built in Toronto, Ontario, Canada by luthier Luis Feu de Mesquita.

Lyle

Ca. 1969-1980. Imported by distributor L.D. Heater of Portland, Oregon. Generally higher quality Japanese-made copies of American designs by unknown manufacturers, but some early ones, at least, were made by Arai and Company. They also had basses and mandolins.

Acoustic or Electric

1969-1980	Various models	$100	$400

Lyon & Healy

In the 1930s, Lyon & Healy was an industry giant. It operated a chain of music stores, and manufactured harps (their only remaining product), pianos, Washburn guitars and a line of brass and wind instruments. See Washburn, American Conservatory, Lakeside, and College brands.

Lyon by Washburn

1990s-present. Budget grade, production, solidbody guitars sold by mass merchandisers such as Target. They also offer basses.

Lyra

1920s. Instruments built by the Oscar Schmidt Co. and possibly others. Most likely a brand made for a distributor.

Lyric

1996-present. Luthier John Southern builds his professional and premium grade, custom, semi-hollow and solidbody guitars in Tulsa, Oklahoma. He also builds basses.

MODEL YEAR	FEATURES	EXC. COND. LOW	HIGH

MODEL YEAR	FEATURES	EXC. COND. LOW	HIGH

M. Campellone Guitars

See listing under Campellone Guitars

Maccaferri

1923-1990. Built by luthier and classical guitarist Mario Maccaferri (b. May 20, 1900, Cento, Italy; d. 1993, New York) in Cento, Italy; Paris, France; New York, New York; and Mount Vernon, New York. Maccaferri was a student of Luigi Mozzani from '11 to '28. His first catalog was in '23, and included a cutaway guitar. He designed Selmer guitars in '31. Maccaferri invented the plastic clothespin during World War II and used that technology to produce plastic ukes starting in '49 and Dow Styron plastic guitars in '53. He made several experimental plastic electrics in the '60s and plastic violins in the late-'80s.

Plastic (Dow Styron)

1950s. Plastic construction, models include Deluxe (archtop, crown logo), Islander (Islander logo), TV Pal (4-string cutaway) and Showtime (Showtime logo).

1950s	Deluxe	$225	$275
1950s	Islander	$225	$250
1950s	Romancer	$225	$250
1950s	Showtime	$225	$250
1950s	TV Pal	$175	$200

Madeira

Late-1970s. Imports serviced and distributed exclusively by Guild Guitars.

Acoustic

1970s-1980s. Acoustic dreadnoughts all with spruce top, models include A-7 (brown mahogany, lowest model), A-12A (12-string, mahogany), A-14 (mahogany), A-14-12 (12-string, mahogany), A-15B (mahogany, all black finish), A-16 (rosewood), A-17M (maple), A-25 (mahogany), A-30M (maple), A-35 (rosewood), A-75 (rosewood) and P-300 (maple).

1970-1980s	Various models	$200	$600

Electric

1970-1980s	Various models	$250	$400

Magnatone

Ca. 1937-1971. Founded as Dickerson Brothers in Los Angeles, California and known as Magna Electronics from '47, with Art Duhamell president. Brands include Dickerson, Oahu (not all), Gourley, Natural Music Guild, Magnatone. In '59 Magna and Estey merged and in '66 the company relocated to Pennsylvania. In '71, the brand was taken over by a toy company.

Cyclops

1930s. Dobro-made resonator guitar.

1930s	Round neck	$1,400	$1,700
1930s	Square neck	$1,700	$2,100

Mark Series

1955-1960. Solidbody series made by Paul Bigsby in small quantities, then taken over by Paul Barth at Magnatone in '59.

1959-1960	Barth design	$1,100	$1,300

Tornado

1965-1966. Offset double-cut body, 3 DeArmond pickups, vibrato.

1965-1966		$700	$1,000

Typhoon

1965-1966. Double-cut solidbody, 3 DeArmond pickups, vibrato.

1965-1966		$600	$850

Zephyr

1965-1966. Double-cut with 2 DeArmond single-coil pickups, metallic finish, vibrato.

1965-1966		$600	$850

Magno-Tone

1930s. Brand most likely used by a music studio (or distributor) on instruments made by others, including Regal-built resonator instruments.

Mai Kai

1910s. Line of Hawaiian guitars built in Los Angeles by the Shireson Brothers.

Mako

1985-1989. Line of budget to lower-intermediate solidbody guitars from Kaman (Ovation, Hamer). They also offered basses and amps.

Solidbody

1985-1989	Various models	$75	$250

Mal n' Sal

See listing for Alternative Guitar and Amplifier Company.

Manuel & Patterson

1993-present. Luthiers Joe Manuel and Phil Patterson build professional, premium and presentation grade, production/custom, flat-top, archtop and solidbody electric guitars in Abita Springs, Louisiana. They also offer mandolins.

Manuel Contreras

1962-1994. Luthier Manuel Gonzalez Contreras worked with José Ramírez III, before opening his own shop in Madrid, Spain, in '62.

Classical or Flamenco

1960-1970s	Higher-end	$2,900	$3,500

Guitarra de Estudio

1970s. Designed as a student model, but with solid cedar top and solid mahogany back and sides.

1970s		$450	$550

Manuel Contreras II

1986-present. Professional grade, production/custom, nylon-string guitars made in Madrid, Spain, by luthier Pablo Contreras, son of Manuel.

C5

1990s-2000s. Solid close-grained cedar top, Indian rosewood back and sides.

1990-2007		$1,200	$1,500

Manuel & Patterson Old Time special

Manuel Contreras II Double Top

Manzer Studio

Maple Lake 2611c

MODEL YEAR	FEATURES	EXC. COND. LOW	HIGH

Manuel Ramirez

See listing under Ramirez, Manuel.

Manuel Rodriguez and Sons, S.L.

1905-present. Professional, premium, and presentation grade, custom flat-top and nylon-string guitars from Madrid, Spain.

Manuel Velázquez

1933-present. Luthier Manuel Velázquez has built his classical guitars in Puerto Rico ('72-'82), New York City, Virginia, and Florida. His son and daughter now build guitars with him.

Manzanita Guitars

1993-present. Custom, steel-string, Hawaiian, and resonator guitars built by luthiers Manfred Pietrzok and Moritz Sattler in Rosdorf, Germany.

Manzer Guitars

1976-present. Luthier Linda Manzer builds her premium and presentation grade, custom, steel-string, nylon-string, and archtop guitars in Toronto, Ontario.

Maple Lake

2003-present. Intermediate grade, production, flat-top and acoustic/electric imported guitars from luthier Abe Wechter. Wechter also builds guitars under his own name.

Mapson

1995-present. Luthier James L. Mapson builds his premium and presentation grade, production/custom, archtops in Santa Ana, California.

Marc Silber Guitar Company

1998-present. Intermediate and professional grade, production, flat-top, nylon-string, and Hawaiian guitars designed by Marc Silber and made in Mexico. These were offered under the K & S Guitars and/or Silber brands for 1992-'98. Silber also has ukuleles.

Marchione Guitars

1993-present. Premium and presentation grade, custom, archtops and solidbodies built by Stephen Marchione originally in New York City, but currently in Houston, Texas.

Marcia

1920s. Instruments built by the Oscar Schmidt Co. and possibly others. Most likely a brand made for a distributor.

Marco Polo

1960-ca. 1964. Imported from Japan by Harry Stewart and the Marco Polo Company of Santa Ana, California. One of the first American distributors to advertise inexpensive Japanese guitars

MODEL YEAR	FEATURES	EXC. COND. LOW	HIGH

and basses. Manufacturers unknown, but some acoustics by Suzuki, some electrics by Guyatone.

Acoustic Hollowbody

| 1960-1964 | Various models | $75 | $200 |

Mark Wescott Guitars

1980-present. Premium grade, custom, flat-tops, built by luthier Mark Wescott in Somers Point, New Jersey.

Marling

Ca. 1975. Budget line guitars and basses marketed by EKO of Recanati, Italy; probably made by them, although possibly imported.

Acoustic

1975. Includes the steel-string S.110, and the dreadnoughts W.354 Western, and W.356 Western.

| 1975 | | $75 | $125 |

Electric Soldibody

1975. Includes the E.400 (semi-acoustic/electric), E.490 (solidbody), E.480 (single-cut-style), and the 460 (Manta-style).

| 1975 | | $100 | $200 |

Martelle

1934. Private brand attributed to Gibson and some to Kay.

De Luxe

1934. Gibson 12-fret round shoulder Jumbo construction, mahogany back and sides, sunburst, Hawaiian or Spanish option.

| 1934 | | $9,000 | $11,000 |

Martin

1833-present. Intermediate, professional, premium, and presentation grade, production/custom, acoustic, acoustic/electric, archtop and resonator guitars. Founded in New York City by Christian Frederick Martin, former employee of J. Staufer in Vienna, Austria. Moved to Nazareth, Pennsylvania in 1839. Early guitars were made in the European style, many made with partners John Coupa, Charles Bruno and Henry Schatz. Scalloped X-bracing was introduced in the late-1840s. The dreadnought was introduced in 1916 for the Oliver Ditson Company, Boston; and Martin introduced their own versions in 1931.

Martin model size and shape are indicated by the letter prefix (e.g., 0, 00, 000, D, etc.); materials and ornamentation are indicated by number, with the higher the number, the fancier the instrument (e.g., 18, 28, 35, etc.). Martin offered electric thinline guitars from '61-'68 and electric solidbodies from '78-'82. The Martin Shenandoah was made in Asia and assembled in U.S. Japanese Martin Sigma ('72-'73) and Korean Martin Stinger ('85 on) imported solidbodies.

Most Martin flat-top guitars, particularly Style 18 and above, came with a standard natural finish, therefore Martin guitar finish coloring is generally not mentioned because it is assumed to be see-through natural. Conversely, Gibson's standard

MODEL YEAR	FEATURES	EXC. COND. LOW	HIGH

finish for their flat-tops during their Golden Era was sunburst. Martin introduced their shaded (sunburst) finish as an option on their Style 18 in 1934 and their Style 28 in 1931. An original Martin shaded factory (sunburst) finish from the 1930's is worth 40% more than the value shown in the Price Guide. A shaded finish option in the 1940s adds 30%, in the 1950s it adds 20%, and in the 1960s it adds 20%. A refinished guitar with a sunburst finish is not included in this analysis, in fact a refinished guitar is generally worth less than one-half that of an original finish guitar. In particular, a refinished sunburst guitar would be worth one-half the value of an original natural finish guitar. The amount of added value associated with a shaded (sunburst) finish for a guitar made between the 1930s and the 1960s also depends on the model. A Style 18 model shaded finish option is more common than some of the other styles, and D-body, OM-body, and 000-body styles can have different premiums for a shaded finish. Braced for steel strings specifications described under certain models are based on current consensus information and data provided by the late Martin employee-historian Mike Longworth, and is for guidance only. Variations from these specs have been found, so "bracing" should be considered on a case-by-case basis.

0-15

1935, 1940-1943, 1948-1961. All mahogany, unbound rosewood 'board, slotted peghead and 12-fret neck until '34, solid peghead and 14-fret neck thereafter, natural mahogany.

1935	2 made, maple/birch	$2,400	$2,800
1940-1943		$2,100	$2,300
1948-1949		$1,900	$2,100
1950-1959		$1,700	$1,850
1960-1961		$1,550	$1,650

0-15 T

1960-1963. Tenor with Style 15 appointments, natural mahogany.

1960-1963		$1,025	$1,100

0-16

1961 only. Six made.

1961		$1,925	$2,100

0-16 NY

1961-1995. Mahogany back and sides, 12 frets, slotted peghead, unbound extra-wide rosewood 'board, natural.

1961-1969		$1,800	$2,100
1970-1979		$1,500	$1,850
1980-1989		$1,450	$1,750
1990-1995		$1,450	$1,750

0-17

1906-1917, 1929-1948, 1966-1968. First version has mahogany back and sides, 3 black soundhole rings, rosewood bound back, unbound ebony 'board, 12 frets, slotted peghead. Second version ('29 and on) is all mahogany, 3 white-black-white soundhole rings, top bound until '30, thin black backstripe, 12 frets and slotted peghead until '34, solid peghead and 14 frets

thereafter, natural mahogany.

1906-1917	Gut braces	$1,900	$2,200
1929-1934	Bar frets, 12 fret-style	$2,400	$2,800
1934-1939	T-frets, 14 fret-style	$2,500	$2,900
1940-1945		$2,400	$2,700
1946-1948		$2,200	$2,400
1966-1968	7 made	$1,900	$2,200

0-17 H

1930, 1935-1941. Hawaiian, mahogany back and sides, 12 frets clear of body, natural.

1930	60 made	$2,400	$2,800
1935-1941		$2,500	$2,900

0-17 S

Early 1930s. Limited production style 17 with spruce top, unique 'guard.

1931		$3,800	$4,200

0-17 T

1932-1960. Mahogany back and sides, tenor, natural.

1932-1949		$1,500	$1,600
1950-1960	Mahogany	$1,500	$1,600

0-18

1898-1996. Rosewood back and sides until 1917, mahogany back and sides after, Adirondack spruce top until 1946, slotted peghead and 12 frets until 1934, solid peghead and 14 frets after 1934, braced for steel strings in 1923, improved neck in late-1934, non-scalloped braces appear late-'44, natural.

1898-1917	Brazilian rosewood	$3,200	$3,800
1918-1922	Mahogany, gut braces	$2,700	$3,200
1923-1939	Steel braces	$3,300	$4,000
1940-1944	Scalloped braces	$3,100	$3,800
1945-1949		$2,800	$3,500
1950-1959		$2,525	$2,825
1960-1969		$2,500	$2,800
1970-1979		$1,900	$2,200
1980-1990s		$1,200	$1,500

0-18 G

1960s. Special order classical nylon-string model, natural.

1961		$1,300	$1,500

0-18 K

1918-1935. Hawaiian, all koa wood, T-frets and steel T-bar neck in late-1934, natural.

1918-1922		$2,800	$3,300
1923-1927		$3,000	$3,400
1928-1935		$3,200	$4,000

0-18 T

1929-1995. Mahogany body, spruce top, tenor, natural.

1929-1939		$2,000	$2,400
1940-1959		$1,900	$2,100
1960-1964		$1,850	$2,200
1965-1969		$1,400	$1,500
1970-1979		$1,200	$1,300
1980-1989		$1,100	$1,200
1990-1995		$1,000	$1,100

Marchione Neck-Through

1936 Martin 0-17

Martin 0-28 Ian Anderson

1936 Martin 00-18

0-21

1898-1948. Rosewood back and sides, Adirondack spruce top until 1946, 12 frets, braced for steel strings in 1923, T-frets and steel T-bar neck in late-1934, non-scalloped braces in late-1944, natural.

MODEL YEAR	FEATURES	EXC. COND. LOW	HIGH
1898-1926	Gut braces	$4,600	$5,500
1927-1943	Steel braces	$5,000	$6,000
1944-1948	Non-scalloped	$4,000	$5,000

0-26

1850-1890. Rosewood back and sides, ivory-bound top, rope-style purfling.

1850-1890		$4,800	$5,700

0-27

1850-1898. Rosewood back and sides, ivory-bound top.

1850-1859	Antique market value	$6,500	$8,000
1890-1898		$5,000	$6,000

0-28

1870s-1931, 1937 (6 made), 1969 (1 made). Brazilian rosewood back and sides, braced for steel strings in 1923, herringbone binding until 1937, natural.

1870-1927		$5,500	$6,800
1928-1931		$6,300	$7,800

0-28 Ian Anderson

2004. Adirondack spruce top, scalloped bracing, Indian rosewood sides and back, slotted headstock, gloss natural finish, limited edition 87 made.

2004		$2,700	$3,100

0-28 K

1917-1931, 1935. Hawaiian, all koa wood, braced for steel strings in '23, natural.

1917	Spruce top option	$6,000	$6,900
1917-1924	Figured koa	$6,000	$6,900
1925-1931	Steel braces	$6,300	$7,800

0-28 T

1930-1931. Tenor neck.

1930-1931		$3,500	$3,700

0-30

1899-1921. Brazilian rosewood back and sides, ivory-bound body, neck and headstock.

1899-1921		$5,600	$7,000

0-34

1880s. Brazilian rosewood.

1880s		$6,000	$7,100

0-42

1870s-1942. Brazilian rosewood back and sides, 12 frets, natural.

1890-1926	Gut braces	$14,500	$15,000
1927-1930	Steel braces	$15,500	$19,000

0-45

1904-1939. Brazilian rosewood back and sides, natural, special order only for '31-'39.

1904-1928	Gut braces	$33,000	$40,000
1929-1930	Steel braces	$38,000	$45,000

00-15

2005		$600	$650

00-16 C

1962-1977, 1980-1981. Classical, mahogany back and sides, 5-ply bound top, satin finish, 12 frets, slotted peghead, natural.

1962-1969		$1,150	$1,400

MODEL YEAR	FEATURES	EXC. COND. LOW	HIGH
1970-1977		$1,100	$1,300
1980-1981	2 made	$1,100	$1,300

00-16 DBFM

2006. Women In Music model, 104 made, 00 size, slotted headstock, flamed maple back.

2006		$1,150	$1,350

00-17

1908-1917, 1930-1960, 1982-1988, 2000-2003. Mahogany back and sides, 12 frets and slotted headstock until '34, solid headstock and 14 frets after '34, natural mahogany, reissued in 2000 with a high gloss finish.

1908-1917	Limited production	$2,300	$2,900
1930-1939		$2,900	$3,500
1940-1944		$2,600	$3,200
1945-1949		$2,400	$2,600
1950-1960		$2,000	$2,300
2000-2003	Reissue model	$1,100	$1,125

00-17 H

1934-1935. Hawaiian set-up, mahogany body, no binding.

1934-1935		$2,900	$3,500

00-17 SO Sing Out!

2000. Limited edition, commemorates the 50th anniversary of Sing Out Magazine, folk era logo inlays including Liberty Bell, folk hammer, and SING OUT inlay on 20th fret, mahogany body, natural gloss finish over mahogany top.

2000		$1,300	$1,375

00-18

1898-1995. Rosewood back and sides until 1917, mahogany after, braced for steel strings in 1923, improved neck in late-1934, war-time design changes 1942-1946, non-scalloped braces in late-1944, Adirondack spruce top until 1946, natural.

1898-1917	Rosewood	$4,500	$5,600
1918-1922	Mahogany	$4,000	$5,000
1923-1939	Steel braces in '23	$5,500	$6,500
1940-1941		$5,200	$6,300
1942-1943	Ebony rod	$5,000	$6,200
1944	Scalloped braces early '44	$4,600	$5,700
1944-1946	Non-scalloped	$3,700	$4,100
1947-1949		$3,200	$3,900
1950-1952		$3,000	$3,200
1953-1959		$2,700	$3,100
1960-1962		$2,700	$3,000
1963-1965		$2,700	$3,000
1966	Black guard late '66	$2,600	$2,700
1966	Tortoise guard early '66	$2,700	$3,000
1967		$2,600	$2,700
1968		$2,600	$2,700
1969		$2,500	$2,600
1970-1979		$1,900	$2,400
1980-1989		$1,200	$1,500
1990-1995		$1,100	$1,300

MODEL YEAR	FEATURES	EXC. COND. LOW	HIGH
00-18 C			

1962-1995. Renamed from 00-18 G in '62, mahogany back and sides, classical, 12 frets, slotted headstock, natural.

MODEL YEAR	FEATURES	EXC. COND. LOW	HIGH
1962-1969		$1,400	$1,500
1970-1979		$1,200	$1,400
00-18 E			

1959-1964. Flat top Style 18, single neck pickup and 2 knobs, heavier bracing, natural.

1959-1964		$2,500	$3,000
00-18 G			

1936-1962. Mahogany back and sides, classical, natural, renamed 00-18 C in '62.

1936-1939		$1,900	$2,300
1940-1949		$1,600	$1,950
1950-1962		$1,350	$1,550
00-18 Gruhn Limited Edition			

1995. Sitka spruce top, C-shaped neck profile, 25 made.

1995		$1,600	$2,000
00-18 H			

1935-1941. Hawaiian, mahogany back and sides, 12 frets clear of body, natural. The Price Guide is generally for all original instruments. The H conversion is an exception, because converting from H (Hawaiian-style) to 00-18 specs is considered by some to be a favorable improvement and something that adds value.

1935-1941		$5,200	$6,500
1935-1941	Converted to Spanish	$5,500	$6,500
00-18 K			

1918-1934. All koa wood.

1918-1934		$6,000	$7,500
00-18 SH Steve Howe			

1999-2000. Limited edition run of 250.

1999-2000		$2,500	$2,600
00-18 V			

2003-present. Mahogany back and sides, spruce top, Vintage Series.

2003-2007		$1,400	$1,600
00-21			

1898-1996. Brazilian rosewood back and sides, changed to Indian rosewood in 1970, dark outer binding, unbound ebony 'board until 1947, rosewood from 1947, slotted diamond inlays until 1944, dot after, natural.

1898-1926	Gut braces	$6,000	$6,600
1927-1931	Steel braces in '27	$7,000	$8,400
1932-1939		$6,700	$8,200
1940-1944	Scalloped braces	$6,500	$7,900
1944-1949	Non-scalloped	$5,300	$5,900
1950-1959		$5,100	$5,700
1960-1965		$4,600	$5,300
1966-1969	Brazilian rosewood, black guard	$4,300	$5,300
1970-1996	Indian rosewood	$1,800	$2,000

MODEL YEAR	FEATURES	EXC. COND. LOW	HIGH
00-21 Custom			

2005-2006. Custom order size 00 style 21, Brazilian rosewood sides and back.

2005-2006		$2,700	$3,100
00-21 Golden Era			

1998. Limited edition, Adirondack spruce top, scalloped braces, rosewood back and sides.

1998		$2,400	$2,500
00-21 H			

Special order limited production Hawaiian.

1914	1 made	$6,600	$7,000
1952	1 made	$6,600	$7,000
1955	1 made	$6,600	$7,000
00-21 NY			

1961-1965. Brazilian rosewood back and sides, no inlay, natural.

1961-1965		$4,500	$4,800
00-21 S			

1968. Slotted headstock, Brazilian rosewood sides and back.

1968		$4,900	$5,500
00-28			

1898-1941, 1958 (1 made), 1977 (1 made), 1984 (2 made). Brazilian rosewood back and sides, changed to Indian rosewood in 1977, herringbone purfling through 1941, white binding and unbound 'board after 1941, no inlays before 1901, diamond inlays from 1901-'41, dot after, natural.

1898-1924	Gut braces	$14,000	$16,000
1925-1931	Steel braces in '25	$17,000	$21,000
1932-1941	Special order	$17,000	$21,000
1958	Special order	$3,300	$3,700
00-28 C			

1966-1995. Renamed from 00-28 G, Brazilian rosewood back and sides, changed to Indian rosewood in '70, classical, 12 frets, natural.

1966-1969	Brazilian rosewood	$4,000	$4,200
1970-1979	Indian rosewood	$1,800	$2,000
00-28 G			

1936-1962. Brazilian rosewood back and sides, classical, natural, reintroduced as 00-28 C in '66.

1936-1939		$5,000	$5,500
1940-1949		$4,500	$5,000
1951-1962		$3,900	$4,900
00-28 K Hawaiian			

1919-1921, 1926-1933. Koa back and sides, Hawaiian set-up.

1919-1921	34 made	$6,700	$7,000
1926-1933	1 made per year	$8,000	$9,000
00-37 K2 Steve Miller			

2001. All koa 12-fret style 00. The 00-37K SM has a spruce top. 68 made of each version.

2001		$4,500	$4,700
00-40 H			

1928-1939. Hawaiian, Brazilian rosewood back and sides, 12 frets clear of body, natural. H models are sometimes converted to standard Spanish setup, in higher-end models this can make the instrument more valuable to some people.

1928-1939		$14,000	$17,000
1928-1939	Converted to Spanish	$14,500	$18,000

Martin 00-18V

1929 Martin 00-40H

Martin 000-1 Series

1953 Martin 000-21

MODEL YEAR	FEATURES	EXC. COND. LOW	HIGH
00-40 K			
Few were made (only 6), figured koa, natural.			
1918	1 made	$24,000	$26,000
1930	5 made	$19,000	$23,000
00-41 Custom			
2005		$3,900	$4,100
00-42			
1898-1942, 1973 (one made), 1994-1996. Brazilian rosewood back and sides, Indian rosewood in 1973, pearl top borders, 12 frets, ivory bound peghead until 1918, ivoroid binding after 1918, natural.			
1898-1926	Gut braces	$16,500	$19,000
1927-1942	Steel braces	$20,000	$24,000
1973	1 made	$2,700	$3,300
1994-1996		$2,300	$2,800
00-42 K			
1919. Koa body, 1 made.			
1919		$25,000	$26,000
00-44 Soloist/Olcott-Bickford Artist Model			
1913-1939. Custom-made in small quantities, Brazilian rosewood, ivory or faux-ivory-bound ebony 'board.			
1913-1939	6 made	$32,000	$38,000
00-45			
1904-1938, 1970-1995. Brazilian rosewood back and sides, changed to Indian rosewood in '70, 12 frets and slotted headstock until '34 and from '70 on 14 frets, and solid headstock from '34-'70, natural.			
1904-1927	Gut braces	$45,000	$53,000
1928-1938	Steel braces	$49,000	$60,000
1970-1979	Reintroduced	$3,300	$3,400
00-45 K			
1919. Koa body, 1 made.			
1919		$45,000	$53,000
00-45 S Limited Edition			
2003. 1902 vintage-pattern with fancy inlays, 00 size style 45, 50 made.			
2003		$11,500	$12,500
00-45 Stauffer Commemorative Limited Edition			
1997. Stauffer six-on-a-side headstock, 45-style appointments, 00-size body, Sitka spruce top, Brazilian rosewood back and sides.			
1997		$8,500	$9,500
000-1 Series			
1995-2005. Solid spruce top with laminated mahogany (000-1) or Indian rosewood (000-1R) sides.			
1995-2002	Indian rosewood	$700	$850
1996-2005	Mahogany	$650	$750
000-15 Auditorium			
1997-present. All solid wood mahogany body, dot markers, natural.			
1997-2000s		$550	$600
000-15 S			
2000. Slotted headstock.			
2000		$800	$850

MODEL YEAR	FEATURES	EXC. COND. LOW	HIGH
000-16 Series			
1989-2000s. Acoustic, mahogany back and sides, diamonds and squares inlaid, sunburst, name changed to 000-16 T Auditorium with higher appointments in '96, in 2000-2005 slotted (000-16 S) and gloss finish (000-16 SGT) were offered.			
1989-1995	000-16	$900	$1,000
1996-1997	000-16 T	$850	$875
2003-2004	000-16 SGT	$875	$900
000-18			
1911-present (none in 1932-1933). Rosewood back and sides until '17, mahogany back and sides from '17, longer scale in '24-'34, 12 frets clear of body until '33, changed to 14 frets in '34. Improved neck late-'34, war-time changes '41-'46, non-scalloped braces in late-'44, switched from Adirondack spruce to Sitka spruce top in '46 (though some Adirondack tops in '50s and '60s), natural. Now called the 000-18 Auditorium.			
1924-1927	12-fret	$13,000	$16,000
1928-1931	12-fret	$15,000	$18,000
1934-1939	Natural	$14,000	$17,000
1940-1941	Natural	$11,000	$12,500
1942-1944	Scalloped braces	$10,000	$12,500
1944-1946	Non-scalloped	$5,500	$6,200
1947-1949	Natural	$5,500	$6,200
1950-1952	Natural	$4,600	$4,900
1953-1959		$4,100	$4,400
1960-1962		$3,400	$4,000
1963-1965		$3,300	$3,600
1966	Black guard late '66	$2,800	$2,900
1966	Tortoise guard early '66	$2,900	$3,000
1967	Last of maple bridgeplate	$2,800	$3,000
1968		$2,500	$3,000
1969		$2,700	$2,800
1970-1979		$2,000	$2,500
1980-1989		$1,400	$1,700
1990-1999		$1,300	$1,600
2000-2007		$1,200	$1,400
000-18 GE			
2006		$2,200	$2,350
000-18 WG Woody Guthrie			
1999. Signed label including artwork and model identification.			
1999		$1,900	$2,200
000-21			
1902-1924 (22 made over that time), 1931(2), 1938-1959, 1965 (1), 1979 (12). Brazilian rosewood back and sides, changed to Indian rosewood in '70, natural.			
1902-1937	Low production mostly gut	$18,000	$20,000
1938-1941	Pre-war specs	$16,000	$19,000
1942-1944	Ebony rod, scalloped braces	$11,000	$13,500
1944-1946	Non-scalloped	$8,500	$9,500
1947-1949	Herringbone, non-scalloped	$6,400	$7,000
1950-1952		$5,700	$6,000
1953-1958		$5,300	$5,700

MODEL YEAR	FEATURES	EXC. COND. LOW	HIGH
1959		$5,200	$5,500
1965	1 made	$5,100	$5,500
1979	12 made	$1,800	$1,900

000-28

1902-present. Brazilian rosewood back and sides, changed to Indian rosewood in '70, herringbone purfling through '41, white binding and unbound 'board after '41, no inlays before '01, slotted diamond inlays from '01-'44, dot after, 12 frets until '32, 14 frets '31 on (both 12 and 14 frets were made during '31-'32), natural.

MODEL YEAR	FEATURES	EXC. COND. LOW	HIGH
1902-1927	Gut/nylon braces	$26,000	$31,000
1928-1938	Steel braces	$32,000	$38,000
1939		$29,000	$35,000
1940-1941		$26,000	$31,000
1942-1944	Scalloped braces	$24,000	$30,000
1945-1946	Herringbone, non-scalloped	$21,000	$25,000
1947-1949	Start of non-herringbone '47	$10,000	$12,500
1950-1952		$9,000	$11,000
1953-1958	Last of Kluson early '58	$8,500	$9,500
1958-1959	Grover tuners late '58	$8,000	$9,000
1960-1962		$7,000	$7,500
1963-1965		$6,100	$7,300
1966	Black guard late '66	$6,000	$7,100
1966	Tortoise guard early '66	$6,100	$7,200
1967	Last of maple bridgeplate	$6,000	$7,000
1968	Rosewood bridge plate	$5,800	$6,600
1969	Last of Brazilian rosewood	$5,000	$6,100
1970-1979	Indian rosewood	$2,000	$2,200
1980-1989	Indian rosewood	$1,500	$2,100
1990-1999	Indian rosewood	$1,500	$1,700
2000-2007		$1,500	$1,600

000-28 C

1962-1969. Brazilian rosewood back and sides, classical, slotted peghead, natural.

1962-1969		$3,700	$4,600

000-28 EC Eric Clapton Signature

1996-present. Sitka spruce top, Indian rosewood back and sides, herringbone trim, natural.

1996-1999		$1,900	$2,200
2000-2007		$2,200	$2,300

000-28 ECB Eric Clapton Brazilian

2003. Limited edition, 2nd edition of EC Signature Series with Brazilian rosewood.

2003		$6,400	$6,600

000-28 G

1937-1955. Special order classical guitar, very limited production.

1937-1940	3 made	$7,800	$9,700
1946-1949	10 made	$6,000	$7,500
1950-1955	4 made	$4,700	$5,700

000-28 Golden Era

1996 only. Sitka spruce top, rosewood back and sides, scalloped braces, herringbone trim, 12-fret model, natural.

1996		$3,000	$3,400

000-28 H

2000-2001. Herringbone top trim.

2000-2001		$1,700	$1,825

000-28 HB Brazilian 1937 Reissue

1997. Pre-war specs including scalloped bracing, Brazilian rosewood.

1997		$5,400	$5,600

000-28 K

1921. Non-catalog special order model, only 2 known to exist, koa top, back and sides.

1921		$28,000	$35,000

000-28 VS

2006. VS Vintage Series, spruce top with aging toner and scalloped bracing, rosewood (not Brazilian) sides and back, slotted diamond markers, ebony pyramid bridge, herringbone top trim, nickel Waverly butterbean tuners.

2006		$2,300	$2,450

000-40

1909. Ivoroid bound top and back, snowflake inlay, 1 made.

1909		$36,000	$45,000

000-40 Q2GN Graham Nash

2003. Limited edition of 147 guitars, quilted mahogany top/back/sides, flying-heart logo on headstock, Graham Nash signature on frets 18-20.

2003		$2,800	$3,000

000-41

1996. Custom shop style 000-41.

1996		$2,600	$2,900

000-42

1918, 1921-1922, 1925, 1930, 1934, 1938-1943. Brazilian rosewood back and sides, natural.

1918-1934	Special order	$40,000	$48,000
1938-1943		$45,000	$55,000
2003	Indian rosewood, 12-fret	$3,700	$4,400

000-42 EC Eric Clapton

1995. Style 45 pearl-inlaid headplate, ivoroid bindings, Eric Clapton signature, 24.9" scale, flat top, sunburst top price is $8320 ('95 price), only 461 made.

1995		$8,300	$8,500

000-42 ECB Eric Clapton

1995	Brazilian rosewood	$12,000	$13,000

000-45

1906, 1911-1914, 1917-1919, 1922-1942, 1971-1993. Brazilian rosewood back and sides, changed to Indian rosewood in '70, 12-fret neck and slotted headstock until '34 (but 7 were made in '70 and 1 in '75), 14-fret neck and solid headstock after '34, natural.

1906-1919		$65,000	$80,000
1922-1927	Gut braces	$81,000	$95,000
1928-1929	Steel braces	$80,000	$95,000
1930-1933		$90,000	$105,000

1927 Martin 000-28

1957 Martin 000-28

1928 Martin 000-45

*1928 Martin 000-45 S
Stephen Stills*

MODEL YEAR	FEATURES	LOW	HIGH
1934-1936	14 frets, C.F.M. inlaid	$97,000	$115,000
1937-1939		$90,000	$110,000
1940-1942		$90,000	$105,000

000-45 JR Jimmie Rodgers Golden Era
1997. Adirondack spruce top, Brazilian rosewood back and sides, scalloped high X-braces, abalone trim, natural, 100 made.

1997		$10,500	$12,500

000-45 S Stephen Stills
2005. Only 91 made.

2005		$7,700	$9,500

000C David Gray Custom
2005-2006. Custom Artist Edition, 000-size cutaway, Italian spruce top, mahogany back and sides, interior label signed by David Gray.

2005-2006		$2,000	$2,100

000C DB Dion The Wanderer
2002. Only 57 made, cutaway acoustic/electric, gloss black finish, Sitka spruce top, scalloped bracing, mahogany sides and back, slotted diamond and square markers, Dion logo on headstock.

2002		$2,300	$2,350

000C Series
1990-present. French-style small soft cutaway (like vintage Selmer), models include; 000C-1E (mahogany body) and 000C-16RGTE (premium, rosewood body).

1990-1995	000C-16	$1,100	$1,200
1996-2000	000C-1E	$1,000	$1,100
2001-2007	000C-16 RGTE	$1,200	$1,300
2004	000C-16 SRNE	$1,300	$1,400

000CXE
2002-present. Acoustic-electric, rounded cutaway, high pressure laminated body, black finish.

2002-2007		$475	$500

000-ECHF Bellezza Nera
2005. Limited edition Eric Clapton and Hiroshi Fujiwara Black Beauty Model, 476 made, Italian Alpine spruce top, Indian rosewood sides and back, black finish, white/blond option.

2005	Black	$3,300	$3,500
2005	White/blond option	$3,000	$3,300

000-JBP Jimmy Buffett Pollywog
2003. Model name and number on label inside back.

2003		$2,200	$2,400

000-M Mahogany Auditorium
2004. Auditorium 000-size, mahogany sides and back.

2004		$700	$725

0000 Custom

2006		$2,250	$2,350

0000-18 Gruhn 35th Anniversary Model
2005. Limited production 0000-size, Golden Era 18 styling.

2005		$2,450	$2,700

0000-28 Series
1997-2000. Several models, jumbo-size 0000 cutaway body, models include; H (herringbone trim), Custom (Indian rosewood, sitka spruce top), H-AG (Arlo Guthrie 30th anniversary, Indian rosewood back and sides, only 30 made), H Custom Shop (herringbone).

1997-2000	0000-28 H	$2,000	$2,300
1998	0000-28 Custom	$2,700	$3,100
1999	0000-28 H-AG	$3,700	$4,300

0000-38 Series
1997-2002. 0000-size, rosewood sides and back, replaced M-38.

1997-2002		$1,925	$2,100

1-17
1906-1917 (1st version), 1931-1934 (2nd version). First version has spruce top, mahogany back and sides, second version has all mahogany with flat natural finish.

1906-1917		$1,900	$2,200
1930-1934		$2,400	$2,800

1-17 P
1928-1931. Mahogany back and sides, plectrum neck, 272 made.

1928-1931		$2,100	$2,500

1-18
1899-1927. Brazilian rosewood or mahogany back and sides.

1918-1927	Mahogany	$2,400	$2,700

1-21
1860-1926. Initially offered in size 1 in the 1860s, ornate soundhole rings.

1860	Antique market value	$5,700	$7,000
1890		$4,500	$5,000
1900-1926		$4,000	$4,600

1-22

1855	Antique market value	$6,500	$8,000

1-26
1850-1890. Rosewood back and sides, ivory-bound top, rope-style purfling.

1855	Antique market value	$6,600	$8,100
1890		$4,800	$5,700

1-27
1880-1907.

1880-1907		$5,000	$6,000

1-28
1880-1923. Style 28 appointments including Brazilian rosewood back and sides.

1880	Antique market value	$6,700	$8,200
1890		$5,000	$6,000

1-30
1860s. Size 1 Style 30 with pearl soundhole trim, cedar neck.

1860s	Antique market value	$6,500	$9,000

1-42
1858-1919. Rosewood back and sides, ivory-bound top and 'board.

1858-1919		$12,500	$14,000

The *Vintage Guitar Price Guide* shows low to high values for items in all-original excellent condition, and, where applicable, with original case or cover.

MODEL YEAR	FEATURES	EXC. COND. LOW	HIGH
1-45			
1904-1919. Only 6 made, slotted headstock and Style 45 appointments.			
1904-1919		$26,000	$31,000
2 1/2-17			
1856-1897, 1909-1914. The first Style 17s were small size 2 1/2 and 3, these early models use Brazilian rosewood.			
1850s	Antique market value	$2,300	$2,800
1890s		$2,300	$2,800
1909-1914		$1,900	$2,200
2 1/2-18			
1865-1923. Parlor-size body with Style 18 appointments.			
1865-1898	Antique market value	$2,400	$2,900
1901-1917	Brazilian rosewood	$2,400	$2,900
1918-1923	Mahogany	$2,300	$2,500
2 1/2-42			
Style 42 size 2 1/2 with Brazilian rosewood.			
1880s		$11,500	$13,000
2-15			
1939-1964. All mahogany body, dot markers.			
1939	Special order	$1,500	$2,000
1951		$1,300	$1,500
2-17			
1910, 1922-1938. 1910 version has spruce top, mahogany back and sides. '22 on, all mahogany body, no body binding after '30.			
1910	6 made	$1,900	$2,200
1922-1930		$2,400	$2,800
2-17 H			
1927-1931. Hawaiian, all mahogany, 12 frets clear of body.			
1927-1931		$2,400	$2,800
2-20			
1855-1899. Rare style only offered in size 2.			
1855-1899		$2,800	$3,400
2-21			
1885-1929. Rosewood back and sides, herringbone soundhole ring.			
1890		$4,500	$5,000
1920		$4,000	$4,600
2-24			
1857-1898.			
1850s	Antique market value	$6,500	$8,000
1890s		$4,800	$5,700
2-27			
1857-1907. Brazilian rosewood back and sides, pearl ring, zigzag back stripe, ivory bound ebony 'board and peghead.			
1850s	Antique market value	$6,500	$8,000
1890s		$5,000	$6,000
1900-1907		$4,200	$4,700
2-28 T			
1929-1930. Tenor neck, Brazilian rosewood back and sides, herringbone top purfling.			
1929-1930		$2,500	$2,700

MODEL YEAR	FEATURES	EXC. COND. LOW	HIGH
2-30			
1902-1921. Similar to 2-27.			
1902-1921	7 made	$4,500	$5,000
2-34			
1870-1898. Similar to 2-30.			
1880s		$5,500	$6,500
2-44			
1940. Style 44, Olcott-Bickford Soloist custom order, only 4 made.			
1940		$22,000	$26,000
3-17			
1856-1897, 1908 (one made). The first Style 17s were small size 2 1/2 and 3. The early models use Brazilian rosewood, spruce top, bound back, unbound ebony 'board.			
1856-1889	Brazilian rosewood	$2,400	$3,000
1890-1897		$2,000	$2,400
1908	1 made	$1,800	$2,100
5-15			
2005-2007. Sapele or mahogany body, shorter scale.			
2005-2007		$550	$675
5-15 T			
1949-1963. All mahogany, non-gloss finish, tenor neck.			
1949-1963		$1,050	$1,300
5-17 T			
1927-1949. All mahogany, tenor neck.			
1927-1949		$1,100	$1,325
5-18			
1898-1989. Rosewood back and sides (changed to mahogany from 1917 on), 12 frets, slotted headstock.			
1918-1922	Gut braces, mahogany	$1,800	$2,200
1923-1939	Steel braces in '23	$2,100	$2,500
1940-1944		$2,000	$2,400
1945-1949		$1,900	$2,300
1950-1959		$1,800	$2,200
1960-1969		$1,700	$2,100
1970-1989		$1,200	$1,500
5-21 T			
1926-1928. Tenor guitar with 21-styling.			
1926-1928		$2,200	$2,500
5-28			
2001-2002. Special edition, 1/2-size parlor guitar size 15 with Terz tuning, Indian rosewood back and sides.			
2001-2002		$2,000	$2,500
7-28			
1980-1995, 1997-2002. 7/8-body-size of a D-model, Style 28 appointments.			
1980-1995		$2,000	$2,500
1997-2002		$2,000	$2,500
7-37 K			
1980-1987. 7/8-size baby dreadnought acoustic, koa back and sides, spruce top, oval soundhole.			
1980-1987		$850	$950

1928 Martin 000CXE

Martin 5-28

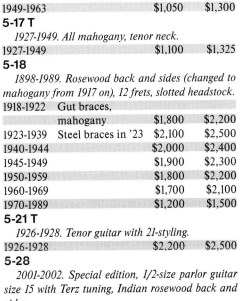

GUITARS

Martin Alternative II Resophonic

Martin Cowboy IV

MODEL		EXC. COND.	
YEAR	FEATURES	LOW	HIGH

Alternative II Resophonic
2004-2007. Textured aluminum top, matching head-stock overlay, high pressure laminate sides and back, spun aluminum cone resonator, Fishman pickup.

2004-2007		$700	$800

Alternative X Midi
2001-2007. Thin 00-size body, solid aluminum top, laminate back and sides, Stratabond aluminate neck, black micarta 'board, micro-dot markers. Roland GK Midi pickup with 13-pin output, additional Fishman Prefix Pro pickup and preamp system, requires Roland GA-20 (or substitute) Midi interface.

2001-2007		$750	$850

ASD-41 Australian Series
2005. Tasmanian Blackwood sides and back, Sitka spruce top, Australian theme appointments and label.

2005		$4,500	$5,000

Backpacker
1994-present. Small-bodied travel guitar, nylon or steel strings.

1994-2007		$100	$165

BC-15E
2004. Natural mahogany top/back/sides, single-cut, on-board electronics.

2004		$1,000	$1,100

C-1
1931-1942. Acoustic archtop, mahogany back and sides, spruce top, round hole until '33, f-holes appear in '32, bound body, sunburst.

1931-1933	Round, 449 made	$2,300	$2,400
1932-1942	F-hole, 786 made	$2,300	$2,400

C-1 R Humphrey
1997-2000. Solid cedar top, laminated rosewood back and sides, satin finish.

1997-2000		$925	$975

C-2
1931-1942. Acoustic archtop, Brazilian rosewood back and sides, carved spruce top, round hole until '33, f-holes appear in '32, zigzag back stripe, multi-bound body, slotted-diamond inlay, sunburst.

1931-1933	Round, 269 made	$3,500	$4,000
1932-1942	F-hole, 439 made	$3,400	$3,900

C-3
1931-1934. Archtop, Brazilian rosewood back and sides, round soundhole until early '33, f-holes after.

1931-1933	Round, 53 made	$5,600	$6,400
1933-1934	F-hole, 58 made	$5,600	$6,400

CEO Series
1997-2006. Chief Executive Officer C.F. Martin IV special editions.

2000-2003	CEO-4, mahogany	$1,350	$1,450
2001-2004	CEO-5, bearclaw top	$1,700	$1,825
2002-2006	CEO-4R, rosewood	$1,550	$1,800

CF-1 American Archtop
2005. 17" body, laminated arched spruce top, X-braced, solid maple sides, laminated arched maple back, maple neck, ebony 'board, dot markers, floating pickup, gold decal.

2005		$2,300	$2,400

MODEL		EXC. COND.	
YEAR	FEATURES	LOW	HIGH

Concept III
2003. U.S.-made, solid spruce top, solid mahogany back and sides, cutaway, on-board electronics, sparkle-mist finish.

2003		$1,625	$1,675

Cowboy Series
2001-present. Inside label identifies model number. Models include Cowboy II (2001, 500 made), Cowboy III ('03, 750 made), and Cowboy IV ('05-'06, 250 made), Cowboy V ('06-'07, 500 made).

2001-2007		$400	$450

C-TSH (Humphrey/Martin)
Late-1990s. Designed by high-end classical guitar luthier Thomas Humphrey for Martin, based on his Millenium model, arched Englemann spruce top, rosewood back and sides.

1998		$2,200	$2,350

Custom Ne Plus Ultra
2005. Very fancy appointments, 0000 M-size body, rhinestone on pearloid peghead.

2005		$4,000	$5,000

D-1
1992-2005. Name first used for the prototype of the D-18, made in 1931, revived for current model with mahogany body, A-frame bracing, available as an acoustic/electric.

1992-1999		$625	$750
2000-2005		$650	$775

D-3-18
1991. Sitka spruce top, 3-piece mahogany back, 80-piece limited edition.

1991		$1,650	$2,000

D12-1
1996-2001. Mahogany, satin finish, 12-string.

1996-2001		$275	$300

D12-18
1973-1995. Mahogany back and sides, 12 strings, 14 frets clear of body, solid headstock.

1973-1979		$1,500	$1,700
1980-1989		$1,400	$1,600
1990-1995		$1,200	$1,400

D12-20
1964-1991. Mahogany back and sides, 12 strings, 12 frets clear of body, slotted headstock.

1964-1969		$1,925	$2,400
1970-1979		$1,400	$1,700
1980-1991		$1,300	$1,500

D12-28
1970-present. Indian rosewood back and sides, 12 strings, 14 frets clear of body, solid headstock.

1970-1979		$1,650	$1,950
1980-1989		$1,500	$1,700
1990-1999		$1,500	$1,675
2000-2007		$1,675	$1,700

D12-35
1965-1995. Brazilian rosewood back and sides, changed to Indian rosewood in '70, 12 strings, 12 frets clear of body, slotted headstock.

1965-1969	Brazilian rosewood	$3,900	$4,100
1970-1979	Indian rosewood	$1,700	$1,950
1980-1989		$1,500	$1,700
1990-1995		$1,500	$1,675

MODEL YEAR	FEATURES	EXC. COND. LOW	HIGH
D12-45			

1970s. Special order instrument, not a standard catalog item, with D-45 appointments, Indian rosewood.

MODEL YEAR	FEATURES	EXC. COND. LOW	HIGH
1970-1979		$6,000	$6,500
D12XM			

1999-2000. 12-string version of the DXM.

1999-2000		$350	$400
D-15			

1970-present. All mahogany body.

1970-2007		$575	$700
D-16 A			

1987-1990. North American ash back and sides, solid spruce top, scalloped bracing, rosewood 'board and bridge, solid mahogany neck.

1987-1990		$950	$1,100
D-16 GT/GTE/D-16 RGT			

1999-present. D-16 T specs, GT with glossy top and mahogany back and sides, RGT with satin top and rosewood back and sides.

1999-2003	GTE, factory pickup	$800	$950
1999-2007	Mahogany, gloss	$700	$750
1999-2007	Rosewood, satin	$750	$800
D-16 H			

1991-1995. Full-size dreadnought, mahogany back and sides with satin finish, herringbone marquetry, vintage X-bracing, scalloped braces, optional acoustic pickup or active preamp system, replaced by D-16 T in '96.

1991-1995		$975	$1,050
D-16 M			

1986, 1988-1990. Mahogany back and sides, non-gloss satin finish.

1988-1990		$850	$1,000
D-16 T			

1995-2002. Solid spruce top, solid mahogany back and sides, scalloped braces, satin finish.

1995-2002		$850	$1,050
D-16 TR			

1995-2002. Indian rosewood version of 16 T.

1995-2002		$1,175	$1,225
D-17			

2000-2005. All solid mahogany back, sides and top, natural brown mahogany finish.

2000-2005		$850	$950
D-18			

1932-present. Mahogany back and sides, spruce top, black back stripe, 12-fret neck, changed to 14 frets in '34.

1932	12-fret neck	$45,000	$52,000
1933	12-fret neck	$38,000	$45,000
1934-1936	14-fret neck	$38,000	$45,000
1937-1939		$28,000	$34,000
1940-1941		$22,000	$27,500
1942-1944	Scalloped braces	$18,500	$23,000
1944-1946	Non-scalloped	$9,500	$16,500
1947-1949		$7,000	$9,500
1950-1952		$6,000	$7,000
1953-1959		$5,500	$6,000
1960-1962		$4,200	$5,000
1963-1965		$3,900	$4,200

MODEL YEAR	FEATURES	EXC. COND. LOW	HIGH
1966	Black 'guard late '66	$3,400	$3,900
1966	Tortoise 'guard early '66	$3,500	$4,100
1967	Last of maple bridgeplate	$3,100	$3,300
1968	Rosewood bridgeplate	$2,950	$3,200
1969		$2,400	$3,000
1970-1979		$1,700	$1,950
1980-1989		$1,400	$1,650
1990-1999		$1,300	$1,450
2000-2007		$1,300	$1,450
D-18 Andy Griffith			

2003. D-18 specs with bear claw spruce top, Andy's script signature on 18th fret.

2003		$2,200	$2,300
D-18 Authentic			

2006-2007. The most authentic pre-war recreation to date including original specs using 'Hide Glue' and gloss lacquer. Adirondack spruce top with forward X-brace and scalloped Adirondack bracing, 14-fret neck.

2006-2007		$4,400	$4,600
D-18 DC David Crosby			

2002. David Crosby signature at 20th fret, Adirondack spruce top, quilted mahogany back and sides, 250 made.

2002		$2,200	$2,500
D-18 E			

1958-1959. D-18 factory built with DeArmond pickups which required ladder bracing (reducing acoustic volume and quality).

1958-1959		$2,900	$3,600
D-18 GE Golden Era			

1995, 1999-present. 1995 version is a copy of a '37 D-18, 272 made. The current model is based on 1934 model.

1995		$2,200	$2,400
1999-2007		$2,100	$2,250
D-18 LE			

1986-1987. Limited Edition, quilted or flamed mahogany back and sides, scalloped braces, gold tuners with ebony buttons.

1986-1987		$1,800	$2,000
D-18 MB			

1990. Limited Edition Guitar of the Month, flame maple binding, Engelmann spruce top signed by shop foremen, X-brace, total of 99 sold.

1990		$1,700	$1,900
D-18 S			

1967-1993. Mahogany back and sides, 12-fret neck, slotted headstock, majority of production before '77, infrequent after that.

1967		$3,200	$3,400
1968		$3,000	$3,300
1969		$2,500	$3,100
1970-1979		$1,800	$2,000
1980-1993		$1,600	$1,700

Martin D12-28

1940 Martin D-18

Martin D-18V

Martin D-25 K2

D-18 V (Vintage)
1992. Guitar of the Month, low-profile neck, scalloped braces, bound, total of 218 sold.

Model Year	Features	Low	High
1992		$1,775	$1,900

D-18 VE
2004-2007. D-18 V with Fishman Ellipse.

| 2004-2007 | | $1,600 | $2,000 |

D-18 VM/D-18 VMS/D-18 V
1996-present. 14-fret Vintage Series, mahogany body, S is for slotted headstock version, M dropped from name in '99.

| 1996-2006 | | $1,800 | $2,000 |

D-19
1977-1988. Deluxe mahogany dreadnought, optional mahogany top, multi-bound but unbound rosewood 'board.

| 1977-1988 | | $1,500 | $1,900 |

D-21
1955-1969. Brazilian rosewood back and sides, rosewood 'board, chrome tuners.

1955-1958	Klusons to early '58	$6,500	$7,500
1958-1959	Grover tuners late '58	$6,400	$7,400
1960-1962		$6,100	$7,100
1963-1965		$5,500	$6,400
1966-1967		$5,400	$6,300
1968-1969		$5,300	$6,000

D-25 K
1980-1989. Dreadnought-size with koa back and sides and spruce top.

| 1980-1989 | | $2,000 | $2,300 |

D-25 K2
1980-1989. Same as D-25K, but with koa top and black 'guard.

| 1980-1989 | | $2,000 | $2,400 |

D-28
1931-present. Brazilian rosewood back and sides (changed to Indian rosewood in '70), '36 was the last year for the 12-fret model, '44 was the last year for scalloped bracing, '47 was the last year herringbone trim was offered, natural. Ultra high-end D-28 Martin guitar (pre-'47) valuations are very sensitive to structural and cosmetic condition. Finish wear and body cracks for ultra high-end Martin flat tops should be evaluated on a case-by-case basis. Small variances within the 'excellent condition' category can lead to notable valuation differences.

1931	12-fret, 1 made	$95,000	$115,000
1932	12-fret, 4 made	$95,000	$115,000
1933	12-fret, 12 made	$95,000	$115,000
1934	12-fret	$95,000	$115,000
1934	14-fret	$95,000	$115,000
1935-1936	12-fret	$95,000	$115,000
1935-1936	14-fret	$95,000	$115,000
1937		$70,000	$95,000
1938		$70,000	$80,000
1939	Early '39, 1.75 neck	$65,000	$75,000
1939	Late '39, 1.68 neck	$60,000	$70,000
1940-1941		$49,000	$60,000
1942-1944	Scalloped braces, metal rod	$45,000	$55,000
1942-1944	Scalloped braces, wood rod	$45,000	$55,000
1944-1946	Herringbone, non-scalloped	$28,000	$35,000
1947-1949	Non-herringbone starting '47	$12,000	$14,000
1950-1952		$11,000	$13,000
1953-1958	Klusons to early '58	$8,500	$11,000
1958-1959	Grover tuners late '58	$7,600	$9,500
1960-1962		$7,400	$7,600
1963-1965		$6,100	$7,300
1966	Black guard late '66	$6,000	$7,100
1966	Tortoise guard early '66	$6,100	$7,200
1967	Last of maple bridgeplate	$6,000	$7,000
1968	Rosewood bridge plate	$5,800	$6,600
1969	Last of Brazilian rosewood	$5,000	$6,100
1970-1979	Indian rosewood	$1,900	$2,200
1980-1989		$1,600	$2,000
1990-1999		$1,500	$1,700
2000-2007		$1,475	$1,600

D-28 (1935 Special)
1993. Guitar of the Month, 1935 features, Indian rosewood back and sides, peghead with Brazilian rosewood veneer.

| 1993 | | $1,800 | $2,200 |

D-28 50th Anniversary
1983. Stamped inside 1833-1983 150th Anniversary, Indian rosewood back and sides.

| 1983 | | $1,700 | $2,100 |

D-28 CW/CWB Clarence White
2002-2004. CW has Indian rosewood back and sides, the CWB Brazilian, only 150 CWBs were to be built.

| 2002-2004 | CW | $2,000 | $2,500 |
| 2002-2004 | CWB | $4,000 | $4,500 |

D-28 DM Del McCourey Signature
2003. Limited edition of 115 instruments, natural.

| 2003 | | $2,500 | $2,700 |

D-28 E
1959-1964. Electric, Brazilian rosewood back and sides, 2 DeArmond pickups, natural.

| 1959-1964 | | $4,500 | $5,000 |

D-28 GE Golden Era
1999-2002. GE Golden Era, Brazilian rosewood, herringbone trim.

| 1999-2002 | | $7,500 | $8,500 |

D-28 Hank Williams Limited Edition
1998. Replica of Hank Williams' 1944 D-28, Brazilian rosewood sides and back, scalloped braces, herringbone, 150 made.

| 1998 | | $5,500 | $6,500 |

MODEL YEAR	FEATURES	EXC. COND. LOW	HIGH

D-28 LSH

1991. Guitar of the Month, Indian rosewood back and sides, herringbone trim, snowflake inlay, zigzag back stripe.

1991		$2,000	$2,150

D-28 LSV

1998. Large soundhole model.

1998		$2,000	$2,150

D-28 Marquis

2004-present. D-28 reissue with specs designed to be close to the original.

2004-2007		$2,400	$2,650

D-28 P

1988-1990. P stands for low-profile neck, Indian rosewood back and sides.

1988-1990		$1,225	$1,475

D-28 S

1954-1993. Rosewood back and sides, 12-fret neck.

1960-1962	Special order	$7,100	$7,600
1963-1965	Special order	$6,200	$7,400
1966-1969	Brazilian rosewood	$5,100	$7,300
1970-1979	Indian rosewood	$2,100	$2,300
1980-1993		$1,600	$2,200

D-28 V

1983-1985. Brazilian rosewood back and sides, Limited Edition, herringbone trim, slotted diamond inlay.

1983-1985		$4,700	$5,200

D-2832 Shenandoah

1984-1992. Dreadnought acoustic, Thinline pickup, spruce top, V-neck, laminated rosewood sides, 3-piece rosewood back.

1984-1992		$700	$800

D-35

1965-present. Brazilian rosewood sides and 3-piece back, changed to Brazilian wings and Indian center in '70, then all Indian rosewood in '71, natural with sunburst option.

1965		$5,900	$6,100
1966		$5,600	$6,000
1967		$5,400	$5,900
1968		$5,200	$5,800
1969	Brazilian rosewood	$5,000	$5,700
1970	Brazilian rosewood	$4,400	$5,500
1970	Indian rosewood	$2,200	$2,500
1971-1979	Indian rosewood	$2,000	$2,100
1980-1989		$1,400	$2,000
1990-1999		$1,500	$1,700
2000-2007		$1,500	$1,600

D-35 Ernest Tubb

2003. Indian rosewood back and sides, special inlays, 90 built.

2003		$3,000	$3,500

D-35 JC Johnny Cash

2006-present. Rosewood back and sides.

2006-2007		$3,200	$3,400

D-35 S

1966-1993. Brazilian rosewood back and sides, changed to Indian rosewood in '70, 12-fret neck, slotted peghead.

1966-1969	Brazilian rosewood	$4,500	$5,500
1970-1979	Indian rosewood	$2,100	$2,500
1980-1993		$2,000	$2,400

D-35 V Brazilian 20th Anniversary

1984.

1984		$3,700	$4,000

D-3532 Shenandoah

1984-1993. Dreadnought acoustic, spruce top, V-neck, laminated rosewood sides, 3-piece rosewood back.

1984-1993		$675	$800

D-37 K

1980-1995. Dreadnought-size, koa back and sides, spruce top.

1980-1995		$2,100	$2,400

D-37 K2

1980-1995. Same as D-37 K, but has a koa top and black 'guard.

1980-1995		$2,100	$2,500

D-40

1997-2005. Rosewood back and sides, hexagon inlays.

1997-2005		$2,100	$2,500

D-40 BLE

1990. Limited Edition Guitar of the Month, Brazilian rosewood back and sides, pearl top border except around 'board.

1990		$8,400	$9,400

D-40 FMG

1995. Figured mahogany back and sides, 150 made.

1995		$3,800	$4,700

D-41

1969-present. Brazilian rosewood back and sides for the first ones in '69 then Indian rosewood, bound body, scalloped braces, natural.

1969	Brazilian rosewood	$16,000	$20,000
1970-1979	Indian rosewood	$2,800	$3,200
1980-1989		$2,500	$2,900
1990-1999		$2,400	$2,900
1990-1999	Sunburst option	$2,500	$3,100
2000-2007		$2,300	$2,700

D-41 BLE

1989. Limited Edition Guitar of the Month, Brazilian rosewood back and sides, pearl top border except around 'board.

1989		$3,300	$3,900

D-41 GJ George Jones

2001. Style 41 appointments, limited edition of 100, label signed by the Opossum.

2001		$3,200	$3,600

D-42

1996-present. Dreadnought, Indian rosewood back and sides, spruce top, pearl rosette and inlays, snowflake 'board inlays, gold tuners, gloss finish.

1996-2007		$2,700	$3,100

1940 Martin D-28

Martin D-35 Ernest Tubb

MODEL YEAR	FEATURES	LOW	HIGH

D-42 JC Johnny Cash
1997. Rosewood back and sides, Cash signature inlaid at 19th fret, 200 made, have label signed by Cash and C.F. Martin IV.

1997		$5,200	$5,500

D-42 K/D-42 K2
2000-present. K has koa back and sides, the all koa body K2 was discontinued in '05.

2000-2007 D-42 K		$3,100	$3,400
2000-2007 D-42 K2		$3,200	$3,600

D-42 LE
1988 only. D-42-style, limited edition (75 sold), scalloped braces, low profile neck.

1988		$3,000	$3,600

D-42 Peter Frampton
2006-2007. Indian rosewood back and sides, Style 45 features.

2006-2007		$4,100	$4,700

D-42 SB
2007. Sunburst finish, sitka spruce top, 45-style appointments.

2007		$2,900	$3,400

D-42 V
1985. Vintage Series, 12 made, Brazilian rosewood, scalloped braces.

1985		$8,600	$9,100

D-45
1933-1942 (96 made), 1968-present. Brazilian rosewood back and sides, changed to Indian rosewood during '69. The pre-WW II D-45 is one of the holy grails. A pre-war D-45 should be evaluated on a case-by-case basis. The price ranges are for all-original guitars in excellent condition and are guidance pricing only. These ranges are for a crack-free guitar. Unfortunately, many older acoustics have a crack or two and this can make ultra-expensive acoustics more difficult to evaluate than ultra-expensive solidbody electrics. Technically, a repaired body crack makes a guitar non-original, but the vintage market generally considers a professionally repaired crack to be original. Crack width, length and depth can vary, therefore extra attention is suggested.

1936	Only 2 made	$280,000	$325,000
1937	Only 2 made	$270,000	$310,000
1938	Only 9 made	$250,000	$290,000
1939	Only 14 made	$245,000	$280,000
1940	Only 19 made	$240,000	$260,000
1941	Only 24 made	$230,000	$250,000
1942	Only 19 made	$200,000	$240,000
1968	Brazilian rosewood	$31,000	$38,000
1969		$28,000	$34,000
1970-1979	Indian rosewood, 105 made	$7,200	$7,800
1980-1989		$6,000	$6,500
1990-1999		$4,600	$5,500
2000-2007		$4,200	$5,200

D-45 (1939 Reissue)
High-grade spruce top, figured Brazilian rosewood back and sides, high X and scalloped braces, abalone trim, natural, gold tuners.

1992		$11,500	$13,000

Martin D-45 Mike Longworth

Martin D-100 Deluxe

D-45 100th Anniversary LE
1996. Limited edition, 1896-1996 C.F. Martin Commemorative Anniversary Model label.

1996		$6,400	$6,600

D-45 150th Anniversary
1983. Brazilian rosewood back and sides, sitka spruce top, 150th logo stamp.

1983		$16,500	$17,500

D-45 200th Anniversary (C.F. Martin Sr. Deluxe)
1996 only. Commemorative model for C.F. Martin Sr.'s birth in 1796, Brazilian Deluxe Edition, natural.

1996		$12,000	$14,000

D-45 Brazilian
1994. Brazilian rosewood.

1994		$11,000	$13,000

D-45 Custom
Various options and models, Brazilian rosewood back and sides.

1991-1992		$10,000	$14,000

D-45 Deluxe
1993 only. Guitar of the Month, Brazilian rosewood back and sides, figured spruce top, inlay in bridge and 'guard, tree-of-life inlay on 'board, pearl borders and back stripe, gold tuners with large gold buttons, total of 60 sold.

1993		$15,000	$18,000

D-45 Gene Autry
1994 only. Gene Autry inlay (2 options available), natural.

1994		$17,000	$19,000

D-45 LE
1987. Limited Edition, 50 made, Guitar of the Month, September '87.

1987		$19,000	$22,000

D-45 Mike Longworth Commemorative Edition
2005-2006. East Indian rosewood back and sides, Adirondack spruce top, 91 made, label signed by Mike's wife Sue and C.F. Martin IV.

2005-2006		$6,900	$8,000

D-45 S
1969-1993. Brazilian rosewood back and sides, 12-fret neck, S means slotted peghead, only 50 made.

1969		$40,000	$41,000
1970-1979		$7,400	$8,500
1980-1993		$6,000	$8,500

D-45 Steven Stills Signature
2002. Limited edition of 91.

2002		$13,000	$14,000

D-45 V
1983-1985, 1999-present. Brazilian rosewood back and sides, scalloped braces, snowflake inlay, natural.

1983-1985		$10,200	$12,300

D-45 VR/D-45 V
1997-present. Vintage specs, Indian rosewood back and sides, vintage aging toner, snowflake inlay. Name changed to D-45 V in '99 (not to be confused with Brazilian rosewood D-45 V of the '80s).

1997-2007		$5,500	$6,500

MODEL YEAR	FEATURES	EXC. COND. LOW	HIGH

D-50/D-50 K/D-50 K2
2003. Ultra high-end D-style solid Koa top, back and side, ultra fancy appointments, 5 made.

2003		$27,000	$34,000

D-62
1989-1995. Dreadnought, flamed maple back and sides, spruce top, chrome-plated enclosed Schaller tuners.

1989-1995		$1,600	$1,800

D-62 LE
1986. Limited Edition, Guitar of the Month October '86, flamed maple back and sides, spruce top, snowflake inlays, natural.

1986		$1,800	$2,100

D-76 Bicentennial Limited Edition
1975-1976. Limited Edition, only 200 made in '75 and 1,976 made in '76, Indian rosewood back and sides, 3-piece back, herringbone back stripe, pearl stars on 'board, eagle on peghead.

1976		$3,000	$3,400

D-100 Deluxe
2004. Guitars have the first 50 sequential serial numbers following the millionth Martin guitar (1,000,001 to 1,000,050), fancy inlay work in pearl on back, 'guard, headstock, 'board and bridge. Herringbone top and rosette inlay, Adirondack spruce top, Brazilian rosewood back

2004		$48,000	$55,000

DC Series
Cutaway versions, E models have electronics.

1991-2000	DC-28	$1,400	$1,450
1997-2005	DC-1E/DC-1M	$725	$900
1998-2005	DC-15E	$925	$1,000
2000-2005	DCX-1E	$500	$550
2000s	DC-16GTE		
	Premium	$1,000	$1,100
2000s	DC-28E	$1,500	$1,550
2000s	DC-Aura	$2,000	$2,200
2005	DC-16E Koa	$1,600	$1,700

Ditson 111
2006. Special Edition by Martin based on their first model made for Ditson in 1916, Adirondack spruce top with aging toner, scalloped braces with forward shifted X-brace, mahogany back and sides, slotted headstock, 12-fret neck, abalone dot inlays.

2006		$3,300	$3,500

DM
1990-present. Solid sitka spruce top, laminated mahogany back and sides, dot markers, natural satin.

1990-2007		$550	$675

DM-12
1996-present. 12-string DM.

1996-2007		$550	$750

DVM Veterans
2002-2008. D-style, spruce top, rosewood back and sides, special veterans ornamentation.

2002-2008		$1,750	$1,950

DXM
1998-present. Wood composite mahogany laminate D body, solid wood neck, decal rosette, screened headstock logo, unique DX bracing.

1998-2007		$325	$375

E-18
1979-1982. Offset double-cut, maple and rosewood laminate solidbody, 2 DiMarzio pickups, phase switch, natural.

1979-1982		$875	$975

E-28
1980-1982. Double-cut electric solidbody, carved top, ebony 'board, 2 humbuckers.

1980-1982		$875	$900

EM-18
1979-1982. Offset double-cut, maple and rosewood laminate solidbody, 2 exposed-coil humbucking pickups, coil split switch.

1979-1982		$875	$975

EMP-1
1998-1999. Employee series designed by Martin employee team, cutaway solid spruce top, ovangkol wood back and sides with rosewood middle insert (D-35-style insert), on-board pickup.

1998-1999		$1,900	$2,100

F-1
1940-1942. Mahogany back and sides, carved spruce top, multi-bound, f-holes, sunburst.

1940-1942	91 made	$1,900	$2,300

F-2
1940-1942. Rosewood back and sides, carved spruce top, multi-bound, f-holes.

1940-1942	46 made	$2,500	$3,200

F-7
1935-1942. Brazilian rosewood back and sides, f-holes, carved top, back arched by braces, multi-bound, sunburst top finish.

1935-1942		$7,000	$9,000

F-9
1935-1941. Highest-end archtop, Brazilian rosewood, Martin inlaid vertically on headstock, 7-ply top binding, 45-style back strip, sunburst.

1935-1941		$11,000	$14,000

F-50
1961-1965. Single-cut thinline archtop with laminated maple body, 1 pickup.

1961-1965		$1,500	$1,700

F-55
1961-1965. Single-cut thinline archtop with laminated maple body, 2 pickups.

1961-1965		$1,600	$2,200

F-65
1961-1965. Electric archtop, double-cut, f-holes, 2 pickups, square-cornered peghead, Bigsby, sunburst.

1961-1965		$1,800	$2,300

Felix The Cat
2004. Felix the Cat logo art, Don Oriolo logo, red body, 756 made, Felix gig bag.

2004	Felix I	$300	$400

Martin EMP-1

1939 Martin F-9

1966 Martin GT-75

Martin HD-28

MODEL YEAR	FEATURES	EXC. COND. LOW	HIGH

GCD-16 CP (Guitar Center)
1998. 15 5/8" Style D.

| 1998 | | $1,900 | $2,100 |

GT-70
1966-1968. Electric archtop, bound body, f-holes, single-cut, 2 pickups, tremolo, burgundy or black finish.

| 1966-1968 | | $1,700 | $1,900 |

GT-75
1966-1968. Electric archtop, bound body, f-holes, double-cut, 2 pickups, tremolo, burgundy or black finish. There is also a 12-string version.

| 1966-1968 | | $1,800 | $2,000 |

Hawaiian X
2002-2004. Hawaiian scene painted on top, similar to the Cowboy guitar model, limited edition of 500.

| 2002-2004 | | $700 | $800 |

HD-18 JB Jimmy Buffett
1998. 424 made, solid mahogany back and sides, herringbone trim, palm tree headstock logo, ebony 'board with Style 42 markers, Buffett's signature inlaid in pearl, label signed by Buffett.

| 1998 | | $2,200 | $2,700 |

HD-28 BLE
1990. Guitar of the Month, Brazilian rosewood back and sides, herringbone soundhole ring, low profile neck (LE), chrome tuners, aging toner finish.

| 1990 | | $4,700 | $5,300 |

HD-28 Custom 150th Anniversary
1983. 150th Anniversary, Martin Custom Shop, Indian rosewood sides and back, "1833-1983 150th Year" stamped on inside backstrip.

| 1983 | | $2,700 | $2,800 |

HD-28 GE Golden Era 1935 Reissue
Late 1990s. Brazilian rosewood sides and back, Adirondack top and bracing.

| 1990s | | $7,200 | $8,000 |

HD-28 GM LSH
1994. Grand Marquis, Guitar of the Month, rosewood back and sides, large soundhole with double herringbone rings, snowflake inlay in bridge.

| 1994 | | $2,400 | $2,700 |

HD-28 KM Keb Mo Signature Edition
2001. 252 made.

| 2001 | | $2,100 | $2,300 |

HD-28 LE
1985. Limited Edition, Guitar of the Month, rosewood back and sides, scalloped bracing, herringbone top purfling, diamonds and squares 'board inlay, V-neck.

| 1985 | | $2,500 | $2,900 |

HD-28 LSV (Vintage Series)
1999-2005. Large Soundhole Vintage, patterned after Clarence White's modified '35 D-28.

| 1999-2005 | | $2,300 | $2,500 |

HD-28 MP
1990. Bolivian rosewood back and sides, scalloped braces, herringbone top purfling, zigzag back stripe, low profile neck.

| 1990 | | $1,550 | $1,900 |

HD-28 P
1987-1989. Rosewood back and sides, scalloped braces, herringbone, low profile neck (P), zigzag back stripe.

| 1987-1989 | | $1,550 | $1,900 |

HD-28 SO Sing Out!
1995. Limited edition, 45 made, Indian rosewood back and sides.

| 1995 | | $2,900 | $3,100 |

HD-28 Standard Series
1976-present. Indian rosewood back and sides, scalloped bracing, herringbone purfling.

1976-1979		$2,100	$2,300
1980-1989		$1,700	$2,100
1990-1999		$1,600	$1,850
2000-2007		$1,500	$1,800

HD-28 V/HD-28 VR
1996-present. 14-fret vintage series, Indian rosewood body, R dropped from name in '99.

| 1996-1999 | | $2,050 | $2,200 |
| 2000-2007 | | $2,000 | $2,200 |

HD-28 VS
1996-present. Slotted headstock, Indian rosewood sides and back.

| 1996-2007 | | $2,200 | $2,450 |

HD-282 R
1994 only.

| 1994 | | $1,625 | $1,700 |

HD-35
1978-present. Indian rosewood back and sides, herringbone top trim, zipper back stripe.

1978-1979		$2,100	$2,200
1980-1989		$1,800	$2,100
1990-1999		$1,800	$2,000
2000-2007		$1,800	$2,000

HD-35 Nancy Wilson
2006-2007. Englemann spruce top, 3-piece back with bubinga center wedge.

| 2006-2007 101 made | | $2,500 | $2,700 |

HD-35 P
1987-1989. HD-35 with low profile neck.

| 1987-1989 | | $1,600 | $1,800 |

HD-40 MK Mark Knopfler Edition
2001-2002. Limited edition of 251 made, Mark Knopfler signature inlay 20th fret, herringbone trim, fancy marquetry soundhole rings.

| 2001-2002 | | $2,600 | $2,800 |

HD-40 MS Marty Stewart
1996. Indian rosewood, 250 made.

| 1996 | | $3,500 | $4,000 |

HD-40 Tom Petty SE
2004-2006. Indian rosewood sides and back, high-end appointments, 274 made, inside label with signature.

| 2004-2006 | | $3,500 | $4,000 |

HDN Negative L.E.
2003. 135 made, unusual appointments include pearloid headstock and black finish, HDN Negative Limited Edition notation on the inside label.

| 2003 | | $2,300 | $2,600 |

The *Vintage Guitar Price Guide* shows low to high values for items in all-original excellent condition, and, where applicable, with original case or cover.

GUITARS

MODEL YEAR	FEATURES	EXC. COND. LOW	HIGH

HJ-28
1992, 1996-2000. Guitar of the Month in '92, regular production started in '96. Jumbo, non-cut, spruce top, Indian rosewood sides and back, herringbone top purfling, with or without on-board electronics.

1996-2000		$1,800	$2,200

HOM-35
1989. Herringbone Orchestra Model, Guitar of the Month, scalloped braces, 3-piece Brazilian rosewood back, bookmatched sides, 14-fret neck, only 60 built.

1989		$4,800	$5,200

HPD-41
1999-2001. Like D-41, but with herringbone rosette, binding.

1999-2001		$2,900	$3,200

J-1 Jumbo
1997-2002. Jumbo body with mahogany back and sides.

1997-2002		$800	$850

J12-16 GT
2000-present. 16" jumbo 12-string, satin solid mahogany back and sides, gloss solid spruce top.

2000-2007		$750	$850

J12-40
1985-1996. Called J12-40 M from '85-'90, rosewood back and sides, 12 strings, 16" jumbo size, 14-fret neck, solid peghead, gold tuners.

1996		$1,850	$2,300

J12-65
1985-1995. Called J12-65M for '84-'90, Jumbo style 65 12-string, spruce top, figured maple back and sides, gold tuning machines, scalloped bracing, ebony 'board, tortoiseshell-style binding, natural.

1985-1995		$1,800	$1,950

J-15
1999-present. Jumbo 16" narrow-waist body, solid mahogany top, sides, and back satin finish.

1999-2007		$600	$675

J-18/J-18 M
1987-1996. J-size body with Style 18 appointments, natural, called J-18M for '87-'89.

1987-1996		$1,375	$1,425

J-40
1990-present. Called J-40 M from '85-'89, Jumbo, Indian rosewood back and sides, triple-bound 'board, hexagonal inlays.

1990-2007		$1,850	$2,300

J-40 Custom
1993-1996. J-40 with upgrades including abalone top trim and rosette.

1993-1996		$2,800	$3,000

J-40 M
1985-1989. Jumbo, Indian rosewood back and sides, triple-bound 'board, hexagonal inlays, name changed to J-40 in '90.

1985-1989		$2,000	$2,300

J-41 Special
2004-2007. East Indian rosewood back and sides, Style 45 snowflake inlays.

2004-2007		$2,450	$2,550

J-65/J-65 E/J-65 M
1985-1995. Jumbo acoustic featuring maple back and sides, gold-plated tuners, scalloped bracing, ebony 'board, tortoise shell-style binding.

1985-1995		$2,000	$2,200

LXM Series
2003-present. Little Martin Series travel guitars.

2003-2007		$200	$250

M-3 H Cathy Fink
2005. Cathy Fink signature model, 0000 (M) size, gloss finish, Adirondack spruce top, rosewood sides, 3-piece back with flamed koa center panel, abalone rosette, torch headstock inlay, herringbone top trim, no Martin logo on headstock.

2005		$2,250	$2,400

M-21 Custom
December 1984. Guitar of the Month, low profile neck M-Series, Indian rosewood back and sides, special ornamentation.

1984		$1,800	$2,000

M-35 SC Shawn Colvin
2002. 120 made, M (0000) size, mahogany sides, 3-piece mahogany/rosewood back, Fishman pickup/preamp, Shawn Colvin & C.F.M. III signed label.

2002		$1,650	$1,750

M-36
1978-1997. Indian rosewood back and sides, bound 'board, low profile neck, multi-bound, white-black-white back stripes.

1978-1997		$1,600	$1,700

M-38
1977-1996. Indian rosewood back and sides, multi-bound, low profile neck, gold-plated tuners, stained top.

1977-1996		$1,825	$2,100

M-42 David Bromberg

2006	83 made	$3,800	$4,100

MC-16 GTE
2002-2004. Acoustic/electric, M-size single cut, gloss finish solid spruce top, satin finish solid mahogany sides and back.

2002-2004		$950	$1,000

MC-28
1981-1996. Rosewood back and sides, single-cut acoustic, oval soundhole, scalloped braces, natural.

1981-1996		$1,700	$2,000

MC-68
1985-1995. Auditorium-size acoustic, rounded cutaway, maple back and sides, gold tuners, scalloped bracing, ebony 'board, tortoiseshell-style binding, natural or sunburst.

1985-1995		$2,000	$2,300

MTV Unplugged Edition
1996, 2003-2004. Body is 1/2 rosewood and 1/2 mahogany (1/2 maple on second version), scalloped bracing, MTV logo on headstock.

1996	MTV-1	$1,100	$1,400
2003-2004	MTV-2	$800	$975

Martin J-40

Martin J-41 Special

Martin OM-18 Golden Era

Martin OM-42

MODEL YEAR	FEATURES	EXC. COND. LOW	HIGH

N-10

1968-1995. Classical, mahogany back and sides, fan bracing, wood marquetry soundhole ring, unbound rosewood 'board, 12-fret neck and slotted peghead from '70.

1968-1969	Short-scale	$1,475	$1,650
1970-1979	Long-scale	$1,375	$1,550
1980-1989	Long-scale	$1,200	$1,475
1990-1995	Long-scale	$1,225	$1,500

N-20

1968-1995. Classical, Brazilian rosewood back and sides (changed to Indian rosewood in '69), multi-bound, 12-fret neck, solid headstock (changed to slotted in '70), natural.

1968-1969	Brazilian rosewood, short-scale	$3,300	$3,500
1970-1979	Indian rosewood, long-scale	$1,650	$1,750
1980-1989	Long-scale	$1,625	$1,725
1990-1995	Long-scale	$1,650	$1,775

OM-18

1930-1934. Orchestra Model, mahogany back and sides, 14-fret neck, solid peghead, banjo tuners (changed to right-angle in '31).

1930-1931	Banjo tuners, small 'guard	$27,000	$33,000
1932-1933	Standard appointments	$26,000	$31,000
1934	Sunburst option	$30,000	$37,000

OM-18 GE Golden Era 1930/Special Edition GE

2003-present. Mahogany back and sides, Brazilian rosewood purfling and binding.

| 2003-2007 | | $1,900 | $2,000 |

OM-18 V

1999-present. Vintage features.

| 1999-2007 | | $1,750 | $1,800 |

OM-18 VLJ/OMC-18 VLJ

2002. 133 made.

| 2002 | | $2,400 | $2,800 |

OM-21 Standard Series

1992-1997. Triple 0-size, 15 1/8", spruce top, rosewood back and sides, natural.

| 1992-1997 | | $1,400 | $1,600 |

OM-28

1929-1933. Orchestra Model, Brazilian rosewood back and sides, 14-fret neck, solid peghead, banjo tuners (changed to right-angle in '31), reintroduced with Indian rosewood in '90.

| 1929-1930 | Small guard, banjo tuners | $40,000 | $50,000 |
| 1931-1933 | Large guard | $38,000 | $46,000 |

OM-28 LE

1985. Limited Edition only 40 made, Guitar of the Month, Indian rosewood back and sides, herringbone top binding, V-neck.

| 1985 | | $2,900 | $3,500 |

OM-28 Marquis

2005-present. Orchestra Model, pre-war appointments, spruce top, ebony 'board and bridge, East Indian rosewood back, sides and headplate.

| 2005-2007 | | $2,775 | $2,900 |

MODEL YEAR	FEATURES	EXC. COND. LOW	HIGH

OM-28 PB Perry Bechtel

1993. Guitar of the Month, signed by Perry Bechtel's widow Ina, spruce top, Indian rosewood back and sides, zigzag back stripe, chrome tuners, V-neck, only 50 made.

| 1993 | | $4,700 | $4,800 |

OM-28 Reissue

1990-1996. Indian rosewood back and sides.

| 1990-1996 | | $1,750 | $2,100 |

OM-28 V

1984-1990, 2001-present.

| 1984-1990 | | $1,800 | $2,200 |
| 2001-2007 | Vintage Series | $1,800 | $2,200 |

OM-28 VR

1990-1998. Orchestra Model, reintroduced OM-28 with rosewood back and sides.

| 1990-1998 | | $1,800 | $2,200 |

OM-42 PS Paul Simon

1997. Bookmatched sitka spruce top, Indian rosewood back and sides, 42- and 45-style features, low profile PS neck, 500 made.

| 1997 | | $4,000 | $4,500 |

OM-42 Reissue

1999-present. Indian rosewood back and sides, Style 45 snowflake inlays, rounded neck profile.

| 1999-2007 | | $2,800 | $3,500 |

OM-45 Custom

2007. High grade appointments, spruce top, Indian rosewood.

| 2007 | | $6,000 | $7,000 |

OM-45 Custom Deluxe

1998-1999. Limited custom shop run of 14, Adirondack spruce and typical Style 45 appointments.

| 1998-1999 | | $11,200 | $14,000 |

OM-45 Deluxe (Special)

1999. 4 made on special order, highly figured Brazilian rosewood.

| 1999 | | $13,000 | $16,200 |

OM-45 Deluxe/OM-45

1930-1933. OM-style, 45 level appointments with pearl inlay in 'guard and bridge, only 14 OM-45 Deluxe instruments made. Regular OM-45 with normal 45-style appointments. Condition is critically important on this or any ultra high-end instrument, minor flaws are critical to

| 1930 | | $270,000 | $325,000 |
| 1931-1933 | | $200,000 | $240,000 |

OM-45 GE Golden Era

2000-2004. Red spruce top, Brazilian rosewood

| 2000-2004 | | $11,200 | $12,800 |

OM-45 Roy Rogers

2006. Based on Roy's 1930 OM-45 Deluxe, Indian rosewood, Limited Edtion of 84 guitars. 14 others were to be built with Brazilian rosewood.

| 2006 | Indian rosewood | $8,300 | $8,700 |

OMC-16RE Aura

2005-present. Orchestra Model cutaway, solid East Indian rosewood back and sides, spruce top, gloss body, pearl rosettes, bound body and 'board.

| 2005-2007 | | $1,200 | $1,300 |

MODEL YEAR	FEATURES	EXC. COND. LOW	HIGH

OMC-28
1990. Guitar of the Month, rounded cutaway, gold tuners, low profile neck, pearl Martin script logo in headstock, label signed by C.F. Martin IV.

1990		$1,800	$2,200

OMC-28 E
2006-present. OMC-28 with Fishman Ellipse.

2006-2007		$1,700	$1,800

OMC-28 Laurence Juber
2004. 133 made.

2004		$2,700	$3,000

OMC-41 Richie Sambora
2008. 200 made, Italian Alpine spruce top, Madagascar rosewood sides and back, combination Style 45 and 41 appointments.

2008		$4,500	$4,900

OMJM John Mayer
2003-present. Indian rosewood sides and back.

2003-2007		$1,900	$2,100

R-17
1934-1942. All mahogany, arched top and back, 3-segment f-holes (changed to 1-segment in '37), 12-fret neck, sunburst.

1934-1942	940 made	$1,300	$1,900

R-18
1933-1942. Spruce arched top (carved top by 1937), mahogany back and sides, 14-fret neck, bound top, sunburst.

1933-1942	1,928 made	$2,100	$2,400

R-18 T
1934-1941. Tenor archtop, 14 3/8" lower bout, 2 f-holes, dot markers, sunburst.

1934-1941		$1,550	$1,800

SPD-16 Series
1997-2004. D-16 Series Special models.

1997-1998	SPD-16R/TR, rosewood, non-cut	$1,300	$1,400
1997-2001	SPDC-16R/TR, rosewood, cutaway	$1,350	$1,450
1998	SPD-16 Special Edition, mahogany	$975	$1,200
1999-2001	SPD-16M, flamed maple	$975	$1,200
2000-2004	SPD-16K, koa	$1,350	$1,450

Stauffer
1830s-ca.1850s. One of C.F. Martin's earliest models, distinguished by the scrolled, six-on-a-side headstock, ornamentation varies from guitar to guitar.

1830s	Plain, no ivory	$7,500	$8,500
1830s	Very fancy, ivory board and bridge	$29,000	$36,000

Stinger
1980s-1990s. Import copy offset S-style electric solidbody.

1980-1990s		$30	$100

SWD Smartwood
1998. D-size, built from wood material certified by the Forest Stewardship Council, sitka top, cherry back and sides, natural satin finish.

1998		$775	$800

Maruha
1960s-1970s. Japanese-made acoustic, classical, archtop and solidbody guitars, often copies of American brands. Probably not imported into the U.S.

Marvel
1950s-mid-1960s. Brand name used for budget guitars and basses marketed by Peter Sorkin Company in New York, New York. Sorkin manufactured and distributed Premier guitars and amplifiers made by its Multivox subsidiary. Marvel instruments were primarily beginner-grade. Brand disappears by mid-'60s. The name was also used on archtop guitars made by Regal and marketed by the Slingerland drum company in the 1930s to early 1940s.

Electric Guitars
1940s-1950s. Various models.

1940-1950s		$200	$600

Marveltone by Regal
1925-1930. Private branded by Regal, Marveltone pearl style logo on headstock.

Guitar
1925-1930. 14" Brazilian.

1925-1930		$3,400	$3,600

Masaki Sakurai
See Kohno brand.

Mason
1936-1939. Henry L. Mason on headstock, wholesale distribution, similar to Gibson/Cromwell, pressed wood back and sides.

Student/Intermediate Student
1936-1939. Various flat-top and archtop student/budget models.

1936-1939		$300	$800

Mason Bernard
1990-1991. Founded by Bernie Rico (BC Rich founder). During this period BC Rich guitars were licensed and controlled by Randy Waltuch and Class Axe. Most Mason models were designs similar to the BC Rich Assassin, according to Bernie Rico only the very best materials were used, large MB logo on headstock. Around 225 guitars were built bearing this brand.

Maton
1946-present. Intermediate and professional grade, production/custom, acoustic, acoustic/electric, hollowbody and solidbody guitars built in Box Hill, Victoria, Australia. Founded by Bill May and his brother Reg and still run by the family. Only available in USA since '82.

Matsuoka
1970s. Ryoji Matsuoka from Japan built intermediate grade M series classical guitars that often featured solid tops and laminated sides and back.

Martin OMC-16RE Aura

Maton MS500/12 - Mastersound

McCollum harp guitar

Megas Athena solidbody

MODEL YEAR	FEATURES	EXC. COND. LOW	HIGH

Mauel Guitars

1995-present. Luthier Hank Mauel builds his premium grade, custom, flat-tops in Auburn, California.

Maurer

Late 1880s-1944. Robert Maurer, of Chicago, was an importer of musical instruments who also began manufacturing his own line of guitars and mandolins in the late 1880s under the Maurer and Champion brands. It is thought that the Larson brothers, Carl and August, worked for him before August bought the company in 1900 and retained the Maurer name. Maurer was the only house brand until 1927 when the Prairie State brand was added, followed by the Euphonon brand a few years later. During most of the years between 1900 and 1944 the brothers also built for W. J. Dyer and Wm. C. Stahl. (See listings for each.)

The Maurer catalog of ca. 1932 lists Style numbers from 487, a student grade parlor guitar with oak back and sides, up to Style 593, the top-of-the-line auditorium size with the full treatment of pearl and abalone trim and a gorgeous tree-of-life fingerboard inlay. The body sizes ran from 12 ¾", 13 ½", 14" and 15". A few larger Maurers were built in the years following the transition to the bigger bodies in the mid-1930s.

12.5" Acoustic Flat-Top (Brazilian)

1910-1930		$4,000	$7,000

13" Acoustic Flat-Top (Brazilian)

Early-1900s. Spruce top, 13 5/8", Brazilian rosewood back and sides, higher-end pearl appointments, slotted headstock.

1910	Natural	$6,000	$9,000

13" Acoustic Flat-Top (Standard)

Early-1900s. Rosewood back and sides, spruce top, 12 3/4", made by Larson Brothers of Chicago.

1910		$3,500	$4,500

14" Flat-Top (Brazilian)

1920s-1930s. Mid-sized (about 14") with Brazilian rosewood back and sides, attractive appointments.

1920s		$9,000	$12,000

14" Flat-Top (Mahogany)

1920s-1930s. Mid-sized (about 14") with mahogany back and sides, standard appointments.

1930s		$3,500	$6,000

15" Flat-Top (Brazilian)

Early-1900s. Higher-end Brazilian rosewood back and sides, tree of life inlay, 15", pearl-bound.

1920s		$10,800	$13,800

May Bell

Late 1920s-1940s. Brand of flat top guitars, some with fake resonators, marketed by the Slingerland drum copy. Most were made by Regal.

McAlister Guitars

1997-present. Premium grade, custom, flat-tops built by luthier Roy McAlister in Watsonville, California.

McCollum Guitars

1994-present. Luthier Lance McCollum builds his premium grade, custom, flat-top and harp guitars in Colfax, California.

McCurdy Guitars

1983-present. Premium grade, production/custom, archtops built by luthier Ric McCurdy originally in Santa Barbara, California and, since '91, New York, New York.

McGill Guitars

1976-present. Luthier Paul McGill builds his premium grade, production/custom, classical, resonator, and acoustic/electric guitars in Nashville, Tennessee.

McGlynn Guitars

2005-present. Luthier Michael J. McGlynn builds his premium and presentation grade, custom, solidbody guitars in Henderson, Nevada.

MCI, Inc

1967-1988. MusiConics International (MCI), of Waco, Texas, introduced the world to the Guitorgan, invented by Bob Murrell. Later, they also offered effects and a steel guitar. In the '80s, a MIDI version was offered. MCI was also involved with the Daion line of guitars in the late '70s and early '80s.

GuitOrgan B-35

1970s (ca. 1976-1978?). Duplicated the sounds of an organ and more. MCI bought double-cut semi-hollow body guitars from others and outfitted them with lots of switches and buttons. Each fret has 6 segments that correspond to an organ tone. There was also a B-300 and B-30 version, and the earlier M-300 and 340.

1970s		$700	$850

McInturff

1996-present. Professional and premium grade, production/custom, solidbody guitars built by luthier Terry C. McInturff originally in Holly Springs, North Carolina, and since '04, in Moncure, North Carolina. McInturff spent 17 years during guitar repair and custom work before starting his own guitar line.

McKnight Guitars

1992-present. Luthier Tim McKnight builds his custom, premium grade, acoustic steel string guitars in Morral, Ohio.

McPherson Guitars

1981-present. Premium grade, production, flat-tops built by luthier Mander McPherson in Sparta, Wisconsin.

Mean Gene

1988-1990. Heavy metal style solidbodies made by Gene Baker, who started Baker U.S.A. guitars in '97, and Eric Zoellner in Santa Maria, California. They built around 30 custom guitars.

MODEL		EXC. COND.	
YEAR	FEATURES	LOW	HIGH

MODEL		EXC. COND.	
YEAR	FEATURES	LOW	HIGH

Megas Guitars

1989-present. Luthier Ted Megas builds his premium grade, custom, archtop and solidbody guitars, originally in San Franciso, and currently in Portland, Oregon.

Melancon

Professional and premium grade, custom/production, solid and semi-hollow body guitars built by luthier Gerard Melancon in Thibodaux, Louisiana. They also build basses.

Mello, John F.

1973-present. Premium grade, production/custom, classical and flat-top guitars built by luthier John Mello in Kensington, California.

Melophonic

1960s. Brand built by the Valco Company of Chicago, Illinois.

Resonator Guitar

Valco-made.

1965		$700	$850

Melville Guitars

1988-present. Luthier Christopher Melville builds his premium grade, custom, flat-tops in Milton, Queensland, Australia.

Mercurio

2002-2005. Luthier Peter Mercurio built his custom/production solidbody guitars, featuring his interchangeable PickupPak system to swap pickups, in Chanhassen, Minnesota.

Mermer Guitars

1983-present. Luthier Richard Mermer builds his premium grade, production/custom, steel-string, nylon-string, and Hawaiian guitars in Sebastian, Florida.

Merrill Brothers

1998-present. Premium grade, production/custom, steel-string and harp guitars built by luthiers Jim and Dave Merrill in Williamsburg, Virginia.

Mesrobian

1995-present. Luthier Carl Mesrobian builds his professional and premium grade, custom, archtop guitars in Salem, Massachusetts.

Messenger

1967-1968. Built by Musicraft, Inc., originally of 156 Montgomery Street, San Francisco, California. The distinguishing feature of the Messengers is a metal alloy neck which extended through the body to the tailblock, plus mono or stereo outputs. Sometime before March '68 the company relocated to Astoria, Oregon. Press touted "improved" magnesium neck, though it's not clear if this constituted a change from '67. Brand disappears after '68. They also made basses.

Electric Hollowbody Archtop

1967-1968. Symmetrical double-cut body shape, metal neck with rosewood 'boards, stereo.

1967-1968	Rojo Red	$2,500	$3,000

Metropolitan

1995-2008. Professional and premium grade, production/custom, retro-styled solidbodies designed by David Wintz reminiscent of the '50s National Res-o-glas and wood body guitars. They feature full-scale set-neck construction and a wood body instead of Res-o-glas. Wintz also makes Robin and Alamo brand instruments.

Meyers Custom Guitars

2005-present. Founded by Donald Meyers in Houma, Louisiana, promoted as 100% on a custom order basis, professional grade classic body style electric models.

Miami

1920s. Instruments built by the Oscar Schmidt Co. and possibly others. Most likely a brand made for a distributor.

Michael Collins Custom Guitars

1975-present. Premium grade, custom/production, classical, flamenco and steel string guitars built in Argyle, New York, by luthier Michael Collins.

Michael Collins Guitars

2002-present. Luthier Michael Collins builds his professional and premium grade, custom, Selmer style, archtop and flat top guitars in Keswick, Ontario. He also builds mandolins.

Michael Dunn Guitars

1968-present. Luthier Michael Dunn builds his production/custom Maccaferri-style guitars in New Westminster, British Columbia. He also offers a harp uke and a Weissenborn- or Knutsen-style Hawaiian guitar, and has built archtops.

Michael Kelly

2000-present. Intermediate and professional grade, production, acoustic, solidbody and archtop guitars imported by Elite Music Brands of Clearwater, Florida. They also offer mandolins and basses.

Michael Lewis Instruments

1992-present. Luthier Michael Lewis builds his premium and presentation grade, custom, archtop guitars in Grass Valley, California. He also builds mandolins.

Michael Menkevich

1970-present. Luthier Michael Menkevich builds his professional and premium grade, production/custom, flamenco and classical guitars in Elkins Park, Pennsylvania.

Mesrobian Session

Metropolitan Glendale Deluxe

GUITARS

Michael Lewis San Rafael

Michael Thames Luis Panormo

Michael Silvey Custom Guitars

2003-present. Solidbody electric guitars built by Michael Silvey in North Canton, Ohio.

Michael Thames

1972-present. Luthier Michael Thames builds his premium grade, custom/production, classical guitars in Taos, New Mexico.

Michael Tuttle

2003-present. Professional and premium grade, custom, solid and hollowbody guitars built by luthier Michael Tuttle in Saugus, California. He also builds basses.

Microfrets

1967-1975, 2004-2005. Professional grade, production, electric guitars built in Myersville, Maryland. They also built basses. Founded by Ralph S. Jones, Sr. in Frederick, Microfrets offered over 20 models of guitars that sported innovative designs and features, with pickups designed by Bill Lawrence. The brand was revived, again in Frederick, by Will Meadors and Paul Rose in '04.

Serial numbers run from about 1000 to about 3800. Not all instruments have serial numbers, particularly ones produced in '75. Serial numbers do not appear to be correlated to a model type, but are sequential by the general date of production.

Instruments can be identified by body styles as follows; Styles 1, 1.5, 2, and 3. An instrument may be described as a Model Name and Style Number (for example, Covington Style 1). Style 1 has a wavey-shaped pickguard with control knobs mounted below the guard and the 2-piece guitar body has a particle board side gasket. Style 1.5 has the same guard and knobs, but no side body gasket. Style 2 has an oblong pickguard with top mounted control knobs and a pancake style seam between the top and lower part of the body. Style 3 has a seamless 2-piece body and a Speedline neck.

Baritone Signature
1971. Baritone version of Signature Guitar, sharply pointed double-cut, with or without f-holes, single- or double-dot inlays.

1971	$500	$700

Baritone Stage II
1971-ca. 1975. Double-cut, 2 pickups.

1971-1975	$500	$700

Calibra I
1969-1975. Double-cut, 2 pickups, f-hole.

1969-1975	$400	$600

Covington
1967-1969. Offset double-cut, 2 pickups, f-hole.

1967-1969	$700	$900

Golden Comet
1969-1971. Double-cut, 2 pickups, f-hole.

1969-1971	$500	$700

Golden Melody
1969-1971, 2004-2005. Offset double-cut, 2 pickups, f-hole, M-shaped metal design behind tailpiece.

1969-1971	$700	$900

Huntington
1969-1975. Double-cut, 2 pickups.

1969-1975	$700	$900

Orbiter
1967-1969. Odd triple cutaway body, thumbwheel controls on bottom edge of 'guard.

1967-1969	$700	$900

Plainsman
1967-1969. Offset double-cut, 2 pickups, f-hole, thumbwheel controls on bottom edge of 'guard.

1967-1969	$900	$1,100

Signature
1967-1969. Double-cut, 2 pickups.

1967-1969	$700	$850

Spacetone
1969-1971, 2004-2005. Double-cut semi-hollow body, 2 pickups.

1969-1971	$700	$850

Stage II
1969-1975. Offset double-cut, 2 pickups.

1969-1975	$650	$850

Swinger
1971-1975. Offset double-cut, 2 pickups.

1971-1975	$700	$900

Wanderer
1969. Double-cut, 2 pickups.

1969	$600	$700

Mike Lull Custom Guitars

1995-present. Professional and premium grade, production/custom, guitars built by luthier Mike Lull in Bellevue, Washington. He also builds basses.

Milburn Guitars

1990-present. Luthiers Orville and Robert Milburn build their premium grade, custom, classical guitars in Sweet Home, Oregon.

Miller

1960s. One of the brand names of guitars built for others by Egmond in Holland.

Minarik

Luthier M.E. Minarik builds his professional and premium grade, custom/production, solid and chambered body guitars in Van Nuys, California.

Minerva

1930s. Resonator and archtop guitars sold through catalog stores, likely made by one of the big Chicago builders of the era.

Mirabella

1997-present. Professional and premium grade, custom archtops, flat-tops, hollowbody, and solidbody guitars built by luthier Cristian Mirabella in Babylon, New York. He also builds basses, mandolins and ukes.

MODEL		EXC. COND.	
YEAR	FEATURES	LOW	HIGH

Mitre

1983-1985. Bolt neck, solidbody guitars made in Aldenville (or East Longmeadow), Massachusetts, featuring pointy body shapes, 2 humbuckers, active or passive electronics and with or without trems. They also offered a bass.

MJ Guitar Engineering

1993-present. Professional and premium grade, production/custom, hollowbody, chambered and solidbody guitars built by luthier Mark Johnson in Rohnert Park, California. He also builds basses.

Mobius Megatar

2000-present. Professional grade, production, hybrid guitars designed for two-handed tapping, built in Mount Shasta, California. Founded by Reg Thompson, Henri Dupont, and Traktor Topaz in '97, they released their first guitars in '00.

Modulus

1978-present. Founded by Geoff Gould in the San Francisco area, currently built in Novato, California. Modulus currently offers only basses but did build professional grade, production/custom, solidbody electric guitars up to '05.

Genesis 2/2T

1996-2005. Double-cut, long extended bass horn alder body, bolt-on carbon fiber/red cedar neck, hum-single-single pickups, locking vibrato (2T model).

1996-2005		$1,200	$1,300

Moll Custom Instruments

1996-present. Luthier Bill Moll builds his professional and premium grade, archtops in Springfield, Missouri. He has also built violins, violas and cellos.

Monarch

Offset double-cut contoured mahogany solidbody, set-neck, single-single-hum pickups, transparent cherry.

2000s		$1,300	$1,600

Taurus Custom

Flame maple top, chambered mahogany body, matching flamed maple headstock, abalone slash inlays, gold hardware.

2000s		$2,200	$2,500

Taurus Standard

1996-2005. Single-cut, carved flamed maple top on chambered mahogany body, dual humbucker pickups, gold hardware, sunburst.

1996-2005		$1,700	$2,000

Monrad, Eric

1993-present. Premium, custom, flamenco and classical guitars built by luthier Eric Monrad in Healdsburg, California.

Monroe Guitars

2004-present. Luthier Matt Handley builds his custom, professional grade, solidbody electric guitars in State Center, Iowa. He also builds basses.

Montalvo

See listing under Casa Montalvo.

Montaya

Late 1970s-1980s. Montaya Hyosung 'America' Inc., Korean acoustic and electric import copies.

Monteleone

1976-present. Presentation grade, production/custom, archtop guitars built by Luthier John Monteleone in Islip, New York.

Eclipse

17" electric archtop, natural orange.

1991-1992		$14,000	$15,000

OM-42

Mid-1970s-1985. Styled like an old Martin OM, spruce top, Brazilian rosewood back.

1975-1985		$9,500	$11,000

Radio City

18" acoustic archtop cutaway, art deco fretboard inlays, golden blond.

1990s		$19,000	$20,000

Montgomery Ward

The mail-order and retail giant offered a variety of instruments and amps from several different U.S. and overseas manufacturers.

Model 8379/H44 Stratotone

Mid-1950s. Private branded Harmony Stratotone, some without logo but with crown-style stencil/painted logo on headstock, many with gold-copper finish, 1 pickup.

1950s		$550	$675

Monty

1980-present. Luthier Brian Monty builds his professional, premium and presentation grade, production/custom, archtop, semi-hollow, solidbody, and chambered electric guitars originally in Lennoxville, Quebec, and currently in Anne de Prescott, Ontario.

Moog

1964-present. Moog introduced its premium grade, production, Harmonic Control System solidbody guitar in 2008. They also offer guitar effects.

Moon (Japan)

1979-present. Professional and premium grade, production/custom, guitars made in Japan. They also build basses.

Moon (Scotland)

1979-present. Intermediate, professional and premium grade, production/custom, acoustic and electric guitars built by luthier Jimmy Moon in Glasgow, Scotland. They also build mandolin family instruments.

Mitre Cobra

Monteleone Eclipse

Moonstone M-80

Mosrite Stereo 350

MODEL YEAR	FEATURES	EXC. COND. LOW	HIGH

Moonstone

1972-present. Professional, premium, and presentation grade production/custom flat-top, solid and semi-hollow electric guitars, built by luthier Steve Helgeson in Eureka, California. He also builds basses. Higher unit sales in the early-'80s. Some models have an optional graphite composite neck built by Modulus.

Eclipse Standard
1979-1983. Figured wood body, offset double-cut, neck-thru, dot markers, standard maple neck, natural finish.

1979-1983		$1,700	$2,100

Explorer
1980-1983. Figured wood solidbody, neck-thru, standard maple neck, natural finish.

1980-1983		$1,700	$2,100

Flaming V
1980-1984. Figured wood body, V-shaped, neck-thru, standard maple neck, natural finish.

1980-1984		$1,700	$2,100

M-80
1980-1984. Figured wood double-cut semi-hollow body, standard maple or optional graphite neck, natural finish.

1980s	Optional graphite neck	$2,500	$3,100
1980s	Standard maple neck	$2,000	$2,500

Vulcan Deluxe
1979-1983. Figured maple carved-top body, offset double-cut, diamond markers, standard maple neck, natural finish.

1979-1983		$1,950	$2,400

Vulcan Standard
1979-1983. Mahogany carved-top body, offset double-cutaway, dot markers, standard maple neck, natural finish.

1979-1983		$1,850	$2,300

Morales

Ca.1967-1968. Guitars and basses made in Japan by Zen-On, not heavily imported into the U.S., if at all.

Solidbody Electric

1967-1968	Various models	$125	$275

More Harmony

1930s. Private branded by Dobro for Dailey's More Harmony Music Studio. Private branding for catalog companies, teaching studios, publishers, and music stores was common for the Chicago makers. More Harmony silk-screen logo on the headstock.

Dobro
1930s. 14" wood body with upper bout f-holes and metal resonator, sunburst.

1930s		$1,200	$1,500

Morgaine Guitars

1994-present. Luthier Jorg Tandler builds his professional and premium grade, production/custom electrics in Germany.

MODEL YEAR	FEATURES	EXC. COND. LOW	HIGH

Morgan Monroe

1999-present. Intermediate grade, production, acoustic, acoustic/electric and resonator guitars made in Korea and distributed by SHS International of Indianapolis, Indiana. They also offer basses, mandolins, banjos, and fiddles.

Morris

1967-present. Intermediate, professional and premium grade, production, acoustic guitars imported by Moridaira of Japan. Morris guitars were first imported into the U.S. from the early '70s to around '90. They are again being imported into the U.S. starting in 2001. They also offer

000 Copy
1970s. Brazilian rosewood laminate body, import.

1970s		$275	$325

D-45 Copy
1970s. Brazilian laminate body.

1970s		$400	$500

Mortoro Guitars

1992-present. Luthier Gary Mortoro builds his premium grade, custom, archtop guitars in Miami, Florida.

Mosrite

The history of Mosrite has more ups and downs than just about any other guitar company. Founder Semie Moseley had several innovative designs and had his first success in 1954, at age 19, building doubleneck guitars for super picker Joe Maphis and protégé Larry Collins. Next came the Ventures, who launched the brand nationally by playing Mosrites and featuring them on album covers. At its '60s peak, the company was turning out around 1,000 guitars a month. The company ceased production in '69, and Moseley went back to playing gospel concerts and built a few custom instruments during the '70s.

In the early-'80s, Mosrite again set up shop in Jonas Ridge, North Carolina, but the plant burned down in November '83, taking about 300 guitars with it. In early-'92, Mosrite relocated to Booneville, Arkansas, producing a new line of Mosrites, of which 96% were exported to Japan, where the Ventures and Mosrite have always been popular. Semie Moseley died, at age 57, on August 7, '92 and the business carried on until finally closing its doors in '93. The Mosrite line has again been revived, offering intermediate and premium grade, production, reissues.

Throughout much of the history of Mosrite, production numbers were small and model features often changed. As a result, exact production dates are difficult to determine.

Brass Rail
1970s. Double-cut solidbody, has a brass plate running the length of the 'board.

1970s		$950	$1,050

MODEL YEAR	FEATURES	EXC. COND. LOW	HIGH

Celebrity 1
Late-1960s-1970s. Thick hollowbody, 2 pickups, sunburst.

1970s		$1,200	$1,350

Celebrity 2 Standard
Late-1960s-1970s. Thin hollowbody, 2 pickups, in the '70s, it came in a Standard and a Deluxe version.

1970s		$1,100	$1,250

Celebrity 3
Late-1960s. Thin hollowbody, double-cut, 2 pickups, f-holes.

1960s		$1,150	$1,350

Combo Mark 1
1966-1968. Bound body, 1 f-hole.

1966-1968		$1,600	$2,000

Custom-Built
1950s. Pre-production custom instruments hand-built by Semie Moseley, guidance pricing only, each instrument will vary. A wide variety of instruments were made during this period. Some were outstanding, but others, especially those made around '60, could be very basic and of much lower quality. Logos would vary widely and some '60 logos looked especially homemade.

1952-1962		$1,500	$15,000

D-40 Resonator Guitar
1960s. Symmetrical double-cut thinline archtop-style body with metal resonator in center of body, 2 pickups, 2 control knobs and toggle switch.

1960s		$1,000	$1,250

D-100 Californian
1960s. Double-cut, resonator guitar with 2 pickups.

1967		$1,500	$1,850

Joe Maphis Mark 1
1960s. Semi-hollow double-cut, 2 single-coils, spruce top, walnut back, rosewood 'board, natural.

1960s		$1,900	$2,200

Joe Maphis Mark XVIII
1960s. 6/12 doubleneck, double-cut, 2 pickups on each neck, Moseley tremolo on 6-string.

1960s		$4,000	$5,000

Mosrite 1988
1988-early-1990s. Has traditional Mosrite body styling, Mosrite pickups and bridge.

1988		$700	$875

Octave Guitar
1965. 14" scale, 1 pickup, Ventures Mosrite body style, single neck pickup, very few made.

1965		$5,700	$7,100

Stereo 350
1974-1975. Single-cut solidbody, 2 outputs, 2 pickups, 4 knobs, slider and toggle, black.

1974-1975		$1,400	$1,650

Ventures Model
1963-1968. Double-cut solidbody, triple-bound body '63, no binding after, Vibramute for '63-'64, Moseley tailpiece '65-'68.

1963	Blue or red, bound	$9,000	$11,000
1963	Sunburst, bound	$8,000	$10,000
1964	Blue or red, Vibramute	$7,000	$7,500
1964	Sunburst, Vibramute	$6,000	$6,500
1965	Blue, red, sunburst, Moseley tailpiece	$3,500	$4,500
1965	Blue, red, sunburst, Vibramute	$5,500	$6,000
1966	Moseley tailpiece	$3,500	$4,300
1967	Moseley tailpiece	$3,300	$4,100
1968	Moseley tailpiece	$3,000	$3,700

Ventures 12-String
1966-1968. Double-cut solidbody, 12 strings.

1966-1968		$2,900	$3,500

Ventures Mark V
1963-1968. Double-cut solidbody.

1963-1968		$2,500	$3,000

Ventures (Jonas Ridge/Boonville)
1982-1993. Made in Jonas Ridge, NC or Booneville, AR, classic Ventures styling.

1982-1993		$2,500	$2,900

Mosrite Ventures

Mossman
1965-present. Professional and premium grade, production/custom, flat-top guitars built in Sulphur Springs, Texas. They have also built acoustic basses. Founded by Stuart L. Mossman in Winfield, Kansas. In '75, fire destroyed one company building, including the complete supply of Brazilian rosewood. They entered into an agreement with C.G. Conn Co. to distribute guitars by '77. 1200 Mossman guitars in a Conn warehouse in Nevada were ruined by being heated during the day and frozen during the night. A disagreement about who was responsible resulted in cash flow problems for Mossman. Production fell to a few guitars per month until the company was sold in '86 to Scott Baxendale. Baxendale sold the company to John Kinsey and Bob Casey in Sulphur Springs in '89.

Flint Hills
1970-mid-1980s. Flat-top acoustic, Indian rosewood back and sides.

1970-1979		$1,700	$1,900

Golden Era
1976-1977. D-style, vine inlay and other high-end appointments, Indian rosewood sides and back.

1976-1977		$3,000	$3,700

Great Plains
1970-mid-1980s. Flat-top, Indian rosewood, herringbone trim.

1970-1979		$1,700	$1,900

Southwind
1976-ca. 1986, mid-1990s-2002. Flat-top, abalone trim top.

1976-1979		$1,800	$2,100

Tennessee
1975-1979. D-style, spruce top, mahogany back and sides, rope marquetry purfling, rope binding.

1975-1979		$1,000	$1,200

1976 Mossman Southwind

Music Man Axis

Myka Sungazer

MODEL YEAR FEATURES	EXC. COND. LOW	HIGH
Tennessee 12-String		
1975-1979.		
1975-1979	$1,000	$1,200
Winter Wheat		
1976-1979, mid-1990s-present. Flat-top, abalone trim, natural finish.		
1976-1979	$1,800	$2,100
Winter Wheat 12-String		
1976-1979. 12-string version of Winter Wheat, natural.		
1976-1979	$1,800	$2,100

MotorAve Guitars

2002-present. Luthier Mark Fuqua builds his professional and premium grade, production, electric guitars originally in Los Angeles, California, and currently in Durham, North Carolina.

Mozart

1930s. Private brand made by Kay.

Hawaiian (Square Neck)

1930s. Spruce top, solid mahogany sides and back, pealoid overlay on peghead with large Mozart inscribed logo, small jumbo 15 1/2" body.

1935-1939	$775	$950

Mozzani

Built in shops of Luigi Mozzani (b. March 9, 1869, Faenza, Italy; d. 1943) who opened lutherie schools in Bologna, Cento and Rovereto in 1890s. By 1926 No. 1 and 2 Original Mozzani Model Mandolin (flat back), No. 3 Mandola (flat back), No. 4 6-String Guitar, No. 5 7-, 8-, and 9-String Guitars, No. 6 Lyre-Guitar.

Muiderman Guitars

1997-present. Custom, premium grade, steel string and classical guitars built by luthier Kevin Muiderman currently in Grand Forks, North Dakota, and previously in Beverly Hills, Michigan, 1997-2001, and Neenah, Wisconsin, '01-'07. He also builds mandolins.

Murph

1965-1967. Mid-level electric semi-hollow and solidbody guitars built by Pat Murphy in San Fernado, California. Murph logo on headstock. They also offered basses and amps.

Electric Solidbody

1965-1966	$550	$675

Electric XII

1965-1967	$550	$675

Music Man

1972-present. Professional grade, production, solidbody guitars built in San Luis Obispo, California. They also build basses. Founded by ex-Fender executives Forrest White and Tom Walker in Orange County, California. Music Man originally produced guitar and bass amps based on early Fender ideas using many former Fender employees.

They contracted with Leo Fender's CLF Research to design and produce a line of solidbody guitars and basses. Leo Fender began G & L Guitars with George Fullerton in '82. In '84, Music Man was purchased by Ernie Ball and production was moved to San Luis Obispo.

Axis

1996-present. Offset double-cut solidbody, figured maple top, basswood body, 2 humbucker pickups, Floyd Rose.

1996-2007	$1,100	$1,250

Edward Van Halen

1991-1995. Basswood solidbody, figured maple top, bolt-on maple neck, maple 'board, binding, 2 humbuckers, named changed to Axis.

1991-1995	$2,000	$2,500

Sabre I

1978-1982. Offset double-cut solidbody, maple neck, 2 pickups, Sabre I comes with a flat 'board with jumbo frets.

1978-1982	$1,200	$1,500

Sabre II

1978-1982. Same as Sabre I, but with an oval 7 1/2" radius 'board.

1978-1982	$1,400	$1,700

Silhouette

1986-present. Offset double-cut, contoured beveled solidbody, various pickup configurations.

1986-2005		$1,000	$1,100
2006	20th Anniversary	$1,000	$1,200

Steve Morse Model

1987-present. Solidbody, 4 pickups, humbuckers in the neck and bridge positions, 2 single-coils in the middle, special pickup switching, 6-bolt neck mounting, maple neck.

1987-2000	$1,100	$1,150

Stingray I

1976-1982. Offset double-cut solidbody, flat 'board radius.

1976-1979	$800	$1,000
1980-1982	$800	$1,000

Stingray II

1976-1982. Offset double-cut solidbody, rounder 'board radius.

1976-1979	$900	$1,100
1980-1982	$900	$1,100

Musicvox

1996-present. Intermediate grade, production, Korean-made retro-vibe guitars and basses from Matt Eichen of Cherry Hill, New Jersey.

Myka

2003-present. Luthier David Myka builds his professional and premium grade, custom/production, solidbody, semi-hollowbody, hollowbody, archtop, and flat top guitars in Seattle, Washington. Until '07 he was located in Orchard Park, New York.

MODEL YEAR	FEATURES	EXC. COND. LOW	HIGH

Nady

1976-present. Wireless sound company Nady Systems offered guitars and basses with built-in wireless systems for 1985-'87. Made by Fernandes in Japan until '86, then by Cort in Korea.

Lightning/Lightning I

1985-1987. Double-cut, neck-thru, solidbody, 24 frets, built-in wireless, labeled as just Lightning until cheaper second version came out in '86.

1985	Fernandes	$550	$650
1986-1987	Cort	$500	$600

Lightning/Lightning II

1986-1987. Cheaper, bolt-neck version of the Lightning I.

1986-1987	Cort	$300	$375

Napolitano Guitars

1993-present. Luthier Arthur Napolitano builds his professional and premium grade, custom, archtop guitars in Allentown, New Jersey.

NashGuitars

2001-present. Luthier Bill Nash builds his professional grade, production/custom, aged solidbody replica electric guitars in Olympia, Washington. He also builds basses.

Nashville Guitar Company

1985-present. Professional and premium grade, custom, flat-top guitars built by luthier Marty Lanham in Nashville, Tennessee. He has also built banjos.

National

Ca. 1927-present. Founded in Los Angeles, California as the National String Instrument Corporation by John Dopyera, George Beauchamp, Ted Kleinmeyer and Paul Barth. In '29 Dopyera left to start the Dobro Manufacturing Company with Rudy and Ed Dopyera and Vic Smith. The Dobro company competed with National until the companies reunited. Beauchamp and Barth then left National to found Ro-Pat-In with Adolph Rickenbacker and C.L. Farr (later becoming Electro String Instrument Corporation, then Rickenbacher). In '32 Dopyera returns to National and National and Dobro start their merger in late-'33, finalizing it by mid-'34. Throughout the '30s, National and Dobro maintained separate production, sales and distribution. National Dobro moved to Chicago, Illinois in '36. In Chicago, archtop and flat top bodies are built primarily by Regal and Kay; after '37 all National resonator guitar bodies made by Kay. L.A. production is maintained until around '37, although some assembly of Dobros continued in L.A. (primarily for export) until '39 when the L.A. offices are finally closed. By ca. '39 the Dobro brand disappears.

In '42, the company's resonator production ceased and Victor Smith, Al Frost and Louis Dopyera buy the company and change name to Valco Manufacturing Company. Post-war production resumes in '46. Valco is purchased by treasurer Robert Engelhardt in '64. In '67, Valco bought Kay, but in '68 the new Valco/Kay company went out of business. In the Summer of '69 the assets, including brand names, were auctioned off and the National and Supro names were purchased by Chicago-area distributor/importer Strum 'N Drum (Noble, Norma brands). The National brand is used on copies in early- to mid-'70s, and the brand went into hiatus by the '80s.

In '88 National Resophonic Guitars is founded in San Luis Obispo, California, by Don Young, with production of National-style resonator guitars beginning in '89 (see following). In the '90s, the National brand also resurfaces on inexpensive Asian imports.

National Resonator guitars are categorized by materials and decoration (from plain to fancy): Duolian, Triolian, Style 0, Style 1, Style 2, Style 3, Style 4, Don #1, Style 97, Don #2, Don #3, Style 35.

National guitars all have serial numbers which provide clues to date of production. This is a complex issue. This list combines information included in George Gruhn and Walter Carter's Gruhn's Guide to Vintage Guitars, which was originally provided by Bob Brozman and Mike Newton, with new information provided by Mike Newton.

Pre Chicago numbers

A101-A450	1935-1936

Chicago numbers

A prefix (some may not have the prefix)	1936-mid-1997
B prefix	Mid-1937-1938
C prefix	Late-1938-1940
G prefix up to 200	Ea. 1941-ea. 1942
G suffix under 2000	Ea. 1941-ea. 1942
G suffix 2000-3000s (probably old parts)	1943-1945
G suffix 4000s (old parts)	Late 1945-mid-1947
V100-V7500	1947
V7500-V15000	1948
V15000-V25000	1949
V25000-V35000	1950
V35000-V38000	1951
X100-X7000	1951
X7000-X17000	1952
X17000-X30000	1953
X30000-X43000	1954
X43000-X57000	1955
X57000-X71000	1956
X71000-X85000	1957
X85000-X99000	1958
T100-T5000	1958
T5000-T25000	1959
T25000-T50000	1960
T50000-T75000	1961
T75000-T90000	1962
G100-G5000	1962

1985 Nady Lightning

Napolitano Primavera

1931 National Duolian

1949 National California

MODEL YEAR	FEATURES	EXC. COND. LOW	HIGH
T90000-T99000	1963		
G5000-G15000	1963		
G15000-G40000	1964		
1 prefix	1965-ea. 1968		
2 prefix	Mid-1968		

Aragon De Luxe
1939-1942. Archtop with resonator (the only archtop resonator offered), spruce top and maple back and sides, light brown.

1939-1942		$8,000	$10,000

Aristocrat 1110/1111
1948-1955. Electric archtop, full body non-cutaway, single neck pickup, 2 knobs, sunburst, early model with triple backslash markers, later with block markers, National-crest headstock inlaid logo, shaded finish (1110) and natural (1111).

1948-1955		$1,000	$1,250

Avalon 1124
1954-1957. Small wood solidbody, 2 pickups, 4 control knobs and switch on top-mounted 'guard, block markers, short trapeze bridge.

1954-1957		$675	$775

Bel-Aire
1953-1961. Single pointed cut archtop, 2 pickups until '57, 3 after, master tone knob and jack, bound body, sunburst.

1953-1961		$950	$1,175

Bluegrass 35
1963-1965. Acoustic, non-cut single-cone resonator, Res-O-Glas body in Arctic White.

1963-1965		$1,000	$1,250

Bobbie Thomas
Ca.1967-1968. Double-cut thinline hollowbody, bat-shaped f-holes, 2 pickups, Bobbie Thomas on 'guard, vibrato.

1967-1968		$450	$550

Bolero 1123
1954-1957. Les Paul-shape, control knobs mounted on 'guard, single pickup, trapeze tailpiece, sunburst.

1954-1957		$700	$825

California 1100
1949-1955. Electric hollowbody archtop, multi-bound, f-holes, trapeze tailpiece, 1 pickup, natural.

1949-1955		$850	$975

Club Combo
1952-1955, 1959-1961. Electric hollowbody archtop, 2 pickups, rounded cutaway.

1952-1955		$900	$1,100
1959-1961		$800	$1,000

Cosmopolitan 1122
1954-1957. Small wood non-cutaway solidbody, dot markers, 1 pickup, 2 knobs on mounted 'guard.

1954-1957		$300	$375

Debonaire 1107
1953-1960. Single rounded-cutaway full-depth 16" electric archtop, single neck pickup, Debonaire logo on 'guard (for most models), large raised National script logo on headstock, sunburst.

1953-1960		$700	$875

Don Style 1
1934-1936. Plain body with engraved borders, pearl dot inlay, 14 frets, single-cone, silver (nickel-plated).

1934-1936		$8,000	$10,000

Don Style 2
1934-1936. Geometric Art Deco body engraving, 14 frets, single-cone, fancy square pearl inlays and pearloid headstock overlay, silver (nickel-plated).

1934-1936		$10,000	$12,500

Don Style 3
1934-1936. Same as Style 2 but more elaborate floral engravings, fancy pearl diamond inlays, 14 frets, single-cone, silver (nickel-plated), only a very few made.

1934-1936		$16,000	$20,000

Duolian
1930-1939. Acoustic steel body, frosted paint finish until '36, mahogany-grain paint finish '37-'39, round neck, square neck available in '33, 12-fret neck until '34 then 14-fret.

1930-1934	Round neck, 12 frets	$2,800	$3,500
1935-1939	Round neck, 14 frets	$2,700	$3,300

El Trovador
1933 only. Wood body, 12 frets.

1933		$2,000	$2,500

Electric Spanish
1935-1938. 15 1/2" archtop with Pat. Appl. For bridge pickup, National crest logo, fancy N-logo 'guard, black and white art deco, sunburst, becomes New Yorker Spanish '39-'58.

1935-1938		$1,000	$1,200

Estralita
1934-1942. Acoustic with single-cone resonator, f-holes, multi-bound, 14-fret, mahogany top and back, shaded brown.

1934-1942		$675	$825

Glenwood
1954-1958. Les Paul-shaped solidbody, wood body, not fiberglass, single-cut, multi-bound, 2 pickups, natural, renamed Glenwood Deluxe with Bigsby in '59.

1954-1958		$1,200	$1,500

Glenwood 95
1962-1964. Glenwood 98 without third bridge-mount pickup.

1962-1964	Vermillion Red/Flame Red	$2,500	$3,100

Glenwood 98
1964-1965. USA map-shaped solidbody of molded Res-O-Glas, 2 regular and 1 bridge pickup, vibrato, pearl white finish.

1964-1965	Pearl White	$3,000	$3,700

Glenwood 99
1962-1965. USA map-shaped solidbody of molded Res-O-Glas, 2 regular and 1 bridge pickups, butterfly inlay.

1962-1963	Snow White	$3,500	$4,000
1964-1965	Sea Foam Green	$4,000	$4,500

MODEL YEAR	FEATURES	EXC. COND. LOW	HIGH

Glenwood Deluxe
1959-1961. Renamed from Glenwood, Les Paul-shaped solidbody, wood body, not fiberglass, multi-bound, 2 pickups, factory Bigsby, vibrato, natural.

1959-1961		$1,500	$1,875

Model 1155
1948-1961. Flat top acoustic with Gibson Jumbo body, mahogany back and sides, bolt-on neck.

1948-1961		$1,200	$1,500

N-600 Series
1968. Offset double-cut solidbody, 1, 2, and 3 pickup models, with and without vibrato.

1968		$500	$550

N-800 Series
1968. Double-cut semi-hollow body, various models with or without Bigsby.

1968	No Bigsby	$600	$650
1968	With Bigsby	$700	$750

Newport 82
1963-1965. Renamed from Val-Pro 82, USA map-shaped Res-O-Glas, 1 pickup, red finish.

1963-1965	Pepper Red	$1,500	$1,800

Newport 84
1963-1965. Renamed from Val-Pro 84, USA map-shaped Res-O-Glas, 1 regular and 1 bridge pickup, Sea Foam Green finish.

1963-1965	Sea Foam Green	$1,800	$2,200

Newport 88
1963-1965. Renamed from Val-Pro 88, USA map-shaped Res-O-Glas, 2 regular and 1 bridge pickup, black finish.

1963-1965	Raven Black	$1,800	$2,200

Pro Dual Pickup
1960s. Non-catalog Jetson-style res-o-glas type body, National logo, 2 pickups, red.

1960s		$1,000	$1,200

Reso-phonic
1956-1964. Pearloid-covered, single-cut semi-solid-body acoustic, single resonator, maroon or white, also a non-cut, square neck version was offered, which is included in these values.

1956-1964	Round neck	$1,200	$1,500
1956-1964	Square neck	$1,100	$1,200

Rosita
1933-1939. Plywood body by Harmony, plain metal resonator, plain appointments.

1933-1939		$1,000	$1,250

Silvo (Electric Hawaiian)
1937-1941. Nickel-plated metal body flat-top, small upper bout, f-holes, square neck, multiple straight line body art over dark background, Roman numeral parallelogram markers, National badge headstock logo, Silvo name on coverplate.

1937-1941	Silver	$3,000	$3,700

Studio 66
1961-1964. Electric solidbody of Res-O-Glas, single-cut, 1 pickup, renamed Varsity 66 in '65.

1961-1962	Sand Buff, bridge pickup	$1,200	$1,500
1963-1964	Jet Black, neck pickup	$1,200	$1,500

MODEL YEAR	FEATURES	EXC. COND. LOW	HIGH

Style 0
1930-1942. Acoustic single-cone brass body (early models had a steel body), Hawaiian scene etching, 12-fret neck '30-'34, 14-fret neck '35 on, round (all years) or square ('33 on) neck.

1930-1934	Round neck, 12-fret	$3,900	$4,500
1933-1942	Square neck	$3,600	$4,300
1935-1942	Round neck, 14-fret	$3,800	$4,500

Style 0 Tenor

1929-1930		$1,700	$1,900

Style 1 Tricone
1927-1943. German silver body tricone resonator, ebony 'board, mahogany square (Hawaiian) or round (Spanish) neck, plain body, 12-fret neck until '34, 14-fret after.

1927-1932	Round neck	$6,000	$7,400
1928-1932	Square neck	$3,500	$4,100

Style 1 Tricone Plectrum
1928-1935. 26" scale versus the 23" scale of the tenor.

1928-1935		$2,200	$2,700

Style 1 Tricone Tenor
1928-1935. Tenor, 4 strings, 23" scale, square neck is Hawaiian, round neck is Spanish.

1928-1935		$2,200	$2,700

Style 2 Tricone
1927-1942. German silver body tricone resonator, wild rose engraving, square (Hawaiian) or round (Spanish) neck, 12-fret neck until '34, 14-fret after.

1930s	Round neck	$10,000	$12,000
1930s	Square neck	$4,400	$5,000

Style 2 Tricone Plectrum
1928-1935. 26" scale versus the 23" scale of the tenor.

1928-1935		$2,400	$3,000

Style 2 Tricone Tenor
1928-1935. Tenor.

1928-1935		$2,400	$3,000

Style 3 Tricone
1928-1941. German silver body tricone resonator, lily-of-the-valley engraving, square (Hawaiian) or round (Spanish) neck, 12-fret neck until '34, 14-fret after, reintroduced with a nickel-plated brass body in '94.

1930s	Round neck	$18,000	$19,000
1930s	Square neck	$5,500	$6,500
1940-1941	Square neck	$5,000	$6,000

Style 3 Tricone Plectrum
1928-1935. 26" scale versus the 23" scale of the tenor.

1928-1935		$4,200	$5,200

Style 3 Tricone Tenor
1928-1939.

1928-1939		$4,200	$5,200

Style 4 Tricone
1928-1940. German silver body tricone resonator, chrysanthemum etching, 12-fret neck until '34, 14-fret after, reissued in '95 with same specs.

1930s	Round neck	$25,000	$27,000
1930s	Square neck	$7,500	$8,500

1933 National El Trovador

1930s National Style N

National Triolian

*National Reso-Phonic
Single-Biscuit Electric*

MODEL YEAR	FEATURES	EXC. COND. LOW	HIGH

Style 35
1936-1942. Brass body tricone resonator, sandblasted minstrel and trees scene, 12 frets, square (Hawaiian) or round (Spanish) neck.

| 1936-1942 | Round neck | $25,000 | $31,000 |
| 1936-1942 | Square neck | $15,000 | $17,000 |

Style 97
1936-1940. Nickel-plated brass body tricone resonator, sandblasted scene of female surfrider and palm trees, 12 frets, slotted peghead.

| 1930s | Round neck | $15,000 | $18,500 |
| 1930s | Square neck | $7,000 | $8,700 |

Style N
1930-1931. Nickel-plated brass body single-cone resonator, plain finish, 12 frets.

| 1930-1931 | | $7,200 | $8,000 |

Triolian
1928-1941. Single-cone resonator, wood body replaced by metal body in '29, 12-fret neck and slotted headstock '28-'34, changed to 14-fret neck in '35 and solid headstock in '36, round or square ('33 on) neck available.

| 1928-1936 | Various colors | $2,900 | $3,100 |
| 1936-1937 | Fake rosewood grain finish | $2,100 | $2,600 |

Triolian Tenor
1928-1936. Tenor, metal body.

| 1928-1936 | | $1,200 | $1,500 |

Trojan
1934-1942. Single-cone resonator wood body, f-holes, bound top, 14-fret round neck.

| 1934-1942 | | $1,225 | $1,525 |

Val-Pro 82
1962-1963. USA map-shaped Res-O-Glas, 1 pickup, Vermillion Red finish, renamed Newport 82 in '63.

| 1962-1963 | | $1,200 | $1,500 |

Val-Pro 84
1962-1963. USA map-shaped Res-O-Glas, 1 regular and 1 bridge pickup, snow white finish, renamed Newport 84 in '63.

| 1962-1963 | | $1,400 | $1,750 |

Val-Pro 88
1962-1963. USA map-shaped Res-O-Glas, 2 regular and 1 bridge pickup, black finish, renamed Newport 88 in '63.

| 1962-1963 | | $1,900 | $2,350 |

Varsity 66
1964-1965. Renamed from Studio 66 in '64, molded Res-O-Glas, 1 pickup, 2 knobs, beige finish.

| 1964-1965 | | $1,100 | $1,350 |

Westwood 72
1962-1964. USA map-shaped solid hardwood body (not fiberglass), 1 pickup, Cherry Red.

| 1962-1964 | | $1,200 | $1,500 |

Westwood 75
1962-1964. USA map-shaped solid hardwood body (not fiberglass), 1 regular and 1 bridge pickup, cherry-to-black sunburst finish.

| 1962-1964 | | $1,500 | $1,850 |

Westwood 77
1962-1965. USA map-shaped solid hardwood body (not fiberglass), 2 regular and 1 bridge pickup.

| 1962-1965 | Blond-Ivory | $1,500 | $1,850 |

National Reso-Phonic
1988-present. Professional and premium grade, production/custom, single cone, acoustic-electric, and tricone guitars (all with resonators), built in San Luis Obispo, California. They also build basses, mandolins and ukuleles. McGregor Gaines and Don Young formed the National Reso-Phonic Guitar Company with the objective of building instruments based upon the original National designs.

Style 1 Tricone
1994-present. Nickel-plated brass body, bound ebony 'board.

| 1994-1999 | | $1,550 | $1,900 |
| 2000-2007 | | $1,775 | $2,200 |

Navarro Custom
1986-present. Professional and premium grade, production/custom, electric guitars built in San Juan, Puerto Rico by luthier Mike Navarro. He also builds basses.

Neubauer
1966-1990s. Luthier Helmut Neubauer built his acoustic and electric archtop guitars in Bubenreuth, Germany.

New Era Guitars
See listing under ARK - New Era Guitars.

New Orleans Guitar Company
1992-present. Luthier Vincent Guidroz builds his premium grade, production/custom, solid and semi-hollow body guitars in New Orleans, Louisiana.

Nickerson Guitars
1983-present. Luthier Brad Nickerson builds his professional and premium grade, production/custom, archtop and flat-top guitars in Northampton, Massachusetts.

Nielsen
2004-present. Premium grade, custom/production, archtop guitars built by luthier Dale Nielsen in Duluth, Minnesota.

Nik Huber Guitars
1997-present. Premium grade, production/custom, electric guitars built in Rodgau, Germany by luthier Nik Huber.

Nioma
1930s. Brand most likely used by a music studio (or distributor) on instruments made by others, including Regal-built resonator instruments.

MODEL YEAR	FEATURES	EXC. COND. LOW	HIGH

Noble

Ca. 1950-ca. 1969. Instruments made by others and distributed by Don Noble and Company of Chicago. Plastic-covered guitars made by EKO debut in '62. Aluminum-necked Wandré guitars added to the line in early-'63. By ca. '65-'66 the brand is owned by Chicago-area importer and distributor Strum 'N Drum and used mainly on Japanese-made solidbodies. Strum 'N Drum bought the National brand name in '69 and imported Japanese copies of American designs under the National brand and Japanese original designs under Norma through the early '70s. The Noble brand disappears at least by the advent of the Japanese National brand, if not before. They also offered amps and basses.

Norma

Ca.1965-1970. Imported from Japan by Strum 'N Drum, Inc. of Chicago (see Noble brand info). Early examples were built by Tombo, most notably sparkle plastic covered guitars and basses.

Electric Solidbody

1965-1970s. Type of finish has affect on value. Various models include; EG-350 (student double-cut, 1 pickup), EG-403 (unique pointy cutaway, 2 pickups), EG-400 (double-cut, 2 pickups), EG-450 (double-cut, 2 split-coil pickups), EG-421 (double-cut, 4 pickups), EG-412-12 (double-cut, 12-string).

1965-1968	Blue, red, gold sparkle	$300	$500
1965-1970s	Non-sparkle	$150	$300

Norman

1972-present. Intermediate grade, production, acoustic and acoustic/electric guitars built in LaPatrie, Quebec. Norman was the first guitar production venture luthier Robert Godin was involved with. He has since added the Seagull, Godin, and Patrick & Simon brands of instruments.

Northworthy Guitars

1987-present. Professional and premium grade, production/custom, flat-top and electric guitars built by luthier Alan Marshall in Ashbourne, Derbyshire, England. He also builds basses and mandolins.

Norwood

1960s. Budget guitars imported most likely from Japan.

Electric Solidbody

1960s. Offset double-cut body, 3 soapbar-style pickups, Norwood label on headstock.

1960s		$150	$175

Novax Guitars

1989-present. Luthier Ralph Novak builds his fanned-fret professional and premium grade, production/custom, solidbody and acoustic guitars in San Leandro, California. He also builds basses.

Noyce

1974-present. Luthier Ian Noyce builds his production/custom, professional and premium grade, acoustic and electric guitars in Ballarat, Victoria, Australia. He also builds basses.

Nyberg Instruments

1993-present. Professional grade, custom, flat-top and Maccaferri-style guitars built by luthier Lawrence Nyberg in Hornby Island, British Columbia. He also builds mandolins, mandolas, bouzoukis and citterns.

Oahu

1926-1985, present. The Oahu Publishing Company and Honolulu Conservatory, based in Cleveland, Ohio was active in the sheet music and student instrument business in the '30s. An instrument, set of instructional sheet music, and lessons were offered as a complete package. Lessons were often given to large groups of students. Instruments, lessons, and sheet music could also be purchased by mail order. The Oahu Publishing Co. advertised itself as The World's Largest Guitar Dealer. Most '30s Oahu guitars were made by Kay with smaller numbers from the Oscar Schmidt Company.

Guitar Models from the Mid-'30s include: 71K (jumbo square neck), 72K (jumbo roundneck), 68B (jumbo, vine body decoration), 68K (deluxe jumbo square neck), 69K (deluxe jumbo roundneck), 65K and 66K (mahogany, square neck), 64K and 67K (mahogany, roundneck), 65M (standard--size, checker binding, mahogany), 53K (roundneck, mahogany), 51 (black, Hawaiian scene, pearlette 'board), 51K (black, pond scene decoration), 52K (black, Hawaiian scene decoration), 50 and 50K (student guitar, brown). The brand has been revived on a line of tube amps.

Graphic Body

1930s. 13" painted artwork bodies, includes Styles 51 and 52 Hawaiian scene.

1930s	Floral, higher appointments	$350	$425
1930s	Hawaiian scene	$350	$425

Round Neck 14" Flat-Top

1930s. Spruce top, figured maple back and sides, thin logo.

1932		$1,000	$1,250

Style 50K Student

Student-size guitar, brown finish.

1935		$200	$250

Style 65M

Standard-size mahogany body, checker binding, natural brown.

1933-1935		$450	$550

Style 68K De Luxe Jumbo

Hawaiian, 15.5" wide, square neck, Brazilian back and sides, spruce top, fancy pearl vine inlay, abalone trim on top and soundhole, rosewood pyramid bridge, fancy pearl headstock inlay, butterbean tuners, ladder-braced, natural. High-end model made for Oahu by Kay.

1935		$3,800	$4,200

Nickerson Guitars Virtuoso

Novax Charlie Hunter

To get the most from this book, be sure to read "Using *The Guide*" in the introduction.

O'Hagan Twenty-Two

Oscar Schmidt OE

MODEL YEAR	FEATURES	EXC. COND. LOW	HIGH

Odessa

1981-1990s. Budget guitars imported by Davitt & Hanser (BC Rich). Mainly acoustics in the '90s, but some electrics early on.

O'Hagan

1979-1983. Designed by clarinetist and importer Jerol O'Hagan in St. Louis Park, Minnesota. Primarily neck-thru construction, most with German-carved bodies. In '81 became Jemar Corporation and in '83 it was closed by the I.R.S., a victim of recession.

SN=YYM(M)NN (e.g., 80905, September '80, 5th guitar); or MYMNNN (e.g., A34006, April 1983, 6th guitar). Approximately 3000 total instruments were made with the majority being NightWatches (approx. 200 Twenty Twos, 100-150 Sharks, 100 Lasers; about 25 with birdseye maple

Electric

1979-1983. Models include; Laser (solidbody, double-cut, maple or walnut body, set-thru neck, 3 single-coil Schaller pickups), Shark (Explorer-looking solidbody) and Twenty Two (V, 2 humbuckers).

1979-1983		$425	$525

Ohio

1959-ca. 1965. Line of electric solidbodies and basses made by France's Jacobacci company, which also built under its own brand. Sparkle finish, bolt-on aluminum necks, strings-thru-body design.

Old Kraftsman

Ca. 1930s-ca. 1960s. Brandname used by the Spiegel catalog company for instruments made by other American manufacturers, including Regal, Kay and even Gibson. The instruments were of mixed quality, but some better grade instruments were comparable to those offered by Wards.

Archtop

1930s-1960s. Various models.

1930s	17", Stauffer-style headstock	$350	$425
1950s		$250	$300
1960s		$250	$300

Flat-Top

1930s-1960s. Various models.

1950s	Prairie Ramblers (stencil)	$250	$300

Thin Twin Jimmy Reed

1952-1958	$700	$875

OLP (Officially Licensed Product)

Intermediate grade, production, guitars based on higher dollar guitar models officially licensed from the original manufacturer. OLP logo on headstock. They also offer basses.

Olson Guitars

1977-present. Luthier James A. Olson builds his presentation grade, custom, flat-tops in Circle Pines, Minnesota.

Omega

1996-present. Luthier Kevin Gallagher builds his premium grade, custom/production acoustic guitars in East Saylorsburg, Pennsylvania.

Oncor Sound

1980-ca. 1981. This Salt Lake City-based company made both a guitar and a bass synthesizer.

Opus

1972-Mid 1970s. Acoustic and classical guitars, imported from Japan by Ampeg/Selmer. In '75-'76, Harmony made a line of acoustics with the Opus model name.

Ormsby Guitars

2003-present. Luthier Perry Ormsby builds his custom, professional and premium grade, solid and chambered electric guitars in Perth, Western Australia.

Orpheum

1897-1942, 1944-early 1970s, 2001-2006. Intermediate grade, production, acoustic and resonator guitars. They also offer mandolins. Orpheum originally was a brand of Rettberg and Lange, who made instruments for other companies as well. William Rettberg and William Lange bought the facilities of New York banjo maker James H. Buckbee in 1897. Lange went out on his own in '21 to start the Paramount brand. He apparently continued using the Orpheum brand as well. He went out of business in '42. In '44 the brand was acquired by New York's Maurice Lipsky Music Co. who used it primarily on beginner to medium grade instruments, which were manufactured by Regal, Kay, and United Guitar (and maybe others). In the early '60s Lipsky applied the brand to Japanese and European (by Egmond) imports. Lipsky dropped the name in the early '70s. The brand was revived for '01 to '06 by Tacoma Guitars.

Auditorium Archtop 835/837

1950s. Acoustic archtop, auditorium size, dot markers, Orpheum shell headpiece, white celluloid 'guard, model 835 with spruce top/back/sides, 837 with mahogany.

1950s		$225	$275

Orpheum Special (Regal-made)

1930s. Slot head, Dobro-style wood body, metal resonator, sunburst.

1930s		$800	$1,000

Thin Twin Jimmy Reed 865E

1950s. Model 865E is the Orpheum version of the generically named Thin Twin Jimmy Reed style electric Spanish cutaway thin solidbody, hand engraved shell celluloid Orpheum headpiece, described as #865E Cutaway Thin Electric Guitar in catalog.

1950s		$700	$875

MODEL YEAR	FEATURES	EXC. COND. LOW	HIGH

Ultra Deluxe Professional 899

1950s. 17" cutaway, 2 pickups, 2 knobs, maple back and sides, top material varies, dot markers, finishes as follows: E-C copper, E-G gold, E-G-B gold-black sunburst, E-B blond curly maple, E-S golden orange sunburst.

1950s	All finishes	$1,200	$1,500

Orville by Gibson

1984-1993. Orville by Gibson and Orville guitars were made by Japan's Fuji Gen Gakki for Gibson. Basically the same models except the Orville by Gibson guitars had real Gibson USA PAF '57 Classic pickups and a true nitrocellulose lacquer finish. The Orville models used Japanese electronics and a poly finish. Some Orvilles were made in Korea and are of a lower quality. These Korean guitars had the serial number printed on a sticker. Prices here are for the Orville by Gibson models.

Electric

1990-1994	Les Paul Standard	$800	$1,000
1990s	Les Paul Jr., double-cut.	$400	$500
1990s	Les Paul Studio J.P.	$750	$900
1990s	MM/Les Paul Jr., single-cut	$300	$375
1990s	SG Les Paul Standard	$550	$650
1993	ES-175	$900	$1,100
1993	ES-335	$800	$1,000
1995	Flying V	$800	$1,000
1995-1998	Les Paul Custom	$800	$1,000

Oscar Schmidt

1879-1938, 1979-present. Budget and intermediate grade, production, acoustic, acoustic/electric, and electric guitars distributed by U.S. Music Corp. (Washburn, Randall, etc.). They also offer basses, mandolins, banjos, ukuleles and the famous Oscar Schmidt autoharp.

The original Oscar Schmidt Company, Jersey City, New Jersey, offered banjo mandolins, tenor banjos, guitar banjos, ukuleles, mandolins and guitars under their own brand and others (including Sovereign and Stella). By the early 1900s, the company had factories in the U.S. and Europe producing instruments. Oscar Schmidt was also an early contributor to innovative mandolin designs and the company participated in the '00-'30 mandolin boom. The company hit hard times during the Depression and was sold to Harmony by the end of the '30s. In '79, Washburn acquired the brand and it is now part of U.S. Music.

Oskar Graf Guitars

1970-present. Premium and presentation grade, custom, archtop, acoustic and classical guitars built in Clarendon, Ontario, Canada by luthier Oskar Graf. He also builds basses and lutes.

Otwin

1950s-1960s. A brand used on electric guitars made by the Musima company of East Germany. Musima also produced guitars under their own brand.

Outbound Instruments

1990-2002. Intermediate grade, production, travel-size acoustics from the Boulder, Colorado-based company.

Ovation

1966-present. Intermediate and professional grade, production, acoustic and acoustic/electric guitars built in the U.S. They also build basses and mandolins.

Ovation's parent company, helicopter manufacturer Kaman Corporation, was founded in 1945 by jazz guitarist and aeronautical engineer Charles Huron Kaman in Bloomfield, Connecticut. In the '60s, after losing a government contract, Kaman began looking to diversify. When offers to buy Martin and Harmony were rejected, Kaman decided to use their helicopter expertise (working with synthetic materials, spruce, high tolerances) and designed, with the help of employee and violin restorer John Ringso, the first fiberglass-backed (Lyracord) acoustic guitars in '65. Production began in '66 and the music factory moved to New Hartford, Connecticut, in '67. Early input was provided by fingerstyle jazz guitarist Charlie Byrd, who gave Kaman the idea for the name Ovation. C. William Kaman II became president of the company in '85. Kaman Music purchased Hamer Guitars in '88, and Trace Elliot amplifiers (U.K.) in '90. On January 1, '08, Fender acquired Kaman Music Corporation and the Ovation brand.

Adamas 1587

1979-1998. Carbon top, walnut, single-cut, bowl back, binding, mini-soundholes.

1979-1998	Black Sparkle	$1,500	$1,800

Adamas 1597

1998-1999. Carbon birch composite top, on-board electronics.

1998-1999	Black	$800	$900

Adamas 1687

1977-1998. Acoustic/electric, carbon top, non-cut, bowl back, mini-soundholes.

1977-1998	Sunburst	$1,700	$1,800

Adamas II 1881 NB-2

1993-1998. Acoustic/electric, single-cut, shallow bowl.

1993-1998	Brown	$1,500	$1,800

Anniversary Electric 1657

1978. Deep bowl, acoustic/electric, abalone inlays, gold-plated parts, carved bridge, for Ovation's 10th anniversary. They also offered an acoustic Anniversary.

1978		$500	$625

Oskar Graf Parlour

Otwin Deluxe

GUITARS

Ovation Breadwinner

1986 Ovation G2S

MODEL YEAR	FEATURES	EXC. COND. LOW	HIGH
Balladeer 1111			
1968-1983, 1993-2000. Acoustic, non-cut with deep bowl, bound body, natural top, later called the Standard Balladeer.			
1976-1983	Natural	$400	$475
Balladeer Artist 1121			
1968-1990. Acoustic, non-cut with shallow bowl, bound body.			
1968-1969	Early production	$450	$550
1970-1990		$350	$425
Balladeer Classic 1122			
1970s. Classical shallow-bowl version of Concert Classic, nylon strings, slotted headstock.			
1970s		$325	$400
Balladeer Custom 1112			
1976-1990. Acoustic, deep bowl, diamond inlays.			
1976-1990	Natural	$400	$500
Balladeer Custom 12-String Electric 1655/1755			
1982-1994. 12-string version of Balladeer Custom Electric.			
1982-1994	Sunburst	$400	$500
Balladeer Custom Electric 1612/1712			
1976-1990. Acoustic/electric version of Balladeer Custom, deep bowl.			
1976-1990	Natural	$500	$575
Balladeer Standard 1661/1761			
1982-2000. Acoustic/electric, deep bowl, rounded cutaway.			
1982-2000		$525	$575
Breadwinner 1251			
1971-1983. Axe-like shaped single-cut solidbody, 2 pickups, textured finish, black, blue, tan or white.			
1971-1983		$825	$900
Celebrity CC-57			
1990-1996. Laminated spruce top, shallow bowl, mahogany neck.			
1990-1996	Black	$200	$225
Celebrity CK-057			
2002-2004. Acoustic/electric rounded cutaway, shallow back.			
2002-2004		$400	$425
Celebrity CS-257 (Import)			
1992-2005. Super shallow bowl back body, single-cut, Adamas soundholes, alternating dot and diamond markers, made in Korea.			
1992-2005	Black	$300	$375
Classic 1613/1713			
1971-1993. Acoustic/electric, non-cut, deep bowl, no inlay, slotted headstock, gold tuners.			
1971-1993	Natural	$450	$550
Classic 1663/1763			
1982-1998. Acoustic/electric, single-cut, deep bowl, cedar top, EQ, no inlay, slotted headstock, gold tuners.			
1982-1998		$550	$650
Classic 1863			
1989-1998. Acoustic/electric, single-cut, shallow bowl, no inlay, cedar top, EQ, slotted headstock, gold tuners.			
1989-1998		$500	$600

MODEL YEAR	FEATURES	EXC. COND. LOW	HIGH
Collectors Series			
1982-present. Limited edition, different model featured each year and production limited to that year only, the year designation is marked at the 12th fret, various colors (each year different).			
1982-2007		$725	$900
Concert Classic 1116			
1974-1990. Deep-bowl nylon string classical, slotted headstock.			
1974-1990		$350	$425
Contemporary Folk Classic Electric 1616			
1974-1990. Acoustic/electric, no inlay, slotted headstock, natural or sunburst.			
1974-1990	Natural	$300	$350
Country Artist Classic Electric 1624			
1971-1990. Nylon strings, slotted headstock, standard steel-string sized neck to simulate a folk guitar, on-board electronics.			
1971-1990		$400	$500
Country Artist Classic Electric 6773			
1995-present. Classic electric, soft-cut, solid spruce top, slotted headstock, Ovation pickup system.			
1995-2007		$400	$500
Custom Ballader 1762			
1992. Rounded cutaway, higher-end specs.			
1992		$700	$750
Custom Legend 1117			
1970s. Non-electrical 2nd generation Ovation, higher-end with abalone inlays and gold hardware, open V-bracing pattern. Model 1117-4, natural.			
1970s		$600	$700
Custom Legend 1569			
1980s. Rounded cutaway acoustic/electric, super shallow bowl, gloss black finish.			
1980s		$650	$800
Custom Legend 1619/1719			
1970s. Acoustic/electric 2nd generation Ovation, electric version of model 1117, higher-end with abalone inlays and gold hardware, open V-bracing pattern.			
1970s		$650	$800
Custom Legend 1759			
1984-2004. Single-cut acoustic/electric.			
1990s		$850	$950
Custom Legend 1769			
1982,1993, 1996-1999. Single-cut acoustic/electric.			
1990s		$1,000	$1,050
Deacon 1252			
1973-1980. Axe-shaped solidbody electric, active electronics, diamond fret markers.			
1973-1980	Sunburst	$700	$800
Deacon 12-String 1253			
1975. Axe-shaped solidbody, diamond inlay, 2 pickups. only a few made.			
1975		$700	$800
Eclipse			
1971-1973. Thinline double cut acoustic-electric archtop, 2 pickups.			
1971-1973		$700	$850

The *Vintage Guitar Price Guide* shows low to high values for items in all-original excellent condition, and, where applicable, with original case or cover.

MODEL YEAR	FEATURES	EXC. COND. LOW	HIGH

Elite 1718
1982-1997. Acoustic/electric, non-cut, deep bowl, solid spruce top, Adamas-type soundhole, volume and tone controls, stereo output.

1982-1997	Sunburst	$700	$800

Elite 1758
1990-1998. Acoustic/electric, non-cut, deep bowl.

1990-1998		$700	$850

Elite 1768
1990-1998. Acoustic/electric, cutaway, deep bowl.

1990-1998	Natural	$700	$850

Elite 1868
1983-2004. Acoustic/electric, cutaway, shallow bowl.

1983-2004	Sunburst	$650	$800

Elite 5858
1991. Super shallow bowl, single cutaway, Adamas-style soundhole, gold hardware, on-board factory OP24 pickup.

1991		$800	$1,000

Elite Doubleneck
1989-1990s. Six- and 12-string necks, can be ordered with a variety of custom options.

1989		$800	$900

Folklore 1614
1972-1983. Acoustic/electric, 12-fret neck on full-size body, wide neck, on-board electronics.

1972-1983		$500	$600

Glen Campbell 12-String 1118 (K-1118)
1968-1982. Acoustic, 12 strings, shallow bowl version of Legend, gold tuners, diamond inlay.

1968-1982		$500	$600

Glen Campbell Artist Balladeer 1127
1968-1990. Acoustic, shallow bowl, diamond inlay, gold tuners.

1968-1990	Natural	$500	$600

Hurricane 12-String K-1120
1968-1969. ES-335-style electric semi-hollowbody, double-cut, 12 strings, f-holes, 2 pickups.

1968-1969		$700	$875

Josh White 1114
1967-1970, 1972-1983. Designed by and for folk and blues singer Josh White, has wide 12-fret to the body neck, dot markers, classical-style tuners.

1967-1970		$600	$700
1972-1983		$500	$600

Legend 1117
1972-1999. Deep bowl acoustic, 5-ply top binding, gold tuners, various colors (most natural).

1972-1999		$550	$600

Legend 12-String 1866
1989-present. Acoustic/electric, cutaway, 12 strings, shallow bowl, 5-ply top binding.

1989-2007	Black	$600	$750

Legend 1717
1990-present. Acoustic/electric, 5-ply top binding, various colors.

1990-2007		$600	$750

Legend 1869
1994. Acoustic/electric, cutaway, super shallow bowl.

1994	Natural	$700	$800

Legend Cutaway 1667
1982-1996. Acoustic/electric, cutaway, deep bowl, abalone, gold tuners.

1982-1996		$650	$750

Legend Electric 1617
1972-1998. Acoustic/electric, deep bowl, abalone, gold tuners, various colors.

1972-1998		$525	$600

Pacemaker 12-String 1115/1615
1968-1982. Originally called the K-1115 12-string, Renamed Pacemaker in '72.

1968-1982		$675	$775

Patriot Bicentennial
*1976. Limited run of 1776 guitars, Legend Custom model with drum and flag decal and 1776*1976 decal on lower bout.*

1976		$700	$800

Pinnacle
1990-1992. Spruce or sycamore top, broad leaf pattern rosette, mahogany neck, piezo bridge pickup.

1990-1992	Sunburst	$450	$500

Pinnacle Shallow Cutaway
1990-1994. Pinnacle with shallow bowl body and single-cut.

1990-1994	Sunburst	$450	$550

Preacher 1281
1975-1982. Solidbody, mahogany body, double-cut, 2 pickups.

1975-1982		$650	$750

Preacher Deluxe 1282
1975-1982. Double-cut solidbody, 2 pickups with series/parallel pickup switch and mid-range control.

1975-1982		$600	$700

Preacher 12-String 1285
1975-1983. Double-cut solidbody, 12 strings, 2 pickups.

1975-1983		$650	$750

Thunderhead 1460
1968-1972. Double-cut, 2 pickups, gold hardware, phase switch, master volume, separate tone controls, pickup balance/blend control, vibrato.

1968-1972	Natural or rare color	$1,000	$1,250
1968-1972	Sunburst	$800	$1,000

Tornado 1260
1968-1973. Same as Thunderhead without phase switch, with chrome hardware.

1968-1973		$800	$1,000

UK II 1291
1980-1982. Single-cut solidbody, 2 pickups, body made of Urelite on aluminum frame, bolt-on neck, gold hardware.

1980-1982		$800	$900

Ultra GS
1985. Double-cut solidbody electrics, 1, 2, or 3 pickups.

1985		$300	$375

Viper 1271
1975-1982. Single-cut, 2 single-coil pickups.

1975-1982		$700	$875

Ovation K-1360

Ovation Tornado

MODEL YEAR	FEATURES	EXC. COND. LOW	HIGH

Viper EA 68
1994-present. Thin acoustic/electric, single-cut mahogany body, spruce top over sound chamber with multiple upper bout soundholes, black.

| 1994-2007 | | $725 | $900 |

Viper III 1273
1975-1982. Single-cut, 3 single-coil pickups.

| 1975-1982 | | $725 | $900 |

P. W. Crump Company
1975-present. Luthier Phil Crump builds his custom flat-top guitars in Arcata, California. He also builds mandolin-family instruments.

Pagan
Guitars made in Germany and imported into the U.S. by a guitar shop.

Palen
1998-present. Premium grade, production/custom, archtop guitars built by luthier Nelson Palen in Beloit, Kansas.

Palmer
Early 1970s-present. Budget and intermediate grade, production acoustic, acoustic/electric and classical guitars imported from Europe and Asia. They also have offered electrics.

Panache
2004-present. Budget grade, production, solid-body electric and acoustic guitars imported from China.

PANaramic
1961-1963. Guitars and basses made in Italy by the Crucianelli accordion company and imported by PANaramic accordion. They also offered amps made by Magnatone.

Acoustic-Electric Archtop
1961-1963. Full body cutaway, 2 pickups.

| 1961-1963 | | $1,400 | $1,500 |

Pantheon Guitars
2000-present. Patrick Theimer created Pantheon which offers premium grade, production/custom, flat-tops built by seven luthiers (including Dana Bourgeois) working in an old 1840s textile mill in Lewiston, Maine.

Paolo Soprani
Early 1960s. Italian plastic covered guitars with pushbutton controls made by the Polverini Brothers.

Paramount
1920s-1942, Late 1940s. The William L. Lange Company began selling Paramount banjos, guitar banjos and mandolin banjos in the early 1920s, and added archtop guitars in '34. The guitars were made by Martin and possibly others. Lange went out of

Parker PM-10N

Patrick James Eggle Etowah

business by '42; Gretsch picked up the Paramount name and used it on acoustics and electrics for a time in the late '40s.

GB
1920s-1930s. Guitar banjo.

| 1920s | | $1,600 | $1,900 |

Style C
1930s. 16" acoustic archtop, maple back and sides.

| 1930s | | $600 | $750 |

Style L
1930s. Small body with resonator, limited production to about 36 instruments.

| 1930s | | $2,500 | $3,100 |

Parker
1992-present. U.S.-made and imported intermediate, professional, and premium grade, production/custom, solidbody guitars featuring a thin skin of carbon and glass fibers bonded to a wooden guitar body. In '05, they added wood body acoustic/electrics. They also build basses. Originally located northwest of Boston, Parker was founded by Ken Parker and Larry Fishman (Fishman Transducers). Korg USA committed money to get the Fly Deluxe model into production in July '93. Parker added a Custom Shop in '03 to produce special build instruments and non-core higher-end models that were no longer available as a standard product offering. In early '04, Parker was acquired by U.S. Music Corp.

Concert
1997 only. Solid sitka spruce top, only piezo system pickup, no magnetic pickups, transparent butterscotch.

| 1997 | | $1,325 | $1,425 |

Fly
1993-1994. There are many Parker Fly models, the model simply called Fly is similar to the more common Fly Deluxe, except it does not have the Fishman piezo pickup system.

| 1993-1994 | | $1,100 | $1,400 |

Fly Artist
1998-1999. Solid sitka spruce top, vibrato, Deluxe-style electronics, transparent blond finish.

| 1998-1999 | | $1,550 | $1,750 |

Fly Classic
1996-1998, 2000-present. One-piece Honduras mahogany body, basswood neck, electronics same as Fly Deluxe.

| 1996-2007 | | $1,100 | $1,400 |

Fly Deluxe
1993-present. Poplar body, basswood neck, 2 pickups, Fishman bridge transducer, '93-'96 models were offered with or without vibrato, then non-vibrato discontinued. The Deluxe normally came with a gig bag, but also offered with a hardshell case, which would add about $50 to the values listed.

| 1993-2007 | | $925 | $1,300 |

MODEL YEAR	FEATURES	EXC. COND. LOW	HIGH

Fly Maple Classic
2000. Classic with maple body (vs. mahogany), transparent butterscotch.

2000		$1,250	$1,450

Fly Supreme
1996-1999. One-piece flame maple body, electronics same as the Fly Deluxe, includes hard molded case.

1990s	Highly flamed butterscotch	$1,950	$2,250

NiteFly/NiteFly NFV1/NFV3/NFV5
1996-1999. Three single-coil pickup NiteFly, Fishman piezo system, bolt neck, maple body for '96-'98, ash for '99. Called the NiteFly in '96, NiteFly NFV1 ('97-'98), NiteFly NFV3 ('98), NiteFly NFV5 ('99).

1996-1999		$550	$650

NiteFly/NiteFly NFV2/NFV4/NFV6/SA
1996-present. Two single-coil and 1 humbucker pickup NiteFly, Fishman piezo system, bolt neck, maple body for '96-'98, ash for '99-present. Called the NiteFly in '96, NiteFly NFV2 ('97-'98), NiteFly NFV4 ('98), NiteFly NFV6 ('99), NiteFly SA ('00-present).

1996-2007		$425	$525

P Series
2000-present. Various models include P-38 (ash body, bolt maple neck, rosewood 'board, vibrato, piezo bridge pickup and active Parker Alnico humbucker and 2 single-coils, gig bag); P-40 (as P-38, but with pickups mounted on body, no 'guard); P-44 (mahogany body, flamed maple top, piezo bridge pickup and 2 special Parker humbuckers).

2000-2007		$375	$450

Tulipwood Limited Edition
1998. Limited build of 35 guitars, standard Deluxe features with tulipwood body.

1998		$1,350	$1,450

Patrick Eggle Guitars
1991-present. Founded by Patrick Eggle and others in Birmingham, England, building solid and semi-solidbody electric guitars. They also build basses. In '95, Eggle left the company to build acoustics.

Patrick James Eggle
2001-present. Eggle co-founded the Patrick Eggle Guitar company in '91 building solidbodies. In '95, he left to do repairs and custom work. In '01 he opened a new workshop in Bedforshire, England, building professional and premium grade, production/custom, archtop and flatop guitars. He has since relocated to Hendersonville, North Carolina.

Paul Berger
1972-present. Acoustic guitars built by luthier Paul Berger originally in Apopka, Florida, and currently in Nazareth, Pennsylvania.

Paul Reed Smith
1985-present. Intermediate, professional and premium grade, production/custom, solid, semi-hollow body, and acoustic guitars made in the U.S. and imported. They also build basses. Paul Reed Smith built his first guitar in '75 as an independent study project in college and refined his design over the next 10 years building custom guitars. After building two prototypes and getting several orders from East Coast guitar dealers, Smith was able to secure the support necessary to start PRS in a factory on Virginia Avenue in Annapolis, Maryland. On '95, they moved to their current location on Kent Island in Stevensville. In 2001 PRS introduced the Korean-made SE Series. Acoustics were added in '08

10th Anniversary
1995. Only 200 made, offset double-cut, carved maple figured top, mahogany body, ebony 'board, mother-of-pearl inlays, abalone purfling, gold McCarty pickups, either 22-fret wide-fat or wide-thin mahogany neck, 10th Anniversary logo, price includes Certificate of Authenticity.

1995	With certificate	$4,800	$6,000

513 Rosewood
Dec.2003-2006. Brazilian rosewood neck, newly developed PRS pickup system with 13 sound settings, hum-single-hum pickups.

2003-2006		$3,400	$3,500

Artist/Artist I/Artist 24
1991-1994. Carved maple top, offset double-cut mahogany body, 24-fret neck, bird markers, less than 500 made. A different Custom 24 Artist package was subsequently offered in the 2000s.

1991-1994		$3,000	$3,600

Artist II/Artist 22
1993-1995. Curly maple top, mahogany body and neck, maple purfling on rosewood 'board, inlaid maple bound headstock, abalone birds, 22 frets, gold hardware, short run of less than 500 instruments.

1993-1995		$2,300	$2,800

Artist III
1996-1997. Continuation of the 22-fret neck with some changes in materials and specs, figured maple tops, short run of less than 500 instruments.

1996-1997	Black Cherry	$2,200	$2,800

Artist IV
1996. Continuation of the 22-fret neck with some upgrades in materials and specs, short run of less than 70 instruments.

1996		$3,000	$3,600

Artist Limited
1994-1995. Like the Artist II with 14-carat gold bird inlays, abalone purfling on neck, headstock and truss rod cover, Brazilian rosewood 'board, 165 made.

1994-1995		$3,000	$3,600

CE 22
1994-2000, 2005-present. Double-cut carved alder body (1995), mahogany '96-'00 and '05-'07, back to alder in '08, bolt-on maple neck with rosewood 'board, dot inlays, 2 humbuckers, chrome hardware, translucent colors, options include vibrato and gold hardware and custom colors.

1994-1995	Alder	$1,100	$1,300
1996-2000	Mahogany	$1,100	$1,300
2005-2007	Mahogany	$1,100	$1,300

PRS 513 Rosewood

PRS CE 22

PRS Custom 22

PRS Custom 24 Brazilian

CE 22 Maple Top
1994-present. CE 22 with figured maple top, upgrade options included gold hardware, custom colors or 10 top.

MODEL YEAR	FEATURES	EXC. COND. LOW	HIGH
1994-1995		$1,275	$1,500
1996-2007		$1,275	$1,400

CE 24 (Classic Electric, CE)
1988-2000, 2005-present. Double-cut, alder body to '95, mahogany '96-'00 and '05-'07, back to alder in '08, carved top, 24-fret bolt-on maple neck, 2 humbuckers, dot inlays, upgrade options included gold hardware, custom colors or 10 top.

1988-1991	Rosewood 'board	$1,400	$1,750
1992-1995	Alder	$1,200	$1,400
1996-2000	Mahogany	$1,100	$1,300
2005-2007	Mahogany	$1,100	$1,300

CE 24 Mahogany
2006-present. CE 24 with mahogany top, upgrade options may include any or all the following: gold hardware, custom colors or 10 top.

2006-2007		$1,400	$1,600

CE 24 Maple Top (CE Maple Top)
1989-present. CE 24 with figured maple top, upgrade options may include any or all the following: gold hardware, custom colors or 10 top.

1988-1991		$1,500	$1,850
1992-1995		$1,200	$1,500
1996-2007		$1,100	$1,350

Corvette
2005-2006. Custom 22 with Velcity Yellow finish, Standard 22 red finish, Z06 inlays, Corvette logo on body.

2006	Standard 22	$1,400	$1,600

Custom (Custom 24/PRS Custom)
1985-present. Double-cut solidbody, curly maple top, mahogany back and neck, pearl and abalone moon inlays, 24 frets, 2 humbuckers, tremolo, options include quilted or 10 Top, bird inlays, and gold hardware.

1985		$5,200	$6,500
1986		$4,000	$5,000
1987		$4,000	$5,000
1988		$3,400	$4,200
1989-1991		$2,000	$2,500
1992-1995		$1,900	$2,100
1996-2004		$1,900	$2,100
1996-2004	Custom 24 Artist	$2,100	$2,400
2005	20th Anniversary	$1,900	$2,200
2006-2007	Plat. metallic finish	$1,800	$1,950

Custom 22
1993-present. Custom 22 with flamed or quilted maple top on mahogany body, 22-fret set-neck, upgrade option is gold hardware, normally the quilt top is higher than flamed top.

1993-1995		$1,800	$2,100
1996-1999		$1,800	$2,100
2000-2007	Custom 22 Artist, bird markers	$2,100	$2,400
2000-2007	Dot marker	$1,800	$2,100

Custom 22 (Brazilian)
2003-2004. Limited run of 500 with Brazilian rosewood 'board, figured 10 top, pearl bird inlays.

2003-2004		$3,400	$3,600

Custom 22/12
December 2003-present. 12-string version, flame or quilt maple top, hum/single/hum pickups.

MODEL YEAR	FEATURES	EXC. COND. LOW	HIGH
2003-2007		$2,500	$3,000

Custom 24 (Brazilian)
2003-2004. Limited run with Brazilian rosewood 'board, figured 10 top, pearl bird inlays.

2003-2004		$2,700	$3,300

Custom 24 (Walnut)
1992. Seamless matched walnut over mahogany, 3 made.

1992		$3,500	$4,300

Dave Navaro Signature
2005-present. Carved maple top, bird inlays, tremolo, white

2005-2007		$1,800	$2,200

Dragon I
1992. 22 frets, PRS Dragon pickups, wide-fat neck, gold hardware, 'board inlay of a dragon made of 201 pieces of abalone, turquoise and mother-of-pearl, limited production of 50 guitars.

1992		$21,000	$25,000

Dragon II
1993. 22 frets, PRS Dragon pickups, wide-fat neck, gold hardware, 'board inlay of a dragon made of 218 pieces of gold, coral, abalone, malachite, onyx and mother-of-pearl, limited production of 100 guitars.

1993		$14,000	$17,000

Dragon III
1994. Carved maple top, mahogany back, 22 frets, PRS Dragon pickups, wide-fat neck, gold hardware, 'board inlay of a dragon made of 438 pieces of gold, red and green abalone, mother-of-pearl, mammoth ivory, and stone, limited production of 100 guitars.

1994		$16,000	$20,000

Dragon 2000
1999-2000. Three-D dragon inlay in body versus neck inlay of previous models, limited production of 50 guitars.

1999-2000		$13,000	$16,000

Dragon 2002
2002. Limited edition of 100 guitars, ultra-inlay work depicting dragon head on the guitar body.

2002		$13,000	$16,000

Dragon Doubleneck
2005. Limited edition 20th Anniversary model, about 50 made.

2005		$16,000	$20,000

EG II
1991-1995. Double-cut solidbody, bolt-on neck, 3 single-coils, single-single-hum, or hum-single-hum pickup options, opaque finish.

1991-1995		$975	$1,200

EG II Maple Top
1991-1995. EG II with flamed maple top, chrome hardware.

1991-1995		$1,200	$1,450

EG 3
1990-1991. Double-cut solidbody, bolt-on 22-fret neck, 3 single-coil pickups.

1990-1991	Flamed 10 top	$1,300	$1,450
1990-1991	Opaque finish	$1,300	$1,450

GUITARS

MODEL		EXC. COND.	
YEAR	FEATURES	LOW	HIGH

EG 4
1990-1991. Similar to EG 3 with single-single-hum pickup configuration, opaque finish.

1990-1991		$1,100	$1,250

Golden Eagle
1997-1998. Very limited production, eagle head and shoulders carved into lower bouts, varied high-end appointments.

1997-1998		$18,000	$22,000

Johnny Hiland
2006-2007. Maple fretboard.

2006-2007		$1,700	$2,000

Limited Edition
1989-1991, 2000. Double-cut, semi-hollow mahogany body, figured cedar top, gold hardware, less than 300 made. In '00, single-cut, short run of 5 antique white and 5 black offered via Garrett Park Guitars.

1989-1991	Various colors, tune-o-matic	$4,000	$5,000
2000	Various colors	$4,000	$5,000

McCarty Model
1994-2007. Mahogany body with figured maple top, upgrade options may include a 10 top, gold hardware, bird inlays.

1994-1995		$1,900	$2,000
1996-1999		$1,800	$1,900
2000-2007		$1,450	$1,625

McCarty Archtop (Spruce)
1998-2000. Deep mahogany body, archtop, spruce top, 22-fret set-neck.

1998-2000		$1,900	$2,200

McCarty Archtop Artist
1998-2002. Highest grade figured maple top and highest appointments, gold hardware.

1998-2002		$3,700	$4,500

McCarty Archtop II (Maple)
1998-2000. Like Archtop but with figured maple top.

1998-2000	Flamed 10 top	$2,400	$2,900
1998-2000	Quilted 10 top	$2,400	$2,900

McCarty Hollowbody I/Hollowbody I
1998-present. Medium deep mahogany hollowbody, maple top, 22-fret set-neck, chrome hardware. McCarty dropped from name in '06.

1998-2007		$2,200	$2,600
2000s	Baggs Piezo option	$2,500	$2,800

McCarty Hollowbody II/Hollowbody II
1998-present. Like Hollowbody I but with figured maple top and back. McCarty dropped from name in '06.

1998-2007		$2,300	$2,700

McCarty Hollowbody/Hollowbody Spruce
2000-present. Similar to Hollowbody I with less appointmentsm spruce top. McCarty dropped from name in '06.

2000-2007		$2,200	$2,600

McCarty Model/McCarty Brazilian
2003-2004. Limited run of 250, Brazilian rosewood 'board, Brazilian is printed on headstock just below the PRS script logo.

1999		$4,000	$5,000
2003-2004		$3,400	$3,600

McCarty Rosewood
2001. PRS-22 fret with Indian rosewood neck.

2005		$2,200	$2,300

McCarty Soapbar/Soapbar Standard
1998-2007. Solid mahogany body, P-90-style soapbar pickups, 22-fret set-neck, nickel-plated hardware, upgrade options may include gold hardware and bird inlays.

1998-1999		$1,400	$1,600
2000-2007		$1,400	$1,600

McCarty Soapbar (Maple)
1998-2007. Soapbar with figured maple top option, nickel hardware.

1998-2007		$1,800	$2,000

McCarty Standard
1994-2006. McCarty Model with carved mahogany body but without maple top, nickel-plated hardware, upgrade options may include gold hardware and bird inlays.

1994-1995		$1,400	$1,600
1996-1999		$1,400	$1,600
2000-2006		$1,400	$1,600

Metal
1985-1986. Solid mahogany body with custom 2-color striped body finish and graphics, 24-fret set-neck, nickel hardware, 2 humbuckers.

1985-1986		$6,700	$8,300

Modern Eagle
2004-2007. Higher-end model based on Private Stock innovations, modern eagle markers, satin nitrocellulose finish, Brazilian rosewood neck.

2004-2007		$4,600	$5,700

Private Stock Program
April 1996-present. One-off custom instruments based around existing designs such as the McCarty Model. Values may be somewhat near production equivalents or they may be higher. The Private Stock option was reintroduced by 2003 and a '03 typical offering might retail at about $7,500, but a '03 Santana I Private Stock might retail at over $15,000, so each guitar should be evaluated on a case-by-case basis.

1996-2007	Hollowbody, typical specs	$5,500	$10,000
1996-2007	Solidbody, typical specs	$5,500	$10,000

PRS Guitar
1985-1986. Set-neck, solid mahogany body, 24-fret 'board, 2 humbuckers, chrome hardware, renamed Standard from '87-'98 then Standard 24 from '98.

1984-1985	Preproduction with provenance	$15,000	$35,000
1985	Sunburst and optional colors	$8,000	$12,500
1986	Sunburst and optional colors	$6,500	$11,000

Rosewood Ltd.
1996. Mahogany body with figured maple top, 1-piece rosewood neck with ultra-deluxe tree-of-life neck inlay, gold hardware.

1996		$9,000	$11,000

PRS McCarty Soapbar

PRS Modern Eagle

PRS Santana SE

Peavey Cropper Classic

MODEL YEAR	FEATURES	EXC. COND. LOW	HIGH

Santana
1995-1998. Mahogany body, slightly wider lower bout than other models, figured maple top, 24-fret set-neck, symmetric Santana headstock, unique body purfling, chrome and nickel-plated hardware, limited production special order.

1995-1998		$4,500	$5,000

Santana II
1998-2007. Three-way toggle replaces former dual mini-switches, special order.

1998-2007		$3,400	$3,900

Santana III
2001-2006. Less ornate version of Santana II.

2001-2006		$2,200	$2,500

SE Series
2001-present. PRS import line.

2001-2005	Santana	$300	$375
2002-2007	Tremonti	$350	$400
2003-2007	Single-cut, humbuckers	$350	$425
2003-2007	Single-cut, Soapbar I	$300	$375
2003-2005	EG	$250	$300
2005	Double-cut, Soapbar II	$350	$400
2005	Standard	$325	$400
2006	Billy Martin	$300	$375

Signature/PRS Signature
1987-1991. Solid mahogany body, figured maple top, set-neck, 24 frets, hand-signed signature on headstock, limited run of 1,000.

1987-1991		$5,100	$5,900

Singlecut
2000-2004, 2005-present. Single-cut mahogany body, maple top, 22-fret 'board, upgrade options may include either or all of the following: 10 top flamed maple, gold hardware, bird inlays.

2000-2004	1st edition, pre-lawsuit	$1,800	$2,000
2000-2004	Artist, maple top	$2,200	$2,400
2006	Artist 20th Anniversary, Brazilian	$2,800	$3,200
2005-2007	2nd issue, post lawsuit	$1,600	$1,900

Singlecut - Satin Standard
2000s. Satin finish.

2000s		$1,200	$1,325

Special
1987-1990, 1991-1993. Similar to Standard with upgrades, wide-thin neck, 2 HFS humbuckers. From '91-'93, a special option package was offered featuring a wide-thin neck and high output humbuckers.

1987-1990	Solid color finish	$2,700	$3,300
1991-1993	Special order only	$3,100	$3,300

Standard
1987-1998. Set-neck, solid mahogany body, 24-fret 'board, 2 humbuckers, chrome hardware. Originally called the PRS Guitar from '85-'86 (see that listing), renamed Standard 24 from '98.

1987-1989	Sunburst and optional colors	$2,900	$3,400

1990-1991	Last Brazilian board	$2,500	$3,000
1992-1995		$1,500	$1,800
1995-1998	Stevensville	$1,400	$1,700

Standard 22
1994-present. 22-fret Standard.

1994-1995		$1,500	$1,800
1995-1999	Stevensville	$1,400	$1,700
2000-2007		$1,400	$1,700

Standard 24
1998-present. Renamed from Standard, solid mahogany body, 24-fret set-neck.

1998-1999		$1,400	$1,700
2000-2007		$1,400	$1,700
2000-2005	20th Anniversary L.E.	$1,500	$1,800

Studio
1988-1991. Standard model variant, solid mahogany body, 24-fret set-neck, chrome and nickel hardware, single-single-hum pickups, special Studio package offered '91-'96.

1988-1991		$1,800	$2,000

Studio Maple Top
1990-1991. Mahogany solidbody, bird 'board inlays, 2 single-coils and 1 humbucker, tremolo, transparent finish.

1990-1991		$2,000	$2,200

Swamp Ash Special
1996-present. Solid swamp ash body, 22-fret bolt-on maple neck, 3 pickups, upgrade options available.

1996-2007		$1,500	$1,800

Tremonti Signature (U.S.A.)
2001-present. Single-cut, contoured mahogany body, 2 humbuckers.

2001-2007	Various options	$1,700	$1,900
2004	Tribal finish, about 60 made	$2,100	$2,300

Pawar
1999-present. Founded by Jay Pawar, Jeff Johnston and Kevin Johnston in Willoughby Hills, Ohio, Pawar builds professional and premium grade, production/custom, solidbody guitars that feature the Pawar Positive Tone System with over 20 single coil and humbucker tones.

PBC Guitar Technology
See Bunker Guitars for more info.

Peavey
1965-present. Headquartered in Meridan, Mississippi, Peavey builds budget, intermediate, professional, and premium grade, production/custom, acoustic and electric guitars. They also build basses, amps, PA gear, effects and drums. Hartley Peavey's first products were guitar amps. He added guitars to the mix in '78.

MODEL YEAR	FEATURES	EXC. COND. LOW	HIGH

Axcelerator/AX
1994-1998. Offset double-cut swamp ash or poplar body, bolt-on maple neck, dot markers, AX with locking vibrato, various colors.

1994-1998		$225	$275

Cropper Classic
1995-2005. Single-cut solidbody, 1 humbucker and 1 single coil, figured maple top over thin mahogany body, transparent Onion Green.

1995-2005		$325	$400

Defender
1994-1995. Double-cut, solid poplar body, 2 humbuckers and 1 single-coil pickup, locking Floyd Rose tremolo, metallic or pearl finish.

1994-1995		$150	$200

Destiny
1989-1992. Double-cut, mahogany body, maple top, neck-thru-bridge, maple neck, 3 integrated pickups, double locking tremolo.

1989-1992		$250	$300

Destiny Custom
1989-1992. Destiny with figured wood and higher-end appointments, various colors.

1989-1992		$350	$425

Detonator AX
1995-1998. Double-cut, maple neck, rosewood 'board, dot markers, hum/single/hum pickups, black.

1995-1998		$175	$200

EVH Wolfgang
1996-2004. Offset double-cut, arched top, bolt neck, stop tailpiece or Floyd Rose vibrato, quilted or flamed maple top upgrade option.

1996-2004	Flamed maple top	$1,200	$1,400
1996-2004	Standard top	$900	$1,100

EVH Wolfgang Special
1997-2004. Offset double-cut lower-end Wolfgang model, various opaque finishes, flamed top optional.

1997-2004	Flamed maple top	$650	$700
1997-2004	Standard basswood finish	$600	$650

Falcon/Falcon Active/Falcon Custom
1987-1992. Double-cut, 3 pickups, passive or active electronics, Kahler locking vibrato.

1987-1992	Custom color	$300	$350
1987-1992	Standard color	$200	$250

Firenza
1994-1999. Offset double-cut, bolt-on neck, single-coil pickups.

1994-1999		$275	$325

Firenza AX
1994-1999. Upscale Firenza Impact with humbucking pickups.

1994-1999		$300	$375

Generation S-1/S-2
1988-1994. Single-cut, maple cap on mahogany body, bolt-on maple neck, six-on-a-side tuners, active single/hum pickups, S-2 with locking vibrato system.

1988-1994		$200	$250

Horizon/Horizon II
1983-1985. Extended pointy horns, angled lower bout, maple body, rear routing for electronics, 2 humbucking pickups. Horizon II has added blade pickup.

1983-1985		$150	$175

Hydra Doubleneck
1985-1989. Available as a custom order, 6/12-string necks each with 2 humbuckers, 3-way pickup select.

1985-1989		$150	$175

Impact 1/Impact 2
1985-1987. Offset double-cut, Impact 1 has higher-end synthetic 'board, Impact 2 with conventional rosewood 'board.

1985-1987		$200	$250

Mantis
1984-1989. Hybrid X-shaped solidbody, 1 humbucking pickup, tremolo, laminated maple neck.

1984-1989		$200	$250

Milestone 12-String
1985-1986. Offset double-cut, 12 strings.

1985-1986		$150	$225

Milestone/Milestone Custom
1983-1986. Offset double-cut solidbody.

1983-1986		$100	$150

Mystic
1983-1989. Double-cut, 2 pickups, stop tailpiece initially, later Power Bend vibrato, maple body and neck.

1983-1989		$150	$225

Nitro I Active
1988-1990. Active electronics.

1988-1990		$200	$250

Nitro I/II/III
1986-1989. Offset double-cut, banana-style headstock, 1 humbucker (I), 2 humbuckers (II), or single/single/hum pickups (III).

1986-1989	Nitro I	$150	$175
1986-1989	Nitro II	$175	$200
1986-1989	Nitro III	$200	$250

Odyssey
1990-1994. Single-cut, figured carved maple top on mahogany body, humbuckers.

1990-1994		$400	$500

Odyssey 25th Anniversary
1990. Single-cut body, limited production.

1990		$550	$675

Omniac JD USA
2005-present. Jerry Donahue-designed single-cut solidbody, 2 single-coils.

2005-2007		$675	$775

Patriot
1983-1987. Double-cut, single bridge humbucker.

1983-1987		$150	$175

Patriot Plus
1983-1987. Double-cut, 2 humbucker pickups, bi-laminated maple neck.

1983-1987		$175	$200

Peavey Generation EXP

Peavey Omniac JD USA

Peavey Rotor EXP

Pedro de Miguel classical

MODEL YEAR	FEATURES	EXC. COND. LOW	HIGH
Patriot Tremolo			
1986-1990. Double-cut, single bridge humbucker, tremolo, replaced the standard Patriot.			
1986-1990		$175	$200
Predator Series			
1985-1988, 1990-present. Double-cut poplar body, 2 pickups until '87, 3 after, vibrato.			
1985-1988		$100	$125
1990-2006		$100	$125
Raptor Series			
1997-present. Offset double-cut solidbody, 3 pickups.			
1997-2007		$75	$90
Razer			
1983-1989. Double-cut with arrowhead point for lower bout, 2 pickups, 1 volume and 2 tone controls, stop tailpiece or vibrato.			
1983-1989		$300	$375
Reactor			
1993-1999. Classic single-cut style, 2 single-coils.			
1993-1999		$250	$300
Rotor Series			
2004-present. Classic futuristic body, elongated upper treble bout/lower bass bout, 2 humbuckers.			
2004-2007	Rotor EX	$200	$250
2004-2007	Rotor EXP	$250	$300
T-15			
1981-1983. Offset double-cut, bolt-on neck, dual ferrite blade single-coil pickups, natural.			
1981-1983		$150	$175
T-15 Amp-In-Case			
1981-1983. Amplifier built into guitar case and T-15 guitar.			
1981-1983		$250	$300
T-25			
1979-1985. Synthetic polymer body, 2 pickups, cream 'guard, sunburst finish.			
1979-1985		$250	$300
T-25 Special			
1979-1985. Same as T-25, but with super high output pickups, phenolic 'board, black/white/black 'guard, ebony black finish.			
1979-1985		$250	$300
T-26			
1982-1986. Same as T-25, but with 3 single-coil pickups and 5-way switch.			
1982-1986		$300	$350
T-27			
1981-1983. Offset double-cut, bolt-on neck, dual ferrite blade single-coil pickups.			
1981-1983		$325	$375
T-30			
1982-1985. Short-scale, 3 single-coil pickups, 5-way select, by '83 amp-in-case available.			
1982-1985	Guitar only	$200	$250
1983-1985	Amp-in-case	$250	$300
T-60			
1978-1988. Contoured offset double-cut, ash body, six-in-line tuners, 2 humbuckers, thru-body strings, by '87 maple bodies, various finishes.			
1978-1988		$350	$425

MODEL YEAR	FEATURES	EXC. COND. LOW	HIGH
T-1000 LT			
1992-1994. Double-cut, 2 single-coils and humbucker with coil-tap.			
1992-1994		$225	$275
Tracer Custom			
1989-1990. Tracer with 2 single/hum pickups and extras.			
1989-1990		$175	$200
Tracer/Tracer II			
1987-1994. Offset scooped double-cut with extended pointy horns, poplar body, 1 pickup, Floyd Rose.			
1987-1994		$175	$200
Vandenberg Quilt Top			
1989-1992. Vandenberg Custom with quilted maple top, 2 humbuckers, glued-in neck, quilted maple top, mahogany body and neck.			
1989-1992		$1,000	$1,250
Vandenberg Signature			
1988-1992. Double-cut, reverse headstock, bolt-on neck, locking vibrato, various colors.			
1988-1992		$500	$550
Vortex I/Vortex II			
1986. Streamlined Mantis with 2 pickups, 3-way, Kahler locking vibrato. Vortex II has Randy Rhoads Sharkfin V.			
1986		$325	$400
V-Type Series			
2004-present. Offset double-cut solidbody, pointed reverse 6-on-a-side headstock, 2 humbuckers.			
2004-2007		$300	$375

Pedro de Miguel

1991-present. Luthiers Pedro Pérez and Miguel Rodriguez build their professional and premium grade, custom/production, classical guitars in Madrid, Spain. They also offer factory-made instruments built to their specifications.

Pegasus Guitars and Ukuleles

1977-present. Premium grade, custom steel-string guitars built by luthier Bob Gleason in Kurtistown, Hawaii, who also builds ukulele family instruments.

Penco

Ca. 1974-1978. Generally high quality Japanese-made copies of classic American acoustic, electric and bass guitars. Probably (though not certainly) imported into Philadelphia during the copy era. Includes dreadnought acoustics with laminated woods, bolt-neck solidbody electric guitars and basses, mandolins and banjos.

Acoustic Flat-Top

1974-1978. Various models.			
1974-1978		$100	$125

Electric

1974-1978. Various copies.			
1974-1978	Solidbody	$200	$250
1974-1978	Thinline Archtop	$200	$250

MODEL YEAR	FEATURES	EXC. COND. LOW	HIGH

Penn

1950s. Archtop and acoustic guitars built by made by United Guitar Corporation in Jersey City, New Jersey, which also made Premier acoustics. Penn was located in L.A.

Pensa (Pensa-Suhr)

1982-present. Premium grade, production/custom, solidbody guitars built in the U.S. They also build basses. Rudy Pensa, of Rudy's Music Stop, New York City, started building Pensa guitars in '82. In '85 he teamed up with John Suhr to build Pensa-Suhr instruments. Name changed back to Pensa in '96.

Classic
1992-Ca. 1998. Offest double-cut, 3 single-coils, gold hardware.

1992-1998		$1,500	$1,850

MK 1 (Mark Knopfler)
1985-present. Offset double-cut solidbody, carved flamed maple bound top, 3 pickups, gold hardware, dot markers, bolt-on neck.

1985-2007		$1,600	$2,000

Suhr Custom
1985-1989. Two-piece maple body, bolt-on maple neck with rosewood 'board, custom order basis with a variety of woods and options available.

1985-1989	Flamed maple top	$1,600	$2,000

Suhr Standard
1985-1991. Double-cut, single/single/hum pickup configuration, opaque solid finish normally, dot markers.

1985-1991		$1,500	$1,850

Perlman Guitars

1976-present. Luthier Alan Perlman builds his premium grade, custom, steel-string and classical guitars in San Francisco, California.

Perry Guitars

1982-present. Premium grade, production/custom, classical guitars built by luthier Daryl Perry in Winnipeg, Manitoba. He also builds lutes.

Petillo Masterpiece Guitars

1965-present. Luthiers Phillip J. and David Petillo build their intermediate, professional and premium grade, custom, steel-string, nylon-string, 12-string, resonator, archtop, and Hawaiian guitars in Ocean, New Jersey.

Petros Guitars

1992-present. Premium grade, production/custom, flat-top, 12-string, and nylon-string guitars built by father and son luthiers Bruce and Matthew Petros in Kaukauna, Wisconsin.

Phantom Guitar Works

1992-present. Intermediate grade, production/custom, classic Phantom, and Teardrop shaped solid and hollowbody guitars assembled in Clats-kanie, Oregon. They also offer basses and the MandoGuitar. Phantom was established by Jack Charles, former lead guitarist of the band Quarterflash. Some earlier guitars were built overseas.

Pheo

1996-present. Luthier Phil Sylvester builds his unique premium grade, production/custom, electric and acoustic guitars in Portland, Oregon.

Pieper

2005-present. Premium grade, custom, solidbody guitars built by luthier Robert Pieper in New Haven, Connecticut. He also builds basses.

Pimentel and Sons

1951-present. Luthiers Lorenzo Pimentel and sons build their professional, premium and presentation grade, flat-top, jazz, cutaway electric, and classical guitars in Albuquerque, New Mexico.

Player

1984-1985. Player guitars featured interchangable pickup modules that mounted through the back of the guitar. They offered a double-cut solidbody with various options and the pickup modules were sold separately. The company was located in Scarsdale, New York.

Pleasant

Late 1940s-ca.1966. Solidbody electric guitars, obviously others, Japanese manufacturer, probably not imported into the U.S.

Electric Solidbody
1940s-1966. Various models.

1950-1966		$125	$150

Prairie State

1927-1940s. A Carl and August Larson of Maurer & Company brand. The early models followed the designs of the equivalent Maurer models, but on average the bodies were ½" thinner. The patented steel rod mechanisms accounted for strengthening the body by running from end block to neck block according to one of the three August Larson patents. On the 12-fret-to-the-body models, the most common patent design reveals a ½" tube fitted lengthwise under the top, with a ¼" straining rod running from the end pin through the neck block and around the heel of the neck. The models built after the conversion to the 14-fret neck usually had only the hollow tube. Any of these configurations led to a guitar with extreme body strength. The effect on the sound of the instrument was a dramatic change lending to an immediate response of bell clear tones and strong sustain. These guitars were used by lap steel players using a high nut as well as fingerstyle players for any type of music. They were usually built with Brazilian rosewood back and sides, laminated necks and patented laminated X-bracing. Some later models were built with beautiful maple.

Perlman Classical

Petros Prairie FS

Premier Deluxe E-621

Rahbek Standard

MODEL YEAR	FEATURES	EXC. COND. LOW	HIGH

1932 Prairie State Catalog Models - description and prices:
Style 225 Concert $65.00
Style 425 Auditorium $70.00
Style 426 Style 425 Steel $70.00
Style 427 Reinforced Neck $75.00
Style 428 Style 427 Steel $75.00
Style 235 Concert with trim $80.00
Style 335 Grand Concert + trim $83.00
Style 435 Auditorium with trim $85.00
Style 340 Grand Concert fancy $90.00
Style 350 Grand Concert fancy $97.00
Style 440 Auditorium fancy trim $93.00
Style 450 Auditorium fancy trim $100.00

Mid-Size Flat-Top (Mid- to Higher-End)
15" spruce X-braced top, Brazilian rosewood back and sides, solid headstock, mid- to high-end appointments.

1920s		$9,000	$15,000

Small Flat-Top (Higher-End)
Spruce top, 13 5/8" scale, Brazilian rosewood back and sides, high-end pearl appointments, slotted headstock, natural.

1920s		$6,000	$9,000

Premier

Ca.1938-ca.1975, 1990s-present. Budget and intermediate grade, production, import guitars. They also offer basses.

Brands originally offered by Premier include Premier, Multivox, Marvel, Belltone and Strad-O-Lin. Produced by Peter Sorkin Music Company in Manhattan, New York City, New York, who began in Philadelphia, relocating to NYC in '35. First radio-sized amplifiers and stick-on pickups for acoustic archtops were introduced by '38. After World War II, they set up the Multivox subsidiary to manufacture amplifiers ca. '46. First flat-top with pickup appeared in '46.

Most acoustic instruments made by United Guitar Corporation in Jersey City, New Jersey. Ca. '57 Multivox acquires Strad-O-Lin. Ca.'64-'65 their Custom line guitars are assembled with probably Italian bodies and hardware, Japanese electronics, possibly Egmond necks from Holland. By ca. '74-'75, there were a few Japanese-made guitars, then Premier brand goes into hiatus.

The rights to the Premier brand are held by Entertainment Music Marketing Corporation in New York. The Premier brand reappears on some Asian-made solidbody guitars and basses beginning in the '90s.

Bantam Custom
1950s-1960s. Model below Special, single-cut archtop, dot markers, early models with white potted pickups, then metal-covered pickups, and finally Japanese-made pickups (least valued).

1950-1960s		$650	$750

Bantam Deluxe
1950s-1960s. Single-cut archtop, fully bound, sparkle knobs, early models with white potted pickups, then metal-covered pickups, and finally Japanese-made pickups (least valued), block markers, single or double pickups (deduct $100 for single pickup instrument).

1950-1960s	Blond	$1,350	$1,500
1950-1960s	Sunburst	$1,250	$1,400

Bantam Special
1950s-1960s. Model below Deluxe, single-cut archtop, dot markers, early models with white potted pickups, then metal-covered pickups, and finally Japanese-made pickups (least valued), single or double pickup models offered (deduct $100 for single pickup instrument).

1950-1960s		$650	$800

Custom Solidbody
1958-1970. Notable solidbody bass scroll cutaway, various models with various components used, finally import components only.

1958-1970	1 pickup	$450	$550
1958-1970	2 pickups	$550	$650
1958-1970	3 pickups	$600	$700

Deluxe Archtop
1950s-1960s. Full body 17 1/4" archtop, square block markers, single-cut, early models with white potted pickups, later '60s models with metal pickups.

1950-1960s	Blond	$1,250	$1,600
1950-1960s	Sunburst	$1,200	$1,450

Semi-Pro 16" Archtop
1950s-early-1960s. Thinline electric 16" archtop with 2 1/4" deep body, acoustic or electric.

1950-1960s	Acoustic	$700	$750
1950-1960s	Electric	$800	$850

Semi-Pro Bantam Series
1960s. Thinline electric archtop with 2 3/4" deep body, offered in cutaway and non-cut models.

1960s		$300	$350

Special Archtop
1950s-1960s. Full body 17 1/4" archtop, less fancy than Deluxe, single-cut, early models with white potted pickups, '60s models with metal pickups.

1950-1960s		$850	$950

Studio Six Archtop
1950s-early-1960s. 16" wide archtop, single pickup, early pickups white potted, changed later to metal top.

1950-1960s		$500	$600

Prestige

Intermediate, professional, and premium grade, production/custom, acoustic, solidbody and hollowbody guitars from Vancouver, British Columbia. They also offer basses.

Queen Shoals Stringed Instruments

1972-present. Luthier Larry Cadle builds his production/custom, flat-top, 12-string, and nylon-string guitars in Clendenin, West Virginia.

MODEL YEAR	FEATURES	EXC. COND. LOW	HIGH

Queguiner, Alain

1982-present. Custom flat-tops, 12 strings, and nylon strings built by luthier Alain Queguiner in Paris, France.

R.C. Allen

1951-present. Luthier R. C. "Dick" Allen builds professional and premium grade, custom hollowbody and semi-hollowbody guitars in El Monte, California. He has also built solidbody guitars.

Rahan

1999-present. Professional grade, production/custom, solidbody guitars built by luthiers Mike Curd and Rick Cantu in Houston, Texas.

Rahbek Guitars

2000-present. Professional and premium grade, production/custom, solidbody electrics built by luthier Peter Rahbek in Copenhagen, Denmark.

Raimundo

1970s-present. Intermediate, professional and premium grade flamenco and classical guitars made in Valencia, Spain, by luthiers Antonio Aparicio and Manual Raimundo.

RainSong

1991-present. Professional grade, production, all-graphite and graphite and wood acoustic guitars built in Woodinville, Washington. The guitars were developed after years of research by luthier engineer John Decker with help from luthier Lorenzo Pimentel, engineer Chris Halford, and sailboard builder George Clayton. The company was started in Maui, but has since moved to Woodinville.

Ramirez, Jose

1882-present. Professional, premium, and presentation grade, custom/production, classical guitars built in Madrid, Spain. The company was founded by Jose Ramirez (1858-1923) who was originally a twelve year old apprentice at the shop of Francisco Gonzales. Jose eventually opened his own workshop in 1882 where he introduced his younger brother Manuel to the business. Manuel split with Jose and opened his own, competing workshop. Jose's business was continued by Jose's son Jose Ramirez II (1885-1957), grandson Jose III (1922-1995), and great grandchildren Jose IV (1953-2000) and Amalia Ramirez. From 1882 various techniques and methods were used including centuries-old traditions and new significant departures from old methods. In the 1930's a larger body instrument with improved fan bracing was developed to meet the needs for more power and volume. Other refinements were developed and the Ramirez 1A Tradicional was soon introduced which found favor with Andres Segovia. The Ramirez company has produced both student and professional instruments, but in the classical guitar field, like the old-

master violin business, a student model is often a very fine instrument that is now valued at $2,000 or more. A student Ramirez instrument is not the same as a student-grade instrument such as a birch body 13" Stella flat top. By the 1980s the Ramirez factory was building as many as 1,000 guitars a year. In the 1980s Ramirez offered the E Series student guitar line that was built for, but not by, Ramirez. In 1991 the company offered the even more affordable R Series which was offered for about $1,300. The A, E, and R Series became the major product offerings but the company also continued to offer a limited number of very high-end instruments that were hand built in the company's shop. In the 1990s the company returned to their 1960s roots and offered the 1A Especial model. In the early 2000s Amalia Ramirez offered a third product line, the SP Series, selling for about $5,800, which was designed as a semi-professional instrument that would fit between the company's concert series and student series instruments. By 2005 the company offered the E, R, and SP lines, in addition to annually making several dozen highest-end master-grade instruments in their old workshop on General Margallo Street. As is typically the case, Ramirez classical guitars do not have a name-logo on the headstock. The brand is identified by a Ramirez label on the inside back which also may have the model number listed.

A/1A

1960s-1990s. Classical.

1960s		$4,200	$5,000
1970s		$4,100	$5,000
1980s		$3,800	$4,700
1990s		$3,700	$4,600

A/2A

1970s		$2,800	$3,500

De Camera

1980s. Classical, cedar top, Brazilian rosewood back and sides.

1980s		$4,500	$5,000

E/1E/Estudio

Intermediate level.

1990s		$1,300	$1,400

E/2E

Red cedar top, Indian rosewood back and sides, Spanish cedar neck, ebony 'board.

2000s		$1,400	$1,700

E/4E

Top of the E Series line, solid red cedar top, solid Indian rosewood back and sides.

2000s		$2,000	$2,500

Flamenco

1920s-1979. European spruce top, cyprus back and sides.

1920s		$4,400	$5,500
1960-1969		$3,400	$4,200
1970-1979		$3,400	$4,200

R1

1991-present. Red cedar top, mahogany sides and back, Spanish cedar neck, ebony 'board.

1991-2007		$900	$1,100

Rahbek Cos-T

Rainsong WS1000

Rarebird Falcon Le Grande

Recording King (TML) Cowboy

MODEL YEAR	FEATURES	EXC. COND. LOW	HIGH
R2			
1991-present. Red cedar top, Indian rosewood back and sides, cedar neck, ebony 'board.			
1990s		$1,000	$1,250
R4 Classical			
1995-present. All solid wood, Western red cedar top, rosewood back and sides.			
1995-2007		$1,600	$2,000
S/S1			
2005-present. Solid German spruce top, African mahogany sides and back, most affordable in Estudio line.			
2005-2007		$800	$975
SP Series			
2002-present. Semi-professional level designed to be between the company's 'concert/professional' series and 'student' series.			
2002-2007		$5,500	$6,000

Ramirez, Manuel

1890-1916. Brother of Jose Ramirez, and a respected professional classical guitar builder from Madrid, Spain. His small shop left no heirs so the business was not continued after Manuel's death in 1916. Manuel was generally considered to be more famous during his lifetime than his brother Jose, and while his business did not continue, Manuel trained many well known Spanish classical guitar luthiers who prospered with their own businesses. During Manuel's era his shop produced at least 48 different models, with prices ranging from 10 to 1,000 pesetas, therefore vintage prices can vary widely. Guitars made prior to 1912 have a label with a street address of Arlaban 10, in 1912 the shop moved to Arlaban 11.

Randy Reynolds Guitars

1996-present. Luthier Randy Reynolds builds his premium grade, production/custom classical and flamenco guitars in Colorado Springs, Colorado.

Randy Wood Guitars

1968-present. Premium grade, custom/production, archtop, flat-top, and resonator guitars built by luthier Randy Wood in Bloomingdale, Georgia. He also builds mandolins.

Rarebird Guitars

1978-2007. Luthier Bruce Clay built his professional and premium grade, production/custom, acoustic, electric solidbody and hollowbody guitars and mini guitars, originally in Arvada, Colorado, and after '05 in Santa Fe, New Mexico. He also built basses.

Rat Fink

2002-present. Lace Music Products, the makers of the Lace Sensor pickup, offered the intermediate grade, production, guitars and basses, featuring the artwork of Ed "Big Daddy" Roth until '05. They continue to offer amps.

Recording King

1936-1941. Brand name used by Montgomery Ward for instruments made by various American manufacturers, including Kay, Gibson and Gretsch. Generally mid-grade instruments. M Series are Gibson-made archtops.

MODEL YEAR	FEATURES	EXC. COND. LOW	HIGH
Carson Robison/Model K			
1936-1939. Flat-top, 14 3/4", mahogany back and sides, renamed Model K in early-'38.			
1936-1939		$1,300	$1,600
Kay 17" flat top.			
1940-1941. Large jumbo, 17" lower bout, pearloid veneer peghead, large Recording King logo.			
1940-1941		$900	$1,100
M-2			
1936-1941. Gibson-made archtop with carved top and f-holes, maple back and sides.			
1936-1941		$900	$1,100
M-3			
1936-1941. Gibson-made archtop, f-holes, maple back and sides, carved top.			
1936-1941		$1,200	$1,500
M-4			
1936-1941. Gibson-made archtop, f-holes, maple back and sides, rope-checkered binding, flying bat wing markers.			
1936-1941		$1,450	$1,750
M-5			
1936-1941. Gibson-made archtop with f-holes, maple back and sides, trapeze tailpiece, checkered top binding.			
1936-1938	16" body	$1,450	$1,750
1939-1941	17" body	$1,550	$1,850
M-6			
1938-1939. M-5 with upgraded gold hardware.			
1938-1939		$1,650	$1,950
Ray Whitley			
1939-1940. High-quality model made by Gibson, round shoulder flat-top, mahogany or Brazilian rosewood back and sides, 5-piece maple neck, Ray Whitley stencil script peghead logo, pearl crown inlay on peghead, fancy inlaid markers.			
1939-1940	Brazilian	$18,000	$22,500
1939-1940	Mahogany	$8,500	$10,000

Recording King (TML)

2005-present. Budget grade, production, acoustic cowboy stenciled guitars designed by Greg Rich for The Music Link, which also offers Johnson and other brand instruments. They also have banjos and ukes.

Regal

Ca. 1884-1966, 1987-present. Intermediate and professional grade, production, acoustic and wood and metal body resonator guitars. They also build basses.

Originally a mass manufacturer founded in Indianapolis, Indiana, the Regal brand was first used by Emil Wulschner & Son. In 1901 new owners changed the company name to The Regal

MODEL YEAR	FEATURES	EXC. COND. LOW	HIGH

Manufacturing Company. The company was moved to Chicago in '08 and renamed the Regal Musical Instrument Company. Regal made brands for distributors and mass merchandisers as well as marketing its own Regal brand. Regal purchased the Lyon & Healy factory in '28. Regal was licensed to co-manufacture Dobros in '32 and became the sole manufacturer of them in '37 (see Dobro for those instruments). Most Regal instruments were beginner-grade; however, some very fancy archtops were made during the '30s. The company was purchased by Harmony in '54 and absorbed. From '59 to '66, Harmony made acoustics under the Regal name for Fender. In '87 the Regal name was revived on a line of resonator instruments by Saga.

Acoustic Hawaiian
1930s. Student model, small 13" body, square neck, glued or trapeze bridge.

1930s	Faux grain painted finish	$175	$350
1930s	Plain sunburst birch top	$125	$175

Concert Folk H6382
1960s. Regal by Harmony, solid spruce top, mahogany back and sides, dot markers, natural.

1960s		$225	$325

Deluxe Dreadnought H6600
1960s. Regal by Harmony, solid spruce top, mahogany back and sides, bound top and back, rosewood 'board, dot markers, natural.

1960s		$225	$350

Dreadnought 12-String H1269
1960s. Regal by Harmony, solid spruce top, 12-string version of Deluxe, natural.

1960s		$225	$350

Esquire
1940s. 15 1/2" acoustic archtop, higher-end appointments, fancy logo art and script pearl Esquire headstock logo and Regal logo.

1940s	Natural	$1,200	$1,400

Model 27
1933-1942. Birch wood body, mahogany or maple, 2-tone walnut finish, single-bound top, round or square neck.

1933-1942		$1,000	$1,300

Model 45
1933-1937. Spruce top and mahogany back and sides, bound body, square neck.

1933-1937		$1,400	$1,600

Model 46
1933-1937. Round neck.

1933-1937		$1,400	$1,600

Model 55 Standard
1933-1934. Regal's version of Dobro Model 55 which was discontinued in '33.

1933-1934		$1,100	$1,300

Model 75
1939-1940. Metal body, square neck.

1939-1940		$1,900	$2,600

Model TG 60 Resonator Tenor
1930s. Wood body, large single cone biscuit bridge resonator, 2 upper bout metal ports, 4-string tenor.

1930s		$1,300	$1,500

Parlor
1920s. Small body, slotted headstock, birch sides and back, spruce top.

1920s		$275	$400

Prince
1930s. High-end 18" acoustic archtop, fancy appointments, Prince name inlaid in headstock along with Regal script logo and strolling guitarist art.

1930s		$1,600	$1,900

RD-45
1994-2006. Standard style Dobro model with wood body, metal resonator, dual screen holes.

1994-2006		$200	$225

Spirit Of '76
1976. Red-white-blue, flat-top.

1976		$400	$500

Reliance
1920s. Instruments built by the Oscar Schmidt Co. and possibly others. Most likely a brand made for a distributor.

Renaissance
1978-1980. Plexiglass solidbody electric guitars and basses. Founded in Malvern, Pennsylvania, by John Marshall (designer), Phil Goldberg and Daniel Lamb. Original partners gradually leave and John Dragonetti takes over by late-'79. The line is redesigned with passive electronics on guitars, exotic shapes, but when deal with Sunn amplifiers falls through, company closes. Brandname currently used on a line of guitars and basses made by Rick Turner in Santa Cruz, California.

Fewer than 300 of first series made, plus a few prototypes and several wooden versions; six or so prototypes of second series made. SN=M(M)YYXXXX: month, year, consecutive number.

Electric Plexiglas Solidbody
1978-1980. Models include the SPG ('78-'79, DiMarzio pickups, active electronics), T-200G ('80, Bich-style with 2 passive DiMarzio pickups), and the S-200G ('80, double-cut, 2 DiMarzio pickups, passive electronics).

1978-1980		$600	$750

Renaissance Guitars
1994-present. Professional grade, custom, semi-acoustic flat-top, nylon-string and solidbody guitars built by luthier Rick Turner in Santa Cruz, California. He also builds basses and ukes.

Reuter Guitars
1984-present. Professional and premium grade, custom, flat-top, 12-string, resonator, and Hawaiian guitars built by luthier John Reuter, the Director of Training at the Roberto-Venn School of Luthiery, in Tempe, Arizona.

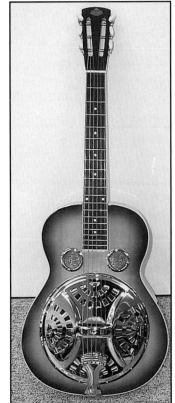

Regal RD-45

Reuter Wolfcaster

GUITARS

Reverend Rick Vito

MODEL YEAR	FEATURES	EXC. COND. LOW	HIGH

Reverend

1996-present. Intermediate grade, production, guitars from luthier Joe Naylor, built in Warren, Michigan and in Korea. Naylor also founded Naylor Amps. Reverend also built basses, amps and effects in the past.

Semi-Hollow Electric

1997-present. Offset double-cut semi-hollowbody, bolt maple neck, various pickup options. Models include Avenger, Commando, Hitman, Rocco, Slingshot and Spy. By '04 the Workhorse Series included the Avenger TL, Commando, and Slingshot Custom, which were all factory-

Year	Model	LOW	HIGH
1997-1999	U.S.-made models	$600	$950
2000-2007	U.S.-made models	$525	$950
2004-2007	Workhorse (USA)	$525	$650

Rex

1930s-1940s, 1960s. Generally beginner-grade guitars made by Harmony and Kay and sold through Fred Gretsch distributors. In the '60s, there were Italian-made electrics bearing the Rex brand. They also had amps.

Acoustic Flat-Top

1940s. Various models.

Year		LOW	HIGH
1940s		$250	$350

Ribbecke Guitars

1972-present. Premium and presentation grade, custom thinline, flat-top, and archtop guitars built by luthier Tom Ribbecke in Healdsburg, California.

Rich and Taylor

1993-1996. Custom acoustic and electric guitars and banjos from luthiers Greg Rich and Mark Taylor (Crafters of Tennessee).

Richard Schneider

1960s-1997. Luthier Richard Schneider built his acoustic guitars in Washington state. Over the years, he collaborated with Dr. Michael A. Kasha on many guitar designs and innovations. Originally from Michigan, he also was involved in designing guitars for Gretsch and Gibson. He died in early '97.

Richter Mfg.

1930s. One of many Chicago makers of the era.

Small 13"

1930s. Typical small 13" lower bout body, slotted headstock, decalmania art over black finish, single dot markers.

Year		LOW	HIGH
1930s		$350	$450

Rick Turner

1979-1981, 1990-present. Rick Turner has a long career as a luthier, electronics designer and innovator. He also makes the Renaissance line of guitars in his shop in Santa Cruz, California. The guitars and basses built in 197-'81 were numbered sequentially

Rick Turner Model One

in the order they were completed and shipped with the second part of the serial number indicating the year the instrument was built. Turner estimates that approximately 200 instruments were made during that period.

Rickenbacker

1931-present. Professional and premium grade, production/custom, acoustic and electric guitars built in California. They also build basses. Founded in Los Angeles as Ro-Pat-In by ex-National executives George Beauchamp, Paul Barth and National's resonator cone supplier Adolph Rickenbacher. Rickenbacher was born in Basel, Switzerland in 1886, emigrated to the U.S. and moved to Los Angeles in 1918, opening a tool and die business in '20. In the mid-'20s, Rickenbacher began providing resonator cones and other metal parts to George Beauchamp and Louis Dopyera of National String Instrument Corporation and became a shareholder in National. Beauchamp, Barth and Harry Watson came up with wooden "frying pan" electric Hawaiian lap steel for National in '31; National was not interested, so Beauchamp and Barth joined with Rickenbacher as Ro-Pat-In (probably for ElectRO-PATent-INstruments) to produce Electro guitars. Cast aluminum frying pans were introduced in '32. Some Spanish guitars (flat-top, F-holes) with Electro pickups were produced beginning in '32. Ro-Pat-In changes their name to Electro String Instrument Corporation in '34, and brand becomes Rickenbacher Electro, soon changed to Rickenbacker, with a "k." Beauchamp retires in '40. There was a production hiatus during World War II. In '53, Electro was purchased by Francis Cary Hall (born 1908), owner of Radio and Television Equipment Company (Radio-Tel) in Santa Ana, California (founded in '20s as Hall's Radio Service, which began distributing Fender instruments in '46). The factory was relocated to Santa Ana in '62 and the sales/distribution company's name is changed from Radio-Tel to Rickenbacker Inc. in '65.

1950s serial numbers have from 4 to 7 letters and numbers, with the number following the letter indicating the '50s year (e.g., NNL8NN would be from '58). From '61 to '86 serial numbers indicate month and year of production with initial letter A-Z for the year (A=1961, Z=1986) followed by letter for the month A-M (A=January) plus numbers as before followed by a number 0-9 for the year (0=1987; 9=1996). To avoid confusion, we have listed all instruments by model number. For example, the Combo 400 is listed as Model 400/Combo 400. OS and NS stands for Old Style and New Style. On the 360, for example, Ric changed the design in 1964 to their New Style with more rounded body horns and rounded top edges and other changes. But they still offered the Old Style with more pointed horns and top binding until the late 1960s. Ric still sometimes uses the two designations on some of their vintage reissues.

MODEL		EXC. COND.	
YEAR	FEATURES	LOW	HIGH

Electro ES-16

1964-1971. Double-cut, set neck, solidbody, 3/4 size, 1 pickup. The Electro line was manufactured by Rickenbacker and distributed by Radio-Tel. The Electro logo appears on the headstock.

1964-1971		$875	$1,000

Electro ES-17

1964-1975. Cutaway, set neck, solidbody, 1 pickup.

1964-1969		$950	$1,150
1970-1975		$800	$950

Electro Spanish (Model B Spanish)

1935-1943. Small guitar with a lap steel appearance played Spanish-style, hollow bakelite body augmented with 5 chrome plates, called the Model B ca. '40.

1935-1936		$3,200	$3,900
1938-1939		$2,800	$3,500
1940-1943		$2,700	$3,300

Model 220 Hamburg

1992-1997. Solidbody.

1992-1997		$700	$800

Model 230 GF

1992.

1992		$1,300	$1,600

Model 230 Hamburg

1983-1991. Solidbody, offset double-cut, 2 pickups, dot inlay, rosewood 'board, chrome-plated hardware.

1983-1991		$650	$750

Model 250 El Dorado

1983-1991. Deluxe version of Hamburg, gold hardware, white binding.

1983-1991		$500	$600

Model 260 El Dorado

1992-1997. Replaces 250.

1992-1997		$600	$700

Model 270

1964-1970.

1964-1970		$2,100	$2,600

Model 310

1958-1970, 1981-1985. Two-pickup version of Model 320.

1960-1971	Vintage	$5,800	$7,200
1981-1985	Reintroduced	$1,000	$1,200

Model 315

1958-1974. Two-pickup version of Model 325.

1960-1971	Vintage	$5,800	$7,200

Model 320

1958-1992. Short-scale hollowbody, 3 pickups, f-holes optional in '61 and standard in '64 and optional again in '79.

1960-1971		$7,800	$9,700
1981-1995		$1,150	$1,400

Model 320/12V63

1986. Short run for Japanese market.

1986		$2,800	$3,100

Model 325

1958-1975, 1985-1992. This was a low production model, with some years having no production. In the mid-'60s, the 325 was unofficially known as the John Lennon Model due to his guitar's high exposure on

the Ed Sullivan Show and in the Saturday Evening Post.

1958-1960	John		
	Lennon specs	$25,000	$31,000
1959-1960		$16,000	$20,000
1961-1963		$16,000	$20,000
1964-1965	Fireglo or black	$9,000	$11,000
1966	Fireglo or black	$8,000	$10,000
1966	Mapleglo	$8,000	$10,000
1967-1968		$7,500	$9,300
1970-1979		$1,700	$2,100
1981-1995		$1,200	$1,500

Model 325 JL

1989-1993. John Lennon Limited Edition, 3 vintage Ric pickups, vintage vibrato, maple body; 3/4-size rosewood neck, a 12-string and a full-scale version are also available.

1989-1993		$2,200	$2,700

Model 325/12V63

1985-1986		$1,800	$2,100
1999		$1,700	$2,000

Model 325C58

2002-present. Copy of the '58 model that John Lennon saw in Germany.

2002-2004		$1,900	$2,100
2005-2007	Hamburg	$2,000	$2,200

Model 325C64

2002-present. Copy of the famous '64 model.

2002-2007		$2,100	$2,200

Model 325V59

1984-2001. Reissue of John Lennon's modified '59 325, 3 pickups, short-scale.

1984-2001		$1,600	$2,000

Model 325V63

1984-2001. Reissue of John Lennon's '63 325.

1987-2001		$1,600	$2,000

Model 330

1958-present. Thinline hollowbody, 2 pickups, slash soundhole, natural or sunburst.

1958-1960	Capri	$6,800	$8,500
1961-1965	330-style body	$3,800	$4,700
1965-1970	330-style body	$3,200	$4,000
1971-1979		$1,450	$1,800
1980-1989		$1,300	$1,600
1990-1999		$1,075	$1,400
2000-2007		$1,075	$1,400

Model 330 F

1958-1969. F-style.

1958-1961	Thick version	$6,800	$8,500
1961-1964	Thin version	$3,800	$4,700
1965-1969	Thin version	$3,200	$4,000

Model 330/12

1965-present. Thinline, 2 pickups, 12-string version of Model 300.

1964		$4,300	$5,300
1965-1970	330-style body	$4,000	$5,000
1971-1979		$1,450	$1,800
1980-1989		$1,400	$1,700
1990-1999		$1,000	$1,200
2000-2007		$1,000	$1,175

Rickenbacker Model 325C58

Rickenbacker 330

GUITARS

Rickenbacker 331 Light Show

1960 Rickenbacker 360 F

MODEL YEAR	FEATURES	EXC. COND. LOW	HIGH

Model 330S/12
1964 (1 made)-1965 (2 made).

1964-1965		$4,000	$5,000

Model 331 Light Show
1970-1975. Model 330 with translucent top with lights in body that lit up when played, needed external transformer. The first offering's design, noted as Type 1, had heat problems and a fully original one is difficult to find. The 2nd offering's design, noted as Type 2, was a more stable design and is more highly valued in the market.

1970-1971	Type 1 1st edition	$13,000	$14,000
1972-1975	Type 2 2nd edition	$16,000	$18,000

Model 335
1961-1970. Thinline, 330-style body, 2 pickups, vibrato, Fireglo. Called the 330VB from '85-'97.

1961-1970		$3,200	$4,000

Model 335 Capri
1958-1960. Thinline, 2 pickups, vibrato. The Capri Model name is technically reserved for the '58 to mid-'60s vintage, these models had a 2" depth. Ca. mid-'60 the body depth was reduced to 1 1/2", Autumnglo, Fireglo or Mapleglo. Rickenbacker dropped the Capri name in '60.

1958-1960		$5,500	$6,800

Model 335 F
1958-1969. F-style.

1958-1961	Thick version	$5,500	$6,800
1961-1964	Thin version	$5,000	$6,200
1965-1969	Thin version	$3,200	$4,000

Model 336/12
1966-1974. Like 300-12, but with 6-12 converter comb, 330-style body.

1966-1974		$3,700	$4,500

Model 340
1958-present. Thin semi-hollowbody, thru-body maple neck, 2 single-coil pickups, sharp point horns, very limited production '58-'65, with first notable volume of 45 units starting in '66.

1958-1960	Capri	$5,500	$6,800
1961-1965	330-style body	$3,700	$4,100
1966-1970	330-style body	$3,000	$3,500
2000-2007		$800	$1,350

Model 340 F
1958-1969. F-style.

1958-1961	Thick version	$5,500	$6,800

Model 340/12
1965-present. 12-string version.

1965-1969	330 body style	$3,200	$4,000
1970-1979		$1,150	$1,400

Model 345
1961-1974. Thinline 330-345 series, version with 3 pickups and vibrato tailpiece.

1961-1965	330-style body	$3,700	$4,100
1965-1969	330-style body	$3,000	$3,500
1970-1974	2 humbuckers, slant frets	$1,150	$1,400

Model 345 Capri
1958-1960. Thinline 330-345 series, version with 3 pickups and vibrato tailpiece. The Capri Model name is technically reserved for the '58 to mid-'60s vintage, these models had a 2" depth. Body depth was reduced to 1 1/2" ca. mid-'60 and Capri name was dropped.

1958-1960		$5,500	$6,800

Model 345 F
1958-1969. F-style.

1958-1961	Thick version	$5,500	$6,800

Model 345 Reissue
2002. Low production, 3 pickups.

2002		$1,800	$1,900

Model 350 Liverpool
1983-1997. Thinline, 3 pickups, vibrato, no soundhole.

1983-1989		$1,300	$1,500
1990-1997		$1,200	$1,400

Model 350 SH
1988-1990. Susanna Hoffs limited edition.

1988-1990		$2,700	$3,300

Model 350/12V63 Liverpool
1994-present. 12-string 350V63.

1994-2007		$1,400	$2,000

Model 350V63 Liverpool
1994-present. Like 355 JL, but without signature.

1994-2007		$1,400	$2,000

Model 355 JL
1989-1993. John Lennon model, signature and drawing on 'guard.

1989-1993		$3,200	$3,500

Model 355/12 JL
1989-1993. 12-string 355 JL, limited production.

1989-1993		$3,000	$3,300

Model 360/360 VB
1958-present. Deluxe thinline, 2 pickups, slash soundhole, bound body until '64.

1958-1960	Capri	$5,500	$6,800
1961-1964	360-style body, OS	$3,700	$4,300
1964-1970	NS, more common	$3,500	$4,300
1965-1970	OS, less common	$7,100	$8,900
1971-1973		$3,000	$3,600
1974-1977		$2,000	$2,400
1978-1979		$1,950	$2,400
1980-1983		$1,700	$1,900
1984-1989	360 VB with vibrato	$1,400	$1,600
1990-1999		$1,300	$1,500
2000-2007		$1,200	$1,500

Model 360 CW
2000. Carl Wilson Limited Edition, 6-string, includes certificate, 500 made.

2000		$2,400	$3,000

Model 360 DCM 75th Anniversary
2006. 360 with 75th Anniversary dark cherry metallic finish, 75 made.

2006		$2,500	$3,000

Model 360 F
1959-1972. F-style.

1959-1961	Thick version	$5,500	$6,800
1961-1964	Thin version	$3,700	$4,100
1965-1972	Thin version	$3,100	$3,600

MODEL YEAR	FEATURES	EXC. COND. LOW	HIGH

Model 360 Tuxedo
1987 only. Tuxedo option included white body, white painted fretboard, and black hardware.

1987		$1,400	$1,700

Model 360 WB
1984-1998. Double bound body, 2 pickups, vibrato optional (VB).

1984-1990		$1,600	$2,000
1991-1998	Non-vibrato WB	$1,350	$1,500
1991-1998	Vibrato option WBVB	$1,350	$1,500

Model 360V64
1991-2003. Reissue of '64 Model 360 old style body without vibrola, has binding with full length inlays.

1991-2003		$2,100	$2,600

Model 360/12
1964-present. Deluxe thinline, 2 pickups, 12-string version of Model 360, Rick-O-Sound stereo.

1964	NS (introduced)	$7,100	$8,800
1964	OS, less common	$13,000	$16,000
1965	NS, more common	$6,600	$8,000
1965	OS, less common	$12,000	$15,000
1965-1966	Harrison exact specs, OS	$17,000	$21,000
1966-1969	NS, more common	$5,000	$5,500
1966-1969	OS, less common	$6,000	$7,500
1970-1979		$2,800	$3,100
1980-1999		$1,650	$2,000
2000-2007		$1,200	$1,500

Model 360/12 CW
2000. Carl Wilson, 12-string version of 360 CW.

2000		$2,400	$3,000

Model 360/12 Tuxedo
1987 only. 12-string version of 360 Tuxedo.

1987		$2,800	$3,100

Model 360/12 VP
2004. VP is vintage pickup.

2004		$2,000	$2,100

Model 360/12 WB
1984-1998. 12-string version of 360 WB.

1984-1998		$2,400	$3,000

Model 360/12C63
2004-present. More exact replica of the Harrison model.

2004-2007		$2,400	$2,500

Model 360/12V64
1985-2003. Deluxe thinline with '64 features, 2 pickups, 12 strings, slanted plate tailpiece.

1985-2003	Black and less common colors	$2,100	$2,600
1985-2003	Common colors	$2,000	$2,500

Model 362/12
1975-1992. Doubleneck 6 & 12, 360 features.

1975-1980		$5,000	$8,000
1981-1990		$4,000	$6,000

Model 365
1958-1974. Deluxe thinline, 2 pickups, vibrato, called Model 360 WBVB from '84-'98.

1958-1960	Capri	$5,500	$6,800
1961-1963		$5,000	$6,200
1964	OS, less common	$3,700	$4,500

MODEL YEAR	FEATURES	EXC. COND. LOW	HIGH
1965-1969	NS, more common	$3,200	$3,600
1965-1969	OS, less common	$3,500	$4,000
1970-1974		$2,400	$3,000

Model 365 F
1959-1972. Thin full-body (F designation), 2 pickups, Deluxe features.

1959-1961	Thick version	$5,500	$6,800
1961-1964	Thin version	$5,500	$6,800

Model 366/12 Convertible
1966-1974. Two pickups, 12 strings, comb-like device that converts it to a 6-string, production only noted in '68, perhaps available on custom order basis.

1966-1968	OS	$4,400	$4,600

Model 370
1958-1990, 1994-present. Deluxe thinline, 3 pickups. Could be considered to be a dealer special order item from '58-'67 with limited production ('58=0, '59=4, '60=0, '61=3, '62-'67=0, then started more regularly in '68).

1958-1960	Capri	$5,500	$6,800
1961-1966		$3,700	$4,100
1968-1969		$3,000	$3,500
1970-1979		$2,600	$3,200
1980-2007		$1,400	$1,600

Model 370 F
1959-1972. F-style, 3 pickups, Deluxe features.

1959-1961	Thick version	$6,000	$7,500
1961-1964	Thin version	$3,800	$4,500

Model 370 WB
1984-1998. Double bound body, 3 pickups, vibrato optional (VB).

1984-1989		$1,800	$2,200
1990-1998		$1,500	$1,700

Model 370/12
1965-1990, 1994-present. Not regular production until '80, deluxe thinline, 3 pickups, 12 strings. Could be considered to be a dealer special order item in the '60s and '70s with limited production.

1966	Special order	$4,000	$5,000
1980-1990		$1,900	$2,300
1994-2007		$1,300	$1,700

Model 370/12 RM
1988. Limited Edition Roger McGuinn model, 1000 made, higher-quality appointments.

1988		$4,000	$4,200

Model 375
1958-1974. Deluxe thinline, 3 pickups, vibrato, called Model 370 WBVB from '84-'98.

1958-1960	Capri	$5,500	$6,800
1961-1964		$4,400	$5,400
1965-1969		$3,200	$3,600
1970-1974		$2,400	$3,000

Model 375 F
1959-1972. F-style, 2 pickups.

1959-1961	Thick version	$5,500	$6,800
1961-1964	Thin version	$3,700	$4,100
1965-1972	Thin version	$3,100	$3,600

Rickenbacker 365

Rickenbacker 362/12

1975 Rickenbacker 481

Rickenbacker 610

MODEL YEAR	FEATURES	EXC. COND. LOW	HIGH
Model 380 L Laguna			
1996-2005. Semi-hollow, oil-finished walnut body, Maple neck and 'board, 2 humbuckers, PZ saddle pickups optional.			
1996-2005		$1,300	$1,600
1996-2005	PZ option	$1,500	$1,800
Model 381			
1958-1963, 1969-1974. Double-cut archtop, 2 pickups, slash soundhole, solid 'guard, reintroduced in '69 with double split-level 'guard.			
1958-1963	Light sporadic production	$8,800	$11,000
1969-1974	Various colors, some rare	$7,000	$8,700
Model 381 JK			
1988-1997. John Kay model, 2 humbucking pickups, active electronics, stereo and mono outputs.			
1988-1997		$3,100	$3,800
Model 381/12V69			
1987-present. Reissue of 381/12, deep double-cut body, sound body cavity, catseye soundhole, triangle inlays, bridge with 12 individual saddles. Finishes include Fireglo, Mapleglo and Jetglo.			
1987-2007		$2,000	$2,400
Model 381V69			
1991-present. Reissue of vintage 381.			
1987-1999		$2,000	$2,500
2000-2007		$1,800	$2,250
Model 400/Combo 400			
1956-1958. Double-cut tulip body, neck-thru, 1 pickup, gold anodized 'guard, 21 frets, replaced by Model 425 in '58. Available in black (216 made), blue turquoise (53), Cloverfield Green (53), Montezuma Brown (41), and 4 in other custom colors.			
1956-1958		$2,800	$3,500
Model 420			
1965-1983. Non-vibrato version of Model 425, single pickup.			
1965-1968		$1,100	$1,400
1969-1983		$1,100	$1,300
Model 425/Combo 425			
1958-1973. Double-cut solidbody, 1 pickup, sunburst.			
1958-1959	425 Cresting Wave	$2,800	$3,500
1960		$2,100	$2,600
1961-1964		$2,000	$2,500
1965-1968		$1,300	$1,600
1969-1973		$1,200	$1,500
Model 425/12V63			
1999-2000. 136 made.			
1999-2000		$1,300	$1,600
Model 425V63			
1999-2000. Beatles associated model, 145 JG black made, 116 BG burgundy transparent made, originally custom ordered by Rickenbacker collectors and they were not part of Rickenbacker's sales literature in the late '90s.			
1999-2000		$1,300	$1,600
Model 430			
1971-1982. Style 200 body, natural.			
1971-1982		$750	$800

MODEL YEAR	FEATURES	EXC. COND. LOW	HIGH
Model 450/Combo 450			
1957-1984. Replaces Combo 450, 2 pickups (3 optional '62-'77), tulip body shape '57-'59, cresting wave body shape after.			
1957-1958	450 Tulip body (Combo)	$3,500	$4,200
1960	Cresting Wave, flat body	$3,400	$3,700
1961	Cresting Wave, super slim	$2,700	$3,300
1962		$2,300	$2,800
1963		$2,200	$2,600
1964		$2,100	$2,500
1965		$2,000	$2,400
1966		$2,000	$2,400
1970-1979	Includes rare color	$1,400	$2,000
1980-1984		$1,150	$1,400
Model 450/12			
1964-1985. Double-cut solidbody, 12-string version of Model 450, 2 pickups.			
1964		$2,300	$2,800
1965		$2,100	$2,600
1966		$2,100	$2,600
1967-1969		$2,000	$2,500
1970-1979	Includes rare color	$1,400	$2,000
1980-1985		$1,150	$1,400
Model 450V63			
1999-2001. Reissue of '63 450.			
1999-2001		$1,275	$1,500
Model 456/12 Convertible			
1968-1978. Double-cut solidbody, 2 pickups, comb-like device to convert it to 6-string.			
1968-1969		$2,500	$3,100
1970-1978		$2,000	$2,500
Model 460			
1961-1985. Double-cut solidbody, 2 pickups, neck-thru-body, deluxe trim.			
1961-1965		$2,800	$3,300
1966-1969		$1,800	$2,300
1970-1979	Includes rare color	$1,300	$1,800
1980-1985		$1,000	$1,300
Model 480			
1973-1984. Double-cut solidbody with long thin bass horn in 4001 bass series style, 2 pickups, cresting wave body and headstock, bolt-on neck.			
1973-1979		$1,200	$1,500
1980-1984		$1,000	$1,350
Model 481			
1973-1983. Cresting wave body with longer bass horn, 2 humbuckers (3 optional), angled frets.			
1973-1983		$1,600	$1,850
Model 483			
1973-1983. Cresting wave body with longer bass horn, 3 humbuckers.			
1973-1983		$1,000	$1,250
Model 600/Combo 600			
1954-1966. Modified double-cut.			
1954-1957	Blond/white	$3,700	$4,200
1956-1959	OT/Blue Turquoise	$3,700	$4,200
1966		$2,900	$3,600

MODEL YEAR	FEATURES	EXC. COND. LOW	HIGH

Model 610
1985-1991. Cresting-wave cutaway solidbody, 2 pickups, trapeze R-tailpiece, Jetglo.

1985-1991		$950	$1,250

Model 610/12
1988-1997. 12-string version of Model 610.

1988-1997		$950	$1,250

Model 615
1962-1966, 1969-1977. Double-cut solidbody, 2 pickups, vibrato.

1962-1965		$2,150	$2,500
1966-1969		$2,050	$2,300
1970-1977		$1,500	$1,800

Model 620
1974-present. Double-cut solidbody, deluxe binding, 2 pickups, neck-thru-body.

1974-1979		$1,300	$1,400
1980-1989		$1,200	$1,300
1990-1999		$1,100	$1,200
2000-2007		$1,100	$1,300

Model 620/12
1981-present. Double-cut solidbody, 2 pickups, 12 strings, standard trim.

1981-1989	Includes rare color	$1,500	$2,000
1990-1999		$1,300	$1,400
2000-2007		$1,300	$1,400

Model 625
1962-1977. Double-cut solidbody, deluxe trim, 2 pickups, vibrato.

1962-1965		$4,500	$5,500
1966-1969		$3,000	$4,000
1970-1977		$2,500	$3,000

Model 650/Combo 650
1957-1959. Standard color, 1 pickup.

1957-1959		$3,500	$5,500

Model 650 A Atlantis
1991-2004. Cresting wave solidbody, neck-thru, 2 pickups, chrome hardware, turquoise.

1991-1999		$750	$1,050
2000-2004		$750	$1,000

Model 650 C Colorado
1993-present. Maple neck and body, neck-thru, 2 pickups.

1993-1999		$750	$1,050
2000-2007		$750	$1,000

Model 650 D Dakota
1993-present. Tulip-shaped neck-thru solidbody, single pickup, chrome hardware, walnut oil-satin finish.

1993-1999		$750	$1,050
2000-2007		$750	$1,000

Model 650 E Excalibur/F Frisco
1991-2003. African Vermilion, gold hardware, gloss finish. Name changed to Frisco in '95.

1991-1999		$800	$1,000
2000-2003		$900	$950

Model 650 S Sierra
1993-present. Tulip-shaped neck-thru solidbody, single pickup, gold hardware, walnut oil-satin finish.

1993-2007		$800	$1,000

Model 660
1998-present. Cresting wave maple body, triangle inlays, 2 pickups.

1998-2007		$1,500	$1,850

Model 660/12
1998-present. 12-string 660.

1998-2007		$1,750	$2,000

Model 660/12 TP
1991-1998. Tom Petty model, 12 strings, cresting wave body, 2 pickups, deluxe trim, limited run of 1000.

1991-1998	With certificate	$2,600	$2,800

Model 800/Combo 800
1954-1966. Offset double-cut, 1 horseshoe pickup until late-'57, second bar type after, called the Model 800 in the '60s.

1954-1959	Blond/white	$4,000	$4,500
1954-1959	Blue or green	$4,000	$4,500
1966		$3,200	$4,000

Model 850/Combo 850
1957-1959. Extreme double-cut, 1 pickup until '58, 2 after, various colors, called Model 850 in the '60s.

1957-1959		$3,800	$4,500

Model 900
1957-1980. Double-cut tulip body shape, 3/4 size, 1 pickup. Body changes to cresting wave shape in '69.

1957-1966		$2,000	$2,200

Model 950/Combo 950
1957-1980. Like Model 900, but with 2 pickups, 21 frets. Body changes to cresting wave shape in '69.

1957-1964		$2,000	$2,200
1965-1980		$1,900	$2,100

Model 1000
1957-1970. Like Model 900, but with 18 frets. Body does not change to cresting wave shape.

1956-1966		$1,800	$1,900
1967-1970		$1,700	$1,800

Model 1993/12 RM
1964-1967. Export 'slim-line' 12-string model made for English distributor Rose-Morris of London, built along the lines of the U.S. Model 360/12 but with small differences that are considered important in the vintage guitar market.

1964	Flat tailpiece	$15,000	$22,000
1965-1967	R tailpiece	$9,000	$12,000

Model 1996 RM
1964-1967. Rose-Morris import, 3/4 size built similiarly to the U.S. Model 325.

1964-1967	Black	$10,000	$14,000
1964-1967	FG and MG	$9,000	$12,000

Model 1996 RM Reissue
2006. Reissue of the Rose-Morris version of model 325, this reissue available on special order in 2006.

2006		$3,000	$3,200

Model 1997 PT
1987-1988. Pete Townsend Signature Model, semi-hollowbody, single F-hole, maple neck, 21-fret rosewood 'board, 3 pickups, Firemist finish, limited to 250 total production.

1987-1988		$3,500	$4,500

Rickenbacker Model 625

Rickenbacker 660

GUITARS

RKS Sunburst

MODEL YEAR	FEATURES	EXC. COND. LOW	HIGH

Model 1997 RM
1964-1967. Export 'slim-line' model made for English distributor Rose-Morris of London, built along the lines of the U.S. Model 335, but with small differences that are considered important in the vintage guitar market, 2 pickups, vibrola tailpiece. Rose-Morris export models sent to the USA generally had a red-lined guitar case vs. the USA domestic blue-lined guitar case.

| 1964-1967 | | $3,500 | $5,500 |

Model 1997 RM Reissue
1987-1995. Reissue of '60s Rose-Morris model, but with vibrola (VB) or without.

| 1987-1995 | | $1,100 | $1,400 |

Model 1997 SPC
1993-2002. 3 pickup version of reissue.

| 1993-2002 | | $1,200 | $1,500 |

Model 1998 RM
1964-1967. Export 'slim-line' model made for English distributor Rose-Morris of London, built along the lines of a U.S. Model 345 but with small differences that are considered important in the vintage guitar market, 3 pickups, vibrola tailpiece.

| 1964-1967 | | $4,500 | $6,000 |

Rigaud Guitars
1978-present. Luthier Robert Rigaud builds his premium grade, custom/production, flat top guitars in Greensboro, North Carolina. He also builds bowed psalterys and harps.

Ritz
1989. Solidbody electric guitars and basses produced in Calimesa, California, by Wayne Charvel, Eric Galletta and Brad Becnel, many of which featured cracked shell mosiac finishes.

RKS
2003-present. Professional and premium grade, production/custom, electric hollowbody and solidbody guitars designed by Ravi Sawhney and guitarist Dave Mason and built in Thousand Oaks, California. They also build basses.

Robert Cefalu
1998-present. Luthier Robert Cefalu builds his professional grade, production/custom, acoustic guitars in Buffalo, New York. The guitars have an RC on the headstock.

Robert Guitars
1981-present. Luthier Mikhail Robert builds his premium grade, production/custom, classical guitars in Summerland, British Columbia.

Robertson Guitars
1995-present. Luthier Jeff Robertson builds his premium grade, production/custom flat-top guitars in South New Berlin, New York.

Robin Ranger Custom

MODEL YEAR	FEATURES	EXC. COND. LOW	HIGH

Robin
1982-present. Professional and premium grade, production/custom, guitars from luthier David Wintz and built in Houston, Texas. Most guitars were Japanese-made until '87; American production began in '88. Most Japanese Robins were pretty consistent in features, but the American ones were often custom-made, so many variations in models exist. They also make Metropolitan (since '96) and Alamo (since '00) brand guitars.

Avalon Classic
1994-present. Single-cut, figured maple top, 2 humbuckers.

| 1994-2000s | | $900 | $1,100 |

Medley Pro
1990s. Solidbody with 2 extreme cutaway horns, hum-single-single.

| 1990s | US-made | $700 | $775 |

Medley Special
1992-1995. Ash body, maple neck, rosewood 'board, 24 frets, various pickup options.

| 1992-1995 | | $500 | $600 |

Medley Standard
1985-present. Offset double-cut swamp ash solidbody, bolt neck, originally with hum-single-single pickups, but now also available with 2 humbuckers.

| 1985-1987 | Japan-made | $400 | $500 |
| 1988-2007 | U.S.-made | $650 | $750 |

Octave
1982-1990s. Tuned an octave above standard tuning, full body size with 15 1/2" short-scale bolt maple neck. Japanese-made production model until '87, U.S.-made custom shop after.

| 1990s | With original case | $725 | $850 |

Raider I/Raider II/Raider III
1985-1991. Double-cut solidbody, 1 humbucker pickup (Raider I), 2 humbuckers (Raider II), or 3 single-coils (Raider III), maple neck, either maple or rosewood 'board, sunburst.

1985-1991	1 pickup	$400	$475
1985-1991	2 pickups	$425	$525
1985-1991	3 pickups	$450	$550

Ranger Custom
1982-1986, 1988-present. Swamp ash bound body, bolt-on maple neck, rosewood or maple 'board, 2 single coils and 1 humbucker, orange, made in Japan until '86, U.S.-made after.

| 1982-1986 | Japan-made | $400 | $500 |
| 1988-2007 | U.S.-made | $750 | $875 |

RDN-Doubleneck Octave/Six
1982-1985. Six-string standard neck with 3 pickups, 6-string octave neck with 1 pickup, double-cut solidbody.

| 1982-1985 | With original case | $700 | $800 |

Savoy Deluxe/Standard
1995-present. Semi-hollow thinline single cut archtop, 2 pickups, set neck.

| 1996-2007 | | $1,200 | $1,400 |

MODEL YEAR	FEATURES	EXC. COND. LOW	HIGH

Soloist/Artisan

1982-1986. Mahogany double-cut solidbody, carved bound maple top, set neck, 2 humbuckers. Renamed Artisan in '85. Only about 125 made in Japan.

1982-1986		$500	$600

Wrangler

1995-2002. Classic '50s single-cut slab body, 3 Rio Grande pickups, opaque finish.

1995-2002		$550	$675

Robinson Guitars

2002-present. Premium and presentation grade, custom/production, steel string guitars built by luthier Jake Robinson in Kalamazoo, Michigan.

RockBeach Guitars

2005-present. Luthier Greg Bogoshian builds his custom, professional grade, chambered electric guitars in Rochester, New York. He also builds basses.

Rockit Guitar

2006-present. Luthier Rod MacKenzie builds his premium grade, custom, electric guitars in Everett, Washington. He also builds basses.

Rogands

Late 1960s. Produced by France's Jacobacci company and named after brothers Roger and Andre. Short-lived brand; the brothers made instruments under several other brands as well.

Roger

Guitars built in Germany by luthier Wenzel Rossmeisl and named for his son Roger. Roger Rossmeisl would go on to work at Rickenbacker and Fender.

Rogue

2001-present. Budget and intermediate grade, production, acoustic, resonator, electric and sitar guitars. They also offer mandolins, banjos, ukuleles, lap steels and basses. They previously offered effects and amps

Roland

Best known for keyboards, effects, and amps, Roland offered synthesizer-based guitars and basses from 1977 to '86.

GR-707 Synth Guitar

1983-1986. Slab-wedge asymmetrical body, bass bout to headstock support arm, 2 humbucker pickups, multi-controls.

1983-1986	Silver	$1,200	$1,400

GS-500 Synth Guitar/Module

1977-1986. Snyth functions in a single-cut solidbody guitar. The GS-300 was the same electronics in a classic offset double-cut body.

1977-1986	Sunburst	$900	$1,100

MODEL YEAR	FEATURES	EXC. COND. LOW	HIGH

Roman & Lipman Guitars

1989-2000. Production/custom, solidbody guitars made in Danbury, Connecticut by Ed Roman. They also made basses.

Roman Abstract Guitars

1989-present. Professional and premium grade, production/custom, solidbody guitars made in Las Vegas, Nevada by Ed Roman.

Roman Centurion Guitars

2001-present. Premium and presentation grade, custom guitars made in Las Vegas, Nevada by Ed Roman.

Roman Pearlcaster Guitars

1999-present. Professional and premium grade, production/custom, solidbody guitars made in Las Vegas, Nevada by Ed Roman.

Roman Quicksilver Guitars

1997-present. Professional and premium grade, production/custom, solid and hollow-body guitars made in Las Vegas, Nevada by Ed Roman.

Roman Vampire Guitars

2004-present. Professional and premium grade, production/custom, solidbody guitars made in Las Vegas, Nevada by Ed Roman.

Rono

1967-present. Luthier Ron Oates builds his professional and premium grade, production/custom, flat-top, jazz, Wiesenborn-style, and resonator guitars in Boulder, Colorado. He also builds basses and mandolins.

Ro-Pat-In

See Rickenbacker.

Rosetti

1950s-1960s. Guitars imported into England by distributor Rosetti, made by Holland's Egmond, maybe others.

Roudhloff

1810s-1840s. Luthier Francois Roudhloff built his instruments in France. Labels could state F. Roudhloff-Mauchand or Roudhloff Brothers. Valuation depends strongly on condition and repair. His sons built guitars under the D & A Roudhloff label.

Small Brazilian

1840s. Solid spruce top, laminated Brazilian sides and back.

1840s		$2,400	$3,000

Rowan

1997-present. Professional and premium grade, production/custom, solidbody and acoustic/electric guitars built by luthier Michael Rowan in Garland, Texas.

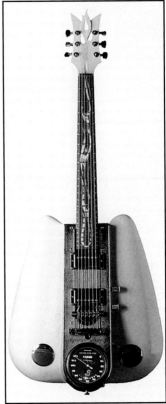

Rockit Limited Edition

Roman Magic Twanger

GUITARS

Running Dog Concert

1976 S.D. Curlee Standard

MODEL		EXC. COND.	
YEAR	FEATURES	LOW	HIGH

Royal

ca. 1954-ca. 1965. Line of jazz style guitars made by France's Jacobacci company, which also built under its own brand.

Royden Guitars

1996-present. Professional grade, production/custom, flat-tops and solidbody electrics built by luthier Royden Moran in Peterborough, Ontario.

RS Guitarworks

1994-present. Professional grade, production/custom, solid and hollowbody guitars built by luthier Roy Bowen in Winchester, Kentucky.

Rubio, German Vasquez

1993-present. Luthier German Vasquez Rubio builds his professional and premium grade, production/custom classical and flamenco guitars in Los Angeles, California.

Ruck, Robert

1966-present. Premium grade, custom classical and flamenco guitars built by luthier Robert Ruck originally in Kalaheo, Hawaii, and currently in Eugene, Oregon.

Custom Classical

1966-present. Premium grade classical with solid spruce top and solid rosewood back and sides.

1990s		$7,200	$9,000

Running Dog Guitars

1994-present. Luthier Rick Davis builds his professional and premium grade, custom flat-tops in Seattle, Washington. He was originally located in Richmond, Vermont.

Ruokangas

1995-present. Luthier Juha Ruokangas builds his premium and presentation grade, production/custom, solidbody and semi-acoustic electric guitars in Hyvinkaa, Finland.

Rustler

1993-ca. 1998. Solidbody electrics with hand-tooled leather bound and studded sides and a R branded into the top, built by luthier Charles Caponi in Mason City, Iowa.

RVC Guitars

1999-present. Professional and premium grade, production/custom, solidbody guitars made in Las Vegas, Nevada by Ed Roman.

RWK

1991-present. Luthier Bob Karger builds his intermediate grade, production/custom, solidbody electrics and travel guitars in Highland Park, Illinois.

MODEL		EXC. COND.	
YEAR	FEATURES	LOW	HIGH

Ryder

1963. Made by Rickenbacker, the one guitar with this brand was the same as their solidbody Model 425.

S. B. Brown Guitars

1994-present. Custom flat-tops made by luthier Steve Brown in Fullerton, California.

S. B. MacDonald Custom Instruments

1988-present. Professional and premium grade, custom/production, flat-top, resonator, and solidbody guitars built by luthier Scott B. MacDonald in Huntington, New York.

S. Walker Custom Guitars

2002-present. Luthier Scott Walker builds his premium grade, production/custom, solid and semi hollow body electric guitars in Santa Cruz, California.

S. Yairi

Ca. 1965-1980s. Steel string folk guitars and classical nylon string guitars by master Japanese luthier Sadao Yairi, imported by Philadelphia Music Company of Limerick, Pennsylvania. Early sales literature called the brand Syairi. Most steel string models have dreadnought bodies and nylon-string classical guitars are mostly standard grand concert size. All models are handmade. Steel string Jumbos and dreadnoughts have Syairi logo on the headstock, nylon-classical models have no logo. The Model 900 has a solid wood body, others assumed to have laminate

S.D. Curlee

1975-1982. Founded in Matteson, Illinois by music store owner Randy Curlee, after an unsuccessful attempt to recruit builder Dan Armstrong. S.D. Curlee guitars were made in Illinois, while S.D. Curlee International instruments were made by Matsumoku in Japan. The guitars featured mostly Watco oil finishes, often with exotic hardwoods, and unique neck-thru-bridge construction on American and Japanese instruments. These were the first production guitars to use a single-coil pickup at the bridge with a humbucker at the neck, and a square brass nut. DiMarzio pickups. Offered in a variety of shapes, later some copies. Approximately 12,000 American-made basses and 3,000 guitars were made, most of which were sold overseas. Two hundred were made in '75-'76; first production guitar numbered 518.

Electric Solidbody

1975-1982. Models include the '75-'81 Standard I, II and III, '76-'81 International C-10 and C-11, '80-'81 Yanke, Liberty, Butcher, Curbeck, Summit, Special, and the '81-'82 Destroyer, Flying V.

1975-1982		$275	$325

MODEL YEAR	FEATURES	EXC. COND. LOW	HIGH

S.S. Stewart

The original S.S. Stewart Company (1878-1904), of Philadelphia, is considered to be one of the most important banjo manufacturers of the late 19th century. The Stewart family was out of the company by the early 1900s, and the brand was soon acquired by Bugellsein & Jacobsen of New York. The brand name was used on guitars into the 1960s.

S101

2002-present. Budget and intermediate grade, production, classical, acoustic, resonator, solid and semi-hollow body guitars imported from China by American Sejung Corp. They also offer basses, mandolins, and banjos.

Sadowsky

1980-present. Professional and premium grade, production/custom, solidbody, semi-hollowbody, archtop, and electric nylon-string guitars built by luthier Roger Sadowsky in Brooklyn, New York. He also builds basses and amps. In '96, luthier Yoshi Kikuchi started building Sadowsky Tokyo instruments in Japan.

Vintage Style

Swamp ash body, Barden pickups, vintage-style gears, bridge, control plate and 'guard, sunburst.

1982-1987		$1,350	$1,700

Saga

Saga Musical Instruments, of San Francisco, California distributes a wide variety of instruments and brands, occasionally including their own line of solidbody guitars called the Saga Gladiator Series (1987-'88, '94-'95). In the 2000s, Saga also offered component kits ($90-$130) that allowed for complete assembly in white wood.

Sahlin Guitars

1975-present. Luthier Eric Sahlin builds his premium grade, custom, classical and flamenco guitars in Spokane, Washington.

Samick

1958-2001, 2002-present. Budget, intermediate and professional grade, production, imported acoustic and electric guitars. They also offer basses, mandolins, ukes and banjos. Samick also distributes Abilene and Silvertone brand instruments.

Samick started out producing pianos, adding guitars in '65 under other brands. In '88 Samick greatly increased their guitar production. The Samick line of 350 models was totally closed out in 2001. A totally new line of 250 models was introduced January 2002 at NAMM. All 2002 models have the new compact smaller headstock and highly styled S logo.

Sammo

1920s. Labels in these instruments state they were made by the Osborne Mfg. Co. with an address of Masonic Temple, Chicago, Illinois. High quality and often with a high degree of ornamentation. They also made ukes and mandolins.

Sand Guitars

1979-present. Luthier Kirk Sand opened the Guitar Shoppe in Laguna Beach, California in 1972 with James Matthews. By '79, he started producing his own line of premium grade, production/custom-made flat-tops.

Sandoval Engineering

1979-present. Luthier Karl Sandoval builds his premium grade, custom, solidbody guitars in Santa Fe Springs, California.

Sano

1944-ca. 1970. Sano was a New Jersey-based accordion company that imported Italian-made solid and semi-hollow body guitars for a few years, starting in 1966. They also built their own amps and reverb units.

Santa Cruz

1976-present. Professional, premium and presentation grade, production/custom, flat-top, 12-string, and archtop guitars from luthier Richard Hoover in Santa Cruz, California. They also build a mandocello. Founded by Hoover, Bruce Ross and William Davis. Hoover became sole owner in '89. Custom ordered instruments with special upgrades may have higher values than the ranges listed here.

Archtop

Early 1980s-present. Originally called the FJZ, but by mid-'90s, called the Archtop, offering 16", 17" and 18" cutaway acoustic/electric models, often special order. Spruce top, curly maple body, ebony 'board, floating pickup, f-holes, sunburst or natural. Many custom options available.

1980-1990s		$4,000	$5,000

D 12-Fret

1994-present. 15 1/2" scale, 12-fret neck, slotted headstock, round shoulders, spruce top, mahogany back and sides, notch diamond markers, herringbone trim and rosette, natural. Special order models will vary in value and could exceed the posted range.

1994-2007		$2,200	$2,300

D Koa

1980s-1990s. Style D with koa back and sides.

1990s		$2,200	$2,300

D/HR (Richard Hoover)

2000	Indian rosewood	$2,400	$2,600

D/PW

2001-present. Pre-war D-style.

2001-2007		$2,000	$2,200

Sadowsky Vintage Style

Sahlin Guitars

Santa Cruz H13

Santa Cruz OM

MODEL YEAR	FEATURES	EXC. COND. LOW	HIGH
F			
1976-present. 15 7/8" scale with narrow waist, sitka spruce top, Indian rosewood back and sides, natural.			
1976-2007		$2,700	$3,300
F46R			
1980s. Brazilian rosewood, single-cut.			
1980s		$4,000	$4,500
FS (Finger Style)			
1988-present. Single-cut, cedar top, Indian rosewood back and sides, mahogany neck, modified X-bracing.			
1988-2000s		$2,500	$3,000
H/H13			
1976-present. Parlor size acoustic, offered in cutaway and non-cut versions, and options included koa, rosewood or maple, special inlays, slotted headstock, and shallow or deep bodies.			
1976-1999		$2,500	$3,100
2000-2007		$2,300	$2,700
OM (Orchestra Model)			
1987-present. Orchestra model acoustic, sitka spruce top, Indian rosewood (Brazilian optional) back and sides, herringbone rosette, scalloped braces.			
1987-1999	Brazilian rosewood	$4,500	$5,500
1987-2007	Indian rosewood	$2,400	$3,000
OM/PW			
2000s. Indian rosewood.			
2000s		$1,900	$2,000
Tony Rice			
1976-present. Dreadnought, Indian rosewood body (Brazilian optional until Tony Rice Professional model available), sitka spruce top, solid peghead, zigzag back stripe, pickup optional.			
1976-1999		$2,400	$3,000
2000-2007		$2,400	$3,000
Tony Rice Professional			
1997-present. Brazilian rosewood back and sides, carved German spruce top, zigzag back stripe, solid peghead.			
1997-2007		$4,800	$6,000
Vintage Artist Custom			
1992-2004. Martin D-42 style, mahogany body, Indian rosewood back and sides, sitka spruce top, zigzag back stripe, solid peghead, scalloped X-bracing, pickup optional.			
1992-2004		$3,000	$3,200
VJ (Vintage Jumbo)			
2000-present. 16" scale, round shouldered body, sitka spruce, figured mahogany back and sides, natural.			
2000-2007		$2,200	$2,500

Saturn

1960s-1970s. Imported, most likely from Japan, solid and semi-hollow body electric guitars and basses. Large S logo with Saturn name inside the S. Many sold through Eaton's in Canada.

MODEL YEAR	FEATURES	EXC. COND. LOW	HIGH
Saturn			
1960s-1970. Solidbody, 4 pickups.			
1960s-1970		$300	$350

Sawchyn Guitars

1972-present. Professional and premium grade, production/custom, flat-top and flamenco guitars and mandolins built by luthier Peter Sawchyn in Regina, Saskatchewan.

Schaefer

1997-present. Premium grade, production, electric archtops handcrafted by luthier Edward A. Schaefer, who was located in Fort Worth, Texas, until '03, then in Duluth, Minnesota until '07, and currently in Bastrop, Texas.

Schecter

1976-present. Intermediate, professional and premium grade, production/custom, acoustic and electric guitars. They also offer basses. Guitar component manufacturer founded in California by four partners (David Schecter's name sounded the best), started offering complete instruments in '79. The company was bought out and moved to Dallas, Texas in the early '80s. By '88 the company was back in California and in '89 was purchased by Hisatake Shibuya. Schecter Custom Shop guitars are made in Burbank, California and their Diamond Series is made in South Korea.

MODEL YEAR	FEATURES	EXC. COND. LOW	HIGH
Diamond Series			
1997-present. Korea-made models, many body style series with names as C, S, Tempest, 00, 007, PT, Hellcat, Ultra, Banshee, Hellraiser, Blackjack, Omen, Damien, Aviation, Semi/Hollow, Baritones, and Double Neck.			
1997-2007	Various models	$250	$500
Electric			
1980s	Various models	$225	$500

Scheerhorn

1989-present. Professional and premium grade, custom, resonator and Hawaiian guitars built by luthier Tim Scheerhorn in Kentwood, Michigan.

Schoenberg

1986-present. Premium grade, production/custom, flat-tops offered by Eric Schoenberg of Tiburon, California. From '86-'94 guitars made to Schoenberg's specifications by Martin. From '86-'90 constructed by Schoenberg's luthier and from '90-'94 assembled by Martin but voiced and inlaid in the Schoenberg shop. Current models made to Schoenberg specs by various smaller shops.

Schon

1986-1991. Designed by guitarist Neal Schon, early production by Charvel/Jackson building about 200 in the San Dimas factory. The final 500 were built by Larrivee in Canada. Leo Knapp also built custom Schon guitars from '85-'87, and '90s custom-made Schon guitars were also available.

MODEL YEAR	FEATURES	EXC. COND. LOW	HIGH
Standard (Canadian-made)			
1987-1991. Made in Canada on headstock.			
1987-1991		$375	$450

GUITARS

MODEL YEAR	FEATURES	EXC. COND. LOW	HIGH

Standard (U.S.A.-made)
1986 only. San Dimas/Jackson model, single-cut, pointy headstock shape, Made in U.S.A. on headstock.

1986		$1,700	$2,100

Schramm Guitars
1990-present. Premium grade, production/custom, classical and flamenco guitars built by luthier David Schramm in Clovis, California.

Schroder Guitars
1993-present. Luthier Timothy Schroeder (he drops the first e in his name on the guitars) builds his premium grade, production/custom, archtops in Northbrook, Illinois.

Schwartz Guitars
1992-present. Premium grade, custom, flat-top guitars built by luthier Sheldon Schwartz in Concord, Ontario.

ScoGo
2001-present. Professional and premium grade, production/custom, solidbody guitars built by luthier Scott Gordon in Parkesburg, Pennsylvania.

Scorpion Guitars
1998-present. Professional and premium grade, custom, solidbody guitars made in Las Vegas, Nevada by Ed Roman.

Scott French
2004-present. Professional grade, custom, electric guitars built by luthier Scott French in Auburn, California. He also builds basses.

Seagull
1982-present. Intermediate grade, production, acoustic and acoustic/electric guitars built in Canada. Seagull was founded by luthier Robert Godin, who also has the Norman, Godin, and Patrick & Simon brands of instruments.

Sebring
1980s-mid-1990s. Entry level Korean imports distributed by V.M.I. Industries.

Seiwa
Early 1980s. Entry-level to mid-level Japanese electric guitars and basses, logo may indicate Since 1956.

Sekova
Mid-1960s-mid-1970s. Entry level instruments imported by the U.S. Musical Merchandise Corporation of New York.

Selmer
1932-1952. France-based Selmer & Cie was primarily a maker of wind instruments when they asked Mario Maccaferri to design a line of guitars for them. The guitars, with an internal sound chamber for increased volume, were built in Mantes-la-Ville. Both gut and steel string models were offered. Maccaferri left Selmer in '33, but guitar production continued, and the original models are gradually phased out. In '36, only the 14 fret oval model is built. Production is stopped for WWII and resumes in '46, finally stopping in '52. Less than 900 guitars are built in total.

Classique
1942. Solid Rosewood back and sides, no cutaway, solid spruce top, round soundhole, classical guitar size, possibly only 2 built.

1942		$6,500	$8,000

Concert
1932-1933. For gut strings, cutaway, laminated Indian rosewood back and sides, internal resonator, spruce top with D hole, wide walnut neck, ebony 'board, only a few dozen built.

1932-1933		$19,200	$21,000

Eddie Freeman Special
1933. For steel strings, 4 strings, laminated Indian rosewood back and sides, cutaway, no internal resonator, solid spruce top, D hole, black and white rosette inlays, walnut 12 fret neck, ebony 'board, 640mm scale, approx. 100 made.

1933		$6,700	$8,300

Espagnol
1932. For gut strings, laminated Indian rosewood back and sides, no cutaway, internal resonator, solid spruce top, round soundhole, wide walnut neck, ebony 'board, only a few made.

1932		$9,500	$11,900

Grand Modele 4 Cordes
1932-1933. For steel strings, 4 string model, laminated back and sides, cutaway, internal resonator, solid spruce top, D hole, walnut neck, ebony 'board, 12 fret, 640mm scale, 2 or 3 dozen made.

1932-1933		$11,000	$13,800

Harp Guitar
1933. For gut strings, solid mahogany body, extended horn holding 3 sub bass strings, 3 screw adjustable neck, wide walnut neck, ebony 'board, only about 12 built.

1933		$15,500	$17,000

Hawaienne
1932-1934. For steel strings, 6 or 7 strings, laminated back and sides, no cutaway, internal resonator, solid spruce top, D hole, wide walnut neck, ebony 'board, 2 or 3 dozen built.

1932-1934		$24,500	$26,000

Modele Jazz
1936-1942, 1946-1952. For steel strings, laminated Indian rosewood back and sides (some laminated or solid mahogany), cutaway, solid spruce top, small oval soundhole, walnut neck, ebony 'board (latest ones with rosewood necks), 14 fret to the body, 670mm scale. Production interrupted for WWII.

1936-1952		$29,200	$31,000

1986 Schecter Yngwie Malmsteen

1968 Sekova Grecian

1937 Selmer Orchestre

*Sheppard Minstral
Grand Concert*

MODEL YEAR	FEATURES	EXC. COND. LOW	HIGH

Modeles de Transition
1934-1936. Transition models appearing before 14 fret oval hole model, some in solid maple with solid headstock, some with round soundhole and cutaway, some 12 fret models with oval hole.

1934-1936		$18,200	$20,000

Orchestre
1932-1934. For steel strings, laminated back and sides, cutaway, internal resonator, solid spruce top, D hole, walnut neck, ebony 'board, about 100 made.

1932-1934		$30,500	$34,000

Tenor
1932-1933. For steel strings, 4 strings, laminated back and sides, internal resonator, solid spruce top, D hole, walnut neck, ebony 'board, 12 fret, 570mm scale, 2 or 3 dozen built.

1932-1933		$6,000	$7,500

Serge Guitars
1995-present. Luthier Serge Michaud builds his production/custom, classical, steel-string, resophonic and archtop guitars in Breakeyville, Quebec.

Sexauer Guitars
1967-present. Premium and presentation grade, custom, steel-string, 12-string, nylon-string, and archtop guitars built by luthier Bruce Sexauer in Petaluma, California.

Shadow
1990s. Made in Europe, copy models such as the classic offset double cutaway solidbody, large Shadow logo on headstock, Shadow logo on pickup cover, student to intermediate grade.

Shanti Guitars
1985-present. Premium and presentation grade, custom, steel-string, 12-string, nylon-string and archtop guitars built by luthier Michael Hornick in Avery, California.

Shelley D. Park Guitars
1991-present. Luthier Shelley D. Park builds her professional grade, custom, nylon- and steel-string guitars in Vancouver, British Columbia.

Shelton-Farretta
1967-present. Premium grade, production/custom, flamenco and classical guitars built by luthiers John Shelton and Susan Farretta originally in Portland, Oregon, and since '05 in Alsea, Oregon.

Sheppard Guitars
1993-present. Luthier Gerald Sheppard builds his premium grade, production/custom, steel-string guitars in Kingsport, Tennessee.

MODEL YEAR	FEATURES	EXC. COND. LOW	HIGH

Shergold
1968-1992. Founded by Jack Golder and Norman Houlder, Shergold originally made guitars for other brands like Hayman and Barnes and Mullins. In '75, they started building guitars and basses under their own name. By '82, general guitar production was halted but custom orders were filled through '90. In '91, general production was again started but ended in '92 when Golder died.

Sherwood
Late 1940s-early 1950s. Archtop and lap steel guitars made for Montgomery Ward made by Chicago manufacturers such as Kay. There were also Sherwood amps made by Danelectro. Value ranges are about the same as Kay model equivalent.

Shifflett
1990-present. Luthier Charles Shifflett builds his premium grade, production/custom, flat-top, classical, flamenco, resophonic, and harp guitars in High River, Alberta. He also builds basses and banjos.

Sho-Bro
1969-1978. Spanish and Hawaiian style resonator guitars made by Sho-Bud in Nashville, Tennessee and distributed by Gretsch. Designed Shot Jackson and Buddy Emmons.

Grand Slam
1978. Acoustic, spruce top, mahogany neck, jacaranda sides and back, and mother-of-pearl inlays, abalone soundhole purfling.

1970s		$475	$550

Resonator
1972-1978. Flat-top style guitar with metal resonator with 2 small circular grilled soundholes.

1972-1978		$775	$850

Siegmund Guitars & Amplifiers
1993-present. Luthier Chris Siegmund builds his professional, premium, and presentation grade, custom/production, archtop, solidbody, and resonator guitars in Los Angeles, California. He founded the company in Seattle, moving it to Austin, Texas for '95-'97. He also builds effects pedals and amps.

Sigma
1970-2007. Budget and intermediate grade, production, import acoustic guitars distributed by C.F. Martin Company. They also offered mandolins and banjos.

DR Series
1970-2003. Various dreadnought models.

1970-2003		$250	$450

GCS Series
1994. Grand concert semi-narrow waist body, laminated spruce top, mahogany back and sides, natural.

1990s		$200	$250

MODEL YEAR	FEATURES	EXC. COND. LOW	HIGH

Signet
1972-Mid 1970s. Acoustic flat-top guitars, imported from Japan by Ampeg/Selmer.

Silber
1992-1998. Solid wood, steel-string guitars designed by Marc Silber, made in Paracho, Mexico, and distributed by K & S Music. Silber continues to offer the same models under the Marc Silber Music brand.

Silvertone
1941-ca. 1970, present. Brand of Sears instruments which replaced their Supertone brand in '41. The Silvertone name was used on Sears phonographs, records and radios as early as the 'teens, and on occasional guitar models. When Sears divested itself of the Harmony guitar subsidiary in '40 it turned to other suppliers including Kay. In '40 Kay-made archtops and Hawaiian electric lap steels appeared in the catalog bearing the Silvertone brand, and after '41-'42, all guitars, regardless of manufacturer, were called Silvertone.

Sears offered Danelectro-made solidbodies in the fall of '54. Danelectro hollowbodies appeared in '56.

By '65, the Silvertones were Teisco-made guitars from W.M.I., but never sold through the catalog. First imports shown in catalog were in '69.

By '70, most guitars sold by Sears were imports and did not carry the Silvertone name.

Currently, Samick offers a line of amps under the Silvertone name.

Amp-In-Case
The 1-pickup guitar, introduced in 1962, came with a smaller wattage amp without tremolo. The 2-pickup model, introduced in '63, came with a higher-watt amp with tremolo and better quality Jensen speaker. Gray tolex covered the guitar-amp case.

1960s	1 pickup, Model 1448	$425	$600
1960s	2 pickups	$500	$900

Belmont
1950s. Single-cut solidbody, double pickup, black.

1958		$525	$650

Espanada
Bigsby, 2 pickups, black.

1960s		$450	$550

Estrelita
Semi-hollowbody archtop, 2 pickups, black, Harmony-made.

1960s		$475	$575

F-66
1964. Similar to Harmony Rocket III, single-cut, thinline electric, 3 pickups, Bigsby.

1964		$500	$600

Gene Autry Melody Ranch
1941-1955. 13" Harmony-made acoustic, Gene Autry signature on belly, cowboy roundup stencil, same as earlier Supertone Gene Autry Roundup.

1941-1955		$375	$450

H-1434 Rocket
1965. Similar to Harmony Rocket H59, sold by Sears, 3 pickups, Bigsby vibrato.

1965		$600	$750

Meteor
Single-cut, 1 pickup, sunburst.

1955		$350	$425

Silhouette
1964-1967		$225	$425

Stratotone Jupiter
1950s. Similar to Kay Thin Twin, single-cut, 2 lipstick pickups, colorful appointments.

1950s		$475	$550

Student-level 13" Flat-Top
Harmony-made, 13" lower bout.

1960s		$40	$50

U-1
1957-1959. Danelectro-made, single pickup, Coke bottle headstock, bronze color.

1957-1959		$650	$800

U-3
1957-1959. Danoelectro-made, 3 pickups, single-cut.

1957-1959		$1,400	$1,650

Ultra Thin Professional
1960s. Harmony-made, thin hollow cutaway, 3 pickups, Bigsby tailpiece.

1960s		$650	$800

Simon & Patrick
1985-present. Intermediate and professional grade, production, acoustic and acoustic/electric guitars built in Canada. Founded by luthier Robert Godin and named after his sons. He also produces the Seagull, Godin, and Norman brands of instruments.

Singletouch
Luthier Mark Singleton builds his professional and premium grade, custom/production, solid and semi-hollow body guitars in Phillips Ranch, California. He also builds basses.

Skylark
1981. Solidbody guitars made in Japan and distributed by JC Penney. Two set-neck models and one bolt-neck model were offered. Most likely a one-time deal as brand quickly disappeared.

Slammer
1999-present. Budget and intermediate grade, production, guitars imported from Indonesia by Hamer. They also offer basses. Not to be confused with Hamer's Korean-made series of guitars from 1990-'97 called Hamer Slammer.

Slammer Series (Import)
1999-2007	Various models	$125	$300

Sho-Bro resonator

Siegmund Outcaster

Smart J-2

Specimen Products Maxwell

MODEL YEAR	FEATURES	EXC. COND. LOW	HIGH

Slingerland

Late 1920s-mid-1940s. The parent company was Slingerland Banjo and Drums, Chicago, Illinois. The company offered other stringed instruments into the '40s. They also marketed the May Bell brand. The guitars were made by other companies, mainly including Regal. Slingerland Drums is now owned by Gibson.

Nitehawk

1930s. 16" archtop, Nitehawk logo on headstock, fancy position neck markers.

1930s		$575	$700

Songster Archtop/Flat-Top

1930s.

1930s	Archtop	$525	$650
1930s	Flat-Top	$900	$1,100

Smart Musical Instruments

1986-present. Luthier A. Lawrence Smart builds his professional and premium grade, custom, flat-top guitars in McCall, Idaho. He also builds mandolin-family instruments.

Smith, George

1959-present. Custom classical and flamenco guitars built by luthier George Smith in Portland, Oregon.

Smith, Lawrence K.

1989-present. Luthier Lawrence Smith builds his professional and premium grade, production/custom, flat-top, nylon-string, and archtop guitars in Thirrow, New South Wales, Australia.

SMK Music Works

2002-present. Luthier Scott Kenerson builds production/custom, professional grade, solidbody electric guitars in Waterford, Michigan. He also builds basses.

Somervell

1979-present. Luthier Douglas P. Somervell builds his premium and presentation grade, production/custom, classical and flamenco guitars in Brasstown, North Carolina.

Somogyi, Ervin

1971-present. Luthier Ervin Somogyi builds his presentation grade, production/custom, flat-top, flamenco, and classical guitars in Oakland, California.

SonFather Guitars

1994-present. Luthier David A. Cassotta builds his production/custom, flat-top, 12-string, nylon-string and electric guitars in Rocklin, California.

Sorrentino

1930s. Private brand made by Epiphone and distributed by C.M.I. Quality close to similar Epiphone models.

MODEL YEAR	FEATURES	EXC. COND. LOW	HIGH

Arcadia

1930s. Lower-end f-hole acoustic archtop similar to Epiphone Blackstone.

1930s		$600	$750

Southwell Guitars

1983-present. Premium grade, custom, nylon-string guitars built by luthier Gary Southwell in Nottingham, England.

Sovereign

Ca. 1899-1938. Sovereign was originally a brand of The Oscar Schmidt Company of Jersey City, New Jersey, and used on guitars, banjos and mandolins starting in the very late 1800s. In the late '30s, Harmony purchased several trade names from the Schmidt Company, including Sovereign and Stella. Sovereign then ceased as a brand, but Harmony continued using it on a model line of Harmony guitars.

Sparrow Guitars

2004-present. Guitars manufactured in China are dismantled and "overhauled" in Vancouver, British Columbia, Canada. From these imports, luthier Billy Bones builds his intermediate and professional grade, production/custom solidbody and hollowbody electric guitars.

Specht Guitars

1991-present. Premium grade, production/custom, acoustic, baritone, parlor, jazz and classical guitars built by luthier Oliver Specht in Vancouver, British Columbia, Canada. He also builds basses.

Specimen Products

1984-present. Luthier Ian Schneller builds his professional and premium grade, production/custom, aluminum and wood body guitars in Chicago, Illinois. He also builds basses, ukes, amps and speaker cabs.

Spector/Stuart Spector Design

1975-1990 (Spector), 1991-1998 (SSD), 1998-present (Spector SSD). Known mainly for basses, Spector offered U.S.-made guitars during '75-'90 and '96-'99, and imports for '87-'90 and '96-'99. Since 2003, they again offer U.S.-professional grade, production, solidbody guitars. See Bass Section for more company info.

SPG

2006-present. Professional grade, custom, solidbody and chambered guitars built by luthier Rick Welch in Farmingdale, Maine and Hanson, Massachusetts. He also builds lapsteels.

MODEL		EXC. COND.	
YEAR	FEATURES	LOW	HIGH

St. Blues

1980-1989, 2005-present. Intermediate and professional grade, production/custom, solidbody guitars imported and set up in Memphis, Tennessee. They also build basses. The original '80s line was designed by Tom Keckler and Charles Lawing at Memphis' Strings & Things.

St. George

Mid to late 1960s. Early Japanese brand imported possibly by Buegeleisen & Jacobson of New York, New York.

St. Moritz

1960s. Guitars and basses imported from Japan by unidentified distributor. Manufacturer unknown, but appears to be Fuji Gen Gakki. Generally shorter scale beginner guitars, some with interesting pickup configurations.

Stahl

1900-1941. William C. Stahl, of Milwaukee, Wisconsin, ran a publishing company, taught stringed instrument classes and sold instruments to his students as well as by mail order across America. His label claimed that he was the maker but most of his products were built by the Larson brothers of Maurer & Co. of Chicago, with the balance mostly from Washburn. The most commonly found Larson-built models are the Style 6 and 7 as seen in the ca. 1912 Stahl catalog. Jimi Hendrix was the proud owner of a Style 8. The Style 6 is a moderately trimmed 15" Brazilian rosewood beauty that is much like the highly sought Maurer Style 551. The Style 7 and 8 are pearl trimmed 13 ½" concert size Brazilians comparable to the Maurer Style 562 ½. The 1912 Stahl catalog Styles 4, 5 and 9 were built by Washburn.

Style 4 Flat-Top
1930s. Mahogany body.

| 1930s | 15", 12-fret | $4,500 | $5,500 |
| 1930s | 15.5", 14-fret | $5,000 | $8,000 |

Style 5 Flat-Top
1930s. Mahogany body.

| 1930s | | $5,000 | $8,000 |

Style 6 Orchestra Special Flat-Top
1930s. 15", Brazilian rosewood body, mid-level trim.

| 1930s | | $7,000 | $9,500 |

Style 7 Special Solo Flat-Top
1930s. 13 1/2" scale, Brazilian rosewood body, white spruce top, pearl trim, fancy appointments.

| 1930s | | $7,000 | $10,000 |

Style 8 Special Solo Flat-Top
1930s. Brazilian rosewood body, finest white spruce top, pearl trim, fancy appointments.

| 1930s | | $8,000 | $9,800 |

Style 9 Artist Special Flat-Top
1930s. Choicest rosewood body, finest white spruce top, fancy appointments.

| 1930s | | $9,000 | $10,000 |

Stambaugh

1995-present. Luthier Chris Stambaugh builds his professional grade, custom/production, solidbody guitars in Stratham, New Hampshire. He also builds basses.

Standel

1952-1974, 1997-present. Amp builder Bob Crooks offered instruments under his Standel brand 3 different times during the '60s. In '61 Semie Moseley, later of Mosrite fame, made 2 guitar models and 1 bass for Standel, in limited numbers. Also in '61, Standel began distributing Sierra steels and Dobro resonators, sometimes under the Standel name. In '65 and '66 Standel offered a guitar and a bass made by Joe Hall, who also made the Hallmark guitars. In '66 Standel connected with Sam Koontz, who designed and produced the most numerous Standel models (but still in relatively small numbers) in Newark, New Jersey. These models hit the market in '67 and were handled by Harptone, which was associated with Koontz. By '70 Standel was out of the guitar biz. See Amp section for more company info.

Custom Deluxe Solidbody 101/101X
1967-1968. Custom with better electronics, 101X has no vibrato, sunburst, black, pearl white and metallic red.

| 1967-1968 | | $1,150 | $1,350 |

Custom Deluxe Thin Body 102/102X
1967-1968. Custom with better electronics, 102X has no vibrato, offered in sunburst and 5 solid color options.

| 1967-1968 | | $1,350 | $1,550 |

Custom Solidbody 201/201X
1967-1968. Solidbody, 2 pickups, vibrola, 2 pointed cutaways, headstock similar to that on Fender XII, 201X has no vibrato, sunburst, black, pearl white and metallic red.

| 1967-1968 | | $950 | $1,150 |

Custom Thin Body 202/202X
1967-1968. Thin body, headstock similar to that on Fender XII, 202X has no vibrato, offered in sunburst and 5 solid color options.

| 1967-1968 | | $1,050 | $1,250 |

Starfield

1992-1993. Solidbody guitars from Hoshino (Ibanez) made in the U.S. and Japan. U.S. guitars are identified as American models; Japanese ones as SJ models. Hoshino also used the Star Field name on a line of Japanese guitars in the late '70s. These Star Fields had nothing to do with the '90s versions and were not sold in the U.S.

Starforce

Ca. 1989. Import copies from Starforce Music/ Starforce USA.

1970s St. George

1968 St. Moritz Stereo

Stefan Sobell Model 1

1968 Stella/Harmony

MODEL YEAR	FEATURES	EXC. COND. LOW	HIGH

Stars

Intermediate grade, production, solidbody guitars made in Korea.

Stauffer

1800s. Old World violin and guitar maker, Georg Stauffer. Valid attributions include signed or labeled by the maker indicating the guitar was actually made by Stauffer, as opposed to attributed to Stauffer or one of his contemporaries. See Martin for listing.

Stefan Sobell Musical Instruments

1982-present. Premium grade, production/custom, flat-top, 12-string, and archtop guitars built by luthier Stefan Sobell in Hetham, Northumberland, England. He also builds mandolins, citterns and bouzoukis.

Steinberger

1979-present. Currently Steinberger offers budget, intermediate, and professional grade, production, electric guitars. They also offer basses. Founded by Ned Steinberger, who started designing NS Models for Stuart Spector in '76. In '79, he designed the L-2 headless bass. In '80, the Steinberger Sound Corp. was founded. Steinberger Sound was purchased by the Gibson Guitar Corp. in '87, and in '92, Steinberger relocated to Nashville, Tennessee.

Headless model codes for '85-'93 are:

First letter is X for bass or G for guitar.

Second letter is for body shape: M is regular offset double-cut guitar body; L is rectangle body; P is mini V shaped body.

Number is pickup designation: 2 = 2 humbuckers, 3 = 3 single coils, 4 = single/single/humbucker.

Last letter is type of tremolo: S = S-Trem tremolo; T = Trans-Trem which cost more on original retail.

Steinegger

1976-present. Premium grade, custom steel-string flat-top guitars built by luthier Robert Steinegger in Portland, Oregon.

Stella

Ca. 1899-1974, present. Stella was a brand of the Oscar Schmidt Company which started using the brand on low-mid to mid-level instruments in the very late 1800s. Oscar Schmidt produced all types of stringed instruments and was very successful in the 1920s. Company salesmen reached many rural areas and Stella instruments were available in general stores, furniture stores, and dry goods stores, ending up in the hands of musicians such as Leadbelly and Charlie Patton. Harmony acquired the Stella brand in '39 and built thousands of instruments with that name in the '50s and '60s. Harmony dissolved in '74. The Stella brand has been reintroduced by MBT International.

MODEL YEAR	FEATURES	EXC. COND. LOW	HIGH

00 Style
Early-1900s. Oak body flat-top.

1908		$725	$875

Flat-Top 15" 12-String
1920s-1930s. Associated with early blues and folk musicians, top of the line for Stella.

1920-1930s		$5,000	$6,200

Flat-Top by Harmony
1950s-1960s. The low end of the Harmony-built models, US-made until the end of the '60s, student level, Stella logo on headstock, playing action can often be very high which makes them difficult to play.

1950-1960s 13"		$50	$60
1950-1960s 14", 12-string		$125	$150

Harp Guitar
Early-1900s.

1915		$2,000	$2,500

Singing Cowboy
Late-1990s. Copy of Supertone (black background)/Silvertone/Harmony Singing Cowboy, import with laminated wood construction and ladder bracing.

2000	Stencil over black	$50	$60

Stetson

1984-ca. 1924. Stetson was a house brand of William John Dyer's St. Paul, Minnesota, music store. They started advertising this brand as early as 1894, but those built by the Larson brothers of Maurer & Co. date from ca. 1904-c. 1924. Most Stetsons were made by the Larsons. Others were built by Harmony (early ones), Washburn and three are credited to the Martin Co.

Parlor Guitar
1910s. Smaller flat-top, Brazilian rosewood sides and back, J.F. Stetson & Co. impressed into inside back center strip.

1910s	Higher-end, fancy	$3,000	$4,000
1910s	Standard, plain	$725	$900

Plectrum
1920s. Brazilian rosewood.

1920s		$1,600	$1,800

Stevenson

1999-present. Professional grade, production/custom, solidbody electric guitars built by luthier Ted Stevenson in Lachine, Quebec. He also builds basses and amps.

Stonetree

1996-present. Luthier Scott Platts builds his professional and premium grade, custom/production, solidbody and chambered electric guitars in Saratoga, Wyoming. He also builds basses.

Strad-O-Lin

Ca.1920s-ca.1960s. The Strad-O-Lin company was operated by the Hominic brothers in New York, primarily making mandolins for wholesalers. Around '57 Multivox/Premier bought the company and also used the name on guitars, making both electrics and acoustics. Premier also marketed student level guitars under the U.S. Strad brand.

MODEL YEAR	FEATURES	EXC. COND. LOW	HIGH

Stratospere

1954-ca. 1958. Solidbody electrics made in Springfield, Missouri by brothers Claude and Russ Deaver, some featuring fanned frets.

Electric Guitar

1954-1958		$800	$1,000

Stromberg

1906-1955, 2001-present. Intermediate and professional grade, production, archtop guitars imported by Larry Davis.

Founded in Boston by master luthier Charles Stromberg, a Swedish immigrant, building banjos and drums. Son Harry joined the company in 1907and stayed until '27. Son Elmer started in 1910 at age 15. The shop was well known for tenor banjos, but when the banjo's popularity declined, they began building archtop orchestra model guitars. The shop moved to Hanover Street in Boston in '27 and began producing custom order archtop guitars, in particular the 16" G-series and the Deluxe. As styles changed the G-series was increased to 17 3/8" and the 19" Master 400 model was introduced in '37. Stromberg designs radically changed around '40, most likely when Elmer took over guitar production. Both Charles and Elmer died within a few months of each other in '55.

Larry Davis of WD Music Products revived the Stromberg name and introduced a series of moderately priced jazz guitars in June, 2001. The models are crafted by a small Korean shop with component parts supplied by WD.

Deluxe

1927-1955. Non-cut, 16" body to '34, 17 3/8" body after '35, also sometimes labeled Delux.

1927-1930		$10,000	$13,000
1931-1955		$12,000	$15,000

G-1

1927-1955. Non-cut, 16" body to '35, 17 3/8" body after '35, sunburst.

1927-1955		$11,500	$14,000

G-3

Early 1930s. Archtop, 16 3/8", 3 segment F-holes, ladder bracing, gold hardware, engraved tailpiece, 8-ply 'guard, 5-ply body binding, laminate maple back, fancy engraved headstock with Stromberg name, less total refinement than higher-end Stromberg models.

1927-1935		$14,000	$15,000

Master 300

1937-1955. 19" non-cut.

1937-1955	Natural	$25,000	$30,000
1937-1955	Sunburst	$20,000	$25,000

Master 400

1937-1955. 19" top-of-the-line non-cut, the most common of Stromberg's models.

1937-1955	Natural	$40,000	$50,000
1937-1955	Sunburst	$36,000	$45,000

Master 400 Cutaway

1949. Only 7 cutaway Strombergs are known to exist.

1949	Natural	$60,000	$75,000

MODEL YEAR	FEATURES	EXC. COND. LOW	HIGH

Stromberg-Voisinet

1921-ca.1932. Marketed Stromberg (not to be confused with Charles Stromberg of Boston) and Kay Kraft brands, plus guitars of other distributors and retailers. Stromberg was the successor to the Groehsl Company (or Groehsel) founded in Chicago, Illinois in 1890; and the predecessor to the Kay Musical Instrument Company. In 1921, the name was changed to Stromberg-Voisinet Company. Henry Kay "Hank" Kuhrmeyer joined the company in '23 and was secretary by '25. By the mid-'20s, the company was making many better Montgomery Ward guitars, banjos and mandolins, often with lots of pearloid.

Joseph Zorzi, Philip Gabriel and John Abbott left Lyon & Healy for S-V in '26 or '27, developing 2-point Venetian shape, which was offered in '27. The first production of electric guitars and amps was introduced with big fanfare in '28; perhaps only 200 or so made. The last Stromberg acoustic instruments were seen in '32. The Kay Kraft brand was introduced by Kuhrmeyer in '31 as the company made its transition to Kay (see Kay).

Archtop Deluxe

1920s-1930s. Venetian cutaways, oval soundhole, decalomania art on top, trapeze tailpiece, light sunburst. Later offered under the Kay-Kraft brand.

1930s		$450	$550

Archtop Standard

1920s-1930s. Venetian cutaways, oval soundhole, no decalomania art, plain top, trapeze tailpiece, light sunburst. Later offered under the Kay-Kraft brand.

1930s		$400	$500

Stroup

2003-present. Luthier Gary D. Stroup builds his intermediate and professional grade, production/custom, arch top and flat top guitars in Eckley, Colorado.

Stuart Custom Guitars

2004-present. Professional and premium grade, production/custom, solid and semi-hollow body guitars built by luthier Fred Stuart in Riverside, California. Stuart was a Senior Master Builder at Fender. He also builds pickups.

Suhr Guitars

1997-present. Luthier John Suhr builds his professional and premium grade, production/custom, solidbody electrics in Lake Elsinore, California. He also builds basses and amps. He previously built Pensa-Suhr guitars with Rudy Pensa in New York.

Superior Guitars

1987-present. Intermediate grade, production/custom Hawaiian, flamenco and classical guitars made in Mexico for George Katechis Montalvo of Berkeley Musical Instrument Exchange. They also offer lap steels and mandolin-family instruments.

1952 Stromberg Master 400

Suhr Standard

To get the most from this book, be sure to read "Using *The Guide*" in the introduction.

GUITARS

1958 Supro Dual-Tone

Supro Folkstar

MODEL YEAR	FEATURES	EXC. COND. LOW	HIGH

Supersound
1958. England's Jim Burns first production brand, about 20 short scale, single-cut solidbodies were produced bearing this name.

Supertone
1914-1941. Brand used by Sears, Roebuck and Company for instruments made by various American manufacturers, including especially its own subsidiary Harmony (which it purchased in 1916). When Sears divested itself of Harmony in '40, instruments began making a transition to the Silvertone brand. By '41 the Supertone name was gone.

Acoustic Flat-Top (High-End Appointments)
1920s	Pearl trim 00-42 likeness	$1,400	$1,750
1920s	Pearl trim, Lindbergh model	$1,375	$1,700

Acoustic Flat-Top 13"
1920-1930s	Non-stencil, plain top	$150	$175
1920-1930s	Stencil top	$200	$225

Gene Autry Roundup
1932-1939. Harmony made acoustic, Gene Autry signature on belly, cowboy roundup stencil, 13" body until '35, then 14".
1932-1939	$275	$325

Lone Ranger
1936-1941. Black with red and silver Lone Ranger and Tonto stencil, silver-painted fretboard, 13 1/2" wide. "Hi-Yo Silver" added in '37, changed to "Hi-Ho Silver" in '38.
1936-1941	$275	$325

Robin Hood
1930s. 13" flat-top similar to Singing Cowboys, but with green and white art showing Robin Hood and his men against a black background.
1933	$350	$400

Singing Cowboys
1938-1943. Stencil of guitar strumming cowboys around chuck wagon and campfire, branded Silvertone after '41.
1938-1943	$275	$325

Supertone Wedge
1930s. Triangle-shaped wedge body, laminate construction, blue-silver Supertone label inside sound chamber, art decals on body.
1930s	$250	$300

Supro
1935-1968, 2004-present. Budget brand of National Dobro Company and Valco. Some Supro models also sold under the Airline brand for Montgomery Ward. In '42 Victor Smith, Al Frost and Louis Dopyera bought National and changed the name to Valco Manufacturing Company. Valco Manufacturing Company name changed to Valco Guitars, Inc., in '62. Company treasurer Robert Engelhardt bought Valco in '64. In '67 Valco bought Kay and in '68 Valco/Kay went out of business. In the summer of '69, Valco/Kay brands and assets

were sold at auction and the Supro and National names purchased by Chicago-area importer and distributor Strum N' Drum (Norma, Noble). TIn the early-'80s, ownership of the Supro name was transferred to Archer's Music, Fresno, California. Some Supros assembled from new-old-stock parts.

Amp builder Bruce Zinky revived the Supro name for a line of guitars built in the U.S. by luthier John Bolin and others. He also offers amps.

Belmont
1955-1964. For '55-'60, 12" wide, single-cut, 1 neck pickup, 2 knobs treble side in 'guard, reverse-stairs tailpiece, No-Mar plastic maroon-colored covering. For '60, size increased to 13 1/2" wide. For '62-'64, Res-o-glas fiberglass was used for the body, a slight cutaway on bass side, 1 bridge pickup, 2 knobs on opposite sides. Polar White.
1955-1962	Black or white No-Mar	$700	$875
1961-1964	Polar White Res-o-glas	$1,025	$1,275

Bermuda
1962 only. Slab body (not beveled), double pickups, dot markers, cherry glass-fiber finish.
1962	$1,000	$1,250

Collegian Spanish
1939-1942. Metal body, 12 frets. Moved to National line in '42.
1939-1942	$1,050	$1,300

Coronado/Coronado II
1961-1967. Listed as II in '62 15 1/2" scale, single-cut thinline, 2 pickups with 4 knobs and slider, natural blond spruce top. Changed to slight cutaway on bass side in '62 when renamed II.
1961-1962	Blond, natural spruce top	$1,200	$1,400
1963-1967	Black fiberglass	$1,550	$1,850

Dual-Tone
1954-1966, 2004-present. The Dual Tone had several body style changes, all instruments had dual pickups. '54, 11 1/4" body, No Mar Arctic White plastic body ('54-'62). '55, 12" body. '58, 13" body. '60, 13 1/2" body. '62, Res-o-glas Ermine White body, light cutaway on bass side.
1954-1961	Arctic White No-Mar	$975	$1,100
1962-1964	Ermine White Res-o-glas	$1,000	$1,100

Folk Star/Vagabond
1964-1967. Molded Res-o-glas body, single-cone resonator, dot inlays, Fire Engine Red. Name changed to Vagabond in '66.
1964-1967	$875	$1,075

Kingston
1962-1963. Double-cut slab body, bridge pickup, glass-fiber sand finish, similar to same vintage Ozark.
1962-1963	$500	$625

MODEL		EXC. COND.	
YEAR	FEATURES	LOW	HIGH

Lexington
1967. Double-cut, wood body, 1 pickup.

1967		$300	$375

Martinique
1962-1967. Single-cut, 13 1/2" wide, 2 standard and 1 bridge pickups, 6 knobs on bass side, 1 knob and slider on treble side, block markers, cataloged as "Supro's finest electric," Val-Trol script on 'guard, Bigsby vibrato tailpiece, blue or Ermine White Polyester Glas.

1962-1967		$1,950	$2,250

N800 Thinline Electric
1967-1968. Thin body, symmetrical double-cut, 2 pickups, copy model, similar to National N800 series models.

1967-1968		$450	$550

Ozark
1952-1954, 1958-1967. Non-cut, 1 pickup, dot inlay, white pearloid body, name reintroduced in '58 as a continuation of model Sixty with single-cut, Dobro tailpiece.

1952-1954	White pearloid	$800	$1,000
1958-1961	Red	$800	$1,000
1962-1967	Jet Black or Fire Bronze	$800	$1,000

Ranchero
1948-1960. Full body electric archtop, neck pickup, dot markers, bound body, sunburst.

1948-1960		$600	$725

Rhythm Master Val-Trol
1959. Val-Trol 'guard.

1959		$1,900	$2,100

Sahara
1960-1964. 13 1/2" body-style similar to Dual-Tone, single pickup, 2 knobs, Sand-Buff or Wedgewood Blue.

1960-1964		$1,000	$1,400

Silverwood/Val-Trol
1960-1962. Single-cut, 13 1/2" wide, 2 standard and 1 bridge pickups, 6 knobs on bass side, 1 knob and slider on treble side, block markers, cataloged as "Supro's finest electric", natural blond, Val-Trol script on 'guard, renamed Martinique in '62.

1960-1962		$1,900	$2,100

Sixty
1955-1958. Single-cut, single pickup, white No-Mar, becomes Ozark in '58.

1955-1958		$500	$625

Special 12
1958-1960. Single-cut, replaces Supro Sixty, neck pickup 'guard mounted.

1958-1960		$500	$625

Strum 'N' Drum Solidbody
1970s. Student-level import, 1 pickup, large Supro logo on headstock.

1970s		$325	$375

Super
1958-1964. 12" wide single-cut body style like mid-'50s models, single bridge pickup, short-scale, ivory.

1958-1964		$500	$575

Super Seven
1965-1967. Offset double-cut solidbody, short scale, middle pickup, Calypso Blue.

1965-1967		$400	$475

Suprosonic 30
1963-1967. Introduced as Suprosonic, renamed Suprosonic 30 in '64, double-cut, single neck pickup, vibrato tailpiece, more of a student model, Holly Red.

1963-1967		$450	$550

Tremo-Lectric
1965. Fiberglas hollowbody, 2 pickups, unique built-in electric tremolo (not mechanical), Wedgewood Blue finish, multiple controls associated with electric tremolo.

1965		$1,450	$1,800

White Holiday/Holiday
1963-1967. Introduced as Holiday, renamed White Holiday in '64, fiberglas double-cut, vibrato tailpiece, single bridge pickup, Dawn White.

1963-1967		$875	$975

Suzuki Takeharu
See listing for Takeharu.

SX
See listing for Essex.

T.D. Hibbs
2005-present. Production/custom, professional grade, steel string and classical guitars built in Cambridge, Ontario, Canada by luthier Trevor Hibbs.

T.H. Davis
1976-present. Professional and premium grade, custom, steel string and classical guitars built by luthier Ted Davis in Loudon, Tennessee. He also builds mandolins.

Tacoma
1995-present. Intermediate, and professional grade, production, acoustic guitars produced in Tacoma, Washington and New Hartford, Connecticut. They also build acoustic basses and mandolins. In October, '04, Fender acquired Tacoma.

C-1C/C-1CE Chief
1997-present. Cutaway flat-top with upper bass bout soundhole, solid cedar top, mahogany back and sides, rosewood 'board. Sides laminated until 2000, solid after, CE is acoustic/electric.

1997-2007		$400	$500
1997-2007	Fishman electronics	$500	$600

DF-21
2001-2003. D-style size and shape, spruce top, maple back and sides.

2001-2003		$675	$800

1959 Supro Ranchero

Tacoma RM6C

GUITARS

Tacoma P-1

Taku Sakashta Karizma

MODEL YEAR	FEATURES	EXC. COND. LOW	HIGH
DM Series			
1997-2006. Dreadnought, solid spruce top, mahogany back and sides, satin finish, natural. Models include DM-8, -9, -10 and -14.			
1997-2006		$325	$400
DR Series			
1997-2006. Dreadnought, solid sitka spruce top, solid rosewood back and sides, natural. Models include DR-20 (non-cut, herringbone trim, abalone rosette), DR-20E (with on-board electronics), DR-8C (cutaway), and DR-38.			
1997-2002	DR-8C	$625	$700
1997-2003	DR-20	$675	$725
1997-2004	DR-20E	$725	$775
2000-2003	DR-38	$700	$1,100
ER Series			
2000-2007. Little Jumbo series, rosewood back and sides, cutaway.			
2003	ER-19C	$1,100	$1,200
JK-50CE4 Jumbo Koa			
1997-2003. Jumbo cutaway, 17" lower bout, sitka spruce top, figured koa back and sides.			
1997-2003		$1,050	$1,300
JR-14C Jumbo Rosewood			
Late-1990s. Jumbo cutaway, 16 5/8" lower bout, gloss spruce top, satin rosewood body.			
1998		$900	$1,050
P-1/P-2 Papoose			
1995-present. Travel-size mini-flat-top, all solid wood, mahogany back and sides (P-1), with on-board electronics (P-1E) or solid rosewood (P-2), cedar top, natural satin finish.			
1995-2007	P-2	$300	$375
1995-2007	P-1	$250	$350
1995-2007	P-1E	$375	$450
Parlor Series			
1997-2003. Smaller 14 3/4" body, solid spruce top, various woods for back and sides.			
1997-2003	PK-30 Koa	$1,000	$1,100
1997-2003	PK-40 Rosewood	$1,000	$1,100
PM-15			
1997-1998. Solid spruce top, solid mahogany back and sides.			
1997-1998		$475	$575
PM-20			
1997-2003. Solid spruce top, solid mahogany back and sides, gloss finish.			
1997-2003		$625	$700

Takamine

1962-present. Intermediate and professional grade, production, steel- and nylon-string, acoustic and acoustic/electric guitars. They also make basses. Takamine is named after a mountain near its factory in Sakashita, Japan. Mass Hirade joined Takamine in '68 and revamped the brand's designs and improved quality. In '75, Takamine began exporting to other countries, including U.S. distribution by Kaman Music (Ovation). In '78, Takamine introduced acoustic/electric guitars. They offered solidbody electrics and some archtops for '83-'84.

MODEL YEAR	FEATURES	EXC. COND. LOW	HIGH
Acoustic Electric (Laminate)			
All laminate (plywood) construction, non-cut, standard features, pickup and preamp.			
1980-1990s		$250	$400
Acoustic Electric (Solid Top)			
Solid wood top, sides and back can vary, cutaway, standard features, preamp and pickup.			
1980-1990s		$450	$900
Acoustic Electric Cutaway (Laminate)			
All laminate (plywood) construction, cutaway, standard features, pickup and preamp.			
1980-1990s		$250	$400
Classical (Solid Top)			
Solid wood (often cedar) top, classical, sides and back can vary.			
1980-1990s		$450	$600
Collectors (Limited Edition)			
Each year a different limited edition collector's guitar is issued. '97 - solid top, koa body, cutaway, natural finish, preamp and pickup. '98 - solid top, rosewood body, cutaway, natural finish, preamp and pickup. '99 - solid top, rosewood body, cutaway, natural finish, preamp and pickup. '00 - solid top, rosewood body, cutaway, natural finish, preamp and pickup. '01 - solid top, rosewood body, cutaway, natural finish, preamp and pickup.			
1990s		$900	$1,100
Solidbody Electric			
1983-1984. Various models.			
1983-1984		$450	$900

Takeharu (by Suzuki)

Mid-1970s. Classical guitars offered by Suzuki as part of their internationally known teaching method (e.g. Violin Suzuki method), various sized instruments designed to eliminate the confusion of size that has been a problem for classroom guitar programs.

Taku Sakashta Guitars

1994-present. Premium and presentation grade, production/custom, archtop, flat-top, 12-sting, and nylon-string guitars, built by luthier Taku Sakashta in Sebastopol, California.

Tama

Ca. 1959-1967, 1974-1979. Hoshino's (Ibanez) brand of higher-end acoutic flat-tops made in Japan. Many of the brand's features would be transferred to Ibanez's Artwood acoustics.

Tamura

1970s. Made in Japan by Mitsura Tamura, the line includes intermediate grade solid wood classical guitars.

Tanara

2000s. Student-level models imported by Chesbro, inside label identifies model and country of origin.

MODEL YEAR	FEATURES	EXC. COND. LOW	HIGH

Taylor

1974-present. Intermediate, professional, premium, and presentation grade, production/custom, steel- and nylon-string, acoustic, acoustic/electric, semi-hollow, and solidbbody guitars built in El Cajon, California. They have also built basses. Founded by Bob Taylor, Steve Schemmer and Kurt Listug in Lemon Grove, California, the company was originally named the Westland Music Company, but was soon changed to Taylor (Bob designed the guitars and it fit on the logo). Taylor and Listug bought out Schemmer in '83. Bob Taylor was the first commercially successful guitar maker to harness CAD/CAM CNC technology for acoustic guitars. They added semi-hollowbodies in '05 and solidbodies in '08.

110 (GB)
2003-present. Solid spruce top, sapele laminated back and sides.

2003-2007		$425	$450

114
2007-present. Grand auditorium, solid sitka spruce top, sapele laminated back and sides.

2007		$425	$450

214
2004-present. Grand auditorium, solid sitka spruce top, Indian rosewood laminated back and sides.

2004-2007		$500	$600

310
1998-2006. Dreadnought-style solid spruce top, sapele-mahogany back and sides.

1998-2006		$800	$950

310ce
1998-present. 310 with Venetian cutaway, on-board electronics.

1998-2007	310ce	$1,100	$1,150
2004	310ce L30 30th Anniversary	$1,150	$1,200

312ce
1998-present. Grand concert Venetian cutaway, solid spruce top, sapele-mahogany back and sides, on-board electronics.

1998-2007		$1,000	$1,250

1998-2006. Mid-size grand auditorium-style, solid spruce top, sapele-mahogany back and sides.

1998-2007		$825	$975

314ce
1998-present. 314 with Venetian cutaway, on-board electronics.

1998-2007		$1,125	$1,200

314cek
2000. Limited edition 314 with flamed koa body.

2000		$1,125	$1,200

315ce
1998-present. Jumbo-style Venetian cutaway, solid spruce top, sapele-mahogany back and sides, on-board electronics.

1998-2007		$1,000	$1,250

355 12-String
1998-2006. Jumbo, solid spruce top, sapele-mahogany back and sides.

1998-2006		$1,000	$1,250

355ce 12-String
1998-present. 355 with cutaway, on-board electronics.

1998-2007		$1,100	$1,275

410
1991-2006. Dreadnought-style, solid spruce top, mahogany back and sides until '98, African ovangkol back and sides after '98.

1991-2006		$1,000	$1,250

410ce
1991-present. 410 with cutaway, on-board electronics.

1991-2007		$1,000	$1,250

412
1991-1998. Grand concert, solid spruce top, mahogany back and sides until '98, African ovangkol back and sides after '98.

1991-1998		$1,000	$1,250

412ce
1998-present. Cutaway electric version replaced the 412 in '98.

1998-2007		$1,000	$1,250

412K
1996. Koa.

1996		$1,000	$1,250

414
1998-2006. Grand auditorium, solid sitka spruce top, ovangkol back and sides, pearl dot inlays, natural.

1998-2006		$1,150	$1,325

414 L10
2005. Limited edition, rosewood sides and back, gloss spruce top, satin finish.

2005		$1,300	$1,500

414ce
1998-present. 414 with cutaway, on-board electronics.

1998-2007		$1,150	$1,325

414K
1997. Sitka spruce, koa.

1997		$1,000	$1,100

414L 30th Anniversary
2004. 30th Anniversary inlays on ebony 'board.

2004		$1,400	$1,500

415
1998-2006. Jumbo, solid sitka spruce top, ovangkol back and sides, pearl dot inlays.

1998-2006		$1,000	$1,250

420
1990-1997. Dreadnought-style, sitka spruce top, Indian rosewood back and sides, natural.

1990-1997		$1,000	$1,250

422K
1991-1998. Grand concert, solid koa construction, satin natural finish.

1991-1998		$1,000	$1,250

Taylor 314ce

1986 Taylor 422K

Taylor 655

Taylor 814 CE

MODEL YEAR	FEATURES	EXC. COND. LOW	HIGH
450 12-String			
1996-1997. Dreadnought, satin finish.			
1996-1997		$1,000	$1,250
455 12-String			
2001-2006. Solid sitka spruce top, ovangkol back and sides, dot markers.			
2001-2006		$1,000	$1,250
455ce 12-String			
2001-present. 455 with cutaway, on-board electronics.			
2001-2007		$1,000	$1,250
455ce LTD 12-String			
2001. Limited edition.			
2001-2003		$1,400	$1,500
510			
1978-2006. Dreadnought, all solid wood, spruce top, mahogany back and sides.			
1978-1979		$1,350	$1,550
1980-2006		$1,250	$1,350
510 Limited			
2002. Limited edition.			
2002		$1,350	$1,575
510ce			
1978-present. 510 with cutaway, on-board electronics.			
1978-1979		$1,550	$1,700
1980-2007		$1,450	$1,650
512			
1978-2000. Grand concert, solid Engelmann spruce top, solid American mahogany back and sides, dot markers.			
1978-2000		$1,425	$1,575
512ce			
1978-present. 512 with cutaway, on-board electronics.			
1978-2007		$1,450	$1,650
512NG Nanci Griffith			
1996-1997. 512ce with sunburst finish.			
1996-19997		$1,800	$1,900
514c			
1990-1998. Grand auditorium, Venetian cutaway, solid spruce or solid red cedar top, mahogany back and sides, no electronics, natural.			
1990-1998		$1,650	$1,800
514ce			
1998-present. 514c with on-board electronics.			
1998-2007		$1,650	$1,800
555 12-String			
1978-2006. Jumbo, solid sitka spruce top, solid mahogany back and sides, higher-end appointments.			
1994-2006		$1,650	$1,800
555ce 12-String			
1994-2006. 555 with cutaway, on-board electronics.			
1994-2006		$1,500	$1,800
610			
1978-1998. Dreadnought, solid spruce top, solid maple back and sides, generally with amber stained finishes.			
1978-1998		$1,475	$1,600

MODEL YEAR	FEATURES	EXC. COND. LOW	HIGH
610ce			
1998-present. 610 with cutaway, on-board electronics.			
1998-2007		$1,500	$1,700
612			
1984-1998. Grand concert, solid spruce top, solid maple back and sides, generally with amber stained finishes.			
1984-1998		$1,575	$1,800
612ce			
1998-present. 612 with cutaway, on-board electronics.			
1998-2007		$1,600	$1,900
614			
1978-1998. Grand auditorium, solid spruce top, solid maple back and sides, generally with amber stained finishes.			
1978-1998		$1,900	$2,000
614ce			
1998-present. 614 with cutaway, on-board electronics.			
1998-2007		$1,950	$2,050
615			
1981-1998. Jumbo, spruce top, flamed maple back and sides, non-cut.			
1981-1998		$1,825	$2,025
655 12-String			
1978-1991, 1996-2006. Solid spruce top, solid maple back and sides, generally with amber stained finishes.			
1978-2006		$1,750	$1,900
655ce 12-String			
1998-present. 655 with cutaway, on-board electronics.			
1998-2007		$1,800	$2,000
710			
1977-2006. Dreadnought-size, rosewood back and sides, spruce top.			
1977-2006		$1,800	$1,900
710BR			
1990s. 710 with Brazilian rosewood.			
1990s		$2,800	$3,200
710ce			
1998-present. 710 with cutaway, on-board electronics.			
1998-2007		$1,900	$1,950
710ce L30 Commemorative			
2004. 30th Anniversary Limited Edition, Englemann spruce top, Indian rosewood body, on-board electronics, 30th Anniversary script logo on headstock, single-cut.			
2004		$1,900	$2,100
712			
1984-2006. Grand concert small body, solid wood, non-cut, rosewood back and sides, spruce top, cedar soundboard.			
1984-2006		$1,800	$1,900
712ce			
2000-present. 712 with cutaway, on-board electronics.			
2000-2007		$1,850	$1,950

The *Vintage Guitar Price Guide* shows low to high values for items in all-original excellent condition, and, where applicable, with original case or cover.

MODEL YEAR	FEATURES	EXC. COND. LOW	HIGH

714
1996-2006. Grand auditorium, 15 7/8" lower bout, solid red cedar top, solid Indian rosewood back and sides.

1996-2006		$1,800	$1,900

714ce
1998-present. 714 with cutaway, on-board electronics.

1998-2007		$1,850	$1,950

755 12-String
1990-1998. Dreadnought-style, 12 strings, solid spruce top, rosewood back and sides, natural.

1990-1998		$1,850	$1,950

810
1975-present. Classic original Taylor dreadnought design - early model.

1975-2007		$1,400	$1,700

810 L30
2004. 30th Anniversary.

2004		$1,600	$1,700

810c
1993-1998. Single-cut version.

1993-1998		$1,500	$1,700

810ce
1996-present. 810 with cutaway, on-board electronics.

1996-2003	Brazilian rosewood option	$3,300	$3,700
1996-2007	Indian rosewood	$1,550	$1,750

812c
1993-1998. Rosewood back and sides, Englemann spruce top, cutaway.

1993-1998		$1,550	$1,700

814
2005-2006. Grand auditorium, cutaway, rosewood back and sides, spruce top.

2005-2006		$2,200	$2,300

814BE
2000. Figured Brazilian rosewood back and sides, Englemann spruce top.

2000		$2,800	$3,000

815
1970s. Jumbo, solid sitka spruce top, Indian rosewood back and sides.

1970s		$2,200	$2,600

815c
1993-1998. Jumbo cutaway, no electronics, solid sitka spruce top, Indian rosewood back and sides.

1993-1998		$1,900	$2,300

815ce
1998-present. 815c with on-board electronics.

1998-2007		$1,900	$2,300

855 12-String
1993-2006. Jumbo, solid sitka spruce top, rosewood back and sides, natural.

1993-2006		$1,900	$2,300

910
1977-present. Dreadnought, maple back and sides until change to Indian rosewood in '86, spruce top, wide abalone-style rosette.

1986-2007		$2,000	$2,500

910ce
1998-present. 910 with cutaway, on-board electronics.

1998-2007		$2,100	$2,600

912c
1993-2002. Grand concert, rosewood back and sides, abalone.

1993-2002		$2,400	$2,600

914ce
2002-present. 914c with on-board electronics.

2002-2007		$2,500	$2,700

Baby
1996-present. 3/4"-size dreadnought, solid spruce top, mahogany laminated back and sides until '99, sapele laminate after.

1996-2007		$175	$225

Baby Mahogany (M)
1998-present. Solid mahogany top version of Baby, mahogany laminated back and sides until '99, sapele laminate after.

1998-2007		$250	$300

Baby Rosewood
2000-2003. Laminated Indian rosewood back and sides version, solid sitka spruce top

2000-2003		$275	$325

Big Baby
2000-present. 15/16"-size dreadnought, solid sitka spruce top, sapele-mahogany laminated back and sides, satin finish, gig bag.

2000-2007		$300	$325

CPSM Chris Proctor Signature
2001. Limited edition, 100 made.

2001		$1,850	$1,900

CUJO-14 CST Walnut
1995. Only 125 made.

1995		$1,500	$1,850

Dan Crary Signature
1986-2000. Dreadnought, Venetian cutaway, thin spruce top, Indian rosewood back and sides, Crary signature on headstock.

1986-2000		$1,400	$1,450

DDSM Doyle Dykes Signature
2000-present. Grand auditorium cutaway acoustic/electric, figured maple body.

2000-2004		$2,500	$2,700

GS Series
2006-present. Grand Symphony Series, various tops and body woods.

2006-2007		$1,500	$3,100

K10
1983-2006. Acoustic dreadnought, koa back and sides, spruce top, distinctive binding.

1983-2006		$1,800	$2,100

K14c
1998-2002. Grand auditorium cutaway, 15 3/4" lower bout, solid cedar top, solid flamed koa body, gloss finish.

1998-2002		$1,900	$2,200

K14ce
2002-present. Figured Hawaiian koa back and sides, abalone top trim, fancy markers.

2002-2007		$2,000	$2,200

Taylor 910

Taylor Baby Mahogany

To get the most from this book, be sure to read "Using *The Guide*" in the introduction.

Taylor NS62ce

Taylor T5 (S1)

MODEL YEAR	FEATURES	EXC. COND. LOW	HIGH
K20			
1983-1992. Non-cut dreadnought-style, koa top/back/sides, abalone rosette.			
1983-1992		$1,300	$1,500
K20c			
1998-2002. K20 with cutaway.			
1998-2002		$1,800	$2,000
K20ce			
2001-present. On-board electronics version.			
2001-2007		$1,900	$2,100
K22			
1984-1992, 1998-2000. Grand concert flamed koa body, artistic pearl headstock and fretboard inlay, natural gloss finish.			
1998-2000		$2,200	$2,300
K22ce			
2003-present. Koa			
2003-2007		$2,200	$2,700
K55 12-String			
2001-2006. Jumbo, spruce top, koa back and sides.			
2001-2006		$2,200	$2,700
LKSM6/12 Leo Kottke			
1997-present. Jumbo 17" body, 6- or 12-string, rounded cutaway, sitka spruce top, mahogany back and sides, gloss finish, Leo Kottke signature.			
1997-2007	12-string	$1,800	$1,900
1997-2007	6-string	$1,700	$1,800
LTG Liberty Tree L.E.			
2002. Limited edition includes DVD and certificate which are important to instrument's value, solid wood grand concert body, high-end art and appointments. Around 400 made.			
2002		$4,800	$5,000
NS Series			
2002-present. Nylon Strung series, models include NS32ce (mahogany body), NS42ce and NS44 (ovangkol body), NS62ce and NS64ce (maple body) and NS74 (Indian rosewood). All models were cutaway electric (ce) by '04.			
2002-2006	NS42ce	$900	$1,100
2002-2006	NS44ce	$900	$1,100
2002-2006	NS52ce	$900	$1,100
2002-2007	NS32ce	$900	$1,100
2002-2007	NS62ce	$900	$1,100
2002-2007	NS64ce	$900	$1,100
2002-2007	NS74ce	$900	$1,100
Pre-Production Model			
1974. Early pre-production custom made (custom order), could be an instrument with the Taylor American Dream label, or may not have a logo or brand.			
1974		$3,000	$7,500
PS Presentation Limited			
2003. Engleman spruce top, quilted maple back and sides.			
2003		$3,900	$4,100
PS12c Presentation			
1996-2004. Presentation Series grand concert 15" lower bout, solid Englemann spruce top, solid AAA flamed koa back and sides, fancy 'Byzantine' vine inlay on fretboard.			
1996-2004		$5,000	$5,500

MODEL YEAR	FEATURES	EXC. COND. LOW	HIGH
PS14BZ Special Edition			
1996. Presentation Series special edition with Englemann spruce top, Brazilian rosewood back and sides, abalone trim.			
1996		$4,500	$5,000
PS14c Special Edition			
1998-2000. Presentation Series special edition with spruce top, AAA koa back and sides.			
1998-2000		$5,100	$5,500
PS15			
1996-present. Presentation Series jumbo, solid Engelmann spruce top, Brazilian rosewood back and sides, scalloped X-bracing, high-end appointments.			
1996-2007		$5,100	$5,500
T5 Series			
2005-present. Semi-hollow thinline body, sapele back and sides, spruce, maple, or koa tops, Custom models have gold hardware and Artist inlays, Standard is chrome with micro-dots.			
2005-2007	Custom (flamed maple)	$1,825	$2,200
2005-2007	Custom (koa top)	$2,100	$2,500
2005-2007	Custom (spruce top)	$1,700	$2,000
2005-2007	Standard (maple top)	$1,700	$1,900
2005-2007	Standard (spruce top)	$1,400	$1,600
W10			
1998-2006. Dreadnought, claro walnut back and sides, optional tops include sitka spruce, Western red cedar, or claro walnut.			
1998-2006		$1,600	$1,800
W14ce			
2000-2006. Grand auditorium, claro walnut back and sides, red cedar top, on-board electronics.			
2000-2006		$1,700	$2,000
WHCM Windham Hill			
2003. Commemorative Model, D-size, spruce top, rosewood sides and back, fancy appointments with Windham Hill logo inlay.			
2003		$1,650	$1,700
XX-RS 20th Anniversary			
1994. Grand auditorium 15 3/4" lower bout, spruce top, Indian rosewood back and sides.			
1994		$2,300	$2,700
XXV-RS 25th Anniversary			
1999-2000. Dreadnought-size, spruce top, sapele back and sides.			
1999-2000		$2,100	$2,300
XXX 30th Anniversary Series			
2004	XXX-KE	$2,500	$2,700
2004	XXX-MS (maple)	$2,300	$2,500
2004	XXX-RS (Indian rosewood)	$2,500	$2,700

Teisco

1946-1974, 1994-present. Founded in Tokyo, Japan by Hawaiian and Spanish guitarist Atswo Kaneko and electrical engineer Doryu Matsuda, the original company name was Aoi Onpa Kenkyujo;

MODEL		EXC. COND.	
YEAR	FEATURES	LOW	HIGH

Teisco was the instrument name. Most imported into U.S. by Chicago's W.M.I. Corporation and Jack Westheimer beginning ca. '63-'64, some early ones for New York's Bugeleisen and Jacobson. Brands made by the company include Teisco, Teisco Del Rey, Kingston, World Teisco, Silvertone, Kent, Kimberly and Heit Deluxe.

In '56, the company's name was changed to Nippon Onpa Kogyo Co., Ltd., and in '64 the name changed again to Teisco Co., Ltd. In January '67, the company was purchased by Kawai. After '73, the brand was converted to Kay in U.S.; Teisco went into hiatus in Japan until being revived in the early-'90s with plexiglass reproductions of the Spectrum 5 (not available in U.S.). Some older Teisco Del Rey stock continued to be sold in U.S. through the '70s.

Electric

1966-1969	1, 2, or 3 pickups	$100	$400
1966-1969	4 pickups or special finishes	$400	$550
1966-1969	Spectrum V	$400	$550
1968-1969	May Queen, black	$525	$600
1968-1969	May Queen, red	$600	$700

Tele-Star

1965-ca.1972. Imported from Japan by Tele-Star Musical Instrument Corporation of New York, New York. Primarily made by Kawai, many inspired by Burns designs, some in cool sparkle finishes. They also built basses.

Electric

1966-1969	1, 2, or 3 pickups	$125	$275
1966-1969	4 pickups or special finishes	$300	$400
1966-1969	Amp-in-case	$175	$300
1969-1970	Double neck 6/4	$500	$650

Tennessee

1970-1993, 1996-present. Luthier Mark Taylor builds his professional and premium grade, production/custom, acoustic guitars in Old Hickory, Tennessee. He also builds mandolins, banjos and the Tut Taylor brand of resophonic guitars. Mark and his father Robert "Tut" Taylor started making the Tennessee brand of acoustic and resophonic guitars, banjos, and mandolins in '71. In '77, Tut left the company and Mark continued on as Crafters of Tennessee. In '93, Mark and Greg Rich started building instruments as Rich and Taylor. In '96, Mark resumed production

Texas

1959-ca. 1965. Line of aluminum neck electric solidbodies and basses made by France's Jacobacci company, which also built under its own brand. One, two, or three pickups.

Teye

2006-present. Luthier Teye Wijterp builds his premium and presentation grade, production/custom, solid and chambered body guitars in Austin, Texas. Some instruments are branded as Electric Gypsy guitars.

TheDon

Guitars made in Germany and imported into the U.S. by a guitar shop.

Thomas Rein

1972-present. Luthier Thomas Rein builds his premium grade, production/custom, classical guitars in St. Louis, Missouri.

Thompson Guitars

1980-present. Luthier Ted Thompson builds his professional and premium grade, production/custom, flat-top, 12-string, and nylon-string guitars in Vernon, British Columbia.

Thorell Fine Guitars

1994-present. Premium grade, custom/production, archtop, flattop and classical guitars built by luthier Ryan Thorell in Logan, Utah.

Thorn Custom Guitars

2000-present. Professional and premium grade, custom/production, solid and hollowbody electrics built by luthiers Bill Thorn and his sons Bill, Jr. and Ron in Glendale, California. They started Thorn Custom Inlay in the early '90s to do custom inlay work for other builders. In '00, they added their own line of guitars.

Threet Guitars

1990-present. Premium grade, production/custom, flat-tops built by luthier Judy Threet in Calgary, Alberta.

Tilton

1850s-late 1800s. Built by William B. Tilton, of New York City. He was quite an innovator and held several guitar-related patents. He also built banjos.

Parlor

1890s. Parlor guitar with various woods.

1850-1860s	Brazilian, fancy binding	$2,400	$2,900
1890s	Diagonal grain spruce top, Brazilian	$1,600	$2,000
1890s	Pearl trim, Brazilian	$2,500	$3,100
1890s	Standard grain spruce top, Brazilian	$1,400	$1,700

Teisco Spectrum 5

1968 Teisco Vamper

Tokai Talbo

Tom Anderson Cobra

Tim Reede Custom Guitars

2004-present. Luthier Tim Reede builds his professional and premium grade, production/custom, archtop, flat top and electric guitars in Minneapolis, Minnesota.

Timeless Instruments

1980-present. Luthier David Freeman builds his professional, premium and presentation grade, custom, flattop, 12-string, nylon-string, and resonator guitars in Tugaske, Saskatchewan. He also builds mandolins and dulcimers.

Timm Guitars

1997-present. Professional grade, custom, flat-top, resonator and travel guitars built by luthier Jerry Timm in Auburn, Washington.

Timtone Custom Guitars

1993-2006. Luthier Tim Diebert built his premium grade, custom, solidbody, chambered-body and acoustic guitars in Grand Forks, British Columbia. He also built basses and lap steels.

Tippin Guitar Co.

1978-present. Professional, premium and presentation grade, production/custom, flat-top guitars built by luthier Bill Tippin in Marblehead, Massachusetts.

Tobias

1977-present. Known mainly for basses, Tobias did offer guitar models in the '80s. See Bass Section for more company info.

TogaMan GuitarViol

2003-present. Premium grade, production/custom, bow-playable solidbody guitars built by luthier Jonathan Wilson in San Fernando, California.

Tokai

1947-present. Japan's Tokai Company started out making a keyboard harmonica that was widely used in Japanese schools. In '65, they started producing acoustic guitars, followed shortly by electrics. In the late '60s, Tokai hooked up with Tommy Moore, a successful instrument merchandiser from Fort Worth, Texas, and by '70 they were producing private label and OEM guitars, sold in the U.S. under the brands of various importers. By the '70s, the Tokai name was being used on the instruments. Today Tokai continues to offer electrics, acoustics, and electric basses made in Japan and Korea.

ASD 403 Custom Edition
Classic offset double-cut solidbody, single-single-hum pickups, locking tremolo.

1980s	$400	$700

AST 56
Classic offset double-cut solidbody style, 3 single-coils.

1980s	$400	$650

ATE 52
Classic single-cut solidbody style, 2 single-coils.

1980s	$400	$650

Goldstar Sound
1984. Replica that replaced the Springy Sound, new less litigiously pointy headstock shape.

1984	$300	$600

Les Paul Reborn
1976-1985. LP replica with Gibson-style 'Tokai' headstock logo and Les Paul Reborn script logo instead of Les Paul Model, renamed Reborn Old in '82, becomes Love Rock in mid-'80s.

1976-1982	Les Paul Reborn	$400	$700
1982-1985	Reborn Old	$300	$600

Love Rock
1980s. Classic single-cut solidbody style, 2 humbuckers, figured tops at the high end.

1980s	$400	$700

Silver Star
1977-1984. Tokai's copy of the post-CBS large headstock model.

1977-1984	$300	$600

Springy Sound
1977-1984. Replica, Tokai logo replaces spaghetti logo, Springy Sound in small block letters follows Tokai logo on headstock, original high-end nitro-finish.

1977-1979	With skunk stripe	$400	$700
1979-1984	No skunk stripe	$400	$700

Tom Anderson Guitarworks

1984-present. Professional and premium grade, production/custom, solidbody, semi-solidbody and acoustic guitars built by luthier Tom Anderson in Newbury Park, California.

Classic
1984-present. Double-cut solidbody, classic 3 pickup configuration, colors and appointments can vary.

1984-2007	$1,400	$1,700

Cobra
1993-present. Single-cut solid mahogany body with figured maple top.

1993-2007	$1,650	$1,900

Drop Top
1992-present. Double-cut solidbody, single-single-hum pickups, various specs.

1992-2007	$1,700	$1,900

Hollow Classic
1996-present. Ash double-cut with tone chambers, 3 pickups.

1996-2007	$1,700	$1,900

TommyHawk

1993-2005. Acoustic travel guitars built by luthier Tom Barth in Succasunna, New Jersey. They also offered a full-scale acoustic/electric model. Barth died in '05.

MODEL		EXC. COND.	
YEAR	FEATURES	LOW	HIGH

Tonemaster
1960s. Guitars and basses, made in Italy by the Crucianelli Company, with typical '60s Italian sparkle plastic finish and push-button controls, bolt-on neck. Imported into the U.S. by The Imperial Accordion Company.

ToneSmith
1997-present. Luthier Kevin Smith builds his professional and premium grade, production/custom, semi-hollow body guitars in Rogers, Minnesota. He also builds basses. He previously built GLF brand guitars and built the line of Vox USA guitars from '98-'01.

Tony Nobles
1990-present. Professional and premium grade, custom, acoustic and electric guitars built by luthier Tony Nobles in Wimberley, Texas. Tony used to write a repair article for Vintage Guitar magazine.

Tony Vines Guitars
1989-present. Luthier Tony Vines builds his premium and presentation grade, custom/production, steel string guitars in Kingsport, Tennessee.

Torres (Antonio de Torres Jurado)
19th Century luthier most often associated with the initial development of the Classical Spanish guitar.

Toyota
1972-?. Imported from Japan by Hershman of New York, New York. At least 1 high-end acoustic designed by T. Kurosawa was ambitiously priced at $650.

Traphagen, Dake
1972-present. Luthier Dake Traphagen builds his premium grade, custom, nylon-string guitars in Bellingham, Washington.

Traugott Guitars
1991-present. Premium grade, production/custom, flat-top and acoustic/electric guitars built by luthier Jeff Traugott in Santa Cruz, California.

Traveler Guitar
1992-present. Intermediate grade, production, travel size electric, acoustic, classical and acoustic/electric guitars made in Redlands, California. They also make basses.

Travis Bean
1974-1979, 1999. Aluminum-necked solidbody electric guitars and basses. The company was founded by motorcycle and metal-sculpture enthusiast Travis Bean and guitar repairman Marc McElwee in Southern California; soon joined by Gary Kramer (see Kramer guitars). Kramer left Travis Bean in '75 and founded Kramer guitars with other partners. Guitar production began in mid-'76. The guitars featured carved aluminum necks with three-and-three heads with a T cutout in the center and wooden 'boards. Some necks had bare aluminum backs, some were painted black. A total of about 3,650 instruments were produced. Travis Bean guitar production was stopped in the summer of '79.

Serial numbers were stamped on headstock and were more-or-less consecutive. These can be dated using production records published by Bill Kaman in Vintage Guitar magazine. Original retail prices were $895 to $1195.

The company announced renewed production in '99 with updated versions of original designs and new models, but it evidently never got going.

TB-500
Aluminum neck, T-slotted headstock, double-cut, 2 single coils mounted in 'guard, 2 controls, dot markers, white.

1975-1976		$3,100	$3,800

TB-1000 Artist
1974-1979. Aluminum neck, T-slotted headstock, double-cut archtop, 2 humbuckers, 4 controls, block inlays.

1974-1979		$3,400	$4,250
1974-1979	Rare colors	$4,250	$5,300

TB-1000 Standard
1974-1979. Similar to TB-1000 Artist, but with dot inlays.

1974-1979		$3,000	$3,700

TB-3000 Wedge
1976-1979. Aluminum neck with T-slotted headstock, triangle-shaped body, 2 humbucking pickups, 4 controls, block markers on 'board.

1976-1979		$3,600	$4,500

Tregan Guitars
2007-present. Solidbody electrics including Bison-style sharp curved horns body style plus other less traditional styles, student and intermediate grade.

Tremblett Archtops
2006-present. Luthier Mark Tremblett builds his professional grade, custom, archtop guitars in Pouch Cove, Newfoundland, Canada.

Trenier
1998-present. Premium grade, production/custom, archtop guitars built by luthier Bryant Trenier in Seattle, Washington. From '02 to '04 he was located in Prague, Czech Republic.

Triggs
1992-present. Luthiers Jim Triggs and his son Ryan build their professional and premium grade, production/custom, archtop, flat-top, and solidbody guitars originally in Nashville Tennessee, and, since '98, in Kansas City, Kansas. They also build mandolins.

Trenier Model 17

Triggs San Salvador

Valencia JF

Trussart Steelcaster

MODEL YEAR	FEATURES	EXC. COND. LOW	HIGH
Acoustic/Electric Archtop			
1992-present. Various archtop cutaway models.			
1992-2007	Byrdland 17"	$3,000	$4,000
1992-2007	Excel 17"	$5,000	$6,000
1992-2007	Jazzmaster	$2,500	$3,000
1992-2007	New Yorker 18"	$6,500	$7,000
1992-2007	Stromberg		
	Master 400	$7,000	$8,000

Trinity River

2004-present. Located in Fort Worth, Texas, luthiers Marcus Lawyer and Ross McLeod import their production/custom, budget and intermediate grade, acoustic and resonator guitars from Asia. They also import basses, mandolins and banjos.

True North Guitars

1994-present. Luthier Dennis Scannell builds his premium grade, custom, flat-tops in Waterbury, Vermont.

True Tone

1960s. Guitars, basses and amps retailed by Western Auto, manufactured by Chicago guitar makers like Kay. The brand was most likely gone by '68.

Electric Archtop (K592 Kay)

1960s. Made by Kay and similar to their K592 double-cut thinline acoustic, 2 pickups, Bigsby tailpiece, burgundy red.

1960s		$525	$650

Fun Time

Early- to mid-1960s. Student 13" flat-top, painted 5-point 'guard, red sunburst finish.

1960s		$60	$75

Imperial Deluxe

Mid-1960s. Harmony-made (Rocket), 3 pickups, trapeze tailpiece, 6 control knobs, block markers, sunburst.

1960s		$625	$700

Jazz King (K573 Kay)

1960s. Kay's K573 Speed Demon, 3 pickups, thinline archtop electric with f-hole, eighth note art on 'guard, sunburst.

1960s		$525	$650

Rock 'n Roll Electric (K100 Kay)

1960s. Kay's K100, slab body, single pickup, but with a bright red multiple lacquer finish.

1960s		$135	$165

Solidbody (K300 Kay)

1960s. Made by Kay and similar to their K300, double-cut, dual pickups and vibrola arm, red.

1960s		$500	$600

Speed Master (K6533 Kay)

1960s. Made by Kay and similar to their K6533 full-body electric archtop Value Leader line, eighth note art 'guard, sunburst.

1960s		$250	$300

Western Spanish Auditorium

Early- to mid-1960s. 15" flat-top, laminate construction, celluloid 'guard, sunburst.

1960s		$175	$200

Trussart

1980-present. Luthier James Trussart builds his premium grade, custom/production, solid and semi-hollow body electric guitars in Los Angeles, California. He also builds basses.

Tucker

2000-present. Founded by John N. "Jack" Tucker, John Morrall, and David Killingsworth, Tucker builds professional and premium grade, production/custom, albizzia wood solidbody guitars in Hanalei, Hawaii. They also build basses.

Tut Taylor

Line of professional and premium grade, production/custom, resophonic guitars built by luthier Mark Taylor of Crafters of Tennessee in Old Hickory, Tennessee. Brand named for his father, dobro artist Tut Taylor. Taylor also builds the Tennessee line of guitars, mandolins and banjos and was part of Rich and Taylor guitars for '93-'96.

TV Jones

1993-present. Professional and premium grade, production/custom, hollow, chambered, and solid body guitars built by luthier Thomas Vincent Jones originally in California, now in Poulsbo, Washington. The instruments have either Jones or TV Jones inlaid on the headstock. He also builds pickups.

U. A. C.

1920s. Instruments built by the Oscar Schmidt Co. and possibly others. Most likely a brand made for a distributor.

Unique Guitars

2003-present. Professional and premium grade, production/custom, solidbody guitars built by luthier Joey Rico in California. He also builds basses. Joey is the son of Bernie Rico, the founder of BC Rich guitars.

Univox

1964-1978. Univox started out as an amp line and added guitars around '68. Guitars were imported from Japan by the Merson Musical Supply Company, later Unicord, Westbury, New York. Many if not all supplied by Arai and Company (Aria, Aria Pro II), some made by Matsumoku. Univox Lucy ('69) first copy of lucite Ampeg Dan Armstrong. Generally mid-level copies of American designs.

Acoustic Flat-Top

1969-1978. Various models.

1970s		$200	$300

Bicentennial

1976. Offset double-cut, heavily carved body, brown stain, 3 humbucker-style pickups.

1976		$850	$1,050

Electric Hollowbody

Various models.

1970s		$300	$450

MODEL YEAR	FEATURES	EXC. COND. LOW	HIGH

Electric Solidbody
Includes Flying V, Mosrite and Hofner violin-guitar copies.

1970s		$275	$675

Guitorgan FSB C-3000
1970s. Double-cut semi-hollow body, multiple controls, Guitorgan logo on headstock, footpedal.

1970s		$975	$1,200

USA Custom Guitars
1999-present. Professional and premium grade, custom/production, solidbody electric guitars built in Tacoma, Washington. USA also does work for other luthiers.

Vaccaro
1997-2002. Founded by Henry Vaccaro, Sr., one of the founders of Kramer Guitars. They offered intermediate and professional grade, production/custom, aluminum-necked guitars designed by Vaccaro, former Kramer designer Phil Petillo, and Henry Vaccaro, Jr., which were made in Asbury Park, New Jersey. They also built basses.

Valco
1942-1968. Valco, of Chicago, was a big player in the guitar and amplifier business. Their products were private branded for other companies like National, Supro, Airline, Oahu, and Gretsch. In '42, National Dobro ceased operations and Victor Smith, Al Frost and Louis Dopyera bought the company and changed the name to Valco Manufacturing Company. Post-war production resumed in '46. Valco was purchased by treasurer Robert Engelhardt in '64. In '67, Valco bought Kay, but in '68 the new Valco/Kay company went out of business.

Valencia
1985-present. Budget grade, production, classical guitars imported by Rondo Music of Union, New Jersey.

Valley Arts
Ca. 1977-present. Professional and premium grade, production/custom, semi-hollow and solid-body guitars built in Nashville, Tennessee. They also make basses. Valley Arts originally was a Southern California music store owned by partners Al Carness and Mike McGuire where McGuire taught and did most of the repairs. Around '77, McGuire and Valley Arts started making custom instruments on a large scale. By '83, they opened a separate manufacturing facility to build the guitars. In '92 Samick acquired half of the company with McGuire staying on for a year as a consultant. Samick offered made-in-the-U.S. production and custom models under the Valley Arts name. In '02, Valley Arts became a division of Gibson Guitar Corp., which builds the guitars in Nashville. Founders Carness and McGuire are back with the company. They reintroduced the line in January, '03.

California Pro (U.S.-made)
1983-2002. Double-cut body, six-on-a-side tuners, single/single/hum pickups, 2 knobs and switch, various colors, serial number begins with CAL.

1983-2002		$850	$1,050
1990-1992	Pre-Samick	$650	$750
1993-1999	Samick owned	$550	$650

Optek Fretlight (U.S.-made)
Double-cut body, about 126 LED lights in fretboard controlled by a scale/chord selector, black opaque.

1990		$525	$625

Standard Pro (U.S.-made)
1990-1993. Double-cut body, six-on-a-side tuners, single/single/hum pickups, 2 knobs and switch, black opaque, serial number begins with VA.

1990-1993		$550	$650

Vantage
1977-present. Budget and intermediate grade, production, acoustic and electric guitars. They also build basses. Instruments from Japan from '77-'90 and from Korea from '90-present.

Vega
1903-1980s, 1989-present. The name Vega means star and a star logo is often seen on the original Vega guitars. The original Boston-based company was purchased by C.F. Martin in '70 and used on imports. In '80, Martin sold the Vega trademark to Korea's Galaxy Trading Company. The Deering Banjo Company, in Spring Valley, California acquired the brand in '89 and uses it (and the star logo) on a line of banjos.

C Series Archtop
1930-1950s. Several different C-model numbers, mid-level archtops including carved solid tops with bookmatched figured maple backs, natural or sunburst.

1930s	Higher models (C-56)	$1,300	$1,600
1930s	Lower models	$900	$1,100
1940s		$900	$1,100
1950s	Cutaway	$1,000	$1,150

Duo-Tron Electric Archtop
1940s-1950s. Mid-level large body non-cut archtop, single pickup, block markers, natural or sunburst.

1940s		$1,225	$1,375
1950s		$1,225	$1,375

FT-90 Flat-Top
1960s. 15" body with narrow waist, dot markers, Vega logo, natural.

1960s		$450	$550

G-30
1960s. D-style with solid spruce top and solid mahogany sides and back, Vega logo with star on headstock, dot markers, natural finish.

1960s		$350	$400

O'Dell
1950s. Full body, single cut, acoustic-electric, 1 pickup, tailpiece controls.

1950s	Sunburst	$1,350	$1,650

TV Jones Spectra-Sonic

Valley Arts Custom Pro

GUITARS

Veillette Acoustic 12

'05 Veleno Original

MODEL YEAR	FEATURES	EXC. COND. LOW	HIGH

Parlor Guitar

Early-1900s. Small parlor-sized instrument, Brazilian rosewood back and sides, styles vary, fancy appointments associated with higher-end models, including binding, purfling and inlays.

| 1900s | Mid-level | $1,100 | $1,350 |
| 1910s | Higher-end | $2,500 | $2,800 |

Profundo Flat-Top

1940s-1950s. Flat-top D-style body, spruce top, mahogany or rosewood back and sides.

| 1940-1950s | Mahogany | $1,100 | $1,300 |
| 1940-1950s | Rosewood | $2,500 | $3,100 |

Solidbody Electric (Import)

1970s-1980s. Solidbody copies of classic designs, Vega script logo on headstock, bolt-on necks.

| 1970s | | $225 | $275 |

Vega, Charles

1993-present. Luthier Charles Vega builds his premium, production/custom, nylon-string guitars in Baltimore, Maryland.

Veillette

1991-present. Luthiers Joe Veillette (of Veillette-Citron fame) and Martin Keith build their professional grade, production/custom, acoustic, acoustic/electric, electric 6- and 12-string and baritone guitars in Woodstock, New York. They also build basses and mandolins.

Veillette-Citron

1975-1983. Founded by Joe Veillette and Harvey Citron who met at the New York College School of Architecture in the late '60s. Joe took a guitar building course from Michael Gurian and by the Summer of '76, he and Harvey started producing neck-thru solidbody guitars and basses. Veillette and Citron both are back building instruments.

Velázquez

1948-1972. Manuel Velázquez, New York, New York, gained a reputation as a fine repairman in the late 1940s. He opened his 3rd Avenue guitar building shop in the early 1950s. By the mid-1950s he was considered by some as being the finest American builder of classical guitars. Velázquez left New York in 1972 and moved to Puerto Rico. He continued building guitars for the Japanese market. He returned to the United States in 1982. By the 2000s he built instruments with this son and daughter.

Veleno

1967, 1970-1977, 2003-present. Premium and presentation grade, production/custom, all-aluminum electric solidbody guitars built by luthier John Veleno in St. Petersburg, Florida. First prototype in '67. Later production begins in late-'70 and lasts until '75 or '76. The guitars were chrome or gold-plated, with various anodized colors. The Traveler Guitar was the idea of B.B. King; only

10 were made. Two Ankh guitars were made for Todd Rundgren in '77. Only one bass was made. Approximately 185 instruments were made up to '77 and are sequentially numbered. In 2003, John Veleno reintroduced his brand.

Original (Aluminum Solidbody)

1973-1976. V-headstock, chrome and aluminum.

| 1973-1976 | | $9,000 | $11,000 |

Traveler Guitar

1973-1976. Limited production of about a dozen instruments, drop-anchor-style metal body.

| 1973-1976 | | $11,000 | $13,500 |

Vengeance Guitars & Graphix

2002-present. Luthier Rick Stewart builds his professional and premium grade, custom/production, solidbody guitars in Arden, North Carolina. He also builds basses.

Ventura

1970s. Acoustic and electric guitars imported by C. Bruno Company, mainly copies of classic American models. They also offered basses.

Acoustic Flat-Top

| 1970s | | $100 | $300 |

Hollowbody Electric

| 1970s | | $300 | $550 |

Verri

1992-present. Premium grade, production/custom, archtop guitars built by luthier Henry Verri in Little Falls, New York.

Versoul, LTD

1989-present. Premium grade, production/custom steel-string flat-top, acoustic/electric, nylon-string, resonator, solidbody, and baritone guitars built by luthier Kari Nieminen in Helsinki, Finland. He also builds basses and sitars.

Victor Baker Guitars

1998-present. Professional and premium grade, custom, carved archtop, flat-top and solidbody electric guitars built by luthier Victor Baker in Philadelphia, Pennsylvania.

Victor Guitars

2002-2008. Luthiers Edward Victor Dick and Greg German build their premium grade, production/custom, flat top guitars in Denver, Colorado.

Victoria

1920s. Instruments built by the Oscar Schmidt Co. and possibly others. Most likely a brand made for a distributor.

Viking Guitars

1998-present. Professional and premium grade, custom, solidbody guitars made in Las Vegas, Nevada by Ed Roman.

MODEL YEAR	FEATURES	EXC. COND. LOW	HIGH

Vincente Tatay
1894-late 1930s. Classical guitars built by luthier Vicente Tatay and his sons in Valencia, Spain.

Vinetto
2003-present. Luthier Vince Cunetto builds his professional grade, production/custom, solid, chambered and semi-hollow body guitars in St. Louis, Missouri.

Vintique
1990-present. Luthier Jay Monterose builds his premium grade, custom/production, electric guitars in Suffern, New York. Vintique also manufactures guitar hardware.

Vivi-Tone
1933-ca. 1936. Founded in Kalamazoo, Michigan, by former Gibson designer Lloyd Loar, Walter Moon and Lewis Williams, Vivi-Tone built acoustic archtop guitars as well as some of the earliest electric solidbodies. They also built amps, basses and mandolins.

Guitar
1930s. Deep archtop-style body with F-holes on the backside and magnetic bridge pickup.

| 1930s | Rare model | $4,000 | $5,000 |
| 1930s | Standard model, sunburst | $2,700 | $3,000 |

Vox
1957-1972, 1982-present. Name introduced by Jennings Musical Instruments (JMI) of England. First Vox products were amplifiers brought to the market in '58 by Tom Jennings and Dick Denny. Guitars were introduced in '61, with an Echo Unit starting the Vox line of effects in '63. Guitars and basses bearing the Vox name were offered from '61-'69 (made in England and Italy), '82-'85 (Japan), '85-'88 (Korea), '98-2001 (U.S.), and they introduced a limited edition U.S.-made teardrop guitar in '07 and the semi-hollow Virage guitars in '08. Vox products are currently distributed in the U.S. by Korg USA. Special thanks to Jim Rhoads of Rhoads Music in Elizabethtown, Pennsylvania, for help on production years of these models.

Ace
Late 1960s. Offset double cut solidbody, 2 single-coils, Ace logo.

| 1967-1968 | | $700 | $900 |

Apollo
1967-1968. Single sharp cutaway, 1 pickup, distortion, treble and bass booster, available in sunburst or cherry.

| 1967-1968 | | $650 | $800 |

Bobcat
1963-1968. Double-cut semi-hollowbody style, block markers, 3 pickups, vibrato, 2 volume and 2 tone controls.

| 1963-1965 | | $900 | $1,000 |

Bossman
1967-1968. Single rounded cutaway, 1 pickup, distortion, treble and bass booster, available in sunburst or cherry.

| 1967-1968 | | $550 | $650 |

Bulldog
1966. Solidbody double-cut, 3 pickups.

| 1966 | | $800 | $1,000 |

Delta
1967-1968. Solidbody, 2 pickups, distortion, treble and bass boosters, vibrato, 1 volume and 2 tone controls, available in white only.

| 1967-1968 | | $1,000 | $1,300 |

Folk XII
1966-1969. Dreadnought 12-string flat-top, large 3-point 'guard, block markers, natural.

| 1966-1969 | | $425 | $525 |

Guitar-Organ
1966. Standard Phantom with oscillators from a Continental organ installed inside. Plays either organ sounds, guitar sounds, or both. Weighs over 20 pounds.

| 1966 | | $1,200 | $1,500 |

Harlem
1965-1967. Offset double-cut solidbody, 2 extended range pickups, sunburst or color option.

| 1965-1967 | | $550 | $625 |

Hurricane
1965-1967. Double-cut solidbody, 2 pickups, spring action vibrato, sunburst or color option.

| 1965-1967 | | $400 | $450 |

Mando Guitar
1966. Made in Italy, 12-string mandolin thing.

| 1966 | | $1,300 | $1,600 |

Mark III
1998-2001. Teardrop reissue, 2 single-coils, fixed bridge or Bigsby. A limited was introduced in '08.

| 1998-2001 | | $700 | $900 |

Mark IX
1965-1966. Solidbody teardrop-shaped, 9 strings, 3 pickups, vibrato, 1 volume and 2 tone controls.

| 1965-1966 | | $1,100 | $1,350 |

Mark VI
1965-1967. Teardrop-shaped solidbody, 3 pickups, vibrato, 1 volume and 2 tone controls.

| 1964-1965 | England, white, Brian Jones model | $3,600 | $4,000 |
| 1965-1967 | Italy, sunburst | $1,450 | $1,750 |

Mark VI Reissue
1998-2001. Actually, this is a reissue of the original Phantom VI (Vox couldn't use that name due to trademark reasons).

| 1998-2001 | | $725 | $900 |

Mark XII
1965-1967. Teardrop-shaped solidbody, 12 strings, 3 pickups, vibrato, 1 volume and 2 tone controls, sunburst. Reissued for '98-'01.

| 1965-1967 | | $1,450 | $1,750 |

Meteor/Super Meteor
1965-1967. Solidbody double-cut, 1 pickup, Super Meteor with vibrato.

| 1965-1967 | Meteor | $450 | $500 |
| 1965-1967 | Super Meteor | $500 | $550 |

Vinetto Legato

Vox Mark VI

Vox Phantom XII

1960s Vox Streamliner

MODEL YEAR	FEATURES	EXC. COND. LOW	HIGH

New Orleans
1966. Thin double-cut acoustic electric similar to ES-330, 2 pickups, a scaled down version of the 3-pickup Bobcat model.

1966		$750	$900

Phantom VI
1962-1967. Five-sided body, 6 strings, 3 pickups, vibrato, 1 volume and 2 tone controls.

1962-1964	English-made	$2,200	$2,400
1965-1967	Italian-made	$1,400	$1,600

Phantom XII
1964-1967. Five-sided body, 12 strings, 3 pickups, vibrato, 1 volume and 2 tone controls. There was also a stereo version with 3 offset pickups.

1964	English-made	$2,400	$2,500
1965-1967	Italian-made	$1,800	$1,900

Phantom XII Stereo
1966. Phantom shape, 3 special offset stereo pickups making 6 pickup conbinations, 3 separate pickup mode selectors, color option.

1966		$2,000	$2,400

Spitfire
1965-1967. Solidbody double-cut, 3 pickups, vibrato.

1965-1967		$500	$575

Starstream
1967-1968. Teardrop-shaped hollowbody, 2 pickups, distortion, treble and bass boosters, wah-wah, vibrato, 1 volume and 2 tone controls, 3-way pickup selector, available in cherry or sandburst.

1967-1968		$1,000	$1,200

Starstream XII
1967-1968. 12 string Starstream.

1967-1968		$1,000	$1,250

Stroller
1961-1966. Made in England, solidbody, single bridge pickup, Hurricane-style contoured body, dot markers, red.

1961-1966		$400	$500

Student Prince
1965-1967. Mahogany body thinline archtop electric, 2 knobs, dot markers, made in Italy.

1965-1967		$375	$450

Super Ace
1963-1965. Solidbody double-cut.

1963-1965		$500	$600

Super Lynx
1965-1967. Similar to Bobcat but with 2 pickups and no vibrola, double-cut, 2 pickups, adjustable truss rod, 2 bass and 2 volume controls.

1965-1967		$750	$850

Super Lynx Deluxe
1965-1967. Super Lynx with added vibrato tailpiece.

1965-1967		$800	$900

Tempest XII
1965-1967. Solidbody double-cut, 12 strings, 3 pickups.

1965-1967		$500	$625

Thunder Jet
1960s-style with single pickup and vibrato arm.

1960s		$575	$675

MODEL YEAR	FEATURES	EXC. COND. LOW	HIGH

Tornado
1965-1967. Thinline archtop, single pickup, dot markers, sunburst.

1965-1967		$375	$425

Typhoon
1965-1967. Hollowbody single-cut, 2 pickups, 3-piece laminated neck.

1965-1967		$425	$525

Ultrasonic
1967-1968. Hollowbody double-cut, 2 pickups, distortion, treble and bass boosters, wah-wah, vibrato, 1 volume and 2 tone controls, 3-way pickup selector, available in sunburst or cherry.

1967-1968		$900	$1,500

Viper
1968. Double-cut, thinline archtop electric, built-in distortion.

1968		$1,000	$1,100

W. J. Dyer
See listing under Dyer.

Wabash
1950s. Acoustic and electric guitars distributed by the David Wexler company and made by others, most likely Kay. They also offered lap steels and amps.

Walker
1994-present. Premium and presentation grade, production/custom, flat-top and archtop guitars built by luthier Kim Walker in North Stonington, Connecticut.

Walker (Kramer)
1981. Kramer came up with idea to offer this brand to produce wood-neck guitars and basses; they didn't want to dilute the Kramer aluminum-neck market they had built up. The idea didn't last long, and few, if any, of these instruments were produced, but prototypes exist.

Wandre (Davoli)
Ca. 1956/57-1969. Solidbody and thinline hollowbody electric guitars and basses created by German-descended Italian motorcycle and guitar enthusiast, artist, and sculptor from Milan, Italy, Wandre Pioli. Brands include Wandre (pronounced Vahn-dray), Davoli, Framez, JMI, Noble, Dallas, Avalon, Avanti I and others. Until '60, they were built by Pioli himself; from '60-'63 built in Milan by Framez; '63-'65 built by Davoli; '66-'69 built in Pioli's own factory.

The guitars originally used Framez pickups, but from '63 on (or earlier) they used Davoli pickups. Mostly strange shapes characterized by neck-thru-tailpiece aluminum neck with plastic back and rosewood 'board. Often multi-color and sparkle finishes, using unusual materials like linoleum, fiberglass and laminates, metal bindings. Often the instruments will have numerous identifying

MODEL YEAR	FEATURES	EXC. COND. LOW	HIGH

names but usually somewhere there is a Wandre blob logo.

Distributed early on in the U.K. by Jennings Musical Industries, Ltd. (JMI) and in the U.S. by Don Noble and Company. Model B.B. dedicated to Brigitte Bardot. Among more exotic instruments were the minimalist Krundaal Bikini guitar with a built-in amplifier and attached speaker, and the pogo stick Swedenbass. These guitars are relatively rare and highly collectible. In '05, the brand was revived on a line of imported intermediate grade, production, solidbodies from Eastwood guitars.

Metal Solidbody

1960s		$3,100	$3,800

Warren

2005-present. Luthier Don Warren builds his professional and premium grade, custom/production, solidbody electric guitars in Latham, New York.

Warrior

1995-present. Professional, premium, and presentation grade, production/custom, acoustic and solidbody electric guitars built by luthier J.D. Lewis in Rossville, Georgia. Warrior also builds basses.

Washburn

1974-present. Budget, intermediate, professional, and premium grade, production/custom, acoustic and electric guitars made in the U.S., Japan, and Korea. They also make basses, amps, banjos and mandolins.

Originally a Lyon & Healy brand, the Washburn line was revived in '74, promoted by Beckman Musical Instruments. Beckman sold the rights to the Washburn name to Fretted Instruments, Inc. in '76. Guitars originally made in Japan and Korea, but production moved back to U.S. in '91. Currently Washburn is part of U.S. Music.

Washburn (Lyon & Healy)

1880s-ca.1949. Washburn was founded in Chicago as one of the lines for Lyon & Healy to promote high quality stringed instruments, ca. 1880s. The rights to manufacture Washburns were sold to J.R. Stewart Co. in '28, but rights to Washburn name were sold to Tonk Brothers of Chicago. In the Great Depression (about 1930), J.R. Stewart Co. was hit hard and declared bankruptcy. Tonk Brothers bought at auction all Stewart trade names, then sold them to Regal Musical Instrument Co. Regal built Washburns by the mid-'30s. The Tonk Brothers still licensed the name. These Washburn models lasted until ca. '49. In '74 the brand resurfaced.

Model 1897

High-end appointments, plentiful pearl, 18 frets, slightly larger than parlor size, natural.

1910		$2,800	$3,500

Model 1915

Brazilian rosewood back and sides.

1928		$2,100	$2,500

Model 5257 Solo

1930s. Jumbo size body, rosewood back and sides, natural.

1930s		$5,600	$6,000

Model 5265 Tenor

1920s. Pear-shaped mahogany body, 4-string tenor.

1920s		$575	$675

Parlor Guitar

Early-1900s. Lower-end, small 12"-13" body, plain appointments.

1900s		$525	$600

Style 188

Rosewood back and sides with full pearl 'board inlaid with contrasting colored pearl, pearl on edges and around soundhole.

1890s		$4,100	$4,800

Style A

1920s. Smaller body, rosewood back and sides, top stencil decoration, natural.

1920s		$3,100	$3,500

Washington

Washington was a brand manufactured by Kansas City, Missouri instrument wholesalers J.W. Jenkins & Sons. First introduced in 1895, the brand also offered mandolins.

Waterstone

2003-present. Intermediate and professional grade, production/custom, electric solid and semi-hollowbody and acoustic guitars imported from Korea by Waterstone Musical Instruments, LLC of Nashville. They also offer basses.

Watkins/WEM

1957-present. Watkins Electric Music (WEM) was founded by Charlie Watkins. Their first commercial product was the Watkins Dominator (wedge Gibson stereo amp shape) in '57. They made the Rapier line of guitars and basses from the beginning. Watkins offered guitars and basses up to '82.

Wayne

1998-present. Professional and premium grade, production/custom, solidbody guitars built by luthiers Wayne and Michael (son) Charvel in Paradise, California. They also build lap steels.

Webber

1988-present. Professional grade, production/custom flat-top guitars built by luthier David Webber in North Vancouver, British Columbia.

Warren AR

Warrior Z Knight

GUITARS

1930s Weissenborn

Weissenborn Style 1

MODEL		EXC. COND.	
YEAR	FEATURES	LOW	HIGH

Weber

1996-present. Premium grade, production/custom, carved-top acoustic and resonator guitars built by luthier Bruce Weber and his Sound To Earth, Ltd. company, originally in Belgrade, Montana, and since '04, in Logan, Montana. They also build mandolins.

Webster

1940s. Archtop and acoustic guitars, most likely built by Kay or other mass builder.

Model 16C

1940s. Acoustic archtop.

1940s		$525	$575

Wechter

1984-present. Intermediate, professional and premium grade, production/custom, flat-top, 12-string, resonator and nylon-string guitars from luthier Abe Wechter in Paw Paw, Michigan. He also offers basses. The Elite line is built in Paw Paw, the others in Asia. Until '94 he built guitars on a custom basis. In '95, he set up a manufacturing facility in Paw Paw to produce his new line and in '00 he added the Asian guitars. In '04, he added resonators designed by Tim Scheerhorn. Wechter was associated with Gibson Kalamazoo from the mid-'70s to '84. He also offers the Maple Lake brand of acoustics.

Weissenborn

1910s-1937, present. Hermann Weissenborn was well-established as a violin and piano builder in Los Angeles by the early 1910s. Around '20, he added guitars, ukes and steels to his line. Most of his production was in the '20s and '30s until his death in '37. He made tenor, plectrum, parlor, and Spanish guitars, ukuleles, and mandolins, but is best remembered for his koa Hawaiian guitars that caught the popular wave of Hawaiian music. That music captivated America after being introduced to the masses at San Francisco's Panama Pacific International Exposition which was thrown in '15 to celebrate the opening of the Panama Canal and attended by more than 13 million people. He also made instruments for Kona and other brands. The Weissenborn brand has been revived on a line of reissue style guitars.

Spanish Acoustic

1920s. High-end Spanish set-up, rope binding, koa top, sides and back, limited production.

1920s		$4,000	$5,000

Style #1 Hawaiian

Koa, no binding, 3 wood circle soundhole inlays.

1926		$2,500	$4,000

Style #2 Hawaiian

Koa, black celluloid body binding, white wood 'board binding, rope soundhole binding.

1926		$3,000	$4,500

MODEL		EXC. COND.	
YEAR	FEATURES	LOW	HIGH

Style #3 Hawaiian

Koa, rope binding on top, 'board, and soundhole.

1925		$3,500	$5,000

Style #4 Hawaiian

Koa, rope binding on body, 'board, headstock and soundhole.

1927		$5,000	$6,000

Tenor

1920		$1,700	$2,000

Welker Custom

Professional and premium grade, production/custom, archtop and flat-top guitars built by luthier Fred Welker in Nashville, Tennessee.

Welson

1960s. Import copy models from accordion maker in Italy, copies range from Jazzmaster-style to ES-335-style, production was not large, Welson logo on the headstock, some sold in the U.S.A. by the Wurlitzer retail stores.

Electric

1960s	Copy models	$225	$350
1960s	Plastic cover, original design	$675	$825

Wendler

1999-present. Intermediate and professional grade, production/custom, solidbody, electro-acoustic guitars from luthier Dave Wendler of Ozark Instrument Building in Branson, Missouri. He also builds basses and amps. In '91, Wendler patented a pickup system that became the Taylor ES system.

Westbury-Unicord

1978-ca. 1983. Imported from Japan by Unicord of Westbury, New York. High quality original designs, generally with 2 humbuckers, some with varitone and glued-in necks. They also had basses.

Westone

1970s-1990, 1996-2001. Made by Matsumoku in Matsumoto, Japan and imported by St. Louis Music. Around '81, St. Louis Music purchased an interest in Matsumoku and began to make a transition from its own Electra brand to the Westone brand previously used by Matsumoku. In the beginning of '84, the brand became Electra-Westone with a phoenix bird head surrounded by circular wings and flames. By the end of '84 the Electra name was dropped, leaving only Westone and a squared-off bird with W-shaped wings logo. Electra, Electra-Westone and Westone instruments from this period are virtually identical except for the brand and logo treatment. Many of these guitars and basses were made in very limited runs and are relatively rare.

From '96 to '01, England's FCN Music offered Westone branded electric and acoustic guitars. The electrics were built in England and the acoustics came from Korea. Matsumoku-made guitars fea-

MODEL		EXC. COND.	
YEAR	FEATURES	LOW	HIGH

ture a serial number in which the first 1 or 2 digits represent the year of manufacture. Electra-Westone guitars should begin with either a 4 or 84.

Weymann

1864-1940s. H.A. Weymann & Sons was a musical instrument distributor located in Philadelphia that marketed various stringed instruments, but mainly known for banjos. Some guitar models made by Regal and Vega, but they also built their own instruments.

Parlor

1904-ca. 1920. Small 14 5/8" body parlor-style, fancy pearl and abalone trim, fancy fretboard markers, natural.

1910		$3,100	$3,400

Style 24

1920s. Mid-size body, 12-fret, slotted peghead, made by Vega for Weymann, mahogany sides and back, natural.

1920s		$800	$1,000

Wilkanowski

Early-1930s-mid-1940s. W. Wilkanowski primarily built violins. He did make a few dozen guitars which were heavily influenced by violin design concepts and in fact look very similar to a large violin with a guitar neck.

Violin-Shaped Acoustic

1930-1945. Violin brown.

1930-1945		$4,800	$6,000

Wilkat Guitars

1998-present. Professional grade, custom handmade, electric guitars built by luthier Bill Wilkat in Montreal, Quebec, Canada. He also builds basses.

Wilkins

1984-present. Custom guitars built by luthier Pat Wilkins in Van Nuys, California. Wilkins also does finish work for individuals and a variety of other builders.

William C. Stahl

See listing under Stahl.

William Hall and Son

William Hall and Son was a New York City based distributor offering guitars built by other luthiers in the mid to late 1800s.

Wilson

1960s-1970s. One of the brand names of guitars built in the 1960s for others by Egmond in Holland. Also a brand name used by England's Watkins WEM in the 1960s and '70s.

Wilson Brothers Guitars

2004-present. Intermediate and professional grade, production, imported electric and acoustic guitars. They also build basses. Founded by Ventures guitarist Don Wilson. VCM and VSP models made in Japan; VM electrics in Korea; VM acoustic in China.

Windsor

Ca. 1890s-ca. 1914. Brand used by Montgomery Ward for flat top guitars and mandolins made by various American manufacturers, including Lyon & Healy and, possibly, Harmony. Generally beginner-grade instruments.

Acoustic Flat-Top

1890s-1914.

1900s		$200	$300

Winston

Ca. 1963-1967. Imported from Japan by Buegeleisen and Jacobson of New York. Manufacturers unknown, but some are by Guyatone. Generally shorter scale beginner guitars. They also had basses.

Worland Guitars

1997-present. Professional grade, production/custom, flat-top, 12-string, and harp guitars built by luthier Jim Worland in Rockford, Illinois.

WRC Music International

1989-mid-1990s. Guitars by Wayne Richard Charvel, who was the original founder of Charvel Guitars. He now builds Wayne guitars with his son Michael.

Wright Guitar Technology

1993-present. Luthier Rossco Wright builds his unique intermediate grade, production, travel/practice steel-string and nylon-string guitars in Eugene, Oregon.

Wurlitzer

Wurlitzer marketed a line of American-made guitars in the 1920s. They also offered American- and foreign-made guitars starting in '65. The American ones were built from '65-'66 by the Holman-Woodell guitar factory in Neodesha, Kansas. In '67, Wurlitzer switched to Italian-made Welson guitars.

Model 2077 (Martin 0-K)

1920s. Made by Martin for Wurlitzer who had full-line music stores in most major cities. Size 0 with top, back and sides made from koa wood, limited production of about 28 instruments.

1922	Natural	$4,500	$5,500

Worland Jumbo

Wright Guitar Technology SoloEtte

Xaviere XV-700

XXL DC model

MODEL YEAR	FEATURES	EXC. COND. LOW	HIGH

Model 2090 (Martin 0-28)
1920s. Made by Martin for Wurlitzer who had full-line music stores in most major cities. Size 0 with appointments similar to a similar period Martin 0-28, limited production of about 11 instruments, Wurlitzer branded on the back of the headstock and on the inside back seam, Martin name also branded on inside seam.

| 1922 | Natural | $6,500 | $8,000 |

Wild One Stereo
1960s. Two pickups, various colors.

| 1967 | | $500 | $600 |

Xaviere
Imtermediate and professional grade, production, solid and semi-hollow body guitars from Guitar Fetish, which also has GFS pickups.

XXL Guitars
2003-present. Luthier Marc Lupien builds his production/custom, professional grade, chambered electric guitars in Montreal, Quebec, Canada.

Yamaha
1946-present. Budget, intermediate, professional, and presentation grade, production/custom, acoustic, acoustic/electric, and electric guitars. They also build basses, amps, and effects. The Japanese instrument maker was founded in 1887. Began classical guitar production around 1946. Solidbody electric production began in '66; steel string acoustics debut sometime after that. Production shifted from Japan to Taiwan (Yamaha's special-built plant) in the '80s, though some high-end guitars still made in Japan. Some Korean production began in '90s.

Serialization patterns:
Serial numbers are coded as follows:
H = 1, I = 2, J = 3, etc., Z = 12
To use this pattern, you need to know the decade of production.
Serial numbers are ordered as follows: Year/Month/Day/Factory Order
Example: NL 29159 represents a N=1987 year, L=5th month or May, 29=29th day (of May), 159=159th guitar made that day (the factory order). This guitar was the 159 guitar made on May 29, 1987.

AE Series
1966-present.

1966-1974	AE-11	$700	$1,100
1973-1977	AE-12	$700	$1,100
1973-1977	AE-18	$800	$1,100
1985-1992	AE-1200	$800	$1,100
1998-2000	AE-500	$300	$375

AES-1500
1990-present. Semi-hollowbody, f-holes, single-cut, 2 humbuckers, maple-center block for sustain, arched sycamore top, maple sides and back, stud and tune-o-matic bridge tailpiece configuration.

| 1990-2007 | | $1,000 | $1,200 |

MODEL YEAR	FEATURES	EXC. COND. LOW	HIGH

APX Series
1987-present. Acoustic/electric, various features.

| 1987-2007 | | $250 | $500 |

CG Series
1984-present. Classical models.

| 1984-2007 | | $100 | $350 |

DW Series
1999-2002. Dreadnought flat-top models, sunburst, solid spruce top, higher-end appointments like abalone rosette and top purfling.

| 1999-2002 | | $200 | $450 |

Eterna Acoustic
1983-1994. Folk style acoustics, there were 4 models.

| 1983-1994 | | $250 | $350 |

FG Series
1970s-present. Economy market flat-top models, laminated sides and back, a 12 suffix indicates 12-string, CE indicates on-board electronics, many models are D-style bodies.

| 1970-2000 | | $150 | $500 |

G Series
1981-present. Classical models.

| 1981-2000 | | $225 | $500 |

GC Series
1982-present. Classical models, '70s made in Japan, '80s made in Taiwan.

| 1982-1999 | | $500 | $750 |

Image Custom
1989-1992. Electric double-cut, flamed maple top, active circuitry, LED position markers.

| 1989-1992 | | $425 | $500 |

L Series
1984-present. Custom hand-built flat-top models, solid wood.

| 1984-1999 | | $500 | $1,000 |

Pacifica
1989-present. Offset double-cut with longer horns, dot markers, various models.

| 1989-1999 | Mid-level models | $150 | $225 |
| 2000-2007 | Mid-level models | $150 | $200 |

RGX Series
1988-1989. Bolt-on neck for the 600 series and neck-thru body designs for 1200 series, various models include 110 (1 hum), 211 (hum-single), 220 (2 hums), 312 (hum-single-single), 603 (3 singles), 612 (hum-single-single), 620 (2 hums), 1203S (3 singles), 1212S (hum-single-single), 1220S (2 hums).

| 1988-1989 | Various models | $200 | $575 |

RGZ Series
1989-1994. Double-cut solidbodies, various pickups.

| 1989-1994 | | $200 | $550 |

SA Series
1966-1994. Super Axe series, full-size and thinline archtop models.

| 1966-1994 | | $500 | $1,100 |

SBG Series
1983-1992. Solidbody models, set necks.

| 1983-1992 | | $225 | $650 |

MODEL		EXC. COND.	
YEAR	FEATURES	LOW	HIGH

SE Series
1986-1992. Solidbody electric models.

1986-1992		$100	$350

SG-3
1965-1966. Early double-cut solidbody with sharp horns, bolt neck, 3 hum-single pickup layout, large white guard, rotor controls, tremolo.

1965-1966		$975	$1,200

SG-5/SG-5A
1966-1971. Asymmetrical double-cut solidbody with extended lower horn, bolt neck, 2 pickups, chrome hardware.

1966-1971		$1,000	$1,200

SG-7/SG-7A
1966-1971. Like SG-5, but with gold hardware.

1966-1971		$1,150	$1,400

SG-20
1972-1973. Bolt-on neck, slab body, single-cut, 1 pickup.

1972-1973		$400	$475

SG-30/SG-30A
1973-1976. Slab katsura wood (30) or slab maple (30A) solidbody, bolt-on neck, 2 humbuckers, dot inlays.

1973-1976		$425	$525

SG-35/SG-35A
1973-1976. Slab mahogany (35) or slab maple (35A) solidbody, bolt-on neck, 2 humbuckers, parallelogram inlays.

1973-1976		$475	$575

SG-40
1972-1973. Bolt-on neck, carved body, single-cut.

1972-1973		$475	$575

SG-45
1972-1976. Glued neck, single-cut, bound flat-top.

1972-1976		$550	$675

SG-50
1974-1976. Slab katsura wood solidbody, glued neck, 2 humbuckers, dot inlays, large 'guard.

1974-1976		$550	$675

SG-60
1972 only. Bolt-on neck, carved body, single-cut.

1972		$525	$600

SG-60T
1973 only. SG-60 with large cast vibrato system.

1973		$575	$675

SG-65
1972-1976. Glued neck, single-cut, bound flat-top.

1972-1976		$625	$700

SG-70
1974-1976. Slab maple solidbody, glued neck, 2 humbuckers, dot inlays, large 'guard.

1974-1976		$625	$700

SG-80
1972 only. Bolt-on neck, carved body, single-cut.

1972		$525	$650

SG-80T
1973. SG-60 with large cast vibrato system.

1973		$575	$700

SG-85
1972-1976. Glued neck, single-cut, bound flat-top.

1972-1976		$625	$700

SG-90
1974-1976. Carved top mahogany solidbody, glued neck, elevated 'guard, bound top, dot inlays, chrome hardware.

1974-1976		$725	$775

SG-175
1974-1976. Carved top mahogany solidbody, glued neck, elevated 'guard, abalone bound top, abalone split wing or pyramid inlays, gold hardware.

1974-1976		$825	$900

SG-500
1976-1978. Carved unbound maple top, double pointed cutaways, glued neck, 2 exposed humbuckers, 3-ply bound headstock, bound neck with clay split wing inlays, chrome hardware. Reissued as the SBG-500 (800S in Japan) in '81.

1976-1978		$500	$600

SG-700
1976-1978. Carved unbound maple top, double pointed cutaways, glued neck, 2 humbuckers, 3-ply bound headstock, bound neck with clay split wing inlays, chrome hardware.

1976-1978		$650	$800

SG-700S
1999-2001. Set neck, mahogany body, 2 humbuckers with coil tap.

1999-2001		$650	$800

SG-1000/SBG-1000
1976-1983 ('84 in Japan), 2007-present. Carved maple top, double pointed cutaways, glued neck, 2 humbuckers, 3-ply bound headstock, unbound body, bound neck with clay split wing inlays, gold hardware. Export model name changed to SBG-1000 in '80. SBG-1000 reissued in'07.

1976-1979	SG-1000	$650	$800
1980-1983	SBG-1000	$650	$800

SG-1500
1976-1979. Carved maple top, double pointed cutaways, laminated neck-thru-body neck, laminated mahogany body wings, 2 humbuckers, 5-ply bound headstock and body, bound neck with dot inlays, chrome hardware. Name used on Japan-only model in the '80s.

1976-1979		$950	$1,000

SG-2000/SG-2000S
1976-1980 (1988 in Japan). Carved maple top, double pointed cutaways, laminated neck-thru-body neck, laminated mahogany body wings, 2 humbuckers, 5-ply bound headstock and body, bound neck with abalone split wing inlays, gold hardware. In '80, the model was changed to the SBG-2000 in the U.S., and the SG-2000S everywhere else except Japan (where it remained the SG-2000). Export model renamed SBG-2100 in '84.

1976-1980		$975	$1,100

Yamaha FG-720

Yamaha Pacifica

Yanuziello electric

Zemaitis S22 Metal-Front

MODEL YEAR	FEATURES	EXC. COND. LOW	HIGH

SG-2100S
1983. Similar to SG-2000 with upgrades such as the pickups.

1983		$1,000	$1,200

SG-3000/SBG-3000/Custom Professional
1982-1992. SG-2000 upgrade with higher output pickups and abalone purfling on top.

1982-1992		$1,300	$1,600

SGV-300
2000-2006. 1960s SG model features.

2000-2006		$250	$300

SHB-400
1981-1985. Solidbody electric, set-in neck, 2 pickups.

1981-1985		$425	$500

SJ-180
1983-1994. Student Jumbo, entry level Folk Series model, laminated top.

1983-1994		$100	$125

SJ-400S
1983-1994. Student Jumbo Folk Series model, solid wood top.

1983-1994		$225	$275

SL Studio Lord Series
1977-1981. LP-style copy models.

1977-1981		$400	$475

SR SuperRivroller Series
1977-1981. Strat copy models.

1977-1981		$200	$225

SSC Series
1983-1992. Solidbody electric models.

1983-1992	SSC-400/SC-400	$350	$425
1983-1992	SSC-500	$325	$400
1983-1992	SSC-600/SC-600	$450	$550

Weddington Classic
1989-1992. Electric solidbody, redesigned set-in neck/body joint for increased access to the higher frets.

1989-1992		$425	$500

Yanuziello Stringed Instruments

1980-present. Production/custom resonator and Hawaiian guitars built by luthier Joseph Yanuziello, in Toronto, Ontario.

Yosco

1900-1930s. Lawrence L. Yosco was a New York City luthier building guitars, round back mandolins and banjos under his own brand and for others.

MODEL YEAR	FEATURES	EXC. COND. LOW	HIGH

Zachary

1996-present. Luthier Alex Csiky builds his professional grade, production, solidbody electric guitars in Windsor, Ontario, Canada. He also builds basses.

Zanini

2007-present. Premium grade, production, electric guitars designed by Luca Zanini of Italy and built by luthier Alex Radovanovic in Switzerland.

Zeiler Guitars

1992-present. Custom flat-top, 12-string, and nylon-string guitars built by luthier Jamon Zeiler in Cincinnati, Ohio.

Zemaitis

1960-1999, 2004-present. Professional, premium, and presentation grade, custom/production, electric and acoustic guitars. Tony Zemaitis (born Antanus Casimere Zemaitis) began selling his guitars in 1960. He emphasized simple light-weight construction and was known for hand engraved metal front guitars. The metal front designs were originally engineered to reduce hum, but they became popular as functional art. Each hand-built guitar and bass was a unique instrument. Ron Wood was an early customer and his use of a Zemaitis created a demand for the custom-built guitars. Approximately 6 to 10 instruments were built each year. Tony retired in '99, and passed away in '02 at the age of 67. In '04, Japan's Kanda Shokai Corporation, with the endorsement of Tony Zemaitis, Jr., started building the guitars again. KSC builds the higher priced ones and licenses the lower priced guitars to Greco.

Celebrity association with Zemaitis is not uncommon. Validated celebrity provenance may add 25% to100% (or more) to a guitar's value. Tony Zemaitis also made so-called student model instruments for customers with average incomes. These had wood tops instead of metal or pearl. Some wood top instruments have been converted to non-Zemaitis metal tops, which are therefore not fully original Zemaitis instruments.

MODEL YEAR	FEATURES	EXC. COND. LOW	HIGH
Acoustic Models			
1965	12-string, 1st year	$21,000	$26,000
1970s	6-string	$14,000	$16,000
1980s	12-string, D-hole	$12,000	$15,000
1980s	12-string, heart-hole	$23,000	$26,000
1980s	6-string, D-hole	$12,000	$14,000
1980s	6-string, heart-hole	$21,000	$26,000
Electric Models			
1980-1990s	Student model, wood top	$12,000	$15,000
1980s	Disc-front	$24,000	$26,000
1980s	Metal-front	$25,000	$27,000
1980s	Pearl-front	$29,000	$35,000
1994	"Black Pearl", very few made	$32,000	$38,000
1995	Disc-front 40th Anniversary	$26,000	$32,000

Zen-On

1946-ca.1968. Japanese manufacturer. By '67 using the Morales brand name. Not heavily imported into the U.S., if at all (see Morales).

Acoustic Hollowbody
1946-1968. Various models.

1950s		$175	$250

Electric Solidbody
1960s. Teisco-era and styling.

1960s		$175	$250

Zeta

1982-present. Zeta has made solid, semi-hollow and resonator guitars, many with electronic and MIDI options, in Oakland, California over the years, but currently only offer upright basses, amps and violins.

Zim-Gar

1960s. Imported from Japan by Gar-Zim Musical Instrument Corporation of Brooklyn, New York. Manufacturers unknown. Generally shorter scale beginner guitars.

Electric Solidbody

1960s		$175	$250

Zimnicki, Gary

1980-present. Luthier Gary Zimnicki builds his professional and premium grade, custom, flat-top, 12-string, nylon-string, and archtop guitars in Allen Park, Michigan.

MODEL YEAR	FEATURES	EXC. COND. LOW	HIGH

Zion

1980-present. Professional and premium grade, production/custom, semi-hollow and solidbody guitars built by luthier Ken Hoover, originally in Greensboro, North Carolina, currently in Raleigh.

Classic
1989-present. Double-cut solidbody, six-on-a-side headstock, opaque finish, various pickup options, dot markers.

1989-2007	Custom quilted top	$725	$800
1989-2007	Opaque finish	$525	$650

Graphic
1980s-1994. Double-cut basswood body, custom airbrushed body design, bolt-on neck, Green Frost Marble finish.

1990s		$875	$950

Radicaster
1987-present. Double-cut basswood body, graphic finish, bolt-on neck, various pickup configurations, marble/bowling ball finish.

1987-2007		$700	$800

The Fifty
1994-present. Single-cut ash solidbody, 2 single coils, bolt-on neck.

1994-2007	Custom figured top	$725	$800
1994-2007	Natural, plain top	$575	$650

Zolla

1979-present. Professional grade, production/custom, electric guitars built by luthier Bill Zolla in San Diego, California. Zolla also builds basses, necks and bodies.

Zon

1981-present. Currently luthier Joe Zon only offers basses, but he also built guitars from '85-'91. See Bass Section for more company info.

Zuni

1993-present. Premium grade, custom, solidbody electric guitars built by luthier Michael Blank in Alto Pass, Illinois and Amasa, Michigan.

ZZ Ryder

Solidbody electric guitars from Stenzler Musical Instruments of Ft. Worth, Texas. They also offer basses.

1994 Zemaitis Pearl-Front

Zion Model 90

BASSES

Alembic Epic

Alleva-Coppolo Standard 4

MODEL YEAR	FEATURES	EXC. COND. LOW	HIGH

A Basses

1976-2002. Luthier Albey Balgochian built his professional grade, solidbody basses in Waltham, Massachusetts. Sports the A logo on headstock.

Solidbody Bass

1990s		$850	$1,100

Acoustic

Ca. 1965-ca. 1987. Mainly known for solidstate amps, the Acoustic Control Corp. of Los Angeles, did offer guitars and basses from around '69 to late '74. The brand was revived a few years ago by Samick for a line of amps.

Black Widow Bass

1969-1970, 1972-1974. Around '69 Acoustic offered the AC600 Black Widow Bass (in both a fretted and fretless version) which featured an unique black equal double-cut body with German carve, an Ebonite 'board, 2 pickups, each with 1 row of adjustable polepieces, a zero fret, and a protective "spider design" pad on back. Also available was the AC650 short-scale. The '72-'74 version had the same body design, but had a rosewood 'board and only 1 pickup with 2 rows of adjustable pole pieces (the '72s had a different split-coil pickup with 4 pole pieces, 2 front and 2 back). Acoustic outsourced the production of the basses, possibly to Japan, but at least part of the final production was by Semie Moseley.

1969-1970		$900	$1,100
1972-1974		$850	$1,075

Aims

Ca. 1974-ca. 1976. Aims instruments, distributed by Randall Instruments in the mid-'70s, were copies of classic American guitar and bass models. Randall also offered a line of Aims amps during the same time.

Airline

1958-1968, 2004-present. Brand for Montgomery Ward. Built by Kay, Harmony and Valco. In '04, the brand was revived on a line of reissues from Eastwood guitars.

Electric Solidbody Bass

1958-1968	Various models	$275	$400

Pocket 3/4 Bass (Valco/National)

1962-1968. Airline brand of double-cut Pocket Bass, short-scale, 2 pickups, 1 acoustic bridge and 1 neck humbucker, sunburst and other colors.

1962-1968		$550	$775

Alamo

1947-1982. Founded by Charles Eilenberg, Milton Fink, and Southern Music, San Antonio, Texas. Distributed by Bruno & Sons.

Eldorado Bass (Model 2600)

1965-1966. Solidbody, 1 pickup, angular offset shape, double-cut.

1965-1966		$275	$325

Titan Bass

1963-1970. Hollowbody, 1 pickup, angular offset shape.

1963-1970		$275	$325

MODEL YEAR	FEATURES	EXC. COND. LOW	HIGH

Alembic

1969-present. Professional, premium, and presentation grade, production/custom, 4-, 5-, and 6-string basses built in Santa Rosa, California. They also build guitars. Established in San Francisco as one of the first handmade bass builders. Alembic basses come with many options concerning woods (examples are maple, bubinga, walnut, vermilion, wenge, zebrawood), finishes, inlays, etc., all of which affect the values listed here. These dollar amounts should be used as a baseline guide to values for Alembic.

Anniversary Bass

1989. 20th Anniversary limited edition, walnut and vermillion with a walnut core, 5-piece body, 5-piece neck-thru, only 200 built.

1989		$2,200	$2,400

Custom Shop Built Bass

1969-present. Various one-off and/or custom built instruments. Each instrument should be evaluated individually. Prices are somewhat speculative due to the one-off custom characteristics and values can vary greatly.

1978	Dragon Doubleneck	$8,100	$9,000
2000	Stanley Clarke Custom	$3,100	$4,500
2004	Dragon 4-string, 4 made	$4,100	$4,400

Distillate Bass

1979-1991. Exotic woods, active electronics.

1979-1991	Distillate 4	$1,700	$2,300
1979-1991	Distillate 5	$1,800	$2,400

Elan Bass

1985-1996. Available in 4-, 5-, 6- and 8-string models, 3-piece thru-body laminated maple neck, solid maple body, active electronics, solid brass hardware, offered in a variety of hardwood tops and custom finishes.

1985-1996	Elan 4	$1,600	$1,900
1985-1996	Elan 5	$1,700	$2,200

Epic Bass

1993-present. Mahogany body with various tops, extra large pointed bass horn, maple/walnut veneer set-neck, available in 4-, 5-, and 6-string versions.

1993-1999	4-string	$1,300	$1,400
1993-1999	5-string	$1,400	$1,500
1993-1999	6-string	$1,500	$1,600
2000-2006	4-string	$1,100	$1,400
2000-2006	5-string	$1,300	$1,500
2000-2006	6-string	$1,400	$1,600

Essence Bass

1991-present. Mahogany body with various tops, extra large pointed bass horn, walnut/maple laminate neck-thru.

1991-1999	Essence 4	$1,500	$1,800
1991-1999	Essence 5	$1,600	$1,900
1991-1999	Essence 6	$1,700	$2,000
2000-2006	Essence 4	$1,500	$2,000
2000-2006	Essence 5	$1,600	$2,100
2000-2006	Essence 6	$1,700	$2,000

BASSES

Exploiter Bass
1980s. Figured maple solidbody 4-string, neck-thru, transparent finish.

		LOW	HIGH
1984-1988		$1,700	$2,000

Persuader Bass
1983-1991. Offset double-cut solidbody, 4-string, neck-thru.

1983-1991		$1,400	$1,500

Series I Bass
1971-present. Mahogany body with various tops, maple/purpleheart laminate neck-thru, active electronics, available in 3 scale lengths and with 4, 5 or 6 strings.

1971-1979	Medium- or long-scale	$4,500	$6,000
1971-1979	Short-scale	$4,500	$6,000
1980-1989	Medium- or long-scale	$4,500	$6,000
1980-1989	Short-scale	$4,500	$6,000
1990-2006	All scales, highly figured top	$4,500	$6,000

Series II Bass
Generally custom-made option, each instrument valued on a case-by-case basis, guidance pricing only.

1971-2000		$6,300	$7,000

Spoiler Bass
1981-1999. Solid mahogany body, maple neck-thru, 4 or 6 strings, active electronics, various high-end wood options.

1981-1986	6-string	$1,800	$2,200
1981-1989	4-string	$1,700	$2,000
1981-1989	5-string	$1,700	$2,100
1990-1999	4-string	$1,700	$2,000

Stanley Clarke Signature Standard Bass
1990-present. Neck-thru-body, active electronics, 24-fret ebony 'board, mahogany body with maple, bubinga, walnut, vermilion, or zebrawood top, 4-, 5-, and 6-string versions.

1990-2006	All scales	$2,000	$4,000

Alleva-Coppolo
1995-present. Luthier Jimmy Coppolo builds his professional and premium grade, custom/production, solidbody basses in Dallas, Texas, for '95-'97, and since in New York City. He also builds guitars.

Alternative Guitar and Amplifier Company
2006-present. Custom/production, intermediate grade, solidbody electric basses made in Piru, California, by luthiers Mal Stich and Sal Gonzales and imported from Korea under the Alternative Guitar and Amplifier Company and Mal n' Sal brands. They also build guitars.

Alvarez
1965-present. Imported by St. Louis Music, they offered electric basses from '90 to '02 and acoustic basses in the mid-'90s.

Electric Bass (Mid-Level)
1990s	Hollowbody	$275	$400
1990s	Solidbody	$225	$400

American Conservatory (Lyon & Healy)
Late-1800s-early-1900s. Mainly catalog sales guitars and mandolins from the Chicago maker. Mid-level Lyon & Healy offering, above their Lakeside brand, and generally under their Washburn brand.

G2740 Monster Bass
Early-mid-1900s. Six-string acoustic flat-top, spruce top, birch back and sides with rosewood stain, natural. Their catalog claimed it was "Indispensable to the up-to-date mandolin and guitar club."

1917		$3,500	$5,000

American Showster
1986-2004. Established by Bill Meeker and David Haines, Bayville, New Jersey. They also made guitars.

AS-57-B Bass
1987-1997. Bass version of AS-57 with body styled like a '57 Chevy tail fin.

1987-1997		$2,500	$3,100

Ampeg
1949-present. Ampeg was founded on a vision of an amplified bass peg, which evolved into the Baby Bass. Ampeg has sold basses on and off throughout its history.

AEB-1 Bass
1966-1967. F-holes through the body, fretted, scroll headstock, pickup in body, sunburst. Reissued as the AEB-2 for '97-'99.

1966-1967		$2,200	$2,500

AUB-1 Bass
1966-1967. Same as AEB-1, but fretless, sunburst. Reissued as the AUB-2 for '97-'99.

1966-1967		$2,000	$2,100

ASB-1 Devil Bass
1966-1967. Long-horn body, fretted, triangular f-holes through the body, fireburst.

1966-1967		$2,700	$3,400

AUSB-1 Devil Bass
1966-1967. Same as ASB-1 Devil Bass, but fretless.

1966-1967		$2,700	$3,400

BB-4 Baby Bass
1962-1971. Electric upright slim-looking bass that is smaller than a cello, available in sunburst, white, red, black, and a few turquoise. Reissued as the ABB-1 Baby Bass for '97-'99.

1962-1971	Solid color	$2,300	$3,200
1962-1971	Sunburst	$2,200	$2,600

BB-5 Baby Bass
1964-1971. Five-string version.

1964-1971	Sunburst	$2,400	$3,400

Ampeg AEB-1

1973 Ampeg Little Stud

1976 Aria Mach 1

Artinger Bass

MODEL YEAR	FEATURES	EXC. COND. LOW	HIGH

Dan Armstrong Lucite Bass
1969-1971. Clear solid lucite body, did not have switchable pickups like the Lucite guitar.

| 1969-1971 | | $3,500 | $3,900 |

Dan Armstrong Lucite Reissue/ADA4 Bass
1998-2001, 2008-present. Lucite body, Dan Armstrong Ampeg block lettering on 'guard. Reissue in '08 as the ADA4

| 1998-2001 | | $900 | $1,100 |

GEB-101 Little Stud Bass
1973-1975. Import from Japan, offset double-cut solidbody, two-on-a-side tuners, 1 pickup.

| 1973-1975 | | $375 | $450 |

GEB-750 Big Stud Bass
1973-1975. Import from Japan, similar to Little Stud, but with 2 pickups.

| 1973-1975 | | $400 | $500 |

Andreas
1995-present. Aluminium-necked, solidbody guitars and basses built by luthier Andreas Pichler in Dollach, Austria.

Angelica
1967-1975. Student and entry-level basses and guitars imported from Japan.
Electric Solidbody Bass
Japanese imports.

| 1970s | Various models | $125 | $200 |

Apollo
Ca. 1967-1972. Entry-level basses imported from Japan by St. Louis Music. They also had guitars and effects.
Electric Hollowbody Bass
Japanese imports.

| 1970s | | $100 | $200 |

Applause
1976-present. Intermediate grade, production, acoustic/electric basses. They also offer guitars, mandolins and ukes. Kaman Music's entry-level Ovation-styled brand. The instruments were made in the U.S. until around '82, when production was moved to Korea.

Arbor
1983-present. Budget grade, production, solidbody basses imported by Musicorp (MBT). They also offer guitars.
Electric Bass

| 1983-1999 | Various models | $150 | $200 |
| 2000-2005 | Various models | $75 | $125 |

Aria/Aria Pro II
1960-present. Budget and intermediate grade, production, acoustic, acoustic/electric, solidbody, hollowbody and upright basses. They also make guitars, mandolins, and banjos. Originally branded as Aria; renamed Aria Pro II in '75; both names

used over the next several year; in '01, the Pro II part of the name was dropped altogether.
Electric Bass

| 1980s | Various models | $250 | $450 |

Armstrong, Rob
1971-present. Custom basses made in Coventry, England, by luthier Rob Armstrong. He also builds mandolins, flat-tops, and parlor guitars.

Artinger Custom Guitars
1997-present. Professional and premium grade, production/custom, basses built by luthier Matt Artinger in Emmaus, Pennsylvania. He also builds builds hollow, semi-hollow, and chambered solid-body guitars.

Asama
1970s-1980s. Japanese line of solidbody basses. They also offered guitars, effects, drum machines and other music products.

Atomic
2006-present. Luthiers Tim Mulqueeny and Harry Howard build their intermediate and professional grade, production/custom, basses in Peoria, Arizona. They also build guitars.

Audiovox
Ca. 1935-ca. 1950. Paul Tutmarc's Audiovox Manufacturing, of Seattle, Washington, was a pioneer in electric lap steels, basses, guitars and amps. Tutmarc is credited with inventing the electric bass guitar in '35, which his company started selling in the late '30s.

Austin
1999-present. Budget and intermediate grade, production, basses imported by St. Louis Music. They also offer guitars, mandolins and banjos.

Austin Hatchet
Mid-1970s-mid-1980s. Trademark of distributor Targ and Dinner, Chicago, Illinois.
Hatchet Bass
Travel bass.

| 1981 | | $350 | $500 |

Avante
1997-2007. Shape cutaway acoustic bass designed by Joe Veillette and Michael Tobias originally offered by Alvarez. Later there was only a lower-priced baritone guitar offered by MusicYo.

Baldwin
1965-1970. The giant organ company got into guitars and basses in '65 when it bought Burns Guitars of England and sold those models in the U.S. under the Baldwin name.

MODEL YEAR	FEATURES	EXC. COND. LOW	HIGH
Baby Bison Bass			
1965-1970. Scroll head, 2 pickups, black, red or white finishes.			
1965-1966		$750	$850
1966-1970	Model 560	$650	$750
Bison Bass			
1965-1970. Scroll headstock, 3 pickups, black or white finishes.			
1965-1966		$1,000	$1,300
1966-1970	Model 516	$1,000	$1,200
G.B. 66 Bass			
1965-1966. Bass equivalent of G.B. 66 guitar, covered bridge tailpiece.			
1965-1966		$750	$875
Jazz Split Sound Bass			
1965-1970. Offset double-cut solidbody, 2 pickups, red sunburst.			
1965-1966	Long-scale	$750	$875
1966-1970	Short-scale	$700	$825
Nu-Sonic Bass			
1965-1966. Bass version of Nu-Sonic.			
1965-1966		$475	$575
Shadows/Shadows Signature Bass			
1965-1970. Named after Hank Marvin's backup band, solidbody, 3 slanted pickups, white finish.			
1965-1966	Shadows	$1,300	$1,500
1966-1970	Shadows Signature	$1,200	$1,300
Vibraslim Bass			
1965-1970. Thin body, scroll head, 2 pickups, sunburst.			
1965-1966		$900	$1,100
1966-1970	Model 549	$800	$900

Barclay

1960s. Generally shorter-scale, student-level imports from Japan. They also made guitars.

MODEL YEAR	FEATURES	EXC. COND. LOW	HIGH
Electric Solidbody Bass			
1960s	Various models	$150	$225

Barrington

1988-1991. Budget to low-intermediate basses, see Guitars Section for company information.

Basone Guitars

1999-present. Professional grade, custom, solid and hollowbody electric basses built by Chris Basaraba in Vancouver, British Columbia, Canada. He also builds guitars.

Bass Collection

1985-1992. Mid-level imports from Japan, distributed by Meisel Music of Springfield, New Jersey. Sam Ash Music, New York, sold the remaining inventory from '92 to '94.

MODEL YEAR	FEATURES	EXC. COND. LOW	HIGH
SB300 Series Bass			
1985-1992. Offset double-cut, bolt neck, ash or alder body, models include 300, 301 (fretless) and 302 (5-string).			
1985-1992		$300	$500

MODEL YEAR	FEATURES	EXC. COND. LOW	HIGH
SB400/SB500 Series Bass			
1985-1992. Offset double-cut, bolt neck, basswood body, active electronics, models include 401, 402 (fretless), 405 (5-string) and 501 (alder body).			
1985-1992		$400	$700

BC Rich

1966-present. Budget, intermediate, and premium grade, production/custom, import and U.S.-made basses. They also offer guitars. Many BC Rich models came in a variety of colors. For example, in '88 they offered black, Competition Red, metallic red, GlitteRock White, Ultra Violet, and Thunder Blue. Also in '88, other custom colors, graphic features, paint-to-match headstocks, and special inlays were offered.

MODEL YEAR	FEATURES	EXC. COND. LOW	HIGH
Bich Bass			
1976-2004. Solidbody, neck-thru, 2 pickups.			
1976-1983	USA	$1,400	$2,000
1984-1989		$1,100	$1,400
1989-1993	Class Axe era	$900	$1,200
1994-1998	2nd Rico-era	$900	$1,200
1999-2004		$900	$1,100
Bich Supreme 8-String Bass			
Late-1970s-early-1980s.			
1978-1982		$1,900	$2,900
Eagle Bass (U.S.A. Assembly)			
1977-1996. Curved double-cut, solidbody, natural.			
1977-1979		$2,000	$2,900
1980-1982		$1,500	$1,800
Gunslinger Bass			
1987-1999. Inverted headstock, 1 humbucker.			
1987-1989		$650	$750
1990-1999		$600	$650
Ironbird Bass			
1984-1998. Kinda star-shaped, neck-thru, solidbody, 2 pickups, active electronics, diamond inlays.			
1980s		$1,000	$1,200
Mockingbird Bass			
1976-present.			
1976	USA, short-horn	$2,600	$3,500
1977-1978	USA, short-horn	$2,300	$3,400
1979-1983	USA, long-horn	$1,800	$2,900
1984-1989	End 1st Rico-era	$1,500	$2,200
1994-2004	New Rico-era	$1,400	$1,900
Nighthawk Bass			
1979-ca.1980. Bolt-neck.			
1978-1982		$725	$800
NJ Series Bass			
1983-2006. Various mid-level import models include Beast, Eagle, Innovator, Mockingbird, Virgin and Warlock. Replaced by NT Series.			
1983-1986		$325	$550
1987-1999		$300	$400
2000-2006		$300	$400
Platinum Series Bass			
1986-2006. Lower-priced import versions including Eagle, Mockingbird, Beast, Warlock.			
1986-1999		$250	$375

Austin AU875

BC Rich Heritage Classic Mockingbird

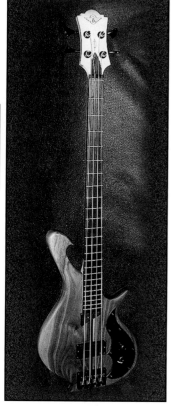

Birdsong Sadhana

Brown's Guitar Factory
Fretted/less

MODEL YEAR	FEATURES	EXC. COND. LOW	HIGH

Seagull/Seagull II Bass
1972-1977. Solidbody, single cut to '75, double Seagull II after.

| 1972-1975 | Initial design | $1,900 | $2,900 |
| 1976-1977 | Seagull II | $1,900 | $2,900 |

ST-III Bass
Available in bolt neck and non-bolt neck (1986 price at $999 & $1299 respectively), black hardware, P-Bass/J-Bass pickup configuration, 2 tone controls, 1 volume control, jumbo frets, ebony 'board.

1987-1989	Bolt-on	$675	$800
1987-1989	Neck-thru	$800	$900
1989-1998		$650	$800

Warlock Bass (U.S.A.)
1981-present. Introduced in '81 along with the Warlock guitar, USA-made, standard bolt-on model, maple body and neck, rosewood 'board, 22/accyruzer jumbo frets, Badass II low profile bridge by '88.

| 1981-1989 | | $1,000 | $1,700 |
| Wave Bass 1980s | | $1,800 | $2,200 |

Beltone
1950s-1960s. Japan's Teisco made a variety of brands for others, including the Beltone line of guitars, basses and amps. Italy's Welson guitars also marketed marble and glitter-finished guitars in the U.S. under this brand.

Benedict
1988-present. Founded by Roger Benedict. Professional and premium grade, production/custom, solidbody basses built by luthier Bill Hager in Cedar, Minnesota. They also build guitars.

Bernie Rico Jr. Guitars
Professional and premium grade, production/custom, solidbody basses built by luthier Bernie Rico, Jr. in Hesperia, California. His father founded BC Rich guitars. He also makes guitars.

Birdsong Guitars
2001-present. Luthiers Scott Beckwith and Jamie Hornbuckle build their intermediate and professional grade, production/custom, solidbody basses in Wimberley, Texas. They also build guitars.

Black Jack
1960s. Entry-level and mid-level imports from Japan. They also offered guitars.
Electric Solidbody Bass
| 1960s | Various models | $100 | $175 |

Blade
1987-present. Intermediate and professional grade, production, solidbody basses from luthier Gary Levinson's Levinson Music Products Ltd. in Switzerland. He also builds guitars.

Bolin
1978-present. See Guitars section for company history, bass models are similar to their guitar styles, such as the NS model, prices are similar to equivalent guitar values.

Bradford
1960s. House brand of W.T. Grant department store, often imported. They also offered guitars.
Electric Solidbody Bass
| 1960s | Various models | $125 | $175 |

Brawley Basses
Solidbody bass guitars designed by Keith Brawley and made in Korea. The company was headquartered in Temecula, California. They also made guitars.

Brian Moore
1992-present. Brian Moore added basses in '97. Currently they offer professional grade, production, solidbody basses. They also build guitars and mandolins.

Brice
1985-present. Budget grade, production, electric and acoustic basses imported by Rondo Music of Union, New Jersey.

Bridgecraft
2000s. Budget to low intermediate level imports.

Brown's Guitar Factory
1982-present. Luthier John Brown builds his professional and premium grade, production/custom, 4-, 5-, and 6-string solid and chambered body basses in Inver Grove Heights, Minnesota. He also builds guitars.

BSX Bass
1990-present. Luthier Dino Fiumara builds his professional and premium grade, production/custom, acoustic, solidbody, semi-solid upright basses in Aliquippa, Pennsylvania.

Bunker
1961-present. Luthier Dave Bunker builds intermediate, professional, and premium grade, production/custom, basses in Port Angeles, Washington. He also builds guitars.

Burns
1960-1970, 1974-1983, 1992-present. Intermediate and professional grade, production, basses built in England and Korea. They also build guitars.
Nu-Sonic Bass
1964-1965. Offset double-cut solidbody, 2 pickups.
| 1964-1965 | | $525 | $675 |
Scorpion Bass
2003-present. Double-cut scorpion-like solidbody.
| 2003-2005 | | $350 | $400 |

MODEL		EXC. COND.	
YEAR	FEATURES	LOW	HIGH

Burns-Weill

1959. Jim Burns and Henry Weill teamed up to produce three solidbody electrics and three solidbody basses under this English brand.

Burrell

1984-present. Luthier Leo Burrell builds his professional grade, production/custom, acoustic and solidbody basses in Huntington, West Virginia. He also builds guitars.

C. P. Thornton Basses

1985-1996. Solidbody basses and guitars built by luthier Chuck Thornton. He currently builds guitars under the C. P. Thornton Guitars brand in Turner, Maine.

Campellone

1978-present. Archtop guitar builder Mark Campellone, of Greenville, Rhode Island, built basses in the '70s.

Canvas

2004-present. Budget and intermediate grade, production, solidbody basses made in China. They also offer guitars.

Carvin

1946-present. Intermediate and Professional grade, production/custom, acoustic and electric basses. They also build guitars and amps.

Chandler

1984-present. Premium grade, production/custom, solidbody 12-string electric basses built by luthiers Paul and Adrian Chandler in Chico, California. They also build guitars, lap steels and effects.

Charles Shifflett Acoustic Guitars

1990-present. Luthier Charles Shifflett builds his premium grade, custom, acoustic basses in High River, Alberta. He also builds flat-top, classical, flamenco, resophonic, and harp guitars, and banjos.

Charvel

1976-present. U.S.-made from '78 to '85 and a combination of imports and U.S.-made post-'85. They also build guitars.

Early Pre-Pro Bass
1980-1981. Pre-mass production basses, made Nov. '80 to '81. Refer to Charvel guitar section for details.

1980-1981	All models	$1,500	$3,500

850 XL Bass
1988-1991. Four-string, neck-thru-body, active electronics.

1988-1991		$450	$550

MODEL		EXC. COND.	
YEAR	FEATURES	LOW	HIGH

CX-490 Bass
1991-1994. Double-cut, 4-string, bolt neck, red or white.

1991-1994		$275	$325

Eliminator Bass
1990-1991. Offset double-cut, active electronics, bolt neck.

1990-1991		$300	$325

Fusion Bass
1989-1991. 4- and 5-string models, active circuitry.

1989-1991	IV	$275	$325
1989-1991	V	$325	$350

Model 1 Bass
1986-1989. Double-cut, bolt neck, 1 pickup.

1986-1989		$325	$400

Model 2 Bass
1986-1989. Double-cut, bolt neck, 2 pickups.

1986-1989		$325	$400

Model 3 Bass
1986-1989. Neck-thru-body, 2 single-coil pickups, active circuitry, master volume, bass and treble knobs.

1986-1989		$325	$400

Model 5 Bass
1986-1989. Double-cut, P/J pickups.

1986-1989		$450	$550

San Dimas Serialized Plated Bass
1981-1982. Soft headstock early models.

1981-1982		$3,000	$3,500

SB-4 Bass
1990s. Offset double cut solid, long bass horn, 2 pickups.

1990s		$300	$325

Star Bass
1980-1981. Unique 4-point solidbody, 1 pickup, considered by Charvel collectors to be Charvel's only original early design.

1980-1981		$2,300	$2,800

Surfcaster Bass
1991-1994. Semi-hollow, lipstick tube pickups.

1991-1994		$750	$925

Cipher

1960s. Student market basses imported from Japan. They also made guitars.

Electric Solidbody Bass
1960s. Japanese imports.

1960s		$175	$225

Citron

1995-present. Luthier Harvey Citron (of Veillette-Citron fame) builds his professional and premium grade, production/custom basses in Woodstock, New York. He also builds solidbody guitars.

Clevinger

1982-present. Established by Martin Clevinger, Oakland, California. Mainly specializing in electric upright basses, but has offered bass guitars as well.

Clevinger Wide Six

Citron AE4

Cort GB-3

Crafter USA BA400EQL

College Line

One of many Lyon & Healy brands, made during the era of extreme design experimentation.

Monster (Style 2089) Bass

Early-1900s. 22" lower bout, flat-top guitar/bass, natural.

Year		Low	High
1915		$3,000	$5,000

Conklin

1984-present. Intermediate, professional, and premium grade, production/custom basses from luthier Bill Conklin, of Springfield, Missouri. Conklin also offers guitars. Conklin instruments are made in the U.S. and overseas.

Conrad

Ca.1968-1978. Student and mid-level copy basses imported by David Wexler, Chicago, Illinois. They also offered guitars, mandolins and banjos.

Model 40096 Acoustical Slimline Bass

1970s. 2 pickups.

Year	Low	High
1970s	$250	$300

Model 40177 Violin-Shaped Bass

1970s. Scroll headstock, 2 pickups.

Year	Low	High
1970s	$300	$400

Model 40224 Bumper Bass

1970s. Ampeg Dan Armstrong lucite copy.

Year	Low	High
1970s	$325	$400

Professional Bass

1970s. Offset double-cut.

Year	Low	High
1970s	$150	$250

Professional Bison Bass

1970s. Solidbody, 2 pickups.

Year	Low	High
1970s	$150	$250

Contessa

1960s. Acoustic, semi-hollow archtop, solidbody and bass guitars made in Germany. They also made banjos.

Coral

1967-1969. In '66 MCA bought Danelectro and in '67 introduced the Coral brand of guitars, basses and amps. The line included several solid and semi-solidbody basses.

Electric Solidbody Bass

Year	Low	High
1967-1969	$600	$650

Corey James Custom Guitars

2005-present. Professional and premium grade, production/custom solidbody basses built by luthier Corey James Moilanen in Davisburg, Michigan. He also builds guitars.

Cort

1973-present. North Brook, Illinois-based Cort offers intermediate and professional grade, production, acoustic and solidbody electric basses built in Korea. They also offer guitars.

Electric Solidbody Bass

Year	Features	Low	High
1973-1999	Various models	$175	$375

Crafter

2000-present. Intermediate grade, production, acoustic/electric bass from Hohner. They also offer guitars.

Crafter USA

1986-present. Intermediate grade, production, solidbody basses made in Korea. They also build guitars and amps.

Crestwood

1970s. Imported by La Playa Distributing Company of Detroit. Product line includes copies of the popular classical guitars, flat-tops, electric solidbodies and basses of the era.

Electric Bass

1970s. Includes models 2048, 2049, 2079, 2090, 2092, 2093, and 2098.

Year	Low	High
1970s	$225	$300

Crown

1960s. Violin-shaped hollowbody electrics, solidbody electric guitars and basses, possibly others. Imported from Japan.

Electric Solidbody Bass

Japanese imports.

Year	Low	High
1960s	$150	$300

CSR

1996-present. Luthiers Roger and Courtney Kitchens build their premium grade, production/custom, archtop and solidbody basses in Byron, Georgia. They also build guitars.

Cumpiano

1974-present. Professional and premium grade, custom steel-string and nylon-string guitars, and acoustic basses built by luthier William Cumpiano in Northampton, Massachusetts.

Curbow String Instruments

1994-present. Premium grade, production/custom, solidbody basses built by luthier Doug Somervell in Morganton, Georgia. They also offer a line of intermediate grade, production, Curbow basses made by Cort. Founded by Greg Curbow who passed away in '05. They also make guitars.

Custom

1980s. Line of solidbody guitars and basses introduced in the early-'80s by Charles Lawing and Chris Lovell, owners of Strings & Things in Memphis.

Custom Kraft

Late-1950s-1968. A house brand of St. Louis Music Supply, instruments built by Valco and others. They also offered guitars.

MODEL YEAR	FEATURES	EXC. COND. LOW	HIGH

Bone Buzzer Model 12178 Bass

Late 1960s. Symmetrical double-cut thin hollow body, lightning bolt f-holes, 4-on-a-side tuners, 2 pickups, sunburst or emerald sunburst.

1968		$325	$400

D'Agostino

1976-early 1990s. Import company established by Pat D'Agostino. Solidbodies imported from EKO Italy '77-'82, Japan '82-'84, and in Korea for '84 on. Overall, about 60% of guitars and basses were Japanese, 40% Korean.

Electric Solidbody Bass

1970s	Various models	$225	$400

Daion

1978-1985. Higher quality copy basses imported from Japan. Original designs introduced in '80s. They also had guitars.

Electric Bass

1978-1985	Various models	$400	$700

Daisy Rock

2001-present. Budget and intermediate grade, production, full-scale and 3/4 scale, solidbody, semi-hollow, and acoustic/electric basses. Founded by Tish Ciravolo as a Division of Schecter Guitars, initial offerings included daisy and heart-shaped electric guitars and basses.

Danelectro

1946-1969, 1997-present. Danelectro offered basses throughout most of its early history. In '96, the Evets Corporation, of San Clemente, California, introduced a line of Danelectro effects; amps, basses and guitars, many reissues of earlier instruments, soon followed. In early '03, Evets discontinued the guitar, bass and amp lines, but revived the guitar and bass line in '05. Danelectro also built the Coral brand instruments (see Coral).

Model 1444L Bass

Ca.1958-ca.1964. Masonite body, single-cut, 2 pickups, copper finish.

1958-1962		$800	$900
1963-1964		$700	$800

Model 3412 Shorthorn Bass

1958-ca.1966. Coke bottle headstock, 1 pickup, copper finish.

1958-1959		$825	$900
1960-1962		$800	$850
1963-1964		$725	$800
1965-1966		$675	$750

Model 3612 Shorthorn 6-String Bass

1958-ca.1966. Coke bottle headstock, 1 pickup, copper finish.

1958-1962		$1,600	$1,800
1963-1964		$1,400	$1,600
1965-1966		$1,300	$1,400

Model 4423 Longhorn Bass

1958-ca.1966. Coke bottle headstock, 2 pickups, copper finish.

1958-1959		$1,900	$2,500
1960-1962		$1,800	$2,400
1963-1964		$1,700	$2,300
1965-1966		$1,600	$2,200

'58 Longhorn Reissue/Longhorn Pro Bass

1997-2003. Reissues of classic Longhorn bass.

1997-2003		$275	$350

UB-2 6-String Bass

1956-1959. Single-cut, 2 pickups.

1956-1959		$1,700	$2,300

Dave Maize Acoustic

1991-present. Luthier Dave Maize builds his premium grade, production/custom, acoustic basses in Cave Junction, Oregon. He also builds flat-tops.

Dean

1976-present. Intermediate and professional grade, production, solidbody, hollowbody, acoustic, and acoustic/electric, basses made overseas. They also offer guitars, banjos, mandolins, and amps.

Baby ML Bass

1982-1986. Downsized version of ML.

1982-1986		$400	$425

Mach V Bass

1985-1986. U.S.-made pointed solidbody, 2 pickups, rosewood 'board.

1985-1986	U.S.-made	$900	$1,100

ML Bass

1977-1986, 2001-present. Futuristic body style, fork headstock.

1977-1983	U.S.-made	$1,400	$1,750
1984-1986	Korean import	$425	$450

Rhapsody Series (USA)

2001-2004. Scroll shaped offset double-cut, various models.

2001-2004	8-string	$300	$350
2001-2004	12-string	$350	$400
2001-2004	HFB fretless	$250	$300

Dean Markley

The string and pickup manufacturer offered a limited line of guitars and basses for a time in the late 1980s.

DeArmond

1999-2004. Electric basses based on Guild models and imported from Korea by Fender. They also offered guitars.

Decca

Mid-1960s. Solidbody basses imported from made in Japan by Teisco and imported by Decca Records, Decca headstock logo, student-level instruments. They also offered guitars and amps.

1968 Custom Kraft Bone Buzzer

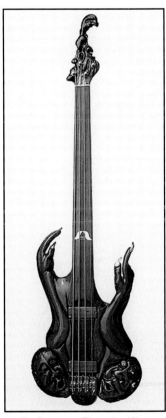

DeGennaro Thunder King

MODEL YEAR	FEATURES	EXC. COND. LOW	HIGH

Dingwall Super J

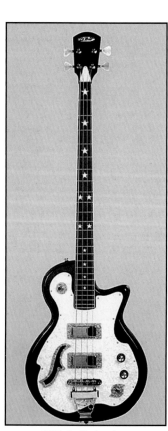
DiPinto Belvedere

DeGennaro
2003-present. Professional and premium grade, custom/production, solidbody basses built by luthier William Degennaro in Grand Rapids, Michigan. He also builds guitars and mandolins.

DeTemple
1995-present. Premium grade, production/custom, solidbody electric basses built by luthier Michael DeTemple in Sherman Oaks, California. He also builds guitars.

Dillon
1975-present. Professional and premium grade, custom, acoustic basses built by luthier John Dillon in Taos, New Mexico. He also builds guitars.

Dingwall
1988-present. Luthier Sheldon Dingwall, Saskatoon, Canada, started out producing guitar bodies and necks, eventually offering complete guitars and basses. Currently Dingwall offers professional to premium grade, production/custom 4-, 5-, and 6-string basses featuring the Novax Fanned-Fret System.

DiPinto
1995-present. Intermediate and professional grade, production retro-vibe basses from luthier Chris DiPinto of Philadelphia, Pennsylvania. He also builds guitars. Until late '99, all instruments built in the U.S., since then built in Korea and the U.S.

Domino
Ca. 1967-1968. Imported from Japan by Maurice Lipsky Music of New York, mainly copies, but some original designs. They also offered guitars.
Electric Bass
1967-1968. Includes the Beatle Bass and Fireball Bass, a Vox Phantom IV copy.
| 1967-1968 | | $325 | $400 |

Dorado
Ca. 1972-1973. Name used briefly by Baldwin/Gretsch on line of Japanese guitar and bass imports.
Electric Solidbody Bass
Japanese imports.
| 1970s | | $175 | $200 |

Dragonfly
1994-present. Professional grade, production/custom, acoustic basses built by luthier Dan Richter in Roberts Creek, British Columbia. He also builds guitars and dulcitars.

Duesenberg
1995-present. Professional grade, production/custom, hollow and semi-hollow basses built by luthier Dieter Goelsdorf in Hannover, Germany. They also build guitars.

Dynacord
1950-present. The German Dynacord company makes audio and pro sound amps, as well as other electronic equipment. In 1966-'67 they offered solidbody guitars and basses from the Welson Company of Italy. They also had the Cora guitar and bass which is the center part of a guitar body with a tube frame in a guitar outline. They also offered tape echo machines.

Earthwood
1972-1985. Acoustic designs by Ernie Ball with input from George Fullerton. One of the first to offer acoustic basses.
Acoustic Bass
1972-1985. Big bodied acoustic bass alternative between Kay double bass and solidbody Fender bass.
| 1972-1985 | | $1,225 | $1,500 |

Eastwood
1997-present. Budget and intermediate grade, production, imported solid and semi-hollowbody basses, many styled after 1960s models. They also offer guitars and mandolins.

EKO
1959-1985, 2000-present. Built by the Oliviero Pigini Company, Italy. Original importers included LoDuca Brothers, Milwaukee, Wisconsin. Since about 2000, production, acoustic and electric EKO basses are again available and made in Italy and China. They also make guitars and amps.
Cobra II Bass
1967-ca.1969. Offset double-cut solidbody, 2 pickups.
| 1967-1969 | | $400 | $450 |
Kadett Bass
1967-1978. Red or sunburst.
| 1967-1978 | | $450 | $550 |
Model 995/2 Violin Bass
1966-ca.1969.
| 1966-1969 | | $550 | $675 |
Model 1100/2 Bass
1961-1966. Jaguar-style plastic covered solidbody, 2 pickups, sparkle finish.
| 1961-1966 | | $550 | $650 |
Rocket IV/Rokes Bass
1967-early-1970s. Rocket-shape design, solidbody, says Rokes on the headstock, the Rokes were a popular English band that endorsed EKO guitars. Marketed as the Rocket IV in the U.S. and as the Rokes in Europe. Often called the Rok. Sunburst, 1 pickup.
| 1967-1971 | | $600 | $750 |

Electra
1971-1984. Imported basses from Japan by St. Louis Music. They also offered guitars.
Electric Solidbody Bass
Japanese imports, various models.
| 1970s | | $275 | $500 |

MODEL YEAR	FEATURES	EXC. COND. LOW	HIGH

MPC Outlaw Bass
1970s. Has 2 separate modules that plug in for different effects, neck-thru-body.

1970s		$500	$600

Emperador
1966-1992. Student-level basses imported by Westheimer Musical Instruments. Early models appear to be made by either Teisco or Kawai; later models were made by Cort. They also had guitars

Electric Solidbody Bass
Japanese imports, various models.

1960s	Beatle violin bass	$275	$425
1960s	Various models	$150	$225

Encore
Late 1970s-present. Budget grade, production, solidbody basses imported by John Hornby Skewes & Co. in the U.K. They also offer guitars.

Hollowbody Bass
1960s. Copy model, greenburst.

1960s		$275	$375

Engelhardt
Engelhardt specializes in student acoustic basses and cellos and is located in Elk Grove Village, Illinois.

Upright Acoustic Bass Viol
Various models.

1970s	EM-1 Maestro	$550	$600
1970s	M-3 3/4	$725	$775
1970s	Supreme	$1,050	$1,150

Epiphone
1928-present. Epiphone didn't add basses until 1959, after Gibson acquired the brand. The Gibson Epiphones were American-made until '69, then all imports until into the '80s, when some models were again made in the U.S. Currently Epiphone offers intermediate and professional grade, production, acoustic and electric basses.

B-5 Acoustic Bass Viol
1950s. 3/4-size laminate construction.

1950s		$3,200	$3,800

EB-0 Bass
1998-present. SG body style, single pickup, bolt-on neck.

1998-2004		$200	$275

EB-1
1998-2000. Violin-shaped mahogany body, 1 pickup,

1998-2000		$275	$325

EB-3 Bass
1999-present. SG body style, 2 pickups.

1999-2005		$300	$350

EBM-4 Bass
1991-1998. Alder body, maple neck, split humbucker, white.

1991-1998		$200	$275

MODEL YEAR	FEATURES	EXC. COND. LOW	HIGH

Elitist Series Bass
2003-2005. Higher-end appointments such as set-necks and USA pickups.

2003-2005	EB-3	$650	$900

Embassy Deluxe Bass
1963-1969. Solidbody, double-cut, 2 pickups, tune-o-matic bridge, cherry finish.

1963-1964		$1,800	$2,300
1965-1966		$1,550	$1,800
1967-1969		$1,400	$1,700

Explorer Korina Bass
2000-2001. Made in Korea, Gibson Explorer body style, genuine korina body, set neck, gold hardware.

2000-2001		$400	$500

Les Paul Special Bass
1997-present. LP Jr.-style slab body, single-cut, bolt neck, 2 humbuckers.

1997-2004		$275	$325

Newport Bass
1961-1970. Double-cut solidbody, 1 pickup (2 pickups optional until '63, two-on-a-side tuners until '63, four-on-a-side after that, cherry.

1961-1962		$1,800	$2,400
1963-1964		$1,600	$2,100
1965-1966		$1,350	$1,600
1965-1966	Custom color	$2,100	$2,600
1967-1969		$1,200	$1,500
1970		$1,150	$1,400

Rivoli Bass (1 Pickup)
1959-1970. ES-335-style semi-hollowbody bass, two-on-a-side tuners, 1 pickup (2 in '70), reissued in '94 as the Rivoli II.

1959		$3,000	$3,500
1960		$2,800	$3,300
1961		$2,400	$2,900
1964		$2,200	$2,700
1965		$1,900	$2,000
1966		$1,800	$1,900
1967-1969		$1,700	$1,800
1970		$1,300	$1,500

Rivoli Bass (2 Pickups)
1970 only. Double pickup Epiphone version of Gibson EB-2D.

1970	Sunburst	$1,900	$2,200

Thunderbird IV Bass
1997-present. Reverse-style mahogany body, 2 pickups, sunburst.

1997-2004		$425	$450

Viola Bass
1995-present. Beatle Bass 500/1 copy, sunburst.

1995-2006		$375	$450

ESP
1975-present. Intermediate, professional, and premium grade, production/custom, electric basses. Japan's ESP (Electric Sound Products) made inroads in the U.S. market with mainly copy styles in the early '80s, mixing in original designs over the years. In the '90s, ESP opened a California-based Custom Shop. They also build guitars.

Eastwood Airline

1967 Epiphone Embassy

BASSES

ESP Surveyor II

1966 Fender Bass V

MODEL YEAR	FEATURES	EXC. COND. LOW	HIGH

B-1 Bass
1990s. Vague DC-style slab solidbody with bolt-on neck, ESP and B-1 on headstock.

1990s		$525	$600

Horizon Bass
1987-1993. Offset double-cut solidbody, 4- and 5-string versions, active electronics, 34" scale

1987-1993	4-string	$400	$500

Essex (SX)
1985-present. Budget grade, production, electric basses imported by Rondo Music of Union, New Jersey. They also offer guitars.

Electric Solidbody Bass

1990s		$75	$100

Evergreen Mountain
1971-present. Professional grade, custom, acoustic basses built by luthier Jerry Nolte in Cove, Oregon. He also builds guitars and mandolins.

Farnell
1989-present. Luthier Al Farnell builds his professional grade, production, solidbody basses in Ontario, California. He also offers his intermediate grade, production, C Series which is imported from China. He also builds guitars.

Fender
1946-present. Intermediate, professional, and premium grade, production/custom, electric and acoustic basses made in the U.S. and overseas. Leo Fender is the father of the electric bass. The introduction of his Precision Bass in late '51 changed forever how music was performed, recorded and heard. Leo followed with other popular models of basses that continue to make up a large part of Fender's production. Please note that all the variations of the Jazz and Precision Basses are grouped under those general headings.

A custom color is worth more than a standard color. The first Precision Bass standard color was blond but changed to sunburst in the late 1950s. The Jazz Bass standard color is sunburst. To understand a custom color, you need to know what the standard color is. Some custom colors are more rare than others. Below is a list of the custom colors offered in 1960 by Fender. They are sorted in ascending order with the most valuable color, Shell Pink, listed last. In the 1960 list, Black and Blond are the least valuable and Shell Pink is the most valuable. A Fiesta Red is typically worth 12% more than a Black or Blond. In the rare color group a Foam Green is normally worth 8% more than a Shoreline Gold. The two very rare colors are often worth 30% more than a Shoreline Gold. In our pricing information we will list the standard color, then the relative value of a common custom color, and then the value of a rare custom color. Remember that the amount of fade also affects the price. These prices are for factory original custom colors with slight or no fade in excellent condition. Fade implies a lighter

MODEL YEAR	FEATURES	EXC. COND. LOW	HIGH

color, but with custom colors a faded example can also be much darker in color. Blue can fade to dark green. White can fade to deep yellow.

The Price Guide lists the standard color, plus the value of a Common Color and the value of a Rare Color. The list below defines which group a color falls into for 1960, and it is in ascending order so, for example, a Daphne Blue should be considered more valuable than a Lake Placid Blue, assuming they are in equal condition.

Common Color: Black, Blond, Olympic White, Lake Placid Blue, Dakota Red, Daphne Blue, Fiesta Red

Rare Color: Shoreline Gold, Inca Silver Burgundy Mist, Sherwood Green, Sonic Blue, Foam Green

Rare (Very Rare) Color: Surf Green, Shell Pink

Ashbory Bass
2003-present. Unique-shaped travel bass, Ashbory logo on body, Fender logo on back of headstock, previously sold under Fender's DeArmond brand.

2005-2006		$150	$175

Bass V
1965-1970. Five strings, double-cut, 1 pickup, dot inlay '65-'66, block inlay '66-'70. Please refer to the beginning of the Fender Bass Section for details on Fender color options.

1965	Common color	$4,000	$5,000
1965	Rare color	$5,000	$7,000
1965	Sunburst	$3,200	$4,000
1966-1967	Common color	$3,100	$4,000
1966-1967	Rare color	$4,000	$5,500
1966-1967	Sunburst, block inlay	$2,300	$2,800
1966-1967	Sunburst, dot inlay	$2,400	$3,200
1968-1970	Common color	$3,000	$3,900
1968-1970	Rare color	$3,900	$5,000
1968-1970	Sunburst	$2,200	$2,700

Bass VI
1961-1975. Six strings, Jazzmaster-like body, 3 pickups, dot inlay until '66, block inlay '66-'75. Reintroduced as Japanese-made Collectable model '95-'98. Please refer to the beginning of the Fender Bass Section for details on Fender color options.

1961-1962	Common color	$10,000	$12,000
1961-1962	Rare color	$12,000	$15,000
1961-1962	Sunburst	$6,300	$7,300
1963-1964	Common color	$8,000	$11,000
1963-1964	Rare color	$11,000	$14,000
1963-1964	Sunburst	$5,000	$6,200
1965	Common color	$5,500	$8,000
1965	Rare color	$8,000	$10,000
1965	Sunburst	$4,000	$4,500
1966	Common color	$4,500	$7,000
1966	Rare color	$7,000	$9,000
1966	Sunburst, block inlay	$3,200	$3,600
1966	Sunburst, dot inlay	$3,300	$3,900
1967-1969	Common color	$4,000	$6,000
1967-1969	Rare color	$6,000	$8,000
1967-1969	Sunburst	$3,000	$3,700

MODEL YEAR	FEATURES	EXC. COND. LOW	HIGH
1970-1971	Common color	$3,500	$5,000
1970-1971	Rare color	$5,000	$7,000
1970-1971	Sunburst	$2,900	$3,600
1972-1974	Natural, walnut	$2,300	$2,600
1972-1974	Other custom colors	$2,800	$3,600
1972-1974	Sunburst	$2,500	$2,800
1975	Natural, walnut	$1,800	$2,200
1975	Olympic White, black, blond	$2,300	$2,800
1975	Sunburst	$2,100	$2,600

Bass VI Reissue
1995-1998. Import, sunburst.

1995-1998		$1,200	$1,400

BG Series Bass
1995-present. Acoustic flat-top bass, single-cut, two-on-a-side tuners, Fishman on-board controls, black.

1995-2006	BG-29	$300	$375
1995-2006	BG-31	$300	$375

Bronco Squier Bass
2007. Squier Bronco logo on headstock, single coil plastic cover pickup, 3/4 body.

2007		$120	$130

Bullet Bass (B30, B34, B40)
1982-1983. Alder body, 1 pickup, offered in short- and long-scale, red or walnut. U.S.-made, replaced by Japanese-made Squire Bullet Bass.

1982-1983		$400	$425

Bullet Squier Bass
1980s. Japanese-made, Squier-branded, replaces Bullet Bass, black.

1980s		$225	$275

Coronado I Bass
1966-1970. Thinline, double-cut, 1 pickup, dot inlay, sunburst and cherry red were the standard colors, but custom colors could be ordered.

1966-1970	Cherry red, sunburst	$900	$1,100
1966-1970	Custom colors	$1,150	$1,400

Coronado II Bass
1967-1972. Two pickups, block inlay, sunburst and cherry red standard colors, but custom colors could be ordered. Only Antigua finish offered from '70 on.

1967-1969	Cherry red, sunburst	$1,400	$1,550
1967-1969	Custom colors	$1,475	$1,800
1967-1969	Wildwood option	$1,475	$1,800
1970-1972	Antigua only	$1,275	$1,550

HM Bass
1989-1991. Japanese-made, 4 strings (IV) or 5 strings (V), basswood body, no 'guard, 3 Jazz Bass pickups, 5-way switch, master volume, master TBX, sunburst.

1989-1991	IV, 4-string	$350	$425
1989-1991	V, 5-string	$375	$450

Jazz Bass
The following are variations of the Jazz Bass. The first four listings are for the main U.S.-made models. All others are listed alphabetically after that in the following order:

Jazz Bass

Standard Jazz Bass
American Standard Jazz Bass
American Series Jazz Bass
American Series Jazz V Bass
50th Anniversary American Standard Jazz Bass
'60s Jazz Bass (Japan)
'62 Jazz Bass
'64 Jazz Bass (Custom Shop)
'75 Jazz Bass American Vintage Series
Aerodyne Jazz Bass
American Deluxe Jazz Bass
American Deluxe FMT Jazz Bass
American Deluxe Jazz V Bass
Custom Classic Jazz IV/Jazz V Bass
Deluxe Jazz Bass (Active)
Deluxe Jazz Bass V (Active)
Deluxe Power Jazz Bass
Foto Flame Jazz Bass
Geddy Lee Signature Jazz Bass
Gold Jazz Bass
Highway One Jazz Bass
Jazz Plus Bass
Jazz Plus V Bass
Jazz Special Bass (Import)
Marcus Miller Signature Jazz Bass
Noel Redding Signature Jazz Bass
Reggie Hamilton Jazz Bass
Roscoe Beck Jazz IV/V Bass
Squier Jazz Bass
Standard Jazz Bass (Later Model)
Standard Jazz Fretless Bass (Later Model)
Standard Jazz V Bass (Later Model)
Ventures Limited Edition Jazz Bass
Victor Baily Jazz Bass

Jazz Bass
1960-1981. Two stack knobs '60-'62, 3 regular controls '62 on. Dot markers '60-'66, block markers from '66 on. Rosewood 'board standard, but maple available from '68 on. With the introduction of vintage reissue models in '81, Fender started calling the American-made version the Standard Jazz Bass. That became the American Standard Jazz Bass in '88 and then became the American Series Jazz Bass in 2000. Renamed back to the American Standard Jazz Bass in '08.

Post '71 Jazz Bass values are affected more by condition than color or neck option. The Jazz Bass was fitted with a 3-bolt neck or bullet rod in late-'74. Prices assume a 3-bolt neck starting in '75. Please refer to the beginning of the Fender Bass Section for details on Fender color options.

1960	Common color	$27,000	$33,000
1960	Rare color	$33,000	$45,000
1960	Sunburst	$20,000	$25,000
1961-1962	Common color, stack knob	$23,000	$28,000
1961-1962	Rare color, stack knob	$28,000	$38,000
1961-1962	Sunburst, stack knob	$19,000	$24,000

1967 Fender Coronado II

1967 Fender Jazz Bass

Fender Aerodyne Jazz Bass

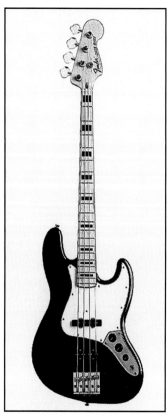

Fender Geddy Lee
Signature Jazz Bass

MODEL YEAR	FEATURES	EXC. COND. LOW	HIGH
1962	Common color, 3 knob	$19,000	$23,000
1962	Rare color, 3 knob	$23,000	$34,000
1962	Sunburst, 3 knob	$15,000	$17,000
1963-1964	Common color	$14,000	$18,000
1963-1964	Rare color	$18,000	$28,000
1963-1964	Sunburst	$11,500	$13,000
1965	Common color	$11,000	$14,000
1965	Rare color	$14,000	$20,000
1965	Sunburst	$8,500	$10,000
1966	Common color	$11,000	$14,000
1966	Rare color	$14,000	$18,000
1966	Sunburst, blocks	$7,000	$8,000
1966	Sunburst, dots	$8,000	$10,000
1967	Common color	$8,000	$10,000
1967	Rare color	$10,000	$14,000
1967	Sunburst	$7,000	$8,000
1968	Common color	$7,500	$9,500
1968	Rare color	$9,500	$13,000
1968	Sunburst	$6,500	$7,000
1969	Common color	$6,000	$7,500
1969	Rare color	$7,500	$12,000
1969	Sunburst	$5,500	$6,000
1970	Common color	$4,300	$5,100
1970	Rare color	$5,100	$6,900
1970	Sunburst	$3,700	$4,000
1971	Common color	$3,600	$4,300
1971	Rare color	$4,300	$5,500
1971	Sunburst	$3,200	$3,400
1972	Common color	$3,200	$3,900
1972	Sunburst	$2,800	$3,100
1973	Natural, walnut	$1,900	$2,300
1973	Other custom colors	$2,700	$3,600
1973	Sunburst	$2,500	$2,900
1974	Natural, walnut	$1,800	$2,200
1974	Other custom colors	$2,500	$3,500
1974	Sunburst, 3-bolt neck, late-'74	$2,300	$2,600
1974	Sunburst, 4-bolt neck	$2,500	$2,900
1975-1977	Black, blond, white, wine, 3-bolt neck	$2,300	$2,800
1975-1977	Natural, walnut, 3-bolt neck	$1,700	$2,200
1975-1977	Sunburst, 3-bolt neck	$2,200	$2,500
1978-1979	Antigua	$2,200	$2,600
1978-1979	Black, blond, white, wine	$2,000	$2,500
1978-1979	Natural	$1,400	$1,900
1978-1979	Sunburst, 3-bolt neck	$1,900	$2,200
1980	Antigua	$2,100	$2,500
1980	Black, white, wine	$1,650	$2,050
1980	Natural	$1,500	$1,800
1980	Sunburst, 3-bolt neck	$1,575	$1,975

MODEL YEAR	FEATURES	EXC. COND. LOW	HIGH
1981	Black and Gold Collector's Edition	$1,400	$2,200
1981	Black, white, wine	$1,400	$1,750
1981	International colors	$1,500	$2,000
1981	Sunburst	$1,500	$1,850

Standard Jazz Bass

1981-1985. Replaced Jazz Bass ('60-'81) and replaced by the American Standard Jazz Bass in '88. Name now used on import version. Please refer to the beginning of the Fender Bass Section for details on Fender color options.

1981-1982	Black, white, wine	$1,400	$1,750
1981-1982	Rare colors	$1,750	$2,200
1982	Gold Edition, top jack	$2,100	$2,600
1982-1984	Top mounted input jack	$900	$1,125
1985	Japan import	$475	$575

American Standard Jazz Bass

1988-2000. Replaced Standard Jazz Bass ('81-'88) and replaced by the American Series Jazz Bass in '00. Various colors.

1988-1989		$850	$1,100
1990-1999		$700	$800

American Series Jazz Bass

2000-2007. Replaces American Standard Jazz Bass. Renamed American Standard in '08.

2000-2007		$650	$750

American Series Jazz V Bass

2000-2007. 5-string version.

2000-2007		$650	$750

50th Anniversary American Standard Jazz Bass

1996. Regular American Standard with gold hardware, 4- or 5-string, gold 50th Anniversary commemorative neck plate, rosewood 'board, sunburst.

1996	IV or V	$850	$1,100

'60s Jazz Bass (Japan)

2001-present. '60s features, rosewood 'board.

2001-2006		$650	$700

'62 Jazz Bass

1982-present. U.S.A.-made, reissue of '62 Jazz Bass. Please refer to the beginning of the Fender Bass Section for details on Fender color options.

1982-1985	Standard colors	$1,150	$1,250
1986-1989	Standard colors	$1,150	$1,250
1990-1999	Rare colors	$1,250	$1,450
1990-1999	Standard colors	$1,150	$1,250
2000-2006	Standard colors	$1,100	$1,175

'64 Jazz Bass (Custom Shop)

1998-present. Alder body, rosewood 'board, tortoise shell 'guard. From June '95 to June '99 Relic work was done outside of Fender by Vince Cunetto and included a certificate noting model and year built, an instrument without the certificate is worth less than the value shown.

1998-1999	Relic (Cunetto)	$1,900	$2,200
2000-2006	Closet Classic option	$1,700	$1,900
2000-2006	N.O.S option	$1,600	$1,800
2000-2006	Relic option	$1,900	$2,100

The *Vintage Guitar Price Guide* shows low to high values for items in all-original excellent condition, and, where applicable, with original case or cover.

BASSES

MODEL YEAR / FEATURES	EXC. COND. LOW	HIGH
'75 Jazz Bass American Vintage Series		
1994-present. Maple neck with black block markers.		
1994-2003	$1,100	$1,175
Aerodyne Jazz Bass		
2003-present. Bound basswood body, P/J pickups, Deluxe Series.		
2003-2004	$500	$550
American Deluxe Jazz Bass		
1998-present. Made in the U.S.A., active electronics, alder or ash body. Alder body colors - sunburst or transparent red, ash body colors - white, blond, transparent teal green or transparent purple.		
1998-1999	$850	$950
2000-2004	$850	$975
American Deluxe FMT Jazz Bass		
2001-2006. Flame maple top version (FMT), active EQ, dual J pickups.		
2001-2006	$975	$1,025
American Deluxe Jazz V Bass		
1998-present. Five-string model, various colors.		
1998-2004	$875	$975
Custom Classic Jazz IV/Jazz V Bass		
2001-2005	$1,000	$1,050
Deluxe Jazz Bass (Active)		
1995-present. Made in Mexico, active electronics, various colors.		
1995-2004	$300	$400
Deluxe Jazz Bass V (Active)		
1995-present. Made in Mexico, various colors.		
1995-2004	$325	$425
Deluxe Power Jazz Bass		
2006. Part of Deluxe Series with Fishman piezo power bridge.		
2006	$575	$625
Foto Flame Jazz Bass		
1994-1996. Japanese import, alder and basswood body with Foto Flame figured wood image.		
1994-1996	$500	$625
Geddy Lee Signature Jazz Bass		
1998-present. Limited run import in '98, now part of Artist Series, black.		
1998-2003	$575	$600
2004-2007	$600	$650
Gold Jazz Bass		
1981-1984. Gold finish and gold-plated hardware.		
1981-1984	$1,175	$1,475
Highway One Jazz Bass		
2003-present. U.S.-made, alder body, satin lacquer finish.		
2003-2004	$550	$600
Jazz Plus Bass		
1990-1994. Alder body, 2 Lace Sensors, active electronics, rotary circuit selector, master volume, balance, bass boost, bass cut, treble boost, treble cut, various colors.		
1990-1994	$625	$800
Jazz Plus V Bass		
1990-1994. Five-string version.		
1990-1994	$650	$825

MODEL YEAR / FEATURES	EXC. COND. LOW	HIGH
Jazz Special Bass (Import)		
1984-1991. Japanese-made, Jazz/Precision hybrid, Precision-shaped basswood body, Jazz neck (fretless available), 2 P/J pickups, offered with active (Power) or passive electronics.		
1984-1991	$450	$500
Marcus Miller Signature Jazz Bass		
1998-present.		
1998-2007 Import	$525	$575
2006 U.S.A Custom Shop	$1,400	$1,600
Noel Redding Signature Jazz Bass		
1997. Limited Edition import, artist signature on 'guard, sunburst, rosewood 'board.		
1997	$550	$650
Reggie Hamilton Jazz Bass		
2005-present. Alder body, C-profile neck, passive/active switch and pan control.		
2005	$600	$675
Roscoe Beck Jazz IV/V Bass		
1997-present. 5-string version offered '97-'06 , 4-string '04-present		
1997-2006 5-string	$1,000	$1,100
2004-2006 4-string	$950	$1,000
Squier Jazz Bass		
1980s-present. Jazz bass import, without cover plates, various colors.		
1980-2000s	$125	$175
Standard Jazz Bass (Later Model)		
1988-present. Imported from various countries. Not to be confused with '81-'88 American-made model with the same name.		
1988-1999	$150	$275
2000-2004	$150	$275
Standard Jazz Fretless Bass (Later Model)		
1994-present. Fretless version.		
1994-2004	$175	$300
Standard Jazz V Bass (Later Model)		
1998-present. 5-string, import model.		
1998-2004	$175	$300
Ventures Limited Edition Jazz Bass		
1996. Made in Japan, part of Ventures guitar and bass set, dark purple.		
1996	$925	$1,000
Victor Baily Jazz Bass		
2002-present. Koa, rosewood and mahogany body, fretless with white fret markers.		
2002-2005	$1,050	$1,150
JP-90 Bass		
1990-1994. Two P/J pickups, rosewood fretboard, poplar body, black or red.		
1990-1994	$450	$550
MB Bass		
1994-1995 Japan	$350	$425
Musicmaster Bass		
1970-1983. Shorter scale, solidbody, 1 pickup. various colors.		
1970-1983	$750	$800

1987 Fender Jazz Special Bass

Fender Victor Bailey Jazz Bass

1953 Fender Precision Bass

1962 Fender Precision Bass (Shoreline Gold)

MODEL YEAR	FEATURES	EXC. COND. LOW	HIGH

Mustang Bass

1966-1982. Shorter scale, solidbody, 1 pickup, offered in standard and competition colors, (competition colors refer to racing stripes on the body).

1966-1969		$1,700	$2,000
1970-1979		$1,375	$1,475
1980-1982		$1,075	$1,375

Mustang Bass (Japan)

2002-present. Alder body, '60s features.

2002-2006		$475	$500

Performer Bass

1985-1986. Swinger-like body style, active electronics, various colors.

1985-1986		$800	$950

Precision Bass

The following are variations of the Precision Bass. The first four listings are for the main U.S.-made models. All others are listed alphabetically after that in the following order:

Precision Bass
Standard Precision Bass
American Standard Precision Bass
American Series Precision Bass
40th Anniversary Precision Bass (Custom Shop)
50th Anniversary American Standard Precision Bass
50th Anniversary Precision Bass
'51 Precision Bass
'55 Precision Bass (Custom Shop)
'57 Precision Bass
'57 Precision Bass (Import)
'59 Precision Bass (Custom Shop)
'62 Precision Bass
'62 Precision Bass (Import)
Aerodyne Classic Precision Special Bass
American Deluxe Precision Bass
American Deluxe Precision V Bass
Big Block Precision Bass
Deluxe P-Bass Special
Elite I Precision Bass
Elite II Precision Bass
Foto Flame Precision Bass
Gold Elite I Precision Bass
Gold Elite II Precision Bass
Highway One Precision Bass
Precision Bass Jr.
Precision Bass Lyte
Precision Special Bass (Mexico)
Precision Special Bass (U.S.A.)
Precision U.S. Deluxe/Plus Deluxe Bass
Precision U.S. Plus/Plus Bass
Squier Precision Special Bass
Squier Precision V Special Bass
Standard Precision Bass (Later Model)
Sting Precision Bass
Walnut Elite I Precision Bass
Walnut Elite II Precision Bass
Walnut Precision Special Bass

MODEL YEAR	FEATURES	EXC. COND. LOW	HIGH

Precision Bass

1951-1981. Slab body until '54, 1-piece maple neck standard until '59, optional after '69, rosewood 'board standard '59 on (slab until mid-'62, curved after), blond finish standard until '54, sunburst standard after that (2-tone '54-'58, 3-tone after '58). Replaced by the Standard Precision Bass in '81-'85, then the American Standard Precision in '88-'00, and the American Series Precision Bass in '00-'08. Renamed American Standard again in '08. Unlike the Jazz and Telecaster Basses, the Precision was never fitted with a 3-bolt neck or bullet rod. Please refer to the beginning of the Fender Bass Section for details on Fender color options.

1951	Butterscotch blond, slab body	$22,000	$27,000
1952	Butterscotch blond, slab body	$18,000	$22,000
1953	Butterscotch blond, slab body	$17,000	$22,000
1954	Blond, slab body	$15,000	$20,000
1955	Blond, contour body	$14,000	$18,000
1956	Blond, contour body	$14,000	$18,000
1956	Sunburst	$13,000	$17,000
1957	Blond, last full year	$14,000	$18,000
1957	Sunburst, anodized guard late '57	$13,000	$17,000
1957	Sunburst, white guard early '57	$13,000	$17,000
1958	Blond option	$13,000	$17,000
1958	Sunburst, anodized guard	$13,000	$17,000
1959	Blond	$13,000	$17,000
1959	Sunburst	$12,000	$16,000
1959	Sunburst, anodized guard	$13,000	$17,000
1960	Blond	$13,000	$16,000
1960	Custom color	$21,000	$26,000
1960	Sunburst	$12,000	$15,000
1961	Common color	$15,000	$19,000
1961	Rare color	$19,000	$25,000
1961	Sunburst	$11,000	$14,000
1962	Common color, curved	$10,000	$14,000
1962	Common color, slab	$13,000	$17,000
1962	Rare color, curved	$14,000	$22,000
1962	Rare color, slab	$17,000	$24,000
1962	Sunburst, curved	$7,500	$9,400
1962	Sunburst, slab	$10,000	$11,500
1963-1964	Common color	$7,500	$11,000
1963-1964	Rare color	$11,000	$21,000
1963-1964	Sunburst	$7,400	$7,500
1965	Common color	$7,500	$10,000
1965	Rare color	$10,000	$16,000
1965	Sunburst	$6,500	$7,400
1966	Common color	$6,700	$8,200

MODEL YEAR	FEATURES	EXC. COND. LOW	HIGH
1966	Rare color	$8,200	$11,000
1966	Sunburst	$6,200	$6,700
1967	Common color	$6,200	$7,500
1967	Rare color	$7,500	$9,500
1967	Sunburst	$5,500	$6,200
1968	Common color	$5,500	$7,000
1968	Rare color	$7,000	$9,000
1968	Sunburst	$5,000	$5,500
1969	Common color	$4,500	$5,500
1969	Rare color	$5,500	$8,500
1969	Sunburst	$4,000	$4,500
1970	Common color	$3,500	$4,500
1970	Rare color	$4,500	$6,500
1970	Sunburst	$3,000	$3,500
1971	Common color	$3,000	$3,600
1971	Rare color	$3,600	$4,500
1971	Sunburst	$2,500	$3,000
1972	Common color	$2,900	$3,500
1972	Sunburst	$2,400	$2,900
1973	Color option	$2,200	$3,300
1973	Natural, walnut	$2,100	$2,400
1973	Sunburst	$2,200	$2,800
1974	Color option	$2,100	$3,200
1974	Natural, walnut	$2,100	$2,400
1974	Sunburst	$2,100	$2,700
1975-1977	Black, blond, Olympic White, wine	$2,100	$2,700
1975-1977	Natural, walnut	$1,600	$2,100
1975-1977	Sunburst	$1,900	$2,300
1978-1979	Antigua	$2,100	$2,500
1978-1979	Black, blond, Olympic White, wine	$1,900	$2,300
1978-1979	Natural, walnut	$1,300	$1,800
1978-1979	Sunburst	$1,600	$2,100
1980	Antigua	$2,000	$2,400
1980	Black, Olympic White, wine	$1,600	$2,000
1980	Natural	$1,400	$1,700
1980	Sunburst	$1,450	$1,800
1981	Black & gold	$1,300	$2,100
1981	Black, Olympic White, wine	$1,300	$1,700
1981	International colors	$1,400	$1,900
1981	Sunburst	$1,500	$1,800

Standard Precision Bass

1981-1985. Replaces Precision Bass, various colors. Replaced by American Standard Precision '88-'00. The Standard name is used on import Precision model for '88-present.

MODEL YEAR	FEATURES	EXC. COND. LOW	HIGH
1981-1984	Top mount jack	$900	$1,100
1985	Japan import	$475	$575

American Standard Precision Bass

1988-2000. Replaces Standard Precision Bass, replaced by American Series Precision in '00.

1988-1989	Blond, gold hardware	$900	$1,150
1988-1989	Various colors	$850	$1,100
1990-2000	Various colors	$700	$800

American Series Precision Bass

2000-2007. Replaces American Standard Precision Bass, various colors. Renamed American Standard in '08.

MODEL YEAR	FEATURES	EXC. COND. LOW	HIGH
2000-2004		$650	$750
2005-2007	S-1 coil switching option	$800	$825

40th Anniversary Precision Bass (Custom Shop)

1991. 400 made, quilted amber maple top, gold hardware.

1991		$1,400	$1,500

50th Anniversary American Standard Precision Bass

1996. Regular American Standard with gold hardware, 4- or 5-string, gold 50th Anniversary commemorative neck plate, rosewood 'board, sunburst.

1996		$850	$1,100

50th Anniversary Precision Bass

2001. Commemorative certificate with date and serial number, butterscotch finish, ash body, maple neck, black 'guard.

2001	With certificate	$900	$1,700

'51 Precision Bass

2003-present. Import from Japan, does not include pickup or bridge covers as part of the package, blond or sunburst.

1994		$450	$500
2003		$350	$425

'55 Precision Bass (Custom Shop)

2003-2006. 1955 specs including oversized 'guard, 1-piece maple neck/fretboard, preproduction bridge and pickup covers, single-coil pickup. Offered in N.O.S., Closet Classic or highest-end Relic.

2003-2006	Closet Classic	$1,700	$1,900
2003-2006	N.O.S.	$1,600	$1,800
2003-2006	Relic	$1,900	$2,100

'57 Precision Bass

1982-present. U.S.-made reissue, various colors.

1982-1989	Standard colors	$1,300	$1,400
1990-1999	Standard colors	$1,200	$1,300

'57 Precision Bass (Import)

1984-1986. Foreign-made, black.

1984-1986		$550	$675

'59 Precision Bass (Custom Shop)

2003-present. Custom Shop built with late-'59 specs, rosewood 'board.

2003	Closet Classic	$1,700	$1,900
2003	N.O.S.	$1,600	$1,800
2003	Relic	$1,900	$2,100

'62 Precision Bass

1982-present. U.S.-made reissue of '62 Precision, alder body.

1982-1989	Mary Kaye Blond, gold hardware	$1,250	$1,350
1982-1999	Rare colors	$1,250	$1,450
1982-1999	Standard colors	$1,150	$1,250
1999	Mars Music custom color	$1,250	$1,450
2000-2006	Standard colors	$1,100	$1,175

1966 Fender Precision Bass

1978 Fender Precision Bass (Antigua)

BASSES

1983 Fender Elite II Precision

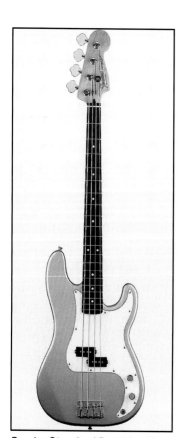

Fender Standard Precision Bass

MODEL YEAR	FEATURES	EXC. COND. LOW	HIGH

'62 Precision Bass (Import)
1984-1986. Foreign-made, black.

1984-1986		$550	$675

Aerodyne Classic Precision Special Bass
2006. Made in Japan, logo states Precision Bass and Aerodyne P Bass, radiused figured maple top, matching headstock, basswood body, P-J pickups, white 'guard.

2006		$500	$550

American Deluxe Precision Bass
1998-present. Made in U.S.A., active electronics, alder or ash body. Alder body colors - sunburst or transparent red. Ash body colors - white blond, transparent teal green or transparent purple.

1998-1999		$850	$950
2000-2004		$850	$975

American Deluxe Precision V Bass
1999-2004. 5-string version.

1999-2004		$850	$975

Big Block Precision Bass
2005-present. Pearloid block markers, black finish with matching headstock, 1 double Jazz Bass humbucker, bass and treble boost and cut controls.

2005-2007		$575	$650

Deluxe P-Bass Special
1995-present. Made in Mexico, P/J pickups, Jazz Bass neck.

1995-2003		$300	$400

Elite I Precision Bass
1983-1985. The Elite Series feature active electronics and noise-cancelling pickups, ash body, 1 pickup, various colors.

1983-1985		$950	$1,000

Elite II Precision Bass
1983-1985. Ash body, 2 pickups, various colors.

1983-1985		$1,000	$1,125

Foto Flame Precision Bass
1994-1996. Made in Japan, simulated woodgrain finish, natural or sunburst.

1994-1996		$500	$625

Gold Elite I Precision Bass
1983-1985. The Elite Series feature active electronics and noise-cancelling pickups, gold-plated hardware version of the Elite Precision I, 1 pickup.

1983-1985		$1,100	$1,150

Gold Elite II Precision Bass
1983-1985. Two pickup version.

1983-1985		$1,150	$1,250

Highway One Precision Bass
2003-present. U.S.-made, alder body, satin lacquer finish.

2003-2004		$550	$600

Precision Bass Jr.
2004-2006. 3/4 size.

2004-2006		$250	$275

Precision Bass Lyte
1992-2001. Japanese-made, smaller, lighter basswood body, 2 pickups, sunburst.

1992-2001		$450	$500

Precision Special Bass (Mexico)
1997-1998. 1 P- and 1 J-pickup. chrome hardware.

1997-1998		$250	$300

Precision Special Bass (U.S.A.)
1980-1983. Gold hardware, matching headstock, active electronics.

1980-1983		$900	$1,100

Precision U.S. Deluxe/Plus Deluxe Bass
1991-1994. P-style bass with P-bass and Jazz bass pickups, concentric knobs, no 'guard models available, various colors.

1991-1994		$650	$700

Precision U.S. Plus/Plus Bass
1989-1992. P-style bass with P- and J-bass pickup, model variations, black.

1989-1992		$675	$750

Squier Precision Special Bass
1999-present. Agathis body, P/J pickups.

1999-2004		$125	$150

Squier Precision V Special Bass
2000-present. 5-string version.

2000-2004		$150	$175

Standard Precision Bass (Later Model)
1987-present. Traditional style, import, currently made in Mexico. Not to be confused with '81-'85 American-made model with the same name.

1987-2000s		$150	$275

Sting Precision Bass
2001-present. Made in Japan, 2-tone sunburst, 1 single-coil, Sting's signature.

2001-2004		$500	$575

Walnut Elite I Precision Bass
1983-1985. The Elite Series feature active electronics and noise-cancelling pickups. Walnut body, 1 pickup, rosewood 'board, natural.

1983-1985		$1,400	$1,700

Walnut Elite II Precision Bass
1983-1985. Two-pickup version.

1983-1985		$1,700	$1,900

Walnut Precision Special Bass
1980-1983. Precision Bass Special with a walnut body, natural.

1980-1983		$1,400	$1,700

Prodigy/Prodigy Active Bass
1992-1995. Poplar body, 1 J- and 1 P-style pickup, active.

1992-1995		$425	$525

Stu Hamm Urge Bass (U.S.A.)
1992-1999. Contoured Precision-style body with smaller wide treble cutaway, J and P pickups, 32" scale.

1992-1999		$800	$900

Stu Hamm Urge II Bass (U.S.A.)
1999-present. J and P pickups, 34" scale.

1999-2004		$800	$900

Telecaster Bass
1968-1979. Slab solidbody, 1 pickup, fretless option '70, blond and custom colors available (Pink Paisley or Blue Floral '68-'69). Please refer to the beginning of the Fender Bass Section for details on Fender color options.

1968	Black	$3,600	$4,400
1968	Blond	$3,500	$4,300
1968	Blue Floral, Paisley	$6,500	$8,000
1968	Lake Placid Blue	$6,000	$7,000

MODEL YEAR	FEATURES	EXC. COND. LOW	HIGH
1969	4-bolt, single-coil	$3,200	$3,900
1970	4-bolt, single-coil	$3,100	$3,800
1971	4-bolt, single-coil	$3,000	$3,700
1972	4-bolt, single-coil	$2,900	$3,600
1973-1974	3-bolt, humbucker	$2,700	$3,300
1973-1974	Rare color, 3-bolt, humbucker	$3,000	$3,600
1975-1976	3-bolt, humbucker	$2,500	$2,900
1977-1979	3-bolt, humbucker	$2,000	$2,500

Fernandes

1969-present. Intermediate and professional grade, production, solidbody basses. Established '69 in Tokyo. Early efforts were classical guitars, but they now offer a variety of guitars and basses.

Electric Bass

1969-2005	Higher-end models	$250	$450
1969-2005	Standard models	$125	$150

Fina

Production acoustic basses built at the Kwo Hsiao Music Wooden Factory in Huiyang City, Guang Dong, mainland China. They also build guitars.

First Act

1995-present. Budget and professional grade, production/custom, basses built in China and their Custom Shop in Boston. They also make guitars, violins, and other instruments.

Fleishman Instruments

1974-present. Premium and presentation grade, acoustic and solidbody basses made by luthier Harry Fleishman in Sebastopol, California. He also offers electric uprights, designed by him and built in China. Fleishman also designs basses for others and is the director of Luthiers School International. He also builds guitars.

Fodera

1983-present. Luthiers Vinnie Fodera and Joseph Lauricella build their professional and premium grade, production/custom, solidbody basses in Brooklyn, New York.

Framus

1946-1975, 1996-present. Professional and premium grade, production/custom, basses made in Germany. They also build guitars and amps.

Atlantic Model 5/140 Bass

1960s. Single-cut thinline with f-holes, 2 pickups, sunburst or blackrose.

1960s		$475	$575

Atlantic Model 5/143 Bass

1960s. Offset double-cut thinbody with f-holes, 2 pickups, 4-on-a-side keys.

1960s		$500	$600

Atlantic Model 5/144 Bass

1960s. Double-cut thinbody with f-holes, ES-335 body style, 2 pickups. Becomes Model J/144 in '70s.

1960s		$525	$650

Charavelle 4 Model 5/153 Bass

1960s. Double-cut thinline with f-holes, 335-style body, 2 pickups, sunburst, cherry red or Sunset.

1960s		$575	$700

De Luxe 4 Model 5/154 Bass

1960s. Double-cut thinline with sharp (acute) hornes and f-holes, 2 pickups, mute, sunburst or natural/ blond. 2nd most expensive in Framus bass lineup in the mid-'60s, although not as famous as the Stone/Bill Wyman bass.

1960s		$600	$700

Electric Upright Bass

1950s. Full-scale neck, triangular body, black.

1958		$1,600	$2,000

Star Series (Bill Wyman) Bass

1959-1968. Early flyer says, Bill Wyman of the Rolling Stones prefers the Star Bass. The model name was later changed to Framus Stone Bass. Single-cut semi-hollow body, 5/149 (1 pickup) and 5/150 (2 pickups), sunburst.

1959-1965	Model 5/150	$1,200	$1,500
1960s	Model 5/149	$900	$1,100

Strato De Luxe Star Model 5/165 Bass

Ca. 1964-ca. 1972. Offset double-cut solidbody, 2 pickups, sunburst. There was also a gold hardware version (5/165 gl) and a 6-string (5/166).

1960s		$525	$625

Strato Star Series Bass

Ca. 1963-ca. 1972. Double-cut solidbody, 5/156/50 (1 pickup) or 5/156/52 (2 pickups), beige, cherry or sunburst.

1960s	Model 5/156/50	$500	$600
1960s	Model 5/156/52	$550	$650

T.V. Star Bass

1960s. Offset double-cut thinbody with f-holes, 2 pickups, short-scale, sunburst or cherry red. Most expensive of the '60s Framus basses, although not as popular as the Bill Wyman 5/150 model.

1960s		$525	$650

Triumph Electric Upright Bass

1956-1960. Solidbody bean pole electric bass, small body, long neck, slotted viol peghead, gold or black.

1956-1960		$1,600	$2,000

Upright Bass Viol

1946	Carved top	$3,600	$4,500

Fresher

1973-1985. Japanese-made, mainly copies of popular brands and not imported into the U.S., but they do show up at guitar shows. They also made guitars.

Solidbody Electric Bass

1970s		$250	$300

Fritz Brothers

1988-present. Luthier Roger Fritz builds his premium grade, production/custom, semi-hollow body basses in Mendocino, California. He also builds guitars.

Fodera Bass

Framus Atlantic

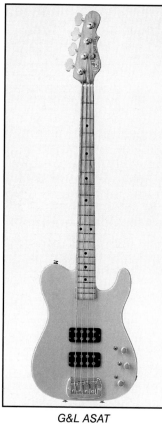

G&L ASAT

G&L L-5000

Fury

1962-present. Founded by Glenn McDougall in Saskatoon, Saskatchewan, Fury currently offers production, solidbody basses. They also build guitars.

Fylde

1973-present. Luthier Roger Bucknall builds his professional and premium grade, production/custom acoustic basses in Penrith, Cumbria, United Kingdom. He also builds guitars, mandolins, mandolas, bouzoukis, and citterns.

G & L

1980-present. Intermediate and professional grade, production/custom, electric basses made in the U.S. In '03, G & L introduced the Korean-made G & L Tribute Series. A Tribute logo is clearly identified on the headstock. They also build guitars.

ASAT Bass

1989-present. Single-cut, solidbody, active and passive modes, 2 humbucking pickups, various colors.

1989-1991	About 400 made	$750	$875
1992-2003		$650	$725

ASAT Commemorative Bass

1991-1992. About 150 made, 4-string ASAT commemorating Leo Fender's life.

1991-1992	$1,800	$2,200

ASAT Semi-Hollow Bass

2001-present. Semi-hollowbody style on ASAT bass.

2001-2003	$800	$900

Climax Bass

1992-1996. Single active humbucker MFD pickup.

1992-1996	$600	$750

El Toro Bass

1983-1991. Double-cut, solidbody, 2 active, smaller, humbucker pickups, sunburst.

1983-1991	$775	$825

Interceptor Bass

1984-1991. Sharp pointed double-cut, solidbody, 2 active, smaller humbucker pickups, sunburst.

1984-1991	$700	$1,000

JB-2 Bass

2001-present. Alder body, 2 Alnico V pickups.

2001-2003	$800	$900

L-1000 Bass

1980-1994. Offset double-cut, solidbody, 1 pickup, various colors.

1980-1994	$650	$800

L-1500 Bass/L-1500 Custom Bass

1997-present.

1997-2003	$700	$850

L-1505 Bass

1998-present. Five-string version, single MFD humbucker pickup.

1998-2003	$600	$750

L-2000 Bass

1980-present. Offset double-cut solidbody, 2 pickups, active electronics. Originally, the L-2000 was available with active (L-2000E) or passive (L-2000) electronics.

1980-1982	$800	$950

1983-1991	Leo signature	$750	$900
1992-2003		$650	$800

L-2000(E) Bass

1980-1982. Offset double-cut, solidbody, 2 pickups, active electronics. Originally, the L-2000 was available with active (L-2000E) or passive (L-2000) electronics.

1980-1982	$800	$1,000

L-2000 Custom Bass

1997. Ash top, wood-grain binding upgrade.

1997	$800	$1,000

L-2000 Fretless Bass

1980-1998. Fretless version.

1980-1982	$900	$1,100

L-2500 Bass

1997-present. Five-string, dual MFD humbucker pickups, figured tops can vary.

1997-2003	$750	$900

L-2500 Custom Bass

1997. Ash top, wood-grain binding upgrade.

1997	$800	$1,000

L-5000 Bass

1988-1993. Offset double-cut, solidbody, G & L Z-shaped split-humbucking pickup, 5 strings, approximately 400 made.

1988-1993	$650	$750

L-5500 Bass

1993-1997. Alder body, 5-string.

1993-1997	$700	$850

L-5500 Custom Bass

1997. Ash top, wood-grain binding upgrade.

1997	$675	$750

LB-100 Bass

1993-2000. Follow-up to earlier Legacy Bass.

1993-2000	$500	$625

Legacy Bass

1992-1993. Offset double-cut solidbody, 1split-coil pickup, renamed LB-100 in '93.

1992-1993	$550	$675

Lynx Bass

1984-1991. Offset double-cut, solidbody, 2 single-coil pickups, black.

1984-1991	$650	$750

SB 1 Bass

1982-2000. Solidbody, maple neck, body and 'board, split-humbucker pickup, 1 tone and 1 volume control.

1982-2000	$550	$650

SB 2 Bass

1982-present. Maple neck with tilt adjustment, 1 split-coil humbucking and 1 single-coil bridge pickups.

1982-2007	$600	$750

G.L. Stiles

1960-1994. Built by Gilbert Lee Stiles primarily in the Miami, Florida area. He also built guitars.

MODEL YEAR	FEATURES	EXC. COND. LOW	HIGH

Gadow Guitars

2002-present. Luthier Ryan Gadow builds his professional and premium grade, custom/production, solidbody basses in Durham, North Carolina. He also builds guitars.

Galveston

Budget and intermediate grade, production, imported acoustic, acoustic/electric and solidbody basses. They also offer guitars and mandolins.

Gibson

1890s (1902)-present. Professional grade, production, U.S.-made electric basses. Gibson got into the electric bass market with the introduction of their Gibson Electric Bass in '53 (that model was renamed the EB-1 in '58 and reintroduced under that name in '69). Many more bass models followed. Gibson's custom colors can greatly increase the value of older instruments. Custom colors offered from '63 to '69 are Cardinal Red, Ember Red, Frost Blue, Golden Mist Metallic, Heather Metallic, Inverness Green, Kerry Green, Pelham Blue Metallic, Polaris White, Silver Mist Metallic.

20/20 Bass

1987-1988. Designed by Ned Steinberger, slim-wedge Steinberger style solidbody, 2 humbucker pickups, 20/20 logo on headstock, Luna Silver or Ferrari Red finish.

1987-1988		$975	$1,100

Electric Bass (EB-1)

1953-1958. Introduced as Gibson Electric Bass in '53, but was called the EB-1 by Gibson in its last year of '58, thus, the whole line is commonly called the EB-1 by collectors, reissued in '69 as the EB-1 (see EB-1 listing), brown.

1953-1958		$5,100	$6,400

EB Bass

1970 only. Renamed from Melody Maker Bass, SG body, 1 humbucker pickup.

1970		$1,350	$1,600

EB-0 Bass

1959-1979. Double-cut slab body with banjo-type tuners in '59 and '60, double-cut SG-type body with conventional tuners from '61 on, 1 pickup. Faded custom colors are of less value.

1959-1960	Cherry, slab body	$4,300	$4,800
1961	Cherry, SG body	$2,100	$2,600
1962	Cherry	$2,000	$2,400
1963-1964	Cherry	$1,900	$2,300
1965	Cherry	$1,600	$1,700
1966	Cherry	$1,550	$1,650
1967	Cherry	$1,500	$1,600
1968	Black	$1,700	$1,800
1968	Burgundy Metallic	$1,700	$1,800
1968	Cherry	$1,500	$1,600
1968	Pelham Blue	$1,800	$2,300
1969	Cherry	$1,400	$1,500
1969	Pelham Blue	$1,800	$2,300
1970-1971	Cherry	$1,350	$1,500
1972-1974	Cherry	$1,300	$1,400
1975-1979	Cherry	$1,000	$1,250

EB-0 F Bass

1962-1965. EB-0 with added built-in fuzz, cherry.

1962		$2,000	$2,400
1963-1964		$1,900	$2,200
1965		$1,600	$1,700

EB-0 L Bass

1969-1979. 34.5 inch scale version of the EB-0, various colors.

1969		$1,400	$1,500
1970-1971		$1,350	$1,400
1972-1979		$1,100	$1,200

EB-1 Bass

1969-1972. The Gibson Electric Bass ('53-'58) is often also called the EB-1 (see Electric Bass). Violin-shaped mahogany body, 1 pickup, standard tuners.

1969-1972		$1,600	$1,900

EB-2 Bass

1958-1961, 1964-1972. ES-335-type semi-hollowbody, double-cut, 1 pickup, banjo tuners '58-'60 and conventional tuners '60 on.

1958	Sunburst, banjo tuners	$4,000	$5,000
1959	Natural, banjo tuners	$4,500	$5,500
1959	Sunburst, banjo tuners	$3,500	$4,300
1960	Sunburst, banjo tuners	$3,000	$3,700
1961	Sunburst, conventional tuners	$2,500	$3,000
1964	Sunburst	$2,500	$2,900
1965	Sunburst	$2,000	$2,500
1966	Cherry, sunburst	$1,900	$2,400
1967-1969	Cherry, sunburst	$2,000	$2,100
1967-1969	Sparkling Burgundy	$2,500	$3,100
1970-1972	Sunburst	$1,400	$1,700

EB-2 D Bass

1966-1972. Two-pickup version of EB-2, cherry, sunburst, or walnut.

1966	Cherry, sunburst	$2,700	$2,800
1967-1969	Cherry, sunburst, walnut	$2,500	$2,600
1967-1969	Sparkling Burgundy	$2,700	$3,200
1970-1972	Cherry, sunburst	$2,100	$2,400

EB-3 Bass

1961-1979. SG-style solidbody, 2 humbuckers, solid peghead '61-'68 and '72-'79, slotted peghead '69-'71, cherry to '71, various colors after.

1961		$5,300	$6,500
1962		$5,100	$6,200
1963		$4,800	$5,800
1964		$4,500	$5,500
1965		$4,000	$5,000
1965	Jack Bruce exact specs	$4,500	$5,500
1966		$2,500	$3,100
1967-1968		$2,400	$3,000
1969		$2,300	$2,700

1964 Gibson EB-0F

Gibson EB-1

BASSES

BASSES

1961 Gibson EB-6

Gibson Flying V Bass

MODEL YEAR	FEATURES	EXC. COND. LOW	HIGH
1970-1971		$1,900	$2,300
1972-1974		$1,800	$2,100
1975-1979		$1,500	$1,800

EB-3 L Bass
1969-1972. 34.5" scale version of EB-3, cherry, natural, or walnut.

1969		$2,300	$2,700
1970-1971		$1,900	$2,300
1972		$1,800	$2,100

EB-4 L Bass
1972-1979. SG-style, 1 humbucker, 34.5" scale, cherry or walnut.

1972-1979		$1,700	$2,000

EB-6 Bass
1960-1966. Introduced as semi-hollowbody 335-style 6-string with 1 humbucker, changed to SG-style with 2 pickups in '62.

1960-1961	Sunburst, 335-style	$8,000	$10,000
1962-1964	Cherry, SG-style	$9,500	$11,500
1965-1966	Cherry, SG-style	$8,000	$9,500

EB-650 Bass
1991-1993. Semi-acoustic single cut, maple neck, laminated maple body with center block, 2 TB Plus pickups.

1991-1993		$1,000	$1,100

EB-750 Bass
1991-1993. Like EB-650, but with Bartolini pickups and TCT active eq.

1991-1993		$1,100	$1,200

Explorer Bass
1984-1987. Alder body, 3-piece maple neck, ebony 'board, dot inlays, 2 humbuckers, various colors.

1984-1987		$1,300	$1,600

Flying V Bass
1981-1982 only. Solidbody, Flying V body.

1981-1982	Blue stain or ebony	$3,000	$3,700
1981-1982	Silverburst	$3,700	$4,500

Gibson IV Bass
1986-1988. Mahogany body and neck, double-cut, 2 pickups, black chrome hardware, various colors.

1986-1988		$600	$675

Gibson V Bass
1986-1988. Double-cut, 5 strings, 2 pickups.

1986-1988		$650	$775

Grabber Bass (G-1)
1974-1982. Double-cut solidbody, 1 pickup, bolt maple neck, maple 'board, various colors.

1974-1982		$850	$1,000

Grabber III Bass (G-3)
1975-1982. Double-cut solidbody, 3 pickups, bolt maple neck, maple 'board, nickel-plated hardware, various colors.

1975-1982		$950	$1,100

L9-S Bass
1973. Natural maple or cherry, renamed Ripper Bass in '74.

1973		$1,000	$1,200

Les Paul Bass
1970-1971. Single-cut solidbody, 2 pickups, walnut finish, renamed Les Paul Triumph Bass '71-'79.

1970-1971		$1,700	$1,900

MODEL YEAR	FEATURES	EXC. COND. LOW	HIGH

Les Paul Deluxe Plus LPB-2 Bass
1991-1998. Upgraded Les Paul Special LPB-1 bass, with carved maple top, trapezoid inlays, TCT active eq and Bartolini pickups. Flame maple top Premium version offered '93-'98.

1991-1998		$1,200	$1,500

Les Paul Signature Bass
1973-1979. Double-cut, semi-hollowbody, 1 pickup, sunburst or gold (gold only by '76). Name also used on LPB-3 bass in '90s.

1973-1975	Sunburst	$2,900	$3,600
1973-1979	Gold	$2,900	$3,600

Les Paul Special LPB-1 Bass
1991-1998. 2 TB-Plus pickups, ebony 'board, dots, slab mahogany body, active electronics, also available as 5-string.

1991-1998		$850	$1,050

Les Paul Special V Bass
1993-1996. Single-cut slab body, 5-string, 2 pickups, dot markers, black/ebony.

1993-1996		$850	$1,050

Les Paul Standard LPB-3 Bass
1991-1995. Like Les Paul Deluxe LPB-2 Bass, but with TB Plus pickups. Flame maple top Premium version offered '93-'95.

1993-1995	Flamed top	$1,000	$1,200

Les Paul Triumph Bass
1971-1979. Renamed from Les Paul Bass.

1971-1979	Various colors	$1,350	$1,650
1973-1974	White optional color	$1,600	$1,800

Melody Maker Bass
1967-1970. SG body, 1 humbucker pickup, Cardinal Red.

1967-1970		$1,500	$1,800

Nikki Sixx Blackbird (Thunderbird) Bass
2000-2002. Thunderbird style, black finish and hardware, iron cross inlays.

2000-2002		$1,000	$1,250

Q-80 Bass
1986-1988. Victory Series body shape, 2 pickups, bolt neck, black chrome hardware, renamed Q-90 in '88.

1986-1988		$550	$675

Q-90 Bass
1988-1992. Renamed from Q-80, mahogany body, 2 active humbuckers, maple neck, ebony 'board.

1988-1992		$550	$675

RD Artist Bass
1977-1982. Double-cut solid maple body, laminated neck, 2 pickups, active electronics, string-thru-body, block inlays, various colors.

1977-1982		$1,500	$1,850

RD Artist Custom Bass
1977-1982. Custom option with bound top, low production.

1977-1982	Sunburst, mild figure	$1,350	$1,650

MODEL YEAR	FEATURES	EXC. COND. LOW	HIGH

RD Standard Bass
1977-1979. Double-cut, solid maple body, laminated neck, 2 pickups, regular electronics, string-thru-body, dot inlays, various colors.

1977-1979		$1,225	$1,375

Ripper Bass
1974-1982. Introduced as L-9 S Bass in '73, double-cut solidbody, glued neck, 2 pickups, string-thru-body, various colors.

1974-1982		$1,000	$1,100

SB Series Bass
1971-1978. The early version, 1971, had oval pickups with wide metal surrounds, these were replaced mid-model with more traditional rectangular pickups with rectangular surrounds. This 2nd version can often fetch a bit more in the market. Various models include 300 (30" scale, 1 pickup), 350 (30" scale, 2 pickups), 400 (34" scale, 1 pickup), 450 (34" scale, 2 pickups). From '75 to '78 the 450 was special order only.

1971-1973	SB-300	$775	$950
1971-1973	SB-400	$775	$950
1972-1974	SB-350	$800	$1,000
1972-1974	SB-450	$800	$1,000
1975-1978	SB-450 special order	$775	$950

SG Reissue Bass
2005-present. Modern version of 1960s EB-3 bass, 2 pickups, '60s specs, mahogany body and neck, Cherry or ebony.

2005-2006		$725	$875

Thunderbird II Bass
1963-1969. Reverse solidbody until '65, non-reverse solidbody '65-'69, 1 pickup, custom colors available, reintroduced with reverse body for '83-'84.

1963	Sunburst, reverse	$9,000	$11,000
1964	Pelham Blue, reverse	$9,000	$11,000
1964	Sunburst, reverse	$6,000	$8,000
1965	Cardinal Red, non-reverse	$7,200	$9,000
1965	Inverness Green, non-reverse	$7,200	$9,000
1965	Sunburst, non-reverse	$4,000	$4,500
1965	Sunburst, reverse	$5,600	$7,000
1966	Cardinal Red, non-reverse	$5,000	$6,000
1966	Sunburst, non-reverse	$3,500	$4,000
1967	Cardinal Red, non-reverse	$4,500	$5,600
1967	Sunburst, non-reverse	$3,500	$4,000
1968	Cardinal Red, non-reverse	$4,400	$5,400
1968	Sunburst, non-reverse	$3,000	$3,500
1969	Sunburst, non-reverse	$2,900	$3,400

Thunderbird IV Bass
1963-1969. Reverse solidbody until '64, non-reverse solidbody '65-'69, 2 pickups, custom colors available, reintroduced with reverse body for '86-present (see Thunderbird IV Bass Reissue).

1963	Sunburst, reverse	$12,000	$14,000
1964	Frost Blue, reverse	$23,000	$25,000
1964	Pelham Blue, reverse	$22,000	$24,000
1964	Sunburst, reverse	$9,600	$12,000
1965	Cardinal Red, non-reverse	$9,600	$12,000
1965	Inverness Green, non-reverse	$9,600	$12,000
1965	Sunburst, reverse	$8,000	$10,000
1965-1966	Sunburst, non-reverse	$6,000	$6,500
1966	White, non-reverse	$7,000	$11,000
1967	Sunburst, non-reverse	$4,700	$5,200
1968	Sunburst, non-reverse	$4,500	$5,000
1969	Sunburst, non-reverse	$4,200	$4,700

Thunderbird IV Bass (Reissue)
1987-present. Has reverse body and 2 pickups, sunburst.

1987-1990		$1,350	$1,450
1991-2002		$1,200	$1,350
1991-2002	Rare color	$1,450	$1,600

Thunderbird 76 Bass
1976 only. Reverse solidbody, 2 pickups, rosewood 'board, various colors.

1976		$2,900	$3,400

Thunderbird 79 Bass
1979 only. Reverse solidbody, 2 pickups, sunburst.

1979		$2,400	$2,800

Victory Artist Bass
1981-1985. Double-cut, solidbody, 2 humbuckers and active electronics, various colors.

1981-1985		$600	$750

Victory Custom Bass
1982-1984. Double-cut, solidbody, 2 humbuckers, passive electronics, limited production.

1982-1984		$600	$750

Victory Standard Bass
1981-1986. Double-cut, solidbody, 1 humbucker, active electronics, various colors.

1981-1986		$500	$625

Godin
1987-present. Intermediate and professional grade, production, solidbody electric and acoustic/electric basses from luthier Robert Godin. They also build guitars and mandolins.

Godlyke
2006-present. Professional and premium grade, production, solidbody basses from effects distributor Godlyke.

Gibson Nikki Sixx Blackbird

Gibson Thunderbird IV reissue

To get the most from this book, be sure to read "Using *The Guide*" in the introduction.

Gold Tone ABG-4

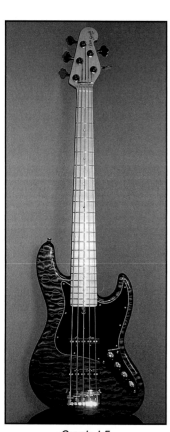

Grosh J-5

Gold Tone

1993-present. Intermediate grade, production/custom acoustic basses built by Wayne and Robyn Rogers in Titusville, Florida. They also offer guitars, lap steels, mandolins, ukuleles, banjos and banjitars.

Goya

1955-present. Originally imports from Sweden, brand later used on Japanese and Korean imports. They also offered basses, mandolins and banjos.

Electric Solidbody Bass

1960s	Various models	$525	$650

Graf

See listing under Oskar Graf Guitars.

Granada

1970s-1980s. Japanese-made electric basses, most being copies of classic American models. They also offered guitars.

Greco

1960s-present. Currently owned by Kanda Shokai, of Japan, and offering solidbody basses. They also offer guitars. Early bass models were copies of popular brands, but by the '70s original designs appear.

Beatle Bass Copy

1970s	$425	$525

Gretsch

1883-present. Intermediate and professional grade, production, solidbody, hollow body, and acoustic/electric basses. Gretsch came late to the electric bass game, introducing their first models in the early '60s.

Broadkaster Bass (7605/7606)

1975-1979. Double-cut solidbody, 1 pickup, bolt-on maple neck, natural (7605) or sunburst (7606).

1975-1979	$725	$875

Committee Bass (7629)

1977-1980. Double-cut walnut and maple solidbody, neck-thru, 1 pickup, natural.

1977-1980	$775	$875

G6072 Long Scale Hollow Body Bass

1998-2006. Reissue of the '68 double-cut hollowbody, 2 pickups, sunburst, gold hardware.

1998-2006	$1,150	$1,250

Model 6070/6072 Bass

1963-1971 (1972 for 6070). Country Gentleman thinline archtop double-cut body, fake f-holes, 1 pickup (6070) or 2 (6072), gold hardware.

1963-1964	6070, with endpin	$2,600	$2,900
1965-1972	6070, no endpin, 1 pickup	$1,900	$2,300
1968-1971	6072, 2 pickups	$1,600	$2,000

Model 6071/6073 Bass

1968-1971 (1972 for 6071). Single-cut hollowbody, fake f-holes, 1 pickup (6071) or 2 (6073), padded back, red mahogany.

1968-1971	6073, 2 pickups	$2,300	$2,900
1968-1972	6071, 1 pickup	$2,100	$2,500

Model 7615 Bass

1972-1975. Offset double-cut solidbody, slotted bass horn (monkey grip), large polished rosewood 'guard covering most of the body, 2 pickups, dot markers, brown mahogany finish. Only bass offered in Gretsch catalog for this era.

1972-1975	$850	$1,000

TK 300 Bass (7626/7627)

1976-1981. Double-cut solidbody, 1 pickup, Autumn Red Stain or natural.

1976-1981	$650	$725

Groove Tools

2002-2004. Korean-made, production, intermediate grade, solidbody basses that were offered by Conklin Guitars of Springfield, Missouri. They also had guitars.

Grosh, Don

1993-present. Professional grade, production/custom, solidbody basses built by luthier Don Grosh in Santa Clarita, California. He also builds guitars.

Guild

1952-present. Guild added electric basses in the mid-'60s and offered them until '02.

Ashbory Bass

1986-1988. 18" scale, total length 30", fretless, silicone rubber strings, active electronics, low-impedance circuitry.

1986-1988	$475	$550

B-4 E Bass

1993-1999. Acoustic/electric single-cut flat-top, mahogany sides with arched mahogany back, multi-bound, gold hardware until '95, chrome after.

1993-1999	$700	$825

B-30 E Bass

1987-1999. Single-cut flat-top acoustic/electric, mahogany sides, arched mahogany back, multi-bound, fretless optional.

1987-1999	$1,325	$1,400

B-50 Acoustic Bass

1976-1987. Acoustic flat-top, mahogany sides with arched mahogany back, spruce top, multi-bound, renamed B-30 in '87.

1976-1987	$1,325	$1,400

B-301/B-302 Bass

1976-1981. Double-cut solidbody, chrome-plated hardware. Models include B-301 (mahogany, 1 pickup), B-301 A (ash, 1 pickup), B-302 (mahogany, 2 pickups), B-302 A (ash, 2 pickups), and B-302 AF (ash, fretless).

1976-1981	B-301	$575	$700
1976-1981	B-302	$625	$750
1977-1981	B-301 A	$625	$750
1977-1981	B-302 A	$675	$800
1977-1981	B-302 AF	$675	$800

B-500 Acoustic Bass

1992-1993. Acoustic/electric flat-top, round soundhole, single-cut, solid spruce top, maple back and sides, dark stain, limited production.

1992-1993	$1,325	$1,400

MODEL YEAR	FEATURES	EXC. COND. LOW	HIGH

Jet Star Bass

1964-1970 (limited production '68-'70). Offset double-cut solidbody, short treble horn, 1 pickup, 2-on-a-side tuners '64-'66 and 4 in-line tuners '66-'70.

1964-1966	2-on-side-tuners	$1,050	$1,300
1967-1970	4 in-line	$875	$1,050

JS I/JS II Bass

1970-1977. Double-cut solidbody, 30" scale, 1 pickup (JS I or 1) or 2 (JS II or 2), mini-switch, selector switch, carved-top oak leaf design available for '72-'76. 34" long scale (LS) versions offered fretted and fretless for '74-'75.

1970-1975	JS I	$600	$700
1970-1977	JS II	$700	$850

M-85 I/M-85 II Bass (Semi-Hollow)

1967-1972. Single-cut semi-hollowbody, 1 pickup (M-85 I) or 2 (M-85 II).

1967-1972	M-85 I	$1,250	$1,500
1967-1972	M-85 II	$1,450	$1,700

M-85 I/M-85 II BluesBird Bass (Solidbody)

1972-1976. Single-cut solidbody archtop, Chesterfield headstock inlay, cherry mahogany, 1 humbucker pickup (I) or 2 (II).

1972-1973	M-85 I	$1,000	$1,200
1972-1976	M-85 II	$1,150	$1,400

MB-801 Bass

1981-1982. Double-cut solidbody, 1 pickup, dot inlays.

1981-1982		$525	$650

SB-201/SB-202/SB-203 Bass

1982-1983. Double-cut solidbody, 1 split coil pickup (201), 1 split coil and 1 single coil (202), or 1 split coil and 2 single coils (203).

1982-1983	SB-201	$625	$750
1982-1983	SB-202	$675	$800
1983	SB-203	$725	$825

SB-502 E Bass

1984-1985. Double-cut solidbody, 2 pickups, active electronics.

1984-1985		$725	$825

SB-601/SB-602/SB-602 V Pilot Bass

1983-1988. Offset double-cut solidbody, bolt-on neck, poplar body. Models include SB-601 (1 pickup), SB-602 (2 pickups or fretless) and SB-602 V (2 pickups, 5-string).

1983-1988	SB-601	$475	$525
1983-1988	SB-602	$525	$625
1983-1988	SB-602 V	$575	$625
1983-1988	SB-602, fretless	$575	$625
1983-1988	SB-605, 5-string	$575	$625

SB-608 Flying Star Motley Crue Bass

1998-2002. Reissue of 2 humbucker version.

1984-1986		$650	$750

Starfire Bass

1965-1975. Double-cut semi-hollow thinbody, 1 pickup, mahogany neck, chrome-plated hardware, cherry or sunburst.

1965-1969	Single-coil	$1,500	$1,725
1970-1975	Humbucker	$1,400	$1,725

Starfire II Bass

1965-1978. Two-pickup version of Starfire Bass.

1965-1969	2 single-coils	$1,600	$1,850
1970-1978	2 humbuckers	$1,500	$1,850

Starfire II Reissue Bass

1984-1985. Pointy 4-point star body, 2 pickups, E version had EMG pickups.

1984-1985		$1,525	$1,700

X-701/X-702 Bass

1982-1984. Body with 4 sharp horns with extra long bass horn, 1 pickup (X-701) or 2 (X-702), various metallic finishes.

1982-1984	X-701	$775	$875
1982-1984	X-702	$875	$950

Guitar Mill

2006-present. Professional grade, production/custom, solidbody basses built by Mario Martin in Murfreesboro, Tennessee. He also builds guitars.

Guyatone

1933-present. Large Japanese maker which also produced instruments under the Marco Polo, Winston, Kingston, Kent, LaFayette, and Bradford brands.

Hagstrom

1921-1983, 2004-present. This Swedish guitar company first offered electric basses in '61.

8-String Bass

1967-1969. Double-cut solidbody, 2 pickups, various colors.

1967-1969		$900	$1,250

F-100 B Bass

1970s. Offset double-cut solidbody, 1 pickup, Fender style headstock.

1970s		$500	$625

Model I B Bass

1965-1966, 1971-1973. Double-cut solidbody, 2 pickups, red.

1965-1966		$550	$650

Model II B/F-400 Bass

1965-1970. Offset double-cut solidbody, 2 pickups, sunburst, called F-400 in U.S., II B elsewhere.

1965-1970		$600	$700

Swede Bass

1971-1976. Single-cut solidbody, block inlays, 2 pickups, cherry.

1971-1976		$700	$875

Swede 2000 Bass (With Synth)

1977. Circuitry on this Swede bass connected to the Ampeg Patch 2000 pedal so bass would work with various synths.

1977		$750	$925

V-IN Bass/Concord Bass

1970s. Bass version of V-IN guitar, 335-style body, 2 pickups, sunburst.

1970s		$625	$775

Guild SB-602

1975 Guild Jet Star II

BASSES

To get the most from this book, be sure to read "Using *The Guide*" in the introduction.

BASSES

Hallmark Vintage Sweptwing

Harmony H-22

MODEL YEAR	FEATURES	EXC. COND. LOW	HIGH

Hallmark

1965-1967, 2004-present. Imported, intermediate grade, production, basses. Hallmark is located in Greenbelt, Maryland. They also make guitars. The brand was originally founded by Joe Hall in Arvin, California, in '65.

Hamer

1975-present. Intermediate and professional grade, production/custom, acoustic and electric basses made in the U.S. and imported. Founded in Arlington Heights, Illinois, by Paul Hamer and Jol Dantzig, Hamer was purchased by Kaman in '88. They also build guitars.

8-String Short-Scale Bass
1978-1993. Double cut solidbody, 1 or 2 pickups, 30.5" scale.

1978-1993		$1,500	$1,700

12-String Acoustic Bass
1985-present. Semi-hollow, long scale, single cut, soundhole, 2 pickups. Import XT model added in the 2000s.

1985-2005		$1,700	$1,900

12-String Short-Scale Bass
1978-1996. Four sets of 3 strings - a fundamental and 2 tuned an octave higher, double cut maple and mahogany solidbody, 30.5" scale.

1978-1996		$1,700	$1,900

Blitz Bass
1982-1990. Explorer-style solidbody, 2 pickups, bolt-on neck.

1982-1984	1st edition	$700	$825
1984-1990		$650	$750

Chaparral Bass
1986-1995, 2000-present. Solidbody, 2 pickups, glued-in neck, later basses have bolt-on neck.

1986-1987	Set-neck	$750	$900
1987-1995	Bolt-on neck	$650	$750

Chaparral 5-String Bass
1987-1995. Five strings, solidbody, 2 pickups, glued-in neck, later basses have 5-on-a-side reverse peghead.

1987-1995		$550	$650

Chaparral 12-String Bass
1992-present. Long 34" scale 12-string, offset double cut. Import XT model added in '01.

1992-2005	USA	$1,800	$2,400
2000-2005	Import	$400	$575

Chaparral Max Bass
1986-1995. Chaparral Bass with figured maple body, glued-in neck and boomerang inlays.

1986-1995		$600	$700

Cruise Bass
1982-1990, 1995-1999. J-style solidbody, 2 pickups, glued neck ('82-'90) or bolt-on neck ('95-'99), also available as a 5-string.

1982-1990	Set-neck	$600	$700
1995-1999	Bolt-on neck	$550	$600

Cruise 5 Bass
1982-1989. Five-string version, various colors.

1982-1989		$600	$700

FBIV Bass
1985-1987. Reverse Firebird shape, 1 P-Bass Slammer and 1 J-Bass Slammer pickup, mahogany body, rosewood 'board, dots.

1985-1987		$575	$675

Standard Bass
1975-1984. Explorer-style bound body with 2 humbuckers.

1975-1979		$1,100	$1,200
1980-1984		$1,000	$1,100

Velocity 5 Bass
2002-present. Offset double-cut, long bass horn, active, 1 humbucker.

2002-2004		$175	$225

Harmony

1892-1976, late 1970s-present. Harmony once was one of the biggest instrument makers in the world, making guitars and basses under their own brand and for others.

H-22/H-27 Bass
Early-1960s-1970s. Single- (H22) or double-cut (H27), hollowbody.

1960-1970s	H-22, 1 pickup	$450	$550
1960-1970s	H-27, 2 pickups	$600	$700

Rocket Bass
1960s-1970s. First models single-cut, later models double-cut, similar to Rocket guitar.

1960-1970s		$450	$550

Hartke

Hartke offered a line of wood and aluminum-necked basses from 2000 to '03.

Hayman

1970-1973. Solid and semi-hollow body guitars and basses developed by Jim Burns and Bob Pearson for Ivor Arbiter of the Dallas Arbiter Company and built by Shergold in England.

Heartfield

1989-1994. Distributed by Fender, imported from Japan. They also offered guitars.

DR-4/DR-5 Bass
1989-1994. Double-cut solidbody, graphite reinforced neck, 2 single-coils, 4 strings, available in 5- and 6-string models.

1989-1994		$300	$375

Heit Deluxe

Ca. 1967-1970. Imported from Japan, many were made by Teisco. They also had guitars.

HenBev

Dec. 2005-present. Luthier Scotty Bevilacqua builds production, premium grade, basses in Oceanside, California. He also builds guitars.

MODEL YEAR	FEATURES	EXC. COND. LOW	HIGH

Höfner

1887-present. Professional grade, production, basses. They also offer guitars and bowed instruments. Hofner basses, made famous in the U.S. by one Paul McCartney, are made in Germany.

JB-59 Upright Jazz Bass

Electric solidbody, 3/4-size, solid mahogany, pickup, preamp.

1980s		$1,200	$1,700

Model (G)5000/1 Super Beatle (G500/1) Bass

1968-present. Bound ebony 'board, gold-plated hardware, natural finish, the version with active circuit is called G500/1 Super Beatle, reissued in '94

1968-1970s		$1,500	$1,850

Model 172 Series Bass

1968-1970. Offset double cut, 6-on-a-side tuners, 2 pickups, 2 slide switches, dot markers, 172-S shaded sunburst, 172-R red vinyl covered body, 172-I vinyl covered with white top and black back.

1968-1970	172-I, white	$500	$550
1968-1970	172-R, red	$500	$550
1968-1970	172-S, sunburst	$525	$575

Model 185 Solid Bass

1962-ca. 1970. Classic offset double-cut solidbody, 2 double-coil pickups.

1962-1970		$400	$475

Model 500/1 Beatle Bass

1956-present. Semi-acoustic, bound body in violin shape, glued-in neck, 2 pickups, sunburst, currently listed as the 500/1 50th Anniversary.

1956-1959		$4,000	$4,400
1960-1961		$4,300	$4,500
1960-1961	Lefty	$4,800	$5,500
1962		$3,800	$4,000
1962	Lefty	$4,300	$5,000
1963		$3,500	$4,000
1963	Lefty	$4,000	$5,000
1964		$3,500	$4,000
1964	Lefty	$4,000	$5,000
1965		$3,000	$3,500
1965	Lefty	$3,500	$4,000
1966		$2,200	$3,100
1966	Lefty	$2,500	$3,500
1967		$2,000	$2,700
1967	Lefty	$2,000	$3,000
1968-1969	Blade pickup	$1,900	$2,200
1968-1969	Lefty, blade pickup	$2,100	$2,400
1970-1973		$1,800	$2,100
1970-1973	Lefty	$1,900	$2,200
1974-1979		$1,550	$1,850

Model 500/1 1964-1984 Reissue Bass

1984. '1964-1984' neckplate notation.

1984		$1,750	$2,150

'63 Model 500/1 Beatle Bass Reissue

1994-present. Right- or left-handed.

1994-2005		$1,300	$2,100

Model 500/2 Bass

1965-1970. Similar to the 500/1, but with 'club' body Hofner made for England's Selmer, sunburst. Club Bass has been reissued.

1965-1970		$2,000	$2,300

Model 500/3 Senator Bass

1962-1964	Sunburst	$1,800	$2,200

Model 500/5 Bass

1959-1979. Single-cut body with Beatle Bass-style pickups, sunburst.

1959		$3,000	$3,500
1960s		$2,400	$2,500

President Bass

Made for England's Selmer, single-cut archtop, 2 pickups, sunburst.

1961-1962		$2,000	$2,400
1963-1965		$1,900	$2,100
1966-1967		$1,600	$1,900
1968-1969		$1,500	$1,800
1970-1972		$1,400	$1,600

Hohner

1857-present. Intermediate and professional grade, production, solidbody basses. Hohner has been offering basses at least since the early '70s. They also offer guitars, banjos, mandolins and ukuleles.

Electric Bass

1980-1990s		$150	$375

Hondo

1969-1987, 1991-present. Budget grade, production, imported acoustic and electric solidbody basses. They also offer guitars, banjos and mandolins.

Electric Solidbody Bass

1970-1990s	Rare models	$275	$550
1970-1990s	Standard models	$150	$275

H 1181 Longhorn Bass

Ca. 1978-1980s. Copy of Danelectro Longhorn Bass, 1 split pickup.

1970-1980s		$350	$425

Hopf

1906-present. From the mid-'50s to the late-'70s, Hopf offered electric basses made in their own factory and by others. Hopf currently mainly offers classical guitars and mandolins.

Hoyer

1874-present. Intermediate grade, production, electric basses. They also build guitars.

Ibanez

1932-present. Intermediate and professional grade, production, solidbody basses. They also have guitars, amps, and effects.

Axstar 50 AXB Bass

1986-1987. Headless solidbody, 1-piece maple neck, rosewood 'board, 2 humbuckers.

1986-1987		$225	$275

1966 Höfner 500/1

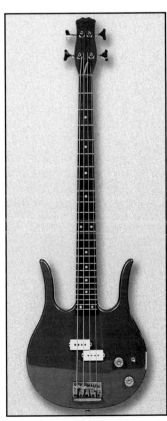

'80s Hondo H 1181

Ibanez SR-500

J.T. Hargreaves Jayhawk

MODEL YEAR	FEATURES	EXC. COND. LOW	HIGH

Axstar 60 AXB Bass
1986-1987. Headless solidbody, 4-string, 1-piece maple neck, ebony 'board, 2 low impedance pick-ups.

1986-1987		$375	$450

Axstar 65 AXB Bass
1986-1987. 5-string version of the 60 AXB.

1986-1987		$375	$450

Axstar 1000 AXB Bass
1986-1987. Headless alder solidbody, 1-piece maple neck-thru-body, ebony 'board, 2 low impedance pick-ups.

1986-1987		$425	$500

BTB500 Series Bass
1999-2000. Offset double-cut ash solidbody, 2 pickups, extra long bass horn, dot markers, natural walnut.

1999-2000		$350	$425

Destroyer X Series Bass
1983-1986. Futuristic-style body, P- and J-style pickups, dot markers, X Series notation on headstock, bolt neck.

1983-1986		$450	$500

Model 2030 Bass
1970-1973. First copy era bass, offset double-cut, sunburst.

1970-1973		$500	$600

Model 2353 Bass
1974-1976. Copy model, offset double-cut, 1 pickup, black.

1974-1976		$500	$600

Model 2364B Bass
1971-1973. Dan Armstrong see-thru Lucite copy with 2 mounted humbucker pickups, clear finish.

1971-1973		$600	$700

Model 2365 Bass
1974-1975. Copy model, Offset double-cut, rosewood 'board, pearloid block markers, sunburst.

1974-1975		$500	$600

Model 2366B/2366FLB Bass
1974-1975. Copy model, offset double-cut, 1 split-coil pickup, sunburst, FLB fretless model.

1974-1975		$500	$600

Model 2385 Bass
1974-1975. Copy model, offset double-cut, 1 pickup, ash natural finish.

1974-1975		$500	$600

Model 2388B Bass
1974-1976. Ric 4001 copy.

1974-1976		$550	$650

Model 2459B Destroyer Bass
1970s. Laminated ash body, copy of Korina Explorer-style.

1977		$550	$650

Musician EQ Bass
1978-1979. Offset double-cut solidbody, 2 pickups, EQ, ash and mahogany body, ebony 'board, dot inlays, became the MC900.

1978-1979		$400	$500

Musician MC800 Bass
1979-1980. Offset double-cut solidbody, 2 pickups, laminated neck.

1979-1980		$350	$425

Musician MC900 Bass
1979-1980. MC800 with on-board 3-band EQ.

1979-1980		$450	$500

Newport Bass
1974-1975. Copy model, cresting wave body, blond.

1974-1975		$600	$700

PL 5050 Bass
Ca. 1985-ca. 1988. Part of the Pro Line Series.

1985-1988		$325	$400

Roadstar Bas
1983-1987. Solidbody basses, various models and colors.

1983-1984	Roadstar	$275	$325
1984-1987	Roadstar II Deluxe	$325	$400
1984-1987	Roadstar II Standard	$250	$300

Rocket Roll Bass
1974-1976. Korina solidbody, V-shape, natural.

1974-1976		$975	$1,200

SB-900 Bass
1990-1993. Ultra slim solidbody.

1990-1993		$350	$425

SR-400 Bass
1993-present. Offset double-cut solidbody, 4-string, long bass horn, 2 pickups.

1993-2003		$300	$375

SR-405 Bass
1994-present. 5-string SR-400.

1994-2003		$300	$375

SR-500 Bass
1993-present. Offset double-cut, 4-string, long bass horn, active pickups, bolt neck.

1993-2005		$350	$425

SR-505 Bass
1993-present. 5-string SR 500.

1993-2005		$350	$425

SR-885 Bass
1991-2003. Offset double-cut solidbody, 5-string, 2 humbuckers.

1991-2003		$350	$425

Studio ST-980 Bass
Late-1970s. Double cut, 8-string, bolt-on neck, walnut-maple-mahogany body.

1979		$500	$550

Imperial
Ca.1963-ca.1970. Imported by the Imperial Accordion Company of Chicago, Illinois. Early guitars and basses made in Italy, but by ca. '66 Japanese-made.

Electric Solidbody Bass

1960s	Various models	$150	$250

Hollowbody Bass
1960s. Hollowbody with sharp double-cuts.

1960s		$200	$275

MODEL YEAR FEATURES	EXC. COND. LOW	HIGH

Infeld

2003-2005. Solidbody guitars and basses offered by string-maker Thomastik-Infeld of Vienna.

Italia

1999-present. Intermediate grade, production, solid and semi-solidbody basses designed by Trevor Wilkinson and made in Korea. They also build guitars.

J Backlund Design

2008-present. Professional and premium grade, production/custom, electric basses designed by J. Bucklund and built in Chattanooga, Tennessee by luthier Bruce Bennett. He also builds guitars.

J.B. Player

1980s-present. Intermediate grade, production, imported, acoustic/electric and solidbody basses. They also offer guitars, banjos and mandolins.

J.T. Hargreaves Basses & Guitars

1995-present. Luthier Jay Hargreaves builds his premium grade, production/custom, acoustic basses, in Seattle, Washington. He also builds guitars.

Jackson

1980-present. Intermediate, professional, and premium grade, production, solidbody basses. They also offer guitars. Founded by Grover Jackson, who owned Charvel.

Concert C5P 5-String Bass (Import)
1998-2000. Bolt neck, dot inlay, chrome hardware.

1998-2000	$150	$200

Concert Custom Bass (U.S.A.)
1984-1995. Neck-thru Custom Shop bass.

1984-1989	$700	$875
1990-1995	$600	$750

Concert EX 4-String Bass (Import)
1992-1995. Bolt neck, dot inlay, black hardware.

1992-1995	$275	$325

Concert V 5-String Bass (Import)
1992-1995. Bound neck, shark tooth inlay.

1992-1995	$425	$500

Concert XL 4-String Bass (Import)
1992-1995. Bound neck, shark tooth inlay.

1992-1995	$325	$400

Kelly Pro Bass
1994-1995. Pointy-cut bouts, neck-thru solidbody, shark fin marker inlays.

1994-1995	$600	$800

Piezo Bass
1986. Four piezo electric bridge pickups, neck-thru, active EQ, shark tooth inlays. Student model has rosewood 'board, no binding. Custom Model has ebony 'board and neck and headstock binding.

1986	$425	$500

Soloist Bass
1996. Pointy headstock, 4-string.

1996	$650	$750

James Tyler

Early 1980s-present. Luthier James Tyler builds his professional and premium grade, custom/production, solidbody basses in Van Nuys, California. He also builds guitars.

Jay Turser

1997-present. Intermediate grade, production, imported semi-hollow and solidbody basses. They also offer guitars and amps.

Jerry Jones

1981-present. Intermediate grade, production, semi-hollow body electric basses from luthier Jerry Jones, and built in Nashville, Tennessee. They also build guitars and sitars.

Neptune Longhorn 4 Bass
1988-present. Based on Danelectro longhorn models, 4-string, 2 lipstick-tube pickups, 30" scale.

1988-2000	$500	$600

Neptune Longhorn 6 Bass
1988-present. 6-string version.

1988-2000	$600	$800

Shorthorn 4 Bass
1990s. Danelectro inspired with Dano Coke bottle headstock, short horns like double cut U-2, 2 pickups, color options.

1990s	$500	$600

Jim Dyson

1972-present. Luthier Jim Dyson builds his intermediate, professional and premium grade, production/custom electric basses in Torquay, Southern Victoria, Australia. He also builds guitars and lap steels.

Johnson

Mid-1990s-present. Budget and intermediate grade, production, solidbody and acoustic basses imported by Music Link, Brisbane, California. They also offer guitars, amps, mandolins and effects.

Juzek

Violin maker John Juzek was originally located in Prague, Czeckoslovakia, but moved to West Germany due to World War II. Prague instruments considered by most to be more valuable. Many German instruments were mass produced with laminate construction and some equate these German basses with the Kay laminate basses of the same era. Juzek still makes instruments.

Kalamazoo

1933-1942, 1965-1970. Kalamazoo was a brand Gibson used on one of their budget lines. They also used the name on electric basses, guitars and amps from '65 to '67.

Jackson C20 Concert

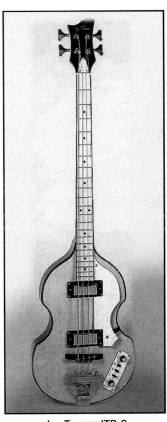
Jay Turser JTB-2

BASSES

'60s Kay Bass

1965 Kay K5915 Pro Model

MODEL YEAR	FEATURES	EXC. COND. LOW	HIGH
Electric Bass			
1965-1967	Bolt-on neck	$375	$450

Kapa

Ca. 1962-1970. Kapa was founded by Koob Veneman in Maryland and offered basses and guitars.

MODEL YEAR	FEATURES	EXC. COND. LOW	HIGH
Electric Bass			
1962-1970	Various models	$300	$500

Kawai

1927-present. Japanese instrument manufacturer Kawai started offering guitars under other brand names around '56. There were few imports carrying the Kawai brand until the late-'70s; best known for high quality basses. Kawai quit offering guitars and basses around 2002.

MODEL YEAR	FEATURES	EXC. COND. LOW	HIGH
Electric Bass			
1970-1980s	Various models	$225	$375

Kay

Ca. 1931-present. Currently, budget and intermediate grade, production, imported solidbody basses. They also make amps, guitars, banjos, mandolins, ukes, and violins. Kay introduced upright acoustic laminate basses and 3/4 viols in '38 and electric basses in '54.

C1 Concert String Bass

1938-1967. Standard (3/4) size student bass, laminated construction, spruce top, figured maple back and sides, shaded light brown.

1938-1949		$2,400	$2,900
1950-1959		$2,200	$2,700
1960-1967		$2,000	$2,500

Jazz Special Electronic Bass

1960-1964		$500	$575

M-1 (Maestro) String Bass

1952-late-1960s. Standard (3/4) size bass, laminated construction, spruce top and curly maple back and sides. Model M-3 is the Junior (1/4) size bass, Model M-1 B has a blond finish, other models include the S-51 B Chubby Jackson Five-String Bass and the S-9 Swingmaster.

1952-1959		$2,400	$3,000
1960-1967		$2,200	$2,700

M-5 (Maestro) String Bass

1957-late-1960s. Five strings.

1957-1967		$2,800	$3,500

Semi-hollowbody Bass

1954-1966. Single or double cut, 1 or 2 pickups.

1954-1966	1 pickup	$250	$450
1954-1966	2 pickups	$350	$550

Solidbody Bass

1965-1968. Single or double cut, 1 or 2 pickups.

1965-1968	1 pickup	$250	$450
1965-1968	2 pickups	$350	$550

KB

1989-present. Luthier Ken Bebensee builds his premium grade, custom, solidbody basses in North San Juan, California. He also builds guitars and mandolins.

MODEL YEAR	FEATURES	EXC. COND. LOW	HIGH

Ken Smith

See listing under Smith.

Kent

1961-1969. Guitars and basses imported from Japan by Buegeleisen and Jacobson of New York, New York. Manufacturers unknown but many early instruments by Guyatone and Teisco.

Electric Bass

1962-1969. Import models include 628 Newport, 634 Basin Street, 629, and 635.

1961-1969	Various models	$125	$375

Kimberly

Late-1960s-early-1970s. Private branded import made in the same Japanese factory as Teisco. They also made guitars.

Violin Bass

1960s		$325	$400

Kinal

1969-present. Luthier Michael Kinal builds and imports his production/custom, professional and premium grade, solidbody electric basses, in Vancouver, British Columbia, Canada. He also builds guitars.

Kingslight Guitars

1980-present. Luthier John Kingslight builds his premium grade, custom/production, acoustic basses in Portage, Michigan (in Taos, New Mexico for '80-'83). He also builds guitars.

Kingston

Ca. 1958-1967. Imported from Japan by Westheimer Importing Corp. of Chicago. Early examples by Guyatone and Teisco. They also offered guitars.

Electric Bass

1960s	Various models	$100	$350

Klein Acoustic Guitars

1972-present. Luthiers Steve Klein and Steven Kauffman build their production/custom, premium and presentation grade acoustic basses in Sonoma, California. They also build guitars.

Klein Electric Guitars

1988-present. Lorenzo German produces his professional grade, production/custom, basses in Linden, California. He also builds guitars.

Klira

Founded in 1887 in Schoenbach, Germany, mainly making violins, but added guitars and basses in the 1950s. The instruments of the '50s and '60s were aimed at the budget market, but workmanship improved with the '70s models.

Electric Bass

1960s	Beatle Bass copy	$425	$525
1960s	Various models	$350	$525

MODEL YEAR	FEATURES	EXC. COND. LOW	HIGH

Knutson Luthiery

1981-present. Professional and premium grade, custom, electric upright basses built by luthier John Knutson in Forestville, California. He also builds guitars, lap steels and mandolins.

Koll

1990-present. Professional and premium grade, custom/production, solidbody and chambered basses built by luthier Saul Koll, originally in Long Beach, California, and since '93, in Portland, Oregon. He also builds guitars.

Kona

2001-present. Budget grade, production, acoustic and electric basses made in Asia. They also offer guitars, amps and banjos.

Kramer

1976-1990, 1995-present. Budget grade, production, imported solidbody basses. They also offer guitars. Kramer's first guitars and basses featured aluminum necks with wooden inserts on back. Around '80 they started to switch to more economical wood necks and aluminum necks were last produced in '85. Gibson acquired the brand in '97.

250-B Special Bass
1977-1979. Offset double-cut, aluminum neck, Ebonol 'board, zero fret, 1 single-coil, natural.

1977-1979		$550	$650

350-B Standard Bass
1976-1979. Offset double-cut, aluminum neck, Ebonol 'board, tropical woods, 1 single-coil, dots. The 350 and 450 were Kramer's first basses.

1976-1979		$750	$800

450-B Deluxe Bass
1976-1980. As 350-B, but with 2 single-coils and blocks.

1976-1980		$800	$1,000

650-B Artist Bass
1977-1980. Double-cut, birdseye maple/burled walnut, aluminum neck, zero fret, mother-of-pearl crowns, 2 humbuckers.

1977-1980		$1,100	$1,300

DMB 2000 Bass
1979. Bolt-on aluminum neck, slot headstock.

1979		$500	$625

DMZ 4000 Bass
1978-1982. Bolt-on aluminum neck, slot headstock, double-cut solidbody, active EQ and dual-coil humbucking pickup, dot inlay.

1978-1981		$525	$750
1982	Bill Wyman-type	$675	$950

DMZ 4001 Bass
1979-1980. Aluminum neck, slot headstock, double-cut solidbody, 1 dual-coil humbucker pickup, dot inlay.

1979-1980		$525	$650

DMZ 5000 Bass
1979-1980. Double-cut solidbody, aluminum neck, slotted headstock, 2 pickups, crown inlays.

1979-1980		$575	$750

DMZ 6000B Bass
1979-1980. Double-cut, aluminum neck, slotted headstock, 2 pickups, crown inlays.

1979-1980		$850	$1,050

Duke Custom/Standard Bass
1981-1983. Headless, aluminum neck, 1 humbucker.

1981-1983		$400	$500

Duke Special Bass
1982-1985. Headless, aluminum neck, 2 pickups, with frets or fretless.

1982-1985		$450	$550

Ferrington KFB-1/KFB-2 Acoustic Bass
1987-1990. Acoustic/electric, bridge-mounted active pickup, tone and volume control, various colors. KFB-1 has binding and diamond dot inlays; the KFB-2 no binding and dot inlays. Danny Ferrington continued to offer the KFB-1 after Kramer closed in '90.

1987-1990		$325	$400

Focus 7000 Bass
1985-1987. Offset double-cut solidbody, P and double J pickups, Japanese-made.

1985-1987		$225	$275

Focus 8000 Bass
1985-1987. Offset double-cut solidbody, Japanese-made.

1985-1987		$250	$300

Focus K-77 Bass
1984. Offset double-cut solidbody, 1 pickup, Japanese-made.

1984		$225	$275

Focus K-88 Bass
1984. Two pickup Focus.

1984		$225	$275

Forum Series Bass
1987-1990. Japanese-made double-cut, 2 pickups, neck-thru (I & III) or bolt-neck (II & IV).

1987-1990	Forum I	$500	$600
1987-1990	Forum II	$400	$500
1987-1990	Forum III	$300	$375
1987-1990	Forum IV	$250	$300

Gene Simmons Axe Bass
1980-1981. Axe-shaped bass, slot headstock.

1980-1981		$2,800	$3,300

Hundred Series Bass
1988-1990. Import budget line, 7/8th solidbody.

1988-1990	710	$225	$275
1988-1990	720	$250	$300

Pacer Bass
1982-1984. Offset double-cut solidbody, red.

1982-1984		$600	$700

Pioneer Bass
1981-1986. First wood neck basses, offset double cut, JBX or PBX pickups, dots, '81-'84 models with soft headstocks, later '84 on with banana headstocks.

1981-1986	Double J, 2 JBX	$600	$750
1981-1986	Imperial, JBX & PBX	$575	$675
1981-1986	Special, 1 PBX	$550	$650
1982-1984	Carrera, JBX & PBX	$600	$750

Ken Smith Black Tiger

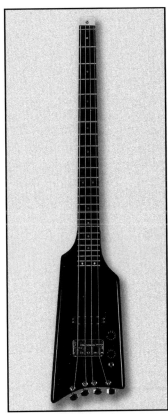

'80s Kramer Duke Standard

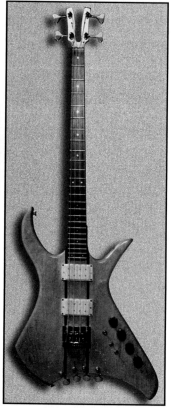

1980 Kramer XL-8

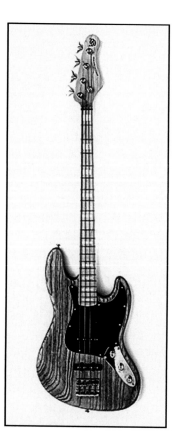

KSD 704

MODEL YEAR	FEATURES	EXC. COND. LOW	HIGH

Ripley Four-String Bass
1985-1987. Four-string version.

| 1985-1987 | | $600 | $750 |

Ripley Five-String Bass
1984-1987. Offset double-cut, 5 strings, stereo, pan pots for each string, front and back pickups for each string, active circuitry.

| 1984-1987 | | $600 | $750 |

Stagemaster Custom Bass (Import)
1982-1985, 1987-1990. First version had an aluminum neck (wood optional). Later version was neck-thru-body, bound neck, either active or passive pickups.

1982-1985	Imperial	$450	$550
1982-1985	Special	$400	$500
1982-1985	Standard	$425	$525
1987-1990	Reintroduced models	$400	$500

Stagemaster Deluxe Bass (U.S.A.)
1981. Made in USA, 8-string, metal neck.

| 1981 | | $1,100 | $1,250 |

Striker 700 Bass
1985-1989. Offset double-cut, Korean-import, 1 pickup until '87, 2 after. Striker name was again used on a bass in '99.

| 1985-1987 | 1 pickup | $175 | $250 |
| 1988-1989 | 2 pickups | $200 | $300 |

Vanguard Bass
1981-1983. V-shaped body, Special (aluminum neck) or Standard (wood neck).

| 1981-1982 | Special | $600 | $700 |
| 1983-1984 | Standard | $625 | $725 |

XKB-10 (Wedge) Bass
1980-1981. Wedge-shaped body, aluminum neck.

| 1980-1981 | | $500 | $625 |

XKB-20 Bass
1981. 2nd version, more traditional double cut body.

| 1981 | | $475 | $575 |

XL Series Bass
1980-1981. Odd shaped double-cut solidbody, aluminum neck.

1980-1981	XL-9, 4-string	$775	$950
1981	XL-24, 4-string	$800	$1,000
1981	XL-8, 8-string	$800	$1,000

ZX Aero Star Series Bass (Import)
1986-1989. Various models include ZX-70 (offset double-cut solidbody, 1 pickup).

| 1986-1989 | | $75 | $100 |

KSD
2003-present. Intermediate grade, production, imported bass line designed by Ken Smith (see Smith listing) and distributed by Brooklyn Gear.

Kubicki
1973-present. Professional and premium grade, production/custom, solidbody basses built by luthier Phil Kubicki in Santa Barbara, California. Kubicki began building acoustic guitars when he was 15. In '64 at age 19, he went to work with Roger

Rossmeisl at Fender Musical Instrument's research and development department for acoustic guitars. Nine years later he moved to Santa Barbara, California, and established Philip Kubicki Technology, which is best known for its line of Factor basses and also builds acoustic guitars, custom electric guitars, bodies and necks, and mini-guitars and does custom work, repairs and restorations.

Ex Factor 4/Factor 4 Bass
1985-present. Solidbody, maple body, bolt-on maple neck, fretless available, 4 strings, 2 pickups, active electronics.

| 1980s | | $800 | $1,000 |

Ex Factor 5/Factor 5 Bass
1985-ca.1990. Solidbody, bolt-on maple neck, fretless available, 5 strings, 2 pickups, active electronics.

| 1980s | | $900 | $1,100 |

Kustom
1968-present. Founded by Bud Ross in Chanute, Kansas, and best known for the tuck-and-roll amps, Kustom also offered guitars and basses from '68 to '69.

Electric Hollowbody Bass

| 1968-1969 | Various models | $950 | $1,100 |

La Baye
1967. Short-lived brand out of Green Bay, Wisconsin and built by the Holman-Woodell factory in Neodesha, Kansas. There was also a guitar model.

Model 2x4 II Bass
1967. Very low production, dual pickups, long-scale, small rectangle solidbody, sometimes referred to as the Bass II.

| 1967 | | $1,200 | $1,500 |

Model 2x4 Mini-Bass
1967. Short-scale, 1 pickup, small rectangle solidbody.

| 1967 | | $1,200 | $1,500 |

Lado
1973-present. Founded by Joe Kovacic, Lado builds professional and premium grade, production/custom, solidbody basses in Lindsay, Ontario. Some model lines are branded J. K. Lado. They also build guitars.

Lafayette
Ca. 1963-1967. Sold through Lafayette Electronics catalogs. Early Japanese-made guitars and basses from pre-copy era, generally shorter scale beginner instruments. Many made by Guyatone, some possibly by Teisco.

Lakland
1994-present. Professional and premium grade, production/custom, solid and hollowbody basses from luthier Dan Lakin in Chicago, Illinois. Lakland basses are built in the U.S. and overseas (Skyline series).

MODEL YEAR	FEATURES	EXC. COND. LOW	HIGH

4 - 63 Classic Bass
1994-2002. Offset double-cut alder body, large bass horn, bolt neck.

| 1994-2002 | | $1,500 | $1,800 |

4 - 63 Deluxe Bass
1994-2002. Like Classic but with figured maple top on ash body.

| 1994-2002 | | $1,700 | $2,000 |

4 - 63 Standard Bass
1994-2002. Like Classic, but with swamp ash body.

| 1994-2002 | | $1,500 | $1,800 |

4 - 94 Classic Bass
1994-present. Offset double-cut alder body with maple top, large bass horn, bolt neck.

| 1994-2000 | | $1,500 | $1,800 |

4 - 94 Deluxe Bass
1994-present. Like Classic but with figured maple top on ash body.

| 1994-2000 | | $1,700 | $2,000 |

4 - 94 Standard Bass
1994-present. Like Classic, but with swamp ash body.

| 1994-2000 | | $1,500 | $1,800 |

Joe Osborn Bass
1998-present. Classic offset double-cut, 4- or 5-string, alder or swamp ash body, 2 pickups.

| 1998-2003 | | $1,850 | $2,050 |

Larrivee
1968-present. Founded by Jean Larrivee in Toronto and currently located in Vancouver, British Columbia, Larrivee has offered several acoustic basses over the years.

Leach
1980-present. Luthier Harvey Leach builds his premium grade, custom, acoustic basses in Cedar Ridge, California. He also builds guitars.

Lehtela
1993-present. Professional and premium grade, custom/production, solidbody basses built by luthier Ari Lehtela in Charlotte, North Carolina. He also builds guitars.

Linc Luthier
Professional and premium grade, custom/production, electric, acoustic and upright basses built by luther Linc Luthier in Upland, California. He also builds guitars and double-necks.

Lipe Guitars USA
1983-1989, 2000-present. Luthier Michael Lipe builds his custom, professional grade, basses in Sunvalley, California. He also builds guitars.

Lotus
Late-1970-2004. Electric basses imported originally by Midco International, and most recently by Musicorp. They also made guitars, banjos and mandolins.

Lowrider Basses
2003-present. Professional grade, production/custom, solidbody basses made in Las Vegas, Nevada by Ed Roman.

LSR Headless Instruments
1988-present. Professional grade, production/custom, solidbody headless basses made in Las Vegas, Nevada by Ed Roman. They also make guitars.

LTD
1995-present. Intermediate grade, production, Korean-made solidbody basses offered by ESP. They also offer guitars.

Lyle
Ca. 1969-1980. Japanese guitars and basses imported by distributor L.D. Heater in Portland, Oregon.

Electric Solidbody Bass
| 1970s | Various models | $100 | $275 |

Lyon by Washburn
1990s-present. Budget grade, production, basses sold by mass merchandisers such as Target. They also offer guitars.

Lyric
1996-present. Luthier John Southern builds his professional and premium grade, custom, basses in Tulsa, Oklahoma. He also builds guitars.

Magnatone
Ca. 1937-1971. Founded as Dickerson Brothers, known as Magna Electronics from '47. Produced instruments under own brand and for many others.

Hurricane Bass
1965-1966. Offset double cut solidbody, 1 single-coil, 4-on-a-side tuners, Magnatone logo on guard and headstock, Hurricane logo on headstock.

| 1965-1966 | | $575 | $700 |

Mako
1985-1989. Line of solidbody basses from Kaman (Ovation, Hamer). They also offered guitars and amps.

Electric Solidbody Bass
| 1985-1989 | Student bass | $75 | $225 |

Mal n' Sal
See listing for Alternative Guitar and Amplifier Company.

Marco Polo
1960- ca.1964. One of the first inexpensive Japanese brands to be imported into the U.S., they also offered guitars.

Solidbody Bass
| 1960s | Various models | $75 | $175 |

Lakland Jerry Scheff Signature

Lowrider Bass

Martin B-40

1982 Martin EB-18

MODEL YEAR	FEATURES	EXC. COND. LOW	HIGH

Marling

Ca. 1975. Budget line instruments marketed by EKO of Recanati, Italy; probably made by them, although possibly imported. They also had guitars.

Electric Solidbody Bass

Models include the E.495 (copy of LP), E.485 (copy of Tele), and the E.465 (Manta-style).

1970s		$75	$175

Martin

1833-present. Professional grade, production, acoustic basses made in the U.S. In 1978, Martin re-entered the electric market and introduced their solidbody EB-18 and EB-28 Basses. In the '80s they offered Stinger brand electric basses. By the late '80s, they started offering acoustic basses.

B-1 Acoustic Bass

2002		$800	$900

B-40 Acoustic Bass

1989-1996. Jumbo-size, spruce top and Indian rosewood back and sides, mahogany neck, ebony 'board, built-in pickup and volume and tone controls. The B-40B had a pickup.

1989-1996	B-40B	$1,500	$1,800
1989-1996	Without pickup	$1,300	$1,600

B-65 Acoustic Bass

1989-1993. Jumbo-size, spruce top, maple back and sides, mahogany neck, ebony 'board with 23 frets, built-in pickup and volume and tone controls, natural.

1989-1993		$1,400	$1,700

BC-15E Acoustic Bass

1999-present. Single cut, sapele or mahogany top, sides, and back, Fishman pickup.

1999-2006		$925	$1,000

EB-18 Bass

1979-1982. Electric solidbody, neck-thru, 1 pickup, natural.

1979-1982		$750	$950

EB-28 Bass

1980-1982. Electric solidbody.

1980-1982		$875	$1,000

SBL-10 Bass

Stinger brand solidbody, maple neck, 1 split and 1 bar pickup.

1980s		$150	$200

Marvel

1950s-mid-1960s. Brand used for budget guitars and basses marketed by Peter Sorkin Company in New York, New York.

Electric Solidbody Bass

1950s	Various models	$125	$300

Messenger

1967-1968. Built by Musicraft, Inc., Messengers featured a neck-thru metal alloy neck. They also made guitars.

Bass

1967-1968. Metal alloy neck. Messenger mainly made guitars - they offered a bass, but it is unlikely many were built.

1967-1968		$2,500	$3,000

Messenger Upright

Made by Knutson Luthiery, see that listing.

Michael Kelly

2000-present. Intermediate grade, production, acoustic/electric basses imported by Elite Music Brands of Clearwater, Florida. They also offer mandolins and guitars.

Michael Tuttle

2003-present. Luthier Michael Tuttle builds his professional and premium grade, custom, solid and hollow body basses in Saugus, California. He also builds guitars.

Microfrets

1967-1975, 2004-2005. Professional grade, production, electric basses built in Myersville, Maryland. They also built guitars.

Husky Bass

1971-1974/75. Double-cut, 2 pickups, two-on-a-side tuners.

1971-1975		$450	$650

Rendezvous Bass

1970. One pickup, orange sunburst.

1970		$500	$700

Signature Bass

1969-1975. Double-cut, 2 pickups, two-on-a-side tuners.

1969-1975		$750	$850

Stage II Bass

1969-1975. Double-cut, 2 pickups, two-on-a-side tuners.

1969-1975		$650	$850

Thundermaster Bass

1969		$750	$850

Mike Lull Custom Guitars

1995-present. Professional and premium grade, production/custom, basses built by luthier Mike Lull in Bellevue, Washington. He also builds guitars.

Mirabella

1997-present. Professional and premium grade, custom, basses built by luthier Cristian Mirabella in Babylon, New York. He also builds guitars, mandolins and ukes.

Mitre

1983-1985. Bolt-neck solidbody basses made in Aldenville (or East Longmeadow), Massachusetts. They also built guitars.

MODEL YEAR	FEATURES	EXC. COND. LOW	HIGH

MJ Guitar Engineering

1993-present. Luthier Mark Johnson builds his professional grade, production/custom, chambered basses in Rohnert Park, California. He also builds guitars.

Modulus

1978-present. Founded by aerospace engineer Geoff Gould, Modulus currently offers professional and premium grade, production/custom, solidbody basses built in California. They also build guitars.

Bassstar SP-24 Active Bass

1981-ca. 1990. EMG J pickups, active bass and treble circuits.

1980s		$1,200	$1,400

Flea 4/Flea Signature Bass

1997-2003. Offset double-cut alder solidbody, also offered as 5-string.

1997-2003		$1,300	$1,600

Genesis Series Bass

1997-1998, 2003-present. Offset double-cut, 2 pickups, 4- or 5-string.

2003-2004	Various models	$1,000	$1,200

Quantum-4 Series Bass

1982-present. Offset double-cut, 2 pickups, 35" scale.

1982-2000		$1,600	$1,800

Quantum-5 Series Bass

1982-present. 5-String version.

1982-2000		$1,700	$1,900

Quantum-6 Series Bass

1982-present. 6-string version.

1982-2000		$1,800	$2,000

Vintage V Series Bass

2002	VJ-4	$1,700	$1,800

Mollerup Basses

1984-present. Luthier Laurence Mollerup builds his professional grade, custom/production, electric basses and electric double basses in Vancouver, British Columbia. He has also built guitars.

Monroe Guitars

2004-present. Professional grade, custom, solidbody electric basses built by Matt Handley in State Center, Iowa. He also builds guitars.

Moon

1979-present. Professional grade, production/custom, basses made in Japan. They also build guitars.

Moonstone

1972-present. Luthier Steve Helgeson builds his premium grade, production/custom, acoustic and electric basses in Eureka, California. He also builds guitars.

Explorer Bass

1980-1983. Figured wood body, neck-thru.

1980-1983		$1,600	$2,000

Vulcan Bass

1982-1984. Solidbody, flat top (Vulcan) or carved top (Vulcan II), maple body, gold hardware.

1982-1984		$1,700	$2,000

Morales

Ca.1967-1968. Guitars and basses made in Japan by Zen-On and not heavily imported into the U.S.

Electric Solidbody Bass

1967-1968	Various models	$125	$200

Morgan Monroe

1999-present. Intermediate grade, production, acoustic/electric basses made in Korea and distributed by SHS International of Indianapolis, Indiana. They also offer guitars, mandolins, banjos, and fiddles.

Mosrite

Semie Moseley's Mosrite offered various bass models throughout the many versions of the Mosrite company.

Brut Bass

Late-1960s. Assymetrical body with small cutaway on upper treble bout.

1960s		$1,100	$1,250

Celebrity Bass

1965-1969. ES-335-style semi-thick double-cut body with f-holes, 2 pickups.

1965-1966	Custom color	$1,250	$1,550
1965-1967	Sunburst	$1,150	$1,250
1968	Red	$1,000	$1,200
1969	Sunburst or red	$950	$1,100

Combo Bass

1966-1968. Hollowbody, 2 pickups.

1966-1968		$1,550	$1,900

Joe Maphis Bass

1966-1969. Ventures-style body, hollow without f-holes, 2 pickups, natural.

1966-1969		$1,800	$2,100

Ventures Bass

1965-1972. Two pickups.

1965	Various colors	$2,800	$3,500
1966	Various colors	$2,500	$3,500
1967-1968	Sunburst	$2,300	$3,300
1967-1968	Various colors	$2,300	$3,500
1969	Sunburst	$2,100	$3,000
1970-1972	Sunburst	$2,000	$2,500

V-II Bass

1973-1974. Ventures-style, 2 humbuckers, sunburst.

1973-1974		$1,900	$2,200

MTD

1994-present. Intermediate, professional, and premium grade, production/custom, electric basses built by luthier Michael Tobias (who founded Tobias Basses in '77) in Kingston, New York. Since '00, he also imports basses built in Korea to his specifications .

Mike Lull M5

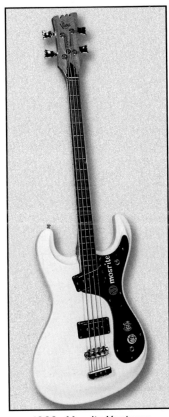

1960s Mosrite Ventures

BASSES

1979 Music Man Sabre Bass

1965 National 85

Murph

1965-1967. Mid-level electric solidbody basses built by Pat Murphy in San Fernado, California. Murph logo on headstock. They also offered guitars and amps.

Music Man

1972-present. Intermediate and professional grade, production, electric basses. They also build guitars.

Cutlass I/Cutlass II Bass

1982-1987. Ash body, graphite neck, string-thru-body.

Year	Features	Low	High
1982-1984	CLF era Cutlass I	$1,200	$1,500
1982-1984	CLF era Cutlass II	$1,400	$1,700
1984-1987	Ernie Ball era Cutlass I	$1,100	$1,200
1984-1987	Ernie Ball era Cutlass II	$1,150	$1,400

Sabre Bass

1978-ca.1991. Double-cut solidbody bass, 3-and-1 tuning keys, 2 humbucking pickups, on-board preamp, natural.

Year	Features	Low	High
1978-1979	CLF era	$1,200	$1,400
1980-1984	CLF era	$1,000	$1,200
1984-1991	Ernie Bass era	$850	$1,000

Stingray Bass

1976-present. Offset double-cut solidbody, 1 pickup, 3-and-1 tuners, string-thru until '80, various colors. In '05, additional pickup options available.

Year	Features	Low	High
1976-1979	CLF era	$2,400	$2,600
1980-1984	CLF era	$2,000	$2,300
1984-1989	Ernie Ball era	$1,200	$1,500
1990-1999		$900	$1,100
2000-2005		$900	$1,000

Stingray 20th Anniversary Bass

1992. 1400 made, flamed maple body.

Year	Features	Low	High
1992		$1,650	$1,850

Stingray 5-String Bass

1987-present. Active electronics, birdseye maple bolt neck, 1 humbucking pickup, 3-band EQ. In '05, additional pickup options available.

Year	Features	Low	High
1987-2005		$950	$1,150

Musicvox

1996-present. Intermediate grade, production, Korean-made retro-vibe guitars and basses from Matt Eichen of Cherry Hill, New Jersey.

Nady

1976-present. Wireless sound company Nady Systems offered guitars and basses with built-in wireless systems for 1985-'87. The neck-thru bass was made by Fernandes in Japan and was only available for about a year.

Nashguitars

2001-present. Luthier Bill Nash builds his professional grade, production/custom, solidbody basses in Olympia, Washington. He also builds guitars.

National

Ca. 1927-present. National offered electric basses in the '60s when Valco owned the brand.

N-850 Bass

1967-1968. Semi-hollow double-cut, art deco f-holes, 2 pickups, block markers, bout control knobs, sunburst.

Year	Features	Low	High
1967-1968		$600	$650

Val-Pro 85 Bass

1961-1962. Res-O-Glas body shaped like the U.S. map, 2 pickups, snow white, renamed National 85 in '63.

Year	Features	Low	High
1961-1962		$1,100	$1,350

National Reso-Phonic

1988-present. Professional grade, production/custom, acoustic and acoustic/electric resonator basses built in San Luis Obispo, California. They also build guitars, mandolins and ukuleles.

Navarro Custom

1986-present. Luthier Mike Navarro builds his production/custom, professional and premium grade, electric basses in San Juan, Puerto Rico. He also builds guitars.

New York Bass Works

1989-present. Luthier David Segal builds his professional and premium grade, production/custom, electric basses in New York.

Noble

Ca. 1950-ca. 1969. Guitars and basses distributed by Don Noble and Company of Chicago. Made by other companies. They also offered amps.

Norma

Ca.1965-1970. Guitars and basses imported from Japan by Chicago's Strum and Drum.

Electric Solidbody Bass

Year	Features	Low	High
1960s	Various models	$125	$275

Northworthy

1987-present. Professional and premium grade, production/custom, acoustic and electric basses built by luthier Alan Marshall in Ashbourne, Derbyshire, England. He also builds guitars and mandolins.

Novax

1989-present. Luthier Ralph Novak builds his fanned-fret professional grade, production/custom, solidbody basses in San Leandro, California. He also builds guitars.

Noyce

1974-present. Production/custom, professional and premium grade, acoustic and electric basses, and semi-acoustic double bass built by luthier Ian Noyce in Ballarat, Victoria, Australia. He also builds guitars.

MODEL YEAR	FEATURES	EXC. COND. LOW	HIGH

O'Hagan

1979-1983. Designed by Jerol O'Hagan in St. Louis Park, Minnesota. He also offered guitars.

Electric Solidbody Bass

1979-1983. Models include the Shark Bass, Night-Watch Bass, NightWatch Regular Bass, and the Twenty Two Bass.

1980s		$400	$500

Old Kraftsman

1930s-1960s. Brand used by the Spiegel Company. Guitars and basses made by other American manufacturers.

Electric Solidbody Bass

1950s	Various models	$250	$400

OLP (Officially Licensed Product)

Intermediate grade, production, guitars based on higher dollar guitar models officially licensed from the original manufacturer. OLP logo on headstock. They also offer guitars.

Oncor Sound

1980-ca. 1981. This Salt Lake City-based company made both a guitar and a bass synthesizer.

Oscar Schmidt

1879-1938, 1979-present. Budget and intermediate grade, production, acoustic basses distributed by U.S. Music Corp. (Washburn, Randall, etc.). They also offer guitars, mandolins, banjos, ukuleles and the famous Oscar Schmidt autoharp.

Oskar Graf Guitars

1970-present. Luthier Oskar Graf builds his premium and presentation grade, custom, basses in Clarendon, Ontario, Canada. He also builds guitars and lutes.

Ovation

1966-present. Intermediate and professional grade, production, acoustic/electric basses. Ovation offered electric solidbody basses early on and added acoustic basses in the '90s. They also offer guitars and mandolins.

Celebrity Series Bass

1990s-2000s. Deep bowl back, cutaway, acoustic/electric.

1990-2000s		$375	$450

Magnum Series Bass

1974-1980. Magnum I is odd-shaped mahogany solidbody, 2 pickups, mono/stereo, mute, sunburst, red or natural. Magnum II is with battery-powered preamp and 3-band EQ. Magnum III and IV had a new offset double-cut body.

1974-1978	Magnum I	$575	$700
1974-1978	Magnum II	$625	$775
1978-1980	Magnum III	$575	$700
1978-1980	Magnum IV	$625	$775

Typhoon II/Typhoon III Bass

1968-1971. Ovation necks, but bodies and hardware were German imports. Semi-hollowbody, 2 pickups, red or sunburst. Typhoon II is 335-style and III is fretless.

1968-1971	Typhoon II	$750	$925
1968-1971	Typhoon III	$800	$1,000

PANaramic

1961-1963. Guitars and basses made in Italy by the Crucianelli accordion company and imported by PANaramic accordion. They also offered amps made by Magnatone.

Electric Bass

1961-1963. Double-cut solidbody or hollowbody, 2 pickups, dot markers, sunburst.

1961-1963	Hollowbody	$400	$500
1961-1963	Solidbody	$400	$500

Parker

1992-present. Premium grade, production/custom, solidbody electric basses. They also build guitars.

Patrick Eggle Guitars

1991-present. Solidbody electric basses built in Birmingham, England. They also build guitars.

Paul Reed Smith

1985-present. PRS added basses in '86, but by '92 had dropped the models. In 2000 PRS started again offering professional and premium grade, production, solidbody electric basses. Bird inlays can add $100 or more to the values of PRS basses listed here.

Bass-4

1986-1992, 2007. Set neck, 3 single-coil pickups, hum-cancelling coil, active circuitry, 22-fret Brazilian rosewood 'board. Reintroduced (OEB Series) in 2000s.

1986-1987		$2,300	$2,800
1988-1992		$1,500	$1,800
2000-2007		$1,400	$1,700

Bass-5

1986-1992. Five-string, set-neck, rosewood 'board, 3 single-coil pickups, active electronics. Options include custom colors, bird inlays, fretless 'board.

1986-1987		$2,300	$2,800
1988-1992		$1,500	$1,800

CE Bass 4

1986-1991. Solidbody, maple bolt neck, alder body, rosewood 'board, 4-string.

1986-1987		$1,200	$1,500
1988-1991		$1,000	$1,200

CE Bass 5

1986-1991. Five-string solidbody, maple bolt neck, alder body, rosewood 'board.

1986-1987		$1,200	$1,500
1988-1991		$1,000	$1,200

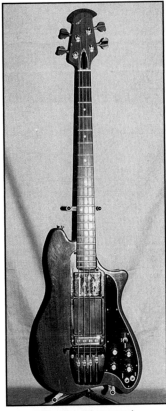

Ovation Magnum I

PRS Bass-4

BASSES

PRS Curly Bass 4

1991 Peavey RJ-IV

MODEL YEAR	FEATURES	EXC. COND. LOW	HIGH

Curly Bass-4
1986-1992. Double-cut solidbody, curly maple top, set maple neck, Brazilian rosewood 'board (ebony on fretless), 3 single-coil and 1 hum-cancelling pickups, various grades of maple tops, moon inlays.

1986-1987		$2,000	$2,300
1988-1992		$1,900	$2,200

Curly Bass-5
1986-1992. Five-string version of Curly Bass-4.

1986-1987		$2,000	$2,300
1988-1992		$1,900	$2,200

Electric Bass
2000-2007. Bolt neck 4-string, offered in regular and maple top versions.

2000-2007	Maple	$1,400	$1,700
2000-2007	Plain	$1,300	$1,600

Peavey
1965-present. Intermediate and professional grade, production/custom, electric basses. They also build guitars and amps. Hartley Peavey's first products were guitar amps and he added guitars and basses to the mix in '78.

Axcelerator Bass
1994-1998. Offset double-cut, long thin horns, 2 humbuckers, stacked control knobs, bolt neck, dot markers.

1994-1998		$300	$350

Cirrus Series Bass
1998-present. Offset double-cut, active electronics, in 4-, 5-string, and custom shop versions.

1998-2006	Cirrus 4	$675	$725
1998-2006	Cirrus 5	$700	$750
1998-2006	Cirrus 6	$725	$775

Dyna-Bass
1987-1993. Double-cut solidbody, active electronics, 3-band EQ, rosewood 'board, opaque finish.

1987-1993		$250	$300

Dyna-Bass Limited
1987-1990. Neck-thru-body, ebony 'board, flamed maple neck/body construction, purple heart strips, mother-of-pearl inlays.

1987-1990		$450	$550

Forum Bass
1994-1995. Double-cut solidbody, rosewood 'board, dot inlays, 2 humbuckers.

1994-1995		$250	$300

Forum Plus Bass
1994. Forum Bass with added active electronics.

1994		$275	$325

Foundation Bass
1984-2002. Double-cut solidbody, 2 pickups, maple neck.

1984-2002		$225	$275

Foundation S Active Bass
1987-1991. Similar to Foundation S Bass with added active circuitry, provides low-impedance output, 2 pickups.

1987-1991		$250	$300

MODEL YEAR	FEATURES	EXC. COND. LOW	HIGH

Foundation S Bass
1986-1991. Two split-coil pickups, maple body, rosewood 'board, black hardware, black painted headstock.

1986-1991		$225	$275

Fury Bass
1986-1999. Double-cut solidbody, rosewood 'board, 1 split-coil humbucker.

1986-1999		$175	$200

Fury Custom Bass
1986-1993. Fury Bass with black hardware and narrow neck.

1986-1993		$250	$300

Fury VI Bass

2002	6-string	$300	$375

Grind Series Bass
2001-present. Offset double-cut, neck-thru, long bass horn, 2 pickups, 4-, 5-, or 6-string.

2001-2006	Grind 4	$225	$275
2001-2006	Grind 5	$250	$300

Milestone Series Bass
1994-present. Import offset double cut, Milestone I ('94) replaced by 1 P-style pickup II ('95-'01), split humbucker IV ('99-'04); 2 single-coil III ('99-present) now just called Milestone.

1994	Milestone I	$75	$100
1995-2001	Milestone II	$75	$100
1999-2004	Milestone IV	$100	$150
1999-2006	Milestone III, Milestone	$100	$150

Millenium Series Bass
2001-present. Offset double-cut, agathis bodies, maple tops, in 4- or 5-string.

2001-2004		$125	$250

Patriot Bass
1984-1988. General J-Bass styling with larger thinner horns, 1 single-coil, maple neck.

1984-1988		$150	$175

Patriot Custom Bass
1986-1988. Patriot with rosewood neck, matching headstock.

1986-1988		$175	$250

RJ-IV Bass
1990-1993. Randy Jackson Signature model, neck-thru-body, 2 split-coil active pickups, ebony 'board, mother-of-pearl position markers.

1990-1993		$325	$400

Rudy Sarzo Signature Bass
1989-1993. Double-cut solidbody, active EQ, ebony 'board, 2 pickups.

1989-1993		$500	$600

T-20FL Bass
1983. Fretless double-cut solidbody, 1 pickup, also available as the fretted T-20 ('82-'83).

1983		$200	$250

T-40/T-40FL Bass
1978-1987. Double-cut solidbody, 2 pickups. T-40FL is fretless.

1978-1987	T-40	$300	$375
1978-1987	T-40FL	$300	$375

MODEL YEAR	FEATURES	EXC. COND. LOW	HIGH

T-45 Bass
1982-1986. T-40 with 1 humbucking pickup, and a mid-frequency rolloff knob.

1982-1986		$300	$375

TL Series Bass
1988-1998. Neck-thru-body, gold hardware, active humbuckers, EQ, flamed maple neck and body, 5-string (TL-Five) or 6 (TL-Six).

1988-1998	TL-Five	$500	$625
1989-1998	TL-Six	$550	$675

Pedulla
1975-present. Professional and premium grade, production/custom, electric basses made in Rockland, Massachusetts. Founded by Michael Pedulla, Pedulla offers various upscale options which affect valuation so each instrument should be evaluated on a case-by-case basis. Unless specifically noted, the following listings have standard to mid-level features. High-end options are specifically noted; if not, these options will have a relatively higher value than those shown here.

Buzz-4/Buzz-5 Bass
1980-present. Double-cut neck-thru solidbody, fretless, long-scale, maple neck and body wings, 2 pickups, preamp, some with other active electronics, various colors, 4-, 5-, 6-, 8-string versions.

1980-1999		$1,250	$1,550

Interceptor Bass
1980s. Double-cut, maple/walnut laminated neck-thru.

1980s		$1,025	$1,250

MVP Series Bass
1984-present. Fretted version of Buzz Bass, standard or flame top, 4-, 5-, 6-, 8-string versions, MVP II is bolt-on neck version.

1984-1990s	MVP-4 flame top	$1,350	$1,500
1984-1990s	MVP-4 standard top	$1,200	$1,350
1984-1990s	MVP-5	$1,200	$1,350
1980s	MVP-6	$1,300	$1,450
1990s	MVP II	$900	$950

Orsini Wurlitzer 4-String Bass
Mid-1970s. Body style similar to late-'50s Gibson double-cut slab body SG Special, neck-thru, 2 pickups, natural. Sold by Boston's Wurlitzer music store chain.

1970s		$1,400	$1,550

Quilt Limited Bass
Neck-thru-body with curly maple centerstrip, quilted maple body wings, 2 Bartolini pickups, available in fretted or fretless 4- and 5-string models.

1987		$1,350	$1,500

Rapture 4/5 Series Bass
1995-present. Solidbody with extra long thin bass horn and extra short treble horn, 4- or 5-string, various colors.

1995-2004		$1,250	$1,400

Series II Bass
1987-1992. Bolt neck, rosewood 'board, mother-of-pearl dot inlays, Bartolini pickups.

1987-1992		$725	$900

Thunderbass 4/5/6 Series Bass
1993-present. Solidbody with extra long thin bass horn and extra short treble horn, 4-, 5- or 6-string, standard features or triple A top.

1993-1999	AAA top	$1,700	$2,000
1993-1999	Standard features	$1,350	$1,650
2000-2005	AAA top	$1,800	$2,000

Penco
Ca. 1974-1978. Generally high quality Japanese-made copies of classic American bass guitars. They also made guitars, mandolins and banjos.

Electric Bass
1974-1978. Various models.

1974-1978		$175	$325

Pensa (Pensa-Suhr)
1982-present. Premium grade, production/custom, solidbody basses built in the U.S. They also build guitars.

Phantom Guitar Works
1992-present. Intermediate grade, production/custom, solid and hollowbody basses assembled in Clatskanie, Oregon. They also build guitars and the MandoGuitar.

Pieper
2005-present. Premium grade, production/custom, solidbody basses with interchangable necks built by luthier Robert Pieper in New Haven, Connecticut. He also builds guitars.

Premier
Ca.1938-ca.1975, 1990s-present. Budget and intermediate grade, production, import basses. They also offer guitars. Originally American-made instruments, but by the '60s imported parts were being used. Current models are imports.

Bantam Bass
1950-1970. Small body, single-cut short-scale archtop electric, torch headstock inlay, sparkle 'guard, sunburst.

1950-1970		$550	$675

Electric Solidbody Bass

1960s	Various models	$375	$450

Prestige
Professional grade, production, acoustic and electric basses from Vancouver, British Columbia. They also offer guitars.

Rarebird Guitars
1978-2007. Luthier Bruce Clay built his professional grade, production/custom, electric solidbody and hollowbody basses originally in Arvada, Colorado, and after '05 in Santa Fe, New Mexico. He also built guitars.

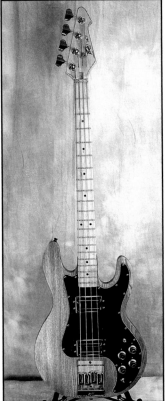

Peavey T-40

Pedulla Buzz 4

BASSES

Reverend Rumblefish PJ

1980 Rick Turner Model 1

MODEL YEAR	FEATURES	EXC. COND. LOW	HIGH

Rat Fink

2002-present. Lace Music Products offered these intermediate grade, production, basses and guitars, featuring the artwork of Ed Big Daddy Roth until '05. They still offer amps.

Regal

Ca. 1884-1966, 1987-present. Intermediate grade, production, acoustic wood body resonator basses from Saga. They also build guitars.

Renaissance

1978-1980. Plexiglass solidbody electric guitars and basses made in Malvern, Pennsylvania.

Plexiglas Bass

1978-1980. Plexiglas bodies and active electronics, models include the DPB bass (double-cut, 1 pickup, '78-'79), SPB (single-cut, 2 pickups, '78-'79), T-100B (Bich-style, 1 pickup, '80), S-100B (double-cut, 1 pickup, '80), and the S-200B (double-cut, 2 pickups, '80).

1978-1980		$600	$725

Renaissance Guitars

1994-present. Professional grade, custom, acoustic and solidbody basses built by luthier Rick Turner in Santa Cruz, California. He also builds guitars and ukuleles.

Reverend

1996-present. Reverend built electric basses in Warren, Michigan, from '98 to '04. They continue to build guitars.

Rumblefish Bass

1998-2004. USA-made, offset double-cut, J-style neck and bridge pickups, 2 volumes, 1 master tone.

1998-2004		$650	$950

Rick Turner

1979-1981, 1990-present. Rick Turner has a long career as a luthier, electronics designer and innovator. He also makes the Renaissance line of guitars in his shop in Santa Cruz, California. Turner estimates that during the three years his company was in business the first time around, only 25 to 30 basses were built, approximately half of which were shipped to Japan.

Rickenbacker

1931-present. Professional grade, production/custom, electric basses. They also build guitars. Rickenbacker introduced their first electric bass in '57 and has always been a strong player in the bass market.

Electric Upright Bass

1936. Cast aluminum neck and body, horseshoe pickup, extension pole.

1936		$4,800	$5,200

MODEL YEAR	FEATURES	EXC. COND. LOW	HIGH

Model 1999 (Rose-Morris) Bass

1964-1967. Export made for English distributor Rose-Morris of London, built along the lines of the U.S. Model 4000 Bass but with small differences that are considered important in the vintage guitar market.

1964-1967		$2,500	$5,500

Model 2030 Hamburg Bass

1984-1997. Rounded double-cut, 2 pickups, active electronics.

1984-1989		$625	$725
1990-1997		$575	$675

Model 2030GF (Glenn Frey) Bass

1992-1995. Limited Edition, double-cut, 2 humbuckers, Jetglo finish.

1992-1995		$1,150	$1,450

Model 2050 El Dorado Bass

1984-1992. Gold hardware, 2 pickups, active.

1984-1992		$800	$900

Model 2060 El Dorado Bass

1992-1997. Gold hardware, 2 pickups, active, double-bound body.

1992-1997		$1,000	$1,200

Model 3000 Bass

1975-1984. Rounded double-cut, 30" scale, 1 pickup, brown sunburst.

1975-1984		$1,100	$1,400

Model 3001 Bass

1975-1984. Same as Model 3000 but with longer 33-1/2" scale, Wine Red.

1975-1984		$800	$1,000

Model 3261 (Rose-Morris Slim-Line) Bass

1967. Export model made for English distributor Rose-Morris, built along the lines of a U.S. equivalent Model 4005 Bass.

1967		$4,000	$6,000

Model 4000 Bass

1958-1985. Cresting wave body and headstock, 1 horseshoe pickup (changed to regular pickup in '64), neck-thru-body.

1958-1959	Autumnglo, Mapleglo	$7,000	$9,000
1960	Fireglo	$6,000	$9,000
1960	Mapleglo	$5,500	$6,000
1961-1965	Fireglo	$5,000	$5,500
1961-1965	Mapleglo	$5,000	$6,000
1967-1969	Various colors	$3,500	$4,000
1970-1972	Various colors	$2,200	$2,800
1973-1979	Various colors	$2,000	$2,200
1980-1985	Various colors	$1,400	$1,500

Model 4001 Bass

1961-1965, 1968-1986. Fancy version of 4000, 1 horseshoe magnet pickup (changed to regular pickup in '64) and 1 bar magnet pickup, triangle inlays, bound neck.

1961-1965	Fireglo	$5,500	$6,500
1963-1965	Mapleglo	$6,000	$7,000
1967-1969	Various colors	$3,600	$4,400
1970-1972	Various colors	$2,500	$3,100
1973-1979	Various colors	$1,950	$2,400
1980-1986	Various colors	$1,700	$2,100

MODEL YEAR	FEATURES	EXC. COND. LOW	HIGH

Model 4001 C64S Bass
2001-present. Recreation of Paul McCartney's 4001 featuring changes he made like a reshaped body and zero-fret 'board.

2001-2006		$1,700	$2,100

Model 4001 CS Bass
1991-1997. Chris Squire signature model.

1991-1997	With certificate	$4,600	$5,500
1991-1997	Without certificate	$4,100	$4,500

Model 4001 FL Bass
1968-1986. Fretless version of 4001 Bass, special order in '60s, various colors.

1968-1970s		$2,100	$3,600

Model 4001 V63 Bass
1984-2000. Vintage '63 reissue of Model 4001S, horseshoe-magnet pickup, Mapleglo.

1984-2000		$2,000	$2,450

Model 4001S Bass
1964-1985. Same as Model 4000, but with 2 pickups, export model.

1980-1985		$1,300	$1,500

Model 4002 Bass
1967-1985. Cresting wave body and headstock, 2 humbuckers, black 'guard, checkerboard binding.

1980-1985		$3,400	$4,200

Model 4003 Bass
1979-present. Similar to Model 4001, split 'guard, deluxe features.

1979-1989		$1,725	$1,850
1990-1999		$1,500	$1,800
2000-2007		$1,200	$1,500

Model 4003 FL Bass
1979-present. Fretless version.

1980s		$1,100	$1,600

Model 4003S Bass
1986-2003. Standard feature version of 4003, 4 strings.

1986-2003		$1,400	$1,600

Model 4003S Redneck Bass
Late 1980s. Red body, 'board and headstock, black hardware.

1980s		$2,300	$2,800

Model 4003S Tuxedo Bass
1987. White body with black 'guard and hardware. 100 made.

1987		$1,600	$2,000

Model 4003S/5 Bass
1986-2003. 5-string 4003S.

1986-2003		$1,400	$1,600

Model 4003S/8 Bass
1986-2003. 8-string 4003S.

1986-2003		$2,500	$3,000

Model 4003S/SPC Blackstar Bass
1989. Black version, black finish, 'board, knobs, and hardware. Also offered as 5-string.

1989		$2,800	$3,400

Model 4004C Cheyenne/Cheyenne II Bass
1993-present. Cresting wave, maple neck-thru-body with walnut body and head wings, gold hardware, dot inlay. Replaced by maple top 4004Cii Cheyenne II in '00.

1993-2004		$1,300	$1,500

Model 4005 Bass
1965-1984. New style double-cut semi-hollowbody, 2 pickups, R tailpiece, cresting wave headstock.

1965-1969	Various colors	$5,600	$7,000
1970-1979	Various colors	$4,000	$4,500
1980-1984	Various colors	$3,800	$4,200

Model 4005 L (Lightshow) Bass
1970-1975. Model 4005 with translucent top with lights in body that lit up when played, needed external transformer.

1970-1975		$13,000	$16,000

Model 4005 WB Bass
1966-1983. Old style Model 4005 with white-bound body.

1966	Mapleglo	$5,800	$6,500
1967-1969	Various colors	$5,700	$6,500
1970-1979	Various colors	$4,000	$4,500
1980-1983	Various colors	$3,900	$4,100

Model 4005-6 Bass
1965-1977. Model 4005 with 6 strings.

1965-1969		$8,000	$10,000
1970-1977		$6,000	$7,000

Model 4005-8 Bass
Late-1960s. Eight-string Model 4005.

1968-1969	Fireglo, Mapleglo	$9,000	$12,000

Model 4008 Bass
1975-1983. Eight-string, cresting wave body and headstock.

1975-1983		$1,600	$2,000

Model 4080 Doubleneck Bass
1975-1992. Bolt-on 6- and 4-string necks.

1975-1979	Jetglo, Mapleglo	$4,500	$5,500
1980-1992		$4,000	$5,000

Ritter Royal Instruments
Production/custom, solidbody basses built by luthier Jens Ritter in Wachenheim, Germany.

RKS
2003-present. Professional and premium grade, production/custom, solidbody basses designed by Ravi Sawhney and guitarist Dave Mason and built in Thousand Oaks, California. They also build guitars.

Rob Allen
1997-present. Professional grade, production/custom, lightweight basses made by luthier Robert Allen in Santa Barbara, California.

Robin
1982-present. Founded by David Wintz and located in Houston, Texas, Robin built basses until 1997. Most basses were Japanese-made until '87; American production began in '88. They continue to build guitars and also make Metropolitan (since 1996) and Alamo (since 2000) brand guitars.

Freedom Bass I
1984-1986. Offset double-cut, active treble and bass EQ controls, 1 pickup.

1984-1986		$525	$575

Rickenbacker 3000

1979 Rickenbacker 4005

BASSES

Robin Freedom

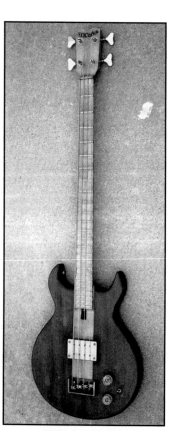

1977 S.D. Curlee

MODEL YEAR	FEATURES	EXC. COND. LOW	HIGH

Freedom Bass I Passive

1986-1989. Non-active version of Freedom Bass, I humbucker. Passive dropped from name in '87.

1986-1989		$525	$575

Medley Bass

1984-1997. Offset deep cutaways, 2 pickups, reverse headstock until '89, then split headstock, back to reverse by '94. Japanese-made until '87, U.S. after.

1984-1987	Japan	$400	$500
1988-1997	USA	$550	$675

Ranger Bass

1984-1997. Vintage style body, dot markers, medium scale and 1 pickup from '84 to '88 and long scale with P-style and J-style pickup configuration from '89 to '97.

1984-1987	Japan	$400	$500
1988-1997	USA	$800	$900

Rock Bass

2002-present. Chinese-made, intermediate and professional grade, production, bolt neck solidbody basses from the makers of Warwick basses.

RockBeach Guitars

2005-present. Professional grade, custom, chambered body basses built by luthier Greg Bogoshian in Rochester, New York. He also builds guitars.

Rockit Guitar

2006-present. Luthier Rod MacKenzie builds his premium grade, custom, electric basses in Everett, Washington. He also builds guitars.

Rogue

2001-present. Budget grade, production, solidbody and acoustic/electric basses. They also offer guitars, lap steels, mandolins, banjos, and ukuleles.

Roland

Best known for keyboards, effects, and amps, Roland offered synthesizer-based guitars and basses from 1977 to '86.

GR-33B (G-88) Bass Guitar Synthesizer

Early-mid 1980s. Solidbody bass with synthesizer in the guitar case, G-88 deluxe bass.

1983-1985		$900	$1,100

Roman & Blake Basses

1977-2003. Professional grade, production/custom, solidbody bass guitars made in Warren, Connecticut by Ed Roman.

Roman & Lipman Guitars

1989-2000. Production/custom, solidbody basses made in Danbury, Connecticut by Ed Roman. They also made guitars.

Roman USA Basses

2000-present. Professional grade, production/custom, solidbody basses made in Las Vegas, Nevada by Ed Roman.

Rono

1967-present. Luthier Ron Oates builds his professional and premium grade, production/custom, acoustic and solidbody basses in Boulder, Colorado. He also builds guitars and mandolins.

Roscoe Guitars

Early 1980s-present. Luthier Keith Roscoe builds his production/custom, professional and premium grade, solidbody electric basses in Greensboro, North Carolina.

S.D. Curlee

1975-1982. S.D. Curlee guitars and basses were made in Illinois; S.D. Curlee International instruments were made in Japan.

Electric Solidbody Bass

1970s	Various models	$275	$325

S101

2002-present. Budget and intermediate grade, production, solidbody basses imported from China. They also offer guitars, mandolins, and banjos.

Sadowsky

1980-present. Professional and premium grade, production/custom, solidbody basses built by luthier Roger Sadowsky in Brooklyn, New York. He also builds guitars. In '96, luthier Yoshi Kikuchi started building Sadowsky Tokyo instruments in Japan; those basses are now available in the U.S.

Vintage Style Bass

1982-1987		$1,350	$1,700

Samick

1958-2001, 2002-present. Budget, intermediate, and professional grade, production, imported acoustic and electric basses. They also offer guitars, mandolins, ukes and banjos.

Saturn

1960s-1970s. Imported, most likely from Japan, solid and semi-hollow body electric basses. Large S logo with Saturn name inside the S. Many sold through Eaton's in Canada. They also had guitars.

Schecter

1976-present. Intermediate and professional grade, production/custom, electric basses made in the U.S. and overseas. They also offer guitars. Schecter Custom Shop basses are made in Burbank, California and their Diamond Series is made in South Korea.

Bass

1980s	Various models	$225	$500

Diamond Series Bass

1997-2006		$250	$550

MODEL YEAR	FEATURES	EXC. COND. LOW	HIGH

Scott French
2004-present. Luthier Scott French builds professional grade, custom, basses in Auburn, California. He also builds guitars.

Shergold
1968-1992. Founded by Jack Golder and Norman Houlder, Shergold originally made guitars for other brands. In '75, they started building guitars and basses under their own name. By '82, general guitar production was halted but custom orders were filled through '90. In '91, general production was again started but ended in '92 when Golder died.

Shifflett
1990-present. Luthier Charles Shifflett builds his premium grade, custom, acoustic basses in High River, Alberta. He also guitars and banjos.

Silvertone
1941-ca.1970, present. Brand used by Sears. Instruments were U.S.-made and imported.

Hornet Bass
1950s-1960s. Fender-shape, 1 lipstick pickup.

1950-1960s		$400	$600

Model 1376L/1373L 6-String Bass
1956-1958. Short scale, 2 pickups

1956-1958		$1,350	$1,650

Simmons
2002-present. Luthier David L. Simmons builds his professional grade, production/custom, 4- and 5-string basses in Hendersonville, North Carolina.

Singletouch
Luthier Mark Singleton builds his professional and premium grade, custom/production, solidbody basses in Phillips Ranch, California. He also builds guitars.

Sinister
2003-present. Intermediate and professional grade, custom/production, solidbody basses built for Sinister Guitars by luthier Jon Kammerer.

Slammer
1999-present. Budget and intermediate grade, production, basses imported by Hamer. They also offer guitars.

Smith
1978-present. Professional and premium grade, production/custom, electric basses built by luthier Ken Smith in Perkasie, Pennsylvania. Earlier models had Ken Smith on the headstock, recent models have a large S logo. He also designs the imported KSD line of basses.

American-Made Bass

1978-2000	Various models	$1,600	$2,200

Custom VI Series Bass
1985-present. Six strings, double-cut, neck-thru-body.

1985-1999		$2,000	$3,000

Imported Bass

1990s	Various models	$450	$550

SMK Music Works
2002-present. Professional grade, production/custom, solidbody electric basses built by luthier Scott Kenerson in Waterford, Michigan. He also builds guitars.

Specht Guitars
1991-present. Luthier Oliver Specht builds his premium grade, production/custom, basses in Vancouver, British Columbia, Canada. He also builds guitars.

Specimen Products
1984-present. Luthier Ian Schneller builds his professional and premium grade, production/custom, aluminum and wood body basses in Chicago, Illinois. He also builds guitars, ukes, amps and speaker cabs.

Spector/Stuart Spector Design
1975-1990 (Spector), 1991-1998 (SSD), 1998-present (Spector SSD). Imtermediate, professional, and premium grade, production/custom, basses made in the U.S., the Czech Republic, Korea, and China. Stuart Spector's first bass was the NS and the company quickly grew to the point where Kramer acquired it in '85. After Kramer went out of business in '90, Spector started building basses with the SSD logo (Stuart Spector Design). In '98 he recovered the Spector trademark.

Bob Series Bass
1996-1999. Offset deep double-cut swamp ash or alder body, bolt neck, various colors, SSD logo on headstock, 4-string (Bob 4) or 5 (Bob 5).

1996-1999	Bob 4	$850	$1,000
1996-1999	Bob 5	$950	$1,100

NS Series Bass
1977-present. Offset double-cut solidbody, neck-thru, 1 pickup (NS-1, made into '80s) or 2 (NS-2), gold hardware.

1977-1984	NS-1	$1,500	$1,700
1977-1984	NS-2	$1,600	$1,900
1985-1990	NS-1, NS-2		
	(Kramer era)	$1,100	$1,300
1990-2000	NS-1, NS-2		
	(SSD era)	$1,200	$1,400

St. Moritz
1960s. Japanese imports, generally shorter-scale, beginner basses. They also offered guitars.

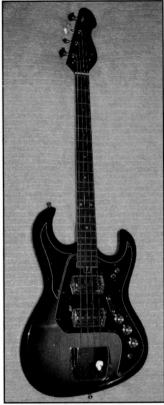

1969 Silvertone Bass

Spector Spectorcore 4

Stambaugh Standard

Steinberger XM-2

MODEL YEAR	FEATURES	EXC. COND. LOW	HIGH

Stambaugh

1995-present. Luthier Chris Stambaugh builds his professional grade, custom/production, solidbody basses in Stratham, New Hampshire. He also builds guitars.

Standel

1952-1974, 1997-present. Amp builder Bob Crooks offered instruments under his Standel brand name three different times during the '60s. See Guitar section for production details. See Amp section for more company info.

Custom Deluxe Solidbody 401 Bass

1967-1968. Custom with higher appointments, various colors.

1967-1968		$1,050	$1,250

Custom Deluxe Thinbody 402 Bass

1967-1968. Custom with higher appointments, various colors.

1967-1968		$1,150	$1,350

Custom Solidbody 501 Bass

1967-1968. Solidbody, 1 pickup, various colors.

1967-1968		$850	$950

Custom Thinbody 502 Bass

1967-1968. Thin solidbody, 2 pickups, various colors.

1967-1968		$950	$1,050

Steinberger

1979-present. Steinberger offers budget and intermediate grade, production, electric basses. They also offer guitars.

Q-4 Bass

1990-1991. Composite neck, Double Bass system, headless with traditional-style maple body, low-impedance pickups.

1990-1991		$850	$1,050

Q-5 Bass

1990-1991. Five-string version of Q Bass.

1990-1991		$900	$1,100

XL-2 Bass

1984-1993. Rectangular composite body, 4-string, headless, 2 pickups.

1984-1989	Black	$1,375	$1,700
1990-1993	Red	$1,125	$1,400

XL-2GR Bass

1985-1990. Headless, Roland GR synthesizer controller.

1985-1990		$1,200	$1,500

XM-2 Bass

1986-1992. Headless, double-cut maple body, 4-string, 2 low-impedance pickups, optional fretted, lined fretless or unlined fretless, black, red or white.

1986-1992		$1,125	$1,400

XP-2 Spirit Bass

2003	Korea	$250	$350

Stevenson

1999-present. Luthier Ted Stevenson, of Lachine, Quebec, added professional grade, production/custom, basses to his product line in '05. He also builds guitars and amps.

Stewart Basses

2000-present. Luthier Fred Stewart builds hi premium grade, custom/production, solidbod basses in Charlton, Maryland. He has also buil guitars since '94.

Stinger

See Martin listing.

Stonetree

1996-present. Luthier Scott Platts builds his pro fessional and premium grade, custom/production solidbody basses in Saratoga, Wyoming. He also builds guitars.

Strad-O-Lin

Ca.1920s-ca.1960s. The Strad-O-Lin mandolin company was operated by the Hominic brothers in New York. Around '57 Multivox/Premier bough the company and added the name to electric and acoustic guitars and basses. Premier also marketed student level guitars under the U.S. Strad brand.

Suhr Guitars

1997-present. In '03, luthier John Suhr added professional grade, production/custom, solidbody basses, to his instrument line built in Lake Elsinore, California. He also builds guitars.

Supro

1935-1968, 2004-present. Supro was a budget brand for the National Dobro Company. Supro offered only two bass models in the '60s. Amp builder Bruce Zinky revived the Supro name for a line of guitars and amps.

Pocket Bass

1960-1968. Double-cut, neck pickup and bridge mounted pickup, semi-hollow, short-scale, black.

1960-1968		$600	$750

Taurus Bass

1967-1968. Asymmetrical double-cut, neck pickup and bridge mounted pickup.

1967-1968		$450	$550

SX

See listing for Essex.

Tacoma

1995-present. Professional grade, production, acoustic basses produced in Tacoma, Washington. They also build acoustic guitars and mandolins.

Thunderchief CB10E4 Bass

2000-present. 17 3/4 flat-top, solid spruce top, solid mahogany back, laminated mahogany sides, rounded cutaway, bolt-on neck, natural satin finish, factory Fishman Prefix Plus pickup system (E4), dot markers.

2000-2006		$675	$750

MODEL		EXC. COND.	
YEAR	FEATURES	LOW	HIGH

Takamine
1962-present. Intermediate, professional and premium grade, production, acoustic and acoustic/electric basses. They also make guitars. They offered solidbody electrics for '83-'84.

Taylor
1974-present. Professional and premium grade, production, acoustic basses built in El Cajon, California.

AB1 Bass
1996-2003. Acoustic/electric, sitka spruce top, imbuia walnut back and sides, designed for 'loose' woody sound.

1996-2003		$1,550	$1,700

AB2 Bass
1996-2003. Acoustic/electric, all imbuia walnut body.

1996-2003		$1,550	$1,700

AB3 Bass
1998-2003. Acoustic/electric, sitka spruce top, maple back and sides.

1998-2003		$1,650	$1,800

Teisco
1946-1974, 1994-present. The Japanese Teisco line started offering basses in '60.

Electric Bass
1968-1969. EB-100 (1 pickup, white 'guard), EB-200B (semi-hollowbody) and Violin bass.

1968-1969	EB-100	$150	$225
1968-1969	EB-200 B	$225	$425
1968-1969	Violin	$425	$475

Tele-Star
1965-ca.1972. Guitars and basses imported from Japan by Tele-Star Musical Instrument Corporation of New York. Primarily made by Kawai, many inspired by Burns designs, some in cool sparkle finishes.

Electric Solidbody Bass

1960s	Various models	$125	$275

Timtone Custom Guitars
1993-2006. Luthier Tim Diebert built his premium grade, custom, solidbody and chambered-body basses in Grand Forks, British Columbia. He also built guitars and lap steels.

Tobias
1977-present. Founded by Mike Tobias in Orlando, Florida. Moved to San Francisco for '80-'81, then to Costa Mesa, eventually ending up in Hollywood. In '90, he sold the company to Gibson which moved it to Burbank. The first Tobias made under Gibson ownership was serial number 1094. The instruments continued to be made by the pre-Gibson crew until '92, when the company was moved to Nashville. The last LA Tobias/Gibson serial number is 2044. Mike left the company in '92 and started a new business in '94 called MTD

where he continues to make electric and acoustic basses. In '99, production of Tobias basses was moved overseas. In late '03, Gibson started again offering U.S.-made Tobias instruments; they are made in Conway, Arkansas, in the former Baldwin grand piano facility. Currently Tobias offers imported and U.S.-made, intermediate and professional grade, production, acoustic and electric basses.

Basic B-4 Bass
1984-1999. 30", 32", or 34" scale, neck-thru-body in alder, koa or walnut, 5-piece laminated neck.

1984-1992		$1,700	$2,100

Classic C-4 Bass
1978-1999. One or 2 pickups, active or passive electronics, 2-octave rosewood 'board, available in short-, medium-, and long-scale models.

1978-1992		$2,000	$2,500

Classic C-5 Bass
1985-1999. 30", 32" or 34" scale, alder, koa or walnut body, bookmatched top, ebony or phenolic 'board, hardwood neck.

1985-1992		$2,000	$2,500

Classic C-6 Bass
Ca. 1986-1999. Flamed maple and padauk neck, alder body, padauk top, ebony 'board, active electronics, 32" or 34" scale.

1986-1992		$2,200	$2,700

Growler GR-5 Bass
1996-1999. 5-string, offset double-cut, bolt neck, various colors.

1996-1999		$850	$1,050

Killer Bee KB-5 Bass
1991-1999. Offset double-cut, swamp ash or lacewood body, various colors.

1991-1999		$1,600	$1,800

Model T Bass
1989-1991. Line of 4- and 5-string basses, 3-piece maple neck-thru-body, maple body halves, active treble and bass controls. Fretless available.

1989-1991		$1,275	$1,600

Signature S-4 Bass
1978-1999. Available in 4-, 5-, and 6-string models, chrome-plated milled brass bridge.

1978-1992		$2,000	$2,400

Standard ST-4 Bass
1992-1995. Japanese-made, 5-piece maple neck-thru, swamp ash body wings.

1992-1995		$1,200	$1,500

Toby Deluxe TD-4 Bass
1994-1996. Offset double-cut, bolt neck.

1994-1996		$600	$750

Toby Deluxe TD-5 Bass
1994-1996. 5-string version.

1994-1996		$625	$775

Toby Pro 6 Bass
1994-1996. Solidbody 6-string, Toby Pro logo on truss rod cover, neck-thru body.

1994-1996		$650	$800

Tacoma Thunderchief

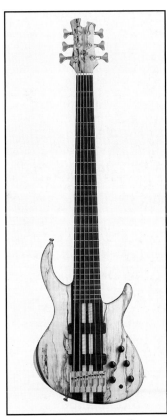

Tobias Signature 6

BASSES

1960 True Tone Bass

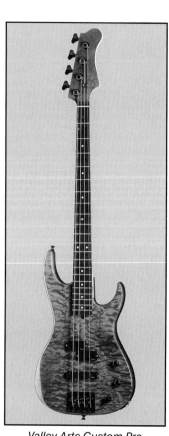

Valley Arts Custom Pro

MODEL YEAR	FEATURES	EXC. COND. LOW	HIGH

Tokai

1947-present. Tokai started making guitars and basses around '70 and by the end of that decade they were being imported into the U.S. Today Tokai offers electrics, acoustics, and electric basses made in Japan and Korea.

Vintage Bass Copies

1970s-1980s. Tokai offered near copies of classic U.S. basses.

1970s		$375	$650

Tonemaster

1960s. Guitars and basses, imported from Italy, with typical '60s Italian sparkle plastic finish and push-button controls, bolt-on neck.

Electric Bass

1960s	Sparkle finish	$500	$625

ToneSmith

1997-present. Luthier Kevin Smith builds his professional and premium grade, production/custom, semi-hollow body basses in Rogers, Minnesota. He also builds guitars.

Traben

2004-present. Intermediate grade, production, solidbody basses imported by Elite Music Brands of Clearwater, Florida.

Traveler Guitar

1992-present. Intermediate grade, production, travel size electric basses made in Redlands, California. They also make guitars.

Travis Bean

1974-1979, 1999. The unique Travis Bean line included a couple of bass models. Travis Bean announced some new instruments in '99, but general production was not resumed.

TB-2000 Bass

Aluminum neck, T-slotted headstock, longer horned, double-cut body, 2 pickups, 4 controls, dot markers, various colors.

1970s		$3,000	$3,700

TB-4000 (Wedge Vee) Bass

1970s. Bass version of Bean's Wedge guitar, few made.

1970s		$3,600	$4,500

Trinity River

2004-present. Intermediate grade, production/custom, acoustic basses imported from Asia by luthiers Marcus Lawyer and Ross McLeod in Fort Worth, Texas. They also import guitars, mandolins and banjos.

True Tone

1960s. Western Auto retailed this line of basses, guitars and amps which were manufactured by Chicago builders makers like Kay. The brand was most likely gone by '68.

MODEL YEAR	FEATURES	EXC. COND. LOW	HIGH

Electric Bass

1960s		$175	$400

Unique Guitars

2003-present. Professional and premium grade, production/custom, solidbody basses built by luthier Joey Rico in California. He also builds guitars.

Univox

1964-1978. Univox started out as an amp line and added guitars and basses around '69. Guitars were imported from Japan by the Merson Musical Supply Company, later Unicord, Westbury, New York. Generally mid-level copies of American designs.

Badazz Bass

1971-ca. 1975. Based on the Guild S-100.

1971-1977		$325	$400

Bicentennial

1976. Carved eagle in body, matches Bicentennial guitar (see that listing), brown stain, maple 'board.

1976		$825	$1,025

Hi Flyer Bass

1969-1977. Mosrite Ventures Bass copy, 2 pickups, rosewood 'board.

1969-1977		$450	$550

'Lectra (Model 1970F) Bass

1969-ca. 1973. Violin bass, walnut.

1969-1973		$450	$550

Model 3340 Semi-Hollow Bass

1970-1971. Copy of Gibson EB-0 semi-hollow bass.

1970-1971		$350	$425

Precisely Bass

1971-ca. 1975. Copy of Fender P-Bass.

1971-1975		$350	$425

Stereo Bass

1976-1977. Rickenbacker 4001 Bass copy, model U1975B.

1976-1977		$450	$550

Vaccaro

1997-2002. They offered intermediate and professional grade, production/custom, aluminum-necked basses built in Asbury Park, New Jersey. They also built guitars.

Valley Arts

Ca. 1977-present. Professional and premium grade, production/custom, solidbody basses built in Nashville, Tennessee. They also make guitars.

Vantage

1977-present. Intermediate grade, production, electric basses imported from Korea (from Japan until '90). They also offer guitars.

Veillette

1991-present. Luthiers Joe Veillette and Martin Keith build their professional and premium grade, production/custom, electric basses in Woodstock, New York. They also build guitars and mandolins.

MODEL YEAR	FEATURES	EXC. COND. LOW	HIGH

Veillette-Citron

1975-1983. Founded by Joe Veillette and Harvey Citron who met at the NY College School of Architecture in the late '60s. Joe took a guitar building course from Michael Gurian and by the Summer of '76, he and Harvey started producing neck-thru solidbody guitars and basses. Veillette and Citron both are back building instruments.

Vengeance Guitars & Graphix

2002-present. Luthier Rick Stewart builds his professional and premium grade, custom/production, solidbody basses in Arden, North Carolina. He also builds guitars.

Ventura

1970s. Import classic bass copies distributed by C. Bruno (Kaman). They also had guitars.

Versoul, LTD

1989-present. Production/custom acoustic/electric and solidbody basses built by luthier Kari Nieminen in Helsinki, Finland. He also builds guitars and sitars.

Vox

1957-1972, 1982-present. The first Vox products were amplifiers brought to market in '58 by Tom Jennings and Dick Denny. By '61 they had added instruments to the line. Guitars and basses bearing the Vox name were offered from 1961-'69 (made in England, Italy), '82-'85 (Japan), '85-'88 (Korea), '98-2001 (U.S.), with a limited edition teardrop bass offered in late '07. Special thanks to Jim Rhoads of Rhoads Music in Elizabethtown, Pennsylvania, for help on production years of these models.

Apollo IV Bass
1967-1969. Single-cut hollowbody, bolt maple neck, 1 pickup, on-board fuzz, booster, sunburst.

1967-1969		$775	$925

Astro IV Bass
1967-1969. Violin-copy bass, 2 pickups.

1967-1969		$775	$950

Clubman Bass
1961-1966. Double-cut 2-pickup solidbody, red.

1961-1966		$450	$550

Constellation IV Bass
1967-1968. Teardrop-shaped body, 2 pickups, 1 f-hole, 1 set of controls, treble, bass and distortion boosters.

1967-1968		$1,000	$1,200

Cougar Bass
1963-1967. Double-cut semi-hollow body, 2 f-holes, 2 pickups, 2 sets of controls, sunburst.

1963-1967		$700	$875

Delta IV Bass
1967-1968. Five-sided body, 2 pickups, 1 volume and 2 tone controls, distortion, treble and bass boosters.

1967-1968		$1,000	$1,200

Guitar-Organ Bass
1966. The 4-string bass version of the Guitar-Organ, Phantom-style body, white.

1966		$1,600	$2,000

Mark IV Bass
1963-1969. Teardrop-shaped body, 2 pickups, 1 set of controls, sunburst.

1963-1965	England, white	$2,400	$3,000
1965-1969	Italy, sunburst	$1,300	$1,400

Panther Bass
1967-1968. Double-cut solidbody, 1 slanted pickup, rosewood 'board, sunburst.

1967-1968		$375	$450

Phantom IV Bass
1963-1969. Five-sided body, 2 pickups, 1 set of controls.

1963-1964	England	$1,900	$2,100
1965-1969	Italy	$1,400	$1,500

Saturn IV Bass
1967-1968. Single-cut, 2 f-holes, 1 set of controls, 1 pickup.

1967-1968		$700	$800

Sidewinder IV Bass (V272)
1967-1968. Double-cut semi-hollow body, 2 f-holes, 2 pickups, 1 set of controls, treble, bass, and distortion boosters.

1967-1968		$1,000	$1,300

Stinger Bass
1968. Teardrop-shaped, boat oar headstock.

1968		$800	$900

Violin Bass
1966. Electro-acoustic bass with violin shaped body, 2 extended range pickups, sunburst.

1966		$1,200	$1,400

Wyman Bass
1966. Teardrop-shaped body, 2 pickups, 1 f-hole, 1 set of controls, sunburst.

1966		$1,200	$1,400

Walker (Kramer)

1981. Kramer came up with idea to offer this brand to produce wood-neck guitars and basses; they didn't want to dilute the Kramer aluminum-neck market they had built up. The idea didn't last long, and few, if any, of these were produced.

Wandre (Davoli)

Ca. 1956/57-1969. Italian-made guitars and basses.

Warrior

1995-present. Professional and premium grade, production/custom, solidbody basses built by luthier J.D. Lewis in Roseville, Georgia. He also builds guitars.

Warwick

1982-present. Professional and premium grade, production/custom, electric and acoustic basses made in Markneukirchen, Germany; founded by Hans Peter Wilfer, whose father started Framus guitars. They also build amps.

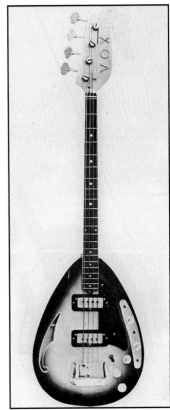

1968 Vox Constellation

Warwick Thumb Bass

BASSES

Wendler electroCoustic Bass

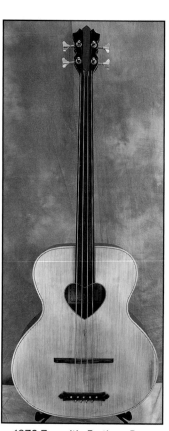

1972 Zemaitis Fretless Bass

MODEL YEAR	FEATURES	EXC. COND. LOW	HIGH

Washburn

1974-present. Intermediate and professional grade, production, acoustic and electric basses. Washburn instruments were mostly imports early on, U.S. production later, currently a combination of both. Washburn also offers guitars, banjos, mandolins, and amps.

Electric Bass

1980-2000s Various models		$250	$500

Waterstone

2002-present. Intermediate and professional grade, production/custom, solid and semi-hollow-body electric basses imported from Korea by Waterstone Musical Instruments, LLC of Nashville. They also offer guitars.

Watkins

1957-present. Watkins Electric Music (WEM) was founded by Charlie Watkins. Their first commercial product was the Watkins Dominator amp in '57. They made the Rapier line of guitars and basses from the beginning. Watkins offered guitars and basses up to '82.

Wechter

1984-present. Professional grade, production/custom acoustic basses built by luthier Abe Wechter in Paw Paw, Michigan. He also offers U.S-made and import guitars.

Wendler

1999-present. Luthier Dave Wendler, of Ozark Instrument Building, builds his intermediate and professional grade, production/custom, solidbody, electro-acoustic basses in Branson, Missouri. He also builds guitars.

Westbury-Unicord

1978-ca. 1983. Japanese guitars and basses imported by Unicord.

Westone

1970s-1990, 1996-2001. Guitars and basses originally imported from Japan by St. Louis Music. Name revived from '96 to '01, by England's FCN Music.

Wilkat Guitars

1998-present. Luthier Bill Wilkat builds his professional grade, custom handmade, electric basses in Montreal, Quebec, Canada. He also builds guitars.

Wilson Brothers Guitars

2004-present. Production electric basses. They also build guitars. Founded by Ventures guitarist Don Wilson.

Winston

Ca. 1963-1967. Guitars and basses imported by Buegeleisen & Jacobson of New York.

Wurlitzer

1970s. Private branded by Pedulla for the Wurlitzer music store chain. Manufacturer and retailer were both based in Massachusetts. Refer to Pedulla listing.

Yamaha

1946-present. Budget, intermediate, professional and premium grade, production, electric basses. They also build guitars. Yamaha began producing solidbody instruments in '66.

Attitude Custom Bass

1990-1994. Part of the Sheehan Series, champagne sparkle.

1990-1994		$675	$800

Electric Bass

1960-1990s Various models		$250	$600

MODEL		EXC. COND.	
YEAR	FEATURES	LOW	HIGH

MODEL		EXC. COND.	
YEAR	FEATURES	LOW	HIGH

Zachary

1996-present. Professional grade, production, solidbody electric basses built by Luthier Alex Csiky in Windsor, Ontario, Canada. He also builds guitars.

Zemaitis

1960-1999, 2004-present. Tony Zemaitis began selling his guitars in '60 and he retired in '99. He emphasized simple lightweight construction and his instruments are known for hand engraved metal fronts. Each hand-built custom guitar or bass was a unique instrument. Approximately 10 custom guitars were built each year. In '04, Japan's Kanda Shokai, with the endorsement of Tony Zemaitis, Jr., started building the guitars again.

Electric Bass

1970s	Heart hole		
	(4 made)	$29,000	$30,000
1980s	1/2 metal		
	& spruce	$15,000	$16,000
1980s	Metal-front		
	4-string	$20,000	$25,000

Zen-On

1946-ca.1968. Japanese-made. By '67 using the Morales brandname. Not heavily imported into the U.S., if at all (see Morales).

Electric Solidbody Bass

1950s	Various models	$175	$250

Zeta

1982-present. Zeta has made professional and premium grade, acoustic and electric basses, many with electronic and MIDI options, in Oakland, California over the years. Currently they only offer upright basses, amps and violins.

Zim-Gar

1960s. Japanese guitars and basses imported by Gar-Zim Musical Instrument Corporation of Brooklyn, New York.

Electric Solidbody Bass

1960s	Various models	$175	$250

Zolla

1979-present. Professional grade, production/custom, electric basses built by luthier Bill Zolla in San Diego, California. Zolla also builds guitars, necks and bodies.

Zon

1981-present. Luthier Joe Zon builds his professional and premium grade, production/custom, solidbody basses in Redwood City, California. Zon started the brand in Buffalo, New York and relocated to Redwood City in '87. He has also built guitars.

Legacy Elite VI Bass

1989-present. Six-string, 34" scale carbon-fiber neck, Bartolini pickups, ZP-2 active electronics.

1990s		$1,100	$1,200

Scepter Bass

1984-1993. Offset body shape, 24 frets, 1 pickup, tremolo.

1984-1993		$1,000	$1,100

ZZ Ryder

Solidbody electric basses from Stenzler Musical Instruments of Ft. Worth, Texas. They also offer guitars.

Zon Sonus Classic

ZZ Ryder Empire

Amps

65Amps London

ADA Viper

Aguilar DB 728

MODEL YEAR	FEATURES	EXC. COND. LOW	HIGH

65amps

2004-present. Founded by Peter Stroud and Dan Boul, 65amps builds tube guitar head and combo amps and speaker cabs in Valley Village, California.

Ace Tone

Late-1960s-1970s. Made by Sakata Shokai Limited of Osaka, Japan, early importer of amps and effects pedals. Later became Roland/Boss.

B-9 Amp

Late-1960s-early-1970s. Solid-state bass amp head.

1960-1970s		$100	$150

Mighty-5 Amp

Late-1960s-early-1970s. Tubes, 50-watt head.

1960-1970s		$75	$100

Acoustic

Ca.1965-ca.1987, 2001-2005. The Acoustic Control Corp., of Los Angeles, California, was mostly known for solidstate amplifiers. Heads and cabinets were sold separately with their own model numbers, but were also combined (amp sets) and marketed under a different model number (for example, the 153 amp set was the 150b head with a 2x15" cabinet). The brand was revived by Samick in '01 for a line of amps.

114 Amp

Ca.1977-mid-1980s. Solidstate, 50 watts, 2x10", reverb, master volume.

1978-1984		$200	$250

115 Amp

1977-1978. Solidstate, 1x12", 50 watts, reverb, master volume.

1977-1978		$250	$300

116 Bass Amp

1978-mid-1980s. Solidstate, 75 watts, 1x15", power boost switch.

1978-1984		$250	$300

120 Amp Head

1977-mid-1980s. Solidstate head, 125 watts.

1977-1984		$200	$250

123 Amp

1977-1984. 1x12" combo.

1977-1984		$175	$200

124 Amp

1977-mid-1980s. Solidstate, 4x10", 5-band EQ, 100 watts, master volume.

1977-1984		$250	$300

125 Amp

1977-mid-1980s. Solidstate, 2x12", 5-band EQ, 100 watts, master volume.

1977-1984		$250	$300

126 Bass Amp

1977-mid-1980s. Solidstate, 100 watts, 1x15", 5-band EQ.

1977-1984		$250	$300

134 Amp

1972-1976. Solidstate, 100-125 watts, 4x10" combo.

1972-1976	125 watts	$250	$300

135 Amp

1972-1976. Solidstate, 125 watts, 2x12" combo, reverb, tremolo.

1972-1976		$275	$325

136 Amp

1972-1976. Solidstate, 125 watts, 1x15" combo.

1972-1976		$275	$325

140 Bass Head

1972-1976. Solidstate, 125 watts, 2 channels.

1972-1976		$200	$250

150 Amp Head

1960s-1976. Popular selling model, generally many available in the used market. Solidstate, 110 watts until '72, 125 watts after.

1968-1976		$200	$250

150b Bass Head

1960s-1971. Bass amp version of 150 head.

1968-1971		$200	$250

153 Bass Amp Set

1960s-1971. 150b head (bass version of 150) with 2x15" 466 cabinet, 110 watts.

1968-1971		$275	$325

165 Amp

1979-mid-1980s. All tube combo, switchable to 60 or 100 watts, brown tolex.

1979-1984		$275	$325

220 Bass Head

1977-1980s. Solidstate, 5-band EQ, either 125 or 160 watts, later models 170 or 200 watts, black tolex.

1977-1984	170 or 200 watts	$200	$250

230 Amp Head

1977-1980s. Solidstate head, 125/160 watts, 5-band EQ.

1977-1984		$200	$250

260 Amp Head

1960s-1971. Solidstate, 275 watt, stereo/mono.

1968-1971		$250	$300

270 Amp Head

1970s. 400 watts.

1970s		$275	$325

320 Bass Head

1977-1980s. Solidstate, 5-band EQ, 160/300 watts, 2 switchable channels, black tolex.

1977-1984		$275	$325

360 Bass Head

1960s-1971. One of Acoustic's most popular models, 200 watts. By '72, the 360 is listed as a "preamp only."

1968-1971		$350	$425

370 Bass Head

1972-1977. Solidstate bass head, 365 watts early on, 275 later.

1972-1977	275 or 365 watts	$350	$650

402 Cabinet

1977-1980s. 2x15" bass cab, black tolex, black grille.

1977-1984		$225	$275

450 Amp Head

1974-1976. 170 watts, 5-band EQ, normal and bright inputs.

1974-1976		$175	$200

MODEL YEAR	FEATURES	EXC. COND. LOW	HIGH

455 Amp Set
1974-1977. 170 watt 450 head with 4x12" cabinet, black.
1974-1977 — $375 — $425

470 Amp Head
1974-1977. 170 watt, dual channel.
1974-1977 — $250 — $300

G20-110 Amp
1981-mid-1980s. Solidstate, 20 watts, 1x10". The G series was a lower-priced combo line.
1981-1985 — $125 — $175

G20-120 Amp
1981-mid-1980s. Solidstate, 20 watts, 1x12".
1981-1985 — $125 — $200

G60-112 Amp
1981-mid-1980s. Solidstate, 60 watts, 1x12".
1981-1985 — $150 — $250

G60-212 Amp
1981-mid-1980s. Solidstate, 60 watts, 2x12".
1981-1985 — $175 — $275

G60T-112 Amp
1981-1987. Tube, 60 watts, 1x12".
1981-1985 — $300 — $350

Tube 60 Amp
1986-1987. Combo, 60 watts, 1x12", spring reverb, bright switch, master volume control, effects loop.
1986-1987 — $300 — $350

ADA
1977-2002. ADA (Analog/Digital Associates) was located in Berkeley, California, and introduced its Flanger and Final Phase in '77. The company later moved to Oakland and made amplifiers, high-tech signal processors, and a reissue of its original Flanger.

Aguilar
1995-present. U.S.-made tube and solidstate amp heads, cabinets, and pre-amps from New York City, New York.

Aiken Amplification
2000-present. Tube amps, combos, and cabinets built by Randall Aiken originally in Buford, Georgia, and since '05 in Pensacola, Florida.

Aims
1970s. Aims amps were manufactured and distributed by Randall Instruments in the mid-'70s. They also offered guitars and basses.

Airline
Ca.1958-1968. Brand for Montgomery Ward, built by Kay, Harmony, and Valco.

Mid to Large Tube Amp
1960s — Various models — $350 — $675

Small to Mid Tube Amp
1960s — Various models — $200 — $350

Alamo
1947-1982. Founded by Charles Eilenberg, Milton Fink, and Southern Music, San Antonio, Texas, and distributed by Bruno and Sons. Alamo started producing amps in '49 and the amps were all-tube until '73; solidstate preamp and tube output from '73 to ca. '80; all solidstate for ca. '80 to '82.

Birch "A" Combo Amp
1949-1962. Birch wood cabinets with A-shaped grill cutout, 2 to 5 tubes. Models include the Embassy Amp 3, Jet Amp 4, Challenger Amp 2, Amp 5, and the Montclair.
1949-1962 — $200 — $250

Bass Tube Amp
1960-1972. Leatherette covered, all tube, 20 to 35 watts, 15" speakers, combo or piggyback, some with Lansing speaker option. Models include the Paragon Special, Paragon Bass, Piggyback Band, Piggyback Bass, Fury Bass, and Paragon Bass (piggyback).
1960-1972 — $200 — $250

Bass Solidstate Preamp-Tube Output Amp
1973-ca.1979. Solidstate preamp section with tube output section, 35 or 40 watts, 15" speakers, combo or piggyback. Models include the Paragon Bass, Paragon Bass Piggyback, Paragon Country Western Bass, Paragon Super Bass, and the Fury Bass.
1973-1979 — $150 — $200

Small Tube Amp
1960-1972. Leatherette covered, all tube, 3 to 10 watts, 6" to 10" speakers, some with tremolo. Models include the Jet, Embassy, Challenger, Capri, Fiesta, Dart, and Special.
1960-1972 — $250 — $300

Mid-power Tube Amp
1960-1970. Leatherette covered, all tube, 15 to 30 watts, 12" or 15" speakers, some with tremolo and reverb, some with Lansing speaker option. Models include Montclair, Paragon, Paragon Band, Titan, and Futura.
1960-1970 — $325 — $400

Twin Speaker Piggyback Tube Amp
1962-1972. Leatherette covered, all tube, up to 45 watts, 8", 10", 12" or 15" speaker configurations, some with tremolo and reverb, some with Lansing speaker option. Models include the Electra Twin Ten, Century Twin Ten, Futuramic Twin Eight, Galaxie Twin Twelve, Galaxie Twin Twelve Piggyback, Piggyback Super Band, Alamo Pro Reverb Piggyback, Futura, Galaxie Twin Ten, Twin-Ten, and Band Piggyback.
1962-1972 — $450 — $550

Small Solidstate Preamp-Tube Output Amp
1973-ca.1979. Solidstate preamp section with tube output section, 3 to 12 watts, 5" to 12" speaker, some with reverb. Models include the Challenger, Capri, Special, Embassy, Dart, and Jet.
1973-1979 — $100 — $125

Aiken Sabre

AMPS

'60s Alamo

Alamo Challenger

MODEL YEAR	FEATURES	EXC. COND. LOW	HIGH

Mid-power Solidstate Preamp-Tube Output Amp

1973-ca.1979. Solidstate preamp section with tube output section, 25 watts, 12" speaker, with reverb and tremolo. Models include the Montclair.

| 1973-1979 | | $125 | $175 |

Twin Speaker Combo (Tube/Hybrid) Amp

1973-ca.1979. Solidstate preamp section with tube output section, 20 or 70 watts, 10", 12" and 15" speaker configurations, some with reverb and tremolo. Models include the 70-watt Paragon Super Reverb Piggybacks, the 45-watt Futura 2x12, and the 20-watt Twin-Ten.

| 1973-1979 | | $250 | $300 |

Solidstate Amp

Ca.1980-1982. All solidstate.

| 1980-1982 | | $50 | $75 |

Alden

Small budget grade solidstate guitar and bass amps from Muse, Inc. of China.

Alden

Alesis

1992-present. Alesis has a wide range of products for the music industry, including digital modeling guitar amps. They also offer guitar effects.

Alessandro

1998-present. Tube amps built by George Alessandro in Huntingdon Valley, Pennsylvania. Founded in '94 as the Hound Dog Corporation, in '98 the company name was changed to Alessandro. The Redbone ('94) and the Bloodhound ('96) were the only models bearing the Hound Dog mark. Serial numbers are consecutive regardless of model (the earliest 20-30 did not have serial numbers). In '98 the company converted to exotic/high-end components and the name changed to Alessandro High-End Products. In '01, he added the Working Dog brand line of amps.

Alessandro Working Dog

Allen Amplification

1998-present. Tube combo amps, heads and cabinets built by David Allen in Walton, Kentucky. He also offers the amps in kit form and produces replacement and upgrade transformers and a tube overdrive pedal.

Aloha

Late-1940s. Electric lap steel and amp Hawaiian outfits made for the Dallas-based Aloha.

Ampeg

1949-present. Ampeg was originally primarily known for their bass amps. In the eastern U.S., Ampeg was Fender's greatest challenger in the '60s and '70s bass amplifier market. St. Louis Music currently offers a line of Ampeg amps.

Allen Old Flame

Amp Covering Dates

Wood veneer	1946-1949.
Smooth brown	1949-1952.
Dot tweed	1952-1954.
Tweed	1954-1955.
Rough gray	1957-1958.
Rough tan	1957-1958.
Cream	1957-1958.
Light blue	1958.
Navy blue	1958-1962.
Blue check	1962-1967.
Black pebble	1967.
Smooth black	1967-1980.
Rough black	1967-1985.

AC-12 Amp

1970. 20 watts, 1x12", accordion amp that was a market failure and dropped after 1 year.

| 1970 | | $350 | $425 |

B-2 Bass Amp

1994-2000. Solidstate, 200 watts, 1x15" combo or 4x8" combo, black vinyl, black grille, large A logo.

| 1994-2000 1x15" | | $500 | $625 |

B-2 R Bass Amp Head

1994-2005. 200 watts, rackmount, replaced by 450 watt B2RE.

| 1994-2005 | | $350 | $425 |

B-3 Amp

1995-2001. Solidstate head, 150 watts, 1x15".

| 1995-2001 | | $400 | $500 |

B-12 N Portaflex Amp

1961-1965. 25 watts, 2x12", 2 6L6 power tubes.

| 1961-1965 | | $1,100 | $1,375 |

B-12X/B-12 XT Portaflex Amp

1961-1969. Tube, 50 watts, 2x12", reverb, vibrato, 2x7027A power tubes.

| 1961-1969 | Style 2 | $1,000 | $1,250 |
| 1965-1969 | Style 1 | $800 | $1,000 |

B-15 N (NB, NC, NF) Portaflex Amp

1960-1970. Introduced as B-15 using 2 6L6 power tubes, B-15 N in '61, B-15 NB in '62, B-15 NC with rectifier tube in '64, B-15 NF with fixed-bias 2 6L6 power tubes and 30 watts in '67, 1x15".

1960-1965		$1,200	$1,500
1966-1970	1x15	$975	$1,200
1967-1968	2x15	$1,000	$1,250

B-15 R Portaflex Amp (Reissue)

1990s. Reissue of '65 Portaflex 1x15", blue check.

| 1990s | | $800 | $875 |

B-15 S Portaflex Amp

1971-1977. 60 watts, 2x7027A power tubes, 1x12".

| 1971-1977 | | $975 | $1,200 |

B-18 N Portaflex Amp

1964-1969. Bass, 50 watts, 1x18".

| 1964-1965 | | $1,200 | $1,500 |
| 1966-1969 | | $975 | $1,200 |

B-25 Amp

1969 only. 55 watts, 2 7027A power tubes, 2x15", no reverb, guitar amp.

| 1969 | | $950 | $1,150 |

B-25 B Bass Amp

1969-1980. Bass amp, 55 watts, 2 7027A power tubes, 2x15".

| 1969-1980 | | $950 | $1,150 |

MODEL YEAR FEATURES	EXC. COND. LOW	HIGH

B-50 R Rocket Bass Amp (reissue)
1996-2005. 50 watts, 1x12" combo, vintage-style blue check cover.

| 1996-2005 | $225 | $275 |

B-100 R Rocket Bass Amp (reissue)
1996-2005. Solidstate, 100 watts, 1x15" combo bass amp, vintage-style blue check cover.

| 1996-2005 | $250 | $325 |

B-115 Amp
1973-1980. 120 watts, solidstate, 1x15" combo.

| 1973-1980 | $275 | $350 |

B-410 Bass Amp
1973-1980. Solidstate, 120 watts, 4x10", black vinyl, black grille.

| 1973-1980 | $375 | $450 |

BT-15 Amp
1966-1968. Ampeg introduced solidstate amps in '66, the same year as Fender. Solidstate, 50 watts, 1x15", generally used as a bass amp. The BT-15D has 2 1x15" cabinets. The BT-15C is a 2x15" column portaflex cabinet.

| 1966-1968 | $325 | $400 |

BT-18 Amp
1966-1968. Solidstate, 50 watts, 1x18", generally used as a bass amp. The BT-18D has dual 1x18" cabinets. The BT-18C is a 2x18" column portaflex cabinet.

| 1966-1968 | $325 | $400 |

ET-1 Echo Twin Amp
1961-1964. Tube, 30 watts, 1x12", stereo reverb.

| 1961-1964 | $900 | $1,100 |

ET-2 Super Echo Twin Amp
1962-1964. Tube, 2x12", 30 watts, stereo reverb.

| 1962-1964 | $1,200 | $1,500 |

G-12 Gemini I Amp
1964-1971. Tube, 1x12", 22 watts, reverb.

| 1964-1971 | $500 | $625 |

G-15 Gemini II Amp
1965-1968. Tube, 30 watts, 1x15", reverb.

| 1965-1968 | $575 | $700 |

G-18 Amp
1977-1980. Solidstate, 1 channel, 10 watts, 1x8", volume, treble, and bass controls,

| 1977-1980 | $100 | $125 |

G-110 Amp
1978-1980. Solidstate, 20 watts, 1x10", reverb, tremolo.

| 1978-1980 | $150 | $175 |

G-115 Amp
1979-1980. Solidstate, 175 watts, 1x15" JBL, reverb and tremolo, designed for steel guitar.

| 1979-1980 | $200 | $225 |

G-212 Amp
1973-1980. Solidstate, 120 watts, 2x12".

| 1973-1980 | $225 | $275 |

GS-12 Rocket 2 Amp
1965-1968. This name replaced the Reverberocket 2 (II), 15 watts, 1x12".

| 1965-1968 | $450 | $550 |

GS-12-R Reverberocket 2 Amp
1965-1969. Tube, 1x12", 18 watts, reverb. Called the Reverberocket II in '68 and '69, then Rocket II in '69.

| 1965-1969 | $550 | $650 |

GS-15-R Gemini VI Amp
1966-1967. 30 watts, 1x15", single channel, considered to be "the accordion version" of the Gemini II.

| 1966-1967 | $550 | $650 |

GT-10 Amp
1971-1980. Solidstate, 15 watts, 1x10", basic practice amp with reverb.

| 1971-1980 | $150 | $175 |

GV-22 Gemini 22 Amp
1969-1972. Tube, 30 watts, 2x12".

| 1969-1972 | $625 | $700 |

J-12 A Jet Amp
1964. Jet Amp with 7591A power tubes.

| 1964 | $300 | $400 |

J-12 D Jet Amp
1966. Jet Amp with new solidstate rectifier.

| 1966 | $300 | $400 |

J-12 Jet Amp
1958-1964, 1967-1972. 20 watts, 1x12", 6V6GT power tubes. Second addition, also known as the Jet II, was like the J-12 D Jet but with 12AX7s.

| 1958-1963 | $450 | $750 |
| 1967-1972 Model reappears | $375 | $425 |

J-12 T Jet Amp
1965. J-12 A with revised preamp.

| 1965 | $300 | $400 |

M-12 Mercury Amp
1957-1965. 15 watts, 2 channels, Rocket 1x12".

| 1957-1959 | $500 | $625 |
| 1960-1965 | $500 | $625 |

M-15 Big M Amp
1959-1965. 20 watts, 2x6L6 power, 1x15".

| 1959 | $600 | $700 |
| 1960-1965 | $600 | $600 |

Model 815 Bassamp Amp
1955. 15 watt combo, 1 channel.

| 1955 | $825 | $1,000 |

Model 820 Bassamp Amp
1956-1958. 20 watt combo, 1 channel.

| 1956-1958 | $875 | $1,050 |

Model 822 Bassamp Amp
1957-1958. 2 channel 820.

| 1957-1958 | $900 | $1,100 |

Model 830 Bassamp Amp
1956-1958. 30 watt combo.

| 1956-1958 | $950 | $1,100 |

Model 835 Bassamp Amp
1959-1961. 35 watt 1x15" combo, 2 channels.

| 1959-1961 | $975 | $1,150 |

R-12 R Reverberocket Amp
1961-1963. Rocket with added on-board reverb.

| 1961-1963 | $625 | $725 |

R-12 R Reverberocket Amp (Reissue)
1996-2007. 50 watts, 2xEL34 power tubes, 1x12" (R-212R is 2x12").

| 1996-2007 | $325 | $400 |

Ampeg B-15-N

AMPS

B-50 R Rocket Bass Amp (reissue)

1959 Ampeg J-12 Jet

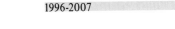
To get the most from this book, be sure to read "Using *The Guide*" in the introduction.

1965 Ampeg R-12-R-T Reverberocket

Ampeg Reverbojet 275

Ampeg SVT-4 Pro

MODEL YEAR	FEATURES	EXC. COND. LOW	HIGH
R-12 R-B Reverberocket Amp			
1964. 7591A power tubes replace R-12-R 6V6 power tubes.			
1964		$625	$725
R-12 R-T Reverberocket Amp			
1965. 7591A or 7868 power tubes, revised preamp.			
1965		$625	$725
R-212 R Reverberocket Combo 50 Amp (Reissue)			
1996-2007. 50 watts, 2x12", all tube reissue, vintage-style blue check cover, vintage-style grille.			
1996-1999		$450	$500
2000-2007		$450	$525
R-12 Rocket Amp			
1957-1963. 12 watts, 1x12", 1 channel.			
1957-1963		$650	$750
R-12 B Rocket Amp			
1964. 12 watts, 1x12", follow-up to the R-12 Rocket.			
1964		$625	$725
R-15 R Superbreverb (Supereverb) Amp			
1963-1964. 1x15 combo, originally called Super-everb, but Fender had a problem with that name.			
1963-1964		$900	$1,000
SB-12 Portaflex Amp			
1965-1971. 22 watts, 1x12", designed for use with Ampeg's Baby Bass, black.			
1965-1971		$650	$775
SBT Amp			
1969-1971. 120 watts, 1x15", bass version of SST Amp.			
1969-1971		$675	$800
SE-412 Cabinet			
1996-1999. 4x12" speakers.			
1996-1999		$300	$350
SJ-12 R/RT Super Jet Amp			
1996-2007. 50 watts, tube, 1x12", SJ-12 RT has tremolo added.			
1996-2007		$300	$325
SS-35 Amp			
1987-1992. Solidstate, 35 watts, 1x12", black vinyl, black grille, large A logo.			
1987-1992		$175	$250
SS-70 Amp			
1987-1990. Solidstate, 70 watts, 1x12".			
1987-1990		$275	$375
SS-70 C Amp			
1987-1992. Solidstate, 70 watts, 2x10", chorus, black vinyl.			
1987-1992		$300	$400
SVT Bass Amp Head			
1969-1985. 300 watt head only.			
1969 Stones World-Tour Assoc.		$2,400	$2,500
1970-1972		$1,900	$2,200
1970-1972	w/set of new tubes	$700	$800
1970-1972	w/set of NOS tubes	$800	$1,000
1973-1979		$1,600	$1,700
1980-1985		$1,500	$1,700
SVT Bass Cabinets			
1969-1985. Two 8x10" cabs only.			
1969		$1,400	$1,500
1970-1985		$1,300	$1,400

MODEL YEAR	FEATURES	EXC. COND. LOW	HIGH
SVT Bass Amp Set			
1969-1985. 300 watt head with matching dual 8x10" cabs.			
1969 Stones World-Tour Assoc.		$3,900	$4,200
1970-1972	Original matching set	$3,500	$3,800
1973-1979	Original matching set	$2,900	$3,400
1980-1985	Original matching set	$2,800	$3,300
SVT Classic Bass Amp Head			
2006		$1,000	$1,200
SVT-II Bass Amp Head			
1989-1994. Rackmount, 300 watts, tube.			
1989-1994		$975	$1,050
SVT-2 Pro Bass Amp Head			
1993-present. 300 watts, rackmount, tube preamp and power section, black metal.			
1993-2007		$725	$900
SVT-3 Pro Bass Amp Head			
1993-present. Tube preamp and MOS-FET power section, 450 watts, rackmount, black metal.			
1993-2007		$525	$600
SVT-4 Pro Bass Amp Head			
1997-present. Rackmount, all tube preamp, MOS-FET power section yielding 1600 watts.			
1997-2007		$700	$825
SVT-5 Pro Bass Amp Head			
2002-2005. Rackmount, all tube preamp, MOS-FET power section yielding 1350 watts.			
2002-2005		$750	$825
SVT-6 Pro Bass Amp Head			
2005-present. Rackmount, all tube preamp, MOS-FET power section yielding 1100 watts.			
2005-2007		$625	$675
SVT-100 T Bass Combo Amp			
1990-1992. Solidstate, ultra-compact bass combo, 100 watts, 2x8".			
1990-1992		$400	$475
SVT-200 T Amp Head			
1987 only. Solidstate, 200 watts to 8 ohms or 320 watts to 4 ohms.			
1987		$400	$500
SVT-350 Amp Head			
1995-2005. Solidstate head, 350 watts, graphic EQ.			
1995-2005		$400	$500
SVT-400 Amp Head			
1987-1997. Solidstate, 2 200 watt stereo amps, rack-mountable head with advanced (in '87) technology.			
1987-1997		$425	$525
SVT-AV Anniversary Edition Amp			
2001		$975	$1,150
V-2 Amp Head			
1971-1980. 60 watt tube head.			
1971-1980		$500	$600
V-2 Amp Set			
1971-1980. 60 watt head with 4x12" cab, black tolex.			
1971-1980		$800	$1,000
V-4 B Bass Amp Head			
1972-1980. Bass version of V-4 without reverb.			
1972-1980		$600	$750

MODEL YEAR FEATURES	EXC. COND. LOW	HIGH

V-4 Stack Amp
1970-1980. 100 watts, with dual 4x12" cabs.

1970-1980 Head and cabs	$1,150	$1,400
1970-1980 Head only	$700	$800

V-4 Cabinet
1970s. Single 4x12" cabinet only.

1970-1980	$375	$450

V-7 SC Amp
1981-1985. Tube, 100 watts, 1x12", master volume, channel switching, reverb.

1981-1985	$575	$700

VH-70 Amp
1991-1992. 70 watts, 1x12" combo with channel switching.

1991-1992	$350	$425

VH-140 C Amp
1992-1995. Varying Harmonics (VH) with Chorus (C), two 70-watt channel stereo, 2x12".

1992-1995	$400	$475

VH-150 Amp Head
1991-1992. 150 watts, channel-switchable, reverb.

1991-1992	$300	$375

VL-502 Amp
1991-1995. 50 watts, channel-switchable, all tube.

1991-1995	$400	$475

VL-1001 Amp Head
1991-1993. 100 watts, non-switchable channels, all tube.

1991-1993	$375	$450

VL-1002 Amp Head
1991-1995. 100 watts, channel-switchable, all tube.

1991-1995	$400	$475

VT-22 Amp
1970-1980. 100 watt combo version of V-4, 2x12".

1970-1980	$625	$775

VT-40 Amp
1971-1980. 60 watt combo, 4x10".

1971-1980	$600	$700

VT-60 Amp Head
1989-1991. Tube head only, 6L6 power, 60 watts.

1989-1991	$350	$450

VT-60 Combo Amp
1989-1991. Tube, 6L6 power, 60 watts, 1x12".

1989-1991	$450	$550

VT-120 Amp Head
1989-1992. 120 watts, 6L6 tube head.

1989-1992	$350	$425

VT-120 Combo Amp
1989-1992. Tube, 6L6 power, 120 watts, 1x12", also offered as head only.

1989-1992	$475	$575

Anderson Amplifiers
1993-present. Tube amps and combos built by Jack Anderson in Gig Harbor, Washington.

Area 51
2003-present. Guitar effects made in Newaygo, Michigan (made in Texas until early '06), by Dan Albrecht. They also build effects.

Aria/Aria Pro II
1960-present. The Japanese instrument builder offered a range of amps from around '79 to '89.

Ariatone
1962. Another private brand made by Magnatone, sold by private music and accordion studios.
Model 810
1962. 12 watts, 1x8, tremolo, brown cover.

1962	$350	$400

Ark
2005-present. Owners Matt Schellenberg and Bill Compeau build professional and premium grade, production/custom amps in Farmington Hills, Michigan (cabinet shop), with all wiring done in Windsor, Ontario, Canada.

Ashdown Amplification
1999-present. Founded in England by Mark Gooday after he spent several years with Trace Elliot, Ashdown offers amps, combos, and cabinets.

Audiovox
Ca.1935-ca.1950. Paul Tutmarc's Audiovox Manufacturing, of Seattle, Washington, was a pioneer in electric lap steels, basses, guitars and amps.

Auralux
2000-present. Founded by Mitchell Omori and David Salzmann, Auralux builds effects and tube amps in Highland Park, Illinois.

Bacino
2002-present. Tube combo amps, heads and cabinets built by Mike Bacino in Arlington Heights, Illinois.

Backline Engineering
2004-present. Gary Lee builds his tube amp heads in Camarillo, California. He also builds guitar effects.

Bad Cat Amplifier Company
1999-present. Founded in Corona, California by James and Debbie Heidrich, Bad Cat offers class A combo amps, heads, cabinets and effects.

Baldwin
Piano maker Baldwin offered amplifiers from 1965 to '70. The amps were solidstate with organ-like pastel-colored pushbutton switches.
Exterminator Amp
1965-1970. Solidstate, 100 watts, 2x15"/2x12"/2x7", 4' vertical combo cabinet, reverb and tremolo, Supersound switch and slide controls.

1965-1970	$500	$600

Model B1 Bass Amp
1965-1970. Solidstate, 45 watts, 1x15"/1x12", 2 channels.

1965-1970	$225	$300

Ashdown Fallen Angel 180

Backline Engineering Zentone 7

Bacino

AMPS

Blue Tone Pro 30M

MODEL YEAR	FEATURES	EXC. COND. LOW	HIGH
Model B2 Bass Amp			
1965-1970. Solidstate, 35 watts, 1x15", 2 channels.			
1965-1970		$200	$275
Model C1 Custom (Professional) Amp			
1965-1970. Solidstate, 45 watts, 2x12", reverb and tremolo, Supersound switch and slide controls.			
1965-1970		$300	$375
Model C2 Custom Amp			
1965-1970. Solidstate, 40 watts, 2x12", reverb and tremolo.			
1965-1970		$300	$375
Professional Deluxe			
1965-1970. Supersound, 1x12.			
1965-1970		$300	$375

Barcus-Berry
1964-present. Pickup maker Barcus-Berry offered a line of amps from '75 to '79.

Barth
1960s. Products of Paul Barth's Barth Musical Instrument Company. Barth was also a co-founder of Rickenbacker.

MODEL YEAR	FEATURES	EXC. COND. LOW	HIGH
Studio Deluxe 958 Amp			
1960s. Small practice combo amp.			
1960s		$200	$300

Basson
2001-present. Speaker cabinets for guitar, bass and PA made by Victor Basson in Carlsbad, California.

Bedrock
1984-1997. Tube amp company founded by Brad Jeter and Ron Pinto in Nashua, New Hampshire. They produced 50 amps carrying the brand name Fred before changing the company name to Bedrock in '86. Around '88, Jay Abend joined the company, eventually becoming President. In '88, Evan Cantor joined the company as an amp designer. In '90, Jeter left Bedrock and, shortly after, Pinto and Abend moved the company to Farmington, Massachusetts. The company closed in '97.

Behringer VT30FX

Behringer
1989-present. Founded in Germany by Uli Behringer, offering a full line of professional audio products. In '98 they added tube, solidstate, and modeling amps. They also offer effects and guitars.

Beltone
1950s-1960s. Japan's Teisco made a variety of brands for others, including the Beltone line of amps. There were also guitars sold under this name made from a variety of builders.

BigDog Amps
2005-2007. Tube head and combo guitar and bass amps and speaker cabinets built in Galveston, Texas, by Steve Gaines.

Callaham EL34 Amp

MODEL YEAR	FEATURES	EXC. COND. LOW	HIGH

Blackstar Amplification
2007-present. Joel Richardson builds his guitar amps and cabinets in Northampton, England. He also offers effects pedals.

Blankenship Amplification
2005-present. Roy Blankenship builds tube head and combo amps and cabinets in North Hollywood, California. He also built amps under the Point Blank brand.

Blue Tone Amplifiers
2002-present. Founded by Alex Cooper in Worcestershire, England, Blue Tone offers amps employing their virtual valve technology.

Bluetron
2004-present. Tube amp heads, combos, and speaker cabinets built by David Smith in Mt. Juliet, Tennessee.

Bogen
1960s. Power and PA tube amps not built for guitar but used by some 1960s/1970s bands.

Bogner
1988-present. Tube combos, amp heads, and speaker cabinets from builder Reinhold Bogner of North Hollywood, California.

Brand X
2004-present. Small solidstate combo amps from Fender Musical Instruments Corporation.

Bruno (Tony)
1995-present. Tube combos, amp heads, and speaker cabinets from builder Tony Bruno of Cairo, New York.

Budda
1995-present. Amps, combos, and cabinets built by Jeff Bober and Scott Sier in San Francisco, California. They also produce effects pedals.

Burriss
2001-present. Bob Burriss builds custom and production guitar and bass tube amps, bass preamps and speaker cabinets in Lexington, Kentucky. He also builds effects.

Byers
2001-present. Tube combo amps built by Trevor Byers, a former Fender Custom Shop employee, in Corona, California. His initial focus was on small early-Fender era and K & F era models.

Callaham
1989-present. Custom tube amp heads built by Bill Callaham in Winchester, Virginia. He also builds solidbody electric guitars.

MODEL YEAR	FEATURES	EXC. COND. LOW	HIGH

Carl Martin

1993-present. In '05, the Denmark-based guitar effects company added tube combo amps.

Carlsbro

1959-present. Guitar, bass, and keyboard combo amps, heads and cabinets from Carlsbro Electronics Limited of Nottingham, England. They also offer PA amps and speaker cabinets.

Carr Amplifiers

1998-present. Steve Carr started producing amps in his Chapel Hill, North Carolina amp repair business in '98. The company is now located in Pittsboro, North Carolina, and makes tube combo amps, heads, and cabinets.

Carvin

1946-present. Founded in Los Angeles by Lowell C. Kiesel who sold guitars and amps under the Kiesel name until late-'49, when the Carvin brand was introduced. They added small tube amps to their product line in '47 and today offer a variety of models. They also build guitars and basses.

Caswell Amplification

2006-present. Programmable tube amp heads built by Tim Caswell in California.

Chicago Blues Box/Butler Custom Sound

2001-present. Tube combo amps built by Dan Butler of Butler Custom Sound in originally in Elmhurst, and now in Lombard, Illinois.

Clark Amplification

1995-present. Tweed-era replica tube amplifiers from builder Mike Clark, of Cayce, South Carolina. He also makes effects.

CMI

1976-1977. Amps made by Marshall for Cleartone Musical Instruments of Birmingham, England. Mainly PA amps, but two tube heads and one combo amp were offered.

CMI Electronics

Late-1960s-1970s. CMI branded amplifiers designed to replace the Gibson Kalamazoo-made amps that ceased production in '67 when Gibson moved the electronics lab to Chicago, Illinois.

Sabre Reverb 1 Amp

Late-1960s-early-1970s. Keyboard amp, 1x15" and side-mounted horn, utilized mid- to late-'60s cabinets and grilles, look similar to mid-late '60s Gibson black tolex and Epiphone gray amp series, black or gray tolex and silver grille.

1970		$125	$150

Comins

1992-present. Archtop luthier Bill Comins, of Willow Grove, Pennsylvania, introduced a Comins combo amp, built in collaboration with George Alessandro, in '03.

Coral

1967-1969. In '66 MCA bought Danelectro and in '67 introduced the Coral brand of guitars, basses and amps. The amp line included tube, solidstate, and hybrid models ranging from small combo amps to the Kilowatt (1000 Watts of Peak Power!), a hybrid head available with two 8x12" cabinets.

Cornell/Plexi

Amps based on the '67 Marshall plexi chassis built by Denis Cornell in the United Kingdom. Large Plexi logo on front.

Cosmosound

Italy's Cosmosound made small amps with Leslie rotating drums in the late '60s and '70s. They also made effects pedals.

Crafter USA

1986-present. Giant Korean guitar and bass manufacturer Crafter also builds an acoustic guitar amp.

Crate

1979-present. Solidstate and tube amplifiers distributed by St. Louis Music.

Solidstate Amp

Various student to mid-level amps, up to 150 watts.

1970s		$50	$125
1980s		$50	$125
1990s		$50	$125

Vintage Club Series Amps

1994-2001. Various tube amps.

1994-1997	5310/VC-5310	$325	$375
1994-1999	30/VC-2110	$225	$275
1994-1999	30/VC-3112	$300	$350
1994-1999	50/VC-50	$250	$300
1994-2001	5212/VC-5212	$325	$375

Cruise Audio Systems

1999-present. Founded by Mark Altekruse, Cruise offers amps, combos, and cabinets built in Cuyahoga Falls, Ohio

Da Vinci

Late-1950s-early-1960s. Another one of several private brands (for example, Unique, Twilighter, Titano, etc.) that Magnatone made for teaching studios and accordion companies.

Model 250 Amp

1958-1962. Similar to Magnatone Model 250 with about 20 watts and 1x12".

1958-1962		$600	$725

Chicago Blues Box Kingston

Crate V100H

Cruise MQ4212

Dean Bassola 40

Demeter TGA-2.1 Inverter

Dinosaur DG-200R

MODEL YEAR	FEATURES	EXC. COND. LOW	HIGH

Danelectro

1946-1969, 1997-present. Founded in Red Bank, New Jersey, by Nathan I. "Nate" or "Nat" Daniel. His first amps were made for Montgomery Ward in '47, and in '48 he began supplying Silvertone Amps for Sears. His own amps were distributed by Targ and Dinner as Danelectro and S.S. Maxwell brands. In '96, the Evets Corporation, of San Clemente, California, reintroduced the Danelectro brand on effects, amps, basses and guitars. In early '03, Evets discontinued the guitar and amp lines, but still offers effects.

Cadet Amp
1955-1969. Tube, 6 watts, 1x6".

1955-1959		$200	$250
1960-1963		$175	$200
1964-1966		$150	$175
1967-1969		$125	$150

Challenger Amp
1950s. Compact lower-power combo amp, golden-brown cover, tan woven cloverleaf-shaped grille, 2 channels, bass and treble control, 2 vibrato controls.

1950s		$350	$375

DM-10 Amp
1960s. Five watts, 1x6".

1960s		$175	$200

DM-25 Amp
1960s. 35 watts, 1x12", reverb and tremolo.

1960s		$400	$475

DS-50 Amp
1967-1969. 50 watts, 3x10" piggyback set, reverb and tremolo, suitable for bass accordion.

1967-1969		$425	$475

DS-100 Amp
1967-1969. 100 watts, piggyback, 6x10" Jensens, reverb, tremolo, suitable for bass accordion.

1967-1969		$525	$575

Model 68 Special Amp
1950s. 20 watts, 1x12", light tweed-fabric cover, light grille, leather handle, script Danelectro plexi-plate logo.

1950s		$400	$500

Model 72 Centurion Amp (Series D)
1954-1957. 1x12" combo, blond tweed, rounded front D cabinet.

1954-1957		$375	$400

Model 89 Amp (Series D)
1954-1957. 1x15" combo, blond tweed, rounded front D cabinet.

1954-1957		$525	$575

Model 98 Twin 12 Amp (Series D)
1954-ca.1957. Blond tweed-style cover, brown control panel, 2x12", vibrato speed and strength, rounded front Series D.

1954-1957		$650	$775

Model 132 Corporal Amp
Early-1960s. Low power, 2x8".

1960s		$350	$400

MODEL YEAR	FEATURES	EXC. COND. LOW	HIGH

Model 142 Viscount Amp
Late-1950s. Combo amp, lower watts, 1x12", light cover, brown grille, vibrato.

1959		$425	$500

Model 143 Viscount Amp
1950s. Small, lower-power compact amp.

1950s		$150	$200

Model 217 Twin 15 Amp
1960s. Combo amp, 100 watts, 2x15" Jensen C15P speakers, black cover, white-silver grille, 2 channels with tremolo.

1962		$500	$600

Model 275 Centurion Amp
1959-1960. 2 6V6 power tubes, approximately 15-18 watts, 1x12", gray cover.

1959-1960		$325	$375

Dean

1976-present. Acoustic, electric, and bass amps made overseas. They also offer guitars, banjos, mandolins, and basses.

Dean Markley

The string and pickup manufacturer added a line of amps in 1983. Distributed by Kaman, they now offer combo guitar and bass amps and PA systems.

K Series Amps
1980s. All solidstate, various models include K-15 (10 watts, 1x6"), K-20/K-20X (10 to 20 watts, 1x8", master volume, overdrive switch), K-50 (25 watts, 1x10", master volume, reverb), K-75 (35 watts, 1x12", master volume, reverb), K-200B (compact 1x12 combo).

1980s	K-15, 20, 20X	$35	$65
1980s	K-200B	$175	$200
1980s	K-50	$40	$75
1980s	K-75	$75	$100

DeArmond

Pickup manufacturer DeArmond starting building tube guitar amps in 1960. By '63, they were out of the amp business. They also made effects. Fender revived the name for a line of guitars in the late '90s.

R-5T Amp
1950s. Low power, 1 6V6, single speaker combo amp.

1950s		$750	$900

R-15T Amp
1950s. Low to mid power, 2 6V6 power section, single speaker.

1950s		$700	$875

Decca

Mid-1960s. Small student-level amps made in Japan by Teisco and imported by Decca Records. They also offered guitars and a bass.

MODEL YEAR	FEATURES	EXC. COND. LOW	HIGH

Demeter

1980-present. James Demeter founded the company as Innovative Audio and renamed it Demeter Amplification in '90. Originally located in Van Nuys, in '08 they moved to Templeton, California. First products were direct boxes and by '85, amps were added. Currently they build amp heads, combos, and cabinets. They also have pro audio gear and guitar effects.

Diaz

Early-1980s-2002. Cesar Diaz restored amps for many of rock's biggest names, often working with them to develop desired tones. Along the way he produced his own line of professional and premium grade, high-end custom amps and effects. Diaz died in '02; his family announced plans to resume production of effects in '04.

Dickerson

1937-1947. Dickerson was founded by the Dickerson brothers in 1937, primarily for electric lap steels and small amps. Instruments were also private branded for Cleveland's Oahu company, and for the Gourley brand. By '47, the company changed ownership and was renamed Magna Electronics (Magnatone).

Oasis Amp
1940s-1950s. Blue pearloid cover, 1x10", low wattage, Dickerson silk-screen logo on grille with Hawaiian background.

1940s		$250	$300

Dinosaur

2004-present. Student/budget level amps and guitar/amp packs, imported by Eleca International.

Divided By Thirteen

Fred Taccone builds his tube amp heads and cabinets in the Los Angeles, California area. He also builds effects.

Dr. Z

1988-present. Mike Zaite started producing his Dr. Z line of amps in the basement of the Music Manor in Maple Heights, Ohio. The company is now located in its own larger facility in the same city. Dr. Z offers combo amps, heads and cabinets.

DST Engineering

2002-present. Jeff Swanson and Bob Dettorre build their tube amp combos, heads and cabinets in Beverly, Massachusetts. They also build reverb units.

Duca Tone

The Duca Tone brand was distributed by Lo Duca Brothers, Milwaukee, Wisconsin, which also distributed EKO guitars in the U.S.

Tube Amp
1950s. 12 watts, 1x12".

1950s		$500	$600

Dumble

1963-present. Made by Howard Alexander Dumble, an early custom-order amp maker from California. Initial efforts were a few Mosrite amps for Semie Moseley. First shop was in '68 in Santa Cruz, California.

Overdrive Special Amp and Cabinet
1970s-1990s. 100 watts, 1x12", known for durability, cabinets vary.

1970s	Black	$20,000	$25,000
1980s	Black	$20,000	$25,000
1990s	Black	$20,000	$25,000

Earth Sound Research

1970s. Earth Sound was a product of ISC Audio of Farmingdale, New York, and offered a range of amps, cabinets and PA gear starting in the '70s. They also made Plush amps.

2000 G Half-Stack Amp
1970s. 100 watts plus cab.

1970s		$450	$550

Original 2000 Model 340 Amp
1970s. Black Tolex, 400-watt head and matching 2x15" cab.

1970s		$375	$450

Revival Amp
1970s. 2x12" tweed twin copy, with similar back mounted control panel, tweed covering, but with solid-state preamp section and 4x6L6 power.

1970		$300	$375

Super Bass/B-2000 Amp
1970s. Tuck & roll black cover, 2 channels - super and normal, volume, bass, mid range, and treble tone controls, no reverb or trem.

1970s	Cabinet	$200	$250
1970s	Head only	$200	$250

Traveler Amp
1970s. Vertical cab solidstate combo amp, 50 watts, 2x12 offset, black tolex.

1977		$200	$250

EBS

1988-present. The EBS Sweden AB company builds professional grade, production bass amps and cabinets in Stockholm, Sweden. They also build effects.

Eden

1976-present. Founded by David Nordschow in Minnesota as a custom builder, Eden now offers a full line of amps, combos, and cabinets for the bassist, built in Mundelein, Illinois. In '02, the brand became a division of U.S. Music Corp (Washburn, Randall). They also produce the Nemesis brand of amps.

Dr. Z Maz 18

DST MarWatt

Eden ENC112

Emery Sound Microbaby

Epiphone Blues Custom

Epiphone Electar Zephyr

MODEL YEAR	FEATURES	EXC. COND. LOW	HIGH

Egnater

1980-present. Tube amps, combos, preamps and cabinets built in Michigan by Bruce Egnater.

EKO

1959-1985, 2000-present. In '67 EKO added amps to their product line, offering three piggyback and four combo amps, all with dark covering, dark grille, and the EKO logo. The amp line may have lasted into the early '70s. Since about 2000, EKO Asian-made, solidstate guitar and bass amps are again available. They also make basses and guitars.

Eleca

2004-present. Student level imported combo amps, Eleca logo on bottom center of grille.

Electar

1996-present. The Gibson owned Electar brand offers tube and solidstate amps, PA gear and wireless systems. Epiphone had a line of Electar amps in the 1930s.

Electro-Harmonix

1968-1981, 1996-present. Electro-Harmonix offered a few amps to go with its line of effects. See Effects section for more company info.

Freedom Brothers Amp

Introduced in 1977. Small AC/DC amp with 2x5 1/2" speakers. E-H has reissued the similar Freedom amp.

1977		$200	$250

Mike Matthews Dirt Road Special Amp

25 watts, 1x12" Celestion, built-in Small Stone phase shifter.

1977		$200	$250

Electromuse

1940s-1950s. Tube amps made by others, like Valco, and usually sold as a package with a lap steel. They also offered guitars.

Amps

Late-1940s. Vertical cabinet with metal handle, Electromuse stencil logo on front of cab.

1948-1949	Lower power	$125	$150

Elk

Late-1960s. Japanese-made by Elk Gakki Co., Ltd. Many were copies of American designs. They also offered guitars and effects.

Custom EL 150L Amp

Late-1960s. Piggyback set, all-tube with head styled after very early Marshall and cab styled after large vertical Fender cab.

1968		$350	$425

Guitar Man EB 105 (Super Reverb) Amp

Late-1960s. All-tube, reverb, copy of blackface Super Reverb.

1968		$300	$375

Twin Amp 60/Twin Amp 50 EB202 Amps

Late-1960s. All-tube, reverb, copy of blackface Dual Showman set (head plus horizontal cab).

1968		$350	$425

Viking 100 VK 100 Amp

Late-1960s. Piggyback set, head styled after very early Marshall and cab styled after very large vertical Fender cab.

1968		$350	$425

Elmwood Amps

1998-present. Jan Alm builds his production/custom, professional and premium grade, guitar tube amps and cabinets in Tanumshede, Sweden.

Elpico

1960s. Made in Europe, PA tube amp heads sometimes used for guitar.

PA Power Tube Amp

1960s. Tubes, 20-watt, metal case, 3 channels, treble and bass control, 2 speaker outs on front panel, Elpico logo on front, small Mexican characterization logo on front.

1960s		$325	$400

Emery Sound

1997-present. Founded by Curt Emery in El Cerrito, California, Emery Sound specializes in custom-made low wattage tube amps.

Emmons

1970s-present. Owned by Lashley, Inc. of Burlington, North Carolina. Amps sold in conjunction with their steel guitars.

Epiphone

1928-present. Epiphone offered amps into the mid-'70s and reintroduced them in '91 with the EP series. Currently they offer tube and solidstate amps.

E-30 B Amp

1972-1975. Solidstate model offered similarly to Gibson G-Series (not GA-Series), 30 watts, 2x10", 4 knobs.

1972-1975		$175	$200

E-60 Amp

1972-1975. Solidstate, 3 watts, 1x10", volume and tone knobs.

1972-1975		$80	$100

E-60 T Amp

1972-1975. E-60 with tremolo, volume, tone, and tremolo knobs.

1972-1975		$85	$110

E-70 Amp

1971-1975. Solidstate, tremolo, 1x10", 3 knobs.

1971-1975		$90	$110

E-1051 Amp

1970s. Tube practice amp, 1x10".

1970s		$150	$175

AMPS

MODEL YEAR	FEATURES	EXC. COND. LOW	HIGH

EA-12 RVT Futura Amp
1962-1967. Low- to mid-power, 4x8", '60s gray tolex, light grille.

1962-1967		$600	$825

EA-14 RVT Ensign Amp
1965-1969. Gray tolex, silver-gray grille, 50 watts, 2x12", split C logo.

1965-1969		$525	$600

EA-15 RVT Zephyr Amp
1961-1965. 14 or 20 watts, 1x15", gray tolex, light grille, split C logo on panel, tremolo and reverb, script Epiphone logo lower right grille.

1961-1965		$475	$575

EA-16 RVT Regent Amp
1965-1969. 25 watts, 1x12", gray vinyl, gray grille, tremolo, reverb. Called the Lancer in first year.

1965-1969		$500	$600

EA-22 RVT Mighty Mite Amp
1965-ca. 1966. 1x12", mid-level power, stereo, reverb, vibrato, old style rear mounted control panel.

1965-1966		$700	$900

EA-26 RVT Electra Amp
1965-1969. Gray tolex, reverb, tremolo, footswitch, 1x12".

1965-1969		$425	$525

EA-28 RVT Pathfinder Amp
Mid-1960s. Similar to Gibson's GA-19 RVT, medium power, 1x12, reverb and tremolo.

1964-1966		$450	$525

EA-32 RVT Comet Amp
1965-1967. 1x10", tremolo, reverb.

1965-1967		$350	$425

EA-33 RVT Galaxie Amp
1963-1964. Gray tolex, gray grille, 1x10".

1963-1964		$425	$475

EA-35 Devon Amp
1961-1963. 1x10" until '62, 1x12" with tremolo in '63.

1961-1963		$475	$525

EA-50 Pacemaker Amp
1961-1969. 1x8" until '62, 1x10" after. EA-50T with tremolo added in '63. Non-tremolo version dropped around '67.

1961-1969		$250	$275

EA-300 RVT Embassy Amp
1965-1969. 90 watts, 2x12", gray vinyl, gray grille, tremolo, reverb.

1965-1969		$675	$725

EA-500T Panorama Amp
1963-1967. 65 watts, head and large cabinet, tremolo, 1x15" and 1x10" until '64, 1x15" and 2x10" after.

1964-1967		$500	$600

EA-600 RVT Maxima Amp
1966-1969. Solidstate Epiphone version of Gibson GSS-100, gray vinyl, gray grille, two 2x10" cabs and hi-fi stereo-style amp head.

1966-1969		$400	$500

Zephyr Amp
1939-1957. Maple veneer cabinet, E logo on front, 1x12" until '54, 1x15" after.

1939-1957		$550	$675

Esteban
2005-2007. Imported brand from China, student budget level compact amps.

Evans Custom Amplifiers
2000s. Intermediate to professional solidstate amps with models designed for jazz and steel guitar players. Evans Custom Amplifiers logo.

Excelsior
The Excelsior Company started offering accordions in 1924 and had a large factory in Italy by the late '40s. They started building guitars and amps around '62. By the early '70s they were out of the guitar business.

Americana Stereophonic High Fidelity Amp
Late 1960s. 50 watts, 1x15", 2x8", 2x3x9" ovals, 2xEL34 power, tube rectifier, large Excelsior logo and small Excelsior The House of Music logo, guitar and accordion inputs, stereo reverb and vibrato.

1968-1969		$900	$1,100

Citation C-15 Amp
1962. Made by Sano, mid power with 2x6V6 power tubes, single speaker combo amp, large Citation by Excelsior logo on front panel.

1962		$500	$600

Fender
1946-present. Leo Fender developed many ground-breaking instruments, but Leo's primary passion was amplifiers, and of all his important contributions to musicians, none exceed those he made to the electric tube amplifier.

Tweed Fender amp circuits are highly valued because they defined the tones of rock and roll. Blackface models remained basically the same until mid-'67. Some silverface circuits remained the same as the blackface circuits, while others were changed in the name of reliability. Price Guide ....values are for all original, excellent condition amps. Small differences in an amp's condition can generate larger differences in selling prices. Non-original speakers will significantly reduce a pre-'68 amp's value. Reconed speakers will reduce the value, but a reconed speaker is preferable to a replacement speaker. Multi-speaker amps generally have matching speaker codes. Different speaker codes require explanation. Fender leather handles are often broken and replaced. A replacement handle drops the value of an amp. Grille cloths should have no tears and a single tear can drop the value of an amp. Each Tweed amp should be evaluated on a case-by-case basis, and it is not unusual for a Tweed amp to have a wide range of values. Alnico speaker replacement is more significant than ce-

'60s Epiphone Pacemaker

Esteban G-10

Fender Acoustasonic SFX II

AMPS

Fender Amp Can

Fender Bandmaster (5E7)

1964 Fender Bandmaster head

MODEL YEAR	FEATURES	EXC. COND. LOW	HIGH

ramic speaker replacement. Fender converted to ceramic about '62. Speaker replacement is of less concern in post-'70 Fender amps.

From 1953 to '67, Fender stamped a two-letter date code on the paper tube chart glued inside the cabinet. The first letter was the year (C='53, D='54, etc.) with the second the month (A=January, etc.).

The speaker code found on the frame of an original speaker will identify the manufacturer, and the week and year that the speaker was assembled. The speaker code is typically six (sometimes seven) digits. The first three digits represent the Electronics Industries Association (E.I.A.) source code which identifies the manufacturer. For example, a speaker code 220402 indicates a Jensen speaker (220), made in '54 (4) during the second week (02) of that year. This sample speaker also has another code stamped on the frame. ST654 P15N C4964 indicates the model of the speaker, in this case it is a P15N 15" speaker. The sample speaker also had a code stamped on the speaker cone, 4965 1, which indicates the cone number. All of these codes help identify the originality of the speaker. The value ranges provided in the Guide are for amps with the original speaker and original speaker cone.

Most Fender speakers from the '50s will be Jensens (code 220). By the late-'50s other suppliers were used. The supplier codes are: Oxford (465), C.T.S. (137), Utah (328). JBL speakers were first used in the late-'50s Vibrasonic, and then in the Showman series, but JBL did not normally have a E.I.A. source code. An amp's speaker code should be reconciled with other dating info when the amp's original status is being verified.

General Production Eras:
Diagonal tweed era
Brown tolex era
Blackface era
Silverface era with raised Fender logo with underlining tail
Silverface era with raised Fender logo without underlining tail
Silverface era with raised Fender logo with small MADE IN USA designation

Nameplate and Logo Attribution:
Fender nameplate with city but without model name (tweed era)
Fender nameplate without city or model name (tweed era)
Fender nameplate with model name noted (tweed era)
Fender flat logo (brown era)
Fender script raised logo (blackface era)

30 Amp
1980-1981. Tube combo amp, 30 watts, 2x10" or 1x12".

1980-1981		$525	$650

75 Amp
1980-1982. Tube, 75 watts, offered as a 1x15" or 1x12" combo, or as head and 4x10" or 2x12" cab.

1980-1982		$575	$700

MODEL YEAR	FEATURES	EXC. COND. LOW	HIGH

85 Amp
1988-1992. Solidstate, 85 watt 1x12" combo, black cover, silver grille.

1988-1992		$225	$275

800 Pro Bass Amp Head
2004-2008. Rack-mount, 800 watts, 5-band EQ.

2004-2008		$475	$550

Acoustasonic 30/30 DSP Amp
2000-present. Small combo, brown tolex, wheat grille. Upgrade model includes DSP (Digital Signal Processor) effects.

2000-2005	30	$200	$225
2000-2005	30 DSP	$325	$375

Acoustasonic Junior/Junior DSP Amp
1998-present. 2x40 watts, 2x8", Piezo horn.

1998-2005		$300	$325

Acoustasonic SFX/SFX II Amp
1998-present. SFX technology, 32 stereo digital presents, 2x80 watts, 1x10" and 1x8", Piezo horn.

1998-2005		$300	$375

AmpCan Amp
1997-present. Cylindrical can-shaped battery powered portable amp.

1997-2004		$100	$125

Bandmaster Amp
1953-1974. Wide-panel 1x15" combo '53-'54, narrow-panel 3x10" combo '55-'60, tolex '60, brownface with 1x12" piggyback speaker cabinet '61, 2x12" '62, blackface '62-'67, silverface '68-'74.

The Fender tweed 4x10" Bassman and tweed 3x10" Bandmaster amps are highly sensitive to condition. Because there are so few that are truly excellent, the price ranges listed may be misleading. Most Bassman amps are at best very good minus (VG-) because their tweed is so damaged and stained. It is also rare to find the original speakers, and if the frames are original, they have often been reconed. 4x10" Bassman and 3x10" Bandmasters that are excellent plus plus (Exc++) may have price ranges that are much higher than the values listed. It is estimated that 90% of the vintage 4x10" Bassman are really only VG or less. Because of the extreme condition factor for these tweed amps, the prices below include amps in very good (VG) condition. Therefore the condition for these listed amps is VG to Exc. Exc+ will be more than the values listed here. As per other high-end collectible, each amp should be taken on a case by case basis.

1953-1954	Tweed, 1x15"	$4,500	$5,000
1955-1958	Tweed, 3x10"	$7,700	$9,500
1959-1960	Matching trio of orig P10Rs	$1,500	$1,700
1959-1960	Old style cab, pink-brown tolex	$9,000	$11,000
1959-1960	Tweed, 3x10"	$9,000	$11,000
1960	Brown tolex, 3x10"	$6,000	$7,500
1961	Rough white & oxblood, 1x12"	$2,450	$2,700
1961-1962	Rough white & oxblood, 2x12"	$2,100	$2,500
1963-1964	Smooth white & gold, 2x12"	$1,900	$2,300

MODEL YEAR	FEATURES	EXC. COND. LOW	HIGH
1964-1967	Black tolex, 2x12"	$1,450	$1,650
1967-1969	Silverface, 2x12"	$775	$900
1970-1974	Silverface, 2x12"	$700	$800

Bandmaster Amp Head
1961-1975. Non-reverb model.

1961-1962	Rough white tolex	$1,000	$1,225
1963-1964	Smooth white tolex	$975	$1,200
1964-1967	Blackface, black tolex	$650	$800
1967-1969	Silverface	$450	$500
1970-1971	Silverface, black tolex	$375	$425

Bandmaster Cabinet
1961-1975. 2x12" speakers.

1961	Blond tolex, 1x12	$825	$1,000
1962-1963	Blond tolex	$725	$900
1964-1967	Blackface horizontal	$450	$550
1967-1970	Silverface vertical	$325	$375

Bandmaster Reverb Amp
1968-1980. 45 watt silverface head with 2x12" cabinet.

1968-1972		$950	$1,100
1973-1980		$850	$1,000

Bandmaster Reverb Amp Head
1968-1980. Reverb, 45 watts.

1968-1972		$575	$700
1973-1980		$450	$550

Bantam Bass Amp
1969-1971. 50 watts, large unusual 1x10" Yamaha speaker.

1969-1971	Original speaker	$475	$575

Bassman Amp
1952-1971. Tweed TV front combo, 1x15" in '52, wide-panel '53-'54, narrow-panel and 4x10" '54-'60, tolex brownface with 1x12" in piggyback cabinet '61, 2x12" cabinet '61-'62, blackface '63-'67, silverface '67-'71, 2x15" cabinet '68-'71. Renamed the Bassman 50 in '72.

The Fender tweed 4x10" Bassman and tweed 3x10" Bandmaster amps are highly sensitive to condition. Because there are so few that are truly excellent, the price ranges listed may be misleading. Most Bassman amps are at best very good minus (VG-) because their tweed is so damaged and stained. It is also rare to find the original speakers, and if the frames are original, they have often been reconed. 4x10" Bassmans and 3x10" Bandmasters that are excellent plus plus (Exc++) may have price ranges that are much higher than the values listed. It is estimated that 90% of the vintage 4x10" Bassman are really only VG or less. Because of the extreme condition factor for these tweed amps, the prices below include amps in very good (VG) condition. Therefore the condition for these listed amps is VG to Exc. Exc+ will be more than the values listed here. As per other high-end collectibles, each amp should be taken on a case by case basis.

1952	TV front, 1x15"	$4,500	$5,000
1953-1954	Wide panel, 1x15"	$4,500	$5,000
1955-1957	Tweed, 4x10", 2 inputs	$7,600	$9,000

MODEL YEAR	FEATURES	EXC. COND. LOW	HIGH
1957-1958	Tweed, 4x10", 4 inputs	$7,000	$9,500
1959-1960	Old style cab, pink-brown tolex	$9,000	$11,000
1959-1960	Tweed, 4x10", 4 inputs	$9,000	$11,000
1961	White 1x12", 6G6, tube rectifier	$2,600	$3,000
1962	Late '62, white 2x12	$2,400	$2,800
1962	White 1x12", 6G6A, s.s. rectifier	$2,500	$2,900
1963-1964	Smooth white 2x12", 6G6A/B	$2,400	$2,800
1965-1966	AA165/AB165, black knobs	$1,550	$1,750
1967-1969	Silverface lg. vertical 2x15"	$800	$925
1970-1971	Silverface 2x15"	$700	$800

Bassman Amp Head
1961-1971. Bassman head only, no cabinet.

1961	White, 6G6, tube	$1,600	$1,800
1962	White, 6G6A, s.s.	$1,300	$1,500
1963-1964	Smooth white, 6G6A/B	$1,300	$1,500
1964	Blackface AA864, white knobs	$750	$850
1965-1967	AA165/AB165, black knobs	$700	$800
1967-1969	Silverface	$600	$650
1970-1971	Silverface, black tolex	$475	$525

Bassman Cabinet
1961-early-1967. Blackface, 2x12" small horizontal cab, replaced in '67 with larger silverface vertical cab.

1961-1963	Blond tolex	$750	$900
1964-1967	Blackface	$450	$550
1967-1970	Silverface verticle	$325	$375

Bassman Amp Parts
The cost of replacement parts for the '59-'60 models.

1959-1960	4 Matching orig P10Q speakers	$2,000	$2,200
1959-1960	New tubes	$100	$125
1959-1960	NOS tubes	$300	$500

Bassman '59 Reissue Amp
1990-present. Tube, 45 watts, 4x10", tweed covering.

1990s		$575	$650

Bassman 10 Amp
1972-1982. 4x10" combo, silverface and 50 watts for '72-'80, blackface and 70 watts after.

1972-1980	50 watts	$475	$550
1981-1982	70 watts	$525	$575

Bassman 20 Amp
1982-1985. Tubes, 20 watts, 1x15".

1982-1985		$400	$450

Bassman 25 Amp
2000-2005. Wedge shape, 1x10", 25 watts, 3-band EQ.

2000-2005		$125	$150

Late-'50s Fender Bandmaster

Late-'50s Fender Bassman

1968 Fender Bassman

Fender Bassman 100

Fender Blues Junior

Fender Champ

MODEL YEAR	FEATURES	EXC. COND. LOW	HIGH
Bassman 50 Amp			
1972-1977. 50 watts, with 2x12" cab.			
1972-1977		$425	$475
1972-1977	Head only	$325	$375
Bassman 60 Amp			
1972-1976, 2000-2005. 60 watts, 1x12". Name reused on solidstate compact combo.			
1972-1976		$425	$525
2000-2005	Combo	$200	$250
Bassman 70 Amp			
1977-1979. 70 watts, 2x15" cab.			
1977-1979		$500	$625
1977-1979	Head only	$400	$450
Bassman 100 Amp			
1972-1977, 2000-present. Tube, 100 watts, 4x12", name reused on solidstate combo amp.			
1972-1977		$500	$625
1972-1977	Head only	$400	$500
Bassman 135 Amp			
1978-1983. Tube, 135 watts, 4x10".			
1978-1983		$550	$650
1978-1983	Head only	$450	$500
Bassman 150 Combo Amp			
2005-present. Solidstate 1x12" combo, 150 watts.			
2005-2006		$300	$350
Bassman 250 Combo Amp			
2006. 250 watts, 2x10".			
2006		$425	$500
Bassman 300 Pro Amp Head			
2002-present. All tube, 300 watts, black cover, black metal grille.			
2002-2006		$700	$750
Bassman 400 Combo Amp			
2000-2004. Solidstate, 350 watts with 2x10" plus horn, combo, black cover, black metal grille.			
2000-2004		$525	$550
Bassman Bassbreaker (Custom Shop) Amp			
1998-2003. Classic Bassman 4x10" configuration. Not offered by 2004 when the '59 Bassman LTD was introduced.			
1998-2003	2x12"	$750	$825
1998-2003	4x10"	$750	$825
Bassman LTD Amp/'59 Limited Edition			
2005. Limited edition with solid pine finger-jointed cabinet, tube rectifier, 45 watts, 4x10", vintage laquered tweed (for original look).			
2005		$825	$900
Blues De Ville Amp			
1993-1996. All tube Tweed Series, 60 watts, 4x10" (optional 2x12" in '94), reverb, high-gain channel, tweed cover (blond tolex optional '95 only).			
1993-1996	Tweed, 4x10"	$525	$550
1994-1996	Tweed, 2x12"	$525	$575
1995	Blond tolex, 4x10"	$525	$575
Blues Deluxe Amp			
1993-2005. All tube Tweed Series, 40 watts, 2 5881 output tubes, reverb, 1x12", tweed covering (blond tolex optional '95 only).			
1993-1999	Tweed	$425	$525
1995	Blond	$450	$525
2000-2005	Tweed	$425	$525

MODEL YEAR	FEATURES	EXC. COND. LOW	HIGH
Blues Junior Amp			
1995-present. All tube, 15 watts, 1x10", spring reverb, tweed in '95, black tolex with silver grille '96 on.			
1995-2006		$300	$350
2003-2006	Ltd. Ed. NOS Lacquer Tweed	$375	$425
Blues Junior Woody Amp			
2002-2003. Exotic hardwood version of Blues Jr., Custom Shop.			
2002-2005		$500	$575
Bronco Amp			
1968-1974, 1993-2001. 1x 8" speaker, all tube, 5 watts until '72, 6 watts for '72-'74, ('90s issue is 15 watts), solidstate, tweed covering (blond tolex was optional for '95 only).			
1968-1974		$325	$375
1993-2001	15 watts, no reverb	$100	$150
Bullet/Bullet 150 Amp			
1994-2005. Solidstate, 15 watts, 1x8", with or without reverb.			
1994-2005	With reverb	$50	$100
1994-2005	Without reverb	$40	$75
Capricorn Amp			
1970-1972. Solidstate, 105 watts, 3x12".			
1970-1972		$225	$275
Champ Amp			
1953-1982. Renamed from the Champion 600. Tweed until '64, black tolex after, 3 watts in '53, 4 watts '54-'64, 5 watts '65-'71, 6 watts '72-'82, 1x6" until '57, 1x8" after.			
1953-1954	Wide panel, 1x6"	$1,000	$1,250
1955-1956	Narrow panel, tweed, 1x6"	$1,150	$1,400
1956-1964	Narrow panel, tweed, 1x8"	$1,400	$1,600
1964	Old cab, black, 1x8", last F51	$1,000	$1,225
1964-1967	New cab, black tolex, 1x8", AA764	$400	$500
1968-1972	Silverface, 1x8"	$375	$450
1973-1982	Silverface, 1x8"	$325	$375
Champ Amp Tubes			
The cost of replacement tubes for the '56-'64 models.			
1956-1964	New tubes	$50	$60
1956-1964	NOS tubes	$90	$110
Champ II Amp			
1982-1985. 18 watts, 1x10".			
1982-1985		$400	$425
Champ 12 Amp			
1986-1992. Tube, 12 watts, overdrive, reverb, 1x12".			
1986-1992	Black	$300	$325
1986-1992	Red, white, gray or snakeskin	$350	$425
Champ 25 SE Amp			
1992-1993. Hybrid solidstate and tube combo, 25 watts, 1x12".			
1992-1993		$200	$250

The *Vintage Guitar Price Guide* shows low to high values for items in all-original excellent condition, and, where applicable, with original case or cover.

MODEL YEAR	FEATURES	EXC. COND. LOW	HIGH

Champion 30/30 DSP Amp
1999-2003. Small solidstate combo, 30 watts, 1x8", reverb.

1999-2003		$115	$140

Champion 110 Amp
1993-2000. Solidstate, 25 watts, 1x10", 2 channels, black tolex, silver grille.

1993-2000		$125	$150

Champion 300 Amp
2004-2007. 30 watt solidstate combo, Dyna-Touch Series, DSP effects.

2004-2007		$125	$150

Champion 600 Amp
1949-1953, 2007-present. Replaced the Champion 800, 3 watts, 1x6", 2-tone tolex, TV front. Replaced by the Champ. Current reissue version is 5 watts.

1949-1953		$950	$1,025

Concert Amp
1960-1965, 1992-1995. Introduced with 40 watts and 4x10", brown tolex until '63, blackface '63-'65. In '62 white tolex was ordered by Webbs Music (CA) instead of the standard brown tolex. A wide range is noted for the rare white tolex, and each amp should be valued on a case-by-case basis. In '60, the very first brown tolex had a pink tint but only on the first year amps. Reissued in '92 with 60 watts and a 1x12".

1960	Brown (pink) tolex	$2,500	$3,000
1960	Brown (pink), tweed grille	$3,200	$3,900
1961-1963	Brown tolex	$2,400	$2,900
1962	White tolex (Webb Music)	$2,500	$3,000
1963-1965	Blackface	$2,000	$2,500

Concert Reverb (Pro Tube Series) Amp
2002-2005. 4x10" combo, reverb, tremolo, overdrive.

2002-2005		$700	$850

Concert 112 Amp
1982-1985. Tube, 60 watts, 1x12".

1982-1985		$575	$700

Concert 210 Amp
1982-1985. Tube, 60 watts, 2x10".

1982-1985		$625	$750

Concert 410 Amp
1982-1985. Tube, 60 watts, 4x10".

1982-1985		$650	$800

Cyber Champ Amp
2004-2005. 65 watts, 1x12", Cyber features, 21 presets

2004-2005		$200	$250

Cyber Deluxe Amp
2002-2005. 65 watts, 1x12", Cyber features, 64 presets.

2002-2005		$400	$425

Cyber Twin Combo Amp
2001-present. Hybrid tube/solidstate modeling amp, 2x65 watts, 2x12".

2001-2006		$550	$600

Deco-Tone (Custom Shop) Amp
2000. Art-deco styling, all tube, 15 watts, 1x12", round speaker baffle opening, uses 6BQ5/ES84 power tubes.

2000		$900	$1,000

Deluxe Amp
1948-1981. Name changed from Model 26 ('46-'48). 10 watts (15 by '54 and 20 by '63), 1x12", TV front with tweed '48-'53, wide-panel '53-'55, narrow-panel '55-'60, brown tolex with brownface '61-'63, black tolex with blackface '63-'66.

1948-1952	Tweed, TV front	$2,300	$2,800
1953-1954	Wide panel	$2,600	$3,000
1955-1956	Narrow panel, sm. Cab	$3,300	$3,600
1956-1960	Narrow panel, lg. cab	$3,800	$4,000
1961-1963	Brown tolex	$1,900	$2,400
1964-1966	Black tolex	$1,850	$2,300

Deluxe Amp Parts
Cost of replacement parts for the '55-'56 Deluxe.

1955-1956	New output or power trans.	$70	$105
1955-1956	New tubes	$50	$80
1955-1956	NOS tubes	$175	$230
1955-1956	Orig P12R Bluebell speaker	$280	$330
1955-1956	Orig. output trans.	$205	$255
1955-1956	Orig. power trans.	$255	$305
1955-1956	Re-coned P12R	$230	$280
1955-1956	Rewind orig. output tran	$205	$255
1955-1956	Rewind orig. power tran	$255	$305

Deluxe Reverb Amp
1963-1981. 1x12", 20 watts, blackface '63-'67, silverface '68-'80, blackface with silver grille option introduced in mid-'80. Replaced by Deluxe Reverb II. Reissued as Deluxe Reverb '65 Reissue.

1963-1967	Blackface	$2,300	$2,800
1967-1968	Silverface	$1,600	$2,000
1969-1970	Silverface	$1,500	$1,800
1971-1972	Silverface	$1,300	$1,500
1973-1980	Silverface	$1,200	$1,300
1980-1981	Blackface	$1,100	$1,300

Deluxe Reverb Amp Parts
Cost of replacement parts for the '63-'67 Deluxe Reverb.

1963-1967	New tubes	$175	$205
1963-1967	NOS tubes	$370	$480
1963-1967	Orig 12K5-2 Oxford speaker	$180	$280

Deluxe Reverb (Solidstate) Amp
1966-1969. Part of Fender's early solidstate series.

1966-1969		$275	$300

Deluxe Reverb '65 Reissue Amp
1993-present. Blackface reissue, 22 watts, 1x12".

1993-1999	Blond (ltd. production)	$650	$800
1993-2005	Black tolex	$600	$650

Fender Champ (5E1)

Fender Concert (6G12)

1955 Fender Deluxe

AMPS

Fender Dual Showman Reverb

Fender Harvard

'70s Fender Musicmaster Bass

Deluxe Reverb II Amp
1982-1986. Updated Deluxe Reverb with 2 6V6 power tubes, all tube preamp section, black tolex, blackface, 20 watts, 1x12".

1982-1986		$725	$800

Deluxe 85 Amp
1988-1993. Solidstate, 65 watts, 1x12", black tolex, silver grille, Red Knob Series.

1988-1993		$200	$225

Deluxe 90 Amp
1999-2003. Solidstate, 90 watts, 1x12" combo, DSP added in '02.

1999-2002		$200	$225
2002-2003	DSP option	$225	$250

Deluxe 112 Amp
1992-1995. Solidstate, 65 watts, 1x12", black tolex with silver grille.

1992-1995		$225	$250

Deluxe 112 Plus Amp
1995-2000. 90 watts, 1x12", channel switching.

1995-2000		$250	$300

Deluxe 900 Amp
2004-present. Solidstate, 90 watts, 1x12" combo, DSP effects.

2004-2005		$250	$350

Dual Professional Amp
1994-2002. Custom Shop amp, all tube, point-to-point wiring, 100 watts, 2x12" Celestion Vintage 30s, fat switch, reverb, tremolo, white tolex, oxblood grille.

1994-2002		$1,425	$1,600

Dual Showman Amp
1962-1969. Called the Double Showman for the first year. White tolex (black available from '64), 2x15", 85 watts. Reintroduced '87-'94 as solidstate, 100 watts, optional speaker cabs.

1962	Rough blond and oxblood	$4,000	$4,900
1963	Smooth blond and wheat	$2,900	$3,300
1964-1967	Black tolex, horizontal cab	$2,200	$2,600
1968	Blackface, large vertical cab	$1,400	$1,500
1968-1969	Silverface	$1,000	$1,150

Dual Showman Amp Head
1962-1969. Dual Showman head with output transformer for 2x15" (versus single Showman's 1x15" output ohms), blackface '62-'67, the late-'67 model logo stipulated "Dual Showman" while the '62-early-'67 head merely stated Showman (could be a single Showman or Dual Showman), '68-'69 silverface.

1962-1963	Blond	$1,700	$2,000
1964-1968	Blackface	$1,200	$1,300
1968-1969	Silverface	$575	$650

Dual Showman Reverb Amp
1968-1981. Black tolex with silver grille, silverface, 100 watts, 2x15".

1968-1972		$1,000	$1,150
1973-1981		$900	$1,100

Dual Showman Reverb Amp Head
1968-1981. Head only.

1968-1972	Includes TFL5000 series	$700	$800
1973-1981		$600	$700

FM 212R
2007. 2x12" combo, FM 212R logo on front and back panel, black tolex, black grille.

2007		$225	$275

Frontman Series Amp
1997-present. Student combo amps, models include 15/15B/15G/15R (15 watts, 1x8"), 25R (25 watts, 1x10", reverb).

1997-2004	25R	$60	$85
1997-2006	15 DSP w/15 FX selections	$60	$95
1997-2006	15/15B/15G/15R	$45	$55

G-Dec Amp
2005-present. Digital, amp and effects presets.

2005-2006	G-Dec (sm. model)	$160	$200

H.O.T. Amp
1990-1996. Solidstate, 25 watts, 1x10", gray carpet cover (black by '92), black grille.

1990-1996		$75	$90

Harvard (Tube) Amp
1956-1961. Tweed, 10 watts, 1x10", 2 knobs volume and roll-off tone, some were issued with 1x8". Reintroduced as a solidstate model in '80.

1956-1961		$1,900	$2,200

Harvard (Solidstate) Amp
1980-1983. Reintroduced from tube model, black tolex with blackface, 20 watts, 1x10".

1980-1983		$75	$125

Harvard Reverb Amp
1981-1982. Solidstate, 20 watts, 1x10", reverb, replaced by Harvard Reverb II in '83.

1981-1982		$125	$150

Harvard Reverb II Amp
1983-1985. Solidstate, black tolex with blackface, 20 watts, 1x10", reverb.

1983-1985		$125	$150

Hot Rod De Ville 212 Amp
1996-present. Updated Blues De Ville, tube, 60 watts, black tolex, 2x12".

1996-2000		$525	$550
2001-2006	Black tolex	$525	$550

Hot Rod De Ville 410 Amp
1996-present. Tube, 60 watts, black tolex, 4x10".

1996-2000		$525	$550
2001-2006	Black tolex	$525	$550
2001-2006	Ltd. Ed. brown tolex	$525	$600

Hot Rod Deluxe Amp
1996-present. Updated Blues Deluxe, tube, 40 watts, 1x12", black tolex. Various covering optional by '98, also a wood cab in 2003.

1996-2000	Black tolex	$400	$450
1996-2000	Blond tolex or tweed option	$425	$475
1996-2001	Brown option	$425	$475
2001-2006	Black tolex	$425	$450
2003	Wood cab	$625	$775

AMPS

MODEL YEAR	FEATURES	EXC. COND. LOW	HIGH
J.A.M. Amp			
1990-1996. Solidstate, 25 watts, 1x12", 4 preprogrammed sounds, gray carpet cover (black by '92).			
1990-1996		$50	$100
Jazz King Amp			
2005-present. 140 watt solidstate 1x15" combo,			
2005		$475	$550
Libra Amp			
1970-1972. Solidstate, 105 watts, 4x12" JBL speakers, black tolex.			
1970-1972		$325	$400
London 185 Amp			
1988-1992. Solidstate, 160 watts, black tolex.			
1988-1992	Head only	$200	$225
London Reverb 112 Amp			
1983-1985. Solidstate, 100 watts, black tolex, 1x12".			
1983-1985		$275	$325
London Reverb 210 Amp			
1983-1985. Solidstate, 100 watts, black tolex, 2x10".			
1983-1985		$300	$350
London Reverb Amp Head			
1983-1985. Solidstate head, 100 watts.			
1983-1985		$200	$250
M-80 Amp			
1989-1994. Solidstate, 90 watts, 1x12". The M-80 series were also offered as head only amp.			
1989-1993		$175	$200
M-80 Bass Amp			
1991-1994. Solidstate, bass and keyboard amp, 160 watts, 1x15".			
1991-1994		$175	$200
M-80 Chorus Amp			
1990-1994. Solidstate, stereo chorus, 2 65-watt channels, 2x12", 90 watts.			
1990-1994		$250	$275
M-80 Pro Amp			
1992. Rackmount version of M-80, 90 watts.			
1992		$150	$175
Model 26 Amp			
1946-1947. Tube, 10 watts, 1x10", hardwood cabinet. Sometimes called Deluxe Model 26, renamed Deluxe in '48.			
1946-1947		$2,100	$2,600
Montreux Amp			
1983-1985. Solidstate, 100 watts, 1x12", black tolex with silver grille.			
1983-1985		$275	$325
Musicmaster Bass Amp			
1970-1983. Tube, 12 watts, 1x12", black tolex.			
1970-1972	Silverface	$325	$350
1973-1980	Silverface	$300	$350
1981-1983	Blackface	$275	$325
PA-100 Amp			
100 watts.			
1970s		$325	$400
Performer 650 Amp			
1993-1995. Solidstate hybrid amp with single tube, 70 watts, 1x12".			
1993-1995		$275	$300

MODEL YEAR	FEATURES	EXC. COND. LOW	HIGH
Performer 1000 Amp			
1993-1995. Solidstate hybrid amp with a single tube, 100 watts, 1x12".			
1993-1995		$300	$325
Princeton Amp			
1948-1979. Tube, 4.5 watts (12 watts by '61), 1x8" (1x10" by '61), tweed '48-'61, brown '61-'63, black with blackface '63-'69, silverface '69-'79.			
1948-1953	TV front	$1,000	$1,200
1953-1954	Wide panel	$1,000	$1,200
1955-1956	Narrow panel, sm. Box	$1,400	$1,600
1956-1961	Narrow panel, lg.box	$1,400	$1,600
1961-1963	Brown, 6G2	$1,200	$1,400
1963-1964	Black, 6G2	$1,100	$1,300
1964-1966	Black, AA964, no grille logo	$1,050	$1,250
1966-1967	Black, AA964, raised grille logo	$1,000	$1,250
1968-1969	Silverface, alum. grille trim	$600	$700
1969-1970	Silverface, no grille trim	$550	$600
1971-1979	Silverface, AB1270	$525	$575
1973-1975	Fender logo-tail	$525	$775
1975-1978	No Fender logo-tail	$500	$575
1978-1979	With boost pull-knob	$500	$575
Princeton Reverb Amp			
1964-1981. Tube, black tolex, blackface until '67, silverface after until blackface again in '80.			
1964-1967	Blackface	$1,600	$1,900
1968-1972	Silverface, Fender logo-tail	$900	$1,100
1973-1979	Silverface, no Fender logo-tail	$875	$1,050
1980-1981	Blackface	$875	$1,050
Princeton Reverb II Amp			
1982-1985. Tube amp, 20 watts, 1x12", black tolex, silver grille, distortion feature.			
1982-1985		$575	$700
Princeton Chorus Amp			
1988-1996. Solidstate, 2x10", 2 channels at 25 watts each, black tolex. Replaced by Princeton Stereo Chorus in '96.			
1988-1996		$225	$300
Princeton 65 Amp			
1999-2003. Combo 1x2", reverb, blackface, DSP added in '02.			
1999-2001		$175	$200
2002-2003	With DPS	$200	$250
Princeton 112/112 Plus Amp			
1993-1997. Solidstate, 40 watts (112) or 60 watts (112 Plus), 1x12", black tolex.			
1993-1994	40 watts	$150	$200
1995-1997	60 watts	$150	$200
Princeton 650 Amp			
2004-present. Solidstate 65 watt 1x12" combo, DSP effects.			
2004-2006		$250	$275

1957 Fender Princeton Amp

1971 Fender Princeton Reverb

Fender Princeton 650

AMPS

1956 Fender Pro

Fender Pro Junior

Fender Rumble 100

Pro Amp

1947-1965. Called Professional '46-'48. 15 watts (26 by '54 and 25 by '60), 1x15", tweed TV front '48-'53, wide-panel '53-'54, narrow-panel '55-'60, brown tolex and brownface '60-'63, black and blackface '63-'65.

MODEL YEAR	FEATURES	EXC. COND. LOW	HIGH
1947-1953	Tweed, TV front	$3,500	$3,900
1953-1954	Wide panel	$3,500	$3,900
1955	Narrow panel (old chassis)	$3,800	$4,000
1955-1959	Narrow panel (new chassis)	$4,100	$4,500
1960	Pink, tweed-era cover	$3,200	$3,800
1961-1965	Brown or black tolex	$2,300	$2,800

Pro Reverb Amp

1965-1982. Tube, black tolex, 40 watts (45 watts by '72, 70 watts by '81), 2x12", blackface '65-'69 and '81-'83, silverface '69-'81.

YEAR	FEATURES	LOW	HIGH
1965-1967	Blackface	$1,900	$2,200
1968	Silverface	$1,600	$2,000
1969-1970		$1,500	$1,800
1971-1972		$1,300	$1,500
1973-1980	Silverface	$1,200	$1,300
1981-1982	Blackface	$1,100	$1,300

Pro Reverb (Solidstate) Amp

1967-1969. Fender's first attempt at solidstate design, the attempt was unsuccessful and many of these models will overheat and are known to be unreliable. 50 watts, 2x12", upright vertical combo cabinet.

1967-1969		$325	$400

Pro Reverb Reissue (Pro Series) Amp

2002-2005. 50 watts, 1x12", 2 modern designed channels - clean and high gain.

2002-2005		$700	$875

Pro 185 Amp

1989-1991. Solidstate, 160 watts, 2x12", black tolex.

1989-1991		$225	$275

Pro Junior Amp

1994-present. All tube, 2xEL84 tubes, 15 watts, 1x10" Alnico Blue speaker, tweed until '95, black tolex '96 on.

1994-1999		$275	$325
2000-2006		$210	$260

Pro Junior 60th Anniversary Woody

2006. Recreation of original Fender model (1946-2006), 15 watts, 1x10, wood cab.

2006		$600	$700

Prosonic Amp

1996-2001. Custom Shop combo, 60 watts, 2 channels, 3-way rectifier switch, 2x10" Celestion or separate cab with 4x12", tube reverb, black, red or green.

1996-2001		$800	$850

Prosonic Amp Head

1996-2001. Amp head only version.

1996-2001		$700	$750

Quad Reverb Amp

1971-1978. Black tolex, silverface, 4x12", tube, 100 watts.

1971-1978		$850	$950

R.A.D. Amp

1990-1996. Solidstate, 20 watts, 1x8", gray carpet cover until '92, black after.

MODEL YEAR	FEATURES	EXC. COND. LOW	HIGH
1990-1996		$65	$75

R.A.D. Bass Amp

1992-1994. 25 watts, 1x10", renamed BXR 25.

1992-1994		$65	$75

Roc-Pro 1000 Amp

1997-2001. Hybrid tube combo or head, 100 watts, 1x12", spring reverb, 1000 logo on front panel.

1997-2001	Combo	$250	$300
1997-2001	Head only	$225	$250

Rumble Bass Amp Head

1994-1998. Custom Shop tube amp, 300 watts.

1994-1998		$2,000	$2,200

Rumble Series Amps

2003-present. Solidstate bass amps, include Rumble 15 (15 watts, 1x8"), 25 (25 watts, 1x10"), 60 (60 watts, 1x12"), and 100 (100 watts, 1x15").

2003-2004	Rumble 100	$200	$225
2003-2004	Rumble 25	$125	$150
2003-2006	Rumble 15	$100	$125

Scorpio Amp

1970-1972. Solidstate, 56 watts, 2x12", black tolex.

1970-1972		$275	$325

SFX Keyboard 200 Amp

1998-1999. Keyboard combo amp, digital effects, black tolex.

1998-1999		$225	$275

SFX Satellite Amp

1997-2001. Hybrid tube combo or head, 100 watts, 1x12", spring reverb.

1998-2000		$225	$250

Showman 12 Amp

1960-1966. Piggyback cabinet with 1x12", 85 watts, blond tolex (changed to black in '64), maroon grille '61-'63, gold grille '63-'64, silver grille '64-'67.

1960-1962	Rough blond and oxblood	$3,800	$4,400
1963-1964	Smooth blond and gold	$2,900	$3,600
1964-1966	Black	$2,100	$2,500

Showman 15 Amp

1960-1968. Piggyback cabinet with 1x15", 85 watts, blond tolex (changed to black in '64), maroon grille '61-'63, gold grille '63-'64, silver grille '64-'67.

1960-1962	Rough blond and oxblood	$3,800	$4,400
1963-1964	Smooth blond and gold	$2,900	$3,600
1964-1967	Blackface	$2,000	$2,400
1967-1968	Silverface	$950	$1,150

Showman 112 Amp

1983-1987. Solidstate, 2 channels, 200 watts, reverb, 4 button footswitch, 5-band EQ, effects loop, 1x12".

1983-1987		$375	$425

Showman 115 Amp

1983-1987. Solidstate, 1x15", 2 channels, reverb, EQ, effects loop, 200 watts, black tolex.

1983-1987		$400	$450

MODEL YEAR	FEATURES	EXC. COND. LOW	HIGH

Showman 210 Amp
1983-1987. Solidstate, 2 channels, reverb, EQ, effects loop, 2x10", 200 watts, black tolex.

1983-1987		$400	$450

Showman 212 Amp
1983-1987. Solidstate, 2 channels, reverb, EQ, effects loop, 2x12", 200 watts, black tolex.

1983-1987		$425	$500

Sidekick 10 Amp
1983-1985. Small solidstate Japanese or Mexican import, 10 watts, 1x8".

1983-1985		$40	$60

Sidekick 100 Bass Amp Head
1986-1993. 100 watt bass head.

1986-1993		$70	$90

Sidekick Bass 30 Amp
1983-1985. Combo, 30 watts, 1x12".

1983-1985		$50	$70

Sidekick Reverb 15 Amp
1983-1985. Small solidstate import, reverb, 15 watts.

1983-1985		$60	$75

Sidekick Reverb 20 Amp
1983-1985. Small solidstate Japanese or Mexican import, 20 watts, reverb, 1x10".

1983-1985		$70	$80

Sidekick Reverb 30 Amp
1983-1985. Small solidstate Japanese or Mexican import, 30 watts, 1x12", reverb.

1983-1985		$80	$90

Sidekick Reverb 65 Amp
1986-1988. Small solidstate Japanese or Mexican import, 65 watts, 1x12".

1986-1988		$90	$100

Squire SKX Series Amps
1990-1992. Solidstate, 15 watts, 1x8", model 15R with reverb. Model 25R is 25 watts, 1x10, reverb.

1990-1992	15 (non-reverb)	$30	$35
1990-1992	15R (reverb)	$35	$45
1990-1992	25R (reverb)	$45	$55

Stage Lead/Lead II Amp
1983-1985. Solidstate, 100 watts, 1x12", reverb, channel switching, black tolex. Stage Lead II has 2x12".

1983-1985	1x12"	$200	$275
1983-1985	2x12"	$225	$300

Stage 100/Stage 1000 Amp
1999-2006. Solidstate, 1x12", combo or head only options, 100 watts, blackface. Head available until 2003.

1999-2006	Combo	$275	$325
1999-2006	Combo stack (2 cabs)	$400	$425
1999-2003	Head only	$150	$175

Stage 1600 DSP Amp
2004-2006. Solidstate, 160 watts, 2x12" combo, 16 digital effects (DSP).

2004-2006		$325	$350

Steel-King Amp
2004-present. Designed for pedal steel, 200 watts, solidstate, 1x15".

2004-2005		$450	$525

Studio Bass Amp
1977-1980. Uses Super Twin design, tube, 200 watt combo, 5-band eq, 1x15".

1977-1980		$475	$500

Studio Lead Amp
1983-1986. Solidstate, 50 watts, 1x12", black tolex.

1983-1986		$225	$275

Super Amp
1947-1963, 1992-1997. Introduced as Dual Professional in 1946, renamed Super '47, 2x10" speakers, 20 watts (30 watts by '60 with 45 watts in '62), tweed TV front '47-'53, wide-panel '53-'54, narrow-panel '55-'60, brown tolex '60-'64. Reintroduced '92-'97 with 4x10", 60 watts, black tolex.

1947-1952	Tweed, TV front	$3,800	$4,700
1953-1954	Tweed, wide panel	$4,100	$5,000
1955	Tweed, narrow panel, 6L6	$5,600	$6,700
1956-1957	Tweed, narrow panel, 5E4, 6V6	$5,200	$6,000
1957-1960	Tweed, narrow panel, 6L6	$6,000	$7,500
1960	Pink, tweed-era grille	$3,000	$3,700
1960	Pink/brown metal knobs	$3,200	$4,000
1960	Pink/brown reverse knobs	$3,200	$4,000
1960-1962	Brown, oxblood grille, 6G4	$2,400	$3,000
1962-1963	Brown, tan/wheat grille, 6G4	$2,300	$2,800

Super (4x10") Amp
1992-1997. 60 watts, 4x10", black tolex, silver grille, blackface control panel.

1992-1997		$650	$750

Super 60 Amp
1989-1993. Red Knob series, 1x12", 60 watts, earlier versions with red knobs, later models with black knobs, offered in optional covers such as red, white, gray or snakeskin.

1989-1993		$400	$450

Super 112 Amp
1990-1993. Red Knob series, 1x12", 60 watts, earlier versions with red knobs, later models with black knobs, originally designed to replace the Super60 but the Super60 remained until '93.

1990-1993		$400	$450

Super 210 Amp
1990-1993. Red Knob series, 2x10", 60 watts, earlier versions with red knobs, later models with black knobs.

1990-1993		$400	$475

Super Champ Amp
1982-1986. Black tolex, 18 watts, blackface, 1x10".

1982-1986		$875	$1,050

Super Champ Deluxe Amp
1982-1986. Solid oak cabinet, 18 watts, upgrade 10" Electro-Voice speaker, see-thru brown grille cloth.

1982-1986		$1,000	$1,200

Fender Pro Series Pro Reverb

1959 Fender Super Amp

1960 Fender Super Amp

AMPS

1969 Fender Super Reverb

Fender Super-Reverb

Fender Twin Amp

MODEL YEAR	FEATURES	EXC. COND. LOW	HIGH

Super Reverb Amp
1963-1982. 4x10" speakers, blackface until '67 and '80-'82, silverface '68-'80.

MODEL YEAR	FEATURES	LOW	HIGH
1963-1967	Blackface	$1,900	$2,200
1968	Silverface, AB763	$1,600	$2,000
1969-1970	Silverface	$1,500	$1,800
1970-1972	Silverface, AA270	$1,400	$1,600
1973-1980	Silverface, no MV	$1,250	$1,350
1981-1982	Blackface	$1,000	$1,200

Super Reverb Solidstate Amp
1967-1970. 50 watts, 4x10".

1967-1970		$375	$450

Super Reverb '65 Reissue Amp
2001-present. 45 watts, all tube, 4x10", blackface cosmetics.

2001-2006		$750	$775

Super Six Reverb Amp
1970-1979. Large combo amp based on the Twin Reverb chassis, 100 watts, 6x10", black tolex.

1970-1979		$850	$950

Super Twin (Non-Reverb) Amp
1975-1976. 180 watts (6 6L6 power tubes), 2x12", distinctive dark grille.

1975-1976		$450	$500

Super Twin (Reverb) Amp
1976-1980. 180 watts (6 6L6 power tubes), 2x12", distinctive dark grille.

1976-1980		$550	$650

Super-Sonic Amp
2000s. Pro Tube Series, all tube, various options, 1x12 combo or 2x12 piggyback, blond and oxblood.

2000s	2x12 piggyback	$925	$1,075
2000s-2007	1x12 combo	$800	$875

Taurus Amp
1970-1972. Solidstate, 42 watts, 2x10" JBL, black tolex, silver grille, JBL badge.

1970-1972		$250	$300

Tonemaster Amp Head
1993-2002. Custom Shop, hand-wired high-gain head, 100 watts, 2 channels, effects loop, blond tolex.

1993-2002		$900	$1,000

Tonemaster Amp Set
1993-2002. Custom Shop, hand-wired head with Tonemaster 2x12" or 4x12" cabinet.

1993-2002	Blond and oxblood	$1,400	$1,600
1993-2002	Custom color red	$1,500	$1,600

Tonemaster 212 Cabinet
1993-2002. Custom Shop extension cabinet for Tonemaster head, blond tolex, Oxblood grille, 2x12" Celestion Vintage 30.

1993-2002		$400	$450

Tonemaster 412 Cabinet
1993-2002. 4x12" Celestion Vintage 30 version.

1993-2002		$425	$500

Tremolux Amp
1955-1966. Tube, tweed, 1x12" '55-'60, white tolex with piggyback 1x10" cabinet '61-'62, 2x10" '62-'64, black tolex '64-'66.

1955-1960	Tweed, 1x12", narrow panel	$3,500	$4,300

MODEL YEAR	FEATURES	EXC. COND. LOW	HIGH
1961	Rough white and oxblood, 1x10"	$2,200	$2,700
1961-1962	Rough white and oxblood, 2x10"	$2,000	$2,400
1962-1963	Rough white and wheat, 2x10"	$1,850	$2,250
1963-1964	Smooth white and gold, 2x10"	$1,775	$2,200
1964-1966	Black tolex, 2x10"	$1,500	$1,875

Twin Amp
1952-1963, 1996-present. Tube, 2x12"; 15 watts, tweed wide-panel '52-'55; narrow-panel '55-'60; 50 watts '55-'57; 80 watts '58; brown tolex '60; white tolex '61-'63. Reintroduced in '96 with black tolex, spring reverb and output control for 100 watts or 25 watts.

1952-1954	Tweed, wide panel	$5,500	$6,400
1955-1957	Tweed, 50 watts	$9,600	$12,000
1958-1959	Tweed, 80 watts	$13,500	$16,500
1960	Brown tolex, 80 watts	$12,000	$15,000
1960-1962	Rough white and oxblood	$6,700	$8,400
1963	Smooth white and gold	$6,000	$7,500

Twin '57 Reissue Amp
2004. Custom Shop '57 tweed, low power dual rectifier model, 40 watts, 2x12", authentic tweed lacquering.

2004		$1,000	$1,200

Twin Reverb Amp
1963-1982. Black tolex, 85 watts (changed to 135 watts in '81), 2x12", blackface '63-'67 and '81-'82, silverface '68-'81, blackface optional in '80-'81 and standard in '82. Reverb reintroduced as Twin in '96.

1963-1967	Blackface	$2,200	$2,600
1968-1972	Silverface, no master vol.	$1,025	$1,100
1973-1975	Silverface, master vol.	$675	$925
1976-1980	Silverface, push/pull	$700	$800
1980-1982	Blackface	$725	$825

Twin Reverb (Solidstate) Amp
1966-1969. 100 watts, 2x12", black tolex.

1966-1969		$350	$425

Twin Reverb '65 Reissue Amp
1992-present. Black tolex, 2x12", 85 watts.

1992-2006	High or low output	$775	$800

Twin Reverb II Amp
1983-1985. Black tolex, 2x12", 105 watts, channel switching, effects loop, blackface panel, silver grille.

1983-1985		$725	$775

Twin "The Twin"/"Evil Twin" Amp
1987-1992. 100 watts, 2x12", red knobs, most black tolex, but white, red and snakeskin covers offered.

1987-1992		$625	$675

Two-Tone (Custom Shop) Amp
2001. Limited production, modern styling, slanted grille, 15 watts, 1x10" and 1x12", 2-tone blond cab, based on modified Blues Deluxe circuit, Two Tone on name plate.

2001		$875	$975

MODEL YEAR	FEATURES	EXC. COND. LOW	HIGH

Ultimate Chorus DSP Amp
1995-2001. Solidstate, 2x65 watts, 2x12", 32 built-in effect variations, blackface cosmetics.

1995-2001		$275	$325

Ultra Chorus Amp
1992-1994. Solidstate, 2x65 watts, 2x12", standard control panel with chorus.

1992-1994		$250	$300

Vibrasonic Amp
1959-1963. First amp to receive the new brown tolex and JBL, 1x15", 25 watts.

1959-1963		$2,200	$2,700

Vibrasonic Custom Amp
1995-1997. Custom Shop designed for steel guitar and guitar, blackface, 1x15", 100 watts.

1995-1997		$700	$800

Vibro-Champ Amp
1964-1982. Black tolex, 4 watts, (5 watts '69-'71, 6 watts '72-'80), 1x8", blackface '64-'68 and '82, silverface '69-'81.

1964-1967	Blackface, AA764	$650	$700
1968-1972	Silverface	$450	$525
1973-1981	Silverface	$350	$450
1982	Blackface	$400	$525

Vibro-King Amp
1993-present. Custom Shop combo, blond tolex, 60 watts, 3x10", vintage reverb, tremolo, single channel, all tube.

1993-2006		$1,200	$1,400

Vibro-King 212 Cabinet
1993-present. Custom Shop extension cab, blond tolex, 2x12" Celestion GK80.

1993-2005		$400	$500

Vibrolux Amp
1956-1964. Narrow-panel, 10 watts, tweed with 1x10" '56-'61, brown tolex and brownface with 1x12" and 30 watts '61-'62, black tolex and blackface '63-'64.

1956-1961	Tweed, 1x10"	$2,500	$2,900
1961-1962	Brown tolex, 1x12", 2x6L6	$2,500	$3,100
1963-1964	Black tolex, 1x12"	$2,500	$3,100

Vibrolux Reverb Amp
1964-1982. Black tolex, 2x10", blackface '64-'67 and '81-'82, silverface '70-'80. Reissued in '96 with blackface and 40 watts.

1964-1967	Blackface	$2,800	$3,300
1968-1972	Silverface	$1,300	$1,600
1973-1982	Silverface or blackface	$1,125	$1,400

Vibrolux Reverb (Solidstate) Amp
1967-1969. Fender CBS solidstate, 35 watts, 2x10", black tolex.

1967-1969		$325	$400

Custom Vibrolux Reverb Amp
1995-present. Part of Professional Series, Custom Shop designed, standard factory built, 40 watts, 2x10", tube, white knobs, blond Tolex and tan grill for '95 only, black Tolex, silver grille after. Does not say Custom on face plate.

1995	Blond and tan	$650	$800
1996-2005	Black and silver	$600	$750

Vibrosonic Reverb Amp
1972-1981. Black tolex, 100 watts, 1x15", silverface.

1972-1981		$1,000	$1,200

Vibroverb Amp
1963-1964. Brown tolex with 35 watts, 2x10" and brownface '63, black tolex with 1x15" and blackface late '63-'64.

1963	Brown tolex, 2x10"	$8,500	$10,500
1963-1964	Black tolex, 1x15"	$4,000	$5,000

Vibroverb '63 Reissue Amp
1990-1995. Reissue of 1963 Vibroverb, 40 watts, 2x10", reverb, vibrato, brown tolex.

1990-1995		$750	$800

Vibroverb '64 Custom Shop Amp
2003-present. Reissue of 1964 Vibroverb with 1x15" blackface specs.

2003-2004		$1,600	$1,700

Yale Reverb Amp
1983-1985. Solidstate, black tolex, 50 watts, 1x12", silverface.

1983-1985		$200	$225

Flot-A-Tone
Ca.1946-early 1960s. Flot-A-Tone was located in Milwaukee, Wisconsin, and made a variety of tube guitar and accordion amps.

Large Amp
Four speakers.

1960s		$550	$675

Small Amp
1x8" speaker.

1962		$275	$325

Framus
1946-1977, 1996-present. Tube guitar amp heads, combos and cabinets made in Markneukirchen, Germany. They also build guitars, basses, mandolins and banjos. Begun as an acoustic instrument manufacturer, Framus added electrics in the mid-'50s. In the '60s, Framus instruments were imported into the U.S. by Philadelphia Music Company. The brand was revived in '96 by Hans Peter Wilfer, the president of Warwick, with production in Warwick's factory in Germany. Distributed in the U.S. by Dana B. Goods.

Fred
1984-1986. Before settling on the name Bedrock, company founders Brad Jeter and Ron Pinto produced 50 amps carrying the brand name Fred in Nashua, New Hampshire.

Fuchs Audio Technology
2000-present. Andy Fuchs started the company in '99 to rebuild and modify tube amps. In 2000 he started production of his own brand of amps, offering combos and heads from 10 to 150 watts. They also custom build audiophile and studio tube electronics. Originally located in Bloomfield, New Jersey, since '07 in Clifton, New Jersey.

Fender Vibroverb

1963 Fender Vibroverb Amp

Framus Dragon

AMPS

348 Fulton-Webb — Gibson Atlas IV

AMPS

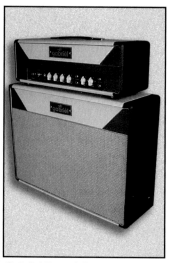
Gabriel Sound Garage Voxer 18

Garcia 60-Watt Combo

GDS 18W S/C

Fulton-Webb
1997-present. Steve Fulton and Bill Webb build their tube amp heads, combos and cabinets in Austin, Texas.

Gabriel Sound Garage
2004-present. Gabriel Bucataru builds his tube amp heads and combos in Arlington Heights, Illinois.

Gallien Krueger
1969-present. Gallien-Krueger has offered a variety of bass and guitar amps, combos and cabinets and is located in San Jose, California.
200G Amp
1980s. Solidstate, black tolex, black grille.

1980s	$275	$325

212GS/212LC Amp
1986-ca.1989. 140-watt mono or 70-watt stereo, 2x12", black carpet.

1986-1989	$350	$425

250ML Amp
1986-1989. Small practice amp, 2x4 1/2", chorus and echo.

1986-1989	$325	$375

700RB Bass Amp
Late 1990s. Rackmount, 380 watts.

1999	$250	$300

2100CEL Digital Stereo Guitar Combo Amp
1989-1991. 200 watts (100 per channel), 2x8", EQ, compression, chorus and reverb.

1989-1991	$300	$375

Garcia
2004-present. Tube amp heads and speaker cabinets built by Matthew Garcia in Myrtle Beach, South Carolina. He also builds effects.

Garnet
Mid 1960s-1989. In the mid '60s, "Gar" Gillies started the Garnet Amplifier Company with his two sons, Russell and Garnet, after he started making PA systems in his Canadian radio and TV repair shop. The first PA from the new company was for Chad Allen & the Expressions (later known as The Guess Who). A wide variety of tube amps were offered and all were designed by Gar, Sr. The company also produced the all-tube effects The Herzog, H-zog, and two stand-alone reverb units designed by Gar in the late '60s and early '70s. The company closed in '89, due to financial reasons caused largely by a too rapid expansion. Gar repaired and designed custom amps up to his death in early 2007.

GDS Amplification
1998-present. Tube amps, combos and speaker cabinets from builder Graydon D. Stuckey of Flint, Michigan. GDS also offers amp kits.

Genesis
Genesis was a 1980s line of student amps from Gibson.
B40 Amp
1984-late-1980s. Bass combo with 40 watts.

1984-1989	$100	$125

G Series Amps
1984-late-1980s. Small combo amps.

1984-1989	G10 (10 watts)	$50	$75
1984-1989	G25 (25 watts)	$75	$100
1984-1989	G40R (40 watts, rvb.)	$125	$150

Genz Benz
1984-present. Founded by Jeff and Cathy Genzler and located in Scottsdale, Arizona, the company offers guitar, bass, and PA amps and speaker cabinets. In late 2003, Genz Benz was acquired by Kaman (Ovation, Hamer, Takamine). On January 1, '08, Fender acquired Kaman Music Corporation and the Genz Benz brand.

George Dennis
1991-present. Founded by George Burgerstein, original products were a line of effects pedals. In '96 they added a line of tube amps. The company is located in Prague, Czech Republic.

Gerhart
2000-present. Production/custom, amps and cabinets from builder Gary Gerhart of West Hills, California. He also offers an amp in kit form.

Germino
2002-present. Intermediate to professional grade tube amps, combos and cabinets built by Greg Germino in Graham, North Carolina.

Gibson
1890s (1902)-present. Gibson has offered a variety of amps since the mid-'30s to the present under the Gibson brandname and others. The price ranges listed are for excellent condition, all original amps though tubes may be replaced without affecting value. Many Gibson amps have missing or broken logos. The prices listed are for amps with fully intact logos. A broken or missing logo can diminish the value of the amp. Amps with a changed handle, power cord, and especially a broken logo should be taken on a case-by-case basis.

Vintage amplifiers are rarely found in original, excellent condition. Many vintage amps have notable wear and have a non-original speaker. The prices shown are for fully original (except tubes and caps) amplifiers that are pleasing clean, and contain no significant wear, blemishes, grille stains, or damage.
Atlas IV Amp
1963-1967. Piggyback head and cab, introduced with trapezoid shape, changed to rectangular cabs in '65-'66 with black cover, simple circuit with 4 knobs, no reverb or tremolo, mid-power with 2 6L6, 1x15".

1963-1965	Brown	$500	$625
1966-1967	Black	$500	$625

MODEL YEAR / FEATURES / EXC. COND. LOW / HIGH

The *Official Vintage Guitar Magazine Price Guide 2009*

The *Vintage Guitar Price Guide* shows low to high values for items in all-original excellent condition, and, where applicable, with original case or cover.

MODEL YEAR	FEATURES	EXC. COND. LOW	HIGH

Atlas Medalist Amp
1964-1967. Combo version with 1x15".

1964-1967		$500	$625

B-40 Amp
1972-1975. 40 watts, 1x12".

1972-1975		$200	$250

BR-1 Amp
1945-1949. 15 watts, 1x12" field-coil speaker, brown leatherette cover, rectangular metal grille with large G.

1945-1949		$500	$575

BR-3 Amp
1946-1947. 12 watts, 1x12" Utah field-coil speaker (most BR models used Jensen speakers).

1946-1947		$450	$475

BR-4 Amp
1946-1947. 14 watts, 1x12" Utah field-coil speaker (most BR models used Jensen speakers).

1946-1948		$450	$550

BR-6 Amp
1946-1954. 10 to 12 watts, 1x10", brown leatherette, speaker opening split by cross panel with G logo, bottom mounted chassis with single on-off volume pointer knob.

1946-1947	Verticle cab	$500	$600
1948-1954	Horizontal cab	$450	$550

BR-9 Amp
1948-1953. Cream leatherette, 10 watts, 1x8". Originally sold with the BR-9 lap steel. Renamed GA-9 in '54.

1948-1953		$425	$525

Duo Metalist Amp
1967-1968. Upright vertical combo cab, tubes, faux wood grain panel, mid-power, 1x12".

1967-1968		$300	$350

EH-100 Amp
1936-1941. Electric-Hawaiian companion amp, 1x10". AC/DC version called EH-110.

1936-1941		$600	$725

EH-125 Amp
1941-1942. 1x12", rounded shoulder cab, brown cover in '41 and dark green in '42, leather handle.

1941-1942		$750	$850

EH-126 Amp
1941-1942. Experimental model, 6-volt variant of EH-125, about 5 made.

1941-1942		$750	$900

EH-135 Amp
1941. Experimental model, alternating and direct current switchable, about 7 made.

1941		$800	$1,000

EH-150 Amp
1935-1941. Electric-Hawaiian companion amp, 1x12" ('35-'37) or 1x10" ('38-'42). AC/DC version called EH-160.

1935	13 3/4" sq. cab	$1,500	$1,650
1936-1937	14 3/4" sq. cab	$1,500	$1,650
1937-1942	15 3/8" round cab	$1,500	$1,650

EH-185 Amp
1939-1942. 1x12", tweed cover, black and orange vertical stripes, marketed as companion amp to the EH-185 Lap Steel. AC/DC version called EH-195.

1939-1942		$1,100	$1,300

EH-195 Amp
1939-1942. EH-185 variant with vibrato.

1939-1942		$1,300	$1,500

EH-250 Amp
1940-1942. Upgraded natural maple cabinet using EH-185 chassis, very few made, evolved into EH-275.

1940-1942		$1,400	$1,600

EH-275 Amp
1940-1942. Similar to EH-185 but with maple cab and celluloid binding, about 30 made.

1940-1942		$1,500	$1,650

Falcon Medalist (Hybrid) Amp
1967. Transitional tube 1x12" combo amp from GA-19 tube Falcon to the solidstate Falcon, Falcon logo and Gibson logo on front panel, brown control panel, dark cover and dark grille, vertical combo cabinet.

1967		$325	$400

Falcon Medalist (Solidstate) Amp
1968-1969. Solidstate combo, 15 watts, 1x12".

1968-1969		$275	$325

G-10 Amp
1972-1975. Solidstate, 10 watts, 1x10", no tremolo or reverb.

1972-1975		$100	$125

G-20 Amp
1972-1975. Solidstate with tremolo, 1x10", 10 watts.

1972-1975		$125	$150

G-25 Amp
1972-1975. 25 watts, 1x10".

1972-1975		$150	$175

G-35 Amp
1975. Solidstate, 30 watts, 1x12".

1975		$175	$225

G-40/G-40 R Amp
1972-1974. Solidstate with tremolo and reverb, 40 watts, 1x12" (G-40) and 2x10" (G-40 R).

1972-1974		$225	$275

G-50/G-50 A/G-50 B Amp
1972, 1975. Solidstate with tremolo and reverb, models G-50 and 50 A are 1x12", 40 watts, model 50 B is a bass 1x15", 50 watts.

1972-1975		$275	$300

G-55 Amp
1975. 50 watts, 1x12".

1975		$300	$325

G-60 Amp
1972. Solidstate with tremolo and reverb, 1x15", 60 watts.

1972		$325	$350

G-70 Amp
1972. Solidstate with tremolo and reverb, 2x12", 60 watts.

1972		$325	$375

G-80 Amp
1972. Solidstate with tremolo and reverb, 4x10", 60 watts.

1972		$375	$400

G-100 A/G-100 B Amp
1975. 100 watts, model 100 A is 2x12" and 100 B is 2x15".

1975		$375	$425

Gerhart Gilmore

Gibson EH-185

Gibson EH-150

AMPS

'55 Gibson GA-5 Les Paul Junior

Gibson GA-5 Skylark

Gibson GA-15

MODEL YEAR	FEATURES	EXC. COND. LOW	HIGH
G-105 Amp			
1975 Solidstate, 100 watts, 2x12", reverb.			
1975		$375	$425
G-115 Amp			
1975. 100 watts, 4x10".			
1975		$400	$450
GA-5 Les Paul Jr. Amp (Reissue)			
2004-present. Class A, 5 watts, 1x8".			
2004-2007		$275	$325
GA-5 Les Paul Jr. Amp			
1954-1957. Tan fabric cover (Mottled Brown by '47), 7" oval speaker, 4 watts. Renamed Skylark in '58.			
1954		$600	$625
1955-1957		$475	$575
GA-5 Skylark Amp			
1957-1968. Gold cover (brown by '63 and black by '66), 1x8" (1x10" from '64 on), 4.5 watts (10 watts from '64 on), tremolo. Often sold with the Skylark Lap Steel.			
1957	Gold, 4.5 watts, 1x8"	$425	$525
1958-1962	Gold, 4.5 watts, 1x8"	$375	$400
1963	Brown, 4.5 watts, 1x8"	$250	$275
1964	Brown, 10 watts, 1x10"	$250	$275
1965-1967	Black, 10 watts, 1x10"	$250	$275
1968	Skylark, last version	$200	$225
GA-5 T Skylark Amp			
1960-1968. Tremolo, 4.5 watts, gold covering and 1x8" until '63, brown '63-'64, black and 1x10" after.			
1961-1962	Gold, 4.5 watts, 1x8"	$400	$425
1963	Brown, 4.5 watts, 1x8"	$325	$350
1964	Brown, 10 watts, 1x10"	$325	$350
1965-1967	Kalamazoo, black, 10 watts, 1x10"	$325	$350
1968	Norlin, vertical cab, 10 watts, 1x10, tubes	$200	$225
GA-5 W Amp			
Late-1960s. Norlin-era, post-Kalamazoo production, 15 watts, small speaker, volume and tone controls.			
1969		$60	$75
GA-6 Amp			
1956-1960. Replaced the BR-6, 8 to 12 watts, 1x12", has Gibson 6 above the grille. Renamed GA-6 Lancer in '60.			
1956-1960		$525	$650
GA-6 Lancer Amp			
1960-1962. Renamed from GA-6, 1x12", tweed cover, 3 knobs, 14 watts.			
1960-1962		$700	$875
GA-7 Amp			
1955-1957. Described as "Les Paul TV Model", a basic old style GA-5 with different graphics, 4 watts, small speaker.			
1955-1957		$475	$525
GA-8 Discoverer Amp			
1962-1964. Renamed from GA-8 Gibsonette, gold fabric cover, 1x12", 10 watts.			
1962-1964		$475	$575

MODEL YEAR	FEATURES	EXC. COND. LOW	HIGH
GA-8 T Discoverer Amp			
1960-1967. Gold fabric cover, 1x10", 9 watts (tan cover, 1x12" and 15 watts by '63), tremolo.			
1960-1962	Tweed, 9 watts, 1x10"	$525	$650
1963-1964	Brown, 15 watts, 1x12"	$425	$475
1965-1967	Black, 15 watts, 1x12"	$375	$425
GA-8 Gibsonette Amp			
1955-1962. Tan fabric cover (gold by '58), 1x10", 8 watts (9 watts by '58). See Gibsonette for 1952-'54. Name changed to GA-8 Discoverer in '62.			
1955	Gibsonette logo on front, square hole	$474	$575
1956-1957	Gibsonette logo on front	$475	$575
1958-1959	Gibson logo on front	$500	$600
1960-1962	Gibson logo upper right front	$500	$600
GA-9 Amp			
1954-1961. Renamed from BR-9, tan fabric cover, 8 watts, 1x10". Often sold with the BR-9 Lap Steel.			
1954-1957	Gibson 9 logo	$475	$575
1958-1961	Tweed, 6V6s	$475	$550
GA-14 Titan Amp			
1959-1961. About 15 watts using 2x6V6 power tubes, 1x10", tweed cover.			
1959-1961		$575	$650
GA-15 RV Goldtone Amp			
1999-2004. 15 watts, Class A, 1x12", spring reverb.			
1999-2004		$325	$425
GA-15 RVT Explorer Amp			
1965-1967. Tube, 1x10", tremolo, reverb, black vinyl.			
1965-1967		$375	$500
GA-17 RVT Scout Amp			
1963-1965. Low power, 1x12", reverb and tremolo.			
1963-1964	Brown	$425	$500
1965	Black	$375	$450
GA-18 Explorer Amp			
1959. Tweed, tube, 14 watts, 1x10". Replaced in '60 by the GA-18 T Explorer.			
1959		$900	$1,000
GA-18 T Explorer Amp			
1959-1964. Tweed, 14 watts, 1x10", tremolo.			
1959		$950	$1,150
1960		$900	$1,100
1961		$875	$1,100
1962		$875	$1,075
1963-1964		$450	$525
GA-19 RVT Falcon Amp			
1961-1966. One of Gibson's best selling amps. Initially tweed covered, followed by smooth brown, textured brown, and black. Each amp has a different tone. One 12" Jensen with deep-sounding reverb and tremolo.			
1961-1962	Tweed, 6V6	$1,000	$1,250
1962-1963	Smooth brown	$600	$650
1964	Textured brown	$450	$525
1965-1966	Black	$425	$450

AMPS

MODEL YEAR	FEATURES	EXC. COND. LOW	HIGH

GA-20 Amp
1950-1962. Brown leatherette (2-tone by '55 and tweed by '60), tube, 12 watts early, 14 watts later, 1x12". Renamed Crest in '60.

1950-1954	Brown, single G logo on front	$525	$600
1955-1958	2-tone salt and maroon	$900	$1,100
1959	2-tone blue and blond	$975	$1,200

GA-20 Crest Amp
1960-1962. Tweed, tube, 14 watts, 1x12".

1960-1962		$975	$1,200

GA-20 RVT Minuteman Amp
1965-1967. Black, 14 watts, 1x12", tube, reverb, tremolo.

1965-1967		$425	$525

GA-20 RVT Amp
2004-2007. 15 watts, 1x12", reverb, tremolo.

2004-2007		$575	$675

GA-20 T Amp
1956-1962. Tube, 16 watts, tremolo, 1x12", 2-tone. Renamed Ranger in '60.

1956-1958	2-tone	$700	$800
1959	New 2-tone	$900	$1,100

GA-20 T Ranger Amp
1956-1962. Tube, 16 watts, tremolo, 1x12", tweed.

1960-1962	Tweed	$900	$1,100

GA-25 Amp
1947-1948. Brown, 1x12" and 1x8", 15 watts. Replaced by GA-30 in '48.

1947-1948		$600	$700

GA-25 RVT Hawk Amp
1963-1968. Reverb, tremolo, 1x15".

1963	Smooth brown	$600	$650
1964	Rough brown	$450	$525
1965-1967	Black	$425	$450
1968	Hawk, last version	$225	$275

GA-30 Amp
1948-1961. Brown until '54, 2-tone after, tweed in '60, 1x12" and 1x8", 14 watts. Renamed Invader in '60.

1948-1954	Brown	$650	$800
1955-1957	2-tone salt and maroon	$925	$1,125
1958-1959	2-tone blue and blond	$1,000	$1,250

GA-30 RV Invader Amp
1960-1961. Tweed, 1x12" and 1x8", 14-16 watts, reverb but no tremolo.

1960-1961		$1,100	$1,300

GA-30 RVT Invader Amp
1962-1967. Updated model with reverb and tremolo, dual speakers 1x12" and 1x8", first issue in tweed.

1962	Tweed	$1,100	$1,300
1963	Smooth brown	$700	$900
1964-1965	Rough brown	$600	$700
1966-1967	Black	$550	$625

GA-30 RVH Goldtone Amp Head
1999-2004. 30 watts, Class A head, reverb.

1999-2004		$600	$725

GA-30 RVS (Stereo) Goldtone Amp
1999-2004. 15 watts per channel, Class A stereo, 2x12", reverb.

1999-2004		$600	$725

GA-35 RVT Lancer Amp
1966-1967. Black, 1x12", tremolo, reverb.

1966-1967		$525	$600

GA-40 Les Paul Amp
1952-1960. Introduced in conjunction with the Les Paul Model guitar, 1x12" Jensen speaker, 14 watts on early models and 16 watts later, recessed leather handle using spring mounting (the handle is easily broken and an unsimilar replacement handle is more common than not). Two-tone leatherette covering, '50s checkerboard grille ('52-early-'55), Les Paul script logo on front of the amp ('52-'55), plastic grille insert with LP monogram, gold Gibson logo above grille. Cosmetics changed dramatically in early/mid-'55. Renamed GA-40 T Les Paul in '60.

1952-1955	Brown 2-tone, LP grille	$1,375	$1,700
1955-1957	2-tone salt and maroon	$1,500	$1,850
1958-1959	2-tone blue and blond	$1,550	$1,875
1959-1960	Tweed	$1,600	$1,900

GA-40 T Les Paul Amp
1960-1965. Renamed from GA-40 Les Paul, 1x12", 16 watts, tremolo. Renamed Mariner in '65-'67.

1961	Tweed	$1,650	$1,950
1962-1963	Smooth brown	$600	$750
1964	Rough brown	$525	$600
1965	Rough brown	$500	$600

GA-45 RVT Saturn Amp
1965-1967. 2x10", mid power, tremolo, reverb.

1965-1967		$525	$600

GA-50/GA-50 T Amp
1948-1955. Brown leatherette, 25 watts, 1x12" and 1x8", GA-50 T with tremolo.

1948-1955	GA-50	$1,375	$1,700
1948-1955	GA-50 T	$1,450	$1,800

GA-55/GA-55 V Amp
1954-1958. 2x12", 20 watts, GA-55 V with vibrato.

1954-1958	GA-55	$1,900	$2,000
1954-1958	GA-55 V	$2,200	$2,500

GA-55 RVT Ranger Amp
1965-1967. Black cover, 4x10", tremolo, reverb.

1965-1967		$600	$825

GA-60 Hercules Amp
1962-1963. 25 watts, 1x15, no-frills 1-channel amp, no reverb, no tremolo.

1962-1963		$625	$675

GA-60 RV Goldtone Amp
1999-present. 60 watts, A/B circuit, 2x12", spring reverb, earliest production in England.

1999-2002		$700	$875

GA-70 Country and Western Amp
1955-1958. 25 watts, 1x15", 2-tone, longhorn cattle western logo on front, advertised to have extra bright sound.

1955-1958		$1,900	$2,000

Gibson GA-30

Gibson GA-40T Les Paul Amp

1955 Gibson GA-55V

To get the most from this book, be sure to read "Using *The Guide*" in the introduction.

1961 Gibson GA-79 RV

*1962 Gibson GA-200
Rhythm King*

Gibson Hawk

MODEL YEAR	FEATURES	EXC. COND. LOW	HIGH

GA-75 Amp
1950-1955. Mottled Brown leatherette, 1x15", 25 watts.

| 1950-1955 | | $1,375 | $1,700 |

GA-75 Recording Amp
1964-1967. 2x10" speakers, no reverb or tremolo, 2 channels, dark cover, gray grille.

| 1964-1967 | | $525 | $625 |

GA-75 L Recording Amp
1964-1967. 1x15" Lansing speaker, no reverb or tremolo, 2 channels, dark cover, gray grille.

| 1964-1967 | | $525 | $625 |

GA-77 Amp
1954-1959. 1x15" JBL, 25-30 watts, 2x6L6 power tubes, 2-tone covering, near top-of-the-line for the mid-'50s.

| 1954-1957 | 2-tone salt and maroon, leather handle | $1,550 | $1,875 |
| 1958-1959 | 2-tone blue and blond, metal handle | $1,575 | $1,900 |

GA-77 Vanguard Amp
1960-1961. 1x15" JBL, 25-30 watts, 2 6L6 power tubes, tweed cover, first use of Vanguard model name.

| 1960-1961 | | $1,650 | $1,950 |

GA-77 RET Vanguard Amp
1964-1967. Mid-power, 2x10", tremolo, reverb, echo.

1964	Rough brown	$575	$700
1965	Rough brown or black	$550	$675
1966-1967	Black	$550	$650

GA-77 RVTL Vanguard Amp
1962-1963. 50 watts, 1x15", Lansing speaker option (L), tremolo, reverb.

| 1962-1963 | | $600 | $750 |

GA-78 Bell Stereo Amp
1960. Gibson-branded amp made by Bell, same as GA-79 series, Bell 30 logo on front, 30 watts, 2x10" wedge cab.

| 1960 | | $2,200 | $2,300 |

GA-79 RV Amp
1960-1962. Stereo-reverb, 2x10", 30 watts.

| 1960-1961 | Tweed | $2,500 | $2,800 |
| 1962 | Gray tolex | $2,400 | $2,700 |

GA-79 RVT Multi-Stereo Amp
1961-1967. Introduced as GA-79 RVT, Multi-Stereo was added to name in '61. Stereo-reverb and tremolo, 2x10", tweed (black and brown also available), 30 watts.

1961	Tweed	$2,500	$2,800
1961-1962	Gray sparkle	$2,100	$2,500
1963-1964	Textured brown	$2,100	$2,500
1965-1967	Black	$2,100	$2,500

GA-80/GA-80 T/Vari-Tone Amp
1959-1961. 25 watts, 1x15", 2 channels, described as "6-in-1 amplifier with improved tremolo," 6 Vari-Tone pushbottons which give "six distinctively separate sounds," 7 tubes, tweed cover.

| 1959-1961 | | $1,700 | $2,000 |

GA-83 S Stereo-Vibe Amp
1959-1961. Interesting stereo amp with front baffle mounted 1x12" and 4x8" side-mounted speakers (2 on each side), 35 watts, Gibson logo on upper right corner of the grille, tweed cover, brown grille (late '50s Fender-style), 3 pointer knobs and 3 round knobs, 4 inputs.

| 1959-1961 | | $2,600 | $3,000 |

GA-85 Bass Reflex Amp
1957-1958. Removable head, 25 watts, 1x12", very limited production.

| 1957-1958 | | $1,000 | $1,200 |

GA-90 High Fidelity Amp
1953-1960. 25 watts, 6x8", 2 channels, advertised for guitar, bass, accordion, or hi-fi.

| 1953-1960 | | $1,375 | $1,700 |

GA-95 RVT Apollo Amp
1965-1967. 90 watts, 2x12", black vinyl, black grille, tremolo, reverb.

| 1965-1967 | | $650 | $700 |

GA-100 Bass Amp
1960-1963. Tweed, 35 watts, 1x12" cabinet, tripod was available for separate head.

| 1960-1963 | | $1,000 | $1,200 |

GA-200 Rhythm King Amp
1957-1962. Introduced as GA-200, renamed Rhythm King in '60, 2-channel version of GA-400. Bass amp, 60 watts, 2x12".

1957-1959	2-tone	$2,000	$2,100
1959-1961	Tweed	$2,175	$2,500
1962	Smooth brown, no trem or reverb	$1,750	$2,175

GA-300 RVT Super 300 Amp
1962. 60 watts, 2x12" combo, reverb, tremolo, smooth brown.

| 1962 | | $1,850 | $2,300 |

GA-400 Super 400 Amp
1957-1962. 60 watts, 2x12", 3 channels, same size as GA-200 cab, 1 more tube than GA-200.

1957-1959	2-tone	$2,100	$2,200
1959-1961	Tweed	$2,300	$2,600
1961	Smooth brown, no trem or reverb	$1,850	$2,300

GA-CB Custom-Built Amp
1951-1953. 25-30 watts, 1x15", the top model in Gibson's '51 line of amps, described as having sound quality found only in the finest public address broadcasting systems, about 47 made, this high-end amp was replaced by the GA-77 and a completely different GA-90.

| 1951-1953 | | $1,400 | $1,700 |

Gibsonette Amp
1952-1954. Gibsonette logo on front, round hole. See GA-8 Gibsonette for later models.

| 1952-1954 | | $450 | $550 |

GSS-50 Amp
1966-1967. Solidstate, 50 watts, 2x10" combo, reverb and tremolo, black vinyl cover, silver grille, no grille logo.

| 1966-1967 | | $350 | $400 |

The *Vintage Guitar Price Guide* shows low to high values for items in all-original excellent condition, and, where applicable, with original case or cover.

MODEL YEAR FEATURES	EXC. COND. LOW	HIGH

GSS-100 Amp
1966-1967. Solidstate, 100 watts, two 24"x12" 2x10" sealed cabs, black vinyl cover, silver grille, 8 black knobs and 3 red knobs, slanted raised Gibson logo. Speakers prone to distortion.

1966-1967	$375	$425

Hawk Amp
1968-1969. Solidstate, upright vertical cab, faux wood grain front panel, 15 watts, 1x10".

1968-1969	$150	$175

LP-1/LP-2 Amp Set
1970. Les Paul model, piggyback amp and cab set, LP-1 head and LP-2 4x12" plus 2 horns cab, large vertical speaker cabinet, rather small compact 190 watt solidstate amp head.

1970	$325	$400

Medalist 2/12 Amp
1968-1970. Vertical cabinet, 2x12", reverb and temolo.

1968-1970	$450	$525

Medalist 4/10 Amp
1968-1970. Vertical cabinet, 4x10", reverb and tremolo.

1968-1970	$450	$550

Mercury I Amp
1963-1965. Piggyback trapezoid-shaped head with 2x12" trapezoid cabinet, tremolo, brown.

1963-1965	$450	$550

Mercury II Amp
1963-1967. Mercury I with 1x15" and 1x10", initially trapezoid cabinets then changed to rectangular.

1963-1964	Brown trapezoid cabs	$550	$650
1963-1964	Head only	$250	$350
1965-1967	Black rectangular cabs	$450	$550

Plus-50 Amp
1966-1967. 50 watts, powered extension amplifier. Similar to GSS-100 cabinet of the same era, 2x10" cab, black vinyl cover, silver grille, slant Gibson logo.

1966-1967	$450	$550

Super Thor Bass Amp
1972-1974. Solidstate, part of the new G-Series (not GA-Series), 65 watts, 2x15", black tolex, black grille, upright vertical cab with front control, single channel.

1972-1974	$325	$375

Thor Bass Amp
1970-1974. Solidstate, smaller 2x10" 50 watt version of Super Thor.

1970-1974	$250	$300

Titan I Amp
1963-1965. Piggyback trapezoid-shaped head and 2x12" trapezoid-shaped cabinet, tremolo.

1963-1965	$475	$525

Titan III Amp
1963-1967. Piggyback trapezoid-shaped head and 1x15" + 2x10" trapezoid-shaped cabinet, tremolo.

1963-1964	Brown	$500	$600
1965-1967	Black	$500	$600

MODEL YEAR FEATURES	EXC. COND. LOW	HIGH

Titan V Amp
1963-1967. Piggyback trapezoid-shaped tube head and 2x15" trapezoid-shaped cabinet, tremolo.

1963-1964	Brown	$525	$625
1965-1967	Black	$525	$625

Titan Medalist Amp
1964-1967. Combo version of Titan Series with 1x15" and 1x10", tremolo only, no reverb, black.

1964-1967	$525	$625

Ginelle
1996-present. Rick Emery builds his tube combo amps in West Berlin, New Jersey.

Gomez Amplificiation
2005-present. Tube combo amps built by Dario G. Gomez in Rancho Santa Margarita, California.

Goodsell
2004-present. Tube head and combo amps built by Richard Goodsell in Atlanta, Georgia.

Gorilla
1980s-present. Small solidstate entry-level amps, distributed by Pignose, Las Vegas, Nevada.

Compact Practice Student Amp
1980s-present. Solidstate, 10 to 30 watts, compact design.

1980s	$25	$40
1990s	$25	$40
2000s	$25	$40

Goya
1955-1996. Goya was mainly known for acoustics, but offered a few amps in the '60s. The brand was purchased by Avnet/Guild in '66 and by Martin in the late '70s.

Green
1993-present. Amp model line made in England by Matamp (see that brand for listing), bright green covering, large Green logo on the front.

Greer Amplification
1999-present. Tube guitar amps and speaker cabinets built by Nick Greer in Athens, Georgia. He also builds effects.

Gregory
1950s-1960s. Private branded amps sold via music wholesalers, by late '60s solidstate models made by Harmony including the 007, C.I.A., Mark Six, Mark Eight, Saturn 80, most models were combo amps with Gregory logo.

Solidstate Amps
1960s	$150	$175

Gretsch
1883-present. In '05, Gretsch again starting offering amps after previously selling them from the 1950s to '73. Initially private branded for them

Gomez Amplification G-Reverb

Green amp

Gretsch Safari

AMPS

*1959 Gretsch Model 6169
Electromatic Twin Western*

*Groove Tubes Soul-O Single
(head)*

Guild 66-J

by Valco (look for the Valco oval or rectangular serialized label on the back). Early-'50s amps were covered in the requisite tweed, but evolved into the Gretsch charcoal gray covering. The mid-'50s to early-'60s amps were part of the Electromatic group of amps. The mid-'50s to '62 amps often sported wrap-around and slanted grilles. In '62, the more traditional box style was introduced. In '66, the large amps went piggyback. Baldwin-Gretsch began to phase out amps effective '65, but solidstate amps continued being offered for a period of time. The '73 Gretsch product line only offered Sonax amps, made in Canada and Sho-Bud amps made in the U.S. In '05, they introduced a line of tube combo amps made in U.S. by Victoria Amp Company.

Artist Amp
1946. Early post-war Gretsch amp made before Valco began to make their amps. Appears to be made by Operadio Mfg. Co., St. Charles, Illinois. Low power small combo amp, Gretsch Artist script logo on grille, round speaker baffle hole.

1946		$200	$250

Electromatic Amp
Late-1950s. Small compact amp, 2x6V6 power, 1x10", volume knob, tone knob, Electromatic logo on back panel.

1957-1958		$500	$625

Model 6150 Compact Amp
Early-1950s-1960s. Early amps in tweed, '60s amps in gray covering, no tremolo, single volume knob, no treble or bass knob, 1x8".

1950s	Brown tweed	$375	$425
1960s	Gray	$375	$425

Model 6151/6151 Compact Tremolo Amp
Late-1940s-late-1960s. 1x8", various covers.

1940s		$375	$450
1950s		$375	$450
1960s		$325	$400

Model 6152 Compact Tremolo Reverb Amp
Ca.1964-late-1960s. Five watts, 11"x6" elliptical speaker early on, 1x12" later.

1964-1966	Elliptical speaker	$600	$725
1966-1969	Round speaker	$575	$700

Model 6154 Super-Bass Amp
Early-1960s-mid-1960s. Gray covering, 2x12", 70 watts, tube.

1960s		$600	$725

Model 6156 Playboy Amp
Early-1950s-1966. Tube amp, 17 watts, 1x10" until '61 when converted to 1x12", tweed, then gray, then finally black covered.

1950s-1960	Tweed, 1x10	$575	$700
1961-1962	Tweed, 1x12"	$650	$800
1963-1966	Black or gray, 1x12"	$650	$800

Model 6157 Super Bass (Piggyback) Amp
Mid-late-1960s. 35 watts, 2x15" cabinet, single channel.

1960s		$500	$550

Model 6159 Super Bass/Dual Playboy (Combo) Amp
Mid-late-1960s. 35 watts, tube, 2x12" cabinet, dual channel, black covering. Replaced by 6163 Chet Atkins Piggyback Amp.

1960s		$675	$825

Model 6160 Chet Atkins Country Gentleman Amp
Early-late-1960s. Combo tube amp, 35 watts, 2x12" cabinet, 2 channels. Replaced by 6163 Chet Atkins Piggyback amp with tremolo but no reverb.

1960s		$650	$800

Model 6161 Dual Twin Tremolo Amp
Ca.1962-late-1960s. 19 watts (later 17 watts), 2x10" with 5" tweeter, tremolo.

1962-1967		$650	$775

Model 6161 Electromatic Twin Amp
Ca.1953-ca.1960. Gray Silverflake covering, two 11x6" speakers, 14 watts, tremolo, wraparound grille '55 and after.

1953-1960		$750	$925

Model 6162 Dual Twin Tremolo/Reverb Amp
Ca.1964-late-1960s. 17 watts, 2x10", reverb, tremolo. Vertical combo amp style introduced in '68.

1964-1967	Horizontal combo style	$750	$825
1968-1969	Vertical combo style	$500	$600

Model 6163 Chet Atkins (Piggyback) Amp
Mid-late-1960s. 70 watts, 1x12" and 1x15", black covering, tremolo, reverb.

1960s		$550	$650

Model 6163 Executive Amp
1959. 1x15, gray cover.

1959		$1,100	$1,300

Model 6164 Variety Amp
Early-mid-1960s. 35 watts, tube, 2x12".

1960s		$550	$650

Model 6165 Variety Plus Amp
Early-mid-1960s. Tube amp, 35 watts, 2x12", reverb and tremolo, separate controls for both channels.

1960s		$600	$700

Model 6166 Fury (Combo) Amp
Mid-1960s. Tube combo stereo amp, 70 watts, 2x12", separate controls for both channels, large metal handle, reverb.

1960s		$600	$700

Model 6169 Electromatic Twin Western Finish Amp
Ca.1953-ca.1960. Western finish, 14 watts, 2-11x6" speakers, tremolo, wraparound grill '55 and after.

1950s		$2,800	$3,500

Model 6169 Fury (Piggyback) Amp
Late-1960s. Tube amp, 70 watts, 2x12", separate controls for both channels.

1960s		$600	$700

Model 6170 Pro Bass Amp
1966-late-1960s. 25 or 35 watts, depending on model, 1x15", vertical cabinet style (vs. box cabinet).

1966-1969		$400	$475

MODEL YEAR	FEATURES	EXC. COND. LOW	HIGH

Model 7154 Nashville Amp
Introduced in 1969. Solidstate combo amp, 4' tall, 75 watts, 2x15", reverb, tremolo, magic echo.

1970s		$500	$550

Model 7155 Tornado PA System Amp
Introduced in 1969. Solidstate piggyback head and cab, 150 watts, 2 column speaker cabs, reverb, tremolo, magic echo.

1970s	2x2x15"	$500	$550
1970s	2x4x15"	$600	$650

Model 7517 Rogue Amp
1970s. Solidstate, 40 watts, 2x12", tall vertical cabinet, front control panel.

1970s		$250	$300

Model G6156 Playboy Amp
2000s. 15 watts, 1x12" combo amp with retro Gretsch styling, made by Victoria.

2005-2007		$750	$950

Model G6163 Executive Amp
2005-2007. Boutique quality made by Victoria for FMIC Gretsch, 20 watts, 1x15", cabinet Uses to the modern retro early '60s Supro Supreme modified-triangle front grille pattern, maroon baffle with white grille, tremolo and reverb.

2005-2007		$850	$1,100

Rex Royal Amp Model M-197-3V
1950s. Small student compact amp, low power, 1x8", Rex Royal logo on grille, Fred Gretsch logo on back panel, single on-off volume knob.

1951		$375	$450

Groove Tubes
1979-present. Started by Aspen Pittman in his garage in Sylmar, California, Groove Tubes is now located in San Fernando. GT manufactures and distributes a full line of tubes. In '86 they added amp production and in '91 tube microphones. Aspen is also the author of the Tube Amp Book. The Groove Tubes brand was purchased by Fender in June, '08.

Guild
1952-present. Guild offered amps from the '60s into the '80s. Some of the early models were built by Hagstrom.

Double Twin Amp
1953-1955. 35 watts, 2x12" plus 2 tweeters, 2-tone leatherette covered cab.

1953-1955		$525	$650

Master Amp
Ca. 1957- Ca. 1957. 2-tone tweed and leatherette combo, tremolo, Guild script logo and smaller block Master logo..

1950s		$400	$500

Maverick Amp
1960s. Dual speaker combo, verticle cab, tremolo, reverb, red/pink control panel, 2-tone black and silver grille.

1960s		$275	$325

Model One Amp
Mid-1970s-1977. 30 watts, 1x12" vertical cab combo, reverb and tremolo.

1970s		$175	$200

Model Two Amp
Mid-1970s-1977. 50 watts, 2x10" vertical cab combo, reverb and tremolo.

1977-1978		$200	$225

Model Three Amp
Mid-1970s-1977. 60 watts, 1x15" vertical cab combo, for bass, organ and guitar.

1977-1978		$225	$250

Model Four Amp
Early-1980s. Six watts.

1980s		$100	$150

Model Five Amp
Early-1980s. 10 watts, 6.25" speaker.

1980s		$125	$150

Model Six Amp
Early-1980s. Same as Model Five but with reverb.

1980s		$175	$200

Model Seven Amp
Early-1980s. Small amp for guitar, bass and keyboard, 12 watts.

1980s		$175	$200

Model 50-J Amp
Early-1960s. 14 watts, 1x12", tremolo, blue/gray vinyl.

1962-1963		$200	$225

Model 66 Amp
1953-1955. 15 watts, 1x12", tremolo, 2-tone leatherette.

1953-1955		$225	$300

Model 66-J Amp
1962-1963. 20 watts, 1x12", tremolo, blue/gray vinyl.

1962-1963		$325	$375

Model 98-RT Amp
1962-1963. The only stand-alone reverb amp from Guild in the early '60s, 30 watts, 1x12", blue/gray vinyl.

1962-1963		$575	$650

Model 99 Amp
1953-1955. 20 watts, 1x12", tremolo, 2-tone leatherette.

1953-1955		$300	$375

Model 99-J Amp
Early-1960s. 30 watts, 1x12", tremolo, blue/gray vinyl.

1962-1963		$350	$425

Model 99-U Ultra Amp
Early-1960s. Piggyback 30-watt head with optional 1x12" or 1x15" cab, cab and head lock together, tremolo, blue/gray vinyl.

1962-1963		$400	$500

Model 100-J Amp
Early-1960s. 35 watts, 1x15", blue/gray vinyl.

1962-1963		$400	$500

Model 200-S Stereo Combo Amp
Early-1960s. 25 watts per channel, total 50 watts stereo, 2x12", tremolo, blue/gray vinyl, wheat grille.

1962-1963		$700	$800

Model RC-30 Reverb Converter Amp
Early-1960s. Similar to Gibson GA-1 converter, attaches with 2 wires clipped to originating amp's speaker, 8 watts, 1x10", blue/gray vinyl.

1962-1963		$400	$450

AMPS

1964 Gretsch 6164 Variety

1971 Guild Maverick

Guild Thunderstar

Guytron GT100

Harry Joyce Custom 50

Headstrong BL 310

MODEL YEAR	FEATURES	EXC. COND. LOW	HIGH

SuperStar Amp
Ca.1972-ca.1974. 50 watts, all tubes, 1x15" Jensen speakers, vertical combo, reverb, tremolo, black vinyl cover, 2-tone black/silver grille.

1972-1974		$350	$425

Thunder 1 (Model 11RVT)/T1 Amp
Introduced 1965. Combo with dual speakers and reverb, light tan cover, 2-tone tan grille.

1965-1968		$425	$525

ThunderStar Bass Amp
1960s. Piggyback bass tube head or combo, 50 watts.

1965-1968		$500	$600

Guyatone
1933-present. Started offering amps by at least the late '40s with their Guya lap steels. In '51 the Guyatone brand is first used on guitars and most likely amps. Guyatone also made the Marco Polo, Winston, Kingston, Kent, LaFayette and Bradford brands.

Guytron
1995-present. Tube amp heads and speaker cabinets built by Guy Hedrick in Columbiaville, Michigan.

Hagstrom
1921-1983. The Swedish guitar maker built a variety of tube and solidstate amps from ca. 1961 into the '70s. They also supplied amps to Guild.

Hanburt
1940-ca. 1950. Harvey M. Hansen built electric Hawaiian guitars in Seattle, Washington, some sold as a set with a small amp. The wooden amps have a large HB in the speaker cutout. He also built at least one mandolin.

Harmony
1892-1976, late-1970s-present. Harmony was one of the biggest producers of guitars, and offered amps as well. MBT International offered Harmony amps for 2000-'02.

H Series Amps
Harmony model numbers begin with H, such as H-304, all H series models shown are tube amps unless otherwise noted as solidstate.

1940-1950s	H-200	$250	$300
1950s	H-204, 18w, 1x12"	$150	$175
1960s	H-303A, 8w, 1x8"	$150	$175
1960s	H-304, low pwr, small spkr	$150	$175
1960s	H-305A, low pwr, small spkr	$150	$175
1960s	H-306A, combo 1x12"	$150	$175
1960s	H306C, piggy-back 2x12"	$425	$500
1960s	H-400, 8w, 1x8"	$100	$150
1960s	H-410A, 10w, 1x10"	$150	$175
1960s	H-415, 20w, 2x10"	$150	$175

MODEL YEAR	FEATURES	EXC. COND. LOW	HIGH
1960s	H-420, 20w, 1x12"	$175	$200
1960s	H-430, 30w, 2x12"	$200	$250
1960s	H-440, 2x12", trem and verb	$600	$725

Solidstate Amps
Dark covering, dark grille.

1970s	Large amp	$75	$125
1970s	Small amp	$50	$75

Harry Joyce
1993-2000. Hand-wired British tube amps, combos, and cabinets from builder Harry Joyce. Joyce was contracted to build Hiwatt amps in England during the '60s and '70s. He died on January 11, 2002.

Hartke
1984-present. Guitar and bass amps, combos and cabinets made in the U.S. Founded by Larry Hartke, since the mid-'80s, Hartke has been distributed by Samson Technologies. Hartke also offered basses in the past.

1-15B-XL Cabinet
1994-present. XL Series, 1x15" rated at 180 watts, larger cab, black cover.

1990s		$225	$275

4.5-XL Cabinet
1994-present. XL Series, 4x10" and 5" driver rated at 400 watts, larger ported cab.

1994-2003		$325	$400

B 30/B 300 Bass Combo Amp
1999-present. Compact practice amp, 30 watts, 1x10", dark cover. Changed to B 300 in '05.

1999-2000		$125	$150

HA 1410 Bass Combo Amp
1994-2004. Solidstate, 140 watts, 2x10", dark cover.

1994-2004		$275	$325

HA 2000 Bass Amp Head
1992-2004. 200 watts, tube preamp, solidstate power section, tube/solidstate switchable.

1992-2004		$275	$325

HA 3500/3500a Bass Amp Head
1990-present. Solidstate, 350 watts, 10-band graphic EQ.

1990-1999		$325	$400
2000-2006		$350	$425

Transporter Series Cabinets
1990s. 1x15" cab rated 150 watts, or 4x10" rated 200-300 watts, black cover, black metal grille.

1990s	150 watts, 1x15"	$225	$275
1990s	200-300 watts, 4x10"	$250	$300

Haynes
Haynes guitar amps were built by the Amplifier Corporation of America (ACA) of Westbury, New York. ACA also made an early distortion device powered by batteries. Unicord purchased the company in around 1964, and used the factory to produce its Univox line of amps, most likely discontinuing the Haynes brand at the same time.

MODEL YEAR	FEATURES	EXC. COND. LOW	HIGH

Jazz King II Amp
1960s. Solidstate, stereo console-style, 2x12", Haynes logo upper left side.

1960s		$350	$425

Headstrong
2002-present. Tube combo amps built by Wayne Jones and Jessica Winterbottom in Asheville, North Carolina. They also offer a range of replacement cabinets for vintage amps.

Heritage
2004-present. Founded by Malcolm MacDonald and Lane Zastrow who was formerly involved with Holland amps. Located in the former Holland facility in Brentwood, Tennessee, they build tube combo and piggyback amps.

Hilgen
1960s. Mid-level amplifiers from Hilgen Manufacturing, Hillside, New Jersey. Dark tolex covering and swiggle-lined light color grille cloth. Examples have been found with original Jensen speakers.

Basso B-2501 Amp
1960s. 25 watts, 1x15" combo, swirl grille, Hilgen crest logo, compact size.

1965		$250	$300

Basso B-2502 Amp
1960s. 25 watts, 1x15" combo, swirl grille, Hilgen crest logo, large cab.

1965		$350	$425

Basso Grande B-2503 Amp
1960s. Brown sparkle cover, piggyback, 2x12".

1965		$400	$500

Champion R-2523 Amp
Mid-1960s. Highest offering in their amp line, piggyback with 2x12" cab, tremolo, reverb, swirl grille cloth.

1965		$450	$550

Galaxie T-2513 Amp
1960s. 25 watts, 2x12" piggyback cabinet, tremolo.

1965		$375	$450

Metero T-2511 Amp
Mid-1960s. Compact 1x12" combo, tremolo.

1965		$325	$400

Pacesetter R-2521 Amp
Mid-1960s. 1x12" combo, tremolo, reverb, swirl grille cloth.

1965		$300	$375

Star T-2512 Amp
1960s. 25 watts, 1x12" combo, tremolo.

1965		$300	$375

Victor R-2522 Amp
Mid-1960s. 1x12" combo, larger cabinet, reverb, tremolo.

1965		$400	$500

HiWatt
Bulldog SA112 Amp
1980s, 1994-present. 50 watts, combo, 1x12".

1980s		$1,000	$1,200
1990s		$700	$1,000

Bulldog SA112FL Amp
1980s-1990s. 100 watts, combo, 1x12".

1980s		$1,000	$1,200
1990s		$700	$1,000

DR-103 Custom 100 Amp Head
1970-late-1980s. Tube head, 100 watts, custom Hiwatt 100 logo on front.

1970-1977		$1,850	$2,300

DR-103 Matching Amp Head/Cabinet
100-watt head, matching SE4122 or SE4123 4x12" cab(s).

1973	Full stack	$4,700	$5,200
1973	Half stack	$3,500	$4,000

DR-201 Hiwatt 200 Amp Head
1970s. 200-watt amp head, Hiwatt 200 logo on front.

1970s		$1,900	$2,600

DR-201 Matching Amp Head/Cabinet
200-watt head, matching SE4122 or SE4151 cab(s).

1970s	Full stack	$5,300	$6,600
1970s	Half stack	$3,600	$5,600

DR-405 Hiwatt 400 Amp Head
1970s. 400-watt amp head.

1970s		$2,000	$4,000

DR-405 Matching Amp Head/Cabinet
400-watt head, matching SE4123, SE 4122, or SE 4129 cabs.

1970s	Full stack	$5,400	$7,750
1970s	SE4122 quad	$8,800	$11,500
1970s	SE4123 quad	$5,000	$10,500
1970s	SE4129 quad	$6,200	$13,100

DR-504 Custom 50 Amp Head
1970-late-1980s, 1995-1999. Tube head amp, 50 watts.

1970s		$1,400	$1,700

DR-504 Matching Amp Head/Cabinet
50-watt head, matching SE4122 or SE4123 4x12" cab(s).

1970s	Full stack	$4,600	$5,100
1970s	Half stack	$3,000	$3,500

Lead 20 (SG-20) Amp Head
1980s. Tube amp head, 30 watts, black cover, rectangular HiWatt plate logo.

1980s		$400	$900

Lead 50R Combo Amp
1980s. Combo tube amp, 50 watts, 1x12", reverb, dark cover, dark grille, HiWatt rectangular plate logo.

1980s		$600	$1,150

PW-50 Tube Amp
1989-1993. Stereo tube amp, 50 watts per channel.

1989-1993		$750	$1,100

S50L Amp Head
1989-1993. Lead guitar head, 50 watts, gain, master volume, EQ.

1989-1993		$650	$900

SA 112 Combo Amp
1970s. 50 watts, 1x12".

1970s		$2,000	$2,400

Heritage Victory

HiWatt DR-504 Custom 50

HiWatt Bulldog SA112

AMPS

Holmes Pro 112

Jackson JG-3

JCA Circuts GR 1.6

MODEL YEAR	FEATURES	EXC. COND. LOW	HIGH
SA 212 Combo Amp			
1970s. 50 watts, 2x12", low production, uses DR 504 chasis in combo form.			
1970s		$2,100	$2,500
SA 412 Combo Amp			
1970s. 50 watts, 4x12" combo.			
1970s		$2,700	$3,300
SE 2150 Speaker Cabinet			
1970s. Veritcal 2x15" cab.			
1970s		$1,600	$2,100
SE 4122 (Lead) Speaker Cabinet			
1971- mid-1980s. 4x12" Fane speakers, 300 watts.			
1970s		$1,600	$2,000
SE 4123 (Bass) Speaker Cabinet			
1970s. Bass version of SE, often used with DR103 head, straight-front cab and stackable, black tolex with gray grille, Hiwatt logo plate in center of grille.			
1970s		$1,600	$1,800
SE 4129 (Bass) Speaker Cabinet			
1970s. SE series for bass, 4x12", often used with DR 201 head.			
1970s		$1,600	$2,700
SE 4151 Speaker Cabinet			
1970s. SE series with 4 x 15".			
1970s		$1,600	$2,900

Hoffman

1993-present. Tube amps, combos, reverb units, and cabinets built by Doug Hoffman from 1993 to '99, in Sarasota, Florida. Hoffman no longer builds amps, concentrating on selling tube amp building supplies, and since 2001 has been located in Pisgah Forest, North Carolina.

Hoffmann

1983-present. Tube amp heads for guitar and other musical instruments built by Kim Hoffmann in Hawthorne, California.

Hohner

1857-present. Matthias Hohner, a clockmaker in Trossingen, Germany, founded Hohner in 1857, making harmonicas. Hohner has been offering guitars and amps at least since the early '70s.

Panther Series Amps
1980s. Smaller combo amps, master volume, gain, EQ.

1980s	P-12 (12 watts)	$70	$100
1980s	P-20 (20 watts)	$75	$125
1980s	P-25R (25 watts)	$75	$125
1980s	PBK-20 bass/keyboard (25 watts)	$75	$150

Sound Producer Series Amps
1980s. Master volume, normal and overdrive, reverb, headphone jack.

1980s	BA 130 bass	$75	$150
1980s	SP 35	$75	$150
1980s	SP 55	$75	$150
1980s	SP 75	$100	$175

Holland

1992-2004. Tube combo amps from builder Mike Holland, originally in Virginia Beach, Virginia, and since 2000 in Brentwood, Tennessee. In 2000, Holland took Lane Zastrow as a partner, forming L&M Amplifiers to build the Holland line. The company closed in '04.

Holmes

1970-late 1980s. Founded by Harrison Holmes. Holmes amplifiers were manufactured in Mississippi and their product line included guitar and bass amps, PA systems, and mixing boards. In the early '80s, Harrsion Holmes sold the company to On-Site Music which called the firm The Holmes Corp. Products manufactured by Harrison have an all-caps HOLMES logo and the serial number plate says The Holmes Company.

Performer PB-115 Bass Amp
60 watts, 1x15", black tolex.

1982		$100	$125

Pro Compact 210S Amp
60 watts, 2x10", 2 channels, active EQ, black tolex.

1982		$100	$125

Pro Compact 212S Amp
2x12" version of Pro.

1982		$125	$150

Rebel RB-112 Bass Amp
35 watts, 1x12", black tolex

1982		$75	$100

Hondo

1969-1987, 1991-present. Hondo has offered imported amps over the years. 1990s models ranged from the H20 Practice Amp to the H160SRC with 160 watts (peak) and 2x10" speakers.

Amps

1970-1990s Various models	$25	$75

Hound Dog

1994-1998. Founded by George Alessandro as the Hound Dog Corporation. Name was changed to Alessandro in 1998 (see that brand for more info).

Hughes & Kettner

1985-present. Hughes & Kettner offers a line of solidstate and tube guitar and bass amps, combos, cabinets and effects, all made in Germany.

Hurricane

1998-present. Tube guitar and harmonica combo amps built by Gary Drouin in Sarasota, Florida. Drouin started the company with harp master Rock Bottom, who died in September, 2001.

Ibanez

1932-present. Ibanez added solidstate amps to their product line in '98. They also build guitars, basses and effects.

MODEL YEAR	FEATURES	EXC. COND. LOW	HIGH

Solidstate Amps
2004-present. Models include Troubadour (TA), Tone Blaster (TB), IBZ Series.

2000s	IBZ Series	$30	$35
2000s	TA Series	$150	$185

Idol
Late-1960s. Made in Japan. Dark tolex cover, dark grille, Hobby Series with large Idol logo on front.
Hobby Series Amps

1968	Hobby 10	$70	$85
1968	Hobby 100	$175	$200
1968	Hobby 20	$100	$125
1968	Hobby 45	$150	$175

Impact
1963-early 1970s. Based in London, England, tube amps made by Don Mackrill and Laurie Naiff for Pan Musical Instrument Company and their music stores. About a dozen different models of combos, piggyback half-stacks and PAs were offered.

Imperial
Ca.1963-ca.1970. The Imperial Accordion Company of Chicago, Illinois offered one or two imported small amps in the '60s.

Jack Daniel's
2004-present. Tube guitar amp built by Peavey for the Jack Daniel Distillery. They also offer a guitar model.

Jackson
1980-present. The Jackson-Charvel Company offered budget to intermediate grade amps and cabinets in the late '80s and the '90s.

Jackson Ampworks
2001-present. Brad Jackson builds his tube amp heads and speaker cabinets in Bedford, Texas.

Jackson-Guldan
1920s-1960s. The Jackson-Guldan Violin Company, of Columbus, Ohio, offered lap steels and small tube amps early on. They also built acoustic guitars.

Jay Turser
1997-present. Smaller, inexpensive imported solidstate guitar and bass amps. They also offer basses and guitars.

JCA Circuits
1995-present. Tube guitar combo amps built by Jason C. Arthur in Pottstown, Pennsylvania.

Jim Kelly
Early 1980s. High-gain, channel-switching tube amps, compact combos and heads, hardwood cabinets available, made by Active Guitar Electronics in Tustin, California, limited production.

JMI (Jennings Musical Industries)
2004-present. Jennings built the Vox amps of the 1960s. They are back with tube amp heads and cabinets based on some of their classic models.

Johnson
Mid-1990s-present. Line of solidstate amps imported by Music Link, Brisbane, California. Johnson also offers guitars, basses, mandolins and effects.

Johnson Amplification
1997-present. Modeling amps and effects designed by John Johnson, of Sandy, Utah. The company is part of Harman International. In 2002, they quit building amps, but continue the effects line.

JoMama
1994-present. Tube amps and combos under the JoMama and Kelemen brands built by Joe Kelemen in Santa Fe, New Mexico.

Juke
1989-present. Tube guitar and harmonica amps built by G.R. Croteau in Troy, New Hampshire. He also built the Warbler line of amps.

Kafel
2004-present. Jack Kafel builds his tube amp heads in Chicago, Illinois.

Kalamazoo
1933-1942, 1965-1970. Kalamazoo was a brand Gibson used on one of their budget lines. They used the name on amps from '65 to '67.

Bass Amp
1965-1967. Enclosed back, 2x10", flip-out control panel, not a commonly found model as compared to numerous Model 1 and 2 student amps.

1965-1967		$200	$250

Lap Steel Amp
1940s. Kalamazoo logo on front lower right, low power with 1-6V6, round speaker grille opening, red/brown leatherette.

1940s		$350	$425

Model 1 Amp
1965-1967. No tremolo, 1x10", front control panel, black.

1965-1967		$150	$175

Model 2 Amp
1965-1967. Same as Model 1 with tremolo, black.

1965-1967		$200	$225

Reverb 12 Amp
1965-1967. Black vinyl cover, 1x12", reverb, tremolo.

1965-1967		$350	$425

AMPS

Johnson Barn Burner

Juke 1210

Kalamazoo Model 2

Kay 703

Kendrick K Spot

Kelemen Reverb-45

AMPS

MODEL YEAR	FEATURES	EXC. COND. LOW	HIGH

Kay

Ca.1931-present. Kay originally offered amps up to around '68 when the brand changed hands. Currently they offer a couple small solidstate imported amps. They also make basses, guitars, banjos, mandolins, ukes, and violins.

K506 Vibrato 12" Amp
1960s. 12 watts, 1x12", swirl grille, metal handle.

1962		$250	$300

K507 Twin Ten Special Amp
1960s. 20 watts, 2x10", swirl grille, metal handle.

1962		$325	$400

Small Tube Amps

1940s	Wood cabinet	$225	$275
1950s	Various models	$150	$175
1960s	Models K503, K504, K505	$150	$175

Kelemen

1994-present. Tube amps and combos under the JoMama and Kelemen brands built by Joe Kelemen in Santa Fe, New Mexico.

Kendrick

1989-present. Founded by Gerald Weber in Austin, Texas, and currently located in Kempner, Texas. Mainly known for their intermediate to professional grade, tube amps, Kendrick also offers guitars, speakers, and effects. Weber has authored books and videos on tube amps.

Kent

Ca.1962-1969. Imported budget line of guitars and amps.

Guitar and Bass Amps
1960s. Various models.

1966	1475, 3 tubes, brown	$50	$60
1966	2198, 3 tubes, brown	$60	$70
1966	5999, 3 tubes, brown	$70	$80
1966	6104, piggyback, 12w	$110	$125
1969	6610, solidstate, small	$25	$30

Kiesel

See Carvin.

King Amplification

2005-present. Tube combo amps, head and cabinets built by Val King in San Jose, California.

Kingston

1958-1967. Economy solidstate amps imported by Westheimer Importing, Chicago, Illinois.

Cat Amps
Mid-1960s. Solidstate Cat Series amps have dark vinyl, dark grilles.

1960s	P-1, 3 watt	$40	$45
1960s	P-2, 5 watts	$40	$50
1960s	P-3, 8 w, P-8 20 w, both 1x8"	$45	$55

Cougar BA-21 Bass Piggyback Amp
Mid-1960s. Solidstate, 60 watts, 2x12" cab, dark vinyl, light silver grille.

1960s		$100	$120

Cougar PB-5 Bass Combo Amp
Mid-1960s. Solidstate, 15 watts, 1x8".

1960s		$45	$55

Lion 2000 Piggyback Amp
Mid-1960s. Solidstate, 90 watts, 2x12" cab.

1960s		$120	$150

Lion 3000 Piggyback Amp
Mid-1960s. Solidstate, 250 watts, 4x12" cab.

1960s		$145	$180

Lion AP-281 R Piggyback Amp
Mid-1960s. Solidstate, 30 watts, 2x8" cab, dark vinyl cover, light silver grille.

1960s		$70	$80

Lion AP-281 R10 Piggyback Amp
Mid-1960s. Solidstate, 30 watts, 2x10" cab.

1960s		$100	$120

Kitchen-Marshall

1965-1966. Private branded for Kitchen Music by Marshall, primarily PA units with block logos. Limited production.

JTM 45 MKII 45-Watt Amp Head
1965-1966. Private branded for Kitchen Music, JTM 45 Marshall with Kitchen logo plate, 45 watts.

1965-1966		$5,600	$6,500

Slant 4x12 1960 Cabinet
1965-1966. Slant front 4x12" 1960-style cab with gray bluesbreaker grille, very limited production.

1965-1966	Black on green vinyl	$4,600	$5,100

KJL

1995-present. Founded by Kenny Lannes, MSEE, a professor of Electrical Engineering at the University of New Orleans. KJL makes tube combo amps, heads and an ABY box.

KMD (Kaman)

1986-ca.1990. Distributed by Kaman (Ovation, Hamer, etc.) in the late '80s, KMD offered a variety of amps and effects.

Koch

All-tube combo amps, heads, effects and cabinets built in The Netherlands.

Komet

1999-present. Tube amp heads built in Baton Rouge, Louisanna, by Holger Notzel and Michael Kennedy with circuits designed by Ken Fischer of Trainwreck fame. They also build a power attenuator.

Kona

2001-present. Budget solidstate amps made in Asia. They also offer guitars, basses, mandolins and banjos.

Krank

1996-present. Founded by Tony Dow and offering tube amp heads, combos and speaker cabinets built in Tempe, Arizona. They also build effects. The company greatly upped its distribution in '03.

Kustom

1965-present. Kustom, a division of Hanser Holdings, offers guitar and bass combo amps and PA equipment. Founded by Bud Ross in Chanute, Kansas, who offered tuck-and-roll amps as early as '58, but began using the Kustom brand name in '65. From '69 to '75 Ross gradually sold interest in the company (in the late '70s, Ross introduced the line of Ross effects stomp boxes). The brand changed hands a few times, and by the mid-'80s it was no longer in use. In '89 Kustom was in bankruptcy court and was purchased by Hanser Holdings Incorporated of Cincinnati, Ohio (Davitt & Hanser) and by '94, they had a new line of amps available.

Prices are for excellent condition amps with no tears in the tuck-and-roll cover and no grille tears. A tear in the tuck-and-roll will reduce the value, sometimes significantly.

Kustom model identification can be frustrating as they used series numbers, catalog numbers (the numbers in the catalogs and price lists), and model numbers (the number often found next to the serial number on the amp's back panel). Most of the discussion that follows is by series number (100, 200, 300, etc.) and catalog number. Unfortunately, vintage amp dealers use the serial number and model number, so the best way is to cross-check speaker and amplifier attributes. Model numbers were used primarily for repair purposes and were found in the repair manuals. In many, but not all cases, the model number is the last digit of the catalog number; for example the catalog lists a 100 series Model 1-15J-1, where the last digit 1 signifies a Model 1 amplifier chassis which is a basic amp without reverb or tremolo. A Model 1-15J-2 signifies a Model 2 amp chassis that has reverb and tremolo. In this example, Kustom uses a different model number on the back of the amp head. For the 1-15J-2, the model number on the back panel of the amp head would be K100-2, indicating a series 100 (50 watts) amp with reverb and tremolo (amp chassis Model 2).

Amp Chasis Model Numbers ('68-'72)

Model 1 Amp (basic)
Model 2 Amp with reverb
Model 3 Amp with Harmonic Clip and Boost
Model 4 Amp with reverb, tremolo, vibrato, Harmonic Clip and Selective Boost
Model 5 PA with reverb
Model 6 Amp (basic) with Selectone
Model 7 Amp with reverb, tremolo, vibrato, boost (different parts)
Model 8 Amp with reverb, tremolo, vibrato, boost (different parts)

Naugahyde Tuck-&-Roll 200 ('65-'67)

The very first Kustoms did not have the model series on the front control panel. The early logo

stipulated Kustom by Ross, Inc. The name was then updated to Kustom Electronics, Inc. 1965-'67 amp heads have a high profile/tall "forehead" area (the area on top of the controls) and these have been nicknamed "Frankenstein models." The '65-'67 catalog numbers were often 4 or 5 digits, for example J695. The first digit represents the speaker type (J = Jensen, etc.), other examples are L995, L1195, L795RV, etc. Some '67 catalog numbers changed to 2 digits followed by 3 digits, like 4-D 140f, or 3-15C (3 CTS speakers), etc. Others sported 5 characters like 4-15J-1, where 4 = 4 speakers, 15 = 15" speakers, J = Jensen, and 1 = basic amp chassis with no effects. The fifth digit indicated amp chassis model number as described above.

Naugahyde Tuck-&-Roll 100/200/400 ('68-'71)

Starting in '68, the Kustom logo also included the model series. A K100, for example, would have 100 displayed below the Kustom name. The model series generally is twice the relative output wattage, for example, the 100 Series is a 50-watt amp. Keep in mind, solidstate ratings are often higher than tube-amp ratings, so use the ratings as relative measurements. Most '68-'70 Kustom catalog numbers are x-xxx-x, for example 1-15L-1. First digit represents the number of speakers, the 2nd and 3rd represent the speaker size, the fourth represents the speaker type (A = Altec Lansing, L = J.B.L., J = Jensen, C = C.T.S. Bass), the fifth digit represents the amp chassis number. The power units were interchangeable in production, so amps could have similar front-ends but different power units (more power and different effect options) and visa versa. Some '68 bass amp catalog numbers were 4 digits, for example 2-12C, meaning two 12" CTS speakers. Again, there were several different numbers used. Kustom also introduced the 200 and 400 amp series and the logo included the series number. The catalog numbers were similar to the 100 series, but they had a higher power rating of 100 equivalent watts (200 series), or 200 equivalent watts (400 series). Kustom U.S. Naugahyde (tuck-&-roll) covers came in 7 colors: black (the most common), Cascade (blue/green), silver (white-silver), gold (light gold), red, blue, and Charcoal (gray). The market historically shows color options fetching more. The market has not noticeably distinguished power and features options. Condition and color seem to be the most important. Gold and Cascade may be the rarest seen colors.

Naugahyde Tuck-&-Roll 150/250/300/500/600 (c.'71-c.'75)

The amp heads changed with a slightly slanted control panel and the Kustom logo moved to the right/upper-right portion of the front panel. They continued to be tuck-&-roll offered in the same variety of colors. The sales literature indicated a 150 series had 150 watts, 250 had 250 watts, etc.

KJL Dirty 30

Koch Studiotone 20-watt

Krank 100 Watt combo

AMPS

AMPS

Kustom 36

Kustom Hustler

Kustom K-100

MODEL		EXC. COND.	
YEAR	FEATURES	LOW	HIGH

Naugahyde Tuck-&-Roll SC (Self Contained) Series

Most SC combo amps were rated at 150 watts, with the 1-12SC listed at 50 watts. They were offered in 7 colors of tuck-and-roll. Again the model numbers indicate the features as follows: 4-10 SC is a 4 x 10", 2-10 SC is a 2x10", etc.

Super Sound Tuck-and-Roll Combo Series

The last tuck-and-roll combo amps with slightly smaller tucks. Amp control panel is noticeably smaller and the Kustom logo is in the right side of the control panel.

Black Vinyl ('75-c.'78)

By '75 ownership changes were complete and the colorful tuck-and-roll was dropped in favor of more traditional black vinyl. The products had a slant Kustom logo spelled-out and placed in a position on the grille similar to a Fender black-face baffle. Models included the I, II, III, and IV Lead amps. Heads with half- and full-stacks were available. Bass amps included the Kustom 1, Bass I, II, III, IV, and IV SRO.

Black Vinyl K logo ('78-'83)

This era is easily recognized by the prominent capital K logo.

Bass V Amp

1990s. Large Kustom Bass V logo upper right side of amp, 35 watts, 1x12", black vinyl.

1990s		$100	$125

Challenger Amp

1973-1975. 1x12" speaker.

1973-1975	Black	$300	$375
1973-1975	Color option	$450	$525

Hustler Amp

1973-1975. Solidstate combo amp, 4x10", tremolo, tuck-and-roll.

1973-1975	Black	$325	$375
1973-1975	Color option	$525	$575

K25/K25 C-2 SC Amp

1960s. SC (self-contained) Series, small combo tuck-and-roll, 1x12", solidstate, reverb, black control panel.

1971-1973	Black	$325	$375
1971-1973	Color option	$425	$525

K50-2 SC Amp

1971-1973. Self-contained (SC) small combo tuck-and-roll, 1x12", reverb and tremolo.

1971-1973	Black	$350	$375
1971-1973	Color option	$450	$550

K100-1 Amp Head

1968-1972. The K100-1 is the basic amp without reverb (suffix 1), 50-watt, solidstate energizer head, offered in black or several color options.

1968-1972	Black	$175	$200
1968-1972	Color option	$275	$325

K100-1 1-15C Bass Amp Set

1968-1972. The K100-1 with 1-15C speaker option with matching 1x15" cab, black tuck-and-roll standard, but several sparkle colors offered, C.T.S. bass reflex speaker.

1968-1972	Black	$325	$350
1968-1972	Color option	$600	$700

MODEL		EXC. COND.	
YEAR	FEATURES	LOW	HIGH

K100-1 1-15L-1/1-15A-1/1-15J-1 Amp Set

1968-1972. K100-1 with matching 1x15" cab, black tuck-and-roll standard, but several colors offered, speaker options are JBL, Altec Lansing or Jensen.

1968-1972	Black	$300	$375
1968-1972	Color option	$600	$700

K100-1 1-D140F Bass Amp

1968-1972. K100-1 with matching 1x15" JBL D-140F cab, black tuck-and-roll standard, but several sparkle colors offered.

1968-1972	Black	$350	$400
1968-1972	Color option	$600	$700

K100-1 2-12C Bass Amp Set

1968-1972. K100-1 with matching 2x12" cab, black tuck-and-roll standard, but several sparkle colors offered, C.T.S. bass reflex speakers.

1968-1972	Black	$375	$425
1968-1972	Color option	$650	$750

K100-2 Reverb/Tremolo Amp Head

1968-1972. K100 50-watt solidstate energizer head with added reverb/tremolo, offered in black or several color options.

1968-1972	Black	$225	$250
1968-1972	Color option	$450	$500

K100-2 1-15L-2/1-15A-2/1-15J-2 Amp Set

1968-1972. K100-2 head and matching 1x15" cab, black tuck-and-roll standard, but several sparkle colors offered.

1968-1972	Black	$375	$450
1968-1972	Color option	$650	$800

K100-2 2-12A-2/2-12J-2 Amp Set

1968-1972. K100-2 head with matching 2x12" cab, black tuck-and-roll standard, but several sparkle colors offered.

1968-1972	Black	$425	$500
1968-1972	Color option	$700	$850

K100-5 PA Amp Head

1968-1972. 50 watts, 2 channels with 8 control knobs per channel, reverb, Kustom 100 logo located above the 4 high-impedance mic inputs.

1968-1972	Black	$225	$250
1968-1972	Color option	$375	$425

K100-6 SC Amp

1970-1972. Basic combo amp with selectone, no reverb.

1970-1972	Black	$300	$350

K100-7 SC Amp

1970-1972. Combo amp with reverb, tremolo, vibrato and boost.

1970-1972	Black	$350	$400
1970-1972	Color option	$600	$700

K100-8 SC Amp

1970-1972. Combo amp with reverb, tremolo, vibrato and boost.

1970-1972	Black	$350	$425
1970-1972	Color option	$600	$725

K100C-6 Amp

1968-1970. Kustom 100 logo middle of the front control panel, 1x15" combo, selectone option.

1968-1970	Black	$300	$350

MODEL YEAR	FEATURES	EXC. COND. LOW	HIGH

K100C-8 Amp
1968-1970. Kustom 100 logo middle of the front control panel, 4x10" combo, reverb, tremolo, vibrato.

| 1968-1970 | Black | $475 | $550 |

K150-1 Amp Set
1972-1975. Piggyback, 150 watts, 2x12", no reverb, logo in upper right corner of amp head, tuck-and-roll, black or color option.

| 1972-1975 | Color option | $425 | $475 |

K150-2 Amp Set
1972-1975. K150 with added reverb and tremolo, piggyback, 2x12", tuck-and-roll, black or color option.

| 1972-1975 | Color option | $550 | $600 |

K200-1/K200B Bass Amp Head
1966-1972. Head with 100 relative watts, 2 channels, 4 controls and 2 inputs per channel, no effects. K200 heads were also offered with Reverb/Tremolo (suffix 2), Harmonic Clipper & Boost (suffix 3), and Reverb/Trem/Clipper/Boost (suffix 4). 1966 and '67 models have the high forehead appearance versus normal appearance by '68.

1966-1967	Black	$225	$250
1966-1967	Color option	$375	$400
1968-1972	Black	$200	$225
1968-1972	Color option	$350	$375

K200-1/K200B Bass Amp Set
1966-1972. K200 head with 2x15" cab.

1966-1967	Black	$325	$400
1966-1967	Color option	$650	$800
1968-1972	Black	$325	$400
1968-1972	Color option	$650	$800

K200-2 Reverb/Tremolo Amp Head
1966-1972. K200 head, with added reverb and tremolo (suffix 2).

1966-1967	Black	$225	$275
1966-1967	Color option	$400	$450
1968-1972	Black	$225	$275
1968-1972	Color option	$400	$450

K200-2 Reverb/Tremolo Amp and Cabinet Set
1966-1972. K200-2 head with 2x15" or 3x12" cab, available with JBL D-140F speakers, Altec Lansing (A) speakers, C.T.S. (C), or Jensen (J).

1966-1967	Black	$400	$475
1966-1967	Blue	$650	$800
1966-1967	Cascade	$675	$825
1966-1967	Charcoal	$650	$800
1966-1967	Gold	$675	$825
1966-1967	Red	$675	$825
1966-1967	Silver	$650	$800
1968-1972	Black	$400	$475
1968-1972	Blue	$650	$800
1968-1972	Cascade	$675	$825
1968-1972	Charcoal	$650	$800
1968-1972	Gold	$675	$825
1968-1972	Red	$650	$800
1968-1972	Silver	$650	$800

K250 Reverb/Tremolo Amp Head
1971-1975. 250 watts, tuck-and-roll cover, Kustom 250 logo on upper right section of control panel, reverb.

| 1971-1975 | Black | $250 | $275 |
| 1971-1975 | Color option | $375 | $450 |

K250 Amp and Cabinet Set
1971-1975. K250 head with 2x15", tuck-and-roll cover.

| 1971-1975 | Black | $375 | $450 |
| 1971-1975 | Color option | $650 | $800 |

K300 PA Amp and Speaker Set
1971-1975. Includes 302 PA, 303 PA, 304 PA, 305 PA, head and 2 cabs.

| 1971-1975 | Color option | $700 | $875 |

K400-2 Reverb/Tremolo Amp and Cab Set
1968-1972. 200 relative watts, reverb, tremolo, with 6x12" or 8x12" cab, available with JBL D-140F speakers, Altec Lansing (A), C.T.S. (C), or Jensen (J). The K400 was offered with no effects (suffix 1), with reverb and tremolo (suffix 2), with Harmonic Clipper & Boost (suffix 3), and Reverb/Trem/Clipper/Boost (suffix 4). The 400 heads came with a separate chrome amp head stand.

| 1968-1972 | Black | $425 | $500 |
| 1968-1972 | Color option | $675 | $825 |

KBA-10 Combo Amp
Late-1980s-1990s. Compact solidstate bass amp, 10 watts, 1x8".

| 1990s | | $25 | $75 |

KBA-20 Combo Amp
Late-1980s-early-1990s. KBA series were compact solidstate bass amps with built-in limiter, 20 watts, 1x8".

| 1989-1990 | | $25 | $75 |

KBA-30 Combo Amp
Late-1980s-early-1990s. 30 watts, 1x10".

| 1989-1990 | | $25 | $75 |

KBA-40 Combo Amp
Late-1980s-early-1990s. 40 watts, 1x12".

| 1989-1990 | | $50 | $75 |

KBA-80 Combo Amp
Late-1980s-early-1990s. 80 watts, 1x15".

| 1989-1990 | | $75 | $125 |

KBA-160 Combo Amp
Late-1980s-early-1990s. Solidstate bass amp with built-in limiter, 160 watts, 1x15".

| 1989-1990 | | $100 | $125 |

KGA-10 VC Amp
1999-2006. 10 watts, 1x6.5" speaker, switchable overdrive.

| 1999-2006 | | $25 | $50 |

KLA-15 Combo Amp
Late-1980s-early-1990s. Solidstate, overdrive, 15 watts, 1x8".

| 1989-1990 | | $50 | $75 |

KLA-20 Amp
Mid-1980s-late-1980s. 1x10", MOS-FET, gain, EQ, reverb, headphone jack.

| 1986 | | $50 | $75 |

Kustom K-100-1-15

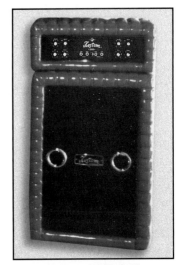

Kustom K250-2-15

Kustom K-400-2

AMPS

AMPS

Lab Series K5

Lace 20-watt

Laney TT 50H

MODEL YEAR	FEATURES	EXC. COND. LOW	HIGH
KLA-25 Combo Amp			
Late-1980s-early-1990s. Solidstate, overdrive, reverb, 25 watts, 1x10".			
1989-1990		$50	$75
KLA-50 Combo Amp			
Late-1980s-early-1990s. Solidstate, overdrive, reverb, 50 watts, 1x12".			
1989-1990		$75	$100
KLA-75 Amp			
Mid-1980s-late-1980s. 75 watts, reverb, footswitching.			
1987		$100	$125
KLA-100 Combo Amp			
Late-1980s-early-1990s. Solidstate, reverb, 100-watt dual channel, 1x12".			
1989-1990		$125	$150
KLA-185 Combo Amp			
Late-1980s-early-1990s. Solidstate, reverb, 185-watt dual channel, 1x12".			
1989-1990		$150	$175
KPB-200 Bass Combo Amp			
1994-1997. 200 watts, 1x15".			
1994-1997		$225	$250
SC 1-12 SC Amp			
1971-1975. 50 watts, 1x12" Jensen speaker.			
1971-1975	Black	$325	$350
1971-1975	Color option	$425	$525
SC 1-15 SC Amp			
1971-1975. 150 watts, 1x15" C.T.S. speaker.			
1971-1975	Black	$325	$350
1971-1975	Color option	$425	$500
SC 1-15AB SC Amp			
1971-1975. 150 watts, 1x15" Altec Lansing speaker.			
1971-1975	Black	$325	$350
1971-1975	Color option	$425	$525
SC 2-12A SC Amp			
1971-1975. 150 watts, 2x12" Altec Lansing speakers.			
1971-1975	Black	$375	$400
1971-1975	Color option	$550	$675
SC 2-12J SC Amp			
1971-1975. 150 watts, 2x12" Jensen speakers.			
1971-1975	Black	$375	$400
1971-1975	Color option	$550	$675
SC 4-10 SC Amp			
1971-1975. 150 watts, 4x10" Jensen speakers.			
1971-1975	Black	$375	$400
1971-1975	Color option	$550	$675

Lab Series

1977-1980s. Five models of Lab Series amps, ranging in price from $600 to $3,700, were introduced at the '77 NAMM show by Norlin (then owner of Gibson). Two more were added later. The '80s models were Lab Series 2 amps and had a Gibson logo on the upper-left front.

MODEL YEAR	FEATURES	EXC. COND. LOW	HIGH
B120 Amp			
Ca.1984. Bass combo, 120 watts, 2 channels, 1x15".			
1984		$75	$100

MODEL YEAR	FEATURES	EXC. COND. LOW	HIGH
G120 R-10 Amp			
Ca.1984. Combo, 120 watts, 3-band EQ, channel switching, reverb, 4x10".			
1984		$175	$200
G120 R-12 Amp			
Ca.1984. Combo, 120 watts, 3-band EQ, channel switching, reverb, 2x12".			
1984		$175	$200
L2 Amp Head			
1977-1983. Head, 100 watts, black covering.			
1977-1983		$75	$100
L3 Amp			
1977-ca.1983. 60 watt 1x12" combo.			
1977-1983		$125	$150
L4 Amp Head			
1977-1983. Solidstate, 200 watts, black cover, dark grille, large L4 logo on front panel.			
1977-1983		$100	$125
L5 Amp			
1977-ca.1983. Solidstate, 100 watts, 2x12".			
1977-1983		$250	$300
L7 Amp			
1977-1983. Solidstate, 100 watts, 4x10".			
1977-1983		$200	$250
L11 Amp			
1977-1983. 200 watts, 8x12", piggyback.			
1977-1983		$300	$375

Lace Music Products

1979-present. Lace Music Products, which was founded by pickup innovator Don Lace Sr., added amplifiers in '96. They also offered amps under the Rat Fink and Mooneyes brands.

Lafayette

Ca.1963-1967. Japanese-made guitars and amps sold through the Lafayette Electronics catalogs.

MODEL YEAR	FEATURES	EXC. COND. LOW	HIGH
Small Tube Amp			
Japanese-made tube, gray speckle 1x12" with art deco design or black 2x12".			
1960s	Black	$150	$175
1960s	Gray speckle	$150	$175

Laney

1968-present. Founded by Lyndon Laney and Bob Thomas in Birmingham, England. Laney offered tube amps exclusively into the '80s. A wide range of solidstate and tube amps are currently offered.

MODEL YEAR	FEATURES	EXC. COND. LOW	HIGH
100-Watt Amp Head			
1968-1969. Similar to short head Plexi Marshall amp cab, large Laney with underlined "y" logo plate on upper left front corner, black vinyl cover, grayish grille.			
1968-1969		$1,400	$1,700
EA-120 Amp			
1990s. 120 watts, 2x10", dark vinyl cover.			
1990s		$375	$425
GC-30 Amp			
1990s. Compact combo amp, 30 watts, dark vinyl cover, reverb, dark see-thru grille.			
1990s		$225	$275

MODEL YEAR	FEATURES	EXC. COND. LOW	HIGH

GS-212 2x12" Cabinet
1980s-1990s. Rated at 150 watts, 2x12", slant front cab, black vinyl cover, metal grille.

1990s		$225	$275

GS-410 4x10" Cabinet
1980s-1990s. 4x10" speakers, straight-front cab, black vinyl cover, metal grille.

1990s		$250	$300

GS-412 4x12" Cabinet
1980s-1990s. Straight-front or slant cab, 4x12" rated at 150 watts, black vinyl cover.

1990s		$325	$400

LC-15 Amp
1990s. Compact practice amp, 15 watts.

1990s		$200	$250

MY-50 Amp Head
All tube head, 50 watts, master volume, 4-stage cascaded preamp, active boosts for treble, middle and bass.

1980s		$250	$300

MY-100 Amp Head
All tube head, 100 watts, master volume, 4-stage cascaded preamp, active boosts for treble, middle and bass.

1980s		$300	$375

Quarter Stack Amp
All tube, 2x12", self-contained, sealed back, foot-switchable reverb and overdrive, effects loop, active tone controls with push/pull switches.

1980s		$350	$400

Legend

1978-1984. From Legend Musical Instruments of East Syracuse, New York, these amps featured cool wood cabinets. They offered heads, combos with a 1x12" or 2x12" configuration, and cabinets with 1x12", 2x12" or 4x12".

A-30 Amp
Late-1970s-early-1980s. Natural wood cabinet, Mesa-Boogie compact amp appearance.

1980s		$350	$425

A-60 Amp
Late-1970s-early-1980s. Mesa-Boogie appearance, wood cabinet and grille, transtube design dual tube preamp with solidstate power section.

1980s		$350	$425

Rock & Roll 50 Combo Amp
1978-1983. Mesa-Boogie-style wood compact combo, either 1x15" or 2x12" options, tube preamp section and solidstate power supply.

1978-1979	2x12" option	$375	$425
1978-1983	1x15" option	$350	$400

Super Lead 50 Amp
Late-1970s-early-1980s. Rock & Roll 50-watt model with added bass boost and reverb, 1x12", hybrid tube and solidstate.

1978-1983		$375	$425

Super Lead 100 Amp
Late-1970s-early-1980s. 100-watt version, 2x12".

1978-1983		$400	$450

Leslie

Most often seen with Hammond organs, the cool Leslie rotating speakers have been adopted by many guitarists. Many guitar effects have tried to duplicate their sound. And they are still making them.

16 Rotating Speaker Cabinet
1960s-1970s. 1x10" or 1x12" rotating speaker (requires an amp head), black vinyl cover, silver grille, Leslie 60 logo on grille.

1960s	1 cab	$550	$650
1970s	1 cab	$450	$550

60 M Rotating Speaker Cabinets
1960s-1970s. Two 1x10" rotating speaker cabs with 45-watt amp, black vinyl cover, light silver grille, Leslie logo upper left on grille.

1960s	2 cabs	$600	$675

103 Amp
Two-speed.

1960s		$250	$300

118 Amp
1x12" Altec speaker.

1960s		$275	$325

125 Amp
Late-1960s. All tube amp with 2-speed rotating 1x12" speaker.

1960s		$250	$300

145 Amp

1960s		$475	$525

Line 6

1996-present. Founded by Marcus Ryle and Michel Doidic and specializing in digital signal processing in both effects and amps.

Little Lanilei

1997-present. Small handmade, intermediate grade, production/custom, amps made by Songworks Systems & Products of San Juan Capistrano, California. They also build a reverb unit and a rotary effect.

Louis Electric Amplifier Co.

1993-present. Founded by Louis Rosano in Bergenfield, New Jersey. Louis produces custom-built tweeds and various combo amps from 35 to 80 watts.

Mack Amps

2005-present. Made in Richmond Hill, Ontario, Canada by amp builder Don Mackrill, the company offers intermediate and professional grade, production, hand wired and hand made amps.

Maestro

Maestro amps are associated with Gibson and were included in the Gibson catalogs. For example, in the '62-'63 orange cover Gibson catalog, tweed Maestro amps were displayed in their own section. Tweed Maestro amps are very similar to Gibson tweed amps. Maestro amps were often associated

Line 6 Duoverb

Line 6 Vetta II

Louis Electric Ferrari

1958 Maestro

*Magnatone Model 112/113
Troubadour Amp*

Magnatone Model 3802

MODEL YEAR	FEATURES	EXC. COND. LOW	HIGH

with accordions in the early-'60s but the amps featured standard guitar inputs. Gibson also used the Maestro name on effects in the '60s and '70s and In 01, Gibson revived the name for a line of effects, banjos and mandolins.

The price ranges listed are for excellent condition, all original amps though tubes may be replaced without affecting value. The prices listed are for amps with fully intact logos. A broken or missing logo may diminish the value of the amp. Amps with a changed handle, power cord, and especially a broken logo, should be taken on a case-by-case basis.

Amp models in '58 include the Super Maestro and Maestro, in '60 the Stereo Maestro Accordion GA-87, Super Maestro Accordion GA-46 T, Standard Accordion GA-45 T, Viscount Accordion GA-16 T, in '62 the Reverb-Echo GA-1 RT, Reverb-Echo GA-2 RT, 30 Stereo Accordion Amp, Stereo Accordion GA-78 RV.

GA-1 RT Reverb-Echo Amp
1961. Tweed, 1x8".

1961		$550	$650

GA-2 RT Deluxe Reverb-Echo Amp
1961. Deluxe more powerful version of GA-1 RT, 1x12", tweed.

1961		$950	$1,000

GA-15 RV/Bell 15 RV Amp
1961. 15 watts, 1x12", gray sparkle.

1961		$800	$950

GA-16 T Viscount Amp
1961. 14 watts, 1x10", gray sparkle. Gibson also had a GA-16 Viscount amp from '59-'60.

1961		$750	$900

GA-45 Maestro Amp
1955-1960. 16 watts, 4x8", 2-tone.

1955-1960		$900	$1,000

GA-45 RV Standard Amp
1961. 16 watts, 4x8", reverb.

1961		$1,100	$1,300

GA-45 T Standard Accordion Amp
1961. 16 watts, 4x8", tremolo.

1961		$950	$1,050

GA-46 T Super Maestro Accordion and Bass Amp
1957-1961. Based on the Gibson GA-200 and advertised to be "designed especially for amplified accordions," 60 watts, 2x12", vibrato, 2-tone cover, large Maestro Super logo on top center of grille.

1957-1960		$1,900	$2,000

GA-78 Maestro Series Amps
1960-1961. Wedge stereo cab, 2x10", reverb and tremolo.

1960-1961	GA-78 RV		
	Maestro 30	$2,200	$2,300
1960-1961	GA-78 RVS	$2,200	$2,300
1960-1961	GA-78 RVT	$2,200	$2,300

MODEL YEAR	FEATURES	EXC. COND. LOW	HIGH

Magnatone
Ca.1937-1971. Magnatone made a huge variety of amps sold under their own name and under brands like Dickerson, Oahu (see separate listings) and Bronson. They also private branded amps for several accordion companies or accordion teaching studios. Brands used for them include Da Vinci, PAC - AMP, PANaramic, Titano, Tonemaster, Twilighter, and Unique (see separate listings for those brands).

Model 108 Varsity Amp
1948-1954. Gray pearloid cover, small student amp or lap steel companion amp.

1948-1954		$300	$350

Model 110 Melodier Amp
1953-1954. 12 watts, 1x10", brown leatherette cover, light grille.

1953-1954		$400	$425

Model 111 Student Amp
1955-1959. Two to 3 watts, 1x8", brown leatherette, brown grille.

1955-1959		$275	$325

Model 112/113 Troubadour Amp
1955-1959. 18 watts, 1x12", brown leatherette, brown grille, slant back rear control panel.

1955-1959		$450	$525

Model 120B Cougar Bass Amp
1967-1968. Initial Magnatone entry into the solidstate market, superseded by Brute Series in '68, 120 watts, 2x12" solidstate bass piggyback amp, naugahyde vinyl cover with polyester rosewood side panels.

1967-1968		$250	$300

Model 120R Sting Ray Reverb Bass Amp
1967-1968. Initial Magnatone entry into the solidstate market, superseded by Brute Series in '68, 150 watts, 4x10" solidstate combo amp, naugahyde vinyl cover with polyester rosewood side panels.

1967-1968		$250	$300

Model 130V Custom Amp
1969-1971. Solidstate 1x12" combo amp.

1969-1971		$200	$225

Model 150R Firestar Reverb Amp
1967-1968. Initial Magnatone entry into the solidstate market, superseded by Brute Series in '68, 120 watts, 2x12" solidstate combo amp, naugahyde vinyl cover with polyester rosewood side panels.

1967-1968		$300	$325

Model 180 Triplex Amp
Mid-to-late-1950s. Mid-level power using 2 6L6 power tubes, 1x15" and 1x8" speakers.

1950s		$500	$625

Model 192-5-S Troubadour Amp
Early-1950s. 18 watts, 1x12" Jensen Concert speaker, brown alligator covering, lower back control panel, 3 chicken-head knobs, Magnatone script logo on front, Troubadour script logo on back control panel.

1950s		$325	$400

Model 194 Lyric Amp
1947-mid-1950s. 1x12" speaker, old-style tweed vertical cab typical of '40s.

1940s		$325	$375

MODEL YEAR FEATURES	EXC. COND. LOW	HIGH

odel 195 Melodier Amp
1951-1954. Vertical cab with 1x10" speaker, pearloid th flowing grille slats.
51-1954 — $325 — $400

odel 196 Amp
1947-mid-1950s. Five to 10 watts, 1x12", scroll grille sign, snakeskin leatherette cover.
40s — $325 — $400

odel 199 Student Amp
1950s. About 6 to 10 watts, 1x8", snakeskin atherette cover, metal handle, slant grille design.
50s — $275 — $325

odel 210 Deluxe Student Amp
1958-1960. 5 watts, 1x8", vibrato, brown leatherette, logo lower right front on grille.
58-1960 — $350 — $375

odel 213 Troubadour Amp
1957-1958. 10 watts, 1x12", vibrato, brown leatherette ver, V logo lower right of grille.
57-1958 — $600 — $650

odel 240 SV Magna-Chordion Amp
1967-1968. Initial Magnatone entry into the solid-ate market, superseded by Brute Series in '68, 240 atts, 2x12" solidstate stereo accordion or organ amp, ugahyde vinyl cover, polyester rosewood side panels, put jacks suitable for guitar, reverb and vibrato, teral combo cab, rear mounted controls.
67-1968 — $325 — $350

odel 250 Professional Amp
1958-1960. 20 watts, 1x12", vibrato, brown atherette with V logo lower right front of grille.
58-1960 — $700 — $800

odel 260 Amp
1957-1958. 35 watts, 2x12", brown leatherette, brato, V logo lower right front corner of grille.
57-1958 — $1,100 — $1,250

odel 262 Jupiter/Custom Pro Amp
1961-1963. 35 watts, 2x12", vibrato, brown atherette.
61-1963 — $800 — $900

odel 280/Custom 280 Amp
1957-1958. 50 watts, brown leatherette covering, own-yellow tweed grille, 2x12" plus 2x5" speakers, uble V logo.
57-1958 — $1,150 — $1,400

odel 280A Amp
1958-1960. 50 watts, brown leatherette covering, own-yellow tweed grille, 2x12" plus 2x5" speakers, logo lower right front.
58-1960 — $1,075 — $1,150

odel 410 Diana Amp
1961-1963. Five watts, 1x12", advertised as a 'studio' w power professional amp, brown leatherette cover, brato.
61-1963 — $400 — $475

odel 413 Centaur Amp
1961-1963. 18 watts, 1x12", brown leatherette cover, brato.
61-1963 — $600 — $700

Model 415 Clio Bass Amp
1961-1963. 25 watts, 4x8", bass or accordion amp, brown leatherette cover.
1961-1963 — $600 — $625

Model 432 Amp
Mid-1960s. Compact student model, wavey-squiggle art deco-style grille, black cover, vibrato and reverb.
1960s — $400 — $475

Model 435 Athene Bass Amp
1961-1963. 55 watts, 4x10", piggyback head and cab, brown leatherette.
1961-1963 — $800 — $1,000

Model 440 Mercury Amp
1961-1963. 18 watts, 1x12", vibrato, brown leatherette.
1961-1963 — $700 — $850

Model 450 Juno/Twin Hi-Fi Amp
1961-1963. 25 watts, 1x12" and 1 oval 5"x7" speakers, reverb, vibrato, brown leatherette.
1961-1963 — $900 — $1,100
1961-1963 Extension cab only — $500 — $550

Model 460 Victory Amp
1961-1963. 35 watts, 2x12" and 2 oval 5"x7" speakers, early-'60s next to the top-of-the-line, reverb and vibrato, brown leatherette.
1961-1963 — $925 — $1,150

Model 480 Venus Amp
1961-1963. 50 watts, 2x12" and 2 oval 5"x7" speakers, early-'60s top-of-the-ine, reverb and stereo vibrato, brown leatherette.
1961-1963 — $925 — $1,150

Model M6 Amp
1964 (not seen in '65 catalog). 25 watts, 1x12", black molded plastic suitcase amp.
1964 — $500 — $575

Model M7 Bass Amp
1964-1966. 38 watts, 1x15" bass amp, black molded plastic suitcase amp.
1964-1966 — $500 — $575

Model M8 Amp
1964-1966. 27 watts, 1x12", reverb and tremolo, black molded plastic suitcase amp.
1964-1966 — $600 — $675

Model M9 Amp
1964-1966. 38 watts, 1x15", tremolo, no reverb, black molded plastic suitcase amp.
1964-1966 — $650 — $700

Model M10/M10A Amp
1964-1966. 38 watts, 1x15", tone boost, tremolo, transistorized reverb section, black molded plastic suitcase amp.
1964-1966 — $750 — $825

Model M12 Bass Amp
1964-1966. 80 watts, 1x15" or 2x12", mid-'60s top-of-the-line bass amp, black molded plastic suitcase amp.
1964-1966 — $650 — $700

Model M14 Amp
1964-1966. Stereo, 75 watts, 2x12" plus 2 tweeters, stereo vibrato, no reverb, black molded plastic suitcase amp.
1964-1966 — $775 — $850

Mgnatone 280

Magnatone 401-A

Magnatone 480 Venus

AMPS

Mako MAK2

Marlboro 560A

Marshall AVT-50

MODEL		EXC. COND.	
YEAR	FEATURES	LOW	HIGH

Model M15 Amp
1964-1966. Stereo 75 watts, 2x12" plus 2 tweeters, stereo vibrato, transistorized reverb, black molded plastic suitcase amp.

1964-1966	$775	$950

Model M27 Bad Boy Bass Amp
1968-1971. 150 watts, 2x15" (1 passive), reverb, vibrato, solidstate, vertical profile bass amp, part of Brute Series.

1968-1971	$275	$300

Model M30 Fang Amp
1968-1971. 150 watts, 2x15" (1 passive), 1 exponential horn, solidstate, vibrato, reverb, vertical profile amp.

1968-1971	$275	$300

Model M32 Big Henry Bass Amp
1968-1971. 300 watts, 2x15" solidstate vertical profile bass amp.

1968-1971	$275	$300

Model M35 The Killer Amp
1968-1971. 300 watts, 2x15" and 2 horns, solidstate, vibrato, vertical profile amp.

1968-1971	$300	$325

Model MP-1 (Magna Power I) Amp
1966-1967. 30 watts, 1x12", dark vinyl, light grille, Magnatone-Estey logo on upper right of grille.

1966-1967	$400	$475

Model MP-3 (Magna-Power 3) Amp
1966-1967. Mid-power, 2x12", reverb, dark vinyl, light grille, Magnatone-Estey logo on upper right of grille.

1966-1967	$450	$550

Model PS150 Amp
1968-1971. Powered slave speaker cabinets, 150 watts, 2x15" linkable cabinets.

1968-1971	$200	$225

Model PS300 Amp
1968-1971. Powered slave speaker cabinets, 300 watts, 2x15" (1 passive) linkable cabinets.

1968-1971	$200	$225

Small Pearloid Amp
1947-1955. Pearloid (MOTS) covered low- and mid-power amps generally associated with pearloid lap steel sets.

1947-1955	$200	$250

Starlet Amp
1951-1952. Student model, 1x8", pearloid cover, low power, single on-off volume control, Starlet logo on back panel, Magnatone logo plate upper left front of grille.

1951-1952	$325	$375

Starlite Model 401 Amp
Magnatone produced the mid-'60s Starlite amplifier line for the budget minded musician. Each Starlite model prominently notes the Magnatone name. The grilles show art deco wavy circles. Magnatone 1960-'63 standard amps offer models starting with 12" speakers. Starlight models offer 10" and below. Model 401 has 15 watts, 1x8" and 3 tubes.

1960s	$225	$275

Starlite Model 411 Amp
Mid-1960s. 15 watts, 1x8", 5 tubes, tremolo (n advertised as vibrato), art deco wavy grille.

1960s	$225	$27

Starlite Model 441A Bass Amp
Early-mid-1960s. Lower power with less than 2 watts, 1x15", tube amp.

1960s	$400	$42

Starlite Model Custom 421 Amp
Early-mid-1960s. Tube amp, 25 watts, 1x10".

1960s	$375	$40

Starlite Model Custom 431 Amp
Early-mid-1960s. Tube amp, 30 watts, 1x10", vibra and reverb.

1960s	$450	$50

Mako
1985-1989. Line of solidstate amps from Kama (Ovation, Hamer). They also offered guitars an basses.

Marlboro Sound Works
1970-1980s. Economy solidstate amps importe by Musical Instruments Corp., Syosset, New Yor Initially, Marlboro targeted the economy compa amp market, but quickly added larger amps an PAs.

GA-2 Amp
1970s. 3 watts, 1x8".

1970s	$15	$2

GA-3 Amp
1970s. 3 watts, 1x8", trem.

1970s	$20	$3

GA-20B Amp
1970s. Bass/keyboard amp, 25 watts, 1x12".

1970s	$30	$7

GA-20R Amp
1970s. 25 watts, 1x12", trem, reverb.

1970s	$30	$7

GA-40R Amp
1970s. 30 watts, 1x12", trem, reverb.

1970s	$60	$10

Model 520B Amp
1970s. 25 watts, 1x15", bass/keyboard amp.

1970s	$60	$10

Model 560A Amp
1970s. 45 watts, 2x10".

1970s	$60	$10

Model 760A Amp
1970s. Guitar/bass/keyboard, 60 watts, 1x15".

1970s	$60	$10

Model 1200R Amp Head
1970s. 60 watts, reverb.

1970s	$60	$10

Model 1500B Bass Amp Head
1970s. 60 watts.

1970s	$60	$10

Model 2000 Bass Amp Set
1970s. 1500B head and 1x12" cab.

1970s	$60	$10

MODEL		EXC. COND.	
EAR	FEATURES	LOW	HIGH

Marshall

1962-present. Drummer Jim Marshall started uilding bass speaker and PA cabinets in his garage 1960. He opened a retail drum shop for his stu- nts and others and soon added guitars and amps. hen Ken Bran joined the business as service anager in '62, the two decided to build their own nps. By '63 they had expanded the shop to house small manufacturing space and by late that year ey were offering the amps to other retailers. Mar- all also made amps under the Park, CMI, Narb, g M, and Kitchen-Marshall brands. Marshall ntinues to be involved in the company.

Mark I, II, III and IVs are generally '60s and 0s and also are generally part of a larger series or example JTM), or have a model number that a more specific identifier. Describing an amp ly as Mark II can be misleading. The most nportant identifier is the Model Number, which arshall often called the Stock Number. To help oid confusion we have added the Model number often as possible. In addition, when appropriate, e have included the wattage, number of channels, aster or no-master info in the title. This should lp the reader more quickly find a specific amp. heck the model's description for such things as vo inputs or four inputs, because this will help ith identification. Vintage Marshall amps do not ways have the Model/Stock number on the front back panel, so the additional identifiers should lp. The JMP logo on the front is common and ally does not help with specific identification. or example, a JMP Mark II Super Lead 100 Watt escription is less helpful than the actual model/ ock number. Unfortunately, many people are not miliar with specific model/stock numbers. VG has ied to include as much information in the title as pace will allow.

Marshall amps are sorted as follows:

AVT Series - new line for Marshall

Club and Country Series (Rose-Morris)-intro- duced in '78

JCM 800 Series - basically the '80s

JCM 900 Series - basically the '90s

JCM 2000 Series - basically the '00s

JTM Series

Micro Stack Group

Model Number/Stock Number (no specific series, basically the '60s, '70s) - including Artist and Valvestate models (Valvestate refers to specific Model numbers in 8000 Series)

Silver Jubilee Series

VT 20 Combo Amp

2001-present. Solidstate, 20 watts, 12AX7 preamp be, 1x10", Advanced Valvestate Technology (AVT) odels have black covering and grille, and gold anel.

001-2007		$200	$225

AVT 50/50H Amp

2001-present. Solidstate, 50 watts, head only or 1x12" combo.

2001-2005	Combo	$275	$325
2001-2007	Head	$250	$300

AVT 100 Combo Amp

2001-present. Solidstate, 100 watts, tube preamp, 1x12".

2001-2007		$400	$450

AVT 150 Series Amp

2001-present. Solidstate, additional features over AVT 100. Combo (100 watts, 1x12"), Half-Stack (150 watts, 4x12") and Head only (150 watts).

2001-2005	Combo	$500	$625
2001-2007	Half-Stack	$650	$800
2001-2007	Head	$375	$425

AVT 275 Combo Amp

2001-2007. Solidstate DFX stereo, 75 watts per side, 2x12".

2001-2007		$550	$650

AVT 412/412A Cabinet

2001-present. Slant half-stack 4x12" cab, 200-watt load, 25-watt Celestions.

2001-2005		$275	$300

AVT 412B Cabinet

2001-present. Straight-front half-stack 4x12" cab, 200-watt load.

2001-2005		$250	$300

Club and Country Model 4140 Amp

1978-1982. Tubes, 100 watts, 2x12" combo, Rose-Morris era, designed for the country music market, hence the name, brown vinyl cover, straw grille.

1978-1982		$775	$875

Club and Country Model 4145 Amp

1978-1982. Tubes, 100 watts, 4x10" combo, Rose-Morris era, designed for the country music market, hence the name, brown vinyl, straw grille.

1978-1982		$775	$875

Club and Country Model 4150 Bass Amp

1978-1982. Tubes, 100 watts, 4x10" bass combo, Rose-Morris era, designed for the country music market, hence the name, brown vinyl cover, straw grille.

1978-1982		$725	$800

JCM 800 Model 1959 Amp Head

1981-1991. 100 watts.

1981-1991		$850	$1,000

JCM 800 Model 1987 Amp Head

1981-1991. 50 watts.

1981-1991		$825	$1,000

JCM 800 Model 1992 Bass Amp Head

1981-1986. Active tone circuit.

1981-1986		$825	$1,000

JCM 800 Model 2000 Amp Head

1981-1982. 200 watts.

1981-1982		$850	$1,000

JCM 800 Model 2001 Amp Head

1981-1982. Bass head amp, 300 watts.

1981-1982		$850	$1,000

JCM 800 Model 2004 Amp Head

1981-1990. 50 watts, master.

1981-1990		$850	$925

Marshall AVT-150

Marshall AVT-275

Marshall Club and Country 4140

AMPS

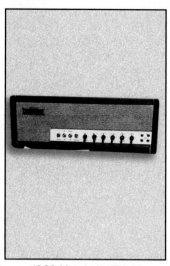
1962 Marshall JTM 45

Marshall Super Tremolo Mk IV

Marshall JCM 2000 DSL 401

AMPS

MODEL YEAR	FEATURES	EXC. COND. LOW	HIGH
JCM 800 Model 2004S Amp Head			
1986-1987. 50 watts, short head.			
1986-1987		$900	$1,050
JCM 800 Model 2005 Amp Head			
1983-1990. 50 watts, split channel.			
1983-1990		$900	$1,050
JCM 800 Model 2005 Limited Edition Full Stack Amp			
1988		$1,700	$1,950
JCM 800 Model 2203 Amp Head			
1981-1990. 100 watts, master volume, reissued in '02.			
1981-1990		$825	$1,025
2007	Reissue	$825	$900
JCM 800 Model 2203 20th Anniversary Half Stack Amp			
1982. 20th Anniversary plate in lower right corner of matching 1960A cab, matching white tolex cover.			
1982		$1,800	$2,200
JCM 800 Model 2204 Amp Head			
1981-1990. 50 watts, 1 channel, 2 inputs, master volume, front panel says JCM 800 Lead Series, back panel says Master Model 50w Mk 2.			
1981-1990		$950	$1,150
JCM 800 Model 2204S Amp Head			
1986-1987. Short head, 50 watts.			
1986-1987		$950	$1,050
JCM 800 Model 2205 Amp Head			
1983-1990. 50 watts, split channel (1 clean and 1 distortion), switchable, both channels with reverb, front panel reads JCM 800 Lead Series.			
1983-1990		$950	$1,150
JCM 800 Model 2205 Limited Edition Full Stack Amp			
Late-1980s. 50-watt head, 1960A slant and 1960B straight front 4x12" cabs.			
1988	Red tolex	$1,800	$2,000
JCM 800 Model 2210 Amp Head			
1983-1990. 100 watts.			
1983-1990		$1,000	$1,200
JCM 800 Model 4010 Combo Amp			
1981-1990. 50 watts, 1x12", reverb, single channel master volume.			
1981-1990		$750	$925
JCM 800 Model 4103 Combo Amp			
1981-1990. Lead combo amp, 100 watts, 2x12".			
1981-1990		$975	$1,100
JCM 800 Model 4104 Combo Amp			
1980-1990. Tube lead amp, 50 watts, 2x12".			
1980-1990	Black	$850	$1,050
1980-1990	White option	$1,050	$1,200
JCM 800 Model 4210 Combo Amp			
1982-1990. 50 watts, 1x12" tube combo, split-channel, single input, master volume.			
1982-1990		$625	$775
JCM 800 Model 4211 Combo Amp			
1983-1990. Lead combo amp, 100 watts, 2x12".			
1983-1990		$675	$825

MODEL YEAR	FEATURES	EXC. COND LOW	HIG
JCM 800 Model 5005 Combo Amp			
1983-1990. Solidstate combo amp, 12 watts, mast volume, 1x10".			
1983-1990		$325	$4(
JCM 800 Model 5010 Combo Amp			
1983-1990. Solidstate combo amp, 30 watts, mast volume, 1x12".			
1983-1990		$375	$4
JCM 800 Model 5150 Combo Amp			
1987-1991. Combo amp, 150 watts, specially d signed 12" Celestion speaker, split channel desig separate clean and distortion channels, presence ar effects-mix master controls.			
1987-1991		$500	$5
JCM 800 Model 5212 Combo Amp			
1986-1991. 2x12" split channel reverb combo.			
1986-1991		$525	$5
JCM 800 Model 5213 Combo Amp			
1986-1991. MOS-FET solidstate combo, 2x12 channel-switching, effects loop, direct output, remo footswitch.			
1986-1991		$425	$4
JCM 800 Model 5215 Combo Amp			
1986-1991. MOS-FET solidstate, 1x15", Accutroni reverb, effects loop.			
1986-1991		$425	$4
JCM 900 2100 Mark III Amp Head			
1990-1993. FX loop, 100/50-watt selectable lea head.			
1990-1993		$675	$7
JCM 900 2100 SL-X Amp Head			
1992-1998. Hi-gain 100 watt head amp, addition 12AX7 preamp tube.			
1992-1998		$700	$8
JCM 900 2500 SL-X Amp Head			
1990-2000. 50 watt version of SL-X.			
1992-1998		$675	$7
JCM 900 4100 Dual Reverb Amp			
1990-2000. 100/50 switchable head, JCM 900 o front panel, black with black front.			
1990-2000	Head & 4x10" cab	$1,150	$1,20
1990-2000	Head only	$675	$7
JCM 900 4101 Combo Amp			
1990-2000. All tube, 100 watts, 1x12" combo.			
1990-2000		$675	$8
JCM 900 4102 Combo Amp			
1990-2000. Combo amp, 100/50 watts switchabl 2x12".			
1990-2000		$725	$8
JCM 900 4500 Amp Head			
1990-2000. All tube, 2 channels, 50/25 watts, EL3 powered, reverb, effects loop, compensated recordin out, master volume, black.			
1990-2000		$625	$7
JCM 900 4501 Dual Reverb Combo Amp			
1990-2000. 50/25 switchable, 1x12".			
1990-2000		$725	$8
JCM 900 4502 Combo Amp			
1990-2000. 50/25 switchable, 2x12".			
1990-2000		$775	$90

MODEL YEAR	FEATURES	EXC. COND. LOW	HIGH

JCM 2000 Series Amps
1998-present. DSL is Dual Single Lead.

1998-2000s	DSL 100 Half Stack (w/1960A)	$1,050	$1,300
1998-2003	DSL 100 head, 100w	$500	$600
1998-2003	DSL 50 head, 50w	$475	$600
1999-2002	DSL 201	$400	$425
2000-2004	DSL 401 1x12 tube combo	$400	$475

JCM Slash Signature Model 2555SL Amp Set
1996. Based on JCM 800 with higher gain, matching amp and cab set, JCM Slash Signature logo on front panel, single channel, Slash Signature 1960AV 4x12" slant cab, black.

1996		$1,700	$2,500

JTM 30 Combo Amp

1999		$400	$475

JTM 45 Amp Head
1962-1964. Amp head, 45 watts. The original Marshall amp. Became the Model 1987 45-watt for '65-'66.

1962-1964		$11,300	$14,000

JTM 45 Amp (Model 1987) Amp Head Reissue
1989-1999. Black/green tolex.

1988-1999		$750	$850

JTM 45 MK IV Model 1961 4x10 Combo Amp
1965-1966. 45 watts, 4x10", tremolo, JTM 45 MK IV on panel, Bluesbreaker association.

1965-1966		$9,100	$11,000

JTM 45 MK IV Model 1962 2x12 Combo Amp
1965-1966. 45 watts, 2x12", tremolo, JTM 45 MK IV on panel, Bluesbreaker association.

1965-1966		$11,100	$13,000

JTM 45 Model 1987 Mark II Half Stack Amp
1965-1966. Matching amp and cab.

1965-1966		$9,100	$11,300

JTM 45 Model 1987 Mark II Lead Amp Head
1965-1966. Replaced JTM 45 Amp ('62-'64), but was subsequently replaced by the Model 1987 50-watt Head during '66.

1965-1966		$7,100	$8,000

JTM 45 Offset Limited Edition Amp Set Reissue
Introduced in 2000. Limited run of 300 units, old style cosmetics, 45-watt head and offset 2x12" cab, dark vinyl cover, light gray grille, rectangular logo plate on front of amp and cab, Limited Edition plate on rear of cab, serial number xxx of 300.

2000		$3,100	$3,400

JTM 50 MK IV Model 1961 4x10 Amp
1965-1972. 50 watts, 4x10", Bluesbreaker association, tremolo, JTM 50 MK IV on front panel to '68, plain front panel without model description '68-'72.

1966-1967		$9,100	$11,000
1968		$8,500	$10,000
1969		$7,500	$8,500
1970		$6,000	$7,500
1971-1972		$5,000	$5,500

JTM 50 MK IV Model 1962 2x12 Amp
1966-1972. 50 watts, 2x12", tremolo, Bluesbreaker association, JTM 50 MK IV on front panel to '68, plain front panel without model description '68-'72.

1966-1967		$11,100	$13,000
1968		$10,500	$12,000
1969		$9,500	$10,500
1970		$7,500	$9,400
1971-1972		$6,000	$6,500

JTM 50 Model 1962 Bluesbreaker Amp Reissue
1989-present. 50 watts, 2x12", Model 1962 reissue Bluesbreaker.

1989-1999		$900	$1,050

JTM 50 Model 1963 PA Amp Head
1965-1966. MK II PA head, block logo.

1965-1966		$4,800	$6,000

JTM 60 Series Amps
1995-1997. Tube, 60 watts, 1x12" (Combo) or 3x10" (Half-Stack).

1995-1997	Combo	$450	$550
1995-1997	Mini Half-Stack	$650	$750

JTM 310 Amp
1995-1997. Tube combo, reverb, 30 watts, 2x10", effects loops, 5881 output sections, footswitchable high-gain modes.

1995-1997		$525	$625

JTM 612 Combo Amp
1995-1997. Tube combo amp, 60 watts, 1x12", EQ, reverb, effects loop.

1995-1997		$525	$625

MG Series Amps
1999-present. Models include 15CD, 15RCD or CDR (solidstate, 15 watts, 1x8"), 15MS (15 watts, micro stack, 1x8" slant and 1x8" straight cabs), 15MSII, (in '02, 10" speakers), 100RCD (Valvestate Series, made in Korea, head, 100 watts), 50DFX (50 watts, 1x12), 100DFX (100 watts, combo), 250DFX (250 watts, combo).

1999-2004	MG15CD	$60	$70
1999-2004	MG15MS/15MSII	$200	$250
2000-2002	MG100RCD	$275	$300
2000-2006	MG15RCD/CDR	$70	$80
2002-2006	MG100DFX	$300	$375
2002-2006	MG250DFX	$300	$375
2002-2006	MG50DFX	$275	$300

Micro Stack 3005 Amp
1986-1991. Solidstate head, 12 watts, 2 1x10" stackable cabs (one slant, one straight). Standard model is black, but was also offered in white, green, red, or the silver Silver Jubilee version with Jubilee 25/50 logo.

1986-1991	Black	$325	$400
1986-1991	Green, red, white	$375	$450
1986-1991	Head only, black	$125	$150
1987-1989	Silver Jubilee/silver	$475	$575

Marshall JCM 2000 TSL 100

Marshall MG15MSII

Marshall 3005 Silver Jubilee

Marshall 1959 Super Lead

1976 Marshall 1959 Super Lead

Marshall 1959 SLP Reissue

MODEL YEAR	FEATURES	EXC. COND. LOW	HIGH

Mini-Stack 3210 MOS-FET Amp Head with 2x4x10"
1984-1991. Model 3210 MOS-FET head with 2 4x10" cabs, designed as affordable stack.

1984-1991		$350	$425

Model 1710 Bass Cabinet
1990s. 1x15" speaker.

1990s		$300	$350

Model 1930 Popular Combo Amp
1969-1973. 10 watts, 1x12", tremolo.

1969-1973		$2,500	$3,000

Model 1935/1935A/1935B Bass Cabinet
1967-1990s. Models 1935, 4x12" bass cab, black, A slant front, B straight front.

1967-1970	75 watts	$2,600	$3,000
1970-1979	100 watts	$1,600	$2,000
1979-1983	260 watts	$600	$800
1983-1986	280 watts	$600	$800
1990s		$300	$350

Model 1936 2x12" Cabinet (JCM 800/900)
1981-present. 2x12" speakers, extension straight-front cab, black.

1981-1999		$325	$350

Model 1937 Bass Cabinet
1981-1986. 4x12", 140 watts.

1981-1986		$625	$775

Model 1958 18-Watt Lead Amp
1965-1968. 18 watts, 2x10" combo, Bluesbreaker cosmetics.

1965		$7,000	$8,500
1965	New tubes	$100	$125
1965	NOS original tubes	$425	$450
1966		$6,500	$8,000
1967		$6,400	$7,700
1968		$6,300	$7,300

Model 1958 20-Watt Lead Amp
1968-1972. 20 watts, 2x10" combo, tremolo.

1968		$6,200	$6,500
1969		$5,500	$5,700
1970		$5,000	$5,200
1971-1972		$4,300	$4,600

Model 1959 Super Lead Amp
1966-1981. Two channels, 100 watts, 4 inputs, no master volume. Plexiglas control panels until mid-'69, aluminum after. See Model T1959 for tremolo version. Early custom color versions are rare and more valuable.

1966-1969	Black, plexi	$5,700	$6,600
1966-1969	Custom color, plexi	$8,500	$9,500
1966-1969	New tubes	$185	$210
1966-1969	NOS original tubes	$775	$900
1969-1970	Black, aluminum	$3,700	$4,600
1969-1970	Custom color, aluminum	$5,200	$6,500
1971-1972	Black, hand-wired, small box	$2,000	$2,500
1971-1972	Custom color, hand-wired	$3,300	$4,000

1973-1975	Black, printed C.B., large box	$1,800	$2,200
1973-1975	Custom color, printed C.B.	$2,000	$2,400
1976-1979	Black	$1,300	$1,600
1976-1979	Custom color	$2,000	$2,300
1980-1981	Black	$1,200	$1,500
1980-1981	Custom color	$1,600	$2,000

Model T1959 Super Lead (Tremolo) Amp Head
1966-1973. Head amp, 100 watts, plexi until mid-'69, aluminum after. Tremolo version of the Model 1959 Amp.

1966-1969	Black, plexi	$6,200	$7,000
1966-1969	Custom color, plexi	$8,000	$10,000
1969-1970	Black, aluminum	$3,900	$4,800
1969-1970	Custom color, aluminum	$5,300	$6,500
1971-1973	Black, hand-wired, small box	$2,400	$3,000
1971-1973	Custom color, hand-wired	$3,000	$3,700

Model T1959 Tubes and Speakers
The cost of replacement tubes and speakers for the '66-'69 models.

1966-1969	New tubes	$150	$170
1966-1969	NOS original tubes	$725	$900
1966-1969	Orig. quad G12M 20w speakers	$1,800	$2,000

Model 1959 Super Lead Matching Full Stack Set
1966-1981 option. Head with 100 watts and matching color slant and straight front 4x12" cabinets.

1966-1969	Black, plexi, weave	$14,600	$18,000
1966-1969	Custom color, plexi, weave	$19,000	$21,000
1969-1970	Black, aluminum, weave	$11,400	$14,200
1969-1970	Custom color, aluminum, weave	$14,000	$16,900
1971-1972	Black, hand-wired, small box, weave	$8,500	$9,000
1971-1972	Custom color, hand-wired, weave	$10,200	$11,000
1973-1975	Black, printed CB, large box, checkerboard	$5,200	$6,000
1973-1975	Custom color, CB, checkerboard	$8,000	$8,500
1976-1979	Black	$4,000	$4,500
1976-1979	Custom color	$6,800	$7,500
1980-1981	Black	$3,300	$3,500
1980-1981	Custom color	$4,800	$5,000

Model 1959 Super Lead Matching Half Stack Set
1966-1981 option. 100 watt head and matching color 4x12" cabinet. Plexiglass control panels made from '65 to mid-'69, followed by aluminum panel. Matching set requires that the head and cab are the

MODEL YEAR	FEATURES	EXC. COND. LOW	HIGH
	exact matching set that came out of the factory as a set. A mismatched set that is of similar color but not built as a set is not applicable for this pricing. As is the case with all vintage amps, the speakers must be the factory original (untouched) speakers.		
1966-1969	Black, plexi, weave	$10,000	$12,000
1966-1969	Custom color, plexi, weave	$14,000	$16,000
1969-1970	Black, aluminum, weave	$8,800	$11,000
1969-1970	Custom color, aluminum, weave	$10,200	$12,700
1971-1972	Black, hand-wired, weave	$5,700	$6,000
1971-1972	Custom color, hand-wired, weave	$7,300	$7,500
1973-1975	Black, printed C.B., large box, checkerboard	$3,400	$4,000
1973-1975	Custom color, printed C.B., large box, checkerboard	$5,700	$6,000
1976-1979	Black	$2,800	$3,000
1976-1979	Custom color	$4,400	$5,000
1980-1981	Black	$2,200	$2,500
1980-1981	Custom color	$3,600	$4,000

Model 1959 SLP Reissue Amp Head
1992-present. SLP refers to Super Lead Plexi.

1990s	Black vinyl	$900	$1,000
1990s	Purple vinyl	$1,150	$1,350
1990s	White limited edition	$1,050	$1,250
2000-2004	Black vinyl	$900	$1,000

Model 1959 SLP Reissue Amp Set
1992-present. 100 watt Super Lead head and matching 4x12" slant cab.

| 1990s | Purple, full-stack, 2x4x12" | $2,600 | $3,500 |
| 1990s | Purple, half-stack, 1x4x12" | $2,000 | $2,800 |

Model 1959HW Amp
2005-present. Hand-wired, 100 watts, 4x12" slant front 1960HW cab (1/2 stack).

| 2005-2006 | Head & half stack | $2,700 | $2,800 |
| 2005-2006 | Head only | $2,000 | $2,200 |

Model 1960 4x12 Speaker Cabinet
1964-1979. Both straight and slant front. The original Marshall 4x12" cab designed for compact size with 4x12" speakers. First issue in '64/'65 is 60-watt cab, from '65-'70 75 watts, from '70-'79 100 watts. After '79, model numbers contained an alpha suffix: A for slant front, B straight.

1966-1970	Black, weave	$2,800	$3,500
1966-1970	Custom color, weave	$4,000	$5,000
1971-1972	Black, weave	$2,400	$2,600
1971-1972	Custom color, weave	$2,900	$3,100
1973-1975	Black, checkerboard	$1,200	$1,400

MODEL YEAR	FEATURES	EXC. COND. LOW	HIGH
1973-1975	Custom color, checkerboard	$2,400	$2,600
1976-1979	Black	$1,000	$1,200
1976-1979	Custom color	$2,000	$2,200

Model 1960A/1960B 4x12 Cabinet
1980-1983 (260 watts), '84-'86 (280 watts, JCM 800 era), '86-'90 (300 watts, JCM 800 era). A for slant front, B straight.

1980-1983	Black	$700	$900
1980-1983	Custom color	$1,000	$1,600
1984-1986	Black	$550	$650
1984-1986	Custom color	$850	$1,300
1986-1990	Black	$500	$600
1986-1990	Custom color	$800	$1,200
2000-2007	Black	$425	$525

Model 1960A/1960B JCM 900 4x12 Cabinet
1990-2000. JCM 900 Series updated to 300 watts, stereo-mono switching, A slant, B straight.

| 1990-2000 | | $425 | $525 |

Model 1960AHW 4x12 Slant Cabinet
2005-present. Half stack slant front cab for HW series.

| 2005-2006 | | $775 | $950 |

Model 1960AV 4x12 Slant Cabinet
1990-present. JCM 900 updated, stereo/mono switching, AV slant, BV straight front.

1990-1999	Black vinyl, black grille	$550	$600
1990s	Red vinyl, tan grille	$650	$800
2000-2006	Black	$550	$600

Model 1960AX/1960BX 4x12 Cabinet
1990-present. Cab for Model 1987X and 1959X reissue heads, AX slant, BX straight.

| 1990-1999 | | $600 | $700 |

Model 1960BV 4x12 Straight Cabinet
1990-present. JCM 900 updated, stereo/mono switching, AV slant, BV straight front.

1990-1999	Black vinyl, black grille	$600	$700
1990s	Red vinyl, tan grille	$800	$850
2000-2007	Black	$650	$800

Model 1960BX 4x12 Straight Cabinet

| 1990-1999 | | $600 | $700 |

Model 1960TV 4x12 Slant Cabinet
1990-present. Extra tall for JTM 45, mono, 100 watts.

| 1990-1999 | | $600 | $700 |
| 2000-2007 | Black | $750 | $950 |

Model 1964 Lead/Bass 50-Watt Amp Head
1973-1976. Head with 50 watts, designed for lead or bass.

| 1973-1976 | | $1,200 | $1,400 |

Model 1965A/1965B Cabinet
1984-1991. 140 watt 4x10" slant front (A) or straight front (B) cab.

| 1984-1991 | | $325 | $400 |

Model 1966 Cabinet
1985-1991. 150 watt 2x12" cab.

| 1985-1991 | | $300 | $350 |

Marshall 1960A slant cab

Marshall 1959 HW stack

Marshall 1960TV 4X12 Cabinet

AMPS

1972 Marshall 1967 Major

Marshall 1974x

Marshall 2060 Mercury

MODEL YEAR	FEATURES	EXC. COND. LOW	HIGH

Model 1967 Pig 200-Watt Amp Head
1967-early-1968 only. Head with 200 watts. The control panel was short and stubby and nicknamed the Pig, the 200-watt circuit was dissimilar (and unpopular) to the 50-watt and 100-watt circuits.

1967-1968		$3,200	$3,600

Model 1967 Major 200-Watt Amp Head
1968-1974. 200 watts, the original Marshall 200 Pig was not popular and revised into the 200 'Major'. The new Major 200 was similar to the other large amps and included 2 channels, 4 inputs, but a larger amp cab.

1968		$3,200	$4,000
1969		$2,600	$3,200
1970		$2,300	$2,800
1971-1974		$1,500	$1,875

Model 1968 100-Watt Super PA Amp Head
1968-1975. PA head with 100 watts, 2 sets of 4 inputs (identifies PA configuration), often used for guitar.

1966-1969	Plexi	$3,200	$3,600
1969-1972	Aluminum	$2,400	$3,000

Model 1973 Amp
1965-1968. Tube combo, 18 watts, 2x12".

1965		$10,000	$11,200
1966		$9,000	$10,000
1967		$8,000	$9,000
1968		$6,000	$8,000

Model 1973 JMP Lead/Bass 20 Amp
1973 only. Front panel: JMP, back panel: Lead & Bass 20, 20 watts, 1x12" straight front checkered grille cab, head and cab black vinyl.

1973		$2,400	$2,600

Model 1974 Amp
1965-1968. Tube combo, 18 watts, 1x12".

1965		$6,200	$7,000
1966		$6,200	$6,500
1967		$5,700	$6,000
1968		$4,500	$5,000

Model 1974X Amp
2004. Reissue of 18-watt, 1x12" combo.

2004	1974CX ext. cab	$425	$450
2004	Combo amp	$1,300	$1,500

Model 1987 50-Watt Amp Head
1966-1981. Head amp, 50 watts, plexiglas panel until mid-'69, aluminum panel after.

1966-1969	Black, plexi	$4,500	$5,600
1966-1969	Custom color, plexi	$7,400	$9,200
1969-1970	Black, aluminum	$3,600	$4,500
1969-1970	Custom color, aluminum	$4,800	$6,000
1971-1972	Black, hand-wired, small box	$2,200	$2,700
1971-1972	Custom color, hand-wired	$2,800	$3,500
1973-1975	Black, printed C.B., large box	$1,600	$2,000
1973-1975	Custom color, printed C.B.	$1,800	$2,200
1976-1979	Black	$1,350	$1,600
1976-1979	Custom color	$1,700	$2,100
1980-1981	Black	$1,200	$1,400
1980-1981	Custom color	$1,400	$1,700

Model 1987 50-Watt Matching Set
Head and matching 4x12" cab, plexiglas control panels from '65 to mid-'69, aluminum panel after.

1966-1969	Black, plexi	$11,000	$13,500
1966-1969	Custom color, plexi	$16,000	$20,000
1969-1970	Black, aluminum	$9,000	$11,000
1969-1970	Custom color, aluminum	$10,500	$13,000
1971-1972	Black, hand-wired, small box	$5,000	$6,000
1971-1972	Custom color, hand-wired	$6,500	$8,000
1973-1975	Black, printed C.B., large box	$4,000	$5,000
1973-1975	Custom color, printed C.B.	$5,500	$6,500
1976-1979	Black	$3,000	$3,700
1976-1979	Custom color	$4,000	$4,700
1980-1981	Black	$2,500	$3,000
1980-1981	Custom color	$3,300	$3,600

Model 1987 50-Watt Matching Full Stack Set
1966-1981. Head and 2 matching 4x12" cabs.

1976-1979	Custom color	$5,000	$5,500

Model 1992 Super Bass Amp Head
1966-1981. 100 watts, plexi panel until mid-'69 when replaced by aluminum front panel, 2 channels, 4 inputs.

1966-1969	Black, plexi	$4,500	$5,600
1966-1969	Custom color, plexi	$7,400	$9,200
1969-1970	Black, aluminum	$3,600	$4,500
1969-1970	Custom color, aluminum	$4,800	$6,000
1971-1972	Black, hand-wired, small box	$2,200	$2,700
1971-1972	Custom color, hand-wired	$2,800	$3,500
1973-1975	Black, printed C.B., large box	$1,600	$2,000
1973-1975	Custom color, printed C.B.	$1,800	$2,200
1976-1979	Black	$1,350	$1,600
1976-1979	Custom color	$1,700	$2,100
1980-1981	Black	$1,200	$1,400
1980-1981	Custom color	$1,400	$1,700

Model 1992 Super Bass Matching Full-Stack Set
Early 1970s. Head and matching cabs, black.

1971-1972		$10,000	$12,000

Model 2040 Artist 50-Watt Combo Amp
1971-1978. 50 watts, 2x12" Artist/Artiste combo model with a different (less popular?) circuit.

1971-1978		$2,000	$2,400

Model 2041 Artist Head/Cabinet Set
1971-1978. 50 watts, 2x12" half stack Artist/Artiste cab with a different (less popular?) circuit.

1971-1978		$2,000	$2,400

MODEL YEAR	FEATURES	EXC. COND. LOW	HIGH

Model 2046 Specialist 25-Watt Combo Amp
1972-1973. 25 watts, 1x15" speaker, limited production due to design flaw (amp overheats).

1972-1973		$900	$1,000

Model 2060 Mercury Combo Amp
1972-1973. Combo amp, 5 watts, 1x12", available in red or orange covering.

1972-1973		$1,400	$1,800

Model 2061 20-Watt Lead/Bass Amp Head
1968-1973. Lead/bass head, 20 watts, plexi until '69, aluminum after. Reissued in '04 as the Model 2061X.

1968-1969	Black, plexi	$3,400	$4,000
1969-1973	Black, aluminum	$2,400	$3,000

Model 2061X 20-Watt Lead/Bass Amp Head Reissue
2004. Reissue of 2061 amp head, 20 watts.

2004		$1,000	$1,200

Model 2078 Combo Amp
1973-1978. Solidstate, 100 watts, 4x12" combo, gold front panel, dark cover, gray grille.

1973-1978		$800	$1,100

Model 2103 100-Watt 1-Channel Master Combo Amp
1975-1981. One channel, 2 inputs, 100 watts, 2x12", first master volume design, combo version of 2203 head.

1975-1981		$1,200	$1,500

Model 2104 50-Watt 1-Channel Master Combo Amp
1975-1981. One channel, 2 inputs, 50 watts, 2x12", first master volume design, combo version of 2204 head.

1975-1981		$1,200	$1,500

Model 2144 Master Reverb Combo Amp
1978 only. Master volume similar to 2104 but with reverb and boost, 50 watts, 2x12".

1978		$1,550	$1,650

Model 2159 100-Watt 2-Channel Combo Amp
1977-1981. 100 watts, 2 channels, 4 inputs, 2x12" combo version of Model 1959 Super Lead head.

1977-1981		$1,600	$2,000

Model 2200 100-Watt Lead Combo Amp
1977-1981. 100 watts, 2x12" combo, early solidstate, includes boost section, no reverb.

1977-1981		$800	$1,000

Model 2203 Lead Amp Head
1975-1981. Head amp, 100 watts, 2 inputs, first master volume model design, often seen with Mark II logo.

1975-1981	Black	$1,200	$1,450
1975-1981	Fawn Beige	$1,600	$1,800

Model 2203(X) JCM800 Reissue Amp Head
2002-present. 100 watts.

2002-2007		$1,300	$1,350

Model 2204 50-Watt Amp Head
1975-1981. Head amp, 50 watts with master volume.

1975-1981		$1,200	$1,425

Model 3203 Artist Amp Head
1986-1991. Tube head version of earlier '84 Model 3210 MOS-FET, designed as affordable alternative, 30 watts, standard short cab, 2 inputs separated by 3 control knobs, Artist 3203 logo on front panel, black.

1986-1991		$450	$500

Model 3210 MOS-FET Amp Head
1984-1991. MOS-FET solidstate head, refer Mini-Stack listing for 3210 with 4x10" stacked cabinets. Early-'80s front panel: Lead 100 MOS-FET.

1984-1991		$300	$350

Model 3310 100-Watt Lead Amp
1988-1991. Solidstate, 100 watts, lead head with channel switching and reverb.

1988-1991		$400	$500

Model 4001 Studio 15 Amp
1985-1992. 15 watts using 6V6 (only model to do this up to this time), 1x12" Celestion Vintage 30 speakers.

1985-1992		$725	$800

Model 4203 Artist 30 Combo Amp
1986-1991. 30-watt tube hybrid combo, 1x12", channel switching.

1986-1991		$550	$600

Model 5002 Combo Amp
1984-1991. Solidstate combo amp, 20 watts, 1x10", master volume.

1984-1991		$175	$200

Model 5005 Combo Amp
1984-1991. Solidstate, 12 watts, 1x10", practice amp with master volume, headphones and line-out.

1984-1991		$150	$175

Model 5302 Keyboard Amp
1984-1988. Solidstate, 20 watts, 1x10", marketed for keyboard application.

1984-1988		$150	$175

Model 5502 Bass Amp
1984-ca.1992. Solidstate bass combo amp, 20 watts, 1x10" Celestion.

1984-1992		$150	$175

Model 6100 30th Anniversary Amp Head
1992-1995. All tube, 3 channels, 100 watts, EQ, gain, contour, full and half power modes, blue vinyl covering, front panel: 6100 LM Anniversary Series. Listed as JCM 900 6100 in '95.

1992-1995		$975	$1,075

Model 6100 30th Anniversary Amp Set
1992-1995. Matching head with 100/50/25 watts and 4x12" cabinet (matching colors), first year was blue tolex.

1992	Blue tolex	$1,600	$2,000
1993-1995	Purple tolex	$1,400	$1,700

Model 6101 LE Combo Amp
1992-1995. 1x12", 100/50/25 switchable watts, blue/purple cover, limited edition.

1992-1995		$1,300	$1,400

Marshall 3203 Artist

AMPS

1985 Marshall 3210 head

Marshall 4101

To get the most from this book, be sure to read "Using *The Guide*" in the introduction.

Marshall 8100 VSH100H head

Marshall MS-2

Matamp 1224

MODEL YEAR	FEATURES	EXC. COND. LOW	HIGH

Model 8008 Valvestate Rackmount Amp
1991-2001. Valvestate solidstate rack mount power amp with dual 40-watt channels.

| 1991-2001 | | $300 | $375 |

Model 8010 Valvestate VS15 Combo Amp
1991-1997. Valvestate solidstate, 10 watts, 1x8", compact size, black vinyl, black grille.

| 1991-1997 | | $125 | $150 |

Model 8040 Valvestate 40V Combo Amp
1991-1997. Valvestate solidstate with tube preamp, 40 watts, 1x12", compact size, black vinyl, black grille.

| 1991-1997 | | $275 | $325 |

Model 8080 Valvestate 80V Combo Amp
1991-1997. Valvestate solidstate with tube 12AX7 preamp, 80 watts, 1x12", compact size, black vinyl, black grille.

| 1991-1997 | | $300 | $350 |

Model 8100 100-Watt Valvestate VS100H Amp Head
1991-2001. Valvestate solidstate head, 100 watts.

| 1991-2001 | | $325 | $375 |

Model 8200 200-Watt Valvestate Amp Head
1993-1998. Valvestate solidstate reverb head, 2x100-watt channels.

| 1993-1998 | | $375 | $425 |

Model 8222 Valvestate Cabinet
1993-1998. 200 watts, 2x12 extention cab, designed for 8200 head.

| 1993-1998 | | $375 | $425 |

Model 8240 Valvestate Stereo Chorus Amp
1992-1996. Valvestate, 80 watts (2x40 watts stereo), 2x12" combo, reverb, chorus.

| 1992-1996 | | $400 | $450 |

Model 8280 2x80-Watt Valvestate Combo Amp
1993-1996. Valvestate solidstate, 2x80 watts, 2x12".

| 1993-1996 | | $450 | $500 |

Model 8412 Valvestate Cabinet
1991-2001. 140 watts, 4x12 extention cab, designed for 8100 head.

| 1991-2001 | | $375 | $425 |

MS-2/R/C Amp
1990-present. One watt, battery operated, miniature black half-stack amp and cab. Red MS-2R and checkered speaker grille and gold logo MS-2C added in '93.

| 1990-2003 | | $30 | $35 |

MS-4 Amp
1998-present. Full-stack version of MS-2, black.

| 1998-2003 | | $35 | $40 |

Silver Jubilee Model 2550 50/25 (Tall) Amp Head
1987-1989. 50/25 switchable tall box head for full Jubilee stack.

| 1987-1989 | | $1,500 | $1,800 |

Silver Jubilee Model 2551 4x12 Cabinet
1987-1988. Matching silver cab for Jubilee 2550 head.

| 1987-1988 | | $600 | $750 |

Silver Jubilee Model 2553 (Short) 2556A (Mini)
1987-1989. Short box, 100/50 watt, two 2x12".

| 1987-1989 | | $1,950 | $2,400 |

Silver Jubilee Model 2553 50/25 (Short) Amp Head
1987-1989. 50/25 switchable small box head for mini-short stack.

| 1987-1989 | | $1,200 | $1,500 |

Silver Jubilee Model 2554 1x12 Combo Amp
1987-1989. 50/25 watts, 1x12" combo using 2550 chasis.

| 1987-1989 | | $1,500 | $1,600 |

Silver Jubilee Model 2555 Amp Head
1987-1989. 100/50 version of 2550 head, cosmetic condition is exceptionally important on this model.

| 1987-1989 | | $2,400 | $2,500 |

Silver Jubilee Model 2555 Amp with Full Stack
1987-1989. Silver vinyl covering, chrome control panel, 100/50 watts with 2 2551A 4x12" cabinets, cosmetic condition is exceptionally important on this model.

| 1987-1989 | | $3,400 | $3,500 |

Silver Jubilee Model 2555 Amp with Half Stack
1987-1989. 100/50 watts, one 4x12", cosmetic condition is exceptionally important on this model.

| 1987-1989 | | $2,900 | $3,000 |

Silver Jubilee Model 2556 4x12 Cabinet
1987-1989. Cab with 4x12" speakers in 3 brand name options.

| 1987-1989 | | $500 | $600 |

Silver Jubilee Model 2556A/AV 2x12 Cabinet
1987-1989. Cab with 2x12" speakers with 3 brand name options.

| 1987-1989 | | $400 | $500 |

Silver Jubilee Model 2558 2x12 Combo Amp
1987-1989. 50/25 watts, 2x12" combo using 2550 chasis.

| 1987-1989 | | $1,500 | $1,875 |

TSL 122 Triple Super Lead Combo Amp
1998-present. 100 watts, 3 channels, 2x12" combo.

| 1998-2004 | | $900 | $1,100 |

Martin

Martin has dabbled in amps a few times, under both the Martin and Stinger brand names.

Model 112 Amp
1959-1960. Branded C.F. Martin inside label, made by Rowe-DeArmond, 1x12 combo, limited production, 2x6V6 power tubes, 2x12AX7 preamp tubes, with tube rectifier, 4 inputs, 3 control knobs.

| 1959-1960 | | $1,250 | $1,600 |

MODEL YEAR	FEATURES	EXC. COND. LOW	HIGH

Stinger FX-1 Amp
1988-1990. 10 watts, EQ, switchable solidstate tube-synth circuit, line out and footswitch jacks.

1988		$100	$125

Stinger FX-1R Amp
1988-1990. Mini-stack amp, 2x10", 15 watts, dual-stage circuitry.

1989		$125	$150

Stinger FX-6B Amp
1989-1990. Combo bass amp, 60 watts, 1x15".

1989		$125	$150

Massie
1940s. Ray Massie worked in Leo Fender's repair shop in the 1940s and also built tube amps. He later worked at the Fender company.

Matamp
1966-present. Tube amps, combos and cabinets built in Huddersfield, England, bearing names like Red, Green, White, Black, and Blue. German-born Mat Mathias started building amps in England in '58 and designed his first Matamp in '66. From '69 to '73, Mathias also made Orange amps. In '89, Mathias died at age 66 and his family later sold the factory to Jeff Lewis.

Green GT-120 Stack Amp
1990s. 120 watt GT head with 4x12" straight front cab.

1993-1999		$1,500	$1,750

Matchless
1989-1999, 2001-present. Founded by Mark Sampson and Rick Perrotta in California. Circuits based on Vox AC-30 with special attention to transformers. A new Matchless company was reorganized in 2001 by Phil Jamison, former head of production for the original company.

Brave 40 112 Amp
1997-1999. 40 watts class A, 1x12", footswitchable between high and low inputs.

1997-1999		$1,100	$1,200

Brave 40 212 Amp
1997-1999. 2x12" version of Brave.

1997-1999		$1,300	$1,400

Chief Amp Head
1995-1999. 100 watts class A, head.

1995-1999		$2,100	$2,200

Chief 212 Amp
1995-1999. 100 watts class A, 2x12", reverb.

1995-1999		$2,400	$2,500

Chief 410 Amp
1995-1999. 100 watts class A, 4x10", reverb.

1995-1999		$2,400	$2,500

Chieftan Amp Head
1995-1999. 40 watts class A head.

1995-1999		$1,400	$1,500

Chieftan 112 Amp
1995-1999. 40 watts class A, 1x12", reverb.

1995-1999		$2,000	$2,250

Chieftan 210 Amp
1995-1999. 40 watts class A, 2x10", reverb.

1995-1999		$2,100	$2,550

Chieftan 212 Amp
1995-1999. 40 watts class A, 2x12", reverb.

1995-1999		$2,200	$2,700

Chieftan 410 Amp
1995-1999. 40 watts class A, 4x10", reverb.

1995-1999		$2,200	$2,700

Clipper 15 112 Amp
1998-1999. 15 watts, single channel, 1x12".

1998-1999		$800	$900

Clipper 15 210 Amp
1998-1999. 15 watts, single channel, 2x10".

1998-1999		$800	$900

Clubman 35 Amp Head
1993-1999. 35 watts class A head.

1993-1999		$1,600	$1,700

DC-30 Standard Cabinet
1991-1999. 30 watts, 2x12", with or without reverb.

1991-1999	Non-reverb	$2,700	$2,800
1991-1999	With reverb	$2,800	$2,900

DC-30 Exotic Wood Cabinet Option
1995-1999. 30 watts, 2x12", gold plating, limited production.

1995-1999	Non-reverb	$4,700	$4,800
1995-1999	With reverb	$5,100	$5,200

EB115 Bass Cabinet
1997-1999. 1x15" bass speaker cabinet.

1997-1999		$350	$400

EB410 Bass Cabinet
1997-1999. 4x10" bass speaker cabinet.

1997-1999		$400	$450

ES/210 Cabinet
1993-1999. 2x10" speaker cabinet.

1993-1999		$400	$500

ES/410 Cabinet
1993-1999. 4x10" speaker cabinet.

1993-1999		$500	$600

ES/412 Cabinet
1993-1999. 4x12" speaker cabinet.

1993-1999		$550	$650

ES/1012 Cabinet
1993-1999. 2x10" and 2x12" speaker cabinet.

1993-1999		$550	$650

ES/D Cabinet
1993-1999. 2x12" speaker cabinet.

1993-1999		$500	$600

ES/S Cabinet
1991-1999. 1x12" speaker cabinet.

1991-1999		$400	$450

HC-30 Amp Head
1991-1999. The first model offered by Matchless, 30 watts class A head.

1991-1999		$2,000	$2,200

HC-85 Amp Head
1992. Only 25 made.

1992		$2,300	$2,600

Hurricane Amp Head
1997. 15 watts class A head.

1997		$1,000	$1,100

Matchless Chief 410

AMPS

Matchless Chieftan

Matchless DC-30

AMPS

Matchless Lightning 15

Matchless Skyliner Reverb

Matchless Spitfire 112

MODEL YEAR	FEATURES	EXC. COND. LOW	HIGH
Hurricane 112 Amp			
1994-1997. 15 watts class A, 1x12".			
1994-1997		$1,200	$1,300
Hurricane 210 Amp			
1996-1997. 15 watts class A, 2x10".			
1996-1997		$1,200	$1,300
JJ-30 112 John Jorgensen Amp			
1997-1999. 30 watts, DC-30 chasis with reverb and tremolo, 1x12" Celestion 30, offered in white, blue, gray sparkle tolex or black.			
1997-1999		$4,100	$4,300
Lightning 15 Amp Head			
1997. 15 watts class A head.			
1997		$800	$900
Lightning 15 112 Amp			
1994-1999. 15 watts class A, 1x12".			
1994-1999	Non-reverb	$1,200	$1,300
1997-1999	With reverb	$1,500	$1,600
Lightning 15 210 Amp			
1996-1997. 15 watts class A, 2x10".			
1996-1997	Non-reverb	$1,400	$1,700
1997	With reverb	$1,500	$1,800
Lightning 15 212 Amp			
1996-1997. 15 watts class A, 2x12".			
1996-1997	Non-reverb	$1,700	$1,800
1997	With reverb	$1,800	$1,900
SC-30 Standard Cabinet Amp			
1991-1999. 30 watts class A, 1x12".			
1991-1999	Non-reverb	$2,300	$2,500
1991-1999	With reverb	$2,600	$2,800
SC-30 Exotic Wood Cabinet Amp			
1995-1999. 30 watts class A, 1x12", gold plating, limited production.			
1995-1999	Non-reverb	$4,400	$4,500
1995-1999	With reverb	$4,900	$5,100
Skyliner Reverb 15 112 Amp			
1998-1999. 15 watts, 2 channels, 1x12".			
1998-1999		$900	$1,000
Skyliner Reverb 15 210 Amp			
1998-1999. 15 watts, 2 channels, 2x10".			
1998-1999		$900	$1,000
Spitfire 15 Amp Head			
1997. 15 watts, head.			
1997		$900	$1,000
Spitfire 15 112 Amp			
1994-1997. 15 watts, 1x12".			
1994-1997		$1,300	$1,450
Spitfire 15 210 Amp			
1996-1997. 15 watts, 2x10".			
1996-1997		$1,400	$1,500
Starliner 40 212 Amp			
1999. 40 watts, 2x12".			
1999		$1,400	$1,500
Superchief 120 Amp Head			
1994-1999. 120 watts, class A head.			
1994-1999		$1,700	$1,800
TC-30 Standard Cabinet Amp			
1991-1999. 30 watts, 2x10" class A, low production numbers makes value approximate with DC-30.			
1991-1999	Non-reverb	$2,400	$2,500
1991-1999	With reverb	$2,900	$3,000

MODEL YEAR	FEATURES	EXC. COND. LOW	HIGH
TC-30 Exotic Wood Cabinet Amp			
1991-1999. 30 watts, 2x10" class A, limited production.			
1991-1999	Non-reverb	$3,000	$3,100
1991-1999	With reverb	$3,500	$4,300
Thunderchief Bass Amp Head			
1994-1999. 200 watts, class A bass head.			
1994-1999		$1,000	$1,200
Thunderman 100 Bass Combo Amp			
1997-1998. 100 watts, 1x15" in portaflex-style flip-top cab.			
1997-1998		$1,300	$1,400
Tornado 15 112 Amp			
1994-1995. Compact, 15 watts, 1x12", 2-tone covering, simple controls--volume, tone, tremolo speed, tremolo depth.			
1994-1995		$800	$900

Maven Peal

1999-present. Amps, combos and cabinets built by David Zimmerman in Plainfield, Vermont (the name stands for "expert sound"). Serial number format is by amp wattage and sequential build; for example, 15-watt amp 15-001, 30-watt 30-001, and 50-watt 50-001 with the 001 indicating the first amp built. S = Silver Series, no alpha = Gold Series.

Mega Amplifiers

Budget and intermediate grade, production, solidstate and tube amps from Guitar Jones, Inc. of Pomona, California.

Merlin

Rack mount bass heads built in Germany by Musician Sound Design. They also offer the MSD guitar effects.

Mesa-Boogie

1971-present. Founded by Randall Smith in San Francisco, California. Circuits styled on high-gain Fender-based chassis designs, ushering in the compact high-gain amp market. The following serial number information and specs courtesy of Mesa Engineering.

.50 Caliber/.50 Caliber+ Amp Head

Jan. 1987-Dec. 1988, 1992-1993. Serial numbers: SS3100 - SS11,499. Mesa Engineering calls it Caliber .50. Tube head amp, 50 watts, 5-band EQ, effects loop. Called the .50 Caliber Plus in '92 and '93.

1987-1988	Caliber	$475	$575
1992-1993	Caliber+	$475	$575

.50 Caliber+ Combo Amp

Dec. 1988-Oct. 1993. Serial numbers FP11,550 - FP29,080. 50 watts, 1x12" combo amp.

1988-1993	$500	$600

20/20 Amp

Jun. 1995-present. Serial numbers: TT-01. 20-22 watts per channel.

1995-2001	$500	$600

MODEL YEAR	FEATURES	EXC. COND. LOW	HIGH

50/50 (Fifty/Fifty) Amp
May 1989-2001. Serial numbers: FF001-. 100 watts total power, 50 watts per channel, front panel reads Fifty/Fifty, contains 4 6L6 power tubes.

1989-2001		$525	$625

395 Amp
Feb. 1991-Apr. 1992. Serial numbers: S2572 - S3237.

1991-1992		$650	$700

Bass 400/Bass 400+ Amp Head
Aug. 1989-Aug. 1990. Serial numbers: B001-B1200. About 500 watts using 12 5881 power tubes. Replaced by 400+ Aug.1990-present, serial numbers: B1200- . Update change to 7-band EQ at serial number B1677.

1989-1990	Bass 400	$875	$1,025
1990-1999	Bass 400+	$875	$1,025

Blue Angel Series Amps
Jun. 1994-2004. Serial numbers BA01-. Lower power 4x10" combo, blue cover.

1994-2004		$750	$850

Buster Bass Amp Head
Dec. 1997-Jan. 2001. Serial numbers: BS-1-999. 200 watts via 6 6L6 power tubes.

1997-2001		$475	$575

Buster Bass Combo Amp
1999-2001. 200 watts, 2x10", wedge cabinet, black vinyl, metal grille.

1999-2001		$500	$600

Coliseum 300 Amp
Oct. 1997-2000. Serial numbers: COL-01 - COL-132. 200 watts/channel, 12 6L6 power tubes, rack mount.

1997-2000		$1,000	$1,200

D-180 Amp Head
Jul. 1982-Dec. 1985. Serial numbers: D001-D681. All tube head amp, 200 watts, preamp, switchable.

1982-1985		$700	$875

DC-3 Amp
Sep. 1994-Jan. 1999. Serial numbers: DC3-001 - DC3-4523. 35 watts, 1x12".

1994-1999	Combo 1x12	$575	$700
1994-1999	Head only	$575	$700

DC-5 Amp
Oct. 1993-Jan. 1999. Serial numbers: DC1024 - DC31,941. 50-watt head, 1x12" combo.

1993-1999	Combo 1x12	$650	$750
1993-1999	Head only	$650	$750

DC-10 Amp Head
May 1996-Jan. 1999. Serial numbers: DCX-001 - DCX-999. Dirty/Clean (DC) 60 or 100 watts (6L6s).

1996-1999		$700	$800

Diesel Bass Cabinets
1994-2003. Designation for regular vinyl covered bass cabs after heavy-duty RoadReady cab option becomes available. Replaced by PowerHouse series.

1994-2003	1x15"	$325	$375

F-50 Amp
2002-Feb. 2007. Combo, 50 watts, 1x12", AB 2 6L6 power.

2002-2007		$675	$825

Formula Preamp
Jul. 1998-2002. Serial numbers: F-01. Used 5 12AX7 tubes, 3 channels.

1998-2000		$450	$500

Heartbreaker Amp Head
1996-2001. 100 watts head only.

1996-2001		$675	$825

Heartbreaker Amp
Jun. 1996-2001. Serial numbers: HRT-01. 60 to 100 watts switchable, 2x12" combo, designed to switch-out 6L6s, EL34s or the lower powered 6V6s in the power section, switchable solidstate or tube rectifier.

1996-2001		$850	$1,050

Lone Star Series Amp
2004-present. Designed by founder Randall Smith with Doug West with focus on boutique-type amp. Class A (EL84) or AB (4 6L6) circuits, long or short head, 1x12" combo, 2x12" combo, and short head 4x10" cab, and long head 4x12" cab.

2004-2007	1x12" combo	$1,250	$1,400
2004-2007	2x12" combo	$1,400	$1,550
2004-2007	4x12"	$675	$750
2004-2007	Head, class A or AB	$1,200	$1,400

M-180 Amp
Apr. 1982-Jan. 1986. Serial numbers: M001-M275.

1982-1986		$575	$650

M-2000 Amp
Jun. 1995-2003. Serial numbers: B2K-01.

1995-2003		$625	$675

Mark I Combo (Model A) Amp
1971-1978. The original Boogie amp, not called the Mark I until the Mark II was issued, 60 or 100 watts, 1x12", Model A serial numbers: 1-2999, very early serial numbers 1-299 had 1x15".

1971-1978	1x12" or 1x15"	$925	$1,000

Mark I Reissue Amp
Nov. 1989-Sept. 2007. Serial numbers: H001- . 100 watts, 1x12", reissue features include figured maple cab and wicker grille.

2000-2007		$825	$850

Mark II Combo Amp
1978-1980. Late-'78 1x12", serial numbers: 3000-5574. Effective Aug. '80 1x15", serial numbers: 300-559 until Mark II B replaced.

1978-1980	1x12" or 1x15"	$750	$900

Mark II B Amp Head
Head only.

1981-1983		$750	$900

Mark II B Combo Amp
1980-1983. Effective Aug. '80 1x12" models, serial numbers 5575 - 110000. May '83 1x15" models, serial numbers 560 - 11000. The 300 series serial numbers K1 - K336.

1981-1983	1x12" or 1x15", tolex cover	$875	$1,000
1981-1983	Custom hard-wood cab	$1,275	$1,375

Mark II C+ Amp Head
1983-1985. 60-watt head.

1983-1985		$1,000	$1,250

Maven Peal Zeetz 0.5>50

Mesa-Boogie Lone Star

Mesa-Boogie Mk 1

AMPS

Mesa-Boogie Mk IV B reissue

Mesa-Boogie Nomad 45

Mesa-Boogie Nomad 100

MODEL YEAR	FEATURES	EXC. COND. LOW	HIGH

Mark II C/Mark II C+ Amp
May 1983-Mar. 1985. Serial numbers 11001-14999 for 60 watts, 1x15", offered with optional white tolex cover. 300 series serial numbers after C+ are in the series K337 - K422.

| 1983-1985 | | $1,700 | $2,100 |
| 1983-1985 | White tolex | $1,800 | $2,200 |

Mark III Amp Head
1985-1999. 100 watts, black vinyl.

| 1985-1990 | | $675 | $825 |
| 1990-1999 | Graphic EQ model | $700 | $850 |

Mark III 1x12 Cabinet
Late-1980s-early-1990s. Typically sized 1x12" extension cab with open half back, black vinyl, black grille, not strictly for Mark III, usable for any Boogie with matching output specs, rated for 90 watts.

| 1988-1990s | | $325 | $400 |

Mark III 4x12 Cabinet
Late-1980s-early-1990s. Half stack 4x12" slant cab with open half back or straight-front cab, not strictly for Mark III, usable for any Boogie with matching output specs, often loaded with Celestion Vintage 30s, small weave grille (not see-thru crossing strips).

| 1988-1990s | Slant or straight | $675 | $750 |

Mark III Combo Amp
Mar. 1985-Feb. 1999. Serial numbers: 15,000 - 28,384. 300 series serialization K500- . Graphic equalizer only Mark III since Aug.'90, 100 watts, 1x12" combo. Custom cover or exotic hardwood cab will bring more than standard vinyl cover cab.

1985-1990	Black	$800	$1,000
1985-1990	Custom color	$1,000	$1,250
1985-1991	Custom hardwood cab	$1,200	$1,500
1990-1999	Graphic EQ, hardwood cab	$1,300	$1,600
1990-1999	Graphic EQ, standard cab	$800	$1,000

Mark IV Head and Half Stack Amp Set
1991-2007. Mark IV head and matching 4x12" slant half stack cab.

| 1991-2007 | | $1,575 | $1,800 |

Mark IV/Mark IV B Combo Amp
May 1990-2007. Changed to Model IV B Feb.'95, serial numbers: IV001. Clean rhythm, crunch rhythm and lead modes, 40 watts, EQ, 3-spring reverb, dual effects loops, digital footswitching.

1991-1999		$1,275	$1,500
1991-1999	Custom hardwood cab	$1,500	$1,850
2000-2007		$1,275	$1,500
2000-2007	Custom hardwood cab	$1,600	$2,000

Mark IV (Rack mount) Amp Head
1999-2007.

| 1999-2007 | | $1,300 | $1,350 |

Maverick Amp Head
1994-Feb. 2005. 35 watts, Dual Rectifier head, white/blond vinyl cover.

| 1994-2005 | | $700 | $800 |

Maverick Half Stack Amp Set
Apr. 1994-2004. Serial numbers: MAV001- . 35 watts, Dual Rectifier head and half stack cab set.

| 1994-2004 | | $1,200 | $1,300 |

Maverick Combo Amp
1997-Feb. 2005. Dual channels, 4 EL84s, 35 watts, 1x12" or 2x12" combo amp, 5AR4 tube rectifier, cream vinyl covering. Serial number: MAV. Also available as head.

| 1997-2005 | 1x12" | $700 | $800 |
| 1997-2005 | 2x12" | $750 | $850 |

M-Pulse 360 Amp
Jul. 2001-2005. Serial numbers: MP3-01- . Rack mount, silver panel.

| 2001-2003 | | $675 | $725 |

M-Pulse 600 Amp
Apr. 2001-present. Serial numbers: MP6-01- . Rack mount bass with 600 watts, tube preamp.

| 2001-2004 | | $825 | $875 |

Nomad 45 Amp Head
1999-Feb. 2005. 45 watts, dark vinyl cover, dark grille.

| 1999-2005 | | $650 | $750 |

Nomad 45 Combo Amp
Jul. 1999-Feb. 2005. Serial numbers: NM45-01. 45 watts, 1x12, 2x12" or 4x10" combo, dark vinyl cover, dark grille.

1999-2005	1x12"	$650	$750
1999-2005	2x12"	$700	$800
1999-2005	4x10"	$750	$850

Nomad 55 Amp Head
1999-2004. 55 watt head only.

| 1999-2004 | | $850 | $900 |

Nomad 55 Combo Amp
Jul. 1999-2004. Serial numbers: NM55-01. 55 watts, 1x12", 2x12" or 4x10" combo.

| 1999-2004 | 1x12" | $850 | $900 |
| 1999-2004 | 2x12" | $800 | $1,000 |

Nomad 100 Amp Head
Jul. 1999-Feb. 2005. 100 watts, black cover, black grille.

| 1999-2005 | | $900 | $1,000 |

Nomad 100 Combo Amp
Jul. 1999-Feb. 2005. 100 watts, 1x12" or 2x12" combo, black cover, black grille.

| 1999-2005 | 1x12" | $900 | $1,000 |
| 1999-2005 | 2x12" | $950 | $1,100 |

Powerhouse Series Bass Cabinets
2004-present.

2004-2007	1x15", 400 watts	$450	$550
2004-2007	2x10", 600 watts	$500	$600
2004-2007	4x10", 600 watts	$550	$650

Princeton Boost Fender Conversion
1970. Fender Princeton modified by Randall Smith, Boogie badge logo instead of the Fender blackface logo on upper left corner of the grille. About 300 amps were modified and were one of the early mods that became Mesa-Boogie.

| 1970 | | $2,100 | $2,600 |

AMPS

MODEL YEAR	FEATURES	EXC. COND. LOW	HIGH
Quad Preamp			
Sep. 1987-1992. Serial numbers: Q001-Q2857. Optional Quad with FU2-A footswitch Aug.'90-Jan.'92, serial numbers: Q2022 - Q2857.			
1987-1992	Without footswitch	$500	$575
1990-1992	With footswitch	$625	$675
Recto Recording Preamp			
2004-present. Rack mount preamp.			
2004-2006		$800	$850
Rect-O-Verb I Amp Head			
Dec. 1998-2001. Serial numbers: R50-. 50 watts, head with 2 6L6 power tubes, upgraded Apr.'01 to II Series.			
1998-2001		$750	$850
Rect-O-Verb/Recto Cabinet			
1998-2001. Slant front 4x12" or 2x12" option cab, black cover, dark grille.			
1998-2001	2x12" option	$450	$525
1998-2001	4x12" slant front	$550	$650
Rect-O-Verb Combo Amp			
Dec. 1998-2001. Serial numbers R50-. 50 watts, 1x12", black vinyl cover, black grille.			
1998-2001		$850	$950
Rect-O-Verb II Amp Head			
Apr. 2001-present. Upgrade, serial number R5H-750.			
2001-2006		$750	$850
Rect-O-Verb II Combo Amp			
April 2001-present. Upgrade R5H-750, 50 watts, AB, 2 6L6, spring reverb.			
2001-2005		$950	$1,100
Road King Dual Rectifier Amp Head			
2002-present. Tube head, various power tube selections based upon a chasis which uses 2 EL34s and 4 6L6, 2 5U4 dual rectifier tubes or silicon diode rectifiers, 50, 100 or 120 watts. Series II upgrades start in '06.			
2002-2006		$2,000	$2,300
Road King Combo Amp			
2002-present. 2x12" combo version, Series II upgrades start in '06.			
2002-2005	Select watts	$1,750	$2,100
2006-2007	Series II	$1,750	$2,100
RoadReady Bass Cabinets			
1994-present. Heavy-duty road case bass cabinets with metal grilles, casters and metal corners.			
1994-2005	1x15"	$375	$450
1994-2005	2x12"	$475	$550
Rocket 440 Amp			
Mar. 1999-Aug. 2000. Serial numbers: R440-R44-1159. 45 watts, 4x10".			
1999-2000		$500	$600
Satellite/Satellite 60 Amp			
Aug. 1990-1999. Serial numbers: ST001-ST841. Uses either 6L6s for 100 watts or EL34s for 60 watts, dark vinyl, dark grille.			
1990-1999		$450	$600
Solo 50 Rectifier Series I Amp Head			
Nov. 1998-Apr. 2001. Serial numbers: R50. 50-watt head.			
1998-2001		$800	$900

MODEL YEAR	FEATURES	EXC. COND. LOW	HIGH
Solo 50 Rectifier Series II Amp Head			
Apr.2001-present. Upgrade, serial numbers: S50-S1709. Upgrades preamp section, head with 50 watts.			
2001-2005		$875	$975
Son Of Boogie Amp			
May 1982-Dec. 1985. Serial numbers: S100-S2390. 60 watts, 1x12", considered the first reissue of the original Mark I.			
1982-1985		$675	$725
Stereo 290 (Simul 2-Ninety) Amp			
Jun. 1992-present. Serial numbers: R0001- . Dual 90-watt stereo channels, rack mount.			
1992-2004		$700	$800
Stereo 295 Amp			
Mar. 1987-May 1991. Serial numbers: S001-S2673. Dual 95-watt class A/B stereo channels, rack mount. Selectable 30 watts Class A (EL34 power tubes) power.			
1987-1991		$600	$725
Stilleto Series Amp Heads			
2004-present. Series includes the Deuce (50 or 100 watts, 4 EL-34s) and Trident (50 or 150 watts, 6 EL-34s).			
2004-2006	Deuce\Trident	$1,075	$1,200
Strategy 400 Amp			
Mar. 1987-May 1991. Serial numbers: S001-S2627. 400 to 500 watts, power amplifier with 12 6L6 power tubes.			
1987-1991		$800	$925
Strategy 500 Amp			
Jun. 1991-Apr. 1992. S2,552- . Rack mount, 500 watts, 4 6550 power tubes.			
1991-1992		$850	$975
Studio .22/Studio .22+ Amp			
Nov. 1985-1988. Serial numbers: SS000-SS11499, black vinyl, black grille, 22 watts, 1x12". Replaced by .22+ Dec. '88-Aug. '93. Serial numbers: FP11,500 - FP28,582. 22 watts.			
1985-1988	.22	$475	$575
1988-1993	.22+	$475	$575
Studio Caliber DC-2 Amp			
Apr. 1994-Jan. 1999. Serial numbers: DC2-01 - DC2-4247 (formerly called DC-2). 20 watts, 1x12" combo, dark vinyl, dark grille.			
1994-1999		$500	$625
Studio Preamp			
Aug. 1988-Dec. 1993. Serial numbers: SP000-SP7890. Tube preamp, EQ, reverb, effects loop.			
1988-1993		$400	$500
Subway/Subway Blues Amp			
Sep. 1994-Aug. 2000. Serial numbers: SB001-SB2515. 20 watts, 1x10".			
1994-2000		$500	$625
Subway Reverb Rocket Amp			
Jun. 1998-Aug. 2001. Serial numbers: RR1000-RR2461. 20 watts, 1x10".			
1998-2001		$500	$625
Subway Rocket (Non-Reverb) Amp			
Jan. 1996-Jul. 1998. Serial numbers: SR001-SR2825. No reverb, 20 watts, 1x10".			
1996-1998		$450	$500

Mesa-Boogie
Road king

Mesa-Boogie
Solo 50

Mesa-Boogie
Son of Boogie combo

Meteoro Bass Head

Mission Aurora Reverb

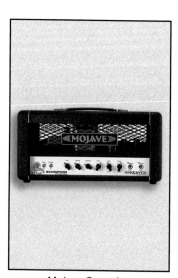

Mojave Scorpion

MODEL YEAR	FEATURES	EXC. COND. LOW	HIGH
Trem-O-Verb Dual Rectifier Amp Head			
Jun. 1993-Jan. 2001. 100-watt head version.			
1993-2001		$1,050	$1,200
1993-2001	Rackmount version	$1,000	$1,150
Trem-O-Verb Dual Rectifier Cabinet			
Late-1980s-early-1990s. Half stack 4x12" slant cab with open half back, or straight-front cab, 2x12" straight-front option, not strictly for this model, useable for any Boogie with matching output specs, often loaded with Celestion Vintage 30s, small weave grille (not see-thru crossing strips).			
1988-1990s	2x12" straight	$550	$600
1988-1990s	4x12" slant or straight	$650	$700
Trem-O-Verb Dual Rectifier Half Stack Amp			
Jun.1993-Jan.2001. 100 watts, head with matching 4x12" slant cab.			
1993-2001		$1,950	$2,200
Trem-O-Verb Dual Rectifier Combo Amp			
Jun.1993-Jan.2001. Serial numbers: R- to about R-21210. 100 watts, 2x12" Celestion Vintage 30.			
1993-2001		$1,100	$1,300
Triaxis Preamp			
Oct. 1991-present. Serial numbers:T0001-. 5 12AX7 tube preamp, rack mount.			
1991-2005		$1,000	$1,200
Triple Rectifier Amp Head			
1997-present. Three-channel amp head.			
1997-2006		$1,250	$1,350
V-Twin Rackmount Amp			
May 1995-Jun. 1998. Serial numbers: V2R-001 to V2R-2258.			
1995-1998		$400	$425
Walk About M-Pulse Bass Amp Head			
Sep. 2001-present. Serial numbers: WK-01-. Lightweight 13 pounds, 2 12AX7s + 300 MOS-FET.			
2001-2005		$650	$775

Meteoro

1986-present. Guitar, bass, harp and keyboard combo amps, heads, and cabinets built in Brazil. They also build effects.

Metropoulos Amplification

2004-present. George Metropoulos builds his professional and premium grade amps in Flint, Michigan.

MG

2004-present. Tube combo guitar amps built by Marcelo Giangrande in São Paulo, Brazil. He also builds effects.

Mission Amps

1996-present. Bruce Collins' Mission Amps, located in Arvada, Colorado, produces a line of custom-made combo amps, heads, and cabinets.

Mojave Amp Works

2002-present. Tube amp heads and speaker cabinets by Victor Mason in Apple Valley, California.

Montgomery Ward

Amps for this large retailer were sometimes branded as Montgomery Ward, but usually as Airline (see that listing).

Lower Power 1x12" Combo Amp

1950s. 1x12" speaker, around 12 watts, includes Model 8439.

	EXC. COND. LOW	HIGH
1950s	$200	$225

Higher Power 1x12" Combo Amp

1950s. 1x12", about 2 6L6 power tubes, includes brown covered Maestro C Series with cloverleaf grille.

	EXC. COND. LOW	HIGH
1950s	$200	$250

Mooneyes

Budget solid state amp line from Lace Music Products. They also offer amps under the Rat Fink and Lace brands. Lace has a Mooneyes guitar model line.

Morley

Late-1960s-present. The effects company offered an amp in the late '70s. See Effects section for more company info.

Bigfoot Amp

1979-ca.1981. Looks like Morley's '70s effects pedals, produced 25 watts and pedal controlled volume. Amp only, speakers were sold separately.

	EXC. COND. LOW	HIGH
1979-1981	$150	$175

Mosrite

1968-1969. Mosrite jumped into the amp business during the last stages of the company history, the company was founded as a guitar company in 1954 and attained national fame in the '60s but by the time the company entered the amp business, the guitar boom began to fade, forcing the original Mosrite out of business in '69.

Model 400 Fuzzrite Amp

1968-1969. Solidstate, 1x15 combo, black tolex with silver grille, reverb and tremolo, large M and Mosrite logo on front panel as well as Fuzzrite and Model 400 designation.

	EXC. COND. LOW	HIGH
1968-1969	$350	$750

Mountain

Mountain builds a 9-volt amp in a wood cabinet. Originally built in California, then Nevada; currently being made in Vancouver, Canada.

Multivox

Ca.1946-ca.1984. Multivox was started as a subsidiary of Premier to manufacture amps, and later, effects. Generally student grade to low intermediate grade amps.

MODEL YEAR	FEATURES	EXC. COND. LOW	HIGH

Murph

1965-1967. Amps marketed by Murph Guitars of San Fernado, California. At first they were custom-made tube amps, but most were later solidstate production models made by another manufacturer.

Music Man

1972-present. Music Man made amps from '73 to '83. The number preceding the amp model indicates the speaker configuration. The last number in model name usually referred to the watts. RD indicated Reverb Distortion. RP indicated Reverb Phase. Many models were available in head-only versions and as combos with various speaker combinations.

Sixty Five Amp
1973-1981. Head amp, 65 watts, reverb, tremolo.

1973-1981		$325	$350

110 RD Fifty Amp
1980-1983. 50 watts, 1x10", reverb, distortion.

| 1980-1983 | | $500 | $525 |

112 RD Fifty Amp
1980-1983. 50 watts, 1x12", reverb, distortion.

| 1980-1983 | | $525 | $550 |

112 RD Sixty Five Amp
1978-1983. 65 watts, 1x12", reverb, distortion.

| 1978-1983 | | $525 | $550 |

112 RD One Hundred Amp
1978-1983. 100 watts, 1x12", reverb, distortion.

| 1978-1983 | | $550 | $625 |

112 RP Sixty Five Amp
1978-1983. 65 watts, 1x12", reverb, built-in phaser.

| 1978-1983 | | $400 | $500 |

112 RP One Hundred Amp
1978-1983. Combo amp, 100 watts, 1x12", reverb, built-in phaser.

| 1978-1983 | | $400 | $500 |

112 Sixty Five Amp
1973-1981. Combo amp, 65 watts, 1x12", reverb, tremolo.

| 1973-1981 | | $500 | $525 |

115 Sixty Five Amp
1973-1981. Combo amp, 65 watts, 1x15", reverb, tremolo.

| 1973-1981 | | $400 | $500 |

210 HD130 Amp
1973-1981. 130 watts, 2x10", reverb, tremolo.

| 1973-1981 | | $500 | $600 |

210 Sixty Five Amp
1973-1981. 65 watts, 2x10", reverb, tremolo.

| 1973-1981 | | $500 | $600 |

212 HD130 Amp
1973-1981. 130 watts, 2x12", reverb, tremolo.

| 1973-1981 | | $500 | $600 |

212 Sixty Five Amp
1973-1981. 65 watts, 2x12", reverb, tremolo.

| 1973-1981 | | $500 | $600 |

410 Sixty Five Amp
1973-1981. 65 watts, 4x10", reverb, tremolo.

| 1973-1981 | | $500 | $600 |

410 Seventy Five Amp
1982-1983. 75 watts, 4x10", reverb, tremolo.

| 1982-1983 | | $500 | $600 |

HD-130 Amp
1973-1981. Head amp, 130 watts, reverb, tremolo.

| 1973-1981 | | $550 | $650 |

RD Fifty Amp
1980-1983. Head amp, 50 watts, reverb, distortion.

| 1980-1983 | | $325 | $350 |

Nady

1976-present. Wireless sound company Nady Systems started offering tube combo and amp heads in '06.

National

Ca.1927-present. National/Valco amps date back to the late-'30s. National introduced a modern group of amps about the same time they introduced their new Res-O-Glas space-age guitar models in '62. In '64, the amp line was partially redesigned and renamed. By '68, the Res-O-Glas models were gone and National introduced many large vertical and horizontal piggy-back models which lasted until National's assets were assigned during bankruptcy in '69. The National name went to Chicago importer Strum N' Drum. Initially, Strum N' Drum had one amp, the National GA 950 P Tremolo/Reverb piggyback.

Bass 70/Bass 75 Amp
1962-1967. 35 watts (per channel), 2x12" (often Jensen) speakers, large control knobs, large National script logo on front control panel, Raven Black tolex with silver and white grille, designed for bass. New model name in '64 with nearly identical features but listed as total of 70 watts, in '62 called Bass 70 but renamed Bass 75 in '64.

| 1962-1963 | Bass 70 | $600 | $700 |
| 1964-1967 | Bass 75 N6475B | $600 | $700 |

Chicago 51 Aztec/Valco Amp
Late-1940s-early-1950s. Low- to mid-power, 2x6L6, 3 oval Rola speakers, 3 baffle openings (1 for each speaker), tweed cover.

| 1940-1950s | | $500 | $725 |

Chicago/Valco 51 Amp
1950s. Vertical tweed cabinet, metal preamps tubes, late-1940s-early-'50s technology, 1x12".

| 1950s | | $500 | $725 |

Dynamic 20 Amp
1962-1963. 17 watts, 2x8" (often Jensen) speakers, two large control knobs, large National script logo on front control panel, Raven Black tolex with silver and white grille, compact student-intermediate amp.

| 1962-1963 | | $550 | $650 |

Glenwood 90 Amp
1962-1967. 35 watts, 2x12" (often Jensen) speakers, large control knobs, large National script logo on front control panel, reverb and tremolo, Raven Black tolex with silver and white grille, top of the line, becomes the nearly identical N6490TR in '64.

| 1964-1963 | | $1,000 | $1,200 |
| 1964-1967 | Model N6490TR | $900 | $1,100 |

Music Man 410 Sixty Five

Nady GTA-1060

National Glenwood 90

AMPS

Naylor Super-Drive Sixty

Nemesis NC-115

Nobels SM-15 Streetman

MODEL YEAR	FEATURES	EXC. COND. LOW	HIGH

Glenwood Vibrato Amp
1964-1967. 70 watts, 2x12", vibrato and reverb.

| 1964-1967 | Model N6499VR | $800 | $900 |

Model 75 Amp
1940s. Vertical tweed combo cabinet, volume and tone knobs, 3 inputs.

| 1940s | | $450 | $500 |

Model 100 Amp
1940. Tube amp, 40 watts, 1x12".

| 1940 | | $450 | $500 |

Model GA 950-P Tremolo/Reverb Piggyback Amp
1970s. Strum N' Drum/National model, solidstate, 50 watts, 2-channel 2x12" and 1x7" in 32" tall vertical cabinet, black.

| 1970s | | $150 | $250 |

Model N6800 - N6899 Piggyback Amps
1968-1969. National introduced a new line of tube amps in '68 and most of them were piggybacks. The N6895 was sized like a Fender piggyback Tremolux, the N6875 and N6878 bass amps were sized like a '68 Fender large cab piggyback with a 26" tall vertical cab, the N6898 and N6899 were the large piggyback guitar amps. These amps feature the standard Jensen speakers or the upgrade JBL speakers, the largest model was the N6800 for PA or guitar, which sported 3x70-watt channels and 2 column speakers using a bass 2x12" + 1x3" horn cab and a voice-guitar 4x10" + 1x3" horn cab.

| 1968-1969 | | $375 | $475 |

Model N6816 (Model 16) Amp
1968-1969. Valco-made tube amp, 6 watts, 1x10" Jensen speaker, 17" vertical cab, tremolo, no reverb, black vinyl cover and Coppertone grille, National spelled out on front panel.

| 1968-1969 | | $300 | $350 |

Model N6820 Thunderball Bass Amp
1968-1969. Valco-made tube amp, about 35 watts, 1x15" Jensen speaker, 19" vertical cab, black vinyl cover and Coppertone grille, National spelled out on front panel.

| 1968-1969 | | $350 | $425 |

Model N6822 (Model 22) Amp
1968-1969. Valco-made, 6 watts tube (4 tubes) amp, 1x12" Jensen speaker, 19" vertical cab, tremolo and reverb, black vinyl cover and Coppertone grille, National spelled out on front panel.

| 1968-1969 | | $350 | $425 |

National Dobro Amp
1930s. Sold by the National Dobro Corp. when the company was still in Los Angeles (they later moved to Chicago). National Dobro plate on rear back panel, suitcase style case that flips open to reveal the speaker and amp, National logo on outside of suitcase. The noted price is for an all-original amp in excellent condition (this would be a rare find), there are other 1930s models included in the price range below.

1930s	Early metal baffle	$500	$600
1930s	Later standard baffle	$450	$500
1930s	Suitcase style	$450	$700

Newport 40 Amp
1964-1967. 17 watts, 2x10", tremolo only.

| 1964-1967 | Model N6440T | $600 | $700 |

Newport 50 Amp
1964-1967. 17 watts, 2x10", tremolo and reverb.

| 1964-1967 | Model N6450TR | $700 | $800 |

Newport 97 Amp
1964-1967. 35 watts, 1x15", rear mounted chasis, tremolo.

| 1964-1967 | Model N6497T | $600 | $700 |

Sportman Amp

| 1950s | 1x10 | $425 | $575 |

Student Practice Amp
1970s. Strum N' Drum era, small solidstate, single control.

| 1970s | | $25 | $35 |

Studio 10 Amp
1962-1967. Five watts, 1x8", 3 tubes, 1 channel, 1 volume control, no tone control, no reverb or tremolo.

| 1962-1963 | | $350 | $450 |
| 1964-1967 | Model N6410 | $350 | $450 |

Tremo-Tone Model 1224 Amp
1956-1959. Small combo, tremolo, dual Rola oval 6x11" speakers, tweed, by Valco, National script logo, flying bird pattern on lower front grille.

| 1956-1959 | | $800 | $1,000 |

Val-Pro 80 Amp
1962-1963. 35 watts, 2x12" (often Jensen) speakers, 8 tubes, large control knobs, tremolo, black cover with white and silver trim, replaced by Glenwood 90 in '64 with added reverb.

| 1962-1963 | | $1,000 | $1,100 |

Val-Trem 40 Amp
1962-1963. 17 watts, 2x10" (often Jensen) speakers, large control knobs, large National script logo on front control panel, Val-Trem logo on back panel, Clear-Wave tremolo, Raven Black tolex with silver and white grille, open back combo amp, becomes Newport 40 in '64.

| 1962-1963 | | $850 | $1,000 |

Val-Verb 60 Amp
1962-1963. 17 watts, 2x10" (often Jensen) speakers, large control knobs, large National script logo on front control panel, Val-Verb logo on back panel, reverb, no tremolo, Raven Black tolex with silver and white grille, open back combo amp.

| 1962-1963 | | $900 | $1,100 |

Westwood 16 Amp
1964-1967. Five watts using 1 6V6 power, 2 12AX7 preamp, 1 5Y3GT rectifier, tremolo, 2x8", dark vinyl cover, silver grille.

| 1964-1967 | Model N6416T | $400 | $500 |

Westwood 22 Amp
1964-1967. 5 watts, 2x8", reverb and tremolo, 1 channel, 6 tubes.

| 1964-1967 | Model N6422TR | $500 | $600 |

MODEL YEAR	FEATURES	EXC. COND. LOW	HIGH

Naylor Engineering

1994-present. Joe Naylor and Kyle Kurtz founded the company in East Pointe, Michigan, in the early '90s, selling J.F. Naylor speakers. In '94 they started producing amps. In '96, Naylor sold his interest in the business to Kurtz and left to form Reverend Guitars. In '99 David King bought the company and moved it to Los Angeles, California, then to Dallas, Texas. Currently Naylor builds tube amps, combos, speakers, and cabinets.

Nemesis

From the makers of Eden amps, Nemesis is a line of made-in-the-U.S., FET powered bass combos and extension cabinets. The brand is a division of U.S. Music Corp.

Nobels

1997-present. Effects manufacturer Nobels Electronics of Hamburg, Germany also offers a line of small practice and portable amps.

Noble

Ca. 1950-ca. 1969. From Don Noble and Company, of Chicago, Illinois, owned by Strum N' Drum by mid-'60s. They also offered guitars and amps.

Mid-Size Tube Amp
1950s. Low- to mid-power tube amp, Noble logo on front.

1950s		$350	$525

Norma

1965-1970. Economy line imported and distributed by Strum N' Drum, Wheeling (Chicago), Illinois. As noted in the National section, Strum N' Drum acquired the National brand in the '70s. Some early amps were tube, but the majority were solidstate.

GA-93 Amp
1969-1970. 6 watts, 1x6".

1969-1970		$55	$75

GA-97 T Amp
1969-1970. 13 watts, 1x8", tremolo.

1969-1970		$60	$85

GA-725 B Amp
1969-1970. Bass amp, 38 watts, 1x10".

1969-1970		$60	$85

GA-918 T Amp
1969-1970. 24 watts, 1x12", tremolo and reverb.

1969-1970		$70	$95

GA-930 P (Piggyback) Amp
1969-1970. 40 watts, 2x12", piggyback.

1969-1970		$80	$125

GA-6240 Amp
1969-1970. 50 watts.

1969-1970		$80	$125

GAP-2 Amp
1969-1970. 3 watts, 1x4".

1969-1970		$55	$75

Oahu

The Oahu Publishing Company and Honolulu Conservatory, based in Cleveland, Ohio, started with acoustic Hawaiian and Spanish guitars, selling large quantities in the 1930s. As electric models became popular, Oahu responded with guitar/amp sets. The brand has been revived on a line of U.S.-made tube amps.

Small Guitar/Lap Steel Amps
1940s-1950s. Various colors

1940-1950s		$275	$450

Oliver

Ca.1966-ca. 1978. The Oliver Sound Company, Westbury, New York, was founded by former Ampeg engineer, Jess Oliver, after he left Ampeg in '65. Tube amp designs were based upon Oliver's work at Ampeg. The Oliver Powerflex Amp is the best-known design, and featured an elevator platform that would lift the amp head out of the speaker cabinet.

Model B-120 Amp Head
1970s. B-120 logo on front panel, 35 watts, all tube head.

1970s		$375	$425

Model G-150R Combo Amp
2 6L6 power tubes, reverb, tremolo, black tolex with black grille, silver control panel, 40 watts, 1x15".

1970s		$525	$600

Model P-500 Combo Amp
All tube combo with 15" motorized amp chassis that rises out of tall lateral speaker cabinet as amp warms up.

1960s		$625	$700

Orbital Power Projector Amp
Late-1960s-early-1970s. Rotating speaker cabinet with horn, Leslie-like voice.

1970s		$625	$700

Sam Ash Oliver Amp Head
Late-1960s-early-1970s. Private branded for Sam Ash Music, about 30 watts using the extinct 7027A power tubes, Sam Ash script logo on front grille.

1960s		$225	$300

Orange

1968-1981, 1995-present. Orange amps and PAs were made in England by Cliff Cooper and Matthew Mathias. The Orange-colored amps were well-built and were used by many notable guitarists. Since '95, Cliff Cooper is once again making Orange amplifiers in England, with the exception of the small Crush Practice Combo amps, which are made in Korea.

Model OR-80 Amp w/4x12 Bottom
1968-1981. 80 watts, 4x12" straight-front cab with Orange crest on grille, orange vinyl and light orange grille.

1968-1981		$2,700	$2,900

Model OR-80 Combo Amp
1968-1981. About 80 watts, 2x12" combo.

1968-1981		$2,300	$2,500

Oahu Holiday

AMPS

Ca. 1950 Oahu 230K Tone Master

Overbuilt Napoleon

AMPS

Palette 1X15 Combo

Park G10

1970s Park 50-watt Lead

MODEL YEAR	FEATURES	EXC. COND. LOW	HIGH

Model OR-120 Graphic Amp Head
1968-1981. 120 watt head only.

1968-1981		$1,900	$2,100

Model OR-120 Graphic Amp Head and Half Stack
1968-1981. 120 watts, 4x12" straight front cab with Orange crest on grille, orange vinyl and light orange grille.

1968-1981		$2,900	$3,300

Model OR-200 212 Twin Amp
1970s. 120 watts, 2x12" combo, orange vinyl, dark grille, Orange crest on grille, reverb and vibrato, master volume.

1970s		$2,400	$2,800

Orpheum
Late-1950s-1960s. Student to medium level amps from New York's Maurice Lipsky Music.

Small/Mid-Size Amps
Late-1950s-1960s. U.S.-made, 2 6V6 power tubes, Jensen P12R 12" speaker, light cover with gray swirl grille.

1959		$200	$225

Ovation
1966-present. Kaman made few amps under the Ovation name. They offered a variety of amps under the KMD brand from '85 to around '94.

Little Dude Amp
1969-ca.1971. Solidstate combo, 100 watts, 1x15" and horn, matching slave unit also available.

1970s		$175	$200

The Kat (Model 6012) Amp
1970s. Solidstate, 2x12" combo.

1970s		$175	$200

Overbuilt Amps
1999-2007. Tube amps and combos built by Richard Seccombe in West Hills, California. He nows works at Fender R&D.

PAC-AMP (Magnatone)
Late-1950s-early-1960s. Private branded by Magnatone, often for accordion studios.

Model 280-A Amp
1961-1963. About 50 watts, 2x12" + 2x5", brown leatherette, light brown grille, stereo vibrato, PAC-AMP nameplate logo.

1961-1963		$900	$1,000

Palette Amps
2003-present. Robert Wakeling builds his tube amp heads and combos and speaker cabinets in Stillwater, Oklahoma.

PANaramic (Magnatone)
1961-1963. Private branded equivalent of '61-'63 Magnatone brown leatherette series, large PANaramic logo. Many Magnatone private brands were associated with accordion companies or accordian teaching studios. PANaramic was a brand name of

PANaramic accordion. They also made guitars.

Audio Guild Ultraflex Amp
1968. Vertical cabinet, pre-amp tubes, 1x12, 1x8.

1968		$125	$150

Model 260/262-style Amp
1961-1963. 35 watts, 2x12", gray vinyl and light grille, vibrato, large PANaramic logo.

1961-1963		$900	$1,000

Model 413-style Amp
1961-1963. 18 watts, 1x12", black leatherette cover, light silver grille, vibrato, large PANaramic logo.

1961-1963		$600	$700

Model 450-style Amp
1961-1963. 20 watts, 1x12", reverb and vibrato, reverb not generally included in an early-'60s 1x12" Magnatone amp, dark vinyl, dark cross-threaded grille, large PANaramic logo.

1961-1963		$900	$1,100

Paris
Master Series Amps
1960s. Compact solid-state combo, 1x12", slanted Paris logo front upper left side of grille, black tolex-style cover, silver grille (like Fender blackface), rear mounted slanted control panel.

1960s		$100	$125

Park
1965-1982, 1992-2000. Park amps were made by Marshall from '65 to '82. Park logo on front with elongated P. In the '90s, Marshall revived the name for use on small solidstate amps imported from the Far East.

G Series Amp
1992-2000. Student compact amps, models include G-10 (10 watts, 1x8"), G-25R (25w, reverb), G-215R (15w, 2x8") and GB-25 (25w, 1x12" bass).

1990s	G-10	$40	$50
1990s	G-25R	$45	$55
1990s	G-215R	$80	$95
1990s	GB-25	$45	$55

Model 75 Amp Head
1967-1971. Head amp, 50 watts, 2xKT88s, small-box plexi (later aluminum), black tolex.

1967-1969	Plexi	$4,500	$5,600
1969-1971	Aluminum	$3,300	$4,100

Model 75 1960 4x12 Slant Cabinet
Early 1970s. Similar to Marshall 1960 4x12" cab.

1970-1971		$1,950	$2,100

Model 1206 50-Watt Amp Head
1981-1982. 50 watts, based upon JCM 800 50-watt made at the same time period.

1981-1982		$850	$1,100

Model 1212 50-Watt 2x12 Combo

1970s		$1,800	$2,000

Model 1213 100-Watt Reverb Combo Amp
1970s. 100 watts, 2x12", reverb, dark vinyl, light grille.

1970s		$2,100	$2,300

MODEL YEAR	FEATURES	EXC. COND. LOW	HIGH

Model 1228 50-Watt Lead Amp Head
1970s. 50 watts, based upon Marshall 50-watt made at the same time period.

1970s		$2,000	$2,200

Model 2046 25-Watt Combo Amp
1970s. 25 watts, 1x15", '70s era blue grille cloth, black tolex, large P Park logo upper center of grille.

1970s		$1,800	$2,000

Paul Reed Smith
1985-present. In the late '80s, PRS offered two amp models. Only 350 amp units shipped. Includes HG-70 Head and HG-212 Combo. HG stands for Harmonic Generator, effectively a non-tube, solid-state amp.

4x12" Straight-Front Cabinet
1989. Straight-front 4x12" black vinyl cab with silver grille, PRS logo front lower right of grille.

1989		$500	$575

HG-70 Amp Head
1989-1990. 70 watts, reverb, effects loop, noise gate. Options include 150-watt circuitry and 4x12" straight and slant cabinets, gray-black.

1989		$500	$575

HG-212 Amp
1989-1990. Combo, 70 watts, 2x12", reverb, effects loop, noise gate. Options include 150-watt circuitry and 4x12" straight and slant cabinets, gray-black.

1989		$575	$650

Peavey
1965-present. Hartley Peavey's first products were guitar amps. He added guitars to the mix in '78. Headquartered in Meridan, Mississippi, Peavey continues to offer a huge variety of guitars, amps, and PAs.

5150 EVH Head/Cabinet Amp Set
1995-2004. Half stack 5150 head and 4x12" cab, large 5150 logo on front of amp.

1995	Head and cab	$1,100	$1,200
1995	Head only	$650	$775
1996-2004	Cab only	$350	$375
1996-2004	Head and cab	$1,000	$1,100
1996-2004	Head only	$625	$700

5150 212 Combo Amp
1995-2004. Combo version of 5150 head, 60 watts, 2x12", large 5150 logo on front panel, small Peavey logo on lower right of grille.

1995-2004		$600	$700

Alphabass Amp
1988-1990. Rack mount all tube, 160 watts, EQ, includes 2x15" Black Widow or 2x12" Scorpion cabinet.

1988-1990		$300	$350

Artist Amp
Introduced in 1975 as 120 watts, 1x12", bright and normal channels, EQ, reverb, master volume.

1970s		$225	$275

Artist 110 Amp
TransTubes, 10 watts.

1990s		$125	$150

Artist 250 Amp
1990s. 100 watts, 1x12", solidstate preamp, 4 6L6 power tubes.

1990s		$200	$250

Artist VT Amp
1990s. Combo amp, 120 watts, 1x12".

1990s		$250	$300

Audition Chorus Amp
2x10-watt channels, 2x6", channel switching, post gain and normal gain controls.

1980s		$100	$125

Audition Plus Amp
1980s. Solidstate, 20 watts, 1x10".

1980s		$65	$75

Audition 20 Amp
1980s-1990s. 20 watts, single speaker combo.

1980-1990s		$50	$60

Audition 30 Amp
1980s-1990s. 30 watts, 1x12" combo amp, channel switching.

1980-1990s		$55	$65

Audition 110 Amp
1990s. 25 watts, 1x10" combo, 2 channels.

1990s		$65	$75

Backstage Amp
1977-mid-1980s. Master gain control, 18 watts, 1x10", 3-band EQ. Name reused in 2000s on small 6.5" speaker, 10 watt amp.

1977-1984		$40	$50

Backstage 30 Amp
30 watts, 1x8".

1980s		$50	$60

Backstage 110 Amp
Repackaged and revoiced in 1988, 65 watts, 1x10", Peavey SuperSat preamp circuitry, new power sections.

1980s		$65	$75

Backstage Chorus 208 Amp
1990s. 150 watts, 2x8", reverb, channel switching.

1990s		$100	$125

Backstage Plus Amp
1980s. 35 watts, 1x10" combo, reverb, saturation effect.

1980s		$65	$75

Bandit 75 Amp
Redesigned and renamed Bandit 112 in 1988. Channel switching, 75 watts, 1x12", 4-band EQ, reverb, post-effects loop, Superstat.

1980s		$175	$200

Bandit 112/Bandit II 112 Amp
1988-present. 80 watts, 1x12", active EQ circuit for lead channel, active controls.

1980s	Bandit	$200	$225
1990s	Bandit II	$225	$250
2000s	Bandit 112	$250	$275

Basic 40 Amp
1980s. 40 watts, 1x12".

1980s		$100	$125

PRS HG-212

Peavey 5150 2x12"

Peavey Bandit

AMPS

To get the most from this book, be sure to read "Using *The Guide*" in the introduction.

Peavey Classic 50/410

Peavey Delta Blues

1978 Peavey TNT-100

MODEL YEAR	FEATURES	EXC. COND. LOW	HIGH

Basic 60 Amp
1988-1995. Solidstate combo amp, 50-60 watts, 1x12", 4-band EQ, gain controls, black.

| 1988-1995 | | $150 | $175 |

Basic 112 Bass Amp
1996-2006. 75 watts, 1x12" bass combo, 2000-era red border control panel.

| 1996-2006 | | $150 | $175 |

Blazer 158 Amp
1995-2005. 15 watts, 1x8", clean and distortion, later called the TransTube Blazer III.

| 1995-2005 | | $50 | $75 |

Bluesman Amp
1992. Tweed, 1x12" or 1x15".

| 1992 | | $275 | $300 |

Bravo 112 Amp
1988-1994. All tube reverb, 25 watts, 1x12", 3-band EQ, 2 independent input channels.

| 1988-1994 | | $225 | $250 |

Classic 20 Amp
Small tube amp with 2xEL84 power tubes, 1x10", tweed cover.

| 1990s | | $225 | $250 |

Classic 30 Amp
1994-present. Tweed combo, 30 watts, 1x12", EL84 tubes.

| 1994-2005 | | $300 | $350 |

Classic 50/212 Amp
1990-present. Combo, 50 watt, 2x12", 4 EL84s, 3 12AX7s, reverb, high-gain section.

| 1990-2005 | | $425 | $500 |

Classic 50/410 Amp
1990-present. Combo amp, 4x10", EL84 power, reverb, footswitchable high-gain mode.

| 1990s | | $425 | $500 |

Classic 120 Amp
1988-ca.1990. Tube, 120 watts.

| 1988-1990 | | $325 | $350 |

DECA/750 Amp
1989-ca.1990. Digital, 2 channels, 350 watts per channel, distortion, reverb, exciter, pitch shift, multi-EQ.

| 1989-1990 | | $250 | $275 |

Decade Amp
1970s. Practice amp, 10 watts, 1x8", runs on 12 volt or AC.

| 1970s | | $35 | $40 |

Delta Blues Amp
1995-present. 30 watts, tube combo, 4 EL84 tubes, 1x15" or 2x8", tremolo, large-panel-style cab, blond tweed.

| 1995-2005 | | $375 | $400 |

Deuce Amp
1972-1980s. 120 watts, tube amp, 2x12" or 4x10".

| 1972-1980s | | $250 | $275 |

Deuce Head Amp
1972-1980s. Tube head, 120 watts.

| 1972-1980s | | $175 | $200 |

MODEL YEAR	FEATURES	EXC. COND. LOW	HIGH

Ecoustic 112 Amp
1996-present. 100 watts, 1x12", guitar input and mic input, brown vinyl, brown grille. Replaced by 112EFX.

| 1996-2007 | | $175 | $200 |

Encore 65 Amp
1983. 65 watt tube combo amp.

| 1983 | | $175 | $200 |

Envoy 110 Amp
1988-present. Solidstate, 40 watts, 1x10", Trans-Tubes.

| 1988-2006 | | $100 | $125 |

Heritage VTX Amp
1980s. 130 watts, 4 6L6s, solidstate preamp, 2x12" combo.

| 1980s | | $175 | $200 |

Jazz Classic Amp
Solidstate, 210 watts, 1x15", electronic channel switching, 6-spring reverb.

| 1980s | | $175 | $200 |

KB Series Amp
1980s. Keyboard amp, 1x15", models include KB-100 (100 watts), and KB-300 (300 watts, with horn).

| 1980s | KB-100 | $175 | $200 |
| 1980s | KB-300 | $200 | $250 |

LTD Amp
1975-1980s. Solidstate, 200 watts, 1x12" Altec or 1x15" JBL.

| 1975-1982 | | $175 | $200 |

Mace Amp Head
1976-1980s. Tube, 180 watts.

| 1980s | | $250 | $300 |

MegaBass Amp
Rack mount preamp/power amp, 200 watts per 2 channels, solidstate, EQ, effects loop, chorus.

| 1980s | | $225 | $275 |

Microbass Amp
1988-2005. 20 watts, 1x8" practice amp, made in China.

| 1988-2005 | | $45 | $50 |

Minx 110 Bass Amp
1987-2005. Solidstate, 35 watts RMS, 1x10" heavy-duty speaker.

| 1987-2005 | | $100 | $125 |

Musician Amp Head
Introduced in 1965 as 120 watt head, upped to 210 watts in '72.

| 1970s | | $150 | $175 |

Nashville 40 Steel Guitar Amp
1982- 2000. 210 watts, 1x15" solidstate steel guitar combo amp.

| 1982-2000 | | $250 | $300 |

Nashville 1000 Steel Guitar Amp
1998-present. 1x15" speaker, solidstate steel guitar combo amp.

| 1998-2007 | | $250 | $300 |

Pacer Amp
1974-1980s. Master volume, 45 watts, 1x12", 3-band EQ.

| 1974-1985 | | $100 | $125 |

MODEL YEAR FEATURES	EXC. COND. LOW	HIGH
ProBass 1000 Amp		
Rack mount, effects loops, preamp, EQ, crossover, headphone output.		
1980s	$150	$175
Rage/Rage 158 Amp		
1988-present. Compact practice amp, 15 watts, 1x8". 158 starts '95		
1988-2007	$75	$90
Reno 400 Amp		
Solidstate, 200 watts, 1x15" with horn, 4-band EQ.		
1980s	$175	$200
Renown 112 Amp		
1989-1994. Crunch and lead SuperSat, 160 watts, 1x12", master volume, digital reverb, EQ.		
1989-1994	$175	$200
Renown 212 Amp		
1989-1994. Crunch and lead SuperSat, 160 watts, 2x12", master volume, digital reverb, EQ.		
1989-1994	$200	$225
Renown 400 Amp		
Combo, 200 watts, 2x12", channel switching, Hammond reverb, pre- and post-gain controls.		
1980s	$250	$300
Revolution 112 Amp		
1992-2002. 100 watts, 1x12" combo, black vinyl, black grille.		
1992-2002	$200	$225
Session 400 Amp		
1980s. 200 watts, 1x15", Session 400 logo on front and back panel, in '88 available in wedge-shaped enclosures slanted back 30 degrees from the floor, 15" EVM, steel amp.		
1980s	$300	$325
Session 500 Amp		
1980s. 250 watts, 1x15", standard black with metal panels appearance.		
1980s	$325	$350
Special 112 Amp		
160 watts, 1x12", channel-switching, effects loops, EQ. In 1988, available in wedge-shaped enclosures slanted back 30 degrees.		
1980s	$250	$275
Special 130 Amp		
1980s. 1x12", 130 watts, transtube, solidstate series.		
1980s	$250	$275
Special 212 Amp		
1995-2005. 160 watts, 2x12", transtube, solidstate series.		
1995-2005	$300	$325
Studio Pro 112 Amp		
Repackaged and revoiced in 1988. Solidstate, 65 watts, 1x12", Peavey SuperSat preamp circuitry, new power sections		
1980s	$175	$200
TKO-65 Bass Amp		
1987-1995. Solidstate, 65 watts, 1x15".		
1987-1995	$150	$175

MODEL YEAR FEATURES	EXC. COND. LOW	HIGH
TKO-75 Bass Amp		
1987-1995. Solidstate, 75 watts, 1x15", EQ, compression and pre-/post-gain controls.		
1987-1995	$175	$200
TNT-150 Bass Amp		
Solidstate, 150 watts, 1x15", EQ, compression, chorus. In 1988, available in wedge-shaped enclosures slanted 30 degrees.		
1980s	$200	$225
Transchorus 210 Amp		
1999. 50 watts, 2x10 combo, stereo chorus, channel switching, reverb.		
1999	$250	$300
Triple XXX Amp Head		
2001-present. Tube head, 120 watts.		
2001-2006	$625	$650
Triumph 60 Combo Amp		
Tube head, effects loop, reverb, 60 watts, 1x12", multi-stage gain.		
1980s	$175	$200
Triumph 120 Amp		
Tube, 120 watts, 1x12", 3 gain blocks in preamp, low-level post-effects loop, built-in reverb.		
1989-1990	$225	$250
Ultra 112 Amp		
1998-2002. 60 watts, 1x12", all tube, 2 6L6 power, black, black grille.		
1998-2002	$300	$325
Ultra 410 Amp		
1998-2002. 60 watts, 4x10".		
1998-2002	$350	$375
Vegas 400 Amp		
1980s. 210 watts, 1x15", reverb, compression feature, parametric EQ. Some musicians prefer as a steel guitar amp.		
1980s	$400	$425
Wiggy 212 Amp		
2001-present. 100-watt head in mono (2x75-watt in stereo) with matching 2x12" cab, 2 EQ, 5-band sliders, rounded amp head.		
2001-2006	$550	$675

Penn

1994-present. Tube amps, combos, and cabinets built by Billy Penn, originally in Colts Neck, New Jersey, currently in Long Branch, New Jersey.

Pignose

1972-present. Made in the U.S. Pignose Industries was started by people associated with the band Chicago, including guitarist Terry Kath, with help from designers Wayne Kimball and Richard Erlund.

MODEL YEAR FEATURES	EXC. COND. LOW	HIGH
7-100 Practice Amp		
1972-present. The original Pignose, 7"x5"x3" battery-powered portable amplifier, 1x5".		
1972-1999	$40	$50
30/60 Amp		
1978-ca.1987. Solidstate, 30 watts, 1x10", master volume.		
1978-1987	$100	$125

Peavey Triple XXX Head

AMPS

Penn Signature amp

Pignose Hog

Port City Dual Fifty

Randall R6-200 ES

Randall RM50

60R Studio Reverb Amp
Solidstate, 30 watts.

1980	$175	$200

Plush
Late 1960s-early 1970s. Tuck and roll covered tube amps made by the same company that made Earth Sound Research amps in Farmingdale, New York.

Tube Amplifiers
Early 1970s. All tube heads and combos including the 450 Super 2x12" combo, 1000/P1000S head, and 1060S Royal Bass combo.

1971-1972	$325	$400

Point Blank
2002-2004. Tube amps built by Roy Blankenship in Orlando, Florida before he started his Blankenship brand.

Polytone
1960s-present. Made in North Hollywood, California, Polytone offers compact combo amps, heads, and cabinets and a pickup system for acoustic bass.

Guitar or Bass Amps

1980-1990s	$275	$325

Port City
2005-present. Daniel Klein builds his amp heads, combos, and cabinets in Rocky Point, North Carolina.

Premier
Ca.1938-ca.1975. Produced by Peter Sorkin Music Company in Manhattan. First radio-sized amplifiers introduced by '38. After World War II, established Multivox subsidiary to manufacture amplifiers ca.'46. By mid-'50s at least, the amps featured lyre grilles. Dark brown/light tan amp covering by '60. By '64 amps covered in brown woodgrain and light tan. Multivox amps were made until around '84.

B-160 Club Bass Amp
1960s. 15 to 20 watts, 1x12" Jensen speaker, '60s 2-tone brown styling, 6V6 tubes.

1963-1968	$425	$475

Model 50 Combo Amp
1940s-1960s. Four to 5 watts, 1x8" similar to Fender Champ circuit with more of a vertical cab.

1950s	$375	$425

Model 76 Combo Amp
1950s. Suitcase latchable cabinet that opens out into 2 wedges, Premier 76 logo on amp control panel, 2-tone brown, lyre grille, 1x12".

1950s	$650	$800

Model 88N Combo Amp
1950s-early-1960s. Rectangular suitcase cabinet, 2-tone tan and brown, Premier and lyre logo, 25 watts, 1x12".

1950-1960s	$650	$800

Model 100R Amp
Combo amp, 1x12", reverb and tremolo.

1960s	$525	$575

Twin 8 Amp
1960s. 20 watts, 2x8", tremolo, reverb.

1964-1966	$625	$700

Twin 12 T-12R Amp
Late-1950s. Early reverb amp with tremolo, 2x12", rectangular cabinet typical of twin 12 amps (Dano and Fender), brown cover.

1950s	$650	$725

Quantum
1980s. Economy amps distributed by DME, Indianapolis, Indiana.

Q Terminator Economy Amps
1980s. Economy solidstate amps ranging from 12 to 25 watts and 1x6" to 1x12".

1980s	$25	$50

Randall
1960s-present. Randall Instruments was originally out of California and is now a division of U.S. Music Corp. They have offered a range of tube and solidstate combo amps, heads and cabinets over the years.

Guitar and Bass Amps
1980s-2000s. Mostly solidstate amps.

1980-1990s	Intermediate-grade	$250	$400
1980-2000s	Student-grade	$100	$250

Rastopdesigns
2002-present. Custom amps built by Alexander Rastopchin in Long Island City, New York. He also builds effects.

Rat Fink
2002-present. Solidstate amp line from Lace Music Products. They also sold guitars and basses under this brand and offer amps under the Mooneyes and Lace brands.

Red Bear
1994-1997. Tube amps designed by Sergei Novikov and built in St. Petersburg, Russia. Red Bear amps were distributed in the U.S. under a joint project between Gibson and Novik, Ltd. Novik stills builds amps under other brands.

MK 60 Lead Tube Amp
1994-1997. Head with 4x12" half stack, Red Bear logo on amp and cab.

1994-1997	$650	$725

Red Iron Amps
2001-present. Paul Sanchez builds his tube amp heads in Lockhart, Texas.

MODEL YEAR FEATURES	EXC. COND. LOW	HIGH

Reeves Amplification

2002-present. Started by Bill Jansen, Reeves builds tube amps, combos, and cabinets in Cincinnati, Ohio, based on the classic British designs of Dan Reeves.

Retro-King Amplifier Company

2004-present. Tube combo and head amps built by Chuck Dean in Marcellus, New York.

Reverend

1996-present. Joe Naylor started building amps under the Naylor brand in '94. In '96 he left Naylor to build guitars under the Reverend brand. From '01 to '05, Reverend offered tube amps, combos, and cabinets built in Warren, Michigan, that Naylor co-designed with Dennis Kager.

Rex

1930s-1950s, 1960s. Generally beginner-grade instruments and amps made by Harmony and Kay and sold through Fred Gretsch distributors. In the '60s, there were Italian-made electrics bearing the Rex brand. See Gretsch for listings.

Rickenbacker

1931-present. Rickenbacker made amps from the beginning of the company up to the late '80s. Rickenbacker had many different models, from the small early models that were usually sold as a guitar/amp set, to the large, very cool, Transonic.

Electro-Student Amp
Late-1940s. Typical late-'40s vertical combo cabinet, 1x12" speaker, lower power using 5 tubes, bottom mounted chassis, dark gray leatherette cover.

1948-1949	$275	$325

Model M-8 Amp
Gray, 1x8".

1950s	$350	$425
1960s	$325	$400

Model M-11 Amp
1950s. 12-15 watts, 1x12", 2x6V6 power. There was a different M-11 offered in the 1930s.

1959	$450	$550

Model M-12 Amp
1950s. 12-15 watts, 1x12", M-12 logo on back panel, brown leatherette. There was a different M-12 offered in the 1930s.

1950s	$450	$600

Model M-15 Amp
1950s-Early 1960s. 1x15" combo, 35 watts, 2 x 6L6 power tubes, model name on top panel.

1950s-1960	$700	$800

Professional Model 200-A Amp
1930s. 15 watts, was sold with the Vibrola Spanish guitar.

1938	$375	$450

RB30 Amp
1986. Bass combo amp, 30 watts, tilted control panel, 1x12".

1986	$150	$175

RB60 Amp
1986. Bass combo amp, 60 watts, tilted control panel, 1x15".

1986	$200	$225

RB120 Amp
1986. Bass combo amp, 120 watts, tilted control panel, 1x15".

1986	$225	$275

Supersonic Model B-16 Amp
4x10" speakers, gray cover.

1960s	$675	$800

TR7 Amp
1978-1982. 7 watts, 1x10", tremolo, solidstate.

1978-1982	$75	$125

TR14 Amp
1978-ca.1982. Solidstate, 1x10", reverb, distortion.

1978-1982	$175	$225

TR35B Bass Amp
1978-ca.1982. Solid-state, mid-power, 1x15".

1978-1982	$225	$250

TR75G Amp
1978-ca.1982. 75 watts, 2x12", 2 channels.

1978-1982	$150	$175

TR75SG Amp
1978-ca.1983. 1x10" and 1x15" speakers.

1978-1982	$200	$225

TR100G Amp
1978-ca.1982. Solidstate, 100 watts with 4x12", 2 channels.

1978-1982	$250	$275

Transonic Amp
1967-1970. Trapezoid shape, 2x12", head and cabinet, Rick-O-Select.

1967-1970	$850	$1,050

Rivera

1985-present. Amp designer and builder Paul Rivera modded and designed amps for other companies before starting his own line in California. He offers heads, combos, and cabinets.

Chubster 40 Amp
2000-present. 40 watts, 1x12" combo, burgundy tolex, light grille.

2000-2003	$825	$900

Clubster 45 Amp
2005-present. 45 watts, 1x12" combo.

2005-2006	$825	$900

Fandango 212 Combo Amp
2001-present. 55 watts, 2x12" tube amp.

2001-2002	$925	$1,075

Knucklehead 55 Amp
1995-2002. 55 watts, head amp, replaced by reverb model.

1995-2002	$725	$875

Reeves Custom 18

Reverend Goblin

Rivera Fandango 2x12"

AMPS

Rivera Suprema R-55 112

Roccaforte 80 watt

Roland AC-100

MODEL YEAR	FEATURES	EXC. COND. LOW	HIGH
Knucklehead 100 Amp	*1995-2002. 100 watt head, head amp, replaced by reverb model.*		
1995-2002		$775	$925
Los Lobottom/Sub 1 Amp	*1999-2004. 1x12" cabinet with 300-watt powered 12" subwoofer.*		
1999-2004		$525	$575
M-60 Amp Head	*1990-present. 60 watts.*		
1990-2006		$575	$625
M-60 112 Combo Amp	*1989-present. 60 watts, 1x12".*		
1989-2006		$675	$725
M-100 Amp Head	*1990-present. 100 watts.*		
1990-2006		$625	$675
M-100 212 Combo Amp	*1990-present. 100 watts, 2x12" combo.*		
1990-2006		$725	$825
Quiana Combo Amps	*2000-present. Combo, 55 watts, 1x12".*		
2000-2002 112		$650	$800
2000-2002 212 or 410		$725	$900
R-30 112 Combo Amp	*1993-2007. 30 watts, 1x12", compact cab, black tolex cover, gray-black grille.*		
1993-2007		$600	$725
R-100 212 Combo Amp	*1993-2007. 100 watts, 2x12".*		
1993-2007		$725	$825
Suprema R-55 112/115 Combo Amp	*2000-present. Tube amp, 55 watts, 1x12" (still available) or 1x15" ('00-'01).*		
2000-2006 1x12" or 1x15"		$975	$1,125
TBR-1 Amp	*1985-1999. First Rivera production model, rack mount, 60 watts.*		
1985-1999		$625	$775

Roccaforte Amps

1993-present. Tube amps, combos, and cabinets built by Doug Roccaforte in San Clemente, California.

Rocktron

1980s-present. Tube and solidstate amp heads, combos and cabinest. Rocktron is a division of GHS Strings and also offers stomp boxes and preamps.

Rodgers

1993-present. Custom tube amps and cabinets built by Larry Rodgers in Naples, Florida.

Rogue

2001-present. They offered student-level solid-state import (Korea) compact amps up to around '06. They also offer guitars, basses, lap steels, mandolins, banjos, ukuleles and effects.

MODEL YEAR	FEATURES	EXC. COND. LOW	HIGH
CG Series Amps	*2001. Solidstate, 20-100 watts.*		
2001		$35	$145

Roland

Japan's Roland Corporation's products include amplifiers and keyboards and, under the Boss brand, effects.

MODEL YEAR	FEATURES	EXC. COND. LOW	HIGH
AC-100 Amp	*1995-present. Acoustic amp, 50 watts, 1x12" and 2x5", chorus, reverb, EQ, effects loop.*		
1995-2000		$325	$350
Bolt 60 Amp	*Early 1980s. Solidstate/tube, 1x12".*		
1980s		$250	$300
Cube 20 Amp	*1978-1982. Portable, 1x8", normal and overdrive channels, headphone jack.*		
1978-1982		$125	$175
Cube 40 Amp	*1978-1980s. Portable, 1x10", normal and overdrive channels, 40 watts.*		
1978-1983		$150	$200
Cube 60/60B Amp	*1978-1980s, 2004-present for Cube 60. 1x12", 60 watts, Cube 60 combo or Cube 60B combo bass amp.*		
1978-1983 Cube 60/60B		$225	$275
Cube 100 Amp	*1978-1982. 100 watts, combo, 1x12".*		
1978-1982		$250	$300
Jazz Chorus Series Amps	*1976-present. Includes the JC-50 (1980s. 50 watts, 1x12"), JC-55 ('87-'94, 50 watts, 2x8"), JC-77 ('87-'94, 80 watts, 2x10"), JC-90 (2x10") and the JC-120 ('76-present, 120 watts, 2x12").*		
1980s JC-50		$250	$300
1987-1994 JC-55		$250	$300
1987-1994 JC-77/90		$275	$325
1987-2000s JC-120		$350	$400
Spirit 30 Amp	*1982-late 1980s. Compact, 30 watts, 1x12".*		
1980s		$100	$150
Studio Bass Amp			
1979		$200	$250
VGA3 V-Guitar Amp	*2003-present. GK digital modeling amp, 50 watts, 1x12" combo.*		
2003-2004		$250	$300
VGA5 V-Guitar Amp	*2001-2004. GK digital modeling amp, 65 watts, 1x12".*		
2001-2004		$300	$350
VGA7 V-Guitar Amp	*2000-present. 65 + 65 watts, 2x12", digital modeling with analog-style controls.*		
2000-2004		$350	$400

Sadowsky

1980-present. From '05 to '07, luthier Roger Sadowsky built a bass tube amp head in Brooklyn, New York. He also builds basses and guitars.

AMPS

MODEL		EXC. COND.	
YEAR	FEATURES	LOW	HIGH

Sam Ash

1960s-1970s. Sam Ash Music was founded by a young Sam Ash (formerly Ashkynase - an Austro-Hungarian name) in 1924. Ash's first store was in Brooklyn, New York, and by '66 there were about four Ash stores. During this time Ash Music private branded their own amp line which was built by Jess Oliver of Oliver Amps and based upon Oliver's Ampeg designs.

Sam Ash Mark II Pro Combo Amp
1960s. 2x12" with reverb combo amp.

1960s		$325	$375

Sano

1944-ca. 1970. Combo, heads and cabinets made in Irvington, New Jersey. Founded by Joseph Zon-Frilli, Louis Iorio, and Nick Sano, with initial offerings of accordion pickups, amplifiers, and all-electric accordions. Sano patented his accordion pickup in '44 and also developed a highly acclaimed stereophonic pickup accordion and matching amp. By '66 the Sano Corporation augmented their all-tube accordion amps with new solidstate circuitry models. In the mid-'60s they offered a new line of amps specifically designed for the guitar and bass market. Sano amps are generally low-gain, low power amplifiers. They also marketed reverb units and guitars.

Model 160R Amp
1960s. Low power, around 15 watts, 1x12", reverb, trem, all-tube 2xEL84 power.

1960s		$225	$250

Savage

1994-present. Tube combos, amp heads and cabinets built by Jeff Krumm at Savage Audio, in Savage, Minnesota.

Sceptre

1960s. Canadian-made. Sceptre script logo on upper left side of grille ('60s Fender-style and placement).

Signet Amp
1960s. Low power, 1x10", Class-A 6V6 power, Signet model name on front panel.

1960s		$150	$175

Schertler

Made in Switzerland, model logo (e.g. David model) on front, intermediate to professional grade, modern designs for modern applications.

Selmer

1930s-1980s. The Selmer UK distributor offered mid- to high-level amps.

Constellation 14 Amp
1965. 14 watts, single speaker combo, gray snake-skin tolex-type cover.

1965		$2,000	$2,500

Futurama Corvette Amp
1960s. Class A low power 1x8", volume and tone controls, plus amplitude and speed tremolo controls, large script Futurama logo on front of amp, Futurama Corvette and Selmer logo on top panel.

1960s		$475	$550

Mark 2 Treble and Bass Amp Head
1960s. About 30 watts (2xEL34s), requires power line transformer for U.S. use, large Selmer logo on grille.

1960s		$575	$700

Truevoice Amp
1961. Truevoice and Selectortone logo on top-mounted chasis, 30-watt combo, 1x15 Goodmans speaker, 2xEL34 power tubes, tremolo, 6 push button Selectortone Automatic.

1961		$2,300	$2,800

Zodiac Twin 30 Amp
1964-1971. Combo amp, gray snakeskin tolex cover.

1964-1971		$2,500	$2,900

Seymour Duncan

Pickup maker Seymour Duncan, located in Santa Barbara, California, offered a line of amps from around 1984 to '95.

84-40/84-50 Amp
1989-1995. Tube combo, 2 switchable channels, 1x12", includes the 84-40 ('89-'91, 40 watts) and the 84-50 ('91-'95, 50 watts).

1989-1995	84-40 or 84-50	$300	$350

Bass 300 x 2 Amp
1986-1987. Solidstate, 2 channels (300 or 600 watts), EQ, contour boost switches, effects loop.

1986-1987		$300	$350

Bass 400 Amp
1986-1987. Solidstate, 400 watts, EQ, contour boost, balanced line output, effects loop.

1986-1987		$275	$325

Convertible 100 Amp
1986-1987. Solidstate, 60 watts, effects loop, spring reverb, EQ, switchable preamp modules.

1986-1987	Head	$300	$375

Convertible 2000 Amp
1988-1995. Solidstate, 100 watts, holds 5 interchangeable modules, 1x12", 2 switchable channels.

1988-1995		$425	$500

KTG-2075 Stereo Amp
1989-1993. Part of the King Tone Generator Series, 2 channels with 75 watts per channel.

1989-1993		$200	$250

Sherwood

Late 1940s-early 1950s. Amps made by Danelectro for Montgomery Ward. There are also Sherwood guitars and lap steels made by Kay.

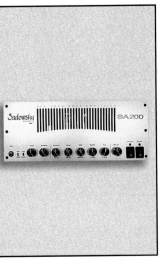

Sadowsky SA200

AMPS

Savage Macht6

Schertler David

To get the most from this book, be sure to read "Using *The Guide*" in the introduction.

Silvertone Model 1471

Silvertone Model 1484

*Smith Custom Amplifiers
Class A 10 Watt*

Sho-Bud

Introduced and manufactured by the Baldwin/Gretsch factory in 1970. Distributed by Kustom/Gretsch in the '80s. Models include D-15 Model 7838, S-15 Model 7836, Twin Tube Model 7834, and Twin Trans Model 7832.

D15 Sho-Bud Double Amp

Introduced in 1970. Solidstate, 100 watts. D-15 is 2 channels, S-15 is 1 channel, both with 1x15" JBL speaker.

Model Year	Features	Low	High
1970s		$300	$350

S15 Sho-Bud Single Amp

Introduced in 1972. 100 watts, 1x15" JBL, solidstate single channel combo.

1970s		$250	$300

Sho-Bass Amp

Introduced in 1972. 100 watts, 1x15", solidstate combo, black grille, black vinyl cover.

1970s		$250	$300

Twin Trans Amp

Introduced in 1972. 100 watts, solidstate combo, 2x12", reverb, black vinyl cover, dark grille, Sho-Bud script logo front upper right.

1970s		$400	$475

Twin Tube Amp

Introduced in 1972. 100 watt tube combo, 4 6L6s, 2x12", reverb, black vinyl cover, dark grille.

1970s		$650	$725

Siegmund Guitars & Amplifiers

1993-present. Chris Siegmund builds his tube amp heads, combos and cabinets in Los Angeles, California. He founded the company in Seattle, moving it to Austin, Texas for '95-'97. He also builds effects pedals and guitars.

Silvertone

1941-ca.1970, present. Brand used by Sears. All Silvertone amps were supplied by American companies up to around '66.

Model 10XL Amp

Mid- Late-1960s. Model 10XL logo on front, tubes, verticle cab, lower power, small speaker.

1960s		$200	$250

Model 40XL Amp

Mid- Late-1960s. Model 1422 40XL was renamed to Model 40XL. Tube combo, low-mid power, 1x12", tremolo, reverb, vertical cab, 2 channels.

1960s		$350	$425

Model 100 Amp

Mid-late-1960s. Solidstate, piggyback amp and 2x12" cabinet with gold-label Jensen speakers.

1960s		$325	$375

Model 150 Amp

Mid-late-1960s. Solidstate, piggyback amp and 6x10" cabinet with gold-label Jensen speakers.

1960s		$450	$525

Model 1300 Amp

1948. Vertical combo cab, treble-clef logo on grille, 2-tone, 3 inputs, 2 controls.

Model Year	Features	Low	High
1948		$375	$450

Model 1331 Amp

Ca.1954-ca.1957. Danelectro-made, luggage tweed, rounded front, a whole series made this style.

1954-1957		$325	$375

Model 1334 Amp

1954-1957. 1x12, tremolo, tube combo.

1954-1957		$325	$375

Model 1336 (Early Twin Twelve) Amp

Ca.1954-ca.1957. Danelectro-made, luggage tweed, rounded front.

1954-1957		$650	$750

Model 1340 (Student Model) Amp

Early-1950s. Tan cover, brown grille with Silvertone logo, brown sides.

1950s		$150	$175

Model 1346 (Twin Twelve) Amp

Ca.1958-ca.1961. Danelectro-made, brown control panel, 2x12", 4 6L6s, vibrato, leather handle, tan smooth leatherette cover, 2 speaker baffle openings.

1958-1961		$600	$750

Model 1391 Amp

1950s. Blond-tan tweed-cloth cover, brown grille, single small speaker, leather handle.

1950s		$200	$225

Model 1392 Amp

1950s. Student amp with tremolo, 5 control knobs, brown cover and brown grille.

1950s		$225	$275

Model 1432 Amp

Late-1950s. 1x12", low- to mid-power, 2 6L6s, late-'50s overhanging top style cabinet.

1950s		$250	$300

Model 1433 Combo Amp

Late-1950s. Tube, 30 watts, 2 6L6s, 1x15", gray cover cabinet with pronounced overhanging top, light colored grille.

1950s		$525	$625

Model 1434 Metalist Twin 12 Amp

Late-1950s. 2x12" combo.

1959		$600	$700

Model 1451 Amp

Late-1950s. Three or 4 watts, 3 tubes, 1x6" or 1x8" speaker, brown sparkle cover, wheat grille, by Danelectro.

1950s	1x6"	$175	$200

Model 1457 Amp-In-Case

1960s. The amp-in-case with the electric Silvertone guitar, this is the higher powered model with tremolo and higher quality speaker.

1965	Amp only (no guitar)	$150	$175

Model 1459 Amp

1960s. Four watts, 1x6" or 1x8".

1960s		$175	$200

Model 1463 Bass 35 Amp

1960s. Solidstate, 2x12", piggyback.

1960s		$325	$350

MODEL YEAR	FEATURES	EXC. COND. LOW	HIGH

Model 1465 Amp Head
Mid-1960s. Rectangular amp head, solidstate, 50 watts, spotted gray cover, used with Twin 12 bottom.
1960s		$225	$250

Model 1471 Amp
1x8" speaker.
| 1960s | | $200 | $225 |

Model 1472 Amp
1960s. 15-18 watts, 2 6V6s provide mid-level power, 1x12", front controls mounted vertically on front right side, dark cover with silver grille, large stationary handle, tremolo.
| 1962-1963 | | $325 | $350 |

Model 1473 Amp
1960s. Mid-power, tubes, 1x15" combo.
| 1960s | | $325 | $375 |

Model 1474 Amp
1960s. Mid-power, mid-level, dual speakers, tube combo amp, gray tolex, gray grille.
| 1960s | | $450 | $500 |

Model 1481 Amp
1960s. Low-power, student amp, 1x6", gray cover, light grille, 2 controls.
| 1960s | | $200 | $250 |

Model 1482 Amp
1960s. Low power, 1x12" combo, gray tolex, silver grille, control panel mounted on right side vertically, tremolo.
| 1960s | | $350 | $425 |

Model 1483 Piggyback Amp
1960s. Mid-power, 1x15" tube amp, gray tolex and gray grille.
| 1960s | | $475 | $550 |

Model 1484 Twin Twelve Amp
1960s. Medium-power, 2x12" piggyback tube amp, classic Silvertone colors--gray cover with light grille.
| 1966 | | $575 | $675 |

Model 1485 Amp
1963. 6x10" (Jensen C-10Q) piggyback, 2 channels, reverb, tremolo, silver-gray tolex-style cover, silver-white grille.
| 1963 | | $700 | $875 |

Simms-Watts
Late 1960s-1970s. Tube amp heads, combos, PA heads and cabinets made in London, England. Similar to Marshall and HiWatt offerings of the era.

Skip Simmons
1990-present. Custom and production tube combo amps built by Skip Simmons in Dixon, California.

Sligo Amps
2004-present. Intermediate and professional grade, production/custom, amps built by Steven Clark in Leesburg, Virginia.

SMF
Mid-1970s. Amp head and cabinets from Dallas Music Industries, Ltd., of Mahwah, New Jersey. Offered the Tour Series which featured a 150 watt head and 4x12" bottoms with metal speaker grilles and metal corners.

SMF (Sonic Machine Factory)
2002-present. Tube amps and cabinets designed by Mark Sampson (Matchless, Bad Cat, Star) and Rick Hamel (SIB effects) and built in California.

Smicz Amplification
Tube combos and extension cabinets built by Bob Smicz in Bristol, Connecticut.

Smith Custom Amplifiers
2002-present. All tube combo amps, heads and speaker cabinets built by Sam Smith in Montgomery, Alabama.

Smokey
1997-present. Mini amps often packaged in cigarette packs made by Bruce Zinky in Flagstaff, Arizona. He also builds Zinky amps and effects and has revived the Supro brand on a guitar and amp.

Snider
1999-present. Jeff Snider has been building various combo tube amps in San Diego, California, since '95. In '99 he started branding them with his last name.

Soldano
1987-present. Made in Seattle, Washington by amp builder Mike Soldano, the company offers a range of all-tube combo amps, heads and cabinets. They also offer a reverb unit.

Astroverb 16 Combo Amp
1997-present. Atomic with added reverb.
1997-2002		$650	$775

Atomic 16 Combo Amp
1996-2001. Combo, 20 watts, 1x12".
| 1996-2001 | | $575 | $700 |

Decatone Combo Amp
1998-2002. 2x12" 100-watt combo, rear mounted controls, still available as a head.
| 1998-2002 | No footswitch | $1,650 | $1,750 |
| 1998-2002 | With Decatrol footswitch | $1,950 | $2,100 |

HR 50/Hot Rod 50 Amp Head
1992-present. 50-watt single channel head.
| 1992-2002 | | $825 | $925 |

HR 100/Hot Rod 100 Amp Head
1994-2001. 100-watt single channel head.
| 1994-2001 | | $975 | $1,075 |

Lucky 13 Combo Amp
2000-present. 100 watts (50 also available), 2x12" combo.
| 2000-2002 | | $1,050 | $1,150 |

Sonic Machine Factory 15 Watter

AMPS

Smokey Amp

Snider combo

Sommatone Roaring 40 2X12

Specimen Horn Amp

Speedster 25-Watt Deluxe

SLO-100 Super Lead Overdrive 100-Watt Amp
1988-present. First production model, super lead overdrive, 100 watts, snakeskin cover head amp, 4x12" cabinet.

1988-1999	Head	$2,000	$2,300
1990s	With cab	$2,600	$2,900

Sommatone
1998-present. Jim Somma builds his tube combo and head amps and cabinets in Somerville, New Jersey.

Sonax
Introduced in 1972. Budget line of solidstate amps offered by Gretsch/Baldwin, made by Yorkville Sound (Traynor) in Toronto, Canada. Introduced with dark grille and dark cover.

530-B Bass Amp
30 watts, 1x12".

1970s	$125	$175

550-B Bass Amp
50 watts, 1x15".

1970s	$150	$200

720-G Amp
Student amp, 20 watts, 2x8", reverb.

1970s	$200	$250

730-G Amp
30 watts, 2x10", reverb and tremolo.

1970s	$300	$350

750-G Amp
50 watts, 2x12", reverb and tremolo.

1970s	$350	$400

770-G Amp
75 watts, 4x10", reverb and tremolo.

1970s	$400	$450

Songworks Systems
See listing under Little Lanilei.

Sonny Jr.
1996-present. Harmonica amplifiers built by harmonica player Sonny Jr. in conjunction with Cotton Amps in Tolland, Connecticut.

Sound City
Made in England from the late-1960s to the late-'70s, the tube Sound City amps were Marshall-looking heads and separate cabinets. They were imported, for a time, into the U.S. by Gretsch.

50 PA Plus Amp
Late-1960s-late-1970s. Similar to 50 Plus but with 4 channels.

1970s	$600	$750

50 Plus/50R Amp Head
Late-1960s-late-1970s. Amp head, labeled 50 Plus or 50 R.

1960-1970s	$700	$850

120/120R Amp Head
Early-late-1970s. The 120-watt head replaced the late-1960s 100-watt model.

1970s	120 no reverb	$750	$925
1970s	With reverb	$800	$1,000

Concord Combo Amp
80 watts, 2x12" Fane speakers, cream, basketweave grille.

1968	$750	$925

L-80 Cabinet
1970s. 4x10" cabinet.

1970s	$525	$600

X-60 Cabinet
1970s. 2x12" speaker cabinet.

1970s	$525	$600

Sound Electronics
Sound Electronics Corporation introduced a line of amplifiers in 1965 that were manufactured in Long Island. Six models were initially offered, all with tube preamps and solidstate power sections. Their catalog did not list power wattages but did list features and speaker configurations.

The initial models had dark vinyl-style covers and sparkling silver grille cloth. The amps were combos with the large models having vertical cabinets, silver script Sound logo on upper left of grille. The larger models used JBL D120F and D130F speakers. Stand alone extension speakers were also available.

Various Model Amps
Mid-1960s. Includes X-101, X-101R, X-202 Bass/Organ, X-404 Bass and Organ, X-505R amps, hi-fi chassis often using 7868 power tubes.

1960s	$375	$450

Southbay Ampworks
2002-present. Tube combo amps and speaker cabinets built by Jim Seavall in Rancho Palos Verdes, CA. He also builds Scumback Speakers.

Sovtek
1992-2000. Sovtek amps were products of Mike Matthews of Electro-Harmonix fame and his New Sensor Corporation. The guitar and bass amps and cabinets were made in Russia.

Mig 50 Amp Head
1994-2000. Tube head, 50 watts.

1994-2000	$350	$475

Mig 60 Amp Head
1994-2000. Tube head, 60 watts, point-to-point wiring.

1994-2000	$450	$550

Mig 100 Amp Head
1992-2000. Tube head, 100 watts.

1992-2000	$475	$575

Mig 100B Amp Head
1996-2000. Bass tube head, 100 watts.

1996-2000	$450	$550

MODEL YEAR	FEATURES	EXC. COND. LOW	HIGH

Space Tone
See Swart Amplifiers.

Specimen Products
1984-present. Luthier Ian Schneller added tube amps and speaker cabinets in '93. He also builds guitars, basses and ukes in Chicago, Illinois.

Speedster
1995-2000, 2003-present. Founded by Lynn Ellsworth, offering tube amps and combos designed by Bishop Cochran with looks inspired by dashboards of classic autos. In '03, Joe Valosay and Jevco International purchased the company and revived the brand with help from former owner Cory Wilds. Amps were originally built by Soldono, but are now built by Speedster in Gig Harbor, Washington.

S.S. Maxwell
See info under Danelectro.

St. George
1960s. There were Japanese guitars bearing this brand, but these amps may have been built in California.

Mid-Size Tube Amp
1965. Low power, 1x10" Jensen, 2 5065 and 2 12AX7 tubes.

1960s		$225	$250

Standel
1952-1974, 1997-present. Bob Crooks started custom building amps part time in '52, going into full time standard model production in '58 in Temple City, California. In '61 Standel started distributing guitars under their own brand and others. By late '63 or '64, Standel had introduced solidstate amps, two years before Fender and Ampeg introduced their solidstate models. In '67 Standel moved to a new, larger facility in El Monte, California. In '73 Chicago Musical Instruments (CMI), which owned Gibson at the time, bought the company and built amps in El Monte until '74. In '97 the Standel name was revived by Danny McKinney who, with the help of original Standel founder Bob Crooks and Frank Garlock (PR man for first Standel), set about building reissues of some of the early models in Ventura, California.

A-30 B Artist 30 Bass Amp
1964-early-1970s. Artist Series, the original Standel solidstate series, 80 watts, 2x15".

1964-1969		$350	$400

A-30 G Artist 30 Guitar Amp
1964-early-1970s. Artist Series, the original Standel solidstate series, 80 watts, 2x15".

1964-1974		$400	$450

A-48 G Artist 48 Guitar Amp
1964-early-1970s. Artist Series, the original Standel solidstate series, 80 watts, 4x12".

1964-1974		$500	$550

A-60 B Artist 60 Bass Amp
1964-early-1970s. Artist Series, the original Standel solidstate series, 160 watts, 4x15".

1964-1974		$475	$525

A-60 G Artist 60 Guitar Amp
1964-early-1970s. Artist Series, the original Standel solidstate series, 160 watts, 4x15".

1964-1974		$500	$550

A-96 G Artist 96 Guitar Amp
1964-early-1970s. Artist Series, the original Standel solidstate series, 160 watts, 8x12".

1964-1974		$550	$600

C-24 Custom 24 Amp
Late-1960s-1970s. Custom Slim Line Series, solidstate, 100 watts, 2x12", dark vinyl, dark grille.

1970s		$400	$450

I-30 B Imperial 30 Bass Amp
1964-early-1970s. Imperial Series, the original Standel solidstate series, 100 watts, 2x15".

1960s		$450	$500

I-30 G Imperial 30 Guitar Amp
1964-early-1970s. Imperial Series, the original Standel solidstate series, 100 watts, 2x15".

1960s		$500	$550

Model 10L8/15L12/25L15 Amp
1953-1958. Early custom made tube amps made by Bob Crooks in his garage, padded naugahyde cabinet with varying options and colors. There are a limited number of these amps, and brand knowledge is also limited, therefore there is a wide value range. Legend has it that the early Standel amps made Leo Fender re-think and introduce even more powerful amps.

1953-1958		$3,000	$4,000

S-10 Studio 10 Amp
Late-1960s-1970s. Studio Slim Line Series, solidstate, 30 watts, 1x10", dark vinyl, dark grille.

1970s		$300	$350

S-50 Studio 50 Amp
Late-1963 or early-1964-late-1960s. Not listed in '69 Standel catalog, 60 watts, gray tolex, gray grille, piggyback.

1964		$400	$450

Star
2004-present. Tube amps, combos and speaker cabinets built by Mark Sampson in the Los Angeles, California area. Sampson has also been involved with Matchless, Bad Cat, and SMF amps.

Starlite
Starlite was a budget brand made and sold by Magnatone. See Magnatone for listings.

Stella Vee
1999-present. Jason Lockwood builds his combo amps, heads, and cabinets in Lexington, Kentucky.

Stevenson
1999-present. Luthier Ted Stevenson, of Lachine, Quebec, added amps to his product line in '05. He also builds basses and guitars.

Standel 100 UL15

Star Gain Star

Stevenson GTA

AMPS

1969 Sunn 100S

Supro Model 50

1950s Supro Comet

MODEL YEAR	FEATURES	EXC. COND. LOW	HIGH

Stimer

Brothers Yves and Jean Guen started building guitar pickups in France in 1946. By the late '40s they had added their Stimer line of amps to sell with the pickups. Early amp models were the M.6, M.10 and M.12 (6, 10 and 12 watts, respectively). An early user of Guen products was Django Reinhardt.

Stinger

Budget line imported by Martin.

Stramp

1970s. Stramp, of Hamburg, Germany, offered audio mixers, amps and compact powered speaker units, all in aluminum flight cases.

Solidstate Amp

1970s. Solid-state amp head in metal suitcase with separate Stramp logo cabinet.

1970s		$500	$550

Sunn

1965-2002. Started in Oregon by brothers Conrad and Norm Sundhold (Norm was the bass player for the Kingsman). Sunn introduced powerful amps and extra heavy duty bottoms and was soon popular with many major rock acts. Norm sold his interest to Conrad in '69. Conrad sold the company to the Hartzell Corporation of Minnesota around '72. Fender Musical Instruments acquired the brand in '85 shortly after parting ways with CBS and used the brand until '89. They resurrected the brand again in '98, but quit offering the name in '02.

601-L Cabinet

1980s. 6x10" plus 2 tweeters cab.

1980s		$350	$400

200S/215B Amp/Cabinet Set

Late-1960s. 60 watts, 2 6550s, large verticle cab with 2x15" speakers.

1969		$1,300	$1,600

Alpha 115 Amp

1980s. MOS-FET preamp section, 1x15", clean and overdrive.

1980s		$250	$275

Alpha 212 R Amp

1980s. MOS-FET preamp section, 2x12", reverb.

1980s		$250	$275

Beta Bass Amp

1978-1980s. 100 watts, solidstate, large "beta bass" logo, 1x15" combo or head only.

1970s	Combo	$550	$650
1970s	Head	$500	$550

Beta Lead Amp

1978-1980s. Solidstate, 100 watts, as 2x12" or 4x10" combo or head only.

1970s	Combos	$600	$650
1970s	Head	$500	$550

Coliseum Lead Full Stack Amp

1970s. Coliseum Lead logo on amp head, two 4x12" cabs.

1970s		$1,300	$1,600

MODEL YEAR	FEATURES	EXC. COND. LOW	HIGH

Concert Bass Amp Head

1970s. Solidstate, 200 watts.

1970s		$550	$650

Concert 215S Bass Amp Set

1970s. Solidstate head, 200 watts, Model 215S tall vertical cabinet with 2x12" Sunn label speakers, dark vinyl cover, silver sparkle grille.

1970s		$1,000	$1,250

Concert Lead 610S Amp Set

1970s. Solidstate, 200 watts, 6x10" piggyback, reverb and built-in distortion.

1970s		$1,000	$1,250

Model T Amp Head

1970s. 100 watt head.

1970s		$1,400	$1,750

Model T Amp Reissue

1990s. Reissue of '70s Model T, 100 watts, with 4x12" cab.

1990s	Head	$650	$700
1990s	Head & cab	$950	$1,100

SB-200 Amp

1985. 200 watts, 1x15", 4-band EQ, master volume, compressor.

1985		$325	$400

Sceptre Amp Head

1968-1970s. Head amp, 60 watts, 6550 power tubes, tremolo, reverb.

1970s		$550	$650

Sentura Amp Head

1970s. Rectifier and power tubes, I and II versions.

1970s	I & II	$550	$650

Solarus Amp

1967-1970s. Tube amp (EL34s), 40 watts (upgraded to 60 watts in '69), 2x12", reverb, tremolo.

1970s		$600	$700

Sonoro Amp Head

Early-1970s. 60 watts, 2 6550s.

1970s		$550	$650

Sorado Amp and Cabinet

1970s. 50 watts, tubes, 2x15" matching cab.

1970s		$1,300	$1,600

SPL 7250 Amp

Dual channels, 250 watts per channel, forced air cooling, switch-selectable peak compressor with LEDs.

1989		$325	$375

Supertone

1914-1941. Supertone was a brand used by Sears for their musical instruments. In the '40s Sears started using the Silvertone name on those products. Amps were made by other companies.

Amp

1930s		$250	$300

Supro

1935-1968, 2004-present. Supro was a budget brand of the National Dobro Company, made by Valco in Chicago, Illinois. Amp builder Bruce Zinky revived the Supro name for a line of guitars and amps.

AMPS

Bantam Amp

1961-1966. Four watts, 3 tubes, 1x 8" Jensen, petite, gold weave Saran Wrap grille, Spanish Ivory fabric cover, red in '64, gray in '66.

		LOW	HIGH
1961-1963	1611S, Spanish ivory	$300	$450
1964-1965	S6411, red cover	$300	$450
1966	Gray cover	$300	$450

Bass Combo Amp

Early 1960s. 35 watts, 2x12", 2 channels (bass and standard), 7 tubes, tremolo, woven embossed black and white tolex that appears grey. The '61 model 1688T has a narrow panel body style somewhat similar to the Fender narrow panel cab style of the late '50s, in '62 the cab panel was removed and the 'no panel' style became the 1688TA model, the new cab was less expensive to build and Supro offered a price reduction on applicable models in '62.

1961	1688T, narrow panel	$500	$700
1962-1963	1688TA, no panel	$500	$700

Big Star Reverb S6451TR Amp

1964. 35 watts, 2x12", reverb and tremolo, 'no panel' cab.

1964	$800	$1,100

Brentwood 1650T Amp

Mid-1950s. Advertised as Supro's "finest amplifier", model 1650T described as the "professional twin speaker luxury amplifier", 2 channels including high-gain, tremolo with speed control.

1956	$500	$700

Combo Amp

1961-1964. 24 watts, 6 tubes, 1x15" Jensen, Rhino-Hide covering in black and white, light grille, tremolo.

1961	1696T, narrow panel	$600	$700
1962-1963	1696TA, no panel	$600	$700

Combo Tremolo S6497T Amp

1964. 35 watts, 1x15", standard 'no panel' cab, tremolo.

1964	$650	$750

Comet 1610B Amp

1957-1959. Grey Rhino-Hide, 1x10".

1957-1959	$400	$550

Comet 1610E Amp

Mid-1950s. Supro's only 1x10" amp from the mid-'50s, 3 input jacks, 2 control knobs, woven tweed and leatherette 2-tone covering.

1956	$400	$550

Coronado Amp

1961-1963. 24 watts, 2x10", tremolo, 2 channels, 6 tubes, Supro logo upper right above grille, black and white mixed tolex appears grey, described as tremolo twin-speaker pro amp, '61 has 'narrow panel' body style, new body style in '62 becomes 1690TA model with grille only

1961	1690T, narrow panel	$650	$700
1962-1963	1690TA, no panel	$650	$700

Corsica Amp

Mid-1960s. Redesigned vertical combo amp, reverb, tremolo, blue control panel, black tolex, silver grille.

1965-1967	$425	$525

Dual-Tone Amp

1961-1965. 17 watts, 6 tubes, 1x12" Jensen, organ tone tremolo, restyled in '64, Trinidad Blue vinyl fabric cover, light color grille.

1961	1624T, narrow panel	$550	$650
1962-1963	1624TA, no panel	$550	$650
1964-1965	S6424T, no panel	$500	$650

Galaxy Tremolo S6488 Amp

1965. 35 watts, 2x12" (often Jensen), 7 tubes, tremolo, multi-purpose for guitar, bass and accordion.

1965	$500	$800

Golden Holiday 1665T Amp

Mid-1950s. Supro's model for the 'semi-professional', 2 oval 11x6" speakers, 14 watts, 6 tubes, tremolo, 2 control knobs, black and tweed cover.

1956	$500	$800

Reverb 1650R Amp

1963. 17 watts, 1x10", 'no panel' grille front style cab, reverb.

1963	$475	$700

Royal Reverb 1650TR Amp

1963-1965. 17 watts, 15 tubes, 2x10" Jensens, catalog says "authentic tremolo and magic-reverberation."

1963-1965	$700	$1,000

Special 1633E Amp

Mid-1950s. Supro's entry level student amp, 1x8", 3 tubes, large Supro stencil logo on grille, 2-tone red and white fabric cover, leather handle, available with matching Special Lap Steel covered in wine-maroon plastic.

1956	$300	$450

Spectator 1614E Amp

Mid-1950s. 1x8", 3 tubes, 2 control knobs, white front with red and black body.

1956	$375	$525

Sportsman S6689 Amp

1966. Piggyback, twin speakers.

1966	$750	$950

Studio 1644E Amp

Mid-1950s. Supro's student model for teaching studios, 2 input jacks for student and instructor or guitar and lap steel guitar, 3 tubes, advertised for "true Hawaiian tone reproduction", covered in royal blue leatherette (in '56), available with a matching Studio Lap Steel covered in blue plastic.

1956-1957	Blue leatherette	$375	$525

Super 1606E Amp

Mid-1950s. Supro advertising states "with features important to women", oval 11x6" Rola speaker, 3 tubes, 1 control knob, 2 inputs, white (front) and grey sides, elliptical baffle soundhole with Supro logo, model number with E suffix common for '50s Supro's.

1956	White front & grey	$375	$525

Super Amp

1961-1963. 4.5 watts, 3 tubes, 1x8", 1606S has contrasting black and white covering with old narrow panel cab, in '63 new 1606B has 'no panel' style cab with lighter (grey) covering.

1961-1962	1606S	$325	$475
1963	1606B	$325	$475

Supro Golden Holiday

Supro Spectator

Supro Super

AMPS

Supro Supreme Twin Speaker

1966 Supro Thunderbolt

SWR Goliath Junior III cab

MODEL YEAR	FEATURES	EXC. COND. LOW	HIGH

Super Six S6406 Amp
1964-1965. Student practice amp, 4.5 watts, 1x8", blue vinyl cover.

1964-1965		$325	$475

Super Six S6606 Amp
1966. Updated version of student compact amp.

1966		$275	$325

Supreme 17 S6400 Amp
1964-1965. 17 watts, 1x10", cab larger than prior models of this type.

1964-1965		$450	$550

Supreme Amp
1961-1963. 17 watts, 1x10", designed for use with Model 600 Reverb Accessory Unit, value shown does not include the Model 600 (see Effects Section for reverb unit). The initial 1600R model was designed with a triangle-like shaped soundhole, in '62 the more typical Supro no panel cab was introduced which Supro called the new slope front design.

1961	1600R	$450	$550
1962-1963	1600S, no panel	$450	$550

Supreme Twin Speaker 1600E Amp
Mid-1950s. 2 oval 11x6" speakers, 5 tubes, 3 input jacks, 2 control knobs, grille logo states "Twin Speaker" but unlike most Supro amps of this era the Supro logo does not appear on the front.

1956		$500	$600

Thunderbolt S6420(B) Bass Amp
1964-1967. 35 watts, 1x15" Jensen, introduced in the '64 catalog as a no frills - no fancy extra circuits amp. Sometimes referred to as the "Jimmy Page amp" based on his use of this amp in his early career.

1964-1967		$750	$950

Thunderbolt S6920 Amp
1967-1968. Redesign circuit replaced S6420B, 35 watts, 1x12".

1967-1968		$400	$450

Tremo-Verb S6422TR Amp
1964-1965. Lower power using 4 12AX7s, 1 5Y3GT, and 1 6V6, 1x10", tremolo and reverb.

1964-1965	Persian Red vinyl cover	$650	$850

Trojan Tremolo Amp
1961-1966. 5 watts, 4 tubes, 1 11"x6" oval (generally Rolla) speaker, '61-'64 black and white fabric cover and Saran Wrap grille, '64-'66 new larger cab with vinyl cover and light grille.

1961	1616T, narrow panel	$375	$525
1962-1963	1616TA, no panel	$375	$525
1964-1966	S6461, blue vinyl cover	$375	$525

Vibra-Verb S6498VR Amp
1964-1965. Billed as Supro's finest amplifier, 2x35-watt channels, 1x15" and 1x10" Jensens, vibrato and reverb.

1964-1965		$1,000	$1,200

Swanpro Amps
2004-present. Robert Swanson builds his tube combo and head amps and cabinets in Denver, Colorado.

Swart Amplifier Co. (Space Tone)
2003-present. Michael J. Swart builds tube combo and head amps and cabinets under the Swart and Space Tone brand names in Wilmington, North Carolina. He also builds effects.

SWR Sound
1984-present. Founded by Steve W. Rabe in '84, with an initial product focus on bass amplifiers. Fender Musical Instruments Corp. acquired SWR in June, 2003.

Baby Blue Studio Bass System
1990-2003. Combo, all tube preamp, 150 watts solidstate power amp, 2x8", 1x5" cone tweeter, gain, master volume, EQ, effects-blend.

1990-2003		$400	$500

Basic Black Amp
1992-1999. Solidstate, 100 watts, 1x12", basic black block logo on front, black tolex, black metal grille.

1992-1999		$350	$425

California Blonde Amp
2000s. Vertical upright combo, 100 watts, 1x12" plus high-end tweeters, blond cover, thin black metal grille.

2003		$400	$500

Goliath III Cabinet
1996-present. Black tolex, black metal grille, includes the Goliath III Jr. (2x10") and the Goliath III (4x10").

1996-2004	2x10"	$200	$250
1996-2004	4x10"	$375	$400

Strawberry Blonde Amp
1998-present. 80 watts, 1x10" acoustic instrument amp.

1998-2003		$350	$425

Studio 220 Bass Amp
1988-1995. 220 watt solidstate head, tube preamp

1988-1995		$250	$300

Workingman's 15 Bass Amp
1995-2005. Combo amp, 1x15", 160 watts, replaced by WorkingPro 15.

1995-2002		$325	$375

Takt
Late-1960s. Made in Japan, tube and solidstate models.

GA Series Amps
1968. GA-9 (2 inputs and 5 controls, 3 tubes), GA-10, GA-11, GA-12, GA-14, GA-15.

1968	GA-14/GA-15	$50	$75
1968	GA-9 through GA-12	$25	$50

Talos
2004-present. Doug Weisbrod and Bill Thalmann build their tube amp heads, combo amps, and speaker cabinets in Springfield, Virginia. They started building and testing prototypes in '01.

MODEL YEAR	FEATURES	EXC. COND. LOW	HIGH

Tech 21

1989-present. Long known for their SansAmp tube amplifier emulator, Tech 21 added solidstate combo amps, heads and cabinets in '96.

Teisco

1946-1974, 1994-present. Japanese brand first imported into the U.S. around '63. Teisco offered both tube and solidstate amps.

Checkmate CM-15 Amp
Late-1960s. Tubes, 15 watts.

1960s		$100	$125

Checkmate CM-20 Amp
Late-1960s. Tubes, 20 watts.

1960s		$125	$150

Checkmate CM-25 Amp
Late-1960s. Tubes, 25 watts.

1960s		$150	$175

Checkmate CM-50 Amp
Late-1950s-early-1960s. Tubes, 2 6L6s, 50 watts, 2x12" open back, reverb, tremolo, piggyback, gray tolex cover, light gray grille.

1960s		$400	$500

Checkmate CM-60 Amp
Late-1960s. Tubes, 60 watts, piggyback amp and cab with wheels.

1960s		$200	$250

Checkmate CM-66 Amp
Late-1960s. Solidstate, dual speaker combo, Check Mate 66 logo on front panel.

1960s		$100	$125

Checkmate CM-100 Amp
Late-1960s. Tubes, 4x6L6 power, 100 watts, piggyback with Vox-style trolley stand.

1960s		$325	$400

King 1800 Amp
Late-1960s. Tubes, 180 watts, piggyback with 2 cabinets, large Teisco logo on cabinets, King logo on lower right side of one cabinet.

1960s		$425	$525

Teisco 8 Amp
Late-1960s. Five watts

1960s		$100	$125

Teisco 10 Amp
Late-1960s. Five watts.

1960s		$100	$125

Teisco 88 Amp
Late-1960s. Eight watts.

1960s		$125	$150

Teneyck

1960s. Solidstate amp heads and speaker cabinets built by Bob Teneyck, who had previously done design work for Ampeg.

THD

1987-present. Tube amps and cabinets built in Seattle, Washington, founded by Andy Marshall.

ThroBak Electronics

2004-present. Jonathan Gundry builds his tube combo guitar amps in Grand Rapids, Michigan. He also builds guitar effects and pickups.

Titano (Magnatone)

1961-1963. Private branded by Magnatone, often for an accordion company or accordion studio, uses standard guitar input jacks.

Model 262 R Custom Amp
1961-1963. 35 watts, 2x12" + 2x5", reverb and vibrato make this one of the top-of-the-line models, black vinyl, light silver grille.

1961-1963		$1,100	$1,250

Model 415 Bass Amp
1961-1963. 25 watts, 4x8", bass or accordion amp, black cover, darkish grille.

1961-1963		$600	$675

Tone King

1993-present. Tube amps, combos, and cabinets built by Mark Bartel in Baltimore, Maryland. The company started in New York and moved to Baltimore in '94.

Tonemaster (Magnatone)

Late-1950s-early-1960s. Magnatone amps private branded for Imperial Accordion Company. Prominent block-style capital TONEMASTER logo on front panel, generally something nearly equal to Magnatone equivalent. This is just one of many private branded Magnatones. Covers range from brown to black leatherette and brown to light silver grilles.

Model 214 (V logo) Amp
1959-1960. Ten watts, 1x12", vibrato, brown leatherette, V logo lower right corner front, large TONEMASTER logo.

1959-1960		$600	$700

Model 260 Amp
1961-1963. About 30 watts, 2x12", vibrato, brown leatherette and brown grille, large TONEMASTER logo on front.

1961-1963		$1,100	$1,250

Model 380 Amp
1961-1963. 50 watts, 2x12" and 2 oval 5"x7" speakers, vibrato, no reverb.

1961-1963		$1,150	$1,400

Top Hat Amplification

1994-present. Mostly Class A guitar amps built by Brian Gerhard originally in Anaheim, California, and since '05 in Fuquay-Varina, North Carolina. They also make an overdrive pedal.

Ambassador 100 TH-A100 Amp Head
Jan.1999-present. 100 watts, Class AB, 4 6L6s, reverb, dark green vinyl cover, white chicken-head knobs.

1999-2004		$1,150	$1,250

Talos Basic

Teisco Checkmate 17

Tone King Galaxy

AMPS

*Torres Engineering
Boogie Mite*

1970 Traynor YBA1 Bass Master

Trainwreck Express

MODEL YEAR	FEATURES	EXC. COND. LOW	HIGH

Ambassador T-35C 212 Amp
1999-present. 35 watts, 2x12" combo, reverb, master volume, blond cover, tweed-style fabric grille.

| 1999-2004 | | $1,150 | $1,250 |

Club Deluxe Amp
1998-present. 20 watts, 6V6 power tubes, 1x12".

| 1998-2004 | | $1,050 | $1,100 |

Club Royale TC-R2 Amp
Jan.1999-present. 20 watts, Class A using EL84s, 2x12".

| 1999-2004 | | $1,200 | $1,300 |

Emplexador 50 TH-E50 Amp Head
Jan.1997-present. 50 watts, Class AB vint/high-gain head.

| 1997-2004 | | $1,350 | $1,600 |

King Royale Amp
1996-present. 35 watts, Class A using 4 EL84s, 2x12".

| 1996-2004 | | $1,250 | $1,500 |

Portly Cadet TC-PC Amp
Jan.1999-2004. Five watts, 6V6 power, 1x8", dark gray, light gray grille.

| 1999-2004 | | $525 | $575 |

Prince Royale TC-PR Amp
Jan.2000-2002. Five watts using EL84 power, 1x8", deep red, light grille.

| 2000-2002 | | $575 | $625 |

Super Deluxe TC-SD2 Amp
Jan.2000-present. 30 watts, Class A, 7591 power tubes, 2x12".

| 2000-2004 | | $1,050 | $1,250 |

Torres Engineering
Founded by Dan Torres, the company builds tube amps, combos, cabinets and amp kits in San Mateo, California. Dan wrote monthly columns for *Vintage Guitar* magazine for many years and authored the book Inside Tube Amps.

Trace Elliot
1978-present. Founded in a small music shop in Essex, England, currently offering guitar and bass amp heads, combos, and cabinets.

TA35CR Acoustic Guitar Amp
1994-1995. Compact lateral-style cab with 2x5", 35 watts, with reverb and chorus, dark vinyl cover, dark grille.

| 1994-1995 | | $325 | $400 |

TA100R Acoustic Guitar Amp
1990-2004. Compact lateral-style cab with 4x5", 100 watts, with reverb, dark vinyl cover, dark grille.

| 1990-2004 | | $525 | $600 |

Vellocette Amp
1996-1998. 15 watt, tube, Class A, 1x10", green cover, round sound speaker hole.

| 1996-1998 | | $375 | $450 |

Trainwreck
1983-2006. High-end tube guitar amp heads built by Ken Fischer in Colonia, New Jersey. Limited production, custom-made amps that are generally grouped by model. Models include the Rocket, Liverpool and Express, plus variations on those themes. Instead of using serial numbers, he gave each amp a woman's name. Due to illness, Fischer didn't make many amps after the mid '90s, but he continued to design amps for other builders. His total production is estimated at less than 100. Each amp's value should be evaluated on a case-by-case basis. Ken wrote many amp articles for *Vintage Guitar*. Fischer died in late 2006.

Custom Built Amp
| 1980s | High-end model | $15,000 | $18,000 |

Traynor
1963-present. Started by Pete Traynor and Jack Long in Canada and made by Yorkville Sound, currently offering tube and solidstate amp heads, combos and cabinets.

Guitar Mate Reverb YGM3 Amp
1969-1979. 40 watts, 1x12", tube amp, black tolex, gray grille.

| 1969-1979 | | $425 | $450 |

Mark III (YGL-3) Amp
1971-1979. All tube, 80 watts, 2x12" combo, reverb, tremolo.

| 1971-1979 | | $400 | $500 |

YBA1 Bass Master Amp Head
1970. 45 watts.

| 1970 | | $475 | $550 |

YBA1A Mark II Bass Master Amp
1970s.

| 1970s | | $475 | $500 |

YBA3 Custom Special Bass Amp Set
1967-1972. Tube head with 130 watts and 8x10" large vertical matching cab, dark vinyl cover, light grille.

| 1967-1972 | | $625 | $700 |

YVM PA Head
1967-1972. Public address head suitable for guitar, 4 inputs on back panel, multiple front panel controls, 2xEL34 power, 4x12AXT preamp section.

| 1970 | | $250 | $275 |

True Tone
1960s. Guitars and amps retailed by Western Auto, manufactured by Chicago guitar makers like Kay.

Hi-Fi 4 (K503 Hot-Line Special) Amp
1960s. Four watts from 3 tubes, gray cabinet, gray grille, metal handle, similar to K503.

| 1960s | | $150 | $175 |

Vibrato 704 Amp
1960s. Solidstate, 10 watts, 1x8", white sides and gray back, gray grille.

| 1960s | | $150 | $175 |

Vibrato 706 Amp
1960s. Solidstate, 15 watts, 1x15", white sides and gray back, brown grille.

| 1960s | | $200 | $225 |

MODEL YEAR	FEATURES	EXC. COND. LOW	HIGH

Tube Works
1987-2004. Founded by B.K. Butler in Denver, Tube Works became a division of Genz Benz Enclosures of Scottsdale, Arizona in 1997. Tube Works' first products were tube guitar effects and in '91 they added tube/solidstate amps, cabinets, and DI boxes to the product mix. In '04, Genz Benz dropped the brand.

Twilighter (Magnatone)
Late-1950s-early-1960s. Magnatone amps private branded for LoDuca Brothers. Prominent block-style capital TWILIGHTER logo on front panel, generally something nearly equal to Magnatone equivalent. This is just one of many private branded Magnatones. Covers range from brown to black leatherette, and brown to light silver grilles.

Model 213 Amp
1961-1963. About 20 watts, 1x12", vibrato, brown leatherette and brown grille.

1961-1963		$600	$650

Model 260R Amp
1961-1963. About 18 to 25 watts, 1x12", vibrato, brown leatherette cover.

1961-1963		$750	$800

Model 280A Amp
Late-1950s-early-1960s. About 35 watts, 2x12", vibrato, brown leatherette cover.

1961-1963		$850	$900

Two-Rock
1999-present. Tube guitar amp heads, combos and cabinets built by Joe Mloganoski and Bill Krinard (K&M Analog Designs) originally in Cotati, California, currently in Rohnert Park. They also build speakers.

Ugly Amps
2003-present. Steve O'Boyle builds his tube head and combo amps and cabinets in Burbank, California and Reading, Pennsylvania.

UltraSound
A division of UJC Electronics, UltraSound builds acoustically transparent amps, designed by Greg Farres for the acoustic guitarist, in Adel, Iowa.

Unique (Magnatone)
1961-1963. Private branded, typically for an accordion company or accordion studio, uses standard guitar input jacks.

Model 260R Amp
1961-1963. Based on Magnatone 260 Series amp, 35 watts, 2x12" but with reverb, black vinyl-style cover with distinctive black diamond-check pattern running through the top and sides.

1961-1963		$900	$1,100

Model 460 Amp
1961-1963. 35 watts, 2x12" and oval 5"x7" speakers, reverb and vibrato make it one of the top models, black vinyl, black grille.

1961-1963		$925	$1,150

Univox
1964-ca.1978. From '64 to early-'68, these were American-made tube amps with Jensen speakers. By '68, they were using Japanese components in American cabinets, still with Jensen speakers. Electronics were a combination of tube and transistors during this time; this type lasted until the mid-'70s. Around '71, Univox introduced a line of all solidstate amps, as well.

Bass Model U130B Amp
1976-1978. 130 watts, 1x15".

1976-1978		$175	$200

Lead Model 65/U65RD Amp
1976-1978. Solidstate, 65 watts, reverb, 1x12" or 2x12"in a vertical cabinet.

1976-1978		$50	$75

Lead Model Tube Amp
1960s. Tube amp, 2x10" or 2x12".

1965-1969		$300	$325

Lead Model U130L Amp
1976-1978. Solidstate.

1976-1978		$175	$200

Valco
Valco, from Chicago, Illinois, was a big player in the guitar and amplifier business. Their products were private branded for other companies like National, Supro, Airline, Oahu, and Gretsch.

Valvetrain Amplification
2005-present. Tube combos, amp heads, and speaker cabinets built by Rick Gessner in Sorrento, Florida. He also builds reverb units.

Vamp
Bass Master Amp Head
1970. 100 watts.

1970		$1,150	$1,400

Vega
1903-present. The original Boston-based company was purchased by C.F. Martin in '70. In '80, the Vega trademark was sold to a Korean company.

A-49 Amp
1960s. Six watts, 1x8", tubes, tan cover.

1960s		$175	$250

Director Combo Amp
1950s. Small to mid-size tube amp, 2-tone cover, 2 volume and 1 tone controls, rear mounted control chassis similar to Fender or Gibson from the '50s.

1950s		$425	$475

Super Amp
Early 1950s. 1 6L6, 1x10", vertical combo amp typical of the era.

1950s		$375	$425

Vesta Fire
1980s. Japanese imports by Shiino Musical Instruments Corp.; later by Midco International. Mainly known for effects pedals.

AMPS

Tube Works 6150 DFX

Two-Rock Jet

Valvetrain 205 Tall Boy

AMPS

VHT Pitbull Super 30

Victor MA-25

Victoria Regal

MODEL YEAR	FEATURES	EXC. COND. LOW	HIGH
Power Amps			
1980s	PT-I	$125	$150
1980s	PT-II	$175	$200
Preamps			
1980s	J-I, J-II	$75	$100

VHT
1989-present. Founded by Steven M. Fryette, VHT builds amps, combos, and cabinets in Burbank, California.

Victor
Late-1960s. Made in Japan.
MA-25 Amp
Late-1960s. Student model, light cover, dark grille, solidstate, 6 controls, 2 inputs, script Victor logo.

1960s		$100	$125

Victoria
1994-present. Tube amps, combos, and reverb units built by Mark Baier in Naperville, Illinois.
Double Deluxe Amp
1994-present. 35 watts, 2x12".

1994-2005		$1,300	$1,400

Model 518 Amp
1994-present. Tweed, 1x8".

1994-2005		$650	$675

Model 5112-T Amp
2001-present. 5 watts, 5F1 circuit, 1x12".

2001-2005		$850	$950

Model 20112 Amp
1994-present. 20 watts, 1x12", tweed.

1994-2005		$950	$1,000

Model 35210 Amp
1994-present. 35 watts, 2x10", tweed.

1994-2005		$1,200	$1,300

Model 35212-T Amp
1990s. 35 watts, 2x12".

1990s		$1,300	$1,400

Model 35310-T Amp
1994-present. 35 watts, 3x10".

1994-2005		$1,500	$1,600

Model 45410-T Amp
1994-present. 45 watts, 4x10" combo, tweed.

1994-2005		$1,500	$1,600

Model 50212-T Amp
2002-present. 50 watts, 2x12" combo.

2002-2005		$1,500	$1,600

Model 80212 Amp
1994-present. 80 watts, 2x12", tweed.

1994-2005		$1,500	$1,600

Regal Amp
2004-2006. Class A with 1 x 6L6, 15 watts, 1x15", brown tolex cover, rear mount controls.

2004-2006		$1,350	$1,450

Regal II Amp
2006-present. Class A, 35 watts, 1x15", tweed or vanilla tolex, rear mount controls.

2006-2007		$1,500	$1,700

Victoriette Amp
2001-present. 20 watts, 1x12" or 2x10", reverb, tremolo in '01.

2001-2005	2x10"	$1,200	$1,300

Victorilux Amp
2001-present. 35 watts, 2x12", 3x10" or 1x15", EL84s, reverb, tremolo.

2001-2005	3x10"	$1,400	$1,500

Vivi-Tone
1933-ca.1936. Founded in Kalamazoo, Michigan, by former Gibson designer Lloyd Loar and others, Vivi-Tone built small amps to accompany their early electric solidbody guitars. They possibly also built basses and mandolins.

V-M (Voice of Music) Corp.
1944-1977. Started out building record changers in Benton Harbor, Michigan. By the early '50s had added amplified phonographs, consoles, and tape recorders as well as OEM products for others. Their portable PA systems can be used for musical instruments. Products sport the VM logo.
Small Portable Amp
1950s. Standard phono input for instrument, phono and microphone controls, wood combo cabinet, 1x10" or 1x12" Jensen.

1950s		$275	$325

Voltmaster
Trapezoid-shaped combo amps and reverb units made in Plano, Texas, in the late 1990s.

Voodoo
1998-present. Tube amp heads and speaker cabinets built in Lansing, New York by Trace Davis, Anthony Cacciotti, and Mike Foster.

Vox
1957-1972, 1982-present. Tom Jennings and Dick Denney combined forces in '57 to produce the first Vox product, the 15-watt AC-15 amplifier. The short period between '63-'65 is considered to be the Vox heyday. Vox produced tube amps in England and also the U.S. from '64 to the early part of '66. English-made tube amps were standardized between '60 and '65. U.S.-made Vox amps in '66 were solidstate. In the mid-'60s, similar model names were sometimes used for tube and solidstate amps. In '93 Korg bought the Vox name and current products are built by Marshall.

A Vox amp stand is correctly called a trolley and those amps that originally came with one are priced including the original trolley, and an amp without one will be worth less than the amount shown. Smaller amps were not originally equipped with a trolley.
AC-4 Amp
1958-1965. Made in England, early Vox tube design, 3.5 watts, 1x8", tremolo.

1958-1965		$1,200	$1,500

MODEL YEAR	FEATURES	EXC. COND. LOW	HIGH

AC-10 Amp

1960-1965. Made in England, 12 watts, 1x10", tremolo, this tube version not made in U.S. ('64-'65).

| 1960-1965 | | $1,850 | $2,300 |

AC-10 Twin Amp

1960-1965. Made in England, also made in U.S. '64-'65, 12 watts (2xEL84s), 2x10".

| 1960-1965 | | $2,400 | $3,000 |

AC-15 TBX Amp

1996-2000. 15 watts, top boost, 1x12" Celestion (lower cost Eminence available).

| 1996-2000 | | $900 | $925 |

AC-15 Twin Amp

1958-1965. Tube, 2x12", 18 watts.

| 1958-1965 | Black Tolex | $3,000 | $3,600 |
| 1960-1965 | Custom colors | $3,400 | $4,200 |

AC-15CC Custom Classic Amp

2006. 15 watts, 1x12" tube combo, master volume, reverb, tremolo, 2-button footswitch, made in China.

| 2006 | | $650 | $725 |

AC-30 Super Twin Amp Head

1960-1965. Made in England, 30-watt head.

| 1960-1963 | Custom colors | $4,000 | $5,000 |
| 1960-1965 | Black, with footswitch | $3,200 | $4,000 |

AC-30 Twin/AC-30 Twin Top Boost Amp

1960-1972. Made in England, 30-watt head, 36 watts 2x12". Top Boost includes additional treble and bass, custom colors available in '60-'63.

1960-1963	Custom colors	$4,900	$5,500
1960-1965		$4,000	$4,900
1966-1972	Tube or solidstate	$2,500	$3,000

AC-30 Reissue Model Amps

1980s-1990s. Standard reissue and limited edtion models with identification plate on back of the amp. Models include the AC-30 Reissue and Reissue custom color (1980s-1990s), AC-30 25th Anniv. (1985-1986), AC-30 30th Anniv. (1991), AC-30 Collector Model (1990s, mahogany cabinet) and the AC-30HW Hand Wired (1990s).

1980s	Reissue	$1,200	$1,500
1985-1986	25th Anniv.	$1,350	$1,650
1990-2000s	Reissue	$1,100	$1,300
1990s	Collector Model	$2,000	$2,200
1990s	Custom colors	$1,400	$1,700
1990s	Hand wired	$2,000	$2,300
1991	30th Anniv.	$1,800	$2,100

AC-30CC Custom Classic Amp

2006. 30 watts, 2x12", tubes, 2-button footswitch, made in China.

| 2006 | | $675 | $725 |

AC-50 Amp Head

1960-1965. Made in England, 50-watt head, U.S. production '64-'65 tube version is Westminster Bass, U.S. post-'66 is solidstate.

| 1960-1965 | | $1,500 | $1,700 |

Berkeley II V108 (Tube) Amp

1964-1966. U.S.-made tube amp, revised '66-'69 to U.S.-made solidstate model V1081, 18 watts, 2x10" piggyback.

| 1964-1966 | | $1,000 | $1,250 |

Berkeley II V1081 (Solidstate) Amp

1966-1969. U.S.-made solidstate model V1081, 35 watts, 2x10" piggyback, includes trolley stand.

| 1966-1969 | | $700 | $800 |

Berkeley III (Solidstate) Amp

1966-1969. Berkeley III logo on top panel of amp.

| 1966-1969 | | $825 | $900 |

Buckingham Amp

1966-1969. Solidstate, 70 watts, 2x12" piggyback, includes trolley stand.

| 1966-1969 | | $850 | $925 |

Cambridge Reverb (Tube) V103 Amp

1964-1966. U.S-made tube version, 18 watts, 1x10", a Pacemaker with reverb, superceded by solidstate Model V1031 by '67.

| 1964-1966 | | $1,000 | $1,200 |

Cambridge Reverb (Solidstate) V1031 Amp

1966-1969. Solidstate, 35 watts, 1x10", model V1031 replaced tube version V103.

| 1966-1969 | | $500 | $600 |

Cambridge 15 Amp

1999-2001. 15 watts, 1x8", tremolo.

| 1999-2001 | | $125 | $150 |

Cambridge 30 Reverb Amp

1999-2002. 30 watts, 1x10", tremolo and reverb.

| 1999-2002 | | $200 | $225 |

Cambridge 30 Reverb Twin 210 Amp

1999-2002. 30 watts hybrid circuit, 2x10", reverb.

| 1999-2002 | | $275 | $325 |

Churchill PA V119 Amp Head and V1091 Cabinet Set

Late-1960s. PA head with multiple inputs and 2 column speakers.

| 1960s | Head and cabs | $750 | $900 |
| 1960s | PA head only | $350 | $400 |

Climax V-125/V-125 Lead Combo Amp

1970-1991. Solidstate, 125 watts, 2x12" combo, 5-band EQ, master volume.

| 1970-1991 | | $475 | $575 |

Defiant Amp

1966-1969. Made in England, 50 watts, 2x12" + Midax horn cabinet.

| 1966-1969 | | $1,300 | $1,600 |

Escort Amp

Late 1960s-1983. 2.5 watt battery-powered portable amp.

| 1968-1986 | | $375 | $425 |

Essex Bass V1042 Amp

1965-1969. U.S.-made solidstate, 35 watts, 2x12".

| 1965-1969 | | $500 | $600 |

Foundation Bass Amp

1966-1969. Tube in '66, solidstate after, 50 watts, 1x18", made in England only.

| 1966 | Tubes | $1,550 | $1,900 |
| 1967-1969 | Solidstate | $600 | $700 |

Kensington Bass V1241 Amp

1965-1969. U.S.-made solidstate bass amp, 22 watts, 1x15", G-tuner.

| 1965-1969 | | $500 | $600 |

Voodoo Witchdoctor Combo

Vox AC-30CC

Vox AC-50 Super Twin

AMPS

Vox Super Beatle

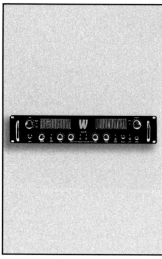

Warwick Quad IV

Washburn WA30

MODEL YEAR	FEATURES	EXC. COND. LOW	HIGH
Pacemaker (Tube) V102 Amp			
1964-1965. U.S.-made tube amp, 18 watts, 1x10", replaced by solidstate Pacemaker model V1021.			
1964-1965		$950	$1,050
Pacemaker (Solidstate) V1021 Amp			
1966-1969. U.S.-made solidstate amp, 35 watts, 1x10", replaced Pacemaker model V102.			
1967-1969		$400	$500
Pathfinder (Tube) V101 Amp			
1964-1965. U.S.-made tube amp, 4 watts, 1x18", '66-'69 became U.S.-made solidstate V1011.			
1964-1965		$800	$900
Pathfinder (Solidstate) V1011 Amp			
1966-1969. U.S.-made solidstate, 25 watts peak power, 1x8".			
1966-1969		$350	$450
Pathfinder 10 Amp			
2002-present. Compact practice amp with 1960s cosmetics, 10 watts, 6.5" speaker.			
2002-2004		$65	$80
Pathfinder 15 Amp			
1998-present. 1960s cosmetics, 15 watts, 1x8".			
1998-2004		$65	$80
Royal Guardsman V1131/V1132 Amp			
1966-1969. U.S.-made solidstate, 50 watts piggyback, 2x12" + 1 horn, the model below the Super Beatle V1141/V1142.			
1966-1969		$1,100	$1,350
Scorpion (Solidstate) Amp			
1968. Solidstate, 60 watts, 4x10" Vox Oxford speaker.			
1968		$550	$650
Super Beatle V1141/V1142 Amp			
1966-1967. U.S.-made 120 watt solidstate, 4x12" + 2 horns, with distortion pedal (V1141), or without (V1142).			
1966-1967		$2,400	$3,000
Viscount V1151/V1152 Amp			
1966-1969. U.S.-made solidstate, 70 watts, 2x12" combo.			
1966-1969		$700	$800
Westminster V118 Bass Amp			
1966-1969. Solidstate, 120 watts, 1x18".			
1966-1969		$600	$650

V-Series

See Crate.

Wabash

1950s. Private branded amps, made by others, distributed by the David Wexler company. They also offered lap steels and guitars.

MODEL YEAR	FEATURES	EXC. COND. LOW	HIGH
Model 1158 Amp			
Danelectro-made, 1x15", 2x6L6 power tubes, tweed.			
1955		$200	$250

Wallace Amplification

2000-present. Production/custom, professional grade, amps built by Brian Wallace in Livonia, Michigan. (Please note: Not affiliated with a 1970's amp company from the United Kingdom also called Wallace that has since gone out of business.)

Warbler

See listing under Juke amps.

Warwick

1982-present. Combos, amp heads and cabinets from Warwick Basses of Markneukirchen, Germany.

Washburn

1974-present. Imported guitar and bass amps. Washburn also offers guitars, banjos, mandolins, and basses.

Watkins

1957-present. England's Watkins Electric Music (WEM) was founded by Charlie Watkins. Their first commercial product was the Watkins Dominator (wedge Gibson stereo amp shape) in '57, followed by the Copicat Echo in '58. They currently build accordion amps.

MODEL YEAR	FEATURES	EXC. COND. LOW	HIGH
Clubman Amp			
1960s. Small combo amp with typical Watkins styling, blue cover, white grille.			
1960s		$525	$575
Dominator V-Front Amp			
Late-1950s-1960s, 2004. 18 watts, 2x10", wedge cabinet similar to Gibson GA-79 stereo amp, tortoise and light beige cab, light grille, requires 220V step-up transformer. Was again offered in '04.			
1959-1962		$1,600	$2,000

Webcor

1940s-1950s. The Webster-Chicago Company built recording and audio equipment including portable amplifiers suitable for record turntables, PAs, or general utility. Low power with one or two small speakers.

MODEL YEAR	FEATURES	EXC. COND. LOW	HIGH
Small Amp			
1950s	1 or 2 speakers	$150	$175

West Laboratories

1965-1970s, 2005-present. Founded by David W. West in Flint, Michigan, moved to Lansing in '68. The '71 catalog included three tube and two solidstate amps, speaker cabinets, as well as Vocal Units and Mini Series combo amps. Amps were available as heads, piggyback half-stacks and full-stacks, with the exception of the combo Mini Series. The Fillmore tube amp head was the most popular model. West equipment has a West logo on the front and the cabinets also have a model number logo on the grille. David West reestablished his company in 2005, located in Okemos, Michigan, with models offered on a custom order basis, concentrating on lower power EL84 designs.

AMPS

MODEL YEAR FEATURES	EXC. COND. LOW	HIGH
Avalon Amp Head		
1971. 50 watts, 2 6CA7 output tubes.		
1971	$525	$600
Fillmore Amp Head		
1971. 200-watts, 4 KT88 output tubes.		
1971	$1,600	$3,000
Grande Amp Head		
1971. 100 watts, 2 KT88 output tubes.		
1971	$850	$1,000

White

1955-1960. The White brand, named after plant manager Forrest White, was established by Fender to provide steel and small amp sets to teaching studios that were not Fender-authorized dealers. The amps were sold with the matching steel guitar. See Steel section for pricing.

White (Matamp)

See Matamp listing.

Woodson

Early 1970s. Obscure builder from Bolivar, Missouri. Woodson logo on front panel and Woodson Model and Serial Number plate on back panel, solidstate circuit, student level pricing.

Working Dog

2001-present. Lower cost tube amps and combos built by Alessandro High-End Products (Alessandro, Hound Dog) in Huntingdon Valley, Pennsylvania.

Yamaha

1946-present. Yamaha started building amps in the '60s and offered a variety of guitar and bass amps over the years. The current models are solidstate bass amps. They also build guitars, basses, effects, sound gear and other instruments.

MODEL YEAR FEATURES	EXC. COND. LOW	HIGH
Budokan HY-10G II Amp		
1987-1992. Portable, 10 watts, distortion control, EQ.		
1987-1992	$75	$100
G50-112 Amp		
1983-1992. 50 watts, 1x12".		
1983-1992	$225	$275
G100-112 Amp		
1983-1992. 100 watts, 1x12" combo, black cover, striped grille.		
1983-1992	$225	$275
G100-212 Amp		
1983-1992. 100, 2x12" combo, black cover, striped grille.		
1983-1992	$275	$325
JX30B Amp		
1983-1992. Bass amp, 30 watts.		
1983-1992	$175	$200
TA-20 Amp		
1968-1972. Upright wedge shape with controls facing upwards, solidstate.		
1968-1972	$150	$175

MODEL YEAR FEATURES	EXC. COND. LOW	HIGH
TA-25 Amp		
1968-1972. Upright wedge shape with controls facing upwards, 40 watts, 1x12", solidstate, black or red cover.		
1968-1972	$175	$200
TA-30 Amp		
1968-1972. Upright wedge shape, solidstate.		
1968-1972	$200	$250
TA-50 Amp		
1971-1972. Solidstate combo, 80 watts, 2x12", includes built-in cart with wheels, black cover.		
1971-1972	$225	$275
TA-60 Amp		
1968-1972. Upright wedge shape, solidstate, most expensive of wedge-shape amps.		
1968-1972	$225	$275
VR4000 Amp		
1988-1992. 50-watt stereo, 2 channels, EQ, stereo chorus, reverb and dual effects loops.		
1988-1992	$275	$325
VR6000 Amp		
1988-1992. 100-watt stereo, 2 channels which can also be combined, EQ, chorus, reverb and dual effects loops.		
1988-1992	$375	$425
VX-15 Amp		
1988-1992. 15 watts.		
1988-1992	$125	$175
VX-65D Bass Amp		
1984-1992. 80 watts, 2 speakers.		
1984-1992	$175	$200
YBA-65 Bass Amp		
1972-1976. Solidstate combo, 60 watts, 1x15".		
1972-1976	$175	$200
YTA-25 Amp		
1972-1976. Solidstate combo, 25 watts, 1x12".		
1972-1976	$175	$200
YTA-45 Amp		
1972-1976. Solidstate combo, 45 watts, 1x12".		
1972-1976	$175	$200
YTA-95 Amp		
1972-1976. Solidstate combo, 90 watts, 1x12".		
1972-1976	$175	$200
YTA-100 Amp		
1972-1976. Solidstate piggyback, 100 watts, 2x12".		
1972-1976	$225	$275
YTA-110 Amp		
1972-1976. Solidstate piggyback, 100 watts, 2x12" in extra large cab.		
1972-1976	$225	$275
YTA-200 Amp		
1972-1976. Solidstate piggyback, 200 watts, 4x12".		
1972-1976	$275	$325
YTA-300 Amp		
1972-1976. Solidstate piggyback, 200 watts, dual cabs with 2x12" and 4x12".		
1972-1976	$425	$450

West Laboratories Picofire

Working Dog Rottweiler

Yamaha VR4000

Zeta AP-12

Zinky 25-Watt

MODEL YEAR	FEATURES	EXC. COND. LOW	HIGH

YTA-400 Amp
1972-1976. Solidstate piggyback, 200 watts, dual 4x12".

1972-1976		$425	$450

Z.Vex Amps
2002-present. Intermediate grade, production amps built by Zachary Vex in Minneapolis, Minnesota with some subassembly work done in Michigan. He also builds effects.

Zapp
Ca.1978-early-1980s. Zapp amps were distributed by Red Tree Music, Inc., of Mamaroneck, New York.

Z-10 Amp
1978-1980s. Small student amp, 8 watts.

1979-1982		$25	$75

MODEL YEAR	FEATURES	EXC. COND. LOW	HIGH

Z-50 Amp
1978-1980s. Small student amp, 10 watts, reverb, tremelo.

1978-1982		$50	$75

Zeta
1982-present. Solid state amps with MIDI options, made in Oakland, California. They also make upright basses and violins.

Zinky
1999-present. Tube head and combo amps and cabinets built by Bruce Zinky in Flagstaff, Arizona. He also builds the mini Smokey amps (since '97), effects, and has revived the Supro brand on a guitar and amp.

Effects

SPEED

WIDTH

AMPLIFIER

Ibanez FLANGER

FL-303

NORMAL/EFFECT

ADA Flanger

EFFECTS

Akai Headrush E2

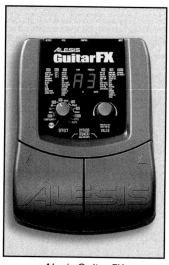

Alesis Guitar FX

MODEL YEAR	FEATURES	EXC. COND. LOW	HIGH

Ace-Tone
1968-1972. Effects from Ace Electronic Industry, which was a part of Sakata Shokai Limited of Osaka, Japan, and and also made organs, amps, etc. Their Ace-Tone effects line was available from '68-'72 and was the precedessor to Roland and Boss.

Fuzz Master FM-1
Distortion and overdrive.

1968-1972		$75	$200

Wah Master WM-1
Filter wah.

1968-1972		$75	$200

Acoustyx
1977-1982. Made by the Highland Corporation of Vermont.

Image Synthesizer IS-1
1977-1982.

1977-1982		$50	$60

Phase Five
1977-ca.1982. Used 6 C cell batteries!

1977-1982		$50	$60

ADA
1975-2002. ADA is an acronym for Analog/Digital Associates. The company was located in Berkeley, California, and introduced its Flanger and Final Phase in '77. The company later moved to Oakland and made amplifiers, high-tech signal processors, and a reissue of its original Flanger.

Final Phase
1977-1979. Reissued in '97.

1977-1979		$400	$450

Flanger
1977-1983, 1996-2002. Reissued in '96.

1977-1979	With control pedal	$400	$450
1977-1979	Without control pedal	$350	$400
1980-1983		$250	$300
1996-2002		$80	$100

MP-1
1987-1995. Tube preamp with chorus and effects loop, MIDI.

1987-1995	Without optional foot controller	$150	$200

MP-2
Ca.1988-1995. Tube preamp with chorus, 9-band EQ and effects loop, MIDI.

1988-1995		$225	$275

Pitchtraq
1987. Programmable pitch transposer including octave shifts.

1987		$225	$275

Stereo Tapped Delay STD-1
Introduced in 1981.

1980s		$150	$200

TFX4 Time Effects
Introduced in 1982, includes flanger, chorus, doubler, echo.

1980s		$150	$200

Aguilar
The New York, New York amp builder also offers a line of tube and solidstate pre-amps.

Akai
1984-present. In '99, Akai added guitar effects to their line of electronic samplers and sequencers for musicians.

Headrush E1
1999-2005. Delay, tape echo simulations, looping recorder.

1999-2005		$180	$190

Alamo
1947-1982. Founded by Charles Eilenberg, Milton Fink, and Southern Music, San Antonio, Texas. Distributed by Bruno & Sons. Mainly known for guitars and amps, Alamo did offer a reverb unit.

Reverb Unit
1965-ca.1979. Has a Hammond reverb system, balance and intensity controls. By '73 the unit had 3 controls - mixer, contour, and intensity.

1965-1970		$275	$350

Alesis
1992-present. Alesis has a wide range of products for the music industry, including digital processors and amps for guitars.

Effects Processors
1992-present. Various digital processors for reverb, echo, etc.

1990s		$125	$200

Allen Amplification
1998-present. David Allen's company, located in Richwood, Kentucky, mainly produces amps, but they also offer a tube overdrive pedal.

Altair Corp.
1977-1980s. Company was located in Ann Arbor, Michigan.

Power Attenuator PW-5
1977-1980. Goes between amp and speaker to dampen volume.

1977-1980		$100	$125

Amdek
Mid-1980s. Amdek offered many electronic products over the years, including drum machines and guitar effects. Most of these were sold in kit form so quality of construction can vary.

Delay Machine DMK-200
1983. Variable delay times.

1983		$100	$125

Octaver OCK-100
1983. Produces tone 1 or 2 octaves below the note played.

1983		$100	$125

MODEL YEAR	FEATURES	EXC. COND. LOW	HIGH

Ampeg

Ampeg entered the effects market in the late-1960s. Their offerings in the early-'60s were really amplifier-outboard reverb units similar to the ones offered by Gibson (GA-1). Ampeg offered a line of imported effects in '82-'83, known as the A-series (A-1 through A-9), and reintroduced effects to their product line in '05.

Analog Delay A-8
1982-1983. Made in Japan.

1982-1983		$75	$125

Chorus A-6
1982-1983. Made in Japan.

1982-1983		$50	$75

Compressor A-2
1982-1983. Made in Japan.

1982-1983		$50	$75

Distortion A-1
1982-1983. Made in Japan.

1982-1983		$50	$75

Echo Jet Reverb EJ-12
1963-1965. Outboard, alligator clip reverb unit with 12" speaker, 12 watts, technically a reverb unit. When used as a stand-alone amp, the reverb is off. Named EJ-12A in '65.

1963-1965		$500	$600

Echo Satellite ES-1
1961-1963. Outboard reverb unit with amplifier and speaker alligator clip.

1961-1963		$500	$600

Flanger A-5
1982-1983. Made in Japan.

1982-1983		$50	$75

Multi-Octaver A-7
1982-1983. Made in Japan.

1982-1983		$50	$100

Over Drive A-3
1982-1983. Made in Japan.

1982-1983		$50	$75

Parametric Equalizer A-9
1982-1983. Made in Japan.

1982-1983		$45	$70

Phaser A-4
1982-1983. Made in Japan.

1982-1983		$50	$75

Phazzer
1975-1977.

1975-1977		$50	$75

Scrambler Fuzz
1969. Distortion pedal. Reissued in '05.

1969		$75	$150

Amplifier Corporation of America

Late '60s company that made amps for Univox and also marketed effects under their own name.

Analog Man

1994-present. Founded by Mike Piera in '94 with full-time production by 2000. Located in Danbury, Connecticut (until '07 in Bethel), producing chorus, compressor, fuzz, and boost pedals by '03. He wrote the book Analog Man's Guide To Vintage Effects.

Aphex Systems

1975-present. Founded in Massachusetts by Marvin Caesar and Curt Knoppel, to build their Aural Exciter and other pro sound gear. Currently located in Sun Valley, California, and building a variety of gear for the pro audio broadcast, pro music and home-recording markets.

Apollo

Ca.1967-1972. Imported from Japan by St. Louis Music, includes Fuzz Treble Boost Box, Crier Wa-Wa, Deluxe Fuzz. They also offered basses and guitars.

Crier Wa-Wa
Ca.1967-1972.

1967-1972		$125	$200

Fuzz/Deluxe Fuzz
Ca.1967-1972. Includes the Fuzz Treble Boost Box and the Deluxe Fuzz.

1967-1972		$125	$200

Surf Tornado Wah Wah
Ca.1967-1972.

1967-1972		$150	$225

Arbiter

Ivor Arbiter and Arbiter Music, London, began making the circular Fuzz Face stompbox in 1966. Other products included the Fuzz Wah and Fuzz Wah Face. In '68 the company went public as Arbiter and Western, later transitioning to Dallas-Arbiter. Refer to Dallas-Arbiter for listings.

Area 51

2003-present. Guitar effects made in Newaygo, Michigan (made in Texas until early '06), by Dan Albrecht. They also build amps.

Aria

1960-present. Aria provided a line of effects, made by Maxon, in the mid-'80s.

Analog Delay AD-10
1983-1985. Dual-stage stereo.

1983-1985		$65	$75

Chorus ACH-1
1986-1987. Stereo.

1986-1987		$40	$50

Chorus CH-5
1985-1987.

1985-1987		$40	$50

Chorus CH-10
1983-1985. Dual-stage stereo.

1983-1985		$40	$50

Compressor CO-10
1983-1985.

1983-1985		$40	$50

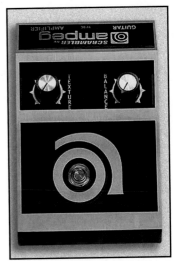

Ampeg Scrambler Fuzz

Aphex Guitar Xciter

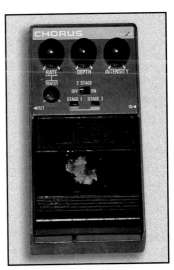

Aria CH-10 Chorus

Arion Stereo Delay SAD-3

Arteffect Bonnie Wah

Automagic British Steel BS-1

MODEL YEAR	FEATURES	EXC. COND. LOW	HIGH
Digital Delay ADD-100			
1984-1986. Delay, flanging, chorus, doubling, hold.			
1984-1986		$65	$75
Digital Delay DD-X10			
1985-1987.			
1985-1987		$65	$75
Distortion DT-5			
1985-1987.			
1985-1987		$40	$50
Distortion DT-10			
1983-1985. Dual-stage.			
1983-1985		$40	$50
Flanger AFL-1			
1986. Stereo.			
1986		$50	$60
Flanger FL-5			
1985-1987.			
1985-1987		$50	$60
Flanger FL-10			
1983-1985. Dual-stage stereo.			
1983-1985		$50	$60
Metal Pedal MP-5			
1985-1987.			
1985-1987		$40	$50
Noise Gate NG-10			
1983-1985.			
1983-1985		$30	$40
Over Drive OD-10			
1983-1985. Dual-stage.			
1983-1985		$40	$50
Parametric Equalizer EQ-10			
1983-1985.			
1983-1985		$40	$50
Phase Shifter PS-10			
1983-1984. Dual-stage.			
1983-1984		$50	$60
Programmable Effects Pedal APE-1			
1984-1986. Compression, distortion, delay, chorus.			
1984-1986		$50	$60

Arion

1984-present. Arion offers a wide variety of budget imported effects.

Guitar and Bass Effects

1984-2007		$15	$45

Arteffect

2006-present. Tom Kochawi and Dan Orr build analog effects in Haifa and Natanya, Israel.

Asama

1970s-1980s. This Japanese company offered solidbody guitars with built-in effects as well as stand-alone units. They also offered basses, drum machines and other music products.

Astrotone

Late 1960s. By Universal Amp, which also made the Sam Ash Fuzzz Boxx.

MODEL YEAR	FEATURES	EXC. COND. LOW	HIGH
Fuzz			
1966. Introduced in '66, same as Sam Ash Fuzzz Boxx.			
1966		$175	$275

ATD

Mid-1960s-early 1980s. Made by the All-Test Devices corporation of Long Beach, New York. In the mid-'60s, Richard Minz and an associate started making effects part-time, selling them through Manny's Music in New York. They formed All-Test and started making Maestro effects and transducer pickups for CMI, which owned Gibson at the time. By '75, All-Test was marketing effects under their own brand. All-Test is still making products for other industries, but by the early to mid-'80s they were no longer making products for the guitar.

PB-1 Power Booster

1976-ca.1980.

1979-1980		$50	$60

Volume Pedal EV-1

1979-ca.1980.

1979-1980		$30	$40

Wah-Wah/Volume Pedal WV-1

1979-ca.1981.

1979-1981		$50	$60

Audio Matrix

1979-1984. Effects built by B.K Butler in Escondido, California. He later designed the Tube Driver and founded Tube Works in 1987. He nows operates Butler Audio, making home and auto hybrid tube stereo amps.

Mini Boogee B81

1981. Four-stage, all-tube preamp, overdrive, distortion.

1981		$100	$135

Audioworks

1980s. Company was located in Niles, Illinois.

F.E.T. Distortion

1982.

1980s		$40	$55

Auralux

2000-present. Founded by Mitchell Omori and David Salzmann, Auralux builds effects and tube amps in Highland Park, Illinois.

Austone Electronics

1997-present. Founded by Jon Bessent and Randy Larkin, Austone offers a range of stomp boxes, all made in Austin, Texas.

Overdrive and Fuzz Pedals

1997-present. Various overdrive and fuzz boxes.

1997-2007		$125	$175

Automagic

1998-present. Wah pedals and distortion boxes made in Germany by Musician Sound Design.

MODEL		EXC. COND.	
YEAR	FEATURES	LOW	HIGH

Avalanche
Brianizer
Late-1980s. Leslie effect, dual rotor, adjustable speed and rates.

1980s		$75	$90

Axe
1980s. Early '80s line of Japanese effects, possibly made by Maxon.

B & M
1970s. A private brand made by Sola/Colorsound for Barns and Mullens, a U.K. distributor.
Fuzz Unit
1970s. Long thin orange case, volume, sustain, tone knobs, on-off stomp switch.

1970s		$275	$325

Backline Engineering
2004-present. Guitar multi-effects built by Gary Lee in Camarillo, California. In '07, they added tube amps.

Bad Cat Amplifier Company
2000-present. Amp company Bad Cat, of Corona, California, also offers guitar effects.

Baldwin
1965-1970. The piano maker got into the guitar market when it acquired Burns of London in '65, and sold the guitars in the U.S. under the Baldwin name. They also marketed a couple of effects at the same time.

Banzai
2000-present. Effects built by Olaf Nobis in Berlin, Germany.

Bartolini
The pickup manufacturer offered a few effects from around 1982 to '87.
Tube-It
1982-ca.1987. Marshall tube amplification simulator with bass, treble, sustain controls.

1982-1987	Red case	$80	$90

Basic Systems' Side Effects
1980s. This company was located in Tulsa, Oklahoma.
Audio Delay
1986-ca.1987. Variable delay speeds.

1986-1987		$75	$100

Triple Fuzz
1986-ca.1987. Selectable distortion types.

1986-1987		$50	$60

BBE
1985-present. BBE, owner of G & L Guitars and located in California, manufactures rack-mount effects and added a new line of stomp boxes in '05.

Behringer
1989-present. The German professional audio products company added modeling effects in '01 and guitar stomp boxes in '05. They also offer guitars and amps.

Beigel Sound Lab
1980. Music product designer Mike Beigel helped form Musitronics Corp, where he made the Mu-Tron III. In 1978 he started Beigel Sound Lab to provide product design in Warwick, New York, where in '80 he made 50 rack-mount Enveloped Controlled Filters under this brand name.

Bell Electrolabs
1970s. This English company offered a line of effects in the '70s.
Vibrato

1970s		$150	$200

Bennett Music Labs
Effects built in Chatanooga, Tennessee by Bruce Bennett.

Bigsby
Bigsby has been making volume and tone pedals since the 1950s. They currently offer a volume pedal.
Foot Volume and Tone Control

1950s		$125	$175

Binson
Late 1950s-1982. Binson, of Milan, Italy, made several models of the Echorec, using tubes or transistors. They also made units for Guild, Sound City and EKO.
Echorec
Ca.1960-1979. Four knob models with 12 echo selections, 1 head, complex multitap effects, settings for record level, playback and regeneration. Includes B1, B2, Echomaster1, T5 (has 6 knobs), T5E, and Baby. Used a magnetic disk instead of tape. Guild later offered the Guild Echorec by Binson which is a different stripped-down version.

1960s	Tube	$500	$1,500

Bixonic
1995-present. Originally distributed by Sound-Barrier Music, Bixonic is currently distributed by Godlyke, Inc.
Expandora EXP-2000
1995-2000. Analog distortion, round silver case, internal DIP switches.

1995-2000		$175	$200

Blackbox Music Electronics
2000-present. Founded by Loren Stafford and located in Minneapolis, Minnesota, Blackbox offers a line of effects for guitar and bass.

Bad Cat 2-Tone

BBE Two Timer

Bixonic Expandora

EFFECTS

Boss Blues Driver BD-2

Boss Digital Delay DD-3

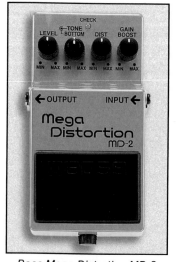

Boss Mega Distortion MD-2

Blackstar Amplification

2007-present. Guitar effects pedals built by Joel Richardson in Northampton, England. He also builds amps.

Blackstone Appliances

1999-present. Distortion effects crafted by Jon Blackstone in New York, New York.

Bon, Mfg

Bon was located in Escondido, California.

Tube Driver 204
1979-ca.1981.

MODEL YEAR FEATURES	EXC. COND. LOW	HIGH
1979-1981	$100	$150

Boss

1976-present. Japan's Roland Corporation first launched effect pedals in '74. A year or two later the subsidiary company, Boss, debuted its own line. They were marketed concurrently at first but gradually Boss became reserved for effects and drum machines while the Roland name was used on amplifiers and keyboards. Boss still offers a wide line of pedals.

Acoustic Simulator AC-2
1997-2007. Four modes that emulate various acoustic tones.

1997-2007	$50	$60

Auto Wah AW-2
1991-1999.

1991-1999	$40	$50

Bass Chorus CE-2B
1987-1995.

1987-1995	$40	$50

Bass Equalizer GE-7B
1987-1995. Seven-band, name changed to GEB-7 in '95.

1987-1995	$40	$50

Bass Flanger BF-2B
1987-1994.

1987-1994	$40	$50

Bass Limiter LM-2B
1990-1994.

1990-1994	$35	$40

Bass Overdrive ODB-3
1994-present.

1994-2007	$40	$50

Blues Driver BD-2
1995-present.

1995-2007	$40	$50

Chorus Ensemble CE-1
1976-1984. Vibrato and chorus.

1976-1984	$145	$245

Chorus Ensemble CE-2
1979-1982.

1979-1982	$45	$95

Chorus Ensemble CE-3
1982-1992.

1982-1992	$45	$95

MODEL YEAR FEATURES	EXC. COND. LOW	HIGH

Chorus Ensemble CE-5
1991-present.

1991-2007	$45	$95

Compressor Sustainer CS-1
1978-1982.

1978-1982	$70	$95

Compressor Sustainer CS-2
1981-1986.

1981-1986	$70	$95

Compressor Sustainer CS-3
1986-present.

1986-2007	$70	$95

Delay DM-2
1981-1984. Analog, hot pink case.

1981-1984	$170	$245

Delay DM-3
1984-1988.

1984-1988	$145	$195

Digital Delay DD-2
1983-1986.

1983-1986	$120	$170

Digital Delay DD-3
1986-present. Up to 800 ms of delay.

1986-1989	$120	$170
1990-2007	$95	$145

Digital Delay DD-5
1995-2005. Up to 2 seconds of delay.

1995-2005	$95	$145

Digital Delay DD-6
2003-2007. Up to 5 seconds of delay.

2003-2007	$55	$70

Digital Dimension C DC-2
1985-1989. Two chorus effects and tremolo.

1985-1989	$135	$145

Digital Metalizer MZ-2
1987-1992.

1987-1992	$80	$90

Digital Reverb RV-2
1987-1990.

1987-1990	$95	$145

Digital Reverb RV-5
2003-present. Dual imput and dual output, four control knobs, silver case.

2003-2007	$60	$95

Digital Reverb/Delay RV-3
1994-2004.

1994-2004	$95	$120

Digital Sampler/Delay DSD-2
1985-1986.

1985-1986	$120	$170

Digital Space-D DC-3/Digital Dimension DC-3
1988-1993. Originally called the Digital Space-D, later changed to Digital Dimension. Chorus with EQ.

1988-1993	$130	$180

Digital Stereo Reverb RV-70
1994-1995. Rack mount, MIDI control, reverb/delay, 199 presets.

1994-1995	$130	$180

MODEL YEAR FEATURES	EXC. COND. LOW	HIGH
Distortion DS-1		
1978-1989, 1990s-present.		
1978-1989	$50	$60
1990-1999	$30	$50
2000-2007	$20	$25
Dr. Rhythm DR-55		
1979-1989. Drum machine.		
1979-1989	$145	$195
Dual Over Drive SD-2		
1993-1998.		
1993-1998	$45	$55
Dynamic Filter FT-2		
1986-1988. Auto wah.		
1986-1988	$70	$95
Dynamic Wah AW-3		
2000-present. Auto wah with humanizer, for guitar or bass.		
2000-2007	$50	$60
Enhancer EH-2		
1990-1998.		
1990-1998	$35	$45
Flanger BF-1		
1977-1980.		
1977-1980	$55	$70
Flanger BF-2		
1980-2005.		
1980-1989	$55	$70
1990-2005	$40	$55
Foot Wah FW-3		
1992-1996.		
1992-1996	$45	$55
Graphic Equalizer GE-6		
1978-1981. Six bands.		
1978-1981	$45	$70
Graphic Equalizer GE-7		
1981-present. Seven bands.		
1982-1989	$70	$95
1990-2007	$45	$65
Graphic Equalizer GE-10		
1976-1985. 10-band EQ for guitar or bass.		
1976-1985	$95	$120
Harmonist HR-2		
1994-1999. Pitch shifter.		
1994-1999	$70	$95
Heavy Metal HM-2		
1983-1991. Distortion.		
1983-1991	$30	$40
Hyper Fuzz FZ-2		
1993-1997.		
1993-1997	$45	$70
Hyper Metal HM-3		
1993-1998.		
1993-1998	$35	$45
Limiter LM-2		
1987-1992.		
1987-1992	$25	$35
Line Selector LS-2		
1991-present. Select between 2 effects loops.		
1991-2007 With adapter	$45	$70

MODEL YEAR FEATURES	EXC. COND. LOW	HIGH
Mega Distortion MD-2		
2003-present.		
2003-2007	$45	$55
Metal Zone MT-2		
1991-present. Distortion and 3-band EQ.		
1991-2007	$45	$70
Multi Effects ME-5		
1988-1991. Floor unit.		
1988-1991	$70	$120
Multi Effects ME-6		
1992-1997.		
1992-1997	$70	$120
Multi Effects ME-8		
1996-1997.		
1996-1997	$70	$120
Multi Effects ME-30		
1998-2002.		
1998-2002	$70	$120
Multi Effects ME-50		
2003-present. Floor unit.		
2003-2007	$170	$195
Noise Gate NF-1		
1979-1988.		
1979-1988	$40	$50
Noise Suppressor NS-2		
1987-present.		
1987-2007	$40	$50
Octaver OC-2/Octave OC-2		
1982-2003. Originally called the Octaver.		
1982-2003	$55	$70
Overdrive OD-1		
1977-1985.		
1977-1979	$95	$170
1980-1985	$70	$145
Overdrive OD-3		
1997-present.		
1997-2007	$45	$70
Parametric Equalizer PQ-4		
1991-1997.		
1991-1997	$45	$70
Phaser PH-1		
1977-1981.		
1977-1981	$70	$95
Phaser PH-1R		
1982-1985. Resonance control added to PH-1.		
1982-1985	$70	$120
Pitch Sifter/Delay PS-2		
1987-1993.		
1987-1993	$95	$120
Reverb Box RX-100		
1981-mid-1980s.		
1981-1985	$70	$95
Rocker Distortion PD-1		
1980-mid-1980s. Variable pedal using magnetic field.		
1980-1985	$45	$70
Rocker Volume PV-1		
1981-mid-1980s.		
1980-1985	$45	$55
Rocker Wah PW-1		
1980-mid-1980s. Magnetic field variable pedal.		
1980-1985	$55	$65

Boss Noise Gate NF-1

EFFECTS

Boss Super Chorus CH-1

Boss Reverb Box RX-100

Boss Tremolo TR-2

Budda Phatman

Burriss Boostier

MODEL YEAR / FEATURES	EXC. COND. LOW	HIGH
Slow Gear SG-1		
1979-1982. Violin swell effect, automatically adjusts volume.		
1979-1982	$325	$375
Spectrum SP-1		
1977-1981. Single-band parametric EQ.		
1977-1981	$325	$375
Super Chorus CH-1		
1989-present.		
1989-2007	$45	$70
Super Distortion & Feedbacker DF-2		
1984-1994. Also labeled as the Super Feedbacker & Distortion.		
1984-1994	$95	$120
Super Over Drive SD-1		
1981-present.		
1981-1989	$45	$85
1990-2007	$30	$50
Super Phaser PH-2		
1984-2001.		
1984-1989	$45	$85
1990-2001	$30	$50
Super Shifter PS-5		
1999-present. Pitch shifter/harmonizer.		
1999-2007	$95	$120
Touch Wah TW-1/T Wah TW-1		
1978-1987. Auto wah, early models were labeled as Touch Wah.		
1978-1987	$95	$120
Tremolo TR-2		
1997-present.		
1997-2007	$65	$75
Tremolo/Pan PN-2		
1990-1995.		
1990-1995	$120	$145
Turbo Distortion DS-2		
1987-present.		
1987-2007	$70	$120
Turbo Overdrive OD-2		
1985-1994. Called OD-2R after '94, due to added remote on/off jack.		
1985-1994	$70	$120
Vibrato VB-2		
1982-1986. True pitch-changing vibrato, warm analog tone, Rise Time control allows for slow attack, four knobs, aqua-blue case.		
1982-1986	$400	$450
Volume FV-50H		
1987-1997. High impedance, stereo volume pedal with inputs and outputs.		
1987-1997	$45	$55
Volume FV-50L		
1987-1997. Low impedance version of FV-50.		
1987-1997	$35	$45
Volume Pedal FV-100		
Late-1980s-1991. Guitar volume pedal.		
1987-1991	$35	$45

Browntone Electronics

2006-present. Foot pedal guitar effects built in Lincolnton, North Carolina by Tim Brown.

Bruno

1834-present. Music distributor Bruno and Sons had a line of Japanese-made effects in the early '70s.

Budda

1995-present. Wahs and distortion pedals by Jeff Bober and Scott Sier in San Francisco, California. They also build amps.

Build Your Own Clone

2005-present. Build it yourself kits based on vintage effects produced by Keith Vonderhulls in Othello, Washington. Assembled kits are offered by their Canadian distributor.

Burriss

2001-present. Guitar effects from Bob Burriss of Lexington, Kentucky. He also builds amps.

Carl Martin

1993-present. Line of effects from Søren Jongberg and East Sound Research of Denmark. In '06 they added their Chinese-made Vintage Series. They also build amps.

Carlsbro

1959-present. English amp company Carlsbro Electronics Limited offered a line of effects from '77 to '81.

Carrotron

Late-1970s-mid-1980s. Carrotron was out of California and offered a line of effects.

MODEL YEAR / FEATURES	EXC. COND. LOW	HIGH
Noise Fader C900B1		
1980-1982.		
1980-1982	$50	$60
Preamp C821B		
1981-ca.1982.		
1981-1982	$55	$65

Carvin

1946-present. Carvin introduced its line of Ground Effects in '02 and discontinued them in '03.

Castle Instruments

Early 1980s. Castle was located in Madison, New Jersey, and made rack-mount and floor phaser units.

MODEL YEAR / FEATURES	EXC. COND. LOW	HIGH
Phaser III		
1980-1982. Offered mode switching for various levels of phase.		
1980-1982	$100	$175

Catalinbread

2003-present. Nicholas Harris founded Catalinbread Specialized Mechanisms of Music in Seattle, Washington, in '02 to do mods and in '03 added his own line of guitar effects.

MODEL		EXC. COND.	
YEAR	FEATURES	LOW	HIGH

Cat's Eye

2001-present. Dean Solorzano and Lisa Kroeker build their analog guitar effects in Oceanside, California.

Chandler

1984-present. Located in California, Chandler Musical Instruments offers instruments, pickups, and pickguards, as well as effects.

Digital Echo

1992-2000. Rackmount, 1 second delay, stereo.

1992-2000		$350	$450

Tube Driver

1986-1991. Uses a 12AX7 tube. Not to be confused with the Tube Works Tube Driver.

1980s	Large Box	$200	$325
1980s	Rackmount	$100	$150
1990s	Rackmount	$100	$150

Chapman

1970-present. From Emmett Chapman, maker of the Stick.

Patch of Shades

1981, 1989. Wah, with pressure sensitive pad instead of pedal. 2 production runs.

1980s		$50	$75

Chicago Iron

1998-present. Faithful reproductions of classic effects built by Kurt Steir in Chicago, Illinois.

Chunk Systems

1996-present. Guitar and bass effects pedals built by Richard Cartwright in Sydney, Australia.

Clark

1960s. Built in Clark, New Jersey, same unit as the Orpheum Fuzz and the Mannys Music Fuzz.

SS-600 Fuzz

1960s. Chrome-plated, volume and tone knobs, toggle switch.

1960s		$150	$200

Clark Amplification

1995-present. Amplifier builder Mike Clark, of Cayce, South Carolina, offers a reverb unit and started building guitar effects as well, in '98.

ClinchFX

2006-present. Hand made pedals by Peter Clinch in Brisbane, Queensland, Australia.

Coffin

Case manufacturer Coffin Case added U.S.-made guitar effects pedals to their product line in 2006.

Colorsound

1967-present. Colorsound effects were produced by England's Sola Sound, which was founded in '62 by former Vox associate Larry Macari and his brother Joe. The first product was a fuzzbox called the Tone Bender, designed by Gary Hurst and sold at Macari's Musical Exchange stores.

The first readily available fuzz in Britain, it was an instant success. In '67, the Colorsound brand was launched. In the late-'60s, wah and fuzz-wah pedals were added, and by the end of the '70s, Colorsound offered 18 different effects, an amp, and accessories. Few early Colorsound products were imported into the U.S., so today they're scarce. Except for the Wah-Wah pedal, Colorsound's production stopped by the early '80s, but in '96 most of their early line was reissued by Dick Denny of Vox fame. Denny died in 2001. Since then, Anthony and Steve Macari build Colorsound effects in London. Mutronics offered a licensed rack mount combination of 4 classic Colorsound effects for a short time in the early 2000s.

Flanger

1970s		$110	$210

Fuzz Phazer

Introduced in 1973.

1970s		$160	$235

Jumbo Tonebender

1974-early 1980s. Replaced the Tonebender fuzz, with wider case and light blue lettering.

1979		$160	$260

Octivider

Introduced in 1973.

1970s		$160	$235

Overdriver

Introduced in 1972. Controls for drive, treble and bass.

1970s		$160	$235

Phazer

Introduced in 1973. Magenta/purple-pink case, slanted block Phazer logo on front.

1970s		$160	$235

Ring Modulator

Introduced in 1973. Purple case, Ring Modulator name with atom orbit slanted block logo on case.

1970s		$260	$285

Supa Tonebender Fuzz

1977-early 1980s. Sustain and volume knobs, tone control and toggle. Same white case as Jumbo Tonebender, but with new circuit.

1970s		$160	$235

Supa Wah-Swell

1970s. Supa Wah-Swell in slanted block letters on the end of the pedal, silver case.

1970s		$160	$235

Supaphase

1970s		$160	$235

Supasustain

1960s		$135	$210

Tremolo

1970s		$160	$210

Tremolo Reissue

1996-present. Purple case.

1996-2007		$110	$135

Cat's-Eye Mista Fuzz

Chandler Tube Driver

Chunk Systems Octavius Squeezer

EFFECTS

Crowther Audio Hot Cake

Cusack Music Tap-A-Whirl

Dallas Arbiter Fuzz Face

MODEL YEAR	FEATURES	EXC. COND. LOW	HIGH

Wah Fuzz Straight
Introduced in 1973. Aqua-blue case, Wah-Fuzz-Straight in capital block letters on end of wah pedal.

| 1970s | | $185 | $260 |

Wah Fuzz Swell
Introduced in 1973. Yellow case, block letter Wah Fuzz Swell logo on front, three control knobs and toggle.

| 1970s | | $260 | $360 |

Wah Swell
1970s. Light purple case, block letter Wah-Swell logo on front.

| 1970s | | $235 | $285 |

Wah Wah
1970s. Dark gray case, Wah-Wah in capital block letters on end of wah pedal.

| 1975 | | $310 | $360 |

Wah Wah Reissue
1996-2005. Red case, large Colorsound letter logo and small Wah Wah lettering on end of pedal.

| 1996-2005 | | $85 | $110 |

Wah Wah Supremo
1970s. Silver/chrome metal case, Wah-Wah Supremo in block letters on end of wah pedal.

| 1975 | | $435 | $485 |

Companion
1970s. Private branded by Shinei of Japan, which made effects for others as well.

Tape Echo
| 1960-1970 | | $350 | $450 |

Wah Pedal
| 1970s | | $125 | $175 |

Conn
Ca.1968-ca.1978. Band instrument manufacturer and distributor Conn/Continental Music Company, of Elkhart, Indiana, imported guitars and effects from Japan.

Strobe ST-8 Tuner
Late-1960s. Brown case.

| 1968 | | $215 | $225 |

Coopersonic
2006-present. Martin Cooper builds his guitar effects in Nottingham, UK.

Coron
1970s-1980s. Japanese-made effects, early ones close copies of MXR pedals.

Cosmosound
Italy's Cosmosound made small amps with Leslie drums and effects pedals in the late '60s and '70s. Cosmosound logo is on top of pedals.

Wah Fuzz CSE-3
1970s. Volume and distortion knobs, wah and distortion on-off buttons, silver case.

| 1970s | | $275 | $350 |

MODEL YEAR	FEATURES	EXC. COND. LOW	HIGH

Creation Audio Labs
2005-present. Guitar and bass boost pedal and re-amplifying gear built in Nashville, Tennessee.

Crowther Audio
1976-present. Guitar effects built by Paul Crowther, who was the original drummer of the band Split Enz, in Auckland, New Zealand. His first effect was the Hot Cake.

Crybaby
See listing under Vox for early models, and Dunlop for recent versions.

CSL
Sola Sound made a line of effects for C. Summerfield Ltd., an English music company.

Cusack Music
2003-present. Effects built in Holland, Michigan, by Jon Cusack.

Dallas/Dallas Arbiter
Dallas Arbiter, Ltd. was based in London and it appeared in the late-1960s as a division of a Dallas group of companies headed by Ivor Arbiter. Early products identified with Dallas logo with the company noted as John E. Dallas & Sons Ltd., Dallas Building, Clifton Street, London, E.C.2. They also manufactured Sound City amplifiers and made Vox amps from '72 to '78. The Fuzz Face is still available from Jim Dunlop.

Fuzz Face
Introduced in 1966. The current reissue of the Dallas Arbiter Fuzz Face is distributed by Jim Dunlop USA.

1968-1969	Red	$900	$1,200
1970	Red	$500	$900
1970-1976	Blue	$400	$800
1977-1980	Blue	$350	$700
1981	Grey, reissue	$300	$600
1990-1999	Red, reissue	$75	$150
2000-2006	Red, reissue	$65	$75

Fuzz Wah Face
| 1970s | Black | $300 | $600 |
| 1990s | Reissue copy | $60 | $75 |

Rangemaster Treble Boost
| 1966 | | $2,500 | $3,500 |

Sustain
| 1970s | | $250 | $550 |

Treble and Bass Face
| 1960s | | $300 | $700 |

Trem Face
Ca.1970-ca.1975. Reissued in '80s, round red case, depth and speed control knobs, Dallas-Arbiter England logo plate.

| 1970-1975 | | $300 | $700 |

Wah Baby
1970s. Gray speckle case, Wah Baby logo caps and small letters on end of pedal.

| 1970s | | $300 | $700 |

MODEL YEAR	FEATURES	EXC. COND. LOW	HIGH

Damage Control

2005-present. Guitar effects pedals and digital multi-effects built in Moorpark, California.

Dan Armstrong

1976-1981, 1991-present. In '76, Musitronics, based in Rosemont, New Jersey, introduced 6 inexpensive plug-in effects designed by Dan Armstrong. Perhaps under the influence of John D. MacDonald's Travis McGee novels, each effect name incorporated a color, like Purple Peaker. Shipping box labeled Dan Armstrong by Musitronics. They disappeared a few years later but were reissued by WD Products from '91 to '02 (See WD for those models). From '03 to '06, Vintage Tone Project offered the Dan Armstrong Orange Crusher. Since '06, a licensed line of Dan Armstrong effects that plug directly into the output of a guitar or bass has been offered by Grafton Electronics of Grafton, Vermont. Dan Armstrong died in '04.

Blue Clipper
1976-1981. Fuzz, blue-green case.

1976-1981		$85	$100

Green Ringer
1976-1981. Ring Modulator/Fuzz, green case.

1970s		$85	$100

Orange Squeezer
1976-1981. Compressor, orange case.

1976-1981		$85	$100

Purple Peaker
1976-1981. Frequency Booster, light purple case.

1976-1981		$85	$100

Red Ranger
1976-1981. Bass/Treble Booster, light red case.

1976-1981		$85	$100

Yellow Humper
1976-1981. Yellow case.

1976-1981		$85	$100

Danelectro

1946-1969, 1996-present. The Danelectro brand was revived in '96 with a line of effects pedals. They also offer the Wasabi line of effects. Prices do not include AC adapter, add $10 for the Zero-Hum adapter.

Chicken Salad Vibrato
2000-present. Orange case.

2000-2007		$20	$25

Cool Cat Chorus
1996-present.

1996-2007		$20	$25

Corned Beef Reverb
2000-present. Blue-black case.

2000-2007		$15	$20

Daddy-O Overdrive
1996-present. White case.

1996-2007		$30	$40

Dan Echo
1998-present.

1998-2007		$40	$45

MODEL YEAR	FEATURES	EXC. COND. LOW	HIGH

Fab Tone Distortion
1996-present.

1996-2007		$30	$40

Reverb Unit

1965		$200	$300

Davoli

1960s-1970. Davoli was an Italian pickup and guitar builder and is often associated with Wandre guitars.

TRD
1970s. Solidstate tremolo, reverb, distortion unit.

1970s		$175	$225

Dean Markley

The string and pickup manufacturer offered a line of effects from 1976 to the early-'90s.

Overlord Classic Tube Overdrive
1988-1991. Uses a 12AX7A tube, AC powered.

1988-1991		$60	$80

Overlord III Classic Overdrive
1990-1991. Battery-powered version of Overlord pedal. Black case with red letters.

1990-1991		$40	$70

Voice Box 50 (Watt Model)
1976-1979.

1976-1979		$75	$125

Voice Box 100 (Watt Model)
1976-1979, 1982-ca.1985.

1976-1979		$75	$125

Voice Box 200 (Watt Model)
1976-1979.

1976-1979		$75	$125

DeArmond

In 1947, DeArmond may have introduced the first actual signal-processing effect pedal, the Tremolo Control. They made a variety of effects into the '70s, but only one caught on - their classic volume pedal. DeArmond is primarily noted for pickups.

Pedal Phaser Model 1900
1974-ca.1979.

1974-1979		$75	$125

Square Wave Distortion Generator
1977-ca.1979.

1977-1979		$100	$150

Thunderbolt B166
1977-ca.1979. Five octave wah.

1977-1979		$50	$100

Tone/Volume Pedal 610
1978-ca.1979.

1978-1979		$75	$125

Tornado Phase Shifter
1977-ca.1979.

1977-1979		$100	$125

Tremolo Control Model 60A/60B
The Model 60 Tremolo Control dates from 1947 to the early-1950s. Model 60A dates from mid- to late-'50s. Model 60B, early-'60s.

1950s	60A	$300	$400
1960s	60B	$150	$300

Dan Armstrong Purple Peaker

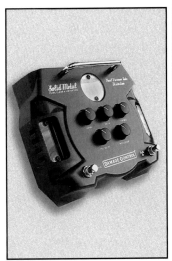

Damage Control Solid Metal

Dean Markley Overlord

Digitech Reverberator XP400

*Digitech Whammy
Pedal WP-I*

DNA Smokey Fuzz

MODEL YEAR	FEATURES	LOW	HIGH
Twister 1930	*1980. Phase shifter.*		
1980		$100	$125
Volume Pedal Model 602	*1960s.*		
1960s		$40	$70
Volume Pedal Model 1602	*1978-ca. 1980s.*		
1970s		$40	$60
Volume Pedal Model 1630	*1978-1980s. Optoelectric.*		
1970s		$40	$60
Weeper Wah Model 1802	*1970s. Weeper logo on foot pedal.*		
1970s		$100	$125

Death By Audio
2001-present. Oliver Ackermann builds production and custom guitar effects in Brooklyn, New York.

DeltaLab Research
Late 1970s-early 1980s. DeltaLab, which was located in Chelmsford, Massachusetts, was an early builder of rackmount gear.

DL-2 Acousticomputer	*1980s. Delay.*		
1980s		$75	$125
DL-4 Time Line	*1980s. Delay.*		
1980s		$75	$125
DL-5	*1980s. Various digital processing effects, blue case, rackmount.*		
1980s		$175	$225
DLB-1 Delay Control Pedal	*1980s. Controls other DeltaLab pedals, chrome, Morley-looking pedal.*		
1980s		$50	$75
Electron I ADM/II ADM	*1980s. Blue case, rackmount effects. Models include the Electron I ADM, and the Electron II ADM.*		
1980s	Electron I ADM	$50	$75
1980s	Electron II ADM	$75	$125

Demeter
1980-present. Amp builder James Demeter and company, located in Van Nuys, California, also build guitar effects.

Denio
Line of Japanese-made Boss lookalikes sold in Asia and Australia.

Diamond Pedals
2004-present. Designed by Michael Knappe and Tim Fifield, these effects are built in Bedford, Nova Scotia, Canada.

Diaz
Early 1980s-2002, 2004-present. Line of effects from the amp doctor Cesar Diaz. Diaz died in '02; in '04, his family announced plans to resume production.

DigiTech
The DigiTech/DOD company is in Utah and the effects are made in the U.S.A. The DigiTech name started as a line under the DOD brand in the early 1980s; later spinning off into its own brand. They also produce vocal products and studio processors and are now part of Harman International Industries.

Digital Delay PDS 1000	*1985-ca.1989. One second delay.*		
1985-1989		$100	$150
Digital Delay and Sampler PDS 2000	*1985-1991. 2 second delay.*		
1985-1991		$125	$175
Digital Delay PDS 2700 Double Play	*1989-1991. Delay and chorus*		
1989-1991		$125	$175
Digital Stereo Chorus/Flanger PDS 1700	*1986-1991.*		
1986-1991		$100	$150
Echo Plus 8 Second Delay PDS 8000	*1985-1991.*		
1985-1991		$175	$200
Guitar Effects Processor RP 1	*1992-1996. Floor unit, 150 presets.*		
1992-1996		$100	$150
Guitar Effects Processor RP 3	*1998-2003. Floor unit.*		
1998-2003		$110	$150
Guitar Effects Processor RP 5	*1994-1996. Floor unit, 80 presets.*		
1994-1996		$120	$175
Guitar Effects Processor RP 6	*1996-1997. Floor unit.*		
1996-1997		$125	$200
Guitar Effects Processor RP 10	*1994-1996. Floor unit, 200 presets.*		
1994-1996		$125	$175
Guitar Effects Processor RP 14D	*1999. Floor unit with expression pedal, 1x12AX7 tube, 100 presets.*		
1999		$300	$350
Guitar Effects Processor RP 100	*2000-2006.*		
2000-2006		$100	$125
Guitar Effects Processor RP 200	*2001-2006. 140 presets, drum machine, Expression pedal.*		
2001-2006		$100	$125
Hot Box PDS 2730	*1989-1991. Delay and distortion*		
1989-1991		$100	$125
Modulator Pedal XP 200	*1996-2002. Floor unit, 61 presets.*		
1996-2002		$100	$125

MODEL		EXC. COND.	
YEAR	FEATURES	LOW	HIGH

Multi Play PDS 20/20
1987-1991. Multi-function digital delay.

1987-1991		$125	$150

Pedalverb Digital Reverb Pedal PDS 3000
1987-1991.

1987-1991		$100	$125

Programmable Distortion PDS 1550
1986-1991.

1986-1991	Yellow case	$50	$75

Programmable Distortion PDS 1650
1989-1991.

1989-1991	Red case	$50	$75

Rock Box PDS 2715
1989-1991. Chorus and distortion.

1989-1991		$50	$75

Two Second Digital Delay PDS 1002
1987-1991.

1987-1991		$100	$125

Whammy Pedal WP I
1990-1993. Original Whammy Pedal, red case, reissued as WP IV in '00.

1990-1993		$375	$475

Whammy Pedal WP II
1994-1997. Can switch between 2 presets, black case.

1994-1997		$200	$275

Whammy Pedal Reissue
2000-present. Reissue version of classic WP-1 with added dive bomb and MIDI features.

2000-2005		$125	$150

DiMarzio

The pickup maker offered a couple of effects in the late-1980s to the mid-'90s.

Metal Pedal
1987-1989.

1987-1989		$50	$75

Very Metal Fuzz
Ca.1989-1995. Distortion/overdrive pedal.

1989-1995		$50	$75

Dino's

1995-present. A social co-op founded by Alessio Casati and Andy Bagnasco, in Albisola, Italy. It builds a line of boutique analog pedals as well as guitars.

Divided By Thirteen

Fred Taccone builds his stomp box guitar effects in the Los Angeles, California area. He also builds amps.

DNA Analogic

2006-present. Line of Japanese-built guitar effects distributed by Godlyke.

DOD

DOD Electronics started in Salt Lake City, Utah in 1974. Today, they're a major effects manufacturer with dozens of pedals made in the U.S. They also market effects under the name DigiTech and are now part of Harman International Industries.

MODEL		EXC. COND.	
YEAR	FEATURES	LOW	HIGH

6 Band Equalizer EQ601
1977-1982.

1977-1982		$45	$65

AB Box 270
1978-1982.

1978-1982		$25	$30

American Metal FX56
1985-1991.

1985-1991		$35	$45

Analog Delay 680
1979-ca. 1982.

1979-1982		$120	$145

Attacker FX54
1992-1994. Distortion and compressor.

1992-1994		$35	$45

Bass Compressor FX82
1987-ca.1989.

1987-1989		$35	$45

Bass EQ FX42B
1987-1996.

1987-1996		$35	$45

Bass Grunge FX92
1995-1996.

1995-1996		$35	$45

Bass Overdrive FX91
1998-present.

1998-2007		$35	$45

Bass Stereo Chorus FX62
1987-1996.

1987-1996		$45	$55

Bass Stereo Chorus Flanger FX72
1987-1997.

1987-1997		$45	$55

Bi-FET Preamp FX10
1982-1996.

1982-1996		$25	$35

Buzz Box FX33
1994-1996. Grunge distortion.

1994-1996		$40	$55

Chorus 690
1980-ca.1982. Dual speed chorus.

1980-1982		$70	$95

Classic Fuzz FX52
1990-1997.

1990-1997		$30	$40

Classic Tube FX53
1990-1997.

1990-1997		$40	$50

Compressor 280
1978-ca.1982.

1978-1982		$40	$50

Compressor FX80
1982-1985.

1982-1985		$40	$50

Compressor Sustainer FX80B
1986-1996.

1986-1996		$40	$50

Death Metal FX86
1994-present. Distortion.

1994-2007		$30	$45

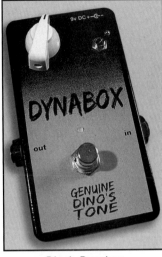

Dino's Dynabox

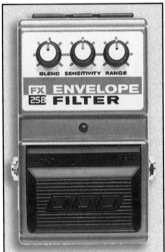

DOD Envelope Filter FX25B

DOD Death Metal FX86

DOD Mixer 240

DOD Noise Gate FX30

DOD Supra Distortion FX55B

MODEL YEAR FEATURES	EXC. COND. LOW	HIGH
Delay FX90		
1984-ca.1987.		
1984-1987	$70	$95
Digital Delay DFX9		
1989-ca.1990.		
1989-1990	$60	$85
Digital Delay Sampler DFX94		
1995-1997.		
1995-1997	$70	$95
Distortion FX55		
1982-1986. Red case.		
1982-1986	$30	$40
Edge Pedal FX87		
1988-1989.		
1988-1989	$20	$40
Envelope Filter 440		
1981-ca.1982. Reissued in '95.		
1981-1982	$60	$70
Envelope Filter FX25		
1982-1997. Replaced by FX25B.		
1982-1997	$40	$60
Envelope Filter FX25B		
1998-present.		
1998-2007	$40	$60
Equalizer FX40		
1982-1986.		
1982-1986	$35	$50
Equalizer FX40B		
1987-present. Eight bands for bass.		
1987-2007	$35	$50
Fet Preamp 210		
1981-ca.1982.		
1981-1982	$35	$50
Flanger 670		
1981-1982.		
1981-1982	$70	$95
Gate Loop FX30		
1980s	$25	$35
Graphic Equalizer EQ-610		
1980-ca.1982. Ten bands.		
1980-1982	$45	$60
Graphic Equalizer EQ-660		
1980-ca.1982. Six bands.		
1980-1982	$35	$50
Grunge FX69		
1993-present. Distortion.		
1993-2007	$30	$45
Hard Rock Distortion FX57		
1987-1994. With built-in delay.		
1987-1994	$30	$45
Harmonic Enhancer FX85		
1986-ca.1989.		
1986-1989	$30	$45
I. T. FX100		
1997. Intergrated Tube distortion, produces harmonics.		
1997	$45	$55
IceBox FX64		
1996-present. Chorus, high EQ.		
1996-2007	$20	$30

MODEL YEAR FEATURES	EXC. COND. LOW	HIGH
Juice Box FX51		
1996-1997.		
1996-1997	$25	$35
Master Switch 225		
1988-ca.1989. A/B switch and loop selector.		
1988-1989	$25	$35
Meat Box FX32		
1994-1996.		
1994-1996	$35	$45
Metal Maniac FX58		
1990-1996.		
1990-1996	$35	$45
Metal Triple Play Guitar Effects System TR3M		
1994.		
1994	$35	$45
Metal X FX70		
1993-1996.		
1993-1996	$35	$45
Milk Box FX84		
1994-present. Compressor/expander.		
1994-2007	$35	$45
Mini-Chorus 460		
1981-ca.1982.		
1981-1982	$45	$70
Mixer 240		
1978-ca.1982.		
1978-1982	$20	$30
Momentary Footswitch		
Introduced in 1987. Temporally engages other boxes.		
1980s	$20	$30
Mystic Blues Overdrive FX102		
1998-present. Medium gain overdrive.		
1998-2007	$20	$25
Noise Gate 230		
1978-1982.		
1978-1982	$25	$35
Noise Gate FX30		
1982-ca.1987.		
1982-1987	$25	$35
Octoplus FX35		
1987-1996. Octaves.		
1987-1996	$35	$40
Overdrive Plus FX50B		
1986-1997.		
1986-1997	$30	$40
Overdrive Preamp 250		
1978-1982, 1995-present. Reissued in '95.		
1978-1982	$100	$300
1995-2007	$25	$40
Overdrive Preamp FX50		
1982-1985.		
1982-1985	$30	$40
Performer Compressor Limiter 525		
1981-1984.		
1981-1984	$50	$55
Performer Delay 585		
1982-1985.		
1982-1985	$55	$70

MODEL YEAR FEATURES	EXC. COND. LOW	HIGH
Performer Distortion 555 *1981-1984.*		
1981-1984	$35	$45
Performer Flanger 575 *1981-1985.*		
1981-1985	$35	$45
Performer Phasor 595 *1981-1984.*		
1981-1984	$40	$50
Performer Stereo Chorus 565 *1981-1985.*		
1981-1985 FET switching	$55	$70
Performer Wah Filter 545 *1981-1984.*		
1981-1984	$45	$70
Phasor 201 *1981-ca.1982. Reissued in '95.*		
1981-1982	$65	$95
Phasor 401 *1978-1981.*		
1978-1981	$65	$95
Phasor 490 *1980-ca.1982.*		
1980-1982	$65	$95
Phasor FX20 *1982-1985.*		
1982-1985	$35	$45
Psychoacoustic Processor FX87 *1988-1989.*		
1988-1989	$35	$45
Punkifier FX76 *1997.*		
1997	$35	$45
Resistance Mixer 240 *1978-ca.1982.*		
1978-1982	$25	$30
Silencer FX27 *1988-ca.1989. Noise reducer.*		
1988-1989	$30	$40
Stereo Chorus FX60 *1982-1986.*		
1982-1986	$35	$45
Stereo Chorus FX65 *1986-1996. Light blue case.*		
1986-1996	$35	$45
Stereo Flanger FX70 *1982-ca.1985.*		
1982-1985	$35	$45
Stereo Flanger FX75 *1986-1987. Silver case with blue trim.*		
1986-1987	$40	$50
Stereo Flanger FX75B *1987-1997.*		
1987-1997	$40	$50
Stereo Phasor FX20B *1986-1999.*		
1986-1999	$40	$50
Stereo Turbo Chorus FX67 *1988-1991.*		
1988-1991	$35	$45

MODEL YEAR FEATURES	EXC. COND. LOW	HIGH
Super American Metal FX56B *1992-1996.*		
1992-1996	$30	$40
Super Stereo Chorus FX68 *1992-1996.*		
1992-1996	$35	$45
Supra Distortion FX55B *1986-present.*		
1986-2005	$25	$35
Thrash Master FX59 *1990-1996.*		
1990-1996	$25	$35
Votec Vocal Effects Processor and Mic preamp *1998-2001.*		
1998-2001	$55	$60
Wah-Volume FX-17 (pedal) *1987-2000.*		
1987-2000	$40	$50

Dredge-Tone

Located in Berkeley, California, Dredge-Tone offers effects and electronic kits.

DST Engineering

2001-present. Jeff Swanson and Bob Dettorre build reverb units in Beverly, Massachusetts. They also build amps.

Dunlop

Jim Dunlop, USA offers the Crybaby, MXR (see MXR), Rockman, High Gain, Heil Sound (see Heil), Tremolo, Jimi Hendrix, Rotovibe and Uni-Vibe brand effects.

MODEL YEAR FEATURES	EXC. COND. LOW	HIGH
Crybaby Bass *1985-present. Bass wah.*		
1985-2007	$75	$100
Crybaby Wah Pedal 535 *1995-present. Multi-range pedal with an external boost control.*		
1995-2007	$70	$90
Crybaby Wah-Wah GCB-95 *1982-present. Dunlop began manufacturing the Crybaby in '82.*		
1982-1989	$55	$75
1990-1999	$45	$70
2000-2007	$40	$50
High Gain Volume + Boost Pedal *1983-1996.*		
1983-1996	$35	$45
High Gain Volume Pedal *1983-present.*		
1983-2007	$40	$50
Jimi Hendrix Fuzz (Round) *1987-1993.*		
1987-1993	$50	$75
Rotovibe JH-4S Standard *1989-1998. Standard is finished in bright red enamel with chrome top.*		
1989-1998	$125	$150

DST Fat Acid Overdrive

Dunlop Rotovibe

Dunlop Jimi Hendrix Fuzz Wah

EFFECTS

EFFECTS

Durham Electronics Mucho Boosto

EBS Valve drive

Eden Analog Detroit

MODEL YEAR	FEATURES	EXC. COND. LOW	HIGH
Tremolo Volume Plus TVP-1			
1995-1998. Pedal.			
1995-1998		$125	$140
Uni-Vibe UV-1			
1995-present. Rotating speaker effect.			
1995-1999		$175	$225
2000-2007		$175	$200

Durham Electronics
2001-present. Alan Durham builds his line of guitar effects in Austin, Texas.

Dynacord
1950-present. Dynacord is a German company that makes audio and pro sound amps, as well as other electronic equipment and is now owned by TELEX/EVI Audio (an U.S. company), which also owns the Electro-Voice brand. In the '60s they offered tape echo machines and guitars. In '94 a line of multi-effects processors were introduced under the Electro-Voice/Dynacord name, but by the following year they were just listed as Electro-Voice.

EchoCord
Introduced in 1959. Tape echo unit.

1960s		$275	$350

Dyno
See Dytronics.

Dytronics
Mid-1970s-early 1980s. The Japanese Dytronics company made a chorus rackmount unit for electric piano called the Dyno My Piano with flying piano keys or a lightning bolt on the front. Another version was called the Tri-Stereo Chorus and a third, called the Songbird, had a bird's head on the front.

CS-5/Dyno My Piano Tri Chorus/Songbird
1970s. Tri-Stereo Chorus, 3 individual chorus settings which can be used all at once. Sold under all 3 brands/models.

1970s		$2,500	$3,000

E Bow
See Heet Sound Products.

EBS
1992-present. Bass and guitar effects built in Stockholm, Sweden by the EBS Sweden AB company. They also build bass amps.

Ecco Fonic
The Ecco Fonic was distributed by Fender in 1958-'59.

Echo Unit
1958-1959. Reverb unit.

1958-1959	With Brown case	$300	$350

Echoplex
The Echoplex tape echo units were first sold under the Maestro brand. After Maestro dropped the Echoplex, it was marketed under the Market Electronics name from the late-'70s to the early-'80s. In the later '80s, Market Electronics was dropped from the ads and they were marketed under the Echoplex brand. Both the Market and Echoplex brands are listed here; for earlier models see Maestro. In '94, Gibson's Oberheim division introduced a rackmount unit called the Echoplex. In '01, it was relabeled as Gibson.

Echoplex EP3
1984-ca. 1988. Solidstate version.

1984-1988		$350	$425

Echoplex EP4
1984-1991. Solidstate version.

1984-1991		$350	$425

Echoplex EP6T
1980-ca.1988. All-tube reissue of the EP2.

1980-1988		$400	$475

Eden Analog
2004-present. Guitar effects pedals built by Chris Sheppard and Robert Hafley in Pelham, Alabama.

Effector 13
2002-present. Devi Ever builds his guitar effects in Minneapolis, Minnesota. He was located in Austin, Texas, until mid '04.

Effectrode
1996-present. Effects pedals built in Corvallis, Oregon by Phil Taylor.

EFX
1980s. Brand name of the Los Angeles-based EFX Center; they also offered a direct box and a powered pedal box/board.

Switch Box B287
1984. Dual effects loop selector.

1984		$25	$35

EKO
1959-1985, 2000-present. In the '60s and '70s EKO offered effects made by EME and JEN Elettronica, which also made Vox effects.

Electra
1971-1984. A guitar brand imported by St. Louis Music, Electra offered a line of effects in the late '70s.

Chorus 504CH
Ca.1975-ca.1980.

1975-1980		$55	$75

Compressor 502C/602C
1975-1980.

1975-1980		$45	$55

Distortion 500D
Ca.1976-ca.1980.

1976-1980		$55	$75

MODEL YEAR	FEATURES	EXC. COND. LOW	HIGH
Flanger (stereo) 605F			
Ca.1975-ca.1980.			
1975-1980		$55	$75
Fuzz Wah			
Ca.1975-ca.1980.			
1975-1980		$75	$125
Pedal Drive 515AC			
Ca.1976-ca.1980. Overdrive.			
1975-1980		$40	$50
Phaser Model 501P			
Ca.1976-ca.1980.			
1975-1980		$50	$60
Phaser Model 875			
1975-ca.1980.			
1975-1980		$50	$60
Roto Phase I			
1975-ca.1980. Small pocket phaser.			
1975-1980		$70	$85
Roto Phase II			
1975-ca.1980. Pedal phasor.			
1975-1980		$80	$95

Electro-Harmonix

1968-1984, 1996-present. Founded by Mike Matthews in New York City, the company initially produced small plug-in boosters such as the LPB-1. In '71, they unveiled the awe-inspiring Big Muff Pi fuzz and dozens of innovative pedals followed. After years of disputes, the nonunion E-H factory became the target of union organizers and a '81 union campaign, combining picketing and harrying of E-H employees, brought production to a halt. Matthews' financier then cut his funding, and in early '82, E.H. filed for bankruptcy. Later that year, Matthews was able to reopen and continue through '84. In '96, he again began producing reissues of many of his classic effects as well as new designs.

MODEL YEAR	FEATURES	EXC. COND. LOW	HIGH
3 Phase Liner			
1981.			
1981		$50	$60
5X Junction Mixer			
1977-1981.			
1977-1981		$30	$40
10 Band Graphic Equalizer			
1977-1981. Includes footswitch.			
1977-1981		$60	$70
16-Second Digital Delay			
Early-1980s, 2004-present. An updated version was reissued in '04.			
1980s	With foot controller	$650	$800
1980s	Without foot controller	$500	$650
1990s		$325	$500
2004-2007		$275	$375
Attack Equalizer			
1975-1981. Active EQ, a.k.a. "Knock Out."			
1975-1981		$150	$200
Attack/Decay			
1980-1981. Tape reverse simulator.			
1980-1981		$200	$225

MODEL YEAR	FEATURES	EXC. COND. LOW	HIGH
Bad Stone Phase Shifter			
1975-1981.			
1970s	Three knobs	$200	$250
1970s	Two knobs, color switch	$175	$225
Bass Micro-Synthesizer			
1981-1984, 1999-present. Analog synthesizer sounds.			
1981-1984		$225	$300
1999-2007		$150	$175
Bassballs			
1978-1984, 1998-present. Bass envelope filter/distortion.			
1978-1984		$200	$225
Big Muff Pi			
1971-1984. Sustain, floor unit, issued in 3 different looks, as described below.			
1970s	Earlier black graphics, knobs in triangle pattern	$350	$425
1970s	Later red/black graphics, 1/2" letters	$225	$425
1980s	Red/black graphics, logo in 1" letters	$150	$250
Big Muff Pi (reissue)			
1996-present. Originally made in Russia, but currently both Russian- and U.S.-made versions are available.			
1996-2007	Russian-made	$40	$45
Big Muff Sovtek			
2000s. Big Muff Pi, Electro Harmonix, and Sovtek logos on an olive green case.			
2000s		$125	$175
Black Finger Compressor Sustainer			
1977, 2003-present. Original has 3 knobs in triangle pattern.			
1977		$125	$225
2003-2007		$75	$100
Clap Track			
1980-1984. Drum effect.			
1980-1984		$40	$60
Clone Theory			
1977-1981. Chorus effect.			
1977-1981	The Clone Theory logo	$150	$175
Crash Pad			
1980-1984. Percussion synth.			
1980-1984		$40	$60
Crying Tone Pedal			
1976-1978. Wah-wah.			
1976-1978		$175	$225
Deluxe Big Muff Pi			
1978-1981. Sustain, AC version of Big Muff Pi, includes a complete Soul Preacher unit.			
1978-1981	Red graphics	$125	$200
Deluxe Electric Mistress Flanger			
1977-1983, 1996-present. AC.			
1977-1979		$150	$250
1980-1983		$125	$175

Effector 13 Disaster Fuzz

Electra Metal 698HM

EFFECTS

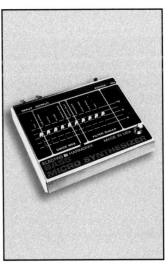

E-H Bass Micro-Synthesizer

To get the most from this book, be sure to read "Using *The Guide*" in the introduction.

E-H Deluxe Memory Man

E-H Frequency Analyzer

E-H Octave Multiplexer

MODEL YEAR	FEATURES	EXC. COND. LOW	HIGH
Deluxe Memory Man			
1977-1983, 1996-present. Echo and delay, featured 4 knobs '77-'78, from '79-'83 it has 5 knobs and added vibrato and chorus.			
1977-1978	Four knobs	$225	$300
1979-1983	Five knobs	$200	$275
1996-2007		$150	$165
Deluxe Octave Multiplexer			
1977-1981.			
1977-1981		$200	$250
Digital Delay/Chorus			
1981-1984. With digital chorus.			
1981-1984		$250	$300
Digital Rhythm Matrix DRM-15			
1981-1984.			
1981-1984		$225	$250
Digital Rhythm Matrix DRM-16			
1979-1983.			
1979-1983		$225	$250
Digital Rhythm Matrix DRM-32			
1981-1984.			
1981-1984		$225	$250
Doctor Q Envelope Follower			
1976-1983, 2001-present. For bass or guitar.			
1976-1983		$150	$200
2001-2007		$30	$35
Domino Theory			
1981. Sound sensitive light tube.			
1981		$50	$100
Echo 600			
1981.			
1981		$175	$225
Echoflanger			
1977-1982. Flange, slapback, chorus, filter.			
1977-1982		$200	$250
Electric Mistress Flanger			
1976-1984.			
1976-1984		$175	$275
Electronic Metronome			
1978-1980.			
1978-1980		$25	$30
Frequency Analyzer			
1977-1984, 2001-present. Ring modulator.			
1977-1984		$200	$250
Full Double Tracking Effect			
1978-1981. Doubling, slapback.			
1978-1981		$100	$150
Fuzz Wah			
Introduced around 1974.			
1970s		$175	$225
Golden Throat			
1977-1984.			
1977-1984		$300	$400
Golden Throat Deluxe			
1977-1979. Deluxe has a built-in monitor amp.			
1977-1979		$300	$400
Golden Throat II			
1978-1981.			
1978-1981		$150	$225

MODEL YEAR	FEATURES	EXC. COND. LOW	HIGH
Guitar Synthesizer			
1981. Sold for $1,495 in May '81.			
1981		$225	$300
Hog's Foot Bass Booster			
1977-1980.			
1977-1978		$70	$90
Holy Grail			
2002-present. Digital reverb.			
2002-2007		$80	$90
Hot Foot			
1977-1978. Rocker pedal turns knob of other E-H effects.			
1977-1978	Gold case, red graphics	$75	$100
Hot Tubes			
1978-1984, 2001-2007. Tube distortion.			
1978-1984		$125	$200
Linear Power Booster LPB-1			
1968-1983.			
1976-1979		$55	$80
1980-1983		$45	$75
Linear Power Booster LPB-2			
Ca.1968-1983.			
1968-1983		$90	$100
Little Big Muff Pi			
1976-1980, 2006-present. Sustain, 1-knob floor unit.			
1976-1980		$150	$175
Memory Man			
1976-1984, 1999-present. Analog delay, newer version in stereo.			
1976-1979		$250	$300
1980-1984		$150	$250
Micro Synthesizer			
1978-1984, 1998-present. Mini keyboard phaser.			
1978-1979		$225	$250
1978-1984		$225	$250
1998-2007		$150	$170
Mini Q-Tron/Micro Q-Tron			
2002-present. Battery-operated smaller version of Q-Tron envelope follower, changed to identical effect in smaller box Micro in '06.			
2002-2007		$40	$45
Mini-Mixer			
1978-1981. Mini mic mixer, reissued in '01.			
1978-1981		$30	$40
MiniSynthesizer			
1981-1983. Mini keyboard with phaser.			
1981-1983		$300	$400
MiniSynthesizer With Echo			
1981.			
1981		$375	$500
Mole Bass Booster			
1968-1978.			
1968-1969		$60	$80
1970-1978		$40	$60
Muff Fuzz			
1976-1983. Fuzz and line boost, silver case with orange lettering.			
1976-1983		$85	$100

MODEL YEAR FEATURES	EXC. COND. LOW	HIGH

Muff Fuzz Crying Tone
1977-1978. Fuzz, wah.
1977-1978 — $150 — $250

Octave Multiplexer Floor Unit
1976-1980.
1976-1980 — $175 — $275

Octave Multiplexer Pedal
1976-1977, 2001-present.
1976-1977 — $150 — $250
2001-2007 — $40 — $45

Panic Button
1981. Siren sounds for drum.
1981 — $30 — $40

Poly Chorus/Stereo Poly Chorus
1981, 1999-present. Same as Echoflanger.
1981 — $175 — $200
1999-2007 — $125 — $150

Polyphase
1979-1981. With envelope.
1979-1981 — $175 — $225

Pulsar
2004-present. Variable wave form tremolo.
2004-2007 — $45 — $55

Pulse Modulator
Ca.1968 -ca.1972. Triple tremolo.
1968-1969 — $250 — $325
1970-1972 — $200 — $250

Q-Tron
1997-present. Envelope controlled filter.
1997-2007 — $125 — $175

Q-Tron +
1999-present. With added effects loop and Attack Response switch.
1999-2007 — $70 — $80

Queen Triggered Wah
1976-1978. Wah/Envelope Filter.
1976-1978 — $125 — $150

Random Tone Generator RTG
1981.
1981 — $40 — $60

Rhythm 12 (Rhythm Machine)
1978.
1978 — $75 — $125

Rolling Thunder
1980-1981. Percussion synth.
1980-1981 — $40 — $50

Screaming Bird Treble Booster
Ca.1968-1980. In-line unit.
1968-1980 — $75 — $100

Screaming Tree Treble Booster
1977-1981. Floor unit.
1977-1981 — $100 — $150

Sequencer Drum
1981. Drum effect.
1981 — $40 — $50

Slapback Echo
1977-1978. Stereo.
1977-1978 — $150 — $200

Small Clone
1983-1984, 1999-present. Analog chorus, depth and rate controls, purple face plate, white logo.
1983-1984 — $150 — $200
1999-2007 — $35 — $40

Small Stone Phase Shifter
1975-1984, 1996-present. Both Russian and U.S. reissues were made.
1975-1979 — $175 — $225
1980-1984 — $125 — $175

Soul Preacher
1977-1983. Compressor sustainer.
1977-1983 — $100 — $150

Space Drum/Super Space Drum
1980-1981. Percussion synthesizer.
1980-1981 — $125 — $175

Switch Blade
1977-1983. A-B Box.
1977-1983 — $45 — $55

Talking Pedal
1977-1978. Creates vowel sounds.
1977-1978 — $350 — $550

The Silencer
1976-1981. Noise elimination.
1976-1981 — $60 — $80

The Wiggler
2002-present. All-tube modulator including pitch vibrato and volume tremolo.
2002-2007 — $100 — $110

The Worm
2002-present. Wah/Phaser.
2002-2007 — $55 — $65

Tube Zipper
2001-present. Tube (2x12AX7) envelope follower.
2001-2007 — $100 — $120

Vocoder
1978-1981. Modulates voice with instrument.
1978-1981 Rackmount — $425 — $525

Volume Pedal
1978-1981.
1978-1981 — $45 — $65

Y-Triggered Filter
1976-1977.
1976-1977 — $140 — $160

Zipper Envelope Follower
1976-1978. The Tube Zipper was introduced in '01.
1976-1978 — $200 — $300

Elk

Late-1960s. Japanese company Elk Gakki Co., Ltd. mainly made guitars and amps, but did offer effects as well.

Elka

In the late '60s or early '70s, Italian organ and synthesizer company Elka-Orla (later just Elka) offered a few effects, likely made by JEN Elettronica (Vox, others).

E-H Pulsar

E-H Q-Tron

E-H Small Clone EH4600

EFFECTS

Empress Effects Tremolo

Eowave Ring O' Bug

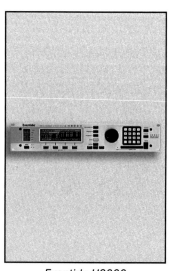

Eventide H8000

MODEL YEAR	FEATURES	EXC. COND. LOW	HIGH

EMMA Electronic
Line of guitar effects built in Denmark.
ReezaFRATzitz RF-1
2004-present. Overdrive and distortion, red case.

2004-2007		$80	$95

Empress Effects
2005-present. Guitar effects pedals built by Steve Bragg and Jason Fee in Ottawa, Ontario.

EMS
1969-1979. Peter Zinnovieff's English synth company (Electronic Music Studios) also offered a guitar synthesizer. The company has reopened to work on original EMS gear.

Eowave
2002-present. Effects built first in Paris and now in Burgundy, France by Marc Sirguy.

Epiphone
Epiphone pedals are labeled G.A.S Guitar Audio System and were offered from around 1988 to '91.
Pedals
Various models with years available.

1988-1989	Chorus EP-CH-70	$35	$45
1988-1989	Delay EP-DE-80	$45	$60
1988-1991	Compressor EP-CO-20	$35	$40
1988-1991	Distortion EP-DI-10	$35	$45
1988-1991	Flanger EP-FL-60	$40	$55
1988-1991	Overdrive EP-OD-30	$35	$45

Ernie Ball
Ernie Ball owned a music store in Tarzana, California, when he noticed the demand for a better selection of strings. The demand for his Slinky strings grew to the point where, in '67, he sold the store to concentrate on strings. He went on to produce the Earthwood brand of guitars and basses from '72-'85. In '84, Ball purchased the Music Man company.
Volume Pedals
1977-present.

1977-2007		$35	$65

Euthymia Electronics
Line of guitar effects built by Erik Miller in Alameda, California.

Eventide
1971-present. This New Jersey electronics manufacturer has offered studio effects since the late '70s.

EXR
The EXR Corporation was located in Brighton, Michigan.
Projector
1983-ca.1984. Psychoacoustic enhancer pedal.

1983-1984		$65	$75

Projector SP III
1983-ca.1984. Psychoacoustic enhancer pedal, volume pedal/sound boost.

1983-1984		$65	$70

Farfisa
The organ company offered effects pedals in the 1960s. Their products were manufactured in Italy by the Italian Accordion Company and distributed by Chicago Musical Instruments.
Model VIP 345 Organ
Mid-1960s. Portable organ with Syntheslalom used in the rock and roll venue.

1960s		$500	$600

Repeater

1969		$100	$150

Sferasound
1960s. Vibrato pedal for a Farfisa Organ but it works well with the guitar, gray case.

1960s		$275	$375

Wah/Volume

1969		$100	$150

Fender
Although Fender has flirted with effects since the 1950s (the volume/volume-tone pedal and the EccoFonic), it concentrated mainly on guitars and amps. Fender effects ranged from the sublime to the ridiculous, from the tube Reverb to the Dimension IV. Presently they offer a reverb unit and retro effects pedals.
Blender Fuzz
1968-1977. Battery operated fuzz and sustain. In '05, Fender issued the Blender Custom.

1968-1969		$350	$375
1970-1977		$275	$300

Contempo Organ
1967-1968. Portable organ, all solidstate, 61 keys including a 17-key bass section, catalog shows with red cover material.

1967-1968		$525	$550

Dimension IV
1968-1970. Multi-effects unit using an oil-filled drum.

1968-1970		$150	$200

Echo-Reverb
1966-1970. Solidstate, echo-reverb effect produced by rotating metal disk, black tolex, silver grille.

1966-1970		$300	$350

Electronic Echo Chamber
1962-1968. Solidstate tape echo, up to 400 ms of delay, rectangle box with 2 controls '62-'67, slanted front '67-'68.

1962-1968		$275	$325

Fuzz-Wah
1968-1984, 2007-present Has Fuzz and Wah switches on sides of pedal '68-'73, has 3 switches above the pedal '74-'84. Current version has switches on sides.

1968-1973	Switches on side	$175	$225
1974-1984	Switches above	$150	$200

MODEL YEAR	FEATURES	EXC. COND. LOW	HIGH
haser			
1975-1977, 2007-present. AC powered, reissued in 7.			
075-1977		$125	$175
everb Unit			
1961-1966, 1975-1978. Fender used a wide variety tolex coverings in the early-'60s as the coverings atched those on the amps. Initially, Fender used ugh blond tolex, then rough brown tolex, followed v smooth white or black tolex.			
961	Blond tolex, Oxblood grille	$1,050	$1,300
961	Brown tolex	$950	$1,100
962	Blond tolex, Oxblood grille	$1,000	$1,300
962	Brown tolex, Wheat grille	$850	$1,000
963	Brown tolex	$850	$1,000
963	Rough blond tolex	$850	$1,000
963	Smooth white tolex	$850	$1,000
964	Black tolex	$850	$1,000
964	Brown tolex, gold grille	$850	$1,000
964	Smooth white tolex	$850	$1,000
965-1966	Black tolex	$750	$950
966	Solidstate, flat cabinet	$250	$325
975-1978	Tube reverb reinstated	$475	$575
Reverb Unit Reissue Models			
1994-present. Reissue spring/tube Reverb Units with arious era cosmetics as listed below.			
990s	'63 brown tolex	$350	$375
990s	'63 white (limited run)	$375	$400
990s	Blackface	$350	$375
990s	Tweed (limited run)	$350	$450
Tone and Volume Foot Pedal			
1954-1984, 2007-present.			
960s		$125	$175
Vibratone			
1967-1972. Leslie-type speaker cabinet made specifically for the guitar, 2-speed motor.			
960s		$750	$850

FlexiSound

FlexiSound products were made in Lancaster, Pennsylvania.

F. S. Clipper

1975-ca.1976. Distortion, plugged directly into guitar jack.

1975-1976		$55	$65

The Beefer

1975. Power booster, plugged directly into guitar ack.

1975		$40	$50

Flip

Line of tube effects by Guyatone and distributed in the U.S. by Godlyke Distributing.

MODEL YEAR	FEATURES	EXC. COND. LOW	HIGH
TD-X Tube Echo			
2004-present. Hybrid tube power delay pedal.			
2004-2007		$90	$100

FM Acoustics

Made in Switzerland.

E-1 Pedal

1975. Volume, distortion, filter pedal.

1975		$70	$80

Foxx

Foxx pedals are readily identifiable by their fur-like covering. They slunk onto the scene in 1971 and were extinct by '78. Made by Hollywood's Ridinger Associates, their most notable product was the Tone Machine fuzz. Foxx-made pedals also have appeared under various brands such .... as G and G, Guild, Yamaha and Sears Roebuck, generally without fur. Since 2005, reissues of some of the classic Foxx pedals are being built in Provo, Utah.

MODEL YEAR	FEATURES	EXC. COND. LOW	HIGH
Clean Machine			
1974-1978.			
1974-1978		$250	$275
Down Machine			
1971-1977. Bass wah.			
1971-1977	Blue case	$250	$275
Foot Phaser			
1975-1977, 2006-present.			
1975-1977		$450	$650
Fuzz and Wa and Volume			
1974-1978, 2006-present.			
1974-1978		$300	$350
Guitar Synthesizer I			
1975.			
1975		$300	$350
O.D. Machine			
1972-ca.1975.			
1972-1975		$150	$200
Phase III			
1975-1978.			
1975-1978		$100	$150
Tone Machine			
1971-1978, 2005-present. Fuzz with Octave.			
1971-1978		$375	$475
Wa and Volume			
1971-1978.			
1971-1978		$200	$225
Wa Machine			
1971-ca.1978.			
1971-1978		$150	$200

Framptone

2000-present. Founded by Peter Frampton, Framptone offers hand-made guitar effects.

Frantone

1994-present. Effects and accessories hand built in New York City.

Foxx Tone Machine

Framptone Amp Switcher

Frantone Sputnik

EFFECTS

Fulltone Choralflange

Fxdoctor Clean Boost

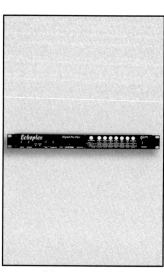

*Gibson Echoplex
Digital Pro Plus*

MODEL		EXC. COND.	
YEAR	FEATURES	LOW	HIGH

Fulltone

1991-present. Fulltone effects are based on some of the classic effects of the past. Fulltone was started in Los Angeles, California by Michael Fuller who says the company was born out of his love for Jimi Hendrix and fine vintage pedals.

Deja Vibe

1991-2002. UniVibe-type pedal, later models have a Vintage/Modern switch. Stereo version also available. Now offerered in Mini version.

1991-2004 Mono	$175	$200

Deja Vibe 2

1997-present. Like Deja Vibe but with built-in speed control. Stereo version also available.

1997-2007 Mono	$200	$225

Distortion Pro

2002-present. Red case, volume and distortion knobs with four voicing controls.

2002-2007	$125	$150

Fat Boost

2001-2007. Clean boost, silver-sparkle case, volume and drive knobs.

2001-2007	$125	$135

Full-Drive 2

1995-present. Blue case, four control knobs.

1995-2007	$120	$145

Octafuzz

1996-present. Copy of the Tycobrahe Octavia.

1996-2007	$85	$100

Soul Bender

1994-present. Volume, tone and dirt knobs.

1994-2007	$100	$125

Supa-Trem

1995-present. Black case, white Supa-Trem logo, rate and mix controls.

1995-2007	$100	$125

Tube Tape Echo TTE

2004-present. EchoPlex style using tape.

2004-2007	$725	$850

Furman Sound

1993-present. Located in Petaluma, California, Furman makes audio and video signal processors and AC power conditioning products for music and other markets.

LC-2 Limiter Compressor

1990s. Rackmount unit with a black suitcase and red knobs.

1990s	$40	$50

PQ3 Parametric EQ

1990s. Rackmount preamp and equalizer.

1998-1999	$110	$150

PQ6 Parametric Stereo

1990s	$135	$175

RV1 Reverb Rackmount

1990s	$110	$150

Fxdoctor

2003-present. Joshua Zalegowski originally built his effects in Amherst, Massachusetts, and in 2005 moved to Boston.

MODEL		EXC. COND.	
YEAR	FEATURES	LOW	HIG

Garcia

2004-present. Guitar effects built by Matthe Garcia in Myrtle Beach, South Carolina. He als builds amps.

George Dennis

1991-present. Founded by George Burgerstei original products were a line of effects pedals. I '96 they added a line of tube amps. The compan is located in Prague, Czech Republic.

Gibson

Gibson did offer a few effects bearing their ow name, but most were sold under the Maestro nam (see that listing).

Echoplex Digital Pro

1994-present. Rackmount unit with digital record ing, sampling and digital delay. Labeled as jus Echoplex until '01 when Gibson name added.

1994-2005	$700	$85(

GA-3RV Reverb Unit

1964-1967. Small, compact, spring reverb unit, blac tolex, gray grille.

1964-1967	$325	$40(

GA-4RE Reverb-Echo Unit

1964-1967. Small, compact, lightweight accessor reverb-echo unit that produces complete reverbera tion and authentic echo, utilizes Gibson's "electroni memory" system for both reverb and echo, black tolex gray grille.

1964-1967	$450	$55(

Godbout

Sold a variety of effects do-it-yourself kits in th 1970s. Difficult to value because quality depend on skills of builder.

Effects Kits

1970s	$20	$3(

Goodrich Sound

Late-1970s. Goodrich was located in Gran Haven, Michigan.

Match Box 33670 Line Boost

Early-1980s. Small rectangular in and out box wit control knob.

1980s	$45	$5!

Volume Pedal 6122

1979-ca.1980. Uses a potentiometer.

1970s	$45	$5!

Volume Pedal 6400ST

1979-ca.1980. Uses a potentiometer.

1970s	$45	$5!

Volume Pedal 6402

1979-ca.1980. Uses photocell.

1970s	$45	$5!

Greer Amplification

1999-present. Guitar stomp box effects built by Nick Greer in Athens, Georgia. He also builds amps.

EFFECTS

MODEL YEAR	FEATURES	EXC. COND. LOW	HIGH

Gretsch

Gretsch has offered a limited line of effects from time to time.

Controfuzz
  Mid-1970s. Distortion.

1970s		$150	$225

Deluxe Reverb Unit Model 6149
  1963-1969. Similar to Gibson's GA-1 introduced around the same time.

1963-1969		$400	$500

Expandafuzz
  Mid-1970s. Distortion.

1970s		$150	$200

Reverb Unit Model 6144 Preamp Reverb
  1963-1967. Approximately 17 watts, preamp functionality, no speaker.

1963-1967		$250	$350

Tremofect
  Mid-1970s. Tremolo effect, 3-band EQ, speed, effect, bass, total, and treble knobs.

1970s		$225	$300

Guild

Guild marketed effects made by Binson, Electro-Harmonix, Foxx, WEM and Applied in the 1960s and '70s.

Copicat
  1960s-1979. Echo.

1970s		$300	$400

DE-20 Auto-Rhythm Unit
  1971-1974. 50 watt rhythm accompaniment unit. Included 20 rhythms and a separate instrument channel with its own volume control. 1x12" plus tweeter.

1971-1974		$200	$300

Echorec (by Binson)
  Ca.1960-1979. This was different stripped-down version of the Binson Echorec.

1960s		$500	$800

Foxey Lady Fuzz
  1968-1977. Distortion, sustain.

1968-1975	Two knobs, made by E-H	$200	$250
1976-1977	3 knobs in row, same as Big Muff	$150	$200

Fuzz Wah FW-3
  1975-ca.1979. Distortion, volume, wah, made by Foxx.

1970s		$150	$175

HH Echo Unit
  1976-ca.1979.

1970s		$200	$300

VW-1
  1975-ca.1979. Volume, wah, made by Foxx.

1970s		$200	$250

Guyatone

1998-present. Imported stomp boxes, tape echo units and outboard reverb units distributed by Godlyke Distributing.

HAO

2000-present. Line of guitar effects built in Japan by J.E.S. International, distributed in the U.S. by Godlyke.

Harden Engineering

2006-present. Distortion/boost guitar effects pedals built by William Harden in Chicago, Illinois. He also builds guitars.

Heathkit

1960s. Unassembled kits sold at retail.

TA-28 Distortion Booster
  1960s. Fuzz assembly kit, heavy '60s super fuzz, case-by-case quality depending on the builder.

1960s		$140	$150

Heavy Metal Products

Mid-1970s. From Alto Loma, California, products for the heavy metal guitarist.

Raunchbox Fuzz
  1975-1976.

1975-1976		$75	$100

Switchbox
  1975-1976. A/B box.

1975-1976		$25	$35

Heet Sound Products

1974-present. The E Bow concept goes back to '67, but a hand-held model wasn't available until '74. Made in Los Angeles, California.

E Bow
  1974-1979, 1985-1987, 1994-present. The Energy Bow, hand-held electro-magnetic string driver.

1974-1979		$50	$60

E Bow for Pedal Steels
  1979. Hand-held electro-magnetic string driver.

1979		$35	$55

Heil Sound

1960-present. Founded by Bob Heil, Marissa, Illinois. Created the talk box technology as popularized by Peter Frampton. In the '60s and '70s Heil was dedicated to innovative products for the music industry. In the late-'70s, innovative creations were more in the amateur radio market, and by the '90s Heil's focus was on the home theater market. The Heil Sound Talkbox was reissued by Jim Dunlop USA in '89.

Talk Box
  1976-ca.1980, 1989-present. Reissued by Dunlop.

1976-1980		$100	$125
1989-1999		$75	$85
2000-2007		$70	$80

High Gain

See listing under Dunlop.

Hohner

Hohner offered effects in the late-1970s.

HAO Rust Driver

Heet E Bow

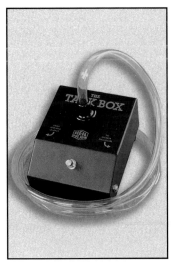

Heil Sound Talk Box

EFFECTS

HomeBrew Compressor Retro

Ibanez Classic Phase PH-99

Ibanez DE7 Delay/Echo

MODEL YEAR	FEATURES	EXC. COND. LOW	HIGH
Dirty Booster			
1977-ca.1978. Distortion.			
1977-1978		$55	$65
Dirty Wah Wah'er			
1977-ca.1978. Adds distortion.			
1977-1978		$65	$75
Fuzz Wah			
1970s. Morley-like volume pedal with volume knob and fuzz knob, switch for soft or hard fuzz, gray box with black foot pedal.			
1970s		$65	$75
Multi-Exciter			
1977-ca.1978. Volume, wah, surf, tornado, siren.			
1977-1978		$60	$70
Tape Echo/Echo Plus			
1970s. Black alligator suitcase.			
1970s		$200	$300
Tri-Booster			
1977-ca.1978. Distortion, sustain.			
1977-1978		$55	$65
Vari-Phaser			
1977-ca.1978.			
1977-1978		$55	$65
Vol-Kicker Volume Pedal			
1977-ca.1978.			
1977-1978		$30	$40
Wah-Wah'er			
1977-ca.1978. Wah, volume.			
1977-1978		$55	$65

HomeBrew Electronics

2001-present. Stomp box effects hand made by Joel and Andrea Weaver in Glendale, Arizona.

Hughes & Kettner

1985-present. Hughes & Kettner builds a line of tube-driven guitar effects made in Germany. They also build amps and cabinets.

Ibanez

Ibanez effects were introduced ca. 1974, and were manufactured by Japan's Maxon Electronics. Although results were mixed at first, a more uniform and modern product line, including the now legendary Tube Screamer, built Ibanez's reputation for quality. They continue to produce a wide range of effects.

60s Fuzz FZ5 (SoundTank)
1991-1992, 1996-1998. Fuzz with level, tone and distortion controls, black plastic case, green label.

1990s		$25	$30

7th Heaven SH7 (Tone-Lok)
2000-2004. Lo, high, drive and level controls, gray-silver case, blue-green label.

2000-2004		$20	$30

Acoustic Effects PT4
1993-1998. Acoustic guitar multi-effect with compressor/limiter, tone shaper, stereo chorus, digital reverb, with power supply.

1993-1998		$75	$100

MODEL YEAR	FEATURES	EXC. COND. LOW	HIGH
Analog Delay AD9			
1982-1984. 3 control analog delay, Hot Pink metal case.			
1982-1984		$200	$27
Analog Delay AD80			
1980-1981. Pink case.			
1980-1981		$225	$30
Analog Delay AD99			
1996-1998. Reissue, 3 control knobs and on/o, switch, winged-hand logo, black case.			
1996-1998		$125	$15
Analog Delay AD100 (Table Unit)			
1981-1983. Stand-alone table/studio unit (not rac, mount) with power cord.			
1981-1983		$200	$25
Analog Delay 202 (Rack Mount)			
1981-1983. Rack mount with delay, doubling, flanger, stereo chorus, dual inputs with tone an, level.			
1981-1983		$200	$25
Auto Filter AF9			
1982-1984. Replaces AF201 model.			
1982-1984		$150	$20
Auto Filter AF201			
1981. Two min-max sliders, 3 mode toggle switches, orange metal case.			
1981		$175	$20
Auto Wah AW5 (SoundTank)			
1994-1999. Plastic case SoundTank series.			
1994-1999		$30	$4
Auto Wah AW7 (Tone-Lok)			
2000-present. Silver case.			
2000-2007		$20	$3
Bass Compressor BP10			
1986-1991.			
1986-1991		$70	$8
Bi-Mode Chorus BC9			
1984. Dual channel for 2 independent speed an, width settings.			
1984		$75	$10
Chorus CS-505			
1980-1981. Speed and depth controls, gray-blu, case, stereo or mono input, battery or external powe, option.			
1980-1981		$100	$12
Chorus Flanger CF7 (Tone-Lok)			
1999-present. Speed, depth, delay, regeneration, controls, mode and crazy switches.			
1999-2007		$35	$4
Classic Flange FL99			
1997-1999. Analog reissue, silver metal case, winged, hand artwork, 4 controls, 2 footswitch buttons.			
1997-1999		$90	$11
Classic Phase PH99			
1995-1999. Analog reissue, silver metal case, winged-hand artwork, speed, depth, feedback, effec, level controls, intense and bypass footswitches.			
1995-1999		$90	$11
Compressor CP5 (SoundTank)			
1991-1998.			
1991-1998		$20	$3

The ***Vintage Guitar Price Guide*** shows low to high values for items in all-original excellent condition, and, where applicable, with original case or cover.

MODEL YEAR FEATURES	EXC. COND. LOW	HIGH
Compressor Limiter CP9		
1982-1984.		
1982-1984	$100	$125
Compressor CP10		
1986-1992.		
1986-1992	$75	$80
Compressor CP830		
1975-1979.		
1975-1979	$100	$125
Compressor II CP835		
1980-1981.		
1980-1981	$100	$125
Delay Champ CD10		
1986-1989. Red case, 3 knobs.		
1986-1989	$125	$150
Delay Echo DE7 (Tone-Lok)		
1999-present. Stereo delay/echo.		
1999-2007	$40	$50
Delay Harmonizer DM1000		
1983-1984. Rack mount, with chorus, 9 control knobs.		
1983-1984	$175	$225
Delay III DDL20 Digital Delay		
1988-1989. Filtering, doubling, slap back, echo S, echo M, echo L, Seafoam Green coloring on pedal.		
1988-1989	$100	$125
Delay PDD1 (DPC Series)		
1988-1989. Programmable Digital Delay (PDD) with display screen.		
1988-1989	$125	$150
Digital Chorus DSC10		
1990-1992. 3 control knobs and slider selection toggle.		
1990-1992	$75	$100
Digital Delay DL5 (SoundTank)		
1991-1998.		
1991-1998	$35	$45
Digital Delay DL10		
1989-1992. Digital Delay made in Japan, blue case, 3 green control knobs, stompbox.		
1989-1992	$100	$125
Distortion Charger DS10		
1986-1989.		
1986-1989	$70	$90
Distortion DS7 (Tone-Lok)		
2000-present. Drive, tone, and level controls.		
2000-2007	$40	$45
Echo Machine EM5 (SoundTank)		
1996-1998. Simulates tape echo.		
1996-1998	$45	$55
Fat Cat Distortion FC10		
1987-1989. 3-knob pedal with distortion, tone, and level controls.		
1987-1989	$50	$75
Flanger FFL5 (Master Series)		
1984-1985. Speed, regeneration, width, D-time controls, battery or adapter option.		
1984-1985	$70	$90
Flanger FL5 (SoundTank)		
1991-1998.		
1991-1998	$25	$35

MODEL YEAR FEATURES	EXC. COND. LOW	HIGH
Flanger FL9		
1982-1984. Yellow case.		
1982-1984	$100	$150
Flanger FL301		
1979-1982. Mini flanger, 3 knobs, called the FL-301 DX in late '81-'82.		
1979-1982	$100	$125
Flanger FL305		
1976-1979. Five knobs.		
1976-1979	$100	$125
Flying Pan FP777		
1976-1979. Auto pan/phase shifter, 4 control knobs, phase on/off button, pan on/off button, silver metal case with blue trim and Flying Pan winged-hand logo.		
1976-1979	$500	$800
Fuzz FZ7 (Tone-Lok)		
2000-present. Drive, tone and level controls, gray-silver case, blue-green FZ7 label.		
2000-2007	$45	$50
Graphic Bass EQ BE10		
1986-1992. Later labeled as the BEQ10.		
1986-1992	$60	$80
Graphic EQ GE9		
1982-1984. Six EQ sliders, 1 overall volume slider, turquoise blue case.		
1982-1984	$60	$80
Graphic EQ GE10		
1986-1992. Eight sliders.		
1986-1992	$60	$80
Graphic Equalizer GE601 (808 Series)		
1980-1981. 7-slider EQ, aqua blue metal case.		
1980-1981	$75	$100
Guitar Multi-Processor PT5		
1993-1997. Floor unit, programmable with 25 presets and 25 user presets, effects include distortion, chorus, flanger, etc, green case.		
1993-1997	$100	$125
LA Metal LM7		
1988-1989. Silver case.		
1988-1989	$55	$65
LoFi LF7 (Tone-Lok)		
2000-present. Filter, 4 knobs.		
2000-2007	$20	$30
Metal Charger MS10		
1986-1992. Distortion, level, attack, punch and edge control knobs, green case.		
1986-1992	$45	$55
Metal Screamer MSL		
1985. 3 control knobs.		
1985	$55	$65
Modern Fusion MF5 (SoundTank)		
1990-1991. Level, tone and distortion controls.		
1990-1991	$45	$50
Modulation Delay DM500		
1983-1984. Rack mount.		
1983-1984	$75	$100

Ibanez DS7 Distortion

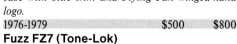

EFFECTS

Ibanez Flanger FL-303 1978

Ibanez Flanger FL-9

EFFECTS

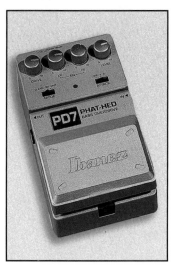

Ibanez Phat Head PD7

Ibanez Tube King TK999

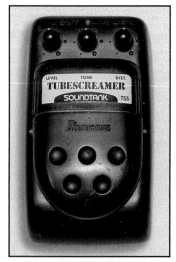

Ibanez TS5 Tube Screamer

MODEL YEAR	FEATURES	EXC. COND. LOW	HIGH
Modulation Delay DM1000			
1983-1984. Rack mount with delay, reverb, modulation.			
1983-1984		$100	$125
Modulation Delay PDM1			
1988-1989. Programmable Digital Modulation pedal.			
1988-1989		$100	$125
Mostortion MT10			
1990-1992. Mos-FET circuit distortion pedal, 5 control knobs, green case.			
1990-1992		$50	$60
Multi-Effect PUE5/PUE5 Tube (Floor Unit)			
1990-1993. Yellow version has tube, blue one does not. Also available in PUE5B bass version.			
1990-1993	Tube	$350	$450
Multi-Effect UE300 (Floor Unit)			
1983-1984. Floor unit, 4 footswitches for super metal, digital delay, digital stereo chorus, and master power, 3 delay modes.			
1983-1984		$275	$350
Multi-Effect UE300B (Floor Unit)			
1983-1984. Floor unit for bass.			
1983-1984		$275	$350
Multi-Effect UE400 (Rackmount)			
1980-1984. Rack mount with foot switch.			
1980-1984		$300	$375
Multi-Effect UE405 (Rackmount)			
1981-1984. Rack mount with analog delay, parametric EQ, compressor/limiter, stereo chorus and loop.			
1981-1984		$300	$375
Noise Buster NB10			
1988-1989. Eliminates 60-cycle hum and other outside signals, metal case.			
1988-1989		$70	$75
Overdrive OD850			
1975-1979.			
1975-1979		$275	$400
Overdrive II OD855			
1977-1979. Distortion, tone, and level controls, yellow/green case, large Overdrive II logo.			
1977-1979		$300	$400
Pan Delay DPL10			
1990-1992. Royal Blue case, 3 green control knobs.			
1990-1992		$100	$125
Parametric EQ PQ9			
1982-1984.			
1982-1984		$125	$175
Parametric EQ PQ401			
1981. 3 sliders, dial-in knob, light aqua blue case.			
1981		$125	$175
Phase Tone PT909			
1979-1982. Blue box, 3 knobs, early models with flat case (logo at bottom or later in the middle) or later wedge case.			
1979-1982		$140	$150
Phase Tone PT999			
1975-1979. Script logo, 1 knob, round footswitch, becomes PT-909.			
1975-1979		$125	$150

MODEL YEAR	FEATURES	EXC. COND. LOW	HIGH
Phase Tone PT1000			
1974-1975. Morley-style pedal phase, light blue case, early model of Phase Tone.			
1974-1975		$200	$300
Phase Tone II PT707			
1976-1979. Blue box, 1 knob, script logo for first 2 years.			
1976-1979		$100	$130
Phaser PH5 (SoundTank)			
1991-1998			
1991-1998		$20	$30
Phaser PH7 (Tone-Lok)			
1999-present. Speed, depth, feedback and level controls.			
1999-2007		$35	$40
Phaser PT9			
1982-1984. Three control knobs, red case.			
1982-1984		$75	$100
Powerlead PL5 (SoundTank)			
1991-1998. Metal case '91, plastic case '91-'98.			
1991	Metal	$25	$40
1991-1998	Plastic	$15	$20
Renometer			
1976-1979. 5-band equalizer with preamp.			
1976-1979		$75	$100
Rotary Chorus RC99			
1996-1999. Black or silver cases available, requires power pack and does not use a battery.			
1996-1999	Black case	$100	$125
Session Man SS10			
1988-1989. Distortion, chorus.			
1988-1989		$70	$80
Session Man II SS20			
1988-1989. 4 controls + toggle, light pink-purple case.			
1988-1989		$70	$80
Slam Punk SP5 (SoundTank)			
1996-1999.			
1996-1999		$35	$40
Smash Box SM7 (Tone-Lok)			
2000-present.			
2000-2007		$30	$35
Sonic Distortion SD9			
1982-1984.			
1982-1984		$75	$100
Standard Fuzz (No. 59)			
1974-1979. Two buttons (fuzz on/off and tone change).			
1974-1979		$175	$200
Stereo Box ST800			
1975-1979. One input, 2 outputs for panning, small yellow case.			
1975-1979		$175	$225
Stereo Chorus CS9			
1982-1984.			
1982-1984		$75	$100
Stereo Chorus CSL (Master Series)			
1985-1986.			
1985-1986		$70	$90

MODEL YEAR FEATURES	EXC. COND. LOW	HIGH
Super Chorus CS5 (SoundTank)		
1991-1998.		
1991-1998	$20	$30
Super Metal SM9		
1984. Distortion.		
1984	$75	$95
Super Stereo Chorus SC10		
1986-1992.		
1986-1992	$75	$100
Super Tube Screamer ST9		
1984-1985. 4 knobs, light green metal case.		
1984-1985	$225	$300
Super Tube STL		
1985.		
1985	$75	$95
Swell Flanger SF10		
1986-1992. Speed, regeneration, width and time controls, yellow case.		
1986-1992	$55	$100
Trashmetal TM5 (SoundTank)		
1990-1998. Tone and distortion pedal, 3 editions 1st edition, 2nd edition metal case, 2nd edition plastic case).		
1990-1998	$15	$20
Tremolo Pedal TL5 (SoundTank)		
1995-1998.		
1995-1998	$45	$95
Tube King TK999		
1994-1995. Has a 12AX7 tube and 3-band equalizer.		
1994-1995 Includes power pack	$150	$200
Tube King TK999US		
1996-1998. Has a 12AX7 tube and 3-band equalizer, does not have the noise switch of original TK999. Made in the U.S.		
1996-1998 Includes power pack	$150	$200
Tube Screamer TS5 (SoundTank)		
1991-1998.		
1991-1998	$20	$25
Tube Screamer TS7 (Tone-Lok)		
1999-present. 3 control knobs.		
1999-2007	$30	$35
Tube Screamer TS9		
1982-1984, 1993-present. Reissued in '93		
1982-1984	$200	$300
1993-2007	$75	$125
Tube Screamer Classic TS10		
1986-1993.		
1986-1993	$200	$225
Tube Screamer TS808		
1980-1982, 2004-present. Reissued in '04.		
1980-1982 Original	$500	$750
2004-2007 Reissue	$50	$115
Turbo Tube Screamer TS9DX		
1998-present. Tube Screamer circuit with added 3 settings for low-end.		
1998-2007	$70	$85
Twin Cam Chorus TC10		
1986-1989. Four control knobs, light blue case.		
1986-1989	$75	$100

MODEL YEAR FEATURES	EXC. COND. LOW	HIGH
Virtual Amp VA3 (floor unit)		
1995-1998. Digital effects processor.		
1995-1998	$55	$75
VL10		
1987-1997. Stereo volume pedal.		
1987-1997	$50	$75
Wah Fuzz Standard (Model 58)		
1974-1981. Fuzz tone change toggle, fuzz on toggle, fuzz depth control, balance control, wah volume pedal with circular friction pads on footpedal.		
1974-1981	$225	$300
Wah WH10		
1988-1997.		
1988-1997	$50	$75

Ilitch Electronics
2003-present. Ilitch Chiliachki builds his effects in Camarillo, California.

Indy Guitarist
See listing under Wampler Pedals.

Intersound
Made by Intersound, Inc. of Boulder, Colorado.
Reverb-Equalizer R100F
1977-1979. Reverb and 4-band EQ, fader.

1977-1979	$75	$100

J. Everman
2000-present. Analog guitar effects built by Justin J. Everman in Richardson, Texas.

Jacques
One-of-a-kind handmade stomp boxes and production models made in France. Production models are distributed in the U.S. by Godlyke Distributing.

JangleBox
2004-present. Stephen Lasko and Elizabeth Lasko build their guitar effects in Springfield, Virginia and Dracut, Massachusetts.

Jan-Mar Industries
Jan-Mar was located in Hillsdale, New Jersey.
The Talker
1976. 30 watts.

1976	$75	$125

The Talker Pro
1976. 75 watts.

1976	$100	$150

Jax
1960s-1970. Japanese imports made by Shinei.
Fuzz Master

1960s	$100	$150

Vibrachorus
Variant of Univibe.

1969	$750	$1,000

Ibanez TS-808

Ilitch Electronics Classic One Dyna Dist Overdrive

Janglebox Compression/Sustain

Keeley Compressor

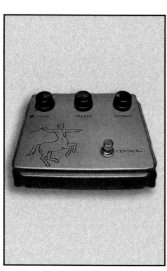

Klon Centaur

Line 6 MM-4

MODEL YEAR	FEATURES	EXC. COND. LOW	HIGH
Wah-Wah			
1960s		$100	$150

Jersey Girl

1991-present. Line of guitar effects pedals made in Japan. They also build guitars.

Jet Sounds LTD

1977. Jet was located in Jackson, Mississippi.
Hoze Talk Box
1977. Large wood box, 30 watts.

1977		$90	$125

JHD Audio

1974-1990. Hunt Dabney founded JHD in Costa Mesa, California, to provide effects that the user installed in their amp. Dabney is still involved in electronics and builds the BiasProbe tool for tubes.
SuperCube/SuperCube II
1974-late 1980s. Plug-in sustain mod for Fender amps with reverb, second version for amps after '78.

1970s		$50	$75

Jimi Hendrix

See listing under Dunlop.

John Hornby Skewes & Co.

Mid 1960s-present. Large English distributor of musical products which has also made their own brands, or self-branded products from others, over the years.

Johnson

Mid 1990s-present. Budget line of effects imported by Music Link, Brisbane, California. Johnson also offers guitars, amps, mandolins and basses.

Johnson Amplification

1997-present. Modeling amps and effects designed by John Johnson, of Sandy, Utah. The company is part of Harman International. In '02, they quit building amps, but continue the effects line.

Jordan

1960s. Jordan effects were distributed by Sho-Bud of Nashville, Tennessee.
Boss Tone Fuzz
1968-1969. Tiny effect plugged into guitar's output jack.

1968-1969		$125	$175
Compressor J-700			
1960s		$75	$100
Creator Volume Sustainer			
1960s		$125	$175
Gig Wa-Wa Volume			
1960s		$125	$150
Phaser			
Black case, yellow knobs.			
1960s	Black case	$125	$150

MODEL YEAR	FEATURES	EXC. COND. LOW	HIGH

Kay

1931-present. Kay was once one of the largest instrument producers in the world, offering just about everything for the guitarist, including effects.
Effects Pedals
1970s. Includes the Wah, Graphic Equalizer GE 5000, Rhythmer, and Tremolo.

1970s		$50	$7

Keeley

2001-present. Line of guitar effects designed and built by Robert Keeley in Edmond, Oklahoma. Keeley Electronics also offers a range of custom modifications for other effects.

Kendrick

1989-present. Texas' Kendrick offers guitars, amps, and effects.
ABC Amp Switcher
1990s.

1990s		$100	$140
Buffalo Pfuz			
1990s.			
1990s		$70	$100
Model 1000 Reverb			
1991-2003. Vintage style, 3 knobs: dwell, tone, and mix, brown cover, wheat grille with art deco shape.			
1991-2003		$400	$450
Powerglide Attenuator			
1998-present. Allows you to cut the output before it hits the amp's speakers, rack mount, metal cab.			
1998-2006		$180	$200

Kent

1961-1969. This import guitar brand also offered a few effects.

Kern Engineering

Located in Kenosha, Wisconsin, Kern offers pre-amps and wah pedals.

Klon

1994-present. Originally located in Brookline, Massachusetts, and now located in Cambridge, Massachusetts, Klon was started by Bill Finnegan after working with two circuit design partners on the Centaur Professional Overdrive.
Centaur Professional Overdrive
1994-present. Gold case.

1990s		$425	$650

KMD (Kaman)

1986-ca. 1990. Distributed by Kaman (Ovation, Hamer, etc.) in the late '80s.
Effects Pedals

1986-1990	Analog Delay	$65	$90
1986-1990	Overdrive	$30	$45
1987-1990	Distortion	$30	$45
1987-1990	Flanger	$30	$50
1987-1990	Phaser	$30	$50
1987-1990	Stereo Chorus	$30	$50

EFFECTS

MODEL YEAR	FEATURES	EXC. COND. LOW	HIGH

Korg

Most of the Korg effects listed below are modular effects. The PME-40X Professional Modular Effects System holds four of them and allows the user to select several variations of effects. The modular effects cannot be used alone. This system was sold for a few years starting in 1983. Korg currently offers the Toneworks line of effects.

PEQ-1 Parametric EQ
1980s. Dial-in equalizer with gain knob, band-width knob, and frequency knob, black case.

1980s		$40	$50

PME-40X Modular Effects

Year	Features	LOW	HIGH
1983-1986	KAD-301 Analog Delay	$60	$70
1983-1986	KCH-301 Stereo Chorus	$25	$35
1983-1986	KCO-101 Compressor	$45	$55
1983-1986	KDI-101 Distortion	$45	$55
1983-1986	KDL-301 Dynamic Echo	$90	$110
1983-1986	KFL-401 Stereo Flanger	$40	$50
1983-1986	KGE-201 Graphic EQ	$25	$35
1983-1986	KNG-101 Noise Gate	$25	$35
1983-1986	KOD-101 Over Drive	$45	$55
1983-1986	KPH-401 Phaser	$45	$55
1983-1986	OCT-1 Octaver	$70	$80

PME-40X Professional Modular Effects System
1983-ca.1986. Board holds up to 4 of the modular effects listed below.

1983-1986		$125	$150

SSD 3000 Digital Delay
1980s. Rack mount, SDD-3000 logo on top of unit.

1980s		$600	$850

Krank

1996-present. Tempe, Arizona, amp builder Krank also builds effects pedals.

Laney

1968-present. Founded by Lyndon Laney and Bob Thomas in Birmingham, England, this amp builder also offered a reverb unit.

Reverberation Unit
1968-1969. Sleek reverb unit, plexi-style front panel, black vinyl cover.

1968-1969		$300	$400

Lehle

2001-present. Loop switches from Burkhard Georg Lehle of Lehle Gitarrentechnik in Voerde, Germany.

D.Loop Signal Router

2004		$150	$175

Line 6

1996-present. Effects from Marcus Ryle and Michel Doidic who were product line designers prior to forming their own design company. A sixth company telephone line was added to their product design business to handle their own product line, thus Line 6. They also produce amps and guitars. All prices include Line 6 power pack if applicable.

DL-4 Delay Modeler
1999-present. Green case.

1999-2007		$175	$225

DM-4 Distortion Modeler
1999-present. Yellow case.

1999-2007		$100	$125

FM-4 Filter Modeler
2001-present. Purple case.

2001-2007		$175	$225

MM-4 Modulation Modeler
1999-present. Aqua blue case.

1999-2007		$150	$185

POD 2.0
2001-present. Updated version of the original Amp modeler.

2001-2007		$150	$200

Little Lanilei

1997-present. Best known for their small hand-made amps, Songworks Systems & Products of San Juan Capistrano, California, also offers effects bearing the Little Lanilei name.

Lock & Rock

2003-present. Line of floor pedal guitar and microphone effects produced by Brannon Electronics, Inc. of Houston, Texas.

Loco Box

1982-1983. Loco Box was a brand of effects distributed by Aria Pro II for a short period starting in '82. It appears that Aria switched the effects to their own brand in '83.

Effects

Year	Features	LOW	HIGH
1982-1983	Analog Delay AD-01	$35	$45
1982-1983	Chorus CH-01	$55	$65
1982-1983	Compressor CM-01	$35	$45
1982-1983	Distortion DS-01	$40	$55
1982-1983	Flanger FL-01	$35	$45
1982-1983	Graphic Equalizer GE-06	$25	$35
1982-1983	Overdrive OD-01	$40	$50
1982-1983	Phaser PH-01	$45	$55

Lovepedal

2000-present. Sean Michael builds his preamps and guitar stomp boxes in Detroit, Michigan.

Lovetone

1995-present. Hand-made analog effects from Oxfordshire, England.

Line 6 POD X3

EFFECTS

Lock & Rock Sour Boost

Lovepedal Meatball

Maestro Boomerang

Maestro Fuzztain

Maestro Theremin

MODEL YEAR	FEATURES	EXC. COND. LOW	HIGH

Ludwig

For some reason, drum builder Ludwig offered a guitar synth in the 1970s.

Phase II Guitar Synth

1970-1971. Oversized synth, mushroom-shaped footswitches.

| 1970-1971 | Vertical silver case | $450 | $600 |

M.B. Electronics

Made in San Francisco, California.

Ultra-Metal UM-10

1985. Distortion.

| 1985 | | $35 | $40 |

Maestro

1950s-1970s, 2001-present. Maestro was a Gibson subsidiary; the name appeared on 1950s accordian amplifiers. The first Maestro effects were the Echoplex tape echo and the FZ-1 Fuzz-Tone, introduced in the early-'60s. Maestro products were manufactured by various entities such as Market Electronics, All-Test Devices, Lowrey and Moog Electronics. In the late-'60s and early-'70s, they unleashed a plethora of pedals; some were beautiful, others had great personality. The last Maestro effects were the Silver and Black MFZ series of the late-'70s. In 2001, Gibson revived the name for a line of effects, banjos and mandolins.

Bass Brassmaster BB-1

1971-ca.1974. Added brass to your bass.

| 1971-1974 | | $450 | $650 |

Boomerang

Ca.1969-ca.1972. Wah pedal made by All-Test Devices.

| 1969-1972 | | $175 | $200 |

Boomerang BG-2

1972-ca.1976. Wah pedal made by All-Test Devices.

| 1972-1976 | | $100 | $125 |

Echoplex EM-1 Groupmaster

Ca.1970-ca.1977. Two input Echoplex, solidstate.

| 1970-1977 | Without stand | $700 | $900 |

Echoplex EP-1

1962/63-mid-1960s. Original model, smaller box, tube, separate controls for echo volume and instrument volume, made by Market Electronics. Though not labeled as such, it is often referred to as the EP-1 by collectors.

| 1960s | Earlier small Green box | $800 | $900 |

Echoplex EP-2

Mid-1960s-ca.1970. Larger box than original, tube, single echo/instrument volume control, made by Market Electronics. Around '70, the EP-2 added a Sound-On-Sound feature.

| 1960s | Larger Green box | $800 | $900 |

Echoplex EP-3

Ca.1970-1977. Solidstate, made by Market Electronics, black box.

| 1970-1977 | | $400 | $550 |

MODEL YEAR	FEATURES	EXC. COND. LOW	HIGH

Echoplex Groupmaster

Ca.1970-ca.1974. Two input Echoplex, solidstate.

| 1970-1977 | With stand | $1,000 | $1,200 |

Echoplex IV (EP-4)

1977-1978. Solidstate, last version introduced by Maestro. See brands Market Electronics and Echoplex for later models.

| 1977-1978 | | $375 | $500 |

Echoplex Sireko ES-1

Ca.1971-mid-1970s. A budget version of the Echoplex, solidstate, made by Market.

| 1971-1975 | | $200 | $300 |

Envelope Modifier ME-1

1971-ca.1976. Tape reverse/string simulator, made by All-Test.

| 1971-1976 | | $150 | $225 |

Filter Sample and Hold FSH-1

1975-ca.1976.

| 1975-1976 | | $475 | $700 |

Full Range Boost FRB-1

1971-ca.1975. Frequency boost with fuzz, made by All-Test.

| 1971-1975 | | $150 | $200 |

Fuzz MFZ-1

1976-1979. Made by Moog.

| 1976-1979 | | $150 | $200 |

Fuzz Phazzer FP-1

1971-1974.

| 1971-1974 | | $200 | $300 |

Fuzz Tone FZ-1

1962-1963. Brown, uses 2 AA batteries.

| 1962-1963 | | $250 | $325 |

Fuzz Tone FZ-1A

1965-1967. Brown, uses 1 AA battery.

| 1965-1967 | | $225 | $300 |

Fuzz Tone FZ-1A (reissue)

2001-present.

| 2001-2007 | | $65 | $70 |

Fuzz Tone FZ-1B

Late-1960s- early-1970s. Black, uses 9-volt battery.

| 1970s | | $150 | $250 |

Fuzztain MFZT-1

1976-1978. Fuzz, sustain, made by Moog.

| 1976-1978 | | $200 | $250 |

Mini-Phase Shifter MPS-2

1976. Volume, speed, slow and fast controls.

| 1976 | | $110 | $125 |

Octave Box OB-1

1971-ca.1975. Made by All-Test Devices.

| 1971-1975 | | $225 | $300 |

Parametric Filter MPF-1

1976-1978. Made by Moog.

| 1970s | | $185 | $200 |

Phase Shifter PS-1

1971-1975. With or without 3-button footswitch, made by Oberheim.

| 1971-1975 | With footswitch | $250 | $300 |
| 1971-1975 | Without footswitch | $150 | $250 |

MODEL YEAR / FEATURES	EXC. COND. LOW	HIGH

Phase Shifter PS-1A
1976.

| 1976 | $150 | $250 |

Phase Shifter PS-1B
1970s.

| 1970s | $150 | $250 |

Phaser MP-1
1976-1978. Made by Moog.

| 1976-1978 | $100 | $120 |

Repeat Pedal RP-1

| 1970s | $200 | $300 |

Rhythm King MRK-2
1971-ca.1974. Early drum machine.

| 1972 | $200 | $300 |

Rhythm Queen MRQ-1
Early 1970s. Early rhythm machine.

| 1970s | $125 | $150 |

Rhythm'n Sound G-2
Ca.1969-1970s. Multi-effect unit.

| 1969-1975 | $200 | $300 |

Ring Modulator RM-1
1971-1975.

| 1971-1975 | With MP-1 control pedal | $650 | $700 |
| 1971-1975 | Without control pedal | $550 | $600 |

Rover Rotating Speaker
1971-ca.1973. Rotating Leslie effect that mounted on a large tripod.

| 1971-1973 | RO-1 model | $1,100 | $1,500 |

Sound System for Woodwinds W-1
1960s-1970s. Designed for clarinet or saxaphone input, gives a variety of synthesizer-type sounds with voices for various woodwinds, uses Barrel Joint and integrated microphone.

| 1960-1970s | $350 | $400 |

Stage Phaser MPP-1
1976-1978. Had slow, fast and variable settings, made by Moog.

| 1976-1978 | $175 | $225 |

Super Fuzztone FZ-1S

| 1971-1975 | $200 | $300 |

Sustainer SS-2
1971-ca.1975. Made by All-Test Devices.

| 1971-1975 | $100 | $150 |

Theramin TH-1
1971-mid-1970s. Device with 2 antennae, made horror film sound effects. A reissue Theremin is available from Theremaniacs in Milwaukee, Wisconsin.

| 1971-1975 | $800 | $1,000 |

Wah-Wah/Volume WW-1
1970s. Wah-Wah Volume logo on end of pedal, green foot pad.

| 1971-1975 | $150 | $250 |

Magnatone
1937-1970s. Magnatone built very competitive amps from '57 to '66. In the early-'60s, they offered the RVB-1 Reverb Unit. The majority of Magnatone amps pre-'66 did not have on-board reverb.

Model RVB-1 Reverb Unit
1961-1966. Typical brown leatherette cover, square box-type cabinet. From '64-'66, battery operated, solidstate version of RVB-1, low flat cabinet.

| 1961-1963 | $275 | $400 |
| 1964-1966 | Battery and solidstate | $200 | $300 |

Mannys Music
Issued by the New York-based retailer.

Fuzz
1960s. Same unit as the Orpheum Fuzz and Clark Fuzz.

| 1960s | $225 | $325 |

Market Electronics
Market, from Ohio, made the famous Echoplex line. See Maestro section for earlier models and Echoplex section for later versions.

Marshall
1962-present. The fuzz and wah boom of the '60s led many established manufacturers, like Marshall, to introduce variations on the theme. They got back into stomp boxes in '89 with the Gov'nor distortion, and currently produce several distortion/overdrive units.

Blues Breaker
1992-1999. Replaced by Blues Breaker II in 2000.

| 1992-1999 | $100 | $130 |

Blues Breaker II Overdrive
2000-present. Overdrive pedal, 4 knobs.

| 2000-2007 | $50 | $65 |

Drive Master
1992-1999.

| 1992-1999 | $70 | $75 |

Guv'nor
1989-1991. Distortion, Guv'nor Plus introduced in '99.

| 1989-1991 | $75 | $100 |

Jackhammer
1999-present. Distortion pedal.

| 1999-2007 | $55 | $65 |

PB-100 Power Brake
1993-1995. Speaker attenuator for tube amps.

| 1993-1995 | $190 | $230 |

Shred Master
1992-1999.

| 1992-1999 | $75 | $100 |

Supa Fuzz
Late-1960s. Made by Sola Sound (Colorsound).

| 1967 | $300 | $400 |

Supa Wah
Late-1960s. Made by Sola Sound (Colorsound).

| 1969 | $300 | $425 |

Vibratrem VT-1
1999-present. Vibrato and tremolo.

| 1999-2007 | $75 | $85 |

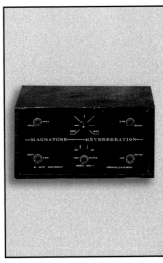
Magnatone RVB-1

Marshall Shred Master

Marshall Blues Breaker II Overdrive

EFFECTS

Maxon AD9 Pro

EFFECTS

MetalPedals.com Demon Drive

Moogerfooger MF-105 MuRF

Matchless

1989-1999, 2001-present. Matchless amplifiers offered effects in the '90s.

AB Box
1990s. Split box for C-30 series amps (DC 30, SC 30, etc.)

MODEL YEAR	FEATURES	LOW	HIGH
1990s		$175	$300

Coolbox
1997-1999. Tube preamp pedal.

1997-1999		$275	$350

Dirtbox
1997-1999. Tube-driven overdrive pedal.

1997-1999		$225	$350

Echo Box
1997-1999. Limited production because of malfunctioning design which included cassette tape. Black case, 8 white chickenhead control knobs.

1990s	Original unreliable status	$300	$400
1990s	Updated working order	$700	$850

Hotbox/Hotbox II
1995-1999. Higher-end tube-driven preamp pedal.

1995-1999		$375	$425

Mix Box
1997-1999. 4-input tube mixer pedal.

1997-1999		$375	$425

Reverb RV-1
1993-1999. 5 controls, tube reverb tank.

1993-1999	Various colors	$1,000	$1,300

Split Box
1990s. Tube AB box.

1997	Standard AB	$275	$325

Tremolo/Vibrato TV-1
1993-1995. Tube unit.

1993-1995		$350	$400

Maxon

1970s-present. Maxon was the original manufacturer of the Ibanez line of effects. Currently offering retro '70s era stomp boxes distributed in the U.S. by Godlyke.

AD-9 Analog Delay
2001-present. Purple case.

2001-2007		$225	$275

CS-550 Stereo Chorus
2000-present. Light blue case.

2000-2007		$100	$130

OD-820 Over Drive Pro
2001-present.

2001-2007		$140	$175

McQuackin FX Co.

1997-present. Analog guitar effects hand made by Rich McCracken II in Augusta, Georgia. He also built them for three years while living in Nashville, Tennessee.

Mesa-Boogie

1971-present. Mesa added pre-amps in the mid '90s.

V-Twin Bottle Rocket
2000-2004.

MODEL YEAR	FEATURES	LOW	HIGH
2000-2004		$100	$150

V-Twin Preamp Pedal
Dec. 1993-2004. Serial number series: V011-. 100 watts, all tube preamp, floor unit, silver case.

1993-1999		$225	$275
2000-2004	Updated bottom tone adj.	$275	$325

MetalPedals.com

2006-present. Brothers Dave and Mike Pantaleone build their guitar effects in New Jersey.

Meteoro

1986-present. Guitar effects built in Brazil. They also build guitar and bass amps.

MG

2004-present. Guitar effects built by Marcelo Giangrande in São Paulo, Brazil. He also builds amps.

Mica

Early 1970s. These Japanese-made effects were also sold under the Bruno and Marlboro brand names.

Tone Fuzz
Silver case, black knobs.

1970s		$200	$250

Tone Surf Wah Siren
1970s. Wah pedal.

1970s		$150	$175

Wailer Fuzz

1970		$75	$100

Wau Wau Fuzz
1970s. Wau Wau Fuzz logo on end of pedal, black.

1970s		$150	$175

Moog/Moogerfooger

Robert Moog, of synth fame, introduced his line of Moogerfooger analog effects in 1998.

Misc. Effects

2004	MF-105 MuRF	$250	$275
2004	Theremin	$250	$275

Moonrock

2002-present. Fuzz/distortion unit built by Glenn Wylie and distributed by Tonefrenzy.

Morley

Late-1960s-present. Founded by brothers Raymond and Marvin Lubow, Morley has produced a wide variety of pedals and effects over the years, changing with the trends. In '89, the brothers sold the company to Accutronics (later changed to Sound Enhancements, Inc.) of Cary, Illinois.

ABY Switch Box
1981-ca.1985. Box.

1981-1985		$25	$35

The *Vintage Guitar Price Guide* shows low to high values for items in all-original excellent condition, and, where applicable, with original case or cover.

MODEL YEAR	FEATURES	EXC. COND. LOW	HIGH
Auto Wah PWA			
1976-ca.1985.			
1976-1985		$25	$35
Bad Horsie Steve Vai Signature Wah			
1997-present			
1997-2007		$65	$70
Black Gold Stereo Volume BSV			
1985-1991.			
1985-1991		$25	$35
Black Gold Stereo Volume Pan BSP			
1985-1989.			
1985-1989		$30	$40
Black Gold Volume BVO			
1985-1991.			
1985-1991		$25	$35
Black Gold Wah BWA			
1985-1991.			
1985-1991		$30	$40
Black Gold Wah Volume BWV			
1985-1989.			
1985-1989		$30	$40
Chrystal Chorus CCB			
1996-1999. Stereo output.			
1996-1999		$25	$30
Deluxe Distortion DDB			
1981-1991. Box, no pedal.			
1981-1991		$40	$60
Deluxe Flanger FLB			
1981-1991. Box, no pedal.			
1981-1991		$55	$65
Deluxe Phaser DFB			
1981-1991. Box, no pedal.			
1981-1991		$40	$60
Distortion One DIB			
1981-1991. Box, no pedal.			
1981-1991		$35	$45
Echo Chorus Vibrato ECV			
1982-ca.1985.			
1982-1985		$150	$225
Echo/Volume EVO-1			
1974-ca.1982.			
1974-1982		$150	$225
Electro-Pik-a-Wah PKW			
1979-ca.1982.			
1979-1982		$55	$65
Emerald Echo EEB			
1996-1999. 300 millisecond delay.			
1996-1999	Green case	$40	$50
Jerry Donahue JD-10			
1995-1997. Multi-effect, distortion, overdrive.			
1995-1997		$80	$90
Power Wah PWA/PWA II			
1992-2006. Wah with boost. Changed to II in '98.			
1992-2006		$40	$50
Power Wah PWO			
Ca.1969-1984, 2006-present. Reissued in '06.			
1969-1984		$60	$70
Power Wah/Boost PWB			
Introduced in 1973, doubles as a volume pedal.			
1970s		$70	$80

MODEL YEAR	FEATURES	EXC. COND. LOW	HIGH
Power Wah/Fuzz PWF			
Ca.1969-ca.1984.			
1969-1984		$75	$125
Pro Compressor PCB			
1978-1984. Stomp box without pedal, compress-sustain knob and output knob.			
1978-1984		$45	$55
Pro Flanger PFL			
1978-1984.			
1978-1984		$100	$125
Pro Phaser PFA			
1975-1984.			
1975-1984		$100	$125
Rotating Sound Power Wah Model RWV			
1974-1982.			
1974-1982		$325	$375
Select-Effect Pedal SEL			
Lets you control up to 5 other pedals.			
1980s		$20	$30
Slimline Echo Volume 600			
1983-1985. 20 to 600 ms delay.			
1983-1985		$45	$55
Slimline Echo Volume SLEV			
1983-1985. 20 to 300 ms delay.			
1983-1985		$50	$60
Slimline Variable Taper Stereo Volume SLSV			
1982-1986.			
1982-1986		$70	$100
Slimline Variable Taper Volume SLVO			
1982-1986.			
1982-1986		$35	$50
Slimline Wah SLWA			
1982-1986. Battery operated electro-optical.			
1982-1986		$55	$75
Slimline Wah Volume SLWV			
1982-ca.1986. Battery operated electro-optical.			
1982-1986		$55	$75
Stereo Chorus Flanger CFL			
1980-ca. 1986. Box, no pedal.			
1980-1986		$60	$70
Stereo Chorus Vibrato SCV			
1980-1991. Box, no pedal.			
1980-1991		$80	$100
Stereo Volume CSV			
1980-ca. 1986. Box, no pedal.			
1980-1986		$30	$45
Volume Compressor VCO			
1979-1984.			
1979-1984		$30	$45
Volume Phaser PFV			
1977-1984. With volume pedal.			
1977-1984		$125	$150
Volume VOL			
1975-ca.1984.			
1975-1979		$30	$45
1980-1984		$25	$40
Volume XVO			
1985-1988.			
1985-1988		$25	$40

Morley ABY

EFFECTS

Morley Jerry Donahue JD10

Morley Volume Boost VBO

To get the most from this book, be sure to read "Using *The Guide*" in the introduction.

Mosferatu

Mu-Tron Octave Divider

Mu-Tron Phasor II

MODEL YEAR	FEATURES	EXC. COND. LOW	HIGH
Volume/Boost VBO			
1974-1984.			
1974-1984		$50	$60
Wah Volume CWV			
1987-1991. Box, no pedal.			
1987-1991		$65	$80
Wah Volume XWV			
1985-ca.1989.			
1985-1989		$65	$80
Wah/Volume WVO			
1977-ca.1984.			
1977-1984		$80	$100

Mosferatu

Line of guitar effects pedals built by Hermida Audio Technology.

Mosrite

Semie Moseley's Mosrite company dipped into effects in the 1960s.

Fuzzrite

1960s. Sanner reissued the Fuzzrite in 1999.

1960s		$175	$225

Multivox

New York-based Multivox offered a variety of effects in the 1970s and '80s.

Big Jam Effects

Multivox offered the Big Jam line of effects from 1980 to ca. '83.

1980-1983	6-Band EQ, Compressor, Phaser, Spit-Wah	$40	$50
1980-1983	Analog Echo/Reverb	$100	$125
1980-1983	Bi-Phase 2, Flanger, Jazz Flanger	$50	$60
1980-1983	Chorus	$45	$55
1980-1983	Distortion	$70	$80
1980-1983	Octave Box	$40	$55
1981-1983	Noise Gate, Parametric EQ	$35	$45
1981-1983	Space Driver, Delay	$60	$70
1982-1983	Volume Pedal	$30	$35

Full Rotor MX-2

1978-ca.1982. Leslie effect.

1978-1982		$300	$350

Little David LD-2

Rotary sound effector in mini Leslie-type case.

1970s	With pedal	$375	$450
1970s	Without pedal	$325	$375

Multi Echo MX-201

Tape echo unit, reverb.

1970s		$200	$250

Multi Echo MX-312

Tape echo unit, reverb.

1970s		$225	$300

Rhythm Ace FR6M

27 basic rhythms.

1970s		$60	$80

MODEL YEAR	FEATURES	EXC. COND. LOW	HIGH

Mu-tron

1972-ca.1981. Made by Musitronics (founded by Aaron Newman), Rosemont, New Jersey, these rugged and unique-sounding effects were a high point of the '70s. The Mu-Tron III appeared in '72 and more products followed, about 10 in all. Musitronics also made the U.S. models of the Dan Armstrong effects. In '78 ARP synthesizers bought Musitronics and sold Mutron products to around '81. A reissue of the Mu-Tron III was made available in '95 by NYC Music Products and distributed by Matthews and Ryan Musical Products.

III Envelope Filter

1972-ca.1981. Envelope Filter.

1972-1981		$500	$600

Bi-Phase

1975-ca.1981. Add $50-$75 for Opti-Pot pedal.

1971-1981	With optical pedal option	$800	$1,200
1975-1981	With 2-button footswitch	$500	$900

C-100 OptiPot Control Pedal

1975-1981	Blue case	$550	$700

C-200 Volume-Wah

1970s		$300	$400

Flanger

1977-ca.1981.

1977-1981		$400	$450

Micro V

Ca.1975-ca.1977. Envelope Filter.

1970s		$200	$250

Octave Divider

1977-ca.1981.

1977-1981		$550	$700

Phasor

Ca.1974-ca.1976. Two knobs.

1974-1976		$200	$300

Phasor II

1976-ca.1981. Three knobs.

1976-1981		$200	$300

Muza

2006-present. Digital guitar effects made in China by Hong Kong's Medeli Electronics Co., Ltd. They also build digital drums.

MXR

1972-present. MXR Innovations launched its line of pedals in '72. Around '77, the Rochester, New York, company changed lettering on the effects from script to block, and added new models. MXR survived into the mid-'80s. In '87, production was picked up by Jim Dunlop. Reissues of block logo boxes can be differentiated from originals as they have an LED above the switch and the finish is slightly rough; the originals are smooth.

6 Band Equalizer

1975-1982.

1975-1979		$70	$85
1980-1982		$60	$70

MODEL YEAR	FEATURES	EXC. COND. LOW	HIGH
6 Band Equalizer M-109 (reissue)			
1987-present. Reissued by Jim Dunlop.			
1987-2007		$30	$40
10 Band Graphic Equalizer M-108			
1975-1981, 2004-present.			
1975-1981	With AC power cord	$80	$100
Analog Delay			
1975-1981. Green case, power cord.			
1975-1979	Earlier 2-jack model	$300	$325
1980-1981	Later 3-jack model	$150	$200
Blue Box			
1972-ca.1978. Octave pedal, M-103.			
1970s	Earlier script logo	$350	$400
1970s	Later block logo	$225	$250
Blue Box M-103 (Reissue)			
1995-present. Reissued by Jim Dunlop. Produces 1 octave above or 2 octaves below.			
1995-2007		$40	$45
Commande Overdrive			
1981-1983. The Commande series featured plastic housings and electronic switching.			
1981-1983		$40	$50
Commande Phaser			
1981-1983.			
1981-1983		$100	$110
Commande Preamp			
1981-1983.			
1981-1983		$40	$50
Commande Stereo Chorus			
1981-1983.			
1981-1983		$60	$70
Commande Stereo Flanger			
1982-1983.			
1982-1983		$70	$80
Commande Sustain			
1981-1983.			
1981-1983		$60	$70
Commande Time Delay			
1981-1983.			
1981-1983		$70	$80
Distortion +			
1972-1982.			
1970s	Earlier script logo	$185	$225
1970s	Later block logo	$85	$110
1980s	Block logo	$80	$95
Distortion + (Series 2000)			
1983-1985.			
1983-1985		$60	$70
Distortion + M-104 (Reissue)			
1987-present. Reissued by Jim Dunlop.			
1987-1990		$55	$65
1991-2007		$45	$55
Distortion II			
1981-1983.			
1981-1983	With AC power cord	$140	$150
Double Shot Distortion M-151			
2003-2005. 2 channels.			
2003-2005		$65	$75

MODEL YEAR	FEATURES	EXC. COND. LOW	HIGH
Dyna Comp			
1972-1982. Compressor.			
1970s	Earlier script logo, battery	$175	$200
1970s	Later block logo, battery	$90	$120
1980s	Block logo, battery	$65	$80
Dyna Comp (Series 2000)			
1982-1985.			
1982-1985		$65	$75
Dyna Comp M-102 (Reissue)			
1987-present. Reissued by Jim Dunlop.			
1987-2007		$35	$40
Envelope Filter			
1976-1983.			
1976-1983		$125	$225
Flanger			
1976-1983, 1997-present. Analog, reissued by Dunlop in '97.			
1976-1979	AC power cord, 2 inputs	$175	$225
1980-1983	AC power cord	$100	$150
1997-2007	M-117R reissue	$60	$70
Flanger/Doubler			
1979	Rack mount	$150	$175
Limiter			
1980-1982. AC, 4 knobs.			
1980-1982	AC power cord	$125	$200
Loop Selector			
1980-1982. A/B switch for 2 effects loops.			
1980-1982		$50	$60
Micro Amp			
1978-1983, 1995-present. Variable booster, white case, reissued in '95.			
1978-1983		$75	$100
1995-2007	M-133 reissue	$40	$45
Micro Chorus			
1980-1983. Yellow case.			
1980-1983		$125	$175
Micro Flanger			
1981-1982.			
1981-1982		$100	$150
Noise Gate Line Driver			
1974-1983.			
1970s	Script logo	$75	$125
1980s	Block logo	$75	$100
Omni			
1980s. Rack unit with floor controller, compressor, 3-band EQ, distortion, delay, chorus/flanger.			
1980s		$425	$475
Phase 45			
Ca.1976-1982.			
1970s	Script logo, battery	$125	$175
1980s	Block logo, battery	$75	$125
Phase 90			
1972-1982.			
1970s	Earlier script logo	$325	$400
1970s	Later block logo	$175	$275
1980s	Block logo	$150	$200

Muza GP300

MXR Distortion +

MXR GT-OD Custom Shop

MXR '74 Vintage Phase 90

MXR Smart Gate M-135

MXR Super Comp M-132

MODEL YEAR	FEATURES	EXC. COND. LOW	HIGH
Phase 90 M-101 (reissue)			
1987-present. Reissued by Jim Dunlop.			
1987-1989	Block logo	$60	$85
1990-2007	Block or script logo	$50	$75
Phase 100			
1974-1982.			
1970s	Earlier script logo	$250	$325
1970s	Later block logo, battery	$175	$275
Phaser (Series 2000)			
1982-1985. Series 2000 introduced cost cutting die-cast cases.			
1982-1985		$60	$85
Pitch Transposer			
1980s		$400	$475
Power Converter			
1980s		$45	$60
Smart Gate M-135			
2002-present. Noise-gate, single control, battery powered.			
2002-2007		$60	$70
Stereo Chorus			
1978-1985. With AC power cord.			
1978-1979		$175	$275
1980-1985		$150	$200
Stereo Chorus (Series 2000)			
1983-1985. Series 2000 introduced cost cutting die-cast cases.			
1983-1985		$55	$75
Stereo Flanger (Series 2000)			
1983-1985. Series 2000 introduced cost cutting die-cast cases, black with blue lettering.			
1983-1985		$60	$80
Super Comp M-132			
2002-present. 3 knobs.			
2002-2007		$40	$55

Nobels

1997-present. Effects pedals from Nobels Electronics of Hamburg, Germany. They also make amps.

ODR-1 Overdrive

1997-present.

1997-2007		$30	$40

TR-X Tremolo

1997-present. Tremolo effect using modern technology, purple case.

1997-2007		$30	$40

Nomad

Fuzz Wah

1960s. Import from Japan, similar looking to Morley pedal with depth and volume controls and fuzz switch, silver metal case and black foot pedal.

1960s		$75	$125

MODEL YEAR	FEATURES	EXC. COND. LOW	HIGH

Olson

Olson Electronics was in Akron, Ohio.

Reverberation Amplifier RA-844

1967. Solidstate, battery-operated, reverb unit, depth and volume controls, made in Japan.

1967		$100	$150

Ovation

Ovation ventured into the solidstate amp and effects market in the early '70s.

K-6001 Guitar Preamp

1970s. Preamp with reverb, boost, tremolo, fuzz, and a tuner, looks something like a Maestro effect from the '70s, reliability may be an issue.

1970s		$100	$125

PAIA

1967-present. Founded by John Paia Simonton in Edmond, Oklahoma, specializing in synthesizer and effects kits. PAIA did make a few complete products but they are better known for the various electronic kit projects they sold. Values on kit projects are difficult as it depends on the skills of the person who built it.

Roctave Divider 5760

Kit to build analog octave divider.

1970s		$70	$85

Park

1965-1982, 1992-2000. Sola/Colorsound made a couple of effects for Marshall and their sister brand, Park. In the '90s, Marshall revived the name for use on small solidstate amps.

Pax

1970s. Imported Maestro copies.

Fuzz Tone Copy

1970s		$125	$150

Octave Box Copy

1970s. Dual push-buttons (normal and octave), 2 knobs (octave volume and sensitivity), green and black case.

1970s		$125	$150

Pearl

Pearl, located in Nashville, Tennessee, and better known for drums, offered a line of guitar effects in the 1980s.

Analog Delay AD-08

1983-1985. Four knobs.

1983-1985		$100	$150

Analog Delay AD-33

1982-1984. Six knobs.

1982-1984		$175	$225

Chorus CH-02

1981-1984. Four knobs.

1981-1984		$75	$100

Chorus Ensemble CE-22

1982-1984. Stereo chorus with toggling between chorus and vibrato, 6 knobs.

1982-1984		$125	$175

MODEL YEAR	FEATURES	EXC. COND. LOW	HIGH
Compressor CO-04			
1981-1984.			
1981-1984		$50	$75
Distortion DS-06			
1982-1986.			
1982-1986		$40	$60
Flanger FG-01			
1981-1986. Clock pulse generator, ultra-low frequency oscillator.			
1981-1986		$75	$100
Graphic EQ GE-09			
1983-1985.			
1983-1985		$40	$55
Octaver OC-07			
1982-1986.			
1982-1986		$100	$250
Overdrive OD-05			
1981-1986.			
1981-1986		$75	$100
Parametric EQ PE-10			
1983-1984.			
1983-1984		$45	$60
Phaser PH-03			
1981-1984. Four knobs.			
1981-1984		$75	$100
Phaser PH-44			
1982-1984. Six knobs.			
1982-1984		$150	$175
Stereo Chorus CH-22			
1982-1984.			
1982-1984	Blue case	$75	$125
Thriller TH-20			
1984-1986. Exciter.			
1984-1986	Black case four knobs	$175	$225

Peavey

1965-present. Peavey made stomp boxes from '87 to around '90. They offered rack mount gear after that.

MODEL YEAR	FEATURES	EXC. COND. LOW	HIGH
Accelerator Overdrive AOD-2			
1980s		$30	$35
Biampable Bass Chorus BAC-2			
1980s		$30	$35
Companded Chorus CMC-1			
1980s		$25	$30
Compressor/Sustainer CSR-2			
1980s		$35	$40
Digital Delay DDL-3			
1980s		$30	$35
Digital Stereo Reverb SRP-16			
1980s		$50	$55
Dual Clock Stereo Chorus DSC-4			
1980s		$30	$35
Hotfoot Distortion HFD-2			
1980s		$25	$30

PedalDoctor FX

1996-present. Tim Creek builds his production and custom guitar effects in Nashville, Tennessee.

Pedalworx

2001-present. Bob McBroom and George Blekas build their guitar effects in Manorville, New York and Huntsville, Alabama. They also do modifications to wahs.

Pharaoh Amplifiers

1998-present. Builder Matt Farrow builds his effects in Raleigh, North Carolina.

Pigtronix

2003-present. Dave Koltai builds his custom guitar effects originally in Brooklyn, and currently in Yonkers, New York and also offers models built in China.

Premier

Ca.1938-ca.1975, 1990-present. Premier offered a reverb unit in the '60s.

MODEL YEAR	FEATURES	EXC. COND. LOW	HIGH
Reverb Unit			
1961-late-1960s. Tube, footswitch, 2-tone brown.			
1960s		$250	$300

Prescription Electronics

1994-present. Located in Portland, Oregon, Jack Brossart offers a variety of hand-made effects.

MODEL YEAR	FEATURES	EXC. COND. LOW	HIGH
Dual-Tone			
1998-present. Overdrive and distortion.			
1998-2007		$165	$175
Throb			
1996-present. Tremolo.			
1996-2007		$165	$175
Yardbox			
1994-present. Patterned after the original Sola Sound Tonebender.			
1994-2007		$90	$125

ProCo

1974-present. Located in Kalamazoo, Michigan and founded by Charlie Wicks, ProCo produces effects, cables and audio products.

MODEL YEAR	FEATURES	EXC. COND. LOW	HIGH
Rat			
1979-1987. Fuzztone, large box until '84. The second version was 1/3 smaller than original box. The small box version became the Rat 2. The current Vintage Rat is a reissue of the original large box.			
1979-1984	Large box	$200	$250
1984-1987	Compact box	$100	$150
Rat 2			
1987-present.			
1987-1999		$50	$75
2000-2007		$40	$50
Turbo Rat			
1989-present. Fuzztone with higher output gain, slope-front case.			
1989-2007		$40	$50
Vintage Rat			
1992-2005. Reissue of early-'80s Rat.			
1992-2005		$40	$50

Pearl CO-04 Compressor

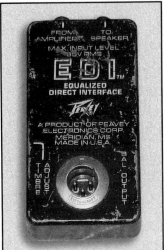

Peavey EDI

ProCo Rat

EFFECTS

EFFECTS

Retroman Dum-Box

Reverend Drivetrain II

Rocktek Metalworker

MODEL YEAR	FEATURES	EXC. COND. LOW	HIGH

Pro-Sound

The effects listed here date from 1987, and were, most likely, around for a short time.

Chorus CR-1

1980s		$25	$40

Delay DL-1
Analog.

1980s		$35	$55

Distortion DS-1

1980s		$20	$35

Octaver OT-1

1980s		$25	$40

Power and Master Switch PMS-1

1980s		$15	$25

Super Overdrive SD-1

1980s		$20	$35

Radial Engineering

1994-present. Radial makes a variety of products in Port Coquitlam, British Columbia, including direct boxes, snakes, cables, splitters, and, since '99, the Tonebone line of guitar effects.

Rapco

The Jackson, Missouri based cable company offers a line of switch, connection and D.I. Boxes.

The Connection AB-100
1988-present. A/B box

1988-2007		$25	$35

Rastopdesigns

2002-present. Alexander Rastopchin builds his effects in Long Island City, New York. He also builds amps.

Real McCoy Custom

1993-present. Wahs and effects by Geoffrey Teese. His first wah was advertised as "the Real McCoy, by Teese." He now offers his custom wah pedals under the Real McCoy Custom brand. He also used the Teese brand on a line of stomp boxes, starting in '96. The Teese stomp boxes are no longer being made.

Red Witch

2003-present. Analog guitar effects, designed by Ben Fulton, and made in Paekakariki, New Zealand.

Retro FX Pedals

2006-present. Guitar effects pedals made in St. Louis, Missouri.

Retroman

2002-present. Joe Wolf builds his retro effects pedals in Janesville, Wisconsin.

Retro-Sonic

2002-present. Tim Larwill builds effects in Ottawa Ontario, Canada.

MODEL YEAR	FEATURES	EXC. COND. LOW	HIGH

Reverend

1996-present. Reverend offered its Drivetrain effects from '00 to '04. They also build guitars.

RGW Electronics

2003-present. Guitar effects built by Robbie Wallace in Lubbock, Texas.

Rockman

See listings under Scholz Research and Dunlop.

Rocktek

1986-present. Imports formerly distributed by Matthews and Ryan of Brooklyn, New York; currently handled by D'Andrea USA.

Effects
1986-present.

1986-2007	Delay, Super Delay	$30	$40
1986-2007	Distortion, 6 Band EQ, Bass EQ, Chorus, Compressor	$15	$25
1986-2007	Overdrive, Flanger, Metal Worker, Phaser, Vibrator, Tremolo	$15	$20

Rocktron

1980s-present. Rocktron is a division of GHS Strings and offers a line of amps, controllers, stomp boxes, and preamps.

Austin Gold Overdrive
1997-present. Light overdrive.

1997-2007		$25	$35

Banshee Talk Box
1997-present. Includes power supply.

1997-2007		$65	$80

Hush Rack Mount
1980s-present.

2000-2007		$50	$100

Hush The Pedal
1996-present. Pedal version of rackmount Hush.

1996-2007		$25	$35

Rampage Distortion
1996-present. Sustain, high-gain and distortion.

1996-2007		$25	$35

Surf Tremolo
1997-2000.

1997-2000		$60	$80

Tsunami Chorus
1996-present. Battery or optional AC adapter.

1996-2007	Battery power	$40	$50
1996-2007	With power supply	$50	$60

Vertigo Vibe
2003-2006. Rotating Leslie speaker effect.

2003-2006	Battery power	$50	$60
2003-2006	With power supply	$60	$70

XDC
1980s. Rack mount stereo preamp, distortion.

1980s		$100	$150

The *Vintage Guitar Price Guide* shows low to high values for items in all-original excellent condition, and, where applicable, with original case or cover.

MODEL YEAR	FEATURES	EXC. COND. LOW	HIGH

Roger Linn Design
2001-present. Effects built in Berkeley, California by Roger Linn.

Roger Mayer Electronics
1964-present. Roger Mayer started making guitar effects in England in '64 for guitarists like Jimmy Page and Jeff Beck. He moved to the U.S. in '69 to start a company making studio gear and effects. Until about 1980, the effects were built one at a time in small numbers and not available to the general public. In the '80s he started producing larger quantities of pedals, introducing his rocket-shaped enclosure. He returned to England in '89.

Axis Fuzz
Early 1980s-present.

1987-2007		$125	$150

Classic Fuzz
1987-present. The Fuzz Face.

1987-2007		$175	$200

Metal Fuzz
Early 1980s-1994.

1987-1994		$125	$150

Mongoose Fuzz
Early 1980s-present.

1987-2007		$175	$200

Octavia
Early 1980s-present. Famous rocket-shaped box.

1981-2007		$150	$200

VooDoo-1
Ca.1990-present.

1990-2007		$175	$300

Rogue
2001-present. Budget imported guitar effects. They also offer guitars, basses, lap steels, mandolins, banjos, ukuleles and amps.

Roland
Japan's Roland Corporation first launched effect pedals in 1974; a year or two later the subsidiary company, Boss, debuted its own line. They were marketed concurrently at first, but gradually Boss became reserved for compact effects while the Roland name was used on amplifiers, keyboards, synths and larger processors.

Analog Synth SPV
1970s. Multi-effect synth, rack mount.

1970s		$700	$900

Bee Baa AF-100
1975-ca.1980. Fuzz and treble boost.

1975-1980		$350	$550

Bee Gee AF-60
1975-ca.1980. Sustain, distortion.

1975-1980		$75	$125

Double Beat AD-50
1975-ca.1980. Fuzz wah.

1975-1980		$175	$200

Expression Pedal EV-5
1970s		$50	$75

Expression Pedal EV-5 Reissue
2000. Black pedal, blue foot pad.

2000		$25	$30

Guitar Synth Pedal GR-33 and Pickup GK-2A
2000-2005. Requires optional GK-2A pickup, blue case.

2000-2005		$475	$550

Human Rhythm Composer R-8
1980s. Drum machine, key pad entry.

1980s		$175	$250

Human Rhythm Composer R-8 MK II
2000s. Black case.

2000s		$300	$400

Jet Phaser AP-7
1975-ca.1978. Phase and distortion.

1975-1978		$225	$250

Phase II AP-2
1975-ca.1980. Brown case.

1975-1980		$125	$175

Phase Five AP-5
1975-ca.1978.

1975-1978		$200	$225

Space Echo Unit
1974-ca.1980. Tape echo and reverb, various models.

1970s	RE-101	$525	$700
1970s	RE-150	$600	$800
1970s	RE-201, RE-301	$650	$800
1970s	RE-501	$700	$900
1970s	SRE-555		
	Chorus Echo	$800	$900

Vocoder SVC-350
Late-1970s-1980s. Vocal synthesis (vocoder) for voice or guitar, rack mount version of VP-330.

1980		$550	$700

Vocoder VP-330 Plus
Late-1970s-1980s. Analog vocal synthesis (vocoder) for voice or guitar, includes 2 1/2 octaves keyboard.

1978-1982		$700	$900

Wah Beat AW-10
1975-ca.1980.

1975-1980		$100	$125

Ross
Founded by Bud Ross, who also established Kustom, in Chanute, Kansas, in the 1970s. Ross produced primarily amplifiers. In about '78, they introduced a line of U.S.-made effects. Later production switched to the Orient.

10 Band Graphic Equalizer
1970s		$80	$100

Compressor
1970s. Gray or black case.

1970s		$200	$300

Distortion
1978-ca.1980. Brown.

1979-1980		$75	$125

Flanger
1977-ca.1980. Red.

1977-1980		$100	$150

Rocktron Vertigo Vibe

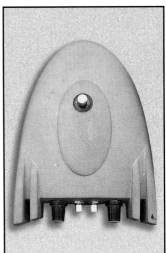
Roger Mayer Octavia

Roland Jet Phaser AP-7

EFFECTS

Scholz Rockman X100

*Seymour Duncan
Shape Shifter SFX-07*

*Siegmund Micro-Tube
Double Drive*

MODEL YEAR FEATURES	EXC. COND. LOW	HIGH
Phase Distortion R1		
1979. Purple.		
1979	$100	$125
Phaser		
1978-ca.1980. Orange.		
1978-1980	$80	$100
Stereo Delay		
1978-ca.1980.		
1978-1980	$125	$175

Rotovibe
See listing under Dunlop.

Sam Ash
1960s-1970s. Sam Ash Music was founded by a young Sam Ash (nee Askynase) in '24. Ash's first store was in Brooklyn, and was relocated in '44. By '66, there were about four Ash stores. During this time, Ash Music private branded their own amps and effects.

Fuzzz Boxx
1966-1967. Red, made by Universal Amplifier Company, same as Astrotone Fuzz.

1967	$200	$225

Volume Wah
Italian-made.

1970s	$175	$200

Sanner
1999. Reissue from Eddie Sanner, who was the engineer behind the 1960s Mosrite Fuzzrite, using the identical circuitry as the original. Issued as a limited edition.

Sano
1944-ca. 1970. Sano was a New Jersey-based accordion company that built their own amps and a reverb unit. They also imported guitars for a few years, starting in '66.

Schaller
1970s. German-made guitar effects.

Scholz Research
1982-present. Started by Tom Scholz of the band Boston. In '95, Jim Dunlop picked up the Rockman line (see Dunlop).

Power Soak

1980s	$100	$160

Rockman

1980s	$70	$130

Rockman X100
Professional studio processor.

1980s	$100	$150

Soloist
Personal guitar processor.

1980s	$50	$80

MODEL YEAR FEATURES	EXC. COND. LOW	HIGH

Seamoon
1973-1977, 1997-2002. Seamoon made effects unti '77, when Dave Tarnowski bought up the remaining inventory and started Analog Digital Associates (ADA). He reissued the brand in '97.

Fresh Fuzz
1975-1977. Recently reissued by ADA.

1975-1977	$150	$200

Funk Machine
1974-1977. Envelope filter. Recently reissued by ADA.

1974-1977	$175	$225

Studio Phase
1975-1977. Phase shifter.

1975-1977	$75	$125

Sekova
Mid-1960s-mid-1970s. Entry level instruments imported by the U.S. Musical Merchandise Corporation of New York.

Seymour Duncan
In late 2003, pickup maker Seymour Duncan, located in Santa Barbara, California, added a line of stomp box guitar effects.

Shinei
Japanese imports. Shinei also made effects for Univox and probably others.

Fuzz Wah

1970s	$125	$175

Resly (Repeat Time) Machine
Black case, 3 speeds.

1970s	$400	$500

Sho-Bud
1956-1980. This pedal steel company offered volume pedals as well.

Volume Pedal

1965	$90	$95

SIB
Effects pedals from Rick Hamel, who helped design SMF amps.

Siegmund Guitars & Amplifiers
1993-present. Los Angeles, California amp and guitar builder Chris Siegmund added effects to his product line in '99.

Snarling Dogs
1997-present. Started by Charlie Stringer of Stringer Industries, Warren, New Jersey in '97. Stringer died in May '99. The brand is now carried by D'Andrea USA.

Sobbat
1995-present. Line of effects from Kinko Music Company of Kyoto, Japan.

MODEL YEAR	FEATURES	EXC. COND. LOW	HIGH

Sola/Colorsound

1962-present. Sola was founded by London's Macari's Musical Exchange in '62. Sola made effects for Vox, Marshall, Park, and B & M and later under their own Colorsound brand. Refer to Colorsound for listings and more company info.

Soldano

1987-present. Seattle, Washington amp builder Soldano also builds a reverb unit.

Songbird

See Dytronics.

South Hawk

Hawk I Fuzz

1975		$100	$125

LTD

1975	Silver case, slider	$100	$125

Speedster

1995-2000, 2003-present. Amp builder Speedster added guitar effects pedals to their product line in '04, built in Gig Harbor, Washington.

Stinger

Stinger effects were distributed by the Martin Guitar Company from 1989 to '90.

Effects

1989-1990	CH-70 Stereo Chorus	$25	$55
1989-1990	CO-20 Compressor	$35	$55
1989-1990	DD-90 Digital Delay	$45	$65
1989-1990	DE-80 Analog Delay	$50	$70
1989-1990	DI-10 Distortion	$40	$65
1989-1990	FL-60 Flanger	$40	$65
1989-1990	OD-30 Overdrive	$40	$65
1989-1990	TS-5 Tube Stack	$45	$65

Studio Electronics

1989-present. Synth and midi developer Greg St. Regis' Studio Electronics added guitar pedal effects to their line in '03.

Subdecay Studios

2003-present. Brian Marshall builds his guitar effects in Woodinville, Washington.

Supro

1935-1968. Supro offered a few reverb units in the '60s.

500 R Standard Reverb Unit

1962-1963. Outboard reverb unit.

1962-1963		$325	$375

600 Reverb Accessory Unit

1961. Independent reverb unit amp combination to be used with Supro Model 1600R amp or other amps, 3 tubes, 1x8" speaker.

1961		$500	$600

MODEL YEAR	FEATURES	EXC. COND. LOW	HIGH

Swart Amplifier

2003-present. Effects pedals built by Michael J. Swart in Wilmington, North Carolina. He also builds amps.

Sweet Sound

1994-present. Line of effects from Bob Sweet, originally made in Trenton, Michigan, currently in Coral Springs, Florida.

Swell Pedal Company

1997-present.

Systech (Systems & Technology in Music, Inc)

1975-late-1970s. Systech was located in Kalamazoo, Michigan.

Effects

1975-1979	Envelope and Repeater	$75	$125
1975-1979	Envelope Follower	$75	$125
1975-1979	Flanger	$75	$125
1975-1979	Harmonic Energizer	$150	$225
1975-1979	Overdrive Model 1300	$75	$125
1975-1979	Phase Shifter Model 1200	$75	$125

T.C. Electronics

1976-present. Brothers Kim and John Rishøj founded TC Electronic in Risskov, Denmark, and made guitar effects pedals for several years before moving into rack-mounted gear. Currently they offer a wide range of pro audio gear.

Booster + Distortion

1980s		$325	$400

Dual Parametric Equalizer

1980s		$275	$350

Stereo Chorus/Flanger

Introduced in 1982, and reissued in '91.

1980s		$175	$225

Sustain + Equalizer

1980s		$225	$300

T.C. Jauernig Electronics

2004-present. Tim Jauernig, of Rothschild, Wisconsin, built effects for several years before launching his T.C. Jauernig brand in '04.

Tech 21

1989-present. Tech 21 builds their SansAmp and other effects in New York City. They also build amps.

Sansamp

1989-present. Offers a variety of tube amp tones.

1989	1st year	$125	$175
1990-2005		$100	$125

XXL Pedal

1995-2000, 2005-present. Distortion, fuzz.

1995-2000		$50	$75

Sobbat FB-1R Fuzz Breaker

Speedster Turbo Charger

Subdecay Liquid Sunshine

EFFECTS

ThroBack stRange Master

ToadWorks John Bull

T-Rex BetaVibe

MODEL YEAR	FEATURES	EXC. COND. LOW	HIGH

Teese

Geoffrey Teese's first wah was advertised as "the Real McCoy, by Teese." He now offers his custom wah pedals under the Real McCoy Custom brand. The Teese brand was used on his line of stomp boxes, starting in '96. The Teese stomp boxes are no longer being made.

Thomas Organ

The Thomas Organ Company was heavily involved with Vox from 1964 to '72, importing their instruments into the U.S. and designing and assembling products, including the wah-wah pedal. Both Thomas Organ and JMI, Vox's European distributor, wanted to offer the new effect. The problem was solved by labeling the Thomas Organ wah the Crybaby. The Crybaby is now offered by Dunlop. Refer to Vox listing for Crybaby Stereo Fuzz Wah, Crybaby Wah, and Wah Wah.

ThroBak Electronics

2004-present. Jonathan Gundry builds his guitar effects in Grand Rapids, Michigan. He also builds guitar amps and pickups.

ToadWorks

2001-present. Guitar effects built in Spokane, Washington by Ryan Dunn and Doug Harrison.

Tonebone

See Radial Engineering listing.

Top Gear

1960s-1970s. Top Gear was a London music store. Their effects were made by other manufacturers.

Rotator
Leslie effect.

1970s		$100	$175

Top Hat Amplification

1994-present. The Fuquay-Varina, North Carolina, amp builder also offers effects.

Tremolo

See listing under Dunlop.

T-Rex

2003-present. Made in Denmark and imported by European Musical Imports.

Tube Works

1987-2004. Founded by B.K. Butler (see Audio Matrix) in Denver, Colorado, Tube Works became a division of Genz Benz Enclosures of Scottsdale, Arizona in 1997 which dropped the brand in 2004. They also offered tube/solidstate amps, cabinets, and DI boxes.

Blue Tube
1989-2004. Overdrive bass driver with 12AX7A tube.

1989-2004		$100	$150

MODEL YEAR	FEATURES	EXC. COND. LOW	HIGH

Real Tube
Ca.1987-2004. Overdrive with 12AX7A tube.

1987-1999		$100	$150

Tube Driver
1987-2004. With tube.

1987-2004	With tube	$100	$150

Tycobrahe

The Tycobrahe story was over almost before it began. Doing business in 1976-1977, they produced only three pedals and a direct box, one the fabled Octavia. The company, located in Hermosa Beach, California, made high-quality, original devices, but they didn't catch on. Now, they are very collectible.

Octavia
1976-1977. Octave doubler.

1976-1977		$1,000	$1,300

Parapedal
1976-1977. Wah.

1976-1977		$750	$950

Pedalflanger
1976-1977. Blue pedal-controlled flanger.

1976-1977		$750	$950

Uni-Vibe

See listings under Univox and Dunlop.

Univox

Univox was a brand owned by Merson (later Unicord), of Westbury, New York. It marketed guitars and amps, and added effects in the late-'60s. Most Univox effects were made by Shinei, of Japan. They vanished in about '81.

EC-100 Echo
Tape, sound-on-sound.

1970s		$75	$150

EC-80 A Echo
Early-1970s-ca.1977. Tape echo, sometimes shown as The Brat Echo Chamber.

1970s		$75	$100

Echo-Tech EM-200
Disc recording echo unit.

1970s		$130	$170

Micro 41 FCM41 4 channel mixer

1970s		$35	$50

Micro Fazer
1970s. Phase shifter.

1970s		$75	$100

Noise-Clamp EX110

1970s		$45	$55

Phaser PHZ1
AC powered.

1970s		$50	$75

Pro Verb
1970s. Reverb (spring) unit, black tolex, slider controls for 2 inputs, 1 output plus remote output.

1970s		$80	$100

Square Wave SQ150
Introduced in 1976, distortion, orange case.

1970s		$75	$125

MODEL YEAR	FEATURES	EXC. COND. LOW	HIGH

Super-Fuzz
1968-1970s. Early transistor effect, made by Shi-nei.

1971	Gray box, normal bypass switch	$400	$700
1973	Unicord, various colors, blue bypass pedal	$400	$700

Uni-Comp
Compression limiter.

1970s		$50	$100

Uni-Drive
1970s		$150	$200

Uni-Fuzz
1960s. Fuzz tone in blue case, 2 black knobs and slider switch.

1960s		$275	$375

Uni-Tron 5
A.k.a. Funky Filter, envelope filter.

1975		$200	$525

Uni-Vibe
Introduced around 1969, with rotating speaker simulation, with pedal.

1960s		$1,200	$1,600
1970s		$900	$1,000

Uni-Wah Wah/Volume
1970s		$100	$125

Vesta Fire
Ca.1981-ca.1988. Brand of Japan's Shiino Musical Instrument Corp.

Effects
1981-1988	Digital Chorus/ Flanger FLCH	$35	$50
1981-1988	Distortion DST	$35	$50
1981-1988	Flanger	$35	$50
1981-1988	Noise Gate	$25	$40
1981-1988	Stereo Chorus SCH	$35	$50

Vintage Tone Project
2003-present. Line of guitar effects made by Robert Rush and company originally in Lafayette, Colorado, and currently in Delmar, New York. They also built reissues of Dan Armstrong's '70s effects from '03 to '06.

VintageFX
2003-present. Effects based on vintage pedals from the '60s and '70s built by Dave Archer in Grand Island, New York.

VooDoo Lab
1994-present. Line of effects made by Digital Music Corp. in California.

Analog Chorus
1997-present.

1997-2007		$100	$120

Bosstone
1994-1999. Based on '60s Jordan Electronics Fuzz.

1994-1999		$70	$75

Microvibe
1996-present. UniVibe swirl effect.

1996-2007		$55	$65

Overdrive
1994-2002. Based on '70s overdrive.

1994-2002		$55	$65

Superfuzz
1999-present.

1999-2007		$75	$90

Tremolo
1995-present.

1995-2007		$55	$75

Vox
1957-present. Vox offered a variety of guitars, amps, organs and effects. Ca. '66, they released the Tone Bender, one of the classic fuzzboxes of all time. A year or so later, they delivered their greatest contribution to the effects world, the first wah-wah pedal. The American arm of Vox (then under Thomas Organ) succumbed in '72. In the U.K., the company was on-again/off-again.

Clyde McCoy Wah-Wah Pedal
Introduced in 1967, reissued in 2001-present. Clyde's picture on bottom cover.

1967	Clyde's picture	$650	$1,000
1968	No picture	$550	$750
2001-2007	Model V-848	$75	$100

Crybaby Wah
Introduced in 1968. The Thomas Organ Company was heavily involved with Vox from '64 to '72, importing their instruments into the U.S. and designing and assembling products. One product developed in conjunction with Vox was the wah-wah pedal. Both Thomas Organ and JMI, Vox's European distributor, wanted to offer the new effect. The problem was solved by labeling the Thomas Organ wah the Crybaby. The original wahs were built by Jen in Italy, but Thomas later made them in their Chicago, Illinois and Sepulveda, California plants. Thomas Organ retained the marketing rights to Vox until '79, but was not very active with the brand after '72. The Crybaby brand is now offered by Dunlop.

1960s	Jen-made	$200	$250
1970	Sepulveda-made	$125	$175

Double Sound
Jen-made, Double Sound model name on bottom of pedal, double sound derived from fuzz and wah ability.

1970s		$200	$250

Flanger
1970s		$200	$250

King Wah
Chrome top, Italian-made.

1970s		$125	$250

Repeat Percussion
Late-1960s. Plug-in module with on-off switch and rate adjustment.

1968		$100	$125

Stereo Fuzz Wah
1970s		$150	$200

Univox Echo-Tech EM-200

Voodoo Lab Tremolo

Vox Clyde McCoy Wah

EFFECTS

Warmenfat Tube Preamp

EFFECTS

Wilson Effects Q-Wah

MODEL YEAR	FEATURES	EXC. COND. LOW	HIGH
Tone Bender V-828			
1966-1970s. Fuzz box, reissued as the V-829 in '93.			
1966-1968	Gray	$400	$950
1969	Black	$300	$650
Tonelab Valvetronix			
2003-present. Multi-effect modeling processor, 12AX7 tube preamp.			
2003-2007		$400	$425
V-807 Echo-Reverb Unit			
Solidstate, disc echo.			
1967		$275	$375
V-837 Echo Deluxe Tape Echo			
Solidstate, multiple heads.			
1967		$350	$450
V-846 Wah			
1969-1970s. Chrome top, Italian-made.			
1969	Transitional		
	Clyde McCoy	$500	$650
1970s		$300	$400
V-847 Wah-Wah			
1992-present. Reissue of the original V-846 Wah.			
1992-2007		$65	$80
Volume Pedal			
Late 1960s. Reissued as the V850.			
1960s		$50	$100

Wampler Pedals

2004-present. Brian Wampler began building effects under the brand Indy Guitarist in 2004, and changed the name to Wampler Pedals in 2007. They are built in Greenwood, Indiana.

Warmenfat

2004-present. Pre-amps and guitar effects built in Sacramento, California, by Rainbow Electronics.

Wasabi

2003-present. Line of guitar effect pedals from Danelectro.

MODEL YEAR	FEATURES	EXC. COND. LOW	HIGH
Washburn			
Washburn offered a line of effects from around 1983 to ca. '89.			
Effects			
1980s	Analog Delay AX:9	$30	$35
1980s	Flanger FX:4	$35	$40
1980s	Phaser PX:8	$40	$45
1980s	Stack in a Box SX:3	$30	$35

Watkins/WEM

1957-present. Watkins Electric Music (WEM) was founded by Charlie Watkins. Their first commercial product was the Watkins Dominator amp in '57, followed by the Copicat Echo in '58.

MODEL YEAR	FEATURES	EXC. COND. LOW	HIGH
Copicat Tape Echo			
1958-1970s, 1985-present. The Copicat has been reissued in various forms by Watkins.			
1960s	Solidstate	$300	$400
1960s	Tube	$700	$1,000

Way Huge Electronics

1995-1998. Way Huge offered a variety of stomp boxes, made in Sherman Oaks, California.

WD Music

Since 1978, WD Music has offered a wide line of aftermarket products for guitar players. From '91 to '02, they offered a line of effects that were copies of the original Dan Armstrong color series (refer to Dan Armstrong listing).

MODEL YEAR	FEATURES	EXC. COND. LOW	HIGH
Blue Clipper			
1991-2002. Fuzz.			
1991-2002		$30	$45
Orange Squeezer			
1991-2002. Signal compressor.			
1991-2002	Light Orange case	$40	$50
Purple Peaker			
1991-2002. Mini EQ.			
1991-2002		$40	$50

Westbury

1978-ca.1983. Brand imported by Unicord.

MODEL YEAR	FEATURES	EXC. COND. LOW	HIGH
Tube Overdrive			
1978-1983. 12AX7.			
1978-1983		$150	$200

MODEL YEAR	FEATURES	EXC. COND. LOW	HIGH

Whirlwind
1980s. Whirlwind called Rochester, New York, home.
Commander
Boost and effects loop selector.

1980s		$75	$100

Wilson Effects
2007-present. Guitar effects built by Kevin Wilson in Guilford, Indiana.

Wurlitzer
Wurlitzer offered the Fuzzer Buzzer in the 1960s, which was the same as the Clark Fuzz.

Xotic Effects
2001-present. Hand-wired effects made in Los Angeles, California, and distributed by Prosound Communications.

Yamaha
1946-present. Yamaha has offered effects since at least the early '80s. They also build guitars, basses, amps, and other musical instruments.
Analog Delay E1005
1980s. Free-standing, double-space rack mount-sized, short to long range delays, gray case.

1980s		$160	$180

Yubro
Yubro, of Bellaire, Texas, offered a line of nine effects in the mid/late '80s.
Analog Delay AD-800
300 ms.

1980s		$75	$125

Stereo Chorus CH-600

1980s		$50	$75

Z.Vex Effects
1995-present. Zachary Vex builds his effects in Minneapolis, Minnesota, with some subassembly work done in Michigan. A few lower-cost versions of his most popular effects are also built in Taipei, Taiwan. In 2002, he began building amps.

Zinky
1999-present. Guitar effects built by Bruce Zinky in Flagstaff, Arizona. He also builds amps and has revived the Supro brand on a guitar and amp.

Zoom
Effects line from Samson Technologies Corp. of Syosset, New York.
1010 Player
1996-1999. Compact multi-effects pedal board, 16 distortions, 25 effects.

1996-1999		$40	$75

503 Amp Simulator
1998-2000.

1998-2000		$25	$40

504 Acoustic Pedal
1997-2000. Compact multi-effects pedal, 24 effects, tuner, replaced by II version.

1997-2000		$25	$40

505 Guitar Pedal
1996-2000. Compact multi-effects pedal, 24 effects, tuner, replaced by II version.

1996-2000		$30	$40

506 Bass Pedal
1997-2000. Compact multi-effects bass pedal, 24 effects, tuner, black box, orange panel. Replaced by II version.

1997-2000		$35	$45

507 Reverb
1997-2000.

1997-2000		$25	$40

Xotic AC Booster

Zinky Master Blaster

EFFECTS

Steels & Lap Steels

Airline Rocket

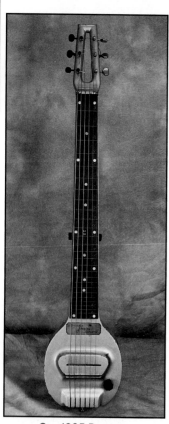

*Ca. 1935 Bronson
Singing Electric*

MODEL YEAR	FEATURES	EXC. COND. LOW	HIGH

Airline

Ca. 1958-1968. Name used by Montgomery Ward for instruments built by Kay, Harmony and Valco.

Lap Steel

1960s	Res-O-Glas/plastic	$475	$575
1960s	Wood	$275	$325

Rocket 6-String Steel

Black and white, 3 legs, Valco-made.

1960s		$325	$400

Student 6 Steel

1950s	Black	$200	$225

Alamo

1947-1982. The first musical instruments built by Alamo, of San Antonio, Texas, were lap steel and amp combos with early models sold with small birch amps.

Hawaiian Lap Steels

1947-ca. 1967. Models include the '50s Challenger and Futuramic Dual Eight, the '50s and early-'60s Embassy (pear-shape) and Jet (triangular), the early-'60s Futuramic Eight and Futuramic Six, and the late-'60s Embassy (triangular Jet).

1950s		$225	$275

Alkire

1939-1950s. Founded by musician and teacher Eddie Alkire, with instruments like his E-Harp Steel built by Epiphone and maybe others (see Epiphone for values).

Aloha

1935-1960s. Private branded by Aloha Publishing and Musical Instruments Company, Chicago, Illinois. Made by others. There was also the Aloha Manufacturing Company of Honolulu which made musical instruments from around 1911 to the late '20s.

Alvarez

Ca. 1966-present. Imported by St. Louis Music from mid-'60s. They also offered guitars, banjos and mandolins.

Model 5010 Koa D Steel-String

1960s		$225	$275

Aria

1960-present. Aria offered Japanese-made steels and lap steels in the '60s.

Laps Steels

1960s		$250	$300

Asher

1982-present. Intermediate, professional and premium grade, production/custom, solidbody, semi-hollow body and acoustic lap steels built by luthier Bill Asher in Venice, California. He also builds guitars.

Audiovox

Ca. 1935-ca. 1950. Paul Tutmarc's Audiovox Manufacturing, of Seattle, Washington, was a pioneer in electric lap steels, basses, guitars and amps.

Lap Steel

1940s		$900	$1,100

Lap Steel and Amp Set

1940s		$1,300	$1,400

Bigsby

1947-1965. All handmade by Paul Arthur Bigsby, in Downey, California. Bigsby was a pioneer in developing pedal steels and they were generally special order or custom-made and not mass produced. The original instruments were made until '65 and should be valued on a case-by-case basis. Models include the Single Neck pedal steel, Double 8 pedal steel, 8/10 Doubleneck pedal steel, Triple 8 pedal steel (all ca. '47-'65), and the '57-'58 Magnatone G-70 lap steel. A solidbody guitar and a pedal steel based upon the original Paul Bigsby designs were introduced January, 2002.

Triple 8-String Neck Steel

1947-1965. Bigsby steel were generally special order or custom-made and not mass produced. Instruments should be valued on a case-by-case basis.

1947-1959	Natural	$3,900	$4,600

Blue Star

1984-present. Intermediate grade, production/custom, lap steels built by luthier Bruce Herron in Fennville, Michigan. He also builds guitars, mandolins, dulcimers, and ukes.

Bronson

George Bronson was a steel guitar instructor in the Detroit area from the 1930s to the early '50s and sold instruments under his own brand. Most instruments and amps were made by Rickenbacker, Dickerson or Valco.

Leilani Lap Steel and Amp Set

1940s. Pearloid lap steel and small matching amp.

1940s		$400	$500

Melody King Model 52 Lap Steel

Brown bakelite body with 5 gold cavity covers on the top, made by Rickenbacker.

1950s		$775	$925

Model B Style

Rickenbacker-made.

1948-1952		$900	$1,100

Singing Electric

1950s. Valco-made.

1950s		$300	$350

Carvin

1946-present. Founded by Lowell C. Kiesel who produced lapsteels under the Kiesel brand for 1947-'50. In late '49, he renamed the instrument line Carvin after sons Carson and Galvin. Until '77, they offered lap, console, and pedal steels with up to 4 necks.

STEELS & LAPS

MODEL YEAR	FEATURES	EXC. COND. LOW	HIGH
Double 6 Steel With Legs			
1960s		$700	$800
Double 8 Steel With Legs			
1960s	Sunburst	$700	$850
Electric Hawaiian Lap Steel			
1950s		$275	$325
Single 8 With Legs			
Large block position markers, 1 pickup, 2 knobs, blond finish.			
1960s		$525	$625

Chandler
1984-present. Intermediate grade, production/custom, solidbody Weissenborn-shaped electric lap steels built by luthiers Paul and Adrian Chandler in Chico, California. They also build guitars, basses and pickups.

Cromwell
1935-1939. Budget model brand built by Gibson and distributed by various mail-order businesses.
Lap Steel
Charlie Christian bar pickup.

1939	Sunburst	$300	$375

Danelectro
1946-1969, 1997-present. Known mainly for guitars and amps, Danelectro did offer a few lap steels in the mid '50s.
Lap Steel

1950s	Common model	$275	$325

Deckly
1970s-1980s. Intermediate and professional grade pedal steel models, Deckly logo on front side of body.

Denley
1960s. Pedal steels built by Nigel Dennis and Gordon Huntley in England. They also made steels for Jim Burns' Ormston brand in the '60s.

Dickerson
1937-1948. Founded by the Dickerson brothers in '37, primarily for electric lap steels and small amps. Besides their own brand, Dickerson made instruments for Cleveland's Oahu Company, Varsity, Southern California Music, Bronson, Roland Ball, and Gourley. The lap steels were often sold with matching amps, both covered in pearloid mother-of-toilet-seat (MOTS). By '48, the company changed ownership and was renamed Magna Electronics (Magnatone).
Lap Steel
1950s. Gray pearloid.

1950s		$300	$375
1950s	With matching amp	$525	$625

Dobro
1929-1942, ca.1954-present. Dobro offered lap steels from '33 to '42. Gibson now owns the brand and recently offered a lap steel.

MODEL YEAR	FEATURES	EXC. COND. LOW	HIGH
Hawaiian Lap Steel			
1933-1942		$375	$450
Lap Steel Guitar and Amp Set			
1930s-1940s. Typical pearloid covered student 6-string lap steel and small matching amp (with 3 tubes and 1 control knob).			
1933-1942	Pearloid	$500	$600

Dwight
1950s. Private branded instruments made by National-Supro. Epiphone made a Dwight brand guitar in the '60s which was not related to the lap-steels.
Lap Steel
1950s. Pearloid, 6 strings.

1950s	Gray pearloid	$400	$500

Electromuse
1940s-1950s. Mainly offered lap steel and tube amp packages, but they also offered acoustic and electric hollowbody guitars.
Lap Steel

1940s		$275	$325

Ellis
2008-present. Professional and premium grade, production/custom, lap steel guitars built by Andrew Ellis in Perth, Western Australia. He also builds guitars.

Emmons
1970s-present. Owned by Lashley, Inc. of Burlington, North Carolina.
Double 10 Steel
1970-1982. Push/pull pedal steel.

1970-1982		$2,500	$2,800

Lashley LeGrande III Steel
2001-present. Double-neck, 8 pedals, 4 knee levers, 25th Anniversary.

2001		$2,500	$2,800

S-10 Pedal Steel
1970-1982. Single 10-string neck pedal steel.

1970-1982		$1,800	$2,200

Student, 3-Pedal Steel
1970s. Single neck.

1970s		$450	$550

English Electronics
1960s. Norman English had a teaching studio in Lansing, Michigan, where he gave guitar and steel lessons. He had his own private-branded instruments made by Valco in Chicago.
Tonemaster Lap Steel
Cream pearloid, 6 strings, 3 legs, Valco-made.

1960s		$375	$450
1960s	Stringtone pitch changer	$625	$750

Chandler Lectraslide

1937 Dobro

Ca. 1947 Fender Princeton

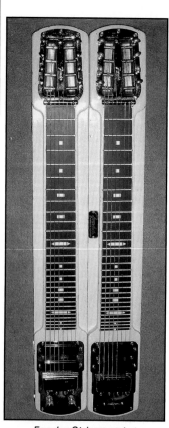

Fender Stringmaster

MODEL YEAR	FEATURES	EXC. COND. LOW	HIGH

Epiphone

1928-present. The then Epiphone Banjo Company was established in '28. Best known for its guitars, the company offered steels from '35 to '58 when Gibson purchased the brand.

Century Lap Steel
1939-1957. Rocket-shaped maple body, 1 pickup, metal 'board, 6, 7 or 8 strings, black finish.

1939-1957		$425	$525

Eddie Alkire E-Harp
1939-1950s. 10-string, similar to Epiphone lap steel with Epi-style logo, offered in lap steel or console.

1939-1950s		$1,200	$1,300

Electar Hawaiian Lap Steel
1935-1937. Wood teardrop-shaped body, bakelite top, black, horseshoe pickup, 6 string.

1935-1937		$500	$600

Electar Model M Hawaiian Lap Steel
1936-1939. Metal top, stair-step body, art deco, black ('36-'37) or gray ('38-'39), 6, 7 or 8 strings.

1936-1939		$400	$475

Kent Hawaiian Lap Steel
1949-1953. Guitar-shaped maple body, 6 strings, lower-end of Epiphone Hawaiian line, Electar script logo below bottom of fretboard.

1949-1953		$325	$400

Solo Console Steel
1939-1954. Maple with white mahogany laminated body, black binding, black metal 'board, 6, 7 or 8 strings.

1939-1954		$525	$625

Triple-Neck Console Steel
1954-1957. neck version of Solo, sunburst or natural finish.

1954-1957		$1,175	$1,450

Zephyr Hawaiian Lap Steel
1939-1957. Maple stair-step body, metal 'board, 6, 7 or 8 strings.

1939-1949	Black, with white top	$650	$750
1950-1957	Sunburst	$625	$700

Fender

1946-present. Fender offered lap and pedal steels from '46 to '80. In 2005 they introduced a new lap steel model under their Folk Music series.

400 Pedal Steel
1958-1976. One 8-string neck with 4 to 10 pedals.

1958-1964		$975	$1,175
1965-1976		$900	$1,100

800 Pedal Steel
1964-1976. One 10-string neck, 6 to 10 pedals.

1964-1976		$1,050	$1,250

1000 Pedal Steel
1957-1976. Two 8-string necks and 8 or 10 pedals.

1957-1964	Natural or sunburst, 8 or 10 pedals	$1,150	$1,425
1965-1976	Natural, 8 or 10 pedals	$1,150	$1,425
1965-1976	Sunburst, 8 or 10 pedals	$1,050	$1,300

2000 Pedal Steel
1964-1976. Two 10-string necks, 10 or 11 pedals sunburst.

1964	10 or 11 pedals	$1,500	$1,800
1965-1976	10 or 11 pedals	$1,400	$1,700

Artist Dual 10 Pedal Steel
1976-1981. Two 10-string necks, 8 pedals, 4 knee levers, black or mahogany.

1976-1981		$900	$1,100

Champ Lap Steel
1955-1980. Replaced Champion Lap Steel, tan.

1955-1959		$750	$925
1960-1969		$750	$900
1970-1980		$625	$775

Champion Lap Steel
1949-1955. Covered in what collectors call mother-of-toilet-seat (MOTS) finish, also known as pearloid. Replaced by Champ Lap Steel.

1949-1955	Tan	$775	$900
1949-1955	White or yellow pearloid	$775	$875

Deluxe Steel
1949-1950. Strings-thru-pickup, Roman numeral markers, became the Deluxe 6 or Deluxe 8 Lap Steel in '50.

1946	Wax	$950	$1,175
1947-1950	Blond or walnut	$950	$1,175

Deluxe 6/Stringmaster Single Steel
1950-1981. Renamed from the Deluxe, 6 strings, 3 legs.

1950-1969	Blond or walnut	$1,300	$1,500
1970-1981	Black or white	$900	$1,100

Deluxe 8/Stringmaster Single Steel
1950-1981. Renamed from the Deluxe, 8 strings, 3 legs.

1950-1969	Blond or walnut	$1,300	$1,500
1970-1981	Black or white	$900	$1,100

Dual 6 Professional Steel
1950-1981. Two 6-string necks, 3 legs optional, blond or walnut.

1952-1981	Blond	$1,300	$1,500
1952-1981	Walnut	$1,050	$1,250

Dual 8 Professional Steel
1946-1957. Two 8-string necks, 3 legs optional, blond or walnut.

1946-1957	Blond	$1,350	$1,650
1946-1957	Walnut	$1,075	$1,325

K & F Steel
1945-1946. Made by Doc Kauffman and Leo Fender, strings-thru-pickup.

1945-1946	Black	$1,550	$1,925

Organ Button Steel
1946-1947.

1946-1947	Wax	$1,000	$1,100

Princeton Steel
1946-1948. Strings-thru-pickup, Roman numeral markers.

1946-1948	Wax	$900	$1,100

STEELS & LAPS

MODEL YEAR	FEATURES	EXC. COND. LOW	HIGH
Stringmaster Steel (Two-Neck)			

1953-1981. The Stringmaster came in 3 versions, having 2, 3 or 4 8-string necks (6-string necks optional).

1953-1954	Blond, 26" scale	$1,900	$2,350
1953-1954	Walnut, 26" scale	$1,600	$2,000
1955-1959	Blond, 24.5" scale	$1,900	$2,350
1955-1959	Walnut, 24.5" scale	$1,600	$2,000
1960-1969	Blond	$1,800	$2,200
1960-1969	Walnut	$1,500	$1,800
1970-1981	Blond or walnut	$1,425	$1,775

Stringmaster Steel (Three-Neck)

1953-1981.

1953-1954	Blond, 26" scale	$2,600	$3,000
1953-1954	Walnut, 26" scale	$2,100	$2,600
1955-1959	Blond, 24.5" scale	$2,600	$3,000
1955-1959	Walnut, 24.5" scale	$2,100	$2,600
1960-1969	Blond	$2,400	$2,800
1960-1969	Walnut	$1,900	$2,300
1970-1981	Blond or walnut	$1,725	$2,150

Stringmaster Steel (Four-Neck)

1953-1968.

1953-1954	Blond, 26" scale	$2,900	$3,600
1953-1954	Walnut, 26" scale	$2,400	$2,900
1955-1959	Blond, 24.5" scale	$2,900	$3,600
1955-1959	Walnut, 24.5" scale	$2,400	$2,900
1960-1968	Blond	$2,600	$3,100
1960-1968	Walnut	$2,100	$2,500

Studio Deluxe Lap Steel

1956-1981. One pickup, 3 legs.

1956-1981	Blond	$850	$1,000

Framus

1946-1977, 1996-present. Imported into the U.S. by Philadelphia Music Company in the '60s. The brand was revived in '96 by Hans Peter Wilfer, the president of Warwick.

Deluxe Table Steel 0/7

1970s	White	$375	$425

Student Hawaiian Model 0/4

1970s	Red	$175	$200

G.L. Stiles

1960-1994. Gilbert Lee Stiles made a variety of instruments, mainly in the Miami, Florida area. See Guitar section for more company info.

Doubleneck Pedal Steel

1970s		$525	$575

Gibson

1890s (1902)-present. Gibson offered steels from '35-'68.

BR-4 Lap Steel

1947. Guitar-shaped of solid mahogany, round neck, 1 pickup, varied binding.

1947	Sunburst	$650	$800

BR-6 Lap Steel

1947-1960. Guitar-shaped solid mahogany body, square neck (round by '48).

1947-1960		$450	$550

MODEL YEAR	FEATURES	EXC. COND. LOW	HIGH
BR-9 Lap Steel			

1947-1959. Solidbody, 1 pickup, tan.

1947-1949	Non-adj. poles	$400	$500
1950-1959	Adj. poles	$450	$550
1950-1959	With matching amp	$725	$875

Century 6 Lap Steel

1948-1968. Solid maple body, 6 strings, 1 pickup, silver 'board.

1948-1968		$550	$650

Century 10 Lap Steel

1948-1955. Solid maple body, 10 strings, 1 pickup, silver 'board.

1948-1955	Black	$575	$675

Console Grand Steel

1938-1942, 1948-1967. Hollowbody, 2 necks, triple-bound body, standard 7- and 8-string combination until '42, double 8-string necks standard for '48 and after.

1938-1942	Sunburst	$1,400	$1,600
1948-1967	Sunburst	$1,400	$1,600

Console Steel (C-530)

1956-1966. Replaced Consolette during '56-'57, double 8-string necks, 4 legs optional.

1956-1966	With legs	$1,200	$1,500

Consolette Table Steel

1952-1957. Rectangular korina body, 2 8-string necks, 4 legs, replaced by maple-body Console after '56.

1952-1957		$1,000	$1,200

EH-100 Lap Steel

1936-1949. Hollow guitar-shaped body, bound top, 6 or 7 strings.

1936-1939		$900	$1,050
1940-1949		$800	$950

EH-125 Lap Steel

1939-1942. Hollow guitar-shaped mahogany body, single-bound body, metal 'board.

1939-1942	Sunburst	$950	$1,150

EH-150 Lap Steel

1936-1943. Hollow guitar-shaped body, 6 to 10 strings available, bound body.

1936	1st offering metal body	$2,700	$3,000
1937-1939	Sunburst	$1,200	$1,500
1940-1943	Sunburst	$1,100	$1,300

EH-150 Lap Steel Matching Set (guitar and amp)

1936-1942. Both electric Hawaiian steel guitar and amp named EH-150, with matching tweed guitar case.

1936-1939	With Christian pickup	$2,500	$3,000
1940-1942		$2,200	$2,700

EH-150 Doubleneck Electric Hawaiian Steel

1937-1939. Doubleneck EH-150 with 7- and 8-string necks.

1937-1939		$2,900	$3,000

Gibson EH-100

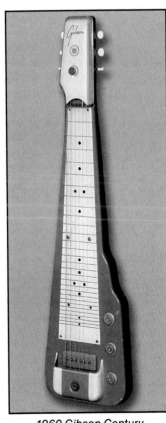

1960 Gibson Century

STEELS & LAPS

1950s Gretsch Electromatic

Gretsch Electromatic

STEELS & LAPS

MODEL YEAR	FEATURES	EXC. COND. LOW	HIGH
EH-185 Lap Steel			
1939-1942. Hollow guitar-shaped curly maple body, triple-bound body, 6, 7, 8 or 10 strings.			
1939-1942	Sunburst, no amp	$1,900	$2,100
1939-1942	Sunburst, with amp	$2,500	$3,000
EH-500 Skylark Lap Steel			
1956-1968. Solid korina body, 8-string available by '58, block markers with numbers.			
1956-1968	Natural	$850	$1,000
EH-500 Skylark Deluxe Lap Steel			
1958-1959. Like Skylark, but with dot markers.			
1958-1959		$1,000	$1,100
EH-620 Steel			
1955-1967. Eight strings, 6 pedals.			
1955-1967	Natural	$900	$1,100
EH-630 Electraharp Steel			
1941-1967. Eight strings, 8 pedals (4 in '49-'67). Called just EH-630 from '56-'67.			
1941-1967	Sunburst	$1,200	$1,400
EH-820 Steel			
1960-1966. Two necks, 8 pedals, Vari-Tone selector.			
1960-1966	Cherry	$1,300	$1,600
Royaltone Lap Steel			
1950-1952, 1956-1957. Volume and tone knobs on treble side of pickup, Gibson silk-screen logo, brown pickup bridge cover.			
1950-1952	Symmetrical body	$775	$925
1956-1957	Guitar-shaped body	$625	$775
Ultratone Lap Steel			
1946-1959. Solid maple body, plastic 'board, 6 strings.			
1940s	White	$850	$1,000
1950s	Dark blue or Seal Brown	$850	$1,000

Gilet Guitars

1976-present. Production/custom, premium grade, lap steels built in Botany, Sydney, New South Wales, Australia by luthier Gerard Gilet. He also builds guitars.

Gold Tone

1993-present. Wayne and Robyn Rogers build their intermediate grade, production/custom lap steels in Titusville, Florida. They also build guitars, basses, mandolins, ukuleles, banjos and banjitars.

Gourley

See Dickerson listing.

Gretsch

1883-present. Gretsch offered a variety of steels from 1940-'63. Gretsch actually only made 1 model; the rest were built by Valco. Currently they offer 2 lap steel models.

Electromatic Console (6158) Twin Neck Steel

1949-1955. Two 6-string necks with six-on-a-side tuners, Electromatic script logo on end cover plates, 3 knobs, metal control panels and knobs, pearloid covered.

1949-1955		$850	$1,000

MODEL YEAR	FEATURES	EXC. COND. LOW	HIGH
Electromatic Hawaiian Lap Steel			
1940-1942. Guitar shaped mahogany body, wooden pickup cover.			
1940-1942		$1,000	$1,300
Electromatic Standard (6156) Lap Steel			
1949-1955. Brown pearloid.			
1949-1955		$500	$575
Electromatic Student (6152) Lap Steel			
1949-1955. Square bottom, brown pearloid, pearloid cover.			
1949-1955		$325	$400
Jet Mainliner (6147) Steel			
1955-1963. Single-neck version of Jet Twin.			
1955-1963		$550	$575
Jet Twin Console (6148) Steel			
1955-1963. Valco-made, 2 6-string necks, six-on-a-side tuners, Jet Black.			
1955-1963		$900	$1,000

Guyatone

1933-present. Large Japanese maker. Brands also include Marco Polo, Winston, Kingston, Kent, LaFayette and Bradford. They offered lap steels under various brands from the '30s to the '60s.

Lap Steels

1960s		$300	$375

Table Steels

Three legs, 2 pickups.

1960s		$450	$525

Hanburt

1940-ca. 1950. Harvey M. Hansen built his electric Hawaiian guitars in Seattle, Washington that were sold through his wife's music instruction studio. His designs were influenced by Seattle's Audiovox guitars. He also built amps and at least one mandolin.

Harlin Brothers

1930s-1960s. Harlin Brothers, of Indianapolis, Indiana, were one of the early designers of pedal steel applications. Prices can vary because some instruments have a reputation of being hard to keep in tune.

Multi-Kord Pedal Steel

1950s	Single neck	$625	$775

Harmony

1982-1976. Founded by Wilhelm Schultz and purchased by Sears in 1916. The company evolved into the largest producer of stringed instruments in the U.S. in the '30s. They offered electric lap steels by '36.

Lap Steels

1936-1959	Various models	$325	$375
1960s	Painted body	$325	$375
1960s	Pearloid body	$325	$375

Hilo

1920s-1930s. Weissenborn-style guitars most likely made by New Jersey's Oscar Schmitt Company, Hilo orange label inside back.

MODEL YEAR	FEATURES	EXC. COND. LOW	HIGH

Hawaiian Steel Guitar
Guitar shaped body, round sound hole, acoustic steel.

| 1930s | | $1,600 | $2,100 |

Hollingworth Guitars
1995-present. Premium grade, production/custom, lap steels built by luthier Graham Hollingworth in Mermaid Beach, Gold Coast, Queensland, Australia. He also builds guitars.

Jackson-Guldan
1920s-1960s. The Jackson-Guldan Violin Company, of Columbus, Ohio, offered lap steels and small tube amps early on. They also built acoustic guitars.

Jim Dyson
1972-present. Production/custom, intermediate, professional and premium grade lap steels built in Torquay, Southern Victoria, Australia by luthier Jim Dyson. He also builds guitars and basses.

K & F (Kaufman & Fender)
See listing under Fender.

Kalamazoo
1933-1942, 1946-1947, 1965-1970. Budget brand produced by Gibson in Kalamazoo, Michigan. They offered lap steels in the '30s and '40s.
Lap Steel
1938-1942, 1946-1947.

1938-1942	No amp	$575	$675
1938-1942	With matching amp	$750	$850
1946-1947		$400	$500

Kay
Ca. 1931-present. Huge Chicago manufacturer Kay offered steels from '36 to '60 under their own brand and others.
Lap Steel

1940s		$325	$375
1950s		$325	$375
1960s		$325	$375

Lap Steel With Matching Amp

| 1940s | Dark mahogany | $500 | $600 |
| 1950s | Green | $500 | $600 |

Kiesel
1946-1949. Founded by Lowell Kiesel as L.C. Kiesel Co., Los Angeles, California, but renamed Carvin in '49. Kiesel logo on the headstock.
Bakelite Lap Steel
1946. Small guitar-shaped bakelite body, 1 pickup, 2 knobs, diamond markers.

| 1946 | | $375 | $450 |

Knutson Luthiery
1981-present. Professional grade, custom, electric lap steels built by luthier John Knutson in Forestville, California. He also builds guitars, basses and mandolins.

Lapdancer
2001-present. Intermediate and professional grade, custom/production, lap steels built by luthier Loni Specter in West Hills, California.

Maestro
A budget brand made by Gibson.
Lap Steel
Pearloid, 1 pickup, 6 strings.

| 1940s | | $325 | $375 |
| 1950s | | $325 | $375 |

Magnatone
Ca. 1937-1971. Magnatone offered lap steels from '37 to '58. Besides their own brand, they also produced models under the Dickerson, Oahu, Gourley, and Natural Music Guild brands.
Lap Steel and Amp MOTS Set
Late-1940s-mid-1950s. Matching pearloid acetate covered lap steel and small amp.

| 1948-1955 | | $575 | $675 |

Lyric Doubleneck Lap Steel
Ca.1951-1958. Model G-1745-D-W, 8 strings per neck, hardwood body.

| 1951-1958 | | $700 | $825 |

Maestro Tripleneck Steel
Ca.1951-1958. Model G-2495-W-W, maple and walnut, 8 strings per neck, legs.

| 1951-1958 | | $1,100 | $1,300 |

Pearloid (MOTS) Lap Steel
1950s. These were often sold with a matching amp; price here is for lap steel only.

| 1950s | | $275 | $325 |

Marvel
1950-mid 1960s. Budget brand marketed by the Peter Sorkin Company of New York.
Electric Hawaiian Lap Steel

| 1950s | | $200 | $250 |

May Bell
See listing under Slingerland.

McKinney
1950s. Private branded for McKinney Guitars by Supro, blue McKinney Guitar logo on headstock.
Lap Steel
Similar to Supro Comet.

| 1950s | White pearloid | $325 | $375 |

Melobar
1967-present. Designed by Walt Smith, of Smith Family Music, Melobar instruments feature a guitar body with a tilted neck, allowing the guitarist to play lap steel standing up. The instrument was developed and first made in Ed and Rudy Dopyera's Dobro factory. Most were available in 6-, 8-, or 10-string versions. Ted Smith took over operations from his father. Ted retired in late 2002. Production ceased in '06, pending a sale of the company, but resumed in '07 under new owners Jim and Carrie Frost.

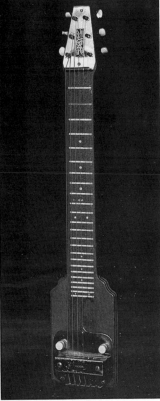
K&F

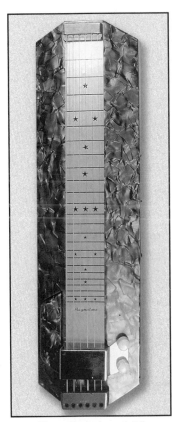
Magnatone (pearloid)

STEELS & LAPS

Melobar X-10

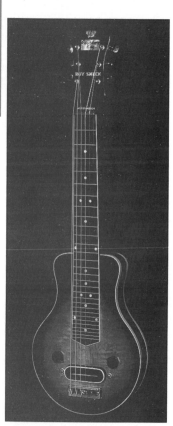

Recording King Roy Smeck

MODEL YEAR	FEATURES	EXC. COND. LOW	HIGH
10-String Electric Steel			
1970s. Double-cut guitar-shaped body, portable Melobar-style. Similar model currently offered as the Skreemr.			
1970s		$750	$900
6-String Electric Steel			
1990s. Solidbody cutaway body shape, portable Melobar-style.			
1990s		$650	$800
Skreemr Electric Steel			
Early 1990s-2006. The classic Melobar in a V (Skreemr SK2000) or double-cut (Skreemr) version, available in 6-, 8- and 10-string versions.			
1990s		$700	$800
V-10 Power-Slide Guitar			
1982-early 1990s. Solidbody, V-shaped body, tilted neck, 10 strings (6- or 8-string models were available). Similar model now called the Skreemr SK2000.			
1980s		$775	$950
X-10 Power-Slide Guitar			
1981-early 1990s. Solidbody, futuristic body shape, tilted neck, 10 strings (6- or 8-string models were available). Called the Power-Slide One in early literature.			
1980s		$775	$950

MSA

1963-1983, 2001-present. Professional and premium grade, production/custom, pedal and lap steel guitars built in Dallas, Texas by Maurice Anderson. The company was dissolved in '83, and reorganized in '01.

National

Ca. 1927-present. Founded in Los Angeles as the National String Instrument Corporation in '27, the brand has gone through many ownership changes over the years. National offered lap steels from '35 to '68.

MODEL YEAR	FEATURES	EXC. COND. LOW	HIGH
Chicagoan Lap Steel			
1948-1961. Gray pearloid, metal hand rest.			
1948-1961		$325	$375
Console (Dual 8) Steel			
1939-1942. Two 8-string necks, parallelogram markers, black top with white sides.			
1939-1942		$1,150	$1,250
Dynamic Lap Steel			
1941-1968. New Yorker-style body, 6 strings, 3 detachable screw-in legs added by '56.			
1941-1965	Lap steel	$475	$550
1956-1968	With legs	$600	$700
Electric Hawaiian Lap Steel			
1935-1937. Cast aluminum round body, 1 pickup, square neck, 6 or 7 strings.			
1935-1937		$625	$775
Grand Console Steel			
1947-1968. 2 or 3 8-string necks, Totem Pole 'board markers, black and white, came with or without legs, National's answer to Fender Stringmaster Series.			
1947-1959	Double neck	$900	$1,100
1947-1959	Triple neck	$1,025	$1,275
1960-1968	Double neck	$650	$775

MODEL YEAR	FEATURES	EXC. COND. LOW	HIGH
New Yorker Lap Steel			
1939-1967. Introduced as Electric Hawaiian model in '35, square end body with stair-step sides, 7 or strings, black and white finish.			
1939-1949		$800	$95
1950-1959		$675	$82.
1960-1967		$575	$67.
Princess Lap Steel			
1942-1947. Strings-thru-pickup, parallelogram markers, white pearloid.			
1942-1947		$375	$42.
Rocket One Ten Lap Steel			
1955-1958. Rocket-shaped, black and white finish.			
1955-1958		$375	$42.
Trailblazer Steel			
1948-1950. Square end, numbered markers black.			
1948-1950		$375	$42.
Triplex Chord Changer Lap Steel			
1944-1958. Maple and walnut body, 2 knobs, natural.			
1944-1958		$500	$57.

Nioma

Regal and others (maybe Dickerson?) made instruments for this brand, most likely for a guitar studio or distributor.

MODEL YEAR	FEATURES	EXC. COND. LOW	HIGH
Lap Steel			
1930s	Pearloid	$250	$300

Oahu

1926-1985. The Oahu Publishing Company and Honolulu Conservatory, based in Cleveland, published a very popular guitar study course. They sold instruments to go with the lessons, starting with acoustic Hawaiian and Spanish guitars, selling large quantities in the '30s. As electric models became popular, Oahu responded with guitar-amp sets. Lap steel and matching amp sets were generally the same color; for example, yellow guitar and yellow amp, or white pearloid guitar and white amp. These sets were originally sold to students who would take private or group lessons. The instruments were made by Oahu, Valco, Harmony, Dickerson, and Rickenbacker and were offered into the '50s and '60s.

MODEL YEAR	FEATURES	EXC. COND. LOW	HIGH
Dianna Lap Steel			
1950s. Oahu and Diana logos on headstock, Oahu logo on fretboard, fancy bridge, pleasant unusual sunburst finish.			
1950s		$475	$550
Hawaiian Lap Steel			
1930-1940s	Rare style, higher-end	$575	$675
1930-1940s	Rare style, student-grade	$425	$525
1930s	Sunburst, student-grade	$300	$350
1930s	Tonemaster with decal art	$350	$425
1940s	Pearloid, Supro-made	$300	$375
1950s	Pearloid or painted	$300	$375

Iolana

1950-1951, Late-1950s. Gold hardware, 2 6-string necks. Early model is lap steel, later version a console.

1950-1951	Lap	$500	$600
1950s	Console	$775	$900

K-71 Acoustic Lap Steel

1930s. Flat top, round sound hole, decals on lower bouts.

1930s		$400	$450

Lap Steel/Amp Set

See also Lap Steel Oahu Amp listing in the Guide's Amp section.

1930-1940s	Pearloid, small rectangular amp	$550	$650
1930-1940s	Sunburst, mahogany	$450	$550
1950s	White Valco Amp, 1x10"	$500	$550
1950s	Yellow Valco amp	$500	$550

Ormston

1966-1968. Pedal steels built in England by Denley and marketed by James Ormston Burns between his stints with Burns London, which was bought by America's Baldwin Company in '65, and the Dallas Arbiter Hayman brand.

Premier

Ca.1938-ca.1975, 1990s-present. Premier made a variety of instruments, including lap steels, under several brands.

Recording King

Ca. 1930-1943. Brand used by Montgomery Ward for instruments made by Gibson, Regal, Kay, and Gretsch.

Electric Hawaiian Lap Steel

1930s		$450	$525

Roy Smeck Model AB104 Steel

1938-1941. Pear-shaped body, 1 pickup.

1940s	No amp	$450	$500
1940s	With matching amp	$725	$875

Regal

Ca. 1884-1954. Regal offered their own brand and made instruments for distributors and mass-merchandisers. The company sold out to Harmony in '54.

Electric Hawaiian Lap Steel

1940s		$250	$300

Octophone Steel

1930s		$400	$450

Reso-phonic Steel

1930s. Dobro-style resonator and spider assembly, round neck, adjustable nut.

1930s		$850	$1,050

Rickenbacker

1931-present. Rickenbacker produced steels from '32 to '70.

Acadamy Lap Steel

1946-1947. Bakelite student model, horseshoe pickup, replaced by the Ace.

1946-1947	$450	$550

Ace Lap Steel

1948-1953. Bakelite body, 1 pickup.

1948-1953	$450	$550

DC-16 Steel

1950-1952. Metal, double 8-string necks.

1950-1952	$1,000	$1,200

Electro Lap Steel

1940s. Large Rickenbacker logo and smaller Electro logo on headstock.

1940s	$975	$1,175

Electro Doubleneck Steel

1940-1953. Two bakelite 8-string necks.

1940-1953	$1,400	$1,500

Electro Tripleneck Steel

1940-1953. Three bakelite 8-string necks.

1940-1953	$1,550	$1,800

Model 59 Lap Steel

1937-1943. Sheet steel body, baked-enamel light-colored crinkle finish, 1 pickup.

1937-1943	$700	$800

Model 100 Lap Steel

1956-1970. Wood body, 6 strings, block markers, light or silver gray finish.

1956-1970	$650	$750

Model 102 Lap Steel

1960s. Wood body, 6 strings, slot head, block markers, natural finish.

1960	$600	$650

Model A-22 Frying Pan Steel

1932-1936	$3,500	$4,000

Model B Steel

1935-1955. Bakelite body and neck, 1 pickup, strings-thru-body, decorative metal plates, 6 strings.

1935-1955	Black	$975	$1,175

Model B-10 Steel

1935-1955. Model B with slot head and 12 strings.

1935-1955	$1,150	$1,425

Model BD Steel

1949-1970. Bakelite body, 6 strings, deluxe version of Model B, black.

1949-1960	$800	$950

Model CW-6 Steel

1957-1961. Wood body, grille cloth on front, 6 strings, 3 legs, renamed JB (Jerry Byrd) model in '61.

1957-1961	Walnut	$750	$850

Model DW Steel

1955-1961. Wood body, double 6- or 8-string necks, optional 3 legs.

1955-1961	8 strings	$900	$1,100

Model G Lap Steel

Ca.1948-1957. Chrome-plated ornate version of Silver Hawaiian, gold hardware and trim, 6 or 8 strings.

1948-1957	$800	$900

Model S/NS (New Style) Steel

1946-early-1950s. Sheet steel body, 1 pickup, gray, gray sparkle or grayburst, also available as a doubleneck.

1946-1949	$850	$1,050

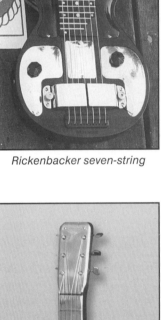

Rickenbacker seven-string

Ca. 1938 Rickenbacker 100/NS Silver Hawaiian

STEELS & LAPS

1947 Rickenbacker Lap Steel

Slingerland Songster

Model SD Steel

1949-1953. Deluxe NS, sheet steel body, 6, 7 or 8 strings, Copper Crinkle finish.

1949-1953	$600	$700

Model SW

1956-1962. Straight body style, 6 or 8 strings, block markers, dark or blond finish.

1956-1962	8 strings	$1,200	$1,500
1956-1962	8 strings with legs	$1,400	$1,700

Silver Hawaiian Lap Steel

1937-1943. Chrome-plated sheet steel body, 1 horseshoe pickup, 6 strings.

1937-1943	$1,175	$1,425

Rogue

2001-present. Budget grade, production, lap steels. They also offer guitars, basses, mandolins, banjos, and ukuleles.

Roland Ball

See Dickerson listing.

Sherwood

Late 1940s-early 1950s. Lap steel guitars made for Montgomery Ward made by Chicago manufacturers such as Kay. They also had archtop guitars and amps under that brand.

Deluxe Lap Steel

1950s. Symmetrical body, bar pickup, volume and tone controls, wood body, sunburst, relatively ornate headstock with script Sherwood logo, vertical Deluxe logo, and lightning bolt art.

1950s	$375	$425

Sho-Bud

1956-1980. Founded by Shot Jackson in Nashville. Distributed by Gretsch. They also had guitar models. Baldwin bought the company in '79 and closed the factory in '80.

Crossover Twin Neck Steel

1967-1970s. Sho-Bud Baldwin double neck, Sho-Bud logo.

1967-1971	$1,500	$1,700

Maverick Pedal Steel

Ca. 1970-1980. Beginner model, burl elm cover, 3 pedals.

1970-1980	$625	$775

Pro I

1970-1980. Three pedals, natural.

1970-1975	Round front	$925	$1,150
1976-1980	Square front	$1,025	$1,250

Pro II

1970-1980. Birdseye maple, double 10-string necks, natural.

1970-1975	Round front	$1,025	$1,275
1976-1980	Square front	$1,100	$1,375

Pro III

1970-1980. Metal necks.

1970-1975	Round front	$1,075	$1,325
1976-1980	Square front	$1,150	$1,425

Super Pro

1977-1980. Doubleneck 10 strings, 8 floor pedals, ● knee levers, Jet Black.

1977-1980	$2,000	$2,50●

Silvertone

1940-1970. Brand name for instruments sold by Sears.

Amp-In-Case Lap Steel

Early 1940s. Lap steel and amp set, amp cabine● doubles as lap case with the lap stored above the amp● amp is in a long vertical cabinet with brown twee● covering, manufacturer appears to be the same a● used by Gibson in the late '30s, low to mid power● 1x10" speaker.

1941-1942	$725	$80●

Six-String Lap Steel

1940s	Valco-made	$350	$42●
1950s	Pearloid	$375	$42●
1950s	Standard finish	$300	$37●
1960s		$300	$37●

Slingerland

1916-present. Offered by Slingerland Banjos and Drums. They also sold the May Bell brand. Instruments were made by others and sold by Slingerland in the '30s and '40s.

May Bell Lap Steel

1930s. Guitar-shaped lap steel with May Bell logo● This brand also had '30s Hawaiian and Spanish guitars.

1930s	$300	$37●

Songster Lap Steel

1930s. Slingerland logo headstock, Songster logo● near nut, guitar-shaped body, sunburst maple top, some with figured maple back, 1 pickup, 2 bakelite brown knobs, dot markers.

1930s	$900	$1,10●

SPG

2006-present. Professional grade, custom, solidbody lapsteels built by luthier Rick Welch in Farmingdale, Maine and Hanson, Massachusetts. He also builds guitars.

Stella

Ca. 1899-1974, present. Stella was a brand of the Oscar Schmidt Company. Harmony acquired the brand in '39. The Stella brand has been reintroduced by MBT International.

Electric Hawaiian Lap Steel

1937	$625	$775

Supertone

1914-1941. Brand name for Sears which was replaced by Silvertone. Instruments made by Harmony and others.

Electric Hawaiian Lap Steel

1930s	Various models	$300	$350

MODEL YEAR	FEATURES	EXC. COND. LOW	HIGH

Supro

1935-1968, 2004-present. Budget brand of the National Dobro Company. Amp builder Bruce Zinky revived the Supro name for a guitar and amp model.

Airline

1952-1962. Asymmetrical body with straight left side and contoured right (treble) side, black pearloid with small white pearloid on right (treble) side, 2 knobs.

1952-1962		$325	$375

Clipper Lap Steel

1941-1943. One pickup, bound rosewood 'board, dot inlay, brown pearloid.

1941-1943		$325	$400

Comet Lap Steel

1947-1966. One pickup, attached cord, painted-on 'board, pearloid.

1947-1949	Gray pearloid	$350	$425
1950-1966	White pearloid	$350	$425

Comet Steel (With Legs)

1950s-1960s. Three-leg 6-string steel version of the lap steel, 2 knobs, Supro logo on cover plate, 1 pickup.

1960s	Black and white	$600	$725

Console 8 Steel

1958-1960. Eight strings, 3 legs, black and white.

1958-1960		$650	$750

Irene Lap Steel

1940s. Complete ivory pearloid cover including headstock, fretboard and body, Roman numeral markers, 1 pickup, 2 control knobs, hard-wired output cord.

1940s		$350	$425

Jet Airliner Steel

1962-1964. One pickup, totem pole markings, 6 or 8 strings, pearloid, National-made.

1962-1964	Red	$225	$275

Professional Steel

Light brown pearloid.

1950s		$325	$400

Special Steel

1955-1962. Pearloid lap steel, student model, large script Special logo near pickup on early models, red until '57, white after.

1955-1957	Red pearloid	$300	$375
1957-1962	White pearloid	$300	$375

Spectator Steel

1952-1954. Wood body, 1 pickup, painted-on 'board, natural.

1952-1954		$200	$225

Student De Luxe Lap Steel

1952-1955. One pickup, pearloid, large script Student De Luxe logo located near pickup, replaced by Special in '55.

1952-1955	Black and white, or red pearloid	$325	$400
1952-1955	Natural or white paint	$200	$250

Studio

1955-1964. Symmetrical body, 2 knobs, priced in original catalog below the Comet, but above the Special, issued in '55 with blue plastic covered body.

1955-1964		$325	$400

Supreme Lap Steel

1947-1960. One pickup, painted-on 'board, brown pearloid until ca.'55, then red until ca.'58, Tulip Yellow after that.

1947-1960		$300	$375

Supro 60 Lap Steel and Amp-in-Case

Late 1930s-early '40s. Supro 60 logo near the single volume knob, long horizontal guitar case which houses a small tube amp and speaker, the case cover folds out to allow for ventilation for the tubes, the amp was made by National Dobro of Chicago.

1939-1941	White pearloid, black amp case	$750	$850

Twin Lap Steel

1948-1955. Two 6-string necks, pearloid covering, renamed Console Steel in '55.

1948-1955		$650	$750

Teisco

1946-1974. The Japanese guitar-maker offered many steel models from '55 to around '67. Models offered '55-'61: EG-7L, -K, -R, -NT, -Z, -A, -S, -P, -8L, -NW, and -M. During '61-'67: EG-TW, -O, -U, -L, -6N, -8N, -DB, -DB2, -DT, H-39, H-905, TRH-1, Harp-8 and H-850.

Hawaiian Lap Steel

1955-1967		$250	$300

Timtone Custom Guitars

1993-2006. Luthier Tim Diebert built his professional grade, custom, lap steel guitars in Grand Forks, British Columbia. He also built guitars and basses.

True Tone

1960s. Brand name sold by Western Auto (hey, everybody was in the guitar biz back then). Probably made by Kay or Harmony.

Lap Steel

1960s. Guitar-shaped, single-cut, 1 pickup.

1960s		$200	$250

Varsity

See Dickerson listing.

Vega

1903-present. The original Boston-based company was purchased by C.F. Martin in '70. In '80, the Vega trademark was sold to a Korean company. The company was one of the first to enter the electric market by offering products in '36 and offered lap steels into the early '60s.

DG-DB Steel

Two necks, 8 strings.

1950s		$725	$800

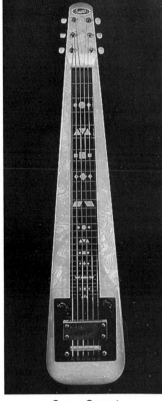

Supro Comet

Timtone Lapdog

Wayne lap steel

MODEL YEAR	FEATURES	EXC. COND. LOW	HIGH
Odell Lap Steel			
White pearloid.			
1950s		$325	$400
Other Lap Steels			
1930s		$350	$425
1940s	Art deco-style	$400	$475

Wabash

1950s. Lap steels distributed by the David Wexler company and made by others. They also offered guitars and amps.

Lap Steel (Hawaiian Scene Tailpiece)
Natural, 12 frets.

1950s		$250	$300

Wayne

1998-present. Luthiers Wayne and Michael Charvel, of Paradise, California, added intermediate-grade production lap steel guitars to their line in '04. They also build guitars.

MODEL YEAR	FEATURES	EXC. COND. LOW	HIGH

White

1955-1960. The White brand, named after plant manager Forrest White, was established by Fender to provide steel and small amp sets to teaching studios that were not Fender-authorized dealers. A standard guitar was planned, but never produced.

6 String Steel
1955-1956. White finish, block markers, 2 knobs, 3 legs. The 6 String Steel was usually sold with the matching white amp Model 80. Possibly only 1 batch of these was made by Fender in October/November '55.

1955-1956		$800	$950
Matching Steel and Amp Set			
1955-1956		$1,600	$1,900

Mandolins

Applause MAE148

Apitius Grand Classic

MANDOLINS

MODEL YEAR	FEATURES	EXC. COND. LOW	HIGH

Airline

Ca. 1958-1968. Brand for Montgomery Ward. Instruments were built by Kay, Harmony and Valco.

Electric Mandolin (Kay K390)

Early-1960s. In '62 the K390 was advertised as the Kay Professional Electric Mandolin. Venetian shape with sunburst spruce top, curly maple back and sides, tube-style pickup, white 'guard, rope-style celluloid binding.

| 1962 | | $350 | $550 |

Mandolin (Lower-End)

1960s. Acoustic, plainer features.

| 1960s | | $200 | $250 |

Allen

1982-present. Premium grade, production resonators, steel-string flat-tops, and mandolins built by Luthier Randy Allen, Colfax, California.

Alvarez

C.1966-present. An import brand for St. Louis Music, Alvarez currently offers intermediate grade, production, mandolins. They also offer guitars, lap steels and banjos.

Model A Mandolin

Classic F-style mandolin features, round soundhole or f-holes. Models include the A700 and A910.

| 1970s | | $425 | $525 |

American Conservatory (Lyon & Healy)

Late-1800s-early-1900s. Mainly catalog sales of guitars and mandolins from the Chicago maker. Marketed as a less expensive alternative to the Lyon & Healy Washburn product line.

Arched Back Mandolin

1910s. Flat back with a mild arch, standard appointments, nothing fancy.

| 1910s | | $325 | $400 |

Bowl Back Mandolin

1917. Bowl back style, 14 ribs, Brazilian.

| 1917 | | $225 | $250 |

Bowl Back Mandolin Style G2603

Early-1900s. Bowl back-style, 28 rosewood ribs (generally more ribs and use of rosewood ribs versus mahogany indicates higher quality), color corded soundhole and edge inlay, inlaid tortoise shell celluloid guard plate underneath strings and below the soundhole, bent top, butterfly headstock inlay.

| 1917 | | $375 | $450 |

Bowl Back Mandolin Style G2604

Early-1900s. Bowl back-style, 42 rosewood ribs (generally more ribs indicated higher quality), extra fancy color corded soundhole and edge inlay around, extra fancy inlaid tortoise shell celluloid guard plate underneath strings and below the soundhole, bent top, butterfly headstock inlay

| 1917 | | $500 | $575 |

MODEL YEAR	FEATURES	EXC. COND. LOW	HIGH

Andersen Stringed Instruments

1978-present. Luthier Steve Andersen builds his premium grade, production/custom mandolins in Seattle, Washington. He also builds guitars.

Andy Powers Musical Instrument Co.

1996-present. Luthier Andy Powers, builds his premium grade, custom, mandolins in Oceanside, California. He also builds guitars and ukes.

Apitius

1976-present. Luthier Oliver Apitius builds his premium and presentation grade, production/custom, mandolins in Shelburne, Ontario.

Applause

1994-present. Applause currently offers intermediate grade, production, mandolins. Kaman Music's entry-level Ovation-styled import brand added mandolins in '94.

Mandolin

| 1990s | | $175 | $200 |

Aria/Aria Pro II

1960-present. Intermediate grade, production, acoustic and electric mandolins from Aria/Aria Pro II, which added Japanese and Korean mandolins to their line in '76.

AM200 Mandolin

1994-present. Pear-shaped A body, plywood.

| 1994-2006 | | $175 | $200 |

AM400 Mandolin

1994-present. F-style, plywood.

| 1994-2006 | | $325 | $375 |

AM600 Mandolin

1994-present. F-style, solid wood.

| 1994-2006 | | $350 | $425 |

PM750 Mandolin

1976-ca. 1982. F-style Loar copy, maple plywood body, sunburst.

| 1976-1982 | | $450 | $550 |

Armstrong, Rob

1971-present. Custom mandolins made in Coventry, England, by luthier Rob Armstrong. He also builds basses, flat-tops, and parlor guitars.

Atkin Guitars

1993-present. Luthier Alister Atkin builds his production/custom mandolins in Canterbury, England. He also builds flat-top guitars.

Austin

1999-present. Budget and intermediate grade, production, mandolins imported by St. Louis Music. They also offer guitars, basses and banjos.

MODEL YEAR	FEATURES	EXC. COND. LOW	HIGH

Bacon & Day

Established in 1921 by David Day and Paul Bacon, primarily known for fine quality tenor and lectrum banjos in the '20s and '30s.

Mandolin Banjo Orchestra

1920s. Mandolin neck and banjo body with open back, headstock with Bacon logo.

1920s		$400	$500

Senorita Banjo Mandolin

1930s		$700	$850

Silverbell #1 Banjo Mandolin

1920s. Fancy appointments, closed-back resonator.

1920s		$950	$1,100

Bauer (George)

1894-1911. Luthier George Bauer built guitars and mandolins in Philadelphia, Pennsylvania. He also built instruments with Samuel S. Stewart (S.S. Stewart).

Acme Professional Mandolin

1890s. Bowl back, 29 ribs, Brazilian, fancy styling.

1890s		$325	$400

Beltone

1920s-1930s. Acoustic and resonator mandolins and banjo-mandolins made by others for New York City distributor Perlberg & Halpin. Martin did make a small number of instruments for Beltone, but most were student-grade models most likely made by one of the big Chicago builders. They also made guitars.

Resonator Mandolin

1930s. F-hole top, banjo-style resonator back.

1930s		$300	$375

Bertoncini Stringed Instruments

1995-present. Luthier Dave Bertoncini mainly builds flat-top guitars in Olympia, Washington, but has also built mandolins.

Bigsby

Ca. 1947-present. Guitar builder Paul Arthur Bigsby also built 6 electric mandolins.

Blue Star

1984-present. Luthier Bruce Herron builds his intermediate grade, production/custom, electric solidbody mandolins in Fennville, Michigan. He also builds guitars, lap steels, dulcimers, and ukes.

Bohmann

1878-ca.1926. Established by Czechoslavakian-born Joseph Bohmann in Chicago, Illinois.

Fancy Bowl Mandolin

1890-1900. Spruce top, marquetry trimmed, inlay, pearl.

1890-1900		$425	$500

Brandt

Early 1900s. John Brandt started making mandolin-family instruments in Chicago, Illinois around 1898.

Mandola

1900s. Spruce top, rosewood body, scroll headstock, pearl and abalone fretboard binding.

1900		$1,150	$1,300

Presentation Mandolin

Spruce top, tortoise shell-bound.

1900s		$775	$950

Breedlove

1990-present. Founded by Larry Breedlove and Steve Henderson. Professional and premium grade, production/custom, mandolins made in Tumalo, Oregon. They also produce guitars.

Alpine Master Class Mandolin

2000s. O-style body, spruce/maple.

2000s		$1,950	$2,100

K-5 Mandolin

Asymmetric carved top, maple body.

1990s		$1,625	$1,800

Olympic Mandolin

Solid spruce top, teardrop-shaped, oval soundhole, highly flamed maple back, sunburst.

1990s		$1,225	$1,400

Quartz OF/OO Mandolin

2000s. Basic A-style body with f-holes.

2000s		$825	$900

Brian Moore

1992-present. Brian Moore offers premium grade, production/custom, semi-hollow electric mandolins. They also build guitars and basses.

Bruno and Sons

1834-present. Established in 1834 by Charles Bruno, primarily as a distributor, Bruno and Sons marketed a variety of brands, including their own; currently part of Kaman. In the '60s or '70s, a Japanese-made solidbody electric mandolin was sold under the Bruno name.

Banjo Mandolin

Open back, 10" model.

1920s		$300	$350

Bowl Back Mandolin

1890s-1920s. Brazilian rosewood, spruce, rosewood ribs.

1920s		$300	$350

Calace

1825-present. Nicola Calace started The Calace Liuteria lute-making workshop in 1825 on the island of Procida, which is near Naples. The business is now in Naples and still in the family.

Lyre/Harp-Style Mandolin

Late-1800s-early-1900s. Lyre/harp-style, 8 strings, round soundhole, slightly bent top. Condition is important for these older instruments and the price noted is for a fully functional, original or pro-restored example.

1900		$1,100	$1,375

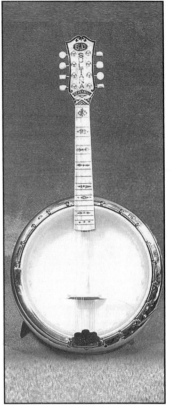

Bacon & Day Silverbell Banjo-Mandolin

Bertoncini F5M

MANDOLINS

MODEL YEAR	FEATURES	EXC. COND. LOW	HIGH

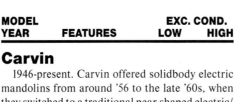

Carvin

1946-present. Carvin offered solidbody electric mandolins from around '56 to the late '60s, when they switched to a traditional pear-shaped electric/acoustic.

MB Mandolin

1956-1968. Solidbody, 1 pickup, single-cut Les Paul shape until '64, double-cut Jazzmaster/Strat shape after. Models include the #1-MB and the #2-MB, with different pickups.

1950s		$800	$975

Clifford

Clifford mandolins were manufactured by Kansas City, Missouri instrument wholesalers J.W. Jenkins & Sons. First introduced in 1895, the brand also offered guitars.

Collings

1986-present. Professional and premium grade, production/custom, mandolins built in Austin, Texas. Collings added mandolins to their line in '99. They also build guitars.

MF Mandolin

1999-present. F-style, carved top and back.

1999-2007		$3,000	$3,400

MF-5 Deluxe Mandolin

2005. Limited production, varnish finish, hand engraved nickel tailpiece unique to each instrument.

2005		$11,200	$14,000

MT Mandolin

1999-present. A-style, 2 f-holes, carved top and back, matte finish, tortoise-bound top.

1999-2004		$1,575	$1,750

MT2 Mandolin

1999-present. MT with high gloss finish, ivoroid body, neck and headstock binding.

1999-2004		$2,400	$2,800

Collings MT2

Conrad

Ca. 1968-1977. Imported from Japan by David Wexler and Company, Chicago, Illinois. Mid- to better-quality copy guitars, mandolins and banjos.

Crafter

2000-present. Line of intermediate grade, production, acoustic and acoustic/electric mandolins from Hohner. They also offer guitars and a bass.

Crestwood

1970s. Copy models imported by La Playa Distributing Company of Detroit.

Mandolin

Includes models 3039 (electric A-style), 3041 (bowl back-style, flower 'guard), 3043 (bowl back-style, plain 'guard), 71820 (A-style), and 71821 (F-style).

1970s		$175	$200

Ditson Style B

Cromwell

1935-1939. Private branded instruments made by Gibson at their Parsons Street factory in Kalamazoo, Michigan. Distributed by a variety of mail order companies such as Continental, Grossman, and Richter & Phillips.

GM-4 Mandolin

1935-1939. Style A, f-holes, solid wood arched top, mahogany back and sides, block capital letter Cromwell headstock logo, dot markers, elevated 'guard, sunburst.

1935-1939		$675	$800

Dan Kellaway

1976-present. Luthier Dan Kellaway builds his production/custom, premium grade, mandolins in Singleton NSW, Australia. He also builds guitars.

D'Angelico

1932-1964. Handcrafted by John D'Angelico. Models include Excel, Teardrop, and Scroll. Appointments can vary from standard to higher-end so each mandolin should be evaluated on a case-by-case basis.

Mandolin

1932-1949. Various models and appointments.

1932-1949	High-end appointments	$18,500	$22,500
1932-1949	Plain styling, lower range	$2,700	$3,300
1932-1949	Plain, non-elevated pickguard	$9,000	$10,000

D'Aquisto

1965-1995. James D'Aquisto apprenticed under D'Angelico. He started his own production in '65.

Mandolin

1970s. Various models and appointments.

1970s	Only 3 made	$27,000	$30,000

Dean

1976-present. Intermediate grade, production, acoustic and acoustic/electric mandolins made overseas. They also offer guitars, banjos, basses, and amps.

Dearstone

1993-present. Luthier Ray Dearstone builds his professional and premium grade, custom, mandolin-family instruments in Blountville, Tennessee. He also builds guitars and violins.

DeCava Guitars

1983-present. Premium grade, production/custom, mandolins built by luthier Jim DeCava in Stratford, Connecticut. He also builds guitars, ukes, and banjos.

MANDOLINS

The *Vintage Guitar Price Guide* shows low to high values for items in all-original excellent condition, and, where applicable, with original case or cover.

MODEL YEAR	FEATURES	EXC. COND. LOW	HIGH

MODEL YEAR	FEATURES	EXC. COND. LOW	HIGH

DeGennaro

2003-present. Professional and premium grade, custom/production, acoustic and electric mandolins built by luthier William Degennaro in Grand Rapids, Michigan. He also builds guitars and basses.

DeLucia, Vincenzo

1910s-1920s. Luthier Vincenzo DeLucia built mandolins in Philadelphia, Pennsylvania.

Mandolin

Early-1900s. High quality material, rosewood body, fine ornamentation.

1910s		$900	$1,100

Dennis Hill Guitars

1991-present. Premium grade, production/custom, mandolins built by luthier Dennis Hill in Panama City, Florida. He has also built dulcimers, guitars, and violins.

Ditson

Mandolins made for the Oliver Ditson Company of Boston, an instrument dealer and music publisher. Turn of the century and early-1900s models were bowl back-style with the Ditson label. The '20s Ditson Style A flat back mandolins were made by Martin. Models were also made by Lyon & Healy of Boston, often with a Ditson Empire label.

Mandola

1920. Bowl back.

1920		$900	$975

Style A Mandolin

1920s. Style A flat back made by Martin, mahogany sides and back, plain ornamentation.

1920s		$775	$900

Victory Mandolin

1890s. Brazilian rib bowl back with fancy inlays.

1890s		$675	$825

Dobro

1929-1942, 1954-present. Dobro offered mandolins throughout their early era and from the '60s to the mid-'90s.

Mandolin

1930s-1960s. Resonator on wood body.

1930s		$1,050	$1,250
1940s		$1,000	$1,250
1960s		$850	$1,050

Dudenbostel

1989-present. Luthier Lynn Dudenbostel builds his limited production, premium and presentation grade, custom, mandolins in Knoxville, Tennessee. He started with guitars and added mandolins in '96.

F-5 Mandolin

1996-2005. Loar-style, about 30 made.

1996-2005		$25,000	$28,000

Dyer

Ca. 1902-1925. W. J. Dyer harp-mandolins, mandolas and mando-cellos were made by the Larson brothers of Maurer & Co., Chicago, from c. 1906 to 1920. Mandolins were offered in styles 25, 35 and 50 with 25 being the plainest and 50 having abalone trim, vine and flowers pickguard inlay and tree-of-life fingerboard inlay. All had mahogany back and sides and select spruce tops. The mandolins are quite rare but the mandola and mando cello are extremely rare. The Larsons also built a few student grade Stetson brand mandolins for Dyer during this time.

Harp-Mandolin Style 35

1920s. Harp-style body with extended upper bass bout horn without drone strings.

1920s		$5,400	$6,600

Eastman

1992-present. Intermediate and professional grade, production, mandolins built in China. Eastman added mandolins in '04. They also build guitars, violins, and cellos.

Eastwood

1997-present. Intermediate grade, production, solidbody electric mandolins. They also offer basses and guitars.

EKO

1961-1985, 2000-present. The Italian-made EKOs were imported by LoDuca Brothers of Milwaukee. The brand was revived around 2000, but does not currently include mandolins.

Baritone Mandolin

1960s. Baritone mandolin with ornate inlays.

1960s		$350	$425

Octave Mandolin

1960s. Octave mandolin with ornate inlays.

1960s		$350	$425

Epiphone

1928-present. Intermediate grade, production, acoustic mandolins. Epiphone has offered several mandolin-family models over the years. Those from the '30s to the '60s were U.S.-made, the later models imported.

Adelphi Mandolin

1932-1948. A-style body, maple back and sides, f-holes, single-bound top and back.

1945-1946		$1,100	$1,300

Mandobird VIII Mandolin

2004-present. Reverse Firebird-style body with mandolin neck, electric, various colors.

2004-2006		$125	$130

MM50 Mandolin

1998-present. Import F-style with The Epiphone logo.

1998-2006		$350	$425

Eastman 915

Epiphone MM50

MANDOLINS

1967 Fender Electric Mandolin

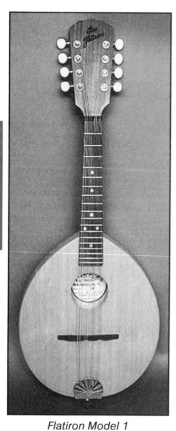

Flatiron Model 1

MODEL YEAR	FEATURES	EXC. COND. LOW	HIGH
Strand Mandolin			
1932-1958. Walnut back and sides, f-holes, multibound, sunburst.			
1944-1947		$1,050	$1,250
Venetian Electric Mandolin			
1961-1970. Gibson-made, pear-shaped body, 4 pole P-90 'dog-ear' mounted pickup, volume and tone knobs, dot markers, sunburst finish.			
1961-1964		$1,400	$1,750
1965-1970		$1,200	$1,500
Zephyr Mandolin			
1939-1958. A-style, electric, f-holes, maple body, 1 pickup, slotted block inlay.			
1950s		$525	$650

Esquire

1930s. Student level instruments with painted Esquire logo and painted wood grain.

MODEL YEAR	FEATURES	EXC. COND. LOW	HIGH
Mandolin			
1930s. Laminate A-style wood body, sunburst.			
1930s		$225	$275

Euphonon

1934-1944. Euphonon was a brand of the Larson Brothers of Chicago. The brand was introduced so Larson could compete in the guitar market with the new larger body 14-fret guitar models. Production also included mandolins, and most models were A-style, with teardrop body and flat backs.

MODEL YEAR	FEATURES	EXC. COND. LOW	HIGH
Mandolin			
1934-1944. Various models and appointments, each mandolin should be evaluated on a case-by-case basis.			
1934-1944	Rosewood	$1,050	$1,300
1934-1944	Rosewood, fancy trim	$3,100	$3,800

Everett Guitars

1977-present. Luthier Kent Everett, of Atlanta, Georgia, mainly builds guitars, but has also built mandolins.

Evergreen Mountain

1971-present. Professional grade, custom, mandolins built by luthier Jerry Nolte in Cove, Oregon. He also builds guitars and basses.

Fairbanks

1875-1904. Primarily known for banjos, Fairbanks also offered mandolins.

Fairbuilt Guitar Co.

2000-present. Professional grade, custom/production, mandolins built by luthiers Martin Fair and Stuart Orser in Loudoun County, Virginia. They also build guitars and banjos.

Fender

1946-present. Intermediate grade, production, acoustic and acoustic/electric mandolins. Fender also offered an electric mandolin for 20 years.

MODEL YEAR	FEATURES	EXC. COND. LOW	HIGH
Mandolin			
1956-1976. Electric solidbody, often referred to as the Mandocaster by collectors.			
1956-1957	Blond	$3,200	$3,400
1958-1959	Sunburst	$2,900	$3,100
1960-1961	Sunburst	$2,700	$3,000
1962-1963	Sunburst	$2,500	$2,800
1964-1965	Sunburst	$2,400	$2,700
1966-1970	Sunburst	$2,200	$2,600
1971-1976	Sunburst	$1,900	$2,000

Fine Resophonic

1988-present. Professional grade, production/custom, wood and metal-bodied resophonic mandolins built by luthiers Mike Lewis and Pierre Avocat in Vitry Sur Seine, France. They also build guitars and ukes.

Flatiron

1977-2003, 2006-present. Gibson purchased Flatiron in 1987. Production was in Bozeman, Montana until the end of '96, when Gibson closed the Flatiron mandolin workshop and moved mandolin assembly to Nashville, Tennessee. General production tapered off after the move and Flatirons were available on a special order basis for a time.

MODEL YEAR	FEATURES	EXC. COND. LOW	HIGH
A-2 Mandolin			
1977-1987	Early, no truss rod, f-holes	$3,000	$3,500
A-5 Mandolin			
Teardrop shape, f-holes, flamed maple body and neck, carved spruce top, unbound ebony 'board, nickel hardware, fleur-de-lis headstock inlay.			
1987-1990	Gibson Montana	$1,800	$2,200
A-5 1 Mandolin			
Carved top and back, dot inlays.			
1983-1985	Pre-Gibson	$2,300	$2,850
A-5 2 Mandolin			
1983-1985	Pre-Gibson	$3,100	$3,850
A-5 Artist Mandolin			
Teardrop shape, f-holes, flamed maple body and neck, carved spruce top, bound ebony 'board, gold hardware, fern headstock inlay.			
1987-1990	Gibson Montana	$2,150	$2,650
A-5 Junior Mandolin			
1987-1990	Gibson Montana	$1,550	$1,900
F-2 Mandolin			
1977-1987	Early, no truss rod	$5,000	$6,000
F-5 Mandolin			
1987-1990	Gibson Montana	$3,000	$3,700
F-5 Artist Mandolin			
F-style body, f-holes, flamed maple body and neck, carved spruce top, x-braced, bound ebony 'board, gold hardware, fern headstock inlay.			
1984-1985	Pre-Gibson	$5,000	$6,000
1987-1990	Gibson Montana	$4,000	$5,000
Festival Series Mandolins			
1988-1995	Style A	$1,400	$1,600
1988-1995	Style F	$2,200	$2,400

MODEL YEAR	FEATURES	EXC. COND. LOW	HIGH

Model 1 Mandolin
Oval shape, spruce top, maple body, rosewood board.

1977-1987	Pre-Gibson	$500	$600
1988-1995	Gibson Montana	$475	$575

Model 2 Mandolin
Oval body, curly maple (MC) or birdseye maple (MB) back and sides, spruce top, ebony 'board.

1977-1987	Pre-Gibson	$600	$750
1977-1995	Flamed koa back and sides	$725	$875
1988-1995	Gibson Montana	$550	$650

Model 2MW Mandola

1977-1987	Pre-Gibson	$725	$875
1988-1995	Gibson Montana	$675	$825

Model 3 Octave Mandolin
Oval shape, birdseye maple (MB) or curly maple (MC) body, spruce top, ebony 'board, longer scale.

1977-1987	Pre-Gibson	$875	$1,075
1988-1995	Gibson Montana	$800	$1,000

Performance Series Mandolins
Spruce top, maple body, nickel hardware.

1990-1995	Cadet	$625	$775
1990-1995	Style A	$900	$950
1990-1995	Style F	$1,700	$1,800

Signature Series Mandolins
Introduced in the 1996 catalog, flamed maple body and neck, carved spruce top, rosewood or ebony board.

1996-2003	A-5	$1,650	$1,800
1996-2003	A-5 Artist	$1,650	$1,800
1996-2003	A-5 Junior	$1,150	$1,300
1996-2003	F-5 Artist (Modified Fern)	$2,800	$3,500

Fletcher Brock Stringed Instruments
1992-present. Custom mandolin-family instruments made by luthier Fletcher Brock originally in Ketchum, Idaho, and currently in Seattle, Washington. He also builds guitars.

Framus
1946-1977, 1996-present. Founded in Erlangen, Germany by Fred Wilfer. In the '60s, Framus instruments were imported into the U.S. by Philadelphia Music Company. They offered acoustic and electric mandolins. The brand was revived in '96.

12-String Mandolin

1960s		$325	$400

Freshwater
1992-present. Luthier Dave Freshwater and family build mandolin family instruments in Beauly, Inverness, Scotland. They also build bouzoukis, dulcimers and harps.

Mandolin/Mandolin Family
2000s. Lateral Freshwater logo on headstock.

2000s		$450	$550

Fylde
1973-present. Luthier Roger Bucknall builds his intermediate and professional, production/custom mandolins and mandolas in Penrith, Cumbria, United Kingdom. He also builds guitars and basses, bouzoukis, and citterns.

G.L. Stiles
1960-1994. Built by Gilbert Lee Stiles in Florida. He also built acoustics, soldibodies, basses, steels, and banjos.

Galiano/A. Galiano
New Yorkers Antonio Cerrito and Raphael Ciani offered instruments built by them and others under the Galiano brand during the early 1900s.

Mandolin
Bowl back, some fancy appointments.

1920s		$325	$400

Galveston
Budget and intermediate grade, production, imported mandolins. They also offer basses and guitars.

Giannini
1900-present. Acoustic mandolins built in Salto, SP, Brazil near Sao Paolo. They also build guitars, violas, and cavaquinhos.

Gibson
1890s (1902)-present. Orville Gibson created the violin-based mandolin body-style that replaced the bowl back-type. Currently Gibson offers professional, premium and presentation grade, production/custom, mandolins.

Special Designations
Snakehead headstock: 1922-1927 with production possible for a few months plus or minus.
Lloyd Loar era: Mid-1922-late 1924 with production possible for a few months plus or minus.

A Mandolin
1902-1933. Oval soundhole, snakehead headstock '22-27, Loar era mid '22 to late '24.

1902-1909	Orange Top	$1,150	$1,400
1910-1918	Orange Top	$1,200	$1,500
1918-1921	Brown	$1,500	$1,900
1922-1924	Loar era	$2,700	$3,300
1925-1933		$2,200	$2,600

A-O Mandolin
1927-1933. Replaces A Jr., oval soundhole, dot inlay, brown finish.

1927-1933		$1,425	$1,725

A-OO Mandolin
1933-1943. Oval soundhole, dot inlay, carved bound top.

1933-1943	Sunburst	$1,450	$1,800

1930s Gibson Style A

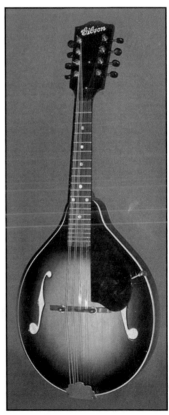

1938 Gibson A-00

MANDOLINS

1950s Gibson A-40

1936 Gibson A-75

MANDOLINS

MODEL YEAR	FEATURES	EXC. COND. LOW	HIGH
A-1 Mandolin			

1902-1918, 1922-1927, 1933-1943. Snakehead headstock '23-'27.

MODEL YEAR	FEATURES	EXC. COND. LOW	HIGH
1902-1918	Orange	$1,400	$1,750
1922-1924	Loar era	$3,000	$3,400
1925-1927	Black	$2,300	$2,800
1927	Not snaked	$2,100	$2,500
1927	Snaked	$2,200	$2,700
1932	Re-introduced, oval	$2,100	$2,500
1933-1943	Sunburst, f-holes	$1,525	$1,875

A-2/A-2Z Mandolin

1902-1908, 1918-1922. A-2Z '22-'27. Renamed A-2 '27-'28. Snakehead headstock '23-'27. Lloyd Loar era mid-'22-late-'24.

MODEL YEAR	FEATURES	EXC. COND. LOW	HIGH
1902-1908	Orange	$1,600	$2,000
1918-1921	Brown	$1,725	$2,150
1922-1924	Loar Era	$3,700	$4,200
1923-1924	Loar era, extra binding	$5,500	$6,000
1925-1928		$2,600	$3,100

A-3 Mandolin

1902-1922. Oval soundhole, single-bound body, dot inlay.

MODEL YEAR	FEATURES	EXC. COND. LOW	HIGH
1902-1917		$1,975	$2,475
1918-1922		$2,350	$2,750

A-4 Mandolin

1902-1935. Oval soundhole, single-bound body, dot inlay, snakehead '23-'27.

MODEL YEAR	FEATURES	EXC. COND. LOW	HIGH
1902-1917	Various colors	$2,350	$2,800
1918-1921	Dark mahogany	$2,800	$3,500
1922-1924	Loar era	$5,100	$6,400
1925-1935	Various colors	$3,100	$3,700

A-5 Mandolin

1957-1979. Oval soundhole, maple back and sides, dot inlay, scroll headstock, sunburst.

MODEL YEAR	FEATURES	EXC. COND. LOW	HIGH
1957-1964		$2,800	$3,000
1965-1969		$2,700	$2,900
1970-1979		$2,000	$2,500

A-5G Mandolin

1988-1996. Less ornate version of the A-5 L, abalone fleur-de-lis headstock inlay.

MODEL YEAR	FEATURES	EXC. COND. LOW	HIGH
1988-1996		$1,550	$1,850

A-5L Mandolin

1988-present. Extended neck, raised 'board, flower-pot headstock inlay, curly maple and spruce, sunburst, based on custom-made 1923 Loar A-5.

MODEL YEAR	FEATURES	EXC. COND. LOW	HIGH
1988-2006		$2,200	$2,400

A-9 Mandolin

2002-present. Spruce top, maple back and sides, black bound top, satin brown finish.

MODEL YEAR	FEATURES	EXC. COND. LOW	HIGH
2002-2004		$1,100	$1,300

A-12 Mandolin

1970-1979. F-holes, long neck, dot inlay, fleur-de-lis inlay, sunburst.

MODEL YEAR	FEATURES	EXC. COND. LOW	HIGH
1970-1979		$1,500	$1,750

A-40 Mandolin

1948-1970. F-holes, bound top, dot inlay, natural or sunburst.

MODEL YEAR	FEATURES	EXC. COND. LOW	HIGH
1948-1949		$1,100	$1,200
1950-1964		$1,075	$1,200
1965-1970		$850	$950

A-50 Mandolin

1933-1971. A-style oval bound body, f-holes, sunburst.

MODEL YEAR	FEATURES	EXC. COND. LOW	HIGH
1933-1941	Larger 11.25" body	$1,350	$1,650
1942-1959	Smaller 10" body	$1,200	$1,500
1960-1965		$1,100	$1,300
1966-1971		$900	$1,000

A-75 Mandolin

1934-1936. F-holes, raised fingerboard, bound top and back.

MODEL YEAR	FEATURES	EXC. COND. LOW	HIGH
1934-1936		$2,400	$2,600

A-C Century Mandolin

1935-1937. Flat back, bound body, oval soundhole, sunburst.

MODEL YEAR	FEATURES	EXC. COND. LOW	HIGH
1935-1937		$3,000	$3,500

A-Junior Mandolin

1920-1927. The Junior was the entry level mandolin for Gibson, but like most entry level Gibsons (re: Les Paul Junior), they were an excellent product. Oval soundhole, dot markers, plain tuner buttons. Becomes A-0 in '27.

MODEL YEAR	FEATURES	EXC. COND. LOW	HIGH
1920-1927	Sheraton Brown	$1,400	$1,750

Army and Navy Special Style DY/Army-Navy Mandolin

1918-1922. Lower-end, flat top and back, round soundhole, no logo, round label with model name, brown stain. Reintroduced as Army-Navy (AN Custom) '88-'96.

MODEL YEAR	FEATURES	EXC. COND. LOW	HIGH
1918-1922		$800	$1,000

AN-Custom (Army-Navy) Mandolin

Mid-1990s. Made in Bozeman, Montana, round teardrop shape, flat spruce top, flat maple back, maple rims, Gibson script logo on headstock.

MODEL YEAR	FEATURES	EXC. COND. LOW	HIGH
1995		$1,300	$1,400

Bella Voce F-5 Mandolin

1989. Custom Shop master-built model, high-end materials and construction, engraved tailpiece with Bella Voce F-5, sunburst.

MODEL YEAR	FEATURES	EXC. COND. LOW	HIGH
1989		$8,400	$9,400

Bill Monroe Model F Mandolin

1992-1995. Limited run of 200.

MODEL YEAR	FEATURES	EXC. COND. LOW	HIGH
1992-1995	Sunburst	$9,000	$10,000

C-1 Mandolin

1932. Flat top, mahogany back and sides, oval soundhole, painted on 'guard, a '32 version of the Army and Navy Special. This model was private branded for Kel Kroydon in the early-'30s.

MODEL YEAR	FEATURES	EXC. COND. LOW	HIGH
1932	Natural	$800	$950

EM-100/EM-125 Mandolin

1938-1943. Initially called EM-100, renamed EM-125 in '41-'43. Style A (pear-shape) archtop body, 1 blade pickup, 2 knobs on either side of bridge, dot markers, tortoise 'guard, sunburst.

MODEL YEAR	FEATURES	EXC. COND. LOW	HIGH
1938-1940	EM-100	$1,550	$1,900
1941-1943	EM-125	$1,450	$1,750

EM-150 Mandolin

1936-1971. Electric, A-00 body, 1 Charlie Christian pickup early on, 1 P-90 later, bound body, sunburst.

MODEL YEAR	FEATURES	EXC. COND. LOW	HIGH
1936-1940	Charlie Christian pickup	$2,300	$2,600
1941-1949	Rectangular pickup	$1,700	$2,000
1949-1965	P-90 pickup	$1,700	$2,000
1966-1971	P-90 pickup	$1,575	$1,725

MODEL YEAR	FEATURES	EXC. COND. LOW	HIGH

EM-200/Florentine Mandolin

1954-1971. Electric solidbody, 1 pickup, gold-plated hardware, 2 control knobs, dot markers, sunburst. Called the EM-200 in '60 and '61.

Year	Features	Low	High
1954-1960	Florentine	$2,800	$3,000
1960-1961	Renamed EM-200	$2,700	$2,900
1962-1971	Renamed Florentine	$2,500	$2,800

F-2 Mandolin

1902-1934. Oval soundhole, pearl inlay, star and crescent inlay on peghead.

Year	Features	Low	High
1902-1909	3-point	$3,800	$4,500
1910-1917	2-point	$3,600	$4,400
1918-1921	2-point	$4,200	$5,200
1922-1924	Loar era	$6,400	$7,000
1925-1934		$4,000	$5,000

F-3 Mandolin

1902-1908. Three-point body, oval soundhole, scroll peghead, pearl inlayed 'guard, limited production model, black top with red back and sides.

Year	Features	Low	High
1902-1908		$4,200	$5,200

F-4 Mandolin

1902-1943. Oval soundhole, rope pattern binding, various colors.

Year	Features	Low	High
1902-1909	3-point	$5,000	$6,000
1910-1917	2-point	$5,900	$7,400
1918-1921	2-point	$6,000	$7,500
1922-1924	Loar era	$7,900	$9,500
1925-1943		$6,100	$6,800

F-5 Mandolin

1922-1943; 1949-1980. F-holes, triple-bound body and 'guard. The '20s Lloyd Loar era F-5s are extremely valuable. Reintroduced in '49 with single-bound body, redesigned in '70.

Year	Features	Low	High
1922	Loar no virzi	$175,000	$208,000
1922	Loar with virzi	$151,000	$189,000
1923	Loar July 9, 1923, side bound	$208,000	$212,000
1923	Loar non-side bound	$200,000	$208,000
1924	Loar no virzi	$175,000	$208,000
1924	Loar with virzi	$151,000	$189,000
1925-1928	Fern, Master Model	$80,000	$90,000
1928-1929	Fern, not Master Model	$70,000	$75,000
1930-1931	Fern peghead inlay	$60,000	$65,000
1932-1935	Fern peghead inlay	$50,000	$60,000
1936-1940	Fern (limited production)	$42,000	$50,000
1940-1943	Fleur-de-lis peghead inlay	$37,000	$45,000
1949	Flower pot, mahogany neck	$12,000	$15,000
1950-1953	Flower pot, maple neck	$8,500	$9,500
1954	Flower pot peghead inlay	$8,000	$9,000
1955-1956	Flower pot peghead inlay	$7,500	$8,500
1957-1959	Flower pot peghead inlay	$7,000	$8,000
1960-1965		$5,500	$6,500
1966-1969	Sunburst	$4,200	$5,200
1970-1980	Sunburst	$3,100	$3,800

F-5 Custom Mandolin

Year	Features	Low	High
1993		$6,250	$6,500

F-5 Master Model Mandolin

2003-present. F-holes, triple-bound body and guard, red spruce top, maple back and sides, flowerpot inlay.

Year	Features	Low	High
2003-2004		$9,000	$11,000

F-5G/F-5G Deluxe Mandolin

1997-present. Two-point style F, Deluxe has a slightly wider neck profile.

Year	Features	Low	High
1997-2003		$2,700	$3,200

F-5L Mandolin

1978-present. Reissue of Loar F-5, gold hardware, fern headstock inlay (flowerpot inlay with silver hardware also offered for '88-'91), sunburst.

Year	Features	Low	High
1978-1984	Kalamazoo-made	$4,000	$4,800
1984-1999		$3,700	$4,600

F-5V Mandolin

1990s. Based on Lloyd Loar's original F-5s of 1922-24, varnish Cremona Brown sunburst finish.

Year	Features	Low	High
1990s		$6,500	$7,500

F-7 Mandolin

1934-1940. F-holes, single-bound body, neck and 'guard, fleur-de-lis peghead inlay, sunburst.

Year	Features	Low	High
1934-1937		$11,000	$13,000

F-9 Mandolin

2002-present. F-5 style, carved spruce top, no inlays, black bound body.

Year	Features	Low	High
2002-2004		$1,800	$2,100

F-10 Mandolin

1934-1936. Slight upgrade of the '34 F-7 with extended 'board and upgraded inlay, black finish.

Year	Features	Low	High
1934-1936		$11,000	$13,000

F-12 Mandolin

1934-1937, 1948-1980. F-holes, bound body and neck, scroll inlay, raised 'board until '37, 'board flush with top '48-on, sunburst.

Year	Features	Low	High
1934-1937		$11,000	$13,000
1948-1959		$4,700	$4,900
1960-1964		$4,100	$4,400
1965-1969		$3,500	$4,000
1970-1980		$2,500	$3,500

H-1 Mandola

1902-1936. Has same features as A-1 mandolin, but without snakehead headstock.

Year	Features	Low	High
1902-1908	Orange	$2,000	$2,200
1918-1921	Brown	$2,200	$2,500
1922-1924	Loar era	$4,000	$4,500
1925-1928		$3,000	$3,500

H-1E Mandola

Late-1930s. Limited number built, electric with built-in adjustable bar pickup, sunburst.

Year	Features	Low	High
1938		$4,000	$4,500

H-2 Mandola

1902-1922. Has same features as A-4 mandolin.

Year	Features	Low	High
1902-1917	Various colors	$2,500	$3,000
1918-1921	Dark Mahogany	$3,200	$3,500

Ca. 1910 Gibson F-4

1927 Gibson F-5

MANDOLINS

Gibson K-2 mandocello

Gilchrist Standard Model 5

MANDOLINS

MODEL YEAR	FEATURES	EXC. COND. LOW	HIGH
H-4 Mandola			
1910-1940. Same features as F-4 mandolin.			
1910-1921		$6,300	$7,700
1922-1924	Loar era	$9,500	$11,000
1925-1940		$8,000	$9,500
H-5 Mandola			
1923-1929 (available by special order 1929-1936), 1990-1991. Same features as the high-end F-5 Mandolin. This is a very specialized market and instruments should be evaluated on a case-by-case basis.			
1923-1924	Loar era	$75,000	$85,000
1925-1928	Fern, Master Model	$42,000	$50,000
1928-1929	Fern, not Master Model	$37,000	$45,000
1990-1991	Limited production	$5,000	$6,000
K-1 Mandocello			
1902-1943. Same features as H-1 mandola, off & on production, special order available.			
1902-1908	Orange	$3,400	$4,100
1918-1921	Brown	$3,900	$4,600
1922-1924	Loar era	$4,700	$5,800
1925-1943		$3,400	$4,000
K-2 Mandocello			
1902-1922. Same features as A-4 mandolin.			
1902-1917	Black or red mahogany	$4,200	$5,000
1918-1922		$4,500	$5,500
K-4 Mandocello			
1912-1929 (offered as special order post-1929). Same features as F-4 mandolin, sunburst.			
1912-1921		$7,000	$8,000
1922-1924	Loar era	$12,000	$15,000
1925-1929		$7,000	$8,500
M-6 (Octave Guitar)			
2002-2006. A-style mandolin body, short-scale 6-string guitar neck.			
2002-2004		$1,400	$1,600
MB-1 Mandolin Banjo			
1922-1923, 1925-1937.			
1922-1923		$800	$1,000
1925-1937		$800	$1,000
MB-2 Mandolin Banjo			
1920-1923, 1926-1937.			
1920-1923		$1,100	$1,300
1926-1937		$1,100	$1,300
MB-3 Mandolin Banjo			
1923-1939		$1,300	$1,500
MB-4 Mandolin Banjo			
1923-1932. Fleur-de-lis inlay.			
1923-1932		$1,600	$1,700
MB-Junior Mandolin Banjo			
Open back, budget level.			
1924-1925		$700	$800
Sam Bush Signature F-5 Mandolin			
2000-present. Artist Series model, carved spruce top, gold hardware, built at Opry Mill plant in Nashville.			
2000-2002		$5,000	$6,000

MODEL YEAR	FEATURES	EXC. COND. LOW	HIGH
SPF-5 Mandolin			
1938. F-style, single bar pickup with volume and tone controls, very limited production, natural.			
1938		$36,000	$39,000
Style J Mando Bass			
1912-1930 (special order post-1930). A-style body, 4 strings, round soundhole, bound top, dot inlay.			
1912-1930		$4,700	$5,800
Style TL-1 Tenor Lute Mandolin			
1924-1926		$2,000	$2,500
Wayne Benson Signature F-5 Mandolin			
2003-2006. Limited edition of 50, solid spruce top, figured maple back, sides and neck, gold hardware, vintage red satin.			
2003-2006		$5,100	$5,400

Gilchrist

1978-present. Premium and presentation grade, custom, mandolins made by luthier Steve Gilchrist of Warrnambool, Australia. Custom ordered but were also initially distributed through Gruhn Guitars, Nashville, Tennessee and then exclusively by Carmel Music Company. Designs are based upon Gibson mandolins built between 1910 and '25.

Model 5 Mandolin

1978-present. Based on the Gibson '22 to '24 Loar-era F-5 mandolin, Gilchrist slant logo, spruce top, flamed maple back, sides, and neck, ebony 'board, multiple binding, sunburst.

1978-1995		$22,000	$25,000
1996-2006		$24,000	$26,000

Givens

1962-1992. Luthier R. L. (Bob) Givens hand-crafted about 800 mandolins and another 700 in a production shop.

A Mandolin

1962-1975. Early production A-style.

1962-1975		$2,250	$2,750

A-3 Mandolin

Mid-1970s-mid-1980s. Distinguished by use of decal (the only model with Givens decal).

1975-1988		$2,100	$2,500

A-4 Mandolin

1988-1993. No 'board binding, simple block-like multiple-line RL Givens inlay, nicer maple.

1988-1993		$1,800	$2,200

A-5 Mandolin

1988-1993. Bound 'board, pearl headstock inlay.

1988-1993		$2,000	$2,400

A-6 (Torch) Mandolin

1988-1992. Torch inlay (the only model with this), gold hardware, snowflake markers.

1988-1992		$3,000	$3,600

A-6 Custom Mandolin

1991-1992. Elaborate customized A-6 model.

1991-1992		$3,700	$4,300

F-5 (Fern) Mandolin

1973-1985. Givens' own version with fern ornamentation.

1973-1985		$3,850	$4,750

MODEL YEAR	FEATURES	EXC. COND. LOW	HIGH

F-5 (Loar) Mandolin
1962-1972. Givens' own version based upon the Loar model F-5.

1962-1972		$3,850	$4,750

F-5 (Torch) Mandolin
1988-1992. Givens F-5 with torch inlay (the only F model with this).

1988-1992		$6,300	$7,700

F-5 (Wheat Straw) Mandolin
1986-1988. Givens F-5-style with wheat straw ornamentation.

1986-1988		$5,300	$6,500

Godin
1987-present. Intermediate grade, production, acoustic/electric mandolins from luthier Robert Godin. They also build basses and guitars.

A-8 Mandolin
2000-present. Single-cut chambered body, acoustic/electric.

2000-2003		$450	$550

Gold Tone
1993-present. Intermediate grade, production/custom mandolins built by Wayne and Robyn Rogers in Titusville, Florida. They also offer guitars, basses, lap steels, ukuleles, banjos and banjitars.

Goodman Guitars
1975-present. Premium grade, custom/production, mandolins built by luthier Brad Goodman in Brewster, New York. He also builds guitars.

Goya
1955-present. Korean-made mandolins. They also build guitars and banjos. Originally made in Sweden, by the late '70s from Japan, then from Korea.

Mandolin

1960s	Japan/Korea	$150	$175
1960s	Sweden built	$275	$325
1970s	Sweden built	$250	$300

Gretsch
1883-present. Gretsch started offering mandolins by the early 1900s. Currently Gretsch does not offer mandolins.

New Yorker Mandolin
Late 1940s-late 1950s. Teardrop shape, f-holes, arched top and back, spruce top, maple back, sides, and neck, rosewood 'board.

1950s		$650	$750

GTR
1974-1978. GTR (for George Gruhn, Tut Taylor, Randy Wood) was the original name for Gruhn Guitars in Nashville, Tennessee (it was changed in '76). GTR imported mandolins and banjos from Japan. An A-style (similar to a current Gibson A-5 L) and an F-style (similar to mid- to late-'20s F-5 with fern pattern) were offered. The instruments were made at the Moridaira factory in Matsumoto, Japan by factory foreman Sadamasa Tokaida. Quality was relatively high but quantities were limited.

A-Style Mandolin
1974-1978. A5-L copy with GTR logo on headstock.

1974-1978		$1,300	$1,550

F-Style Mandolin
1974-1978. F-5 Fern copy with slant GTR logo on headstock, sunburst, handmade in Japan.

1974-1978		$2,200	$2,600

Harmony
1982-1976. Founded by Wilhelm Schultz in 1892, and purchased by Sears in 1916. The company evolved into one of the largest producers of stringed instruments in the U.S. in the '30s.

Baroque H35/H835 Electric Mandolin
Late 1960s-early 1970s. Electric version of Baroque H425 with single pickup and two controls.

1969-1970	H35	$350	$400
1971-1976	H835	$325	$375

Baroque H425/H8025 Mandolin
F-style arched body, extreme bass bout pointy horn, close grained spruce top, sunburst.

1969-1970	H425	$300	$350
1971-1976	H8025	$300	$350

Lute H331/H8031 Mandolin
1960s-1970s. A-style, flat top and back, student level.

1960s	H331	$150	$175
1970s	H8031	$150	$175

Monterey H410/H417/H8017 Mandolin
1950s-1970s. A-style arched body with f-holes, sunburst.

1950-1970s	All models	$150	$175

Heiden Stringed Instruments
1974-present. Luthier Michael Heiden builds his premium grade, production/custom mandolins in Chilliwack, British Columbia. He also builds guitars.

Heritage
1985-present. Started by former Gibson employees in Gibson's Kalamazoo, Michigan plant, Heritage offered mandolins for a number of years.

H-5 Mandolin
1986-1990s. F-style scroll body, f-holes.

1980s		$3,100	$4,000

Höfner
1887-present. Höfner has offered a wide variety of instruments, including mandolins, over the years. They currently do not offer a mandolin.

Gold Tone GM-110

1960s Harmony Monterey

MANDOLINS

Ibanez M5225

Johnson MF100 Savannah

MANDOLINS

Model 545/E545 Mandolin

1960s. Pear-shaped A-style with catseye f-holes, block-style markers, engraved headstock, Genuine Hofner Original and Made in Germany on back of headstock, transparent brown.

MODEL YEAR	FEATURES	EXC. COND. LOW	HIGH
1968-1969	545 (acoustic)	$325	$400
1968-1969	E545 (acoustic-electric)	$425	$500

Hohner

1857-present. Intermediate grade, production, acoustic and acoustic/electric mandolins. They also offer guitars, basses, banjos and ukuleles.

Holst

1984-present. Premium grade, custom, mandolins built in Creswell, Oregon by luthier Stephen Holst. He also builds guitars.

Hondo

1969-1987, 1991-present. Budget grade, production, imported mandolins. They also offer banjos, basses and guitars. Hondo also offered mandolins from around '74 to '87.

Mandolin

1974-1987. Hondo offered F-style, A-style, and bowl back mandolin models.

MODEL YEAR	FEATURES	EXC. COND. LOW	HIGH
1970s	Acoustic	$100	$125
1970s	Acoustic-electric	$150	$175

Hopf

1906-present. Professional grade, production/custom, mandolins made in Germany. They also make basses, guitars and flutes.

Howe-Orme

1897-ca. 1910. Elias Howe patented a guitar-shaped mandolin on November 14, 1893 and later partnered with George Orme to build a variety of mandolin family instruments and guitars in Boston.

Mandola

1897-early-1900s. Guitar body-style with narrow waist, not the common mandolin F- or S-style body, pressed (not carved) spruce top, mahogany back and sides, flat-top guitar-type trapeze bridge, decalomania near bridge.

MODEL YEAR	FEATURES	EXC. COND. LOW	HIGH
1890s		$1,450	$1,700

Mandolinetto

1890s. Guitar body, mandolin neck and tuning, 'guard below oval soundhole, slightly arched top, Brazilian rosewood sides and back, dot/diamond/oval markers.

MODEL YEAR	FEATURES	EXC. COND. LOW	HIGH
1890s		$1,900	$2,000

Ianuario Mandolins

1990-present. Professional and premium grade, custom, mandolins built by luthier R. Anthony Ianuario in Jefferson, Georgia. He also builds banjos and violins.

Ibanez

1932-present. Ibanez offered mandolins from '65 to '83. In '04 they again added mandolins to the product line.

Model 511 Mandolin

MODEL YEAR	FEATURES	EXC. COND. LOW	HIGH
1974-1979		$275	$325

Model 513 Mandolin

1974-1979. A-5 copy with double cutaways, oval sound hole, dot markers, sunburst.

MODEL YEAR	FEATURES	EXC. COND. LOW	HIGH
1974-1979		$400	$475

Model 514 Mandolin

1974-1979. Arched back, spruce, rosewood, dot inlays, sunburst.

MODEL YEAR	FEATURES	EXC. COND. LOW	HIGH
1974-1979		$400	$475

Model 524 Artist Mandolin

1974-1978. F-5 Loar copy, solid wood carved top and solid wood carved top and solid wood back, sunburst.

MODEL YEAR	FEATURES	EXC. COND. LOW	HIGH
1974-1978		$875	$925

Model 526 (electric) Mandolin

1974-1978. A-style body, single pickup, two control knobs, sunburst.

MODEL YEAR	FEATURES	EXC. COND. LOW	HIGH
1974-1978		$375	$450

Model 529 Artist Mandolin

1982-1983. F-5 Loar era copy, solid wood carved top and solid wood spruce top and solid maple sides and back, sunburst.

MODEL YEAR	FEATURES	EXC. COND. LOW	HIGH
1982-1983		$900	$1,100

Imperial

1890-1922. Imperial mandolins were made by the William A. Cole Company of Boston, Massachusetts.

Bowl Back Mandolin

MODEL YEAR	FEATURES	EXC. COND. LOW	HIGH
1890s		$300	$350

J.B. Player

1980s-present. Budget grade, production, imported mandolins. They also offer basses, banjos and guitars.

J.R. Zeidler Guitars

1977-2002. Luthier John Zeidler built premium grade, custom, mandolins in Wallingford, Pennsylvania. He also built guitars.

John Le Voi Guitars

1970-present. Production/custom, mandolin family instruments built by luthier John Le Voi in Lincolnshire, United Kingdom. He also builds guitars.

Johnson

Mid-1990s-present. Budget and intermediate grade, production, mandolins imported by Music Link, Brisbane, California. Johnson also offers guitars, amps, basses and effects.

MA Series A-Style Mandolins

Mid-1990s-present. Import, A-style copy. Several levels offered; the range shown is for all value levels.

MODEL YEAR	FEATURES	EXC. COND. LOW	HIGH
1990s		$125	$150

MODEL YEAR	FEATURES	EXC. COND. LOW	HIGH

MF Series F-Style Mandolins

Mid-1990s-2006. Import, F-style copy. Several levels offered; the range shown is for all value levels.

1990s		$175	$200

K & S

1992-1998. Mandolins and mandolas distributed by George Katechis and Marc Silber and handmade in Paracho, Mexico. They also offered guitars and ukes.

Kalamazoo

1933-1942, 1946-1947, 1965-1970. Budget brand produced by Gibson in Kalamazoo, Michigan. They offered mandolins until '42.

Kalamazoo/Oriole A-Style Mandolin

1930s. Kalamazoo and Oriole on the headstock, KM/A-style.

1930s		$825	$900

KM-11 Mandolin

1935-1941. Gibson-made, A-style, flat top and back, round soundhole, dot inlay, sunburst.

1935-1941		$750	$900

KM-21 Mandolin

1936-1940. Gibson-made, A-style, f-holes, arched bound spruce top and mahogany back, sunburst.

1936-1940		$850	$975

KMB Mandolin/Banjo

1930s. Banjo-mandolin with resonator.

1930s		$500	$525

Kay

1931-present. Located in Chicago, Illinois, the Kay company made an incredible amount of instruments under a variety of brands, including the Kay name. From the beginning, Kay offered several types of electric and acoustic mandolins. In '69, the factory closed, marking the end of American-made Kays. The brand survives today on imported instruments.

K68/K465 Concert Mandolin

1952-1968. Pear-shape, close-grain spruce top, genuine mahogany back and sides, natural. Renamed the K465 in '66. Kay also offered a Venetian-style mandolin called the K68 in '37-'42.

1952-1968		$200	$250

K73 Mandolin

1939-1952. Solid spruce top, maple back and sides, A-style body, f-holes, cherry sunburst.

1939-1952		$200	$250

K390/K395 Professional Electric Mandolin

1960-1968. Modified Venetian-style archtop, 1 pickup, f-hole, spruce top, curly maple back and sides, sunburst finish. Renamed K395 in '66.

1960-1968		$400	$500

K494/K495 Electric Mandolin

1960-1968. A-style archtop, single metal-covered (no poles) pickup, volume and tone control knobs, sunburst. The K494 was originally about 60% of the price of the K390 model (see above) in '65. Renamed K495 in '66.

1960-1968		$375	$425

Kay Kraft

1931-1937. First brand name of the newly formed Kay Company. Brand replaced by Kay in '37.

Mandola

1937		$750	$850

Mandolin

1931-1937. Kay Kraft offered Venetian- and teardrop-shaped mandolins.

1931-1937		$400	$450

KB

1989-present. Luthier Ken Bebensee builds his premium grade, production/custom, mandolins in North San Juan, California. He also builds guitars and basses.

Kel Kroydon (by Gibson)

1930-1933. Private branded budget level instruments made by Gibson. They also had guitars and banjos.

KK-20 (Style C-1) Mandolin

1930-1933. Flat top, near oval-shaped body, oval soundhole, natural finish, dark finish mahogany back and sides.

1930-1933		$725	$875

Kent

1961-1969. Japanese-made instruments. Kent offered teardrop, A style, and bowlback acoustic mandolins up to '68.

Acoustic Mandolin

1961-1968. Kent offered teardrop, A-style, and bowlback acoustic mandolins up to '68.

1961-1968		$125	$150

Electric Mandolin

1964-1969. Available from '64-'66 as a solidbody electric (in left- and right-hand models) and from '67-'69 an electric hollowbody Venetian-style with f-holes (they called it violin-shaped).

1964-1969		$175	$200

Kentucky (Saga M.I.)

1977-present. Brand name of Saga Musical Instruments currently offering budget, intermediate, and professional grade, production, A- and F-style mandolins. Early models made in Japan, then Korea, currently made in China.

KM Series Mandolins

1980s	KM-180 A-style	$275	$325
1980s	KM-650 F-style	$650	$800
1980s	KM-700 F-style	$650	$800
1980s	KM-800 F-style	$650	$800
1990s	KM-200S A-style	$325	$375
1990s	KM-250S A-style	$475	$575
1990s	KM-500S A-style	$575	$700
1990s	KM-620 F-style	$600	$750
1990s	KM-675	$375	$450
2000s	KM-140 A-style	$110	$120
2000s	KM-150 A-style	$125	$145
2000s	KM-620 F-style	$325	$375
2000s	KM-630 F-style	$350	$425

Kalamazoo A-style

Kentucky KM160

MANDOLINS

Larson Harp-Mandolin

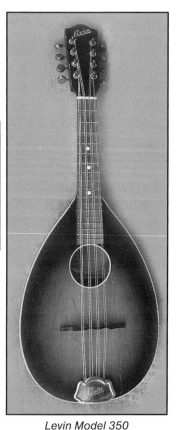

Levin Model 350

MODEL YEAR	FEATURES	EXC. COND. LOW	HIGH
2000s	KM-700 F-style	$375	$450
2000s	KM-800 F-style	$400	$475

Kimble
2000-present. Luthier Will Kimble builds his premium grade, custom/production, mandolins, mandocellos, and mandolas in Cincinnati, Ohio.

Kingston
Ca. 1958-1967. Mandolins imported from Japan by Jack Westheimer and Westheimer Importing Corporation of Chicago, Illinois. They also offered guitars and basses.
Acoustic Mandolin

1960s		$150	$175

EM1 Electric Mandolin
1964-1967. Double-cut solidbody electric, 15.75" scale, 1 pickup.

1960s		$175	$200

Knutsen
1890s-1920s. Luthier Chris J. Knutsen of Tacoma/Seattle, Washington.
Harp Mandolin
1910s. Harp mandolin with tunable upper bass bout with 4 drone strings, and standard mandolin neck. The mandolin version of a harp guitar.

1910s		$4,500	$5,500

Knutson Luthiery
1981-present. Professional and premium grade, custom, acoustic and electric mandolins built by luthier John Knutson in Forestville, California. He also builds guitars, basses and lap steels.

Kona
2001-present. Budget grade, production, acoustic mandolins made in Asia. They also offer guitars, basses, banjos and amps.

La Scala
Ca. 1920s-1930s. A brand of the Oscar Schmidt Company of New Jersey, used on guitars, banjos, and mandolins. These were often the fanciest of the Schmidt instruments.

Lakeside (Lyon & Healy)
1890-early-1900s. Mainly catalog sales of guitars and mandolins from the Chicago maker. Marketed as a less expensive alternative to the Lyon & Healy Washburn product line.
Style G2016 12-String Mandolin
1890-early-1900s. 12-string, 18 mahogany ribs with white inlay between, celluloid guard plate, advertised as "an inexpensive instrument, possessing a good tone, correct scale, and durable construction."

1890-1910		$300	$375

Lakewood
1986-present. Luthier Martin Seeliger built his professional grade, production/custom, mandolins in Giessen, Germany up to '07. He continues to build guitars.

Larson Brothers (Chicago)
1900-1944. Made by luthiers Carl and August Larson and marketed under a variety of brands including Stetson, Maurer, Prairie State, Euphonon, Dyer, Stahl and others. The Larson name was not used as a brand name but has been adopted as a reference to any instrument of the brands they built.

Laurie Williams Guitars
1983-present. Luthier Laurie Williams builds his premium grade, custom/production, acoustic mandolins on the North Island of New Zealand. He also builds guitars.

Levin
1900-1973. Acoustic mandolins built in Sweden. Levin was best known for their classical guitars, which they also built for other brands, most notably Goya. They also built ukes.

Lewis
1981-present. Luthier Michael Lewis builds his premium and presentation grade, custom/production, mandolin family instruments in Grass Valley, California. He also builds guitars.

Lotus
Late-1970s-2004. Acoustic mandolins imported by Musicorp. They also offered banjos and guitars.

Lyle
Ca. 1969-1980. Instruments imported by distributor L.D. Heater of Portland, Oregon. Generally Japanese-made copies of American designs. They also had basses and guitars.
TM-200 Mandolin

1970s	A-style	$125	$150

Lyon & Healy
1864-ca. 1945. Lyon & Healy was a large musical instrument builder and marketer, and produced under many different brands.
Style A Mandocello
1910-1920s. Scroll peghead, symmetrical 2-point body, natural.

1910s		$5,400	$6,600
1920s		$5,400	$6,600

Style A Professional Mandolin
1918-1920s. Violin scroll peghead, natural.

1918-1920s		$3,500	$4,000

Style B Mandolin
1920. Maple back and sides, 2-point body, natural.

1920		$1,600	$2,000

MODEL YEAR	FEATURES	EXC. COND. LOW	HIGH

Style C Mandolin

1920s. Like Style A teardrop Gibson body style, oval soundhole, carved spruce top, carved maple back, natural.

1920s		$1,700	$2,000

Lyra

1920s-1930s. Private brand made by Regal, Lyra name plate on headstock.

Style A (Scroll) Mandolin

1920s-1930s. Scroll on upper bass bout.

1925-1935		$425	$500

Maccaferri

1923-1990. Mario Maccaferri made a variety of instruments over his career. He produced award-winning models in Italy and France until he fled to the U.S. due to WW II. He applied the new plastic to a highly successful line of instruments after the war. A mandolin was about the only stringed instument they didn't offer in plastic. His Europe-era instruments are very rare.

Mandolins/Mandolas made by Maccaferri: 1928-ca. '31: No. 1 Mandolone, No. 2 Mandoloncello, No. 3 Mandola Baritono, No. 4 Mandola Tenore, No. 5 Mandola Soprano, No. 6 Mandolino, No. 7 Quartino.

Mann

2002-present. Luthier Jonathan Mann builds his professional grade, production/custom, acoustic and electric mandolins in Joelton, Tennessee.

Manuel & Patterson

1993-present. Professional and premium grade, production/custom, carved top mandolins built by luthiers Joe Manuel and Phil Patterson in Abita Springs, Louisiana. They also build guitars.

Martin

1833-present. Martin got into the mandolin market in 1895 starting with the typical bowl back designs. By 1914, Gibson's hot selling, innovative, violin-based mandolin pushed Martin into a flat back, bent top hybrid design. By '29, Martin offered a carved top and carved back mandolin. Most models were discontinued in '41, partially because of World War II. Production resumed and standard models are offered up to 1993. From '94 to '02 mandolins are available on a custom order basis only. Martin offered a Backpacker mandolin up to '06.

Style 0 Mandolin

1905-1925. Bowl back-style, 18 rosewood ribs, solid peghead.

1905-1925		$800	$900

Style 00 Mandolin

1908-1925. Bowl back-style, 9 rosewood ribs (14 ribs by '24), solid peghead.

1908-1925		$650	$800

Style 000 Mandolin

1914 only. Bowl back, solid peghead, dot inlay, 9 mahogany ribs.

1914		$575	$675

Style 1 Mandolin

1898-1924. Bowl back, German silver tuners, 18 ribs.

1898-1924		$900	$1,000

Style 2 Mandolin

1898-1924. Bowl back, 26 rosewood ribs, higher appointments than Style 1.

1898-1924		$1,100	$1,200

Style 2-15 Mandolin

1936-1964. Carved spruce top, maple back and sides, f-hole, single-bound back, solid headstock.

1936-1964		$1,300	$1,500

Style 2-20 Mandolin

1936-1941. Carved spruce triple-bound top and bound maple back and sides, f-hole, dot inlay.

1936-1942		$2,400	$2,900

Style 2-30 Mandolin

1937-1941. Carved spruce top and maple back and sides, multi-bound, f-holes, diamond and square inlays.

1937-1941		$3,400	$3,700

Style 4 Mandolin

1907	30 rosewood ribs	$2,200	$2,500

Style 5 Mandolin

1898-1920. Bowl back, vine inlay, abalone top trim.

1898-1899		$2,300	$2,600
1900-1909		$2,300	$2,600
1910-1920		$2,300	$2,600

Style 6 Mandolin

1898-1921. Bowl back, top bound with ivory and abalone, vine or snowflake inlay.

1898-1921		$2,400	$2,700

Style 20S Mandolin

1949-1957. 30 made, special ordered for Carlos De-Filipis, decorative point on each side of body, oval sound hole, carved spruce top, carved curly maple back.

1949-1957		$2,150	$2,300

Style A Mandolin

1914-1995. Flat back, oval soundhole, dot inlay, solid headstock.

1914-1919		$975	$1,100
1920-1939		$1,000	$1,200
1940-1949		$950	$1,000
1950-1959		$875	$1,000
1960-1969		$850	$1,000
1970-1995		$750	$900

Style AK Mandolin

1920-1937. Koa wood version of Style A, flat back.

1920-1937		$1,300	$1,450

Style B Mandolin

1914-1946, 1981-1987. Flat back with bent top, spruce top and rosewood back and sides, herringbone back stripe, multi-bound.

1914-1919		$1,400	$1,500
1920-1939		$1,350	$1,650
1940-1946		$1,200	$1,500
1981-1987		$900	$1,100

Martin 2-15

1931 Martin Style B

MANDOLINS

1920 Martin Style C

Michael Kelly Legacy Plus

MANDOLINS

MODEL YEAR	FEATURES	EXC. COND. LOW	HIGH

Style BB Mandola
1917-1921, 1932-1939. Brazilian rosewood, herringbone trim, features like Style B mandolin. This is the only Mandola offered.

1917-1921		$1,700	$2,100

Style C Mandolin
1914-1934. Flat back.

1914-1934		$2,800	$3,000

Style D Mandolin
1914-1916. Flat back.

1914-1916		$4,600	$5,200

Style E Mandolin
1915-1937. Flat back, rosewood back and sides, bent spruce top, Style 45 snowflake fretboard inlay and other high-end appointments. Highest model cataloged.

1915-1919		$4,600	$5,300
1920-1937		$4,100	$4,800

Maurer
Late 1880s-1944. Brand started by Robert Maurer in Chicago, and continued by Carl and August Larson from 1900 to 1944. Early models were bowl-backs ranging from one model with 9 ribs to one with 50. Flat-backs were made as early as 1912. All were handmade with quality mahogany, rosewood or maple and appointments range from plain to presentation-grade. The Larsons built the same line for the Stahl label with some variations. Maurer Mandolins from the 1930s include Style 30 Flat Model, Style 40, Octave Mandola Style 45, Mandocello Style 50, and Mandola Tenor.

Mandolin
1920-1930. Brazilian rosewood, birdseye maple, bowl back.

1920-1930	Fancy, higher-end	$2,900	$3,600
1920-1930	Standard	$1,200	$1,400

May Flower
Ca. 1901-1910. H. J. Flower's Chicago-based May Flower Music Company offered bowl back mandolins that he may or may not have built. There were also May Flower harp guitars built by others.

Bowl Back Mandolin
1901-1910. Mid-level bowl back-style with 19 rosewood ribs and mid-level appointments.

1901-1910		$1,000	$1,200

Menzenhauer & Schmidt
1894-1904. Founded by Frederick Menzenhauer and Oscar Schmidt International. Menzenhauer created the guitar-zither in the U.S. He had several patents including one issued in September 1899 for a mandolin-guitar-zither. Control of operations quickly went to Oscar Schmidt.

12-String Mandolin
1890s. Bowl back mandolin with 3 strings per course that were tuned in octaves, designed during an experimental era for mandolin-related instrumetns, 13 rosewood ribs, spruce top, inlays.

1890s		$250	$300

MODEL YEAR	FEATURES	EXC. COND. LOW	HIGH

Michael Collins Guitars
2002-present. Luthier Michael Collins builds his professional and premium grade, production/custom, mandolins in Keswick, Ontario. He also builds guitars.

Michael Kelly
2000-present. Intermediate and professional grade, production, imported, acoustic and acoustic/electric mandolins. They also offer guitars and basses.

Michael Lewis Instruments
1992-present. Luthier Michael Lewis builds his premium grade, custom, mandolins in Grass Valley, California. He also builds guitars.

Mid-Missouri/The Big Muddy Mandolin Company
1995-present. Intermediate grade, production, acoustic and electric mandolins and mandolas built by luthier Michael Dulak in Columbia, Missouri. In late '06, they changed their name to The Big Muddy Mandolin Company.

M Series Mandolins
1995-present. Teardrop A-style body, solid spruce top, solid maple, mahogany or rosewood back and sides.

1995-1999	M-0	$300	$375
1995-1999	M-1	$350	$425
1995-1999	M-2	$400	$475
1995-1999	M-3	$450	$525
1995-1999	M-4	$525	$650

Mirabella
1997-present. Professional and premium grade, custom, mandolins built by luthier Cristian Mirabella in Babylon, New York. He also builds guitars, basses and ukes.

Mix
2007-present. Carbon fiber mandolins built by Peter Mix, Will Kimball, and Matt Durham of New Millennium Acoustic Design (NewMAD) in Waterville, Vermont.

Monteleone
1971-present. Primarily a guitar maker, luthier John Monteleone also builds presentation grade, custom, mandolins in West Islip, New York.

Grand Artist Mandola
1979-present. 15 7/8" scale until '90, then 17".

1990-1995		$20,000	$23,000

Grand Artist Mandolin
1977-present. Style F body, spruce top, curly maple back and sides, dot markers, currently offered in a Standard and Deluxe model.

1977-1989		$22,000	$24,000
1990-2003		$21,000	$23,000

MODEL YEAR	FEATURES	EXC. COND. LOW	HIGH

Radio Flyer Mandolin
1996-present. Style F body, currently offered in a Standard and Deluxe model.

1996-2000		$26,000	$28,000

Style B Mandolin
1982-1990s. Long A body style with long f-holes, flamed curly maple back and sides, elongated fretboard over body, sunburst.

1982-1990		$15,000	$17,000

Moon (Scotland)
1979-present. Intermediate and professional grade, production/custom, acoustics and acoustic/electric mandolins and mandolas built by luthier Jimmy Moon in Glasgow, Scotland. They also build guitars.

Morales
Ca.1967-1968. Japanese-made, not heavily imported into the U.S.

Electric Mandolin
1967-1968.

1967-1968		$275	$325

Morgan Monroe
1999-present. Intermediate and professional grade, production, acoustic mandolins made in Korea and distributed by SHS International of Indianapolis, Indiana. They also offer guitars, basses, banjos, and fiddles.

Morris
1967-present. Imported by Moridaira of Japan, Morris offered copy-era mandolins during the 1970s, including the popular F-5 style copy. They also build guitars.

Mozzani
Late-1800s-early-1900s. Founder Luigi Mozzani was an Italian (Bologna) master luthier and renowned composer and musician. There are original Mozzani-built mandolins and also factory-built instruments made later at various workshops.

Mandolin
Factory-built bowl back model.

1920s		$300	$375

Original Bowl Back Mandolin
Late-1800s-early-1900s. Handcrafted by Luigi Mozzani, about 24 ribs, soundhole ornamentation, snowflake-like markers.

1904		$1,125	$1,375

Muiderman Guitars
1997-present. Custom, premium grade, mandolins built by luthier Kevin Muiderman currently in Grand Forks, North Dakota, and previously in Beverly Hill, Michigan, 1997-2001, and Neenah, Wisconsin, '01-'07. He also builds guitars.

MODEL YEAR	FEATURES	EXC. COND. LOW	HIGH

National
Ca.1927-present. The National brand has gone through many ownership changes and offered resonator mandolins from around 1927 to '41. Currently, National does not offer a mandolin.

Style O Mandolin
1931-early-1940s. Metal body with Hawaiian scenes, single-cone resonator.

1930s		$3,000	$3,750

Style 1 Mandolin
1928-1936. Plain metal body, tri-cone resonator.

1928-1936	Single cone	$2,200	$2,500
1928-1936	Tricone version	$3,700	$4,000

Style 2 Mandolin
1928-1936. Metal body with rose engraving, tri-cone resonator.

1928-1936	Single cone	$4,300	$5,000
1928-1936	Tricone version	$6,600	$6,900

Style 3 Mandolin

1930s	Single cone	$5,600	$6,400
1930s	Tricone version	$6,600	$6,900

Style 97 Mandolin
1936-1940. Metal body, tri-cone resonator.

1936-1940		$5,600	$7,000

Triolian Mandolin
1928-1940. Metal body with palm trees, single-cone resonator.

1928-1940	Single cone	$1,900	$2,350

National Reso-Phonic
1988-present. Successors to the National name, with the designs and patented amplifying resonator assemblies of the original National models, they offer professional grade, production, mandolins from their shop in San Luis Obispo, California. They also build guitars, basses and ukuleles.

Northworthy
1987-present. Professional and premium grade, production/custom, mandolin-family instruments built by luthier Alan Marshall in Ashbourne, Derbyshire, England. He also builds guitars.

Nouveau (Gibson)
1986-1989. Mandolin bodies and necks made in Japan, assembled and finished in U.S. Became Nouveau (by Epiphone) in '88 and the brand was discontinued in '89. They also made guitars.

C7 Mandolin
1986-1987. F-style, white wood body and neck.

1986-1987		$1,900	$2,100

Nugget
1970s-present. Luthier Mike Kemnitzer builds his premium grade mandolins in Central Lake, Michigan.

Moon Master Series

National Style 2

MANDOLINS

Paris Swing John Jorgenson

Ratliff R-5

MANDOLINS

MODEL YEAR	FEATURES	EXC. COND. LOW	HIGH

Nyberg Instruments

1993-present. Professional grade, custom, mandolins and mandolas built by luthier Lawrence Nyberg in Hornby Island, British Columbia. He also builds guitars, bouzoukis and citterns.

O'Dell, Doug

See listing under Old Town.

Old Hickory

2005-present. Budget grade, production, imported F- and A-style acoustic mandolins from Musician's Wholesale America, Nashville, Tennessee. They also offer banjos.

Mandolins

2005	AC-100 mid-level	$65	$80
2005	FC-100 highest level	$125	$150
2005	M-1 lowest level	$40	$50

Old Kraftsman

1930s-1960s. Brand name used by the Siegel Company on instruments made by Kay and others (even Gibson). Quality was mixed, but some better-grade instruments were offered.

Mandolin

1950s		$275	$325

Old Town

1974-2007. Luthier Doug O'Dell built his professional and premium grade, production/custom acoustic and electric mandolins in Ohio.

EM-10 Electric Mandolin

1980s-2006. Double-cut, flamed maple top, 1 pickup, 2 control knobs.

1980s		$1,700	$2,000

Old Wave

1990-present. Luthier Bill Bussmann builds his professional and premium grade, production/custom, mandolins and mandolas in Caballo, New Mexico. He has also built guitars and basses.

Orpheum

1897-1942, 1944-early 1970s, 2001-present. Currently intermediate grade, production, mandolins. They also offer guitars. An old brand often associated with banjos, 1930s branded guitars sold by Bruno and Sons. 1950s branded guitars and mandolins sold by Maurice Lipsky Music, New York, New York.

Electric Mandolin Model 730 E

1950s. Private branded for Maurice Lipsky. Cataloged as a student model designed for ensemble playing. A-style body, single neck bar pickup, 2 side-mounted knobs, spruce top, maple back and sides, dot markers, sunburst.

1950s		$550	$650

Model No. 1 Mandolin-Banjo

1920s		$550	$650

Model No. 2 Mandolin-Banjo

1920s. Mandolin neck on small banjo body, fancy headstock and fretboard inlay, carved heel.

1920s		$550	$650

Oscar Schmidt

1879-ca. 1939, 1979-present. Currently offering budget and intermediate grade, production, mandolins. They also offer guitars, basses, banjos, ukuleles and the famous Oscar Schmidt autoharp. The original Schmidt company offered innovative mandolin designs during the 1900-'30

Mandolin Harp Style B

1890s. More zither-autoharp than mandolin, flat autoharp body with soundhole.

1890s		$150	$175

Sovereign Mandolin

1920s. Bowl back, bent top, rope-style binding, mahogany ribs, dot inlay, plain headstock, natural.

1920s	Fancy appointments	$600	$750
1920s	Standard appointments	$225	$275

Ovation

1966-present. Known for innovative fiberglass-backed bowl back acoustic and acoustic/electric guitars, Ovation added mandolins in '94 and currently offers intermediate and professional grade, production, mandolins and mandocellos. They also offer guitars and basses.

MSC148 (Celebrity) Mandolin

1994-present. Single-cut, small Ovation body, Ovation headstock, red sunburst.

1990s		$350	$425

P. W. Crump Company

1975-present. Luthier Phil Crump builds his custom mandolin-family instruments in Arcata, California. He also builds guitars.

Paris Swing

2005-present. Intermediate grade, production, imported acoustic mandolins from The Music Link, which also offers instruments under the Johnson and other brands.

Penco

Ca. 1974-1978. Japanese-made copies of classic American mandolins. They also made guitars, basses and banjos.

Phantom Guitar Works

1992-present. Intermediate grade, production, solidbody MandoGuitars assembled in Clatskanie, Oregon. They also build guitars and basses.

Phoenix

1990-present. Premium grade, production/custom, mandolins built by luthier Rolfe Gerhardt (formerly builder of Unicorn Mandolins in the '70s) in South Thomaston, Maine. Gerhardt's Phoenix

MODEL YEAR	FEATURES	EXC. COND. LOW	HIGH

company specializes in a 2-point Style A (double-cut) body style.

Premier

Ca.1938-ca.1975, 1990s-present. Brand produced by Peter Sorkin Music Company in New York City. Around '57 the company acquired Strad-O-Lin and many of their mandolins were offered under that brand. By '75, the Premier brand went into hiatus. The Premier brand currently appears on Asian-made solidbody guitars and basses.

Ramsey

1990s. Built by luthier John Ramsey of Colorado Springs, Colorado.

Randy Wood Guitars

1968-present. Premium and presentation grade, custom/production, mandolins, mandolas, and mandocellos built by luthier Randy Woods in Bloomingdale, Georgia. He also builds guitars.

Ratliff

1982-present. Professional and premium grade, production/custom, mandolin family instruments built in Church Hill, Tennessee.

R-5 Mandolin

1990s-present. F-5 style, carved spruce top, figured maple back and sides.

1995-2004		$2,000	$2,400

Recording King

1929-1943. Montgomery Ward house brand. Suppliers include Gibson, Kay, Regal, and Gretsch.

Mandolin

1929-1940. Gibson-made, A-style body, sunburst.

1930s		$500	$600

Regal

Ca.1884-1954. Large Chicago-based manufacturer which made their own brand name and others for distributors and mass merchandisers. Absorbed by the Harmony Company in 1955.

Mandolin

1920s	Flat-top A-style	$400	$475
1930s	Sunburst, standard model	$400	$500
1930s	Ultra Grand Deluxe model	$800	$1,000

Octophone Mandolin

1920s. Octave mandolin, long body with double points, round soundhole.

1920s		$775	$925

Resonator Mandolin

1950s		$450	$550

Rickenbacker

1931-present. Rickenbacker had the Electro Mandolin in the late '30s and introduced 4-, 5- and 8-string electric models in 1958 and currently offers one model.

Model 5002V58

1997-present. Symmetrical solidbody with small lap steel appearance, 1 pickup, 2 knobs, reissue of '50s 8-string.

1997-2002		$975	$1,200

Rigel

1990-2006. Professional and premium grade, production/custom mandolins and mandolas built by luthier Pete Langdell in Hyde Park, Vermont.

A-Plus Series Mandolins

1990s-2006. A-style body, carved spruce top, maple back and sides, dot markers.

1990s	F-holes	$1,200	$1,400
1990s	Oval soundhole	$1,100	$1,300

Classic S Mandolin

2000s. Double cutaway, f-holes.

2000s		$1,700	$1,900

Model G-110 Mandolin

1990-2006. Maple neck, back and sides, red spruce top, f-holes, sunburst.

1990s		$2,100	$2,300

Roberts

1980s. Built by luthier Jay Roberts of California.

Tiny Moore Jazz 5 Mandolin

1980s. Based on Bigsby design of the early-1950s as used by Tiny Moore, five-string electric, sunburst.

1985		$1,550	$1,925

Rogue

2001-present. Budget grade, production, imported mandolins. They also offer guitars, basses, ukes, and banjos.

Rono

1967-present. Luthier Ron Oates builds his professional grade, production/custom, electric mandolins in Boulder, Colorado. He also builds basses and guitars.

Ryder

1991-present. Luthier Steve Ryder builds his professional grade, production/custom solid and semi-hollowbody electric mandolins, mandola and octave mandolins in South Portland, Maine.

S. S. Stewart

1878-1904. S.S. Stewart of Philadelphia was primarily known for banjos. Legend has it that Stewart was one of the first to demonstrate the mass production assembly of stringed instruments.

Mandolin Banjo

Early-1900s. Mandolin neck and a very small open back banjo body, star inlay in headstock.

1900s		$400	$450

1976 Regal Bicentennial

Rigel A-Plus Oval Deluxe

MANDOLINS

Sawchyn F-Style

Stella pear-shape

MODEL		EXC. COND.	
YEAR	FEATURES	LOW	HIGH

Samick

1958-2001, 2002-present. Budget and intermediate grade, production, imported acoustic and acoustic/electric mandolins. They also offer guitars, basses, ukes and banjos.

Sammo

1920s. Labels in these instruments state they were made by the Osborne Mfg. Co. with an address of Masonic Temple, Chicago, Illinois. High quality and often with a high degree of ornamentation. They also made ukes and guitars.

Sawchyn

1972-present. Intermediate and professional grade, production/custom, mandolins built by luthier Peter Sawchyn in Regina, Saskatchewan. He also builds flat-top and flamenco guitars.

Sekova

Mid-1960s-mid-1970s. Entry level, imported by the U.S. Musical Merchandise.
Electric Mandolin
1960s-1970s. Kay-Kraft-style hollowbody with f-holes, 1 pickup and Sekova logo on the headstock.

1965-1970s		$275	$325

Sigma

1970-2007. Budget and intermediate grade, production, import mandolins distributed by C.F. Martin Company. They also offered guitars and banjos.
SM6 Mandolin
1970s-present. Made in Korea.

1980s		$200	$250

Silvertone

1941-ca.1970. Brand name used by Sears on their musical instruments.
Mandolin
1941-ca.1970. Arched top and back, sunburst.

1940s		$180	$225
1950s		$175	$200

Smart Musical Instruments

1986-present. Premium and presentation grade, custom, mandolin family instruments built by luthier A. Lawrence Smart in McCall, Idaho. He also builds guitars.

Sovereign

Ca. 1899-ca. 1938. Sovereign was originally a brand of the Oscar Schmidt company of New Jersey. In the late '30s, Harmony purchased several trade names from the Schmidt Company, including Sovereign. Sovereign then ceased as a brand, but Harmony continued using it on a model line of Harmony guitars.
Mandolin
1920s. Old-style bent top.

1920s		$275	$325

Stahl

The William C. Stahl music publishing company claimed their instruments were made in Milwaukee, Wisconsin, in the early-1900s, but the Larson Brothers of Maurer & Co., Chicago, built a line of mandolin orchestra pieces them. Models followed their Maurer line. Models included Style 4 (22 ribs) to Style 12 Presentation Artist Special. The more expensive models were generally 44-rib construction.
Arched Back Presentation Mandolin
1910s. Brazilian rosewood back and sides, very fancy abalone appointments.

1910s		$2,325	$2,900

Bowl Back Mandolin (Deluxe Professional)
1910's. Rosewood, 40 ribs.

1910s		$1,000	$1,250

Bowl Back Mandolin (Mid-Level)
1910s. Pearl floral design on 'guard, 32 ribs.

1910s		$400	$500

Flat Back Mandolin

1920s	Rosewood sides/back	$2,300	$2,700

Stathopoulo

1903-1916. Original design instruments, some patented, by Epiphone company founder A. Stathopoulo.
A-Style Mandolin
1903-1916. A-style with higher-end appointments, bent-style spruce top, figured maple back and sides.

1912		$900	$1,100

Stefan Sobell Musical Instruments

1982-present. Luthier Stefan Sobell builds his premium grade, production/custom, mandolins in Hetham, Northumberland, England. He also builds guitars, citterns and bouzoukis.
10-String Mandolin

1982-1990s		$2,900	$3,600

Stella

Ca. 1899-1974, present. Stella was a brand of the Oscar Schmidt Company which was an early contributor to innovative mandolin designs and participated in the 1900-'30 mandolin boom. Pre-World War II Stella instruments were low-mid to mid-level instruments. In '39, Harmony purchased the Stella name and '50s and '60s Stella instruments were student grade, low-end instruments. The Stella brand has been reintroduced by MBT International.
Banjo-Mandolin
1920s. One of several innovative designs that attempted to create a new market, 8-string mandolin neck with a banjo body, Stella logo normally impressed on the banjo rim or the side of the neck.

1920s		$200	$250

MODEL YEAR	FEATURES	EXC. COND. LOW	HIGH

Bowl-Back Mandolin
1920s. Typical bowl back, bent top-style mandolin with models decalomania, about 10 (wide) maple ribs, dot markers.

1920s		$175	$200

Pear-Shape Mandolin
1940s-1960s. Harmony-made lower-end mandolins, pear-shaped (Style A) flat back, oval soundhole.

1940s	Natural	$200	$250
1950s		$200	$250
1960s	Sunburst	$200	$250

Stelling
1974-present. Mainly known for banjos, Stelling also build premium grade, production/custom mandolins in Afton, Virginia.

Sterling
Early-1900s. Distributed by wholesalers The Davitt & Hanser Music Co.

Stiver
Professional and premium grade, custom/production, mandolins built by luthier Lou Stiver in Pennsylvania.

Strad-O-Lin
Ca.1920s-ca.1960s. The Strad-O-Lin company was operated by the Hominic brothers in New York, primarily making mandolins for wholesalers. In the late '50s, Multivox/Premier bought the company and used the name on mandolins and guitars.

Baldwin Electric Mandolin
1950s. A-Style, single pickup, tone and volume knobs, spruce top, maple back and sides, Baldwin logo on headstock.

1950s	Natural	$400	$450

Junior A Mandolin
1950s. A-Style, Stradolin Jr. logo on headstock, dot markers.

1950s	Sunburst	$250	$350

Stromberg-Voisinet
1921-ca.1932. Marketed Stromberg (not to be confused with Charles Stromberg of Boston) and Kay Kraft brands, plus instruments of other distributors and retailers. Became the Kay Musical Instrument Company. By the mid-'20s, the company was making many better Montgomery Ward guitars, banjos and mandolins, often with lots of pearloid. The last Stromberg acoustic instruments were seen in '32.

Summit
1990-present. Professional and premium grade, production/custom mandolins built by luthier Paul Schneider in Hartsville, Tennessee. He was originally located in Mulvane, Kansas.

Superior
1987-present. Intermediate grade, production/custom mandolin-family instruments made in Mexico for George Katechis Montalvo of Berkeley Musical Instrument Exchange. They also offer guitars.

Supertone
1914-1941. Brand used by Sears before they switched to Silvertone. Instruments made by other companies.

Mandolin
Spruce top, mahogany back and sides, some with decalomania vine pattern on top.

1920s		$225	$275
1930s	Decalomania vine pattern	$225	$275

Supro
1935-1968, 2004-present. Budget line from the National Dobro Company. Amp builder Bruce Zinky revived the Supro name for a guitar and amp model.

T30 Electric Mandolin

1950s		$525	$625

T. H. Davis
1976-present. Premium grade, custom, mandolins built by luthier Ted Davis in Loudon, Tennessee. He also builds guitars.

Tacoma
1995-present. Tacoma offered intermediate, professional and premium grade, production, electric and acoustic mandolins up to '06. They also build guitars and basses.

M Series Mandolins
1999-2006. Solid spruce top, typical Tacoma body-style with upper bass bout soundhole, E (i.e. M-1E) indicates acoustic/electric.

1999-2004	M2, rosewood	$375	$450
1999-2006	M1, mahogany	$350	$425
1999-2006	M1E, mahogany	$350	$425
1999-2006	M3/M3E, maple	$600	$725

Tennessee
1970-1993, 1996-present. Luthier Mark Taylor builds his professional and premium grade, production/custom, mandolins in Old Hickory, Tennessee. He also builds guitars, banjos and the Tut Taylor brand of resophonic guitars.

Timeless Instruments
1980-present. Luthier David Freeman builds his intermediate grade, mandolins in Tugaske, Saskatchewan. He also builds guitars and dulcimers.

Triggs
1992-present. Luthiers Jim Triggs and his son Ryan build their professional and premium grade, production/custom, mandolins in Kansas City, Kansas. They also build guitars. They were located in Nashville, Tennessee until '98.

2000 Summit J.M. model

Triggs Mando

MANDOLINS

1921 Vega Style L Whyte Laydie mandolin-banjo

MODEL YEAR	FEATURES	EXC. COND. LOW	HIGH

Trinity River

2004-present. Production/custom, budget and intermediate grade, mandolins imported from Asia by luthiers Marcus Lawyer and Ross McLeod in Fort Worth, Texas. They also import guitars, basses and banjos.

Unicorn

1970s-late 1980s. Luthier Rolfe Gerhardt (currently luthier for Phoenix Mandolins) founded Unicorn in the mid-'70s. Gerhardt built 149 mandolins before selling Unicorn to Dave Sinko in '80. Sinko closed Unicorn in the late-'80s.

Vega

1903-present. The original Boston-based company was purchased by C.F. Martin in '70. Vega means star and a star logo is often seen on the original Vega instruments. In '80, the Vega trademark was sold to a Korean company. The Deering Banjo Company, in Spring Valley, California acquired the brand in '89 and uses it (and the star logo) on a line of banjos.

Lansing Special Bowl Mandolin
1890s. Spruce top, abalone, vine inlay.

1890s		$450	$550

Little Wonder Mandolin Banjo
Maple neck, resonator.

1920s		$450	$550

Mando Bass Mandolin
1910s-1920s. Large upright bass-sized instrument with bass tuners, body-style similar to dual-point A-style, scroll headstock.

1910-1920s		$2,800	$3,500

Mandolin Cittern
1910s. 10-string (five double strings tuned in 5ths), vague A-style with oval soundhole and cylinder back, natural.

1910s		$1,800	$2,200

Style 202 Lute Mandolin
Early-1900s. Basic A-style with small horns, natural spruce top, mahogany sides and cylinder back, dot markers.

1910s		$1,100	$1,350

Style 205 Cylinder Back Mandolin
1910s-1920s. Rounded tube cylinder shape runs the length of the back.

1910s		$1,600	$1,800
1920s		$1,300	$1,600

Style A Mandolin

1910s		$475	$575

Style F Mandolin
1910s. Scroll upper bass bout, oval soundhole, Vega and torch inlay in headstock.

1910s		$800	$950

MODEL YEAR	FEATURES	EXC. COND. LOW	HIGH

Style K Mandolin Banjo

1910-1930s		$425	$525

Style L Banjo Mandolin/Whyte Laydie
1910s-1920s. Open back banjo body and mandolin 8-string neck.

1910-1920s		$1,100	$1,350

Super Deluxe Mandolin

1910s	Sunburst	$675	$800

Tubaphone Style X Mandolin Banjo

1923		$675	$800

Veillette

1991-present. Luthiers Joe Veillette and Martin Keith build their professional grade, production/custom, mandolins in Woodstock, New York. They also build basses and guitars.

Vinaccia

Italian-made by Pasquale Vinaccia, luthier.

Bowl Back Mandolin
High-end appointments and 'guard, 30 rosewood ribs.

1900-1920s		$2,000	$2,500

Vivi-Tone

1933-ca. 1936. Lloyd Loar's pioneering guitar company also built early electric mandolins and mandocellos in Kalamazoo, Michigan.

Electric Mandocello
1933-1935. Traditonal guitar-arch body, Vivi-Tone silkscreen logo on headstock.

1933-1935		$5,500	$6,500

Electric Mandola
1933-1935. Traditonal European teardrop/pear-shaped top, Vivi-Tone silkscreen logo on headstock.

1933-1935		$4,500	$5,500

Electric Mandolin
1933-1935. Vivi-Tone silkscreen logo on headstock.

1933-1935		$4,000	$5,000

Waldo

1891- early 1900s. Mandolin family instruments built in Saginaw, Michigan.

Bowl Back Mandolin
1890s. Alternating rosewood and maple ribs, some with script Waldo logo on pickguard.

1890s		$175	$200

Ward

Depression era private brand made by Gibson's Kalamazoo factory.

Style A Mandolin
1930s. Style A body with round soundhole and flat top and back, dot markers, mahogany back and sides, silkscreened Ward logo.

1935	Sunburst	$275	$325

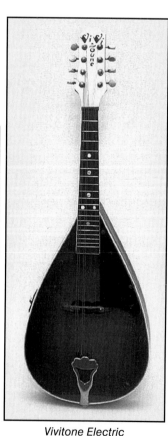

Vivitone Electric

MANDOLINS

MODEL YEAR	FEATURES	EXC. COND. LOW	HIGH

Washburn (Lyon & Healy)

1880s-ca.1949. Washburn was founded in Chicago as one of the lines for Lyon & Healy to promote high quality stringed instruments, ca. 1880s. The rights to Washburn were sold to Regal which built Washburns by the mid-'30s until until ca. '49. In '74 the brand resurfaced.

Bowl Back Mandolin
1890s-1900s. Lyon and Healy sold a wide variety of bowl back mandolins, Brazilian ribs with fancy inlays and bindings.

MODEL YEAR	FEATURES	LOW	HIGH
1890s	Fancy inlays and bindings	$700	$875
1890s	Plain appointments	$300	$350
1900s	Fancy inlays and bindings	$700	$875
1900s	Plain appointments	$300	$350
1900s	Standard appointments	$300	$350

Style A Mandolin
1920s. Brazilian rosewood.

1920s		$800	$1,000

Style E Mandolin
1915-1923. Brazilian rosewood.

1915-1923		$1,000	$1,200

Washburn (Post 1974)

1974-present. Currently, Washburn offers imported intermediate and professional grade, production, mandolins.

Mandolin/Mandolin Family
1974-present.

1974-2005		$375	$450

Washington

Washington mandolins were manufactured by Kansas City, Missouri instrument wholesalers J.W. Jenkins & Sons. First introduced in 1895, the brand also offered guitars.

Weber

1996-present. Intermediate, professional, and premium grade, production/custom, mandolins, mandolas, and mandocellos. Many former Flatiron employees, including Bruce Weber, formed Sound To Earth, Ltd., to build Weber instruments when Gibson moved Flatiron from Bozeman, Montana, to Nashville. Originally in Belgrade, Montana, and since '04, in Logan, Montana. They also build guitars.

Aspen #1 Mandolin
1997-present. Teardrop A-style, solid spruce top, maple sides and back, mahogany neck.

1990s		$750	$825

Aspen #2 Mandolin
1997-present. Like #1, but with maple neck.

2000s		$925	$1,025

Beartooth Mandolin
1997-present. Teardrop A-style, solid spruce top, curly maple sides, back, and neck.

2000s		$1,800	$2,000

Fern Mandolin
1997-present. F-style, top of the product line.

2000s		$3,200	$3,600

Yellowstone Mandolin
1997-present. F-style, solid spruce top, curly maple sides, back, and neck, sunburst.

1997-2006		$2,000	$2,200

Weymann

1864-1940s. H.A. Weymann & Sons was a musical instrument distributor located in Philadelphia. They also built their own instruments.

Keystone State Banjo Mandolin
1910s. Maple rim and back, ebony fretboard.

1910s		$325	$400

Model 20 Mando-Lute
1920s. Lute-style body, spruce top, flamed maple sides and back, rope binding, deluxe rosette, natural.

1920s		$600	$700

Model 24 Mandolin Banjo
1920s		$350	$425

Model 40 Mandolin Banjo
1910s-1920s. Mandolin neck on a open banjo body with a larger sized 10" head.

1920s	10" or 11" rim	$450	$550

Model 50 Mando-Lute
1920s		$600	$700

Wurlitzer

The old Wurlitzer company would have been considered a mega-store by today's standards. They sold a wide variety of instruments, gave music lessons, and operated manufacturing facilities.

Mandolin
1920s	Koa	$525	$650

Mandolin Banjo
1900s. Mandolin neck on open back banjo body, plain-style.

1900s		$225	$275

Yosco

1900-1930s. Lawrence L. Yosco was a New York City luthier building guitars, round back mandolins and banjos under his own brand and for others.

Zeta

1982-present. Zeta has made professional grade, acoustic/electric mandolins in Oakland, California over the years, but currently only offer upright basses, amps and violins.

Washburn M1S

Weber Absaroka

MANDOLINS

Ukuleles

Aero Uke

Beltona The Blue Uke

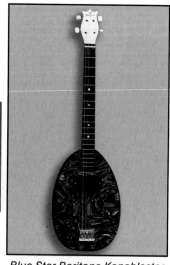

Blue Star Baritone Konablaster

UKULELES

MODEL YEAR	FEATURES	EXC. COND. LOW	HIGH

Aero Uke

1920s. Never branded, but almost certainly produced by Chicago's Stromberg-Voisenet Company, the precursor of Kay, the Aero Uke is an instrument quite unlike any other. With its spruce-capped body resembling an old-timey airplane wing and a neck and headstock that approximate a plane's fuselage, this clever '20s offering cashed in on the Lindbergh craze (like the Harmony Johnny Marvin model with its airplane-shaped bridge), and must have been a big hit at parties.

Aero Ukulele
Airplane body.

1927	Black deco on wing	$2,500	$3,000
1927	Gold deco on wing	$2,700	$3,200

Aloha

1935-1960s. The Aloha brand turns up on numerous vastly different ukes. In fact, the variety of features exhibited by Aloha ukuleles leads the modern observer to believe that the ukes that bear this headstock decal were made by as many as a dozen different manufacturers, each with access to the same logo. Many were undoubtedly Island-made, with all koa bodies and some with fancy rope binding; others bear unmistakable mainland traits. Some of these have a more traditional look and are stamped Akai inside the soundhole, while still others, strongly resembling mainland C.F. Martins in design, typically sport a decal of the Sam F. Chang curio shop on the reverse of the headstock.

Akai Soprano Ukulele
Koa construction.

1930s		$500	$700

Soprano Ukulele
Koa body, plain.

1950s		$500	$700

Andy Powers Musical Instrument Co.

1996-present. Luthier Andy Powers, builds his professional grade, custom, ukuleles in Oceanside, California. He also builds guitars and mandolins.

Applause

1976-present. Kaman Music's entry-level Ovation-styled import brand Applause currently offers budget and intermediate grade, production, soprano and tenor ukuleles.

Bear Creek Guitars

1995-present. Intermediate and professional grade ukuleles built by luthier Bill Hardin in Kula, Hawaii. He also builds guitars.

Beltona

1990-present. Production metal body resonator ukuleles made in New Zealand by Steve Evans and Bill Johnson. Beltona was originally located in England. They also build guitars.

Blue Star

1984-present. Intermediate grade, production, custom, acoustic and electric ukuleles built by luthier Bruce Herron in Fennville, Michigan. He also builds guitars, mandolins, dulcimers and lap steels.

Bruno

1834-present. This New York distributor certainly subcontracted all of its ukulele production to other manufacturers, and as a result you'd be hard pressed to find two identical Bruno ukes.

Soprano Ukulele

1920s	Koa, rope soundhole	$350	$450
1930s	Koa, rope bound body	$400	$600

Chantus

1984-present. Professional grade, production/custom, ukuleles built in Austin, Texas, by luthier William King. He also builds guitars.

DeCava Guitars

1983-present. Professional grade, production/custom, ukuleles built by luthier Jim DeCava in Stratford, Connecticut. He also builds guitars, banjos, and mandolins.

Del Vecchio Dimonaco

With a design patterned after the pioneering work of Dobro and National, this Brazilian company produced a full line of resonator instruments, all constructed of native Brazilian rosewood, from the 1950s onward.

Resonator Ukulele
Brazilian rosewood.

1950s		$750	$900

Ditson

1916-1930. Don't be fooled. While some of the ukes that were commissioned by this East Coast music publisher and chain store were actually manufactured by C.F. Martin, Martin was by no means the sole supplier. The Martin-made instruments often bear a Martin brand as well as a Ditson one, or, barring that, at least demonstrate an overall similarity to the rest of the ukes in the regular Martin line, both inside and out. The most telling and desirable feature of these Martin-made Ditsons is a dreadnaught-style wide waisted body design.

Soprano Ukulele

1922	as Martin Style 1 K	$2,000	$2,500
1922	as Martin Style 1 M	$1,200	$1,400
1922	as Martin Style 2 K	$2,500	$3,000
1922	as Martin Style 2 M	$1,500	$1,700
1922	as Martin Style 3 K	$3,000	$4,000
1922	as Martin Style 3 M	$2,500	$3,000
1922	as Martin Style 5 K	$10,000	$15,000
1922	as Martin Style O	$1,000	$1,200

MODEL YEAR	FEATURES	EXC. COND. LOW	HIGH

Dobro

1929-1942, ca. 1954-present. The ukulele version of the popular amplifying resonator instruments first produced in California, the Dobro uke was offered in 2 sizes (soprano and tenor), 2 styles (f-holes and screen holes), and 2 colors (brown and black). Models with Dobro headstock decals are often outwardly indistinguishable from others bearing either a Regal badge or no logo at all, but a peek inside often reveals the presence of a sound well in the belly of the former, making them the more desirable of the two.

Resonator Ukulele
Wood body.

Year	Features	Low	High
1930s	F-holes, Regal-made	$500	$1,000
1930s	Screen holes	$750	$1,000

Douglas Ching

1976-present. Luthier Douglas J. Ching builds his professional grade, production/custom, ukuleles currently in Chester, Virginia, and previously in Hawaii ('76-'89) and Michigan ('90-'93). He also builds guitars, lutes and violins.

Earnest Kaai

Hawaiian Earnest Kaai was many things (teacher, songbook publisher, importer/exporter) during the early part of the 20th century, but ukulele manufacturer was certainly one job that he couldn't add to his resume. Still, scads of ukes proudly bear his name, in a variety of different styles and variations. Even more puzzling is the fact that while some appear to actually have been island-made, an equal number bear the telltale signs of mainland manufacture. Some Kaai labeled ukes may have been made by the Larson Brothers of Chicago.

Soprano Ukulele
Koa body.

Year	Features	Low	High
1925	No binding, decal on headstock	$300	$400
1930	No binding, rope inlaid soundhole	$500	$700
1935	Pearl inlaid top and soundhole	$1,500	$2,000
1935	Rope binding on top and back only	$700	$900

Epiphone

Ca. 1873-present. Epiphone made banjo ukes in the 1920s and '30s and recently got back into the market with koa and mahogany models.

Favilla

1890-1973. The small New York City family-owned factory that produced primarily guitars also managed to offer some surprisingly high quality ukes, the best of which rival Martin and Gibson for craftsmanship and tone. As a result, Favilla ukuleles are a real value for the money.

Baritone Ukulele

Year	Features	Low	High
1950s	Plain mahogany body	$500	$750

MODEL YEAR	FEATURES	EXC. COND. LOW	HIGH

Soprano Ukulele

Year	Features	Low	High
1950s	Mahogany body, triple bound	$500	$750
1950s	Plain mahogany body	$500	$700
1950s	Teardrop-shaped, birch body	$300	$500
1950s	Teardrop-shaped, stained blue	$400	$600

Fender

Fender offered Regal-made ukuleles in the 1960s, including the R-275 Baritone Ukulele.

Fin-der

1950s. The pitch of this short-lived plastic ukulele was apparently the ease of learning, since the included instructional brochure helped you to "find" your chords with the added help of rainbow color-coded nylon strings.

Diamond Head Ukulele
Styrene plastic, in original box.

Year	Low	High
1950s	$150	$250

Fine Resophonic

1988-present. Intermediate and professional grade, production/custom, wood and metal-bodied resophonic ukuleles built by luthiers Mike Lewis and Pierre Avocat in Vitry Sur Seine, France. They also build guitars and mandolins.

Flamingo

1950s. If swanky designs hot-foil stamped into the surface of these '50s swirly injection molded polystyrene ukes didn't grab you, certainly the built-in functional pitch pipe across the top of the headstock would. And I ask you, who can resist a ukulele with a built-in tuner?

Soprano Ukulele

Year	Features	Low	High
1955	Brown top, white 'board	$150	$200
1955	White top, brown 'board	$150	$200

Gibson

1890s (1902)-present. A relative late-comer to the uke market, Gibson didn't get a line off the ground until 1927, fully nine years after Martin had already been in production. Even then they only produced three soprano styles and one tenor version. Worse still, they never made any ukes in koa, sticking to the easier-to-obtain mahogany.

Nonetheless, Gibson ukuleles exhibit more unintentional variety than any other major maker, with enough construction, inlay, binding, and cosmetic variations to keep collectors buzzing for many a year to come. In general, the earliest examples feature a Gibson logo in script, later shortened to just Gibson. Post-war examples adopted the more square-ish logo of the rest of the Gibson line, and, at some point in the late '50s, began sporting ink-

ca. 1916 Earnest Kaai

Epiphone Masterbilt UKE-500M

Fine Resophonic Model 3

UKULELES

Gibson TU-1

Gibson Uke-1

Graziano Concert

UKULELES

MODEL YEAR	FEATURES	EXC. COND. LOW	HIGH

stamped serial numbers on the back of the head-stock like their guitar and mandolin brethren.

ETU 1 Ukulele
Electric tenor, unbound body, square black pickup, 88 made.

1949		$3,500	$5,000

ETU 3 Ukulele
Electric tenor, triple bound body, rectangle pickup, rare.

1953		$5,000	$7,500

TU-1 Ukulele
Tenor, called the TU until 1 added in 1949, mahogany body, sunburst finish.

1930s		$850	$1,100

Uke-1 Ukulele
Soprano, plain mahogany body.

1927		$1,000	$1,250
1966	Red SG guitar-like finish	$750	$900

Uke-2 Ukulele
Soprano, mahogany body.

1934	Triple bound	$750	$1,000

Uke-3 Ukulele
Soprano, dark finish.

1933	Diamonds and squares inlay	$1,500	$1,750
1935	Diamond inlay, short 'board	$800	$1,200
1935	Rare curved designs inlay	$2,000	$2,500

Gold Tone
1993-present. Wayne and Robyn Rogers build their intermediate grade, production/custom ukuleles in Titusville, Florida. They also offer guitars, basses, lap steels, mandolins, banjos and banjitars.

Graziano
1969-present. Luthier Tony Graziano has been building ukuleles almost exclusively since '95 in his Santa Cruz shop. Like many, he sees the uke as the instrument of the new millennium, and his entirely handmade, custom orders can be had in a variety of shapes, sizes, and woods.

Gretsch
1883-present. The first (and most desirable) ukuleles by this New York manufacturer were actually stamped with the name Gretsch American or with interior brass nameplates. Subsequent pieces, largely inexpensive laminate-bodied catalog offerings, are distinguished by small round Gretsch headstock decals, and a lack of any kerfed linings inside the bodies.

Plain Soprano Ukulele
Natural mahogany body, no binding.

1950s		$100	$150

Round Ukulele
Round body, blue to green sunburst.

1940		$150	$200

MODEL YEAR	FEATURES	EXC. COND. LOW	HIGH

Soprano Ukulele

1940s	Koa wood body, fancy 'board inlay	$750	$900
1940s	Mahogany body, fancy 'board inlay	$650	$800
1940s	Unbound body, engraved rose in peghead	$800	$1,000
1950s	Darker finish, bordered in dark binding	$300	$450

Guild
1952-present. By rights this fine East Coast shop should have produced a full line of ukes to complement its impressive flat and carved-top guitar offerings. Alas, a lone baritone model was all that they could manage. And it's a darned shame, too.

B-11 Baritone Ukulele
1963-1976. Mahogany body, rosewood 'board.

1960s		$500	$750

Harmony
1892-1976, late 1970s-present. This manufacturer surely produced more ukuleles than all other makers put together. Their extensive line ran the gamut from artist endorsed models and ukes in unusual shapes and materials, to inexpensive but flashy creations adorned with eye-catching decals and silk screening. The earliest examples have a small paper label on the back of the headstock, and a branded logo inside the body. This was replaced by a succession of logo decals applied to the front of the headstock, first gold and black, later green, white, and black. By the '60s Harmony had become so synonymous with ukulele production that they were known around their Chicago locale as simply "the ukulele factory," as in, "Ma couldn't come to the bar-b-que on-a-counta she got a job at the ukulele factory."

Baritone Ukulele
Bound mahogany body.

1960s		$250	$350

Concert Ukulele
Mahogany body, bound, concert-sized.

1935		$250	$300

Harold Teen Ukulele
Carl Ed cartoon decals on front.

1930	Gray-blue	$400	$500
1930	Red	$400	$500
1930	Yellow	$400	$550

Johnny Marvin Tenor Ukulele
Sports an airplane bridge.

1930s	Flamed koa	$700	$900
1930s	Sunburst mahogany	$500	$600

Roy Smeck Concert Ukulele
Concert-sized, sunburst spruce top.

1935		$400	$500

Roy Smeck Ukulele
Mahogany body.

1955	Plastic 'board	$150	$200
1955	Wood 'board	$350	$450

MODEL YEAR	FEATURES	EXC. COND. LOW	HIGH
Roy Smeck Vita Ukulele	*Pear-shaped body, seal-shaped f-holes.*		
1926		$750	$1,000
Tiple Ukulele	*Multicolored binding, 10 steel strings.*		
1935		$600	$850
Ukulele			
1930	Koa body, unbound	$250	$500
1935	Plain mahogany body, unbound	$300	$400

Hilo Bay Ukuleles

2003-present. Intermediate grade, production, tenor ukuleles made in Cebu City, Philippines for Hilo Guitars and Ukuleles of Hilo, Hawaii.

Hohner

1857-present. They currently offer budget grade, tenor, baritone, standard, pineapple, and concert ukuleles. They also have guitars, basses, banjos, and mandolins.

Johnson

Mid-1990s-present. Budget ukuleles imported by Music Link of Brisbane, California. They also offer guitars, amps, mandolins and effects. Most notable of the Johnson ukes are the National metal-bodied uke copies, which come surprisingly close to the look and feel of the originals, at an unfathomably low price.

K & S

1992-1998. Ukes distributed by George Katechis and Marc Silber and handmade in Paracho, Mexico. They also offered guitars. In '98, Silber started marketing the ukes under the Marc Silber Guitar Company brand and Katechis continued to offer instruments under the Casa Montalvo brand.

Kala

2005-present. Mike Upton's Petaluma, California company offers budget and intermediate grade, production, ukuleles.

Kamaka

Part of the second wave of ukulele builders on the Hawaiian islands (after Nunes, Dias, and Santos) Kamaka distinguished itself first with ukes of extremely high quality, subsequently with the most enduring non-guitar-derived designs, the Pineapple Uke, patented in 1928. Kamaka is the only maker which has been in continuous production for nearly a hundred years, offering Hawaiian-made products from native woods in virtually every size and ornamentation. In the early '70s, Kamaka began rubber stamping the full date of manufacture on the end of the neck block of each uke, visible right through the sound hole. Now don't you wish that every manufacturer did that?

MODEL YEAR	FEATURES	EXC. COND. LOW	HIGH
Concert Ukulele	*Koa body, extended rosewood 'board.*		
1975		$600	$750
Lili'u Ukulele	*Concert-sized koa body.*		
1965	8 strings	$800	$1,000
1985	6 strings	$800	$1,000
Pineapple Ukulele			
1925	Pearl inlay on top and/or 'board	$3,500	$4,000
1925	Pineapple art painted onto top or back	$2,500	$3,000
1930	Monkeypod wood, plain, unbound	$1,500	$1,700
1930	Rope bound top only, koawood body	$2,500	$3,000
1935	Rope bound soundhole only	$1,500	$1,700
1960	Koa body, unbound, 2 Ks logo	$1,200	$1,500
1970	Koa body, extended rosewood 'board	$1,000	$1,200
Soprano Ukulele	*Traditional uke shape, plain koa body.*		
1920		$600	$800
Tenor Ukulele	*Koa body, extended rosewood 'board.*		
1955		$600	$750

Kanile'a Ukulele

1998-present. Joseph and Kristen Souza build their intermediate, professional and premium grade, production/custom, ukuleles in Kaneohe, Hawaii.

Kay

1931-present. Kay offered banjo ukuleles in the 1920s and again in the late '50s; they offered ukuleles from '66-'68 and currently offer budget grade, production, imported ukuleles. They also make amps, guitars, banjos, mandolins, basses, and violins.

Kent

1961-1969. Large, student quality ukes of laminated construction were offered by this Japanese concern throughout the '60s.

Baritone Ukulele
Mahogany body, bound top, bound back.

1960s		$150	$200

Knutsen

1890s-1920s. While Christopher Knutsen was the inventor of flat-topped harp instruments featuring an integral sound chamber on the bass side of the body, he almost certainly left the manufacturing to others. Striking in both concept and design, Knutsen products nonetheless suffer from compromised construction techniques.

Hilo Baritone

Kala KA-KB

Kamaka Pineapple Uke Style-1

UKULELES

Kumalae Style 1

Lanikai LU11

Leonardo Nunes

MODEL YEAR	FEATURES	EXC. COND. LOW	HIGH
Harp Taro Patch Ukulele			
Koa body, large horn chamber, 8 strings, unbound.			
1915		$4,000	$5,500
Harp Ukulele			
Koa body, large horn chamber.			
1915	Bound	$4,000	$5,000
1915	Unbound	$3,500	$5,000

Kumalae

Along with Kamaka, Kumalae was also of the second wave of Hawaiian uke makers. Jonah Kumalae's company quickly snagged the prestigious Gold Award at the Pan Pacific Exhibition in 1915, and the headstock decals and paper labels aren't about to let you forget it, either. Many assume that these all date from exactly that year, when in fact Kumalaes were offered right up through the late 1930s.

MODEL YEAR	FEATURES	EXC. COND. LOW	HIGH
Soprano Ukulele			
Figured koa body.			
1919	Bound top, back, 'board	$1,000	$1,200
1920	Rope bound top/back	$800	$1,000
1927	As 1919 but with fiddle-shaped peghead	$1,200	$1,500
1930	Unbound body	$800	$1,000
1933	Rope bound soundhole only	$800	$1,000
Tenor Ukulele			
Koa body, unbound top and back.			
1930		$1,000	$1,500

Lanikai

2000-present. Line of budget and intermediate grade, production, koa or nato wood, acoustic and acoustic/electric, ukuleles distributed by Hohner.

Larrivee

1968-present. This mainstream guitar manufacturer has an on-again off-again relationship with the ukulele, having occasionally produced some superb examples in various sizes, woods and degrees of ornamentation. They introduced three ukulele models in '00. They also build guitars.

Le Domino

This line of striking ukuleles turned the popularity of domino playing into a clever visual motif, displaying not only tumbling dominos on their soundboards and around their soundholes, but 'board markers represented in decal domino denominations (3, 5, 7, 10, 12, etc.). The ukuleles were, in fact, produced by at least two different companies - Stewart and Regal - but you can scarcely tell them apart.

MODEL YEAR	FEATURES	EXC. COND. LOW	HIGH
Concert Ukukele			
Concert size, black-finish, white bound, dominos.			
1932		$1,300	$1,600

MODEL YEAR	FEATURES	EXC. COND. LOW	HIG
Soprano Ukukele			
Domino decals.			
1930	Black finish, white bound	$500	$70
1940	Natural finish, unbound	$150	$25

Leonardo Nunes

Leonardo was the son of Manuel, the self professed inventor of the ukulele. Whether actually the originator or not, Dad was certainly on the ship that brought the inventor to the islands in 1879. Leonardo, instead of joining up and making Manuel & Son, set out on his own to produce ukes that are virtually indistinguishable from Pop's. All constructed entirely of koa, some exhibit considerable figure and rope binding finery, making them as highly desirable to collectors as Manuel's.

MODEL YEAR	FEATURES	EXC. COND. LOW	HIG
Radio Tenor Ukulele			
Koa body, bound top, back and neck.			
1935		$2,000	$2,500
Soprano Ukulele			
Figured koa body.			
1919	Bound top/ back/'board	$800	$1,200
1920	Rope bound top/back	$900	$1,200
1927	Bound body/ 'board/head	$1,500	$1,750
1930	Unbound body	$750	$900
1933	Rope bound soundhole only	$750	$900
Taro Patch Fiddle			
Koa body, unbound top and back.			
1930		$2,000	$2,250
Tenor Ukulele			
Koa body, unbound top and back.			
1930		$1,000	$1,250

Levin

1900-1973. Ukuleles built in Sweden. Levin was best known for their classical guitars, which they also built for other brands, most notably Goya. They also built mandolins.

Loprinzi

1972-present. Intermediate and professional grade, production/custom, ukuleles built in Clearwater, Florida. They also build guitars.

Lyon & Healy

1880s-ca.1949. During different periods several different makers constructed ukes bearing this stamp – often with an additional Washburn tag as well. After initial production by Lyon & Healy, instrument manufacture then apparently bounced between Regal, Stewart, and Tonk Brothers all within a span of only a few short years. Adding to the confusion, ukes surface from time to time bearing no maker's mark that can be reasonably attributed to Lyon & Healy. Suffice it to say that

UKULELES

MODEL YEAR	FEATURES	EXC. COND. LOW	HIGH

...he best of these ukes, those displaying the highest degrees of quality and ornamentation, rival Gibson and Martin for collectability and tone and beauty.

Bell-Shaped Ukulele
Mahogany body.

1927		$2,000	$2,500

Camp Ukulele
Round nissa wood body, black binding.

1935		$200	$300

Concert Ukulele
Mahogany body, bound top and back.

1930		$2,000	$3,000

Shrine Ukulele
Triangular body.

1927	Koa, abalone binding	$3,000	$5,000
1930	Mahogany, green binding	$1,500	$2,000
1933	Koa, green binding	$2,500	$3,500

Soprano Ukulele (Koa Body)

1927	Bound top, pearl rosette	$2,500	$3,500
1934	Bound top/back	$1,000	$1,500
1935	Pearl bound top/back	$10,000	$15,000

Soprano Ukulele (Mahogany Body)

1930	Unbound	$650	$800
1932	Bound top/back	$650	$800

Tenor Ukulele
Mahogany body, bound top and back.

1933		$1,500	$2,500

Maccaferri

1923-1990. Between the time he designed the Selmer guitar that became instantly synonymous with Django's gypsy jazz and his invention of the plastic clothespin, guitar design genius and manufacturing impresario Mario Maccaferri created a line of stringed instruments revolutionary for their complete plastic construction. The ukuleles were by far the greatest success, and most bore the tiny Maccaferri coat of arms on their tiny headstock.

Baritone Ukulele
Polystyrene cutaway body.

1959		$200	$300

Islander Ukulele
Polytyrene plastic body, crest in peghead.

1953		$200	$300

Playtune Ukulele
Polystyrene body.

1956		$200	$300

TV Pal Deluxe Ukulele
Extended 'board.

1960		$200	$300

TV Pal Ukulele
Polystyrene plastic body.

1955		$200	$300

Magic Fluke Company

1999-present. Budget grade, production, ukuleles made in New Hartford, Connecticut. With a clever design, exceptional quality, dozens of catchy finishes, and surprisingly affordable prices, it's little wonder that these little wonders have caught on. Riding – if not almost single-handedly driving the coming third wave of uke popularity (the '20s and '50s were the first and second), Dale and Phyllis Webb of the Magic Fluke, along with Phyllis' brother, author Jumpin' Jim Beloff, are downright ukulele evangelists. The Fluke is the first new uke that you're not afraid to let the kids monkey with.

Manuel Nunes

The self-professed father of the ukulele was at least one of the first makers to produce them in any quantity. Beginning after 1879, when he and the first boat load of Portuguese settlers landed in Hawaii, until at least the 1930s, Manuel and his son Leonardo (see Leonardo Nunes section) produced some of the most beautiful and superbly crafted ukes offered by any Island maker.

Soprano Ukulele
Koa body.

1919	Figured koa body, bound top, back, 'board	$1,500	$2,500
1920	Rope bound top/back	$1,000	$1,500
1927	Bound body, 'board/head	$1,500	$2,500
1930	Unbound body	$600	$800
1933	Rope bound soundhole only	$800	$1,000

Taro Patch Fiddle
Koa body.

1930	Rope bound top/back	$2,500	$3,000
1930	Unbound top/back	$1,500	$2,500

Tenor Ukulele
Koa body, unbound top and back.

1930		$1,000	$1,500

Marc Silber Guitar Company

1998-present. Mexican-made ukes from designer Marc Silber of Berkley, California. He also offers guitars. His Frisco Uke takes its inspiration from the inimitable Roy Smeck Vita Uke (see Harmony), but without the whimsy of the original.

Martin

1833-present. The C.F. Martin Company knew they wanted in on the uke craze, and toyed with some prototypes as early as 1907 or so, but didn't get around to actually getting serious until '16. The first of these were characterized by rather more primitive craftsmanship (by stringent Martin standards), bar frets, and an impressed logo in the back of the headstock. By '20, koa became available as a pricey option, and by the early '30s, regular frets and the

Loprinzi MRS

Marc Silber Frisco

Martin S-O

UKULELES

Martin Style O

Martin Style 2-K

National Concert uke

familiar Martin headstock decal had prevailed. Martin single-handedly created the archetype of the mainland uke and the standard by which all competitors are measured.

Martin has recently re-entered the ukulele market with its budget Mexican-made model S-0, the Backpacker Uke, as well as a limited edition of the ornate, and pricey, 5K.

Style O Ukulele
Unbound mahogany body.

Year	Features	Low	High
1920	Wood pegs	$700	$800
1953	Patent pegs	$700	$800

Style 1 Taro Patch Ukulele
Mahogany body, 8 strings, rosewood bound.

Year	Features	Low	High
1933		$1,250	$1,750

Style 1 Ukulele
Mahogany body.

Year	Features	Low	High
1940	Rosewood bound top only	$800	$900
1950	Tortoise bound top only	$800	$900
1960s	Tortoise bound top only	$800	$900

Style 1-C Concert Ukulele
Concert-sized mahogany body, bound top.

Year	Features	Low	High
1950		$1,500	$1,700

Style 1-C K Concert Ukulele
Concert-sized koa body, bound top.

Year	Features	Low	High
1950		$2,500	$3,500

Style 1-K Taro Patch Ukulele
Style 1 with koa wood body.

Year	Features	Low	High
1940		$1,500	$2,500

Style 1-K Ukulele
Koa body, rosewood bound top.

Year	Features	Low	High
1922	Wood pegs	$1,500	$2,000
1939	Patent pegs	$1,500	$2,000

Style 1-T Tenor Ukulele
Tenor-sized mahogany body, bound top only.

Year	Features	Low	High
1940		$1,500	$2,000

Style 2 Taro Patch Ukulele
Mahogany body, 8 strings, ivoroid bound.

Year	Features	Low	High
1931		$1,500	$2,000

Style 2 Ukulele
Mahogany body, ivoroid bound top and back.

Year	Features	Low	High
1922		$1,200	$1,500
1935		$1,200	$1,500
1961		$1,200	$1,500

Style 2-K Taro Patch Ukulele
Style 2 with koa wood body.

Year	Features	Low	High
1937		$1,750	$2,500

Style 2-K Ukulele
Figured koa body, bound top and back.

Year	Features	Low	High
1923		$2,500	$3,000
1939	Patent pegs	$2,500	$3,000

Style 3 Taro Patch Ukulele
Mahogany body, 8 strings, multiple bound.

Year	Features	Low	High
1941		$2,000	$3,500

Style 3 Ukulele
Mahogany body.

Year	Features	Low	High
1925	Kite inlay in headstock	$2,500	$3,000

Year	Features	Low	High
1940	B/W lines in ebony 'board	$2,500	$3,000
1950	Extended 'board, dots	$2,500	$3,000

Style 3-C K Concert Ukulele
Same specs as 3K, but in concert size.

Year	Features	Low	High
1930		$15,000	$20,000

Style 3-K Taro Patch Ukulele
Style 3 with koa wood body.

Year	Features	Low	High
1929		$3,000	$5,000

Style 3-K Ukulele
Figured koa body.

Year	Features	Low	High
1924	Bow-tie 'board inlay	$3,500	$5,000
1932	B/W lines, diamonds, squares	$3,500	$5,000
1940	B/W lines and dot inlay	$3,500	$5,000

Style 3-T K Tenor Ukulele
Same specs as 3K, but in tenor size.

Year	Features	Low	High
1930		$15,000	$20,000

Style 51 Baritone Ukulele
Mahogany body, bound top and back.

Year	Features	Low	High
1966		$1,250	$1,750

Style 5-K Ukulele
Highly figured koa body, all pearl trimmed.

Year	Features	Low	High
1926		$15,000	$20,000

Style 5-M Ukulele
1941 only. Same as 5K, but mahogany body, extremely rare.

Year	Features	Low	High
1941		$25,000	$35,000

Style T-15 Tiple Ukulele
Mahogany body, 10 metal strings, unbound.

Year	Features	Low	High
1971		$800	$1,000

Style T-17 Tiple Ukulele
Mahogany body, 10 strings, unbound top and back.

Year	Features	Low	High
1940		$1,000	$1,200

Style T-18 Tiple Ukulele
Mahogany body, 10 strings, spruce top.

Year	Features	Low	High
1925		$1,500	$1,700

Style T-28 Tiple Ukulele
Rosewood body, 10 strings, bound top and back.

Year	Features	Low	High
1947		$2,500	$3,500

Maurer

The Larson brothers of Maurer & Co., Chicago, built a few ukes and one known taro patch from 1915 into the 1930s. Their small tops and backs are built-under-tension in the Larson tradition. A few of them have surfaced with the Hawaiian teacher/player's Ernest Kaai label and were probably bought from Bill Stahl, Milwaukee.

Ukulele
Abalone bound koa body, fancy headstock shape.

Year	Features	Low	High
1920s		$7,000	$11,000

Michael Dunn Guitars

1968-present. Luthier Michael Dunn builds a Knutsen-style harp uke in New Westminster, British Columbia. He also builds guitars.

UKULELES

MODEL YEAR	FEATURES	EXC. COND. LOW	HIGH

Mirabella

1997-present. Professional grade, custom ukuleles built by luthier Cristian Mirabella in Babylon, New York. He also builds guitars, basses and mandolins.

National

Ca. 1927-present. To capitalize on the success of their amplifying guitars, the Dopyera brothers introduced metal-bodied ukuleles and mandolins as well. Large, heavy, and ungainly by today's standards, these early offerings nonetheless have their charms. Their subsequent switch to a smaller body shape produced an elegant and sweet-sounding resonator uke that soon became much sought after.

Style 1 Ukulele
Nickel body.

1928	Tenor, 6" resonator	$2,000	$3,000
1933	Soprano	$2,000	$3,000

Style 2 Ukulele
Nickel body, engraved roses.

1928	Tenor	$3,000	$4,000
1931	Soprano	$3,500	$5,000

Style 3 Ukulele
Nickel body, lilies-of-the-valley.

1929	Tenor	$4,000	$5,000
1933	Soprano	$5,000	$7,500

Style O Ukulele
Metal body, soprano size, sandblasted scenes.

1931		$2,000	$3,000

Triolian Ukulele

1928	Tenor, sunburst painted body	$2,000	$3,000
1930	Soprano, sunburst painted body	$2,000	$3,000
1934	Soprano, wood-grained metal body	$2,000	$3,000

National Reso-Phonic

1988-present. Successors to the National name, with the designs and patented amplifying resonator assemblies of the original National models, they offer professional grade, production, single cone ukuleles from their shop in San Luis Obispo, California. They also build guitars, basses and mandolins.

Oscar Schmidt

1879-1938, 1979-present. The same New Jersey outfit responsible for Leadbelly's 12-string guitar offered ukes as well during the same period. Many of these were odd amalgams of materials, often combining koa, mahogany, and spruce in the same instrument. Since 1979, when the name was acquired by the U.S. Music Corp. (Washburn, Randall, etc.), they have offered a line of budget grade, production, Asian-made ukes. They also offer guitars, basses, mandolins, and banjos.

Soprano Ukulele
Spruce top, bound mahogany body.

1930		$300	$500

Pegasus Guitars and Ukuleles

1977-present. Professional grade, custom, ukulele family instruments built by luthier Bob Gleason in Kurtistown, Hawaii, who also builds steel-string guitars.

Polk-a-lay-lee

1960s. These inexplicably shaped oddities were produced by Petersen Products of Chicago ca. the mid-'60s, and anecdotal Midwestern lore has it that their intent was to be offered as giveaways for the Polk Brothers, a local appliance chain. This may be how they ended up, although the gargantuan original packaging makes no reference to any such promotion. The box does call out what the optional colors were.

Many have noted the striking resemblance to the similarly named wares of the Swaggerty company (see Swaggerty) of California, who also offered brightly colored plywood-bodied ukes in comically oversized incarnations, but who was copying whom has yet to be determined.

Ukulele
Long boat oar body, uke scale, brown, natural, red, or black.

1965		$300	$500

Recording King (TML)

2005-present. The Music Link added budget grade, production, stenciled ukuleles designed by Greg Rich. They also have banjos and guitars.

Regal

Ca. 1884-1966, 1987-present. Like the other large 1930s Chicago makers, Harmony and Lyon & Healy, the good ukes are very, very good, and the cheap ukes are very, very cheap. Unlike its pals, however, Regal seems to have produced more ukuleles in imaginative themes, striking color schemes, and in more degrees of fancy trim, making them the quintessential wall-hangers. And lucky for you, there's a vintage Regal uke to suit every décor.

Carson Robison Ukulele
Top sports painted signature, cowboy scene.

1935		$800	$1,000

Jungle Ukulele
Birch body, covered in leopard skin fabric.

1950		$1,000	$1,200

Resonator Ukulele
Black body, f-holes, see Dobro uke.

1934		$700	$1,000

Soprano Ukulele (Birch)
Birch body.

1931	Brown sunburst	$200	$300
1931	Nautical themes, various colors	$175	$250
1945	Painted body, victory themes	$1,000	$1,500

Oscar Schmidt

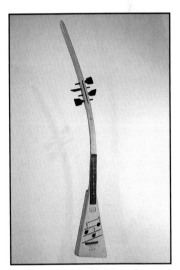

Petersen Polk-A-Lay-Lee

Regal Jungle Uke

UKULELES

Rogue Hawaiian Soprano

Samick UK70

Silvertone

MODEL YEAR	FEATURES	EXC. COND. LOW	HIGH
Soprano Ukulele (Koa)			
Koa body, multicolored rope bound top.			
1930		$300	$500
Soprano Ukulele (Mahogany)			
Mahogany body.			
1930	Multiple bound top	$500	$800
1935	Spruce top, inlays	$500	$700
1940	Extended 'board	$200	$300
Tiple Ukulele			
1930	Birch body stained dark, black binding	$400	$500
1935	Spruce top, mahogany body, fancy binding	$500	$700
Wendall Hall Red Head Ukulele			
Koa body, celebrity decal on headstock.			
1935		$500	$700

Renaissance Guitars

1994-present. In '05 luthier Rick Turner added a line of acoustic and acoustic/electric ukuleles built in Santa Cruz, California. He also builds guitars and basses.

Rogue

2001-present. Budget grade, production, imported ukuleles. They also offer guitars, basses, lap steels, mandolins, banjos, effects and amps.

S. S. Stewart

Not much is known about the ukuleles of this Philadelphia firm, except that they were most certainly sub-contracted from another maker or makers.

Soprano Ukulele
Mahogany body, bound top and back.

1927		$300	$400

Samick

1958-2001, 2002-present. Budget grade, production, imported ukuleles. They also offer guitars, basses, mandolins and banjos.

Sammo

Flashy internal paper labels trumpet that these ukes (mandolins and guitars, too) were products of the Osborne Mfg. Co. Masonic Temple, Chicago-Illinois and what the heck any of that means is still open to modern speculation. Your guess is as good as mine. Still, the high quality and often opulent degree of ornamentation that the instruments exhibit, coupled with even the vaguest implication that they were made by guys wearing fezzes and/or men who ride around in tiny cars at parades is all the reason we need to buy every one we see.

Soprano Ukulele

1925	Figured maple body, 5-ply top, back binding	$600	$800

MODEL YEAR	FEATURES	EXC. COND. LOW	HIGH
1925	Unbound koa body, fancy headstock shape	$600	$800

Silvertone

1941-ca. 1970, present. Silvertone was the house brand of Sears & Roebuck and most (if not all) of it ukes were manufactured for them by Harmony.

Soprano Ukulele
Mahogany body, Harmony-made.

1950	Sunburst	$200	$300
1950	Unbound	$200	$300
1955	Bound	$200	$300
1960	Green	$200	$300

Slingerland

Slingerland started marketing ukes around 1916 Banjo ukuleles bearing this brand (see Slingerland Banjo uke section below) were certainly made by the popular drum company (banjos being little more than drums with necks, after all). Slingerland standard ukuleles, on the other hand, bear an uncanny resemblance to the work of the Oscar Schmidt company.

Soprano Ukulele
Koa body, rope bound top and soundhole.

1920		$350	$500

Specimen Products

1984-present. Luthier Ian Schneller builds his professional grade, production/custom, ukuleles in Chicago, Illinois. He also builds guitars, basses, amps and speaker cabs. Schneller has built some of the most offbeat, endearing - and high quality - custom ukuleles available.

Sterling

The miniscule reference buried deep within the headstock decal to a T.B. Co. can only mean that the Sterling ukulele somehow fits into the mind-numbing Tonk Bros./Lyon & Healy/Regal/S.S. Stewart manufacturing puzzle. Nonetheless, the brand must have been reserved for the cream of the crop, since the Sterling ukes that surface tend to be of the drop-dead-gorgeous variety.

Soprano Ukulele
Flamed koa, multiple fancy binding all over.

1935		$2,500	$3,500

Stetson

Popular misconception - to say nothing of wishful thinking and greed - has it that all instruments labeled with the Stetson brand were the work of the Larson Brothers of Chicago. While a few Stetson guitars and a very few mandolins may be genuine Larson product, the ukuleles surely were made elsewhere.

Soprano Ukulele
Mahogany body, single bound top and back.

1930		$400	$500

MODEL YEAR	FEATURES	EXC. COND. LOW	HIGH

Supertone

1914-1940s. For whatever reason, Supertone was the name attached to Sears' musical instruments before the line became Silvertone (see above). These, too, were all Harmony-made.

Soprano Ukulele (Koa)
Koa body, Harmony-made.

1935	Rope bound	$300	$500
1943	Unbound	$300	$500

Soprano Ukulele (Mahogany)
Mahogany body, Harmony-made.

1930	Unbound	$300	$500
1940	Bound	$300	$500

Swaggerty

Not enough is known of this West Coast company, except that their product line of unusually shaped 4-stringed novelty instruments oddly mirrors those made by Petersen Products in Chicago at the same time (see Polk-a-lay-lee). The two companies even seem to have shared plastic parts, such as 'boards and tuners. Go figure.

Kook-a-Lay-Lee Ukulele
Green plywood body, twin necks.

1965		$300	$500

Singing Treholipee
Orange plywood body, long horn.

1965		$300	$500

Surf-a-Lay-Lee Ukulele
Plywood body, long horn, green, yellow, or orange.

1965		$300	$500

Tabu

The Tabu brand on either the back of a ukulele's headstock or inside its soundhole was never an indication of its original maker. Rather, it was intended to assure the purchaser that the uke was, indeed of bona fide Hawaiian origin. So rampant was the practice of mainland makers claiming Island manufacture of their wares that in the late 'teens Hawaii launched a campaign to set the record straight, and – lucky for you – a nifty little brand was the result. The Tabu mark actually was used to mark the ukes of several different makers.

Soprano Ukulele
Figured koa body.

1915	Rope bound	$800	$1,300
1915	Unbound	$800	$900

Tombo

This venerable Japanese harmonica manufacturer jumped on two bandwagons at once with its mid-Sixties introduction of a solid body electric ukulele. The Tombo Ukulet shares a tenor scale length and single coil pickup with Gibson's ETU electric tenor ukes, but the Tombo's thin, solidbody design is decidedly more Fender than jumping flea. Completing the imitation-is-the-sincerest-form-of-flattery theme is a snazzy Silvertone-esque case with onboard amplifier.

MODEL YEAR	FEATURES	EXC. COND. LOW	HIGH

Ukulet
Solid body, amp-in-case, red sunburst or white finish.

1967	Red sunburst	$800	$1,200
1968	White	$1,000	$1,500

Turturro

Unlike manufacturers like Regal and Harmony who were content to produce novelty ukes by merely spray painting or applying decals with eye-catching motifs, New York manufacturer Nicola Turturro issued novelty ukuleles from his own patented designs. The most well-known is the Turnover Uke, a playable two-sided contraption strung as a 4-string uke on one side, and an 8-string mandolin on the other.

Peanut Ukulele
Ribbed peanut shaped body.

1928		$500	$700

Turnover Ukulele
Two-sided uke and mandolin.

1926		$500	$700

Vega

Famous for their banjos, the Vega name was applied to a sole baritone uke, tied with the endorsement of 1950s TV crooner Arthur Godfrey.

Arthur Godfrey Baritone Ukulele
Mahogany body, unbound.

1955		$500	$700

Washburn

See Lyon & Healy.

Weissenborn

1910s-1937. The mainland maker famous for their hollow-necked Hawaiian guitars was responsible for several uke offerings over the course of its 20-or-so-year run. Like their 6-stringed big brothers, they were the closest thing to Island design and detail to come from the mainland.

Soprano Ukulele
Figured koa body.

1920	Rope bound	$1,500	$2,000
1920	Unbound	$1,500	$2,000

Weymann

Renowned for fine tenor banjos, Weyman affixed their name to a full line of soprano ukes of varying degrees of decoration, quite certainly none of which were made under the same roof as the banjos. Most were C.F. Martin knock-offs.

Soprano Ukulele

1925	Mahogany, unbound	$800	$1,000
1930	Koa, fancy pearl vine 'board inlay	$1,500	$2,000

Specimen Electric Soprano

Supertone Soprano

Tombo Ukulet

UKULELES

Gibson BU 3

Ludwig Banjo Uke

MODEL YEAR	FEATURES	EXC. COND. LOW	HIGH

Wm. Smith Co.

1920s. Like Ditson, the Wm. Smith Co. was a company for which C.F. Martin moonlighted without getting much outward credit. The South American cousin of the uke, the tiple, with its 10 metal strings and tenor uke sized body, was first produced exclusively for Smith by Martin starting around 1920, before being assumed into the regular Martin line with appropriate Martin branding.

Tiple Ukulele
1920. Mahogany body, spruce top, ebony bridge.

1920		$800	$1,000

Banjo Ukuleles
Bacon

This legendary Connecticut banjo maker just couldn't resist the temptation to extend their line with uke versions of their popular banjos. As with Gibson, Ludwig, Slingerland, and Weyman, the banjo ukuleles tended to mimic the already proven construction techniques and decorative motifs of their regular banjo counterparts. In materials, finish, and hardware, most banjo ukes share many more similarities with full sized banjos than differences. The banjo ukes were simply included as smaller, plainer, variations of banjos, much as concert, tenor, and baritone options fleshed out standard ukulele lines.

Banjo Ukulele
Walnut rim, fancy 'board inlays.

1927		$1,500	$1,750

Silver Bell Banjo Ukulele
Engraved pearloid 'board and headstock.

1927		$1,500	$2,500

MODEL YEAR	FEATURES	EXC. COND. LOW	HIGH

Dixie

With chrome plated all-metal design, there's only one word for these banjo ukes – shiny. Their bodies, necks, and frets are die cast together in zinc (think Hot Wheels cars and screen door handles) the Dixie must have made the perfect indestructible instrument for Junior's birthday back in the 1960s. Similar to one made by Werko.

Banjo Ukulele
One-piece, all-metal construction.

1960		$250	$300

Gibson

BU-1 Banjo Ukulele
Small 6" head, flat panel resonator.

1928		$500	$650

BU-2 Banjo Ukulele
8" head, dot inlay.

1930		$800	$1,000

BU-3 Banjo Ukulele
8" head, diamond and square inlay.

1935		$1,300	$1,500

BU-4 Banjo Ukulele
8" head, resonator and flange.

1932		$1,500	$2,000

BU-5 Banjo Ukulele
8" head, resonator and flange, gold parts.

1937		$2,500	$3,500

Le Domino

Banjo Ukulele
Resonator, decorated as Le Domino uke.

1933		$350	$500

UKULELES

MODEL YEAR	FEATURES	EXC. COND. LOW	HIGH

Ludwig

The Ludwig was then, and is today, the Cadillac of banjo ukes. British banjo uke icon George Formby's preference for Ludwig continues assuring their desirability, while the fact that they were available in only a couple of models, for a few short years, and in relatively small production numbers only adds to the mystique.

Banjo Ukulele
Flange with crown holes.

1927	Gold-plated parts	$4,000	$4,500
1928	Nickel-plated parts	$3,500	$4,500
1930	Ivoroid headstock overlay w/ art deco detail	$4,500	$5,000

Wendell Hall Professional Banjo Ukulele
Walnut resonator, flange with oval holes.

1927		$2,500	$3,500

Lyon & Healy
Banjo Ukulele
Walnut neck and resonator, fancy pearl inlay.

1935		$1,500	$2,000

Paramount

1920s-1942, Late 1940s. The William L. Lange Company began selling Paramount banjos, guitar banjos and mandolin banjos in the early 1920s. Gretsch picked up the Paramount name and used it on guitars for a time in the late '40s.

Banner Blue Banjo Ukulele
Brass hearts 'board inlay, walnut neck.

1933		$1,250	$1,500

Regal
Banjo Ukulele
Mahogany rim, resonator, fancy rope bound.

1933		$300	$500

MODEL YEAR	FEATURES	EXC. COND. LOW	HIGH

Richter

Allegedly, this Chicago company bought the already-made guitars, ukes, and mandolins of other manufacturers, painted and decorated them to their liking and resold them. True or not, they certainly were cranked out in a bevy of swanky colors.

Banjo Ukulele
Chrome-plated body, 2 f-holes in back.

1930		$250	$400
1930	Entire body/ neck painted	$250	$400

Slingerland
May Bell Banjo Ukulele
Walnut resonator with multicolored rope.

1935		$300	$600

Werko

These Chicago-made banjo ukuleles had construction similar to the Dixie brand, and except for the addition of a swank layer of blue sparkle drum binding on the rim, you would be hard pressed to tell them apart.

Banjo Ukulele
Chrome-plated metal body and neck.

1960		$200	$300

Weymann
Banjo Ukulele
Maple rim, open back, ebony 'board.

1926		$1,500	$2,000

Richter Banjo Uke

Werko Banjo Uke

UKULELES

Banjos

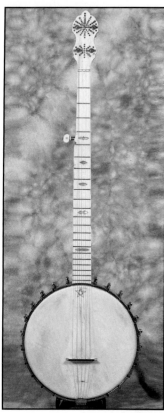

1924 Bacon & Day

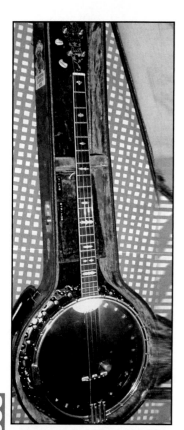

Bacon & Day Silver Bell #1

BANJOS

MODEL YEAR	FEATURES	EXC. COND. LOW	HIGH

Banjo collectors, hobbyists, and dealers often think nothing of changing the neck on a banjo; a banjo may have a true vintage neck or a new replacement neck. So, our all original parts concept that applies to the rest of this Price Guide doesn't always apply to vintage banjos.

The banjo market operates somewhat differently than many of the other markets that are covered in the Guide. The prices shown are guidance prices only and each instrument should be evaluated on a case by case basis.

Acme

1893-early 1900s. Banjos made for Sears by S.S. Stewart, and later George Bauer, both of Philadelphia.

The Pearl
1908. Open back, 5-string, pearl fretboard.

MODEL YEAR	FEATURES	EXC. COND. LOW	HIGH
1908		$1,150	$1,250

Alvarez

Ca. 1966-present. An import brand for St. Louis Music, Alvarez currently offers intermediate grade, production, banjos. They also offer guitars, lap steels and mandolins.

Bacon & Day

1921-1967. David Day left Vega to join up with Fred Bacon in '21. Gretsch purchased Bacon & Day in '40, and ran the Bacon line until '67.

Blue Bell

MODEL YEAR	FEATURES	EXC. COND. LOW	HIGH
1922-1939	Tenor	$1,400	$1,600

Blue Ribbon 17

1933-1939	Tenor	$600	$750

Ne Plus Ultra

1920s	#5, tenor	$13,500	$16,500
1920s	#6, tenor	$9,000	$11,000
1920s	#7, tenor	$13,500	$16,500
1920s	#8, tenor	$16,000	$20,000
1920s	#9, tenor	$13,500	$16,500
1930s	Tenor	$9,000	$11,000
1950s	Tenor	$2,900	$3,100
1960s	Tenor	$2,800	$3,000

Senorita

1930s	Plectrum, pearloid, resonator	$1,000	$1,250
1950s	4-string	$750	$925

Silver Bell Series

1920-1930s	#1, 5-string	$3,800	$4,500
1920s	#2, tenor	$1,950	$2,400
1920s	#3, tenor	$2,000	$2,500
1920s	#5, 5-string	$5,500	$6,500
1920s	Montana #3, tenor	$3,500	$3,800
1922-1939	#1, tenor/plectrum	$1,550	$1,900
1933-1939	Montana #1, tenor	$1,500	$2,000
1933-1939	Montana #3, plectrum	$4,800	$5,200
1933-1939	Symphonie #1, tenor	$3,000	$3,400

Sultana #1

1933-1939	Tenor	$2,000	$2,500

MODEL YEAR	FEATURES	EXC. COND. LOW	HIGH

Super

1920-1923	Tenor, non-carved neck	$1,150	$1,400
1927	5-string, carved neck	$3,900	$4,100
1927	5-string, non-carved neck	$2,900	$3,100

Baldwin

1966-1976. Baldwin was one of the largest piano retailers in the Midwest and in 1965, they got into the guitar market. In '66 they bought the ODE Banjo company. From '66 to '71 the banjos were labeled as Baldwin; after that ODE was added below the Baldwin banner. In '76 Gretsch took over ODE production.

Ode Style C

1968	Bluegrass, 5-string	$1,300	$1,500

Barratt

1890s. Made by George Barratt in Brooklyn, New York.

5-String

1890s	Victorian era	$375	$450

Benary and Sons

1890-1899. Manufactured by the James H. Buckbee Co. for music instrument wholesaler Robert Benary.

Celebrated Benary
1890-1899. 5-string, open back, plain appointments.

1890-1899		$500	$600

Boucher

1830s-1850s. William Boucher's operation in Baltimore is considered to be one of the very first banjo-shops. Boucher and the Civil War era banjos are rare. The price range listed is informational guidance pricing only. The wide range reflects conservative opinions. 150 year old banjos should be evaluated per their own merits.

Double Tack

1840s		$16,000	$19,000

Single Tack

1840s		$12,000	$15,000

Bruno and Sons

1834-present. Established by Charles Bruno, primarily as a distributor, Bruno and Sons marketed a variety of brands, including their own.

Royal Artist Tenor

1920s	Figured Resonator	$675	$750

Buckbee

1863-1897. James H. Buckbee Co. of New York was the city's largest builder. The company did considerable private branding for companies such as Benary, Dobson, and Farland.

MODEL YEAR	FEATURES	EXC. COND. LOW	HIGH

5-String
1890-1897. 5-string, open back, plain appointments.

| 1890-1897 | Higher-end models | $1,600 | $2,000 |
| 1890-1897 | Lower-end models | $800 | $1,000 |

Cole
1890-1919. W.A. Cole, after leaving Fairbanks & Cole, started his own line in 1890. He died in 1909 but the company continued until 1919.

Eclipse
| 1890-1919 | Flower inlays, dots | $2,000 | $2,500 |
| 1890-1919 | Man-in-the-moon inlays | $3,250 | $3,800 |

Deering
1975-present. Greg and Janet Deering build their banjos in Spring Valley, California. In 1978 they introduced their Basic and Intermediate banjos. They also offer banjos under the Vega and Goodtime brands.

Ditson
1916-1930. The Oliver Ditson Company of Boston offered a variety of musical instruments.

Tenor
1920. 4-string, resonator with typical appointments.

| 1920 | | $575 | $700 |

Dobson, George
1870-1890. Marketed by George C. Dobson of Boston, Massachusetts. Brothers Henry, George, and Edgar Dobson were banjo teachers and performers. They designed banjos that were built for them by manufactures such as Buckbee of New York.

Matchless
| 1880s | 5-string | $750 | $875 |

Epiphone
1873-present. Epiphone introduced banjos in the early 1920s, if not sooner, offering them up to WW II. After Gibson bought the company in '57, they reintroduced banjos to the line, which they still offer.

EB-44 Campus
1960s. Long neck, folk-era 5-string banjo.

| 1960s | | $700 | $850 |

EB-99 5-String
| 1970s | Higher-end, import | $450 | $500 |

Electar (Electric)
| 1930s | Tenor | $1,300 | $1,400 |

Recording A
Ca. 1925-ca. 1935. Epiphone Recording logo on headstock, flamed maple neck and resonator, fancy pearl inlay markers

| 1920s | Tenor | $1,400 | $1,750 |

Recording B
Ca. 1925-ca. 1935.

| 1930s | Tenor | $1,600 | $2,000 |

Recording Concert C Special
1930s. Tenor, maple body, fancy appointments, resonator.

| 1930s | | $3,200 | $4,000 |

TB-100
Mid 1960s.

| 1960s | Tenor | $850 | $950 |

Fairbanks/Vega Fairbanks/ A.C. Fairbanks
1875-1919. From 1875 to 1880, A. C. Fairbanks built his own designs in Boston. In 1880, W. A. Cole joined the company, starting Fairbanks & Cole, but left in 1890 to start his own line. The company went by Fairbanks Co. until it was purchased by Vega in 1904. The banjos were then branded Vega Fairbanks (see Vega listings) until 1919.

Acme (F & C)
1880-1890. 5-string, open back, fancy markers.

| 1880-1890 | | $900 | $1,000 |

Electric 5-String Series
1890s	F & C	$5,300	$6,300
1890s	Imperial	$6,500	$7,500
1890s	No. 3	$5,500	$6,800
1890s	No. 6	$6,500	$7,500

Electric Banjeaurine
| 1890s | 5-string | $3,900 | $4,300 |

Regent
| 1900-1904 | 5-string | $3,300 | $3,700 |

Senator No. 1/Fairbanks 3
| 1900-1904 | 5-string | $1,400 | $1,600 |

Special #0
| 1890-1904 | | $875 | $1,075 |

Special #2
| 1890-1904 | 5-string | $1,100 | $1,200 |

Special #4
| 1900-1904 | 5-string | $1,200 | $1,500 |

Whyte Laydie #2
| 1901-1904 | 5-string | $3,600 | $4,500 |

Whyte Laydie #7
| 1901 | 1st year | $10,000 | $12,500 |
| 1902-1904 | | $8,200 | $8,600 |

Farland
Ca. 1890-1920s. Buckbee and others made instruments for New York banjo teacher and performer A. A. Farland.

Concert Grand
| 1900-1920 | 5-string | $1,400 | $1,700 |

Grand Artist No. 2
1890s-1910. Ornate floral markers, open back, 5-string.

| 1890-1910 | | $1,800 | $2,100 |

Fender
1946-present. Fender added banjos to their product mix in the late 1960s, and continues to offer them.

Allegro
Late 1960s-1970s.

| 1960s | Tenor or 5-string | $1,100 | $1,300 |

1904 Cole Eclipse Banjeaurine

Fairbanks & Cole (Acme)

BANJOS

1927 Gibson Granada

Gibson RB-3

MODEL YEAR	FEATURES	EXC. COND. LOW	HIGH
Artist			
1960-1970s	5-string	$1,500	$1,700
FB-58			
1999-present. Import from Korea, style and design similar to '60s-'70s Fender banjos.			
1999-2005	5-string	$400	$500
Leo Deluxe			
1980-1988. Fancy inlay, Japanese-made.			
1980s		$1,600	$1,800

Framus

1946-1977, 1996-present. The new Framus company, located in Markneukirchen, Germany, continues to offer banjos.

MODEL YEAR	FEATURES	EXC. COND. LOW	HIGH
5-String Model			
1960s		$250	$300

Gibson

1890s (1902)-present. Gibson started making banjos in 1918, and continues to manufacture them. Vega and Gibson were the only major manufacturing companies that offered banjos in their product catalog in the '50s.

  RB prefix = regular banjo (5-string)
  TB prefix = tenor banjo (4-string, tenor tuning)
  PB prefix = plectrum banjo (4-string, plectrum tuning)

The prices shown are guidance prices only and each instrument should be evaluated on a case by case basis.

MODEL YEAR	FEATURES	EXC. COND. LOW	HIGH
All American			
1930-1937. Tenor banjo, fancy appointments, historic art, gold hardware.			
1930-1937		$15,000	$17,000
Bella Voce			
1927-1931. Tenor banjo, fancy appointments, flower-pattern art, gold hardware.			
1927-1931		$14,200	$17,800
Earl Scruggs Standard			
1984-present. 5-string, high-end appointments, Standard added to model name in '92.			
1980s		$2,950	$3,150
1990s		$2,950	$3,150
2000s		$2,900	$3,100
ETB Electric Tenor			
1938-1941. Electric Tenor Banjo, Charlie Christian pickup.			
1934-1941		$2,600	$3,200
Flint Hill Special			
2005-2006. Earl Scruggs style, 5-string.			
2005-2006		$4,200	$4,700
Florentine Plectrum			
1925-1930	2 piece flange	$13,000	$16,000
Florentine Tenor			
1927-1937. High-end appointments, gold hardware.			
1927-1935	40 hole	$13,000	$18,000
Granada Earl Scruggs			
With high-end replacement tone ring.			
1988-1999		$3,350	$3,750

MODEL YEAR	FEATURES	EXC. COND. LOW	HIGH
Granada FE			
2004. Flying eagle inlay.			
2004		$3,350	$4,200
Granada RB			
1925-1939. 5-string banjo with either a 2 piece flange (1925-1930), or a 1 piece flange (1933-1939).			
1925-1926	Ball bearing	$30,000	$35,000
1927-1930	40 hole arched	$35,000	$40,000
1933-1939	Flat head tone ring	$200,000	$250,000
Granada RB Pot and Reneck			
1933-1939. Original pot and replacement neck.			
1933-1939	Flat head tone ring	$41,000	$50,000
Granada TB			
1925-1939. Tenor banjo with either a 2 piece flange (1925-1930), or a 1 piece flange (1933-1939).			
1925-1926	Ball bearing	$10,000	$15,000
1927-1930	40 hole arched	$15,000	$20,000
1933-1939	Flat head tone ring	$125,000	$165,000
PB-1			
1926-1930s. PB stands for Plectrum Banjo.			
1920s		$1,125	$1,400
PB-3			
1923-1937. Laminated maple resonator Mastertone model, plectrum neck and tuning.			
1925-1927		$2,700	$3,100
PB-4			
1925-1940. Plectrum banjo with either a 2 piece flange (1925-1932), or a 1 piece flange (1933-1940).			
1925-1927	Ball bearing tone ring	$3,000	$3,600
1928-1932	Archtop	$3,500	$4,000
1933-1940	Archtop	$9,000	$11,000
1933-1940	Flat head tone ring	$75,000	$80,000
PB-100			
1969-1979		$900	$1,000
RB Jr.			
1924-1925. 5-string, budget line, open back.			
1924-1925		$1,200	$1,400
RB-00			
1932-1942.			
1933-1939		$2,000	$2,500
RB-1			
1922-1940.			
1922-1930		$3,600	$4,500
1930-1932	1 piece flange	$3,700	$4,400
1933-1939	Diamond flange	$3,700	$4,400
RB-1 reissue			
1993		$1,700	$1,900
RB-2			
1933-1939		$8,900	$9,500
RB-3			
1923-1937. Reissued in 1988.			
1927-1928	5-string	$17,000	$18,000
1960s	Reno	$2,700	$3,000
RB-3 reissue			
1988-present. Currently called the RB-3 Wreath.			
1988-1999		$2,600	$2,800
2000s		$2,300	$2,600

BANJOS

The *Vintage Guitar Price Guide* shows low to high values for items in all-original excellent condition, and, where applicable, with original case or cover.

RB-4

1922-1937. 5-string banjo with either a 2 piece flange (1925-1931), or a 1 piece flange (1933-1937). Trap or non-trap door on earlier models (1922-1924).

MODEL YEAR	FEATURES	EXC. COND. LOW	HIGH
1922-1924	Trap or non-trap door	$2,600	$3,100
1925-1931	Archtop, resonator	$20,000	$24,000
1933-1937	Archtop	$40,000	$50,000
1933-1937	Flat head tone ring	$100,000	$125,000

RB-4/R-4/Retro 4

1998-2003		$2,900	$3,300

RB-6

1927-1937. 5-string banjo with fancy appointments.

1927-1933	Archtop	$19,000	$25,000

RB-11

1931-1942.

1933-1939		$7,200	$9,000

RB-75 J.D. Crowe

1999-2006.

1999		$3,300	$3,700

RB-100

1948-1979. Maple resonator.

1948-1965		$1,650	$2,000
1966-1979		$1,000	$1,900

RB-150

1948-1959		$1,200	$1,400

RB-170

1960-1973. 5-string, no resonator, dot markers, decal logo, multi-ply maple rim.

1960-1973		$1,000	$1,100

RB-175

1962-1973. 2000s. Open back, long neck typical of banjos of the 1960s. Models include the RB-175, RB-175 Long Neck, RB-175 Folk.

1962	RB-175	$1,050	$1,100
1962-1964	Long Neck	$1,050	$1,100
1965-1969	Folk	$1,000	$1,100
1970-1973	RB-175	$1,000	$1,100

RB-250

1954-present.

1954-1965		$2,500	$3,000
1966-1969	Flat head tone ring	$2,400	$2,900
1970s	Mastertone	$1,850	$2,100
1980s	Mastertone	$1,850	$2,150
1990s		$2,000	$2,200
2002-2003	Reissue	$2,100	$2,300

RB-800

1971-1986		$2,700	$3,000

TB

1918-1923. Renamed TB-4.

1919		$1,100	$1,300

TB-00

1932-1942.

1939		$2,600	$2,800

TB-1

1922-1939. Tenor banjo with a 1 piece flange.

1922-1924	Trap door	$800	$900
1925	No resonator	$800	$900
1926	Maple resonator, shoe-plate	$800	$1,000
1933-1939	Simple hoop tone ring	$3,400	$4,200

TB-2

1922-1937.

1922-1928	Wavy flange	$800	$1,000
1933-1939	Pearloid board	$3,800	$4,600

TB-3

1925-1939. Tenor banjo with either a 2 piece flange (1925-1931), or a 1 piece flange (1933-1939).

1925-1926	Ball-bearing tone ring	$2,300	$2,700
1927-1931	40 or no hole ring	$3,500	$3,700
1933-1939	40 or no hole ring	$10,000	$12,500
1933-1939	Flat head tone ring	$67,000	$83,000
1933-1939	Wreath, archtop	$16,100	$17,900

TB-4

1922-1937.

1922-1924	Trap door	$1,650	$1,800
1925-1937	40 or no hole ring	$12,500	$14,000

TB-5

1922-1924	Trap door	$1,850	$2,100
1927-1931	40 or no hole ring	$13,100	$15,000

TB-6

1927-1939	40 or no hole ring	$13,000	$15,000
1933-1939	Flat head tone ring	$50,000	$100,000

TB-11

1933-1939		$3,900	$4,800

TB-12

Introduced in 1937. Produced in limited quantities in the late '30s. One piece flange, flat head tone ring, double bound walnut resonator, price levels include both original and conversion instruments, conversions with original flat head tone rings are somewhat common in the

1937	Top tension pot assembly	$65,000	$80,000

TB-18

1937. Rare model.

1937	Flat head top tension	$70,000	$85,000

TB-100

1948-1979.

1963-1967		$1,000	$1,250

TB-250

1954-1996.

1954-1965		$2,500	$3,000
1966-1969	Mastertone	$2,400	$2,900
1970s	Mastertone	$1,850	$2,100

Trujo Plectrum

1928-1934		$3,400	$3,600

Gold Tone

1993-present. Professional and premium grade, production/custom banjos and banjitars built by Wayne and Robyn Rogers in Titusville, Florida. They also offer guitars, basses, lap steels, mandolins and ukuleles.

Gibson PB-4

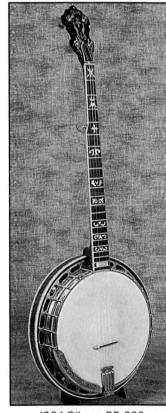

1964 Gibson RB-800

BANJOS

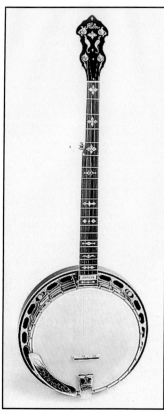

Huber Lexington

Kay KBJ24

MODEL YEAR	FEATURES	EXC. COND. LOW	HIGH

Gretsch

1883-present. Gretsch offered banjos in the '20s and again in the '50s and '60s.

Broadkaster

1920s-1939. Tenor or 5-string banjo with pearloid head and board.

1920s	Tenor	$725	$875
1932-1939	5-string	$950	$1,150
1932-1939	Tenor	$575	$700

Model 6536 Folk

1960s. Open-back, 5-string, long-neck style.

1964		$475	$525

New Yorker

1960s. New Yorker on headstock, 5-string or tenor.

1930-1960s		$550	$650

Orchestella

1925-1929. Tenor or 5-string banjo with gold engravings.

1925-1929	5-string	$2,800	$3,300
1925-1929	Tenor	$900	$1,100

Tenor Short-Scale

1925-1929	Plain styling	$200	$300
1950s	Plain styling	$250	$300

GTR

1974-1978. GTR (for George Gruhn, Tut Taylor, Randy Wood) was the original name for Gruhn Guitars in Nashville, and they imported mandolins and banjos from Japan.

5-String Copy

1974-1978		$850	$1,050

Harmony

1892-1976, late 1970s-present. Huge, Chicago-based manufacturer of fretted instruments, mainly budget models under the Harmony name or for many other American brands and mass marketers.

Electro

1950s. Electric banjo, wood body, 1 pickup.

1950s	5-string	$675	$800

Holiday Folk

1960s		$150	$275

Roy Smeck Student Tenor

1963		$175	$275

Sovereign Tenor

1960s		$125	$200

Hondo

1969-1987, 1991-present. Budget grade, production, imported banjos. They also offer guitars, basses and mandolins.

Howard

1930s. Howard script logo on headstock.

Tenor

1930s	Open back	$325	$425

MODEL YEAR	FEATURES	EXC. COND. LOW	HIGH

Huber

1999-present. Premium grade, production, 5-string banjos built by luthier Steve Huber in Hendersonville, Tennessee.

Ianuario Mandolins

1990-present. Professional and premium grade, custom, banjos built by Luthier R. Anthony Ianuario in Jefferson, Georgia. He also builds mandolins and violins.

Ibanez

1932-present. Ibanez introduced their Artist line of banjos in 1978 in a deal with Earl Scruggs, but they were dropped by '84.

Model 591

1978-1984. Flat head, 5-string copy.

1978-1984		$1,000	$1,100

J.B. Player

1980s-present. Budget grade, production, imported banjos. They also offer basses, mandolins and guitars.

John Wesley

Introduced in 1895 by Kansas City, Missouri instrument wholesalers J.W. Jenkins & Sons, founded by cello builder John Wesley Jenkins. May have been built by Jenkins until circa 1905, but work was later contracted out to others.

Kalamazoo

1933-1942, 1965-1970. Budget brand built by Gibson. Made flat-tops, solidbodies, mandolins, lap steels, banjos and amps.

Banjos

1935-1940	KPB, plectrum	$300	$900
1935-1941	KRB, 5-string	$500	$1,200

Kay

Ca. 1931 (1890)-present. Kay was a huge manufacturer and built instruments under their name and for a large number of other retailers, jobbers, and brand names.

Silva

1950s. Top of the line 5-string, Silva verticle logo along with Kay logo on headstock, block markers.

1950s		$750	$900

Student Tenor

1950s		$175	$225

Kel Kroydon

1930-1933. Private branded budget level instruments made by Gibson. They also had guitars and banjos. The name has been revived on a line of banjos by Tom Mirisola and made in Nashville.

Banjos

1933-1933	Conversion	$4,000	$4,500
1933-1937	Tenor	$3,500	$4,400

BANJOS

MODEL YEAR	FEATURES	EXC. COND. LOW	HIGH

Keystone State
1920s. Brand of banjos built by Weymann.
Style 2
1920s. Tenor, resonator, fancy appointments.

1920s		$1,200	$1,350

Kona
2001-present. Budget grade, production, banjos made in Asia. They also offer guitars, basses and amps.

Lange
1920s-1942, Late 1940s. The William L. Lange Company began selling Paramount banjos, guitar banjos and mandolin banjos in the early 1920s. Gretsch picked up the Paramount name and used it on acoustics and electrics for a time in the late '40s. See Paramount for more listings.
Tourraine Deluxe

1920s	Tenor	$400	$500

Leedy
1989-1930. Founded in Indianapolis by U. G. Leedy, the company started making banjos in 1924. Leedy was bought out by C. G. Conn in '30.
Olympian

1930	Tenor	$600	$700

Solotone

1924-1930	Tenor	$850	$1,050

Ludwig
The Ludwig Drum Company was founded in 1909. They saw a good business opportunity and entered the banjo market in '21. When demand for banjos tanked in the '30s, Ludwig dropped the line and concentrated on its core business.
Bellevue
1920s. Tenor, closed-back banjo with fancy appointments.

1920s		$850	$1,050

Big Chief
1930. Carved and engraved plectrum banjo.

1930		$7,250	$7,700

Capital
1920s. Tenor banjo, resonator and nice appointments.

1920s		$900	$1,100

Columbia

1920s	Tenor, student-level	$500	$550

Commodore
1930s. Tenor or plectrum, with gold hardware and fancy appointments.

1930s	Tenor	$1,700	$2,000
1932	Plectrum	$2,500	$3,000

Deluxe
1930s. Engraved tenor, with gold hardware.

1930s		$2,500	$3,000

Dixie

1930s	Tenor	$400	$500

Kenmore Plectrum

1920s	Open back	$600	$750

Kenmore Tenor

1920s	Resonator	$475	$575

Kingston

1924-1930	Tenor	$450	$550

Standard Art Tenor
1924-1930. Tenor banjo with fancy appointments.

1924-1930		$3,900	$4,100

The Ace
1920s. Tenor banjo, resonator and nickel appointments.

1920s		$1,150	$1,350

Luscomb
1888-1898. John F. Luscomb was a well-known banjo player who designed a line of instruments for Thompson & Odell of Boston.
5-String

1890s	Open back	$750	$800

Matao
1970s. High quality builder from Japan. Matao logo on headstock.
Bluegrass

1970s	5-string	$275	$350

Mitchell (P.J.)
1850s. Early gut 5-string banjo maker from New York City.
Gut 5-String

1850s		$4,000	$4,500

Morgan Monroe
1999-present. Intermediate and professional grade, production, banjos made in Korea and distributed by SHS International of Indianapolis, Indiana. They also offer guitars, basses, mandolins, and fiddles.

Morrison
Ca. 1870-ca. 1915. Marketed by New Yorker James Morrison, made by Morrison or possibly others like Buckbee. After 1875, his instruments sported the patented Morrison tone ring.
5-String

1885-1890		$700	$800

ODE/Muse
1961-1980. Founded by Charles Ogsbury in Boulder, Colorado, purchased by Baldwin in '66 and moved to Nashville. Until '71 the banjos were branded as Baldwin; afterwards as Baldwin ODE. Gretsch took over production in '76. Muse was a retail store brand of banjos produced by ODE from '61 to '66. In '71, Ogsbury started the OME Banjo Company in Colorado.
Model C
1976-1980. 5-string banjo, resonator and fancy markers.

1976-1980		$1,600	$1,900

Kel Kroyden conversion

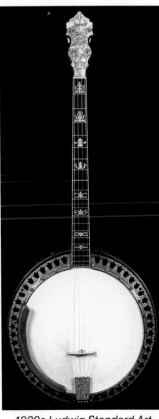

1920s Ludwig Standard Art Tenor Banjo

BANJOS

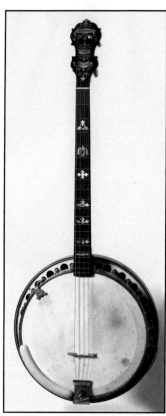

Paramount Aristrocrat Special

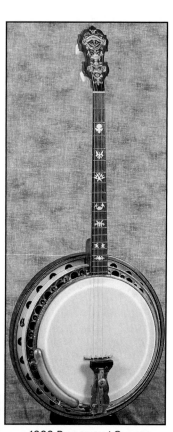

1933 Paramount Super

MODEL YEAR	FEATURES	EXC. COND. LOW	HIGH
Model D			
1970s-1980. 5-string banjo, resonator and gold engravings.			
1970s		$2,200	$2,700

Old Hickory

2005-present. Budget grade, production, imported banjos from Musician's Wholesale America, Nashville, Tennessee. They also offer mansolins.

Orpheum

1897-1922. Lange and Rettberg purchased the J.H. Buckbee banjo factory in 1897 and started making banjos under the Orpheum label. William Lange took control in 1922 and changed the name to Paramount.

MODEL YEAR	FEATURES	EXC. COND. LOW	HIGH
Model #2			
1920-1922	5-string	$2,300	$2,800
1920-1922	Tenor	$1,100	$1,350
Model #3			
1910s	5-string	$2,500	$3,000
1910s	Tenor	$1,200	$1,300

Oscar Schmidt

1879-ca. 1939, 1979-present. Currently offering budget and intermediate grade, production, banjos. They also offer guitars, basses, mandolins, ukuleles and the famous Oscar Schmidt autoharp.

Paramount

1921-1935. William Lange and his Paramount company are generally accredited with commercializing the first modern flange and resonator in 1921.

MODEL YEAR	FEATURES	EXC. COND. LOW	HIGH
Aristocrat			
1921-1935	Plectrum	$2,200	$2,700
1921-1935	Tenor	$2,100	$2,600
Aristocrat Special			
1921-1935. Plectrum or tenor with fancy appoinments.			
1921-1935	Plectrum	$2,500	$3,000
1921-1935	Tenor	$2,400	$2,900
Artists Supreme			
1930s. High-end appointments, 19-fret tenor, engraved gold-plated hardware.			
1930s	Tenor	$5,200	$5,800
Junior			
1921-1935	Plectrum	$875	$1,075
1921-1935	Tenor	$750	$925
Leader			
1921-1935	Plectrum	$1,175	$1,450
1921-1935	Tenor	$1,125	$1,400
Style 1			
1921-1935	Plectrum	$800	$1,000
1921-1935	Tenor	$725	$900
Style 2			
1921-1935. Tenor banjo, resonator and plain appointments.			
1921-1935		$525	$650

MODEL YEAR	FEATURES	EXC. COND. LOW	HIGH
Style A			
1921-1935. Models include the Style A Tenor, Plectrum, and the 5-string (with resonator and fancy appointments).			
1921-1935	5-string	$2,000	$2,500
1921-1935	Plectrum	$1,400	$1,700
1921-1935	Tenor	$1,300	$1,600
Style B			
1921-1935. Models include the Style B Tenor, and the Plectrum (with resonator and fancy appointments).			
1921-1935	Plectrum	$1,800	$2,200
1921-1935	Tenor	$1,700	$2,100
Style C			
1921-1935. Models include the Style C Tenor, Plectrum, and the 5-string (with resonator and fancy appointments).			
1921-1935	5-string	$3,600	$4,400
1921-1935	Plectrum	$2,050	$2,300
1921-1935	Tenor	$1,825	$1,875
Style D			
1921-1935	Plectrum	$2,300	$2,800
1921-1935	Tenor	$2,200	$2,700
Style E			
1921-1935	Plectrum	$2,900	$3,400
1921-1935	Tenor	$2,700	$3,200
Style F			
1921-1935	Plectrum	$3,400	$4,100
1921-1935	Tenor	$3,300	$4,000
Super/Super Paramount			
1921-1935	Plectrum	$4,500	$4,700
1921-1935	Tenor	$4,400	$4,600
Trooper			
1921-1935	Plectrum	$700	$800
1921-1935	Tenor	$600	$700

Penco

Ca. 1974-1978. Japanese-made banjos imported into Philadelphia. They also offered guitars, basses and mandolins.

MODEL YEAR	FEATURES	EXC. COND. LOW	HIGH
Deluxe Tenor			
1970s	Japan	$200	$250

Recording King

1929-1932, 1936-1941. Brand name used by Montgomery Ward for instruments made by various American manufacturers, including Kay, Gibson and Gretsch.

MODEL YEAR	FEATURES	EXC. COND. LOW	HIGH
Studio King Tenor			
1929-1932	40 hole archtop, Gibson	$8,500	$9,000

Recording King (TML)

2005-present. Intermediate and professional grade, production, banjos imported by The Music Link, which also offers Johnson and other brand instruments. They also have guitars and ukes.

Regal

Ca. 1884-1966, 1987-present. Mass manufacturer Regal made brands for others as well as marketing its own brand. In '87 the Regal name was revived by Saga.

BANJOS

MODEL YEAR	FEATURES	EXC. COND. LOW	HIGH

Bicentennial '76
1976. Part of a series of Regal instruments with Bicentennial model logo on headstock (similar to the '76 Regal guitar model), blue finish on neck and headstock, large '76 on banjo head, American-Eagle USA art on back of resonator. Another style with red finish neck and fife and drum art on back of the resonator.

1976	5-string	$375	$425

Rogue
2001-present. Budget grade, production, imported banjos. They also offer guitars, basses, lap steels, mandolins, and ukuleles.

S.S. Stewart
1878-1904. S.S. Stewart of Philadelphia is considered to be one of the most important and prolific banjo manufacturers of the late 19th century. It's estimated that approximately 25,000 banjos were made by this company. The brand name was used on guitars into the 1960s.

20th Century
1890s		$1,550	$1,650

American Princess
1890s	5-string, 10" rim	$600	$1,200

Banjeaurine
1890. 5-string banjo, 10" head with an open back.
1890		$1,300	$1,600

Champion
1895	Open back 5-string	$1,000	$1,300

Orchestra
1890s	5-string, various styles	$1,300	$2,500

Piccolo
1880s	5-string, 7" rim	$1,000	$1,200

Special Thoroughbred
1890s-1900s. Open back, 5-string, carved heel.
1890-1900s		$1,200	$2,000

Universal Favorite
1892	11" head	$1,000	$1,150

Samick
1958-2001, 2002-present. Budget and intermediate grade, production, imported banjos. They also offer guitars, basses, ukes and mandolins.

Silvertone
1941-ca. 1970, present. Brand of Sears instruments which replaced their Supertone brand in '41. Currently, Samick offers a line of amps under the Silvertone name.

5-String Copy
1960s		$200	$350

Slingerland
1930s-mid-1940s. The parent company was Slingerland Banjo and Drums, Chicago, Illinois. The company offered other stringed instruments into the '40s. Slingerland Drums is now owned by Gibson.

Deluxe
1920s	Tenor, higher-end	$1,800	$2,000

May Bell
1920-1930s	Various styles	$500	$900

Student/Economy
1930s		$400	$500

Stelling
1974-present. Founded by Geoff Stelling, building premium and presentation grade, production/custom banjos in Afton, Virginia. They also build mandolins.

Studio King
1930s. Banjos made by Gibson, most likely for a mail-order house or a jobber.

Studio King
1933-1937	Original 5-string	$2,300	$2,500
1933-1937	Tenor	$1,200	$1,300

Superb
1920s. Private brand made by Epiphone.

Mayfair Tenor
1920s	Resonator	$400	$500

Supertone
1914-1941. Brand used by Sears, Roebuck and Company for instruments made by various American manufacturers, including its own Harmony subsidiary Harmony. In '40, Sears began making a transition to the Silvertone brand.

Prairie Wonder
1925. 5-string, open back banjo.
1925		$425	$525

Tennessee
1970-1993, 1996-present. Luthier Mark Taylor builds his professional and premium grade, production/custom, banjos in Old Hickory, Tennessee. He also builds guitars, mandolins and the Tut Taylor brand of resophonic guitars.

Thompson & Odell
1875-1898. Boston instrument importers Thompson & Odell started building banjos in the 1880s. They sold the company to Vega in 1898.

Artist
1880s	5-string, fretless	$775	$950

Tilton
1850s-late 1800s. Built by William B. Tilton, of New York City. He was quite an innovator and held several instrument-related patents. He also built guitars.

Toneking
1927. Private brand of the NY Band Instruments Company, Toneking logo on headstock.

Tenor
1927		$325	$400

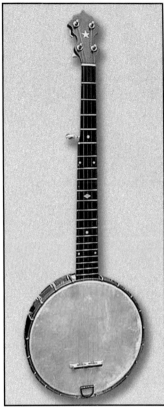

S.S. Stewart American Princess

Slingerland May Bell tenor

BANJOS

Vega Little Wonder

Vega 22-fret plectrum

Trinity River

2004-present. Luthiers Marcus Lawyer and Ross McLeod from Fort Worth, Texas, import their intermediate grade, production/custom, banjos from Asia. They also import guitars, basses and mandolins.

Univox

1964-1978. Instruments imported from Japan by the Merson Musical Supply Company, later Unicord, Westbury, New York.

Tenor

MODEL YEAR	FEATURES	EXC. COND. LOW	HIGH
1970s	Import	$200	$225

Van Eps

1920s. Designed by virtuoso banjo artist Fred Van Eps and sold through Lyon & Healy.

Recording 5-String

1920s		$575	$675

Vega

1903-1980s, 1989-present. Vega of Boston got into the banjo business in 1904 when it purchased Fairbanks. Vega and Gibson were the only major manufacturing companies that offered banjos in their product catalog in the 1950s. The Deering Banjo Company acquired the brand in '89 and uses it on a line of banjos.

Artist Professional #9

1923-1929	Tenor	$2,500	$2,700

Earl Scruggs STII

1969	5-string, resonator	$1,500	$1,700

Folk Ranger FR-5

1960s	5-string, open back	$450	$500

Folk Wonder

1960s	5-string	$1,200	$1,400

Folklore SS-5

5-string, open back, long neck folk banjo.

1966		$1,200	$1,300

Imperial Electric

1921	5-string	$2,200	$2,300

Lady's Banjo

1913		$800	$1,000

Little Wonder

MODEL YEAR	FEATURES	EXC. COND. LOW	HIGH
1920s	Guitar Banjo	$700	$800
1920s	Plectrum	$650	$800
1920s	Tenor	$600	$700
1930s	Tenor	$600	$700
1950s	5-string	$1,450	$1,600

Pete Seeger

1958-1966. 5-string, long neck banjo.

1958-1964	Folk era	$4,700	$5,800
1965-1966		$3,300	$4,100

Professional

1960. 5-string banjo with a Tubaphone tone ring.

1960	Pro II, slits	$1,300	$1,400
1960	Professional, holes	$1,300	$1,400

Ranger

1960s. Standard appointments, dot markers.

1966	5-string	$600	$700

Regent

1920s. 5-string banjo with an open back and dot markers.

1920s		$2,000	$2,200

Style 9

1920s. Tenor banjo with fancy appointments.

1920s		$1,700	$2,100

Style M

1920s. Tenor banjo, models include the Style M and the Style M Tubaphone.

1920s	Style M	$1,900	$2,100
1920s	With Tubaphone TR	$1,100	$1,200

Style N

1910-1920s		$450	$600

Style X

1926	Tenor	$2,500	$2,700

Tubaphone #3

1910-1919	Professional grade option	$3,500	$4,400
1918-1929	5-string	$2,900	$3,000
1923-1929	Tenor, Plectrum, Special	$1,500	$2,900

Tubaphone #9

1929	5-string	$8,400	$8,600

The *Vintage Guitar Price Guide* shows low to high values for items in all-original excellent condition, and, where applicable, with original case or cover.

MODEL YEAR	FEATURES	EXC. COND. LOW	HIGH

Tubaphone Deluxe

1920s. Higher-end appointments, carved heel, Deluxe logo on tailpiece.

| 1923 | 5-string | $10,500 | $12,500 |

V.I.P. Tenor

1970s. 4-string, open back, fancy engraved pearl markers, on-board electronics.

| 1970 | | $1,500 | $1,800 |

V-45

1970. Plectrum banjo, flat head tone ring, fancy appointments.

| 1970s | | $2,800 | $3,000 |

Vegaphone De-Luxe

| 1929 | Plectrum | $2,900 | $3,100 |

Vegaphone Professional

1920s	Plectrum	$1,250	$1,500
1930s	Tenor	$1,025	$1,275
1960s	5-string	$925	$975

Vegavox I Tenor

1930s-1962. Vox-style deep resonator, alternating block/dot markers.

| 1930s | | $1,900 | $2,000 |
| 1956-1962 | | $1,500 | $1,800 |

Vegavox IV

1956-1962. IV logo on truss rod cover, high-end appointments, 4-string plectrum neck.

| 1956-1962 | Plectrum or tenor | $3,000 | $4,500 |

Whyte Laydie #2

| 1923-1928 | 5-string | $3,400 | $3,800 |

Whyte Laydie #7

1905	5-string	$9,000	$10,000
1909		$8,500	$9,000
1921		$8,500	$9,000

Whyte Laydie Style R

1920-1930s. Tenor banjo with closed back.

| 1920-1930s | | $1,200 | $1,250 |

Wonder Tenor

1973. Made by C.F. Martin (brand owner in the '70s), closed back resonator style.

| 1973 | | $550 | $650 |

MODEL YEAR	FEATURES	EXC. COND. LOW	HIGH

Washburn (Lyon & Healy)

1880s-ca.1949. Washburn was the brand name of Lyon & Healy of Chicago. They made banjos from 1880-1929.

5-String

| 1896 | Old 1890s style | $950 | $1,000 |

Irene

| 1920s | 5-string | $750 | $800 |

Washburn (Post 1974)

1974-present. Currently, Washburn offers imported intermediate and professional grade, production, banjos.

Weymann

1864-1940s. The Weymann company was founded in 1864 and got seriously into the banjo manufacturing business in 1917. They manufactured banjos until around 1930.

Plectrum

| 1924-1928 | Style A | $800 | $1,000 |

Tenor

1924-1928	Style #1	$1,350	$1,650
1924-1928	Style #2	$1,400	$1,700
1924-1928	Style #4	$2,600	$3,200
1924-1928	Style #50	$500	$600
1924-1928	Style #6	$4,300	$5,300
1924-1928	Style A, low pro model	$775	$850

Wilson Brothers

1920s-1930s. Private branded by Lyon & Healy.

Tenor

| 1920-1930s | Resonator | $400 | $500 |

Yosco

1900-1930s. Lawrence L. Yosco was a New York City luthier building guitars, round back mandolins and banjos under his own brand and for others.

Style 3

| 1920s | Tenor | $1,250 | $1,400 |

1927 Vega Vegaphone De-Luxe

Washburn 5183 tenor

BANJOS

BIBLIOGRAPHY

'50s Cool: Kay Guitars, by Jay Scott, 1992, Seventh String Press, Inc.

50 Years of Fender, by Tony Bacon, 2000, Miller Freeman Books.

50 Years of Gretsch Electrics, by Tony Bacon, 2005, Backbeat Books.

Acoustic Guitars and Other Fretted Instruments, A Photographic History, by George Gruhn and Walter Carter, 1993, GPI Books.

Acoustic Guitar magazine, various issues, String Letter Publishing.

Acquired of the Angels, by Paul William Schmidt, 1998, Scarecrow Press.

American Basses, by Jim Roberts, 2003, Backbeat Books.

American Guitars, An Illustrated History, by Tom Wheeler, 1992, Harper Collins.

American's Instrument, The Banjo in the Nineteenth Century, by Philip F. Gura and James F. Bollman, 1999, University of North Carolina Press.

Ampeg - The Story Behind The Sound, by Gregg Hopkins and Bill Moore, 1999, Hal Leonard Publishing.

Amps! The Other Half of Rock 'n' Roll, by Ritchie Fliegler, 1993, Hal Leonard publishing.

Analog Man's Guide to Vintage Effects, by Tom Hughes, 2004, Musicians Only Publishing.

The Bass Book, A Complete Illustrated History of Bass Guitars, by Tony Bacon and Barry Moorhouse, 1995, Miller Freeman Books.

The Boss Book, 2001, Hal Leonard Publishing.

The Burns Book, by Paul Day, 1990, PP Publishing and The Bold Strummer.

Classic Guitars U.S.A., by Willie G. Moseley, 1992, Centerstream.

The Classical Guitar Book, by Tony Bacon, et al., 2002, Balafon Books.

The Complete History of Rickenbacker Guitars, by Richard R. Smith, 1987, Centerstream.

Cowboy Guitars, by Steve Evans and Ron Middlebrook, 2002, Centerstream.

Custom Guitars, A Complete Guide to Contempory Handcrafted Guitars, 2000, String Letter Publishing.

The Custom Guitar Shop and Wayne Richard Charvel, by Frank W/m Green, 1999, Working Musician Publications.

A Desktop Reference of Hip Vintage Guitar Amps, by Gerald Weber, 1994, Kendrick Books.

Electric Guitars and Basses, A Photographic History, by George Gruhn and Walter Carter, 1994, GPI Books.

Elektro-Gitarren Made in Germany, by Norbert Schnepel and Helmuth Lemme (German, with English translation), 1987, Musik-Verlag Schnepel-Lemme oHG.

Epiphone: The Complete History, by Walter Carter, 1995, Hal Leonard publishing.

Epiphone: The House of Stathopoulo, by Jim Fisch & L.B. Fred, 1996, Amsco Publications.

The Fender Amp Book, by John Morrish, 1995, Balafon Books and GPI Books.

Fender Amps: The First Fifty Years, by John Teagle and John Sprung, 1995, Hal Leonard Publishing.

The Fender Bass, by Klaus Blasquiz, 1990, Mediapresse.

The Fender Bass, An Illustrated History, by J.W. Black and Albert Molinaro, 2001, Hal Leonard Publishing.

The Fender Book, by Tony Bacon and Paul Day, 1992, Balafon and GPI Books.

Fender: The Sound Heard 'Round the World, by Richard R. Smith, 1995, Garfish Publishing.

The Fender Stratocaster, by Andre Duchossoir, 1988, Mediapresse.

The Fender Telecaster, by Andre Duchossoir, 1991, Hal Leonard Publishing.

G&L: Leo's Legacy, by Paul Bechtoldt, 1994, Woof Associates.

Gibson Electrics, The Classic Years, by A. R. Duchossoir, 1994, Hal Leonard Publishing.

Gibson's Fabulous Flat-Top Guitars, by Eldon Whitford, David Vinopal, and Dan Erlewine, 1994, GPI Books.

Gibson Guitars: 100 Years of An American Icon, by Walter Carter, 1994, W. Quay Hays.

Gibson Guitars: Ted McCarty's Golden Era: 1948-1966, by Gil Hembree, 2007, Hal Leonard Publishing Corporation.

The Gibson Les Paul Book, A Complete History of Les Paul Guitars, by Tony Bacon and Paul Day, 1993 Balafon Books and GPI Books.

The Gibson Super 400, Art of the Fine Guitar, by Thomas A. Van Hoose, 1991, GPI Books.

Gibson Shipping Totals 1948-1979, 1992, J.T.G.

The Gretsch Book, by Tony Bacon & Paul Day, 1996, Balafon Books and GPI Books.

Gruhn's Guide to Vintage Guitars, 2nd Edition, by George Gruhn and Walter Carter, 1999, Miller Freeman Books.

The Guild Guitar Book: The Company and the Instruments 1952-1977, by Hans Moust, 1995, GuitArchives Publications.

Guitar Identification: Fender-Gibson-Gretsch-Martin, by Andre Duchossoir, 1983, Hal Leonard Publishing Corporation.

Guitar People, by Willie G. Moseley, 1997, Vintage Guitar Books.

Guitar Player magazine, various issues, Miller Freeman.

Guitar Stories, Vol. I, by Michael Wright, 1994, Vintage Guitar Books.

Guitar Stories, Vol. II, by Michael Wright, 2000, Vintage Guitar Books.

Guitar World magazine, various issues, Harris Publications.

The Guitars of the Fred Gretsch Company, by Jay Scott, 1992, Centerstream.

Guitars From Neptune, A Definitive Journey Into Danelectro-Mania, by Paul Bechtoldt, 1995, Backporch Publications.

Guitar Graphics, Vol. 1 (Japanese), 1994, Rittor Music Mooks.

The Guru's Guitar Guide, by Tony Bacon and Paul Day, 1990, Track Record and The Bold Strummer.

The History and Artistry of National Resonator Instruments, by Bob Brozman, 1993, Centerstream.

The History of Marshall, by Michael Doyle, 1993, Hal Leonard Publishing.

The History of the Ovation Guitar, by Walter Carter, 1996, Hal Leonard publishing.

The History of Yamaha Guitars, by Mark Kasulen & Matt Blackett, 2006, Hal Leonard Corporation.

Ibanez, the Untold Story, by Paul Specht, Michael Wright, and Jim Donahue, 2005, Hoshino (U.S.A.) Inc.

The Larson's Creations, Guitars & Mandolins, by Robert Carl Hartman, 2007, Centerstream.

The Martin Book, by Walter Carter, 1995, Balafon Books and GPI Books.

Martin Guitars, A History, by Mike Longworth, 1988, 4 Maples Press.

Martin Guitars: An Illustrated Celebration of America's Premier Guitarmaker, by Jim Washburn & Richard Johnston, 1997, Rodale Press, Inc.

Musicial Merchandise Review magazine, various issues, Symphony Publishing.

The Music Trades magazine, various issues, Music Trades Corporation.

The Official Vintage Guitar Magazine Price Guide, all editions.

The PRS Guitar Book, by Dave Burrluck, 1999, Outline Press, London.

The Rickenbacker Book, by Tony Bacon & Paul Day, 1994, Balafon Books and GFI Books.

Six Decades of the Fender Telecaster, by Tony Bacon, 2005, Backbeat Books.

Stellas & Stratocasters, by Willie G. Moseley, 1994, Vintage Guitar Books.

Stompbox, by Art Thompson, 1997, Miller Freeman Books.

The Tube Amp Book, 4th Edition, by Aspen Pittman, 1993, Groove Tubes.

The Ultimate Guitar Book, by Tony Bacon and Paul Day, 1991, Alfred A. Knopf.

Vintage Guitar magazine, various issues, Vintage Guitar, Inc.

VG Classics magazine, various issues, Vintage Guitar, Inc.

The Vox Story, A Complete History of the Legend, by David Peterson and Dick Denney, 1993, The Bold Strummer, Ltd.

Washburn: Over One Hundred Years of Fine Stringed Instruments, by John Teagle, 1996, Amsco Publications.

Various manufacturer catalogs, literature, and web sites.

DEALER DIRECTORY A GEOGRAPHICAL GUIDE

AUSTRALIA
Guitar Emporium
Darren Garth
155 Victoria Avenue
Albert Park, Victoria,
Australia, 3206
Phone 61.3.9696.8032
emporium@ozemail.com.au
www.guitaremporium.com.au

Ric's Vintage Guitars
Australia's Number 1 Vintage
 Guitar Dealer
Richard Zand-Vliet
84 King Street
Perth
West Australia
Phone: international +61 8
 94815008
Phone: local 08-94815008
ric@ricsvintageguitars.com
www:ricsvintageguitars.com

CANADA
Capsule Music
Mark or Peter Kesper
921 Queen St. W.
Toronto, Ontario M6J 1G5
Phone: 416-203-0202
contact@capsulemusic.com
www.capsulemusic.com

Folkway Music
Mark Stutman
163 Suffolk Street West
Guelph, Ontario N1H 2J7
Phone: 519-763-5524
info@folkwaymusic.com
www.folkwaymusic.com

SD Custom Guitar Works
Atelier de Lutherie SD
6610 Blvd des-Galeries-D'Anjou
 (Ste. 102)
Montreal (Anjou), Quebec
Phone 514-543-3888
info@MontrealCustomGuitars.
 com
www.MontrealCustomGuitars.
 com

The Twelfth Fret Inc.
Grant MacNeill and David Wren
2132 Danforth Avenue
Toronto, Ont., Canada M4C 1J9
Phone: 416-423-2132
Fax: 416-423-0012
sales@12fret.com
www.12fret.com

ENGLAND
Ampaholics
Paul Goodhand-Tait
P.O. Box 542
Surrey, GU1 12F, England
Phone: +44-1483-825102
ampaholics@aol.com
www.ampaholics.org.uk

Watford Valves & Speakers
Derek Rocco
Bricket Wood, Street Albans.
Herts. England AL2 3TS
Phone: 44-1923-893270
Fax: 44-1923-679207
sales@watfordvalves.com
www.watfordvalves.com

ITALY
Real Vintage
Nino Fazio
via Manzoni, 13
98057 Milazzo ME, Italy
Phone: +39-090-40646
realvintage@realvintage.it
www.realvintage.it

UNITED STATES
Arizona
The Bass Place
David Goldenfarb
1440 Scottsdale Rd.
Tempe, AZ 85281
Phone: 480-423-1161
dave@thebassplace.com
www.thebassplace.com

Arkansas
Blue Moon Music, Inc.
Les Haynie
3107 North College Ave.
Fayetteville, AR 72703-2609
Phone: 479-521-8163
blumnmus@aol.com

Antique Electronic Supply
Brian Campanella
6221 South Maple Avenue
Tempe, AZ 85283
Phone: 480-820-5411
Fax: 800-706-6789
info@tubesandmore.com
www.tubesandmore.com

California
Buffalo Bros. Guitars
Steve Mendoza
4901 El Camino Real
Carlsbad, CA 92008
Phone: 760-434-4567

Fax: 760-434-4347
bb_info@buffalobrosguitars.com
www.buffalobrosguitars.com

California Vintage Guitar and Amps
5244 Van Nuys Blvd.
Sherman Oaks, CA 91401
Phone: 818-789-8884
sales@californiavintageguitaran-
damp.com
www.californiavintageguitaran-
damp.com

Eric Schoenberg Guitars
Eric Schoenberg
106 Main Street
Tiburon, CA 94920
Phone: 415-789-0846
eric@om28. com
www.om28.com

Freedom Guitar, Inc.
Dewey L. Bowen
6334 El Cajon Boulevard
San Diego, CA 92115
Phone: 800-831-5569
Fax: 619-265-1414
info@freedomguitar.com
www.freedomguitar.com

Fretted Americana
23901 Calabasas Rd., Ste 2024
Calabasas, CA 91302
Phone: 818-222-4113
Fax: 818-222-6173
vgm@frettedamericana.com
www.frettedamericana.com

Gryphon Stringed Instru-ments
Richard Johnston
211 Lambert Ave.
Palo Alto, CA 94306
Phone: 650-493-2131
VintageInstruments@gryphon-
strings.com
www.gryphonstrings.com

Guitar Center (CA)
7425 Sunset Boulevard
Hollywood, CA 90046
Phone: 323-874-2302
       323-874-1060
Fax: 323-969-9783
www.vintageguitars.net

Guitar Heaven (CA)
Frank Benna
1934 Oak Park Blvd.

Pleasant Hill, CA 94523-4602
Phone: 925-938-5750
guitarheaven@sbcglobal.net
www.guitarheaven.com

Guitars West
Gary Hernandez
41110 Sandalwood Cir., Ste 113
Murrieta, CA 92562
Cell: 619-988-9777
Store: 951-894-3072
guitarswest@hughes.net
www.guitarswest.net

Mahar's Vintage Guitars
Chuck Mahar
PO Box 598
Forest Ranch, CA 95942-0598
Phone: 530-894-2228
s-source@pacbell.net
www.maharsvintageguitars.com

Norman's Rare Guitars
Norman Harris
18969 Ventura Blvd.
Tarzana, CA 91356-3229
Phone: 818-344-8300
Fax: 818-344-1260
normsgtrs@aol.com
www.normansrareguitars.com

Players Vintage Instruments
P.O. Box 445
Inverness, CA 94937-0445
Phone: 415-669-1107
Fax: 415-669-1102
info@vintageinstruments.com
www.vintageinstruments.com

Soest Guitar Shop
Steve Soest
760 North Main Street Suite D
Orange, CA 92668
Phone: 714-538-0272
Fax: 714-532-4763
soestguitar@earthlink.net
www.soestguitar.com

Sylvan Music
Al Markasky
1521 Mission St.
Santa Cruz, CA 95060
Phone: 831-427-1917
info@sylvanmusic.com
www.sylvanmusic.com

TrueTone Music
Ken Daniels
714 Santa Monica Blvd.
Santa Monica, CA 90401

Phone: 310-393-8232
310-260-1415
sales@truetonemusic.com
www.truetonemusic.com

Virtual Vintage Guitars
Jason C. Allen
Phone: 949-635-9797
sales@virtualvintageguitars.com
www.virtualvintageguitars.com

Florida
Andy's Guitars
Andy Eder
1208 North Monroe Street
Tallahassee, FL 32303
Phone: 850-224-9944
Fax: 850-224-5381
info@andysguitars.com
www.andysguitars.com

Crescent City Music
Allen Glenn
111 North Summit Street
Crescent City, FL 32112
Phone/Fax: 386-698-2873
Phone: 386-698-2874
Cell: 386-559-0133
ccag@alletel.net
www.crescentcitymusic.biz

Grampa's Music
Reese Smith
804-A Anastasia Blvd.
St. Augustine, FL 32080
Phone: 904-819-5797
grampas@localnet.com
www.grampasmusic.com

Greene Acres Guitars
Bob Greene
5416 26th St. West
Bradenton, FL 34207
Phone: 941-756-7333
greeneacresguitars@gmail.com
www.greeneacresguitars.com

Gulfcoast Guitars
Dave Lipstein
1927 Beach Rd.,
Engelwood, FL 34223-5709
Phone: 941-474-1214
gcg@ewol.com
www.guitars.net

Kummer's Vintage Instruments
Timm Kummer
Phone: 954-752-6063
prewar99@aol.com
www.kummersvintage.com

Legends Music, Inc.
Kent Sonenberg
4340 West Hillsborough Avenue
Tampa, FL 33614
Phone: 813-348-0688
Fax: 813-348-0689

ksonenbl@tampabay.rr.com
www.legendsguitars.com

Old Goat Guitars
Mark Humphrey
Phone: 941-356-1206
mhumphrey9@comcast.net
www.oldgoatguitars.com

Georgia
Atlanta Vintage Guitars
Frank Moates
561 Windy Hill Road
Smyrna, GA 30080
Phone: 770-433-1891
Fax: 770-433-1858
atlantavintage@bellsouth.net
www.atlantavintageguitars.com

Southern Guitars
Robbie Cantrell or Jimmy Miller
105 South Dixie Ave.
Cartersville, GA 30120
Phone: 770-386-1314
Fax: 770-386-1350
info@southernguitars.com
www.southernguitars.com

Hawaii
Coconut Grove Music
Frank Kam
418 Kuulei Road
Kailua, HI 96734
Phone: 808-262-9977
Fax: 808-263-7052
cgmusic@lava.net
www.coconutgrovemusic.com

Illinois
Chicago Music Exchange
Scott Silver
3316 N. Lincoln Ave.
Chicago, IL 60657
Phone: 773-525-7775
Fax: 773-477-2775
sales@chicagomusicexchange.com
www.chicagomusicexchange.com

Guitar Works Ltd
Steve or Terry
709 Main Street
Evanston, IL 60202
Phone: 847-475-0855
Fax: 847-475-0715
guitarworksltd@aol.com
www.guitarworksltd.com

Make 'n Music
Teddy
1455 W. Hubbard St.
Chicago, IL 60622
Phone: 312-455-1970
info@makenmusic.com
www.makenmusic.com

Music Gallery
Frank
2558 Greenbay Road

Highland Park, IL 60035
Phone: 847-432-6350 / 847-432-8883
MusicGlry@aol.com
www.musicgalleryinc.com

RWK Guitars
P.O. Box 1068
Highland Park, IL 60035
Phone: 847-432-4308
Bob@RWKGuitars.com
www.RWKGuitars.com

Kansas
Overland Express Guitars
David Schaefer
Overland Park, KS as well as Missouri & Iowa
Phone: 913-469-4034
Fax: 913-469-9672
dave@overlandexpress.com
www.overlandexpress.com

Kentucky
Guitar Emporium
1610 Bardstown Road
Louisville, KY 40205
Phone 502-459-4153
Fax: 502-454-3661
guitar-emporium@mindspring.com
www.guitar-emporium.com

Louisianna
International Vintage Guitars
Steve Staples
646 Tchopitoulas St.
New Orleans, LA 70130-3212
Phone: 504-524-4557
Fax: 504-524-4665
guitars@webcorral.com
www.webcorral.com

Maryland
Garrett Park Guitars, Inc.
Rick Hogue
302 S. Truman Pkway, Ste. F
Annapolis, MD 21401
Phone: 410-571-9660
Fax: 410-573-0502
gpguitars@gmail.com
www.gpguitars.com

Guitar Exchange
Bruce Sandler
740 Frederick Road
Baltimore, MD 21228
Phone: 410-747-0122
Fax: 410-747-0525

Jim's Guitars Inc.
Jim Singleton
706 Frederick Rd.
Baltimore, MD 21228-4501
Phone: 866-787-2865
Fax: 410-744-0010
info@jimsguitars.com
www.jimsguitars.com

Main Street Vintage Co.
Patrick Grissinger
Baltimore, MD
Phone: 888-335-1959
msvco.patrick@mac.com
www.mainstreetvintageco.com

My Old Guitars and Amps and New Old Stock Tubes
PO Box 50063
Baltimore, MD 21211
Phone: 410-705-8980
marspoolshack@gmail.com
www.myoldguitarsandampsandnewoldstocktubes.com

Nationwide Guitars, Inc.
Bruce Rickard
P.O. Box 2334
Columbia, MD 21045
Phone: 410-997-7440
Fax: 410-997-7440
nationwideguitars@comcast.net
www.nationwideguitars.com

Southworth Guitars
Gil Southworth
Phone/Fax: 703-759-4433
southworthguitar@aol.com
www.southworthguitars.com

Massachusetts
Bay State Vintage Guitars
Craig D. Jones
295 Huntington Avenue, Room 304
Boston, MA 02115
Phone: 617-267-6077

Cold Springs Electrical Works
Norm Moren
332 Rock Rimmon Road
Belchertown, MA 01007
Phone: 413-323-8869
norm@coldspringselectricalworks.com
www.coldspringselectricalworks.com

Lucchesi Vintage Instruments
Shane LoSelle
108 Cottage St.
Easthampton, MA 01027
Phone: 413-527-6627
info@lucchesivintageinstruments.com
www.lucchesivintageinstruments.com

Michigan
Elderly Instruments
Stan Werbin
1100 North Washington
P.O. Box 14210 -VGF
Lansing, MI 48901
Phone: 517-372-7890
Fax: 517-372-5155
elderly@elderly.com
www.elderly.com

Huber & Breese Music
33540 Groesbeck Highway
Fraser, MI 48026
Phone: 586-294-3950
Fax: 586-294-7616
info@huberbreese.com
www.huberbreese.com

Lakeshore Guitars
Rich Baranowski
Troy, MI
Phone: 248-879-7474
richbaronow@wowway.ncom
www.lakeshoreguitars.com

mygear.com
Phone: 888-508-GEAR
www.mygear.com

Minnesota
Solidbodyguitar.com
Bruce Barnes
2436 Highway 10
Mounds View, MN 55112
Phone: 763-783-0080
Fax: 763-783-0090
solidbodyguitar@quest.net
www.solidbodyguitar.com

Willie's American Guitars
254 Cleveland Avenue South
St. Paul, MN 55105
Phone: 651-699-1913
Fax: 651-690-1766
info@williesguitars.com
www.williesguitars.com

Missouri
Eddie's Guitars
Ed Putney
7362 Manchester Rd.
St. Louis, MO 63143-3108
Phone: 314-781-7500
Fax: 314-781-7510
eddiesguitars@sbcglobal.net
www.eddiesguitars.com

Fly By Night Music
Dave Crocker
103 South Washington
Neosho, MO 64850-1816
Phone: 417-451-5110
Show number: 800-356-3347
crocker@joplin.com
www.texasguitarshows.com

Hazard Ware Inc./ Killer Vintage
Dave Hinson
P.O. Box 190561
St. Louis, MO 63119
Phone: 314-647-7795
        800-646-7795
Fax: 314-781-3240
www.killervintage.com

Silver Strings Music
Ed Seelig
8427 Olive Blvd.

St. Louis, MO 63132
Phone: 314-997-1120
ed@silverstringsmusic.com
www.silverstringsmusic.com

Nevada
AJ's Music In Las Vegas
Peter Trauth
2031 W. Sunset Rd.
Henderson, NV 89014-2120
Phone: 702-436-9300
Fax: 702-436-9302
ajsmusic@earthlink.net
www.ajsmusic.com

Cowtown Guitars
2797 South Maryland Parkway,
Ste. 14
Las Vegas, NV 89109
Phone: 702-866-2600
Fax: 702-866-2520
www.cowtownguitars.com

New Hampshire
Retro Music
Jeff Firestone
38 Washington Street
Keene, NH 03431
Phone/Fax: 603-357-9732
retromusic@verizon.com
www.retroguitar.com

New Jersey
Golden Age Fretted Instruments
John Paul Reynolds
309 South Avenue W.
Westfield, NJ 07090
Phone: 908-301-0001
Fax: 908-301-1199
info@goldenageguitars.com
www.goldenageguitars.com

Lark Street Music
479 Cedar Lane
Teaneck, NJ 07666
Phone: 201-287-1959
Larkstreet@aol.com
www.larkstreet.com

New Jersey Guitar & Bass Center
Jay Jacus
995 Amboy Avenue
Edison, NJ 08837
Phone: 732-225-4444
Fax: 732-225-4404
NJGtrBass@aol.com
www.newjerseyguitarandbasscenter.com

Pick of the Ricks
Chris Clayton
121 Holly St.
Lindenwold, NJ 08021
Phone: 856-782-7300
sales@pickofthericks.com
www.pickofthericks.com

New York
Bernunzio Uptown Music
John or Julie Bernunzio
122 East Ave.
Rochester, NY 14604
Phone: 585-473-6140
Fax: 585-442-1142
info@bernunzio.com
www.bernunzio.com

Carmine Street Guitars
Home of famous Kustom Kelly
 Guitar
Rick Kelly
42 Carmine St.
New York, NY 10014
Phone: 212-691-8400
kellyguitars@yahoo.com
www.carminestreetguitars.com

Imperial Guitar and Soundworks
Bill Imperial
99 Route 17K
Newburgh, NY 12550
Phone: 845-567-0111
igs55@aol.com
www.imperialguitar.com

Laurence Wexer Ltd.
Larry Wexer
251 East 32nd Street #11F
New York, NY 10016
Phone: 212-532-2994
larrywexer@aol.com
www.wexerguitars.com

Ludlow Guitars
164 Ludlow Street
New York, NY 10002
Phone: 212-353-1775
Fax: 212-353-1749
ludlowguitars@gmail.com
www.ludlowguitars.com

Mandolin Brothers, Ltd.
629 Forest Avenue
Staten Island, NY 10310
Phone: 718-981-3226/8585
Fax: 718-816-4416
mandolin@mandoweb.com
www.mandoweb.com

Michael's Music
Michael Barnett
29 West Sunrise Highway
Freeport, NY 11520
Phone: 516-379-4111
Fax: 516-379-3058
michaelsmusic@optonline.net
www.michaelsmusic.com

Music Services
Gary Blankenburg
2008 Wantagh Ave.
Wantagh, NY 11793-3921
Phone: 516-826-2525
vcoolg@verizon.net
www.verycoolguitars.com

My Generation Guitars
John DeSilva
Syosset, NY
Phone: 516-993-9893
info@mygenerationguitars.com
www.mygenerationguitars.com

Rivington Guitars
Howie Statland
125 Rivington St.
New York, NY 10002
Phone: 212-505-5313
www.rivingtonguitars.com

Rudy's Music
Rudy Pensa
169 West 48th Street
New York, NY 10036
Phone: 212-391-1699
info@rudysmusic.com
www.rudysmusic.com

Rumble Seat Music
Eliot Michael
121 West State St.
Ithica, NY 14850
Phone: 607-277-9236
Fax: 607-277-4593
rumble@rumbleseatmusic.com
www.rumbleseatmusic.com

Stutzman's Guitar Center
David Stutzman
4405 Ridge Rd. West
Rochester, NY 14626
Phone: 585-352-3225
Fax: 585-352-8614
info@stutzmansguitarcenter.
 com
www.stutzmansguitarcenter.
 com

We Buy Guitars
David Davidson
705A Bedford Ave.
Bellmore, NY 11710
Phone: 516-221-0563
Fax: 516-221-0856
webuyguitars1@aol.com
www.webuyguitars.net

We Buy Guitars
Richie Friedman
705A Bedford Ave.
Bellmore, NY 11710
Phone: 516-221-0563
Fax: 516-221-0856
webuyguitars@aol.com
www.webuyguitars.net

We Buy Guitars
Tom Dubas
705A Bedford Ave.
Bellmore, NY 11710
Phone: 516-221-0563
Fax: 516-221-0856
webuyguitars2@aol.com
www.webuyguitars.net

North Carolina

Bee-3 Vintage
Gary Burnette
PO Box 19509
Asheville, NC 28815
Phone: 828-298-2197
bee3vintage@hotmail.com
www.bee3vintage.com

Coleman Music
Chip Coleman
1021 S. Main St.
China Grove, NC 28023-2335
Phone: 704-857-5705
CGColemuse@aol.com
www.colemanmusic.com

Legato Guitars
Bill Fender
1121C Military Cutoff Rd. #342
Wilmington, NC 28405
Phone: 910-686-3264
By Appointment Only
legatoguitars@ec.rr.com
www.legatoguitars.com

Maverick Music
Phil Winfield
8425 Old Statesville Rd., Ste 19
Charlotte, NC 28269-1828
Phone: 704-599-3700
Fax: 704-599-3712
sales@maverick-music.com
www.maverick-music.com

North Dakota

Nightlife Music
Rick or Jory Berge
1235 S. 12th St.
Bismarck, ND 58504
Phone: 701-222-0202
sales@nightlifemusic.com
www.nightlifemusic.com

Stringbean Music
Phil Feser
510-E. Main Ave.
Bismarck, ND 58501
Phone: 701-250-8699
phil@stringbeanmusic.com
www.stringbeanmusic.com

Ohio

DHR Music
PO Box 43209
Cincinnati, OH 45243
Phone: 513-272-8004
Fax: 513-530-0229
dhrmusic@hotmail.com
www.dhrmusic.com

Fretware Guitars
Dave Hussung
400 South Main
Franklin, OH 45005
Phone: 937-743-1151
Fax: 937-743-9987

guitar@erinet.com
www.fretware.cc

Gary's Classic Guitars
Gary Dick
Cincinnati, OH
Phone: 513-891-0555
Fax: 513-891-9444
garysclssc@aol.com
www.garysguitars.com

Mike's Music
Mike Reeder
2615 Vine Street
Cincinnati, OH 45219
Phone: 513-281-4900
Fax: 513-281-4968
www.mikesmusicohio.com

Oklahoma

MandoAiki
Ed Cunliff
3433 Baird Dr.
Edmond, OK 73013
Phone: 405-341-2926
mandoaiki@yahoo.com
www.mandoaiki.com

Martin Vintage Guitars
Russ Martin
612 Riverwalk Ct.
Norman, OK 73072
Phone: 405-824-1868
russ@martinvintageguitars.com
www.martinvintageguitars.com

Strings West
Larry Briggs
P.O. Box 999
20 E. Main Street
Sperry, OK 74073
Phone: 800-525-7273
Fax: 918-288-2888
larryb@stringswest.com
www.stringswest.com

Oregon

McKenzie River Music
Bob November
455 West 11th
Eugene, OR 97401
Phone: 541-343-9482
Fax: 541-465-9060
www.McKenzieRiverMusic.com

Pennsylvania

Guitar-Villa – Retro Music
John Slog
216A Nazareth Pike
Bethlehem, PA 18020
Phone: 610-746-9200
qtown2@nni.com
www.guitar-villa.com

JH Guitars
Jim Heflybower
Pennsylvania
Phone: 610-363-9204

Fax: 610-363-8689
JHGuitars@msn.com
www.jhguitars.com

Rhoads Music
Your Vox and Rickenbacker
  authority
Jim Rhoads
123 W. Libhart Alley
Elizabethtown, PA 17022
Phone: 717-361-9272
Fax: 717-361-9272
rhoadsmusi@aol.com
www.rhoadsmusic.com

Vintage Instruments Inc.
Fred W. Oster
1529 Pine Street
Philadelphia, PA 19102
Phone: 215-545-1100
vintagefred@aol.com
www.vintage-instruments.com

Rhode Island

PM Blues Guitar Heaven
Paul Moskwa 401-722-5837
bluespm@aol.com
www.pmblues.com

Tennessee

Gruhn Guitars
George Gruhn
400 Broadway
Nashville, TN 37203
Phone: 615-256-2033
Fax: 615-255-2021
gruhn@gruhn.com
www.gruhn.com

Rick's Guitar Room
Rick Mikel
4422 Dayton Blvd.
Chatanooga, TN 37415
Phone: 423-870-5335
ricksguitarroom@bellsouth.net
www.ricksguitarroom.com

Texas

Charley's Guitar Shop
Clay and Sheila Powers
2720 Royal Ln. Ste.100
Dallas, TX 75229-4727
Phone: 972-243-4187
Fax: 972-243-5193
shop@charleysguitar.com
www.charleysguitar.com

Eugene's Guitars Plus
Eugene Robertson
2010 South Buckner Boulevard
Dallas, TX 75217-1823
Phone: 214-391-8677
pluspawnguitars@yahoo.com
www.texasguitarshows.com

Hill Country Guitars
Kevin Drew Davis
111 Old Kyle Rd. #200

Wimberley, TX 78676-9701
Phone: 512-847-8677
Fax: 512-847-8699
info@hillcountryguitars.com
www.hillcountryguitars.com

Texas Amigos Guitar Shows
Arlington Guitar Show (The 4
  Amigos)
Contact: John or Ruth Brink-
  mann
Phone: 800-473-6059
Fax: 817-473-1089
web: www.texasguitarshows.com

Chicago/Austin Guitar Show
Dave Crocker
Phone: 800-356-3347
Fax: 817-473-1089
crocker@joplin.com
www.texasguitarshows.com

California World Guitar Shows
Larry Briggs
Phone: 800-525-7273
Fax: 918-288-2888
larryb@stringswest.com
www.texasguitarshows.com

**Van Hoose Vintage Instru-
ments**
Thomas Van Hoose
2722 Raintree Drive
Carrollton, TX 75006
Phone: (days) 972-250-2919 or
  (eves) 972-418-4863
Fax: 972-250-3644
tv0109@flash.net
www.vanhoosevintage.com

Waco Vintage Instruments
John Brinkman
1275 North Main Street, Ste #4
Mansfield, TX 76063
Phone: 817-473-9144
Guitar Show Phone: 888-473-6059

Utah

**Intermountain Guitar and
Banjo**
Leonard or Kennard
712 East 100 South
Salt Lake City, UT 84102
Phone: 801-322-4682
Fax: 801-355-4023
guitarandbanjo@earthlink.com
www.guitarandbanjo.net

Virginia

Callaham Guitars
Bill Callaham
217 Park Center Dr.
Winchester, VA 22603
Phone: 540-678-4043
Fax: 540-678-8779
callaham@callahamguitars.com
www.callahamguitars.com

Vintage Sound
Bill Holter
P.O. Box 11711
Alexandria, VA 22312
Phone: 703-914-2126
Fax: 703-914-1044
bhvsound@vintagesound.com
www.vintagesound.com

Washington

Emerald City Guitars
Jay Boone
83 South Washington in Pioneer
Square
Seattle, WA 98104
Phone: 206-382-0231
jayboone@emeraldcityguitars.com

Guitarville
Billy
19258 15th Avenue North East

Seattle, WA 98155-2315
Phone: 206-363-8188
Fax: 206-363-0478
gv@guitarville.com
www.guitarville.com

Mark's Guitar Shop
Nate Corning
318 W. Garland
Spokane, WA 99205
Phone: 866-219-8500
       509-325-8353
marksguitarshop@qwest.net
www.marksguitarshop.com

Wisconsin

Bizarre Guitars
Brian Goff
2501 Waunona Way
Madison, WI 53713
Phone: 608-235-3561

bdgoff@sbcglobal.net

Cream City Music
Joe Gallenberger
12505 W. Bluemound Rd.
Brookfield, WI 53005-8026
Phone: 414-481-3430
joeg@warpdrivemusic.com
www.warpdrivemusic.com

Dave's Guitar Shop
Dave Rogers
1227 South 3rd Street
La Crosse, WI 54601
Phone: 608-785-7704
Fax: 608-785-7703
davesgtr@aol.com
www.davesguitar.com

Top Shelf Guitar Shop
2358 S. Kinnickinnic Ave.

Milwaukee, WI 53207
Phone: 414-481-8677
topshelfguitars@sbcglobal.net
www.topshelfguitarshop.com

Vintage Paper
Mike Mair
41 Means Dr., Ste. A
Platteville, WI 53818
Phone: 608-348-3057
Fax: 608-348-7918
vpaper@mhtc.net
www.vintagepaper.com

MANUFACTURER DIRECTORY

ACME Guitar Works
www.acmeguitarworks.com

Aero Instrument Pickups
15 Years of Building Custom
Pickups
2798 Kaumana Dr.
Hilo, HI 96720
Phone: 808-969-6774
www.aeroinstrument.com

Alfieri Guitar Repair
Repairs & Restorations
Don Alfieri
POB 2132
New Hyde Park, NY 11040
Phone: 516-410-2926
www.alfieriguitars.blogspot.com

Allparts
13027 Brittmoore Park Drive
Houston, TX 77041
Phone: 713-466-6414
allpartgtr@aol.com
www.allparts.com

Amplikat
Erik Scott
Fresno, CA
Phone: 559-277-5380
Fax: 559-440-9220
sales@amplikat.com
http://amplikat.com

Analog Man Guitar Effects
Mike Piera
36 Tamarack Avenue #343
Danbury, CT 06811
Phone: 203-778-6658
AnalogMike@aol.com

www.analogman.com

Antique Electronic Supply
Brian Campanella
6221 South Maple Avenue
Tempe, AZ 85283
Phone: 480-820-5411
Fax: 800-706-6789
info@tubesandmore.com
www.tubesandmore.com

Asher Guitars and Lap Steels
Bill Asher
Venice, CA
Phone: 877-466-9524
info@asherguitars.com
www.asherguitars.com

Bacino Amplification
Mike Bacino
Arlington Heights, IL. 60005
Phone: 847-736-4987
mike@bacinoamp.com
www.bacinoamp.com

Bad Cat Amps
James Heidrich
PMB #406, 2621 Green River
Road
Corona, CA 92882
Phone: 909-808-8651
Fax: 909-279-6383
james@badcatamps.com
www.badcatamps.com

Bill Lawrence Pickups
Bill or Becky Lawrence
1785 Pomona Road, Unit D
Corona, CA 92880
Phone: 951-371-1494

Fax: 951-647-2651
becky@billlawrence.com
billlawrence.com

Bluetron Amps
Smitty
11123 Lebanon Park
Mt. Juliet, TN 37122
Phone: 615-232-0300
smitty@bluesamps.com
www.bluetron.com

Butler Custom Sound/Chicago Blues Box
1040 N. Dupage
Lombard, IL 60148
Phone: 630-268-2670
www.chicagobluesbox.com

Callaham Guitars
Bill Callaham
108 Rugby Place
Winchester, VA 22603
Phone: 540-955-0294
Fax: 540-678-8779
callaham@callahamguitars.com
www.callahamguitars.com

Campbell American Guitars
Dean Campbell
PO Box 460
Westwood, MA 02090
Phone: 617-620-8153
Fax: 508-785-3577
sales@campbellamerican.com
www.campbellamerican.com

Carmine Street Guitars
Home of famous Kustom Kelly
Guitar

Rick Kelly
42 Carmine St.
New York, NY 10014
Phone: 212-691-8400
kellyguitars@yahoo.com
www.carminestreetguitars.com

Carr Amplifiers
Steve Carr
433 West Salisbury St.
Pittsboro, NC 27312
Phone: 919-545-0747
Fax: 919-545-0739
info@carramps.com
www.carramps.com

CE Distribution
Noreen Cravener
6221 South Maple Avenue
Tempe, AZ 85283
Phone: 480-755-4712
Fax: 480-820-4643
info@cedist.com
www.cedist.com

Chandler Musical Instruments
Paul or Adrian
975 East Ave. #111
Chico, CA 95926
Phone: 530-899-1503
info@chandlerguitars.com
www.chandlerguitars.com
www.pickguards.us

Demeter Amplification
James Demeter
6990 Kingsbury Rd.
Templeton, CA 93465
Phone: 818-994-7658
Fax: 818-994-0647

fo@demeteramps.com
www.demeteramps.com

LS Effects, Inc.
51 Perinton Parkway
airport, NY 14450
www.dlseffects.com

ST Engineering
ob Dettorre/Jeff Swanson
Clipper Way
everly, MA 01915
hone: 508-364-9578
　　978-578-0532
ob@dst-engineering.com
eff@dst-engineering.com
www.dst-engineering.com
www.swansoncabinets.com

Durham Electronics
Alan Durham
Austin, TX USA 78704
hone: 512-581-0663
ales@durhamelectronics.com
www.durhamelectronics.com

Emery Sound
Curtis Emery
Phone: 510-236-1176
www.emerysound.com

Eric Schoenberg Guitars
Eric Schoenberg
06 Main Street
Tiburon, CA 94920
Phone: 415-789-0846
eric@om28.com
www.om28.com

Falk Guitars
Dave Falk
PO Box 7732
Amarillo, TX 79114-7732

Phone: 816-678-3255
dave@falkguitars.com
www.falkguitars.com

Fuchs Audio Technology
Annette Fuchs
407 Getty Ave.
Clifton, NJ 07015
Phone: 973-972-4420
sales@fuchsaudiotechnology.com
fuchsaudiotechnology.com

Gadotti Guitars
Jeff Smith
Phone: 812-486-5836
Fax: 812-254-6476
jsmith@gadottiguitars.ws
www.gadottiguitars.com

Goodsell Electric Instrument Co., LLC
Richard Goodsell
781 Wheeler St. Studio 8
Atlanta, GA 30318
678-488-8176
richardgoodsell@bellsouth.net
www.superseventeen.com

J. Backlund Designs
Bruce Bennett or Kevin Maxfield
100 Cherokee Blvd. N., Ste. 123
Chattanooga, TN 37405
Phone: 423-643-4999
　　423-316-4628
info@bennett-maxfieldmusic.com
www.jbacklunddesigns.com

Mercury Magnetics
Paul Patronette
Chatsworth, CA
Phone: 818-998-7791
Fax: 818-998-7835
paul@mercurymagnetics.com

www.mercurymagnetics.com

Mirabella Guitars & Restorations
Cris Mirabella
P.O. Box 482
Babylon, NY 11702
Phone: 631-842-3819
Fax: 631-842-3827
mirguitars@aol.com
www.mirabellaguitars.com

Reeves Amplification
Phone: 513-615-8923
sales@reevesamps.com
www.reevesamps.com

Rocky Mountain Slide Co.
Doc Sigmier
PO Box 1426
Salida, CO 81201-1426
Phone: 719-530-0696
docsigmier@yahoo.com
www.rockymountainslides.com

Savage Audio Inc.
Jeff Krumm
12500 Chowen Ave. S. Ste. 112
Burnsville, MN 55337
(952)894-1022
(952)894-1536 FAX
www.savageamps.com
www.savageaudio.com
email: savrok@prodigy.net

Skip Simmons Amplifier Repair
Phone: 707-678-5705
www.skipsimmonsamps.com

Tone Tubby
53 Joseph Ct.
San Rafael, CA 94903

Phone: 415-479-2124
Fax: 415-479-2132
abs@abrown.com
www.abrown.com

Torres Engineering
Amps Guitars & Pickups
www.torresengineering.com

Tradition Electric Guitars & Basses
Sales & Warehouse Operations
Fort Worth, TX
Toll Free: 888-361-5838
Fax: 817-923-6600
traditionguitars@gmail.com
trb50@sbcglobal.net
www.traditionguitars.com

Trem King Fixed Bridge Vibrato
Sales & Warehouse Operations
3124 Sandage Ave.
Fort Worth, TX 76109
Toll Free: 866-324-6300
Fax: 817-923-6600
info@tremking.com
www.tremking.com

Tungsten Amplification
Adam Palow
Grand Island, FL
Phone: 352-250-3939
info@tungstenamp.com
www.TungstenAmp.com

Virtuoso Polish and Cleaner
The Virtuoso Group, Inc.
P.O. Box 9775
Canoga Park, CA 91309-0775
Phone: 818-992-4733
virtuosopolish@sbcglobal.net
www.virtuosopolish.com

INDEX

Bold Page numbers indicate first listing

Bold Page numbers indicate first listing

Bold Page numbers indicate first listing

Bold Page numbers indicate first listing

Bold Page numbers indicate first listing

530

The Official Vintage Guitar Magazine Price Guide 2009

Bold Page numbers indicate first listing

Bold Page numbers indicate first listing

Bold Page numbers indicate first listing